The Fly Tier's
Benchside Reference
to Techniques and Dressing Styles

Ted Leeson and Jim Schollmeyer

All inquiries should be addressed to:
Frank Amato Publications, Inc.
P.O. Box 82112 • Portland, Oregon 97282 • 503-653-8108

Book Design: Amy Tomlinson and Tony Amato
Photography: Jim Schollmeyer

Printed in Hong Kong, China
5 7 9 10 8 6

ISBN: 1-57188-126-3   UPC: 0-66066-00325-6

Acknowledgments

Collecting and assembling the fly-tying techniques presented in this book would not have been possible without the assistance and cooperation of many other people. It is a pleasure to acknowledge their contributions.

We are indebted to Darrel Martin, who not only allowed us to draw extensively from his own research into fly-tying methods, but offered as well valuable insights during the early stages of this project.

We are also grateful to John Betts, who generously consented to let us reproduce techniques from his extensive work on both historical tying methods and the use of synthetic materials.

Our sincere thanks to English tyer Oliver Edwards, whose support for this project was invaluable, both in making available many of his unusual tying methods and in acting as liaison to a number of tyers in Europe.

We would also like to thank Veli Autti of Finland, Henning von Monteton of Germany, Roman Moser of Austria, and Neil Patterson of England for efforts, above and beyond the call, in acquainting us with their techniques. And thanks to Olav Koster of Holland for his interest and goodwill.

A number of editors and publishers helped facilitate our research efforts, and we are grateful for their assistance: the staff at Frank Amato Publications; Jim Butler of *Fly Rod & Reel* magazine; Nick Lyons at Lyons Press; Jim Pruett at Pruett Publishing Company; John Randolph at *Fly Fisherman* magazine; Art Scheck at *Fly Tyer* and *American Angler* magazines; Judith Schnell at Stackpole Books; Mark Koenig at Angler's Book Supply; and Dick Stewart.

We are indebted as well to the many tyers who kindly gave us permission to include their techniques and tying methods in this book and who provided help of various and indispensable kinds. Thanks to Al and Gretchen Beatty; A.K. Best; Bill Black; Gary Borger; Richard Bunse; Keith Burkhart, scrounger extraordinaire, at the Valley Flyfisher; Al Caucci; Jack Dennis; Larry Duckwall; Ken Ferguson and Bill Black at Spirit River, Inc.; René Harrop; Chris Helm; Mark Hoy; Dave Hughes; Ken Iwamasa; Gary LaFontaine; Eric Leiser; Ken Menard; Joe Messinger, Jr.; Skip Morris; Dick Nelson; Tom Nixon; Boyd Pfeiffer; Sandy Pittendrigh; John Rodriguez; Tatsuhiro Saido; John Schaper; Shane Stalcup; Randy Stetzer and Rod Robinson at Kaufmann's Fly Shop; a very special thanks to Dick Talleur; Gene Trump; Mike Tucker; the helpful people at Umpqua Feather Merchants; Gary Warren; and Tom Whiting of Whiting Farms.

Our gratitude as well to the many other tyers—too numerous to mention individually—who have shared with us their techniques at expositions and demonstrations over the years, beginning long before this book was ever imagined. Observing them has shown to us that some of the most creative technical innovations in the craft are the product of local tyers, who are enduring proof—were any needed—that you don't need to be famous to be good.

Thanks as well to Tony Amato and Amy Tomlinson who brought imagination, patience, and good humor to the considerable task of preparing the manuscript for publication.

Finally, the deepest appreciation to our wives, Debbie Schollmeyer and Betty Campbell, who encouraged and supported this project at every step. Thank you both.

Table of Contents

Chapter 11
Wingcases and Overbodies

Chapter 12
Wings

Introduction

Our purpose in writing *The Fly Tier's Benchside Reference* has been to collect, systematize, and present a wide range of fly-tying methods—both those that have appeared in the literature of the craft, and those shown to us by others. Because of its explicit emphasis on technique, this book differs in a number of ways from other instructional tying texts that you may have seen or used, and a few words of explanation are in order.

The vast majority of fly-tying books approach the subject by focusing on a selection of specific fly patterns and the procedures used to dress them. Many such works—a number of them excellent—have been written, and their value lies in stressing finished flies, in guiding the tyer to the completion of usable patterns. But books of this type do have their limitations. They must of necessity restrict themselves to a particular set of tying techniques appropriate to the patterns presented, and in the process, they must exclude a more comprehensive range of methods that would enable the tyer to dress a much greater variety of fly designs and styles. Certainly the techniques used to dress one pattern can be adapted to others, but even so, most books focus on a relatively small number of dressing methods. The larger world of fly-tying techniques remains unexplored for the simple reason that it is not the goal of such books to explore it.

The Fly Tier's Benchside Reference, however, is an attempt to map out that larger territory of fly-tying techniques, and in so doing it reverses the approach taken by more conventional tying texts. As even a quick glance through these pages will reveal, there are very few finished flies pictured here. Our goal instead is to provide detailed instructions for a wide variety of techniques used in fly tying, in essence furnishing the reader with a reservoir of methods, procedures, and dressing styles that can be drawn upon to tie a full range of trout patterns. Rather than leading the tyer through complete instructions for a small number of selected flies, this book provides a collection of techniques with which virtually any trout fly can be dressed.

Though little emphasis is placed on finished flies here, in other ways this book closely resembles the type of tying reference that is devoted exclusively to finished flies—the pattern book. And in fact *The Fly Tier's Benchside Reference* was compiled with exactly this resemblance in mind. We have attempted to design a book that does for fly-tying techniques what pattern books do for fly dressings—that is, to provide tyers with a collection of options and alternatives for accomplishing a particular purpose. Where a pattern directory, for example, might provide half-a-dozen different dressings for a blue-wing olive dun, this book shows a variety of different ways to fashion the wings, body, tails and other components in each of those dressings. In this regard, *The Fly Tier's Benchside Reference* is intended to supplement or complement many existing books, both pattern directories and conventional instructional texts, by providing more detail in the procedures and offering a greater range of tying techniques from which to choose. And like a pattern book, this one is primarily a collection of existing information rather than a body of original material. Like fly patterns, techniques tend to be scattered throughout the literature of tying, in books, magazines, videotapes, newsletters, and more recently, electronic media. As a pattern directory draws together fly dressings from a wide range of sources and organizes them into a useful format, this book attempts the same task with the techniques and methods used to tie trout flies, assembling and arranging them into a practical reference.

As with most reference works, this one is intended to serve a range of users. The beginning or novice tyer may find it most useful for the detail of its instruction. Basic tying operations, the preparation and handling of materials, thread placement and tension, and hand positioning often prove troublesome for less experienced tyers. But because these procedures are second nature to more practiced fly dressers, they are apt to be taken for granted or overlooked in many instructional sources, particularly those such as magazines, in which space is at a premium. We have attempted here to accommodate the needs of novice tyers by providing, in text and photographs, complete and detailed instructions for all the techniques presented, from the most basic to the most advanced. Since there are relatively few finished flies in this book, the beginning tyer may find the information here most helpful when used in conjunction with a more conventional tying text, consulting the appropriate techniques presented here as each fly component is tied.

More experienced tyers, from intermediate to advanced, will find broader applications for the material contained in these pages. Many of the tying methods detailed here are presented in groups that will acquaint the tyer with a variety of different ways to dress the same fly component. For instance, Chapter 8: "Tails and Trailing Shucks" demonstrates ten approaches to tying split tails. Though many of these techniques produce tails that are similar or identical, tyers who already employ a specific method for dressing split tails may find additional or alternate procedures that are easier, faster, or better suited to certain materials, fly styles, hook sizes, or tying situations than the method they currently use. In this respect, the book is aimed at enlarging the tyer's repertoire for more technical flexibility in a broader variety of tying situations.

Tyers with a basic grasp of fly proportions and the sequence in which individual fly components are dressed on the hook, should find this book useful in reproducing fly patterns that they have seen in fly shops, magazines, and particularly in books of fly patterns. Indeed, one of our principal goals in compiling these techniques and organizing the book by fly component has been to assist tyers in successfully translating a photograph or sample pattern into a finished fly. Doing so is simply a matter of identifying the style of each fly component—for instance, triple tail, biot body, and hackle-tip spentwing—and choosing from among the techniques that can be used to dress each part of the pattern.

Along these same lines, more inventive or innovative tyers may well find this book most helpful in designing their own fly patterns and creating dressings with the appearance and characteristics best suited to the specific conditions that they encounter in their fishing. To this end, we have not only provided dressing instructions for a wide range of component styles, but have endeavored as well to identify the advantages, drawbacks, performance characteristics, and the range of materials suited to each style. A tyer can thus select a set of individual fly components—a tail style, body, wing design, and so on—to construct a fly pattern that incorporates the desired attributes: realism, buoyancy, a high-floating or flush-riding profile, absorbency, durability, lifelike movement, visibility to the angler, ease of tying, and so forth. Well chosen combinations of the various components and materials presented in these pages can aid the tyer in custom designing patterns to address specific fishing conditions.

By the same token, the information provided here can assist tyers in modifying or substituting components on existing patterns. For instance, anglers who value the effectiveness of the No-hackle Dun design but dislike its lack of durability, may find that the instructions provided here for dressing the same basic pattern with wings of poly yarn or feather-tips, instead of quill, will improve the durability of the fly without diminishing its attractiveness to fish.

And finally we very much hope that tyers of all skill levels, from beginner to expert, will discover here tying techniques that they have not encountered before. In the interests of comprehensiveness and utility for a full range of tyers, we have presented a number of common tying techniques along with many variations of these methods. But one of our main objectives has been to acquaint tyers with less widely known, less commonly employed, more innovative, and newer dressing techniques and styles.

Though many of the methods shown here can be used or adapted to dress patterns for species other than trout, this book focuses specifically on the tying of trout flies. As a result, we have excluded certain types of techniques. Those used to dress specialized components of Atlantic salmon patterns, for instance, have been omitted. Similarly, we've excluded methods typically used in saltwater or warmwater patterns: wooden or foam-bodied poppers; flies with diving lips fashioned from plastic, shaped deer hair, or other materials; flies tied with pre-formed bodies; some of the more elaborate body patterns often found on deer-hair bass bugs (though hair spinning and stacking techniques as they pertain to trout flies are certainly presented); and flies with bodies formed from epoxy, silicone adhesives, and hot glue. We have omitted as well tying procedures that can be performed only with a true rotary vise; the specialized equipment required makes such techniques properly a study of their own and one, we think, that has not been adequately explored in the literature of fly tying. Since the methods shown in this book are aimed at practical fly tying, we have not presented techniques used to produce the ultra-realistic flies often fashioned for display—a version of the craft that, as Dick Talleur has remarked, lies closer to model-making than fly tying.

There is one category of trout-fly tying that is not well represented here. We had originally intended to include "historical" tying techniques, those recorded in the angling literature of centuries past, but no longer in widespread use. Limitations of space, however, forced us to narrow the scope of the book. Many older techniques, of course, form the foundation of modern tying, and these are certainly included, as are a selection of other historical techniques, primarily those revived by tyer/historians Darrel Martin and John Betts. But in the end, when it became necessary to choose, we elected to present more contemporary or newer techniques and dressing styles from both North American and European tyers rather than those of a distant past; the pages allotted simply would not accommodate both.

Despite these exclusions, a vast territory still remains, and surveying it raises an interesting and certainly pertinent question: "What exactly constitutes a 'technique' in fly tying?" In one sense there are but a small handful of tying "techniques"—one, for instance, by which materials are affixed to the hook; one in which materials are wrapped around the hook; and so on. And it is at least arguable that there is no significant difference between winding a tinsel rib, for example, and wrapping a dry-fly hackle, that in fact they are the same technique. But fly tying exists in its details, and to paint the subject with a brush so broad practically generalizes it out of existence, and ultimately offers far too little in the way of useful information. At the other extreme, it might be argued that no two tyers work in precisely identical fashions, differing very slightly in the details of material and thread handling, and thus each in fact possesses a unique set of tying methods. Valid as this may be as a theoretical view, practically speaking many of these small variations among tyers are insignificant. A book structured around this very narrow construction of fly-tying technique would be impossibly large and tediously repetitive.

In compiling *The Fly Tier's Benchside Reference* we have attempted to take the middle ground between these two extremes, presenting a wide range of tying approaches that still acknowledge smaller or more subtle variations in technique, and at the same time grouping together or combining similar methods to minimize redundancy. In determining which technical distinctions are major ones, which are secondary, and which from a practical standpoint are immaterial, we have tried to make choices that are instructive and useful to the tyer and that preserve the rich variety of dressing methods from which the craft of fly tying has been shaped.

How to Use This Book

This book is structured around individual fly components, with each chapter presenting a group of methods devoted to dressing a part of the finished fly—the tail, body, wings, and so forth. Each technique contains what we have termed a "main sequence," a series of instructional photographs with *blue* backgrounds designated as "Step 1," "Step

2," and so on. This main sequence of photographs is a complete and self-contained set of step-by-step procedures for dressing a specific fly component. A large number of methods, however, also contain what we have called "alternate steps " or "alternate sequences." These are photographed against a *green* background and designated with both a number and lower-case letter, as for instance, "Step 2a" or "Step 5a."

The relation between the instructional steps in the main sequence and those in the alternate sequence varies, depending upon the requirements of the particular technique. For instance, a method may contain "Step 1," "Step 2," "Step 2a," "Step 3," and so on. In this case, Step 2a may picture a variation preferred by some tyers of the procedure shown in Step 2; an additional or optional procedure; or a way of executing Step 2 using a material other than that pictured in the main sequence. In some cases, an alternate procedure cannot be conveniently explained in a single photograph, and so a short sequence of alternate steps is used: "Step 2a," "Step 2b," "Step 2c," for example. Again, the alternate photographs, on a green background, demonstrate a variation of the main technique or an alternate or optional set of steps. In both of these cases, the alternate photographs are intermixed with the main-sequence photographs in order to indicate the point in the tying procedure at which the alternate approach may be used.

Some methods have, in addition to the main sequence, a complete and independent set of alternate sequence photographs. These may picture a variation of the technique shown in the main sequence, a related method for producing the same fly component, or a procedure for dressing a different version of the component shown in the main set of photographs. Typically, this alternate procedure (again, shown against a green background) will be labeled "Step 1a," "Step 2a," "Step 3a," and so on, and the entire sequence of photographs will be placed at the end of the main sequence, where the progression of steps can be more easily followed.

One point is worth noting here: the use of a technique in the main sequence does not suggest that it is the best, or preferred, or most widely used method, or that alternate procedures are somehow secondary or minor. Instead, the decision to present one tying approach as a main sequence and another as an alternate was largely a matter of efficiency, of which technique was most easily presented as a version of the other.

In the headnote that accompanies each method in the book, we have tried to present objectively the advantages and disadvantages of each technique, the materials to which it is best suited, and the fly style or tying situation in which it is most useful. Such information is provided to give the tyer some indication of the circumstances under which the method may be most profitably employed. We have, however, refrained from recommending or favoring one method over another for the simple reason that there is no one "right" way to tie flies. As we hope this book demonstrates, there are many different ways to dress the same fly component, and which is "best" in any given situation rests primarily on the style and preference of the tyer.

Many of the procedures used in different fly-tying techniques overlap, and in assembling this book we have tried to balance two, often competing, claims: thoroughness of instruction and economy of presentation. To begin each and every method by explaining how to de-barb the hook, affix the thread to the shank, prepare the materials, and so forth, would be impractically repetitive. At the same time to omit such procedures altogether would make the instructions incomplete. We have, therefore, included in the first four chapters information about materials and hook preparation, techniques for thread handling, and methods for mounting and trimming materials. Tyers unfamiliar with such procedures may wish to consult these chapters for basic information, while more experienced tyers may discover in them lesser-known or unusual techniques that will prove valuable. Similarly, the introductions to chapters and chapter divisions often contain useful ideas about specific component styles, handling and preparing materials, as well as other tying-related matters, and readers may benefit from consulting these sections prior to tying.

As tying procedures overlap, so techniques often build upon one another. For example, dressing hackle-tip spentwings first requires tying a pair of upright wings. Rather than repeat the entire procedure for dressing upright wings in the method devoted to spentwings—or duplicate instructions in any method that would require it—we have adopted instead a system of cross references. A cross reference will appear as part of a tying sequence and point the reader to a relevant procedure that has already been detailed elsewhere in the book. This is, admittedly, an imperfect solution, since it may require the tyer to consult two different portions of the book in order to execute one technique. We have tried to keep these cross references to a minimum, and in many cases, they direct the reader to relatively commonplace procedures; experienced tyers may find that they can pass over many of these references.

In order to facilitate cross-referencing, as well as to indicate the substance of the technique, each method has a title. In some instances, naming a method, such as **Method #53: Feather Streamer Wings**, was a simple matter of enlisting familiar tying terminology. In other cases, the titles proved more of a problem. Some tying methods simply have no formal names, and so it was necessary to devise titles. At many points in the book, several methods are devoted to dressing a single component, such as triple tails, and it was necessary to name the methods in a way that distinguished among the various techniques. Finally, titling the methods accurately sometimes required stepping outside of conventional tying terminology. For example, the reader will find no method here entitled "hair wings," though this component is in fact covered extensively. The reason for this apparent omission is that other materials such as feather barbs, synthetic yarns, and other fibers can all be used to fashion wings using the method typically employed with hair. The title "hair wings" would thus be unnecessarily restrictive and misleading, and so we have settled for the less familiar but more accurate "bundled-fiber wings" as a way of more precisely identifying the range of materials suited to the technique. An index—where, for example, the reader will find "hair wings" listed—has been included in part to help translate familiar tying terms into the vocabulary used here. This kind of adjustment is necessary in only a handful of instances, and even a few short sessions with this book should make its structure and terminology clear and easy to follow.

While a few of the techniques described here are of our own devising, the vast majority come from other tyers, and whenever possible, we have attempted to give credit to specific individuals for tying methods that they have developed. In some cases, the source of a technique, particularly a more modern one such as Mike Tucker's liquid-filled bodies or the hair-stacking technique devised by Joe Messinger, Sr., is easily established. More often, however, the origin of a technique is difficult to determine, particularly methods such as direct dubbing or collar hackling that have long been used. We have avoided speculating about the sources of such procedures; they are matters best left to more skilled historians. Many methods and component styles are linked to specific individuals who may or may not have devised them; split dry-fly tails and thorax hackling, for example, are commonly associated with Vince Marinaro, though it is entirely possible that these dressing approaches pre-date him. In such cases, we have identified the tyer who, while perhaps not the originator of the method, has brought a technique or dressing style to the attention of a larger fly-tying audience. Making such determinations is not always a simple matter, and doubtless the book contains some errors in this respect; we hope they are few in number. But our primary goal here is not tracing the precise historical lineage of every method, but rather to acknowledge the individuals who have established particular techniques in the literature of tying and to indicate to the reader additional sources for further information.

Though the research that informs this book has been extensive, the finished product could not in any legitimate sense be called complete or comprehensive. Such a thing, we are convinced, is impossible in just the same way that a complete pattern directory is impossible. New techniques, like new fly patterns, are being devised even as this book goes to press. But we do hope that the collection of methods presented in these pages will enlarge the reader's technical repertoire and increase both the enjoyment and effectiveness of tying.

CHAPTER 1

The Anatomy and Selection of Fly-tying Materials

While a comprehensive discussion of fly-tying materials is well beyond the scope of this book, the structure and selection of some materials have a direct bearing on the ease and success with which certain tying techniques are executed and on the quality of the finished fly. For example, a fly pattern may call for a body of spun deer hair. But deer hair, even that of high quality, varies considerably in its tying characteristics, and an improperly chosen material will not only produce a poor finished fly, but make spinning or stacking techniques difficult or impossible to perform. Not all materials show this kind of variation, but a handful of the more commonly used ones do. Typically, they are materials with a broad range of applications; depending on the fly pattern, a given material might be used for wings, tails, bodies, hackles, or other fly components, and the tying characteristics deemed desirable may differ with each use. To simplify cross-referencing, we are presenting this particular group of materials in one chapter. Other materials with more specific and local uses, such as foam for bodies or synthetic winging films, are discussed in the corresponding sections of this book.

The aim of this chapter, then, is to examine briefly the basic structure of some of the more widely employed materials as a way of addressing their tying properties and uses. Such information is also useful in identifying criteria for selecting materials of high quality and of the proper type for a given tying application. Finally, because fly-tying terminology is often inconsistent (and at times inaccurate), this chapter introduces some of the terms that are used throughout the remainder of the book.

Furs and Hairs

Furs and hairs are among the most commonly used materials in fly tying, and while the terms are often employed interchangeably, there is still some consistency in usage based on the structure of the natural material. Despite its fairly uniform appearance to the eye, a patch of animal fur is composed of different types of fibers. While these can in fact be divided into a number of taxonomic subgroups, from the standpoint of practical tying, we need go no further than two basic categories: "underfur" (or what tyers generally mean when they refer simply to "fur") and "guard hairs" (or to tyers, simply "hair").

Underfur is short, relatively fine, and often quite soft, at least compared with longer, coarser guard hairs of the same animal. The chief use of underfur is in dubbing, since the thinner, more supple fibers twist more readily around the tying thread in direct dubbing methods. Moreover, on many species of animals, the surface of the underfur is sheathed in overlapping, scale-like structures that not only grip the tying thread, but grip one another, and make spinning the dubbing reasonably easy. Underfurs are sometimes used for tails on subsurface patterns, and very occasionally for downwings; but in general, the microscopic scales on the surface and the often corkscrewed or kinked shape (which make it difficult to align the hair fibers in a stacker) and the short length limit its use for other fly components. Underfurs can differ significantly from one species of animal to another; the underfur of rabbit, beaver, mink, and otter, for instance, are popular with tyers since the high ratio of underfur to guard hairs means an abundance of soft, supple, easily dubbed material. On other animals, such as deer or calf, the underfur is seldom, if ever, used for dubbing. Even among the underfurs suitable for dubbing, there are differences in texture and thickness that make the material more or less easily worked, but the behavior of all these underfurs during tying is more alike than different.

In terms of tying technique, there is considerably greater variation in types of guard hairs. These thicker, longer, often distinctly tapered hairs are generally less abundant on the body of the animal and can vary enormously in texture, from the stiff bristles on a porcupine to the much softer guard hairs of a rabbit, and the applications of guard hairs in tying are correspondingly more varied. Some guard hairs, particularly those that are softer,

can be mixed with underfur for dubbing to give a bristled, "spikey" appearance to the fly body. Bundles of guard hairs without underfur can be used for tails, wings, wingcases, legs, and even hackle. Though guard hairs from different species of animals may be quite unlike in appearance, length, texture, and abundance, from the standpoint of tying technique, the most significant distinction to be drawn is between, what are termed in this book, "solid" hairs and "hollow" ones.

Solid Hair

Structurally, solid hairs are not actually solid, but rather, under the pressure of tying thread, they behave as though they were. Such hairs are incompressible and do not flare or deform as they are wrapped with thread. The surface of the fibers themselves tends to be rather smooth, almost slippery, and when gathered in a bundle, these hairs will slide and roll against one another. Except for those varieties that have a crinkly texture, such as calf tail, solid hairs slide readily in a hair stacker and the tips are easily aligned.

The animals that have solid guard hairs are so numerous that they are perhaps best identified by exclusion—virtually all species commonly used in tying except for deer, elk, moose, antelope, and caribou, which have predominantly hollow guard hairs. (Porcupine quills, which are hollow, represent a very specialized type of guard hair; on the hide, they are mixed with a much larger number of solid fibers.) The uses to which various solid hairs may be put depend primarily on four characteristics: length, stiffness, uniformity, and abundance.

The stiffest hairs, such as bristles from boar, peccary, and javelina, are used primarily in small quantities for tailing material on floating patterns, where the resilience of the material supports the fly well in the surface film. These hairs, however, are rather thick, and a bundle large enough to form the wing on a fly would produce an excessively bulky tie-in; moreover, these very stiff hairs tend to be sparsely distributed on the hide, and gathering a quantity sufficient for winging is somewhat impractical. Because of their stiffness, these solid hairs are sometimes wrapped to produce a quill-type body, or used for legs or antennae.

A substantial number of solid hairs are of moderate stiffness, and these have broadest range of tying applications. Guard hairs from the body fur of bear; badger; raccoon; woodchuck; fox; calf; some types of elk, moose,

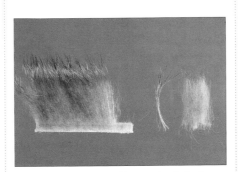

The strip of rabbit hide on the left shows the differences in length, thickness, and texture between the guard hairs (middle) and the underfur (right).

and deer (discussed below); and a number of others fit this category. Guard hairs from many animal tails – raccoon, fox, bucktail, squirrel, monga ringtail, calf, and mink – are particularly useful, as the guard hair tends to be more thickly distributed, while the under-fur is less dense, which simplifies gathering larger quantities of guard hair. These moder-ately stiff, solid hairs tend to be reasonably uniform in length and thickness, tapered to a pleasing point, and often attractively marked and colored. Stiff enough to give good sup-port when tied as dry-fly tails, they are also thin enough in diameter to be used for wing-ing both dry flies and streamers without pro-ducing a prohibitive amount of bulk in the fly head or body. Solid hairs resist water absorp-tion, making them suitable for dry-fly wings. On streamers, wings fashioned from this moderately stiff, resilient hair maintain their shape and preserve the silhouette of the fly.

Because of their similarity in structure, these solid guard hairs share certain han-dling and tying characteristics. Generally smooth and straight, these hairs stack easily to align the tips, though crinkled hairs such as calf tail require combing first to untangle the fibers. Their slickness and incompress-ibility, however, make them slippery under tying thread; a significant amount of pres-sure and a twisted thread are often necessary to secure even a moderate quantity to the hook shank. Even then, many tyers apply some adhesive – head cement or liquid CA glue (see "Adhesives" on page 12) – to the mounting point of the hair before, during, or after securing it to the hook shank to prevent the slick hairs from pulling out. Thick bun-dles of such solid hairs are difficult to secure even with cement, and when larger quanti-ties of material are needed, most tyers will use two or more smaller bundles rather than a single large one. Finally, because these solid fibers are incompressible, they build bulk on the hook shank quickly and require angle-cutting to form a smooth tapered or spliced underbody.

For various reasons, the solid guard hairs from some animals are poorly suited for tail-ing and winging. Guard hairs on the body fur of muskrat, otter, squirrel, and most small mammals, for instance, are too short to han-dle easily. Rabbit guard hairs are poorly shaped, with broad, flattened tip sections, and thinner shafts. Beaver guard hairs are often inconsistent in their conformation, though they can sometimes be used for tail-ing when a small amount of material is required, as in tying split- or triple-tails, for instance. But in general, the guards hairs from all of these animals are either discarded or mixed with the underfur for dubbing.

The quality of fur patches sold for fly tying varies and depends upon the age and condition of the animal, the season of har-vest, and the care taken in processing. When buying material primarily for dubbing, look for a dense, rich, lustrous coat of underfur that indicates a patch or pelt in prime condi-tion, as this will furnish an ample supply of high-quality dubbing.

There are additional factors when select-ing material on which the guard hairs are the primary consideration. The guard hairs should have no broken tips, as these make poor tails and most tyers find them aestheti-cally displeasing when used in wings. In gen-eral, longer guard hairs are more useful than shorter ones since they can be employed on a wider range of hook sizes. The density of the guard hairs determines the amount of useful material; density seems to be a particular problem with calf body hair, which is too often sold in sparse, anemic patches. When purchasing tails, look for large specimens which indicate a mature animal (deer tails are an exception here), since these offer more material and longer hair. Squirrel tails demand particular attention, since sparse, undersize tails are not uncommon.

Finally, there appears to be little differ-ence in quality between hair on a hide that has been tanned and hair on a dried hide. Tanned hides are somewhat simpler to han-dle when cutting small clumps of fur for dub-bing or bundles of guard hairs. Dried hides are more easily cut into strips for use in fur chenilles and dubbing brushes.

Hollow Hair

Hollow hairs are also guard hairs, and the varieties used in tying come from deer, elk, moose, caribou and antelope. As solid hairs are not actually solid, so hollow hair is not actually hollow, at least in the same way that a drinking straw is hollow. Rather, the shaft of the hair (excluding the tip) is honey-combed with small, hollow chambers, and in its structure most closely resembles closed-cell foam. And indeed, unlike solid hair, hol-low hair is spongy, quite compressible, and not particularly stiff.

Because of its unusual structure, hollow hair has two important properties for the fly tyer. First, these hollow chambers make the hair quite buoyant, and as a result, it is an excellent material for wings, tails, and bodies on floating flies. Second, when these cham-bers are collapsed under the pressure of tying thread, the hair on either side of the compres-sion point flares upward, and in some cases will stand almost perpendicular to the hook shank. The degree to which hair will flare depends upon the diameter of the fiber, the size of the internal chambers, and their wall thickness, which in turn may be influenced by a number of factors: which part of the hide the hair was taken from; the species, subspecies, and sometimes sex of the animal; its diet and health; the season of harvest; and even its geo-graphical origin. And this is where the matter of selecting hollow hair grows a bit compli-cated. As Chris Helm, master deer-hair tyer writes, "Fly-tying instructions that say 'use deer hair' are about as specific as a recipe that instructs you to 'cook food.'"

First of all, not all the hair on deer, elk, or similar animal is actually hollow; much of the hair from the tail, mask, and lower leg is virtually solid, and the tying methods used to dress it are identical to those for solid hair. In tying with hollow hair, the particular proper-ties deemed desirable depend to a great extent upon the particular application. For spinning fly bodies, coarser, "hollower" hair flares to the greatest degree, concealing the wraps of tying thread and producing a dense, uniform, buoyant body. For tying wings and tails, however, hair with less flare is more desirable. In short, the best results in tying are obtained when hollow hairs are chosen for a specific application or fly component.

Before proceeding to specifics about particular types of hair, it is worth examin-ing a bit more closely the general categories of use for deer hair, since not all tyers pre-fer the same type of hair for the same pur-pose, at least in all cases, and the accompa-nying chart of uses depends to some extent on the tying characteristics identified below. Most tyers in fact do agree about the prop-erties of good spinning hair. It should flare fully and readily, and hair that does so under the least thread pressure is often con-sidered premium material, since hair that requires excessive pressure to flare may ultimately be cut by the tying thread. For tailing dry flies, many tyers favor a hair that flares very little. Under thread pressure, hair of this type will remain consolidated into a neat bundle instead of producing an unruly brush at the rear of the fly. Tyers such as Chris Helm, to whom we are indebted for much of the information that follows, prefer tailing hair that is almost solid. Such hair is more easily kept under control, though it lacks the buoyancy of hollow hair. Other tyers prefer a hair that flares a bit more for better floatation, and they use techniques (presented in Chapter 8: "Tails and Trailing Shucks") to prevent such hair from flaring excessively.

In upright dry-fly wings, a bit more flare is generally considered desirable. Under thread pressure, such hair will spread to a moderate degree, fanning to a winglike sil-houette; too much flare, however, will splay the fibers radically, and any impression of two distinct wings will be lost. In tying downwings, on caddis patterns for example, still a bit more flare is usually deemed appropriate. Hair that flares upward from the hook shank at an angle of about 45 degrees nicely represents the tent-shaped silhouette of a caddis and incorporates a sufficient por-tion of the hollow hair to give the fly good buoyancy. Perhaps the one exception here is in Al Troth's original Elk Hair Caddis, which called for bleached cow elk – a hair that flares extremely well and produces a bushier, less caddis-like wing, but one with superior floatation.

There is substantial disagreement among tyers concerning the best material for hol-low-hair arc wings of the style used on Comparaduns. Al Caucci and Bob Nastasi's original dressing called for hair from a deer mask, which is almost solid, flares little, lacks buoyancy, and is stiff enough to make vertical posting difficult. Caucci has gradu-ally moved away from this material to hairs that flare slightly more, and many tyers pre-fer a hair similar to that used for caddis wings – one that flares to about 45 degrees. This material is sufficiently buoyant to float the fly, but does not flare so drastically that it makes controlling the wing shape difficult. Other tyers prefer a hair that flares readily and fully; under thread pressure, such material will stand nearly perpendicular to the shank, which greatly simplifies posting the wing upright. These very hollow fibers give superior floatation, though consolidating the wing into the traditional narrow, fanlike shape can be more difficult. The hair designated on the table as suitable for Comparaduns flares easily and fully. If you prefer a hair that flares somewhat less, choose a type designated on the table as suitable for "caddis" or "downwings." For hair that flares even less, choose a type designated for use in "tails" or "upright wings."

Perhaps the trickiest hair to locate is that useful for Muddler Minnows or other flies that incorporate a natural-tip collar and clipped head. Hair that flares too readily will produce a collar that stands almost perpendicular to the hook shank, though it will make a nice, full head. Conversely, hair that does not flare much will produce a pleasing swept-back collar, but a poor head. The best material is one that flares under thread pressure just at the mounting point so that the collar angles back nicely toward the rear of the fly, while the butts of the hair flare easily into a dense head.

Shown in the following group of photographs are four types of hollow hair, each of which is tied to a hook shank in a way that typifies its use.

Pictured here is a coarse hair, mule deer in this particular case. Under thread pressure it flares quite dramatically and is useful for spinning and stacking.

Notice the very fine texture of this hair from a Florida whitetail. It flares only a small amount – notice in particular how little the hair tips are raised from the shank. This kind of hair is easily formed into nicely shaped tails and upright wings.

Here is a very short, fine hair, taken from a whitetail deer. Notice that when affixed to the hook, it flares only moderately, raising the hair tips to about 45 degrees to the hook shank. It makes nicely formed, buoyant downwings for caddis and other flies.

Shown here is a different type of mule deer hair. Note the long, very uniform hair shafts that taper abruptly to a tip. If this hair is mounted in the transitional zone from hollow to solid, it will produce a well-formed Muddler collar from the hair tips, while the butts flare nicely for creating a clipped head.

The following chart shows the various types of hollow hair and their uses.

TYPE	USES	COMMENTS
ANTELOPE		
Body	Spinning/stacking	Most buoyant of all hollow hairs; flares easily but brittle and easily cut with thread
CARIBOU		
Body	Spinning smaller bodies; small upright and caddis wings if tips are intact	Good texture for smaller bodies and wings
ELK		
Mane	Primarily tails, especially on larger flies	Very fine, almost solid, but long
Rump	Extended bodies	Coarse, but only moderate flare; broken tips common
Hock	Tails; upright and downwings	Stiff; flares to about 45 degrees; short and best suited to small flies; spins poorly
Bull	Tails; wings on stoneflies and larger caddis	Flares to about 45 degrees; longer than hock for larger flies; spins poorly
Cow	Caddis wings; spinning/stacking for larger bodies	Produces more fully flared caddis wings; spins well
Yearling	Comparaduns, Humpies, some spinning but good for small flies	Uniform diameter fibers, short tip; moderately long
DEER		
Mask	Tails	Very hard, almost solid; winging material for tyers who prefer no flare; can be curved
Rump/Belly	Spinning/stacking	Flares well; very long and best suited to larger flies
Tail	Tails; streamer downwings; upright wings on larger flies	Hair on upper 3/4 of tail virtually solid, no flare – best for wings. Hair near base of tail is coarse, with moderate flare
Body/Back		
Short, fine	Tails; upright and downwings on smaller flies; small Muddler heads	Moderate flare
Short, coarse	Small Comparaduns	Flares fully
Long, fine	Wings and tails on larger patterns	Flaring characteristics variable
Long, coarse	Spinning/stacking; Muddler heads	Flares fully
MOOSE		
Body	Tails; wings on larger flies	Stiff; moderately coarse; little flare
Mane	Tails; quill-type bodies	Coarse, virtually no flare

The following photos picture three types of hair that represent the range of characteristics preferred by different tyers for forming hollow-hair arc wings used on Comparaduns.

Shown here is a short, coarse whitetail hair that flares very fully; it produces a very high volume, buoyant wing, with a low-bulk tie-in. The wing shape, however, can be difficult to control because of the extreme flare, and it often yields a broad, brushlike wing.

This elk hair has a moderate flare that gives good buoyancy and moderately bulky tie-in. The wing shape is somewhat more easily controlled during tying, as the fibers are more readily consolidated into a narrow fanlike wing.

Elk mane hair flares very little; it produces a very narrow fan-shaped wing. Posting the stiff material upright can be difficult; the tie-in bulk is substantial; and the wing is not particularly buoyant. Some hair from a deer mask and legs will yield approximately the same type of wing.

For most species of hollow-haired animals, selecting hair is not as complicated as it may appear. Among antelope, moose, caribou, cow elk, bull elk, and yearling elk, there is a certain uniformity among animals. As Chris Helm observers, "one antelope is pretty much like another; one moose like another, and so on." While hair from different parts of these animals are required to accomplish different purposes, as indicated on the chart, the tyer can be fairly confident that a given type of hair will achieve the purpose regardless of which individual animal it comes from, which makes generalizations more reliable. That is, most moose body hair, for example, will exhibit the same tying characteristics regardless of the moose in question. There are always slight variations, and the quality of the hair – the number of broken tips, for instance, or damage done during processing – may vary, but its general behavior under the pressure of tying thread will be fairly constant.

Not so with deer hair. Helm, who handles hundreds of deer pelts a year, emphasizes that almost every deer is an individual. Given that there are 8 subspecies of mule deer and 17 of whitetail distributed throughout every geographical region of the country, it is perhaps no surprise that generalizing about the properties of deer hair, even from specific parts of the animal, is an uncertain and imprecise business. The neck hair, for instance, of two whitetails of the same age and sex, harvested from the same geographical region, can vary in their tying properties. Thus buying deer hair on the basis of species alone, such as "Texas whitetail," may not yield a hair suitable to your purposes, even if the last patch of Texas whitetail you bought was perfect.

According to Helm, however, here are some general guidelines that can be observed. Coarse, stiff hair, whether it is long or short, typically spins and flares well for making fly bodies. The finer the hair, as a rule, the less it will flare and the more satisfactory it becomes for wings and tails. This is, of course, not inflexibly true as some fine hairs, for example, flare quite well. A limited amount of information can be gained from visually inspecting hair – color, the general condition of the material, the general texture of the hair. The fingers can tell a bit more. Hair that feels stiff and resilient, like a paintbrush, will usually flare well; hair that is soft, with an almost fur-like feel, will flare less.

There is one last consideration that is often overlooked in discussions of deer hair, and that is the length of the hair relative to the size of the fly tied. Evaluating this relationship can provide important information about the behavior of the hair when it is actually tied. Though most deer hair is hollow, it is not uniformly so. The base or butt of most hair, that is, the end nearest the skin, is the hollowest and on any give type of hair, this portion will flare most readily. As you move away from the hair butt, the hair becomes more dense and less apt to flare, until you reach a point near the tip where the hair is virtually solid and will not flare at all.

The behavior of the hair, then, depends to a great extent on the point at which the tying thread crosses it.

Determining such tying characteristics in a patch of hair is quite simple. Cut, clean, and stack a bundle of hair. Mount it near the butts behind the eye of a long-shanked hook, and observe the degree of flare, particularly in the hair tips – the portion of the hair generally of greatest concern to trout-fly tyers. Then regrasp the tips, wrap the thread tightly

Here, bundles of deer hair from the same patch of hide have been mounted at various distances from the hair tips. The hair is approximately 1½" long.

If a bundle of hair is mounted on a hook shank with thread crossing the material about ¾" to 1" from the tip, as shown on the fly at the upper left, it will flare quite readily.

The same hair mounted ½" from the tip may flare to about 45 degrees, making an excellent wing for a #14 Deer Hair Caddis, as shown on the fly in the upper right.

If the same hair is mounted about ¼" from the tip, it will not flare sufficiently for a caddis wing, but it makes an excellent tail on a #18 hook, as shown at the lower left.

This increasing density of the hair toward the tip is one reason that shorter hairs are used to tie smaller flies – the mounting point on the hair is well down the shaft, into the hollower portion of the hair, which provides a certain degree of flare and buoyancy.

a few turns toward the rear of the hook; release the tips and check them again. By repeating this process of wrapping a few turns and checking the flare until you reach the hair tips, you can get a good idea of the tying properties of the hair throughout its length and use the material for the appropriate purposes.

There is another approach to the problem of the varying hollowness within the shaft of the deer hair itself. Al Beatty, a tyer well-known for his hair-wing and tail techniques, has offered a most interesting observation about the increasing density of deer hair from base to tip in relation to its coloration. If you inspect a single deer hair, you will see a black tip followed by a cream-colored band; below the cream band, the deer hair becomes dark gray, and finally light gray. Beatty notes that if more than half of the hair shaft is dark gray, then the material is suitable for wings and tails; that is, the dark gray indicates the portion of the hair that is becoming more dense, less hollow, and thus less apt to flare. By contrast, the greater the length of hair that is light gray in color, the more likely it is to flare fully and readily, making a poor wing material but a good one for spun bodies. This rule of thumb, in our experience, is not entirely reliable, as some hair, such as that found on certain parts of the Florida whitetail, contains virtually no dark gray coloration, yet it does not flare particularly well. Still, in a large number of cases, Beatty's guideline holds and can provide important information when visually inspecting the hair.

Finally, when it comes to selecting an individual patch of hair used primarily for

Al Beatty's method of selecting hair relies on the color of the fiber. The sample of deer hair shown on the left has a long portion of dark gray fiber; when bound to the hook shank, it exhibits only a moderate flare and is useful for wings, as shown on the fly at the left.

The hair on the right exhibits a long section of light gray fiber; when bound to the hook shank, it will flare readily, as shown on the fly at the right.

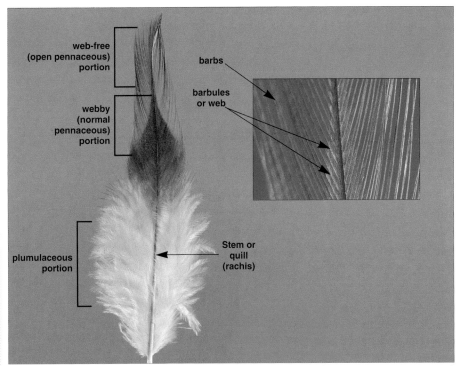

The parts of a typical feather are identified here by both the common names used in tying, and the scientific terms in parentheses.

winging and tailing, look for that which shows no broken tips, since intact tips will give the best results. In hair for flaring and spinning, this is far less crucial, since the tips are ultimately trimmed away, and on certain types of hair, broken tips are difficult to avoid. Elk rump and caribou frequently have broken tips, and antelope, which is quite brittle, is almost never found with intact tips. Second, look for hair that is straight; it will stack more easily and produce a more regular shape when dressed on the hook. (Waviness in hair is perfectly acceptable, usually indicating a winterkilled deer.) Some short hairs, especially hock, show a natural curvature, but provided it isn't excessive, this poses little problem. Third, if possible, look for hollow hair that has a minimum of underfur. The quantity varies widely with the species or individual animal, time of harvest, and location of hair on the hide. While underfur has nothing to do with the actual performance of the hollow hair, an excessive quantity of underfur, especially if it is long, can be laborious to remove. Lastly, there is some disagreement among experts about the effect of tanning on the quality of hollow hair. Chris Helm maintains that tanning can damage the hair; others claim that proper tanning procedures have no effect. A tyer inclined to play it safe might go with untanned if all other quality factors were equal.

Feathers

Like furs and hairs, feathers have an enormously broad range of tying applications and can be used to dress nearly every part of a fly. As tyers know, feathers vary significantly in appearance and tying characteristics, depending on the species of bird or part of the body from which the feather is taken. Still, there are enough anatomical similarities to make a brief look at feather structure helpful in both clarifying terms and understanding the tying characteristics of various feather types.

The photo above right shows a typical feather – this one taken from the body of a rooster.

The central feature of the feather is a semi-rigid structure known to anatomists as the "rachis," but more commonly among tyers as the "quill." In this book, we generally use the term "stem," primarily to minimize confusion and distinguish the stem from other uses of "quill" in fly tying – a wing quill or peacock quill, for example. Stems vary widely in thickness, taper, and particularly in cross-sectional shape, which explains why some feathers, particularly among the hackles, wrap in an orderly manner, while others tend to twist, roll, or lean; the cross-sectional stem shape prevents certain feathers from lying against the hook shank in the orientation desired by the tyer.

The particular type of feather shown in the photo above is a "pennaceous" feather, a category of feather commonly used in fly dressing. It consists generally of two portions. The "plumulaceous" portion is defined by the fluff near the base of the stem, and these fluffy fibers are called "plumulaceous" barbs; in certain types of feathers such as ostrich plumes, peacock tails, and sometimes marabou feathers – where these plumula-

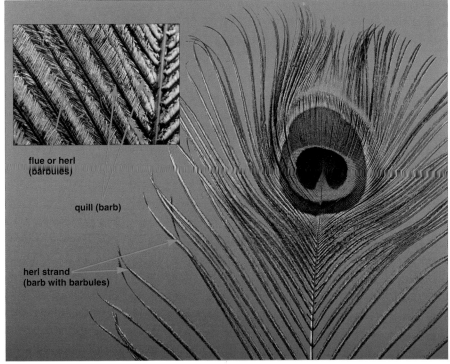

The parts of this peacock eye feather are identified using both common tying terms and anatomical ones.

ceous barbs are long and distinct – they are often termed "herl" by tyers.

The "pennaceous" portion of the feather lies above the fluff on the stem and generally forms the visible, sheathlike covering of plumage on the body and wings of the bird. It is the portion of the feather most commonly used in tying and is composed of two rows of parallel fibers called "pennaceous barbs," or among tyers, simply "barbs." Collectively, the barbs on one side of the stem are called a "vane," and in most feathers, the two vanes are symmetrical.

Projecting from both sides of most barbs are tiny hairlike structures called "barbules," shown on the inset photo. On the vane of the feather, these barbules often interlock, holding the barbs in a smooth, flat, panel-like shape. The portion of the feather on which the barbs interlock is termed by anatomists the "normal pennaceous portion," and among tyers the "webby" portion, particularly in reference to a body or hackle feather. Some barbs, or portions of barbs, lack these hairlike barbules and do not interlock; sections of these barbs are called the "open pennaceous portion" of the feather, or to tyers, the "web-free" area, and it is perhaps most observable in high-grade genetic rooster hackle, which is bred to be predominantly open pennaceous or web-free.

Though peacock and ostrich feathers look very different from the body feather shown above, the same structures are present. However, tyers often use a slightly different vocabulary to describe them.

The particular configuration and characteristics of these parts on a feather – stems, barbs, and barbules – determine its fly-tying uses and suitability.

Hackle

Hackle feathers of all types, whether dry- or wet-fly quality, from domestic or imported sources, can show considerable variation in quality. But the main emphasis of this section falls on dry-fly hackle, primarily because of the importance of these feathers in the performance of a finished fly and the often considerable expense of obtaining them. Dry fly hackle is found on roosters, and apart from pre-packaged feathers (a rather expensive alternative) and strung feathers (usually of inferior quality), hackle comes to the tyer in 2 forms – capes and saddles. Hackle capes are the skinned neck and shoulders of the bird, and indeed are called "necks." Capes are a particularly convenient format for the tyer, since the feathers are arranged from the very smallest sizes at the tip to the very largest sizes at the butt. Feathers of like sizes grow adjacent to one another on the skin in crosswise "bands," which simplifies selecting several hackles of the same size.

The "saddle" comes from the back of the bird and usually contains a smaller number of much longer feathers, and a smaller proportion of the total number of saddle feathers are of dry-fly quality. Even top-grade dry-fly saddles contain a significant number of very long, heavily webbed feathers called "schlappen," that are completely unsuited to dry

flies. (They do, however, make superior wet-fly hackle, particularly on palmered patterns, as very long, fully webbed feathers can in fact be difficult to obtain.) Decades ago, saddle hackles were commonly regarded as a second-rate dry-fly material, but breeding efforts over the past 20 years or so have produced saddle feathers that are now often superior to cape feathers. For a given feather size, saddle hackles often have greater barb density, thinner stems, and longer useable lengths – important hackle characteristics discussed below – than do cape feathers.

In the matter of hackle selection, one of the most basic distinctions to be drawn – aside from the division between dry-fly hackle and wet-fly hackle – is that between "genetic hackle," which is bred domestically for specific use in fly tying, and hackle which, quite simply, is not. Into this latter category fall capes and saddles labeled as "Indian," "Chinese," or perhaps most often, "Imported." These capes and saddles are physically smaller than the genetic variety, contain fewer and shorter feathers, offer a smaller range of feather sizes, and are available in a more limited selection of colors. A small percentage of imported capes are in fact of good dry-fly quality, but the days when fly shops bought capes by the bale, and a tyer could pick through the lot searching for one of superior quality, are pretty much a thing of the past. Thanks, in fact, to the quality standards brought to the market by genetic hackle, most retailers are familiar enough with evaluating hackle that a prime imported neck will rarely escape notice and will be priced accordingly. Even so, imported capes and saddles cost significantly less than genetic stock and do appeal for that reason. But in most cases, the hackles are so short that two feathers are quite often needed under circumstances that require only a single genetic feather, and in this respect, the "economy" can be a false one. In fact, many fly shops no longer offer imported dry-fly necks as an alternative, and in this they merely reflect the fact that most tyers prefer to use genetic hackle, regardless of the price tag; the quality is higher and more consistent, the range of colors wider, and the feathers themselves easier to tie.

Imported hen capes and saddles for wet-flies show many of the same drawbacks as

Shown here are various types of rooster hackle. From left to right, they are: a genetic cape, an imported cape, a genetic saddle patch, and an imported saddle patch. Notice the greater size and feather count on the genetic varieties.

Shown here are various types of hen hackle. From left to right, they are: a genetic cape, an imported cape, a genetic saddle patch, and an imported saddle patch. Again, the genetic types have a greater size and quantity of feathers.

the dry-fly material – such as small size, low feather count, and short feathers – but in general they are more satisfactory than imported dry-fly material, primarily because of the less stringent demands placed upon feathers used in subsurface patterns. In almost all regards, genetic hen capes and saddles are superior, but many tyers find that the additional price commanded by these prime feathers is not justified by the difference they yield in the finished fly. As a result, imported wet-fly material, particularly hen saddles, are widely available in fly shops and are useful not only for hackle, but for feather-tip wings, wing cases, legs, and a variety of other purposes.

When it comes to choosing capes and saddles, there are really two sets of criteria to bear in mind: one that pertains to the quality of individual feathers, and one that refers to the quality of capes and saddles as a collection of feathers. Tyers who use genetic hackle may feel that assessing the quality of feathers, capes, and saddles is relatively unimportant, since the breeder has already graded the material and since most genetic hackle is of at least reasonably good quality. Nonetheless, there are good reasons for evaluating the hackle you buy and use. First, chickens are not manufactured by machine, and as living organisms they do differ, partly from genetics and partly from rearing. Second, as explained below, breeder grading can be deceptive; there are several criteria that determine the quality of feathers, capes, and saddles, and in grading, different breeders may have different priorities among these criteria. One, for instance, may place a high value on useable feather length and manage his flock with that in mind. Another may regard feather length as far less important than thin-stemmed feathers or uniform color. This oversimplifies the case somewhat, but the fact remains that all capes of the same grade do not contain feathers with the same characteristics. Neither of these breeder is "right" or "wrong," and the object in evaluating hackle is to end up with feathers that meet your own highest priorities.

Feather Characteristics

The primary purpose of dry-fly hackle is to float, or assist in floating, the fly; it may have as well some imitative functions, but these are largely secondary matters. Strictly speaking, hackle doesn't "float" a fly since the material itself isn't particularly buoyant. Rather, it supports the fly on the surface of the water. Thus the hackle, whether collar or parachute style, primarily serves a structural purpose in the dressing, and the qualities that distinguish a good hackle feather from a poor one are themselves structural matters.

Of primary consideration in selecting dry-fly hackle is the stiffness (sometimes called "hardness") of the feather. One significant measure of stiffness is the amount of "web" on the feather – as noted earlier, a minimum of web in the portion of the feather that will actually be dressed on the fly – usually the upper ½ of a neck feather and the upper ½ to ⅔ of a saddle feather.

In hen feathers for wet-fly hackling, precisely the opposite is true – the more heavily webbed, the better, and premium feathers have web that extends right to the tips of the barbs. Such barbs absorb water readily, are quite soft, and have good movement underwater. Though occasionally found on hen necks, feathers of this type are seen more often on hen saddles.

hackled less heavily than dry flies; fewer wraps are needed and a shorter useable length poses no real difficulties. The one exception is in palmer hackles on wet flies or streamers; heavily webbed feathers with long sweet spots are rare in smaller sizes.

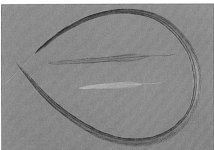

Notice the difference in useable length among these 3 types of rooster hackles. The cream hackle at the bottom is from an imported cape and has about half the useable length of the brown genetic rooster neck hackle above it.

The long dun feather encircling the other two is from a Hoffman rooster saddle. It has 6 or 7 times the useable length of even a top-quality genetic neck feather.

The pair of feathers at the left are rooster neck hackles. The feather at the extreme left is a prime dry-fly hackle, showing very little web. Next to it is a rooster hackle that has an unacceptable amount of web, visible as a black band along the feather stem; this would make a poor dry-fly hackle.

The next pair of feathers are hen neck feathers. The black one at the top is webbed only near the stem; the barb tips are web-free, making this a poor feather for wet-fly hackle. The dark, shadowlike, webby portion could, however, be used to make cut or burned feather-tip wings. The gray feather beneath it is a prime hen hackle; notice the web that extends right to the tips of the barbs, making this an excellent feather for hackling or winging.

The next two feathers are rooster saddles. Both contain too much web to make good dry-fly hackle, but could be used for palmer hackling wet flies and streamers.

The badger hackle, third from the right, is like many rooster saddle feathers – wide, with some web, and a springy stem. Many tyers prefer this type of hackle for feather-tip streamer wings.

The feather second from the right is a versatile, fully webbed hen saddle. It is long enough to be palmered; it can be wrapped collar style; and it is especially useful for tying Matuka-type streamer wings.

The feather at the extreme right is a schlappen. It is long enough for palmer hackling even the longest fly bodies and can be used as well to make streamer wings with a dense appearance and sharp silhouette.

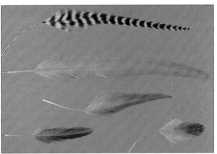

There are differences in useable length among wet-fly hackles as well. The grizzly feather at the top is the type of heavily webbed hackle found on even top-grade rooster saddles. The length makes this excellent for palmering subsurface patterns such as Woolly Buggers.

The gray feather is a schlappen, which offers perhaps the longest useable length of any wet-fly feather; the barbs, however, are typically sized for larger flies.

The green feather is a rooster saddle that is often sold as strung hackle. It has just enough length to palmer a fly.

Hen necks and saddles yield the shortest feathers. The neck feather at the lower left and the saddle feather at the lower right are excellent for collar hackling, but too short to palmer.

term used to describe the small barbules located on the sides of the barbs. It appears as a tapering, shadowlike band on either side of the feather stem. Webbing is undesirable on dry-fly hackle for a couple of reasons. First, webby barbs are usually less stiff than web-free ones and will bend or collapse under the weight of the fly, giving at best poor support. Second, web absorbs water and in fact may transfer it through capillary action to other barbs or even fly components that are not actually in contact with the water. Absorbed water adds weight to the fly, making greater structural demands on the hackle; moreover, fly components that have become wet more easily break the surface tension that in part supports the fly. Virtually every hackle feather contains some web, and a small amount is certainly tolerable. The primary concern is in selecting hackle with a

A second criterion related to webbiness is "useable length." Each dry-fly feather has a section of barbs along the stem that are relatively web-free and are consistent in length – a section that Dick Talleur calls the "sweet spot." Barbs below this section are too long or webby to incorporate into the fly, while those above it are too short or sparsely distributed. This section of feather is suited for hackling, and as a rule, feathers with a longer useable length are more convenient and more economical for the tyer since an adequate number of hackle wraps may be obtained from a single feather rather than mounting and wrapping two feathers with shorter sweet spots. Longer feathers are necessary as well for palmer hackling.

Hen hackle, especially genetic types, tends to have a much shorter useable length than rooster hackle, but wet flies are generally

A feather characteristic often overlooked by tyers deals with specific properties of the barbs – their thickness, shape, straightness, and uniformity. The diameter of feather barbs can vary considerably from one neck or saddle to another. Very thin barbs simply do not possess the stiffness or strength of thicker ones and poorly support a fly. To provide adequate aggregate stiffness in the hackle, more of these thin barbs are required, which means more wraps of hackle and greater bulk in the fly, and it may necessitate using two hackles instead of one. Barbs that are thick at the base but taper to very fine, hairlike tips have essentially the same problem. The best barbs are thick, relatively uniform in diameter throughout their length, and taper abruptly to a point. Such characteristics in hackle barbs are difficult to see, and a small hand magnifier is especially useful in assessing them.

More easily observed is the straightness of the barbs. Many feathers are slightly "cupped" from front to back; the front side of the feather is slightly convex and the rear slightly concave. A small degree of cupping does no harm at all, but severely cupped feathers can tie poorly. The same is true with barbs that arc toward the tip. In all hackle feathers, of course, the barbs *lean* toward the tip, but some barbs actually *curve* in that direction, and in our experience, such feathers are much more apt to twist or roll during tying.

Finally, the barbs on both sides of the feather stem must be of equal length. Uneven barb length is not terribly common, but it does occur from time to time, particularly with saddle feathers, with feathers from the sides of a cape, and with very small neck feathers, usually about #20 and smaller.

The tyer should take note of the barb density or barb count of the feather – that is, how many barbs grow on a given length of stem, say, an inch. It's not practical to count the barbs, but you can get a reasonable sense of the barb density by observing how close together the barbs grow from the feather stem. A high-density feather will put more barbs beneath the hook with each turn of hackle, thus providing better support and floatation. Conversely, if the barb density is low, each wrap of hackle distributes a relatively small number of barbs around the hook shank. Even if the barbs themselves are of good quality, extra wraps of hackle are required to produce adequate support for the fly. Again, weight and bulk are added, and two hackle feathers may be necessary to dress the fly. On most feathers, in fact, barb density varies – it is greater nearer the butt of the feather and lower near the tip. Provided that web or stem thickness, as discussed below, does not become a problem, the tyer is better off taking more wraps from the butt end of the feather than trying to squeeze a few more turns from the tip.

Wet-fly feathers vary in barb density as well, and a high barb-count is always desirable. But since wet-fly hackle is generally applied more sparsely, low barb density is a relatively minor matter.

Again, a hand magnifier is useful in evaluating barb density, especially since webby hackle will appear to the unaided eye as denser than it really is.

A final, and significant, consideration in choosing hackle – stem thickness – really has less to do with the performance of the finished fly on or in the water than with accommodating the tyer. Thin-stemmed feathers are far easier to wrap than thick-stemmed ones and show less tendency to twist or lean. They allow the tyer to place the turns of hackle closer together for a more densely hackled fly with fewer wraps of the feather.

By observing the preened barbs at the base of these feathers, you can see that the dry-fly hackle at the left has barbs growing closer together than the feather next to it; the greater barb density makes this a prime feather.

The hen hackle, second from the right, shows a similar density in the barb count as compared to the feather at the extreme right. Again, this grizzly feather will lay more barbs around the hook shank for each turn of the feather.

To put it all together, the best dry-fly hackle feathers have thick, stiff, web-free barbs growing densely along a thin feather stem. Most of the genetic hackle necks available today are at least satisfactory in these regards, and often very good. But the feathers that come closest to fulfilling the ideal are more often found on high-quality saddles. For a given hackle size – say, #12 – a top-quality saddle feather will have a higher barb count, a longer useable length, and a thinner stem than a top-grade neck feather. However, while the quality of individual saddle feathers may exceed that of neck feathers, saddles have other limitations.

First, they contain relatively few useable feathers when compared to a neck, though in most instances they are priced proportionately lower. Second, they offer a limited range of sizes; saddles typically contain feathers that will dress 2 or 3 different hook sizes, as compared to a neck which may dress 8 or 10 sizes. And finally, the feathers on most saddles are suitable for dressing dry flies approximately in the #8 to #12 range – useful for larger imitations or bigger attractor flies, but not particularly helpful for smaller patterns. There are, of course, exceptions to this last point, most notably the Hoffman saddles from Whiting Farms. These saddles contain feathers in much smaller sizes, from about #14 to as small as #20, with useable feather length that runs as high as 10 inches.

For most tyers, though, the decision to purchase either a cape or a saddle is, in the end, less a question of feather quality than of individual use. Tyers who will be dressing flies through a broad range of hook sizes will probably find that a neck will give them the best value, since most of the feathers can be used. Those who tie heavily in a restricted range of sizes, either #8 to #12 or #14, or #14 to #18 or #20, may find better value in a saddle, since many of the feathers on a neck would go unused.

Cape and Saddle Quality

Feather quality is, of course, the primary determinant in choosing a cape or a saddle,

but there are other considerations that pertain to the cape or saddle as a collection of feathers. Foremost among these is a high feather count – the number of hackles a neck or saddle actually contains – and particularly a high count in the sizes the tyer has most need of. Unfortunately, the physical dimensions of a neck or saddle do not always indicate the number of feathers it contains. The skin that holds the feathers is sometimes stretched during processing so that even a sparsely feathered neck can appear large in size. A better method for assessing feather count, at least when comparing two necks or saddles, is to turn them over and take note of the small bumps on the skin. Each of these bumps is the base of a feather, and while it's certainly impractical to count them, you can compare the general density of the bumps and gain some sense of how the relative feather counts stack up.

The skin side of this rooster cape shows small "bumps," each of which represents a hackle feather. These bumps can give you an idea, when comparing necks, of the relative feather count.

There is one important qualification about feather count: it is useful only in comparing capes or saddles of the same type, that is, two genetic capes, two imported necks, two saddle patches. While evaluating feather count will give an approximate sense of the number of useable hackles, it does not always give an indication of the number of flies that those feathers will tie – and that, of course, is the tyer's chief concern. For example, a good-quality genetic rooster cape should contain anywhere from roughly 600-800 useable feathers; for average dry-fly purposes, this neck should tie an equivalent number of flies, since most genetic feathers are long enough to produce the required number of hackle wraps. An imported number of neck will typically contain about half the number of feathers, let us say 400, but typically these feathers are so short that two of them are required for the same number of hackle wraps produced by a single genetic feather. Such a neck will tie about 200 flies. With saddle hackles, particularly the Hoffman variety, the situation is reversed. A saddle patch may contain only 150 useable feathers, but on a good-quality patch, many of them will be long enough to hackle two or more flies. (Many Hoffman saddle feathers will dress 4-8 flies.) Thus feather count is only a relative indicator, best used in comparing hackle of similar types from similar sources.

Some information about feather count can be gleaned as well by gently squeezing the neck or saddle from back to front. A heavily feathered patch will feel thick and cushiony rather than thin and flat.

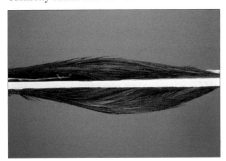

Some indication of the number of feathers on a neck can be obtained by assessing its thickness. The neck at the top is rather thin, and contains fewer feathers than the full, cushiony neck at the bottom.

Genetic necks are sorted by the breeder into grades #1 through #3, and some useful information can be gained from these numbers. A few of the grading criteria, such as feather count, pertain to the neck or saddle as a whole, but more often the numbers reflect the characteristics of the individual feathers – stiffness, barb density, length, and so on – and as such are important indicators of quality. From the tying standpoint, however, other criteria are less significant. Many breeders (like many tyers) put a premium on the color of the cape or saddle, its shade, consistency, and the absence of "splashing" – slight variations of color usually at or near the feather base. Similarly, a neck earns high marks if it contains no "chipped" feathers, those with broken tips, or no pinfeathers. In short, a grade #1 cape or saddle is as perfect as they come.

But precise color and color consistency tend to be a much overrated factor in hackle selection. And chipped or splashed feathers tie up as well as perfect ones, and even pinfeathers, provided they are not excessive in number, pose no problem. A neck that has been downgraded to a #2 or #3 for these "flaws" can be an excellent value for the tyer.

Tailing Barbs

Hackle barbs are frequently used for tailing flies. Selecting tailing material for subsurface patterns is rarely a problem, as the webby barbs used to tail such patterns are abundant and serve no structural purpose on the fly. Dry-fly tails are a different matter since the tailing fibers assist in floatation. As a rule, those criteria that govern barb quality on feathers used for dry-fly hackle apply equally to tailing barbs. Stiff, glossy, web-free fibers with no hooks or curves provide the maximum support for the fly with a minimum of bulk, and in this regard, thicker barbs are more useful, particularly on larger flies. With smaller, lighter hooks, somewhat thinner barbs are at least satisfactory, and generally, the larger hackles on a neck or saddle will provide tailing barbs for flies in sizes 16 and smaller.

One of the unfortunate consequences of

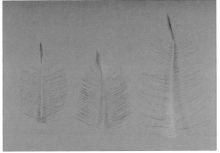

The feather on the left is well suited for tailing; notice the straight, thick, web-free barbs. The feather in the middle has barbs that curve toward the feather tip; when they are consolidated into a bundle for tailing, these barbs curve in different directions, and forming a neat tail is difficult. The feather on the right has very thin, hairlike tips, many of which show "hooks" at the end; such barbs give poor support to a fly.

modern hackle breeding is that the general drive for short hackle barbs has made the long, thick, stiff barbs suitable for tailing larger flies difficult to come by. Even the largest feathers on a neck, and often on a saddle, rarely provide much suitable material, since these feathers tend to be more heavily webbed. Thus, in selecting necks, some tyers place a high value on the presence of "spade" hackle – the very short, abruptly tapering feathers at the shoulders of the cape.

The curved lines here show the location of spade hackle when it is present on a cape.

Good spade feathers are typically rather short, but they have long, stiff, web-free barbs and make excellent dry-fly tailing material.

The feather on the left is a spade hackle as it appears on the neck. The spade on the right shows the barbs preened outward; while the feather itself is rather short, the barbs are long, thick, and web-free – excellent tail material.

Not all necks possess spade in the same quantity; a single neck may not have an equal quantity of spade on each shoulder;

and some have no spade hackle at all. And again, modern breeding has somewhat reduced the size of spade feathers as well. Still, spade feathers are the most readily available source of good tailing barbs, and in selecting a neck it is worth assessing the quality, quantity, and size of the spade feathers when comparing capes. Many tyers pluck and bag the spade hackle separately to have the material ready at hand. When tailing a dry fly, it's best to use the shortest hackle barbs that will do the job. To tail a #16 fly with barbs long enough for a #12 is a waste of the long, stiff material that can be hard to come by.

Wing Feathers

The wing feathers used for trout flies typically come from waterfowl, particularly ducks, though feathers from other birds are sometimes employed. Starling feathers are occasionally used, as are those from game birds such as pheasant and grouse, which have attractively marked wing feathers; all of these feathers can be small, however, and are best reserved for smaller patterns. Shoulder feathers from geese and swans are used for married wings on larger patterns, but as a rule, the larger wing feathers are too coarse for winging flies in typical trout sizes.

A bird wing contains many types of feathers; for our purposes, and as shown on the accompanying photograph, the wing feathers can be divided into two major categories – the flight feathers and the wing coverts. We are concerned here primarily with the flight feathers, which are commonly used for tying quill wings. On some birds, covert feathers may be suitable for this purpose, and these instances are noted below.

Like the body feather pictured on page 5, a flight feather has a stem with barbs projecting outward from either side. The first few primaries at the wing tip are interesting in this regard, since the vanes on either side of the quill are highly asymmetrical. On one side of the stem is the "quill" portion of the feather, used to tie wings, and on the other side are the "biots," which are quite different in texture and shape. These wide, flat, tightly overlapping barbs add rigidity to the leading edge of the feather and prevent it from twisting when the bird is in flight. As shown in the second photo on pg. 10, the underside of the primaries shows a glossy sheen or glaze on a portion of the feather next to the stem. This "ventral ridge," as it is termed, is formed from thick barb bases. The flight feathers on some birds have very small ventral ridges, or none at all, but they are generally pronounced in waterfowl and are related to the need for rigidity or flex in various parts of the airfoil. From the tyer's standpoint, the ventral ridge is a pithy, spongy section of the vane, unsuited to making wings. When cutting sections of barbs for winging, you can include this spongy base to help you hold and manipulate the material, but it should not actually be incorporated into the finished wing, as it tends to split easily.

Wing feathers have somewhat specialized barbules. They are longer and more

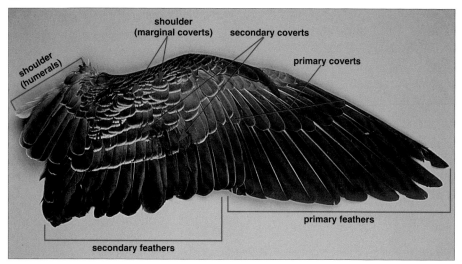

Like a human arm, a bird wing consists of three jointed sections, which correspond in human anatomy to the upper arm, the forearm, and the hand (which on a bird are the bones of the wing tip). These last two sections, the wing tip and the forearm, contain most of the feathers used to tie quill wings. The rearmost feathers attached to the wing tip, which are the longest on the wing, are called by both anatomists and fly tyers "primary feathers," though occasionally tyers distinguish between a "pointer," which is the very tip feather, and the remaining primaries. The rearmost feathers on the forearm section are called "secondary feathers." Collectively, the primaries and secondaries are termed "flight feathers," and they are partially covered, on both the top and bottom of the wing, with successive, overlapping rows of smaller feathers called "coverts."

The glossy ventral ridge shown on this first primary feather, or "pointer," is unsuited to tying. Note how it limits the useable material in the narrow, upper half of the feather.

highly developed than those on body feathers and account for the interesting characteristic that every tyer has probably observed in wing feathers – the ability to separate the barbs and rejoin them again into a smooth, seamless vane. To some extent, this is characteristic of all pennaceous barbs, but it's more pronounced and visible on wing feathers because the barbules and hooklets are more specifically shaped for the purpose. Tyers take advantage of this ability to separate and rejoin wing-feather barbs to form married wings, using strips of different colored barbs from different birds to form a single, multicolored segment of barbs for winging. (More details about feathers for married wings can be found in **Method #41: Married Quill Wings**, p. 288.)

Both primaries and secondaries can be used to make quill wings. The primaries, excluding the feather or two at the very wing tip, are generally considered the most desirable. The tip feathers tend to be somewhat coarse, and because of the abrupt narrowing of the vane, may contain relatively little useable material. The inner primaries, however,

are more regularly shaped, with more useable material, and less likely to show torn or ragged edges.

Secondary feathers can make very good winging material, but they are somewhat less reliable. They often have barbs that curve very noticeably toward the feather tip, and a section of these barbs may produce a wing that seems narrow, with a long, sweeping taper at the tip and an excessively pointed appearance. Secondary feathers may also be severely curved or "cupped" from front to back. In many cases, though, the secondaries make quite acceptable material. The barb texture is usually finer than that of primary feathers, making secondaries useful for a wider range of hook sizes. Moreover, the vanes on the secondaries (and sometimes covert feathers) are often quite symmetrical, and an especially well-formed secondary may have vanes so uniform that a pair of wings can be cut from a single feather – one wing from each side of the stem – rather than using a pair of feathers from opposing wings, as is normally the case.

Finally, some coverts may be suitable for

On this pair of secondary feathers, note the curve of the barbs toward the tip of the feather, which can produce excessively pointed wings on a fly, but note the greater symmetry overall and the very small ventral ridge.

making quill wings, though this depends largely upon the individual bird. Wing coverts are arranged in rows on both the top and underside of the wing. The row nearest the trailing edge of the wing contains the largest feathers; they decrease in size as the rows of coverts get closer to the leading edge. On a duck, coverts in this rearmost row may be the only ones large enough for winging a fly, and even then, they may be restricted to very small patterns. On a larger bird, such as a goose, the wing coverts may in fact be the only feathers suitable for winging trout flies, since the large flight feathers are rather coarsely textured. Where primaries and secondaries are curved from front to back, and a pair of dry-fly wings formed from sections of these feathers will flare away from one another to form two distinct wings, covert feathers are rather flat. Conventional quill dry-fly wings formed from these wings will show little outward flare. However, provided they are large enough, covert feathers can make excellent wet-fly wings and side-mounted quill wings of the type used on No-Hackle Duns; in these cases, curvature is relatively unimportant.

It is necessary that quill wings be tied from opposing feathers, that is, one from the

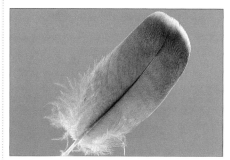

Notice the symmetry on this large covert feather. Two wings can be cut from this single feather, one from each side of the stem.

left wing and one from the right. A pair of quill segments from the same wing will not provide the opposing curvature that produces a divided wing silhouette. If one segment is reversed to provide this opposing curvature, the wings will not be uniform in appearance – one wing will point forward, the other rearward. The exceptions here, as noted above, are with some secondary and covert feathers, which are sometimes sufficiently symmetrical to furnish both wing segments from the same feather.

The two feathers used for winging a fly should be matched as closely as possible in size, texture, degree of curvature, and color, and the best way to achieve this match is to select feathers from the same bird – one from each wing, from the same relative position. That is, the second primary feather from one wing is paired with the second primary from the other, the fourth left secondary with the fourth right secondary, and so on. Mating feathers like this is a simple matter if whole wings are used. If purchasing individual pairs of feathers, inspect them to ensure that they are properly matched. Finally, feathers used for quill wings should have a clean, smooth outer edge. If the barb ends are frayed, tattered, or broken, the wing will not produce a sharp, pleasing silhouette.

Marabou

Most tyers know that the material called "marabou" does not come from the (now prohibited) marabou stork, but rather from turkeys. Some smaller marabou feathers, particularly "grizzly marabou," and feathers marketed under the name "Chickabou" are obtained from chickens.

Anatomists term these marabou-like feathers "semiplumes," and despite their downy appearance, they are not true down feathers, which are often sparsely barbed and seldom used by tyers. Semiplumes are characterized by long, thin, flexible barbs, and in the case of marabou, unusually long barbules, that give both the barbs and the feathers a frondlike appearance. Moreover, these plumulaceous barbules lack hooklets, and do not interlock like the barbs on flight feathers; rather, the barbs look and feel fluffy.

Marabou is sold to tyers in two forms: long feathers, 4" to 7", with stout, rigid stems, called "plumes"; and much shorter

The feather on the left is a marabou plume; at the right is a shorter blood feather.

feathers, 1" to 3", with thinner, flexible stems, called "bloods" or "shorts."

Marabou plumes are more difficult to work with (and some tyers refuse to use them at all) because the barbs must be cut from the stem and consolidated into a bundle before they are tied on the shank. Typically, 2 or 3 such bundles are required. Moreover, barbs on a plume are often of uneven length and can produce a ragged trailing edge on a tail or wing, though the tips can be trimmed or broken to a more uniform length. However, the barbs on plumes have a couple of characteristics that some tyers find desirable. On high-grade plumes, the barbs are unusually fluffy, owing to extremely long barbules, and some tyers think that tails and wings formed from these barbs are livelier in the water and give the impression of greater bulk. Second, the barbs tend to be broad at the base, and a bundle of such barbs is slightly rigid at the butt end, which can help the wing or tail hold its shape.

Blood feathers are more convenient to use because it is not necessary to remove the barbs from the much thinner stem. The tip of the stem may be trimmed away, but usually, the short barbs at the base of the stem are stripped away, and the remainder are simply

preened toward the feather tip. Because the barbs are of very nearly equal length, a neat bundle is easily formed in this way, and the entire feather is tied to the shank; as with plume barbs, however, two or more bundles are sometimes required. The drawback to blood feathers is that the barbules are often short, sometimes almost threadlike at the tip of the barb (a problem also seen in lower-quality plumes), and thus the impression of bulk and liveliness is reduced. Still, their tying convenience makes marabou bloods the more popular of the two feather types. Occasionally, one finds blood feathers with extremely long, fluffy barbules that resemble those found on top-grade plumes. This is prime material; unfortunately, locating it is largely a matter of luck since suppliers rarely grade marabou.

When selecting marabou, either bloods or plumes, look for the fullest feathers with dense, long barbules extending to the very tip of the barb. When selecting blood feathers, look for those that have thin stems as well, since these create less bulk on the hook shank.

CDC

In a somewhat amusing inversion of vocabularies, the feathers found by the preen oil gland of a bird go by the somewhat exotic tying term "cul de canard," or "CDC," while avian anatomists simply call them "oil gland feathers." Regardless of their name, tyers prize them for the superior floatation that they give to a fly. Many birds have them, but those used in tying come from waterfowl, primarily ducks, which have an unusually large number of these feathers. CDC feathers are located on the skin surrounding the oil gland, and particularly around the ducts; oil collects on these feathers, where it is transferred easily to the bird's bill and then used to preen and waterproof other plumage. Indeed, on a live bird, those feathers nearest the oil ducts may be matted with oil and so saturated that they require cleaning before they are suitable for tying.

Despite their function in distributing preen oil, CDC feathers are not "impregnated" with oil, as is commonly claimed. Rather, it is the structure of the feather itself, particularly the barbules, that provide floatation. First, CDC barbules radiate from all sides of the barb – a bit like a bottle brush or palmered fly body. Second, the barbules have a flattened and corkscrewed shape, like a twisted ribbon. These characteristics promote floatation in two ways. The large number of long, twisted barbules greatly increases the surface area of the feather that is in contact with the water and supports the fly in the film. Second, the shape of the barbules traps air, preventing them from sinking; even if part of the feather becomes submerged, air bubbles clinging to the barbules provide buoyancy. When a bundle of CDC barbs is used to tie a wing, for instance, the effect is magnified, as the close proximity of the barbs produces an interlacing network of barbules, that further increases surface area and provides an even more effective matrix in which

to trap air bubbles. This tendency to trap air bubbles also makes CDC useful on subsurface patterns – particularly emergers, since nymphs and pupae often generate a bubble of gas to help them ascend to the surface.

CDC feathers are available in two forms. The most widely distributed is a semiplume, much like marabou but considerably smaller. Barb length varies considerably, and the barbs are often broken, presumably by the action of the bird's bill in gathering preen oil. The tips of such feathers can be tied as a bundle, or barbs can be stripped from the stem, consolidated, and tied as a clump. They can also be tied in as feather-tip wings, a style used in many of René Harrop's patterns.

The second type of CDC is a plumule, a downlike feather that has virtually no stem at all. These are marketed, appropriately, as "puffs." The barbs on a plumule are very nearly of equal length, though they tend to be short, and such a feather can be tied in at the base as a single tuft, requiring very little preparation. However, on both semiplumes and plumules, barb density is low and more than one feather is often required.

Finally, CDC should never be treated with a paste-type floatant, since it mats the barbules and destroys the unusual properties

The CDC feather on the left has a tip that is "squared off" and the stem is rather fine. The tip of this feather can be tied in as a wing; the barbs could also be stripped and bundled for winging material.

The feather in the middle is a short, tuft-like plume. All the barbs extend to the tip of the feather and the stem is quite fine; it can simply be tied in at the base for a wing.

The feather on the right has a rounded tip and a thicker stem. Tying in the tip of this feather for a wing would prove unsuitable, since the barbs at the tip are of unequal length; the best way to use this feather is to strip the barbs.

of the material. Some fishermen argue that no type of floatant at all – even natural preen oil – is necessary or desirable on CDC feathers.

Afterfeathers

Afterfeather is often incorrectly identified by fly tyers as "filoplume" (or "philoplume") or sometimes, a bit more accurately, as "aftershaft." The afterfeather is not actually a separate feather, but rather a projection branching from the lower stem on the underside of a larger feather, as shown in the accompanying photo.

Afterfeathers are a feature of many feathers on the body of the bird, and sometimes on the wing and tail feathers, though these

12

On the left is a pheasant body feather with the afterfeather attached. On the right is a detached afterfeather; the barbs have been preened outward to better show their short length and downy texture.

are often little more than a short tuft of very sparse barbs and not useful in tying.

Afterfeathers are fully plumulaceous, but vary widely in size and shape, depending upon the species of bird. Those most commonly used by tyers are the longer, narrow afterfeathers that consists of a stem (strictly speaking, this portion is the "aftershaft"), and short barbs covered entirely with very soft, fuzzy, non-interlocking barbules. A true mature filoplume, by contrast, is a hairlike feather almost completely lacking in barbs that, to our knowledge, has no fly-tying applications.

For most tyers, the preferred source of afterfeathers is the skin of the ring-necked pheasant, where they are attached to the base of body feathers. These afterfeathers tend be longer – about 1 ½" – than those found on other bird skins used in tying. The patches often sold as "game hen saddles" frequently contain a good quantity of afterfeathers as well, though these are generally shorter and hence of more limited use. Genetic capes and saddles, both rooster and hen, usually lack useable afterfeathers. When tying with any body feathers on the skin, it is always worth keeping an eye out for afterfeathers and setting them aside for use later.

The lower section of a hackle or body feather that contains very fluffy barbs – that is, the plumulaceous portion of the feather – can make an acceptable substitute for afterfeather in applications where the feather is not wrapped – as in tuft gills, for instance. The barbs, however, will probably need to be broken or trimmed to length, as they tend to be much longer than those found on afterfeathers.

Hooks

The hook is the foundation of the tyer's craft, the armature on which ideas take shape in feathers and fur. There are literally hundreds of different hook styles from different manufacturers, and a discussion of their individual uses, the advantages and drawbacks of different types, and the relative merits of different brands are beyond the scope of this book. Readers interested in information about hook styles, sizing, strength, and design rationales should consult the instructive and comprehensive treatments of the subject in the following works: Dick Stewart, *The Hook Book*; Darrel Martin, *Micropatterns* and *Fly-Tying Methods*; Dick

Talleur, *Mastering the Art of Fly Tying* and *The Versatile Fly Tyer*.

We are concerned here only with the basic anatomy of the hook, since its various parts are often used as reference points in sizing and mounting materials.

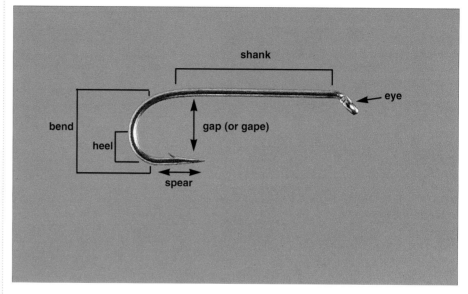

Adhesives

In recent years, adhesives have come to play a greater role in fly tying than was once the case, probably owing to the simple availability of a wide range of useful glues. Saltwater tyers in particular have devised a number of interesting glue techniques, though for the most part, this book does not cover silicone heads and bodies, mother-of-epoxy (MOE) methods, and hot-glue techniques, since these are not, at least at present, important in trout-fly tying.

Even so, there is still a significant range of tying adhesives, each with its particular virtues and uses. The adhesives described here are used in tying methods throughout the book. A few more specialized glues, restricted to only one tying technique, are described in the corresponding methods.

Head Cements

This category includes head cements sold for tying, lacquers, varnishes, and even fingernail polish, all of which can be thinned with readily available solvents. Of particular note are the newer water-based formulations, which dry to a waterproof finish. These, however, do take considerably longer to dry – a matter of hours as compared to minutes for most conventional cements. Head cements are generally best used as a sealant or finish for various parts of the fly, as their adhesive strength is not especially high. Still, as a light-duty glue, used for instance to secure a parachute hackle to a post, they are adequate.

Perhaps the most important property of head cement is its viscosity. Thinned cements are useful when penetration of the adhesive is desired – to secure the thread on a finished fly head, reinforce a quill body, and so forth. Thinned cements are often used during tying procedures, since they dry fairly quickly. Thicker cements, because they

penetrate poorly, are generally used where the build-up of finish is desired, such as forming a smooth, glossy head on a fly. Many tyers keep both types on hand to accommodate various needs.

Most head cements and lacquers can be thinned with lacquer thinner, and even thick cements require the occasional addition of solvent because the bottles, once open, are rarely airtight. Clear nail polish is soluble in acetone, though colored polishes may use a combination of solvents, and using a commercial nail-polish remover to thin them is the safest course. Dispensing the solvent with an eye dropper or a plastic syringe of the type available at hobby stores is the best way of ensuring control over viscosity. A small bottle of solvent at hand is always useful for cleaning up drips and removing glue from fingertips.

Epoxy

Epoxies have a somewhat limited use in trout-fly tying and are restricted primarily to finishing nymph cases on Poxyback nymphs, finishing some overbodies, forming very smooth, hard heads on flies, and gluing eyes, though they are certainly excellent for these purposes. Epoxy is quite viscous and penetrates poorly, but forms a very strong bond and a durable finish. Still, epoxy isn't particularly convenient, since it must be mixed; when a slow-curing variety is used on the head of the fly, the hook must be rotated continually to prevent the glue from dripping or sagging. Quick-setting epoxies do not require this rotation, but their short pot-life limits their use during actual tying. Resin, hardener, and mixed (but not dry) epoxy can be cleaned up with lacquer thinner or acetone.

Flexible Cement

Unlike head cements and epoxies, flexible cements remain pliable when dry. They are used primarily for reinforcing wingcases, overbodies, grasshopper wings, streamer eyes, and other components that may be too fragile in their natural state to survive rough treatment in the jaws of a trout. Their adhesive power is generally good, and viscous types can be used to glue doll eyes and shoulder/cheek assemblies for streamers.

There are quite a wide variety of flexible cements and a few are sold specifically for fly tying, including a water-based formula. These tend to be thinner cements, with better penetration. When used to reinforce a section of quill for a grasshopper, for example, they actually glue the barbs together as opposed to more viscous cements that tend to lay a coating over the material. They make a good head cement but may require thinning.

Pliobond is a medium viscosity adhesive that was once much favored among tyers, and it is still useful. It does not shrink much during drying, and feathers reinforced with this glue will not curl or wrinkle much. When dry, Pliobond is quite flexible and strong, though many tyers find it excessively gummy and harder to handle than other flexible cements. Moreover, when thickly applied, it can lend a faint amber cast to lighter-colored material, and the best solvent, methyl ethyl ketone, is more difficult to obtain than other solvents.

Silicone cement comes in tubes for sealing aquariums, plumbing fixtures, and so on, and it is useful for reinforcing fly components such as wingcases and overbodies, but it can be used to glue doll eyes and assemble cheeks and shoulders on streamers. Straight from the tube, silicone cements are quite viscous and form a strong, flexible, waterproof bond. The chief drawback is that silicone cements take a long time to dry; some types take 24 hours to cure fully. Drying time can be shortened by thinning the cement, and most silicone glues are soluble in acetone, though as always, it's best to check the label to determine what solvent is used in manufacturing. Thinning, however, does reduce the amount of actual adhesive applied, and two coats may be required.

Cements sold under the name Shoe Goop and Goo live up to their names; they are viscous and very sticky. But their adhesive properties are outstanding, and they're quite durable. For most uses, however, they require at least some thinning, and tuluol or acetone is generally the solvent.

Vinyl cements and sealers are among the most useful glues to the tyer. Like silicone glues, they are packaged in tubes, though they are generally not as viscous. They dry to a clear finish. Vinyl cements are slightly less flexible than silicone types when dry, and they can shrink slightly and curl feathers. Their chief virtues are a relatively short drying time, good adhesive strength, and simplicity of use. Most vinyl cements are soluble in acetone, and thinned, they make an excellent flexible reinforcement for nymph wingcases, hopper wings, and so forth.

Thick flexible glues that come in tubes can be made more widely useable by squeezing a tablespoon or two into a small glass jar; add a small amount of the appropriate solvent and shake until dissolved. Continue adding solvent a bit at a time and shaking until the desired viscosity is reached.

Cyanoacrylate (CA) Glue

Though many brands are available, one of the first on the market, Super Glue, has more or less conferred its name generically on the rest. CA glues offer superb adhesion and have a variety of applications, depending upon the viscosity used.

Liquid CA glue is extremely thin and penetrates well; it can be used in any application where thinned head cement would be employed. It dries clear, does not shrink, and is extremely hard, making it a good head cement, coating for quill and tinsel bodies, and so on. Liquid CA glue, however, does work best as an actual adhesive when there is a large contact area between the surfaces being joined. For added security in tying slippery downwings – those made from squirrel tail, for example – or securing a parachute hackle to a post, or other applications where fibers are drawn tightly into a bundle, its penetrating and adhesive qualities are virtually unmatched. Moreover, liquid CA glue dries very quickly. Its major drawback is packaging. Most types come in tubes, and precisely dispensing a controlled amount of glue is difficult. A partial, but not entirely satisfactory solution, is to squeeze the tube until a small droplet forms, then transfer the drop to a dubbing needle.

Gel-type CA glues are considerably more viscous and will form a strong bond even if the contact area between surfaces is small. The cement fills any gaps as it dries. It has a wide range of uses – securing parachute hackle, gluing underbodies, barbell and doll eyes, cementing the bases of stiff-fibered wings such as arc wings and upright hair wings, pre-assembling streamer cheeks and shoulders, finishing fly heads – just about anything. Though it is packaged in a tube, its greater viscosity makes dispensing it less troublesome. The major disadvantage with gel-type CA glue is the longer drying time. Both types of CA glue can be cleaned up with acetone.

Spray Fixative

Spray fixatives—Tuffilm is a common brand—are manufactured for artists and draftsman to protect drawings against smudging. For tyers, they are useful in reinforcing more delicate feathers that would mat and lose their shape if smeared with flexible cement. Quill wings are often treated in this way, and tyers will often spray an entire feather to be used for wingcases or grasshopper wings. The dried cement is slightly flexible, though not as pliable as other flexible cements, and the degree of reinforcement achieved with spray fixative is only moderate. When treating feathers, it's best to mist them lightly, a couple of times if necessary; spray fixatives are very thin, and applying it thickly causes the feathers to mat and the adhesive to drip. When forming streamer cheek/shoulder assemblies or gluing eyes to feathers, many tyers mist the feather components with spray fixative to provide a more uniform gluing surface and get a more reliable bond.

CHAPTER 2

Preparing Hooks

Preparing the hook for tying typically involves three procedures—debarbing, sharpening, and securing the hook in the vise.

De-barbing Hooks

The simplest and best solution to the problem of debarbing hooks is to avoid it altogether—that is, to use hooks manufactured without barbs. Such hooks have the strongest points, since the structural soundness of the wire is not compromised by the barb cut. Barbless hooks, however, are available in only a limited selection of styles and sizes and tend to be expensive—a fact that perplexes many tyers. In most hook making, the barb itself actually simplifies certain manufacturing operations, most notably forming the hook bend. Thus barbless hooks require alternate production techniques, which can make them more costly. Hence most tyers prefer to remove the barbs themselves.

Method #1:
Parallel De-barbing Pinch

Many tyers prefer this method because the hook "spear" (the straight portion between the point and bend) is fully supported by one jaw of the pliers, minimizing the risk of fracturing or breaking the hook. Moreover, the barb is forced both downward and toward the hook bend—a direction precisely opposite to that in which the barb was cut—and advocates believe that pressure of this type lays the barb down flattest (particularly on larger hooks) and produces the least stress on the hook spear.

This method, however, can be tricky with small hooks, which are difficult to handle and require a very fine-tipped pliers.

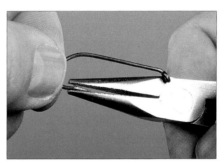

Step 1. Hold the hook by the bend and position the jaws of a pair of flat needle-nose pliers over the barb. Only the flat hook spear should make contact with the jaw face. Inserting the hook too far into the jaws may cause pressure to be applied to the hook bend, risking breakage.

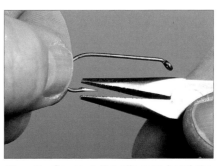

Step 2. Squeeze the pliers to bend the barb down. Use the lightest pressure that will still do the job. Most barbs will not bend completely flat, and excessive pressure can weaken the hook spear or point.

Method #2:
Perpendicular De-barbing Pinch

This is the most common technique, though the risk of breaking, or worse yet, fracturing a hook that may break later, is increased. And because the barb may break off or curl rather lay flat, the results are sometimes questionable. Where barbless hooks are required, some game officials will test a hook by pushing the spear through a piece of flannel. If it can be withdrawn without snagging, it is considered barbless. Hooks debarbed by the method described here may not always pass muster.

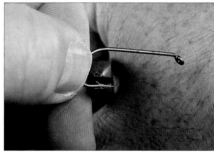

Step 1. Hold the hook by the bend, and position the plier jaws crosswise over the barb. Again, be careful—especially with small hooks—that the pliers do not contact any part of the bend. Pressure here can break the hook.

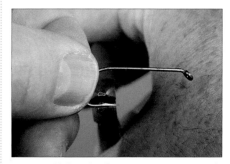

Step 2. Using the lightest pressure possible, mash the barb down. If the barb should break rather than bend, set the hook aside and file off the barb as described below.

Method #3:
Filing Barbs

Using a file to remove hook barbs has a couple of advantages. It exerts the least stress on the hook wire, which makes it particularly desirable for small hooks, and the barb can be completely removed, which gives the best hook penetration when fishing. Filing, however, is the slowest method of debarbing and is normally used on larger hooks.

Use a thin file that is tapered toward one or both edges to get sufficient working room in small hook gaps. Use a very sharp, fine-toothed file for small hooks to prevent catching the barb in the teeth; a coarser one will cut more quickly on larger hooks.

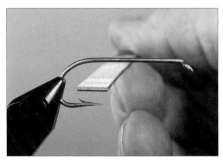

Step 1. Mount the hook in a vise, clamping it near the upper end of the bend. This position minimizes the possibility of nicking the vise jaws with the file.

Step 2. Remove the barb by stroking the file perpendicular to the hook shank, or with the file angled very slightly toward the bend. If you file toward the point, the barb will "stick" in the file teeth. If you angle the file too far toward the bend, it has a tendency to skate sideways. You can nick the bend and weaken the hook this way.

Sharpening Hooks

While virtually all fly tyers affirm the importance of sharpening hooks, most, if pressed, will concede that they rarely do it. For the most part, dry-fly and nymph hooks smaller than #8 or #10 are useably sharp as they come from the box. The marginal gains in penetration efficiency that come from sharpening the hook seem to many tyers not worth the effort and time.

Larger hooks can be a different matter.

These require more force to penetrate on the hookset merely because of the larger diameter of the hook wire; overcoming the effects of a blunt or rough hook point requires additional force, and makes hooksetting more difficult and less certain. Still, some brands of large hooks are sufficiently sharp right from the package; others are not. The venerable Thumbnail Test is still a good way to determine the condition of the hook point.

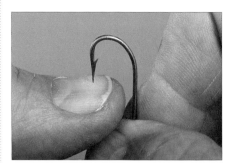

Grasp the hook by the shank, and rest the point squarely against your thumbnail. Pull down on the shank very lightly. A sharp hook point will seat itself in surface of the nail; a dull one won't. Now try to slide the hook point across the top of the thumbnail. A sharp hook will "stick" and resist moving. A dull one will move easily, slipping across the nail, sometimes leaving a light scratch as it does so. Chances are, if one hook in a box is dull, the rest are.

Method #4:
Sharpening Hooks

Dull hooks can be sharpened with a whetstone or file, but the ceramic sharpeners designed specifically for fishing give excellent results on all but the very largest hooks. Whatever the tool, however, the procedure is the same.

Step 1. Clamp the hook in the vise as shown above in **Method #3: Filing,** Step 1. Placing the hook low in the vise gives more working room and visibility and lessens the likelihood of scratching the vise jaws. Larger hooks can be held in the hand while sharpening.

Tilt the stone or file slightly to match the taper of the hook point. Lightly stroke across the tapered surface of the point. Sharpening in this direction will prevent a

metal burr from forming on the point.

It's important to note that most hooks are dull primarily because of the finish (usually a bronzing compound) applied to them before hardening. A roughness or uneven buildup in this finish inhibits hook penetration. In most cases, "sharpening" simply removes this finish to expose the hook point beneath. The finish cuts quickly and takes very little pressure.

Your goal is not to hone off a lot of metal or re-shape the point, but merely to scrape away the outer coating of finish. When this has been achieved, the exposed metal on the hook point will appear quite shiny.

Reposition the stone or file 2 or 3 times to dress other surfaces of the hook point. One light pass in each position is usually all that's required.

Mounting the Hook

Many older tying books recommend mounting a hook by placing it deep in the jaws so that the hook point is covered. The rationale was that the tying thread wouldn't snag on the point of a hook mounted in this fashion—which is undeniably true. Most modern tyers, however, find that this arrangement severely diminishes working room at the rear of the hook, particularly on small flies.

Moreover, the spear of most hooks is actually tapered. The wire is thicker near the bend and thinner near the point. When a hook is clamped so that the point is covered, the vise jaws actually contact only the thickest part of the hook, near the bend. Under heavy thread pressure, the thinner point can flex or wobble slightly inside the jaws and break.

Instead, the following method is now standard:

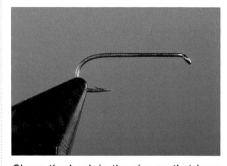

Clamp the hook in the vise so that jaws grip the hook at the bottom of the bend—at the "heel," as it's called. The shank should be parallel to the work surface, and the jaws tips extended just beyond the hook wire. Jaw tension should be adjusted so that downward pressure applied at the eye does not cause the hook to slip or rotate.

A hook mounted in this way maximizes working room around the shank and minimizes the possibility of breaking a hook point if the shank is flexed sideways.

CHAPTER 3

Thread Handling

Threads

Thread manufactured from synthetic materials have replaced silk threads as the standard among modern tyers. Silk thread is still used by some tyers seeking to replicate traditional fly patterns and for fabricating pre-dubbed strands using some older techniques since the rougher texture of silk more readily traps and twists dubbing materials. But most tyers have abandoned it; aside from being more expensive, silk is not as strong as synthetic materials, and over time, it will deteriorate, even on the spool, weakening it further.

Synthetic threads are manufactured in a variety of sizes, designated by a somewhat archaic system of zeros originally used in the sewing industry to indicate thread thickness. Size 000—almost universally abbreviated as 3/0—is, for example, thicker (and usually stronger) than size 000000, or 6/0. Heavier threads are designated by letters, with the thinnest of these designated as size A. Of the wide variety of thread sizes, only some are routinely employed by trout-fly tyers. The choice of thread size depends on both the particular tying application and the proclivities of the individual tyer, and differences in thread selection are common enough to make generalizations a bit tenuous. As a rough rule, the thickest and strongest threads typically used in trout-fly tying, size A and 3/0, are usually reserved for larger patterns where greater quantities of material are affixed to the hook shank, and corresponding greater thread pressure and strength are required to secure them; for spinning deer hair, where considerable thread pressure is used; and for applications where the quick build-up of thread bulk is desirable. Size 6/0 was once considered the "all-purpose" tying thread for trout flies, a useful compromise between strength and low bulk, and it is still used by a very large number of tyers, particularly for flies in sizes 4-12. Recently, however, many tyers have turned to 8/0 threads; the thinness of the strand minimizes bulk, particularly in dry flies, and the small decrease in strength is not significant when dressing most materials in the quantities used on flies of size 12 and smaller. Sizes 12/0 and 14/0 are used for the smallest flies, where minimizing bulk takes precedence over thread strength, though in the continuing trend toward lighter threads, many tyers are now employing

these thinner strands in the middle range of hook sizes. Every thread size and type has its advocates, but in general, tyers use the thinnest thread that is strong enough for the application.

Most of the threads available in the trout-fly sizes are manufactured from either nylon or polyester. Nylon thread is, perhaps, marginally weaker than polyester and exhibits more stretch. Some tyers regard stretch as an advantage, since the force of contraction exerted by a wrapped thread tends to "squeeze" the materials to the hook shank. Others claim that elasticity makes precise thread control in mounting materials more difficult. Polyester threads are more durable and less prone to degrade over time; while this is rarely a consideration in a finished fly, nylon thread on a spool will eventually weaken.

Many threads are available in waxed and unwaxed versions. Waxed threads are given a light coating of wax during manufacturing, though the exact type and quantity of wax varies. Waxed threads are rarely coated thickly enough to make them noticeably better for dubbing, but they do resist fraying and the lubricating properties of wax can be an aid in forming finishing wraps such as the whip-finish. Unwaxed threads lack this treatment, and some tyers find that the absence of adhesive wax allows the thread filaments to separate more easily, giving a bit greater latitude in controlling the thread shape, as for instance, in flattening it. In the end, however, the differences between the two types are minor.

The technique almost universally used in fly tying today is the "continuous thread" method, in which a single, continuous length of thread is bound to the hook shank, affixes all the materials, and is tied off at the finish. Between tying steps, the thread and materials are held in place by tension, usually supplied by the weight of the hanging bobbin, rather than knots. Thus, except for certain specialized techniques, thread-handling methods—that is, tying procedures which involve only the thread—can be divided in the four categories discussed in this chapter: mounting the thread; controlling the twist or shape; tying half hitches; and forming finishing wraps at the head of the fly. Since even experienced tyers occasionally break thread during fly dressing, a method is also shown for salvaging a partially completed fly when the thread is broken.

Method #1:

Single-wrap Thread Mount

This widely used method is preferred by many for its speed and simplicity in securing thread to the hook shank.

A length of wire is used in place of tying thread for a clearer illustration.

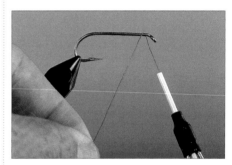

Step 1. Secure the hook in the vise. Strip 6" of thread from the bobbin. The cut end of the thread, or "tag," is held in the left hand; the bobbin holding the "working thread" is held in the right. Fold the thread over the top of the hook shank at the tie-in position. The tag-end of thread should be about 4" long.

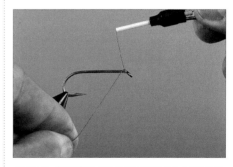

Step 2. Holding the thread under a moderate tension, bring the thread around the hook, angling it toward the hook bend. Keep the tag end beneath the hook, and the working thread will trap it against the hook shank. (Note the direction of the wrap. The bobbin moves away from the tyer as it passes over the hook shank, and toward the tyer as it passes under the hook shank. Wrapping in this direction maintains the direction of twist used in manufacturing the thread (see "Thread Twist and Shape," p. 20).

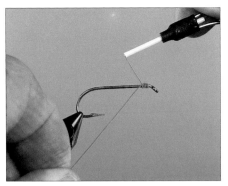

Step 3. Continue winding 4 or 5 tight wraps toward the bend, binding the tag as you go.

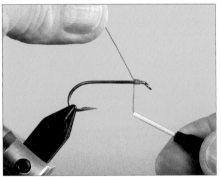

Step 3a. For closely spaced wraps that create a smooth foundation on the shank, elevate the tag as shown. Each new turn of thread will slide down this "ramp" and abut the previous wrap.

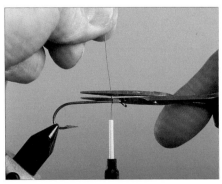

Step 4. The tag end can now be trimmed with a scissors. With threads of 6/0 or lighter, however, there is a quicker method. Grasp the tag firmly in the left hand, and jerk it abruptly toward the hook eye. If the thread is pulled sharply, parallel to the hook shank, it should break off neatly next to the last wrap. This method is unreliable with strong threads of 3/0 and heavier, and should never be tried with Kevlar thread, which can cut fingers.

Method #2:
Double-wrap Thread Mount

Some tyers find this thread-mounting variation simpler to execute, since reversing the thread direction is easily accomplished once a few initial wraps are taken. It is particularly useful with thick threads on thin hook shanks or very slippery thread, though it does build extra bulk.

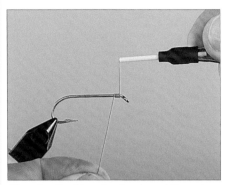

Step 1. Position the hook and thread as described in **Method #1: Single-wrap Thread Mount**, Step 1, p. 17. Instead of angling the thread backward toward the hook bend, take 5 closely spaced wraps toward the hook eye.

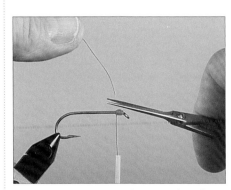

Step 2. Now reverse the wrapping direction and wind the thread back to the tag. Trim or break as described in **Method #1; Single-wrap Thread Mount**, Step 4.

The Half-hitch

In most continuous-thread tying, the thread is not knotted after each material. However, during certain tying procedures, such as spinning deer hair, a half-hitch is used to secure the thread and lock the material in position. Half-hitches can be used in place of a whip-finish to secure the thread when tying is complete and to form the head of the finished fly – an approach that is particularly useful when fly components, such as parachute hackle, obstruct the hook shank and make whip-finishing somewhat cumbersome.

Method #3:
Two-finger Half-hitch

This method gives the tyer an unobstructed view of the thread for good positioning of the knot.

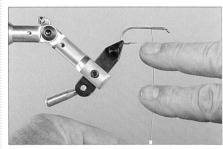

Step 1. With the bobbin hanging at the half-hitch point, place the first two fingers of your right hand against the thread as shown. The thread should cross the index finger very near the tip.

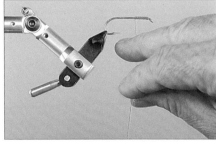

Step 2. Pinch the thread lightly between thumb and forefinger.

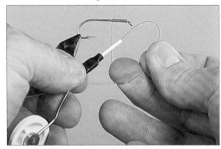

Step 3. Rotate your hand so that the palm is facing you. It's important to maintain a slight pressure against the loop with the middle finger to keep slack from developing between the middle finger and hook shank.

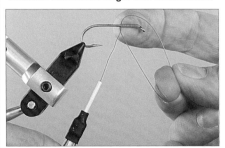

Step 4. Place the loop around the hook eye, and using the index finger, pinch the working thread (that which runs down to the bobbin) against the hook immediately adjacent to the last turn of thread on the shank. Note that the index finger pinches both the thread that forms the hatch hitch and the thread wraps already on the shank. This prevents thread on the shank from unraveling.

3

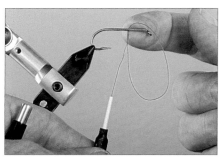

Step 5. Withdraw your middle finger from the loop.

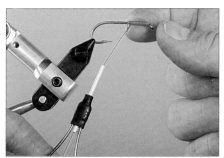

Step 6. Pull slowly on the working thread to tighten the knot. Maintain pressure against the hook shank with the index finger until the knot is secured.

Method #4:
Single-finger Half-hitch

This version of the knot is quick to execute, but the small loop that is formed restricts this method to half hitches placed near the hook eye. It's used primarily to finish the fly head.

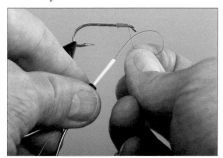

Step 1. Pinch the thread near the hook eye with thumb and forefinger. Use the left hand to form a small loop in the thread as shown.

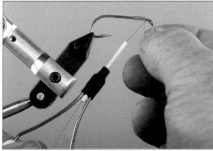

Step 2. Maintaining tension on the bobbin, pass the loop over the eye of the hook and position it above the half-hitch point.

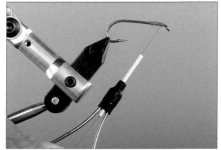

Step 3. Pull on the bobbin, and allow the loop to close. Continue to pinch the loop until it slips from your fingers and tightens against the hook shank.

Method #5:
Half-hitch Tool

A half-hitch tool is typically a smooth, tapered rod with a hole drilled into the face of the tip. Using one is virtually identical to the procedure described in **Method #4: Single-finger Half-hitch,** except that the loop is formed around the barrel of the tool rather than pinched between the fingers. The smooth barrel allows for quick loop formation and accurate knot positioning near the hook eye, as shown in the main sequence.

Half-hitches can also be used to complete the head of the fly as an alternative to the whip-finish, and this approach is often taken when the shank behind the hook eye is not easily accessible for whip-finishing, as for instance, on parachute flies. A series of individual half-hitches can be used, but many tyers find it more efficient to form a series of half-hitches simultaneously, as shown in the alternate sequence.

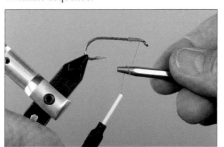

Step 1. Hold the half-hitch tool against the thread, and using the bobbin, cast a loop around the barrel.

Step 1a. To form a series of half-hitches simultaneously, simply repeat Step 1 casting the desired number of loops—three are shown here—around the barrel of the tool.

The half-hitches are transferred to the hook as shown in Steps 2 and 3.

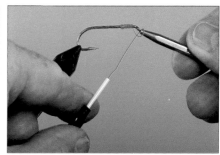

Step 2. Maintaining tension on the bobbin with the left hand, slide the half-hitch tool to the hook.

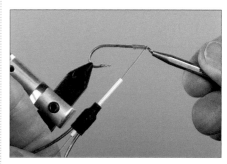

Step 3. Insert the hook eye into the hole in the end of the tool. Pull the working thread toward the hook bend, sliding the loop off the tool tip and seating the knot.

Method #6:
Dubbing Needle Half-hitch

This technique provides superior control in forming the loop size, and so is useful in tying half-hitches in the middle of the hook shank, where the loop may need to pass over materials already mounted nearer the eye. The use of a dubbing needle (or scissor points) to seat the knot makes for very precise placement.

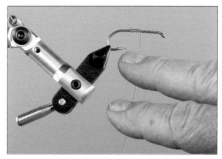

Step 1. Place the first two fingers of the right hand against the thread as shown. There should be about 5" of thread between bobbin and hook shank.

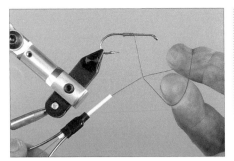

Step 2. Rotate your hand so that a loop is formed around your two fingers, and the fingers are pointing upward.

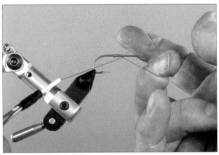

Step 3. Spread your fingers apart so that the crossed threads that form the loop touch the hook shank at the half-hitch point.

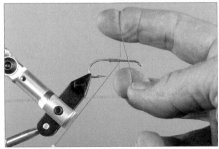

Step 4. While holding the bobbin to maintain tension on the thread, raise your fingers so that the eye of the hook is passed through the loop and your index finger is held directly above the half-hitch point.

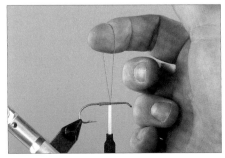

Step 5. Pull upward with your index finger so that the bobbin is drawn upward and the barrel touches the hook shank. Withdraw your middle from the loop and release the bobbin.

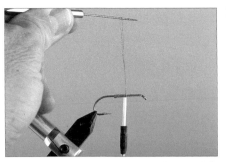

Step 6. With a dubbing needle in your left hand, transfer the loop from your fingertip to the needle.

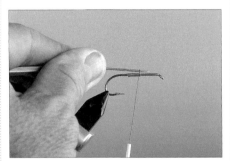

Step 7. Pull downward on the bobbin, guiding the loop with the dubbing needle to seat the knot at the desired point.

Thread Twist and Shape

From the standpoint of tying technique, the structure of thread is perhaps its most significant attribute. Most tying threads are not monofilament strands (that is, they do not resemble tippet material) but rather, they are composed of dozens of thin filaments. The way in which these filaments are handled during manufacturing determines the structure of the thread. In heavier threads, for instance, groups of filaments are first spun together into yarns, and the yarns are then twisted into a thread; this multi-ply construction most closely resembles ordinary rope.

In most threads used for trout-fly tying, however, the filaments are treated differently. All of the filaments may be twisted gently into a cord that is roughly oval in cross section; because they are consolidated by only a light twist, the filaments are easily untwisted or separated. In some threads, the filaments may be left untwisted altogether so that the resulting strand, sometimes called "flat" thread, resembles fly-tying floss.

Controlling this twist—increasing or decreasing it—alters the cross-sectional shape of the thread and to some extent its tying properties, strength, and appearance on the hook shank. There is, naturally, disagreement among tyers about the ideal shape of the thread for tying. Some prefer a thread with a relatively tight twist; others prefer it flattened. But most agree that changing the thread shape to accommodate specific tying procedures gives the best results.

A thread with a relatively tight twist is roughly circular in cross section, and offers some distinct advantages during tying. First, it builds up bulk quickly in a small area, as for instance, building a thread bump for split or fanned dry-fly tails, or fashioning the head

of a fly. Second, it concentrates wrapping pressure at very small point on the hook shank. Thus it's useful for mounting materials that require precise placement—dry-fly wings, for example—or materials like deer hair that are intended to collapse at the mounting point and flare. Finally, adjacent wraps of twisted thread form a rough, "corrugated" foundation on the hook shank and provide a non-slip base on which materials can be mounted.

However, a very tightly twisted thread will tend to twist around itself, or "furl," when it is not under tension, and can prove troublesome in slack-wrap mounting techniques (see "Mounting and Trimming Materials," p. 25). Excessive twist will also weaken a thread, making it more apt to break under wrapping pressure.

Tightening thread to increase the twist is a simple matter of spinning the bobbin clockwise, as shown in **Method #7: Controlling Thread Twist**, p. 21.

By the same token, a flattened thread has useful tying properties as well. First, it is low in bulk and hence desirable in any procedure where thread buildup must be kept to a minimum, as in binding down wing-butts on a dry fly, for example, or with very small hooks. Second, a flat thread lays down smoothly with no ridges or bump, and so is useful in operations that demand a smooth, uniform layer of thread—forming a foundation for a quill body, for instance. Third, flattened thread distributes the pressure of a wrap over a larger surface area; more of the material being wrapped contacts the hook shank, maximizing the binding force while minimizing bulk.

Flat thread has its drawbacks, though. It does not mount materials with great precision of placement. And if the thread is completely untwisted, it will begin to separate; individual filaments will begin to "stray" along the hook shank, making thread control more difficult. When working near the bend the hook, such filaments can catch on the hook point and break, weakening the thread.

Apart from its role in specific tying procedures, flattening the thread has one other important function. The mere act of winding thread around the hook shank or using it to affix material introduces "wrapping twist" into the thread. Each wrap puts a single twist in the thread. For a right-handed tyer, the thread twists in a clockwise direction (when viewed looking down at the bobbin tube)—the same direction that most threads are twisted during manufacturing.

Thus, as you wrap, the thread continually twists tighter and tighter. Eventually, the thread can become so tightly twisted that its strength is significantly diminished and the risk of breakage increases. Thus most tyers periodically untwist the thread during tying by counterspinning the bobbin as explained in **Method #7: Controlling Thread Twist**, p. 21.

Note that each wrap produces one twist regardless of the length of the tying thread. For example, if you take a 2-inch piece of thread and wrap it 10 times around the

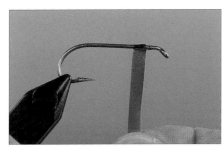

Any material will twist as it is wrapped. Here, a piece of flat ribbon is used to represent the tying thread. The material is mounted without twist.

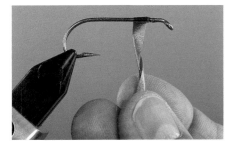

After one revolution around the hook shank, the material is twisted once.

shank, you will have introduced ten twists, or 5 twists per inch. If you use a 5-inch piece of thread and wrap it 10 times around the shank, you will have again introduced ten twists, but they are distributed over a longer length of thread—in this case giving 2 twists per inch.

Thus shorter threads, which wrap more rapidly and accurately, also twist more quickly and require more frequent counterspinning. Longer threads are less convenient to wrap, but maintain their "shape" longer and require less frequent counterspinning.

Method #7:
Controlling Thread Twist

During tying, the amount of twist in the thread can be increased or decreased by spinning the bobbin. Doing so will alter the twist in the entire length of thread between the hook shank and the spool, and this technique is particularly useful for removing the "wrapping twist" that naturally accrues during tying.

Step 1. To flatten the thread, spin the bobbin barrel counterclockwise (as viewed from above, looking down at the bobbin tube). Closely observe the point at which the tying thread meets the hook shank. When the thread is untwisted, it will flatten and spread slightly. A piece of floss is used here for illustration.

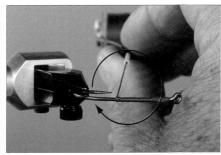

Step 2. To tighten the thread, spin the bobbin clockwise (when viewed from above looking down at the bobbin tube).

Method #8:
Thread Flattening

Producing a twisted thread during tying is seldom a problem, since the act of wrapping the thread continually increases its twist. More often, there is a necessity to flatten the thread for specific tying operations.

Many tyers, for instance, prefer to mount a flattened thread to reduce bulk, and two techniques for doing so are shown in the main sequence.

At times, it is useful to produce a short section of flattened thread without untwisting the entire length between hook shank and spool, as occurs with counterspinning. A method for flattening the thread immediately adjacent to the hook shank is shown in the alternate photo. Floss is used in the following demonstrations to illustrate the procedures more clearly.

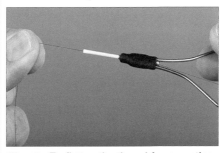

Step 1. To flatten the thread for mounting, strip 4 or 5 inches of thread through the bobbin tube. Draw the thread through tightly pinched thumb and forefinger a few times to remove the twist. Take care not to drag the thread over your fingernails or it may fray.

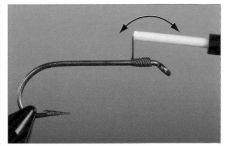

Step 1a. You can flatten a small portion of thread during any stage of tying by applying tension to the thread and rocking the bobbin back and forth to splay the filaments and flatten the thread.

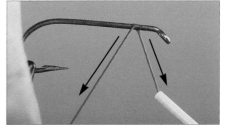

Step 1b. To flatten the thread for mounting, position it for tie-in as described in **Method #1: Single-wrap Thread Mount**, Step 1, p. 17. "Saw" the thread back and forth over the hook shank to flatten a small section.

The thread can now be affixed to the hook shank.

Finishing Wraps

Finishing wraps are those used to tie off the thread at the completion of a dressing and to form a neat head on the fly. Any of the half-hitch methods previously described above (see "The Half-hitch," p. 18) can be used to finish a fly. But half-hitches are not always easy to place accurately, and thus may not form a smooth, neat head—particularly on larger flies—and a large number of tyers employ some version of the whip-finish, described below.

Regardless of the method used to form it, a whip-finish is essentially a series of half hitches, formed in succession, and tightened all at once when the last hitch is completed. Since the working thread is bound beneath several wraps, the whip-finish is more secure than a number of individual half hitches. It also allows a greater precision in placing thread wraps and controlling the shape of the finished head.

Some tyers are adamant about whip-finishing by hand, while others insist on a tool, and interestingly enough, proponents of both approaches claim the same virtues for their chosen method—ease, speed, and precision in forming the head. Suffice it to say that both techniques give excellent results.

Method #9:
Hand Whip-finish

This whip-finish technique requires no tools, though forming the fly head does take some practice. It can be used in conjunction with **Method #13: Dubbed Whip-finish**, p. 24, to create a dubbed head that conceals the finish wraps.

Step 1. Strip about 6" of thread from the bobbin. Form a loop around the first fingers of the right hand.

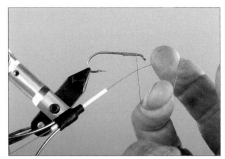

Step 2. Rotate your hand so the palm points upward. Note that the thread coming from the bobbin is in front of the thread descending from the hook.

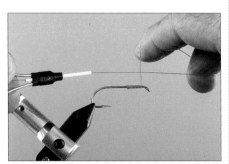

Step 3. Bring your fingers above the hook shank, and turn them so that your palm points downward. Note the crossed threads above the hook shank. The horizontal thread from the bobbin is behind the vertical thread coming from the hook.

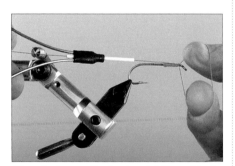

Step 4. Lower the horizontal thread to lie along the hook shank. Twist your wrist so the index finger guides the vertical thread around the back of the hook shank, binding down the horizontal thread. The palm of your hand should be facing you.

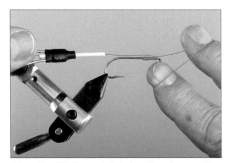

Step 5. While maintaining tension on the loop with your fingers, rotate your wrist again so that the back of your hand is facing you. Your fingers should change position by turning inside the loop, but the loop itself should remain stationary.

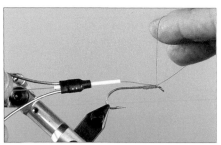

Step 6. Raise your fingers above the hook shank again. Note that hand and thread position are identical to those pictured in Step 3 except that the horizontal thread is now bound to hook shank with one wrap.

Step 7. Repeat Steps 4-6 four more times. Each turn of the hand around the hook shank binds down the horizontal thread with another wrap.

Step 8. After 5 wraps, hold the thread beneath the hook shank and remove your middle finger from the loop. With thumb and forefinger, pinch the loop.

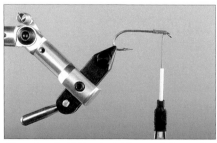

Step 9. Pull the bobbin to tighten the whip-finish. Using thumb and forefinger to keep the loop closed as you take up thread with left hand will prevent hackle fibers or other materials from becoming trapped in the fly head.

Method #10:

One-finger Whip-finish

Though quicker than the hand whip, this method does not place the thread quite as accurately, and takes some practice to master. In its mechanics, this knot is identical to that shown in **Method #9: Hand Whip-finish**, p. 21, but here the index finger alone applies tension to both threads that form the whip-finish loop.

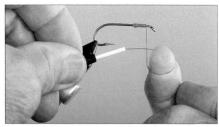

Step 1. Form a loop of thread over the tip of your index finger. Note that the thread from the bobbin passes over the thread from the hook shank.

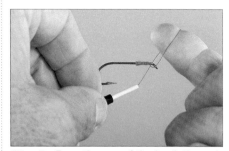

Step 2. Pass the eye of the hook through the loop.

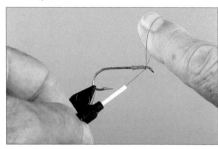

Step 3. Rotate your hand so that your finger slides inside the loop and is pointing away from you.

Step 4. Curl your finger underneath the hook shank and bring it up the near side so that your fingertip is pointing directly at you, as shown. One key to a successful whip is to maintain tension on the thread that passes over the pad of your fingertip as you make this wrap.

Notice that you've now trapped the thread from the bobbin beneath a wrap made from the loop thread.

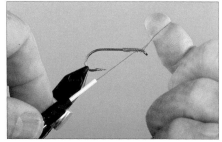

Step 5. Pass the loop around the hook eye again.

Step 6. Rotate your hand so that the index finger is above the hook shank and pointing away from you.

This position is identical to that pictured in Step 3. Repeat Steps 4-6 four more times. As thread is wrapped on the hook shank, the loop will tighten around your finger, and you will need to draw more thread from the bobbin to continue wrapping. Rock or pull your fingertip against the loop, drawing additional thread beneath the wraps on the hook shank.

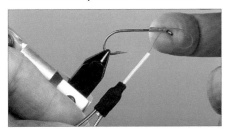

Step 7. When you're ready to tighten the knot, pinch the wraps lightly with your middle finger. Remove your index finger from the loop and pull on the bobbin.

Some tyers find that a whip-finish tool greatly simplifies the formation of the fly head and knot. Because the tool is smoother and less bulky than your fingertips, the visibility of the tying thread during the process is much improved, and wraps can be placed with great precision. There are two basic types of tool, the "orbiting whip-finisher" and the "rotating whip-finisher."

Method #11:
Orbiting Whip-finisher

Orbiting finishers (like the Matarelli tool pictured here) have a sleeved handle that allows the hook and arm to rotate freely inside the sleeve. During use, the handle of the tool is moved in a circle (or "orbits") the hook shank. This type of tool can be used by either left- or right-handed tyers, and can be used in conjunction with **Method #13: Dubbed Whip-finish**, p. 24, to form a dubbed head that conceals the finish wraps.

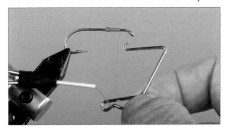

Step 1. Hold the whip-finisher above the handle to prevent it from turning. Loop the thread in the guide notch on the arm.

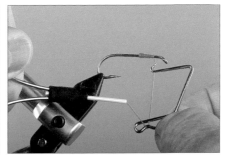

Step 2. Catch the thread near the hook shank in the hook of the tool. Note that the point of tool hook is *behind* the thread.

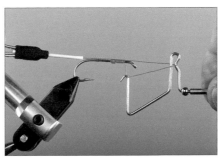

Step 3. Shift your right fingers to hold the tool by the handle sleeve. Now raise the bobbin so the bobbin thread lies along the top of the hook shank. The tool will spin inside the sleeve to the position pictured.

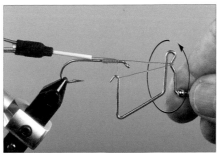

Step 4. While holding only the handle sleeve, move the handle in a circle around the hook shank. The guide notch on the arm should remain stationary and in line with the hook eye.

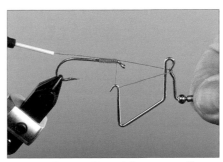

Step 5. Repeat Step 4 four more times. The thread between the tool hook and hook shank will shorten. Gently rock the tool back and forth, and pull against the thread with tool hook. This motion will draw thread from the bobbin. When enough additional thread has been gained, continue winding.

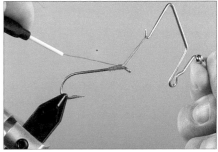

Step 6. To finish the knot, slip the thread out of the guide notch so that the loop is held only with the tool hook. Pull on the bobbin, using the tool hook to guide the thread into position and seat the knot.

Method #12:
Rotating Whip-finisher

This tool has a solid, unsleeved handle that is held stationary along the axis of the hook shank, and rotated with the thumb and forefinger. As the thread shortens, the spring arm bends toward the hook eye, feeding thread and maintaining tension. This tool can be used in conjunction with **Method #13: Dubbed Whip-finish**, p. 24, to create a dubbed head that conceals the finish wraps.

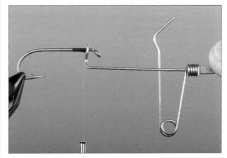

Step 1. Hold the tool parallel to the hook shank, and place the curved portion of the tool that is directly below the tip against the hook shank at the whip-finish point.

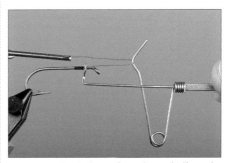

Step 2. Pull the tying thread directly toward you. Bring the tying thread across the curved tool tip and loop it around the spring arm, as shown. Finally, draw the thread back to the bend of the hook. Put just enough tension on the thread to flex the spring arm very slightly.

Note that in bringing the bobbin to the rear of the hook, the thread passes *behind* the very point of the whip finisher.

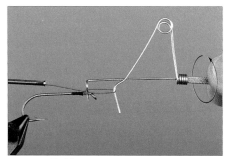

Step 3. Holding the tool exactly parallel to the hook shank, rotate the handle on its own axis as shown, casting the desired number of wraps on the hook shank.

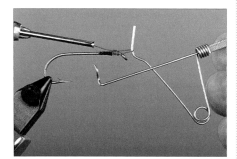

Step 4. Maintaining tension on the thread, elevate the handle of the tool slightly. The tool point will slip free of the tying thread, which remains looped around the spring arm.

Pull the thread until the spring arm is drawn against the hook shank.

Slip the spring arm free of the thread, and pull the whip-finish securely closed.

Method #13:
Dubbed Whip-finish

A small amount of dubbing can be applied to the thread before finishing the fly head. When the whip-finish is completed, the fly will have a dubbed head that conceals the thread wraps used to finish the fly. This approach can be used anywhere a dubbed head is desired, but it is particularly useful in two instances: on very small flies, where there may be limited room for both a dubbed head and standard whip-finish; and on bead-head flies, where standard whip-finishing produces a band of thread wraps behind the bead that some tyers find unsightly.

This technique can be used in conjunction with **Method #9: Hand Whip-finish**, p. 21; **Method #11: Orbiting Whip-finisher**, p. 23, and **Method #12: Rotating Whip-finisher**, p. 23. It is not well-suited to **Method #10: One-finger Whip-finish**.

We're using an orbiting whip-finisher in the following procedure; since its use has already been demonstrated, the instructions are abbreviated.

Step 1. Immediately prior to whip-finishing, apply dubbing thinly to about ½" of the tying thread immediately below the hook shank, as shown.

Do not attempt to dub too long a section of thread, or closing the whip-finish will be difficult. If more dubbing is needed, on the head of a large fly for example, form a smaller head by using the procedure shown here, then add additional dubbing by repeating the procedure until the desired quantity of dubbing has been applied.

Step 2. Form the finishing wraps using the desired method, in this case the procedure shown in **Method #11: Orbiting Whip-finisher**, Steps 1-5, p. 23.

In forming the wraps, make certain that all the dubbed thread is applied to the hook shank.

Step 3. Pull the whip-finish closed, and the thread wraps are concealed beneath the dubbing.

Method #14:
Salvaging Broken Thread

Even the experts break thread during tying once in a while, snagging it on the hook point or applying too much pressure. If a thread breaks as you're tying, all may not be lost.

If the tag of broken thread is long enough, immediately cast a half-hitch around the hook shank to prevent the thread from unwinding and fly components from loosening. Then re-mount the thread, wrapping over the half-hitch, and clipping any thread tags that remain.

If the thread is too short to half-hitch, you can use the following procedure. In either case, many tyers keep a second loaded bobbin ready at hand to rescue a broken thread.

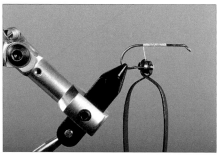

Step 1. To rescue a broken thread that is too short to half-hitch, quickly clip the broken end in a hackle pliers. If slack wraps developed on the hook shank when the thread broke, carefully use the hackle pliers to unwind the slack wraps.

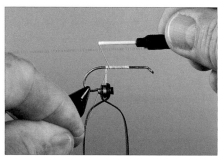

Step 2. Re-thread the bobbin if necessary, and using **Method #1: Single-wrap Thread Mount**, p. 17, reattach the bobbin thread to the hook shank ahead of the broken thread. We're using a red thread to salvage the broken yellow one.

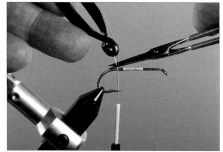

Step 3. Wind the thread back toward the bend, capturing the broken thread beneath the wraps. Clip both tags.

CHAPTER 4

Mounting and Trimming Materials

There are a relatively small number of basic ways to attach fly-tying materials to a hook shank, but there are an almost unlimited number of slight variations, as individual tyers develop tricks of thread tension and positioning that help compensate for the limpness, springiness, slipperiness, or general misbehaviors of specific materials. Some of the techniques that follow are long-time standards (or variations of them); a few are traceable to specific tyers; and still others represent the fruit of observing dozens of tyers over the years and the methods they repeatedly employ.

The following techniques are generalized methods, used in a wide variety of tying situations with a broad range of materials, and we've attempted to described the circumstances under which they are most commonly used. Other mounting techniques, however, are considerably more specialized and may pertain to only a single method or material. Mounting hollow hair by spinning it around the hook shank, for example, is restricted to a very small group of materials—deer, elk, caribou, and antelope. This technique, and other equally specialized ones, are presented in tying methods throughout the book.

Foundations

It is possible, and in some instances desirable, to mount materials on a bare hook shank, but unless you are intending to spin materials around the shank or trying to hold bulk to an absolute minimum, binding materials over a thread foundation gives better results. Hook wire is slippery and encourages materials to roll around the shank. A tying-thread foundation offers a high-friction surface for a better grip on materials.

To lay a foundation on a bare shank, use a tightly twisted thread rather than a flat one. A smooth thread will form a slippery base; a twisted one will create a corrugated surface that will help hold materials in place. A few wraps of thread should span the mounting point, and the rest of the foundation should be laid along that portion of the hook where the material will be bound down.

Some tyers lay a thread foundation over the entire hook shank prior to mounting any materials. Certainly a serviceable approach, it does, however, require extra time and adds bulk to the fly. Generally, in the normal course of tying, the thread wraps used to mount and secure one material can, at the same time, be used to form a foundation for the next material and many tyers take advantage of the economy of this approach.

Here is a thread foundation for hair wings on a dry fly. The hair butts extend toward the hook bend and most of the thread foundation has been laid in this direction.

Quill wings for a wet fly are mounted with butts forward; thus, the foundation is laid toward eye of hook.

Finally, some flies may require mounting a material directly on top of another with no intervening thread wraps—as for example, mounting a section of goose quill for a wing-case directly on the dubbed body of a nymph. In these cases, the roughness of the foundation material takes the place of the thread base, and additional wraps of thread aren't ordinarily required.

Lock-wraps

A large number of the mounting techniques presented in this chapter can be employed in conjunction with lock-wraps. Lock-wraps are thread-handling procedures that bind materials to the hook shank with added security. They are most commonly used with very slippery materials—tinsel, floss, hackle stems, quills, some yarns, and a variety of others. Most of these materials are relatively thin fibers or strands; the effectiveness of lock-wraps diminishes when bulky bundles of material, such as hair for wings, are used. Lock-wraps are especially helpful when the mounted material is wrapped around the hook shank, since wrapping torque is the most common cause of materials slipping beneath the mounting wraps and

pulling free. But this is not always the case; slippery materials such as Krystal Flash or Flashabou, incorporated into a wing or tail, can be secured with lock-wraps as well. Lock-wraps are also extremely useful in tying off materials after they have been wrapped around the hook shank.

Since it would be impractical to illustrate every lock-wrap with every mounting technique shown in this chapter, they are presented as generalized techniques in the method that follows. But they can be used with almost any mounting procedure shown in this chapter, or any time a material is tied off.

Method #1:

Lock Wraps

This method presents 3 basic lock-wraps.

The "L-lock" presented in Steps 1-2 is useful for most materials, but is most often used with those that are somewhat brittle, such as hackle stems or quills, since the material is not folded back on itself in a way that would damage it. This lock-wrap is also extremely useful in tying off almost any material, since the thread wraps elevate the tag and make it more accessible for clipping.

The technique shown in Step 3, the "kink-lock," is an extension of the "L-lock" and can again be used with virtually any material, though it is perhaps most commonly employed when mounting hackles, since the wrap does not strain the somewhat fragile stem.

The "fold-lock" shown in the alternate sequence is used for very flexible, slippery materials such as tinsel, Krystal Flash, Flashabou, and so on. These materials are strong and supple, and folding them over does not risk breaking the material.

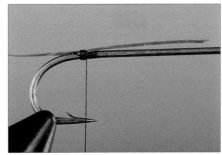

Step 1. Here, a piece of tinsel to be used for ribbing is mounted at the rear of the shank with 3 or 4 ordinary thread wraps.

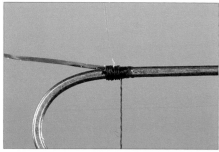

Step 2. To form the "L-lock," elevate the tag of material and take 2 or 3 thread wraps ahead of the tag, around the hook shank only. Tightly abut these thread wraps against the base of the tag.

As shown here, the mounting wraps and the lock-wraps pinch the material tightly to prevent slippage. At the same time, they lift the tag for ease in clipping.

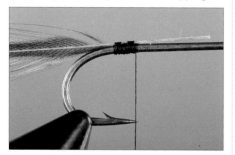

Step 3. To form the "kink-lock," form the "L-lock" shown in Steps 1-2.

Draw the tag of material forward—we're using a hackle stem here—and bind it down ahead of the lock-wraps with additional turns of thread.

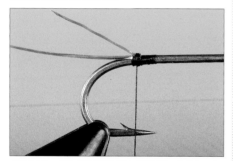

Step 1a. To execute the "fold-lock," begin as in Step 1. Then simply fold the material back over the mounting wraps and secure with additional turns of thread.

Taut-thread Mounting Techniques

Taut-thread techniques are those in which some degree of tension is maintained on the tying thread throughout the mounting procedure. Most tyers employ them more frequently than slack-loop methods because they are, in general, less complicated and faster, offering greater visibility of the material and more control over its placement on the hook shank. Most materials can be mounted under a taut thread, though some—bunches of hair or slips of wing quill, for instance—tend to separate under thread tension and migrate around the shank as the thread is wrapped. These materials are best mounted with the slack-loop methods described later in this chapter.

Method #2:
The Soft Wrap

This is perhaps the simplest and most common mounting technique in fly tying, and it is most often used to mount materials on top of the hook along the axis of the shank—tails, for instance; yarn, floss, or tinsel for bodies; and so on. The technique involves a very light tension on the thread (hence the "soft" wrap), and in fact, many tyers put so little tension on the thread that the procedure virtually becomes a slack-loop method. This variation is presented in the alternate photo sequence below.

Step 1. Lay a foundation and position the thread at the mounting point.

Position the material, in this case a length of yarn for the fly body, atop the shank.

Using a very light pressure on the thread, take one wrap over the yarn. As shown here, there's just enough tension to place the thread accurately and keep it from slipping, but not so much pressure that the material is moved or disturbed from the mounting point.

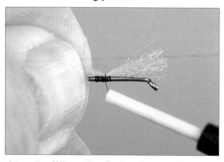

Step 2. When the first soft wrap is complete, pull the bobbin directly toward you, and apply more tension. This will cinch the material to the shank.

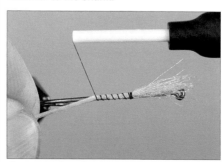

Step 3. Continue binding the material down, in this case toward the rear of the hook. As shown in this top view, pulling the material slightly toward you while wrapping will help compensate for its tendency to be drawn around the shank. Held

---

off-center like this, the material will be pulled by thread pressure to the top of the shank and secured there.

On materials where the mounting area is relatively short—as with tails, for instance—you can secure the material with adjacent, touching wraps. For binding materials over a longer length of shank, a more open spiral, as shown here, is more efficient.

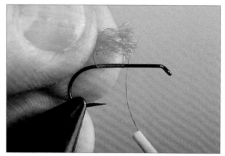

Step 1a. If the material moves off the mounting point or begins to twist around the shank—as may be the case with extremely soft materials such as hen-hackle barbs used as a tail—try this version.

Position the material above the hook shank, and pinch your index finger against the far side of the hook shank. With no tension on the thread, form a loop of slack over the material.

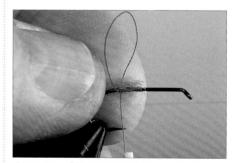

Step 2a. Slip the tying thread between your index finger and the hook shank. The loop is now completed.

Step 3a. Maintain pressure on the side of the hook shank with your index finger. Your finger will act as a "backstop" to keep the material on top of the hook shank when it tries to roll under thread pressure.

Pull the bobbin directly toward you to tighten the loop and secure the material.

Additional wraps can be made as shown in Step 3.

4

Method #3:

The Angle Wrap

This method is practical with a wide variety of materials, but is particularly well-suited to slippery materials (such as bunched rooster hackle barbs for tailing); very limp ones (such as very fine tinsel); and crinkled, crooked, or otherwise unruly materials that tend to splay at the butt end when bunched (a clump of calf tail or rabbit guard hairs). In all these cases, a soft loop, even with very light thread tension, can disturb the materials from the mounting point.

Step 1. Lay a thread base and leave the thread at the mounting point. With your left hand, position the material—we're using calf tail here—so that the tie-down point is directly above the thread, as shown in this top view. The material should cross the hook shank at roughly a 45-degree angle.

Using moderate tension on the thread, take one wrap over the material. Note that because the hair is angled, thread pressure will be exerted more along the axis of the material, rather than across it as in the soft wrap. The longitudinal stiffness is usually greater than lateral stiffness, and hence the material resists the tendency to roll around the hook. Moreover, you can apply additional resistance by "pushing" the material against the thread as you take the wrap, further helping to keep it atop the hook shank.

Step 2. For materials that are to be bound along the length of the hook shank, as in this tailing material, you must now perform two operations simultaneously.

With the thread still under moderate tension, begin another wrap around the material directly behind the first. As the thread crosses the material, use your left hand to "swing" the hair into alignment with the hook shank, as shown here from the top. The material will pivot beneath the

first thread wrap and remain on top of the hook. The second wrap begins to secure it in this parallel orientation.

Step 3. Use the left fingers to keep the material in place on top of the shank, and continue wrapping to the desired point. Lifting the material slightly with the left hand helps keep it centered atop the shank.

Method #4:

The Bottom Wrap

Many tyers prefer to mount certain materials, especially ribbings, on the bottom of the hook shank. The first wrap of ribbing crosses the body on the top of the hook shank, giving a neater, more uniform appearance. This version of the angle wrap is well-suited to tying materials beneath the hook. Since such materials are typically wound around the hook in subsequent procedures, the technique describes mounting materials in such a way that they remain at angle to the hook shank.

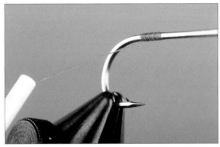

Step 1. Lay a thread base, and leave the thread at the mounting point. Take the bobbin and pull it toward your lap. The thread should be positioned at angle about 30 degrees below the horizontal.

Step 2. Hold the material—in this case a piece of vinyl ribbing, against the bottom of the hook, making a 45-degree angle with the shank.

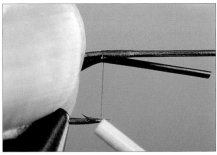

Step 3. Take one wrap of thread, again using your left hand to "push" against the material if it begins to roll to the top of the shank.

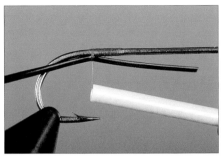

Step 4. Take another wrap, using a controlled tension on the thread to swing the tag end of material into alignment with the hook shank. Now you can bind down the tag and clip it.

Method #5:

The Compensation Wrap

Most tyers eventually discover this technique for themselves. The material is held against the hook shank at a position that is slightly offset from the mounting point, and thread pressure is used to pull or drag the material to the proper position on the shank. Thus the tyer compensates for the tendency of the material to migrate around the hook under a taut thread. The method requires some experience, as the amount of compensation varies with the type and quantity of material. Once mastered, however, the technique is fast and efficient. Here, hackle barbs are used to fashion a dry-fly tail, but the method is suited to a wide range of materials, particularly softer ones, which are easily displaced by the thread and thus fussier to mount with more conventional techniques.

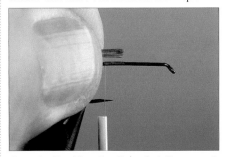

Step 1. Position the thread at the mounting point. With the left thumb and forefinger, pinch the material directly behind the mounting point.

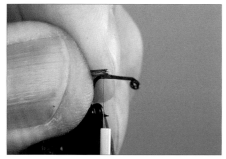

Step 2. Position the material against the near side of the hook shank. The exact point of placement varies with the specific type and quantity of material, but as a starting point, try placing the material against the side of the shank at the 10 o'clock position (as viewed from the hook eye).

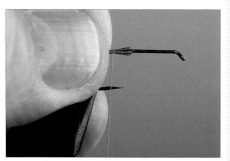

Step 3. Under very light tension, take one wrap around the material over the mounting point.

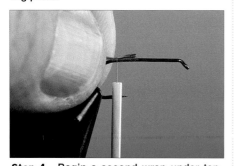

Step 4. Begin a second wrap under tension. As the wrap passes over the material, increase the tension on the thread, "dragging" or "rolling" the material to the top of the hook shank. When the material is centered on top of the shank, ease off on the tension slightly to prevent moving the material farther, and continue the wrap. If the material will not roll far enough even under heavy thread tension, unwrap the thread and reposition the material closer to the top of the shank, and try again.

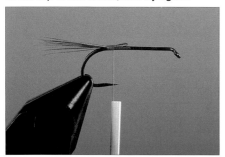

Step 5. Take 2 or 3 tight adjacent wraps toward the hook eye to secure the tailing material. The material butts can now be trimmed and bound down.

Method #6:
The Taut Distribution Wrap

Like the preceding technique, this one takes advantage of the way that thread tension pushes materials around the shank and is used to spread or distribute fibers uniformly around the shank. The most common application, and the one described below, is in creating collar style hackle from bundles of barbs or solid hair, but it is also useful in bulletheads and pulled bodies.

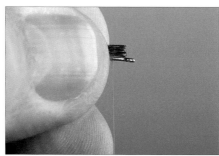

Step 1. Position the tying thread at the mounting point. Note that no foundation has been laid ahead of thread. The bare wire better allows materials to slip around the shank. Hold the material (in this case, a clump of hen-hackle barbs) atop the hook shank.

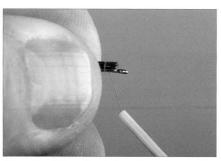

Step 2. Bring the tying thread over the hook shank under moderate tension, contacting the material at the mounting point.

Step 3. Continue wrapping the thread slowly, but do not grip the barbs tightly. Instead let thread tension pull some of the barbs around the shank. Gently roll the hackle fibers around the hook shank with the thumb and forefinger of the left hand. This motion, along with thread tension, will distribute the material evenly around the shank.

If the material builds up too thickly in one spot, unwind the thread slightly. Increase thread tension and wrap over the thick area again, and if necessary, use the left fingers to coax the material a bit more forcefully.

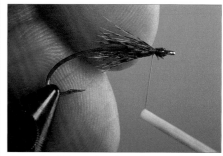

Step 4. When the thread wrap is complete, the fibers will uniformly encircle the hook shank. They can then be secured with extra thread wraps taken toward the eye of the hook.

Note: Some materials will roll more readily and evenly than others. If you've made a complete wrap and material is distributed around the shank, but not as uniformly as you'd like, try this. Release the material in the left fingers. With the thread under moderate tension, take one wrap (immediately adjacent to the first) toward the hook *bend*, allowing the material to redistribute itself around the shank. This additional wrap will often thin out thick spots and fill in the sparse ones.

Method #7:
The Cradle Loop

This mounting procedure is useful for the precise placement of materials since it allows you to adjust their position after a thread wrap has been taken, but before the material has been secured. It is particularly helpful in accurately mounting somewhat fussier materials such as quill strips or hackle tips for winging, as pictured here. However, the method has its limitations. It is rather slow, and since the material must be held by both ends, it is restricted to those materials with tag ends long enough to grasp.

Step 1. Position the thread at the mounting point. With the left hand, hold the material against the top of the hook directly above the mounting point.

Step 2. Take a wrap of thread as closely as possible over the mounting point. Let the bobbin hang.

Step 3. Maintaining a grip with the left fingers, grasp the tips of the material with the right fingers and use both hands to raise the material slightly above the hook shank.

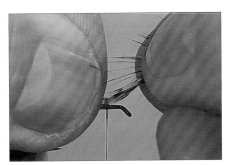

Step 4. With the material in this position, it is now possible to slide it gently beneath the thread to adjust it for accurate mounting. Note here that we've slipped the wings slightly forward.

When moving the material, elevate one end to help slide the thread, rocking the material gently. The object is to move the material to the desired position without disturbing the thread from the mounting point.

Step 5. When the material has been adjusted so that the thread crosses directly over the correct mounting point, lower the material to the top of the hook shank. Hold the tips and bind down the butts of the material.

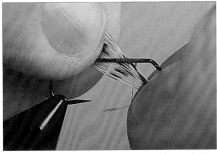

Step 1a. This alternate version of the technique can also be used. Position the material below the hook shank as shown. The fingers should pinch the material on either side of the mounting point.

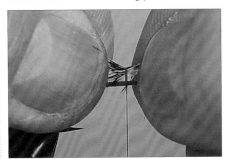

Step 2a. Lift the material, bringing it up the far side of the hook and slipping it beneath the thread and up to the top of the hook. Once the material is in this position, proceed to Step 4.

Method #8:

The Lash Mount and Crisscross Wrap

The lash mount and crisscross wrap are not actually two separate techniques; rather, they are two very similar methods of thread handling used for different purposes.

The lash mount, shown in the main sequence below, is used to mount materials that are affixed perpendicular to the hook shank—certain styles of legs and eyes and, most commonly, spentwings formed from yarn or other bundled materials, as shown in the following demonstration, Steps 1-3.

Crisscross wraps, though similar in execution, have a different purpose. They are used to secure, divide, or position materials already mounted on the hook shank. Such materials may be affixed with a lash mount, and the crisscross wrap shown in Steps 4-5 is in fact used to secure the yarn wing mounted at the beginning of the sequence. But crisscross wraps are also used to separate a material that has already been mounted and raised perpendicular to the hook, as in a pair of upright, divided hair wings, or they can be used to divide and position material mounted along the top of the hook shank, such as a bundle of hackle fibers used to form spentwings. These more specialized uses of crisscross wraps are demonstrated as they are required by methods that appear in later chapters.

The crisscross technique described here is sometimes called the "figure-eight wrap,"

but this term is more commonly used to identify a particular method for dividing and securing rolled or hair wings on a dry fly, and we have followed this more conventional terminology throughout the book.

The material—poly yarn is used here—can also be mounted using the procedure described in **Method #3: The Angle Wrap**, Steps 1-2, p. 27, and this approach is perhaps the most common.

Extremely soft or loosely bundled material, however, may resist angle wrapping, and the following sequence shows a different method of affixing such materials.

Another commonly used method for mounting softer materials is shown in alternate Steps 1a-2a.

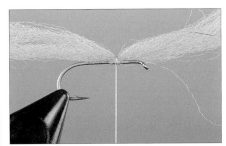

Step 1. Lay a foundation over the mounting area, and position the thread at the mounting point.

Position the material atop the hook shank so that it is centered over the mounting point.

Affix the material with two wraps of thread under moderately light tension, as shown.

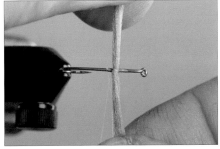

Step 2. With the left fingers, grasp the end of the material nearest the hook bend. With the right fingers, grasp the end of the material nearest the hook eye.

Moving both hands simultaneously, rotate the material counterclockwise until it is perpendicular to the hook shank.

Step 3. Using moderate tension, bring the tying thread up behind the near wing, over the original mounting wraps, and down ahead of the far wing.

The material is now mounted; to secure it, use the crisscross wrap shown in Steps 4-5.

Step 4. The crisscross that secures the material is virtually identical to the mounting wrap. We've colored the tying thread black to better show the wrap.

In Step 3 the thread was left beneath the shank ahead of the far wing. Most crisscross wraps, regardless of purpose, begin from this position.

Using fairly heavy tension, bring the thread beneath the shank and up ahead of the near wing. Cross the thread over the top of the shank between the wings, and down behind the far wing.

Step 5. Maintain tension on the thread. Bring it beneath the shank and up behind the near wing. Cross the thread over the top of the shank, and down ahead of the far wing. Notice the "X"-shaped wrap between the wings.

Repeat Steps 4-5 to secure the material tightly to the shank.

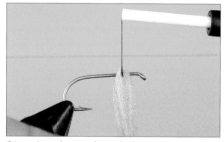

Step 1a. Lay a foundation and position the thread as in Step 1.

Hold the thread vertically above the hook shank. Fold the material around the thread so that the two ends point toward you.

Then slide the material down the thread until it contacts the hook shank.

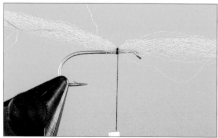

Step 2a. Maintain tension on the ends of the yarn, and wrap the thread around the shank, securing the yarn to the top.

Take one more wrap of thread over the first, and proceed to Step 3.

Slack-loop Mounting Techniques

As the name suggests, slack-loop methods are those in which the tyer employs a slack wrap of thread around the material and hook shank prior to applying tightening pressure. The slack allows the tyer to position the thread in such a way that a uniform tension is exerted directly toward the hook shank when the thread is tightened. A thread that is wrapped under direct tension applies a lateral pressure to materials, pushing them ahead of the thread and causing them to roll around the hook shank. A perpendicular pressure applied by slack-loop methods counteracts this tendency to roll and enables the tyer to hold materials at a specific location—on the top of the hook shank, for instance, or on either side.

These techniques are most commonly used with "bunched" materials—a clump of bucktail or hackle fibers, for instance—or those composed of many strands or fibers, such as a marabou blood feather or piece of poly yarn. Slack loops are especially useful with slippery materials like squirrel tail and synthetic hairs.

One problem encountered in slack-loop methods is a tendency for the thread to curl up on itself, or "furl," when thread tension is relaxed, making it difficult to form the loop. This furling is the result of excessive twist in the tying thread. To remedy the problem, counterspin the bobbin (see **Method #7: Controlling Thread Twist**, p. 21) to untwist the thread.

Method #9:

The Pinch Wrap

This is one of the most commonly used techniques in fly tying for mounting materials on top of the hook shank. Its virtues are perhaps best illustrated in the mounting of quill wings, shown here in the wet-fly style, but it can be used to position and secure almost any material.

Step 1. Position the wings with right hand over the thread base so that the mounting point on the wings is directly over the bobbin thread.

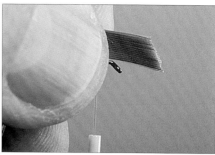

Step 2. Without moving the quills, lightly pinch the wings and the hook shank with the left thumb and forefinger. Note that the mounting point of the wings remains directly over the thread. It's important to pinch the hook shank; pressure applied by the fingers to the thread wraps will keep them from unraveling when slack is introduced in the following steps.

Step 3. Raise the thread vertically, and slide it between your thumb and the quill on the near side of the shank.

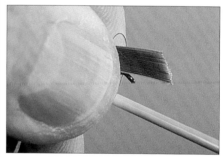

Step 4. Maintaining the pinch, form a small slack loop on the top of the quills, and pass the thread downward between your forefinger and the quill on the far side of the shank.

Step 5. Maintain a firm pinch on the wings, and pull down on the bobbin thread. Since the loop tightens toward the center of the hook shank and the material is pinched in position, the wings will cinch down neatly atop the shank.

4

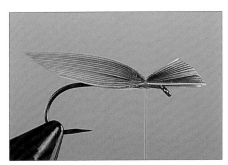

Step 6. Briefly release the material and inspect it to make sure that it's properly positioned. Small adjustments can be made at this point.

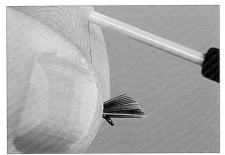

Step 7. Pinch the material again as described in Step 2, and repeat Steps 3-5. One repetition (for a total of two pinch wraps) is usually sufficient most materials, but large quantities of materials or very slippery ones may require additional pinch wraps to secure them.

Step 8. Maintaining the pinch on the material, slide your fingers backward far enough to expose the thread wraps. Secure the material butts with 4 or 5 tight, adjacent wraps, toward the hook eye.
    Clip and bind down the excess.

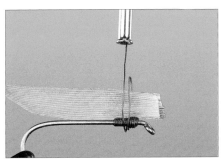

Step 1a. In one commonly practiced variation of this technique, the slack loop is formed as in Steps 1-4. The tying thread is brought beneath the hook shank and back up the near side of the shank. The bobbin is then held above the hook shank, as shown.
    Two strands of thread now cross the quill on the near side of the shank; they should be positioned directly atop one

another, and both are pinched by the thumb.
    In this variation, the thread is pulled directly upward (rather than downward, as shown in Step 5) to close the slack loop and secure the material. Both approaches give about the same results, but some tyers find that the method shown in this step promotes a more symmetrical tightening tension that better prevents materials from twisting around the hook shank. It can be especially useful in mounting larger quantities of material or very slippery ones.

Method #10:
The Bobbin Loop

The bobbin-loop method presented below is a slight variation on a technique described by Darrel Martin in *Fly-Tying Methods*. This approach is particularly useful with fussy materials that are difficult to keep aligned atop the hook shank. The bobbin tube is used to tighten the loop, equalizing the thread tension on both sides and applying an almost perfectly perpendicular pressure on the material.
    Though quill wings are used for illustration, the technique can be used with any material. It is, however, best reserved for attaching highly compressible or small amounts of material, since the thread tension required to cinch down thick bunches of hair is difficult to apply with a bobbin tube and could damage it.

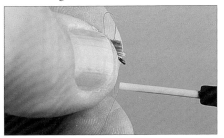

Step 1. This technique begins by forming a slack loop as shown in **Method #9: The Pinch Wrap**, Steps 1-4, p. 30.
    After the loop is formed above the shank, maintain your pinch on the material. Extend your middle finger beneath the hook shank, and loop the thread around it. Use just enough tension to keep the loop from slipping off your fingertip.

Step 2. Bring the tying thread up between your thumb and the quill on the near side of the hook shank. This wrap should lie on top of the thread already beneath your thumb.

Step 3. Bring the tying thread down a second time between your index finger and the quill on the far side. Two wraps of thread now pass over the quill at the mounting point.

Step 4. Continue pinching the material to maintain its position as a little slack may develop in this next operation. Insert the bobbin tube in the loop below the hook shank and withdraw your middle finger.

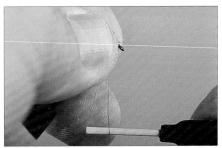

Step 5. Pull down on the bobbin tube directly beneath the mounting point. The material will tighten against the hook shank.

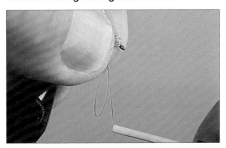

Step 6. Maintain the pinch so that the wraps do not loosen. Slip the bobbin tube from the loop and pull down on the bobbin to close the loop and secure the material.

Step 7. With two wraps at the mounting point, you're ready to bind down the butts.

Method #11:
The Langley Loop

This method originated in England with fly tyer Ken Langley and the details of the procedure come to us courtesy of Darrel Martin. Though the technique was developed primarily for winging flies, it can be used with a wide variety of materials. It affords an unusually clear and unobstructed view of the hook shank and tying thread, making possible an extremely precise placement of materials.

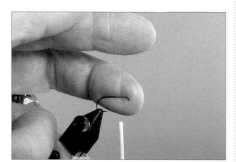

Step 1. Lay a thread base. Extend your index finger over, and parallel to, the hook shank. Loop the tying thread over the index finger, and use your middle finger to pinch the thread tightly against the hook shank, forming a loop. Notice the "V" of thread formed at the mounting point. The higher your index finger is positioned, the narrower this "V" will be.

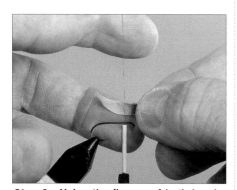

Step 2. Using the fingers of both hands, slip the material into the "V"—again, quill wings are used to demonstrate. It's important to maintain tension on the loop with the index finger.

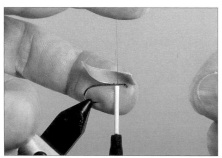

Step 3. When you're satisfied with their placement, release the quills. They will be held in place by the pinch of the thread "V", allowing you to view their position and adjust it if necessary.

Step 4. Maintaining the pinch on the far side of the hook shank with the middle finger, use your thumb to pinch the material on the near side of the shank. Carefully slip your index finger from the loop.

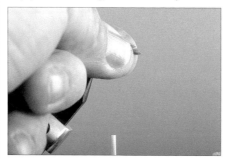

Step 5. Draw the thread downward to tighten the loop and secure the materials.

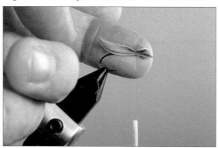

Step 6. Withdraw your thumb, but keep pressure on the material and mounting point with your middle finger. Observe the wings.

Step 7. If all is well, form another loop as described in Step 1, and position it directly ahead of the first loop.

Step 8. Again, pinch both sides of the material and draw the loop tight.

Form and tighten a third loop. Then trim and bind the butts.

Method #12:
The Noose Loop

This technique is commonly employed to help position bunches of hair on top of the hook shank and prevent them from rolling under thread pressure. It's especially useful when using slippery hair, like squirrel tail, or hairs such as deer and elk that flare.

Step 1. Lay a thread base and position the material above the mounting point.

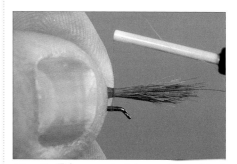

Step 2. Take one slack loop of thread just around the material butts, not the hook shank. Note that this loop is formed in the same direction as the thread is normally wrapped. Put just enough tension on the thread to hold it in position at the mounting point.

Step 2a. Some tyers form this noose loop in reverse. Bring the thread first beneath the bundle, around the back, over the top, and down the near side. The thread is then slipped beneath the bundle and down the far side of the hook shank.

Proponents of this variation claim that it provides better control of the material and keeps it more reliably atop the shank.

Step 3. Lay the material against the hook and pinch your index finger tightly against the far side of the hook shank.

Pull down on the bobbin to tighten the noose, bundle the material on top of the hook and secure it. It's imperative to keep a tight pinch against the hook with your index finger, as the direction of thread tension will encourage the material to roll around the shank. Your finger should act as a backstop to prevent this.

Step 4. Pinch the material directly behind the mounting point and secure the butts with tight, adjacent wraps.

Method #13:
The Side Pinch

Pinch wraps can be used to affix a material to the side of a hook shank for forming certain styles of tails, antennae, legs, and for streamer shoulders. Because the technique involves a one-finger pinch, it is generally unsuitable for bunched or stranded materials, since it is difficult maintain control of many fibers with a single finger. The following sequence illustrates the technique using feathers for a streamer cheek, but the procedures are identical for any material at any position along the hook shank.

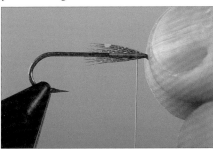

Step 1. With the thread foundation laid and the bobbin hanging at the mounting point, hold the material on the far side of the hook, positioning it precisely at the point you wish to mount it.

Step 2. Pinch the material, lightly but firmly, between your index finger and the hook shank.

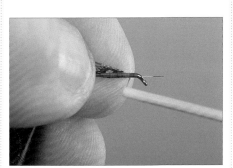

Step 3. Bring the tying thread over the top of the hook shank, and slip it between your fingertip and the feather. Do not release the bobbin or tighten the thread. There should be a small slack loop on the near side of the hook shank. The loop size pictured has been exaggerated here for better visibility.

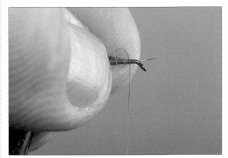

Step 4. If need be, adjust the position of the thread so that it crosses the feather at the mounting point. Maintain firm pressure on the feather with your fingertip and pull the bobbin directly toward you. This will apply a perpendicular force on the feather and keep it from twisting around the hook.

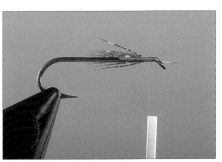

Step 5. Take one or two more wraps to secure the material.

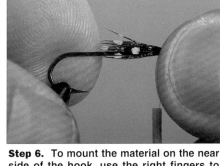

Step 6. To mount the material on the near side of the hook, use the right fingers to position the feather so that the tip is aligned with the feather on the far side.

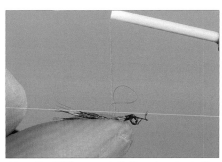

Step 7. With your left thumb, pinch the feather against the near side of the shank.

Slip the thread between your thumb and the feather. Since your thumb will obscure the view of the thread position, look down from above the hook shank—as in this top view—to make certain that the thread contacts the feather at the mounting point. Note that a slack loop is formed on the far side of the hook.

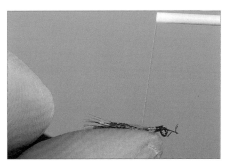

Step 8. Draw the bobbin directly away from you to tighten the loop and secure the material.

Method #14:
The Double Side Pinch

Some materials behave predictably enough that you can mount matching pieces of material at the same time. Here, a goose biot tail for a stonefly nymph is used to demonstrate, but the technique is the same for virtually any material.

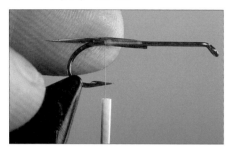

Step 1. Cut matching pieces of biot. Position one on the far side of the shank, and pinch it with the tip of your index finger at the mounting point.

Step 2. Hold the second biot on the near side, matching its length with the first.

Step 3. Pinch the second biot with the tip of your thumb at the mounting point.

It's difficult to relax finger pressure enough to slip the thread into position without disturbing the placement of the biots or dropping them. Instead, spread your fingertips slightly by pinching the biots with the pads of the thumb and forefinger, as shown here from above. Note that the mounting point on the biots, directly above the thread, is now exposed.

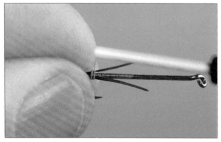

Step 4. Loop the thread loosely around the hook shank at the mounting point.

Applying a slight bit of tension after the loop is formed will allow you to seat the thread at the right mounting position. The bobbin should be above the hook shank.

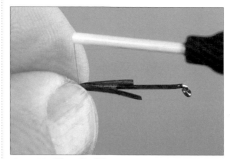

Step 5. Now "roll" your fingertips forward so that the thread and biots are once again pinched at the mounting point.

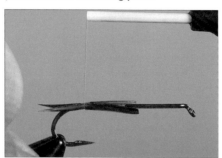

Step 6. Pull up on the bobbin to tighten the loop. If one or both biots is incorrectly positioned, slacken the thread pressure very slightly, adjust the material, and re-tighten the thread.

Trimming Materials

Proper trimming of materials during tying contributes to the ease and efficiency of thread handling, to accurate proportioning, to a neat appearance, and in many cases, to the durability of the finished fly. As many fly tyers and instructional texts have urged, sharp, fine-pointed scissors—whatever their particular design—are essential. Smaller flies require finer points for working in close quarters; larger patterns require more substantial blades for cutting materials that are often greater in volume and coarser in texture. Most accomplished tyers have at least one pair of each type and scrupulously restrict them to operations for which they are suited. They never, for example, use small, fine-pointed scissors for cutting clumps of hair, which can dull them quickly.

Scissor blades can be either smooth or serrated, and as always, different tyers have different preferences. As a very general rule, smooth blades offer a somewhat closer, more precise cut. Scissors with at least one serrated blade, however, have an advantage in cutting slippery materials like hackle barbs and hair. The teeth on the blade trap these materials and prevent them from sliding toward the tip as the scissors are closed, giving a good grip when large quantities of material are cut or when only the very tips of the scissors are used. Some tyers feel that serrated blades also stay sharper longer.

Method #15:
The Basic Trim

Materials that are flat, small in diameter, or generally low in bulk—tinsel, hackle stems and tips, feather barbs, quills, and so on—can be cut simply by clipping them off. The best results are obtained if materials are cut as closely as possible to the tie-down wraps.

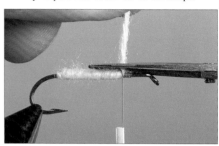

Step 1. For a close trim, raise the tag of material so that it is perpendicular to the hook shank. Lay the scissors against the thread wraps and clip. This position affords the most working room and gives unobstructed access to the base of the material.

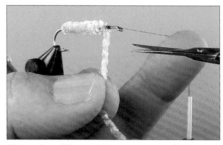

Step 1a. When trimming materials near the underside or far side of the shank, there is a risk of inadvertently cutting the tying thread. To avoid this problem, use the thumb and forefinger of the left hand to draw tag of material away from the hook shank for clipping.

Use the middle finger of the left hand to push the thread away from the hook shank and keep it clear of the scissor tips.

Method #16:
The Knife Cut

When an exceptionally close trim is desired—for minimum bulk on a small dry fly, for instance—some tyers use the following technique. It is used with very thin, fine, or flat materials—tying thread, tinsel, quills, and so on—and requires very sharp scissor blades.

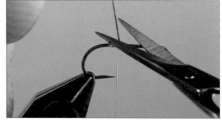

Step 1. Raise the tag end of material so that it stands at 90 degrees to the shank. If you inspect a pair of scissors, you'll see that the

4

interior surfaces—those that meet when the scissors are closed—are flat. Lay the flat of the blade against the fly body so that the cutting edge of the scissors contacts the tag of material right at the thread wrap.

Pull the tag of material into the blade. Lightly stroke the material with the scissor blade, using it as a knife to shear the tag off at the wraps.

Method #17
The Angle Cut

Bulkier materials pose a particular problem for the tyer. A straight, vertical cut leaves an abrupt "ledge" in the material.

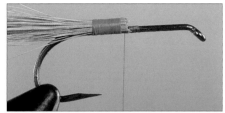

If a ledge is left close to the tie-down wraps, there's insufficient room for securely binding down the material, and it may pull out. Moreover, this ledge or step produces a sudden change in diameter on the hook shank. Attaching or wrapping subsequent materials over this step may prove difficult. If left beneath the body, this step may produce an unnatural profile.

Thick clumps or pieces of material are generally cut at an angle to provide a smooth transition and a greater binding surface for the thread.

The angle-cutting methods described here produce a wedge in which the point of the taper rests against the hook shank, forming a kind of "ramp." A couple of general points are worth noting:

First, angle cuts require some manipulation of the material butts, and it is important that, prior to trimming, the material is bound tightly to the shank so that it doesn't move during cutting.

Second, when grasping butts of the material, try to hold them so that they form a tight clump. This enables you to exert uniform tension on each fiber or strand of material and makes for a smooth taper.

Angle-cutting can be used for any thick or bulky material—yarns, hairs, sections of wing quill, thick ribbings, bundled fibers, etc. Here, a calf tail wing post is used to illustrate the technique.

Step 1. If the butts of the material are long enough to hold, pinch them with your

thumb and forefinger, and raise them just enough to sneak the scissor blades around them. When you make the cut, you want the butts of the material to be as parallel to the hook shank as possible.

Position the scissors at the desired angle. The trimming angle is to some degree dependent on the purpose—forming an underbody, mating with other materials, etc. However, angles steeper than 45 degrees do not hold thread wraps well; the wraps tend to slide down the taper and bunch up. A shallower angle gives more security when wrapping with thread, but does produce greater bulk on the hook shank.

Note the orientation of the scissors; you're trimming from the bottom of the butts to the top. This cutting direction gives a reliable control over the length of the taper. If you cut "down" on a material, you risk nicking the scissor blades on the hook shank.

Step 2. Maintain a light, uniform tension on the material butts, and cut smoothly.

Step 1a. If the butts of the material aren't long enough to hold securely—as with the calf body hair used here for tailing—work a dubbing needle beneath the material. Pry the butts up from the shank.

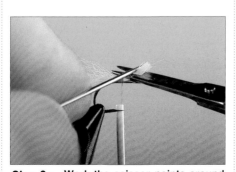

Step 2a. Work the scissor points around the material, cradling the butts. Use the dubbing needle to press the butts lightly into the "V" of the scissors for better control while cutting. Proceed to trim.

Method #18:
The Bend Cut

This alternative technique for making angle cuts is best used with larger clumps of material. It avoids the awkward hand position sometimes required with other angle cutting methods.

Step 1. Grasp the butts of the material and bend them upward so that they are perpendicular to the shank. Notice that the portion of the hair clump that rests against the hook shank forms an arc that is larger in diameter than the arc made by the hairs on top of the clump. When the material is trimmed parallel to the hook shank, this differential in diameter will produce a taper.

Rest the scissor points on the binding wraps, parallel to the hook shank.

Step 2. Lightly pull the butts into the "V" of the scissors, and trim. The length of the taper is controlled by the degree of bending. A very tight bend of 90 degrees or more will produce a shorter taper. A shallower bend will give a longer one.

Method #19:
Pre-trimming Materials

It is often more efficient, and sometimes necessary, to trim materials before they are mounted—an approach widely used by more experienced tyers. Because you aren't hampered by the hook shank or thread wraps, the material is more easily manipulated for simpler, more accurate cutting. On very small flies, for instance, where working room is limited, pre-trimming is especially useful. The method, however, is pretty much restricted to materials mounted with the butts toward the hook eye—tails, ribbing, body materials—where you grip the portion of material that will be incorporated into the fly. Materials mounted in the other direction, such as the wing post pictured in **Method #17: The Angle Cut**, p. 35, are difficult to pre-trim since the shortened butts do not provide enough material to grip securely during mounting.

Here, a clump of squirrel hair tied in for a tail is used to demonstrate the technique.

Step 1. Hold the material against the shank to determine the mounting point.

Step 2. With the left fingers, grasp the hair tips about ⅛" behind the mounting point.

Step 3. Determine the angle and length of the taper that you desire, and trim.

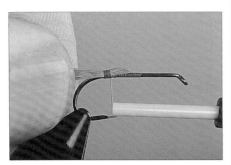

Step 4. Bind the material at the mounting point and take continuous wraps forward to secure the butts.

Method #20:
The Slide Mount

Stranded materials with fibers that tend to fray or stray are difficult to mount very close to the tip, since the thread will not trap all the fibers on top of the hook shank. For such materials—untwisted yarns, bundled synthetics, crooked hairs, and the like—the slide mount works well.

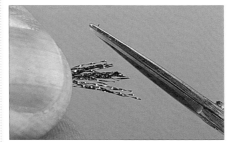

Step 1. Grip the material about ¼" behind the mounting point and trim the end. Thinner bunches of material can be clipped to an even length; thicker bunches can be pre-trimmed with an angle cut, as is this bundle of Krystal Flash.

Step 2. Rest the material against the shank, and take two light wraps very near the fingertips, where the strands are tightly bundled.

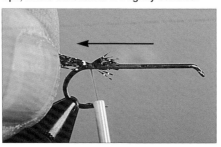

Step 3. Maintain some tension on the bobbin, and slide the material beneath the thread back toward the hook bend so that the mounting point on the strands is directly under the thread wraps. The tension of the bobbin helps prevent the thread from being drawn backward.

Step 4. Pull on the bobbin to tighten the mounting wraps, and proceed to bind down the butts.

Method #21:
Trimming Wire

Trimming wire used for bodies or ribbing, or lead wire for weighting hooks, poses little problem for the tyer, but much distress to the tools. Nothing dulls scissors faster than cutting metals.

There are two solutions here. First, simply reserve a pair of old scissors for the sole purpose of cutting metal materials. Heavy-gauge wires may require the use of fine-tipped wire cutters. Or you can use one of the techniques shown here that don't require scissors at all.

Step 1. Lead wire can be trimmed by wiggling it, as shown in Step 1a, but thicker wires take some time to break. It is faster to use your thumbnail to shear off the lead.

When the lead is in place and bound down, trap the tag of lead between your thumbnail and the hook shank. Your left hand should hold the lead wraps to keep them from moving. Using the shank as a backstop, press down with your nail. The lead is soft enough to mash and separate.

Step 1a. This approach works best with finer wires, such as those used for ribbing. The wire should be tied off against the shank very tightly.

Grasp the tag end and wiggle it up and down. The metal will soon fatigue and break close to the binding wraps. While the wire can be wiggled back and forth, it may loosen slightly and ultimately break beneath the tie-off wraps, where it can pull free. Wiggling the wire up and down levers it around the edge of the frontmost wrap, where it will break.

Binding down the tag end of wire can pose a problem at times, since trimming often leaves a sharp edge that will easily cut tying thread. To avoid this problem, cover the cut end of the wire with loose wraps of thread that conceal the sharp edge. Then wrap more tightly over the wire tag. The loose wraps act as a kind of cushion for the tighter wraps and prevent the thread from breaking.

CHAPTER 5

Weighting Hooks

Wire, strips, and tapes made of lead or non-toxic metals can be applied to the hook shank to add weight to subsurface flies. In some cases, these materials are affixed to the hook shank in ways that deliberately shape the silhouette of the finished fly, and thus overlap to some extent with the contents of Chapter 6: "Underbodies." However, the methods included here are those that take as their primary goal adding weight to the fly—a fair distinction since all of the body profiles produced by methods in this chapter can also be produced without adding weight to the fly, in which case the primary purpose becomes creating a specific shape in the underbody.

Other materials, too, can be used to add weight to the fly—metal or glass beads, preformed "dumbbell" eyes, and bead chain—but since these materials are also representa-

tional components of the finished fly, their use is presented later, in Chapter 15: "Heads, Collars, and Eyes."

It can be useful to know the relative amount of weight added to a fly using various materials. The following chart presents this information. For ease of comparison, all the materials customarily used to add weight to a fly, including beads and eyes, are included.

RELATIVE WEIGHTS OF HOOK-WEIGHTING MATERIALS
(Values expressed in percents)

WIRE[1]	.039" (4)	.032" (5)	.025" (6)	.020" (8)	.015" (11)
Lead	100	54	43	28	13
Copper	80	40	32	21	10
Brass	75	38	30	20	9
Tin	64	33	27	17	8

BEADS[2]	7/32"	3/16"	5/32"	1/8"	3/32"
Lead split shot[3]	(AAA, 3/0) 377	(AB) 306	(BB) 211	N/A	N/A
Tin split shot[3]	(AAA, 3/0) 322	(AB) 251	(BB) 197	N/A	N/A
Tungsten	N/A	305	224	102	48
Brass	N/A	113	83	38	15
Copper/ Nickel	N/A	113	83	38	15
Glass[4]		74 (X-Large)	22 (Large)	11 (Medium)	4 (Small)

BARBELL EYES[5] (per pair)	7/32"	3/16"	5/32"	1/8"	3/32"
Lead	659 (Large)	462 (Medium)	323 (Small)	188 (X-small)	107 (Mini)
Brass	436	341	238	99	60
Bead chain	N/A	N/A	126	71	39

This chart indicates the *relative* weights of materials commonly used to add weight to flies. The standard of reference on the chart is one inch of .039" lead wire (5 amp fuse wire), which will provide about 4 turns (shown in parentheses on the chart) around a hook shank of this same diameter. On the chart, this weight is expressed as 100%. All other values on the chart are expressed in relation to this reference point.

Thus the value for a 5/32" copper bead, shown on the chart as "83," indicates that this bead is 83% the weight of the one-inch length of .039" lead wire. Similarly, the relative weight of a piece of size AB tin split shot is "251," that is, 251% or approximately 2 ½ times the weight of the reference wire.

To compare any values on the chart, simply construct a

ratio. To find the relative weight of, for instance, a ⅛" brass bead (38 on the chart) and a 3/16" glass bead (74 on the chart), express them as a ratio: 38/74=.51; that is, the brass bead weighs about half as much as the larger glass bead.

[1] The weight values given are for one inch of wire; the number in parentheses indicates the approximate number of turns that this one inch of wire will provide around a hook shank of the same diameter.

[2] The metal beads, excluding lead, are counterdrilled "Brite Beads" sold by Spirit River, Inc. The brass beads are marketed as "Real Gold," though the material is brass. Copper and nickel beads are plated brass. Tapered-hole beads are similar in weight; straight-hole beads are slightly heavier.

[3] The sizes of both lead and tin shot are typically specified by letters rather than diameters. These sizes are indicated in parentheses. Diameters are approximate since the shot is not uniformly shaped. The type of shot indicated here is round, not the removable style with "tabs."

[4] The glass beads shown here are marketed by Spirit River Inc., as "Hi-Lite Glass Beads." They are sold by size, indicated in parentheses, rather than diameter.

[5] The lead eyes here are sold by Umpqua Feather Merchants, which designates the eyes by the sizes shown in parentheses. The metal eyes are "Dazl-Eyes" sold by Spirit River, Inc. Other brands of metal barbell eyes are similar in weight.

Wrapped Wire

Wrapping wire around a hook shank is the most common method of weighting hooks. It can be accomplished with or without a thread foundation, but the most satisfactory results are obtained if: a) the wrapped wire is bound securely with tying thread to prevent it from shifting or rolling when applying the overbody materials, b) tying thread is used to build a taper from the wire to the hook shank at both front and rear ends of the wire, providing a "ramp" for wrapping the overbody and minimizing the possibility of gaps or thin spots, and c) sufficient room is left between the wire and the hook eye for binding materials and finishing the fly. Waste can be minimized if you wrap wire directly from a small spool rather than cutting individual lengths for each fly.

Lead wire is overwhelmingly the most popular material for weighting hooks, both for its rapid sink-rate and for the ease with which this relatively soft material can be handled. For flies that sink more slowly, however, or for fishing areas in which lead is prohibited, hooks can be weighted with wire of other metals—primarily copper and brass, which can be obtained in various diameters from hardware stores and electrical supply houses, and to a lesser extent, tin.

Wires of all materials are generally applied in the same fashion, with a couple of exceptions. Lead wire is soft enough to be pinched off, pulled apart, or cut with a razor blade when the lead underbody is complete. Trimming harder wires requires a pair of fine-tipped cutters. And caution must be exercised when overwrapping hard wire; cutters can leave a sharp edge that can sever the tying thread. (For details on cutting wire and managing sharp edges, see **Method #21: Trimming Wire**, p. 36.)

The best results are obtained by using wire that is no more than slightly larger than the diameter of the hook shank. Thick wires are difficult to wrap around thin hook shanks and often do not hold securely.

In any of the following wrapped-wire methods, a drop of gel-type CA glue can be applied to the area of the shank that will be weighted. The wire is wrapped directly over the glue, giving a quick, secure bond to the shank. Use restraint, however, in applying the adhesive; the wraps of wire will push the glue along the shank—possibly to an area that you wish to keep free of adhesive.

Lastly, some patterns are weighted by constructing the finished fly body itself of wire; techniques for doing so are presented in **Method #74: Single-layer Wire Body**, p. 162; **Method #75: Double-layer Wire Body**, p. 162; and **Method #76: Thorax-wrapped Wire Body**, p. 162.

Method #1:

The Eye-anchor Wrap

This technique is simple, fast, and sure, but restricted to wires small enough to pass through the hook eye.

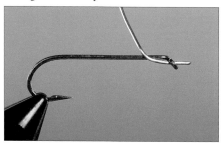

Step 1. If desired, lay a thread underbody on the shank, and leave the bobbin at the rear of the hook. This method, however, works well with a bare hook shank, as is used here.

Insert the wire through the hook eye so that just a short tag protrudes.

Angle the wire down the hook shank, as shown, to the point where you wish the wire wraps to begin.

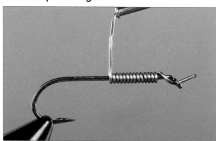

Step 2. Wrap the wire in tight, touching wraps to the end of the underbody.

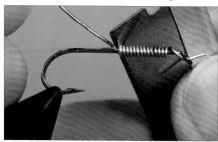

Step 3. If using lead, pinch the wire between your thumbnail and the hook shank to shear it off. Lead wire can also be cut with a razor blade. Trim wires of other metals with wire cutters.

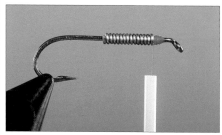

Step 4. Pinch or cut the tag of wire at the head of the underbody.

Mount the tying thread directly against the front of the wire wraps, and winding back and forth across the hook shank, build up a taper. (If the tying thread is already attached and positioned at the rear of the shank, build the rear taper first.)

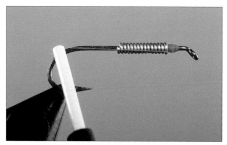

Step 5. Pull the tying thread to the back of the wire wraps; do not wrap the thread back, as it will merely slip between the turns of wire and separate them slightly. (If you have built the rear taper first, pull the thread from back to front and build the front taper.)

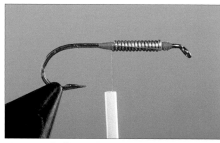

Step 6. Build a similar taper at the rear of the wire wraps. Abut the thread tightly against the wire to squeeze it between the two thread tapers and hold it in place.

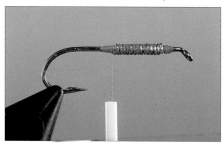

Step 7. Working back and forth across the shank, overwrap the wire with tying thread to secure it.

Method #2:

The Direct Wrap

This technique will work with wire of any diameter, as well as with the flat lead strips—of the type used to add weight to a leader, or those cut from lead tape. Using a bobbin to hold the lead wire, as shown in the following demonstration, minimizes waste.

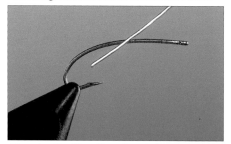

Step 1. Position the wire at the rear of the thread foundation, crossing the hook shank with a short tag protruding, as shown.

5

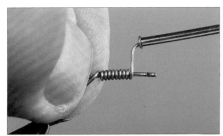

Step 2. Grasp the tag with your left hand, and with your right hand simply wrap the wire in tight, adjacent turns.

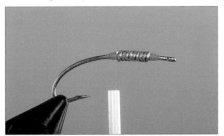

Step 3. Finish the underbody by pinching or cutting the wire, forming tapers, and overwrapping as described in **Method #1: The Eye-anchor Wrap**, Steps 4-7, p. 38.

Method #3:
The Bound-tag Wrap

Though a bit slower than other methods, this technique uses tying thread to anchor the wire, freeing both hands for wrapping. This method works best with a cut length of wire. Flat lead strips can be wrapped with this method by angle-cutting the end and securing the point to the hook shank.

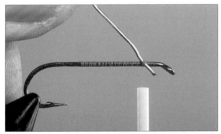

Step 1. A foundation of thread on the shank helps to secure the wire in mounting. Using an angle wrap, bind the wire at the front of the underbody, leaving a small tag.

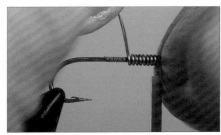

Step 2. With the right hand, pinch the wire at the mounting point.

With the left hand, wrap the wire toward the hook bend. Note the short bobbin thread, which minimizes interference from the bobbin when wrapping the wire.

Once a few turns of wire are applied, both hands can be used for faster wrapping.

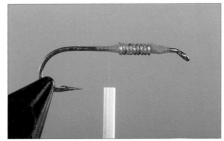

Step 3. Cut or pinch off the wire at front and rear, form tapers, and overwrap the body as described in **Method #1: The Eye-anchor Wrap**, Steps 4-7, p. 38.

Method #4:
The Double-layer Wrap

Two layers of wire can be wrapped to give the fly extra weight or thicken the body profile. This approach is particularly useful when tying heavily weighted flies from non-toxic wires such as copper and brass, which are less dense than lead and require more wraps to produce an equivalent weight.

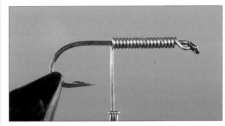

Step 1. Using any of the methods previously described, wrap a wire underbody, but do not trim the excess material.

Step 2. When the rear of the underbody is reached, angle the wire toward the hook eye and wrap a second layer of wire over the first. Note that the second layer ends a few wraps behind the front of the first layer. Staggering the layers will help taper the wire underbody and facilitate wrapping other materials over it.

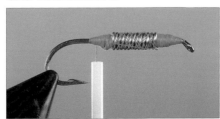

Step 3. Pinch or cut the wire at the front of the body. Form the front and rear tapers, and secure the wire with thread, as described in **Method #1: The Eye-anchor Wrap**, Steps 4-7, p. 38.

Wrapping subsequent materials will be easier if thread is used to build a taper not only from the first layer of wire to the hook shank, but from the second layer of wire to the first.

Method #5:
The Thorax Wrap

A double layer of wire can be used to widen a nymph underbody at the thorax, adding weight and shaping the body in one operation. This method is well-suited to producing rather heavily weighted flies when lead wire is used; with lighter wires, such as copper or brass, the underbody shape is built up quickly without producing an excessively heavy fly.

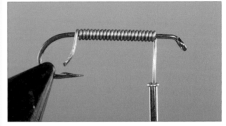

Step 1. Using **Method #2: The Direct Wrap**, p. 38, apply a layer of wire from the hook bend to the eye.

Step 2. Angle the wire back toward the bend, and add a second layer only over the thorax portion of the fly.

Step 3. Cut or pinch the wire, build tapers, and overwrap as described in **Method #4: The Double-layer Wrap**, Step 3.

Method #6:
Flattened Wire

Lead-wire bodies wrapped using any of the methods described in this chapter can be broadened slightly with a pair of pliers to produce a wider, flatter body shape. Non-toxic wires, because they are harder, do not lend themselves to this technique quite as readily as lead, though some degree of flattening can be achieved even with these materials.

The key to flattening lead-wire bodies is to use restraint. As the wire is squeezed in the plier jaws, it is pinched against the hook wire, and overly aggressive pressure will force the hook shank completely through the lead, cutting the wire and ruining the underbody.

Both single and multiple layer bodies made of wire can be flattened. The amount of "spread" obtainable on the body depends largely on the thickness of the wire used.

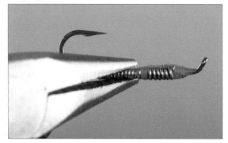

Step 1. Wrap a wire underbody using any of the methods described above.

Use a pair of flat-jawed needle-nose pliers, and position the hook crosswise in the jaws. Beginning at one end of the wire underbody, gently squeeze the wire to flatten it. Again, do not use too much pressure; only a small, but still perceptible, flattening is possible without breaking the wire.

Because the plier jaws close at an angle, they will not compress the wire uniformly across the body. Thus you should work down one side of the hook first, as shown above.

Step 2. Reverse the hook in the pliers and gently squeeze and flatten the wire on the other side.

Lashed and Lead-tape Weight

Wire or lead strips can be lashed to the hook shank to add weight to a fly (though the amount of weight added is generally less than that obtained by wrapping wire) and at the same to broaden the body profile. The material can be lashed to the full length of the hook shank, to the thorax portion only, or to only one side of the shank, depending on the silhouette desired in the finished fly.

Wire, which is readily obtainable in a variety of diameters, is the most widely used material. Since lashed wires are not wrapped, it is possible to use less malleable types of material. Fly designer and tyer George Grant, for instance, used brass pins for lashed underbodies on his woven-body flies. The method for lashing wire to the hook shank is identical to that for lashing other, unweighted materials to form underbodies, and the technique for doing so is detailed in **Method #8: Lashed Underbody**, p. 45. When using this method, lead wire can be cut with a razor blade to produce the necessary tapers. Other wires must

be trimmed with a pair of fine-tipped wire cutters.

The use of lead strips, of the type sold for adding weight to the leader, can increase the range of profiles created by lashed weight. Because they are flat and thin, lead strips can be trimmed, and then mounted edgewise, to create a broad, flat profile, as shown in the method that follows.

Though not commonly sold for fly tying, adhesive-backed lead tape is widely available at golf pro-shops where it is used to weight club shafts. This tape can be used in two ways. It can be sandwiched around the hook shank, using its own adhesive to hold it in place. This technique is identical to that for forming underbodies from lightweight metal tape and is detailed in **Method #11: Metal-tape Underbody**, p. 48. Or it can be used to fashion strips for lashing.

Sold by the foot, lead tape is typically 3/4" in width. With a straightedge and a razor blade, however, it can be trimmed to form narrower strips. These can be affixed to one another by joining their adhesive sides, making a strip of double thickness for lashed-strip underbodies.

Method #7:
Lashed Weight

Lead strips—both those used for adding weight to a leader or those formed from adhesive lead tape—can be lashed to a hook shank to form flattened or asymmetrically shaped weighted underbodies.

It's simplest to cut the strips to shape before mounting them on the hook shank. The sequence below pictures lead strips lashed to form a widened abdomen on a dragonfly nymph.

Step 1. Stack two lead strips. With heavy-duty fly tying scissors—preferably a pair reserved exclusively for cutting lead, metal tape, and so on—cut the underbody sections to the desired shape.

Here, the ends of the strips will be tapered for the nymph underbody.

Step 2. Lay a foundation of thread on the hook, and position the bobbin at the front end of the underbody.

Lay one of the lead strips against the far side of the hook shank, as shown in this top view. Pinch it tightly near the tip, and begin binding it down with tying thread.

Step 3. Lash the strip to the shank using firm wraps, but not overly tight ones that will curl or deform the lead.

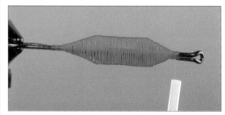

Step 4. Take the second strip, lay it on the near side of the shank, and lash it alongside as you did the first.

Step 5. Give the lashed underbody a coat of CA glue.

Step 6. A wide range of lashed styles are possible. Pictured here, from top to bottom are: a widened-thorax underbody for nymphs; a single, curved lashing for scud or shrimp patterns; lead lashed for a Zonker-style streamer. The hook at the bottom has wire lashed to the sides of the shank that is subsequently overwrapped with a layer of wire for extra weight. When overwrapping a lashed weight with wire, the key is to keep the lashed wires short on the front and rear ends, to ensure room for dressing the head and tail of the fly.

CHAPTER 6

Underbodies

Underbodies are essentially shaped foundations on the hook shank over which the final body materials are applied. Underbodies serve various functions—to provide a smooth base for winding flat body materials like peacock quill or tinsel; to give a specific, usually lifelike, shape or contour to the body that would be difficult or impossible to achieve with the body materials alone; or to provide a smooth, even foundation over the butt ends of materials already bound to the hook shank. Underbodies are often used as well to build bulk quickly on larger patterns, where the application of the finished body material alone—dubbing, for instance—would be tedious and time-consuming. Some underbodies are formed with metal wire or strips of lead, but their principal purpose is less to give shape to the body than add weight to the fly, and the techniques for dressing these materials are presented separately in Chapter 5: "Weighting Hooks."

Underbodies can be fashioned from almost any material, but tyers tend to choose those that are relatively inexpensive and easily applied, like wool yarn or floss, and those that contribute in some way to the performance of the finished fly. Thus dry-fly underbodies might be made from a non-absorbent or buoyant material like poly yarn, which assists floatation. Nymph underbodies might be wrapped from wool yarn or soft leather since these materials absorb water and do not inhibit sinking.

Whatever the material, underbodies should be formed with both restraint and forethought. In applying materials, bear in mind that the overbody will add some bulk to the finished fly. A heavy-handed application of underbody material may eventually produce a fly with a disproportionately bulky body. On streamers, and particularly on nymphs, terminate the underbody well short of the tailing point and hook eye. There must enough space to mount and tie off subsequent materials.

Underbody materials that build bulk rapidly are rarely used on hooks smaller than size 10 or 12, since most ordinary body materials build up quickly enough on smaller hooks to shape the fly body without the extra step of constructing an underbody.

Wrapped Underbodies

The most common type of underbody is fashioned from material wrapped around the hook shank, since tyers generally find this pro-cedure to be quick, easy, and accurate. It does, however, limit the underbody to a few basic shapes, all of which are symmetrical about the hook shank and circular in cross-section.

Floss, Yarn, Chenille, and Foam Underbodies

A number of materials used to form underbodies are also used to fashion fly bodies, and chief among these are floss, yarn, and to a lesser extent, foam and chenille. The techniques for fashioning underbodies with these materials are in fact identical to those used to form bodies, and the specific applicable methods are indicated below.

Floss is typically used as an underbody on dry flies since it builds bulk rather slowly, giving the tyer good control over the precise underbody shape and providing a firm foundation for subsequent body materials. Of particular note are the newer flosses that have an almost loosely woven texture when slack. They are slightly elastic, and when wrapped tightly, they form a smooth, flat band quite similar in appearance to traditional floss but with none of the fiber separation or straying that is often a problem with the more conventional material.

Yarns are generally used on larger flies, particularly nymphs, and streamers to a lesser extent. Wool yarns build bulk rapidly, allow a moderate degree of control over underbody shape, and provide a firm foundation. The surface is usually rough in texture and helps grip body materials, such as dubbing, that are applied over it. Yarns spun from absorbent materials such as wool and many synthetics are generally used on subsurface patterns. Poly yarn is better suited to dry flies since it is slightly buoyant, resists water absorption, and has a finer texture to give better control over the body shape. Floss and yarn can be dressed as underbodies using the techniques shown in **Method #5: Single-layer Floss Body**, p. 102; **Method #6: Double-layer Floss Body**, p. 103; **Method #7: Bullet-taper Floss Body**, p. 104; and **Method #8: Reverse-taper Floss Body**, p. 104.

Chenille has more limited applications in wrapping underbodies and is primarily used underneath woven Mylar tubing of the type used to form bodies on Zonkers and other streamer patterns. For this purpose, however, it is very useful. The fluffy fiber-spread of a single layer of chenille is usually adequate to fill out the interior of the tubing and give the body an impression of bulk without adding weight or requiring much tying time. Such an underbody can be formed using the procedure described in **Method #1: Simple Chenille Body**, p. 99.

Foam is occasionally used as an underbody on both floating and subsurface patterns. Closed-cell foam is used on dry flies, where it gives an unsual amount of buoyancy to the pattern; open-cell foam, which absorbs water, is used on sinking patterns. (For information on types of foam, see p. 190.) Both types build bulk rather quickly on the hook shank, and they would probably be used more widely if not for a single drawback—foam cannot be wrapped very tightly around the shank. Closed-cell foam wrapped under excessive tension compresses, and the small air-filled cells that give the material its buoyancy can rupture, greatly reducing the floatation it lends a fly. Open-cell foam can be wrapped under fairly high tension, but the volume of the material greatly decreases, and in the end, tightly wrapped foam of this type builds bulk no more quickly, and is no more absorbent, than yarn, and it is somewhat more troublesome to tie since it tears readily. Thus foam underbodies must be wrapped under moderate tension, and this can result in a somewhat loose, spongy underbody, which makes it difficult to apply a layer of body material over it. Better success can be had by using foam as the core of a pulled body. The procedure for wrapping foam is the same as that explained in **Method #108: Wrapped Foam Body**, p. 193.

The important point to bear in mind when wrapping foundations of these materials is to keep them undersize and allow the overbody material to bring the fly body into its proper final dimensions.

Thread Underbodies

Probably the simplest type of underbody is one formed from tying thread. Since thread does not build up bulk very quickly, it's generally used in two applications—for underbodies on very small flies, and for underbodies on larger flies with very slim profiles.

Method #1:

Straight Thread Underbody

This basic technique produces a smooth, untapered foundation—typically for bodies made of flat, ribbonlike materials such as tinsel and floss, or bodies made of thin-diameter materials such as wire.

Generally, the tail will be mounted, the body material tied in at the tailing point, and the thread foundation wrapped to the body tie-off point. (Double-layered tinsel bodies are an exception, as shown in **Method #71: Double-layer Tinsel Body**, p. 160.)

Step 1. With the tail in place, mount the body material—floss, in this case—at the tailing point.

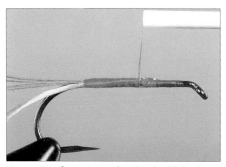

Step 2. Counterspin the bobbin (see **Method #7: Controlling Thread Twist**, p. 21) to produce a flat, flosslike strand. Wrap the thread forward. Adjacent wraps should slightly overlap one another.

Note that both body and tailing material are bound over length of the shank to help maintain a uniform underbody diameter. Work for a smooth, even foundation, pausing often to counterspin the bobbin to maintain a flat thread.

Stop the thread at the body tie-off point and wind the body material forward.

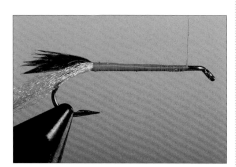

Step 1a. With larger hooks or certain materials, such as these turkey quills, the tailing butts may not extend the entire length of the shank. In this case, taper the tail butts by angle-cutting, and tie in the body material. The thread underbody will have a gradual taper, but will provide a good foundation provided that it is smooth.

Method #2:
Tapered Thread Underbody

Since flat materials (such as peacock quill), or those of uniform diameter (such as twisted yarn) will not naturally produce a tapered body, tying thread can be used to shape the underbody and give the finished fly the proper profile.

The taper shown in the following demonstration is used on adult mayfly patterns, but other shapes are certainly possible. The key is to form smooth, even layers of the thread over the thickest part of the taper.

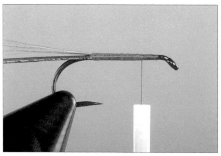

Step 1. With tail and body material mounted, form a smooth, uniform-diameter foundation, and stop the thread at the body tie-off point.

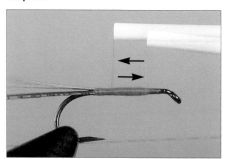

Step 2. Maintaining a flat thread, wrap back about ⅔ of the way to the hook bend, and return the thread to the tie-off point.

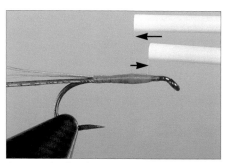

Step 3. Again with a flat thread, wrap back about ⅓ the distance to the hook bend, and return to thread to the tie-off point.

Leather and Latex Underbodies

It does sound a little kinky, but both of these materials are useful in forming underbodies. They can be cut to specific sizes and shapes, making them practical for a wide range of hook sizes and body styles. Since

these materials are, in varying degrees, elastic, they must be stretched as they are wrapped. The elasticity helps them conform to the hook shank, and once wrapped, the underbody can be altered in shape by overwinding with tying thread, using a heavy pressure to reduce the underbody diameter, or a lighter pressure to preserve it. The finished underbody, however, may be somewhat compressible and too "spongy" for the secure mounting of materials on top of the foundation. Thus some tyers will cover the entire underbody in tying thread to make it more solid and give a firmer base for attaching subsequent materials.

Both leather and latex are especially useful in forming underbody foundations for woven-body flies.

Method #3:
Leather Underbody

Thin, soft, pliable leathers make good medium- to high-bulk underbodies without adding excessive weight. Because it absorbs water readily, leather is generally used for subsurface patterns like the dragonfly nymph pictured in the following sequence. Soft-tanned leather, about ¹⁄₁₆" thick, or less, works well. An ordinary chamois (either natural or synthetic) of the type used to wash automobiles serves the purpose nicely.

Step 1. Cover the hook shank with a secure foundation of heavy tying thread, and position the thread at the rearmost point of the underbody.

Cut a strip of leather (we're using chamois here) that is about ⅓ the width of the hook gap. Taper one end to a point, as shown.

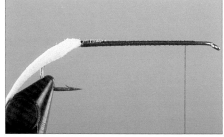

Step 2. Mount the leather strip by the point. Make certain that the leather is mounted over the thread foundation, and secure it with tight, closely spaced wraps. A solid underbody requires pulling and stretching the leather, and tight wraps are necessary to prevent the material from rolling around the hook shank.

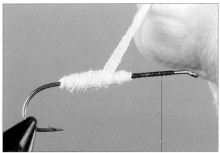

Step 3. Pull the leather tightly (notice the stretch) and begin wrapping it around the shank. To build bulk, wrap the leather in closely overlapping turns.

The underbody shown here will have a pronounced abdomen and a smaller thorax to rough out the shape of the dragonfly nymph, but many other profiles are possible depending upon the placement of the wraps and degree of overlap.

Step 4. Wrap to the tie-off point, decreasing the overlap to narrow the body. Leave plenty of room for the head of the fly, and bind down the leather strip with several tight wraps of thread.

To trim the material, stretch the leather toward the hook eye and clip it close to the shank. Bind down the tag with tight wraps of thread, and you are ready to apply the overbody material.

Method #4:
Latex Underbody

The type of latex sold in sheets for fly tyers is a versatile underbody material (and a versatile body material as well—see "Latex, Plastic, and Vinyl Bodies," p. 164). Because it can be stretched quite thin, it is suitable for underbodies on hooks as small as #10 or #12. Latex floats—but just barely—and is non-absorbent, making it suitable for underbodies on dry flies, emergers, and nymphs that float or sink slowly.

Latex can be cut to shape—usually into strips for underbodies—with a pair of scissors. Very sharp shears are better than fly-tying scissors, but smooth, even cuts are still tricky. In *Modern Fly Dressings for the Practical Angler*, Poul Jorgensen recommends sandwiching the latex sheet between stiff pieces of paper or cardboard—a file folder works nicely. Rule lines on the paper and cut the "sandwich" with a pair of shears or lever-type paper cutter.

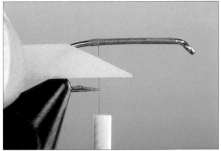

Step 1. Wrap a thread foundation along the hook shank. Cut a latex strip whose width is about ¾ the width of the hook gap. Trim one end to a point as shown.

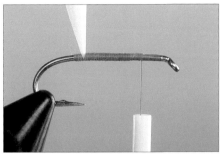

Step 2. Tie in the point of the latex strip about ⅛" ahead of the mounting point for the body material.

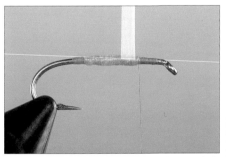

Step 3. Keep the latex flat and stretch it tightly. Begin wrapping the underbody. The stretched latex becomes quite thin and builds bulk slowly.

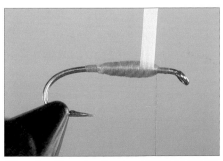

Step 4. At parts of the underbody where you wish to increase the diameter abruptly—as in the thorax area of this mayfly nymph—wind the latex back and forth across the hook shank, gradually building thickness with each pass.

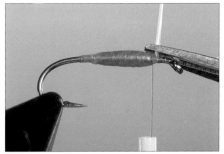

Step 5. When the underbody is complete, advance the latex strip to the front end of the underbody, and bind it down to the hook shank. Note that the thread foundation extends beyond the underbody; the latex strip should be bound down on top of this foundation. Note as well that the underbody ends well back from the hook eye, leaving sufficient room to tie down subsequent materials.

Trim the latex by stretching it forward and clipping it close to the hook shank.

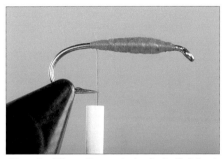

Step 6. When the underbody is finished, wrap a layer of thread over the front taper of the underbody. Spiral the tying thread to tail, and wrap a layer of thread over the rear portion. These thread bases will aid in securing subsequent materials.

Method #5:
Compressed Underbody

Though often discussed in older tying books, this technique is seldom mentioned in modern texts. It is, nonetheless, quite useful, particularly for creating flattened underbodies on smaller hooks, which are difficult to dress with the lashing methods more typically used for flat underbodies. In fact, the method is best reserved for hooks size 10 and smaller, since only a limited amount of "spread" is obtainable on the underbody by compressing it with pliers.

The selection of underbody material is important. It must absorb the head cement (which eliminates waxed tying thread); it must be limp rather than springy (which rules out most synthetic yarns); it should be somewhat compressible (which argues for stranded or twisted materials over monofilament types); and it must strong enough to resist cutting or breaking under pressure (which excludes most flosses). Thin cotton or wool yarns work well, though other materials may be acceptable.

The adhesive can be either head cement or CA glue; both have their advantages. If using head cement, dilute it with solvent to a very thin consistency. It must penetrate to the core of the underbody wrappings so that the underbody will maintain its shape and adhere well to the hook shank. In either case, keep a container of solvent close at hand—lacquer thinner for most head cements, acetone for CA glue. When you've finished forming the underbody, immediately wipe the down the plier jaws with solvent to remove any adhesive.

One of the most interesting versions of this technique is one rarely practiced anymore, owing primarily to the difficulty in obtaining a key material—acetate floss. An underbody of the type pictured in the following sequence is wrapped from acetate floss. A few drops of acetone are applied with an eye dropper or small syringe. In 15-30 seconds, the outer layer of floss partially dissolves and softens into an almost plastic-like putty. It can then be flattened with pliers. For a still flatter body, apply a few more drops of acetone to saturate the inner layers of floss, and flatten again. The underbody will usually harden in about 25-30 minutes, depending on its size. Once hard, it resembles a rigid plastic.

Acetate floss can create an extremely broad, flat body, since the floss filaments dissolve and bond to one another, and they will not cut when squeezed by the plier jaws. In fact, with repeated applications of acetone, and repeated shaping with pliers, it is possible to make a nymph thorax, for instance, that is quite wide but only very slightly thicker than the hook shank. Consequently, relatively little floss need be applied to the hook since virtually all the material is squeezed to the sides of the shank.

The drawback to this technique, aside from handling acetone, which like any solvent should always be used with care, is the long hardening time.

Acetate floss is still available—very occasionally—and should you locate some, it would be worth picking up a spool and giving this most unusual technique a try.

In the following demonstration, however, more readily obtainable wool yarn and head cement are used, though the procedure for using floss and acetone is identical.

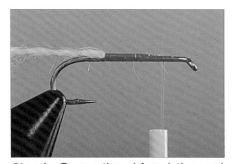

Step 1. Form a thread foundation, and bind down the underbody material *very tightly* to the hook shank. It's important that these thread wraps be very secure to prevent the underbody from twisting around the shank.

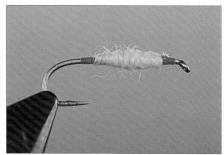

Step 2. Wrap the material to form an underbody of the desired shape (see "Floss, Yarn, Chenille, and Foam Underbodies," p. 41). Wrap the first layer of yarn tightly around the shank; subsequent layers can applied under a bit less tension, since a slight looseness in the material will promote a broader spread on the finished underbody. Keep the underbody slightly shorter than what you desire for the finished length. When the material is compressed with pliers, it will lengthen as well as widen.

Secure the thread at the front of the underbody with a few half-hitches, and clip it off.

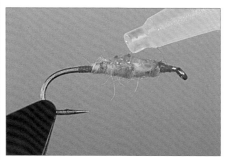

Step 3. Saturate the underbody with adhesive. It should be soaked but not dripping.

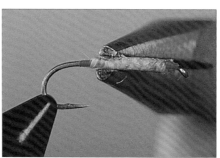

Step 4. With the pliers, squeeze the underbody so that it widens, forming "shoulders" in a horizontal plane. Use moderate pressure, working up and down the hook, from eye to bend and back again several times. Using excessive pressure may cut the underbody material. Flatten it gradually. Use the pliers near the tip to prevent getting adhesive into the hinge of the plier jaws, especially if using CA glue.

After flattening the body, apply a bit more adhesive, as you will have squeezed much of the glue out to the edges of the underbody.

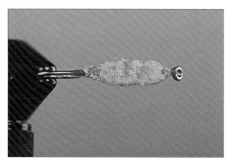

Step 5. Let the finished underbody dry thoroughly.

Mated Underbodies

Creating smooth underbody foundations is often complicated by the presence of materials already bound to the hook shank. The bound-down butts of wing, tail, and body materials can produce bumps and irregularities on the hook shank that show up as an improper or uneven shape on the finished body. It can be a particular problem on dry flies that incorporate body materials such as quill or floss which, unlike dubbing, have little bulk with which to even out the body silhouette as they are wrapped. The solution here is to integrate the butts of materials already bound to the shank into a uniform underbody foundation.

Method #6:
Spliced Underbody

On dry flies, wing and tail butts can be "spliced" at an angle to create a smooth underbody. While some tyers prefer to mount dry-fly wings first and others prefer to begin with the tails, this technique is most effective when the material with the greater bulk is mounted first.

Step 1. Mount the wings—here we're using calf body hair—and trim with angle cut (see **Method #17: The Angle Cut**, p. 35, and **Method #18: The Bend Cut**, p. 35). Bind down the wing butts.

Step 2. Wrap the tying thread to the tailing position and mount the tail. A contrasting color of calf tail is used here for a greater visibility in demonstrating the technique. Do not trim the tail butts.

Step 3. Bind the down the butts with flattened tying thread. Pause occasionally, if necessary, to reposition the butts on top of the hook shank.

Continue wrapping the tail butts until they are bound down over the tips of the taper-cut wing butts, as shown here.

Step 4. Pull the tail butts upward and slightly forward so that they match the wing-butt taper. Lay the scissors across the top of the hook shank.

Step 5. Clip the tail butts flush with the wing-mounting wraps, as shown here.

When the tail butts are covered with thread, a smooth, even underbody will be formed.

Note that in this case, where both tail and wing materials are relatively thick, the underbody will be of a nearly uniform diameter. Had thinner clump hackle barbs been used for the tail, the underbody would assume a more tapered shape.

Method #7:
Abutted Underbody

This approach is used most often on weighted flies with bulky tailing materials such as bucktail, marabou, synthetic hairs, or twisted Mylar.

Step 1. Mount the tail and bind it securely to the shank. Use plenty of thread and very tight wraps. Clip the butts perpendicular to the hook shank.

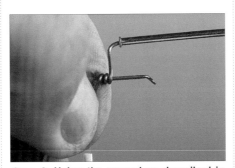

Step 2. Using the procedure described in **Method #2: The Direct Wrap**, p. 38, begin wrapping lead wire from the tail, closely abutting the end of the marabou.

Step 3. Wrap the lead along the desired length of hook shank, and trim the ends.

Secure the lead wire with wraps of tying thread, and build a thread taper at the front of the lead wraps as shown in **Method #1: The Eye-anchor Wrap**, Step 5, p. 38. (We've omitted these steps for a clearer illustration.)

The overbody material can be mounted and applied over this relatively uniform-diameter underbody.

Lashed, Molded, and Metal-tape Underbodies

With the exception of the flattened shape produce by **Method #5: Compressed Underbody**, p. 43, wrapped underbodies share one common feature—they produce a foundation that is radially symmetrical, that is, one that's circular in cross-section. But a large number of aquatic food forms—many nymphs, most fishes—do not exhibit this type of symmetry. Rather, their cross-sectional profiles tend to be more elliptical, some nearly round, others narrower, still others quite flattened, and tyers use a number of techniques to reproduce these shapes, which in general are restricted to subsurface patterns.

Method #8:
Lashed Underbody

One of the most commonly imitated aquatic insects is the mayfly nymph, and those species often categorized as "crawlers" tend to have broad, flat bodies, particularly in thorax area. Lashing materials to the side of the hook shank widens the profile without adding thickness to the body.

Any material that is relatively non-compressible can be used, and selection depends largely on the characteristics of the finished fly. Lead wire offers a quick sink-rate. For slower-sinking flies, sections of sinking fly line can be used, and where no weight is desired, lengths of ordinary monofilament line. Rigid wires, such as sections cut from ordinary straight pins, are sometimes employed as well.

As a general rule, choose a material that is approximately the same diameter or thickness as the hook shank. Materials that are appreciably smaller add little width to the underbody, and those that are much larger are difficult to lash. Lashed underbodies are practical for hooks down to about size 12.

Step 1. Select two pieces of lashing material—we're using pieces of fly line here—each about an inch longer than the hook. Place them together as shown, and with a sharp razor blade trim the ends at an angle no steeper than 45 degrees. Cutting the pieces at the same time like this will ensure that this angle, which forms the front taper of the underbody, is the same on both pieces.

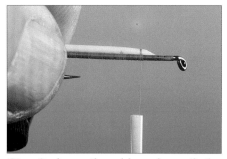

Step 2. Lay a thread base beneath the underbody area. Position one of the lashing strips along the far side of the hook shank, as shown in this top view. Note the placement: plenty of room is left between the lashing and the hook eye for binding down materials and finishing the fly. Take one complete wrap, under moderate tension, around the material. Note the thread placement slightly behind the tapered areas.

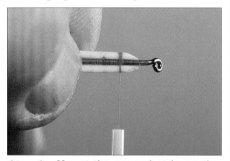

Step 3. Mount the second strip on the near side of the hook shank directly opposite the first. Note in this top view that the tapered ends angle down to the hook shank. The lashing materials should lie in a horizontal plane with the shank.

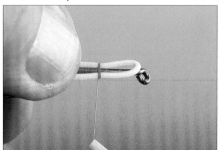

Step 3a. On larger hooks, with more working room, you can mount both sides at once. Fold the lashing material back on itself, forming a loop. Position the material as shown, with the loop toward the hook eye, and bind down with 3 or 4 tight wraps of the thread.

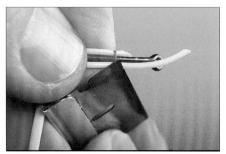

Step 3b. With a sharp razor blade, trim both sides at an angle, using the hook shank as a backstop. Note that there is no thread foundation beneath the cutting area.

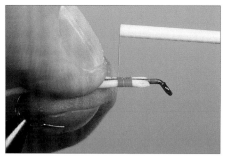

Step 4. Use thumb and forefinger to pinch the lashing strips and hook shank together in a horizontal plane, and continue binding the material toward the bend. Do not use excessive thread pressure or the lashings will roll around the shank.

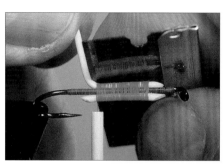

Step 5. When most of the underbody area has been covered, stop wrapping. Grab the tags of material, and with a sharp razor blade, trim them at the desired angle.

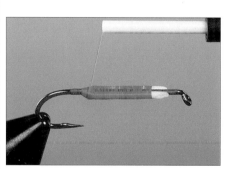

Step 6. Bind down the butts, again using your thumb and forefinger to ensure that the material stays in a horizontal plane.

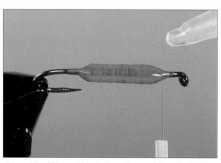

Step 7. Wrap the tying thread back to the head and bind the down the front taper. Put a drop of glue—head cement will work, CA glue will work better—over the underbody, and let it dry.

You can form bodies of varying shapes with this technique, lashing material to part, most, or all of the hook shank. A steep rear taper will make an abrupt underbody transition; a more gradual angle cut will produce a longer taper on the abdomen.

Method #9:
Frame Underbody

In this method, shown to us by Finnish tyer Veli Autti, a shaped hook wire and a length of monofilament are used to construct an underbody frame for use on baitfish patterns.

The main sequence shows how this frame can be used to contain a cut section of foam for floating minnow patterns. The alternate sequence demonstrates the construction of an open frame. This underbody can be left hollow, for slow sinking flies, or lead wire can be lashed or wrapped on the hook for faster-sinking patterns.

This underbody design relies on a particular hook design. The "swimming nymph" hook used in the following demonstration is available from a couple of different manufacturers, but an ordinary streamer hook hand-formed to the shape shown will serve as well.

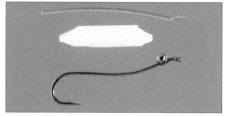

Step 1. Shown here are the components required for a frame underbody with a foam insert.

At the top is a length of monofilament (about .030"); note that the front has been flattened with pliers to facilitate mounting.

In the middle is a strip of closed-cell foam, trimmed to shape for the insert.

At the bottom is swimming nymph hook. Autti dresses this fly with bead-chain eyes (see **Method #7: Barbell Eyes**, p. 431); other types of eyes can be used, or they can be omitted altogether.

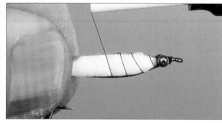

Step 2. Using a series of crisscross wraps, lash the flatted end of the mono between the barbell eyes.

Trap the trimmed foam between the shank and the mono, as shown. Wrap the tying thread toward the rear of the hook. Use firm, but not overly tight thread pressure, to compress the foam slightly and trap it in position. Pinch the foam between the left fingers during wrapping to keep it in the proper orientation.

Step 3. When the rear of the fly is reached, bind the mono securely to the

shank and trim it to leave a tag about ⅛" long, as shown at the rear of the fly.

At the rear of the hook, mount an over-body material; shown here is length of pearlescent Mylar tubing that has been frayed into strands.

When the body material is mounted, wrap the thread forward over the foam foundation, making a series of "X" wraps against the side, as are visible here.

At this point, the foam can be colored with waterproof markers if desired, and the eyes painted, as shown.

Wrap the overbody material forward and secure it behind the bead-chain eyes.

Step 4. At the top is a finished fly of this type tied by Veli Autti. Additional body coloration has been added, and a fur-strip wing tied over the top (see Steps 2a-3a below).

Pictured at the bottom is a fly dressed over the hollow underbody formed in the alternate sequence. It has a body of woven Mylar tubing, and a "sewn Matuka" wing attached as shown in the alternate steps.

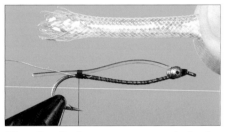

Step 1a. To form an open underbody, attach the mono as explained in Step 2. Raise the tag of monofilament and advance the tying thread to the rear of the body. Secure the mono there with tight thread wraps. Note that a length of silver wire is attached at the rear of the hook; this is needed for dressing the wing.

As shown here, the body is dressed "Zonker-style" with pearlescent woven Mylar tubing (see **Method #77: Woven-tubing Body**, p. 163), and colored with waterproof markers.

Step 2a. Autti dresses this fly with a fur-strip wing, but to get a secure mount over the monofilament on the underbody, he uses a special technique.

The wing is first mounted at the front of the hook using the technique shown in **Method #69: Fur-strip Downwing**, p. 317, and shown here.

Step 3a. Using a dubbing needle, part the hair on the fur strip directly over the thread wraps securing it to the shank. Take a tight wrap of wire over the exposed hide.

Using the wire like a sewing needle, push the end through the back side of the Mylar tubing and out the front side. The wire should pass *beneath* the monofilament that is under the tubing.

Make a second division in the fur, and wrap the wire over the exposed hide once again.

Continue this sewing procedure, lashing the fur strip to the top of the body, making sure that the wire passes beneath the mono each time it is pushed through the body material.

The finished fly is shown in Step 4.

Method #10:
Molded Underbody

Molded underbodies are a useful style, though one not commonly employed by most tyers. They are most practical on larger hooks, as some finger room is required to shape the material, but the plasticity of molding compounds allows even complex underbody shapes to be formed.

The two materials that form the most satisfactory underbodies are epoxy putty and a tungsten-based moldable epoxy sold by Loon Outdoors under the name Hardbody Epoxy. Epoxy putty is widely available at hardware stores, is simple to use, and has a working time of about 30 minutes. It adds only a modest amout of weight to the hook, though heavier flies can be made by molding the material over a foundation of lead wire; if desired, lead strips or lengths of lead wire can be pressed into the pliable epoxy and formed into the underbody. Loon's tungsten putty, by contrast, is quite heavy—about 75% the weight of lead.

We're using commercial epoxy putty in the following demonstration, but the technique for forming Loon Hardbody Epoxy is identical except that no thread foundation on the hook is required.

Step 1. The particular type of epoxy putty used here comes in a single bar containing both resin and hardener. Other types are available, some in tape or ribbon form,

others with separate bars of resin and hardener; their use is identical, however.

Cut off the amount of material needed to form the desired number of underbodies, and knead it thoroughly for 2-3 minutes.

Step 2. Wrap a thread foundation on the portion of the hook shank to be covered with the underbody. Whip-finish or half-hitch the thread, and clip it off.

Pinch off the amount of putty required for the underbody, but be conservative—it takes less than it might seem.

Shaping a full-length underbody is easier if the putty is first rolled into a cylinder; if forming an underbody on only a portion of the shank, roll the putty into a ball.

Press the hook into the formed putty.

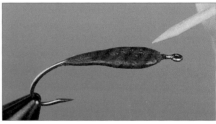

Step 3. Squeeze the putty to completely encase the hook shank.

A few points in the final forming of the underbody are worth noting. First, after encasing the hook shank in the putty, wipe or wash your hands. Some material will rub off on your fingers during kneading and cause your fingertips to stick to the putty as you're forming the underbody. Working with the material is significantly easier with clean fingertips.

Second, mount the hook in a vise for final shaping; it's simpler to work around the hook this way.

Third, a few tools can come in handy. A single-edge razor blade is useful for removing excess material. A few toothpicks and a small container of water are also helpful. The toothpick can be used to smooth surfaces, create "shoulders" on a nymph thorax, and perform various other operations that are a bit too fine for the fingertips. Dipping the toothpick in water will prevent it from sticking to the epoxy.

Using your fingers and whatever tools seem helpful, work the underbody to its final shape.

Step 4. The underbody formed in this sequence, for a stonefly nymph, is at the left. On the right, Loon Hardbody has been used to create an abodmen underbody for a weighted dragonfly nymph.

Method #11:
The Metal-tape Underbody

The adhesive-backed metal tape—sometimes called "Zonker tape"—sold in fly shops is a highly versatile underbody material. It can be trimmed to a variety of shapes, form asymmetrical bodies, and cover large areas of the hook shank quickly. Zonker tape is rather light and adds little weight to the fly; for a more heavily weighted pattern, adhesive-backed lead tape, described in "Lashed and Lead-tape Weight," p. 40, can be used. The method for dressing lead tape is identical to that shown in the following procedures.

There are two demonstrations shown below. Steps 1a-1h show the use of metal tape in creating the underbody for a typical nymph pattern. Steps 2a-2d illustrate its use in fashioning streamer underbodies, where the metal tape is typically used as a foundation for woven-tubing bodies made of Mylar or reflective plastics. The Zonker is perhaps the best-known example, followed by the Janssen Minnow, but many other shapes are possible. Regardless of the style, however, the underbody must be sized so that the woven tubing will still pass over it and so that the hook gap will not be excessively reduced.

Step 1a. Cover the underbody area with a foundation of tying thread.

Cut two identical squares of metal tape. The sides should be roughly equal to the length of the hook shank. Peel away the backing tape from one square; press the adhesive side of this square to the metal side of the second square. This double thickness of material will add rigidity to the fly. (Note: for small hooks, a single layer of material may be used.)

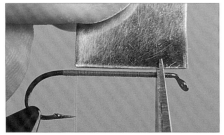

Step 1b. Position the material against the hook shank and make a small cut to mark the underbody length. Trim the tape to this dimension.

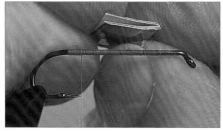

Step 1c. Before peeling the adhesive backing away, fold the material in half crosswise, creasing it along the center. This crease will aid in folding the material evenly.

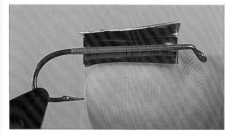

Step 1d. Remove the backing and straddle the underside of the hook shank with half of the tape, as shown. Press upward lightly so that the metal tape sticks to the underside of the shank.

Apply a coating of liquid or gel-type CA glue to the thread wraps.

Step 1e. Fold the top half of the material down, and press the adhesive surfaces together tightly. With pliers or fingernails, work the tape tightly against the hook shank for a good bond.

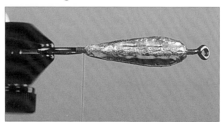

Step 1f. Trim the material parallel to the shank so that the width of the tape is equal to the widest portion of the underbody. Then use scissors to trim the front and rear tapers to the desired shape. A short rear taper will produce a fly with a wide thorax; a long rear taper (as shown here) will widen the abdomen as well.

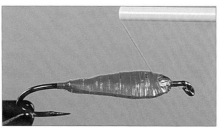

Step 1g. Wrap the tying thread over the tape. Thread pressure should be firm, but

not so tight that it folds or wrinkles the tape. When the thorax area is reached, use crisscross wraps, as shown, to lay the thread over the front taper.

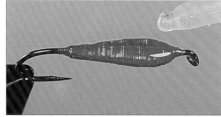

Step 1h. Bring the thread to the hook eye and tie it off with a couple half-hitches. Clip off the thread.

Cover the entire underbody with CA glue and allow it to dry.

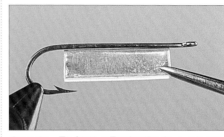

Step 2a. To form a Zonker body, cut a rectangle of metal tape. One edge should be exactly equal to the length of the underbody, the other edge should 1 ½ times the hook gap. Crease the material as described in Step 1c.

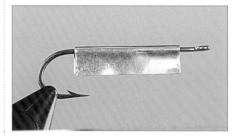

Step 2b. Remove the backing and position the crease over the top of the hook shank. Firmly press the adhesive sides together, using pliers or thumbnail to work the tape tightly against the hook shank.

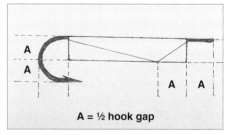

A = ½ hook gap

Step 2c. To form a Zonker body, trim the tape to the proportions shown on this chart.

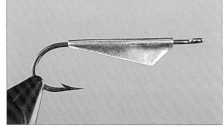

Step 2d. Here, the Zonker body is trimmed to shape.

CHAPTER 7

Wiggle Bodies, Tandem Hooks, and Weed Guards

Wiggle bodies, tandem hooks, and weed guards obviously serve quite different purposes, but they do share a common feature—many of the techniques for fashioning them involve wire or monofilament loops, or shaped wires, that are affixed to the hook shank. Many tyers, suspicious of the difficulty, are reluctant to attempt these techniques. While they are somewhat more involved than ordinary tying procedures, on the whole they are not difficult. Success, however, is best assured by using the proper tools and materials.

For cutting and shaping wire, two tools are essential—first, a pair of high-quality, flat-jawed, fine-point needle-nose pliers. The inexpensive type often sold for bending down hook barbs have jaws that are too soft and often fail to meet precisely at the tips. Second, a pair of small wire cutters, again of good quality. These should be of the "side-cutter" type, where the cutting edges meet on one side of the jaw and allow for trimming wire flush against a surface. A third tool is helpful, but not necessary—a pair of small, fine-pointed, round-jawed needle-nose pliers. All of these tools are most easily obtained at an electronic supply house.

Materials are the second consideration, and choosing the proper ones will greatly improve the ease of tying as well as the durability and performance of the finished fly.

Materials

Wiggle-body hinges, tandem-hook connections, and weed guards can all be made from ordinary monofilament fishing line, and as a rule, the stiffest material is the best. On wiggle bodies and weed guards, stiff mono forms loops that hold their shape well; on tandem hooks, it makes a more rigid connection. Probably the best material for these purposes are the new fluorocarbon of PVDF (polyvinylidenfluoride) monofilaments. They are stiff, strong, impervious to deterioration by sunlight and water, and exceptionally abrasion resistant. However, stiff nylon monofilament such as Mason (hard type) and Maxima are also satisfactory.

Wire is generally stronger and more durable than monofilament. Three types of wire are used in the techniques presented in this chapter, and they differ enough in their characteristics to warrant a brief explanation here.

The wire used for making hinges on wiggle bodies must possess two somewhat contradictory characteristics. It must be stiff, hard, and springy enough to avoid deforming easily and to make a durable fly, but it must be malleable enough to bend and form without much difficulty. Moreover, it must obtainable in relatively fine diameters. The brass, silver, and copper wires ordinarily used in fly tying are too soft for this application. They can be bent by the jaws of a fish or by a snag, and even a small amount of repeated flexing can break them.

We experimented with a large number of different wires and in the end found only two that were really suitable. The first is the type of single-strand wire sold for making spinner shafts. Such wire provides a good compromise between hardness and flexibility, and it is readily obtainable through catalogs that carry lure-making components. The drawback is that this wire is normally available in diameters down to about .011"—about the largest practical size for making wire-hinged bodies on small fly patterns, such as mayfly nymphs. Larger flies, like articulated leeches, allow for the formation of somewhat larger wire loops; hence diameters up to about .014" are practical, and spinner wire is a good choice for this application.

One of the best and most easily obtainable wires for making wiggle bodies comes from an unlikely source—single-strand wire guitar strings sold in music stores. The wire used is hard but sufficiently malleable to shape easily, and it's available in a wide variety of diameters, particularly thinner ones. Strings for electric guitars are made as fine as .008"; from there, the diameters increase to sizes that are outside the useful range. Though somewhat more costly than spinner wire, they are not prohibitively expensive. An inexpensive string is less than a dollar, and at nearly 3 feet long, it can easily form a couple dozen wiggle-body hinges. Harpsichord wire is also ideal for making articulated bodies, though it is more difficult to obtain.

Because of its great strength, wire is also desirable for many tandem-hook techniques. The best choice here is the multi-strand steel wire (Sevenstrand is one brand) sold in the general tackle market for making wire leaders. Where single-strand wire will eventually fatigue and break with repeated flexing, multi-strand wire can endure the abuse. Such wire is sold in both uncoated and nylon-coated versions. Either type can be used, though in tandem-hook riggings where the wire passes through the eye of the trailer hook, the uncoated version allows a larger diameter, and thus stronger, wire to be used. The choice of diameters depends upon the size of the trailing hook, but in general choose the largest wire that will still pass through the hook eye (or the largest diameter that will allow two strands of wire to fit through the eye in those methods that require it).

For making weed guards, there is really only one choice—music wire (Bright Music Wire is a specific type). Fashioned from tempered steel, it differs from guitar string wire. It is harder and springier and, consequently, somewhat more difficult to shape into small loops for wiggle-body hinges (though it is possible to do so with the very smallest diameters). But its resilience makes it ideal for weed guards, and the relatively simple bending operations are not hampered by the hardness of the wire. Music wire is available in both straight cut-lengths, usually of 24" or 36", which are preferable, and in coils, which are less desirable because the wire must first be straightened. It is manufactured in a range of usable diameters (see the chart on p. 61 for recommendations). The one problem is in obtaining it, especially in thinner diameters. Hardware stores and hobby shops may carry a limited selection, but the best bet is probably a machinery supply house.

All of the techniques described below offer strong connections, but they are not indestructible. Repeated flexing can eventually fatigue even stranded wire, and it's prudent to inspect wire connections periodically for fraying or wear. Monofilament is easy to work, but such synthetics have a limited life. Repeated soaking and drying, long exposure to sunlight, nicks from snags or toothy jaws can all weaken the material. Checking the mono from time to time is the best insurance against mishap.

Wiggle Bodies

Extended bodies are used on a wide variety of both floating and subsurface fly patterns, but the extensions themselves fall into two basic categories. Fixed extensions are secured in some manner to the hook shank and are immobile; techniques for dressing this style are detailed in the section "Extended Bodies," p. 204. Some subsurface aquatic food forms, however, are strong swimmers, and an extended body that undulates, wriggles, or flutters best reproduces the characteristic movements of such organisms. Articulated, or "wiggle" bodies are fashioned by adding a "hinged" section to a hook.

Both the hook and extension are dressed, and the hinge allows the rear section of the fly to wiggle freely underwater. No anglers have argued more strenuously for the effectiveness of articulated bodies, or developed more useful designs, than Doug Swisher and Carl Richards in their books *Selective Trout* and *Emergers*. While they advocate this style primarily to imitate certain mayfly nymphs, it can also be used on damselfly nymph, leech, and baitfish patterns.

A hookless extension added to the rear of the main hook is the most common form of wiggle body. It is also possible, however, to create hookless front extensions or a pair of articulated hooks. In these latter designs, however, the articulated rear section is designed to bear the weight of a hooked fish and requires a stronger hinge material and stouter attachment. Thus the methods for making articulated rear hooks are presented separately.

If you're highly partial to articulated bodies with wire-loop hinges, or plan to tie lots of them, you might consider investing in a "spinner tool"—a jig used to twist and form wire used for spinner shafts. These tools can quickly form closed loops with a barrel twist—a kind of wire snell—for the body extension, and can also fashion open loops for the front half of the hinge that is bound to the main hook shank. Such devices, however, are best suited to larger-diameter wires for bigger flies.

Hookless Rear Extensions

Bodies with articulated rear sections are typically used in dressing wiggle nymphs and other smaller patterns, as a solid hookup requires that the trout take the entire fly. As the size of fly increases, so do chances that a trout may nip only the hookless rear body extension, probably failing to become hooked and possibly damaging the dressing.

Method #1:
Single-strand Hinge

With a hinge made from a single strand of heavy tying thread or round rubber leg material, this wiggle body is perhaps the simplest in design. It is particularly useful on smaller patterns, where other hinge methods may prove too bulky. The single-strand hinge provides extremely good movement in the water, but is less durable than hinges fashioned from monofilament or wire.

The body extension is formed from a hook shank or short length of wire, the selection of which is important. To wiggle properly, the articulated section must be light, so choose a hook with a shank that is just long enough to dress the body extension—no longer. The hook wire should be 1X-fine or finer. If plain wire is used (see "Materials," p. 49), select a diameter that is just rigid enough to mount in a vise and dress without

bending. Since most tyers are more apt to have a proper hook at hand rather than suitable wire, a hook is used to demonstrate the procedure.

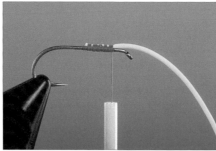

Step 1. Mount the body-extension hook in a vise, and lash a 3-inch piece of heavy tying thread (3/0 will work on smaller patterns; size "A" or "E" nylon, Dacron thread, or even light fly line backing for larger ones), or a length of rubber leg material, as shown here. Note that the lashing ends well behind the hook eye.

Step 2. Cover the hook shank with a tight thread foundation, and coat it with head cement or CA glue. The adhesive helps prevent the body from slipping when the hook is clipped at the bend and eye.

At this point, dress the body extension. (We've omitted this step for clearer illustration.)

Clip the hook off at the top of the bend. Then clip off the hook eye.

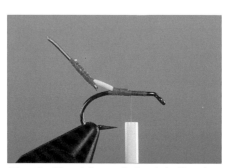

Step 3. Mount the main hook in the vise, and lash the tag of rubber leg material or tying thread to the top. If the extension is lashed very close to the main shank, the abdomen will have an upswept profile, as shown. Leaving a bit of slack in the rubber or tying thread will produce a straighter body.

The remainder of the fly is dressed as usual.

Method #2:
Single-loop Hinge

Like the single-strand method, this technique involves dressing a body extension on a light hook. But in this case, the hook eye is left intact and is threaded on a small loop of tying thread or monofilament tippet material which is bound to the shank of the main hook. This method produces a slightly greater gap between body sections, but is stronger than the single-strand hinge.

The hook used for the body extension should be as light as possible, and it must have a ring-eye or straight eye to articulate freely. The loop material, whether heavy tying thread or monofilament, should pass easily through the eye of the body-extension and allow plenty of play for wiggling.

Step 1. Lash a piece of heavy tying thread or monofilament tippet material of the desired diameter to the top of the main hook shank. Wrap it tightly and clip the excess.

Dress the body extension on the desired hook (we have omitted this step for a clearer illustration), and clip the hook at the top of the bend as described in **Method #1: Single-strand Hinge**, Step 2.

Thread the free end of the mono through the hook eye of the body extension.

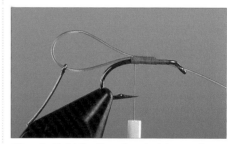

Step 2. Fold the tippet material over, forming a loop. Lash the free end of the loop directly atop the mono already bound to the hook shank. Take two or three wraps under moderate tension, but do not bind tightly. The loop may be large at this point.

Step 3. Take the end of the loop material and pull it smoothly to draw the loop

closed. Bind down the tag of monofilament to secure the loop.

Note that the loop is vertical, that is, at a right angle to the hook eye of the body extension. This ensures maximum movement in the body extension.

Coat the thread wraps securing the loop material with liquid or gel-type CA glue.

The loop should not be made too small, or the body will not wiggle properly. An overly large loop will interfere with the body profile. In general, the finished loop should be slightly larger than the outside diameter of the hook eye on the body extension.

The front hook can now be dressed.

Method #3:
Double-loop Mono Hinge

Because it incorporates two loops of monofilament material, this technique is quite versatile. Both the diameter of the monofilament and the size of the loops can be adjusted to accommodate a wide variety of hook sizes. Forming large loops will produce an extremely free-swinging body extension.

The body extension can be fashioned from a clipped hook or a piece of stiff music wire of the appropriate diameter, as shown in the following sequence.

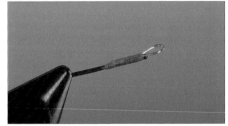

Step 1. Select a short length of wire for the body extension (or clip the eye from a hook). Secure it in the vise and lash a piece of monofilament to one side of the shank.

Proceed to form a loop as described in **Method #2: Single-loop Hinge**, Steps 2-3, p. 50. The difference here, though, is that this loop is formed in a horizontal plane; that is, it has the same orientation as the eye on a ring-eye hook.

Finally, dress the body extension. (Again, we have omitted this dressing for clarity of illustration.)

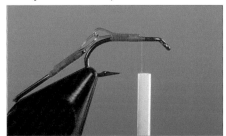

Step 2. Lash a piece of monofilament to the top of the main hook shank. Thread the free end of the mono through the loop on the body extension.

Form a loop on the main hook shank as described in **Method #2: Single-loop Hinge**, Steps 2-3, p. 50. Note that the two loops are perpendicular to one another.

The front hook can now be dressed.

Method #4:
Double-loop Wire Hinge

This technique makes possible a strong and lightweight rear extension, offers great durability in the hinge, and creates a body that wiggles quite freely. With light wire, an unobtrusive hinge and freely wiggling body extension can be fashioned for small nymphs. It produces a precise, even elegant body, but is somewhat more complicated than other methods.

Larger streamer or leech patterns can be made with wire of .012", or even slightly larger, but wires much thicker are difficult to bend and shape. On smaller flies, wire of about .008" in diameter is suitable, though wires much thinner than this are too flexible for easy dressing of the body extension. The body extension can also be formed from a light, ring-eye hook, which simplifies the technique. This option is presented as an alternate step below.

To make this hinge you need a cylindrical form around which to bend the wire and create an "eye." The diameter of the eye, and hence of the bending form, varies with hook size, and there is some latitude here. As a starting point, try forming a hinge eye that is slightly smaller in diameter than the outside of the hook eye.

The bending form can be any hard, metal, cylindrical object, but for most flies, you probably won't need to look further than a selection of ordinary sewing needles. These are available in a variety of diameters, are tapered (which is an advantage), and are inexpensive.

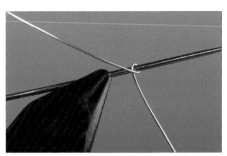

Step 1. Select a piece of wire and clip a piece about 3 inches long. Secure a needle of the desired diameter in the vise. Bend the wire around the needle, and cross the wire ends, pulling tightly to snug the wire around the needle shank to form a circular eye.

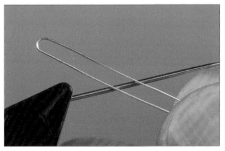

Step 2. Slip the bent wire off the needle, and "uncross" the wire tags, pulling gently to form a U-shaped or "hairpin" bend. The wire tags should be parallel, as shown.

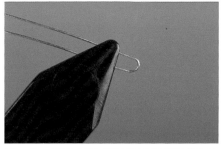

Step 3. Clamp the wire loop in the vise as shown. The length of the loop that extends beyond the jaw tips is somewhat critical. The exposed length of the wire should be about twice the diameter of the loop.

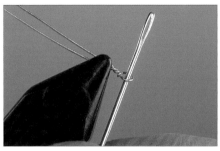

Step 4. Insert the needle through the loop and take 1 ½ to 2 turns, screwing a twist into the wire that locks both tags together. Do not take more than 2 turns or the wire will begin to deform or break.

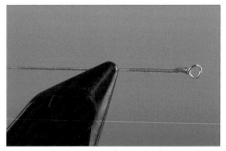

Step 5. Remove the formed wire eye from the vise and clip one tag of the wire. Leave the other one long, and clip it in the vise as shown.

The durability of the finished fly is increased if you cover the wire with tying thread and coat with a film of CA glue, as shown. The cemented threads will not slip off the wire when the excess tag is clipped flush with the body. At this point, however, do not clip the wire tag.

Dress the rear extension on this wire; we've omitted this step for a clearer illustration.

Step 6. Form a second loop of wire, identical to the one formed in Step 1. Slip the dressed body extension onto this loop, and clamp the loop in the vise as described in Step 3, and shown here.

Step 6a. Alternately, the body extension can be formed from a light, ring-eye hook. First, dress the body extension, but do not yet clip off the hook at the bend.

Insert the second wire loop formed in Step 5 through the hook eye, and clamp the loop in the vise. Position the body extension, handling it by the hook bend, so that the hook eye is trapped in the wire loop away from the vise jaws.

Step 7. Again, insert the needle through the new loop. If necessary, adjust the body extension so that the wire eye is trapped in the bend of the new loop, away from the vise jaws. Handle the body extension by the wire tag.

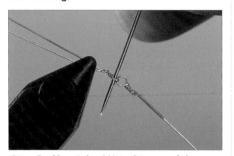

Step 8. Now take 1½ to 2 turns of the needle to create a second eye. Note: the finished eye should lie in a horizontal plane, as shown here. This orientation simplifies correct mounting on the hook shank.

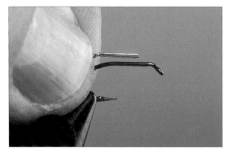

Step 9. With wire cutters, clip the tag from the body extension. Trim the doubled wires on the front hinge-eye so that they are about ¾ the length of the hook shank.

If the extension is dressed on a ring-eye hook as shown in Step 6a, clip off the hook just beyond the rear of the body. Apply a drop of CA glue to the clipped tag of hook wire to help secure the body materials.

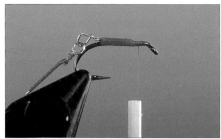

Step 10. Lay the doubled wires side-by-side along the shank of the hook, so that the eye is vertical. Leave enough overhang at the rear of the hook so that the hinge is unobstructed and the body extension swings freely.

Bind down the wires with tying thread. The cut ends of the wire will be quite sharp. To avoid cutting the thread, take loose wraps over the cut ends at first. These will provide a "cushion" for the tighter wraps you can take subsequently.

When the wires are secured, coat the wraps with CA glue or head cement. Dress the remainder of the fly.

Method #5:
Bead-chain Wiggle Body

This is a technique of our own devising in which a length of bead chain is used to form a flexible wiggle-body extension. It is useful primarily for stillwater patterns or those fished on a retrieve. The weight of the metal beads give a good "swing" to the body extension when the fly is stripped through the water.

The beads add weight to the rear of the pattern and must be counterbalanced with weight at the front of the hook or the fly will tilt tail-down during pauses in the retrieve. This counterbalancing weight can be added in different ways. The first is simply to bind to the hook shank a length of chain equal to that forming the wiggle extension, as shown in the following demonstration. Or it can be added with a pair of barbell eyes or lead wire wrapped or lashed on the hook shank. The weight equivalency chart on p. 37 gives some idea of the approximate amount of weight necessary to balance bead chain of any given length.

The equipment setup for this method is a bit more involved than usual, but the tying itself is fairly simple. During tying, the chain must be strung horizontally—either by using two vises as shown in **Method #128: Double-vise Core Extension**, p. 212, or by using an extended body tool (the preferred approach) shown in **Method #129: Extended Body Tool**, p. 212.

Step 1. Dressing the fly is made simpler if the vise jaws are positioned vertically.

Mount the hook and lash a section of

bead chain atop the shank. Here, the counterbalance weight is supplied by the chain; five beads are lashed to the shank to off-set the weight of the five beads that will form the wiggle extension on this leech-type pattern. Fewer beads can be mounted on the hook if the counterweight is supplied by barbell eyes or lead wire. When the chain is lashed to the shank, apply CA glue to the thread wraps.

Using either a double-vise arrangement or an extended body tool, mount the bead chain so that it stretches horizontally, as shown. Here, we're using the spring-hook on the extended-body tool to hold a pair of hackle pliers that grip the end of the bead chain.

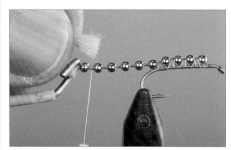

Step 2. Locate the rearmost bead that will form the body extension. Bear in mind that materials affixed to the bead extension can be mounted no closer together than between every other pair of beads. Wherever materials are mounted, the chain no longer wiggles and becomes a stiff point in the extension. The shank between some pairs of beads, particularly those closest to the rear of the hook, must be left free in order to have movement in the extension.

Attach the tying thread between the last two beads on the extension.

Cut a clump of the desired body material. Soft, mobile hairs such as rabbit underfur work well, as do the marabou barbs used here. Synthetic hairs are suitable as well.

Position the material atop the thread foundation.

Step 3. Mount the material. It can be lashed to the top of the bead chain or, as shown here, distributed around it.

The short shank on which the materials are actually mounted is designed to "float" between the beads for flexibility in the chain. When the thread pressure is applied, this shank may well rotate; using your left fingers to put tension on the chain or hold the rearmost bead during mounting will prevent this shank from turning and give a stationary foundation for tying.

Affix the material with tight wraps and clip the butts. When the material is secure, clip the tying thread and secure it with a couple of half-hitches, as shown.

Clip the thread and apply a *small* drop of head cement or CA glue to the wraps, being careful not to let the cement bleed onto parts of the chain that must be left free to wiggle.

Step 4. Move to the next mounting position on the extension, at least 2 beads ahead of the first, and secure a second bundle of material.

Step 5. Remount the tying thread on the hook and dress the desired type of body, and finish the fly as usual. Here, as shown on the fly at the top, additional clumps of marabou have been secured atop the hook shank to complete the body.

The fly in the middle shows a leech pattern tied from black bead chain and marabou.

On the fly at the bottom, only two beads on the chain extension are lashed to the hook; the counterbalancing weight is supplied by brass barbell eyes. The body on this pattern is chenille and hackle tied in the Woolly Bugger style.

Hookless Front Extensions

When using larger patterns, or imitations in which the articulation point falls nearer the head than the tail, it is often necessary to position the hook at the rear of the fly by creating a hookless front extension. The constraints are obvious—since the hook is behind the articulation point, all the force exerted by a fighting fish is transferred to the hinge, which must be especially strong and durable.

In order to articulate freely, the eye of the rear hook must be in a horizontal plane.

The simplest solution is to use a hook with a ring or straight eye. Some hook styles, however, are unavailable in this configuration, and a suitable substitute can be made from a hook with a turned-down eye.

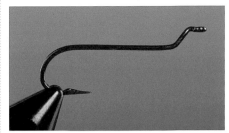

With a needle-nose pliers, grip the hook shank a short distance behind the eye and bend it upward until the eye is parallel to the hook shank. Be careful not to bend the eye off to one side; a correctly bent hook should lie flat on a tabletop

It is not advisable to simply straighten the hook eye into a horizontal plane, making a ring-eye from a turned-down eye. The hook wire has already been bent once to form the turned-down eye; bending it again in the opposite direction may fatigue and weaken the metal.

Method #6:

Single-loop Front Extension

This technique closely resembles the one shown in **Method #2: Single-loop Hinge**, p. 50, differing primarily in the selection of materials. The front extension is typically made from a hook shank, and since weight is generally not a consideration on these larger patterns, choose a hook that is 1X strong (or larger) with a shank equal to the desired length of the front extension.

The hinge should be made of wire. It is possible to make a monofilament hinge, but not recommended. The front hook will be clipped off at the top of the bend, leaving a rough edge, and a monofilament hinge flexed against this edge will soon break. Though in fact the clipped hook-wire will be reshaped to minimize such a possibility, some risk remains.

Multi-strand wire (see "Materials," p. 49), is the best choice; we're using coated wire in the following demonstration, but uncoated gives good results as well. The wire should be the largest diameter that will pass through the rear hook eye and still allow the hook to move easily.

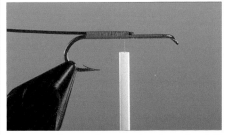

Step 1. Dress the rear hook and set it aside.

To make the front extension, clamp the desired hook in a vise. Beginning at the middle of shank, bind down the wire along the top of the hook shank, working toward the bend. Raise the tag, clip it, and use a needle-nose pliers to flatten the end and smooth out rough edges.

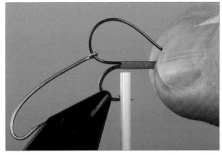

Step 2. Bind down the tag and wrap the thread tightly over the wire, leaving the bobbin at the rearmost wrap.

Pass the wire through the eye of the rear hook, and double it back to form a large loop.

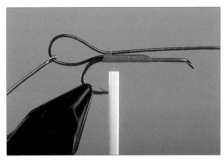

Step 3. Take 6 or 7 wraps over the wire, binding it on top of the wire already lashed to the shank, so that the loop is vertically oriented.

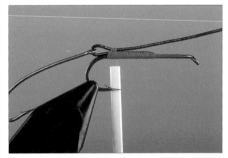

Step 4. Pull the tag of wire and close the loop to the desired size.

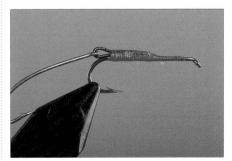

Step 5. Take tight thread wraps to the midway point of the shank. Clip the wire tag, flatten the end, and bind down. Wrap another tight layer of thread over the wires, and coat the windings with CA glue.

When the glue dries, dress the front hook.

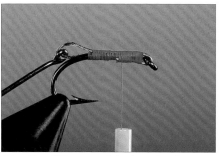

Step 5a. If the eye of the front hook extension is large enough, one or both wire tags can be inserted through the eye, doubled back along the underside of the shank, and bound with tying thread. This provides extra insurance against wire slippage.

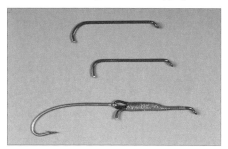

Step 6. Clip the hook in the middle of the bend, as shown on the hook at the top.

With a needle nose pliers, bend the tag of hook wire downward to form a right angle beneath the hinge, as shown on the hook in the middle.

Clip off the wire, leaving about a ⅛" tag, as shown on the bottom. Reshaping the hook wire like this will prevent the hinge wire from snagging any rough edges.

Method #7:

Formed-wire Front Extension

A very strong and reliable connection can be obtained by making the front extension from a hook and bending the shank into a loop for the wiggle-body hinge. Such an extension can be made with a pair of needle-nose pliers, but the shank is more easily bent with a forming jig of the type shown below.

A forming jig can be made simply by clipping or sawing the heads off two finishing or wire nails and driving them into a block of wood. The nails should project about ¼" or so from the wood.

The diameter of the nails determines the size of the loop formed, and in general it is best to use a nail that is slightly thick-er than the hook wire. The distance between the nails should be slightly greater than the diameter of the hook wire. Placing the nails near the edge of the wood block gives your fingers more room to shape the hook, though a pair of pliers may still be required.

The hook used for the front extension should have at least a 4XL shank. Hooks with shorter shanks do not have enough material to form the loop easily.

The hook for the rear portion of the fly should be a ring-eye style (or a down-eye hook re-shaped as shown on p. 53) and should have an eye large enough to slip over the loop of the front extension and swing freely.

Some brands of hooks are too brittle to tolerate the degree of bending required by this technique and will simply break. We're using Mustad #9674 in the following demonstration, though other types may work; trial and error will quickly establish whether a given hook is suitable.

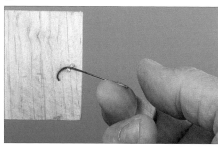

Step 1. Take the hook that is used for the front extension, and clip it off at the bottom of the bend. Leaving most of the hook bend intact helps in forming the loop in the correct plane.

Place the clipped hook between the nails, as shown. Notice that the hook is lying flat on its side against the wood. Maintaining this position throughout the bending is necessary to forming the loop properly.

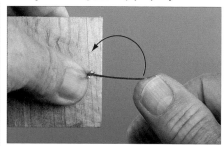

Step 2. With your left thumb, press down on the bend of the hook, as shown, to keep the hook flat against the wooden block.

With the right fingers, push on the eye of the hook to lever it around the nail.

Step 3. Continue bending the hook until a complete loop is formed; pliers may be required to finish the bending.

Notice that the front portion of the hook shank is bent beyond the clipped end. In order to form the loop in this way, you will need to raise the hook eye slightly so that it can be passed above the clipped end of the hook wire.

Step 4. Remove the hook from the forming jig. Notice that the loop is slightly offset, and the clipped end still maintains the arc of the original hook bend.

With a pair of cutters, clip the arc at its lowest point. It helps to clip this tag of material from top to bottom, as shown, rather than side to side. The sharp edge created by clipping in this direction is less likely to cut the tying thread later in the procedure.

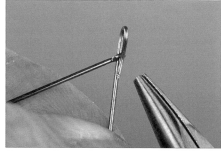

Step 5. Dress the hook used for the rear portion of the fly; we've omitted the dressing for a clearer illustration.

Slip the eye of the rear hook onto the loop of the front extension.

With a pair of needle-nose pliers, straighten the clipped end of hook wire so that it lies atop the shank of the front extension, as shown.

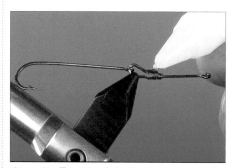

Step 6. To complete the fly, mount the front extension in the vise, as shown. Bind down the clipped end of the front extension to the shank. The clipped hook wire has sharp edges and can cut the tying thread. A very strong thread, such as Kevlar, can be used or, as shown here, a thin wire can be wrapped to close the loop.

After binding the loop closed, apply a drop of gel-type CA glue to secure the wraps.

The front extension can now be dressed.

Tandem Hooks, Trailing Hooks, and Stingers

While some anglers use the terms interchangeably and others draws distinctions among them, "tandem hooks," "trailing hooks," and "stingers" all involve a second hook fastened behind, and usually in line with, the first. And they all serve the same purpose. On patterns where some portion of the dressing extends beyond the hook bend—flies with brushed bodies, long body-extensions, or long streamer wings, for example—the second hook increases the chances of taking fish that nip only at the rearmost portion of the fly.

In general, a tandem-hook fly is one in which both hooks are actually incorporated into the dressing. Both hook shanks and the ligature that connects them may be sheathed in woven tubing, for instance, to form a single, long body—a method commonly, but not exclusively, employed by saltwater tyers. Or each hook may be dressed independently, as is done with some trolling flies.

A "trailing hook" or "trailer" is not usually dressed, but is positioned in such a way that it is at least partially concealed by materials extending back from the front hook. The term "stinger" is often loosely used for any dual-hook arrangement, but if there is any consistency in its application, it seems most often to refer to a small hook—as small as #16 or #18—tied as a trailer.

Tandem hooks may be either fixed or articulated, and the technique for forming the articulated style is identical to that described above in **Method #6: Single-loop Front Extension**, p. 53, except of course that the front hook is not clipped. Trailing hooks and stingers are fixed; since they are not dressed there is little to be gained from an articulated joint.

Method #8:
Wire-loop Trailing Hook

A tandem or trailing hook can be affixed with a length of wire. Multi-strand wire works best, as the single-strand type cannot endure the repeated flexing that this type of connection must withstand (see "Materials," p. 49). The double thickness of wire used in this technique makes it the strongest tandem-hook connection.

This method is generally reserved for larger hooks, since the eye of the trailing hook must be of sufficient diameter to accommodate a double thickness of wire. Hooks with turned-down eyes or turned-up eyes give the best results, forming the straightest connection with the front hook and minimizing the tendency for the finished fly to twist in the water. The loop-eye hooks traditionally used on steelhead and salmon patterns are ideal, as the eye is quite large in relation to the hook size, allowing the use of smaller trailing hooks or larger diameter wire.

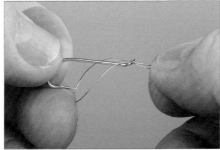

Step 1. Clip a length of wire about 6" long and double it over. Insert both ends through the eye of the hook leaving a large loop. For a hook with a turned-up eye, as is used here, pass the loop over the hook bend and around the point so that it is underneath the shank. For a hook with a turned-down eye, pass the loop around the point and over the bend so that it is on top of the shank.

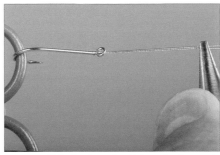

Step 2. Grip both ends of the wire in a pair of pliers, and hold the hook in the finger loop of a pair of tying scissors. Pull firmly and repeatedly to seat the wire against the hook eye.

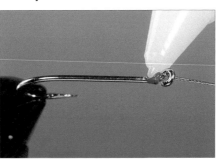

Step 3. Attach the tying thread directly behind the wire loop. Wrap two or three layers of thread over the wire loop. These wrappings will prevent the loop from sliding back along the hook shank. Whip-finish and coat the wrappings with CA glue.

If the rear hook is to be dressed, do so at this point.

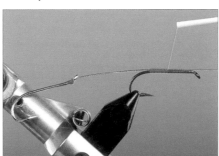

Step 4. Mount the front hook in the vise and lay a foundation of tying thread. Hold the two tags of wire on top the shank, and bind them down working from the hook bend to the eye.

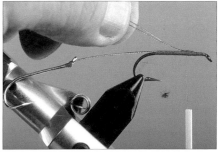

Step 5. As the tying thread nears the eye, release one of the wires, and bind the other toward the eye with a few more wraps of thread.

Fold both wires back along the hook shank, and bind them down a short distance toward the hook bend. Note that the folds are staggered, which helps create a tapered foundation for the body.

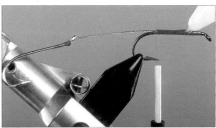

Step 6. Clip the wires, bind down the ends, and coat the wrappings with CA glue. The front hook is now ready for dressing.

Method #9:
Single-strand Trailing Hook

This technique is used when the eye of the trailing hook is too small to admit a double thickness of wire. This connection can be made with either wire, as shown in the main sequence, or monofilament line as shown in the alternate sequence. The mono works best on hooks with eyes large enough to accommodate at least 15-pound monofilament, though heavier can be used. Using thinner mono for smaller hooks may not provide the necessary strength, and in such cases wire is preferred.

Trailing hooks with turned-up or turned-down eyes provide the straightest connection. On small hooks, turned-up eyes are recommended since the wire is lashed to the top of the shank and won't interfere with the hook gap.

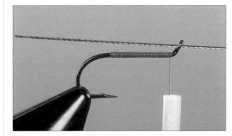

Step 1. Mount the trailing hook and form a foundation of thread. Pass the wire or mono through the eye of the hook.

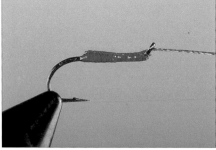

Step 2. If using wire, proceed to bind the wire to the shank. When the bend is reached, double the wire over, and wrap back about halfway to the eye. Clip the wire, bind down, and coat wraps with CA glue.

If the rear hook is to be dressed, do so at this point.

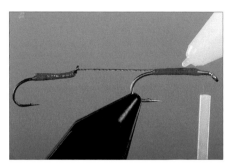

Step 3. Mount the front hook in the vise and lay a thread foundation. Bind the wire to the front hook shank as described in Step 2, and coat the wraps with CA glue.

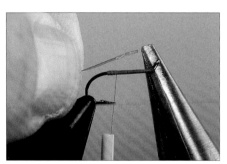

Step 1a. If using monofilament, take a pair of needle-nose pliers and flatten the end. The flattened section should be about half the length of the hook shank. This simplifies binding the mono, and the slight "shoulder" created will prevent it from slipping through the wrappings.

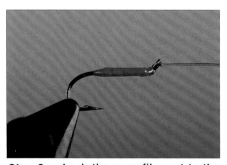

Step 2a. Lash the monofilament to the hook, covering it with two or three layers of thread. Coat the wraps with CA glue.

If the rear hook is to be dressed, do so at this point.

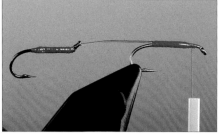

Step 3a. Clip the mono to length. Flatten the end as shown in Step 1a, and bind it atop the hook. Coat the wraps with CA glue.

Method #10:

Snelled Trailing Hook

A simple connection can be made by knotting a trailer hook to a piece of monofilament. Knots tied to the eye of the hook do not work well, as the trailer hook can hinge around them. Knots attached to the shank of the hook are more secure and offer a straighter connection. Again, hooks with eyes that are turned up or turned down give the straightest connection.

Snelling is not difficult, and all that is really involved here is forming a whip-finish around the shank of the hook. We're using red cord instead of monofilament for greater visibility in the following demonstration.

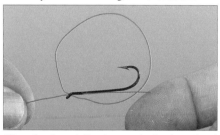

Step 1. Insert the tag end of a length of monofilament through the hook eye. The tag extending through the eye should be about 12 inches long.

Make a loop with the tag and pass it through the hook eye in the same direction as the tag was initially inserted.

Note in the photo that, after the tag is passed through the eye a second time, it is positioned against the hook shank.

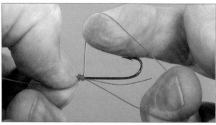

Step 2. With the left fingers, pinch the hook eye and monofilament simultaneously.

Insert the index and middle fingers of the right hand into the loop, with the palm of your hand facing you, as shown.

From here, construct a whip-finish as described in **Method #9: Hand Whip-finish**, Steps 4-6, p. 22.

Repeat the procedure to form at least six wraps around the hook shank.

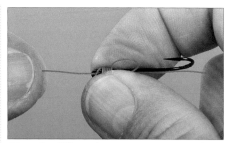

Step 3. When the wraps are complete, withdraw your fingers from the loop and pinch the wraps to prevent them from unraveling.

Pull outward on the line extending from the hook eye to close the loop.

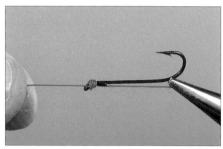

Step 4. To seat the knot firmly, grasp the tag with a pair of needle-nose pliers, and pull the two lengths of line in opposite directions.

This trailing hook (dressed if desired) can now be affixed to the front hook as explained in **Method #9: Single-strand Trailing Hook**, Step 3a.

Method #11:

Nail-knot Trailing Hook

A simple nail-knot—familiar to most fly fishermen—can also be used to snell a trailing hook. We're using red cord rather than monofilament for better visibility.

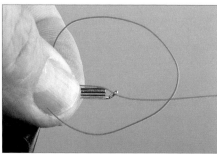

Step 1. Mount the hook in a vise, and lay the tube of an empty fly-tying bobbin along the hook shank behind the eye.

Inert the end of the monofilament through the hook eye. Using about 10 inches of material, form a loop in the mono, as shown.

7

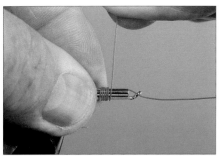

Step 2. Under moderate tension, wrap the tag of material in close turns around the hook shank and bobbin, working toward the hook eye.

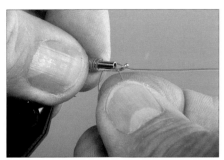

Step 3. When 6 or 7 wraps are made, use the thumb and forefinger of the left hand to pinch the wraps against the bobbin tube to prevent them from unraveling.

Insert the tag of material into the bobbin tube. Continue feeding the monofilament into the tube until only a small loop remains in front, as shown.

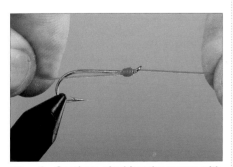

Step 4. Continue pinching the wraps with the left fingers. Use the right fingers to withdraw the bobbin tube from beneath the wraps of mono.

Pull the ends of the mono outward in opposite directions to seat the nail knot firmly behind the hook eye.

This trailing hook (dressed if desired) can now be affixed to the front hook as explained in **Method #9: Single-strand Trailing Hook**, Step 3a, p. 56.

Method #12:
Fixed-hook Trailer

Using a hook with an extra-long shank (4XL-6XL) makes possible a trailing hook without the use of wire or monofilament. This is the most reliable tandem hook connection, particularly useful on larger, thinner streamers since the relatively small ratio of hook gap to shank length allows the construction of long, narrow bodies. The method does add extra weight to the pattern, which may or may not be desirable.

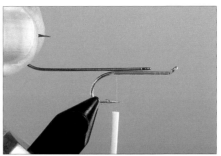

Step 1. Mount the front hook in the vise, and wrap the shank tightly with 2 or 3 layers of heavy tying thread—Kevlar is a good choice for this procedure.

Select a hook for the trailer. A 6XL shank allows the longest rear extension, and a ring-eye hook offers the least interference when applying body materials to the front hook. A ring-eye hook used for the extension can be mounted with the hook point up or down. However, a down-eye hook can be used if the trailer is to be mounted with the point upward.

Lay the trailer hook on top of the front hook. The amount of overhang can be adjusted to provide the correct dimension for the finished fly, but at least ¼ of the shank on the trailer hook should be bound to the front hook in order to get a secure connection.

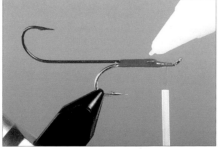

Step 2. Bind the two hooks, shank-to-shank, again with 2 or 3 layers of heavy thread wraps. Coat the wrappings with CA glue.

Weed Guards

Though weedless hooks are traditionally associated with warmwater angling, stillwater trout fishermen are turning to them as a way of coping with the weeds, brush, and heavy cover that are home to many food organisms in lakes and ponds. The techniques for producing weed guards for weed-

less hooks vary with the size, weight, and specific dressing of the fly.

On nearly all subsurface patterns, snagging can be reduced if the hook rides with the point up. Weighting the shank heavily with wraps of lead wire will cause the finished fly to flip upside down and reduce the possibility of catching the hook point on obstructions. The specialized "keel hook," generally used for streamer patterns, is designed specifically to ride point-up when dressed. A suitable substitute can be made by bending a long-shank hook.

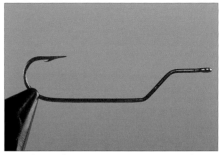

Bending a ring-eye streamer hook will produce this keel-style hook. Long-shank hooks, however, must be used. A shorter shank will place the angle-bend too close to the hook point and obstruct the gap.

Using large or heavy flies, or fishing in thicker cover, generally necessitates a hook guard affixed to the fly. Hook guards employ a length of relatively stiff material extending from behind the hook eye back to the point. When the hook guard hits a weed or submerged obstruction, the fly is pushed upward slightly and slides across the snag on the surface of the guard. The hook-guard material must be sufficiently stiff to remain unyielding against the force of a retrieved fly, but at the same time flexible enough to bend and expose the hook point to a striking fish. Thus the choice of materials for the guard depends to some extent on both the fly and the fish. Smaller, lighter patterns are more easily deflected from obstacles and can be dressed with more flexible, less obtrusive hook guards, which are also better suited to hooking fish that strike gently. Larger, heavier patterns require more substantial guards, and these are best for trout that strike more aggressively.

Few anglers are as well versed in fashioning hook guards as warmwater tyer Tom Nixon. A number of the techniques below are the result of his experimentation and innovation with bass flies, and they can be successfully adapted to trout patterns.

Hair, Hackle, and Synthetic-fiber Hook Guards

These materials, which are naturally rather flexible, become more supple as they absorb water and are well-suited to small or lightly weighted hooks. Hair and hackle guards can also be incorporated into the fly design for an unobtrusive, "disguised" hook guard. Though materials here vary, most of the methods described below allow you to mount the hook guard as the very last step in dressing the fly, making them less cumbersome than wire or monofilament techniques that sometimes require you to work around a hook guard mounted early in the tying sequence.

Method #13:
Beard Hook Guard

This is perhaps the simplest of all hook guards and is most often used in conjunction with a weighted or keel hook that rides point-up. The beard can be made from any relatively stiff material—bucktail, moose mane, Krystal Flash, and some synthetic fly-tying hairs. The quantity of material depends upon the size and weight of the fly. Lighter flies obviously require less material; heavier ones need a thicker bundle.

Step 1. Dress the fly as usual, leaving extra space behind the eye to bind down the hook-guard material. Leave the tying thread attached and invert the hook in the vise.

Step 2. Select a clump of material for the guard and determine its length. If the material is to be used solely as a hook guard, the tips should project beyond the hook point a distance equal to about ½ the hook gap, though longer is acceptable. If the guard doubles as the wing on a fly designed to ride upside-down, the material should be sized accordingly.

Bind it to the hook shank over a base of tying thread as you would a hair streamer wing (see **Method #57: Solid-fiber Downwing**, p. 305).

Step 3. Wrap the thread toward the bend, forcing the guard material against the end of the fly body. This will push the hook-guard material upward, so that it slants back and conceals the hook point. Most of the guard material should be ahead of the point.

Clip the material and whip finish.

Step 1a. Alternately, a half-beard style can be constructed, which is less conspicuous in the finished pattern. In this case, dress the fly body to the midpoint of the hook shank. Invert the hook in the vise.

Step 2a. Select a clump of material and size it as described in Step 2.

Bind the material to the shank, and secure it as described in Step 3.

Dress the remainder of the fly as usual.

Method #14:
Hackle Hook Guard

Using stiff hackle at or near the hook eye will help "brush" it away from underwater obstacles. While the hackle need not be top-grade, dry-fly quality, it should have stiff, glossy barbs with little web (see "Hackle," p. 6). Barb length should be at least 1 ½ to 2 times the hook gap, or longer if the hackle is to be slanted rearward or tied on an extra-long shank.

Step 1. Dress the fly as usual, leaving space behind the eye for the hackle. Here, a Woolly Bugger is palmered with a soft saddle hackle; a stiff hackle will be wrapped at the head for a weed guard.

Select a hackle with the appropriate barb length, and tie it in as you would a hackle for a dry-fly collar (see **Method #2: Single-hackle Mounts**, p. 347), except that the feather is mounted with the shiny (or convex) side facing the hook eye.

Step 2. Wrap the hackle in close, touching wraps, as shown in **Method #4: Single-hackle Dry-fly Collar**, p. 351. The more wraps, the greater the cumulative stiffness and hence snag resistance..

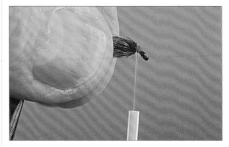

Step 2a. If desired, stroke the hackle barbs toward the bend with the left hand, and take a few wraps of thread against the base of the barbs, much as you would to form a collar-style wet fly hackle (see **Method #5: Single-hackle Wet-fly Collar**, Steps 3-4, p. 353).

Step 3a. A fly hackled in this manner offers a more streamlined profile and less water resistance, and angles the barbs toward the hook point to help "slide" the fly over obstacles.

Step 4a. To further decrease water resistance or to improve the fly profile, the hackle can be clipped close to the shank on the top and sides, essentially forming a beard-hackle guard.

Method #15:
Nylon Brush Guard

This technique is a variation of a method we first saw described by Tom Nixon. Though a bit more time-consuming than other techniques, it is not difficult and is quite versatile. The diameter of monofilament can be chosen for precisely the right degree of stiffness on any hook size or fly type. Determining the proper diameter may require a bit of simple experimentation, but as a starting point try using 1X tippet material for hooks #2-#4; 2X for hooks #6-10; 3X for hooks #12-#14.

Tom Nixon describes this technique using three separately knotted strands of monofilament mounted under the hook shank. This variation is slightly simpler to tie but produces somewhat greater bulk at the head of the fly.

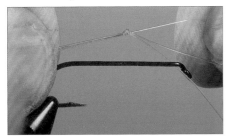

Step 1. Cut three 3-inch strands of the desired monofilament, and hold them in a bundle so that the tips are approximately aligned. Tie a simple overhand knot in the bundle and pull tightly. Then tug each strand individually to make sure it is seated snugly.

Step 2. Dress the fly as usual, leaving space at the head to mount the hook guard. Lay a base of thread behind the hook

eye. Position the monofilament bundle crosswise atop the hook shank so that the knot is centered on the top of the shank and the tip ends of the mono point downward.

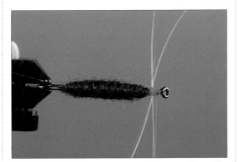

Step 3. Mount the monofilament bundle using the lash mount (see **Method #8: Lash Mount and Crisscross Wrap**, p. 29). Begin using light wraps that crisscross directly over the center of the knot. Gradually increase thread tension to secure the material. The knot should be completely covered with thread and remain on top of the shank, as shown in this top view.

When the mono is secure, take one half hitch behind the hook eye.

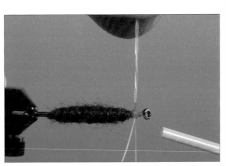

Step 4. Invert the hook in the vise. Grasp the three strands of monofilament on the far side of the hook shank in the fingers of your left hand and hold them together. Beginning at the base of the bundle, take 6 to 8 tight, adjacent wraps of thread toward the tip of the bundle—in essence, laying a thread foundation on the strands, as shown in this top view.

Now wrap the thread back down over this foundation to the hook shank.

Step 5. Repeat Step 4 with the three strands on the near side of the shank, taking 6 to 8 wraps up the bundle, then wrapping back down to the shank.

When this bundle is secured, take two turns of thread ahead of the knot, around the hook shank only.

Step 6. Hold all six fibers in the fingers of your left hand and pull them directly upward. Carefully begin taking horizontal wraps around the base of both monofilament bundles to gather them into a single brushlike post that projects vertically upward from the shank. The thread foundation you've wrapped on each bundle gives a non-slip foundation for these horizontal wraps.

Step 7. When the weed guard is secure, whip-finish the fly.

Clip the nylon brush to length—about 1½ times the hook gap—and coat the knot wraps with CA glue or head cement.

Method #16:
Nelson Point Guard

Dick Nelson, originator of the Aztec fly, adapted this monofilament-loop technique from a similar method used on popping bugs and made it practical for streamers. This low-profile guard offers little wind resistance in casting and protects the hook point on both sides. Again, the diameter of the monofilament and the loop length are contingent on the size and weight of the hook, but because the loop forms a rather long "lever," it must be quite stiff in order to push the fly away from snags. Thus monofilament from 25-60 pound test is necessary. The technique presented below, a slight variation of Nelson's original method, helps in determining the loop size.

The size of the monofilament loop is the most critical part of this method. When the loop is folded backward, it should pass just in front of the hook point and not catch on it.

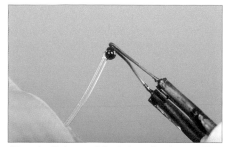

Step 1. Select a 6-inch length of monofilament of the appropriate diameter. Using a butane lighter, or a hot-tip tool as shown here, melt a ball on one end as explained in **Method #7: Barbell Eyes**, p. 431.

Step 2. Dress the fly as usual, and let the bobbin hang directly at the mounting point for the weed guard. Position the melted ball against the far side of the shank, and bind it down with crisscross wraps so that the monofilament hangs vertically below the shank.

Step 3. To size the loop, double the mono around a dubbing needle positioned directly in front of the hook point. With the thumb and forefinger of the right hand, pinch the unbound end of the monofilament directly at the mounting point.

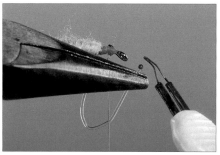

Step 4. Now that you've determined the mounting point for the second side of the loop, you must trim the monofilament, leaving enough tag to melt a second ball about the same size as the first. As a general rule, a tag of about ¼" is sufficient.

Grip the monofilament at the mounting point in a pair of needle-nose pliers. Trim it, leaving a tag of the desired length, and melt a second ball.

Step 5. Mount this second ball on the near side of the hook shank. Use only 3 or wraps of thread, as you may need to remove the guard.

Step 6. Test for size by folding the loop to the underside of the shank. It should pass just in front of the hook point.

If the loop is too long, unwrap the end tied to the near side of the shank, and melt the tag a bit more to shorten the length. Re-attach and test.

If the loop is too short, you must, regrettably, start over.

When the loop is correct, you may wish to unwrap the thread, remove the mono guard, and measure its exact length. Keep a record of the length of the monofilament along with the size and style of hook. These notes will eliminate the necessity of custom-fitting every individual hook guard.

Step 7. When the loop size is correct, take a few wraps of thread at the base of the loop underneath the hook shank. If all is well, the hook point should be centered in the loop when you "sight down" the hook shank from the eye. If the point isn't centered, adjust the loop by pulling one side or the other, twisting it, or taking additional wraps of the thread as necessary to make the loop symmetrical.

Whip finish and apply CA glue or head cement to the loop wraps.

Monofilament-Loop Weed Guards

Weeds guards in this category differ from the Nelson Point Guard described above in that the loop encircles the hook longitudinally and is affixed at both the front and rear. Thus it must be partially mounted before the fly is dressed.

Again, the stiffest material with smallest diameter is desirable, and only experimentation can really settle the question of what diameter to use with a given fly style and hook size. On small, light flies monofilament as thin as .013" may give satisfactory results; larger, heavier flies may require mono diameters of .030" or thicker.

Method #17:
Single-loop Guard

This popular technique is noteworthy for its simplicity. Though the weed guard is partially attached at the beginning of the dressing, the free tag can be held in a material clip away from the tying field for ease in dressing the fly.

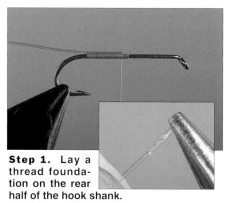

Step 1. Lay a thread foundation on the rear half of the hook shank.

Select a 5-inch length of the desired monofilament. Bind it over the thread base, beginning at the middle of the shank, working toward the bend, and then back to the middle. Wrap carefully to make certain that the monofilament stays centered on top of the hook shank.

Keeping monofilament, especially larger diameters, centered on top of the hook shank is easier if you flatten the section to be bound with a needle-nose pliers, as shown in the inset photo.

Step 2. Dress the fly as usual, leaving room at the head to tie off the weed guard. Position the bobbin at the tie-off point.

Make a large loop in the monofilament, and feed the free end through the hook eye. Take three or four moderately tight wraps to bind the mono to the underside of the hook shank, well behind the eye.

Now pull the free end of the monofilament to adjust the loop size. The distance between the lower portion of the loop and the bottom (or spear) of the hook should be ¼ to ⅓ the hook gap.

Step 3. When the loop is adjusted to the proper size, bind down the monofilament, working carefully to keep it centered underneath the shank. The hook shank and weed guard should all be positioned in one flat plane.

Clip off the excess mono, making certain that it does not obstruct the hook eye and interfere with tying the fly to a tippet. Cover the wraps with CA glue or head cement.

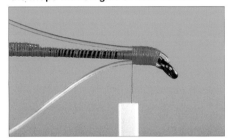

Step 3a. For extra security on large hooks, adjust the loop size, and then bend the monofilament (which passes through the hook eye) back along the top of the hook shank, so that the tag points toward the bend. Use tight wraps to bind the doubled-over section of mono to both the top and bottom of the hook shank. Clip the tag and coat the wraps.

Note that this approach is practical only when the eye of the hook is large enough to accommodate both the weed guard monofilament and the tippet to which the fly is tied.

Method #18:
Double-loop Guard

This style of weed guard comes from a somewhat unlikely source—fly tyer Ken Iwamasa, who is best known for his delicate, realistic mayfly duns. Because the double loop protects the hook point on both sides, it's especially effective in very heavy cover.

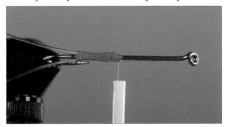

Step 1. Lay a thread base on the rear half of the hook shank. Cut two 5-inch lengths of the desired monofilament. Bind one piece tightly against the far side of the hook shank, and the second piece to the near side of the hook shank, as shown in this top view.

Coat the wraps with CA glue or head cement.

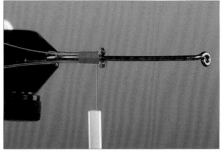

Step 1a. For extra security in the weed guard, you can also use a lighter or hot-tip tool to melt a small ball on one end of each piece of mono as described in **Method #7: Barbell Eyes**, p. 431.

Bind in monofilament sections as described in Step 1. The melted ends prevent the monofilament from slipping out beneath the wraps.

Step 2. Dress the fly as usual, leaving space at the head to tie-off the weed guard.

Beginning with the monofilament on the far side of the hook, form a large loop around the hook bend, and bind the mono with 3 or 4 moderately tight wraps to the far side of the hook shank, directly behind the eye. Adjust the loop size as described above in **Method #17: Single-loop Guard**, Step 2, p. 60.

Step 3. Now take the monofilament on the near side of the shank, and proceed as described above in Step 2, binding the tag and sizing the loop. The two loops should be identical in size.

Bind both pieces of monofilament tightly to the shank with additional wraps. Clip the excess and coat the wraps with CA glue or head cement.

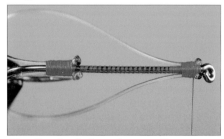

Step 3a. Again for extra security, you can melt a ball on each end of the monofilament. Using a pair of needle-nose pliers, grip the monofilament exactly at the tie off point, and clip it, leaving a ¼" tag. Melt this tag to form a ball, and tie it in on the side of the hook shank.

Wire Weed Guards.

Wire weed guards offer excellent snag protection and superior durability. They do have drawbacks, however. They are somewhat more involved to tie, and the stiffness of the wire makes them most appropriate for larger streamer patterns and aggressive fish.

Finding the right wire can pose a difficulty as well. The most suitable is springy, fine-diameter, tempered-steel wire—Bright Music Wire, single-strand spinner wire, or guitar string wire are all acceptable. (See "Materials," p. 49 for further details about selecting wire.)

The wire should also be matched to the hook used. The following chart, reprinted with the kind permission of Tom Nixon, specifies wire diameter in relation to the hook size for the 4 types of weed guards shown in the methods that follow.

SHANK LENGTH	HOOK SIZE	METHOD #18	METHOD #19	METHOD #20	METHOD #21
Standard	1/0	.014"	.010"	.010"	.010"
Standard	1	.012"	.010"	.008"	.010"
Standard	2	.012"	.008"	.008"	.008"
Standard	4	.010"	.008"	.007"	.008"
Standard	6	.008"	.006"	.006"	.006"
4XL	1	.018"	.012"	.010"	.012"
4XL	2	.018"	.011"	.010"	.011"
4XL	4	.014"	.010"	.008"	.010"
4XL	6	.012	.009"	.008"	.009"
4XL	8	.010"	.008"	.007"	.008"
4XL	10	.010"	.008"	.006	.008"

This chart specifies the wire diameters used for weed guards in relation to hook-shank length and hook size.

Method #19:
Single-Wire Guard

This is the simplest of all wire guards, and because it uses only a single strand of wire, is the most practical for smaller hook sizes. It has the added advantage of being affixed to the hook shank as the last tying step, and thus offers no obstruction while dressing the fly.

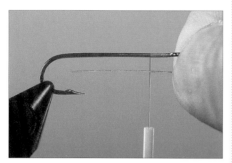

Step 1. Select a piece of wire according to the chart above. Clip a length that reaches to from the *front* of the hook eye back about ¼" past the hook point.

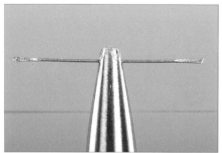

Step 2. With a pair of pliers, flatten both ends of the wire for about ⅛" to ¼" inch. The flats should be in the same plane.

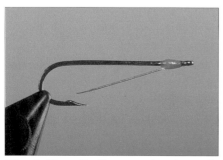

Step 3. Dress the fly as usual; we've omitted the dressing for a clearer illustration.
Bind one end of the wire directly beneath the head of the fly, mounting it directly against the thread wraps used to form the fly head. Use 2 or 3 tight layers of thread. Coat with CA glue.

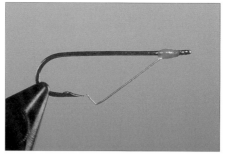

Step 4. When the glue has dried, use a pair of needle-nose pliers to bend the free end of the wire at an angle, as shown, so that the flat of the wire shields the hook point.

Method #20:
Split-wire Guard

This style offers good snag protection, is relatively easy to tie, and is attached after the fly is dressed.

Step 1. Select the wire according to the chart on p. 61. Cut a length about 4" long. Straddle the hook bend with the wire, and bend the wire to double back on itself.

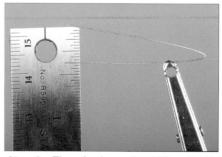

Step 2. The wire loop should be slightly splayed so that the tag ends are about ⅜" apart.

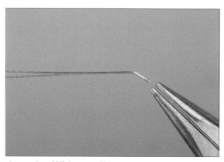

Step 3. With needle-nose pliers, grip the wire loop and bend it down to form an elbow at about a 35-degree angle. The short, bent portion should be about ³⁄₁₆" long.

Step 4. Dress the fly as usual; we've omitted the dressing for greater clarity.
Mount the wire loop on the underside of the hook, directly against the wraps used to form the fly head. Secure the loop with 2 or 3 tight layers of thread. Coat with CA glue.

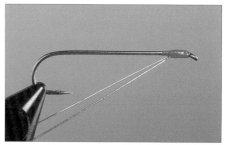

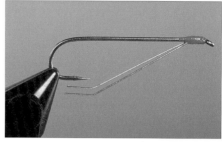

Step 5. When the glue has dried, bend the wire and clip it as shown in the photo. Cut the wires about ¼" behind the hook point, and if needed, gently bend them so that they flank the hook point, about ³⁄₁₆" off to either side.

Method #21:
Stirrup Guard

Like most wire weed guards, this one is an import from the world of lure-making. Because of the design, it is restricted to hooks with eyes large enough to accommodate two pieces of wire as well as the tippet material from the leader—that is to say, larger hooks. Tom Nixon describes mounting this guard early in the tying procedure, but it can be mounted last, as explained below, which greatly simplifies dressing the fly. You should, however, leave a small space between the fly head and hook eye in order to ensure sufficient room to bind down the wire tags.

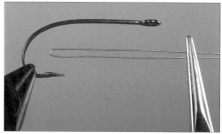

Step 1. Select a piece of wire according the chart on p. 61, and cut a 4-inch section.
Straddle the bend of the hook with the wire, and bend the wire double, as described above in **Method #20: Split-wire Guard**, Step 1, p. 62. In this case, however, the tag ends are bent parallel, as shown in the photo.

7

Step 2. The loop end is now bent in two stages. With a needle-nose plier, grip the doubled wire about ¼" from the loop and bend an elbow to 45 degrees, as shown at the left.

Next, grip the doubled wire about ⅛" from the loop, and bend a second elbow, also about 45 degrees. The finished shape is shown at the right.

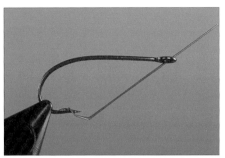

Step 3. Insert both tags of wire through the hook eye from underneath, and clip the loop over the hook point as shown.

Step 4. Pinch the hook point and wire loop tightly in the fingers of the left hand to hold them immobile.

With the right hand, bend both wires back toward the hook bend, levering them around the inside of the hook eye. Be careful handling the cut ends of the wire, which are sharp.

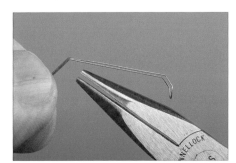

Step 5. Remove the weed guard from the hook. Position a needle-nose pliers at the bend you've just created, and bend the wires against the plier jaws to give a distinct edge to this elbow. Bend only a shallow angle.

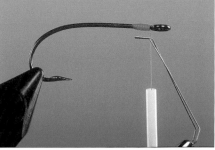

Step 6. Measure the wire tags against the fly head. Position the bend directly behind the hook eye, and clip the tags at the rearmost end of the fly head.

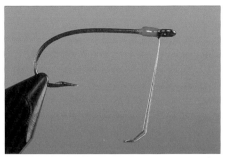

Step 7. Reinsert the tags through the hook eye from underneath. Make certain that wires stay parallel and do not cross one another.

Bind the wires with 2 or 3 tight layers of thread that extend from the back of the fly head to the rear of the hook eye. A heavy tying thread will give the best results.

Tie off with a few half hitches, and coat the wraps with CA glue.

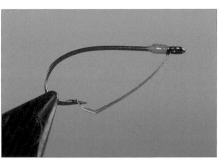

Step 8. When the glue is dry, bend the guard backward and clip the loop over the hook point.

Method #22:

Snagless Sally Guard

This is Tom Nixon's adaptation of the hook guard used on the Snagless Sally, a casting lure.

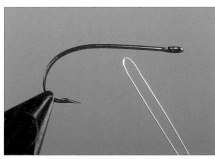

Step 1. Select a wire according to the chart on p. 61, and cut a 4" section.

Straddle the hook shank with the wire, and bend the wire back on itself as described in **Method #20: Split-wire Guard**, Step 1, p. 62.

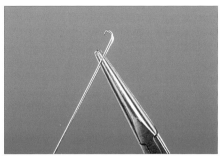

Step 2. Using needle-nose pliers with fine points, grip the wire loop to make a bend 1/32" from the end. Bend the wire around the pliers, doubling it back on itself to form a "U" as shown.

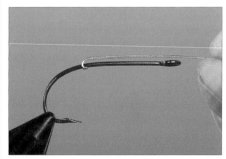

Step 3. At this point, Nixon recommends tying in all materials that are mounted at the bend of the hook. Do not wrap any materials; merely secure them to the hook. Slip the wire loop around the hook shank from underneath, as shown.

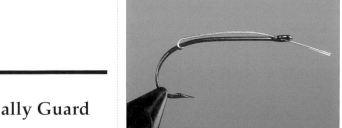

Step 4. Position the loop at the bend of the hook, and feed both wire tags down through the hook eye.

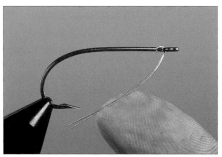

Step 5. Pull the tags while pushing on the loop to bring the weed guard behind the hook eye. It will be somewhat loose. Clip the tags so that they extend about ¼" past the hook point.

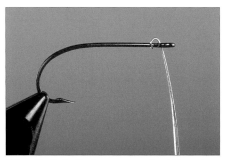

Step 6. Note that you can adjust the wires to minimize interference in the tying field. With the wires in this position, dress the remainder of the fly.

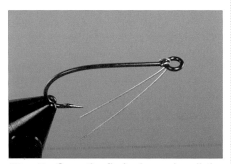

Step 7. Once the fly is dressed, pull the wire tags down and back, reseating the wire loop against the hook shank. Adjust the spread of the wire tags to straddle the hook point evenly.

This weed guard is not rigidly fixed, but rather has some "play" back and forth.

CHAPTER 8

Tails and Trailing Shucks

Tails on fly patterns perform various functions. On subsurface patterns, they are largely a component of imitation. On dry flies and some emergers, they perform the additional function of supporting the fly on the water. How well they accomplish these purposes is a matter of tail design and material.

Tyers have proven themselves remarkably inventive in devising tails; in addition to the more customary tailing styles, there are techniques for dressing tails in combination with other fly components or tailing very particular types of patterns. These more specialized methods are presented in other sections of the book. For instance, a tail may be formed by using the tips of feather barbs used to fashion the fly body, and the techniques for forming such tails are presented in **Method #27: The Multiple-herl Body**, p. 118; **Method #28: Core-twisted Herl Body**, p. 119; and **Method #30: Flat-wrapped Barb Body**, p. 121. Tails can also be fashioned from the wingcase material (see **Method #4: Bundled-fiber Wingcase**, p. 232) or overbody materials (**Method #8: Bundled-fiber Overbody**, p. 237). Bead bodies require a special approach to tailing, shown in **Method #96: Tailed Bead Body**, p. 183, and many types of extended bodies involve their own special tailing methods, which are presented throughout the section on "Extended Bodies," p. 204.

This chapter, however, presents those techniques in which the tailing material is mounted as a separate and distinct step in the tying procedure apart from other fly components, and in which the tail method is not dependent on a particular body material (such as beads) or style (such as an extended body). Tying trailing shucks is, for the most part, nearly identical to tying other types of tails, varying primarily in the materials used. These are presented at the end of the chapter.

Tailing Styles and Proportions

On subsurface patterns, tails largely serve the purposes of imitation or attraction and have no structural function in the dressing. Thus there is considerable variation in the selection of materials, styles, and proportions for tailing sinking flies, and these depend upon an individual tyer's perception of the specific way and degree in which a tail contributes to the performance of a pattern. And in fact some tyers, Gary LaFontaine for example, go so far as to omit tails on most nymph patterns, believing that they are at best a minor representational component not worth the extra tying steps. Most tyers, however, include tails, but differ widely in their ideas about tail material, length, and, on bundled-fiber tails, the number of fibers used. The methods presented in this chapter for tailing subsurface flies illustrate what are probably the most typical and commonly used, but by no means obligatory, proportions.

Tails on floating flies, however, present a somewhat different problem. Not only is there a greater range of tailing styles from which to choose and a more specific set of criteria for tailing materials, but tail proportion also plays a more important role in fly performance. Thus using hackle barbs, hairs, or synthetic fibers to form tails on dry flies raises questions about proportion—how many fibers should be used to dress the tail and how long should these fibers be?

The tail length traditionally recommended for dry flies is 1 to 1½ times the length of the hook shank—a proportion that originated, in part, from a somewhat inaccurate explanation of how collar-hackled dry flies float. In the past, hackle and tail lengths were established under the theory that a dry fly rests on the surface film supported by the tips of the hackle and the tips of the tail fibers, so that the hook spear rests on or slightly above the water. But as discussed later in this section—and we are hardly the first to point his out—dry flies rarely float in this manner under actual fishing conditions. Still, this recommended tail length has endured in fly tying, not only for collar-hackled flies, but for flush-floating patterns such as parachute flies, in which there is no essential relation between tail and hackle lengths, and even for flies such as No-Hackle Duns and Comparaduns, which lack hackle altogether.

That this particular tail proportion persists, even though the rationale for it based on supporting a collar-hackled dry fly is largely faulty, suggests that tyers have found it useful in other respects. And indeed, two reasons suggest themselves. First, on the average, a tail that is 1 to 1½ times the shank length does in fact roughly approximate the relative length of tail and body on many species of mayflies—the type of imitation most frequently dressed with tails and the one that has lent its proportions to many attractor-style flies that have no particular counterpart in nature. And second, experience has simply established that this tail length is generally adequate for supporting a fly in the surface film. Tails that are much shorter provide insufficient support for the fly at the rear, particularly if the body is fashioned from quill, floss, or other material that does not lend floatation to the fly. Tails that are much longer merely add bulk and wind resistance to the fly and may appear disproportionate from the representational standpoint.

Even so, there is much variation among tyers, who alter the tail length for representational purposes or simply for a better sense of aesthetic proportion. If there is any general trend among modern tyers, we would hazard a guess that there is a tendency to dress tails that are slightly longer rather than shorter. But the recommended tail length of 1 to 1½ times the shank length is still a serviceable guideline and one used in the demonstrations in this chapter.

Unlike tail length, tail thickness or density—that is, the number of fibers used for tailing—is closely related to the style of tail, and the matter is perhaps best addressed by looking at how a tail helps float a fly in the first place, and then at specific tail designs.

Hackle barbs, solid hairs, and synthetic fibers have little or no inherent buoyancy; tails made of hollow hairs differ in this respect and are discussed later in this section. These solid fibers don't actually "float" a fly in the conventional sense, but rather support it in or on the surface film. Such materials typically possesses tapered, resilient fibers—they are stiff, but springy. Under the weight of a fly, the fibers yield slightly to the surface film without penetrating it. Once these solid tail materials break the surface film, they contribute little or nothing to the support of the fly. Thus the amount of support they provide depends upon both the stiffness and resilience of the tailing material and the amount of contact area between the tail and the surface film. That is, the support given the fly depends upon how many tail fibers, and how much of each fiber, are in contact with the surface film.

This contact area is virtually always along the length of the underside of the tailing fibers. This is true even of collar-hackled dry flies. As mentioned earlier, and discussed more fully in the section on "Collar Hackle," p. 346, only in rare circumstances are such flies supported on the tips of the hackle and tail. Under most actual fishing conditions, the hackle tips penetrate the surface film, and the body of the fly drops closer to the water; the tail meets the water at a very shallow angle or quite often, lies full length on the surface film. The rear of the fly, then, is not supported by the tip of the tail, but rather by part or all of the underside of the tail fibers and often by the body itself. This is easily observed in everyday fishing; it is more difficult, for example, to keep afloat a collar-style dry fly with a quill body than it is one with a dubbed body. If the two flies did indeed ride on their "tiptoes," as is commonly alleged, there would be no difference in their floatation. But in reality, the hackle penetrates the surface film and part or all of the body of the fly rests on the water. The fibers on a dubbed body trap small bubbles of air, and assist floatation; the smooth, hard quill surface traps no air, and the fly is more apt to sink. Thus when looking at tail design from the standpoint of actual fishing, it is most useful to view a dry fly, even one with a collar hackle, as resting on the water with the rear of the body and the entire length of the tailing in contact with the surface film.

There are four basic styles of dry-fly tails, and probably the simplest in design and easiest to dress is the straight bundled tail—a clump of fibers mounted as a bundle in line with the hook shank. Such a tail produces a relatively small contact area; only some of the tail fibers—those on the underside of the tail—actually touch the surface film. The fibers on top of the tail, however, lend a kind of structural reinforcement so that the aggregate stiffness of the tail fibers is sufficient to float the fly. What's worth noting here is that increasing the number of fibers in a straight bundled tail does little to increase the number that are in contact with the surface film; it only increases the overall stiffness of the tail—which is necessary, but only to a point. You need only enough of these to give structural support; additional tailing material only adds unnecessary bulk to the fly.

How many tail fibers is this? Again, it depends on the stiffness of the fibers (which is a function of the particular material) and the overall weight they must support (which is a function of hook size and diameter). A useful answer must relate these two variables. We get some help from the materials here. Stiffer fibers tend to be thicker, so fewer of them are needed to achieve a given support strength. More flexible ones tend to be thinner, so more of them are needed for the same support. But within reasonable limits, using materials suitable for dry-fly tailing, the overall volume of material is roughly constant. Experimentation suggests that, for a straight bundled dry-fly tail made of hackle barbs or solid hair, the thickness of a pinched bundle of tail fibers should be about 1 to 1 ½ times the thickness of the hook shank. This should at least provide a starting point—you may, for instance, prefer a clump that is twice the thickness of the hook shank—but once you've established a ratio that is satisfactory to you, it should work on nearly all patterns incorporating this style of tail.

One exception here is in tailing bushy, heavily hackled dry flies such as Wulffs, Humpies, and most hair-wing patterns. Typically, these are dressed with more tail material, and Montana tyer Al Beatty offers a useful guideline. Beatty takes a clump of

fibers—either solid or hollow hairs—and holding them between the fingertips of both hands, gives them one-half of a twist. On a properly sized bundle, the thickness of the twisted fibers is equal to the outside diameter of the hook eye. This approach produces a bundle of untwisted fibers that is about 3-4 times the diameter of the hook wire.

Straight bundled tails are typically used on collar-hackled dry flies, and the tail stiffness is an advantage; since only a portion of the fly body may rest against the surface film to assist floatation, added demands are made on the tail to support the fly. But this tail style has its disadvantages as well; it provides no lateral support, and many flies will roll on their sides if not stabilized by the tail. Moreover, as fly tyer John Betts has shrewdly observed, a straight bundled tail may be perceived by the fish as simply part of a long body. Thus from the trout's point of view, the imitation may appear too large in relation to the natural insect.

Both of these problems are addressed by split tails, which use two bundles of fibers arranged in a "V" shape. The split tail, a design made popular Vince Marinaro in *A Modern Dry Fly Code*, is generally used on very low- or flush-floating flies. Two clumps of tailing material offer an increase in contact area over a straight bundled tail with the same number of fibers. The two fiber bundles distribute the weight of the fly through more material, diminishing the force applied to each half of the tail, which in turn reduces the need for stiffness and decreases the number of tailing fibers necessary. Moreover, because they act like "pontoons," split tails provide greater lateral stability than a straight, bundled tail and prevent the fly from leaning or rolling on its side. Finally, split tails better approximate the divided tails of natural mayflies and offer the trout a more realistic silhouette—an advantage in circumstances that make a sparse, low-floating fly a necessity in the first place.

Split tails require less material than straight, bundled tails. Again, the quantity is variable, but experience indicates that a clump of barbs about ¾ to 1 times the thickness of the hook wire is sufficient. On some flies, however, particularly parachute patterns which obtain most of their floatation from the hackle, tyers will frequently use only one or two fibers for each side of the tail. A very sparse tail like this more closely approximates the tail of the natural insect, and increasing the number of fibers does not materially add to the support of a parachute pattern.

Though we've been speaking primarily of dry flies, split tails are also used on nymph patterns, primarily mayflies and stoneflies; though the materials used on subsurface flies often differ from those used on floating patterns, many of the dressing techniques are the same.

The triple tail is, in a sense, a logical extension of the representational impulse behind split tails, and for both nymphs and dry flies that imitate three-tailed species of mayflies, it is the most realistic of all designs. The general approach—three widely

split tail fibers—theoretically offers good stability on floating patterns, but in the interests of realism, most tyers dress this tail with three individual fibers. While each fiber is completely engaged in supporting the fly, the small number of fibers provides a relatively low total contact area and will support a fly only in relatively placid waters. However, mayfly spinners are the patterns most often tailed in this style; such low-floating flies are generally dressed sparsely and fished in calmer waters, and thus do not require a high degree of support. It is, we imagine, possible to dress triple tails from three bundles of material rather than three individual fibers, and such a tail would give excellent stability and floatation. This rarely seems to be done, however. Like the split tail, the triple tail is occasionally used on nymph patterns, and the techniques for tailing subsurface flies are identical to those used for floating flies.

In the fan tail, individual tailing fibers are distributed in an arc around the tie-in point, forming a fan shape. Used almost exclusively for floating flies, this design effectively distributes the weight of the fly through all of tailing fibers, since each fiber is fully in contact with the surface film. It requires less material than a bundled tail and affords excellent stability, though it is, at least arguably, less realistic than a split or triple tail. From the standpoint of supporting the fly, the fan tail may well be the most functional of all, but it's not often employed by tyers—perhaps owing to the perceived difficulty of tying. This is, however, in large measure a misconception. Fan tails can be fashioned from a bundle of material about ½ to ¾ the thickness of the hook shank.

So far, we've been discussing tails of hackle barbs, solid hairs, and synthetics. But hollow hairs are quite frequently used for straight bundled tails on more heavily dressed flies of conventional, collar-hackle design. Tails made of hollow hair actually help float a fly in two ways. Like solid fibers, they are a structural member of the dressing; they rest on the surface film, and their stiffness supports the fly. But because they are hollow, the hairs contribute to the actual buoyancy of the fly; should the tail penetrate the surface film, the air trapped inside the hollow tail material can help refloat the fly—a property that makes such tails particularly desirable in fast or rough water, where turbulence may wash water over the fly or momentarily submerge it. Moreover because hollow hair tends to flare when tied, hollow-hair tails often spread slightly when they are mounted on a hook, putting more fibers in contact with the surface film, broadening the platform of support and improving the floatation of the fly.

Hollow hair, however, has its drawbacks. It doesn't possess much structural strength or resilience, and more fibers may be needed to make a tail with sufficient aggregate stiffness to support fly. Thus it is not often used on sparsely dressed patterns and is not particularly well suited to split, triple, or fan tails. Because such hair lacks resilience, the fibers may bend and kink, usually at the tie-in point. Once the hairs develop a crease, the effective stiffness is further diminished, and the hairs may in fact become permanently bent out of position. Moreover, most hollow hairs tend to be rather thin-walled and not very durable. They fray or break easily. On a straight, bundled tail with many fibers, this is of little concern. On the split or fan style, a broken tail can render a pattern useless.

Tailing Materials and Their Preparation

Tyers use a wide variety of materials for tailing flies. Some of them—like marabou, biots, or slips of wing quill, for instance—tend to be used in only one or two basic configurations, and the techniques for preparing them are relatively simple. Thus the details of handling and preparing such materials are presented in the corresponding instructional sequences.

A few materials, yarns used for trailing shucks or short bundled tails on streamer patterns and synthetic tailing materials such as Microfibbets, require no preparation at all. On dry flies, synthetic tailing materials have become quite popular and a word about their use is in order. These very straight fibers with tapering tips are stiff and springy, perfectly uniform, long, durable, and relatively easy to handle; from these standpoints, they make an excellent tailing material. They are, however, thicker than hackle barbs and most hairs, completely incompressible, and somewhat heavy. Thus they build up weight and bulk fairly quickly on the hook shank and are best suited to sparser tails. Synthetic tailing fibers are almost never used for straight bundled tails, but they are commonly employed for split or triple tails that use only one or two fibers to form each tail section. Though this limits the material in one respect, for sparsely dressed patterns synthetic fibers are an excellent material, and many tyers prefer them to hackle barbs or hair.

A few materials, however—most notably hackle barbs, barbs from body feathers, and hairs—are used quite frequently for tailing flies in a number of styles. (For more information on materials suitable for tailing, see "Solid Hair," p. 1; "Hollow Hair," p. 2; and "Tailing Barbs," p. 9.) Moreover, these same materials are often employed on other parts of the fly—wings, wingcases, shellbacks, even bodies. In order to minimize repetition and facilitate cross-referencing, the techniques for preparing these materials are presented separately in the following three methods.

Method #1: Preparing Feather Barbs

Preparing feather barbs for almost any tying purpose—tails, wings, wingcases, legs, and so on—usually requires separating a bundle of fibers of the proper thickness, aligning the tips of the barbs so that they will be of equal length on the finished fly, and

clipping or stripping them from the stem.

The main sequence shows one common approach to bundling and aligning hackle barbs. The method is simple if a relatively small number of barbs are needed. When a greater number of fibers are required—for tailing a larger pattern or tying bundled-fiber spentwings—this approach can be cumbersome, as two or more separate bundles must be clipped and the tips of the bundles aligned. The method shown in the alternate sequence, "barb gathering" as Dick Talleur calls it, bundles and aligns barbs from both sides of the feather and thus doubles the number of fibers that are gathered at one time. It is particularly efficient when larger amounts of material are needed. In order to produce a bundle of fibers with the tips properly aligned, however, the barbs on either side of the stem must be equal in length.

Both procedures are demonstrated with a feather used for dry-fly tailing, but the technique is identical when using a wet-fly hackle or other webby feather for tailing subsurface patterns, fashioning bundled-fiber wings, and so forth.

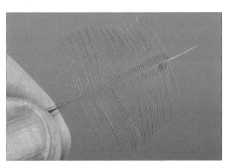

Step 1. To prepare hackle barbs for tailing, hold the feather by the very tip. With thumb and forefinger, pinch the feather stem near the tip, and lightly stroke downward toward the butt so that the barbs stand out from the stem. Repeat this process until the barbs are standing perpendicular to the stem.

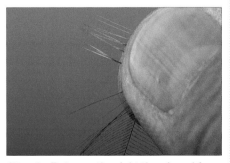

Step 2. Between the right thumb and forefinger, pinch at the base a section of adjacent barbs that you wish to use for tailing.

On some feathers, simply standing the barbs perpendicular to the stem will align the tips. On other feathers, it will not. If necessary, pull or preen the entire section of barbs in whatever direction will align the tips. You may need to preen the tips, check the alignment, and readjust them 2 or 3 times until the tips are even; this is particularly true of webby feathers used for subsurface patterns.

Taking time to align the tips precisely makes for a neat tail, and it's especially

necessary when tailing small flies, where any unevenness in the tail fibers will be quite apparent on the finished fly.

Step 3. When the tips are aligned, pinch them in the left thumb and forefinger, and clip them with scissors next to the stem. Some tyers prefer to pull the barbs toward the butt, peeling them from the stem rather than cutting them. This can work, but the force necessary sometimes pulls the tips out of alignment.

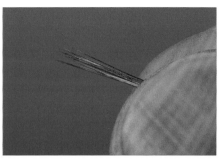

Step 4. Grasp the base of the barbs with the right thumb and forefinger and gather them into a bundle.

A hair stacker can also be used to align the tips of dry-fly hackle barbs or to mix barbs of different colors for a single tail (see **Method #3: Stacking and Aligning Hair**, Steps 1a-1e, p. 69). For best results, use a hair stacker with a small diameter and clip off any web on the butt of the barbs, which hinders stacking.

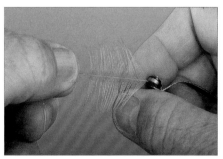

Step 1a. Barb gathering is virtually identical to the technique for folding hackle described in **Method #1: Preparing Hackle Feathers**, Step 4a, p. 345.

Begin by stroking the barbs perpendicular to the feather stem as described in Step 1.

Clip the butt of the feather in a pair of hackle pliers, and loop the pliers over the ring finger of the right hand.

Grasp the tip of the feather in the left fingers, and position the feather with the dull side facing upward.

Pinch the right thumb and forefinger together beneath the feather, as shown.

Step 2a. Draw the right thumb and forefinger upward, pinching the feather barbs on both sides of the stem, and folding the barbs together so that the tips are aligned, as shown.

Only a section of barbs will have the tips aligned; those near the edges of your fingers will be angled or uneven. Carefully grasp the tips of the aligned fibers and clip them as shown in Step 3.

Method #2:

Preparing and Cleaning Hair

When using hair to tail subsurface patterns, many tyers simply clip a small clump of fur from the hide, with both guard hairs and underfur included, and mount it on the hook shank.

On dry flies (and some nymph patterns), however, only the guard hairs are suitable tailing material, and these must be separated from the underfur. There are three methods shown below, each identified by a number/letter combination, where the number specifies the tying sequence and the letter indicates the step within that sequence. That is, Steps 1a-1c constitute one method, Steps 2a-2c a second method, and so on. These techniques are often used in combination, particularly when the underfur is long and more difficult to remove.

These same cleaning techniques are used when a bundle of guard hair is needed for wings, bodies, or other fly components.

After the underfur is removed, the guard hairs can, if necessary have the tips aligned by either of the techniques shown in **Method #3: Stacking and Aligning Hair**, p. 69.

Step 1a. This approach works best with hair that has relatively short underfur. Here, a mink tail is used to demonstrate the technique.

Fold or bend the material to raise and separate the hairs. With the right thumb and forefinger, pinch a small clump of fur at the base, close to the hide. Use the left fingers to preen away stray or splayed hair at the edges, so that you are pinching a well-defined clump.

Slide the tips of the right thumb and forefinger against one another, moving back and forth, pinching and sliding the hair to flatten the clump. You want to produce a thin, wide band of hair.

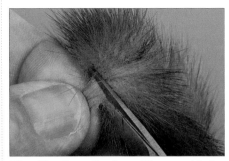

Step 1b. Grasp the tips of the guard hairs with the left hand. Grip just far enough down the clump to trap the tips of the longer guard hairs, but little underfur. Clip this pinch of fur close to the hide.

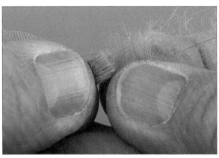

Step 1c. With the right hand, gently pinch the clump at the base and slide out the fibers of underfur.

Step 2a. This approach works best on material with longer guard hairs, such as the deer hair shown here.

Clip a bundle of hair as explained in Step 1a. Note here that the hide has been cut into a strip about ½" wide. Many tyers prepare hair by cutting the hide into strips like this. The narrow strip simplifies gathering the hair into a clump, and when tying several flies of the same style, it is easier to repeatedly clip hair bundles of the same size and thus maintain consistency in the finished flies.

Step 2b. Grasp the hair about ¼ of the way down the tip, and pull out any short underfur and loose guard hair.

Step 2c. A small comb will remove most or all of the remaining underfur. Such combs are sold specifically for fly tying, but a small mustache comb or plastic flea comb will also serve the purpose. The only real requirement is that the teeth be relatively fine; an overly coarse comb will not capture the fine guard hairs.

In your left fingers, hold the bundle of hair by the tips. Bring the comb briskly downward through the butts of the hair. This is less a combing action than a kind of "chopping" stroke. Repeat 3 or 4 times until the underfur is removed.

Step 3a. One cleaning method takes advantage of the softness of the underfur and requires no tools. It is best suited to material with long guard hairs.

Clip a bundle of hair as explained in Step 1a.

Holding the clump of fur by the very tips, position it as shown about 2 inches from your lips. Blow sharply and directly into the base of the clump 2 or 3 times.

Step 3b. The fine underfur will be driven by air pressure to the tip end of the clump.

8

Step 3c. Transfer the clump to the right hand, and use the left fingers to preen the underfur out past the guard-hair tips.

Method #3:
Stacking and Aligning Hair

For many tying applications, the hair tips must be aligned. In dry-fly tails, aligning the hair ensures that each fiber will contribute to the support of the fly; in wings, aligning the hair tips helps produce the proper shape or silhouette.

The most common approach to aligning hair, and the one that produces the most even tips, is to use a hair stacker. These tools come in a variety of sizes, but large diameter stackers are the most versatile, since they can accommodate both small and large quantities of material. Whatever the size of the hair stacker, however, do not overload it. Very large clumps of hair stack poorly and are better prepared in two or more smaller bunches.

The use of a stacker is demonstrated in Steps 1a-1e. Static electricity can sometimes be a problem, causing hairs to cling to the inside of the stacker. If this proves to be a difficulty, apply a commercial anti-static product; wipe the stacker with an anti-static sheet or mist it with an anti-static spray. Both products are widely sold for use in laundering clothes.

It is possible to align hair tips by hand, without the use of a hair stacker, as demonstrated in Steps 2a-2c. This method is less precise than using a stacker and doesn't produce perfectly aligned tips. Some tyers prefer the approach, particularly when preparing hair for wings; the slight unevenness in the hair tips, they feel, gives a more lifelike silhouette on the finished fly.

Step 1a. Clip and clean a bundle of hair using one of the techniques shown in **Method #2: Preparing and Cleaning Hair**,

p. 68. Insert the guard hairs, tip first, into the barrel of a hair stacker.

Note, however, that some hairs, particularly those from animal tails—bucktail and calf tail—are rather crinkly in texture and the hairs tend to tangle or cling to one another. To prepare them for stacking, use a small, fine-toothed comb to untangle and separate the fibers. Comb the hair butts, then reverse your grip and comb the tips. The hair will stack much more easily when prepared in this way.

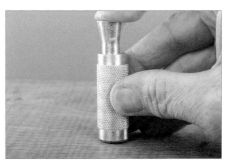

Step 1b. Hold the hair stacker as shown, making sure to cover the opening completely with your index finger. Tap the bottom of the stacker sharply against a table-top 3 or 4 times to force all the hair tips to the base of the stacker, thus aligning them. Small quantities of hair, or very slippery hair, require only a few taps; coarser hair, or larger amounts, may require repeated and vigorous taps.

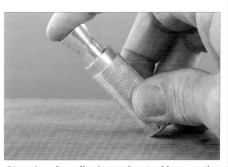

Step 1c. As a final step in stacking, particularly when using smaller quantities of material, tilt the stacker at a 45-degree angle as shown, and tap it against the tabletop a few times. This helps consolidate materials into an even-tipped bundle.

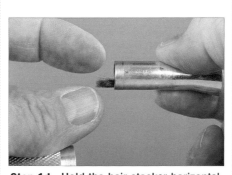

Step 1d. Hold the hair stacker horizontally, as shown, and remove the barrel with the right hand. Do this gently to avoid disturbing the hairs. Grasp the hair tips with the left hand and remove them.

Step 1e. The tips have been aligned and are ready to mount.

Step 2a. To align the hair by hand, clip and clean a bundle of hair using one of the techniques shown in **Method #2: Preparing and Cleaning Hair**, p. 68.

Flatten the clump slightly, and grasp the hair butts in your right fingers. Pluck out any unusually long hairs.

Step 2b. With the left fingers, grip the longest hairs by the very tips, and pull them from the bundle. Note in the photo that the left thumb traps the tips of these long hairs against the first joint of the left index finger. This finger position simplifies rejoining the bundles.

Do not discard the hair in the right hand.

Step 2c. Carefully lay the shorter hairs in the right hand on the first joint of your left index finger, adjacent to the bundle of longer hairs so that the tips of both clumps are even.

Some types of hair may be sufficiently aligned at this point; you can simply grasp the aligned bundle by the hair butts and it's ready for mounting

If the tips are not sufficiently aligned, repeat Steps 2b-2c until the hair tips are even.

Bundled Tails

Bundled tails are those composed of undivided bundles of material—barbs from hackle, body, and tail feathers; sections of wing quill; solid and hollow hairs; synthetic fibers; and even yarns. It is probably the most commonly used and versatile style of tail; some version of it is regularly employed on dries, wets, nymphs, and streamers.

Four techniques are commonly used for mounting bundled tailing materials: **Method #2: The Soft Wrap**, p. 26, which is suitable for any material but segments of wing quill; **Method #3: The Angle Wrap**, p. 27, which is most practical with straight-fibered materials like hackle barbs and hair; **Method #5: The Compensation Wrap**, p. 27, which is best suited to hackle barbs and solid hairs; and **Method #9: The Pinch Wrap**, p. 30, which can be used with any material. Each of these methods is also presented in a somewhat shortened form in one of the tying sequences that follow.

Straight Tails

Straight bundled tails extend straight outward from the mounting point and are affixed directly in line with hook shank. The style is among the easiest to tie and the most popular for a wide variety of applications.

Method #4:
Solid-fiber Bundled Tail

This method is suitable for hackle barbs, and all synthetic fibers, hairs, and yarns that are essentially solid rather than hollow.

Though for dry-fly tails, many modern tyers are turning more and more to split or fan tails, this style still has its devotees, primarily because of the simplicity of dressing it. This straight bundled tail is quite widely used on both nymph and streamer patterns.

The following sequence demonstrates the technique using dry-fly hackle barbs, but other materials are dressed in an identical fashion.

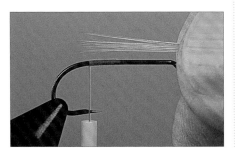

Step 1. Establishing the proper mounting point is important, as tails of this type should be affixed to the straight part of the hook shank.

Position the tying thread about one thread-width ahead of the point where the hook begins to bend.

Select and prepare a clump of the desired tailing material. If using feather barbs, see **Method #1: Preparing Feather**

Barbs, p. 67; if using solid hair, see **Method #3: Stacking and Aligning Hair**, p. 69. Synthetic materials generally require no preparation.

With the butts of the tail material in your right thumb and forefinger, measure the tail against the hook shank to determine the proper length. The tips of thumb and forefinger should pinch the material exactly at the mounting point.

This dry-fly tail is sized to be equal in length to the hook shank. Nymph and streamer tails are typically shorter, sized to ¼ to ½ the shank length.

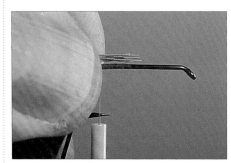

Step 2. Transfer the material to your left hand, so that the tips of the left thumb and forefinger pinch the material at the mounting point.

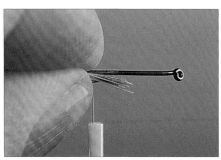

Step 3. To mount barbs with a compensation wrap (see **Method #5: The Compensation Wrap**, p. 27), position the tailing fibers against the near side of the hook shank, as shown here from the top. If viewed from the eye of the hook, the tailing material would be at approximately the 10 o'clock position.

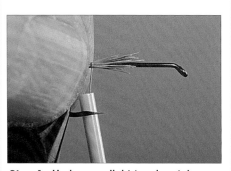

Step 4. Under very light tension, take one wrap around the material over the mounting point.

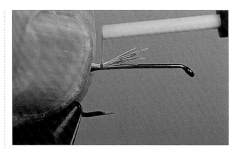

Step 5. Begin a second wrap under tension. As the wrap passes over the tail material, increase the tension on the thread, "dragging" or "rolling" the tail bundle to the top of the hook shank. When the tail is centered on top of the shank, ease off on the tension slightly to prevent moving the material farther, and continue the wrap.

Step 6. Take 3 or 4 tight adjacent wraps toward the hook eye to secure the tailing material. The tail butts can now be trimmed according to the type of underbody being formed.

Method #5:
Hollow-hair Tail

Since they add buoyancy to the fly, hollow-hair tails are used almost exclusively on floating patterns. Tyers differ in the types of hollow hair preferred for tailing; an explanation of the various types of hollow hair and their applications can be found in the section "Hollow Hair," p. 2.

Because most hollow hairs flare at least to some degree under thread pressure, they cannot be mounted in precisely the same way as solid fibers. Instead, tight wraps secure the hair to the hook shank, while a series of somewhat looser wraps helps consolidate and bundle the material into a straight tail.

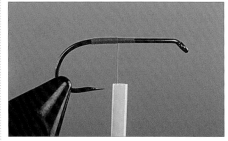

Step 1. Wrap the thread from the middle of the shank to the bend, laying a foundation, then spiral the thread back about ⅓ of the distance to the hook eye.

Select and prepare a bundle of tailing material as described in **Method #3: Stacking and Aligning Hair**, p.69.

Step 2. Size the tail by laying the hair atop the hook shank, as shown in **Method #4: Solid-fiber Bundled Tail**, Step 1, p. 70.

Transfer the clump to the left hand so that the fingertips grip the material directly above the tying thread. Unlike other methods, this one requires mounting the material near the middle of the shank and binding it down by wrapping toward the bend.

Step 3. A well-waxed tying thread helps simplify some of the later steps, so if desired, wax the thread at this point. It will be awkward to do so later.

Use the soft-wrap technique (see **Method #2: The Soft Wrap**, p. 26) to take a wrap of thread around the hair at the mounting point.

Tighten the wrap. It is important to pinch the hair securely as you tighten the thread to keep the fibers grouped on top of the hook shank. Do not release the hair in your left fingers.

Step 3a. Some tyers prefer to trim the hair butts a short distance ahead of the mounting point *before* mounting the bundle. This simplifies binding the butts down later and keeps excess material out of the tying field. However, some underbodies may require that the butts be trimmed to a specific shape or angle after the tail is mounted, so pre-trimming may not be practical on all dressings.

Step 4. Take 3 or 4 more tight, adjacent wraps toward the bend. Again, pinch the hair tightly in the left fingertips; elevating the clump slightly as you wrap will help keep the hairs grouped and centered on top of the shank.

Step 5. Take another turn around the hair, toward the bend, but this time relax the tension slightly on the thread. You may need to leave a slight gap between this wrap and the preceding ones, or the angle of the hair fibers may cause this wrap to slide forward, down on top of the preceding ones. Here is where a well-waxed thread helps maintain the proper thread position.

Step 6. Take another wrap toward the bend, relaxing the tension still further. The point of these looser wraps is to bundle the hair and gather together the flared fibers.

Step 7. Continue taking thread wraps toward the hook bend, slackening thread pressure with each wrap. Stop when the tying thread is directly above the rearmost wrap of the thread foundation.

Maintain the thread pressure used on the last wrap and take one turn of thread toward the hook eye. Release the hair tips

from the left fingers and check the amount of flare. If the fibers splay too much, grip the hair tips in your left hand, unwrap the rearmost turn of thread, and wrap it again using less tension. Release the tips and check the amount of flare.

Step 7a. When the tying thread approaches the bend of the hook, some tyers prefer to take one turn of tying thread, under light tension, directly around the hair bundle only (not the hook shank) to help gather and consolidate the fibers. This variation is especially useful when large bundles of hair are used.

Step 8. When the hairs are bundled satisfactorily, begin wrapping back toward the mounting point, increasing thread pressure as you go. Do not hold the hair tips during these wraps, but rather, observe them as you wind the thread toward the eye. If they begin to flare, relax the thread tension.

When you reach the mounting point, trim the hair butts and bind them with thread. If desired, apply a drop of head cement to the thread wraps.

Angled Tails

When dressing bundled tails (usually from solid fibers), many tyers prefer to angle the tail upward, elevating it slightly. In trout fishing, this type of tail is generally used on dry flies, but some wet flies, primarily those modeled on salmon or steelhead patterns, may use a short elevated or "posted" tail.

The value of angling the tail of a dry fly upward is the subject of some debate. Devotees of raised tails argue that the style best imitates the tail position of a natural mayfly dun. Others claim that dressing the tail in this way, particularly on flush-floating flies, pulls the tailing material away from the surface film and decreases the amount of support afforded the rear of the fly. In our observations, elevating the tail fibers does initially take them out of contact with the surface. As a consequence, the rear of the fly body sinks lower into the surface film, particularly if the body material absorbs water;

as the body drops lower, the base of the tail fibers are pulled back into contact with the surface film. This increases support for the fly, but diminishes the amount of tail elevation and thus, to some degree, reduces the imitative value of the raised tail.

Elevated tails are perhaps most practical on parachute patterns. A raised tail on a parachute dun will angle upward, but little is lost in the way of supporting the fly since the radial fibers of horizontal hackle are more than enough to keep the fly from sinking.

In one unusual design that comes from English tyer Neil Patterson, a dry-fly tail is angled downward. The function of such a tail is to invert the fly so that it rides with the hook point upward. For further explanation, see **Method #8: Funneldun Tail**, p. 73.

Step 3. Release the fibers, and trim the tail butts to shape for the underbody. If desired, a drop a head cement can be applied to the wrappings to help hold the tail in position.

Method #6:
Bent Tail

This simple method of raising the tail relies on the fact that most natural tailing materials, when bent, will take a "set" and remain in position. This technique can be used with any natural material, though it is best suited to bundles of fibers that are not excessively thick. Thinner clumps of material are handled more easily and predictably. Tails formed with this method will tend to splay a bit, which improves both their ability to support the fly and their silhouette.

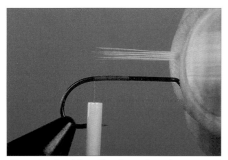

Step 1. Position the thread at the mounting point. Select, prepare, and size a bundle of tailing material as described in **Method #1: Preparing Feather Barbs**. p. 67.

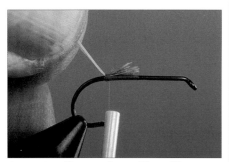

Step 2. Mount the tailing fibers as explained in **Method #4: Solid-fiber Bundled Tail**, Steps 2-5, p. 70.

Maintain tension on the thread and elevate the tail fibers about 45 degrees above the hook shank. Hold the tail in this position while you take 3 or 4 tight adjacent wraps toward the hook eye.

Method #7:
Base-Wrap Tail

Though this method involves a few more steps than the preceding one, it secures the fibers at an angle and permanently fixes the tail in an elevated position. The technique can be used with any material and is well suited to thicker clumps.

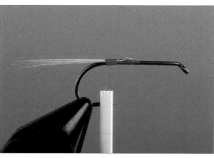

Step 1. Mount and secure a tail using the procedure shown in **Method #4: Solid-fiber Bundled Tail**, p. 70.

Spiral the thread back to the rearmost wrap.

Step 2. Cast a slack loop of thread around the base of the tailing material *only* (not the hook shank). Begin by bringing the thread over the base of the tail to the far side of the shank; then slip the tying thread beneath the tail tip. The procedure is simpler if you adjust the bobbin to shorten the working thread to a length of about 2 inches.

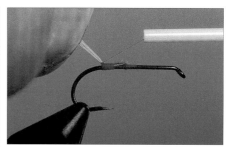

Step 3. When the wrap is completed, grip the tips of the tail fibers in the left fingers and pull gently on the bobbin to close and seat the slack loop around the base of the tail fibers.

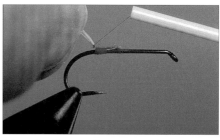

Step 4. Now make a second slack loop around the tail fibers identical to the first. This will help consolidate them into a well-defined bundle.

Pull very gently on the bobbin toward the hook eye, maintaining just enough tension to keep the two loops closed.

Step 5. Grip the tips of the tail fibers in the left hand and elevate the tail to the desired angle. Pass the bobbin over the top of the shank and hold it as shown. Adjust the tension on the thread, pulling just hard enough to hold the tail bundle in position. Release the tail-fiber tips to check the angle. If they begin to straighten, raise them again and increase thread tension to hold them in place.

Always adjust thread tension while holding the tip of the tail. Pulling on the bobbin without a secure grip on the tail will pull the fibers out of alignment.

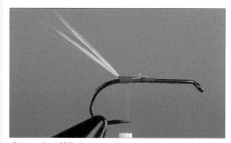

Step 6. When you can release the tail fibers and hold the tail at the desired angle using only thread tension, maintain this precise thread pressure and take 3 wraps of thread toward the hook eye. This locks the tying thread at the right tension to keep the tail elevated. If desired, put a drop of head cement on the rearmost wraps.

Method #8:
Funneldun Tail

The Funneldun tail is one of the key components in Neil Patterson's Funneldun design. Because the tail is mounted on the curved, rather than the straight portion, of the shank, it angles downward. When a fly with a collar-style or Funneldun hackle lands on the surface in the conventional position, with the hook point down, the downward angling tail holds the hook high above the surface film—so high, in fact, that the center of gravity of the hook is well above the water. This position is unstable, and the hook will pivot around the tip of the tail until the center of gravity is at the lowest possible point. Thus the hook turns upside down and rides with the point upward.

Patterson designed this tail to be used with a specific type of hackle, shown in **Method #14: Funneldun Hackle**, p. 362, but it can be used with a conventional collar style hackle (see any of the methods under "Collar Hackle," p. 346), in which case the hackle should be at least one size larger than would normally be used for the hook. Whatever the hackle style used, it should have the barbs on top of the shank trimmed away to form an open "V" above the shank, as shown in **Method #14: Funneldun Hackle**, Steps 6-7, p. 362.

The only trick to tying the Funneldun tail is in locating the mounting point. Flies with this tail style are designed to ride upside down supported on the tips of the hackle and the tips or shafts of the tail fibers; the rear of the fly body remains on or slightly above the surface film. If the tail is mounted too far down the hook bend and angles steeply downward, the fly will turn over but the rear of the body will penetrate the surface. If the tail is not tied far enough down the hook bend, the fly will not roll over. The exact mounting point depends upon tail length, hackle length, and hook style, since not all hook bends are shaped identically. Experimentation is the only real way to determine the mounting point, but the following demonstration gives a rough guideline on where to begin.

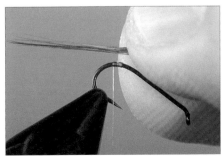

Step 1. Beginning near the end of the hook shank, lay a thread foundation a short distance down the bend.

Mounting the tail is simplified if the hook is tilted slightly in the vise jaws so that the thread does not slip down the hook bend. Note that the front portion of the hook point is visible beyond the jaw tips; this provides a reference point for mounting the tail.

Prepare a bundle of hackle fibers as explained in **Method #1: Preparing Feather Barbs**, p. 67. Grasp the barbs so that they project beyond the right fingertips the desired distance. Depending upon the hook style and the tyer's preference, the tail length may be anywhere from 1½ times the shank length (as shown here) to 5 times the shank length (as shown in Step 6).

Position the bundle atop the bend, as shown.

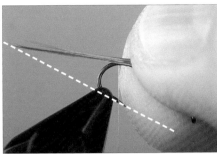

Step 2. Move the bundle up or down the bend until the tips just reach an imaginary line drawn through the hook spear, as shown.

This position may not work for all hook types or hackle styles, but it is a starting point for experimentation.

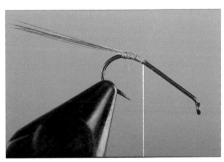

Step 3. Grasp the tips of the tail fibers with the left fingers, being careful not to alter their position relative to the hook bend.

Bind them to the shank with tight, consecutive wraps of thread moving toward the hook eye. Clip and secure the butts.

Step 4. Spiral the thread back to the rearmost mounting wrap.

Take one turn of thread around the hook shank, *beneath* the tail fibers. Snug this wrap into the base of the tail fibers to flare them slightly, but do not tighten this wrap so much that the tail fibers are raised upward and out of position.

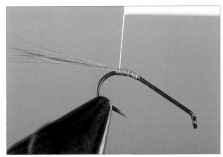

Step 5. When the tail fibers are spread slightly, take a wrap or two of thread ahead of the tail to lock in the "flaring wrap."

Step 6. This Funneldun, dressed by Neil Patterson, shows the proper position and function of the tail in the pattern.

Marabou Tail

Marabou is commonly used for bundled tails on both streamer and nymph patterns and is valued for its sinuous, lifelike movement under water. The material is used as well for wings, gills, legs, and even fly bodies, as demonstrated in other sections of this book. To facilitate cross-referencing from these other sections, procedures for preparing marabou feathers and barbs are presented in a separate method. Because the same techniques are often used to prepare CDC barbs, this material is included in the following method as well.

Method #9:
Preparing Marabou and CDC

Perhaps the most common way of using both marabou and CDC feathers, particularly for wings and tails, is to consolidate a bundle of barbs in which the tips are aligned.

While CDC feathers vary in size, their overall structure tends to be fairly uniform. With marabou, however, two rather different types of feathers are available to the tyer: blood feathers and plumes (see "Marabou," p. 11). Each requires a slightly different procedure for preparation.

Four techniques are shown below, each identified by a number/letter combination, where the number specifies the tying sequence and the letter indicates the step within that sequence. That is, Steps 1a-1e constitute one method, Steps 2a-2c a second method, and so on.

Step 1a. To prepare a marabou blood feather, as shown here, or a CDC feather, preen all the barbs toward the tip of the feather. Pinch the barb tips in the left fingers as shown. Note the short barbs at the sides of the quill. These must be removed, as they contribute little to the tail and serve only to build up unnecessary bulk on the hook shank.

Step 1b. Beginning at the base of the stem, strip away any fluff and short barbs. On CDC feathers, these lower barbs can be preened back toward base of the feather and prepared using one of the subsequent procedures in this section.

Step 1c. The barbs are now of approximately equal length, and the feather is ready to tie in.

Step 1d. Some marabou barbs, particularly those on blood feathers, have very thin tips that lack the fluffiness that is desirable in the material. Thus many tyers prefer to remove these tips to give the tail a fullness along its entire length.

To accomplish this—or any other purpose that requires trimming the marabou—it is best to break the tips rather than cutting them with scissors. Breaking the tips produces barbs that are slightly uneven in length and hence more natural in appear-

ance than those cut to a straight, uniform length.

To break the marabou, simply bundle the barbs and with the right hand grasp them near tips. With the left hand, break or tear the thin tips off as shown. CDC feathers can treated in exactly the same way to produce a bundle in which the tips are more evenly aligned.

Step 1e. Some marabou blood feathers (and occasionally CDC) have thicker stems than others, and many tyers feel that a thick stem that is incorporated into a tail or wing diminishes the flexibility and liveliness of the marabou in the water.

The feather stem can be trimmed away simply by preening back the barbs toward the butt of the feather to expose the tip end of the feather stem, and breaking or clipping off the feather tip. The length of the stem that is trimmed away varies with the length of the tail or wing, but is generally only ¼"-¾"; clipping away too much of the feather tip may remove a significant number of feather barbs from the bundle.

The approach shown below allows the tyer to take advantage of the barbs on a marabou plume, which are often quite full and attractive. CDC feathers can be prepared in this way as well, though they are often stripped, rather than cut, from the quill, as shown in **Method #36: Stalcup CDC Parachute Hackle**, Steps 1-3, p. 391.

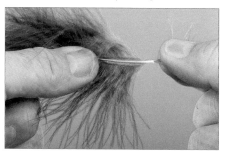

Step 2a. To prepare a clump of marabou barbs from a thick quill, strip away the fluff at the base of the feather until you reach a point where the barbs are of uniform length.

Step 2b. Pinch the feather lengthwise as shown, and clip the barbs close to the stem.

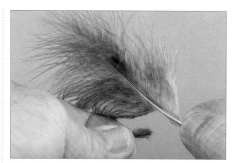

Step 2c. Bundle them by pinching the butt ends with thumb and forefinger to form a clump.

Two or more such clumps may be require to form a tail with sufficient density. On some quills (such as the one pictured) the stem becomes quite thin and flexible at the tip. Reserve this portion of the feather; it can be prepared and mounted in exactly the same fashion as a blood feather.

Step 3a. This method for preparing marabou can be used with blood feathers, but it's more commonly employed with the longer plumes. Some tyers prefer it since the barbs need not be clipped from the stem prior to mounting. This method is also a good way to take advantage of the butt portion of CDC feathers in which the tips have already been used as shown in Steps 1a-1c above,

Clip away the tip of the plume. If this tip portion contains good quality barbs, reserve it for tying as you would a blood feather.

Preen most of the barbs toward the base of the feather, leaving sections of barbs on each side of the stem tip, forming a "V". It's important that the barbs used to make this "V" are all of equal length. Provided that the barbs are of the same length, the quantity of material left at the tip of the feather can be adjusted according to the particular tying need.

Step 3b. Preen this "V" of remaining barbs straight out from the feather tip, and pinch the base of the barbs directly against the tip of the feather stem.

This clump of fibers can be mounted as though it were a blood feather, or it can be mounted using the technique shown in **Method #10: Marabou Tail**, Steps 1a-3a.

In either case, note that the tip of the feather stem itself is not incorporated into the bundle when it is affixed to the hook shank; instead, the barbs are trimmed beyond the stem tip. Thus the maximum useable length of the barbs may be somewhat shorter than that obtained by trimming the barbs from the stem as shown in Steps 2a-2c.

Step 3c. Once this bundle of barbs is mounted, the excess stem at the tip of the feather can be trimmed away at the point indicated by the dotted line. The tipmost barbs can be then be preened outward to form another "V" section of barbs.

Provided the barbs stay reasonably uniform in length, you can continue forming "V" sections of barbs right down to the base of the plume.

Step 4a. This quick technique for preparing a CDC feather was shown to us by German tyer Henning von Monteton, who uses it for tying his Stackwing patterns. It can be used with marabou plumes as well, provided the feather stem is thin enough to cut easily.

Take a CDC feather, as shown on the left. Strip away any very short barbs at the base, and trim away the very tip portion. Then cut the feather into 3 or 4 sections, as shown in the middle.

Finally, stack these sections atop one another. Pinch the stacked stems at the base and preen the barbs forward, as shown at the right.

The tips are not exactly aligned, but the feather can be tied in for a wing as it is, or the longer barbs broken off, as shown in Step 1d, to align the tips. In either case, however, the feather stems are not incorporated into the fly; rather, the barbs are mounted, and the stems are trimmed away.

Method #10:
Marabou Tail

Marabou tails can be tied in any length and density, but the material, fluffy and full as it may appear when dry, collapses when wet to a much smaller volume. Thus tyers tend to dress marabou tails rather heavily, and since the material is somewhat slippery, heavy thread pressure and the strongest thread practical for the dressing helps secure these thicker bundles.

The main sequence shows forming a tail from a blood feather. The alternate sequence shows how a tail, in this case a short one, can be dressed using a marabou plume.

Step 1. Lay a thread base on the rear ⅓ of the hook shank. (If the butts of the marabou are to be bound along the entire length of the shank as an underbody, lay a thread foundation along the whole shank.) Position the tying thread at the rear of the hook.

Prepare a blood feather as explained in **Method #9: Preparing Marabou and CDC**, Steps 1a-1e, p. 74. (If a plume is used, consult Steps 2a-2c or 3a-3c of that method.)

The light, supple barbs can make marabou somewhat unruly, and tying is somewhat simplified if the material is dampened slightly before mounting. Some tyers keep a small bowl of water with a sponge in it on the tying bench for this purpose. Wet the thumb and forefinger of the left hand, and preen the barbs from base to tip. They should be just damp enough to stick together, not soaking wet.

Other tyers use a spray bottle of water to "mist" the barbs before mounting. This method dampens the feather more uniformly and keeps your fingers drier.

Step 2. Size the tail according to the pattern. Pinch it directly behind the mounting point tightly, and position it above the rearmost thread wrap.

Take one wrap under moderate pressure. Use the left hand to keep the material centered on top of the hook shank, and tighten the wrap.

Step 3. Take 7 or 8 tight, consecutive wraps toward the hook eye, securing the material to the shank.

On smaller patterns, one clump of marabou may be sufficient. Larger hooks may require another bundle for a tail of sufficient density. If this is the case, reposition the thread at the mounting point. Prepare a second bundle of material and bind it directly on top of the first, using the procedure described in Steps 1-3.

Step 4. Trimming the butts of the material depends largely on the style of underbody desired.

The marabou (one or more clumps) can be angle-cut for a tapered underbody, as shown at the top.

The marabou can be bound along the length of the hook shank to create a uniform-diameter underbody, as shown in the center.

Or, as shown at the bottom, the clumps can be trimmed perpendicular to the hook shank to create a smooth underbody when lead wire is used to weight the fly, as explained in **Method #7: Abutted Underbody**, p. 45.

Step 1a. To form a tail from a marabou plume, lay a thread foundation and position the tying thread as described in Step 1.

Prepare a marabou plume as explained in **Method #9: Preparing Marabou and CDC**, Steps 3a-3b, p. 74.

Consolidate the "V" of barbs at the feather tip into a bundle, and position the bundle atop the shank over the mounting point. Mounting the marabou barbs very close to the tips can be troublesome, since they are quite soft and difficult to control. Thus, though we're tying a short tail in this demonstration, the marabou is mounted well back from the barb tips, as shown here. Tail length will be adjusted in the next step.

Step 2a. Take two wraps under moderately light tension over the clump of marabou.

With the left fingers, maintain moderate pressure on the bobbin to prevent the thread from shifting position when the tail is pulled to size.

With the right fingers, pull the clump of marabou toward the hook eye until the tail is of the desired length.

Step 3a. Use heavy thread pressure to secure the tail with tight, adjacent wraps.

Bind the butts along the length of the hook shank, or clip them using one of the approaches shown in Step 4.

Method #11:
Quill Tail

A few patterns—the Muddler Minnow, for instance—use segments of wing or tail feathers for tailing the fly. Duck, goose, and turkey can all be used, but if the butt of the material is to be bound along the entire length of the hook shank to form a smooth underbody, as shown in this demonstration, the material selected should be long enough for the purpose.

A number of techniques shown in Chapter 4: "Mounting and Trimming Materials" can be used to mount tails formed from quill segments: **Method #7: The Cradle Loop**, p. 28; **Method #10: The Bobbin Loop**, p. 31; **Method #11: The Langley Loop**, p. 32. We're using **Method #9: The Pinch Wrap**, p. 30, though the instructions that follow are much abbreviated since this technique has already been detailed.

Some tyers prefer to mount a pair of quill segments to form the tail; others prefer only a single segment since, unlike quill wings, two segments of tail material are not required for balance or profile. In either case, the width of the quill segment(s) used is about one-half the hook gap.

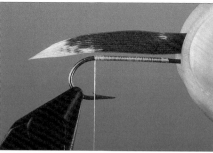

Step 1. Lay a thread foundation over the tail-mounting area. If the butts of the material are to be bound along the hook shank, as we're doing here, lay a thread foundation over the entire shank.

Cut a segment of wing or tail barbs (or cut and pair two segments) as explained in "Preparing Quill Wings," p. 243.

Position the segment atop the hook shank as shown. Customarily, the pointed tip of the feather points downward and the tail length is approximately equal to the hook gap.

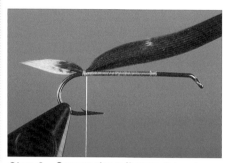

Step 2. Secure the tail material using a pinch wrap.

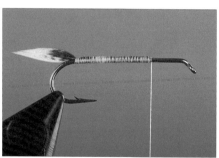

Step 3. Clip and secure the butts or, as shown here, bind them along the length of the hook shank. This approach is best when the fly body is fashioned from tinsel, floss, or other material that requires a smooth, uniform foundation.

Divided Tails

Divided tails are those in which individual fibers or bundles of material are distinctly separated—to improve floatation, to better imitate the natural food form, or both (see "Tailing Styles and Proportions," p. 65). Three styles of divided tails are commonly used: split tails, which use two bundles (or at times, two individual fibers) spread at an angle; triple tails, usually made of three individual fibers; and fan tails, which use a clump of fibers distributed in fan shape at the rear of the body.

Split Tails

Split tails are perhaps most often used on low- or flush-floating dry flies and are generally fashioned from hackle barbs, hairs, or synthetic tailing fibers. Such tails do, however, appear on many nymph patterns as well. On small hooks, the bundles may contain only a few fibers each, and on the smallest hooks may in fact consist of only a single fiber on each side of the shank. In most instances, the techniques for dressing split tails are identical regardless of the number of tailing fibers used and the type of fly, floating or subsurface, that is dressed. In a few cases, however, tying techniques can differ slightly depending on tail density and fly style, and these variations are explained in the methods that follow.

Method #12:
Dubbing Ball Split Tail— Side Mount

Though this technique is occasionally used in dressing nymphs, its widest application is on floating patterns. Since dry-fly tailing material is typically stiff and straight, the tyer cannot rely on any natural curvature or flare of the material to achieve separation of the tailing bundles. Some physical divider is necessary, and a small ball of dubbing is frequently used to separate the tail bundles, which are affixed to the sides of the hook shank. Though this approach is slightly more involved than the procedure explained in **Method #13: Dubbing Ball Split Tail— Top Mount**, p. 77, it forms a symmetrical, lower-bulk mount for thin or sparse patterns with thin or sparse bodies.

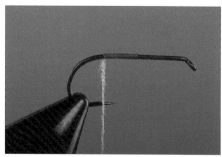

Step 1. Lay a short foundation and leave the thread at the tailing point. Spin a small amount of dubbing on the thread near the shank and compact it tightly. Loose or stray fibers or excessively spikey dubbing may interfere with the proper positioning of the tail.

8

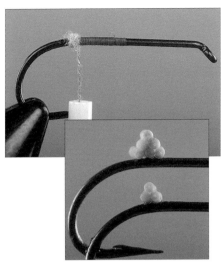

Step 2. Wrap the dubbing tightly to form a small ball at the tailing point. Do not wrap the dubbing toward the hook eye, but rather wind it over itself to shape a compact ball.

This is most easily achieved by wrapping the dubbing in an "X" pattern over the top of the shank, thus building height without creating too much width. A rough rule of thumb is to make this ball about 2 times the diameter of the hook shank, though this dimension is variable. A smaller ball generally produces a narrower angle between the tail sections; a larger ball gives a wider angle.

Note, however, that because the dubbing ball forms the very tip of the body, it establishes the thinnest point on the body profile. A tapered body that begins with an overly large ball may eventually become excessively thick at the front and out of proportion for the imitation.

Since dubbing balls are an extra step in the tying procedure and somewhat bulky, many tyers prefer to use a bump of tying thread at the tailing point instead.

To form a thread bump, spin the bobbin to twist the tying thread tightly; this is important for a compact bump. To wind the bump using the fewest turns of thread possible, and hence reduce bulk at the tip of the body, the thread wraps must be "stacked" in a somewhat orderly fashion. If you simply attempt to wind the thread over itself, the wraps will slide off to one side as the bump gets higher.

In the inset photo, short sections of thick tubing are mounted on the shank to show more clearly the appearance of the thread wraps in cross section. For hook sizes about #10 to #14, a "triangular" bump of six thread wraps, stacked as shown at the top, is usually sufficient. For hook sizes #16 and smaller, a stack of three wraps as shown on the bottom is generally enough. The number of wraps, however, does depend on the desired angle between the tail sections and the thickness of the tying thread.

Part of the thread bump will be visible on the finished fly, so it is advisable to use tying thread of a color that matches the tailing fibers and/or the body material.

Once the thread bump is formed, tying in the tail is identical to the method described for using the dubbing ball.

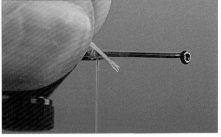

Step 3. Position the thread about one thread-wrap's distance ahead of the dubbing ball.

Select, prepare, and size a bundle of tailing material, such as the hackle barbs shown here, using one of the methods described in "Tailing Materials and Their Preparation," p. 67. Remember that this bundle forms only one-half of the tail, so use an appropriate quantity of material.

Lay the bundle on top of the hook shank, directly above the tying thread, at a 45-degree angle as shown in this top view.

Step 4. Using a relatively flat thread, take one wrap over the mounting point of the bundle.

Begin a second wrap. As you cross the material a second time, increase the thread pressure to "drag" the fibers to the far side of the hook shank. When it is properly positioned, the bundle should lie horizontally against the far side of the hook shank, as shown here from the top. The tail angle may be rather narrow at this point; it will be adjusted in a subsequent step.

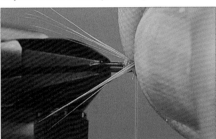

Step 5. Take a second bundle of material identical to the first, and lay it across the hook shank so that the fiber tips are equal in length to those of the first bundle, as shown in this top view.

Step 6. Pinch the tip of the bundle with the left fingers, and carefully reposition the butts of fibers on the underside of the shank, as shown in this top view.

The idea here is to keep the tips as stationary as possible so that the mounting point on the fibers is still adjacent to the tying thread. In doing so, you will maintain the correct length for this second tail section.

Step 7. Take a wrap of thread toward the dubbing ball, binding this bundle to the near side of the shank. When the wrap is complete, maintain tension on the bobbin and release the fiber tips. As shown here, view the two bundles from above the hook shank to check for length and alignment.

Step 8. When the second bundle is properly positioned, spin the tying thread to twist it tightly. Take one more wrap toward the dubbing ball, using the thread to force the bundles against the dubbing, which will spread them to a wider angle, as shown in this top view.

Counterspin the bobbin to flatten the thread again, and bind down the tail butts.

Method #13:

Dubbing Ball Split Tail— Top Mount

In this technique, the tail bundles are affixed to the top of the hook shank. Though slightly simpler than the procedure shown in **Method #12: Dubbing Ball Split Tail—Side Mount**, p. 76, it produces somewhat greater thread bulk at the rear of the fly. Synthetic tail fibers, in this case Microfibbets, are used to demonstrate the technique, though hackle barbs or hair can certainly be used.

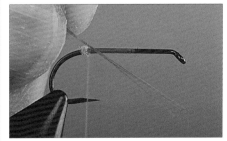

Step 1. Prepare a dubbing ball or thread bump as described above in **Method #12:**

Dubbing Ball Split Tail—Side Mount, Steps 1-2, p. 76.

Grasp the tailing fibers in the left fingers; lay them across the side of the shank at a 45-degree angle, as shown, and establish the desired tail length.

Raise the fiber tips slightly upward to compensate for the thread torque, which will pull the fibers to the top of the shank.

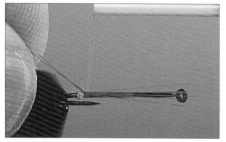

Step 2. Take one thread wrap, adjusting the tension so that the bundle is drawn to the top of the shank. When the bundle is correctly positioned with the tail fibers lying horizontally atop the shank, as shown in this top view, take another wrap toward the hook eye to hold the material in place.

Step 3. Prepare a second bundle, size it against the first to ensure that the two tail bundles are of equal length, and transfer it to the left hand as shown. This time, tilt the tips slightly downward to compensate for the thread torque.

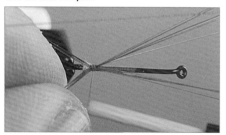

Step 4. Take a turn of thread directly over the wrap taken in Step 2, and allow the thread pressure to pull the fibers to the top of the shank, as shown in this top view.

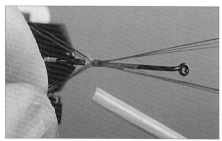

Step 5. Now take a wrap of thread toward the dubbing ball to further secure the fibers, as shown here from the top. As the thread crosses each bundle, grip the fibers by the tips to hold bundle in position.

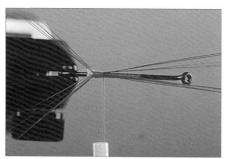

Step 6. Twist the thread tightly, and as shown in this top view, take one wrap tight against the dubbing ball, forcing the bundles to spread to the desired angle. Untwist the thread, and bind down the fiber butts.

Method #14:
Dubbing Ball Split Tail— Bundle Mount

In this technique, generally credited to René and Bonnie Harrop, all the tailing fibers are mounted in a single bundle, and divided in half as the tying thread is wrapped down the shank. This method simplifies mounting the material, but dividing the fibers evenly can be a bit tedious, and somewhat difficult on small flies. Still, some tyers prefer it as a reliable method that produces nicely symmetrical tails.

Step 1. Create a dubbing ball or thread bump as described in **Method #12: Dubbing Ball Split Tail—Side Mount**, Steps 1-2, p. 76.

Wrap a thread foundation over the rear ⅓ of the hook shank, and position the thread at the front of this foundation.

Select, prepare, and size a bundle of tailing material, such as the hackle barbs shown here, using one of the methods described in "Tailing Materials and Their Preparation," p. 67. Bind the bundle to the top of the shank with 3 or 4 tight, adjacent wraps taken toward the dubbing ball.

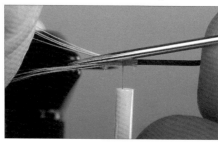

Step 2. Grasp the tips of half the fibers—as nearly as possible, try to grasp the tips

of the fibers on the far side of the shank. If necessary, use a dubbing needle to help divide the bundle in half, as shown in this top view.

Step 3. Pull the tips on the far side of the hook shank away from the hook shank and slightly upward. Holding the fibers in this position, take a wrap of tying thread toward the dubbing ball. The bundle should now be partially separated from the remaining fibers.

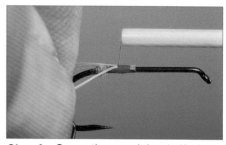

Step 4. Grasp the remaining half of the fibers; pull them toward you and slightly downward. Take another wrap of thread toward the dubbing ball to help secure the fibers in this position.

Step 5. Repeat Steps 3 and 4 a couple more times, wrapping the thread back to the dubbing ball and pulling the fibers further outward each time the tying thread crosses a bundle. With each wrap of thread, the bundles should become more compact, more distinct, and more widely separated, as shown in this top view.

Step 6. When you reach the dubbing ball, take one turn of tightly twisted thread, forcing the fibers against the dubbing and spreading them to the desired angle, as seen here from the top.

Method #15:
Loop-split Tail

In this technique, a separate loop of tying thread is used to divide a bundle of tail fibers. It is perhaps the simplest of all procedures for creating split-tails, but generally does not produce tightly consolidated tail bundles. Rather, the fibers on each half of the tail are slightly spread. It is, however, one of the better split-tail techniques for small flies, where the short tail fibers can be difficult to handle with the fingers, as is required by other methods shown in this section. It is also useful when the total number of fibers used to form the tail is small.

Hackle barbs are probably the tailing material most commonly used with this method, but synthetic fibers and hair also give good results.

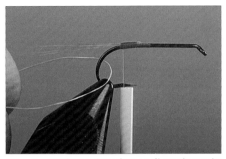

Step 1. Begin by dressing a tail as shown in **Method #4: Solid-fiber Bundled Tail**, p. 70.

Position the tying thread just ahead of the rearmost thread wrap securing the tail fibers, as shown.

Clip a 6" length of tying thread, and loop it around the hook bend, as shown. The thread size can make a slight difference. Thicker threads generally produce a wider tail spread, especially when a large number of tailing fibers are used. Thinner threads produce a narrower angle between the tails unless a relatively small number of fibers are used.

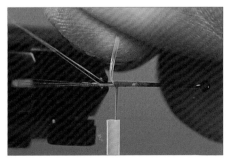

Step 2. With the right fingers, grasp the tips of half the fibers—those on the far side of the shank—and pull them outward, as shown in this top view.

With the left fingers, pull the thread loop and tighten it around the hook bend.

Maintaining this tension, hold the thread loop at about a 45-degree angle with the hook shank so that it is positioned between the two bundles of tailing fibers, as shown.

Step 3. Maintain tension on the loop; slide it up the hook bend and between the two bundles of tail fibers. Bring the loop threads forward toward the hook eye and, finally, down atop the hook shank, as shown here from the top.

Secure the loop threads with 2 or 3 thread wraps under moderate tension.

Step 4. To split the tails more widely, grasp the two loop threads and pull them forward simultaneously. This draws the loop into the base of the tail fibers and forces them outward, as shown in this top view.

Step 5. When the desired angle between the tails is obtained, bind the loop threads tightly to the top of the hook shank, as shown in this top view.

Clip the loop threads and bind down the tags.

Method #16:
Thread-split Tail

Because this technique does not require the formation of either a dubbing ball or thread bump, it creates a low-bulk mount for sparse dressings.

The following sequence demonstrates how a split tail is formed from a single bundle of fibers. The procedure does, however, necessitate dividing the bundle into equal halves. Because of the finger room required to manipulate the two tail bundles, the tech-

nique is best suited to tails on larger patterns.

On smaller patterns, manipulating the material is simpler if the tailing fibers are first separated into a fan shape, which makes them easier to divide and grasp. This fan shape can be produced using any of the techniques shown in the section on "Fan Tails," p. 85; of these, **Method #28: Thread-jam Fan Tail**, p. 86, is perhaps the fastest for the purposes of tying a split tail. Alternately, some materials can be temporarily bent into a fan shape, as shown in Step 1a.

Since the tying thread will be partially visible on the finished fly, it is best to use a thread color that matches the tail and/or body color.

Hackle barbs and hair can both be used with this technique. We're using the synthetic fiber Microfibetts here; in order to show the thread wraps and tailing material more clearly, the bundle of fibers is much thicker than would normally be used.

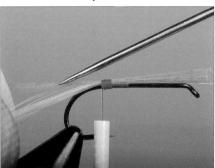

Step 1. Begin by dressing a tail as shown in **Method #4: Solid-fiber Bundled Tail**, p. 70.

Position the tying thread at the rearmost thread wrap securing the tail fibers, as shown.

With your fingers or dubbing needle, divide the bundle of fibers in half. Grip the tips of half the fibers—those on the near side of the shank—and pull them slightly toward you.

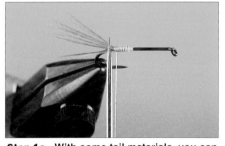

Step 1a. With some tail materials, you can flare the tail fibers temporarily to make them easier to divide.

Once the bundled tail is dressed as shown in Step 1, use your thumbnail or, as shown here, a dubbing needle to push into the base of the tail fibers from behind. This will raise and spread the tail fibers. The spread won't be perfectly uniform, but the tail fibers should be sufficiently spread to simplify grasping and dividing them.

Some types of tail fibers, however, such as stiff hairs, tend to spring back to their original position, and this approach is of limited usefulness. It works best with fibers that will temporarily crimp, such as hackle fibers and synthetics such as Microfibetts, and tails that are dressed rather sparsely; thicker tail bundles are difficult to flare in this manner.

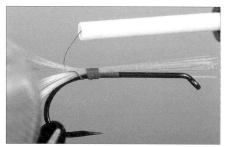

Step 2. The tying thread should be twisted, though not tightly, into a cord. Pass the thread over the base of the bundle on the near side the hook and beneath the bundle on the far side of the hook. Maintain a grip on the fiber tips on the near side of the shank.

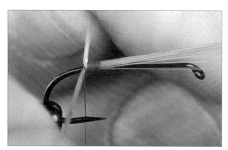

Step 3. Pull the bobbin toward the hook eye to snug this wrap into the base of the fibers on the far side of the shank.

Using the fingertips of both hands, pull the two bundles apart, bending them to keep them separated.

Step 4. Bring the tying thread underneath the shank, and upward between the base of the near bundle and the hook shank.

What's actually done in Steps 3-4 is that a wrap of thread is taken around only the hook shank, behind the two fiber bundles. The sharp-eyed reader may recognize that the approach shown here is quite similar to the one taken in **Method #15: Loop-split Tail**, p. 79. In that method, a separate loop of thread was used to force the tail halves apart; here the loop is formed from the tying thread itself.

Step 5. Pull the thread gently toward the hook eye to help snug this wrap against

the base of the fibers on the near side.

Take one or two wraps toward the hook eye to secure the thread. The tails may be slightly splayed or misaligned at this point. If so, carefully preen them into position, pulling them by the tips to set them in a horizontal plane and to form the proper angle between them, as shown here from the top.

When the tails are properly positioned, apply a drop of head cement to the wraps.

Method #17:
Clipped Split Tail

Fly tyer Skip Morris has solved the split-tail problem with this direct and straightforward approach—simply clipping the center fibers from a fan tail. The fibers on the outer edges are left, forming "V"-shaped tails.

Step 1. Tie a fan tail using any of the methods described in the section on "Fan Tails," p. 85. Of these methods, **Method #26: Thread-torque Fan Tail**, p. 85, and **Method #27: Reverse-wrap Fan Tail**, p. 86, will generally give the best results since they produce a widely fanned tail.

Since some of the fibers will be lost to trimming, use a slightly thicker bundle of tailing material than you would if the fan tail were to be left intact. We're using a very thick bundle of Microfibetts here to demonstrate the method; in actual tying, a sparser bundle would be appropriate.

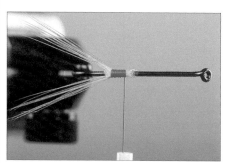

Step 2. With a pair of sharp, fine-pointed scissors, trim the fibers in the middle of the tail close to the mounting wraps.

The clipped fiber butts can be left exposed, as shown here, or on flies with dubbed bodies, a crisscross wrap of sparsely dubbed thread can be placed between the tail bundles to conceal the clipped butts.

Method #18:
Two-fiber Split Tail

In the interests of more precise representation, many tyers dress some dry-fly and nymph patterns with split tails formed from a single fiber on either side of the hook shank. A wide variety of materials are suitable, and when using hackle barbs, solid hairs, or synthetic fibers such as Microfibetts, any of the preceding techniques for forming split tails can be employed; the procedure shown in **Method #29: Hockley Tail**, p. 87, is also suitable. But since many of these techniques are designed to help consolidate bundles of fibers, they are often unnecessarily elaborate for dressing a single fiber on each side of the hook shank. Most tyers, then, employ somewhat simpler methods, and these depend to some extent on the particular materials used.

Some nymph tailing materials such as some biots, clipped feather stems, and even some feather barbs possess a natural curvature. When properly mounted, the tail fibers will automatically flare away from one another and give separation to the tailing fibers without the use of a dubbing ball or thread bump. Other materials such as hollow hair and rubber leg material will flare under thread pressure; when mounted on the sides of the shank, they will flare away from one another, again making the use of a thread bump or dubbing ball unnecessary. Thus both of these types of material can be dressed rather simply by binding them to the sides of the hook shank using **Method #13: The Side Pinch**, p. 33, or **Method #14: The Double Side Pinch**, p. 34. (Note: rubber leg material can be also be used to form tails as shown in **Method #19: Split Rubber Tail**, p. 81, a technique that some tyers find a bit simpler for this material.)

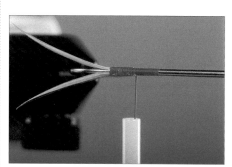

For materials with a natural curvature, such as the goose biots shown here, it is not necessary to form a thread bump or dubbing ball at the tailing point if the material is mounted so that the fibers curve away from one another. The individual fibers are mounted with the convex side against the hook shank and the tips flaring outward.

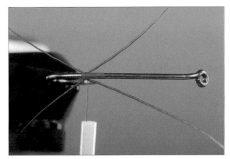

Similarly, when using materials that flare under thread pressure, such as the moose body hair shown here, no thread bump or dubbing ball is required. Binding these fibers to the side of the hook shank will cause them to splay outward, forming a well-defined split tail.

Many fibers used to tail nymphs lack natural curvature or flare, and thus require a thread bump or dubbing ball to separate them; they can be dressed using the procedure in the following demonstration.

Two-fiber split tails are often used on dry flies as well. On very small hooks, such tails are sufficient to support the rear of the fly; on larger hooks, they provide only minimal support and are used chiefly for more realistic tails on patterns that obtain most of their floatation from some other component of the fly: a buoyant dubbing, for example, a parachute hackle, or a hollow-hair arc wing of the type used on Comparaduns. Such tails are typically fashioned from hackle fibers or a synthetic tailing material such as Microfibetts, but stiff solid hairs like the guard hairs from mink tail, beaver, or nutria are quite good. Even at their best, however, single-fiber tails are somewhat fragile.

The following sequence shows Microfibetts tied against a thread bump formed at the tailing point. A dubbing ball can be formed instead, as shown in Step 4a, if desired, but the greater bulk of the dubbing ball generally isn't necessary for flaring only two tail fibers. Part of the thread bump will be visible on the finished fly, so choose a color of thread that matches the tailing material or body.

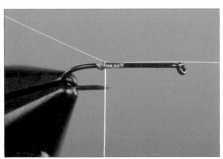

Step 1. Form a small thread bump at the tailing point as described in **Method #12: Dubbing Ball Split Tail—Side Mount**, Step 2a, p. 76.

Position one fiber on top of the hook shank. Take one wrap of thread over the material, tight against the thread bump, and use the tension on the tying thread to "roll" this fiber to the far side of the hook shank, as shown in this top view.

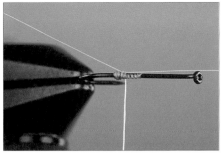

Step 2. When the fiber is correctly positioned, take another wrap of thread to hold the material in place.

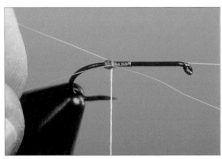

Step 3. Hold the second fiber against the near side of the shank, and take one wrap of thread directly ahead of the thread bump to hold the material in place. If this fiber is too long or too short, gently pull on the butt or tip, adjusting the length to equal that of the first fiber.

Step 4. When the tail fibers are of equal length, bind down the second fiber with another wrap. Flatten the tying thread and take 2 more wraps toward the eye of the hook, binding down and securing the fiber butts, as shown in this top view.

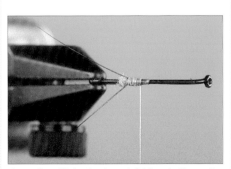

Step 4a. If desired, a dubbing ball can be used to separate the tailing fibers and give a more finished appearance to the rear of the body. The method for dressing the tails is identical to that shown in the main sequence.

Method #19:
Split Rubber Tail

Rubber leg material is often used to create tails on larger nymph patterns and, to a lesser extent, on some large dry flies. Such tails can be fashioned using the technique described above in **Method #18: Two-fiber Split Tail**, p. 80, but the material does permit a more direct method as shown in the following sequence.

Rubber tails can also be dressed in conjunction with rubber legs as shown in **Method #2: Loop-lashed Legs**, Step 6a, p. 410.

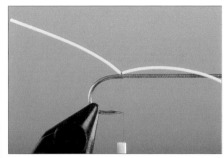

Step 1. Lay a thread foundation to the end of the hook shank, and advance the thread 4 or 5 wraps toward the hook eye.

Cut a 2-inch length of rubber leg material and center it lengthwise over the tying thread. Bind it to the top of the shank as shown.

Step 2. Take the tag that points toward the hook eye and fold it toward the bend. Bind it in this position with a few tight wraps of the thread. The rubber tails may be asymmetrical and uneven at this point. They will be positioned in the next steps.

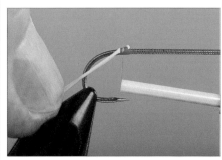

Step 3. Grasp both tags of the rubber and pull them toward the hook bend and slightly downward. One tail should be on each side of the shank.

While maintaining tension on the tails, take two or three tight wraps of thread toward the hook bend. These wraps secure the tails to each side of the shank.

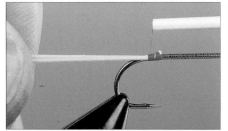

Step 4. Now pull the tails so that they project straight back from the shank; try to stretch them with equal tension on each piece of material.

Bind them tightly in this position. Placing significant tension on the material as it is bound to the shank causes the tails to flare widely on the finished fly. Less tension will produce a narrower angle between them.

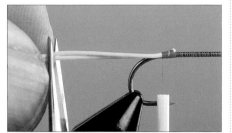

Step 5. Maintain your hold on the tails, but relax the tension. Clip both tails at once to ensure that they are of equal length.

Method #20:
Trimmed-feather Split Tail

This is an old technique for forming split tails of feather barbs. Because the barbs remain attached to the quill, the method is quite simple, as there's no need to handle individual fibers. This technique is typically used with a soft, webby feather—a hen saddle hackle, a flank or body feather—to form tails on nymph patterns. It can also be used on smaller dry flies that do not require thick bundles of tail fibers, but binding the feather stem to the shank does add bulk to the fly body.

Step 1. Position the thread at the tailing point. Select a feather with barbs of equal length on each side of the stem. Beginning at the feather tip, move down the quill until you reach the first barbs that are of the correct length for the tail you wish to form. Clip off the tip of the quill at this point.

Some tyers leave the feather tip intact during mounting and trim it away after the feather is affixed to the shank in Step 5. Both approaches work equally well.

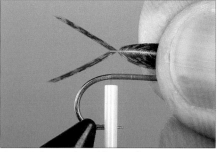

Step 2. Leave 3 or 4 barbs (or more can be left for thicker tails, fewer for sparser tails) on the stem, and preen the remaining barbs toward the base of the quill as shown. Do not strip these fibers from the quill, as they aid in mounting and securing the feather.

Step 2a. Some tyers coat the two barb clumps with head cement to form a single, thick fiber on each side of the stem.

The cement can be applied instead after the tail is mounted in Step 5.

Step 3. Position the feather horizontally on top of the hook shank, with the small exposed portion of quill directly over the tailing point. Traditionally, the barb tips, which are naturally curved, point upward.

Step 4. Take a wrap of thread over the bare quill. Use moderate tension, as excessive pressure will cause the feather to twist. Release the feather and check its position.

If the feather is not centered, or is cocked to one side, adjust it to the position shown in this top view.

Step 5. When the feather is correctly positioned, bind down the quill with tight, adjacent wraps toward the hook eye.

Note, in this top view, that the preened back feather barbs are bound to the shank along with the feather stem. This helps prevent the feather from rolling under thread pressure and keeps the tails properly positioned.

Method #21:
Split Feather Tail

A few streamer patterns, those representing sculpins in particular, use split feather tails to reproduce the silhouette and movement of a natural baitfish tail. Soft, webby, naturally curved feathers are generally used—hen neck or saddle, body, or flank feathers. The feathers should be symmetrical and have nicely rounded tips.

The following sequence illustrates the tying of a true split tail, in which the feathers are mounted with the convex sides together, causing them to flare outward and away from one another. This style provides a good profile and encourages the tails to pulse in the current. Some tyers, however, prefer to mount the feathers with the concave sides together, forming a straight, almost rigid tail. Others place both feathers in the same orientation, forming a tail that curves to one side only.

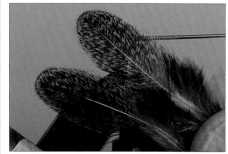

Step 1. Lay a thread foundation over the tailing area, and position the thread at the tail-mounting point.

Select two feathers—these are from a hen saddle—that are matched in size and curvature. The best way to obtain such a match is to pluck adjacent feathers from the skin.

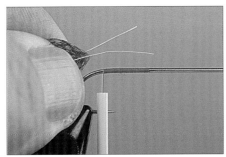

Step 2. Determine the tail length, and strip away the excess barbs from the base of the quill.

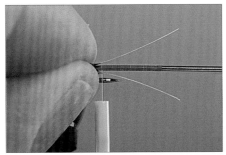

Step 3. Place the feathers with the convex sides together (or in whatever orientation you prefer), and pinch them just behind the bare quill. While it is possible to mount these feathers on the top of the hook shank, bare quills tend to roll under thread pressure and twist the feather. They are more easily and reliably mounted on the sides of the hook.

Straddle the shank with the bare quills as shown, one on the near side, one on the far side.

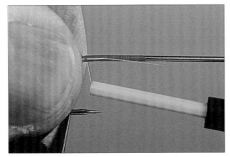

Step 4. Pinch the feathers tightly against the hook shank. Take two wraps of thread under moderate tension, crossing the bare quill just at the base of the barbs. Do not trap any barbs under the thread.

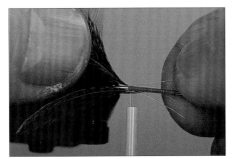

Step 5. Release the feathers and check the alignment. If one or both feathers have twisted, you can readjust the position by holding the tip and butt of the feather, as shown, and gently pulling, twisting, or rocking it into alignment.

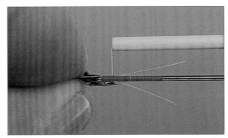

Step 6. When the feathers are correctly positioned—that is, vertically oriented and symmetrically flared when viewed from above—pinch them tightly again at the mounting point and wrap the tying thread forward in firm, adjacent wraps.

Triple Tails

Triple tails are probably used most often on patterns imitating mayfly spinners, since the naturals of many species possess three long tails that lie flat in the surface film when the fly is spent. They are, however, also used on mayfly duns and occasionally on nymphs. As a rule, triple tails are dressed from three individual fibers and contribute only minimally to floatation on all except the smallest patterns. Moreover, they can be somewhat fragile and fussy to dress, and thus tyers tend to reserve them for patterns to be fished under especially exacting conditions—low, flat, clear waters or particularly finicky trout.

Dry-fly tails can be fashioned from hackle fibers or hairs, though Microfibetts are popular for this tailing style as their stiffness and uniformity make them easy to handle. Nymph tails can be made from hackle barbs or quills, hairs, or the straight, resilient barbs of pheasant tail feathers.

In addition to the methods demonstrated in this section, triple tails can also be tied using the procedure shown in **Method #29: Hockley Tail**, p. 87.

Method #22:

Three-fiber Tail

This technique meets the problem head-on: each of the three fibers is mounted individually. Because this method uses more thread than other techniques, it is really best suited to thin or compressible tail materials or larger hooks, where the extra wraps will not produce a disproportionate bulk. In the following demonstration, Microfibetts are used.

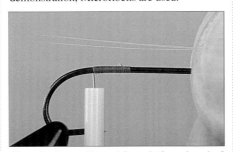

Step 1. Lay a thread foundation ahead of the tailing area, and position the thread ahead of the tail-mounting point a distance

of about 4 or 5 thread wraps, as shown. To minimize bulk, the first fiber will be bound to the bare hook shank behind the rearmost wrap of the thread foundation.

Select three tailing fibers of equal thickness. Place the first fiber against the top of the shank. If the fiber is curved at all, it should be positioned with the concave side up, so that the tail sweeps upward.

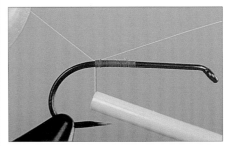

Step 2. Mount the fiber directly atop the shank with four tight wraps toward the hook bend. Use the left hand to keep the material centered on top of the hook shank.

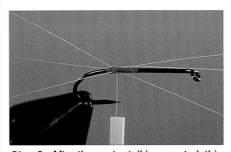

Step 3. After the center tail is mounted, this technique becomes identical to the method for forming a two-fiber split tail. Form a thread bump, and use it to flare a fiber outward on each side of the shank as shown in **Method #18: Two-Fiber Split Tail**, p. 80.

Method #23:

Loop-split Triple Tail

Like split tails, triple tails can be fashioned by using a separate loop of tying thread to divide and flare the fibers. Since the basic procedure has been demonstrated for forming split tails, as shown in **Method #15: Loop-split Tail**, p. 79, the following instructions are abbreviated. Readers seeking more detail should consult that earlier method.

Nearly any tailing material is suitable, but as in other triple-tail methods, many tyers prefer synthetic fibers, such as the

Microfibetts used in the following sequence, for their stiffness and durability.

Step 1. Mount the tying thread at the rear of the hook shank, and wrap a short thread foundation toward the hook eye.

Lay three tailing fibers atop the hook shank, and secure them by wrapping back toward the hook bend. Stop at the rearmost wrap of the original thread foundation. The fibers should lay side by side rather than in a bundle.

Cut a 6-inch length of tying thread, and loop it around the hook bend. Bring one end of the loop up between the center fiber and the fiber on the far side of the shank. Bring the other end of the loop up between the center fiber and the fiber on the near side of the shank, as shown.

Some tailing fibers, particularly short ones on small flies, can be difficult to separate with the fingertips; they can be partially separated, as shown in **Method #16: Thread-split Tail**, Step 1a, p. 79.

Step 2. Pull the two ends of the loop toward the hook eye, forcing the sides of the loop between the tailing fibers and flaring the outside fibers, as shown.

Step 3. Maintain tension on the loop ends, and bind them to the top of the shank with two moderately tight thread wraps.

At this point, the spread of the tail can be adjusted by pulling one or both loop ends to achieve the desired amount of flare and to ensure that the tail is symmetrically shaped.

When the tail is properly adjusted, bind the two ends of the loop tightly to the top of the shank, and clip the tags.

Method #24:
Thread-spread Triple Tail

Though this technique can require some delicate thread work, particularly on small patterns, it produces almost no thread bulk, making it well-suited to thin-bodied flies, small hooks, or hard and incompressible tailing materials such as Microfibetts.

Step 1. Position the thread ahead of the tailing point a distance of about 4 or 5 thread wraps, as shown. To minimize bulk, all three fibers will be bound around the bare hook shank behind the rearmost wrap.

Select three fibers of equal thickness, and bundle them with the tips even. Use a hair-stacker if necessary. Position them on top of the hook shank as shown.

Step 2. Take two tight wraps over the material, toward the hook bend. After the second wrap, check the fibers. They should lie next to one another in a row across the top of the shank, as shown in this top view. If they are stacked on top of another instead, relax the tension on the thread slightly, and "rock" the thread back or forth, or in and out, to flatten the bundle of fibers into a single layer.

When the fibers are flat, continue binding with tight wraps to the end of the hook shank.

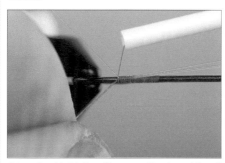

Step 3. Hold the fiber on the far side of the hook shank by the tip, and bend it toward the hook eye. If possible, bend it far enough to kink the fiber a little, so that it remains in a slightly bent position when the tip is released.

Grip the two remaining fibers by the tips, and pull them toward you slightly. Take a turn of thread over the two near fibers, but under the fiber on the far side of the shank.

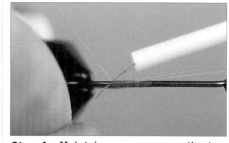

Step 4. Maintain your grasp on the two near fibers, as tightening the thread may pull them to the far side of the shank. Now gently pull the bobbin toward the hook eye, forcing the thread wrap into the base of the fiber on the far side of the shank and pushing it outward.

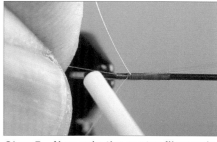

Step 5. Now grip the center fiber only. Bring the bobbin beneath the hook shank and up between the center fiber and the fiber on the near side of the shank, as shown in this top view.

Step 6. Again, gently pull the bobbin toward the hook eye to force the thread into the base of the fiber on the near side, causing it to flare outward. Use your left fingers to keep the middle fiber centered on the hook and in line with the shank. Pull or tug this fiber as necessary to counteract any thread pressure that would cause it to roll or bend.

Step 7. Maintain pressure on the thread and preen or bend the tails to make them symmetrical. When the tail is properly adjusted, take 2 thread wraps ahead of the tail to lock the fibers in position.

Method #25:
Fiber-spread Triple Tail

We were shown this method by a tyer who simply said he "saw it in a magazine." Eventually, we tracked it down as originating with New Jersey tyer Andrew Gennaro. It's an unusual and innovative technique that allows for precise adjustment of the tail position. It does, however, produce medium to high bulk at the tailing point, and the manipulation required at the butt end of the material makes it practical only with longer tailing fibers.

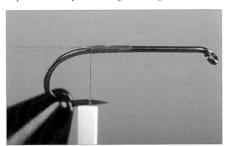

Step 1. Lay a thread foundation and position the tying thread at the tailing point.

Select three, very long fibers of equal thickness. Mount them directly on top of the rearmost thread wrap, rocking the thread as necessary to flatten the fibers into a single layer on top of the hook shank as described above in **Method #24: Thread-spread Triple Tail**, Step 2, p. 84.

When the bundle is flattened, bind it toward the hook eye with 4 or 5 tight wraps.

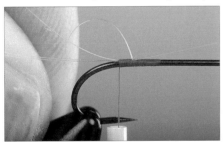

Step 2. Clip off the butt end of one of the fibers. Take the butt end of one of the remaining fibers and fold it toward the rear of the hook and down between the center fiber and the fiber on the far side of the shank as shown. It may be easiest to use the right hand to form the fiber butt into a loop and pass it over the tip of the far fiber.

A small forceps or hemostat may be useful in this procedure, particularly if the fiber butts are short.

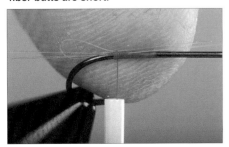

Step 3. Fold the fiber butt under the hook shank and pinch it there with the left index finger. Take a turn of thread to hold it in position. Do not pull on the fiber butt to tighten the loop yet.

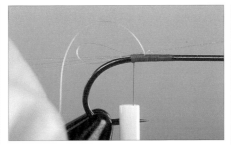

Step 4. Take the second fiber butt and fold it toward the rear of the hook and down between the center fiber and the fiber on the near side

Step 5. Fold it back under the hook shank and secure with one turn of thread.

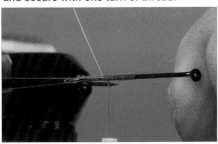

Step 6. Take one of the fiber butts and gently pull it, sliding it beneath the thread wraps. One of the outside tail fibers will flare away from the hook shank, as shown in this top view.

Step 7. Take the other fiber butt and pull on it gently to flare the other side of the tail. Adjust both fiber butts as needed to produce the desired tail shape, shown here from the top.

When the tail configuration is satisfactory, bind the fiber butts to the shank with tight thread wraps and clip the excess.

Fan Tails

Fan-shaped tails give excellent support and stability to a dry fly, and offer a good compromise between the representational accuracy of split tails and the tying ease of straight bundled tails.

Fan tails are generally fashioned from natural materials; synthetics, like Microfibetts, build up too much bulk. In order to fan the tail fibers, a physical separation, a

thread bump or dubbing ball, is necessary to help divide the fibers and hold them in place. A thread bump or ball of dubbing will also elevate the tail fibers, and to some extent, the degree of elevation can be controlled. A larger bump of thread or dubbing ball, or one closely abutting the rear base of the tail, will produce a greater elevation; a smaller bump or one placed further back from the tail will reduce the elevation, but will also slightly decrease the spread of the tail. A thread bump used to fan the fibers will remain partially visible on the finished fly. It is least conspicuous when made of a thread color that matches the tailing and/or body material.

Method #26:
Thread-torque Fan Tail

Though it takes a little practice to master, this technique essentially fans and elevates a bundle of tail fibers with one wrap of thread. It's quite efficient but does take a delicate touch with the thread and sensitivity to wrapping pressure.

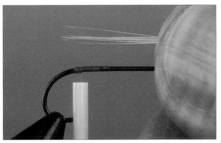

Step 1. Form a thread bump at the rear of the shank as described in **Method #12: Dubbing Ball Split Tail—Side Mount**, Step 2, p. 76.

Select, prepare, and size a bundle of tailing material using one of the methods described in "Tailing Materials and Their Preparation," p. 67.

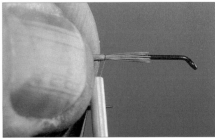

Step 2. Position the tailing fibers against the near side of the hook shank. If viewed from the eye of the hook, the tailing material would be at approximately the 10 o'clock position.

Spin the bobbin as necessary to twist the thread tightly (it may already be twisted from forming the thread bump).

Take one wrap, under moderate pressure, around the bundle about one thread-wrap's distance *ahead* of the bump. This wrap should not disturb the position of the fibers or be forced against the thread bump. Rather, it snugs the bundle against the hook shank.

Step 3. The tail is formed in this step. With the thread still twisted, begin a wrap that crosses the tailing fibers between the thread bump and the first mounting wrap, taken in Step 2.

As the thread makes contact with the tail fibers, increase tension and pull the bobbin directly away from you and slightly downward. This motion will "drag" the tailing fibers from the 10 o'clock position to the top of the shank and spread them over the thread bump.

A rather precise thread control is needed to roll all the fibers to the top of the shank, distribute them evenly over the thread bump, and elevate them. To aid this process, check the tail position during wrapping. Once the thread has crossed all the fibers, you can release the tips briefly without losing any fibers. Observe the progress. If the fibers haven't rolled far enough, try increasing the thread pressure. If they appear as though they will roll too far, relax the tension.

Step 4. When you've completed the wrap and the tail is fanned to your satisfaction, maintain the same tension on the bobbin and take one wrap toward the hook eye to hold the tail in position.

At this point it is possible to remedy any small inconsistencies in the tail by pulling the fibers into position. Frequently, the tail will arc over the bump and appeared curved when viewed from the rear of the hook; the fibers at the extreme edges should be pulled upward so that all the tail fibers form a flat, slightly elevated, plane. Such adjustments are relatively simple at this point since the fibers are somewhat mobile under the thread wraps.

Step 5. When the tail is in position, as shown in this top view, bind down the butts and trim.

Method #27:
Reverse-wrap Fan Tail

We are indebted to Oregon fly tyer Skip Morris for this simple and reliable method for fanning tail fibers.

Step 1. Form a ball of dubbing (or thread bump if you prefer) at the rear of the shank as described in **Method #12: Dubbing Ball Split Tail—Side Mount**, Steps 1-2, p. 76.

Spiral the tying thread about 6 turns forward, or about ¼ the distance to the hook eye.

Select, prepare, and size a bundle of tailing material using one of the methods described in "Tailing Materials and Their Preparation," p. 67.

Bind the hackle fibers with 3 tight wraps toward the hook bend. The fibers should be securely fastened.

Grip the fiber tips and pull them downward over the dubbing ball, spreading them evenly across the top and sides of the ball. If the fibers are not uniformly distributed, rock them from side to side to spread them evenly.

Step 2. Maintain the fibers in this spread position, and wrap tightly toward the bend. The last wrap should force the base of the fibers tightly against the dubbing ball to secure and elevate the tail.

Check the tail position by viewing it from the rear of the hook. If the tail is arced, adjust the outer fibers as described in **Method #26: Thread-torque Fan Tail**, Step 4, p. 85.

Method #28:
Thread-jam Fan Tail

This technique forces thread wraps up under a straight bundled tail to flare the fibers. The method is relatively fast, and though it doesn't generally produce a broad tail spread, it doesn't significantly elevate the tail either. It is best suited to more sparsely dressed tails.

Step 1. Mount a bundle of tailing fibers as described in **Method #4: Solid-fiber Bundled Tail**, p. 70.

Position the tying thread at the rearmost thread wrap.

Step 2. Spin the bobbin to twist the thread. Take one wrap around the bend of the shank only, beneath the fibers.

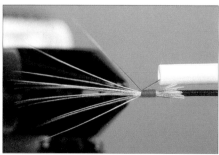

Step 3. Pull the bobbin toward the hook eye to force this wrap of thread into the base of the tailing fibers where they meet the hook shank. The thread wrap should flare the tailing fibers.

You can increase the flare by carefully using your thumbnail to push the thread wrap deeper into the base of the fibers, or you can repeat Step 2 to add another wrap of thread around the shank.

8

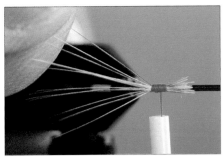

Step 4. When the desired spread is obtained, take one wrap over the tailing bundle toward the hook eye to hold the tail fibers in position.

If the tail is not uniformly spread, use your fingertips to spread and preen the fibers to the desired shape.

Then take one more tight wrap to secure the tail.

Method #29:
Hockley Tail

This technique first saw print in the work of noted tyer John Betts, who first saw it demonstrated by Baltimore tyer Bud Hockley. Though it takes essentially the same approach as that used in **Method #28: Thread-jam Fan Tail**, p. 86, the use of a dubbing needle allows the formation of a larger-diameter thread bump for a greater spread and elevation of the tail fibers.

This is a versatile technique that can be used to produce split tails, triple tails, or fan tails. Since the steps for forming these three tail styles are essentially identical, we are presenting them only once, in demonstrating the construction of fan tail, where the greater number of tailing fibers gives a somewhat clearer illustration of the method. Procedures to adapt the technique for split or triple tails are noted as required in the steps that follow.

Hockley tailing offers a number of advantages. Since the tail fibers are first mounted as a bundle, the method does not require the sometimes cumbersome mounting of individual fibers when dressing split or triple tails. Moreover, the thread bump beneath the tailing fibers is formed one wrap at a time, thus allowing a tyer to take the minimum number of wraps required to divide or fan the tail. Finally, this technique is particularly useful for dressing split or triple tails on nymph patterns, where the tail fibers are often short and the material soft, making them difficult to handle with other methods.

Though the procedure may appear a bit involved, it's one of those fly-tying techniques that is easier to execute than to describe. We're using Microfibetts for the fan tail in the following demonstration for better visibility; normally, this material would be used only for split or triple tails.

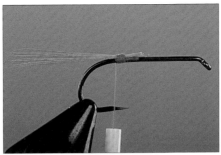

Step 1. Position the thread ahead of the tail-mounting point a distance of about 4 or 5 thread wraps, as shown. Select, prepare, and size a bundle of tailing material using one of the methods described above in "Tailing Materials and Their Preparation," p. 67.

A split tail can be formed from two fibers or from an even-numbered quantity of fibers that will later be divided into two bundles. A triple tail can be formed by mounting three individual fibers or a number that will later be divided into three bundles.

Mount the bundle of fibers, taking tight, adjacent wraps down the shank, stopping short of the hook bend,

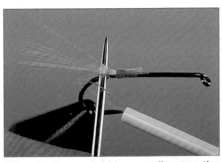

Step 2. Lay a dubbing needle atop the hook shank behind the tail. Gently push the side of the needle into the base of the fibers to elevate them slightly.

Take two wraps of thread around the shank of the needle, passing the wraps behind the fiber tips, "as though," Betts explains, "you were beginning to lash the needle to and across the hook."

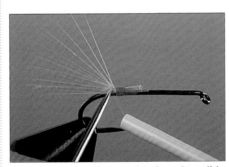

Step 3. Put tension on the thread to slide the wraps down the needle. Use the needle point to guide the thread wraps up underneath the tail, as close to the base of the fibers as possible. These wraps create a thread bump to spread and elevate the tail.

Fan tails on small hooks, or split or triple tails formed from 2 or 3 fibers may be sufficiently fanned at this point.

Larger hooks may require enlarging the bump as described in the following steps.

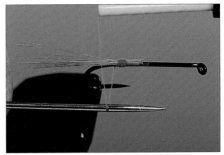

Step 4. Position the needle on the near side of the hook, parallel to the shank. Bring the tying thread around the needle and under the tail. Maintain tension on the bobbin as shown.

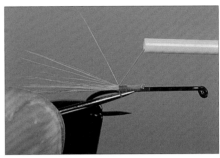

Step 5. Angle the needle toward the base of the fibers as shown. Put tension on the thread to slide the wrap off the needle point and directly on top of the two wraps created in Step 3.

Step 6. Repeat Steps 4-5 until the tail fibers are fanned to the desired spread.

If forming a split or triple tail from more than 2 or 3 fibers, the tail material can be consolidated into separate bundles by taking crisscross wraps between the tail bundles. For split tail, use the procedure shown in **Method #16: Thread-split Tail**, p. 79; for triple tails, use the procedure shown in **Method #24: Thread-spread Triple Tail**, p. 84.

Fur-strip Tails

Narrow, supple strips of fur on the hide are often used to form tails on streamer patterns, particularly those that represent sculpins. Like marabou, fur-strips are highly mobile under water and impart a lifelike action to the fly, but the strip of hide to which the fur is attached helps the tail maintain its shape better than the much limper marabou.

Fly-tying terminology poses something of a problem in speaking of fur-strip tails, since such tails are often dressed in conjunction with other parts of the fly. For example, a fur-strip wing of the type typically used on Zonker patterns can be left long to form a "tail" and "wing" from a single piece of material. The strip of fur over the top of the fly is referred to by tyers as a "wing," even though Zonkers and similar streamers typically imitate baitfish, which clearly have no wings. By the same token, some tyers will lash a strip of fur to a thread-covered or weighted hook shank, leaving a long flexible "tail" to produce a simple leech pattern. In this case, the entire fur strip is intended to represent the body of the leech, even though its most prominent feature is the long, flowing strip of fur projecting rearward from the tailing point. Thus while the actions and, to some extent, profiles of all these different fly styles are fairly similar, the terms used to describe the fur-strip component differ, depending on the type of imitation tied.

While it would have been possible to group the technically similar methods used to tie these components into a single section, we have chosen to place them instead into sections of the book that correspond more closely to ordinary tying terminology. Thus fur-strip tails that are fashioned from the same piece of material used to fashion wings are presented in **Method #70: Fur-strip Downwing**, p. 318, since this entire component is most commonly called a wing. For the same reason, fur-strip "tails" that are essentially an extension of a fly body are presented in **Method #56: Lashed Fur-strip Body**, p. 143. Readers seeking a particular style of fur-strip tail dressing may wish to consult these other methods.

The following method demonstrates techniques for dressing fur-strips at the tailing point of the fly.

Method #30:

Fur-strip Tail

The main sequence, Steps 1-2, show the construction of a simple fur-strip tail commonly used on sculpin patterns and, in conjunction with **Method #55: Wrapped Fur-strip Body**, p. 142, for leech patterns. Tails with shorter fur are often tied with this technique to dress strip nymphs. Step 3 of the main sequence shows an approach taken by Gary Borger to produce a very simple fur-strip tail for leech patterns.

The alternate sequence shows the method for creating a "double" tail, using two fur strips to widen the profile and increase the bulk of the tail.

Any fur can be used, but rabbit fur is widely employed since it is available in a variety of colors and can be purchased in pre-cut strips. Squirrel, muskrat, or other shorter furs are better proportioned to smaller hooks. In any case, the hide must be tanned rather than dried in order to obtain a flexible tail.

Step 1. Select or cut a length of longitudinally cut fur (see "Fur Strips", p. 142). The technique for cutting such strips is presented in **Method #42: Hide-strip Chenille**, Steps 1 and 2a, p. 132. The width of the fur strip varies with hook size, but in general, a strip about ³⁄₁₆"-¼" wide is sufficient for hooks in the #2-#6 range.

Trim the fur strip to a length about ¼" longer than the desired length of the finished tail.

At the front end of the strip, that is, the end at which the fur curves or slopes away from the edge of the hide, shave the fur from about ¼" of the hide, as shown here.

If desired, the front of the strip can be trimmed to a point for a tapering underbody, as shown in **Method #70: Fur-strip Downwing**, Step 1, p. 318. However, flies tied with fur-strip tails are often weighted, and leaving the front of the strip untrimmed, as shown here, makes a smoother underbody when lead wire is wrapped on the hook (see **Method #7: Abutted Underbody**, p. 45).

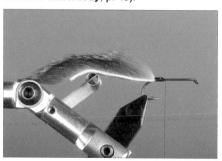

Step 2. Lay a thread foundation over the tailing area and position the thread at the tail-mounting point.

Position the fur strip atop the shank, as shown, and use heavy thread pressure to bind the shaved portion of the strip to the top of the shank.

Step 3. Gary Borger's version of the fur-strip tail is about as simple as they come, though the style is designed to be used on patterns weighted with wraps of lead wire or barbell eyes attached to the top of the shank, which will cause the fly to ride with the hook point up.

Cut a strip of fur as described in Step 1, but do not shave the front end.

Use a dubbing needle to poke a hole through the hide about ¼" from the front of the strip.

Insert the hook point through the hole, as shown here. Because the fly rides upside down, the fur side of the strip faces upward.

Step 1a. To create a tail of double thickness, cut a fur strip and shave the tip as explained in Step 1. Cut a second strip about ¼"-½" shorter; the exact length depends upon the hook size, as explained in Step 3a.

Use a relatively viscous adhesive—vinyl, silicone, or gel-type CA glue—to join the strips. Smearing glue on the underside of the strip may get adhesive on the fur; instead, apply the glue in a series of "dots" on the underside of shorter strip. The glue points here are represented by black dots on the hide.

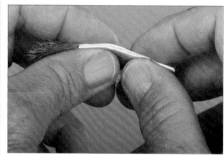

Step 2a. Press the fur strips firmly together, taking care not to get any glue on the fur. Allow the tail to dry.

Step 3a. The shaved portion of the top fur strip is mounted as shown in Step 2, but the double thickness of fur produces a much fuller tail.

Note the position of the bottom strip; it is set back far enough to clear the hook bend.

Trailing Shucks

Tying tailing fibers to imitate the trailing shucks of newly emerged flies is essentially identical to tying straight bundled dry-fly tails. The primary differences are in tailing materials, tail density, and sometimes tail position.

For forming shucks, tyers often use a reflective, translucent material to reproduce the hollow nymphal skin. There is a marked tendency these days to use synthetic fibers like Antron and Z-lon, but webby hen hackle or body feathers, and even CDC feathers, are sometimes used.

Tail density varies with fly style. Dry flies tied with trailing shucks use the same quantity of material as they would if tied with rooster hackle barbs or solid hair. Floating nymphs and emergers tend to use sparser tails, about ½ to ⅓ the density of a dry-fly tail. On such patterns, many tyers prefer tailing fibers of uneven length to imitate the irregular shape of the shuck.

On some patterns, most notably midge pupae, the shuck is tied in at the curved portion of the hook to imitate the profile of the natural.

Method #31:

Straight Shuck

Probably no one has done more to popularize this style of trailing shuck than Craig Mathews in his Sparkle Dun and X-Caddis designs.

To tie this type of shuck, follow the procedure described in **Method #4: Solid-fiber Bundled Tail**, p. 70. The one difference here is that synthetic tailing material need not be sized before tying in. A longer bundle can be secured the shank and cut to exact length afterward.

Whether made of natural or synthetic materials, this type of shuck can be bound in at the bend of the hook so that it curves downward.

The fly at the top has a shuck tied at the bend of a midge pupa pattern to imitate the curvature the natural insect.

A straight shuck on a floating nymph, or the emerger pattern dressed with feather barbs shown at the right, will project beneath the water like the shuck on an emerging natural.

The fly at the left shows a straight shuck used on a dry fly, in this case an X-Caddis.

Method #32:

Combination Shuck

In *Production Fly Tying*, A.K. Best argues persuasively for the use of a trailing shuck along with a dry-fly tail for patterns that float in or on the surface film. The style gives good floatation and may have a representational function in imitating both the tails and the shuck of a freshly hatched fly.

Step 1. Tie in a bundle of fibers for the shuck (Antron is used here), as explained in **Method #4: Solid-fiber Bundled Tail**, p. 70. The shuck should be relatively short—about 1 hook gap. The material can be mounted on the straight portion of the shank, or just where the shank begins to curve so that the fibers project downward through the surface film.

Step 2. For the tail, Best recommends stiff hackle fibers that are slightly elevated.

At the rearmost thread wrap, mount a bundled tail of the normal length using the technique shown in **Method #6: Bent Tail**, p. 72.

Method #33:

Bead Trailing Shuck

This is a technique of our own devising for using glass beads to form an extended trailing shuck on both emerging mayfly and caddis patterns. The use of an Antron sheath gives added reflectivity, a hollow shape, and translucence to the shuck. Because the beads add weight, the rear of the fly sinks below the surface film, like an emerging natural. To keep the fly afloat, a buoyant emerger wing of hollow hair or CDC is recommended.

Clear or very pale-colored beads

enclosed in the Antron sheath give the appearance of an empty shuck from which the fly has emerged. Beads that match the body color of the natural give the appearance of an insect still withdrawing its abdomen from the shuck. The diameter of the beads should be approximately as wide as the abdomen of the insect that is being imitated.

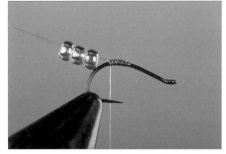

Step 1. Lay a thread foundation over the trailing shuck area. The shuck can be mounted at the rear of the hook shank or, as shown by this foundation, slightly down the bend of the hook. If mounting the shuck on the bend, it helps to tilt the hook in the vise, as shown.

Cut a 6" length of monofilament tippet material. The size of the tippet material should be matched to the beads used. Chose largest diameter tippet material that will still allow two pieces of the monofilament to pass through the bead hole.

Using a pair of needle-nose pliers, flatten about ¼" of one end of the monofilament.

Bind the flattened section to the hook shank, and position the tying thread at the rearmost mounting wrap, as shown.

Thread the desired number of beads onto the monofilament, and snug them up against the hook shank, as shown.

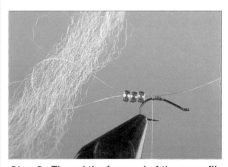

Step 2. Thread the free end of the monofilament back through all the bead holes, forming a loop beyond the rearmost bead, as shown.

Take 2 or 3 moderately tight thread wraps over the free end of the mono, binding it to the top of the hook shank, as shown.

Clip a 2" length of material to form the sheath; we're using Antron yarn here. Comb through the fibers to separate and untangle them. All the fibers can be used on larger patterns. On smaller flies, less sheath material is needed, and some of the fibers can be removed and discarded.

Center the combed fibers inside the loop, as shown.

90

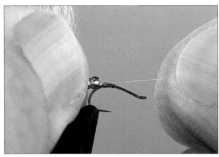

Step 3. Pull the free end of the mono until the loop is almost closed.

Pinch the beads in the left fingers, as shown. Pull tightly on the tag of monofilament. This will cinch the Antron fibers into the rear bead and secure them.

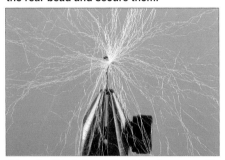

Step 4. Bind down the tag of mono with several tight thread wraps, and clip the excess. Position the tying thread directly ahead of the front most bead.

Using your fingers or a small comb, spread the fibers so that they are uniformly distributed in a circle behind the rearmost bead, as shown in this rear view.

Step 5. Separate out 4-6 fibers, and hold them in your left fingers, as shown. These will be used to imitate the tails on the shuck and provide some resistance on the beads when preening the shuck fibers forward.

With your right fingers, pull the yarn fibers forward. Keep them uniformly distributed around the beads and apply even tension on all of the fibers to form a smooth, even sheath.

Step 6. With tight thread wraps, bind the yarn to the hook shank ahead of the front-most bead, as shown.

Step 7. Clip the excess yarn, and bind down the butts. Trim the trailing the fibers to the desired length.

The remainder of the emerger pattern can now be dressed.

The fly at the top shows the bead shuck dressed in this demonstration; the 2 flies at the bottom show different applications of this shuck style.

CHAPTER 9

Ribbing and Gills

Ribbing and gills are typically dressed over the abdomen or body of a fly, and the techniques used to form them often overlap. They are sometimes, for example, dressed in conjunction with one another, as when ribbing is used to secure the gill material, and in some instances, the difference between the two is merely one of terminology, as when gills are formed by ribbing certain types of material over the body. Because of these similarities, the two components are presented together in this chapter.

Ribbing

Ribbing is a versatile fly component; it is frequently incorporated into dry, nymph, and streamer patterns; it can be made highly conspicuous or almost invisible; and it has a variety of different purposes.

Ribbing can have an imitative function on the fly, usually in creating the impression of body segments, or producing realistic markings, on the abdomen. It can have a structural purpose when it is added to reinforce more fragile materials such as quill bodies and palmered hackles, or when it is used to affix other components, such as gills or overbodies, to the hook. Or it can simply be used to adorn the fly, adding flash, color, or sparkle. In many instances, the ribbing material performs two or more these functions simultaneously.

Virtually any strand of relatively thin material can be used to form the ribbing. The most commonly used are tinsel, wire, and plastic or vinyl cords such as Swannundaze and V-Rib, but tying thread, monofilament tippet material, stripped feather stems and quills, twisted mylars such as Krystal Flash, floss, and latex strands can also be used.

Despite the wide versatility of this component, the actual number of ribbing methods is quite small, making it perhaps the most straightforward technique in all of fly tying. Ribbing materials can be wrapped in the same direction as the body material; they can be wrapped in the opposite direction ("counter-ribbing"); and if hollow tubing is used to form the body, an internal rib can be created, as shown in **Method #81: Internal-ribbed Tubing Body**, p. 166.

Method #1:

Ribbing

In ribbing, a strand of rib material is wrapped in the same direction as the body material. Its most typical applications are in creating body segments or adding flash to a fly, but it is also used to tie-off and reinforce reverse palmer hackle as explained in **Method #17: Reverse Palmer Hackle**, p. 365.

The appearance of the finished ribbing depends to some extent on the type of body and the way in which body materials are applied. For instance, on a body that is loosely dubbed to give the fly a somewhat rough, shaggy appearance, ribbing will "bite" or "sink" into the body and be partially or fully obscured by the body materials, forming a very inconspicuous rib. The same dubbing twisted tightly around the thread will create a denser, less compressible body, and the ribbing material will lie atop the dubbing, forming a much more prominent rib. Neither type of rib is "right" or "wrong," though in dubbing a body, some care should be taken to make the body texture consistent so that the rib itself is uniform in appearance over the entire body length, as shown in the main sequence, where Swannundaze is ribbed over a dubbed body.

One problem encountered with bodies formed of chenille and similar materials (and to some extent with dubbing) is that thinner ribbing strands may tend to lodge between the wraps of body material, falling into the cracks as it were, where the rib is neither visible nor structurally significant. The problem can be solved by taking care to space the wraps of rib material farther apart than the body wraps, or by using the approach shown in **Method #2: Counter-ribbing**, p. 92.

The main sequence shows a common technique that can be used with any ribbing material. The alternate sequence shows a useful approach to ribbing bodies with the tying thread. In this technique, the body material is wrapped toward the rear of the hook, then ribbed with the tying thread. When the ribbing crosses the body wraps, the two materials make an "X" shape, which prevents the ribbing from slipping between the wraps of body material. Though this is not a true counter-ribbing technique since both materials are wrapped in the same direction around the hook shank, the effect produced is similar to counter-ribbing. This approach is most often

employed when a highly visible rib is desired, usually over a dubbed or floss body.

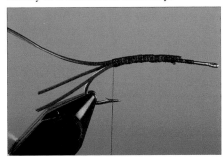

Step 1. Dress the tail or trailing shuck if one is used.

Mount the ribbing material; the rearmost wrap securing the rib material should be placed directly atop the rearmost tail-mounting wrap. Thicker ribs, such as the Swannundaze shown here, can be bound along the length of the shank to help form a smooth underbody.

Step 2. Dress the body of the fly, taking care to place a turn of body material over the mounting wraps securing the ribbing so that no thread wraps show on the finished fly.

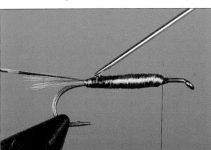

Step 3. (Optional) The rib material gets little "bite" on very smooth or hard materials such as quill, tinsel, or the floss shown here, and it can slide out of position, particularly on tapered bodies.

To better secure such ribbing, use a small brush or a dubbing needle to apply a coat of thinned head cement to the body material. On non-absorbent materials such as quill, a single thin coat is all that is required. On absorbent materials like floss, you may need to continue applying cement until the body is nearly saturated and the surface layer of the floss holds enough cement to adhere to the ribbing.

After the cement is applied, wrap the rib forward as described in Step 4.

If desired, a second coat of thinned cement can be applied over the finished body and ribbing.

Step 4. Wrap the ribbing material forward in an open spiral. There are really two simple keys to forming a neat, attractive rib. First, maintain a consistent tension on the ribbing material so that the ribbing strand compresses evenly into the surface of the body, making segmentations of a uniform depth. Second, work for a uniform spacing between ribbing wraps.

The number of wraps of the rib material is almost completely a matter of individual taste, though in general the gaps between the ribbing wraps are wider than the ribbing material itself. When ribbing material is used for reinforcement, such as fine wire over a palmered hackle, placing the wraps somewhat closer together gives greater durability in the finished fly.

Step 5. After the rib is complete, secure the ribbing strand at the front of the body, clip the excess, and bind with thread.

Step 1a. To rib a body with the tying thread, mount the tail, and advance the tying thread to the front edge of the abdomen. If using dubbing, as shown here, begin dubbing the body back toward the tail-mounting point.

(If using floss or a similar type of stranded material, secure the body material at the front of the abdomen. Return the thread to the tail-mounting point, and wrap the body material toward the rear of the hook.)

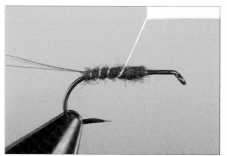

Step 2a. When the body is complete, simply spiral the thread forward to create the rib.

(If using a separate body material like floss, tie off the strand at the tail-mounting point, clip the excess, and spiral the thread forward.)

Method #2:
Counter-ribbing

Counter-ribbing involves applying the ribbing material in a direction opposite to that in which the body material is wrapped. The method is typically used to reinforce materials already dressed on the hook—usually quill, herl, or feather-barb bodies, or palmered hackle as shown in the alternate sequence. Because the ribbing is counter-wrapped, it cannot lodge between wraps of any material beneath it; rather the rib lies crosswise atop other materials, securing them to the shank.

The following sequence shows one common use of counter-ribbing—reinforcing a palmer hackle.

Step 1. Here, a tail and a strand of ribbing material have been mounted at the rear of the shank. A yarn body has been dressed, and the hackle wrapped from the rear of the fly forward. A conventional rib would lie on the body alongside the feather stem rather than crossing the stem to help secure it.

Step 2. Bring the rib material toward you over the top of the shank, and wrap it forward in this direction.

When counter-ribbing over palmered hackle, it helps to wiggle the rib material from side to side as you wrap. This wiggling motion helps slip the ribbing strand between the feather barbs so that it is seated directly against the hackle stem without trapping any barbs.

Step 3. When the counter-ribbing is complete, pull the rib strand directly toward you, as shown.

With the right hand, maintain moderate tension on the rib material; with the left hand, take 2 or 3 tight wraps over the rib material at the tie-off point. It is important to maintain tension on the ribbing material. Because it is counter-wrapped, thread torque from the tie-off wraps will push against the direction of the counter-rib and tend to loosen the rib material if it is not held taut.

Step 4. When the ribbing is secured with a few tight wraps, clip the excess and bind down the tag tightly with additional thread wraps.

Gills

Gills, particularly on nymph patterns, are not an anatomical feature that most American tyers typically seek to imitate in much detail. There are few exceptions, however. The prominent abdominal gills on large burrowing mayfly nymphs such as *Hexagenia* are sufficiently conspicuous that they are a part of many nymph patterns that represent these species. On midge pupae, many tyers simulate gills by tying a peacock or ostrich herl collar at the head of the fly using the technique shown in **Method #26: Single-herl Body**, p. 117. And Mike Mercer's Poxyback series of nymphs are characterized in part by the inclusion of tuft gills at the rear of the thorax. But for the most part, American tyers are content to tease out a few strands of dubbing between turns of ribbing on a nymph abdomen to suggest the delicate, feathery gills on some species.

European tyers, by contrast, particularly English tyer Oliver Edwards, take greater pains to imitate gills on subsurface patterns, and their dressings often tend to be more realistic in appearance than American designs. We are indebted to Edwards who has kindly consented to let us reproduce some of the innovative and unusual gill techniques he demonstrates in his book *Flytyers Masterclass.*

Flies with bead bodies require special gilling techniques shown in **Method #97: Feather-gill Bead Body**, p. 183; and **Method #98: Dubbed-gill Bead Body**, p. 184.

Method #3:
Tuft Gills

"Tuft" gills are fashioned from clumps or bundles of material, often applied at the rear of a nymph thorax, though they can be tied between abdominal segments as well. Some tyers also use this style on streamer patterns, particularly sculpins, applying a bit of red material at the base of the fly head to suggest the gills on a baitfish.

Nymph gills are generally delicate, mobile structures, best imitated by soft, fluffy material that has movement in the water. Marabou is commonly used, and CDC can make excellent gills provided it is not used in quantities that inhibit the sinking of the fly. But one of the best materials to tie tuft gills is the plumulaceous portion of a feather—the very soft, fluffy, short barbs found near the base of the stem (see "Feathers," p. 5). Much like marabou in appearance, these barbs have very fine stems and are quite flexible and lively under water. Other materials, such as very soft barbs from body or flank feathers, can also be used.

The techniques for tying tuft gills are virtually identical to those for tying bundled-fiber legs, and so the instructions provided in the following sequences are abbreviated. Readers seeking a more detailed explanation should consult **Method #7: Side-mounted Bundled-fiber Legs**, p. 416. Other techniques, particularly **Method #8: Gathered-fiber Legs**, p. 417, and **Method #10: Wingcase-split Legs**, p. 419, can also be adapted to form tuft gills.

The main sequence demonstrates forming tuft gills by mounting individual clumps of material at the rear of thorax. The alternate sequence shows tuft gills mounted between abdominal segments.

Step 1. All components that lie behind the thorax are dressed, and the wingcase (if one is used) is mounted.

Strip or clip a small clump of gill material—we're using the fluff from the base of a hen hackle—and pinch it at the mounting point.

Once the mounting point is established, you may wish to dampen extremely soft materials to consolidate them and simplify handling.

Step 2. Transfer the clump to the left fingers, and mount it directly in front of the abdomen on the near side of the hook shank. The projecting gill fibers should be about half the length of the abdomen.

When the first clump is secure, mount a second one on the far side of the shank.

Step 3. Dress the thorax, using the left fingers to hold the gill fibers against the sides of the abdomen as the thorax material is wrapped.

Take a wrap of thorax material tight against the base of the wingcase; this will help keep the clumps of gill material separate and flare them outward.

Step 4. Fold and secure the wingcase as explained in **Method #1: Folded-strip Wingcase**, Steps 5-7, p. 230.

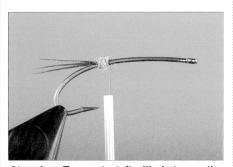

Step 1a. To create tuft gills between the abdominal segments, dress the tail of the fly, and use the body material, such as the dubbing shown here, to create the rearmost body segment. Position the tying thread 3 or 4 thread-wraps ahead of this body segment.

Step 2a. Select a feather to form the gills. We're using the fluffy barbs at the base of a pheasant body feather. In this technique, two gills tufts are formed simultaneously—one from the barbs on each side of the stem.

Prepare the feather by clipping away the tip, leaving just the fluffy barbs at the base, as shown in the middle. Preen most the remaining barbs toward the feather base, leaving a "V" of barbs at the tip of the stem, as shown on the right. To produce a uniform pair of gills, the barbs on each side of the stem should be of equal length. If necessary, preen the barbs in "V" upward into a clump, and break off the very end of the clump so that the barb tips are even.

Step 3a. Straddle the section of barbs over the hook shank so that the point of "V" lies over the tying thread.

Using light tension, take 2 wraps of thread over the feather stem.

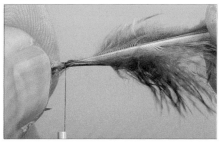

Step 4a. With the left fingers, lightly pinch the two clumps of gill material against the sides of the rearmost abdominal segment. Pinching the barbs helps keep each clump in position on the side of the shank when the gills are drawn to size.

With the right hand, pull the feather stem beneath the thread wraps, shortening the gill fibers until they reach the desired length.

Step 5a. When the gills are properly sized, clip the excess feather and bind the butts of the gill material.

Take another wrap of body material to form the next abdominal segment.

Step 6a. Repeat Steps 3a-5a until gills are formed between all abdominal segments.

Method #4:
Ribbed Gills

Using certain types of ribbing material is one of the simplest ways of creating abdominal gills on nymph patterns. Though perhaps less precisely imitative than other styles, ribbed gills are quick and easy to dress, and still create a credible impression of gill filaments.

Ribbed gills can be fashioned in two ways. The main sequence shows the most direct approach, which is to spiral the gill strand over the fly body. The most commonly used materials for this technique are peacock and ostrich herl, and hackle feathers trimmed (either before or after wrapping) to leave a short stubble on the stem. These materials, however, are rather fragile, and ribbed gills fashioned from them are usually reinforced with a second, counter-wrapped ribbing material. Wire is often used, but if you wish to conceal the second rib material, a very thin, clear monofilament tippet material or tying thread of a color to match the fly body can also be used.

The alternate sequence shows the opposite approach. Here, a fluffy underbody of wrapped herl is dressed on the hook shank, and the body material is spiraled over this foundation. Gills fashioned in this way require no reinforcement, as the body material protects the fragile quill. However, the method has some limitations. Clipped hackle works poorly with this approach, and when using herl, the body diameter must be narrow enough that the herl barbules project beyond the body wraps to create the impression of gills. Overwrapping thick body materials for larger flies may end up concealing the gill material altogether.

Step 1. Prepare the gill material. For herls, merely strip away the barbules from the last ¼" of the base of the quill, as shown on the left.

Hackle feathers can be trimmed before they are mounted by preening the barbs outward perpendicular to the feather stem, as shown in the middle, and then clipping them close to the stem, as shown on the right. Many tyers, however, find it simpler to wrap the feather first and then trim the barbs to size afterward.

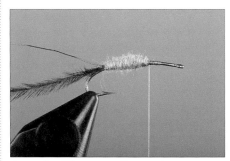

Step 2. Tie any tails on the pattern. Mount a length of reinforcement ribbing material, such as the wire shown here. Mount the gill material—we're using ostrich herl.

Dress the abdomen, and position the tying thread at the front edge of the body material.

Step 3. Using the technique explained in **Method #1: Ribbing**, Step 4, p. 91, wrap the gill material forward. In wrapping herls, make sure that the quill lays flat against the body material and does not twist as the ribbing progresses.

Using the counter-ribbing procedure shown in **Method #2: Counter-ribbing**, p. 92, counter-wrap the reinforcement material, securing the gill strand to the abdomen.

Step 4. If desired, the herl can be trimmed to a more realistic profile. Here, the gill material on the top and bottom of the fly has been clipped close to the body, leaving longer gill filaments projecting from the sides.

Step 1a. To form gills by wrapping the body material over the gill material, first dress any tails on the pattern. Mount the body material, such as the Vernille shown here, atop the tail-mounting wraps.

Using one of the techniques shown in **Method #26: Single-herl Body**, p. 117; **Method #27: Multiple-herl Body**, p. 118; **Method #28: Core-twisted Herl Body**, p. 119; or **Method #29: Loop-twisted Herl Body**, p.120—dress a foundation of herl on the hook shank. The foundation should be dressed over the portion of the hook shank on which you wish the gills to appear. Here, the herl foundation covers the abdomen of a nymph.

When the foundation is complete, tie off the herl, bind down the excess and position the tying thread at the front edge of the herl.

Step 2a. Spiral the body material over the herl, spacing the wraps just far enough apart to allow the herl barbules to project outward beyond the body.

Method #5:
Lashed Gills

Lashed gills are formed by binding a section of feather or herl lengthwise along the hook shank to form a continuous series of abdominal gills. Ostrich and peacock herls are often used, but smaller rhea and emu feathers will also work, though the barbs on these feathers may be disproportionately long and require trimming after the gills are dressed. Two excellent materials for forming lashed gills are the plumulaceous portion of a thin-stemmed feather (see "Feathers," p. 5) and afterfeather (see "Afterfeather," p. 11), which is used in the following demonstration.

The main sequence shows a technique for forming lashed gills on a nymph pattern dressed on a straight-shanked hook. In the demonstration, an afterfeather is tied along the top of the body so that the barbs form a row of gills on each side of the abdomen. On smaller patterns with narrower abdomens, peacock or ostrich herl can be tied in the same way. The method shown in the main sequence can also be used to lash a strand of gill material (usually herl) down each side of the abdomen when the fly is dressed on a straight-shank hook.

The alternate sequence comes from the work of Oliver Edwards, who lashes strands of ostrich herl to form the delicate gills on a *Hydropsyche* larva, though the technique can certainly be adapted to other patterns as well. Though similar to the method shown in the main sequence, this technique is designed to dress gills on a curved-shank hook of the type often used to tie scuds. The curved shank requires a slightly different approach to lashing, as 3 strands of material—2 lengths of herl and the ribbing—must be handled simultaneously.

Step 1. Mount any tails used on the pattern, and secure a length of ribbing material over the tail-mounting wraps. The ribbing will be used to lash the gill material to the top of the shank. The afterfeather used here for the gills is a rather fragile material, and a very thin wire ribbing can easily sever it. Thicker wire, heavier tying thread, Krystal Flash, or monofilament ribbing better protects the delicate afterfeather stem.

Lashed gills are generally tied with an overbody atop the gill material (see "Overbodies," p. 235). The overbody not only gives a realistic color or mottling to the top of the abdomen, but protects the lashed feather stem and helps position the gills horizontally.

Mount the overbody material using one of the techniques explained in **Method #7: Strip Overbody**, Steps 1-2, p. 236, or **Method #8: Bundled-fiber Overbody**, Step 1, p. 237.

Finally, mount the gill material. Here, an afterfeather is positioned atop the shank with the butt of the feather extending beyond the tail of the fly and the barbs projecting horizontally. The material is secured over the tail mounting wraps, and bound toward the hook eye.

Lateral gills can also be formed by mounting a strand of herl on each side of the shank, as shown in Step 1a.

Note: when working with fragile, thin-stemmed materials such as afterfeather and herl, do not attempt to bind down the feather too close to the tip. You need only enough length in the gill material to reach to the front of the abdomen, and less stem breakage occurs if the material is tied in well back from the tip.

Step 2. Dress the abdomen of the fly and position the tying thread at the front of the body material.

Step 3. Draw the gill material forward so that the stem is centered directly along the top of the abdomen. Pull the stem straight, but do not apply too much pressure; thin stems can readily break where they are folded. Note that the barbs will form gills projecting outward on either side of the shank.

If a strand of herl is mounted on each side of the shank, draw both strands forward, laying the quills flat against the sides of the abdomen so that all of the fuzzy barbules project downward, as shown in Step 4a.

Secure the gill material at the front of the abdomen with tight thread wraps. Clip the excess and bind down.

Step 4. Fold the overbody material forward and secure it at the front of the abdomen as explained in **Method #7: Strip Overbody**, Steps 5-6, p. 236, or **Method #8: Bundled-fiber Overbody**, Steps 2-4. p. 237.

Step 5. Here we've removed the overbody for a clearer view of the gill lashing. Normally, the overbody would remain in

place and be secured to the abdomen along with the gill material.

Wrap the ribbing material forward, slipping it between the feather barbs to bind only the stem to the top of the abdomen.

Work the ribbing forward in a uniform spiral in order to make the gills on either side of the abdomen symmetrical in size. Do not wrap the ribbing material with too much force or you may break the gill material.

Step 6. When the front of the abdomen is reached, tie off the ribbing; clip and bind the excess. The fly on the left shows the ribbed gills produced in this sequence. The gill material here can flare slightly upward because there is no overbody material. The fly on the right, dressed with a strip overbody, shows how the overbody material helps position the gills along the sides of the abdomen.

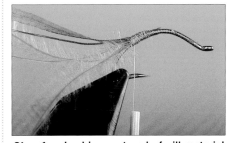

Step 1a. Lashing a strand of gill material to each side of a curved shank, as we're doing here using ostrich herl, requires a slightly different preparation.

Secure the tails and two strands of rib material. Mount a strand of herl on each side, and slightly toward the bottom, of the shank; finally mount the overbody material.

With a curved hook shank, it is impractical to lash the overbody and two strands of gill material to the shank simultaneously. There are two many pieces of material to control easily with one hand. Thus the overbody and gills are secured separately, each with its own ribbing material. Here, a length of wire will be used to lash the latex-strip overbody, and a piece of thin monofilament will be used to lash the gills in position.

Step 2a. Dress the fly body and position the tying thread at the front of the body material.

Step 3a. On a curved shank, the overbody material must be held in position with the right hand as it is bound to the shank.

Fold the overbody material forward and keep it centered atop the shank with the right hand. With the left hand, wrap the overbody ribbing—wire is used here—over the top of the overbody, securing it to the shank as shown.

When the ribbing is on the far side of the shank, it is momentarily transferred to the right fingers. The left hand can then be repositioned in front of the vise stem to retrieve the ribbing material and continue wrapping.

Step 4a. Continue binding the overbody until the front of the fly body is reached. Tie off both the overbody and rib material, and clip the excess.

Fold the strands of herl forward, so that they lie slightly toward the bottom of the hook at the rear of the abdomen. Since the hook is curved, it is not possible to secure the gill material at the front of the body as was done in the main sequence. Instead, the strands of herl must be held in the right fingers as the ribbing is wrapped with the left hand.

Notice that the fuzzy barbules on the herl do not project from the center of the quill; rather, they are attached to one edge of the quill. When folding the herl forward, place the quill flat against the side of the fly body, with the fuzzy edge of the quill facing downward. Positioned in this orientation, the body material will force all the fuzzy barbules downward, as shown here, for fuller gills.

Step 5a. With the strands of herl held in position with the right hand, grasp the gill ribbing—monofilament is used here—in the left fingers. Take one wrap around the gills and body, following exactly the path of the ribbing material used to lash the overbody. Slip the ribbing material between the herl barbules, taking care not to trap them. The mono should be seated against the quill only, binding it to the body of the fly.

Step 6a. Once during each wrap, when the left hand is on the far side of the fly, you will need to release the herl strands from the right hand.

Maintain tension on the mono, and transfer it momentarily to the right fingers so that you can reposition the left hand in front of the vise stem to continue wrapping.

Once the ribbing material is transferred back to the left hand, re-grasp the herl strands with the right fingers, and continue ribbing, laying each turn of monofilament atop the turn of wire used to secure the overbody.

Step 7a. When the gills and ribbing reach the front edge of the body, tie them off and bind the excess.

Method #6:
Woven Gills

This unusual technique—another gilling method devised by Oliver Edwards and presented in *Flytyers Masterclass*—is designed to produce two rows of gills on part or all of a nymph abdomen. Edwards uses this technique to dress dorsal gills on the rear portion of an articulated body for a jointed *Ephemera* nymph, but the gill style can be used on a variety of imitations and placed anywhere around the abdomen.

This is not, in the strict sense, a "weave," but the alternate manipulations of body and gill material do have the feel of weaving. The method is best suited to larger hook sizes.

Step 1. Prepare the gill material. Edwards uses marabou to form the gills, as we're

doing here. But rhea or emu feathers, or the fluffy plumulaceous base of a body or hackle feather, can also be used.

An important requirement in the feather used for gills is proper stem thickness. If the stem is too thin—as can be the case with marabou blood feathers (see "Marabou," p. 11)—the material is difficult to handle; if the stem is too thick—the butt portion of large marabou plume, for example—the stem is difficult to bind to the hook shank and may add unwanted bulk to the body. As a rule, a stem that is roughly the same diameter as the hook shank works well.

A small marabou plume, such as the one shown here on the left, is excellent for the purpose. Snip the stem to produce a one-inch section, as shown on the right. On the narrow end of the stem, clip off a few feather barbs from each side, leaving a stubble. This tag will be used to mount the feather.

Step 2. Dress the tails and mount the body material, such as the 3-ply Antron yarn used here. Dubbing can be used to dress the body, but it must be very tightly twisted around the thread. Moreover, the tight twist must be scrupulously maintained during tying, as a cordlike body material is necessary to make the gills flare away from the body.

Place the marabou section along the top of the hook shank so that the barbs nearest the rear of the fly are positioned at the point where the first set of gills are to be formed.

Tie the feather in tightly by the clipped tag of stem prepared in Step 1.

If a separate body material, such as yarn, is used, lift the marabou feather and advance the tying thread to the tie-off point for the abdomen. If the body is to be dubbed, return the thread to the rear of the shank.

Step 3. Twist the body material, clockwise when viewed from above, until it forms a fairly tight cord. This is the direction that the material will naturally twist during wrapping, and twisting clockwise helps preserve the twist as the body material is applied.

Wrap the body material forward until

you reach the rearmost barbs of the marabou, twisting the yarn as necessary to maintain a uniform cord. With the right hand, pull the body material directly toward you, as shown in this top view.

Step 4. With the left fingers, separate a small clump of the marabou barbs at the rear of the feather on the near side of the stem. The size of the clump determines the appearance of the finished gills. Here, we've separated out about 3 individual barbs; a small number of barbs for each clump in the procedure will produce 2 rows of rather distinct, individual gills. Larger clumps will tend to merge together, producing a denser cluster of gills with little separation between them.

Some tyers find marabou easier to work with if it is dampened slightly to help consolidate the fibers.

Draw the clump back along the near side of the body and slightly toward the top, as shown.

Step 5. Wrap the body material over the barb clump to the top of the hook shank, closely abutting the previous wrap of body material. Abutting the wraps helps flare the marabou outward. When viewed from the hook eye, this first clump of marabou should angle outward from the shank at about the 11 o'clock position.

Step 6. While the body material is still atop the hook shank, use the left fingers to separate out a clump of barbs, identical in size to the first, on the far side of the shank.

Draw these barbs rearward along the far side of the body, and slightly toward the top.

Step 7. Continue wrapping the body material around the shank until it is once again pulled directly toward you.

This second clump of material should angle out from the hook shank at about the 1 o'clock position. That is, the pair of gill clumps should form a "V" on the top of the hook shank.

Note the instructions given here are for producing two rows of dorsal gills. If desired, the gills can in fact be mounted to project outward from the sides of the body or to slant downward.

The materials and hand positions are now identical to those shown in Step 4.

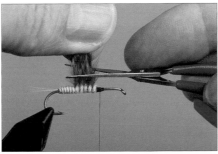

Step 8. Repeat Steps 4-7, forming additional pairs of gills until the desired number have been dressed (Edwards usually dresses 4 or 5 pairs) until the rear of the thorax is reached.

Tie off the body material, clip the excess marabou quill, and bind down with thread.

To trim the gills, preen all the clumps upward with the left fingers.

Step 9. Trim the gills parallel to the abdomen.

Method #7:

Twisted Gills

Gills on the abdomen or body of a fly can be fashioned by twisting or wrapping a strand of herl around a strand of body material, causing the fuzzy herl barbules to flare outward.

The main sequence shows a simple approach to the twisting technique that uses a single-strand core. The alternate sequence shows a version of this approach that uses a spun loop of body material.

Step 1. This method is really a version of the technique shown in **Method #28: Core-twisted Herl Body**, p. 119, and readers seeking a more detailed explanation of the procedure may wish to consult that method.

Dress any tails on the pattern, and mount any ribbing material used.

Secure the body material—we're using Vernille here—directly atop the tail-mounting wraps. Mount a strand of herl by the tip on top of the body material.

Step 2. Pull both the body material and herl strand downward under an equal, light tension.

You can clip the strands together at the bottom with a hackle pliers, as shown here, or you can omit the pliers and twist the strands with your fingers.

Twist the two strands together. The amount of twist depends upon the final effect desired in the finished body. A looser twist will put the wraps of gill material farther apart for a sparser appearance. A tighter twist will give fuller, more closely spaced gills and a more segmented body.

Step 3. Wrap the desired length of hook shank with the twisted strands. As you wrap, use the left fingers to preen back the herl barbules from previous wraps so that they are not trapped beneath turns of body material.

Step 1a. This is a version of the technique shown in **Method #29: Loop-twisted Herl Body**, p. 120. Readers seeking a fuller explanation, particularly regarding the use of the dubbing hook, may wish to consult that method.

Dress any tails on the pattern and mount any ribbing material used.

Select a body material. It can be a single strand of material such as floss or Vernille, a yarn such as the Antron used here, or a bundle of strands, such as Krystal Flash. Bring the ends of the strand together to form a loop, and secure the ends atop the tail-mounting wraps.

Mount a strand of herl by the tip atop the body material, and advance the tying thread to the body tie-off point.

Step 2a. Pull the loop downward, insert the dubbing hook through the loop, and capture the strand of herl, maintaining your grasp on the butt end of the herl strand, as explained in **Method #29: Loop-twisted Herl Body**, Steps 3-5, p. 120.

Step 3a. Twist the strands together as explained in **Method #29: Loop-twisted Herl Body**, Steps 5-6, p. 120.

Step 4a. Wrap the twisted strands forward, using the left fingers to preen back the herl barbules as explained in Step 3.

Method #8:
Wrapped-core Gills

This technique, from English tyer Oliver Edwards, is used to form gills over a core of body material. Edwards uses Flexibody—a flat, flexible sheet material; we're using Larva Lace tubing. Solid plastic cords that are somewhat flattened in cross section, such as Swannundaze and V-rib, are also suitable. The gills formed by this technique closely resemble the ones formed in **Method #7: Twisted Gills**, p. 97, but they are wrapped around the body material rather than twisted together with it. As a result, the body material maintains its normal shape rather than becoming corded.

Step 1. Mount the body material. If the material is bulky, such as the Larva Lace shown here, bind it along the length of the hook shank to create a smooth underbody, as shown.

When the body material is mounted, clip the end in a hackle pliers, as shown.

Secure a piece of ostrich herl by the tip directly over the rearmost mounting wrap on the body material.

Advance the tying thread to the front edge of the body.

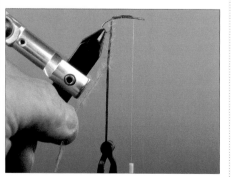

Step 2. Spiral the herl down the body material, as shown.

With a relatively open spiral, of the type pictured here, the body material will be plainly visible on the finished fly. More closely spaced wraps of herl will produce denser gilling, but partially obscure the body.

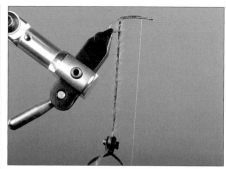

Step 3. When a sufficient length of body material has been wrapped with herl, clip the herl in the hackle pliers, as shown.

Step 4. Wrap the combined body/gill material forward. When the front edge of the body is reached, secure the material, clip the excess, and bind down the butts with thread.

Bodies

Since virtually every fly pattern has a body, it isn't surprising that tyers have devised an enormous number of techniques and styles, using almost every conceivable material, for this particular fly component. In order to make locating a particular body-dressing technique simpler, this chapter is divided into sections based on distinctions commonly used in tying. Fly tyers are not entirely consistent in their categorizations of styles and techniques—a fact that is reflected in the chapter divisions. Some sections are organized around a single material, such as "Foam Bodies." Others center around a group of materials, such as "Chenille, Floss, and Yarn Bodies," which are tied in a similar fashion. Some sections focus on a single category of techniques, such as "Woven Bodies," while others present a particular body style, such "Extended Bodies." If the organizational logic of the chapter, then, is somewhat hybrid in this respect, for ease of use it nonetheless seemed best to observe the kinds of divisions and distinctions in body dressings most widely used among tyers.

SECTION ONE

Chenille, Floss, and Yarn Bodies

Because they are manufactured as continuous strands, chenille, floss, and yarn require virtually no preparation at all, are among the most straightforward of tying materials to use, and are dressed on the hook in similar ways. Thus they are presented together in this section.

Chenille

Chenilles are manufactured of relatively short fibers of natural or synthetic material trapped between two twisted threads. The result is a fuzzy strand of uniform density and diameter that produces an even, brushlike body when wrapped around a hook shank. In a poll of fly tyers, chenille might well be chosen as the simplest of all materials to use—it handles easily, quickly, and consistently; properly wrapped, it provides a solid foundation for ribbing material or palmered hackle; it is durable and inexpensive.

The variety of chenilles available make the material quite versatile as well. Highly reflective synthetic fibers used in materials such as Estaz and Ice Chenille make flashy, conspicuous bodies. Others like Vernille, Ultra Chenille, and Micro Chenille are not actually conventional chenilles at all, but rather, flocked yarns. Instead of using a twisted thread, they are made with an adhesive-coated core to which very soft, fine fibers are electrostatically attracted. Flocked yarns produce dense bodies on tiny flies. Still others like New Dub employ sparse fibers on semi-rigid cores that yield a spikey appearance and can be used on extended-body patterns (see "Extended Bodies," p. 204). The easy handling of chenille makes it well suited for wrapping multiple strands to produce banded, striped, and variegated bodies, and it is among the favorite materials for woven bodies (see "Woven Bodies," p. 195).

Method #1:
Simple Chenille Body

Most chenilles are absorbent, and while a few dry-fly patterns do incorporate the material, it is used predominantly on wet flies, nymphs, and streamers.

Chenille can be handled in three ways during tying. The simplest, and probably the most common method is to clip a length of material suitable for 3 or 4 flies; the cut strand is then wrapped. This approach does have a couple of shortcomings, though. First, it involves a certain waste of material, as tag ends too short for a fly body must be discarded. Moreover, the repeated handling of the chenille often causes the thread core to loosen, and the fibers begin to shed. The last body tied from a cut length of chenille is often noticeably sparser than the first.

Tyers use a couple of approaches to avoid these problems.

Some tyers wind chenille on empty thread spools and mount them in a materials bobbin. On a bobbin, the chenille is wrapped much like tying thread. The handling of material with fingertips is minimized and waste is virtually eliminated.

Other tyers simply use the card on which the chenille is wrapped as a kind of bobbin, trapping the material in the slit used to secure the tag end.

Both of these techniques, however, are slightly more cumbersome than using a cut length of chenille, since the thread bobbin hanging from the hook poses an obstacle that must be maneuvered around when wrapping the body.

Step 1. Use the thumbnail to scrape away the short fibers from the end of the chenille, exposing about ¼" of the thread core. This core is bound to the shank for a low-bulk tie-in.

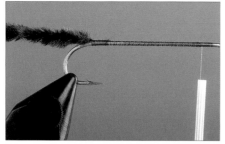

Step 2. Bind down the thread core, directly adjacent to the unstripped, fuzzy portion of the material. Take several tight wraps of thread over the tag of the thread core, and advance the thread to the tie-off point of the body.

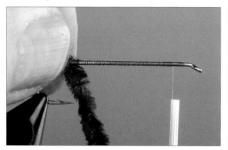

Step 3. Take a wrap of chenille around the shank. Before taking a second wrap, use the fingers of the left hand to preen the chenille fibers back toward the hook bend. This prevents the fibers from becoming bound down under the next wrap of material, and allows the turns of chenille to be placed quite close together, producing a dense, uniform body.

Step 4. Continue wrapping the chenille, using the left fingers to preen back the fibers on every wrap.

Step 5. When the tie-off point is reached, hold the chenille vertically as shown. With the left hand, bring the tying thread over the top of the chenille, wiggling the bobbin slightly to slip the tying thread between the fibers and seat it directly against the thread core. Care in seating the thread prevents trapping fibers in the tie-off wraps and minimizes bulk.

When the first wrap of thread is secured, take a second tight wrap toward the hook eye. Clip the chenille and bind down the tag.

Method #2:
Striped Chenille Body

This technique produces a body from two strands of material spiraled simultaneously along the shank to make stripes. Striped chenille bodies can be used to imitate specific naturals or simply to produce the broken color pattern that is often characteristic of living creatures. We're using highly contrasting materials to illustrate the technique, which produces a boldly striped body, but more subtle color combinations—browns and olives, for instance—can produce quite lifelike effects.

Note as well that different sizes, textures, or types of chenilles can be combined with this method to give the body a segmented or ribbed appearance, or to introduce a bit of flash.

A similar type of body, with distinctly separated bands of color, can be produced by **Method #111: The Banded Weave,** p. 195.

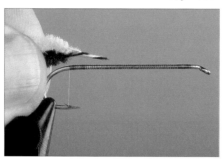

Step 1. Prepare the two pieces of chenille by stripping the ends as shown in **Method #1: Simple Chenille Body**, Step 1, p. 99. Twist the thread cores together as shown.

Step 2. Bind down the combined cores at the rearmost thread wrap.

Hold the two strands close to the hook shank to keep them as close together as possible. Wrap the strands simultaneously, keeping an equal and even tension on each strand.

Step 3. When the tie-off point is reached, bind down both strands at once, using the procedure described above in **Method #1: Simple Chenille Body**, Step 5.

Method #3:
Variegated Chenille Body

Chenilles can be blended to create variegated colors or mixed textures. Since the method involves twisting strands of chenille together, it produces an extra-thick body. For a thinner body, use a narrower size of chenille for one or both strands.

The following sequence illustrates the technique using two strands of chenille. Three strands, and theoretically even more, can also be used, but correspondingly thinner chenilles should be chosen to avoid excessive bulk in the body.

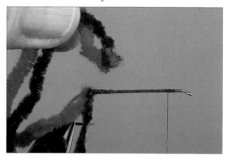

Step 1. Take two strands of chenille, and tie them together with a square knot at one end. Clip the free ends to an even length. Prepare the two pieces of chenille by stripping the free ends to expose the cores as shown in **Method #1: Simple Chenille Body**, Step 1, p. 99.

Twist the thread cores together, and bind down the combined cores at the rearmost thread wrap. The chenille forms a loop, as shown here.

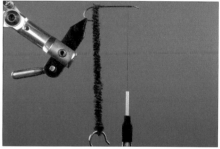

Step 2. Use a dubbing hook or whirl (see "The Dubbing Loop," p. 129) to twist the two strands of chenille together. A loose twist will produced a tightly banded body. A tighter twist will intermix the fibers more fully and give a mottled or variegated color, as shown here.

Step 2a. You can also twist the strands by hand, or clip them in a hackle pliers—in which case, they need not be knotted together. This alternate technique, however, is slower and involves more handling of the chenille.

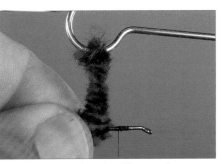

Step 3. Wrap the chenille exactly as you would a single strand, using the left hand to preen back the fibers as you wrap (see **Method #1: Simple Chenille Body**, Step 3, p. 99).

Step 4. Wrap to the tie-off point. Since the chenille strands are under some tension from the twisting, make certain to bind them down very tightly before clipping.

(The excess chenille retains its twist after it is has been clipped. If sufficiently long strands have been used, a second fly body can be fashioned simply by attaching the material to another hook when needed, thereby eliminating the need to knot and twist another pair of chenille strands.)

Method #4:

Lashed Chenille Body

Though limited to relatively few dressings—most notably the San Juan Worm (presented in the following sequence) and a few extended-body patterns—this technique is nonetheless useful and produces a fishable fly quite quickly. Most tyers select a thread to match the color of chenille.

Twisted chenille gives poor results with this technique since the thread cores may unravel and destroy the fly body. Tyers generally use some type of flocked yarn such as the Vernille used in the following demonstration.

Step 1. Cut a section of material equal to the length of the body you wish to create.

In order to produce a body silhouette that more accurately reproduces the profile of a midge larva—the type of imitation most frequently dressed in this style—many tyers touch each end of the material to the side of a flame, as shown, to give it a slightly pointed shape.

Other tyers, however, omit this step, in which case a longer piece of material can be used and cut to its final length in Step 4 when the fly is complete.

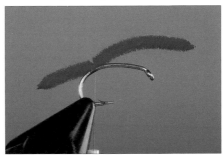

Step 2. Secure the thread at the hook bend. Bind the strand of material atop the rearmost thread wrap, leaving a "tail" of the desired length projecting from the rear. Use only 2 or 3 tight thread wraps to bind the chenille down in order to minimize interference with the body profile.

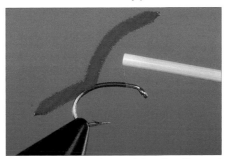

Step 3. Raise the front of the chenille, and wrap the thread forward, completely covering the hook shank in smooth, even wraps. Stop about 4 thread-wraps distance behind the hook eye.

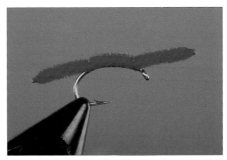

Step 4. Pull the chenille firmly so that it hugs the top of the shank, and bind down tightly with 2 wraps of thread.

Whip finish with two wraps. If a long piece of material was initially mounted, clip the front and rear ends to the desired length.

Floss

Though silk flosses are still occasionally seen, most are now made of synthetics such as nylon and rayon. Flosses vary in their specifics from one manufacturer to another, and in fact, what constitutes a "floss"

depends largely on how you define the term. Traditional flosses, of the type long used in tying, consist of one or more bundles of very straight, thin filaments. The filaments themselves, or bundles of them, are sometimes loosely twisted to consolidate the strand, sometimes not. These traditional flosses are sold in two basic formats. In single-strand floss, the fine filaments are consolidated into one strand of material. Multi-strand flosses are essentially composed of two or more pieces of single-strand floss, usually wound on a spool as a single length of material. Of the multi-strand flosses, the four-strand type is perhaps the most common.

There are some slight differences in handling single- and multi-strand flosses, but their chief distinction is that single-strand floss is used for smaller fly bodies where the smaller volume of a single strand makes it easier to control the build-up of material on the hook shank. It's possible to wrap a larger body with single-strand floss, but the number of wraps necessary makes the process a tedious one, and the excessive handling required may eventually fray the floss. And since the single-strand type is relatively narrow, producing smooth bodies over a long hook shank can be difficult. For larger hooks, four-strand is preferable, since it applies material more rapidly and evenly over long distances. Four-strand floss has an additional advantage—it can be separated into lengths of single-, double-, or triple-strand floss to dress hooks of intermediate sizes.

As a general rule, hooks with standard-length shanks are most efficiently dressed according to the following rough guidelines.

Hooks #16 and smaller . . . . 1 strand
Hooks #12-#14 . . . . 2 strands
Hooks #8-#10 . . . . 3 strands
Hooks larger than #8 . . . . . 4 strands

When using extra-long hooks, be guided by the *effective* hook-shank length rather than the hook gap size. That is, a #14 4XL hook actually has a shank length equivalent to a standard #6 hook, and thus would be most easily dressed using 4 strands of floss.

There are other types of floss, or perhaps "floss-like" materials would be a better description. Uni-Floss and Danville's Depth Ray Nylon are representative of the type; the filaments used to manufacture them are extremely fine, and the strands themselves quite thin in diameter, making them best suited to smaller flies or applications, such as the band on a Royal Coachman, where smaller amounts of material are used. Some types are available only in fluorescent colors, and tend to have good color retention when wet.

Some of these materials are often called "stretch flosses" and sold under the name "Nylon-Stretch" or "Uni-Stretch." The filaments that compose the strand are curly or kinked, and when the strand is under no tension, it more closely resembles a loose yarn than traditional floss. Under tying pressure, however, the curl straightens out and the material looks and behaves much like ordinary floss. Despite the name, the material itself has little elasticity; rather, under tension, the curl in the material is removed and the strand elongates, giving the impression of stretching. Many tyers find this type of floss to be more forgiving, more easily worked—with less filament stray or fraying—and more durable than traditional flosses.

One of the most critical factors in forming attractive floss bodies is the creation of a smooth underbody with no ledges, edges, bumps, or abrupt changes in diameter. This requires a judicious trimming of materials to create gradual, even tapers, or to match clipped butts for an unbroken underbody (see "Mounting and Trimming Materials," p. 25, and "Underbodies," p. 41). Binding down material butts or underbody materials with a flat tying thread will provide a smooth foundation for the floss.

Floss is one of the fly-tying materials that can change character substantially when it becomes wet. It darkens in color and thin layers of material become somewhat translucent. Because of this translucence, the color of the hook shank has a strong influence on the appearance of the body when it's wet. A bronzed or black hook, then, will further darken the color of a wet floss body. In some cases, of course, this may be desirable; in others, it may not. To more nearly preserve the true color of the floss when wet, some tyers wrap floss over a very thin underbody; thread matched in color to the floss or tinsels are the most common.

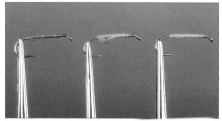

This photo shows the effect of various types of underbodies when floss is wet. From left to right, the hooks above show: no underbody; an underbody of silver tinsel; an underbody of pearl Flashabou.

Many tyers dislike tying floss bodies, finding the material somewhat fussy to work with, and there is some justification for this claim. The very fine filaments that make up a strand of floss are easily frayed or broken; unless wrapping tension and twist are not properly controlled, the filaments can begin to separate, and the material can spread or stray along the hook shank and generally get out of control. Nonetheless, floss is not particularly difficult to work with if a few precautions are exercised.

Most difficulties in floss handling can be traced to three sources—first, an uneven or rough underbody that will not allow the smooth application of material; second, rough skin on the fingertips that snags and frays the floss filaments; and third, trying to build up body tapers too rapidly, creating a "ledge" at the edge of the body that causes the floss to separate.

Such problems, of course, have their solutions. Forming smooth, uniform underbodies with a minimum of bumps, edges, and irregularities greatly facilitates wrapping floss and improves the finished product. Using a pumice stone to smooth out rough or calloused fingertips helps prevent the delicate floss filaments from fraying, as does the use of hand lotion worked into the fingertips. And forming tapers gradually will prevent the floss from separating.

Like other materials, floss can be wrapped using only your fingers, a method that gives perhaps the most sensitive control over the floss, particularly with the multi-strand types. The drawback is that floss is quite delicate, and even smooth fingers can fray or break the individual filaments. To minimize fraying, many tyers dampen the floss slightly before mounting and wrapping. Wetting the material (not soaking it) consolidates the filaments and lubricates the strand to simplify handling, though fibers on damp floss are slightly more difficult to flatten into a smooth body since the moisture causes them to stick together slightly.

Other tyers prefer to use spooled floss on a floss bobbin, particularly with multi-strand materials. This method completely eliminates the handling of floss and holds fraying to a minimum. However, control over the shape of the floss is somewhat diminished since the tyer loses fingertip sensitivity in wrapping the material. And like all bobbin-wrapped materials, the floss will twist with each wrap around the shank, making it necessary to counterspin the bobbin and flatten the floss back into a ribbon-like shape. Perhaps the most pronounced drawback is that the thread bobbin, positioned at the tie-off point, hangs in the working field. You must maneuver the floss bobbin around it, which is inconvenient, or you must tie off and clip the thread, reattaching it when the body is complete—which adds time to the tying and bulk to the body. Finally, using a bobbin restricts the tyer to using the full number of strands on the spooled floss. The strands cannot be divided to tie smaller fly bodies. Still, tyers use both techniques successfully, and both are illustrated below.

Finally, floss will discolor easily if the fingers are slightly dirty, sweaty, or oily, so it's wise to make certain that your hands are clean and stay clean during tying. A number of tyers have recommended keeping a container of pre-moistened towlettes handy at the bench for just this purpose.

As indicated in the section on "Yarn," p. 105, the techniques for dressing yarn bodies are virtually identical to those used for floss, and thus yarn can be substituted in any of the following methods.

Method #5:
Single-layer Floss Body

This technique involves mounting the material at the tailing point and wrapping the body with one layer of floss. The low bulk produced makes it useful for small flies, and it is the quickest way to form a floss body. The single layer of wraps, however, gives the tyer only a limited control over the body shape and is limited primarily to forming bodies of uniform diameter or with very slight tapers. Forming bodies with more pronounced tapers requires a a somewhat different technique and is presented below in "Tapered Floss Bodies," p. 104. In the following sequence, single-strand floss is wrapped using only the fingers. However, multi-strand floss and/or a bobbin may be used instead, and the techniques for doing so are described below in **Method #6: Double-layer Floss Body,** p. 103.

When a floss-body requires a tail (as below), leave the tail butts long, and bind them to the hook shank along with the tag of floss to create a smooth underbody.

Step 1. The tail here is mounted. Notice the butts are left long.

Dampen the end of the floss, wetting a section equal to the length of the hook shank. This will simplify tying it in. Bind the floss to the hook shank directly atop the rearmost thread wraps with two turns of thread, as shown in the photo. Dick Talleur offers a helpful recommendation here—gently tug the floss, sliding a very small length of it from beneath the wraps. This aligns the floss filaments for a good first wrap.

Note that the tying thread is quite flat. As you bind the floss and tail's butts to the shank, counterspin the bobbin as necessary to keep the thread flat and the underbody smooth.

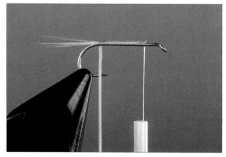

Step 2. Here a smooth underbody is formed. Pull the floss downward, as shown, to flatten the material into a ribbon-like shape.

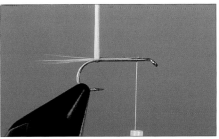

Step 3. With the floss in this position, take the first turn over the rearmost thread wraps.

Notice the position of the floss; it is perpendicular to the hook shank. Maintaining this orientation as you wind will minimize the unruly straying of floss fibers.

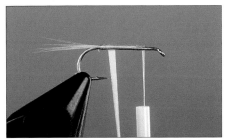

Step 4. Maintain tension on the floss to keep the fibers consolidated in flat ribbon, but use only the minimum pressure necessary to accomplish this. Excess tension on the floss may cause some of the fine filaments to break.

Begin wrapping forward in smooth, slightly overlapping wraps.

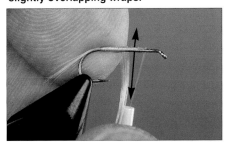

Step 5. If an unevenness or bump appears in the body, it can be smoothed as follows. Pinch the floss lightly against the far side of the hook shank with the left forefinger. With the right hand, slacken the tension on the floss slightly so that the previous wrap of floss loosens around the hook shank. Then tug gently on the floss, "bouncing" it a few times against the hook shank. This will cause the fibers to spread and smooth out any small inconsistencies.

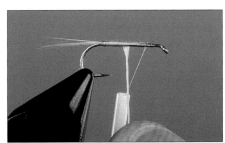

Step 6. If the floss filaments begin to separate and individual fibers begin to stray from the main strand, try the following. Unwrap one turn of the floss, and use the fingertips of your left hand to gently twist the spread floss close to the hook shank as shown. (Do not twist too tightly or some fibers may break.) Take one wrap of floss

while holding the twist to regroup the filaments. Then release the twist and continue wrapping in smooth, overlapping turns.

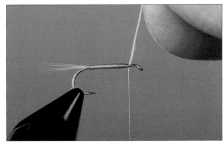

Step 7. Continue wrapping toward the hook eye. If the wraps overlap uniformly, as shown here, the body will have a consistent diameter. To form a slight taper, gradually increase the amount of overlap as you wrap forward, causing the material to build up and form a tapered body. Do not, however, try to build up a steep taper, as the floss will separate when it crosses the edge of the body during tie-off.

As the tie-off point is reached, begin twisting the floss slightly to narrow the ribbon. This will simplify binding and clipping the tag end.

Tie off the floss, clip, and bind down the tag.

Method #6:
Double-layer Floss Body

This technique is somewhat slower than the single-layer body because the hook shank is traversed twice with the floss. It is, however, better suited to flies that require more bulk or a longer body and gives the tyer more latitude in controlling the taper since the double wrap allows thickness to be gradually and selectively built along one area of the shank.

In the following sequence, four-strand floss is used with a bobbin.

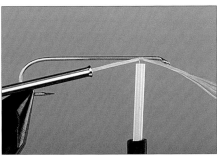

Step 1. Position the tying thread at the exact point where the front of the body will end. This position is important, as the thread provides a reference point.

Lay the floss against the shank, with the tag end toward the eye. Many tyers prefer to mount the floss underneath the shank, as shown here.

Take 4 tight, adjacent turns of thread toward the hook bend. The floss tag need not be clipped at this point. Note that the tube of the thread bobbin is very close to the hook shank, a position that will minimize its interference when winding the floss.

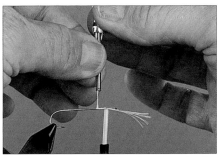

Step 2. Begin winding the floss body. This is most easily accomplished by transferring the bobbin from one hand to another as it passes around the hook shank—much as you would wrap a cut length of material. Winding the bobbin with one hand only introduces twist into the floss that must be periodically removed.

The four strands of floss should lie adjacent to one another as shown, forming a single, ribbon-like strand. The floss wraps should be flat and slightly overlapping. Smooth out any inconsistencies in the body by "bouncing" the floss against the shank as described above in **Method #5: Single-layer Floss Body**, Step 5. Control the width of the floss by twisting or untwisting the bobbin to keep the material from spreading and straying as described above in **Method #5,** Step 6.

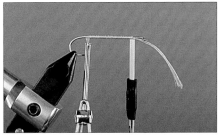

Step 3. When the rear of the body is reached, carefully reverse the direction of wrapping. This rearmost wrap of material should be tight and not steeply angled back toward the hook eye or slack will develop in the floss.

Step 4. Wrap the floss back to the eye of the hook in smooth overlapping wraps. Stop wrapping when the tying thread is reached.

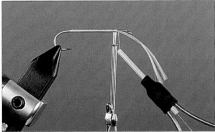

Step 5. Unwind the thread wraps holding the tag of floss. The bobbin thread is now at the original mounting position, marking the front end of the body.

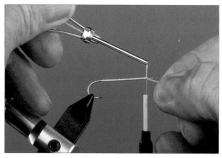

Step 6. Take a wrap or two of the working floss over the floss tag, and end with the floss bobbin above the hook shank as shown.

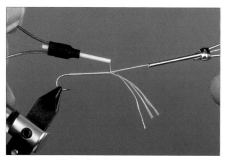

Step 7. Bind the floss to the top of the shank. Since the material was originally mounted at the bottom, tying off on the top will produce a nicely symmetrical front to the body.

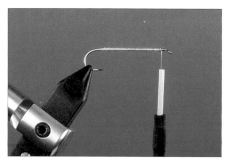

Step. 8. Clip both ends of the floss and bind the butts.

Tapered Floss Bodies

As noted earlier, slight tapers can be introduced into a single- or double-layer floss body by increasing the amount of overlap on the wraps as they are wound around the hook, thus increasing bulk at the desired point. If this technique is used to form more pronounced tapers, however, the floss begins to separate and stray. Other approaches must be used.

The most satisfactory way to create a more steeply tapered mayfly body, thickest at the front and tapering toward the rear, is to wrap the floss over a tapered underbody, usually formed by either tying thread alone (see **Method #2: Tapered Thread Underbody**, p. 42) or by a combination of wing and tail butts (see **Method #6: Spliced Underbody**, p. 44, and **Method #7: Abutted Underbody**, p. 45). Forming a taper of this type using floss alone usually gives poor results, as the floss filaments will begin to separate at the wide front portion of the body.

Building bullet-shaped tapers for streamer bodies or reverse tapers for caddis bodies (which are thickest at the rear) can be accomplished with floss only. The success of these techniques relies on mounting the floss at what will become the thickest point of the body, and gradually building floss layers of increasing length until the tie-off point is reached.

Method #7:
Bullet-taper Floss Body

This method is used to form symmetrically tapered streamer bodies. The sequence below shows an average taper, in which the floss body is built from 2 layers of material laid on the shank. A body that is thicker in the middle can be produced by forming a larger number of shorter layers of floss at the middle of the shank before extending the floss wraps to the ends of the body.

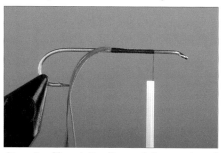

Step 1. Mount the floss at the center of the hook shank, since this will be the thickest part of the body. Advance the tying thread to the tie-off point for the front end of the body.

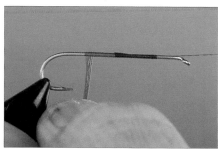

Step 2. Wrap the floss about halfway to the hook bend. Here, and in subsequent wrapping steps, control the floss width and smoothness by adjusting the twist of the floss and "bouncing" it against the hook as described above in **Method #5: Single-layer Floss Body**, Steps 5 and 6, p. 103.

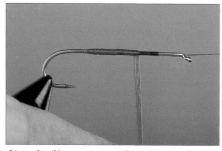

Step 3. Now reverse direction, and wrap the floss halfway to the hook eye.

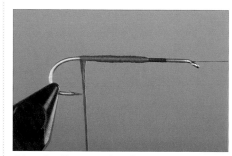

Step 4. Reverse the direction again, and wrap the floss all the way to the rear end of the body.

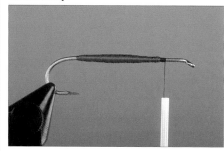

Step 5. Reverse the direction and wrap to the front end of the body. Tie off and clip the tag.

Method #8:
Reverse-taper Floss Body

This technique produces a body that is thickest at the rear and tapers to a thin front end—a profile widely used on imitations of caddis pupae and adults.

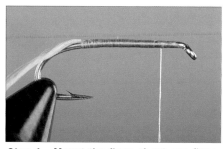

Step 1. Mount the floss about one floss-wrap ahead of the rearmost point of the body. Bind the tag to the shank about halfway to the hook eye, creating a slightly thicker underbody on the rear half of the hook. Advance the tying thread to the tie-off point for the front of the body.

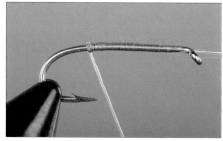

Step 2. To form the thick, rear portion of the body, the floss must be twisted tightly into a cord. Take one wrap of the twisted floss behind the mounting point, toward the hook bend.

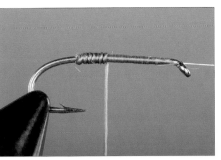

Step 3. Maintain a twist on the floss, and begin wrapping forward, over the mounting point and toward the hook eye. Take adjacent wraps until the rear ⅓ of the hook shank is covered. The rear part of the body will be bumpy at this point. You'll smooth it out later.

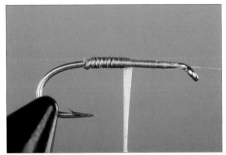

Step 4. Relax the twist some so that the floss begins to flatten, and wrap smoother turns of floss to the halfway point of the hook shank.

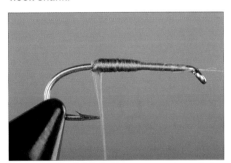

Step 5. When the halfway point of the shank is reached, the floss should be flat. Now reverse direction, winding back to the rear end of the body, covering the previous wraps of material with smooth, even wraps of the flattened floss. Keep the material flat, but narrow, by adjusting the twist, and smooth the body by "bouncing" the floss as described above in **Method #5: Single-layer Floss Body**, Steps 5 and 6, p. 103.

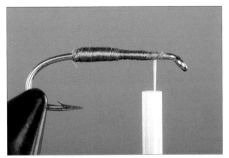

Step 6. When the rear of the body is reached, reverse the direction of wrapping, and wind smooth, even wraps of floss to the front tie-off point.
Bind the floss and clip the tag.

Yarn

Natural yarns, particularly wool, are among the oldest of fly-tying materials, though they have declined some in popularity. Modern tyers seem to prefer the greater versatility of fur dubbing for fly bodies. The one exception here is mohair yarn, which is commonly employed on leech patterns for stillwater fishing. Nonetheless, natural yarns do make effective bodies and underbodies. The material is easy to wrap; builds up bulk quickly on large patterns; is inexpensive; and is available in a wide variety of sizes, colors, and textures.

Synthetic yarns, on the other hand, particularly Antron and polypropylene, are stock items for virtually every modern tyer. Antron and other trilobal filaments are valued for their high reflectivity under water. Poly yarn is non-absorbent and slightly buoyant, making it ideal for dry flies, particularly large or bulky ones such as adult stoneflies or grasshoppers, where the large volume of body material contributes to floatation.

Though many yarns, especially natural fibers, produce bodies with a somewhat fuzzy or furry appearance—much like a dubbed body—the handling and tying of yarn most closely resembles the techniques used for floss. Structurally, the materials are similar—a strand composed of many thin filaments. And they tend to behave in much the same way when wrapped—spreading against the hook shank under wrapping pressure—though yarns far less so than flosses. Like floss, yarn is available in single-strand or multi-ply types, although the tyer has a much greater range of options in this regard when using yarns. Thin crewel yarns can be used to fashion small fly bodies or underbodies; thicker, multi-ply knitting yarns are suitable for larger flies, and the strands can be separated or combined to accommodate any hook size. Single-strand yarns like poly and spooled Antron can be divided lengthwise to proportions suitable for a variety of hook sizes.

Smooth yarn bodies, those with an even texture and almost seamless appearance, can be produced by using any of the preceding techniques shown for floss bodies. There are, however, a few differences between the materials that are worth noting. Forming smooth bodies requires that the filaments within the yarn strand are not twisted or tangled and thus will lie on the shank in flat, ribbonlike wraps. Single-ply yarns such as poly and spooled Antron can be untangled if necessary by running a small comb or dubbing needle lengthwise through the yarn strand to separate the filaments. Multi-strand yarns, used for larger bodies, are mounted on the hook shank and then untwisted so that the individual plies lay side-by-side in a flat band.

Since many types of yarn, particularly those of natural fibers, are more tightly consolidated than strands of floss, the yarn has far less tendency to spread and stray than floss, making the bodies less fussy to wrap. However, "bouncing" the material to help smooth out inconsistencies, as shown in **Method #5: Single-layer Floss Body**, Step 5, p. 103, has somewhat less effect on yarn than on floss. Because the surface of most yarns is

rougher in texture than floss, it tends to "grip" itself, with less propensity to slip when building a taper. Thus it is possible to construct steeper tapers by simply layering the material as you wrap forward (or backward) on the hook shank. Finally, since yarn is generally thicker than floss, greater care must be taken in binding it to the hook shank at the tie-off point so that it will not slip.

Smooth yarn bodies are generally used on streamers and, to a lesser extent dry flies. But yarn is so well suited to producing more realistic bodies with a segmented appearance that many tyers prefer to use the material for twisted bodies of the type shown in the following two methods.

Method #9:
Twisted Yarn Body

This technique produces a body with pronounced segmentation. The twisted poly yarn body shown in the following demonstration is typically used on grasshopper or adult stonefly patterns. A similar body of Antron, wrapped on a smaller hook, is used on many midge pupae and chironimid patterns. If the Antron is spooled, a bobbin can be used to wrap the material.

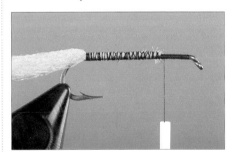

Step 1. Position the tying thread at the rearmost point of the body.
Lay the yarn atop the hook, and bind it tightly along the length of the shank to the body tie-off point, as shown.

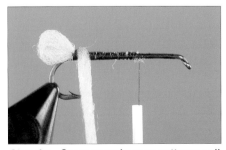

Step 1a. Some grasshopper patterns call for a loop of material left at the butt. To create this tag, mount the tying thread at the rearmost point of the body and wrap forward, laying a thread foundation up to the body tie-off point.
Lay the yarn atop the hook shank and bind it securely with thread wraps, moving toward the rear of the hook.
Double the yarn to form a loop of the desired size, and secure the loop at the rearmost point of the body with several tight thread wraps, as shown.
When the loop is secure, advance the thread back to the body tie-off point.

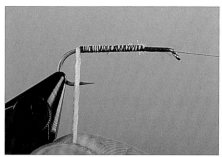

Step 2. Holding the yarn about 2 or 3 inches from the hook shank, twist it into a tight cord. The direction of twist should be clockwise when viewed from above. Twisting in this direction will keep the material tightly corded as you wrap the body.

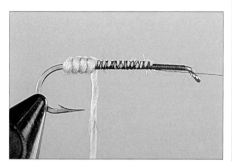

Step 3. Begin wrapping the body in tight, adjacent wraps.

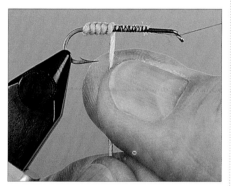

Step 4. If the material begins to loosen, or you wrap all of the twisted section, reposition your hands and twist a new length of yarn.

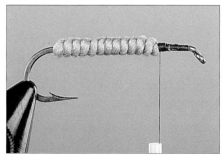

Step 5. Wrap the yarn to the front of the body, tie it off, clip the tag and bind it with thread.

Method #10:

Tapered Twisted Yarn Body

Segmented bodies that are also tapered can be fashioned from yarn. The key here is to begin by wrapping a smooth, tapered underbody from untwisted yarn. Once the underbody is complete, the yarn is tightly corded and wrapped to give a segmented finished body. Since both the smooth underbody and twisted body add bulk, using a relatively thin piece of yarn will keep the body from becoming disproportionately thick. As a rule of thumb, the strand of yarn, when twisted, should be about the diameter of the hook shank.

Two types of tapers are presented here. The main sequence shows the type of taper commonly used for mayfly bodies—on both the adult fly, and the nymph shown in the following demonstration. The alternate sequence illustrates the method for creating a reverse taper of the type frequently used for both caddis pupae and adults.

Step 1. Position the tying thread at the tie-off point of the body. Mount the yarn, with the tag pointing toward the hook bend, using 2 wraps of thread.

Maintain tension on the bobbin, and draw the yarn toward the hook eye until the tag extends about ⅓ the length of the body.

Secure the yarn tag with several tight thread wraps.

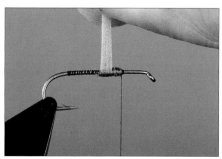

Step 2. Untwist the yarn to flatten it to a ribbon-like strand, and begin taking closely overlapping wraps to form the front portion of the taper.

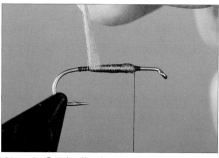

Step 3. Gradually decrease the amount of overlap on the yarn wraps as you reach the middle of the hook shank, thinning out the taper. Untwist the yarn as necessary to keep it flat.

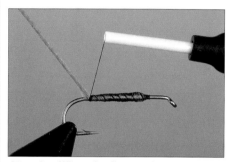

Step 4. When the flattened yarn reaches the tailing point, spiral the tying thread down the underbody. Bind the yarn down at the rearmost point of the body with 3 or 4 tight wraps of thread.

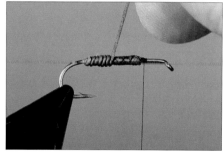

Step 5. Spiral the thread back to the front of the body. Tightly twist the yarn (clockwise when viewed from above) into a cord, and begin wrapping forward.

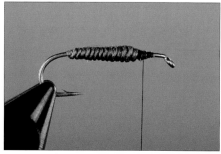

Step 6. Continue wrapping to the tie-off point. Tie off the yarn at the front of the body; clip and bind down the excess.

10

SECTION 1

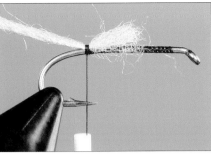

Step 1a. To form a reverse taper, position the thread at the rearmost point of the body. Mount the yarn, with tag pointing toward the hook eye, with two wraps of thread. Maintain tension on the bobbin and draw the yarn toward the hook bend until the tag extends about ½ the length of the body.

Step 4a. When the middle of the hook is reached, reverse the wrapping direction. Maintain a flat yarn and wrap back to the rearmost point of the body.

Secure the yarn with a few tight thread wraps.

Spiral the thread forward to the body tie-off point.

Step 2. Wrap the yarn in tight, adjacent wraps to the front of the body. Tie off, clip, and bind down the tag.

Step 3. The fibers of mohair must now be teased or picked out to give the body the impression of somewhat greater bulk and to give the fly an undulating action in the water.

With the point of a dubbing needle, a dubbing teaser, a small brush, or a piece of Velcro "hook" material as shown here, tease out fibers from the exterior of the yarn body. Work all around the hook shank, from one end to the other, to achieve a relatively even density of teased fibers.

Do not try to raise up too many fibers; the yarn consists merely of twisted fibers, and pulling too many strands from the core may cause the yarn to break.

Step 5a. Tightly twist the yarn into a cord, as in Step 5, and wrap it forward.

Tie off the body as shown in Step 6.

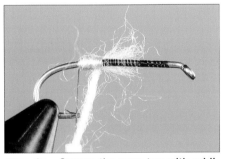

Step 2a. Secure the yarn tag with additional tight thread wraps.

Untwist the yarn to flatten it, and begin taking closely overlapping wraps to form the rear portion of the taper.

Method #11:

Leech Yarn Body

Rough, fuzzy, mohair yarn is a simple and very popular material to use for leech bodies, most notably the Canadian Blood Leech pattern from Brian Chan. The noteworthy point of this technique is less the wrapping of the yarn than the treatment of the material afterward.

Step 4. At this point, Brian Chan recommends immersing the fly for a few moments in hot water. This will remove some of the kinks from the teased fibers.

After immersing the fly, comb the wet fibers backward into a flowing "capsule" around the hook shank.

When the material dries, the teased yarn will be less crinkled or curled and will sweep rearward around the fly.

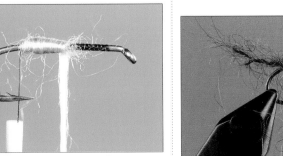

Step 3a. Gradually decrease the amount of overlap on the yarn wraps, thinning out the taper as you approach the middle of the hook shank. Untwist the yarn as necessary to keep it flat

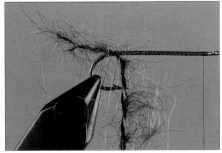

Step 1. Tie in the yarn at the rearmost point of the body. Frequently a tag is left at the back, as shown, to form a tail. Advance the thread to the tie-off point.

Quill, Quill-Style, and Biot Bodies

The term "quill" is one of the most ambiguous in fly tying. It can refer to a complete feather—usually a flight feather from the wing, as in a "duck quill"; a section cut from such a feather for winging a fly, as in a "slip or segment of quill"; or the central stem of any feather. For the purposes of tying bodies, the term "quill" applies to a different group of materials: the stem of rooster hackle with the barbs removed; a strip of material peeled from the outer layer of a large feather stem; a length of peacock or ostrich herl with the fuzzy barbules or "flue" removed; and even certain stiff hairs such as porcupine or moose mane that are similar to quill in appearance. The techniques for tying these quill and quill-like materials are presented in this section.

Quills can produce thin-profile fly bodies that appear distinctly segmented, and they are generally used on mayfly or nymph patterns. Tying quills, however, can be somewhat more involved than other body materials, as the quills often require some advance preparation. Moreover, they can demand delicate handling, and the resulting fly body may be fragile unless reinforced. And finally, the short length of some quill materials restricts their use to smaller flies. Still, quill bodies have a beautifully smooth, slightly glossy surface with a strikingly lifelike, segmented appearance.

Selecting and Preparing Quill-body Materials

Peacock herl suitable for quill bodies can be found on both the "eyed" feather and on the tapered, eyeless sword feathers. Which type to choose depends on the characteristics you desire in the material. Traditionally, tyers have used herl from the eyed portion of a feather for quills. These quills often show a distinct longitudinal stripe; one edge of the quill is dark in color, the other light, and when wrapped, the material produces a distinct banding that gives the body a segmented look. The tradeoff, however, is that herl from the eye is often very thin and short, making it somewhat more delicate to work with and more appropriate for smaller flies. The first few inches of herl below the eye is usually wider and stronger, and hence easier to tie. It may, however, lack the banding that produces the most distinct appearance of segmentation.

Quills from peacock sword feathers also tend to be more uniform in color. But this herl may run to 7" inches or even longer, making it better for large flies, and the added length allows a tyer to mount the material well below the thin tip, where most quills split or break when wrapping.

High-quality quills, of either type, come from mature feathers. Such feathers are typically large, long, and full, with bushy herl and an obvious metallic sheen. Herls and quills from thin, ratty, anemic-looking peacock feathers tie poorly.

Ostrich herl, prepared like peacock with the flue or barbules removed, is also a satisfactory quill-body material. Unlike quill from a peacock eye, however, ostrich lacks the longitudinal stripe that produces a segmented appearance, and the resulting body is more uniform in color. Many tyers find that such a body is easily duplicated by other materials that are less fragile and require less preparation. Still, ostrich is available in a variety of dyed colors, and the quills are suitable for dressing bodies.

Hackle-quill bodies can be made from rooster saddle or the large feathers on the butt of a rooster neck. (Hen hackle is usually too short.) Many tiers find that quill bodies are an excellent use for the neck or saddle hackles that are too large or webby for dry flies. Traditional patterns usually call for quills from reddish-brown or ginger necks, though grizzlies and other variants can yield interesting bodies, and light-colored quill are easily dyed.

Long hackle feathers with gradually tapering stems are the best. The thick butt section of most hackle stems has a soft, pithy core, making it unsuitable for tying, and it frequently lacks the coloration of the upper portion of the quill. Since some of the quill will thus be unusable, a long feather will guarantee enough good material to wrap the body.

In order to make a useable quill, the flue or barbs must first be removed. Tyers have devised a number of methods for preparing herls and hackles, and the particular method employed generally depends upon the quantity of material needed and the degree to which a tyer is willing to become involved in procedures that can get a trifle messy.

Method #12:
Hand-stripped Quills

The barbules from herls and the barbs from hackle can be removed by hand—the simplest and most direct approach. The technique, however, can be somewhat tedious, and occasionally, a quill is broken. Still, for small quantities of material, it is the most efficient technique. Herls can be stripped using either of the methods shown in the first two photographs.

Ordinarily, hackle stems should not be stripped of their barbs, since this process also peels away the thin outer covering of the quill that contains the color. A hackle stripped this way will produce a quill with longitudinal white stripes. However, strip-ping barbs is a practical approach if the feather stem is subsequently colored, by dyeing or by using a waterproof marker, as shown in the alternate sequence.

Select a herl and remove the flue by gently stripping it with your thumbnail. Stroke the herl from tip to butt, against the "grain" of the flue. Several light strokes are better than fewer hard strokes, since the quill is fragile.

Or you can use an eraser instead. Hold the herl by the tip against a tabletop, and rub the eraser from tip to butt. A coarse ink eraser works better than a pencil eraser.

Step 1a. To strip a hackle feather, grasp it by the very tip, and peel away short sections of barbs on both sides of the stem. Work gently when stripping barbs from the tip portion of the feather.

Step 2a. To color a hackle quill, simply draw it between the tip of a waterproof marker and a work surface. Make several passes to ensure that the entire quill is tinted.

After coloring the material, allow the ink to dry so that the color doesn't bleed when the hackle quills are soaked for tying or stored in a solution (see "Soaking and Storing Stripped Quills," below).

Method #13:
Bleach-stripped Quills

It's both tedious and time consuming to hand-strip a large number of peacock or hackle quills. Instead, you can chemically dissolve, or "burn" flues and barbs using ordinary household bleach. The burning solution should be no more than 50% bleach. More dilute solutions, water/bleach ratios of 3/1 or even 4/1, take longer but give better control over the process and decrease the likelihood of damaging or bleaching out the quills by overexposure to the solution.

Several eyes—up to two-dozen or so—can be prepared at once using the procedure shown in the main sequence. It's best, however, to strip only enough material to last 2 or 3 months and prepare a fresh batch when more quills are required.

The alternate sequence shows how hackle feathers are prepared and stripped using a bleach solution.

Step 1. Fill a wide-mouth quart jar with a solution made of 2 cups of bleach and 2 cups of tap water (or a more dilute solution if you choose). Fill a second jar with tap water only.

Take a peacock eye (or several eyes if desired), and immerse it in the bleach solution. Small bubbles will begin to form on the feather. Swish it gently. After 20 or 30 seconds, enough bubbles will form that the solution almost seems to fizz. A white foam will gather on the surface of liquid.

Step 2. After 30 seconds or so, the color will bleach from the eye. Remove the feather, and rinse it under running water. Placing the eye in the jar of clean water will fluff out the flue and allow you to see if any fibers remain on the quill.

If any flue remains, return the eye to the bleach for about 10 seconds; rinse and inspect. Repeat if necessary. Short immersions are best, as the process moves rather quickly—between 1 and 2 minutes total (with a 50% bleach solution)—and you want to expose the quills to the bleach for the minimum time necessary to dissolve the flue.

When the quill is clean, thoroughly rinse the eye under running water.

Some tyers recommend rinsing the stripped peacock eyes or hackle quills in a solution of 2 or 3 tablespoons of baking soda dissolved in a quart of water. This allegedly neutralizes any residual effect of the bleach. We have frequently omitted this step, however, with no ill effect on the material.

Step 1a. Prepare hackles by bundling the desired amount of material at the butt with a rubber band. Hackles of different length and thickness, and feathers from different necks, burn at different rates. When bundling material, select hackles of roughly the same size and all from the same neck or saddle.

If you are preparing a reasonably small number of hackles, it helps to trim the barbs close to the stem before burning, leaving only a stubble next to the quill. This trimming promotes an even rate of burning along the length of the quill and speeds up the process.

Using a forceps or hemostat, grip the bundle at the butt and swish it in the bleach solution. Let it sit submerged for 5-10 minutes.

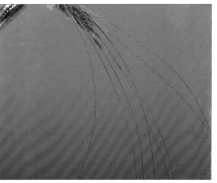

Step 2a. Check the progress of the feathers by immersing them in a jar of clean water as described in Step 2. Hackle barbs are sterner stuff than peacock flue, and the burning process takes much longer—from 15-30 minutes (with a 50% bleach solution), depending on the feather.

Because the fluff and webby barbs at the base of the feather are finer in texture, they will dissolve more quickly than those near the tip. When the butt portion of the feather stem is clean, tyer A.K. Best recommends removing the feathers, preparing a new batch of bleach solution, and immersing only the portion of the feathers that have barbs remaining. This prevents damaging the cleaned quill. On smaller batches of material that burn more quickly than large ones, we've found this step unnecessary.

Re-check the material at short intervals. In most cases, the barbs at the very tip of the feather are the last to disappear, and it isn't necessary to dissolve these. This portion of the feather is usually trimmed away when the feather is mounted, and the additional time needed to completely dissolve the tip barbs may damage the clean feather stem.

When most of the barbs are dissolved, thoroughly rinse the bundle of quills under running water.

Soaking and Storing Stripped Quills

Regardless of the method used to strip the quills or hackle stems, the prepared material should be soaked in water before using. Soaking renders the quills soft and pliable; they are easier to wrap around a hook shank and less prone to break or split. Peacock quills in particular profit from this treatment, since the soaked quills wrap more tightly and tie off with less bulk. Unused quills can be stored in a covered jar of water and kept for several months.

Though older tying books recommend storing quills in a solution of glycerine and water, A.K. Best, in his book *Production Fly Tying*, argues against this method on the grounds that bodies tied from quills that have been stored in a glycerine solution tend to absorb water. Dick Talleur, however, does recommend storing stripped quills and hackle stems in a solution of 75% water and 25% hair conditioner, which preserves the material and renders it quite pliable.

Method #14:
Paraffin-coated Quills

Some tyers object to burning peacock eyes, arguing that the bleach solution diminishes the light/dark contrast on the quill, and hence the appearance of segmentation on the body, and that it makes the quills brittle. Properly burned quills—that is, those treated for the absolute minimum time required to dissolve flue and rinsed thoroughly and immediately afterward—are generally satisfactory. Still, bleaching can be a bit messy and involved, and so some tyers prefer hand-stripping quills that have first been coated with paraffin.

The paraffin technique shown in the following sequence does offer some distinct advantages. Paraffin-coated eyes are easy to store in a zip-loc bag, and they keep almost indefinitely. A single quill can easily be removed, and the oils in the paraffin keep the quills soft and pliable.

Step 1. Bring about a quart of water to boil in a small pan. Drop in a piece of paraffin about 1"x1"x1½". Keep the water at a slow boil until the paraffin has melted. Since the paraffin is lighter than water, it will rise and form a thin film on the water.

Turn off the heat and let the pan stand for about 5 minutes. Dip the eye through the film of wax and withdraw it. Repeat 2 or 3 times, turning the eye over each time to lay a thin coating of wax on the herl.

Step 2. Lay the waxed eye on a piece of waxed paper or tin foil and let cool.

Step 3. Using scissors, cut off a quill, and with thumb and forefinger, strip away the paraffin. The herl comes away completely and easily with the wax, leaving a clean, flexible quill.

Tying Peacock Quills

Most quill bodies are wrapped after the wings, tail, (and separate underbody material, if used) have been mounted, and there is one important key for clean, attractive results—getting a smooth, even foundation on which to wrap the quill. To a great extent, the choice of winging and tailing materials determines both the body profile and the techniques used to achieve a smooth underbody (see "Underbodies," p. 41). When you wish to keep bulk to a minimum, use the finest thread possible, particularly with small flies. Using 8/0 or 12/0 thread prevents an unnecessary buildup of material.

Most quill bodies—but peacock especially—are fragile. The durability is greatly increased if the finished body is reinforced. The various techniques for doing so are presented separately in the section "Reinforcing Quill Bodies," p. 116.

Method #15:
Single-quill Body

Using a single strand of material is the most common way of forming bodies from peacock quill. The length of the material, however, is often a limiting factor in the size of the body that can be dressed.

As noted earlier, a smooth underbody is the key to a neat quill body, and using a minimum of thread wraps is the best way to ensure a slender profile. In the following demonstration, we've mounted a pair of feather-tip wings; the tail fibers have been mounted as explained in Step 1, and will be secured along with the tip of the quill to minimize thread wraps and form a smooth body foundation.

Step 1. Tie in the desired type of wings; clip and bind the butts. Wind the thread in close, even wraps to the tailing point.

Mount the desired style of tail, using a flat, untwisted thread and taking just enough wraps, perhaps only 2 or 3, to position and hold the tail in place. Do not trim the excess tail material. The tying thread should be positioned just slightly forward of the rearmost tail-mounting wrap.

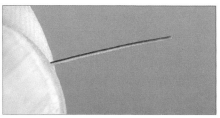

Step 2. Select a stripped quill from a peacock eye. Note the light and dark edges.

Step 3. If the body is to be reinforced using the approach shown in **Method #25: Wrapped Thread Reinforcement**, p. 116, the silk thread should be mounted now, with only one wrap of tying thread.

Place the quill on top of the hook shank, slanting toward the rear, as shown. Note that the quill is not mounted at the very tip, but rather a short way down the stem. The very thin tip section is often too fragile to endure even a light wrapping pressure and can easily break.

The butt end of the quill should be pointing away from you, making a 45-degree angle with the hook shank. Take only one wrap of thread around the quill.

Step 4. With a flattened tying thread, bind the tail butts and the tip of the quill down together (and the silk thread, if one is used). The thread wraps should barely overlap at the edges. The idea here is to form the smoothest possible foundation for the quill. Continue wrapping until you reach the tie-off point for the body.

Step 5. If the quill is relatively long, it can be wrapped using only the fingers.

With shorter quills, it is helpful to clamp the butt end of the quill in a pair of hackle pliers, as shown here. The pliers should be in line with the quill rather than gripping it crosswise, which can break the quill during wrapping.

Step 6. The first wrap of quill is actually toward the rear of the hook, where it will

cover the rearmost thread wrap. Since the quill is already angled toward the tail, its position will encourage this first "backward" wrap. Take one turn of quill to the rear.

After one complete wrap, the quill will be angled toward the hook eye, in just the right position to continue winding the body.

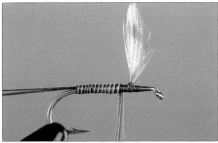

Step 7. Wind the quill forward, placing wraps precisely adjacent to one another. Do not overlap the edges of the quill or the segmentation effect will be diminished or lost.

Wrap the quill while maintaining a consistent and firm, but not overly tight, tension. Slackening tension may cause the wraps of quill to loosen slightly and reduce the durability of the body.

Step 8. Wrap the quill to the tie-off point, secure it, clip the tag, and bind the excess.

Method #16:
Multiple-quill Body

Large hooks or thick bodies may require more wraps of material than are obtainable from a single quill. Using two quills wrapped side-by-side solves this problem and can also make very short quills useable.

Step 1. Prepare wings, tail (and underbody, if used) as described above in **Method #15: Single-quill Body**, Step 1, p. 110. Here we've used hair wings and a floss underbody. If the body is to be reinforced with thread as shown in **Method #25: Wrapped Thread Reinforcement**, p.

116, mount the silk thread using one wrap of the tying thread.

Select two stripped quills, and grasp them side-by-side so that the light and dark bands alternate. Mount them together as described above in **Method #15: Single-quill Body**, Step 3, p. 110. With a flattened tying thread bind down the tailing butts and the tips of the quills (and the silk thread if one is used for reinforcement) to form a smooth underbody.

Step 2. Hold the quills side-by-side to form a flat "ribbon" or band, as shown. Longer quills can be held and wrapped in the fingers; shorter ones should be gripped in hackle pliers.

Take one turn toward the rear of the hook to cover the exposed tail-mounting wraps, and begin wrapping the quills forward, as explained in **Method #15: Single-quill Body**, Steps 6-7, p. 110. Take care to hold the quills flat, so they do not overlap one another as they are wrapped.

Step 3. Wrap the quills to the tie-off point and bind them down.

Method #17:
Hackle-quill Body

Unlike flat peacock quills, stripped hackle stems are roughly oval in cross-section. Because the diameter gradually increases from tip to butt, winding a hackle quill produces a naturally tapered body. Thus an underbody with little or no taper should be used if possible. Excessive taper in the underbody will be exaggerated further by the wrapped hackle stem, and the finished body may appear poorly proportioned.

Two (or more) hackle stems can be wrapped simultaneously to create some interesting quill bodies. However, since this method more closely resembles the technique for tying moose mane and horsehair quill-style bodies, it is detailed in **Method #22:**

Multiple-strand Quill-style Body, p. 115.

The finished body can be made more durable by using one of the approaches explained in **Method #24: Varnish Body Reinforcement**, p. 116.

Step 1. Dress the wings and tail, and mount the hackle stem as explained in **Method #15: Single-quill Body**, Steps 1-3, p. 110. Mounting the hackle stem is identical to mounting a peacock quill with one exception: the stem is tied in directly over the rearmost wrap on the tail. Hackle stem is bulky and taking the first wrap of material toward the rear of the fly, as is done with flat quill, will produce a bump at the back of the body.

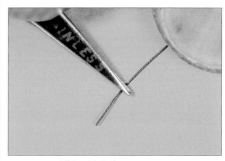

Step 1a. With thick feather stems or very small flies, there may be some difficulty tying in the quill without forming an uneven bump of thread. To solve this problem, lay the quill flat against a table, and run the side of your scissors down the last half-inch of quill at the tip. Apply pressure as go, flattening the hackle stem.

Tie in the quill just where the flattened portion ends. This procedure also helps keep the body profile thin.

Step 2. With a flattened tying thread, bind the quill and tail butts with smooth, even wraps.

Position the thread at the tie-off point.

Step 3. Wind the quill forward, leaving no gaps between the wraps of material.

Tie off the stem, clip the excess at an angle, and bind down the tag with tying thread.

Method #18:
Feather-stem Quill Strips

Long strips of quill can be peeled from the stems of wing or tail feathers from any number of birds—goose, turkey, duck, peacock, and almost any game bird—and used for flies with bodies too large or long to wrap with stripped hackle or peacock. Undyed feathers work best; dyeing feathers tends to make the outer layer of the stem weak and brittle, though some dyed feathers do give satisfactory results.

Step 1. Select a wing or tail feather. It doesn't matter if barbs or biots have been removed for another purpose, but the stem should show no nicks, cracks, or evidence that it has been bent.

Position the feather as shown, with the glossy side of the stem facing up.

Hold a sharp single-edged razor blade near the tip of the stem at a very shallow angle. Push inward and downward to nick the stem and raise a small flap of material.

Step 2. With a tweezers, hemostats, or your fingernails, grasp this flap; pull outward and downward to peel a thin layer of the outer stem covering.

When an inch or two of material has been separated, reposition your fingers closer to the feather stem, and continue

---

peeling slowly. Always work close to the feather stem; pulling from the very tip of the quill strip may cause it to break.

Step 3. Shown here is a completed feather-stem quill strip. Generally, the width of the strip will follow the taper of the feather stem, so that the peeled quill will be narrow at one end and wide at the other.

The resulting material is thin and tough. It can be used either dry or wet.

Tying bodies of stripped stem quill is identical to the procedure for tying peacock quill described in **Method #15: Single-quill Body**, p. 110. If the material is too wide, or the tip too blunt to tie in easily, the quill strip can be split lengthwise or tapered with scissors.

Biots

Biots are actually highly specialized barbs that form a vane on the leading edge of a bird's flight feathers (see "Wing Feathers," p. 9).

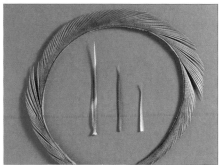

The circular material is a strip of biots peeled from the flight feather of a goose. Inside the strip are, from left to right, a single turkey biot, a goose biot, and a duck biot. Biots are quite short in comparison to other quill materials. Turkey biots, the longest, rarely exceed 1 ¼"; a very good goose biot is an inch long, and duck biots considerably shorter.

Biots taper rather abruptly and the butt end is relatively wide, which makes tying off a biot somewhat more cumbersome than tying off other quill-type materials. Nonetheless, biots make a handsome bodies and can give two distinct kinds of segmentation depending on how they are wrapped, as noted below.

Natural, undyed biot is quite flexible and strong, and can usually be tied without soaking it first. Commercially dyed biot strips, however, are often brittle and prone to splitting when tied. Soaking them before use or storing them in water can improve the handling characteristics, particularly when tying off and trimming the material. They can be stored in a jar of water for several months. A fly body wrapped from a wet biot will be

---

quite translucent at first, but will regain its original color when dry.

Like other quill materials, undyed biots can be colored with waterproof marking pens and have the added advantage of easy storage since they require no soaking. But owing primarily to the efforts of René Harrop, biots have become a widely used material, and dyed biots are available in a wide assortment of colors. Many tyers prefer them to other quill materials, particularly peacock, for their superior durability.

Method #19:
Stripping Biots

Most tyers purchase biots that have already been stripped, and often dyed. But flight feathers that a tyer may already have are an excellent source of biots, particularly in natural colors. Though individual biots can be cut from the feather stem, it's easier to remove all the biots in a single strip, which is easier to store and use.

Step 1. With a very sharp single-edge razor blade, shave away a half-inch section of biots near the tip of the feather to gain a little working room. These biots are generally too short to be useable.

Step 2. Work the edge of a razor blade into the stem beneath biots. Slowly and carefully draw the razor toward you, peeling the biots away on a thin strip of the stem.

Step 3. A peeled biot strip is shown here. These strips are more conveniently stored than whole feathers and simplify removing the biots for tying.

Method #20:
Biot Body

Individual biots are asymmetrical. One side of the biot contains a tiny row of fringe-like barbules. You may be able to see these barbules, particularly on an undyed biot, but they are more easily detected in the following manner. Hold an individual biot by the tip. With thumb and forefinger, lightly pinch and stroke the biot from tip to butt. The barbules will appear as a fuzz or roughness on one edge. A wrapped biot can produce either smooth body or one with a fringed rib, depending upon which direction this edge faces during mounting. As explained in Steps 1 and 1a, however, there are easier ways to establish the proper mounting orientation than inspecting each individual biot for the row of fringed barbules.

Turkey biots are probably the most popular material because they are the longest, most easily handled, and well-suited to larger hooks. Shorter biots, such as those from goose or even duck feathers, are better proportioned to smaller flies, though they are more difficult to wrap. These biots are generally narrower than turkey biots, producing a closer segmentation for smaller bodies and are less bulky when the body is tied off.

The main sequence that follows shows the procedure for wrapping a smooth biot body that is similar in appearance to those obtained with other quills. Because the technique involves overlapping wraps to conceal the fringe of barbules and make the body smooth, however, the coverage area on the hook shank is reduced, and forming extremely long bodies is not practical. Smooth biot bodies can be reinforced using either of the techniques described under "Reinforcing Quill Bodies," p. 116.

The alternate sequence demonstrates the procedure for fashioning a biot body with a fringe-like ribbing. Because the wraps do not overlap, slightly more material is available and longer bodies are possible. Ribbed biot bodies of this type are best reinforced using the technique pictured **Method #24: Varnish Body Reinforcement**, Step 1, p. 116.

you will notice an indentation or notch at the base of the biot. This notch may be shallow or deep, depending on the material. The direction that this notch is positioned during mounting determines whether the body will be smooth or fringed, as shown in Steps 2 and 1a.

If the biot is clipped from the strip with scissors, the very base of the biot that contains the notch remains on the strip and, obviously, cannot be used as a guide to mounting orientation. In this case, observe the biot, and you will notice that it is slightly curved or cupped from side to side, as shown by the biots on the right. On some biots this cross-sectional curvature is quite pronounced; on others, it is less conspicuous. The convex side of the biot tends to be glossier or shinier and darker or more distinctly marked than the concave side. Again, as shown in Steps 2 and 1a, the curvature of the biot can also be used as a guide for mounting orientation.

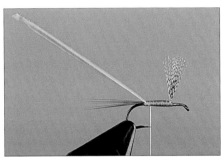

Step 2. Dress the wings, tail (and underbody, if used) as described above in **Method #15: Single-quill Body**, Step 1, p. 110. Smooth biot bodies tie up best if a tapered underbody is used. Slight tapers can be fashioned from tying thread (as shown here); to form bulkier underbodies or steeper tapers, see "Underbodies," p. 41.

Select a biot and bind it to the near side of the hook shank, slightly ahead of the rearmost thread wrap. The biot should form a 45-degree angle with the tail and should be mounted about ⅛" from the tip.

To form a smooth body, the biot should be mounted so the notch faces downward, as shown here. If using a clipped biot, mount it so that the convex side of the biot faces the tyer.

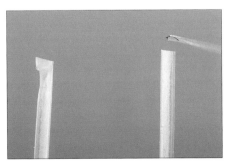

Step 1. There are two basic ways to determine the mounting orientation of the biot. Most tyers peel an individual biot from the end of a strip of material, since this maximizes its handling and tying length. If you inspect a peeled biot, as shown on the left,

Step 3. Advance the tying thread to the body tie-off point, binding down the biot tip as you go. Use a flattened thread to maintain a smooth underbody.

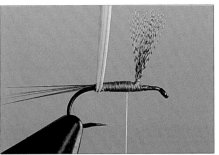

Step 4. Clip the butt of the biot in hackle pliers (straight on, not crosswise), and take one turn of the biot around the rearmost thread wraps and stop. Notice that the leading edge of the biot has ridge of hairlike barbules projecting upward.

Step 5. Take another turn of biot, overlapping the material so that the fringe of barbules on the first wrap is completely covered by the edge of material on the second wrap.

Step 6. Continue wrapping, always overlapping the previous wrap just enough to hide the barbule fringe. The first wraps will be spaced close together; as the biot gets wider, each wrap will cover an increasing length of hook shank. The body should appear smooth.

Step 7. Wrap to the tie-off point. The biot will be rather wide at at the butt end, and it's easiest to take a complete wrap of tying thread, under light tension, around the biot. Then, apply pressure to the thread to snug it evenly around the biot to form a smooth tie-off. Once the biot is secured in this way, take additional tight wraps to bind it to the shank.

Clip and bind the excess.

Step 1a. To create a ribbed biot body, prepare the hook and mount the biot as shown in Step 2, but position the biot with the notch facing up, as shown here.

If using a clipped biot, mount it with the concave side facing the tyer.

Step 2a. Bind down the biot tip, creating a smooth underbody.

Wrap the biot, but do not overlap the wraps. Successive turns should be placed edge-to-edge so that the barbule fringe raised with each wrap of material is not concealed.

Step 3a. Continue wrapping and tie off as explained in Step 7.

Quill-type Materials

Though moose mane, horsehair, and porcupine are not "quills" in the sense that we've been using the term—that is, as portions of a feather—they nonetheless produce segmented bodies that are quite quill-like in appearance, and so their use is explained in this chapter. Included in this section as well are bodies fashioned from two stripped hackle stems (see **Method #22: Multiple-strand Quill-style Body**, p. 115) since the technique for wrapping them so closely resembles that used for moose, porcupine, and horsehair. Hackle stems should be prepared as described in **Method #12: Hand-stripped Quills**, p. 108, or **Method #13: Bleached-stripped Quills**, p. 109. Since one or both hackle stems can by colored by dyeing or using a waterproof marking pen, some interesting bandings and segmentations can be produced that are largely unavailable with other materials.

Moose mane (moose body hair is sometimes used as well) contains both white and dark hairs. Moose hairs tend to flatten when wrapped, and so the finished body most closely resembles peacock quill, though the segmentation obtained from individual hairs is not as distinct. Thus light and dark hairs are often tied in combination to produce a banded body.

Horsehair (from the tail) comes in a variety of colors, and these can be used individually or in combination. Since horsehair is solid, and will not flatten when wrapped, horsehair bodies closely resemble those tied from stripped hackle stems—both have a distinct, three-dimensional segmentation. Unlike a hackle stem, however, horsehair maintains a uniform diameter along its length and will not form a taper naturally as it is wrapped. The desired taper must be formed from the underbody or thread foundation. Light-colored hair can be dyed or tinted with a marking pen.

Porcupine actually contains two kinds of hair suitable for quill bodies. The first are long, thin, hairlike fibers (not the stiff, sharp quills used for defense); these are often white, but may be brown, or a mixture of the two colors. These solid hairs can be wrapped like stripped hackle stems and produce much the same type of body, though like horsehair, they have little or no natural taper. The second type of hair is the quill itself. These are larger in diameter, longer, and hollow, and must be flattened before tying. Quills vary in size; the long, thick ones are best reserved for large hooks, while the shorter, thinner ones are suitable for smaller bodies. Porcupine quills are used by tyers perhaps far less often than their virtues merit. The material produces tough, durable, attractive bodies, can be tinted or dyed, is relatively easy to work, and is often long enough to dress large patterns.

At the left is a patch of porcupine hide as it is sold to tyers. The three fibers at the right are a short quill (left) and a long quill (middle), both of which are hollow and require preparation as shown below. The long fiber at the right is a solid hair; it is also suitable for quill-style bodies and requires no preparation.

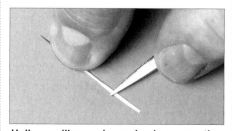

Hollow quills require a simple preparation before tying. To prepare a quill, select one on the hide and clip it off at the base. Don't try to pull it from the hide, as the quills are designed to break off.

Lay the quill against a smooth surface, and use the back of a pair of scissors to flatten the quill.

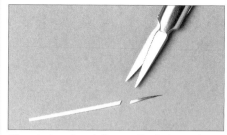

The dark-colored tip, particularly on large quills, is quite stiff and ties poorly. Clip off the tip at an angle as shown. The quill is now ready for coloring with a waterproof marker or tying in as is.

Though quill-style bodies are probably used most often on dry flies, they are effective on nymph patterns as well. Solid fibers such as horsehair, hackle stem, and porcupine hair make especially attractive bodies.

Method #21:
Single-strand Quill-style Body

Single strands of moose, horsehair, or either type of porcupine hair (see the preceding explanation) can be used to form quill-type bodies.

We're using horsehair in the following demonstration, a material, like porcupine, that was once more widely used than it is today. It is perhaps undervalued by modern tyers, though the material is, admittedly, not widely available in fly shops. Still, it is quite strong, can be tinted or dyed, and the long strands are easily handled.

Quill-style bodies fashioned from fibers that will flatten, such as moose hair or porcupine quill, can be reinforced using either of the techniques shown in the section, "Reinforcing Quill Bodies," p. 116. Bodies from solid fibers are best reinforced using **Method #24: Varnish Body Reinforcement**, p. 116. Overwrapping solid-fiber bodies with silk thread may obscure the ridged, three-dimensional segmentation produced by these materials.

Step 1. Dress the wings, tail (and separate underbody material, if used) as described above in **Method #15: Single-quill Body**,

Step 1, p. 110. If moose mane is used, clip the very fine tip from the hair before mounting, as it may break during wrapping. Mount the tip of the material—we're using horsehair here—directly atop the rearmost thread wrap.

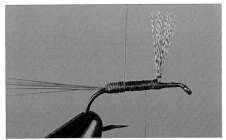

Step 2. Take the first turn of material to cover the rearmost thread wrap. Then wrap forward in adjacent, touching wraps to the tie-off point.

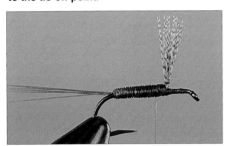

Step 3. Secure the body material, clip, and bind down.

Method #22:

Multiple-strand Quill-style Body

Bodies of this type can be wrapped from moose mane, horsehair or stripped hackle quills; the technique is identical regardless of the material. Since the body is fashioned from two or more strands of material, it's important that the individual strands are of equal thickness to prevent an uneven, lumpy appearance in the body. Hackle quills should match in taper and be trimmed so that the tips have an equal diameter at the tie-in point.

As always with quill materials, preparing a smooth underbody or thread foundation is the key to a uniform, attractive body.

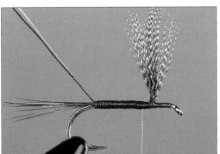

Step 1. Dress the wings, tail (and separate underbody material, if used) as described in **Method #15: Single-quill Body**, Step 1, p 110. Holding the two strands of material together, tie them in side-by-side, directly

on the top of the rearmost thread wrap.

Using strands of contrasting color, such as the moose mane shown here, produces a body with distinct banding.

Step 2. Wind the materials forward, maintaining the side-by-side orientation to produce the segmented effect. Keep the two strands of material as close together as possible when wrapping to avoid any gaps in the body.

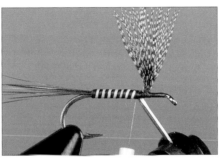

Step 3. Wrap the entire body. Clip the strands in a hackle pliers if they become to short to handle with your fingers.

Tie off the strands; trim and bind down the excess.

Method #23:

Ribbed Quill-style Body

The method shown here is preferred by professional tyer A.K. Best and is adapted from his book *Production Fly Tying*. The appearance of segmentation is produced by a contrasting strand of material essentially wrapped as ribbing over the primary body material. This approach gives the tyer greater control over the relative widths of the body-color bands. In the following demonstration, for instance, the width of the dark-colored bands is controlled by the spacing of the lighter-colored ribbing. By the same token, the width of the light band can be controlled by using the lighter material as the primary body material and ribbing with a dark strand. Body texture, too, can be altered. Using a solid hair such as porcupine or horsehair for the contrasting ribbing strand will make a body with ridged or humped segments.

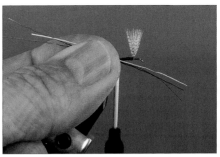

Step 1. Dress the wings, tail (and separate underbody material, if used) as described in **Method #15: Single-quill Body**, Step 1, p. 110.

Select two strands of a dark-colored quill-type material and one of a lighter color—we're using black and white moose hair in this demonstration.

Align the tips and clip the butts so that the strands are of equal length. Clip an additional inch from the butt of the white hair.

Step 2. Position the two black hairs on top of the hook shank so that the tips extend just to the tie-off point of the body. Secure them with two adjacent turns of thread.

Step 3. Now mount the white hair at the point where you left the thread in Step 2, that is, slightly ahead of the two black hairs. Bind down all three hair tips with smooth wraps of thread, making sure the hairs remain on top of the hook.

Step 4. Using the technique shown in **Method #22: Multiple-strand Quill-type Body**, grasp the two black hairs only (made easier by the fact that they are longer) and

take one turn behind the white hair.

Take the next wrap directly in front of the white hair, and continue wrapping to the tie-off point.

Secure the black hairs with a couple of turns of thread.

Step 5. Now take the white hair and spiral it forward to the tie-off point. Note that the spacing of these wraps determines the relative widths of the black and white bands; here, they are of equal width.

Secure the white hair, clip the butts, and bind down.

Reinforcing Quill Bodies

Because quills, especially peacock, tend to be thin or brittle or both, quill bodies are fragile; even the raspy teeth of a small trout can destroy them unless they are reinforced. The two techniques described below require head cement or CA glue. If head cement is used over the wrapped quill, it should be thinned with solvent until it is quite runny; if CA glue is used, it should be the liquid type. Thinner cement penetrates more readily, avoiding any buildup that might obscure the body segmentation. For underbody varnishing, a thin coat of thickened head cement or gel-type CA glue is better, as the more viscous consistency will not easily penetrate the underbody and ensure that the cement contacts both the quill and underbody.

Method #24:

Varnish Body Reinforcement

The easiest way of reinforcing quill or quill-type bodies is to secure the body material with head cement or CA glue. The simplest approach is to apply a drop of adhesive over the wrapped body as the very last step in tying the fly, that is, after all the fly components have been dressed and the head cemented. Applying cement immediately after the body is wrapped requires that you wait until the adhesive dries before completing the fly.

Coating a wrapped body with cement, however, results in a glossy finish that may or may not be desirable. The technique shown in the following photo is useful when you wish to avoid this glossy shine or when

tying a ribbed biot body (see **Method #20: Biot Body**, p. 113), where a finish coat of cement will mat down the fringe of barbules that produce the rib.

Step 1. After mounting wings and tail, and fashioning the underbody, tie in the quills. Apply a thin film of head cement or CA glue to the entire underbody (or a foundation of tying thread if no underbody is used).

Immediately wrap the quills to the tie-off point, using a just enough tension to seat the quills against the wet cement, but not so much pressure that adhesive is squeezed out between the body wraps. The varnish will essentially glue the quills to the underbody.

Method #25:

Wrapped Thread Reinforcement

This technique was popular when silk thread was widely used; it is employed less often now that such thread is less easily obtained. Still, it remains the strongest reinforcement—if you can find the proper materials. It requires a fine-diameter, white silk thread which is wrapped over the quill body and varnished. When the head cement dries, the thread becomes nearly invisible and doesn't obscure the segmented effect of the quill. None of the modern synthetic threads we've tried can reproduce this effect, as they remain visible through the varnish.

On nymph patterns, where weight is not a consideration, some tyers substitute fine wire for the silk.

Step 1. Tie in the quills, and along with them, bind in a 6-inch piece of fine, white silk thread. (A thicker, nylon tying thread is pictured here for better visibility.) Wrap and tie off the body.

Counterwrap the thread from tail to head; that is, the direction of wrapping

(counterclockwise when viewed from the eye of the hook) is opposite the direction in which the quill was wrapped.

Step 1a. Another version of this technique involves binding in the silk thread after the quill body is completed. The thread is then wrapped (in the usual direction, not counterwrapped) down to the tail and brought back up the hook shank, producing a crisscross pattern of thread across the quill.

Step 2. Apply a thin layer of head cement or CA glue to the body. When it dries, the thread will become nearly transparent.

SECTION THREE

Herl, Barb, and Feather Bodies

Strictly speaking, the title of this section is somewhat redundant, since all the bodies presented in this section are in fact fashioned from feather barbs of various types—the herl of peacock and ostrich, for example; fibers from pheasant and turkey tails; marabou and CDC. However, because the bodies produced by these materials are often quite different in appearance, and because some dressing styles use only the feather barbs while others incorporate the feather stems as well, tyers often differentiate among these materials, and we have preserved those distinctions here.

Herl Bodies

The term "herl" is generally used to designate a feather barb that is long, narrow, and flat with dense, fuzzy barbules (see p. 5). To confuse matters, these barbules are themselves sometimes called "herl," though they are more commonly termed "flue." Neither the barbs nor the barbules interlock, and so the herl stands out from the feather stem in individual, frondlike strands. The herls most commonly used in tying come from peacock, ostrich, and emu, though strands of marabou separated from the feather stem look and behave much like these other herls and are included in this section as well.

Peacock herl has long been a favorite among tyers and fishermen; for whatever reason—its color, reflectivity, its movement in the water—the material seems especially attractive to trout. Thus a large number of fly patterns, both floating and subsurface, incorporate it as a body material.

The peacock herl generally regarded as most desirable is that which has dense barbules on a thin, narrow quill. The barbules or flue differ in length from feather to feather, and the length determines the hook size to which the material is suited. Herl with shorter flue is better proportioned for smaller flies, and such material is easy to come by. Peacock sword feathers and smaller peacock eyes generally contain an abundance of short-flued herl. More difficult to obtain is peacock herl with long, bushy barbules that produce thick, fuzzy bodies with a minimum of bulk from the quill. Occasionally, a peacock sword feather that is suitable in this regard can be found, and such feathers are prized because the strands of herl themselves can be quite long and used to dress larger bodies. Typically, though, long-flued herl is found on a peacock eye feather, along a section of the feather that begins at the base of the eye and extends two or three inches down both sides of the stem. Herl from the eye itself has sparse barbules and makes poor bodies, though stripped quills from the eye make excellent quill bodies.

Herl below this two- or three-inch "prime" section has shorter barbules and wider quills. Since herl from the prime section has the longest barbules, tyers tend to reserve it for the largest flies, and in fact tying a small fly with it may produce a body that is disproportionately thick for the hook size.

It is somewhat curious that top-quality peacock herl is among the more difficult materials to come by. The best herl comes from wide, mature feathers, with dense barbules on long quills, and it is a lucky tyer who finds a reliable source for feathers of this type. The smaller, narrower feathers more typically available are usually serviceable, however. Strung herl, which has been removed from the feather stem and sewn at the base into long strings, is generally of lesser quality, though it can be an economical choice when large quantities of material are needed.

Peacock herl has one peculiar and interesting property—exposure to sunlight will change its color from greenish yellow or greenish blue, to a metallic shade of purple or magenta, in some cases almost deep violet. Such material makes bodies that are both attractive and effective. To "age" the herl and produce this color, simply stand the feathers upright near a window where they will receive indirect sunlight. (Direct sunlight may damage the feather.) The color change occurs gradually over weeks. Conversely, storing feathers in a dark place helps preserve the original color of the material.

The thick, lush strands of herl that are often difficult to find with peacock herl occur in abundance on ostrich plumes. In fact, tying with ostrich sometimes presents the opposite problem—finding strands of herl with barbules short enough to dress small fly bodies. A somewhat softer material than peacock, ostrich herl is generally used on patterns fished subsurface or in the surface film. Unlike peacock, ostrich is easily dyed, and the wide selection of colors makes the material suitable for a variety of patterns. The techniques for tying peacock and ostrich herl, however, are essentially identical. Because of the difficulty of finding ostrich herl with shorter barbules, some tyers use larger rhea and emu feathers. Smaller in overall size than ostrich plumes, they contain shorter herls with shorter flue and are suited to smaller patterns.

Finally, barbs from marabou feathers, with their long and soft barbules, possess a distinctly herl-like structure (see "Marabou," p. 11) and can be tied using many of the same techniques as other herls. Marabou herl, however, has unusually thin barbs that are so fragile that the material is rarely tied using only a single strand.

Method #26:

Single-herl Body

This technique involves winding a single strand of herl, much as you would for a stripped quill body. A good quality herl produces a dense, uniform, fuzzy body with a minimum of quill bulk on the hook shank, making the method a common one for dressing dry-fly bodies, most notably Coachman-type flies. Since the tyer is somewhat limited by the length of the herl strand, longer fly bodies may require more than one strand of material. Multiple strands are wrapped in sequence—the first piece of herl is mounted, wrapped, and tied off; the second then mounted, wrapped, and tied off; and so on until the body is complete.

Herl bodies tied in this manner are rather fragile, and as such are often reinforced with a piece of very thin tying thread, or fine wire as shown in the following sequence.

Ostrich, emu, and rhea herls can all be dressed in this fashion, though they are more typically used for dressing collar-style gills on midge pupae than for bodies. Most marabou barbs are too fragile to be wrapped in this manner. Tyer Jack Gartside employs this single-herl technique using afterfeather (see "Afterfeather," p. 11) to create very full, soft-textured nymph bodies.

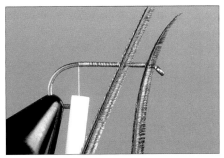

Step 1. Position the tying thread at the rearmost point of the body.

Select a long piece of herl with dense barbules, and trim away the very fine tip. If you attempt to mount the herl untrimmed, the fragile tip section may break as you begin wrapping. The piece of herl shown at the right is untrimmed; the one on the left is trimmed for mounting.

If you observe the herl closely, you'll notice that the barbules are not centered on the quill. Rather, they project outward from one edge of the quill—the edge that faces you when you look at the front of the eyed feather. The strand of herl on the left is shown from the back side; notice that the shiny quill is quite prominent. The strand on the right is shown from the front; the barbs project from the front of the quill, and the quill itself is less conspicuous on this side of the herl. Noting the orientation of the barbs is crucial to tying a herl body of the desired density.

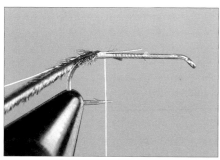

Step 2. If a reinforcement is desired, mount a piece of thread, or fine wire as shown here, with one wrap of the tying thread.

Strip the barbules from about ¼" of the quill tip. For a dense body, mount the herl so that the edge of the quill containing the barbs faces the hook bend.

Step 3. With a flattened thread, wrap a smooth, thin underbody to the tie-off point.

Begin wrapping the herl. Adjacent wraps should overlap so that the fuzzy barbules on one wrap of material butt up against the barbules on the previous wrap, and the bare quill is concealed.

Step 4. Continue wrapping the herl in close, overlapping turns until the body is complete.

If the herl strand is used up before the body is finished, as is the case here, mount a second strand—remembering to orient the quill properly, as described in Step 2—next to the first. The first turn of this new herl strand should overlap the tie-off point of the previous strand to produce a smooth, seamless body.

Step 5. When the body is complete, counterwrap the wire or thread; that is wrap it forward in a direction opposite to that in which the herl was wrapped (see **Method #2: Counter-ribbing**, p. 92), wiggling the material as you wrap to seat it tightly against the quill without binding down any barbules.

When the front edge of the herl body is reached, tie off the reinforcement material, and clip the excess.

Step 6. The herl body at the top has been dressed using the procedure described in this sequence; in this case, we've left off the wire for a clearer illustration. Notice that the wraps of material closely overlap and produce a dense, full body. This style is preferred by most anglers for most herl-body applications. The hook on the bottom is wrapped with herl that has been mounted with the flat quill section facing the hook bend. When the herl is wrapped, the bands of quill make it impossible to place the barbules close together, and a much sparser body is created.

Method #27:
Multiple-herl Body

This technique is most commonly used with marabou barbs or herl, since the very thin quills do not produce excessive bulk, and it produces a somewhat denser body than is obtainable with thicker-quilled herl materials. Because each turn of the herls binds down some of the barbules, the body produced has a slightly ribbed appearance. It is most often used on nymph patterns, particularly damselflies.

Marabou barbs with thin tips, of the type shown in the following demonstration, will produce a tapered body, narrower at the rear and wider at the front. Barbs with barbules that are equally long from tip to butt will produce a body with a more uniform diameter. Barbs from both marabou plumes and blood feathers (see "Marabou," p. 11) can be

used. Mixing colors of barbs will produce a body with a striped or variegated appearance.

If desired, this type of body can be reinforced with a counterwrapped rib as described in **Method #26: Single-herl Body**, p. 117.

Step 1. Preen the barbs on a marabou feather outward so that the tips are even. Select a clump of 5 or more barbs (though in careful hands, fewer may be used) and cut them at the base.

Step 2. To form a tail from the marabou tips, position the tying thread at the tailing point. Mount the marabou clump to form tails of the desired length, using only 3 or 4 tight wraps of thread.

Lift the marabou herl and advance the thread to the tie-off point.

Step 2a. If a different tail material is desired, or tail omitted entirely (as it is here), tie in the clump of barbs at the rearmost point of the body with the tips pointing toward the hook eye. Advance the tying thread to the tie-off point, binding down the marabou tips as you go.

Step 3. Grasp the marabou and pull gently, applying an even tension on all the strands. Begin winding, covering the thread with the first wrap of material.

Step 4. Continue winding, and attempt to keep the marabou in a flat, ribbonlike shape rather than allowing it to twist or gather into a single strand. Doing so will create a more uniform body with evenly spaced bands of spikey barbules.

Step 5. Tie off the marabou and clip the excess.

Method #28:
Core-twisted Herl Body

This technique employs a core of tying thread, fine wire, or other material that is twisted together with the herl to make a strong, durable body. It can be used with any number of herl strands, but larger amounts of material can become a bit unruly in handling, and the method is generally used with 5 herl strands or fewer. When a greater quantity of herl is required, **Method #29: Loop-twisted Herl Body**, p. 120, is more often employed. This twisted herl body need not be ribbed with wire or thread for durability, though ribbing may certainly be added if desired.

Twisting the material effectively shortens its length. On large flies it may be necessary to wrap and tie off one set of herl strands, then mount and wrap a second set to complete the body. On nymph patterns, some tyers prefer to use the tips of the herl for tails, and this technique is presented in the alternate sequence below.

Mixing colors of herl will produce a body with a variegated appearance, and mixing types of herl can give some interesting body textures.

The core strand can be varied as well. Tyer Gary LaFontaine touch-dubs the core strand (see **Method #37: Dusting and Touch Dubbing**, p. 127) to give an unusual mixed texture to the body. Krystal Flash, synthetic hair, round or oval tinsel, Antron yarn—indeed, almost any stranded material that will withstand twisting can be used.

Step 1. Position the tying thread at the rearmost point of the body. Mount a 6-inch length of thread or fine wire with one wrap of tying thread, and let the bobbin hang.

Note that if the herl body is the first material applied to the hook (that is, no tail or ribbing is used on the pattern), mount the tying thread near the bend by holding a 6-inch tag of thread in the left hand. This will serve as the core material and eliminate the need to tie it in separately.

Select the desired number of herl strands—we're using 4 here—of approximately equal length, and hold them so that the tips are even. Trim or break off the fine, fragile tip portions.

Mount the herl strands as a group directly over the thread wrap holding the core material.

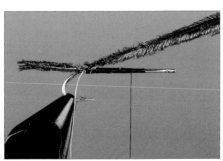

Step 1a. If the herl tips are used to form the tail, do not trim or break them. Align them carefully, and mount them at a point that will provide tails of the desired length. Use only 2 or 3 firm wraps of thread. Lift the herl away from the shank and wind the thread forward to the tie-off point.

Step 2. With a flattened thread, wrap a smooth, even underbody to the tie-off point.

Gather and gently draw down all the strands of herl and the core material simultaneously. Try to place a uniform tension on all the strands.

Grip all the strands at the butt ends, using a hackle pliers. The E-Z Hook type pictured here works especially well.

Step 2a. Some tyers prefer to use their hands instead of hackle pliers. In this case, the strands are gently pulled down and spun with the fingers, using the procedure described in the next step.

Step 3. Spin the hackle pliers to twist the materials together. They should be spun clockwise (when viewed from above), as this direction will help maintain the twist while wrapping.

The herl strands (like any material spun in this fashion) will begin to twist first next to the hook shank. When one inch or so is spun into a tight, fuzzy chenille, stop twisting and begin wrapping. Do not attempt to spin the entire strand tightly at once. Since the twist is tightest at the hook shank, excessive spinning may cause this thinnest portion of the material to break.

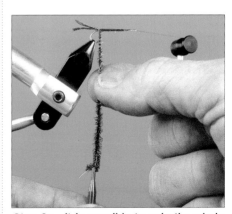

Step 3a. It is possible to spin the whole strand at once in the following way. After you've twisted about 1-2 inches of herl, pinch the herl below the twist, as shown, and begin spinning again. This procedure helps distribute the twist evenly over the length of the strand. Continue pinching and spinning, working down the strand, until all the herl is tightly twisted.

Step 4. Begin wrapping the material as you would chenille—in close turns, preening back the barbules on each wrap in order to avoid trapping any barbules against the hook shank and to place each wrap of material as close as possible to the preceding one.

Step 5. When you've wrapped the tightly twisted portion of the strand, stop and spin the hackle pliers again to twist another inch or so of material.

Step 6. Continue wrapping, pausing to twist the material as needed to produce a tight, bushy strand. Since the quill becomes wider near the butt end, it forms a greater proportion of the twisted strand, and the fuzzy barbules may begin to appear sparse at this point no matter how tightly you twist the material. If the body is not yet complete, it may be necessary to mount and wrap a second set of strands to maintain a dense, uniform body.

Method #29:
Loop-twisted Herl Body

Though it closely resembles a dubbing loop, the loop in this technique furnishes a double-strand twisting core; the herl is not completely trapped inside the loop, and the butt of herl bundle, not the loop itself, is actually spun. The method is particularly well-suited to twisting a large number of strands—5 or more—but it will work with fewer.

Ostrich herl and a thread loop are used in the following sequence, but a variety of materials can be used. Almost any type of

herl is suitable, though fine-stemmed marabou barbs must be mounted well back from the fragile tips and even then must be handled carefully. Herls of different colors and textures can be mixed to produce some interesting effects in the body. The loop can be fashioned from wire, Mylar strands such as Krystal Flash or Flashabou, or almost any strand of material strong enough to endure twisting but fine enough to prevent excessive bulk in the body.

This method produces the most durable of all herl bodies. Reinforcement is not required, though ribbing, of course, can be used if desired.

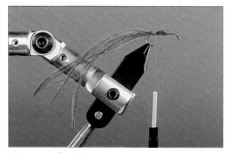

Step 1. Position the tying thread at the rearmost point of the body. Prepare the desired number of herl strands by aligning and trimming the fine tips as described above in **Method #28: Core-twisted Herl Body**, Step 1, p. 119.

Bind in the bundle of herl directly atop the rearmost thread wrap with 2 or 3 tight turns of thread. Then wrap the thread back to the mounting point of the herl.

If the herl tips are to be used as tails, prepare and tie in the herl as described in **Method #28: Core-twisted Herl Body**, Step 1a, p. 119.

Step 2. Form a loop by taking a turn of thread around your left index finger, returning the thread to the mounting point of the herl, and taking a couple of wraps around the shank. This loop should be about one inch *shorter* than the herl bundle.

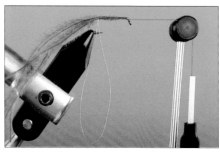

Step 2a. If you wish to form the loop from a separate material such as the wire shown here, tie in both ends of the material over the rearmost thread wrap. But again, the loop must be shorter than the herl strands.

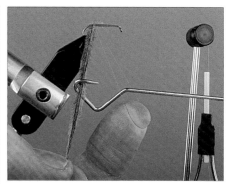

Step 3. When the loop is formed, advance the thread to the tie-off point, binding the tips of the herl to the shank as you go.

Insert the middle finger of your left hand into the loop to hold it open. Pinch the herl butts between left thumb and forefinger. Insert a dubbing hook through the loop, and grab all the herl strands, but do not release them from the left fingers.

The tool shown here is a Cal Bird Dubbing Tool, which is designed in part precisely for this application. Any dubbing hook, however, and some dubbing whirls can be used (see "Dubbing Loops," p. 129).

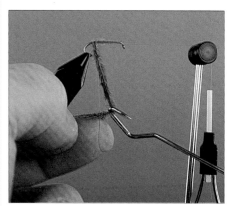

Step 4. Maintain your grasp on the herl butts, and pull them partially through the loop as shown.

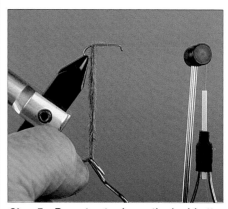

Step 5. Do not yet release the herl butts. Lower the handle of the dubbing tool as shown. Notice that the hook is pulling down on the herl strands only. The butts held in the left hand are being pulled snugly against the thread loop, which is outside the tool.

Begin spinning the tool, clockwise as viewed from above.

Step 6. After you've taken 2 or 3 turns of the tool, the herl will be locked in the thread, and you can release the butts from the left fingers.

Step 7. Wrap the body as described above in **Method #28: Core-twisted Herl Body**, Steps 3-6, p 119. Again, do not try to twist the entire length of the strands tightly all at once, especially if a wire loop is used. Rather, alternate twisting and wrapping, or use the pinch-and-twist procedure described in **Method #28**, Step 3a, p. 119.

When the body is complete, tie off the twisted strand and clip the excess.

Feather Barb Bodies

Barbs from the tail feathers of turkeys and various pheasants, primarily ring-necked and golden, are among the most widely used for wrapping bodies, since they are sufficiently long to dress hooks down to about size 12. Tails from gamebirds such as grouse are sometimes employed on smaller patterns. Tail-feather barbs, however, are fragile, and the finished bodies will easily cut or fray in the jaw of a hooked trout. Some method of reinforcement is generally used.

Tail feathers to be used for body material should come from mature birds, as they offer the longest, strongest, and most attractively marked barbs.

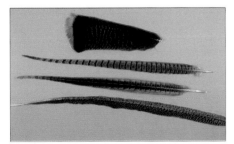

On a turkey tail feather (top), material is usually selected from lower on the quill so that the barbs used for the body contain none of the black or white bars at the feather tip, but rather are mottled throughout their length.

The barbs on a ring-necked pheasant tail (front view, second from top) tend to separate at their tips, unlike those on a turkey feather, and produce a "frayed" edge to the feather. Any of these barbs can be used, but the color of the finished body may vary depending on which are chosen. The pheasant tail feather seen from the rear (third from the top) shows a distinct dark band flanking the quill. When this portion of the barb is wrapped, the body color will change from a light brown to nearly black. To maximize the quantity of dark material in the finished body, choose barbs from nearer the tip, where the band is wider and darker. To maximize the quantity of light-brown material, choose barbs from nearer the base, where the dark band is narrow and less distinct.

The golden pheasant tail feathers (bottom) are more uniform, and the barbs evenly marked throughout the feather.

Method #30:
Flat-wrapped Barb Body

In this technique, a section of tail feather barbs are wrapped as a single, flat band to make a very thin body with subtle segmentation, and a short, spikey fuzz produced by the barbules. The low bulk makes this an excellent body for small flies. Since the material is held flat when wrapping, it isn't feasible to produce a tapered body with the material alone; any shape in the body must be created by an underbody.

Often, the tips of the barbs are used to form the tails, and the body is wrapped from the remainder of the material. This method is presented as an alternate technique below. Flat-wrapped bodies are almost always reinforced; wire is used in the following demonstration, but other materials—Krystal Flash, tying thread, fine monofilament, and so on—can also be used.

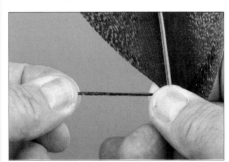

Step 1. With a dubbing needle, separate a section of barbs on the feather. The number of barbs depends mainly on fly size, though if the barb tips are to be used for tailing, the number depends as well on the number of tail fibers you wish to use. In general, 3 or 4 strands are ample for a #16 hook. Larger or smaller hooks require correspondingly more or fewer barbs.

Pinching the barb section by the base, stroke the material in a direction that will even the tips—usually toward the base of the feather stem. If using turkey (as shown here) or other feathers in which the barbs interlock, try to preen the barbs so that they

remain interlocked. The idea here is to manipulate the material to produce a flat strip of interlocking barbs with aligned tips.

Clip the section of barbs close to the quill.

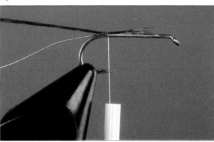

Step 2. Position the tying thread at the middle of the hook shank. Mount a length of fine wire for ribbing, and wrap the tying thread back to the rearmost point of the body, binding the wire to the shank as you go.

If a tail (omitted here) is used, mount the tailing material using only two tight wraps to secure it to the shank.

Mount the section of barbs directly atop the rearmost thread wrap, but do not mount them by the very tips. Rather, leave a tag of material about equal in length to the tail of the fly. Mounting the barbs at this slightly thicker point will prevent the fragile tips from breaking as you wrap. Try to keep the section of barbs flat, rather than bunched, when you tie them in.

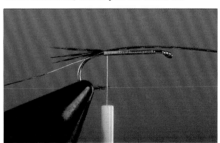

Step 2a. If you wish to fashion tails from the barb tips, mount the wire in the middle of the hook shank, and bind it down by wrapping back to the tailing point. Affixing the wire in this manner will keep thread bulk from building up at the tailing point. Mount the barbs at a point that will provide tails of the proper length. Again, attempt to keep the barb section on top of the hook shank and flat.

Tie-in the tail directly atop the rearmost thread wraps securing the wire. Use only 2 firm wraps of thread to avoid producing a bump beneath the body. When the 2 wraps are taken, lift the quill section and advance the tying thread along the shank to the tie-off point in smooth, even wraps.

Step 3. Bind in the tips with smooth, even wraps and advance the thread to the tie-off point.

Grasp the section of barbs by the base, keeping them flat between your fin-

122

gertips. Begin wrapping, and maintain an even tension on all barbs. An unequal pressure may break one of the barbs or cause others to become slack.

Take the first turn of material over the rearmost thread wraps, and wind forward smoothly in edge-to-edge, non-overlapping wraps.

Step 4. Bind and clip the butts at the tie-off point.

Counterwrap the ribbing material. It is important to wrap the wire in a direction opposite that of the body material (see **Method #2: Counter-ribbing**, p. 92) so that it overwraps and secures the barbs instead of slipping between them.

When the rib is complete, tie off the ribbing material and trim the excess.

Method #31:
Twisted Barb Body

This technique produces a slightly thicker, more durable body, with distinct segmentations. Twisting the material, however, does shorten its effective length, and the barbs will not yield a body as long as can be obtained with **Method #30: Flat-wrapped Barb Body**, p. 121. You can compensate by using a greater number of barbs which will produce a longer, but thicker, body. Or you can create the body in stages—twisting, wrapping, and tying off one set of barbs, then mounting and continuing the body with another set.

This method permits many variations. A simple twisted barb body is considerably more durable than a flat-wrapped one, though many tyers still choose to reinforce it in some way. It can be counterwrapped with a rib as described in the **Method #30: Flat-wrapped Barb Body**, p. 121. Or the barbs can be twisted around a thread or wire core, as shown below. Since this technique is virtually identical to tying a twisted herl body, the instructions here are abbreviated. Readers should consult **Method #28: Core-twisted Herl Body**, p. 119 for more detailed instructions. Again, the barbs may be incorporated as tails or used in conjunction with a separate tailing material.

The most famous version of this technique was used by Frank Sawyer to tie the popular and effective Pheasant Tail Nymph. Sawyer used fine wire, instead of thread, to dress the entire fly. The barb tips were used as tails, and the barbs twisted with the wire to fashion the body.

In the following sequence, the barb tips are used for tailing and then twisted around a thread core for the body. With other dressings or materials, however, you can omit the tails and substitute wire, Krystal Flash, monofilament or other material strands for the core as circumstances or preferences dictate. The tying technique is the same in any case.

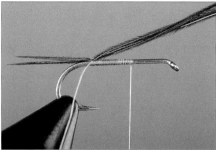

Step 1. Mount the tying thread in the middle of the hook shank, leaving a 6-inch tag. Wind the thread to the tailing point, trapping the tag against the hook shank as you go.

Mount the barbs to form a tail as described in **Method #30: Flat-wrapped Barb Body**, Step 2a, p. 121. For this type of body, however, it is not necessary to keep the barb section flat. Rather, mount it as a bundle of material.

Step 2. Gently draw the barbs and thread tag downward, and clip them at the base with hackle pliers or an E-Z Hook. Spin the material (clockwise as viewed from above). Take only a few twists—barbs are fragile at the tip and easily broken. Spin the material just enough to twist the top ¼" or so, then wrap the spun barbs on the shank, covering the rearmost thread wrap.

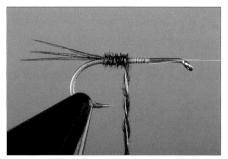

Step 3. Continue forming the body by alternately twisting and wrapping. Do not try to spin a long section of material all at once or it may break.

Step 4. Wrap to the tie-off point, bind down, and clip the butts.

On longer hooks, it may be necessary to mount a second bundle of barbs to complete the body.

Feather Bodies

The distinguishing feature of this dressing style is that the feather barbs are not removed from the quill before they are wrapped. The most widely used feathers for creating bodies of this type are marabou and CDC. Other types of body or flank feathers, however—mallard, teal, wood duck—may prove suitable for the following methods, though there appears to be little experimentation in this direction among tyers.

On marabou bodies of this style, blood feathers are used (see "Marabou," p. 11). Commonly, the tip of the blood feather is used to fashion the tail, and the remainder wrapped forward to create the body—an efficient technique for dressing Woolly Buggers, where the marabou replaces chenille as a body material, and for damselfly nymphs. On smaller patterns, like damsel nymphs, one feather may wrap an entire body; on larger flies, two or more feathers wrapped in sequence may be necessary.

To write about marabou bodies is to bump up against yet another ambiguity in fly-tying terminology. In the techniques detailed below, the marabou barbs are tied in as a bundle with the quill attached and wrapped to form the body. It is, however, possible to wrap a marabou feather much like a hackle feather, winding the quill around the shank so that a collar of barbs encircles the shank. If the entire shank is wrapped in this manner, the result might be called a marabou "body." It might also reasonably be called a palmered marabou "hackle." Given the overall impression of the material, long and flowing toward the hook bend, it might also reasonably be called a marabou "wing," and indeed it is termed so by tyer Jack Gartside who devised this use of marabou for winging his Soft-Hackle Streamer. In this book, it is termed a marabou "hackle" since the dressing technique is virtually identical to other hackling methods (see **Method #6: Marabou Collar Hackle**, p. 353).

Whole CDC feathers may be wrapped to create dry-fly bodies. Perhaps most notable among these is the caddis pattern developed by Slovenian tyer Marjan Fratnick. CDC feathers, however, are quite short, and a single feather will wrap only a relatively small hook; larger bodies require more than one feather.

Method #32:
Flat-wrapped Feather Body

We're using CDC to demonstrate this technique, though marabou may also be used, in which case the tips of the feather may be used for tailing the fly (see **Method #33: Twisted Feather Body**, Step 2).

Step 1. When using CDC, selecting the proper feather is important. Choose a feather with long barbs that extend to the tip of the quill in order to give the longest possible length to the body.

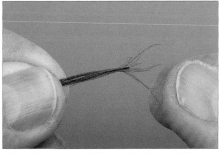

Step 2. Preen all the barbs toward the tip of the feather. Pinch the feather by the very tip, trapping all the longest barbs between your left fingers.

With your right hand, begin at the butt of the feather, preening back all the shorter barbs. When you're finished, the barbs pinched in the left fingertips should be very nearly the same length.

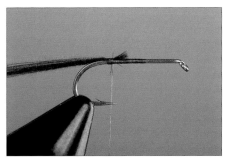

Step 3. Position the tying thread at the rearmost point of the body, and tie in the feather by the very tip as shown. Advance the thread to the body tie-off point.

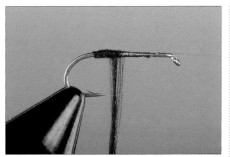

Step 4. Preen the short barbs toward the feather base and pinch them against the quill to keep them out of the way when wrapping the feather.

Wrap the feather forward in adjacent, edge-to-edge wraps. Make certain that the material covers the hook shank with no gaps, but in order to maximize body length, do not overlap the material.

Step 5. Bind down the feather at the tie-off point and clip the excess.

Method #33:
Twisted Feather Body

Twisting the feather as you wrap gives greater strength and bulk to the body. It does, however, shorten the effective length of the material, and so more than one feather may be required to complete the body. The technique yields an unusually soft, chenille-like body with a lifelike appearance. Here we're using marabou to tie both the tail and body. To dress a body only, tie in the marabou as described in **Method #32: Flat-wrapped Feather Body**, Step 3.

Step 1. The marabou blood feather is prepared in much the same way as the CDC feather shown above in **Method #32: Flat-wrapped Feather Body**, Steps 1-2. Stroke

all the barbs toward the tip; in the left fingers, pinch all the barbs that reach the feather tip. With the right fingers, preen the shorter barbs back toward the base of the feather. The left fingers should now be pinching a clump of barbs that are equal in length. Note that dampening the feather slightly when preparing it in this fashion will help keep the soft barbs under control.

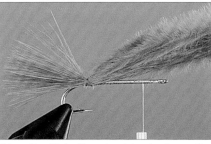

Step 2. Strip the short barbs from the stem. Position the tying thread at the tailing point.

Mount the marabou on top of the hook shank to form a tail of the desired length. Tie in the marabou with 3 or 4 very tight, adjacent wraps of thread.

Lift the feather and advance the thread to the tie-off point.

Step 3. Grasp the butt of the feather quill, and twist it slightly. Twist gently and only enough to consolidate the barbs into a bundle and to flare the barbules.

Step 4. Wrap the feather forward, pausing to retwist it as necessary to maintain a uniform appearance and texture in the body.

Step 5. Bind down the feather at the tie-off point. If necessary, mount a second feather (with tips pointing toward the hook eye), and continue wrapping the body.

Dubbed Bodies

The term "dubbing" refers both to a material and a set of techniques used to apply it to a hook. The dubbing material itself may be composed of natural furs, synthetic fibers or filaments, clipped feather barbs, or any combination of these, while the dubbing process most often (but not always) involves twisting such materials around a core strand that is subsequently wrapped around the shank.

Dubbing materials vary widely, from short fibers to long ones, soft to stiff, fine to coarse, and the texture of the material governs the appearance of the finished fly body and, to a certain extent, the techniques by which the dubbing is most easily handled. Fine, soft materials are quite compressible and compact easily when dubbed, giving the tyer good control for producing smooth, tapered bodies, or well-defined segmentation. Stiff or coarse materials, especially short-fibered ones such as hare's ear, produce rougher, bristled, "spikey" bodies, of a somewhat less uniform appearance.

Dubbing is one of the oldest of fly-tying materials, and in its long history, tyers have devised a number of useful and unusual techniques for dressing it. Related groups of these techniques are presented in the sections that follow. In many of these methods, the tyer has options in handling the material that influence the shape and texture of the finished body. To avoid repetition in the instructional sequences, these options are illustrated at the end of each related group of tying methods.

Preparing Dubbing Materials

Probably a majority of tyers use pre-packaged dubbing materials, and these require no preparation, with two exceptions. Many synthetic dubbings are manufactured in long strands, which can be inconvenient to use; the fiber length makes it difficult to control the amount of dubbing material being applied to the thread. They can be handled more easily by pinching off a small piece and cutting randomly through the clump 3 or 4 times with tying scissors to shorten the fibers and simplify the application of precise quantities of material. And for very small flies, almost any dubbing material must be cut in this fashion to permit spinning the tiny amounts required on small hooks.

Many tyers prefer to prepare their own dubbing from furs and hairs on patches of hide. The fur must first be cut from the skin with scissors or a single-edge razor blade. Cutting small pinches of fur from the hide will allow you to remove the longer, stiffer guard hairs for a finer dubbing of underfur (see "Furs and Hairs," p. 1). Leaving some, or all, of the guard hairs mixed with underfur will give a somewhat rougher texture to the dubbed body.

Once the desired amount of fur is removed from the hide, it must be mixed to ensure a uniform texture and color throughout, and to randomize the fibers for easier application to the tying thread.

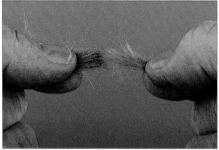

To mix small quantities of dubbing, pinch a ball of shaved fur between the thumb and forefinger of the right hand. With the thumb and forefinger of the left hand, pull the clump of fur in half. Stack the two halves into a single clump, and repeat the process, pulling and stacking until the dubbing is thoroughly blended. Make certain that there are no clumps or pills of material, as they will interfere with the application of the dubbing to the thread.

Natural or synthetic yarns, silk or nylon floss, CDC, marabou—almost any strand or fiber can be made into dubbing as well. Simply cut the material to the desired length, and mix as you would fur. If the material is composed of twisted fibers, like yarn, first fray the end with scissor points, a dubbing needle, or a fine comb; then cut the fibers to length and mix.

Rather than using dubbing that has been dyed to a uniform color, many tyers prefer to blend materials of different shades to better approximate the appearance of the living insect or to reproduce the subtle highlights and glints of color that are often characteristic of the naturals. Interesting and lifelike effects can also be produced by combining materials of different textures. Color-blending small amounts of dubbing can be accomplished by using the "pull-and-stack" method described above.

This process, however, is tedious and time-consuming with larger amounts of material (though it can be done), and two alternate procedures are commonly employed. Many tyers use a water-mixing process. Fill a quart jar about half full of water, and add the dubbing to it. Close the jar and shake vigorously until the fibers are well mixed and no clumps of material are visible. Then strain the mixture through a sieve, screen, or piece of cheesecloth, and spread the dubbing out to dry.

Other tyers prefer the quicker results obtained with a commercially available "electric dubbing mixer"—really no more than a small coffee or spice grinder. Put the material into the mixing container, and blend in short pulses. The material is more easily blended and removed if the mixing container is first treated with an anti-static spray or wiped with an anti-static cloth, both of which are sold as laundry products. Larger amounts of material can be mixed in a kitchen blender, though best results are obtained by using a small volume (usually 8-ounce) container that is available as an accessory for most blenders. Large quantities of material can be blended dry, but smaller quantities may require the addition of a little water in the blender to ensure thorough mixing. Note, however, that these devices chop, as well as mix, the fibers, and thus may change the texture of the original material.

Direct Dubbing

Direct dubbing involves twisting or spinning the dubbing material around a core strand, usually tying thread; it is the most common of all dubbing techniques and suitable for all but the very stiffest fibers.

To help the dubbing fibers grip the core strand and spin readily, wax is often used. Stiff fibers, particularly short ones, resist twisting, and a thin film of wax on the thread will help them adhere. Waxes are available in various consistencies. "Hard" waxes provide the least adhesion, but also leave the least residue on your fingertips; it's best suited to softer or finer-textured dubbing materials. Very coarse or stiff dubbings may require a "soft" or tacky wax, which adheres well to both the fibers and the core strand and simplifies spinning the material. In either case, apply wax sparingly; use as little as you can get away with.

As explained in "Threads," p. 17, some tying thread is "pre-waxed." The type and quantity of wax used on these threads are rarely such that they provide much assistance in dubbing. Instead, the function of the wax is primarily to help consolidate and lubricate the filaments that compose the thread.

Many tyers, however, avoid using wax with all but the most stubborn materials. While wax gives good adhesion between material and thread, it tends to rub off on fingertips, giving an undesirable stickiness that interferes with handling other materials in subsequent steps of dressing the fly. Most fibers, particularly soft ones, can be dubbed without using wax. Moistening the fingertips slightly will help provide some grip on the dubbing when spinning without wax. On dry-fly bodies, a tiny dab of paste floatant smeared on the fingertips accomplishes the same purpose and helps waterproof the body at the same time.

Regardless of whether wax is used or not, a couple general principles govern efficient direct dubbing. First, apply dubbing sparsely, in small pinches. Thick clumps of material do not adhere firmly to the thread and do not spin well. Second, do not dub along more thread than it takes to wrap the body. It's easier to add dubbing to complete the body than it is to remove excess material.

Method #34:

Thread-core Direct Dubbing

Twisting dubbing material around a core of tying thread is one of the most basic and widely used procedures in fly tying, yet nearly every tyer approaches the process in a slightly different way, using some small variation in material handling or finger placement. Even so, there are three basic approaches to the process.

These 3 methods are shown below, each identified by a number/letter combination in which the number specifies the tying sequence and the letter indicates the step within that sequence. That is, Steps 1a-1f constitute one methods; Steps 2a-2d another, and so on.

The first method involves spinning each pinch of material as it is applied to the thread. This approach is necessary if an unwaxed thread is used, though it is suitable as well for a waxed thread. It also gives good control over the body shape. Since each pinch of material is twisted before the next is applied, the tyer can see the dubbing strand taking shape in increments and can add or subtract material on each subsequent application of dubbing to fashion a body of the desired profile.

The approach shown in the second sequence below involves applying all the dubbing material to the thread before the fibers are twisted. It requires a waxed thread to hold each pinch of dubbing in place while the next is added. This technique is perhaps slightly faster than the preceding one because of the efficiency in handling the material. And because all the material is twisted continuously down the thread, it is less prone to produce irregularities in the thickness of the dubbed strand.

The last approach involves twisting the material as it is drawn directly from a clump held in the fingers. The primary advantage of this approach is speed, and it is especially well-suited to covering a long length of thread with a relatively thin layer of dubbing. It is, however, practical only with medium-to long-fibered dubbings since it relies on fiber length to maintain a continuous skein of material between the clump of dubbing held in the fingers and the tying thread. And because it takes a somewhat sensitive touch with the dubbing material to maintain a skein of the proper consistency, this technique takes a bit more practice than the previous two methods.

In all of these techniques, body shape, density, and texture can be controlled as explained in "Controlling the Shape and Texture of Direct-dubbed Bodies," p. 128.

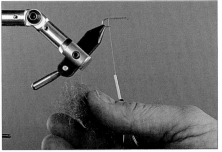

Step 1a. Position the tying thread a few wraps ahead of the point at which the fly body begins, and leave about 4 inches of bare thread between the bobbin and hook shank.

Hold the bobbin in your palm as shown, leaving thumb and forefinger free to hold a clump of dubbing material. For very stiff dubbing material, wax the thread as shown in Step 2a.

Step 1b. With the thumb of your left hand, "tease" a small amount of dubbing over the top of your right forefinger. This teasing motion loosens the dubbing, making it less dense and compacted, and simplifies applying small quantities sparsely to the thread.

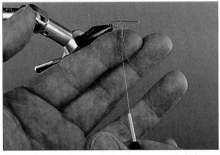

Step 1c. Pull the bobbin very slightly to apply a small amount of tension on the tying thread. Pick up the teased dubbing in your left hand and press it against the back of thread, just below the hook shank. The thread should cross the middle of the pad of your forefinger.

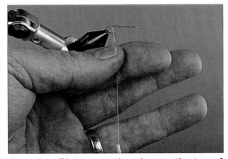

Step 1d. Place your thumb over the top of the thread, pinching the material. Now roll or "spin" the dubbing by pinching it tightly and sliding the thumb in one direction and

the forefinger in the opposite direction. The material should twist around the thread, forming a yarn-like strand. If the material has not compacted into a yarn, reposition your fingers and repeat the rolling motion. It is important to roll the material in *one* direction only. Do not spin it back and forth.

The dubbing can be twisted around the thread either clockwise or counterclockwise, but the two directions will produce slightly different results. Dubbing spun clockwise (when viewed from above) follows the direction of twist in the thread. When wrapped around a hook, the thread will twist, locking in the dubbing fibers and producing a somewhat tighter body. Dubbing twisted around the thread in a counterclockwise direction produces the opposite effect, loosening slightly when the strand is wrapped and giving a less compacted body. Often, the differences are small; what is most important is that all the dubbing be twisted in the same direction, either all clockwise or all counterclockwise.

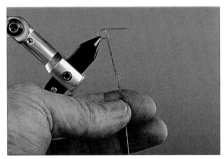

Step 1e. Tease out another pinch of dubbing and position it directly below the first. Roll the dubbing as described in Step 1d, making certain to spin the material in the same direction. The dubbing should be sparsely and evenly distributed, with no visible gaps between the two pinches of dubbing. It should appear as a single, uniform, yarn-like strand.

If you see thin spots, apply a bit more dubbing. If there are clumps of material on the thread, tease them apart and redistribute the material uniformly. Continue this process until the desired amount of thread is covered.

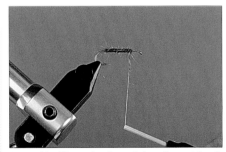

Step 1f. Wrap the bare tying thread back to the rearmost point of the body.

Wrap the dubbed thread forward to create a body of the desired profile. Dubbing twisted over a thread core gives the tyer some latitude in wrapping and allows compensating for some inconsistencies in the dubbed strand. Normally, the dubbed thread is wrapped forward in tight, adjacent wraps. If however, there is a thin spot in the dubbing that produces a narrowing of the body, a second wrap of material can be taken directly atop the first to help fill out this portion of the body profile. Likewise, a thick spot on the dubbed thread can be wrapped forward in a more open spiral to "stretch" or elongate the dubbing to avoid building a bulky spot in the body. And as explained in "Controlling the Shape and Texture of Direct-dubbed Bodies," p. 128, the dubbed thread can be wrapped back and forth across the hook shank to build body bulk or taper.

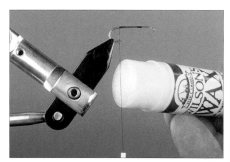

Step 2a. In this approach, all the dubbing is applied before any material is twisted, and thus it's necessary to prepare the thread by lightly stroking it with fly-tying wax. Use wax sparingly, leaving no clumps or beads of wax on the thread. Coverage should be thin and uniform.

Step 2b. Tease out a sparse pinch of dubbing as explained in Step 1c, and touch it to the back of the tying thread. Since wax has been applied, the dubbing will adhere to the thread, allowing you to release it and prepare another pinch of material.

Step 2c. Repeat Step 2b, taking another pinch of dubbing and touching it to the thread directly below the first pinch. It should adhere to the wax and remain in place.

Continue adding small amounts of dubbing, each pinch very slightly overlapping the one above it, until the desired length of thread is covered.

Step 2d. When dubbing has been added to the desired length of thread, pinch the material nearest the hook shank between the left thumb and forefinger. Roll the dubbing as described above in Step 1d.

When the first section of material is compacted around the thread, move your fingers down to the next section of material, and twist it in the same direction as the first. Continue working down the thread, spinning one section of material at a time until all the dubbing is twisted onto the thread. The dubbed strand should be uniform in appearance, with no thin spots or clumps.

Wrap the body as explained in Step 1f.

Step 3a. This "twist-and-feed" method requires a dubbing with medium to long fibers. While it can be accomplished with an unwaxed thread, most tyers will find it easier with a waxed thread, at least until some proficiency is acquired.

Begin by teasing out a light skein of material about 1" long. Position the tip of the teased dubbing against the back of the tying thread, as shown, holding the skein of fibers at about 45 degrees to the thread.

Note that the right fingertips are quite close to the thread in this technique.

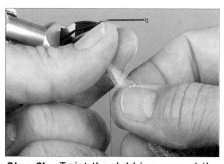

Step 3b. Twist the dubbing around the thread as explained in Step 1d. Pinch the material firmly and twist it tightly, since this technique is not well-suited to repeatedly spinning the material to tighten the dubbing.

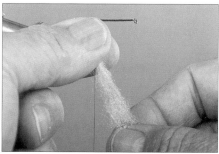

Step 3c. Maintain the pinch on the dubbed thread with the left fingers, and gently pull the clump of dubbing away from the tying thread, drawing out more dubbing fibers. If necessary, you can use the left fingers to help pull material from the clump to form a skein of the desired density.

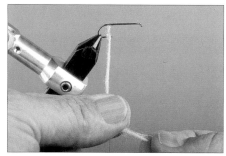

Step 3d. Spin this next portion of the skein around the thread. Maintaining a pinch on the thread, draw out another skein of dubbing.

Continue twisting and feeding the dubbing until the desired length of thread is covered. When enough dubbing is applied, pull the clump of material away from the thread, breaking the skein, and twist the last loose fibers around the thread.

Method #35:

Wire-core Direct Dubbing

Though not commonly practiced, dubbing can be applied to wire, oval tinsel, or almost any threadlike material, and some very interesting effects can be obtained. Dubbing on wire, as shown in the main sequence, adds strength, flash, and some weight to a fly pattern, and is particularly well adapted to smaller flies. Virtually any type of wire—gold, silver, colored craft wires—in almost any diameter can be used.

Using oval tinsel, shown in the alternate sequence, produces a bulkier but lighter body with a muted metallic glitter beneath the translucent color of the dubbing.

The trick with both core materials is to dub sparsely and loosely; a thick, tight dubbing will completely cover the core, eliminating any flash in the fly body and thus negating one of the advantages of a wire or tinsel core.

Techniques for both short, coarse dubbings and soft, long-fibered ones are presented. Body shape and texture can be altered using a number of the options described in "Controlling the Shape and Texture of Direct-dubbed Bodies," p. 128.

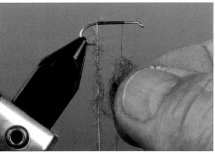

Step 1. Here dubbing is applied to a gold wire. Bind the wire to the hook shank at the frontmost point of the body, and spiral the thread to the tie-off point. Lay a thin film of very tacky wax on the wire.

For short-fibered dubbing, like the hare's ear shown here, pinch off a small quantity of material, and touch the dubbing to the wire; it will adhere to the wax. Do not twist or spin the dubbing.

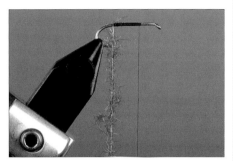

Step 2. Continue adding small pinches of fur until the desired length of wire is covered.

Step 3. Wind the body forward as usual. Place the wraps of wire close together for a denser body (pictured here), or wind it in an open spiral for a sparser one.

Step 1a. Very soft, long-fibered dubbings create a different effect. Here, the core is a medium oval tinsel that has been waxed; the dubbing is a superfine poly.

Again, touch a very sparse pinch of dubbing to the waxed core. Continue adding small pinches of material until the desired length of tinsel is covered.

Step 2a. Roll the dubbing very lightly and loosely around the core. Do not twist the tinsel, merely spin the dubbing around it. Properly applied, the material should form a soft "haze" around the tinsel core.

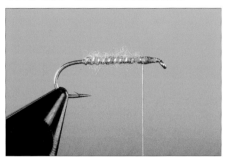

Step 3a. Wind the body, closely spacing the wraps for a dense body, or loosely spiraling them (as shown here) for a sparser one.

Method #36:
Lead-core Direct Dubbing

One of the more unusual versions of direct dubbing involves applying material to a lead wire, thus fashioning a dubbed and weighted body in one operation. The objective here is to cover the wire with dubbing so that the lead does not show through. It requires a light touch since the lead wire itself cannot be twisted or it will break. Thinner-diameter lead wires are more fragile than thicker ones and more difficult to work with. Softer, longer-fibered dubbings are easier to manipulate in this technique than coarse, short materials.

This approach is especially useful in dubbing nymph thoraxes on patterns where both bulk and weight are desired in this portion of the body.

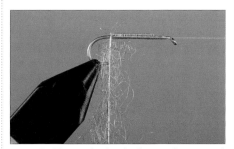

Step 1. Mount the lead wire as shown, and advance the thread to the tie-off point. Wax the wire. Apply small pinches of dubbing until the desired length of wire is covered.

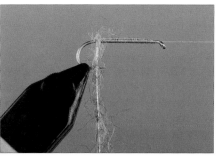

Step 2. Beginning near the hook shank, roll the dubbing (but not the lead wire) to distribute the fibers around the core. Work down the wire until all the dubbing is loosely twisted around the core.

Step 3. Wrap the body; tie off and clip the dubbing strand.

Method #37:
Dusting and Touch-Dubbing

These two approaches to dubbing are very simple and useful methods for applying material to a thread core, though they do not appear to be in general use among tyers.

Dusting, shown in Step 1, is unusual in that material is applied by spinning a waxed thread rather than the dubbing. The dubbing material used for this method must be finely chopped; long strands will give poor results. Coarse materials can be used, but softer ones adhere more readily to the thread. The resulting body is rather sparse with a spikey appearance, and it is particularly useful on smaller patterns. (Two similar techniques for dusting wire cores are presented in **Method #46: Single-wire Spun Dubbing**, p. 135, and **Method #47: Double-wire Spun Dubbing**, p. 135, where a vise is used to spin the core since twisting fine-diameter wire with the fingers alone is quite difficult.)

Touch-dubbing is similar to dusting in that the dubbing is applied to thread using the adhesive power of the wax only. When short fibers are used—the type of material advocated by tyer Gary LaFontaine and shown in Step 1a—the dubbing is generally not twisted after it is applied; it produces a somewhat bushy body when wrapped. LaFontaine also advocates touch-dubbed thread as a core strand for twisting herl, as explained in **Method #28: Core-twisted Herl Body**, p. 119.

The approach shown in alternate Step 2a, using a longer-fibered dubbing, is favored by tyer Al Beatty for applying the material to the thread. It is then twisted with the fingers in the conventional fashion. Soft dubbings with medium-length fibers give the best results; stiff, coarse dubbings adhere poorly when they are brushed against a waxed thread.

The techniques are demonstrated using tying thread, but other core materials such as tinsel or Krystal Flash can also be used.

In all of these techniques, the dubbing fibers are distributed rather uniformly on the thread; any taper is introduced into the body during wrapping, as explained in "Controlling the Shape and Texture of Direct-dubbed Bodies," p. 128.

Step 1. Attach the thread to the hook and apply a tacky wax. If necessary, use your fingers to smooth the wax into a thin, uniform film on the thread.

With the thumb and forefinger of your right hand, grasp the tying thread about 3" below the hook shank. Spin the thread *back and forth* between your fingers, and lightly touch it with the dubbing. Continue spinning the thread, and move the clump of dubbing slowly down the tying thread to coat it with a uniform layer of dubbing fibers.

Because the wax alone holds the fibers, only a limited amount of dubbing can be applied this way. Once the layer of wax is covered with material, no more fibers will adhere to that portion of the thread.

Wrapping the body with the strand shown will produce a somewhat bushy body. If a tighter body is desired, roll the dubbed thread between your fingers, in one direction only, to compact the fibers around the thread.

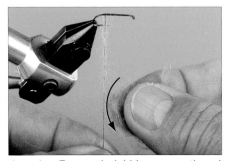

Step 1a. For touch-dubbing, wax a thread as described in Step 1.

With the right hand, brush the dubbing downward against the thread; the fibers will adhere to the wax. To make sure that all sides of the thread are evenly covered with material, either brush the dubbing around the perimeter of the thread or use the left fingers to rotate the thread a half-turn or so in either direction as the material is applied.

Step 2a. Soft, longer-fibered dubbings are applied exactly as in Step 1a. Note, however, that such dubbing adheres more loosely to the thread, and must be twisted using the technique explained in **Method #34: Thread-core Direct Dubbing**, Step 2d, p. 126.

Controlling Body Texture and Shape in Direct Dubbing

There are a number of ways in which the texture, density, and profile of the fly body are governed. The following photographs show options, variations, or simple one-step procedures that give the tyer control over the shape and appearance of the finished body.

Dubbing that is twisted tightly and compactly around the thread will produce a relatively dense body with a well-defined shape.

Dubbing that is spun more loosely will give a less dense, translucent body with an irregular surface.

You can add bristle or spike to any body by picking out some strands of dubbing with a needle, small brush, or a dubbing teaser, a tool designed specifically for this purpose. A strip of the "hook" portion of a "hook-and-loop" material such as Velcro also does an admirable job.

On the fly shown here, dubbing fibers have been picked out on the underside of the body using a dubbing needle.

Many fly patterns call for bodies that are tapered to match the profile of the natural insect. Body shape can be controlled in a number of ways.

If the dubbing is applied uniformly along a thread core, form the taper as you make the body by winding the dubbing back over itself slightly to increase the diameter at the thicker portions of the body. The upper hook illustrates the taper for a typical mayfly body, the lower hook for a caddis.

This technique, however, is not well-suited to dubbing strands with wire or tinsel cores that show through the dubbed fibers. These should be wrapped in evenly spaced, non-overlapping turns to maintain a uniform appearance of the core material, and tapering the body is best accomplished by one of the following methods.

You can shape the body by varying the quantity of dubbing applied to the thread, gradually increasing (or decreasing) the amount of material to make a tapered yarn.

On roughly dubbed or bristled bodies, you can use scissors to trim the body to the desired shape.

10

For very small flies, size 20 and beyond, you can create tapered bodies by taking advantage of the natural taper of furs still attached to the hide.

Cut a tiny pinch of fur from the skin and remove the guard hairs. Notice that the material is thick at the base, narrowing to fine tips. Align the fur parallel to the thread. Placing the fur tips nearest the hook shank, as shown here, will produce a typical mayfly-body taper. Putting the fur butts nearest the shank will give the reverse taper typical of caddis.

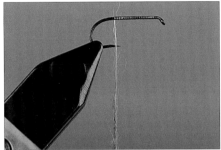

Maintaining this orientation, twist the fibers around the thread. The resulting strand of dubbing will maintain the natural taper of the fur clump and produce a tapered body when wrapped.

Dubbing Loops

Dubbing-loop (or "spinning-loop") methods can be used with any material, but they are a distinct advantage 1) when handling coarse, wiry, long-fibered dubbings, 2) when forming thick, bulky bodies that require large amounts of material, 3) when a very tight yarn is desired for producing distinct segmentation on the fly body, 4) or conversely, when forming very bushy, brushlike bodies. The double thickness of thread employed in this technique adds extra bulk, making it generally less suitable for small flies or bodies with a very thin profile.

Dubbing loops can, to a limited degree, be spun using the fingers alone, but the high degree of twist required to produce the tightly spun bodies for which dubbing loops are generally valued cannot be achieved using the fingertips alone. Almost universally, tyers use some type of spinning tool. A number of such devices—of distinctly different designs—are commercially available, but you can use a hook-type or E-Z Hook hackle pliers, a hooked piece of stiff wire (a half-straightened paper clip, for instance), or a crochet hook. Tools made especially for the purpose, however, are generally more convenient to use.

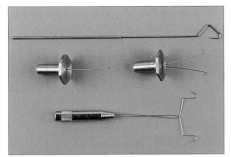

Tools designed specifically to form and spin dubbing loops can make the procedure simpler and more efficient. Shown here are a few different tool designs.

At the top is a Cal Bird hook, a simple and effective design that is also useful in forming herl bodies as explained in **Method #29: Loop-twisted Herl Body**, p. 120.

In the middle are two dubbing whirls, a single-hook type (left) and a double-arm type (right). They are manufactured with heavy bases and are designed to be spun, a bit like a top, rather than twirled between the fingers like a dubbing hook.

At the bottom is a double-armed dubbing twister. Like the double-arm whirl, this tool uses a pair of wire spreader arms to hold the loop open for inserting material. When the dubbing is positioned inside the loop, the tool is pulled downward; the arms close and trap the dubbing between the loop threads.

Regardless of the tool, however, a few basic principles govern the construction of dubbing loops. As a rule, don't attempt to form loops more than 5 or 6 inches in length. On excessively long loops, the thread will twist unevenly, and the resulting strand of dubbing will not be uniform in texture. For large bodies, use 2 shorter loops rather than a single long one. Dub the rear of the body and tie off the loop; form a new loop and complete the body. Second, once the dubbing is tightly compacted, wrap the body. Additional twisting can cause the thread to break. When dubbing very coarse materials, or applying large quantities of dubbing, use a heavy tying thread—3/0 or heavier—as these can withstand more twisting. Finally, try to apply only as much dubbing as you need. Ideally, the last bit of dubbing will be used on the last wrap of the body, leaving only bare thread on the loop to be bound down and clipped. A neater, more compact tie-off will result.

Many variations of the dubbing loop are possible, as the loop can be fashioned from a material other than tying thread. Perhaps the most popular of these is wire, which adds both weight and flash to the fly. When using wire cores, however, many tyers prefer to construct dubbing brushes using one of the techniques shown in "Dubbing Brushes," p. 133, since these procedures are generally a bit simpler and can produce strands of material long enough for two or more flies. Still wire-core dubbing loops are frequently used and make quite pleasing bodies. Other materials—tinsels, Mylars such as Krystal Flash, Antron yarn, and so on can also be used to form the core inside which the dubbing fibers are twisted, as noted in **Method #72: Twisted-tinsel Body**, p. 160.

Method #38:
Trap-loop Dubbing

The trap loop, formed to pinch or trap dubbing material between the two thread strands, is the most basic and widely used type of dubbing loop. Any of the dubbing-loop tools described above can be used to twist the loop; we're using an ordinary crochet hook in the following demonstration.

Steps 1-2 show one of the more common ways of forming the loop. This method is fast, but the loop threads actually meet atop the hook shank; beneath the shank, there is a gap between the threads. Dubbing material positioned in this area may not be effectively trapped and held in place since the threads do not pinch it tightly. Steps 1a-2a show an alternate technique in which the loop threads meet beneath the shank; finer or shorter dubbing materials in particular are more tightly held.

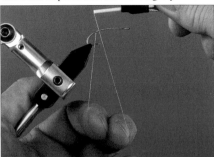

Step 1. Wrap the tying thread to the rearmost point of the body. Pull off about 8-12" of thread from the bobbin, pass it around the first two fingers of the left hand to form a loop, and bring the thread back to the hook shank.

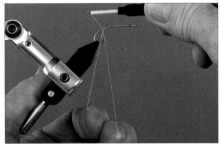

Step 2. Keep your fingers in the loop and secure the tying thread to the shank directly on top of the other end of the loop.

Spiral the thread forward to the body tie-off point.

Step 3. Apply a little wax to one side of the loop. Take the proper amount of dubbing and distribute it along the waxed thread. You can spread it evenly (as illustrated) for a uniform dubbing yarn, or vary the quantity along the thread to make a tapered body.

Step 2. Form a loop around your fingers using either approach shown in **Method #38: Trap-loop Dubbing**, p. 129.
  Spin the second dubbing material on the bare thread.

Step 3. Twist the dubbing to the desired degree of compactness. Spinning loosely will form a body with alternating bands of color; a tight twist will blend the colors for a more variegated appearance.

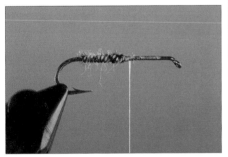

Step 4. Wrap the body, tie off the strand, and clip the excess.

Fur Chenilles

Dubbing loops can be used to spin unblended fur cut directly from the hide. The fur is carefully positioned in the loop so that both guard hairs and underfur are intact and placed perpendicular to the thread. When the loop is spun the hair flares evenly to create a cylindrical strand of dubbing so uniform that it resembles a length of manufactured chenille.

Fur chenilles are typically used for bodies on larger nymph or streamer patterns, as long-fibered hairs are easiest to handle. Chenilles suitable for smaller flies can be made from short-fibered furs such as mole, though these are somewhat fussier to handle. With practice, however, it can be done. Narrow-diameter chenilles for smaller flies can also be made by inserting only the tips of the fur into the dubbing loop, though such bodies will be composed almost entirely of

guard hairs and thus be somewhat spikey. Bodies spun from fur chenilles can also be trimmed to a variety of shapes as shown in **Method #67: Clipped Bodies**, p. 155.

There are a number of options in mounting and manipulating the dubbing material in order to vary the size, shape, and texture of the body. These alternative procedures, presented as a group in "Controlling Body Texture and Shape of Fur Chenille Bodies," p. 133, can be used with any of the methods in this section.

Method #41:

Fur Chenille Dubbing Loop

The technique shown here is the most basic method of forming fur-strip chenilles. Though not difficult, handling the fur strip takes a light touch and a bit of practice since the fur must be clipped from the hide and transferred to the loop while maintaining the original position of all the fibers. Handling the fur can be simplified by using a paper clamp, as shown in the main sequence, but longer furs can be handled using only your fingers, as shown in the alternate sequence.

A version of this technique can also be used to form hair hackles as explained in **Method #22: Spun-hair Collar Hackle**, p. 370.

Step 1. Take a patch of hide and fold it in half. Use a dubbing needle to tease up a single, sparse row of fur fibers. With your fingers or a small comb, preen the fibers to a smooth, uniform row that stands outward, perpendicular to the hide.

Step 2. With a paper clamp, trap the fibers about halfway down their length. Take care not to bend or disturb the fibers when pinching them in the jaws of the paper clamp.

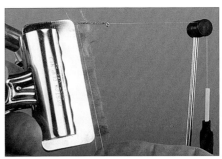

Step 3. Cut the trapped strip of fur close to the hide.
  Form a loop using either procedure described in **Method #38: Trap-loop Dubbing**, p. 129. Position the fur strip between the threads and pull the loop closed.

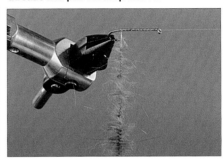

Step 4. Spin the loop to create a bushy fur chenille.

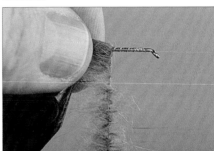

Step 5. As you wrap the fur chenille forward, preen the fur on previous wraps backward to avoid trapping the longer fibers beneath subsequent winds.

Step 6. Shown here is the finished body.

Step 1a. Long-fibered furs can be trapped by forming "scissors" with the first two fingers of the left hand, as shown.

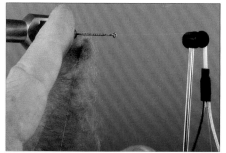

Step 2a. Clip the fur and insert the butts of the strip into the loop as shown.

Method #42:
Hide-strip Fur Chenille

Fur chenilles can be formed by using a very thin strip of fur still on the hide. This method requires a little more preparation, but several fur strips can be cut at a sitting, and if several flies are to be tied, this technique may ultimately be more efficient. The placement of hide strips is quite precise, making it easier to adjust the diameter of the fur chenille, particularly on smaller flies. This approach is considerably more practical than the paper-clamp technique (shown in **Method #41: Fur Chenille Dubbing Loop**, p. 131) when handling very short furs, such as mole, that are typically used on smaller flies.

This technique is simpler if the hide is not tanned but rather dried so that it remains stiff. Dried skins are more easily cut into strips, and the rigidity of the material is an advantage when positioning the fur in the dubbing loop. Tanned hides require a bit more care to cut and position, but they can be used. In either case, the strips should be no wider than about ³⁄₃₂". Thicker strips of fur do not spin well; they twist unevenly, and slicker types of hair can slip from the loop.

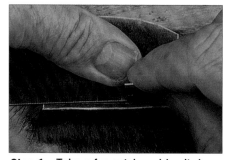

Step 1. Take a fur patch and lay it down skin-side up. Position a straightedge along the patch, exposing a strip on the edge about ¹⁄₁₆" wide. With a very sharp single-edge razor blade, score the skin about halfway through. Do not cut all the way through the hide or the fur underneath will be damaged. Score several parallel cuts if additional strips are desired.

Step 2. For dried skins, bend the hide along the cut. Beginning at one end, carefully separate the strip from the rest of the hide.

Step 2a. Tanned hides are a bit more difficult to work with. After scoring the skin, hold one edge in a paper clamp, or a clipboard as shown here. Push the tip of the razor blade through the center of cut and with a rocking or sawing motion, separate half the strip from the rest of the hide.

Reverse the skin in the clip and complete the cut.

Step 3. Form a dubbing loop using either procedure described in **Method #38: Trap-loop Dubbing**, p. 129. Wax one or both threads.

Trap the fur strip between the threads, very close to the hide. You can spin the dubbing tool two or three times to help lock in the strip, but do not spin it so much that the hide begins to twist or you will have difficulty cutting it away from the fur.

Step 4. By gently pulling on either the hair tips or the hide strip, you can adjust the amount of fur that extends beyond the threads. For thick, large-diameter bodies, allow most of the fur to protrude, as shown here. For thinner, or small fly bodies, allow only the tips to protrude.

Step 5. With a pair of scissors, carefully cut away the strip of hide. Serrated scissors work best, since the serrations trap the hairs and help prevent slippage. In any event, the scissors should be very sharp. The hair strip is only lightly held in the loop, and the excessive force required by dull scissors can cause the strip to shift position.

Step 6. Spin the loop. The result is a very uniform chenille, with a dense underfur body and sparse guard hair bristles.

The fur chenille is wrapped as explained in **Method #41: Fur Chenille Dubbing Loop**, Step 5, p. 131.

Method #43:
Split-thread Dubbing

This technique involves forming a dubbing loop by splitting a single piece of tying thread, applying the dubbing, and retwisting the thread into a single strand. The procedure yields a very low-bulk dubbing loop that is ideal for small fly bodies or very sparsely dubbed ones. It is also an excellent way to spin small amounts of dubbing for specialized purposes—such as spinning a short fur chenille for dressing the head of a caddis pupa.

There are limitations, however. As a rule, it's best suited to smaller quantities of dubbing and shorter loops; lots of dubbing and long loops require a significant amount of twisting, which can break a single strand of thread. Moreover, the application of dubbing must be judicious. Excess dubbing cannot be trimmed away since it is spun inside the working thread. Both short, spikey dubbings and long-fibered, soft ones can be employed with this method. Almost any thread is suitable, though splitting threads much finer than 6/0 is somewhat difficult.

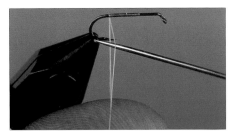

Step 1. Position the thread at the rearmost point of the body, and spin the bobbin counterclockwise to flatten the thread. Drape the thread over your left index finger so that it forms a flat, ribbonlike strand.

With a dubbing needle, carefully split the thread into two halves.

Step 2. Insert a finger in the loop to hold it open. Wax one or both of the threads, and apply a small quantity of dubbing.

For short, stiff dubbings, just touch the clump of material to the waxed thread and let some of the fibers adhere. For long-fibered dubbings, place a loose skein of material between the threads.

Step 3. Remove your finger and allow the loop to close. Spin the bobbin (clockwise when viewed from above) to twist the thread into a tight yarn.

Controlling Body Texture and Shape of Fur Chenille Bodies

The texture of bodies formed from fur-chenille dubbing loops and dubbing brushes is governed by the proportion of guard hairs to underfur in the fur chenille. These proportions can be altered in the following ways:

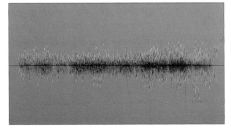

For a spikey, narrow-diameter body, position the fur strip (or clamped hair, if using a paper clamp) close to the tips. Trim the fur close to the wire.

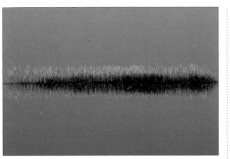

For a soft, dense body of underfur, trap the fur strip about ⅓ of the way up the fibers from the base. Carefully trim the side of the fur containing the guard hairs so that it is equal in length to fiber butts projecting from the other side of the wires. Spin as usual.

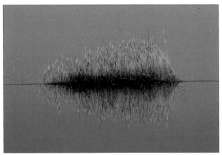

Tapered fur chenilles and dubbing brushes can be made by mounting the fur strip at a slight angle to the loop strands. Trim by cutting the butts of the hair parallel to the loop strands, and spin. The finished chenille will be tapered.

Note: Positioning the strip at an extreme angle will cause the narrow part of the chenille to be composed almost entirely of guard hairs, and it will appear quite sparse in relation to the thicker end, which contains underfur. The result is that when the chenille is wrapped, the body taper will appear quite exaggerated.

Dubbing Brushes

The dubbing brush is a natural extension of the thread-core dubbing or spinning loop. However, while tyers have used dubbing loops for some time, by all indications the dubbing brush is a comparatively recent idea. Darrel Martin, who first saw dubbing brush techniques demonstrated by tyers in the Czech Republic, is largely responsible for introducing them to American fly dressers. Many tyers are now using brushes, primarily on subsurface patterns.

A dubbing brush is essentially a chenille—made from either fur strips or chopped fibers—spun in a dubbing loop made of wire rather than thread. It is a small, but highly significant, alteration. The wire adds durability, weight, and flash to the fly body. Perhaps most importantly, a wire core will not untwist once the dubbing loop is spun. Hence dubbing brushes can be made in advance and stored until needed. Sufficiently long brushes can be used to wrap 2 or 3 fly bodies, making them an efficient investment in time.

Almost any non-stranded wire will serve for the core material—gold, silver, copper, tin, colored craft wire—provided it is not too thick. Large-diameter wires spin quickly but will not tighten to make a dense chenille. However, if you're seeking a sparse chenille with an ample amount of flashy core showing, a thicker wire will serve the purpose. As always in fly tying, some experimentation is necessary. The maximum wire size for producing a dense twist depends to some extent on the type and quantity of fur used, but in general, wires up to .012" in diameter work best.

It is possible to make a dubbing brush in much the same way as a dubbing loop, by binding in a loop of wire at the rearmost point of the body and spinning the dubbing material as explained in **Method #38: Trap-loop Dubbing**, p. 129, or by spinning fur chenilles as described in **Method #41: Fur Chenille Dubbing Loop**, p. 131, and **Method #42: Hide-strip Fur Chenille**, p. 132. However, dubbing brushes can be made more easily and precisely by using either a rotary-capable vise, as demonstrated in the methods shown in this section, or a dubbing board (see "Dubbing Boards," p. 136).

There are a few specialized vises, designed for prolonged hand-rotation and geared for higher turning speeds that simplify and expedite the process of spinning dubbing brushes. But any fly-tying vise capable of true centerline rotation can be used. The only other piece of equipment needed is a wire spinning hook that can be clamped in the vise jaws.

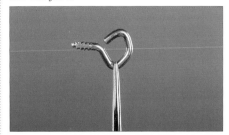

An ordinary screw eye, bent open slightly, will serve for a spinning hook; filing flats on the shank gives a more secure hold in the vise.

The techniques for regulating the texture and shape of the dubbing-brush chenilles are identical to those presented in "Controlling Body Texture and Shape of Fur Chenille Bodies," p. 133. Such bodies can also be trimmed to shape as shown in **Method #67: Clipped Bodies**, p. 155.

Method #44:

Wire-core Dubbing Brush

The following sequence illustrates the construction of a hide-strip dubbing brush using a rotary vise. A paper clamp can also be used to hold the fur as described in **Method #41: Fur Chenille Dubbing Loop**, p. 131, though this does limit the length of the dubbing brush to the width of the clamp jaws.

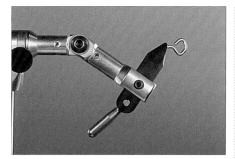

Step 1. Position the head of a rotary vise horizontally, and mount the spinning hook in the jaws as shown.

Step 2. Cut a length of core wire about 18" long. Medium-gauge wires handle more easily than very thin ones and are recommended for your first attempts.

Fold the wire in half and slip the fold over the spinning hook. Hold both wires about 1" from the hook, and spin the vise 3 or 4 times to lock in the wire.

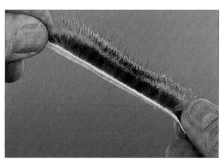

Step 3. Cut a fur strip as explained in **Method #42: Hide-strip Fur Chenille**, p. 132, and preen the hairs so that they stand perpendicular to the hide.

Step 4. Apply a thin film of high-tack wax to both wires, covering all sides. Pull the wires toward you, as shown in this top view, so that they are at nearly a right angle to vise head. Mount the fur strip on the lower wire; it should stick to the wax.

Bring the upper wire down to the fur, trapping it. If necessary, you can tug on the skin lightly in order to position the hide strip parallel to the wires.

Step 5. Holding the wire ends in your right hand, spin the vise a few times to lock in the fur, but not enough to cause the hide to twist, or trimming will be difficult.

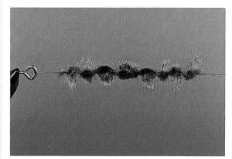

Step 6. With a pair of sharp serrated scissors, carefully trim away the hide strip, cutting parallel to the wire as shown in **Method #42: Hide-strip Fur Chenille**, Step 5, p. 132.

Hold the free ends of the wire securely, and spin the vise head, allowing the wire between the hook and your hand to twist. The hair will begin to curl and flare. The tighter the twist, the denser and more brushlike the dubbing.

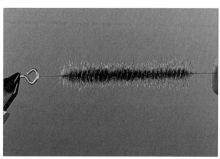

Step 7. A completed dubbing brush—this one of squirrel hair. To form a fly body, bind the wire core of the brush to the hook shank, and wrap as you would chenille. Stroke back the hairs on previous wraps as you wind to avoid binding down the fur.

When larger-diameter wires or thick strips of fur are used, or when the dubbing brush is not tightly spun, fibers in the brush may shed when the material is handled during wrapping—in much the same way that ordinary synthetic chenille will shed when handled repeatedly. Wrapping the dubbing brush around the shank locks in the fur, and thus losing fibers from the finished body is not a problem. To avoid shedding when tying the dubbing brush, wrap the brush using a pair of hackle pliers or a dubbing hook inserted into the loop that was formed at one end of the brush during spinning.

Method #45:

Lead-core Dubbing Brush

One of the more interesting variations of the dubbing brush employs a core of lead wire, allowing you to form a weighted chenille and eliminating the need to weight the hook prior to dressing the fly.

Lead wire, particularly fine-diameter material, is a bit trickier to spin than other metal wires because of its extreme malleability. Over-twisting or overly aggressive handling can cause thin wire to break. On the other hand, because lead twists easily and tightly, somewhat thicker wires—up to .025"—are practical. The brush itself will look somewhat sparse, but the core will be hidden once the body is wrapped on the hook.

The following technique gives the best results with lead wire, and again we are indebted to Darrel Martin for his discussion of the method. Both the hide-strip technique (shown below) and the paper-clamp technique (illustrated in **Method #41: Fur Chenille Dubbing Loop**, p. 131) can be used.

Step 1. Cut a 12" length of lead wire of the desired diameter. Mount it by taking two wraps of wire around the hook, and then secure it with a few turns of the vise as described in **Method #44: Wire-core Dubbing Brush**, Steps 1-2, p. 133. The extra wraps around the spinning hook give greater strength and prevent the wire from shearing.

Step 2. Wax the wires, mount a strip of fur between them, and trim off the hide as described above in **Method #44: Wire-core Dubbing Brush**, Steps 3-5, p. 133.

Step 3. Spin the vise slowly and smoothly. As it twists, the wire will shorten. Avoid the tendency to pull tight with the right hand,

or with the hackle pliers used here. Use a light touch. Holding the wire too tightly, pulling outward as the twisting wire draws inward, can cause the soft lead to break.

Continue spinning until the desired texture is reached. For the densest possible brush, continue twisting until the lead breaks—either at the spinning hook or at your fingers.

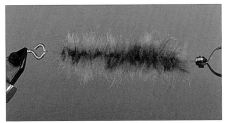

Step 4. Shown here is a finished lead-core dubbing brush—this one of rabbit fur. To tie the brush in, clip the core, flatten the end slightly, and bind it to the hook shank.

Wrap the brush forward, stroking back the fur on previous wraps to avoid trapping the hair against the shank.

Method #46:

Single-wire Spun Dubbing

Though the finished product of single-wire spinning is similar to a direct-dubbed wire (see **Method #35: Wire-core Direct Dubbing**, p. 126), the technique itself is actually a version of the dubbing brush since the method involves spinning the wire rather than the material. And like a dubbing brush, it requires the use of a rotary-capable vise. Like all wire-core dubbings, this one adds a bit of flashiness, toughness, and weight to a fly. It is particularly well-suited to smaller or very sparse flies, since the method does not produce much bulk in the dubbing strand.

Single-wire spinning offers a couple of advantages over direct dubbing. Long lengths of dubbed wire, suitable for many fly bodies, can be fashioned at once, and many wires can be spun at a sitting to be stored for later use—both of which help justify the slightly involved setup of equipment that is necessary.

If care is taken, lead wires down to about .015" can be dubbed using this method, eliminating the need to weight the hook before dubbing. Long-fibered dubbings work best. Lead wire, however, is soft and somewhat fragile; it must be handled gently and not overspun.

The following procedures are adapted from Darrel Martin's *Micropatterns*.

Step 1. Spinning wire requires a rotary vise and spinning hook (see **Method #44:**

Wire-core Dubbing Brush, p. 133). In addition, an anchor for the free end of the wire is also needed.

You can use a second vise, fitted with a second hook, as pictured here, or use the arrangement pictured in Step 1a.

Step 1a. Instead of a second vise, you can use a nail, tack, or rubber button mounted on the edge of the wooden block of the same height as the vise jaws.

It is also possible to use a nail, tack, or button mounted on the edge of the tying bench, but if this arrangement is used, the vise head must be tilted so that the stretched wire is directly on the rotational centerline.

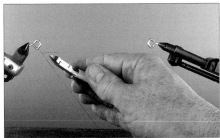

Step 2. Loop the left end of the wire over the spinning hook, and take a few turns with the vise to secure it as explained in **Method #44: Wire-core Dubbing Brush**, Step 2, p. 134.

Clip off the tag end of wire.

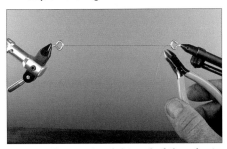

Step 3. Fasten the right end of the wire to the hook on the second vise (as shown here) or to the anchor tack affixed to the block shown in Step 1a. Trim the excess wire.

Step 4. Apply a thin film of high-tack wax to the wire. If necessary, use your fingers to spread an even coating on the wire.

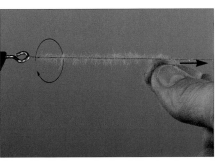

Step 5. Take a pinch of finely chopped dubbing in your right thumb and forefinger. Spin the vise with your left hand and touch the dubbing to the spinning wire. Move your hand slowly along the wire, distributing dubbing as you go. A thin dusting of material should coat the core.

To dress a fly body, simply secure one end of the wire to the hook shank and wrap forward as you would a length of yarn.

Step 5a. For long-fibered dubbings, put a pinch of material between thumb and forefinger and tease a sparse amount beyond the fingertips. Again, touch the dubbing to the spinning wire. Feed strands of material through the fingertips, moving down the wire and spinning a uniform layer of fibers. Material can be applied sparsely, so that the wire shows through, or it can be spun more densely to cover the core completely.

Method #47:

Double-wire Spun Dubbing

This technique is actually a combination of single-wire spinning and the dubbing brush. Bodies of double-spun wire are more durable and less delicate to handle than those fashioned by single-wire spinning, and the double thickness of core material adds extra weight and flash.

Step 1. Set up the equipment to spin a single-wire body as described **Method #46: Single-wire Spun Dubbing**, Steps 1-4, except do not trim the wire after affixing it to the spinning hook. Leave a tag a few inches longer than the stretched wire.

Using either a short- or long-fibered dubbing, fashion a single-spun wire body as described above in **Method #46: Single-wire Spun Dubbing**, Steps 5-6, p. 135.

When the single-spun wire body is completed, carefully take the tag of wire, stretch it parallel to the dubbed wire.

Step 2. Affix the tag to the anchor.

Continue spinning both strands of wire together until the desired body texture is achieved.

Dubbing Boards

Virtually all the dubbing-brush methods previously described (with the exception of single- and double-spun wire) can be accomplished with a dubbing board or dubbing block—essentially a horizontal platform on which dubbing brushes can be twisted. Some dubbing boards, in fact, enable you to spin types of dubbing brushes that are difficult, or impossible, to achieve with rotary-capable vises.

Dubbing boards are an old idea given their fullest articulation in American fly-tying literature in *The Art of Tying the Wet Fly* by Vernon Hidy and Jim Leisenring, who pre-spun dubbed bodies on silk cores—a method detailed at the end of this section. However, an even earlier book, Rube Cross's *The Complete Fly Tier*, contains a photograph of a dubbing board.

There are two basic types of dubbing board—the flat board, described below, and the grooved board, detailed in **Method #49: Grooved Dubbing Board**, p. 137.

Method #48:
Flat Dubbing Board

At the time of this writing, dubbing boards are not commercially available, but they are quite simple to make, as shown in Step 1. They vary in size, depending upon the length of brush you wish to make, though a board 4" wide and 7" long is fairly typical. Fine, fragile wires will tolerate less twisting than thicker wire, and a shorter board, about 5" long, may work best in such cases. Thick wire, which can be twisted very tightly without breaking, can be used satisfactorily on longer boards.

The requirements for a flat dubbing board are few—the surface must have the proper texture and there must be a way to anchor the wire at each end to hold it taut. In order to hold the dubbing in place as you apply it to the board, the surface texture must be slightly rough. Jim Leisenring and Vernon Hidy used a piece of leather, and covering the board with a piece of chamois, suede, velvet, or velour is still quite practical. A particularly

modern solution was shown to us by Oregon tyer and guide Ray Slusser, who makes his dubbing boards from an ordinary piece of unsanded particle board. The rough surface holds the dubbing in place while it is being applied. The board can be painted to provide better contrast for the dubbing material, which simplifies the uniform application of fibers.

Dubbing boards can be used with short or long dubbing fibers or to make fur chenilles. As shown in the main sequence, they excel at creating brushes made of chopped dubbing—a process that is more difficult with a rotary vise.

The alternate sequence shows the technique for using fur cut directly from the hide to form a chenille with both guard hairs and underfur combined.

Step 1. There's not much to making a dubbing board. To anchor the wire, a nail is driven into one end of the board, and the nail head is clipped off. A small slit is cut into the other end of the board (with a razor), directly in line with the nail, to center and secure the wire. A second slit is cut in the side of the board to hold the wire tag while dubbing is applied.

Set up the dubbing board by wrapping the core material a few times around the nail. You can get more convenient access to the nail if the board is elevated slightly—by placing it on top of a thick book, for example, as shown here.

At this point, the core material can be waxed if desired. Wax helps secure short, coarse dubbing fibers to the wire, but is not really necessary with longer fibers. Secure the wire firmly in the slit at the end of the board.

Hang a dubbing hook or twister from the wire as shown. Bring the excess wire to the slit in the side of the board and secure it there. Note that the wire is used directly from the spool here, a practice that minimizes waste.

Step 2. Take a clump of chopped dubbing and tease out a small amount. Press the dubbing directly over the wire at the top of the board. The roughened surface of the board (and any wax used) will help the material stay in position. Attempt to center the dubbing over the wire.

Step 3. Take another clump of dubbing and apply it below the first. Try to distribute the dubbing evenly along the wire.

Continue applying pinches of material until the wire is covered.

Step 4. Pull lightly outward and downward on the handle of the dubbing hook or twister to maintain tension on the wire.

Remove the wire from the slit on the side of the board, and lay it directly on top of the dubbed wire. Wrap the wire with a few turns around the nail to secure it. Clip the wire from the spool.

Step 5. Gently pull the dubbing hook outward, putting a light tension on the wire.

Begin spinning the dubbing hook. As the wire begins to twist, gently lift the dubbing hook to remove the wire from the slit at the bottom of the board.

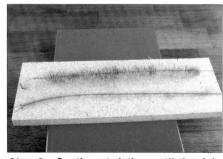

Step 6. Continue twisting until the dubbing brush reaches the desired texture. Remove the wire from the nail and clip the excess. The photo here shows both the chopped dubbing from the main sequence (at the bottom) and the fur chenille from the alternate sequence (at the top).

Step 1a. If spinning fur chenille, cut a small clump of fur from the hide. Position it crosswise over the top end of the wire. Place your fingertip over the dubbing, and using a light pressure, drag the fur a short distance down the wire. The fur can be thinly or thickly distributed, depending on the desired density of the finished dubbing brush. But in either case, spread the fur in an even layer to produce a uniform brush with no thick or thin spots.

Step 2a. Cut another clump of fur. Position it below the first, and spread it along the wire.

Continue with additional applications of material until the wire is covered in a uniform layer.

Spin the brush as explained in Steps 4-6.

Method #49:
Grooved Dubbing Board

Flat dubbing boards of the type described in **Method #48: Flat Dubbing Board**, p. 136 pose one problem—fashioning very narrow-diameter dubbing brushes from finely chopped fibers; the method of application tends to produce stray fibers that increase the diameter of the brush. One solution is to cut a groove in the dubbing board to help eliminate these stray fibers.

Grooved dubbing boards are identical to flat dubbing boards, with two exceptions. First, a channel is cut down the center of the board with a table saw or router. The width of the groove determines, at least approximately, the diameter of the finished dubbing brush. The depth of the groove influences the density. A deep channel, which will hold lots of dubbing, will produce a fuller brush; a shallow groove, which holds less dubbing, will give a sparser one.

The second difference is the surface of the board. While the bottom of the groove should be left rough, the surface of the board should be quite smooth to help facilitate brushing material into the channel. If desired, it can be painted to give better contrast with the dubbing material.

Grooved dubbing boards can be used

There are a couple of ways to make a grooved dubbing board. On the left, a groove has been cut into a piece of particle board, and the top surface sanded smooth and varnished. Note that two grooves of different widths and depths have been cut here. A single dubbing board could in fact have a number of different channels cut to produce dubbing brushes of different sizes.

On the right, a smooth material—plastic, sanded hardwood, formica, or Masonite (as used here) is cut into slats. These are affixed to the top of the particle board, leaving a channel between them. Again, two channels of different widths have been formed.

The anchor nail and slits on a grooved board differ slightly from those on a flat board. As shown on the left, the anchor nails (with the heads removed) are driven into the end of the board, directly in line with the center of the channel. Directly above the nail, a slit is cut into the center of the channel. This method for mounting the anchor nails must be used in order to hold the entire length of wire against the bottom of the groove in the board; the slit helps keep the wire centered in the groove.

At the bottom of the dubbing board, a piece of heavy rubber is mounted, as shown on the right. A slit is cut in the rubber directly in line with the center of the channel; the high-friction rubber holds the wire securely.

Finally, a slit is cut in the side of the board, just as on a flat dubbing board.

with both finely chopped dubbing, shown in the main sequence, or longer-fibered dubbings, shown in the alternate steps.

Step 1. Mount the core material as described in **Method #48: Flat Dubbing Board**, Step 1, p. 136, using either a waxed or unwaxed wire.

Begin applying dubbing into the groove. There are two basic ways to do this, depending on the texture of the material.

With finely chopped dubbing, as shown here, it is easiest to fill the groove from the side. Hold a clump of dubbing in the right hand to one side of the groove. With the left forefinger, tease out some dubbing, drag it over the surface of the

board and into the groove from the side. Pack it lightly with your fingertip.

Tease out a bit more dubbing, and pull it across the surface of the board into the groove next to the first pinch of dubbing. Continue until the entire groove has been filled. Distributing the fibers evenly in the groove will produce dubbing brushes with a consistent texture.

Step 1a. For longer-fibered dubbings, it is easiest to draw small quantities of material lengthwise into the groove. Center the clump of dubbing in your right hand over the channel. With your left fingers, draw out small pinches of material and pack them into the groove. Move the right hand along the groove, while your left hand continues to draw out and pack material until all the wire is covered.

Step 2. When the entire groove is filled, lay the bare wire over the dubbed one as described in **Method #48: Flat Dubbing Board**, Step 4, p. 136, and begin twisting the dubbing as described in Step 5.

There is, however, one slight difference. As the wire nearest the dubbing tool begins to twist and lock in the fibers, raise the dubbing tool slightly, pulling the twisted section of wire from the groove. As you continue spinning and more of the wire twists, raise that twisted section from the groove as well. Eventually, the entire length of wire will be removed from the channel, and stretched between the anchor nail and the dubbing twister. Raising the dubbing tool to free the twisted wire from the groove makes twisting the brush into its final form much simpler.

Pre-dubbed Thread

While dubbing boards can be used to make dubbing brushes with wire cores, their earliest use seems to have been in fashioning pre-dubbed bodies twisted on silk thread cores—a technique that goes at least as far back as the late 19th century in the work of Selwyn Marryat and Francis Francis. The technique is practiced only infrequently by modern tyers, primarily those who desire the authentic dressing for the "flymph" patterns designed by Vernon Hidy and James Leisenring, which incorporate bodies dressed in this manner.

The principal drawback is that pre-dubbed threads, unlike wire dubbing brushes, will unravel unless the ends of the thread are trapped in such a way to prevent them from untwisting. This is usually accomplished by stretching the dubbed thread over a card of rigid paper, and securing the twisted ends in slots cut into the edge of the card. Despite this extra step, however, the technique is still practical.

A dubbing board or block allows for a somewhat greater control over the density and placement of material than does the dubbing-loop technique shown in **Method #38: Trap-loop Dubbing**, p. 129. The horizontal work surface simplifies spreading and arranging the material to the desired shape and thickness, and producing tapered dubbing strands is quite simple. Moreover, colors of dubbing material are mixed easily during twisting. And for dry-fly bodies, or patterns on which the flash or weight of a wire core is undesirable, pre-dubbed thread is a logical choice.

There are two basic approaches here. The first uses a dubbing board with a doubled thread and closely resembles the construction of a wire-core dubbing brush. The second, and in all likelihood the older method, uses a single strand of thread for the core and requires no dubbing block.

Method #50:
Hidy/Leisenring Pre-dubbed Thread

While this technique did not originate with Hidy and Leisenring, their work was instrumental in bringing the method to the attention of American tyers. While Leisenring spun-dubbed bodies by laying the thread across his knee, as shown in the alternate sequence, his pupil and friend, Dick Clark, devised a dubbing block to make the process more efficient. Both flat dubbing boards and grooved boards are suitable for pre-dubbed thread. Silk thread is the traditional material, but synthetics work as well.

The main sequence shows the method for pre-dubbing thread strands using one of Hidy's own blocks. Note that the dubbing is laid on a piece of leather. One side is white and one black, and the leather is reversible to provide a contrasting background for various colors of dubbing.

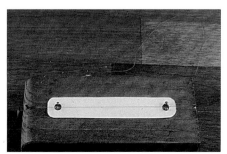

Step 1. Wax the tying thread. If using a flat board mount the thread as shown in **Method #48: Flat Dubbing Board**, p. 136; for grooved

boards, use the technique shown in **Method #49: Grooved Dubbing Board**, p. 137.

In Hidy's dubbing block, the tag end of the thread is secured in a slit at one end of the board. The thread is stretched along the middle of the board and secured in a slit at the other end. Finally, the thread is passed behind the anchor nail, and secured in the slit on the side of the board.

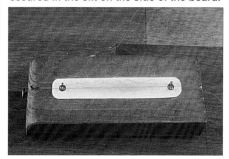

Step 2. Tease out the desired amount of dubbing into an elongated skein. Making the skein thinner at the ends and thicker in the middle will produce a tapered body when the dubbing is wrapped on the hook.

Center the skein of dubbing on top of the waxed thread.

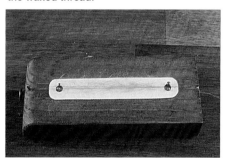

Step 3. Remove the thread from the side slit, lay the bare thread directly atop the dubbing, and secure it in the bottom slit. The fur is now caught between the two strands of thread.

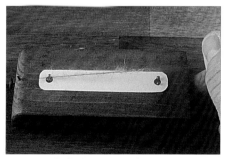

Step 4. Pull the thread from the bottom slit, and spin it (in one direction only) between thumb and forefinger. The twisting thread will compact the dubbing.

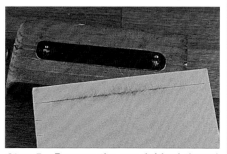

Step 5. Remove the pre-dubbed thread from the spinning block, and store it on a cardboard or plastic card as shown.

Step 1a. To form a pre-dubbed thread without the use of a dubbing board, lay a length of waxed thread along your knee, as shown.

Tease out a skein of dubbing as shown in Step 2, and lay the skein on the lower half of the thread.

Step 2a. Fold the upper half of the thread over the lower half, trapping the dubbing between the two strands.

Step 3a. Spin the body by twisting the ends of the loop in opposite directions.

The dubbed thread can be stored in a card, as shown in Step 5.

Method #51:
Pre-dubbed Single Thread

Pre-spun strands of dubbing can be made with a single thread as the core. Both of the approaches shown are older methods, best suited to softer-fibered materials; short, stiff furs are difficult to spin with these techniques.

The method shown in the main sequence was used by Catskill tyer Reuben Cross and is very fast—faster, even, than the direct dubbing method used by most tyers—though it is best suited to producing bodies with a rougher texture. The alternate sequence shows a technique used by many tyers, most notably the late Polly Rosborough; it produces a more tightly compacted dubbing strand.

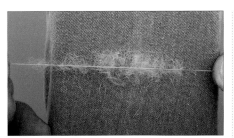

Step 1. Spread a clump of soft-fibered dubbing about 2" long and 1" wide crosswise on your knee. The thickness of the clump determines, in part, the density of the dubbed strand. A thick clump will produce a bulkier body; a sparser clump gives a narrower one.

Lay a film of tacky wax on an 8" length of tying thread. Grasp the thread in both hands, as shown, so that the distance between your fingertips is about 4 inches.

Maintain a light but firm tension on the thread, and lay it atop the dubbing. Spin the thread, using either one hand, or both hands twisting in opposite directions.

Immediately, the waxed thread will begin to pick up the dubbing fibers and twist them around the thread. To increase the density of the body, press the thread more firmly into the dubbing clump.

Continue twisting. As one section of the thread is sufficiently covered with spun material, slide the thread across the clump of material so that bare sections of the thread pick up and twist additional dubbing.

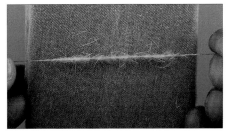

Step 2. Shown here is the finished strand.

If desired, twisted strands can be stored on cards as in **Method #50: Hidy/Leisenring Pre-dubbed Thread,** Step 5, p. 138. But generally, a dubbed strand of this type was spun for immediate use. If the twist is relaxed momentarily in order to mount the strand on a hook shank, the dubbing will be held in place by the wax; after the strand is mounted, it is re-twisted. Alternately, the bare thread on one end of the dubbed strand can be mounted like tying thread, and the dubbing wrapped to form a body without ever relaxing the twist.

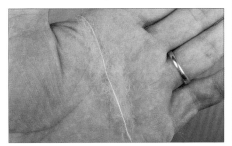

Step 1a. A more tightly dubbed strand can be produced by spinning the material between your palms.

Tease out a skein of dubbing about 3" long. The width and thickness of the skein are variable and determine the thickness of the finished body. A broader or thicker skein of material produces a bulkier body;

less material gives a sparser one. The skein can also be formed into an elongated football-shape to produce a dubbing strand that tapers at both ends.

Lay the skein crosswise in the palm of your left hand, as shown.

Place an 8" length of thread, coated with a film of tacky wax, down the center of the dubbing.

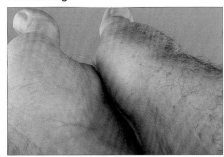

Step 2a. Place the palms of your hands together under moderate pressure. Slide the palm of your right hand toward the fingertips of your left hand, rolling the dubbing and thread together between your palms.

Spin the dubbing in one direction only; do not roll it back and forth between your palms.

Step 3a. If the dubbing is not tightly compacted, place the strand in the center of the left palm, and repeat Step 2a.

Shown here is the finished strand. It can be stored or used immediately.

Dubbing Noodles

Dubbing-noodle techniques involve forming a yarn or "noodle" of dubbing material that can be wrapped directly around the hook shank or twisted with thread-loop core and then wrapped. It is one of the quickest ways of forming a dubbed body and is particularly well suited to large, bulky flies—stonefly nymphs, for example—because substantial quantities of material can be applied rather rapidly.

There is a limitation however. The technique can only be employed with longer-fibered dubbing materials. Natural hairs such as Angora goat, camel, and some types of seal fur are ideal, though these are somewhat coarse and, again, generally restricted to larger flies. Long-fibered synthetics, on the other hand, come in a variety of textures, and some of the soft, fine ones are certainly suitable for smaller flies, as is long-fibered rabbit fur. However, as the volume of material required for the body decreases, so do the gains in efficiency offered by the dubbing-noodle method. That is, you can direct dub a #14 hook about as quickly as you can dress it with a dubbing noodle.

In the two techniques shown here, a thin noodle of material is formed as the body is wrapped by drawing fibers from a "reservoir" of dubbing material held in the right hand. When long-fibered dubbing is used, in which the hairs or filaments are intertwined, dubbing that is wrapped around the shank will draw after it additional fibers from a clump held in the hand, and a continuous supply of material is available.

The main sequence shows the most common approach, suitable for long-fibered materials of all types. It can produce both uniform-diameter and tapered bodies. The alternate sequence shows a technique devised by California tyer Bob Johns that uses a pinch of sheep's wool cut directly from the hide to produce a tapered body.

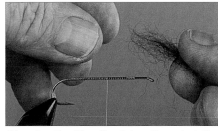

Step 1. Position the tying thread at the middle of the hook shank.

Take a ball of well-mixed, long-fibered dubbing in your right hand, and tease out a small amount of material. It should extend about 1" beyond your index finger.

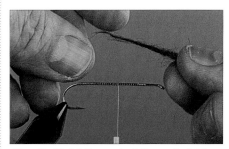

Step 2. Twist the end of the material to a point. Notice as you twirl the material that it begins to form a yarn—this is the "noodle." Make certain to twist the material clockwise, as viewed from above, looking down at the point.

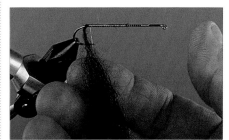

Step 3. Bind the point of the noodle to the hook shank, wrapping the thread back to the rearmost point of the body and securing the dubbing noodle as you go.

Strip off about 6" of thread from the bobbin and drape it across your palm. Place the ball of loose dubbing over the thread.

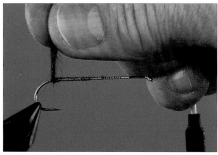

Step 4. Begin to wrap the body by grasping both the noodle and the tying thread together between your thumb and forefinger. Do not pinch the noodle tightly, because additional fibers of dubbing must be able to slide out between your fingers.

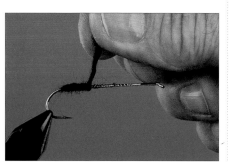

Step 5. As you wind the body, the fibers being wrapped around the hook will pull additional material from the dubbing ball in your hand. Feed this material evenly through your fingers as you wrap.

Step 6. At the tie-off point, separate the tying thread from the dubbing ball as shown. Bind down the dubbing noodle and clip the excess material.

Step 1a. This technique, which uses sheep's wool cut from the hide, is well-suited to smaller bodies.

To form a wool noodle, use a comb to brush the wool outward until the individual fibers are separated and standing perpendicular to the hide.

Carefully cut away a section of the fur at the base of the hide.

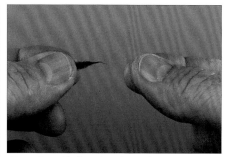

Step 2a. Twist the tips of the material (clockwise when looking down at them) into a point.

Step 3a. Cut away the very fine tip of the twisted fur.

Bind the twisted tip to the hook shank as described in Step 3, and advance the thread to the tie-off point of the body.

Twist the wool a few more times; take care not to pull on the fibers—just twist them.

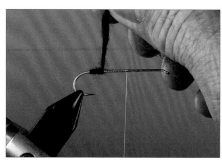

Step 4a. Begin wrapping the wool around the shank. With each wrap of the material, twist the wool fibers one time. This will maintain a tight yarn and produce a nicely segmented body.

Step 5a. Tie off the wool at the completion of the body. It must be bound in tightly to maintain the twist. Clip the excess material.

Method #53:

Two-color Dubbing Noodle

With the dubbing noodle, you can easily dress a body in which the front and rear portions are different colors—without forming a second noodle for the second color.

Step 1. Form a noodle and partially wind the rear portion of the body, as shown in **Method #52: Twisted Dubbing Noodle**, p. 139. When you are a few wraps away from the color-transition point, stop.

Pull the excess material from the bottom of the noodle, leaving a "frayed" end about an inch long. Take a dubbing ball of the second color, and loosely tease out about an inch of material.

Step 2. Overlap the two colors, and twist slightly to form a continuous length of dubbing material.

Step 3. Wrap the second color, and tie off the body as explained in **Method #52: Twisted Dubbing Noodle**, Step 6.

Controlling the Shape and Texture of Dubbing-noodle Bodies

The shape of the body depends upon the amount of material you let slide through your fingers as you wrap it around the hook shank. Tapered bodies are easy to form because the "drawing" action of the dubbing fibers encourages it naturally. The dubbing being fed to the hook shank will pull from your hand an ever-increasing amount of material. If you do nothing to inhibit this process the noodle will get progressively thicker and form a tapered body.

To produce a straight, untapered body, you'll need to counteract the tendency of the noodle to grow in volume.

As the dubbing-noodle technique will naturally produce a tapered body, so will it naturally produce a segmented one. Any material wound around a hook shank will twist, and as the noodle twists, it tightens to produce a dense yarn that will give distinct segmentation.

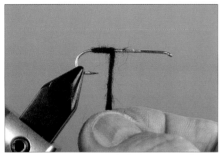

Form and mount a dubbing noodle as shown in **Method #52: Twisted Dubbing Noodle**, Steps 1-4, p. 139. Wrap a few turns on the hook shank.

As the amount of material being drawn between your fingers begins to increase, stop. Gently pull the dubbing, "stretching" it along the length of the thread to reduce the density of distribution.

Continue wrapping. As the volume of dubbing begins to increase again, repeat the process.

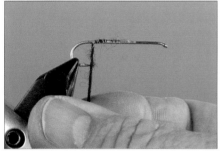

For a segmented body, form the point of the dubbing noodle around the thread. Twist tightly until a noodle about one inch long is formed.

Begin wrapping the body. When the material is secured, pause, and use your fingers to roll the material into a tight cord around the thread. Then proceed. Hold your fingers close to the hook shank; working with a very short noodle will promote a tighter twist.

To form a smooth body, you must compensate for the natural twist that comes with winding. Form the point of the noodle by twisting the fibers counterclockwise (as viewed looking down at the point). Mount the material and begin wrapping. Because the noodle has been formed against the direction of natural twist, it will unwind during the first few wraps, producing a smooth body.

After a few wraps, the fibers will begin to twist. Relax tension on the dubbing, and let it unwind. Continue wrapping, again relaxing tension every time the material begins to twist into a tight yarn.

Method #54:
Dubbing Noodle Loop

One of the most common uses of dubbing noodles is to insert them into a dubbing loop. Because the dubbing material is pre-rolled into a yarnlike strand, the additional twisting provided by the dubbing loop will compact the material quite tightly to produce a distinctly segmented body. Again, only longer-fibered materials are really practical with this method. Yarns formed with very short-fibered dubbings will break apart as you try to handle them.

Step 1. Position the thread at the rearmost point of the body, and form a dubbing loop as described in **Method #38: Trap-loop Dubbing**, p. 129.

Tease out an elongated skein of long-fibered dubbing; for a tapered body, it should be thinner at the ends and thicker in the middle.

Step 2. Lay the skein across the palm of your left hand (or your pant leg), and place

the palm of your right hand over the dubbing.

Compress the dubbing between your two palms (or palm and pant leg), and push the right hand forward, rolling the dubbing beneath the palm. If the material is quite slippery, it helps to moisten the palms of the hands to provide additional grip.

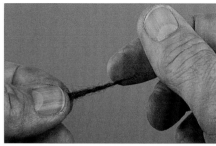

Step 3. If the dubbing has not rolled into a sufficiently tight noodle, reposition the material at the base of the left palm, and repeat Step 2. Spin the dubbing in one direction only; do not roll it back and forth. It may be necessary to twist the ends of the noodle separately to form tight points.

Step 4. Insert the noodle into the dubbing loop. It may be difficult to trap the noodle between the two threads along its entire length. Just make sure that the two points of the noodle are sandwiched inside the loop. Any part of the noodle that projects outside of the thread loop will be drawn into position as the loop is twisted.

Step 5. Twist the dubbing loop as described in **Method #38: Trap-loop Dubbing**, Step 5. p. 129. The material will compact into a tight strand.

Step 6. Wrap the body. Note the segmented effect produced.

Fur-Strip and Hide-Strip Bodies

Fur Strip Bodies

Strips of fur on the hide can be wrapped or lashed to form bodies on larger flies, particularly streamer and leech-type patterns favored by lake anglers. The wrapped-body style was first popularized by Charlie Brooks in his Assam Dragon. Brooks used seal fur, though almost any type is suitable for the technique provided that the hide is tanned. Longer, softer furs, however, are generally preferred as they give a lifelike, undulating action in the water. Rabbit fur is perhaps the most widely used type today.

Fur strips can also be lashed to, rather than wrapped around, a hook shank. As explained in "Fur-strip Tails," p. 87, conventional tying terminology poses a bit of a problem, as 2 or more fur-strip components—usually bodies, wings, and tails—are often dressed from the same piece of material. What the finished component is actually called often depends less on tying technique than on the specific pattern being dressed. For instance, a strip of fur mounted atop the shank, as in a Zonker pattern, is generally termed a "wing" by tyers, even though it helps create the body profile and forms the tail as well. We have followed that fly-tying custom, and thus this particular fur-strip technique is presented in the **Method #70: Fur-strip Downwing**, p. 318. On a very similar type of dressing used for leech patterns, the fur strip is used to represent the body of the leech, and thus the technique for dressing it is included in this section. But tyers working with fur strips may wish to consult the section on "Fur strip Tails," p. 87, and the method for tying fur-strip wings for additional, related techniques.

Fur, particularly from the back and sides of an animal, generally has a distinct orientation or grain. The hair tips slant toward the tail of the animal. Thus fur on strips cut from the pelt side-to-side (called a "cross-cut strip") will have a different orientation than fur on a strip cut lengthwise, end-to-end (called a "longitudinal cut"). When wrapped, the two types of strips will produces bodies with different profiles. Most tyers tend to use cross-cut strips for wrapped bodies and longitudinally cut strips for lashed bodies, wings, and tails.

At the top is a longitudinally cut strip of rabbit fur. Notice that the fur tips slope lengthwise *along* the strip. At the bottom is a cross-cut strip; notice that the fur tips slant *across* the hide and lean to one side.

The thickness of the hide has some bearing on the ease with which the fur strip is handled. A thick hide is more difficult to mount, wind, and tie off on wrapped bodies, and gives less action to a fly with a lashed body. If you have a choice in the matter, use a fur strip with the thinnest hide you can find.

Rabbit fur is generally available in pre-cut strips. Those labeled "rabbit strips" or often "Zonker strips" are longitudinally cut. Those labeled "cross-cut rabbit" or sometimes "bunny hackle" are cross-cut strips. You can also cut strips from a tanned hide, and the procedure for doing so is explained in **Method #42: Hide-strip Fur Chenille**, p. 132.

Method #55:

Wrapped Fur-strip Body

Cross-cut rabbit strips are used with this technique (as shown in the main sequence below) to produce streamer patterns such as the Bunny Leech. Using longitudinally cut strips (presented in the alternate photos) will produce a sparser body with a broader silhouette underwater. The bulk of the material and the length of the fur generally restrict this method to larger hooks.

Step 1. Lay a foundation of tying thread, beginning behind the eye and ending at the rear of the shank. Any tailing materials are tied in at this point, and the thread is positioned at the rearmost tailing wrap.

Select or cut a strip of cross-cut fur (we're using rabbit here). The strip must be tied in so that the natural slant of the fur points toward the hook bend. Position the fur strip above the hook shank so that the fur tips point downward; the end of the strip near the hook eye is the mounting end.

Binding in the strip by wrapping over the fur will produce a bulky tie-in and a potentially insecure one, as the hair is slippery. With scissors, clip the hair close to the skin at the mounting end of the strip, leaving a ⅛" tag of sheared hide. Trim this tag to form a point as shown.

Step 1a. To determine the mounting end for a longitudinally cut strip, place the strip skin-side down on the tying bench with the hair tips pointing directly away from you. The end of the strip closest to you is the end to be mounted on the hook.

Clip the fur and trim a point on the strip as described in Step 1.

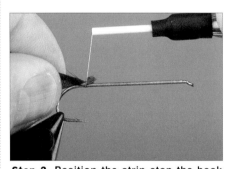

Step 2. Position the strip atop the hook shank, directly above the rearmost thread wrap. The point you trimmed on the mounting end should point directly at the hook eye.

Take 3 or 4 tight turns of thread over the widest part of the point. Then advance the thread toward the hook eye in close, very tight wraps, binding down the tag of sheared hide as you go.

Position the thread at the body tie-off point.

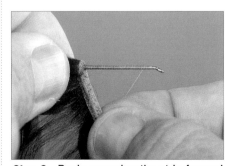

Step 3. Begin wrapping the strip forward in firm, snug turns.

There are two points to bear in mind here. First, as you wrap, use the fingers of the left hand, as shown, to preen the hairs back toward the hook bend to prevent them from becoming trapped under the hide strip. You'll need to reposition your fingers every half-turn or so, as new wraps of material are laid down. Second, the wraps should slightly overlap; on each new wrap, the edge of the hide should just touch the base of the fur on the previous wrap. This overlap not only gives a denser body, but helps maintain the slant of the hair toward the hook bend, preserving the slimmer profile.

Continue wrapping until the tie-off point is reached.

Step 3a. If longitudinally cut fur is wrapped in overlapping turns, it will yield a body fairly similar to that produced by cross-cut fur.

To produce a body with a broader silhouette, wrap the longitudinally cut fur strip in close, adjacent, non-overlapping turns, as shown here. Again, use your left hand to preen the hair back and prevent it from becoming trapped underneath the wrapped hide.

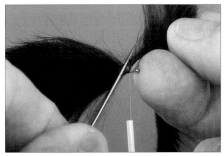

Step 4. When the tie-off point is reached, hold the fur strip across the top of the hook shank as shown. Use a dubbing needle to part the fur that lies directly above the tying thread. You are trying to create a small gap in the fur so that the first tie-off wraps lie directly against the hide rather than on the hair. It may help to dampen the fur slightly to maintain the gap that is exposed.

Step 5. Take 3 or 4 tight turns of thread in the gap, directly against the hide. Clip the end of the fur strip, leaving a tag of about 1/8". If there is any fur on the tag, clip it close to the skin.

Step 6. Bind down the tag of hide, and the body is complete. The top fly has been dressed with a cross-cut strip; notice that the hair slants rearward, creating a body with a slimmer profile. The lower fly has been wrapped with a longitudinally cut strip; the hair stands out almost perpendicular to the shank, giving the impression of greater bulk.

Method #56:
Lashed Fur-strip Body

Though restricted primarily to leech imitations, this fur-strip technique nonetheless produces a highly effective body. This body style, in which the fur strip is mounted on the underside of the shank, is intended to be dressed with a pair of barbell eyes lashed atop the shank. The eyes will cause the hook to ride point-up, which puts the fur strip on the top side of the fly when it is fished. Mounting the strip of body material on the underside of the shank minimizes the tendency for the long, trailing strip to become fouled in the hook bend—a common problem when this body style is tied atop the shank.

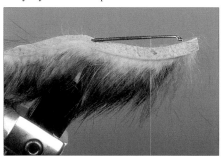

Step 1. Wrap a thread foundation along the rear 3/4 of the hook shank, and position the tying thread at the front of the foundation. (If desired, a simple body—chenille, for example—can be used instead of the thread foundation.)

Select a piece of longitudinally cut fur strip about 2-3 times the hook length.

Use a dubbing needle to pierce a hole through the strip about one hook-length behind the mounting end (to determine the mounting end, see **Method #55: Wrapped Fur-strip Body**, Step 1a, p. 142).

Push the hook point through the hole, and slide the strip up the hook bend, as shown.

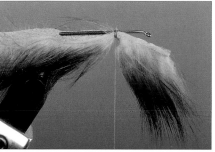

Step 2. Draw the front tag of the strip forward, beneath the hook shank.

Tie off the fur-strip as explained in **Method #55: Wrapped Fur-strip Body**, Steps 4-5, p. 143.

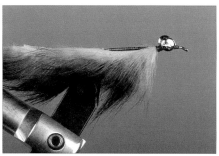

Step 3. Clip the excess fur strip and bind it down.

A pair of barbell eyes of the desired material can now be added (see **Method #7: Barbell Eyes**, p. 431), as shown.

Hide-strip Bodies

Strips or pieces of tanned hide are sometimes used in fly tying. Because they are easily cut, even into fairly complex shapes, they can be used to form overbodies—on crayfish patterns for instance—but are more often used to fashion bodies on leech-type patterns, as shown below. The techniques developed for tying hide strips are largely the work of tyer and fly designer Dave Whitlock, who uses the material for both trout and bass patterns.

The selection of material for forming hide-strip bodies is important to both the ease of handling and the performance of the fly. Thin, flexible hides, such as ordinary chamois, tie in with little bulk and give a more pronounced undulation in the water. Chamois, or other thin leathers, can easily be colored with waterproof marking pens to give the desired shade or produce mottled or spotted effects.

In recent years, a number of synthetic substitutes—Bugskin and Syn-Sham, for instance—have become available, and these are at least the equal of natural materials. They tend to be thinner, more flexible, and easier to shape than natural leathers; they absorb water more quickly and are available in a greater range of colors. They are, however, more expensive.

Method #57:

Hide-strip Body

Here we're using chamois to form a leech body, using an approach devised by Dave Whitlock. This method requires that an underbody of dubbing or chenille first be dressed on the hook shank to act as a foundation for the contact cement required by this technique.

A similar type of body can be constructed without the use of contact cement by using the procedure shown in **Method #56: Lashed Fur-strip Body**, p. 143. in which the hook point is inserted through the strip of hide.

Step 3. On the underside of the chamois strip, brush a thin band of contact cement. Apply cement only to that portion of the chamois that will be in contact with the underbody. Allow the cement to dry.

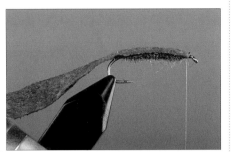

Step 4. Place the cemented portion of the chamois against the top of the underbody, and press down tightly to get a good adhesive bond.

Step 1. Prepare a thin underbody of dubbing or chenille. The tying thread should be positioned behind the hook eye. Apply a thick coat of contact cement to the top of the underbody.

Step 5. Bind down the front edge of the chamois body, forming a head with the tying thread. Whip finish and clip.

Step 2. Cut a strip of chamois to the desired body shape. Here we're cutting an elongated teardrop for a leech body, but other designs—split tails, for example—are certainly possible.

Both natural and synthetic materials can be cut with scissors or razor blade, though it may help to form a cardboard template and trace the shape onto the material. The only real requirement is that the front of the body be kept relatively narrow, to facilitate mounting.

At this point, any coloring to the body should be applied with waterproof marking pens.

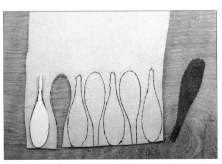

Step 5a. If desired, a narrow body can be ribbed with tying thread, forming body segments and helping secure the chamois. In this case, the thread is secured at the rear of the body with a whip-finish or half-hitches.

SECTION SIX

Spun, Flared, Stacked, and Clipped Bodies

This section contains two basic categories of techniques. One set of methods concerns mounting materials—primarily hollow hair, wool, marabou, and certain synthetic fibers—in a way that causes them to stand outward perpendicular to the shank. The second group of techniques is concerned with shaping such materials into finished bodies. These shaping methods can be used as well with materials that have been mounted using procedures described elsewhere in this book, particularly fur-chenille bodies shown in **Method #41: Fur Chenille Dubbing Loop**, p. 131; **Method #42: Hide-strip Fur Chenille**, p. 132; and **Method #44: Wirecore Dubbing Brush**, p. 133. Bodies formed from wrapped hackle using methods shown in "Collar Hackle," p. 346, can also be shaped using some of these techniques.

Spun Bodies

Hollow hair, such as that from deer, elk, antelope, and caribou (see "Hollow Hair," p. 2) is the only natural material suitable for true spinning, as the hollow, cell-like interior structure accounts for the two properties that are of most interest to the tyer: the tendency for the hair to flare or splay when compressed at one point, and its great buoyancy. While hollow-hair bodies are more often associated with bass bugs and poppers, they nonetheless have a well-established and useful place in the tying of trout flies. Spun-hair bodies are used on such patterns as the Irresistible and the Goddard Caddis, and spinning techniques can be used to fashion heads on some patterns, most notably the Muddler Minnow and sculpin imitations (see **Method #1: Clipped Head**, p. 425).

Of hair suitable for spinning, deer hair is unquestionably the most popular—it is easy to work, widely obtainable, and available in a variety of natural and dyed colors. Modern deer-hair tying owes much to the work of Dave Whitlock, who both pioneered and popularized many of the techniques and applications in use today. And in fact Whitlock is one of a small group of tyers, including such names as Darwin Atkin; Tim England; Chris Helm; the Joe Messingers, Sr. and Jr.; Jimmy Nix; and Frank Wentik, who have helped make working with deer hair a distinct, almost independent sub-speciality of fly tying.

Hollow hairs vary widely in their characteristics, and suitable spinning hair depends not only on the species of animal, but its geographical origin, season of harvest, and most importantly, the part of the animal from which the hair is obtained. (For a more detailed discussion of such hair, see "Hollow Hair," p. 2.) Using the proper type of material is the principal consideration in producing high-quality bodies.

The other matter in regard to spinning deer hair is the thread. Spinning and securing hair requires significant thread pressure, and the material itself can be slightly abrasive—both of which argue for a strong thread. On smaller hooks that require smaller amounts of hair, 6/0 thread can be used, and in skilled hands, threads as light as 8/0 are practical. For larger trout flies that use heavier hooks, thicker bundles of hair, and more thread pressure, 3/0 or even heavier size A may prove more satisfactory. Regardless of the size of the thread, it should be kept tightly corded by spinning the bobbin to twist the thread.

Note that an entire fly pattern need not be dressed using these heavier threads; the thread can be mounted immediately prior to spinning, then tied off and clipped after the body is fashioned. Other fly components can be tied using threads of a more customary size.

Method #58:

Spinning Hollow Hair

The technique described here can be used with any hollow hair suitable for spinning (see "Hollow Hair," p. 2).

The manner in which the first bundle of hair is mounted and spun depends to some extent on the hook size. If you attempt to spin a clump of long hairs at the rearmost point of the body, the hair tips will catch on the hook point, spear, and bend and interfere with proper spinning. Thus this first clump of hair must be kept short—no longer than twice the hook gap. Clipped to this length, the hair will spin cleanly around the shank without obstruction. On larger hooks with larger gaps, this approach presents little problem, since the clump of material, even when trimmed to the appropriate length, is still long enough to handle easily. The details of this method are presented in the main sequence that follows.

Small hooks require a different approach. They have small gaps, and trimming the hair to a length of twice the hook gap may leave the clump of fibers so short that they are difficult to handle. In this case, the bundle is mounted off-center, and the technique for doing so is presented in the alternate sequence.

The main sequence also demonstrates one possibility of creating color effects with spun deer hair—the banded body. Two other types of color mixing are illustrated in the photograph that follows Step 9.

Step 1. Position the tying thread at the rearmost point of the body. If a tail is used (as it is here), bind the excess tailing material with a flattened tying thread to lay the smoothest possible foundation on the hook shank, as this will aid in spinning the hair. If no tail is used, attach the tying thread directly at the rearmost point of the body, leaving the rest of the shank bare.

Prepare a clump of hair by removing the underfur as described in **Method #2: Preparing and Cleaning Hair**, p. 68. For spinning, the hair need not be stacked. The quantity of hair to use is, to a great degree, a matter of experience. Too large a clump will not bind securely to the hook shank, and the hairs may come loose. Too little hair requires that a large number of clumps be mounted and spun in order to complete the body, which is unnecessarily time-consuming.

As a rule of thumb, try using a clump of hair that, when cleaned and compacted between the fingertips, as shown above, is roughly ½ the hook gap. In general, working with smaller bundles gives better results than with larger ones when tying trout flies. Thin hook wires will bend easily under the kind of pressure required to flare thick clumps of hair. But hair varies considerably in its spinning properties, and experimentation and experience are the best guides.

Step 2. For hooks with larger gaps, trim off the tips of the hair so that the bundle is no longer than twice the hook gap. Hold the bundle by the end in the left fingertips as shown, and position it atop the hook shank so that the bundle is centered directly above the rearmost thread wrap.

For hooks with small gaps, see Steps 1a-4a.

Step 3. Take two complete wraps of thread, directly on top of one another, around the middle of the hair bundle. The thread should be just tight enough to snug against the hair, but not so tight that the hair begins to flare or is disturbed from its position on the top of the shank.

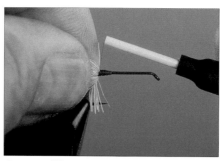

Step 6. When the hair is securely bound to the shank, draw the tying thread to the front of the bundle. Preen back the hair as shown, and take 3 or 4 tight wraps of thread against the base of the hair, as shown. This helps consolidate the bundle and fix its position on the shank.

Step 8a. A number of hair-compacting tools are available to the tyer, but like the Brassie Hair Packer shown here, all such tools slip over the hook eye and compact the hair at the base.

Use the fingers of the left hand as a "backstop" against which to push the tool. Unless you counteract the force of the tool this way, you may push the hair down around the hook bend.

Step 4. This is really the crucial step in spinning hair. Apply tension to the thread, and as you do so, begin taking another wrap around the middle of the bundle. As you apply pressure to the thread and begin to wrap, the hair will begin to flare and want to spin and "follow" the thread around the shank.

When you feel the hair wanting to spin down the far side of the hook shank, slowly release the hair from the left fingers. At the same time, increase tension on the tying thread and continue wrapping the thread, allowing the hair to roll around the hook shank.

Step 7. Prepare and clean another bundle of hair. Trim the tips off, but length is not critical now since the hook spear and point offer no obstacle to spinning.

Mount the second bunch and spin it just as you did the first, repeating Steps 2-6.

Note that in this photo, we've used a contrasting color of hair for the second bundle—both to differentiate it from the first bundle, and to show how banded bodies can be fashioned by using hairs of different colors.

Step. 9. Continue mounting and spinning clumps of hair, and periodically compacting them until the desired length of hook shank is covered.

Then secure the thread with a series of half-hitches or a whip-finish to prevent the thread from unraveling. Clip the thread.

The spun body is now ready for trimming using one of the techniques shown in "Shaping Spun, Stacked, and Wrapped Bodies," p. 155.

Step 5. Continue wrapping the thread slowly, increasing tension to just below the breaking point. (Hair is slippery and must be bound tightly to the shank.) The hair should flare quite dramatically, and distribute itself evenly around the shank.

Continue wrapping slowly. After two or three wraps, enough friction will build up against the hook shank so that the hair will no longer spin and it will be firmly affixed.

Step 8. When the second bundle is in place, the hair should be compacted. Such compression helps form a dense and uniform body.

Compacting hair can be accomplished by flanking the hair with the fingertips of both hands, and pushing inward at the base of the spun hair from both sides. Take care that the fingertips of the right hand don't push into the hook point.

Hair can also be compacted using a hair-packing took as shown in Step 8a.

Spinning a body by using clumps of hair that are themselves composed of smaller bundles of differently colored hair will produce a mottled or blotched effect, as shown on the left.

Mixing cleaned hairs of different colors in a hair stacker to randomize the fibers will produce a body of blended shades and tones, as shown on the right.

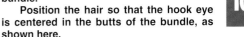

Step 1a. For hooks with smaller gaps, trim off the tips so that the bundle is about ¾" to 1" long. Hold the bundle near the middle with the fingers of the right hand. Position it atop the hook shank so that the length of hair that extends back behind the tying thread, toward the bend, is slightly less than one hook gap. This short end of the bundle will spin around the shank without catching on the hook point.

Step 2a. Take 2 complete wraps of thread, directly on top of one another, around the bundle. Let the bobbin hang as shown.

Step 3a. Reach the left hand in front of the vise stem to grab the bobbin. (If you grasp it from behind the vise, you won't be able to make the thread wrap that is required shortly.) Pull down on the bobbin until the hair begins to flare.

Step 4a. Begin taking a wrap of thread, increasing pressure as you go. When you feel the hair begin to slip and start to spin, relax pressure on the hair butts with the right hand. But do not completely release them. Rather, use your right fingertips to help work the hair around the shank, dis-

tributing it evenly. Keep the long end of the bundle loosely trapped in a "cage" made by the fingertips of the right hand. The hair should be loose enough to spin inside the fingertips, but not so loose that it flares and catches on the hook point.

Continue wrapping the thread slowly, and increasing tension. The hair should flare. When it is evenly distributed around the shank, take a very tight turn of thread to bind it securely to the shank.

After this first bundle is mounted, the remainder of the fly can be dressed as explained in Step 6.

Flared Bodies

Flared bodies are actually a kind of hybrid. In appearance they resemble spun bodies, since the hair is ultimately spread radially around the shank, and so the method can be used to create banded as well as single-color bodies. From the standpoint of technique, flaring more closely resembles stacking since the thread flares the hair, but thread pressure does not spin the material around the shank. (A similar technique can be used to dress solid fibers, as shown in **Method #63: Wrapped-around Wool Stacking**, p. 151, but strictly speaking, this application is really a stacking technique since the solid-fibers do not flare.)

The hairs and threads suitable for flaring are identical to those used for spinning bodies.

Method #59:

Flaring Hollow Hair

In flaring hair, the tyer positions the bundle of material so that the hair is distributed around the shank prior to mounting and then secures, but does not spin, the hair with thread.

This approach is perhaps most commonly used in dressing hollow-hair heads (see **Method #1: Clipped Head**, p. 425), but it can be used to fashion bodies as well. The technique is simpler than spinning or stacking hair, though if the hair bundle is not reasonably well-centered around the hook shank, the resulting body may not be uniform in density since the thread pressure does not redistribute material as it does in spinning. Larger bundles of material can be difficult to handle with this technique, though this is not typically a consideration with most trout flies.

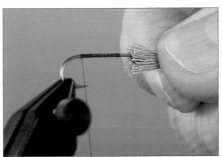

Step 1. Prepare a hook and a bundle of hollow hair as explained in **Method #58: Spinning Hollow Hair**, Step 1, p. 145. Clip

the tips of the hair to form a straight even bundle.

Position the hair so that the hook eye is centered in the butts of the bundle, as shown here.

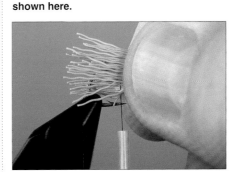

Step 2. Slide the hair lengthwise down the hook, keeping the shank centered inside the bundle.

With the left hand, apply a downward tension on the tying thread; this will make it easier to slide the hair past the thread as the bundle is pushed farther down the shank.

Push the bundle down the shank until it extends about halfway beyond the tying thread.

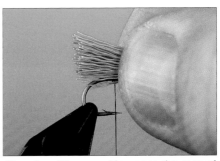

Step 2a. When working near the rear of the hook shank, especially a long one, it is often easier to position the hair atop the shank, then use your fingers to push the hair downward and work it around the shank until it is evenly distributed.

Step 3. Transfer the bundle to the left fingers, again taking care to keep the hook shank centered inside of the bundle.

Take 2 or 3 wraps of thread, directly atop one another, around the center of the hair. The thread should be just tight enough to snug against the hair, but not so tight that the hair begins to flare.

When the wraps are complete, pull firmly downward on the thread, but do not release your grip on the hair. Instead, use the left fingers to counteract any tendency of the hair to spin.

If necessary, take one or more additional tight wraps around the center of the hair bundle, until you can feel with your left fingers that the hair is firmly secured and resists spinning under thread pressure.

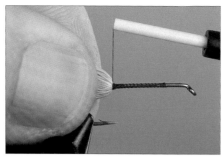

Step 4. Release the hair, and draw the tying thread to the front of the flared clump.

Preen the hair toward the bend, and take 3 or 4 tight wraps against the base of the hair, as shown.

Repeat Steps 1-4 until the desired length of hook shank is covered. After each subsequent application of hair, the material can be compressed with the fingers or a packing tool as shown in **Method #58: Spinning Hollow Hair**, Steps 8 and 8a, p. 146.

The completed body can be shaped using the techniques shown in "Shaping Spun, Stacked, and Wrapped Bodies," p. 155.

Stacked Bodies

In some respects, the procedures for stacking materials and those for spinning represent opposite approaches. Where spinning requires that materials move freely around the hook shank, stacking is designed to hold them securely in one spot. Despite this difference, however, the bodies produced by the two methods are nearly identical in density, texture, and general appearance.

Stacking, however, does allow a wider latitude in the final color scheme of the fly body. Like spinning, stacking can form vertical bands of color, but it can also produce horizontal bands, half-bands, "parr marks," spots, halos, gills, eyes and other specialized effects. Most of these are really of more interest to bass-fly tyers, and hence will not be detailed here, but some interesting streamer and dry-fly bodies can be fashioned by employing simpler color arrangements.

For the trout-fly tyer, one of the chief advantages of stacking techniques is that they are practical with materials that don't flare, that is, materials other than the hollow hairs. Not only is the tyer's range of materials expanded, but wool, yarn, and marabou can be used to fashion the type of fast-sinking, clipped bodies that are impossible to achieve with buoyant deer hair. Simple color arrangements can be produced with these solid-fiber materials, but because they don't flare, they tend to lack the precise definition between colors that allows forming more complex patterns—spots, halos, and so on. These materials are discussed in more detail in the section "Stacked Wool, Yarn, and Marabou," p. 151.

Stacked Hollow Hair

The types of hairs suitable for stacking are identical to those used in spinning and flaring (see "Spun Bodies," p. 145). Two basic approaches to stacking deer hair are

presented below. The conventional stacking method is used by most tyers, as both the horizontal orientation of the hook shank and the thread-handling techniques are most familiar.

The more unusual Messinger Method was devised in the 1920s by Joe Messinger, Sr., who originated the Messinger Bucktail Frog, a bass fly, and more to our purposes, the Irresistible, a standard trout pattern for decades.

Method #60:
Stacking Hollow Hair

For trout-fly tyers, the primary advantage in stacking hair is in constructing bodies on which the dorsal and ventral sides are of different colors, as shown in the following demonstration. In general, there is little to be gained in stacking hair for bodies formed from a single color of material, since both spinning and flaring take less time and involve preparing fewer batches of material.

The keys to attractive stacked bodies—those with sharp, straight divisions of color—are consistency in the quantity, mounting, and positioning of the bundles of hair, and manipulating the thread so that hairs at the color-transition point do not intermix. To help in achieving such bodies, first, clean the hair thoroughly; small amounts of underfur left in the bundle will catch on the thread and drag stray hairs around the shank. Second, do not use overly large clumps of hair; they are difficult to secure with the relatively few thread wraps used in stacking. Finally, use a strong thread to apply lots of tension. Each wrap of thread tends to mix the colors of hair; use a minimum of wraps with maximum tension on each.

Step 1. Prepare a hook and a bundle of hair as explained **Method #58: Spinning Hollow Hair**, Step 1, p. 145. In this case, however, the clump of hair will form only one-half of the first body section, so only half as much material is required.

The tips of the hair can be clipped, but tyer Skip Morris recommends mounting the hair with tips intact, as shown here. When the hair bundles are pulled back in Step 6, the longer tips on the underside hair make them easier to preen back separately to keep the colors from mixing.

The color of hair forming the underside of the body—white in this case—is mounted first. With the left fingers, center the clump of hair directly atop the tying thread. Note that hair tips extend over the hook eye.

Take 2 turns of thread, directly atop one another, over the center of the hair bundle. The wraps should be just snugged against the hair.

Step 2. Apply downward pressure to the bobbin. As the hair begins to flare, release your grip and let thread tension draw the hair to the underside of the shank.

Step 3. When the hair reaches the underside, press against the middle of the bundle firmly with your left index finger to prevent the hair from shifting.

Pull tightly on the bobbin to secure the hair. Take one more wrap of thread over the center of the bundle, and tighten very firmly.

Step 4. Prepare another bundle of the same size, using the hair that will form the top color.

Center it above the tying thread and take two snug wraps around the middle.

Step 5. Pull very firmly downward on the bobbin to flare this clump. Use your left hand to keep the hair atop the shank.

Take one more wrap of thread around the center of both bundles. As you wrap, wiggle the thread from side to side to seat it between the hairs.

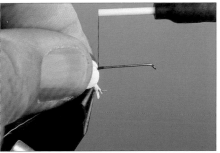

Step 6. Preen all the hair back toward the hook bend, keeping the colors separated as much as possible. The longer hair on the underside of the shank will help you draw this clump back separately.

Draw the tying thread forward, and take 2 or 3 wraps directly ahead of the flared hair, as shown.

Step 7. Repeat Steps 1-6, mounting additional bundles. For a denser body, compress the hair as shown in **Method #58: Spinning Hollow Hair,** Steps 8 and 8a, p. 145.

When the desired length of hook shank is covered, shape the body using any of the methods shown in "Shaping Spun, Stacked, and Wrapped Bodies," p. 155.

Method #61:
Messinger Stacking

This method involves mounting the hook vertically in the vise and securing individual clumps of hair by knotting each to the shank separately—a distinctly different approach than the continuous-thread method almost universally used by tyers today. Joe Messinger, Jr., son of the originator and renowned tyer from Morgantown, West Virginia, has carried on the tradition and generously furnished instructions for our own presentation of the technique.

This approach allows for a precise placement of materials, gives good lateral color separation, and builds an unusually durable body. The unconventional approach may strike many tyers as complicated, but it is conceptually quite simple. It takes practice—particularly the unfamiliar thread-handling, but once mastered, it is an efficient technique. This method may also have the distinction of being one of the few, if not only, fly-tying method in which the tyer's teeth are an integral part of the process.

The technique requires a vise in which the jaws can be positioned vertically, and the

vise head can be rotated 180 degrees. In C-clamp vises, this merely requires adjusting the tension on the vise stem so that the jaws don't slip downward, but the stem will still rotate. On vises with a metal base, the stem will turn in the socket on the base.

Thread selection is very important since heavy knotting tension is used. For trout flies in sizes smaller than #8 or so, Messinger recommends knotting the hair with size A rod-winding thread; on larger flies, he prefers cotton-covered polyester button-and-carpet thread for its strength and ability to hold a knot well.

The following demonstration shows the technique for dressing a two-color body for an Irresistible—a pattern designed by Joe Messinger, Sr.—but the technique is suitable for any hollow-hair body. For greater clarity of illustration, we're tying the body on a much larger hook than usual.

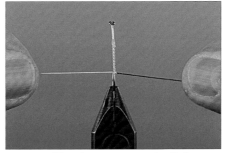

Step 1. Tie whatever type of tail the pattern requires (we've omitted it here) using ordinary tying thread. Secure the tail tightly, tie-off the thread with a whip-finish or a few half-hitches, and clip.

A sturdy thread foundation is necessary for the hair. If the tail has been mounted with size 6/0 thread or larger, the foundation can be wrapped immediately after the tail is secured; the thread should be twisted tightly to form the foundation. Here, a thicker, more visible thread is used.

To form the foundation, mount the thread at the frontmost point of the body; the thread should be positioned accurately, since it furnishes a reference point for finishing the body. Wrap the thread down the shank in an open spiral. When the rearmost thread wrap securing the tail is reached, reverse the wrapping direction, and wrap forward in an open spiral, creating a crisscross foundation on the shank, as shown here. When the frontmost wraps are reached, secure the thread with a whip-finish or half-hitches and clip it. Coat the foundation with a thin film of head cement or CA glue.

Position the vise jaws vertically, and mount the hook vertically so that the hook point faces away from the tyer, as shown. Because this technique requires holding one end of the thread in the teeth, the vise jaws must be elevated. Raise the jaws so that the hook is at about mid-chest level.

Strip off about 2 arm-lengths of knotting thread from the spool. You can clip this thread, but Messinger does not; leaving one end attached to the spool—what is called the "standing thread"—helps distinguish it during knotting from the free end—or "tag end"—of the thread. Being able to distinguish these separate sections of the thread is important during tying.

With hard, non-tacky wax, wax about two feet of thread at the tag end. Place the thread spool off to one side of the vise.

This next step can be omitted after some proficiency is gained, but it simplifies things a bit for the novice. Form a loose overhand knot in the thread about one foot from the tag end. Slip the knot over the hook eye and slide it down the shank. Tighten the knot on the far side of the shank (the side facing away from the tyer) directly over the lowermost thread wrap securing the tail. The tag end of the thread should project to the tyer's right. The tag end of the thread shown here is colored black to better distinguish it from the white standing end during the tying sequence.

It is important in forming this knot that the tag end be long enough, since no additional thread is available once tying begins. There must be enough tag thread to handle conveniently and finish the body.

Step 2. Prepare a bundle of hair—deer hair is used here—as explained in **Method #2: Preparing and Cleaning Hair,** p. 68. This hair will form the top of the fly body.

Grasp the standing (white) thread in your teeth, and the (black) tag in your right hand to form a "V" of thread at the hook shank, as shown.

In your left hand, grasp the hair bundle lengthwise (not crosswise) so that the fingertips are positioned at the center of the bundle.

Position the hair against the hook shank so that the center of the bundle is in the "V" of the thread, as shown.

Step 3. Bring the tag of thread over the center of the hair bundle, over the standing thread, and transfer it momentarily to the last two fingers of the left hand, as shown. Note here that the right hand has been repositioned behind the vise, ready to regrasp the tag end of the thread.

Step 4. Transfer the tag of thread back to the right hand.

Pull firmly on the tag to flare the hair. At the same time, use your neck to pull back and apply countertension on the standing thread held in your teeth. This countertension will prevent the hair from being drawn around the shank.

When flaring the hair like this, pinch the bundle tightly in the left fingers to hold it on the near side of the shank and prevent it from spinning.

Step 5. Bring the tag of thread around the back of the hook shank, and forward toward the tyer.

In this step, an overhand knot is formed around the bundle. The trick is to form it with the right hand only, since the hair cannot yet be released.

Hold the tag in the right thumb and forefinger. Lay the tag over the standing thread—which is still held under moderate tension in the teeth—to form a loop. With the last two fingers of the right hand, reach through the loop and capture the tag, as shown.

Step 6. Pull the tag through the loop, forming an overhand knot.

Pull the tag to seat the knot directly atop the thread wrap used to flare the hair in Step 4.

When the knot is partially seated, you can remove the thread from your teeth and use both hands to pull the knot tight. Note that the threads are pulled directly outward from the shank, and that the tag end is to the tyer's right.

Step 7. Rotate the vise 180 degrees, so that the hook point now faces the tyer. Straighten the threads, which have now reversed position. The tag end is now on the left, the standing thread on the right.

With the left fingers, preen the flared hair back away from the hook shank, as shown.

Take the tag end of the thread, which is now on the left, and bring it behind the hook so that it passes between the hook shank and the preened-back hair, and extends to the right.

Bring the standing thread between the hook shank and hair, so that it is now on the left.

Step 8. Pull the threads downward against the base of the hair. Tug them slightly or rock them to compact the hair downward.

The thread is now is the same position as in Step 1.

Step 9. Additional bundles of hair are mounted in the same way as the first. There are a few differences, shown in the steps that follow, but since the basic technique has been demonstrated, these steps are abbreviated.

Prepare a second clump of hair of a color to be used for the belly of the fly.

Replace the standing thread in your teeth, grasp the tag in your right hand, and form a "V" of thread as described in Step 2.

With the left fingers, position the second clump of hair in the "V". Note here, however, that as the left fingertips position the hair, the rear portion of the pads on the left thumb and forefinger pinch around the shank and press downward and back on the flared hair from the first bundle. Pushing the flared hair away from the tyer like this helps seat the second bundle close to the first and promotes good color separation between the bundles.

Step 10. Take a loop of thread around the second bundle of hair, and flare it as described in Steps 3-4.

Maintain tension on the tag end, and elevate it slightly so that it touches the pad of your thumb. Bring the thread around the back of the hook shank, following the contour of your fingertips. That is, as the thread is brought round to the front of the shank, it should be in contact with the left fingers at all times. In this photo, the thread has passed the thumb and is being "dragged" over the tip of the index finger as it comes to the front of the shank.

Carefully following the contour of the fingers like this helps slip the thread between the hook shank and the flared hair from the first bundle. Handled in this way, the thread will not drag hair from the first bundle to the front of the shank, and good color separation will be maintained.

Step 11. Once the thread has been brought to the front of the shank, secure it with an overhand knot seated directly on the thread wrap used to flare the hair, as shown in Steps 5-6.

Step 12. Again, rotate the vise 180 degrees. The thread ends will now be reversed.

Use the left fingertips to preen back the flared hair from the second bundle.

Bring the tag end of the thread to the right, as explained in Step 7. As you do so, work it between the two hair colors. That is, slip it upward between the two bundles, then behind the hook shank, over the preened-back hair, and down between the bundles on the right side of the shank.

Do the same with the standing thread, bringing it to the left side of the shank.

Grasp the threads, and pull downward to compact the hair as shown in Step 8.

Repeat Steps 9-12 until the end of the thread foundation, which marks the front edge of the body, is reached.

After the last bundle of hair has been mounted and compacted, tie a square knot against the near side of the hook shank to secure the knotting thread. Clip the threads.

The body can now be shaped using the techniques described in "Shaping Spun, Stacked, and Wrapped Bodies," p. 155.

Shown here are two finished Irresistibles tied by Joe Messinger, Jr. Note the dense, finely grained bodies and the distinct lateral color separation.

Stacked Wool and Yarn

Unlike hollow hair, wools and yarns are solid, and under thread pressure, they exhibit virtually no flare. Other measures must be taken to raise the fibers perpendicular to the hook shank. Moreover, where hollow hair is generally quite straight, some of these other fibers tend to be wavy or crinkled, a characteristic that causes them to cling together and interlock, and so they must be prepared in a way that separates the fibers to maximize the fullness of the body. When properly prepared and stacked, however, these materials can make dense, finely grained bodies that take trimming detail well and are extremely durable.

In general, stacked wool and yarn can produce most of the same color effects as stacked hair—two-tone bodies, mottles, bands, and so on—by blending or combining colors in advance or by applying clumps of material selectively on the shank.

There are two types of wool suitable for stacking. The first is ram's wool on the hide. Often sold as "sculpin wool," it is available in a variety of natural and dyed colors and can be obtained from fly-tying suppliers and shops. The hair length varies from 1-3", but is generally long enough to create bodies on even large flies.

The second material is wool that has been spun into a thick, loose rope. Its principal use is for yarn spinning and weaving, and is available from shops that specialize in supplies for those crafts. The material has a number of virtues. The loose rope, with fibers already aligned, is a convenient format for the tyer. Moreover, the tyer isn't restricted to sheep's wool; a number of other types and textures are available—angora goat and camel among them. Finally, material in this

form is significantly less expensive than wool patches. There are, however, two drawbacks. First, wool ropes of this type are generally sold only in natural colors—various shades of brown, tan, and cream—and while they are useful and attractive, some of the fly-tying standards, like black and olive, are difficult to come by. These materials, however, dye quite well, and the rope strands make handling during dyeing a simple matter. The second drawback is that the fibers are often somewhat straight, and such materials don't provide the same impression of bulk in the body as do more crinkly or kinked materials such as wool on the hide.

Synthetic yarns can also be stacked provided they have certain characteristics—they must be straight (not spun, twisted, or worsted), relatively fine-fibered, and manufactured into thick ropes. The material sold as "Glo-Bug Yarn" or "Egg Yarn" meets these criteria and is the synthetic best suited to stacked bodies. It's obtainable in a variety of colors, though most of these are bright or fluorescent shades best suited to attractor-type patterns.

Wools and yarns of this type are both coarse and slippery—a combination that demands a strong tying thread to secure them firmly. On smaller patterns using small bundles of material, 6/0 thread may prove sufficient, but in most cases thread that is 3/0 or stronger will give better results. Only a few wraps are used to secure the hair or yarn, so you must work close to the breaking strength of the thread.

The techniques detailed in this section can be used with wool on the hide, wool or fur ropes, or egg yarn. The tying procedures are identical regardless of material, though wool on the hide and some wool ropes require a bit of advance preparation.

Method #62:
Preparing Stacking Wool

All patches of wool on the hide and some wool ropes require preparation to untangle and separate the hairs. This is a simple matter of combing out the fur.

Step 1. Wool patches are more easily prepared and cut into clumps for tying if the patch is cut (from the hide side) into strips about ½" to ¾" wide.

Using a comb with widely spaced teeth, comb the hair from skin to tips thoroughly to straighten out any tangles and remove any debris caught in the wool.

Step 2. Cut a clump of wool of the desired size close to the skin. Hold the wool by the tips, pinching the clump tightly at the middle. Then run the comb a few times through the butts of the hair to straighten any tangles and remove any short fibers.

Step 3. Clip off the tips of the hair so that the clump is about 1 to 1½ inches long. Trimming the tips gives a bundle of hair that is relatively uniform in density.

Where a wool patch can be brushed quite vigorously because the hairs are attached to the hide, wool ropes used by yarn spinners and weavers must be treated a little more delicately. The individual hairs are not anchored, and excessive combing will eventually pull out all the hair from the rope and form it into a ball of fur on the brush or comb—an excellent way to make dubbing, but not too useful for stacked bodies.

With wool ropes, the comb should be run through the end of the bundle just a few times to straighten any twists or tangles.

Method #63:
Wrap-around Wool Stacking

In this method, only one clump of material is mounted at any given point on the shank; thus somewhat lower thread tension can be used, making this technique well-suited to small hooks that might bend under excessive tying pressure. Colors can be alternated with this technique to form banded bodies.

There are two approaches to this kind of stacking. The one shown in the main sequence resembles, in the handling of material, the procedure shown in **Method #59: Flaring Hollow Hair**, p. 147, though solid fibers will not actually flare. The approach shown in the alternate steps is useful when smaller quantities of material are used, as it allows for a more precise placement and uniform distribution of fewer fibers.

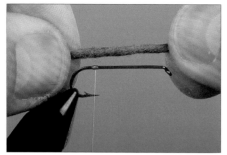

Step 1. With the thread at the rearmost point of the body, lay a foundation of 5 tight thread wraps toward the eye. Position the thread in the middle of this foundation.

Prepare a clump of wool (or other suitable material) as described in **Method #62: Preparing Stacking Wool**, p. 151. The quantity of material, naturally, varies with hook size and the wool texture. As a rough guide, try this: momentarily twist the material into a tight yarn; the resulting strand should be 2 to 4 times the thickness of the hook wire. Crinkled hairs, such as wool from patches, give better coverage on the shank and less material is required. Straight fibers, such as many yarn ropes, require a thicker bundle. This is only a rough guideline, however, as both materials and preferences in body density vary.

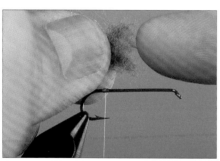

Step 2. Holding the clump of wool as shown, with the butts outward, use your little finger to form a small depression or dimple in the center of one end of the bundle. The "collar" of hair that is formed around this dimple should be evenly distributed.

Step 3. Holding the clump as shown, press the hook eye into the dimple, and slide the clump down the hook shank.

When you reach the tying thread, hold the bobbin with your left hand to keep the thread in position on the shank. Wiggle the bobbin to work the thread between the wool fibers until the clump is centered over the mounting point.

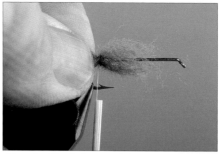

Step 4. Pinch the wool tightly against the shank directly behind the mounting point to hold it in position as the thread is wrapped.

Take one turn of thread under light pressure around the fibers and pull the bobbin tightly. Maintain your hold on the bundles, and take a second turn directly atop the first.

Release the wool for a moment and apply tension to the bobbin. If the hair begins to slip around the shank, take another tight turn around the bundle.

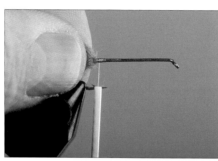

Step 5. With the bobbin beneath the shank, work the thread straight between the hairs and toward the hook eye.

When the thread is clear of the bundle, use your left fingers to preen the wool toward the hook bend. Take two or three tight wraps at the base of the hair to hold it in position.

Advance the thread 5 more wraps toward the eye to lay a foundation for the next clump, and then position the thread at the middle of this foundation.

Step 6. Prepare another clump of wool and position it for mounting. As you push the bundle of fibers over the hook eye and into position, notice how the new bundle "mushrooms" against the fibers already on the hook. Make sure the fibers on this new clump are evenly distributed, then preen all the material behind the mounting point back toward the hook bend to give a clear field for wrapping the thread.

Step 7. Secure the bundle as you did in Step 4.

Add additional clumps until the desired length of hook shank is covered. For denser bodies, compact the bundles as described in **Method #58: Spinning Hollow Hair**, Steps 8 and 8a, p. 146.

When the last bundle is mounted. Secure the thread with a few half-hitches and clip it.

Step 8. The body can now be shaped as explained in **Method #67: Clipped Bodies**, p. 155.

Here the body has been clipped to form the abdomen for a dragonfly nymph.

Step 1a. You can also mount the wool by first flattening the bundle against the tying bench, making a band or strip of fibers that is uniform in density.

Step 2a. Center the strip of fibers over the mounting point.

With the left fingers positioned on the clump just behind the mounting point, pinch the wool around the hook shank to make a uniform layer of fibers.

Proceed to Step 4.

Method #64:
Single-stacked Wool

While this technique in fact uses two clumps of wool tied in at one point on the hook shank, the wool bundles are mounted individually; hence they are "single-stacked" as opposed to the simultaneous mounting of two or more bundles as described in **Method #65: Multi-stacked Wool,** p. 153.

The method described in the following sequence gives a good coverage and density of material. Two-tone bodies can be fashioned by mounting materials of different colors on the top and bottom of the shank. Regardless of the color scheme, however, the bundles of material used should be of consistent size.

Step 1. With the thread at the rearmost point of the body, lay a foundation of 5 tight thread wraps toward the eye. Position the thread in the middle of this foundation.

Prepare a clump of wool of the desired size as described above in **Method #62: Preparing Stacking Wool,** p. 151.

Step 2. Position the bundle atop the hook shank, centered over the mounting point. Using light tension, take one wrap around the middle of the wool clump.

Begin a second wrap. As the thread crosses the material, apply pressure on the bobbin. The tension will cause the bundle to begin rotating around the hook shank. Use the fingers of your left hand to help push the clump to the underside of the hook shank and center it there.

Step 3. Pinch the wool bundle to help hold it in place, and pull tightly on the thread to seat the material securely.

Take another wrap of thread directly atop the other two.

Step 4. Take a second clump of wool and center it over the mounting point. Under light tension, place one wrap of thread around it.

Step 5. Place your finger on the far side of the hook shank against the material to act as a "backstop." Pull tightly on the thread, holding the material on top of the shank with your finger.

Take another tight wrap or two to lock in the wool.

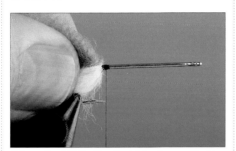

Step 6. With the bobbin beneath the shank, work the thread straight between the hairs and toward the hook eye.

When the thread is clear of the bundle, preen the wool toward the hook bend. Take two or three tight wraps at the base of the hair to hold it in position.

Advance the thread 5 more wraps toward the eye to lay a foundation for the next pair of wool clumps, and then position the thread at the middle of this foundation.

Step 7. Repeat Steps 2-6, mounting bundles of material above and below the shank until the desired body length is reached. For denser bodies, compact the bundles as described in **Method #58: Spinning Hollow Hair,** Step 8 or 8a, p. 146. When the last material has been applied, secure the thread with half-hitches and clip it.

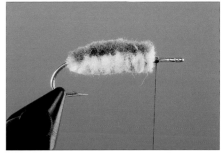

Step 8. Trim the body to the desired shape as explained in **Method #67: Clipped Bodies,** p. 155.

Method #65:
Multi-stacked Wool

With this technique, you can apply large quantities of material to the hook shank at one time. However, securing two or more clumps of material at once requires significant thread pressure—which requires a very strong thread and a sturdy hook. Hence the technique is best used with larger flies.

Mixing wool bundles of different colors can produce some interesting mottled patterns. Bright, contrasting colors are used in the following sequence to give a clearer illustration of the finished effect; on actual fly patterns, combinations of more muted tones produce very lifelike markings on baitfish patterns, particularly sculpins, and on larger nymphs.

Step 1. With the thread at the rearmost point of the body, lay a foundation of 5 tight thread wraps toward the eye. Position the thread in the middle of this foundation.

Prepare 2 or more clumps of wool of the desired size as described above in **Method #62: Preparing Stacking Wool,** p. 151. We're using three pieces of material here.

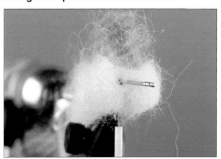

Step 2. Position the clumps of material so that they are centered over the mounting point, and adjust them so that they are symmetrical around the hook shank.

Step 3. Holding the material tightly in place with the left hand, take 3 or 4 very tight wraps of thread around the middle of all the clumps. The wraps of thread should be placed directly on top of one another.

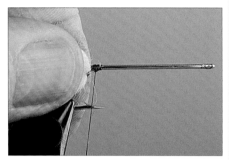

Step 4. With the bobbin beneath the shank, work the thread straight between the hairs and toward the hook eye. When the thread is clear of the bundle, pull the wool toward the hook bend. Take two or three tight wraps at the base of the hair to hold it in position.

Advance the thread 5 more wraps toward the eye to lay a foundation for the next group of wool bundles, and then position the thread at the middle of this foundation.

Step 5. Repeat Steps 2-4 until the desired length of hook shank is covered. For a mottled effect, shift the positions of the different colored bundles each time a group of wool clumps is mounted. For denser bodies, compact the bundles as described in **Method #58: Spinning Hollow Hair**, Step 8 or 8a, p. 146.

When the last material is applied, secure the thread with a few half-hitches and clip it.

Step 6. Trim the body to the desired shape as explained in **Method #67: Clipped Bodies**, p. 155.

Stacked Marabou and CDC

Like wools and yarns, marabou barbs can be stacked by binding bundles of material to the hook in a way that surrounds the shank. They can then be clipped to shape. The result is a soft, lifelike body that absorbs water and sinks readily, and has good natural movement in the water. Marabou barbs, however, are not particularly dense fibers, and it takes a large number of them to cover the hook shank, making this a somewhat tedious technique with large hooks. Still, the appearance and behavior of the finished body cannot be duplicated with other materials. Using bundles of differently colored marabou barbs will produce a mottled body.

While marabou bodies are used primarily on subsurface patterns, dry flies can be dressed using bodies of stacked CDC barbs, which provides excellent floatation on surface patterns. Finally, however, there is little to be gained in buoyancy or effort if a stacked CDC body is trimmed into a very narrow profile of the type used on mayfly adults. Such bodies are better fashioned from CDC barbs that are chopped and dubbed. However, for broader silhouettes, such as the wedge shape of a caddis, stacked CDC is ideal, and indeed English tyer Taff Price incorporates this technique in his Riffle Sedge design.

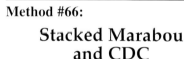

Method #66:

Stacked Marabou and CDC

The best results are obtained by using the fullest, fluffiest marabou barbs you can find. Blood feathers will work, but barbs from marabou quills are often more suitable (see "Marabou," p. 11). Excessive thread pressure isn't required, so thinner threads can be used.

The following sequence shows the technique for stacking barbs; marabou is used in the demonstration, but CDC barbs are handled in an identical fashion.

Note that a very similar type of body can be formed from either marabou or CDC spun on a dubbing board (see **Method #48: Flat Dubbing Board**, p. 136) or on a pre-dubbed thread (see **Method #50: Hidy/Leisenring Pre-dubbed Thread**, p. 138). Though a thread-core dubbing loop (see **Method #38: Trap-loop Dubbing**, p. 129) can be used, it is more difficult to apply the barbs densely inside the loop. The resulting "feather-barb chenille" is wrapped around the shank and then clipped to shape. Spinning barbs in advance like this, however, does not give the tyer quite the same control over the distribution of color, but it is faster.

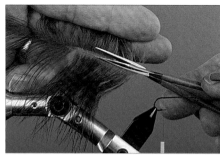

Step 1. Position the tying thread at the tailing point. Using the left fingers in a "scissor" fashion as shown, clip a clump of barbs from the stem of a marabou feather. The exact quantity varies with the hook size and texture of the feather, but 35 to 45 individual barbs—or approximately 1 ½ inches along the quill—is about right.

Step 2. Bundle the barbs by pinching the butts together.

Step 3. Mount this clump atop the hook shank at the tailing position using 4 or 5 tight wraps of thread. Clip the butts neatly.

Note the position the thread—about 3 wraps ahead of where this first clump of marabou is mounted. This is the mounting point for the second clump.

Step 4. Clip a second bundle of marabou barbs, and bind them tightly to the far side of the hook shank, as shown in this top view. Clip the butts neatly, and position the thread about 3 wraps ahead of where this second bundle was mounted.

Step 5. Clip a third bundle of marabou barbs, and bind them to the near side of the shank. Clip the butts, and leave the thread about 3 wraps ahead of where this third bundle was mounted.

Step 6. Compact the bundles by pushing with the fingertips from both front and rear, as shown. Note that no barbs have been mounted beneath the shank. In mounting and compacting the barbs, enough of them will migrate to the underside of the shank to provide coverage.

Step 7. Repeat Steps 3-6, alternately mounting bundles on the top, far side, and near side of the shank. After each group of 3 bundles is mounted, compact them on the shank.

When the desire length of hook shank is covered, secure the thread with a few half-hitches and clip.

Step 8. Trim the body to the desired shape as shown in **Method #67: Clipped Bodies**, p. 155.

Shaping Spun, Stacked, and Wrapped Bodies

Though a fly pattern may occasionally call for a body of spun or stacked material that is left untrimmed—cased caddis, for instance, which are sometimes fashioned from unclipped deer hair, or leeches from untrimmed marabou—most bodies constructed by spinning, flaring, or stacking are eventually shaped in some manner. Moreover, other body materials are sometimes trimmed as well, particularly fur chenilles spun in dubbing loops or dubbing brushes and wrapped-hackle bodies.

The most common and versatile approach to shaping bodies is to clip them to the desired profile using scissors. Bodies of virtually any material can be trimmed this way, but it is imperative that the scissors be quite sharp. Dull tools will merely bend the body material in the direction that pressure is applied, cutting the ends at an angle and leaving a rough, uneven, or badly shaped body. Serrated scissors are best, as the small notches trap the body fibers and prevent them from slipping forward. To cut rounded contours on a body, scissors with curved blades are the most efficient and accurate.

Bodies formed from very densely packed materials—primarily hollow hair and wool—can be trimmed using a razor blade. Provided they are very sharp, razor blades cut smoothly and effortlessly and are capable of shaving very small amounts of material from the body. Many tyers rough-cut a hair or wool body to shape with scissors, and finish it using a razor blade.

An unusually smooth and uniform surface can be created on a body of spun or stacked hollow hair by using a flame to shape the material. This approach is used largely to smooth out corners or remove bumps or high spots from the body after it has been cut to nearly its final dimensions using a scissors or razor. With care, wool can be flame-shaped, but the method is not really practical with other materials.

Method #67:
Clipped Bodies

The basic approach to clipping bodies is the same regardless of the material or final profile; first, the body is roughed-out into some symmetrical shape—usually square, rectangular, or circular in cross section—and then carefully trimmed into its final dimensions. The key here is to work evenly around the hook shank, checking your progress often, to maintain the symmetry of the body. Hasty or overly aggressive trimming is a little like cutting the legs off a table to make them even; if you're not careful, eventually there'll be nothing left.

There is one important point worth noting when trimming hollow hair. Such materials are generally used in a fly body to promote floatation, and buoyancy can be affected by the way the body is clipped. While larger fly bodies present little problem in this respect, smaller bodies often require trimming the hair quite close to the shank to achieve the proper proportions. The hair near the shank is quite compressed, both by the tying thread and by the compacting of hair bundles during the tying process. This kind of compression can flatten or rupture the hollow cells inside the hair, and the upshot is that the hair very close to the shank offers little buoyancy. A very closely trimmed body will not float as well as a thicker one.

To sidestep this problem, it's best to trim small flies asymmetrically by cropping the bottom of the body quite close to the hook shank and forming the body contour from the hair above the shank. The hair on top of the shank will thus be kept as long as possible and aid floatation. Trimming like this also keeps the hook gap clear, which aids in hooking with very small flies.

The main sequence that follows (Steps 1a-1g) shows the general technique for scissor-trimming any material. In this demonstration, a deer-hair body is clipped to the tapered profile used for Irresistible patterns, but the method is identical regardless of body shape or material.

The short demonstrations that follow the main sequence, identified by letter/number combinations—Steps 2a-2b, 3a-3b, and so on—illustrate other types of clipped bodies that can be formed. Fur chenilles and wrapped hackle are used in the demonstrations, but hair and wool bodies can be trimmed to these shapes as well. Still other body shapes have been shown in the preceding methods in this section.

Step 1a. It is certainly possible to trim the entire fly while holding the hook in your hand, but the first rough cuts are often more easily achieved if the hook is held in a vise, since this gives an accurate sense of the orientation of the hook—where the bottom and top are—which is sometimes difficult to determine when the hook point is obscured by untrimmed hair.

Place the hook upside-down in the vise. (Note that angling the vise head toward you at 45 degrees gives a better view when trimming.)

If some of the hair projects forward toward the hook eye, use the scissors to trim it perpendicular to the hook shank, creating a flat face at the front of the body.

Step 1b. Position the scissors parallel to the hook shank, and cut the bottom of the body flat.

Step 1c. Remount the hook in the vise so that it is right-side up. Again with the scissors parallel to the shank, trim both sides to an equal length.

Then trim the hair on the top parallel to the shank.

With any body profile or any material, use the rough-cuts to form the body into a symmetrical shape—in this case, a body that is square in cross section.

Step 1d. Trim the corners of the square. Cut from head to tail, giving the body its taper and beginning to round it at the same time.

Step 1e. Remove the hook from the vise. (We're leaving it mounted only for a clearer demonstration.) Larger hooks can simply be held by the bend. For smaller hooks, clamp them in a hackle pliers, E-Z Hook, or hemostats to give more working room.

Using the scissor points, trim away any hairs that project from the rear of the body.

Step 1f. Skilled deer-hair tyers, such as Tim England, who dress patterns for display, recommend steaming the fly at this point to return the hair to its original position and stiffen it, which helps in final trimming. To steam the fly, clamp it in a pair of hemostats and hold it over the spout of a boiling kettle, turning the fly to make sure all sides of the body are exposed to the steam. This process provides the foundation for a very smooth, uniform body on exhibition-grade flies, but is really optional on more workmanlike patterns that are to be fished.

Step 1g. Now smooth the body out, trimming to final shape. Trim lengthwise along the shank, turning the fly often to maintain a uniform, symmetrical body.

The following 3 sequences show clipped bodies formed from fur chenilles using the techniques shown in "Dubbing Loops," p. 129, and "Dubbing Brushes," p. 133. Bodies of this type can also be formed from feather barbs and from strands of long-fibered synthetic chenilles such as Plushille.

Step 2a. Shown here is a dubbing brush spun from hare's mask. Ultimately, the stiff guard hairs are used to represent the legs on a nymph, and the material must be mounted in the dubbing brush so that these hairs will be of the proper length.

Step 2b. To form a mayfly nymph, the abdomen of the fly is trimmed flat on top and bottom, and narrowed at the sides. The long hair atop the thorax is trimmed short, the wingcase is formed from a drop of epoxy as explained in **Method #6: Epoxy and Varnish Wingcases**, p. 234.

Step 3b. Shown here is a dubbing brush of olive rabbit fur with a gold-wire core. Again, guard hairs are used for legs and the material is mounted in the dubbing loop so as to obtain the correct proportions.

Step 3b. To form a scud, the fur on the top and sides of the shank is trimmed close to expose the wire core, which gives a segmented appearance and a bit of flash to the body. The shellback is formed from a coat of epoxy.

Step 4a. Here, brown rabbit fur is spun in a dubbing brush.

10

Step 4b. To form the bulky abdomen of a dragonfly nymph, the body is trimmed flat on the top and bottom.

Step 4c. The sides are rounded to form a teardrop shape.

Palmered hackle can be clipped to produce a variety of body shapes. There are two keys to getting good results. First, wrap the body as uniformly and densely as possible, taking care that no barbs are trapped beneath the hackle stems when they are wrapped. Such bodies are best obtained by using **Method #7: Multiple-hackle Collar**, p. 354, except the hackles are wrapped over the body portion of the hook shank. Using three or more feathers will give the best results.

The second key is choosing a hackle consistent with the purpose.

Step 5a. Shown here are three webby and absorbent hen saddles feathers wrapped around the shank and trimmed to form the body for a small dragonfly nymph.

Step 5b. Shown at the right are three dry-fly hackles wrapped on a hook. The hackles can be clipped to form a mayfly taper (shown in the middle) that can be used in place of deer hair on flies such as the Irresistible. Or they can be clipped with a reverse taper (shown on the right) to create a body much like that of a Goddard Caddis.

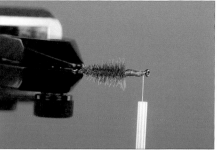

Step 5c. Dry-fly hackle can also be used to form sparse nymph bodies with a segmented, gilled appearance. Here the wrapped hackle is trimmed flat on top and bottom, then tapered on the sides.

Method #68:
Razor-trimmed Bodies

Many tyers prefer to shape hollow-hair with a razor blade. The process is fast and relatively easy, though it takes a surer and steadier hand than scissor-trimming, particularly when working close to the hook shank. One small slip here can cut the tying thread and destroy the body.

Razor-cutting works best on densely compacted bodies, where the hair offers some resistance against the blade when cutting. For razor cutting, single-edge, injector-type blades are a good choice, as are double-edge safety blades, though these should be cut lengthwise to form two separate cutting edges and help protect the fingers.

Preferences vary when it comes to positioning the vise and hook. Some tyers angle the eye of the hook toward them. Others prefer to face the fly head-on and cut from the eye to the bend. Still others mount the hook vertically, and cut downward.

Step 1. "Sight down" the hook shank from eye to bend, and position the razor blade to make a flat cut down the bottom of the body. Trim the hair by using a sawing, slicing, or rocking motion.

Step 2. Trim the three other sides to form a square body.

Step 3. Now cut along the corners of the body, tapering and rounding the fly. Be extremely careful when cutting the narrow end of the body if it tapers right down to the hook shank. Nicking the thread will prove disastrous. You can trim the narrow end with scissors instead.

At this point, you may wish to steam the hair as described above in **Method #67: Clipped Bodies**, Step 1f, p. 156.

Step 4. Now work carefully and systematically around the body, removing corners and rough edges, shaping the body into its final form.

Method #69:
Flame-shaped Bodies

A few brave souls use a match, lighter, or hot-tip tool to give final shape to hollow-hair bodies. The heat singes the hair evenly and accurately. Unlike scissors or razor blades that push against the hair and move it slightly during trimming, heat does not disturb the material and shapes it exactly in position on the hook shank. Flame-shaping is performed only as the final operation. The body must first be trimmed to nearly finished form with scissors or razor.

The pitfall here is obvious. A little too much enthusiasm will transform the fly into a deer-hair Hindenburg. It takes a steady hand. The singed hair will discolor slightly. On natural-hair bodies, the discoloration can give an interesting and lifelike effect. But on dyed hair, it dulls the overall color impression a bit.

Step 1. Trim the fly to its nearly finished form with scissors or razor blade. Clamp it in a hemostat, hackle pliers, or rotary vise—this procedure requires that the fly be rotated during shaping.

A butane lighter works best here, as it produces less soot than a match. Regardless, the heat source must, *at all times*, be held above the fly, since only the bottom of the flame is used to shape the body.

Carefully lower the heat source toward the body, stopping when the hair begins to singe. Use a light touch here, as the hair singes very readily and quickly.

Step 2. Move the flame along the body, maintaining a uniform distance from the hair to shape the body evenly.

Step 3. When one portion of the body has been shaped, rotate the hook and begin shaping another section.

Continue turning and shaping until the body reaches the desired proportions.

Step 4. With a small brush, such as a toothbrush, gently sweep the body free of the charred particles.

Tinsel, Wire, and Woven-Tubing Bodies

Tinsels, wires, and woven tubings all form bodies with flashy or reflective surfaces; they may add some sparkle to general attractor patterns, imitate the shimmer of baitfish scales on streamers, or replicate the glossy segmentation on some nymphs. Because these materials add no buoyancy to the fly, their use is restricted almost exclusively to subsurface patterns.

Flat Tinsel Bodies

The most common type of flat tinsels are those with metallic finishes, usually gold or silver, and virtually all the tinsels in widespread use today are made of Mylar, a plastic-like material that is superior to the older metal tinsels in almost every regard. It does not tarnish; it won't kink or break during wrapping; and it handles far more easily. The one drawback is that Mylar tinsel is less durable than the metal type—a problem that some tyers remedy by coating tinsel bodies with clear head cement or CA glue.

Probably the most practical type of metallic tinsel is the spooled Mylar variety that is silver on one side and gold on the other, thus serving double duty for the tyer. Tinsels of this sort come in a variety of sizes. The smallest, usually labeled #16 or #18, are typically reserved for ribbing flies. Size #14 is a medium width suitable for wrapping bodies on smaller hooks or ribbing larger ones. And wider tinsels, size #12 or below, are used to create tinsel bodies on larger hooks. Flat tinsels are available in a smooth finish for a body with a uniform appearance, and in an embossed finish, which gives the body a broken, scale-like effect.

Though spooled metallics are the most familiar types of tinsel, this category does include other materials. There are a large, and increasing, number of materials made of narrow Mylar strips given colored, reflective, or even holographic coatings, and sold under names such as Flashabou, Krystal Flash, Accent Flash, Prismatic Tinsel, Fly Flash, and so on. These are sold in bundled hanks and can be used in exactly the same way as conventional tinsels to produce bodies that range from the interesting to the outrageous. Mylar strip materials like these are available in an enormous variety of colors and finishes, and present only two real drawbacks to the tyer. First, they are generally available in only one width—roughly the equivalent of #14 or #16 tinsel, depending on the brand—which makes wrapping larger hooks somewhat tedious; second, some types are rather elastic, and care must be taken not to stretch the material when wrapping or an uneven body may result.

Both conventional tinsels and Mylar strip materials can be used as ribbing materials, and may be used to dress a hook shank beneath a floss body to compensate for the translucence of the floss when it becomes wet.

Tinsel bodies are relatively easy to create, though they must be wrapped over very smooth underbodies (see "Underbodies," p. 41). This is particularly true of Mylar tinsels, since the material is thin enough to conform tightly to any bumps or irregularities in the underbody and will produce a correspondingly uneven body. Tinsel can be wrapped over underbodies with a slight taper, but those with abrupt edges or steeper tapers—particularly lead wire underbodies—are generally unsuitable. On weighted patterns, tyers often substitute Mylar tubing for the tinsel.

Method #70:

Single-layer Tinsel Body

This technique, advocated by Dick Talleur for its simplicity, is perhaps best suited to wider tinsels, since the initial wraps of material must cover the thread at the mounting point. Thinner tinsels may show some unevenness here.

Step 1. If the pattern requires it, mount the tail, making sure that the excess tailing material is bound smoothly to the hook shank. Tailing materials, like the bucktail used here, that extend the entire length of the hook shank will produce the most uniform underbodies.

Since the first wrap of tinsel will be taken behind the mounting point, position the tying thread one "tinsel-width" ahead of the rearmost point of the body.

Step 2. Cut a length of tinsel and mount it on the near side of the hook shank. Bind it in with 3 or 4 tight wraps of flattened tying thread. When the tinsel is secure, advance the *flattened* thread evenly to the tie-off point.

Step 3. To begin wrapping, raise the tinsel vertically. It will fold over itself, or create a "pleat" as Dick Talleur describes it, behind the mounting point. Use your thumbnail to crease and flatten the fold, thus giving a neat appearance to the first wrap.

Step 4. The first wrap of tinsel is placed directly over the fold or pleat to hide it.

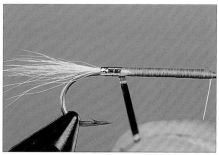

Step 5. Wrap the tinsel forward in adjacent, edge-to-edge wraps with no gaps. The easiest way to achieve this is to take a turn of tinsel that very slightly overlaps the previous wrap. Then slide the tinsel forward slightly. It will slip off the previous wrap and seat itself nicely alongside.

Step 6. Continue wrapping forward. Bind the tinsel at the tie-off point and clip the excess. If desired, coat the body with head cement or CA glue.

Method #71:

Double-layer Tinsel Body

This classic technique for applying tinsel ensures a body with no gaps, and the double layer of material helps hide small inconsistencies in the underbody.

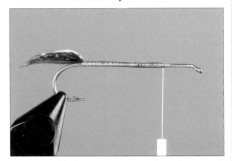

Step 1. If the pattern requires it, mount the tail, making sure that the excess tailing material is bound smoothly to the hook shank. Here, a slip of turkey wing quill is used, as it would be to dress a Muddler Minnow.

Position the thread at the body tie-off point.

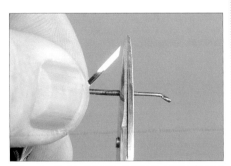

Step 2. Cut a length of tinsel, and clip the end at a 45-degree angle as shown.

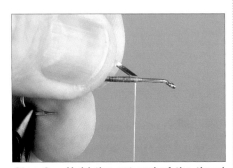

Step 3. Hold the cut end of the tinsel against the hook shank and parallel to it.

While holding the tinsel in the orientation shown here, bind the tip with 3 or 4 tight wraps of thread. Positioning the tinsel in this fashion ensure a smooth first wrap, since the tinsel is mounted so that it angles toward the hook bend, in the direction of wrapping.

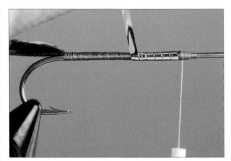

Step 4. Wrap the tinsel back in adjacent, edge-to-edge wraps with no gaps. The easiest way to achieve this is to take a turn of tinsel that very slightly overlaps the previous wrap. Then slide the tinsel backward slightly. It will slip off the previous wrap and seat itself neatly alongside.

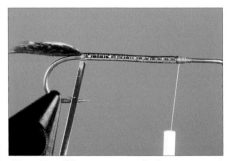

Step 5. When you reach the rearmost point of the body, reverse the direction of wrapping. The rearmost turn of tinsel should cover the tying thread that mounts the tail.

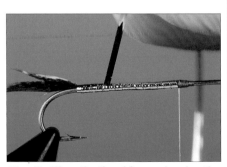

Step 6. Wrap the tinsel forward, using the technique described in Step 4.

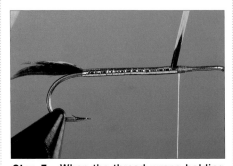

Step 7. When the thread wraps holding the tip of the tinsel are reached, stop wrapping the tinsel.

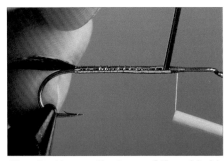

Step 8. Unwrap the turns of thread holding the tinsel tip, and wrap the body tinsel forward, covering the tip.

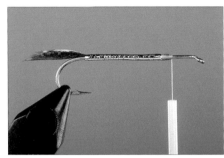

Step. 9. When the tip is covered, tie off the tinsel and clip the excess.

Method #72:

Twisted-tinsel Body

Twisted bodies can be made from tinsel-like Mylar materials, either the twisted type, like Krystal Flash, or flat varieties like Flashabou. They are useful when highly reflective, colored bodies are desired. Entomologist and fly-tyer Rick Hafele uses this style extensively—for bodies on midge pupae, small nymphs such as *Baetis*, and even as a substitute for Antron dubbing on LaFontaine's Sparkle Pupa patterns. The body is quick to tie, very durable, and quite effective.

The main sequence shows the basic wrap for a bundle of tinsel strands. The alternate sequence shows a faster technique using a spun loop of strands.

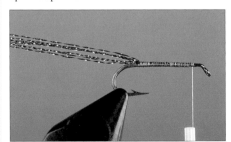

Step 1. Position the tying thread at the rearmost point of the body.

Select the desired quantity of body material—we're using Krystal Flash here. The specific number of strands depends on how bulky the finished body should be. Three strands (about the minimum) will produce a very slim body; ten or twelve strands a thick one.

Mount the material atop the hook shank at the last thread wrap. Bind the butts down to form a smooth, even underbody.

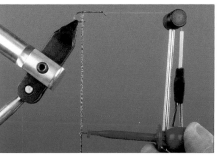

Step 2. Draw all the strands downward together, and twist them.

For a Krystal Flash body with a segmented appearance, spin the strands counterclockwise (when viewed from above), which follows the direction of twist already in the material and will produce a tightly corded strand. For a flatter body, spin the material clockwise, which removes the twist in the strands.

If using a material that is not manufactured with a twist, spin it clockwise for a tightly twisted body; spun in this direction, the material will maintain its twist during wrapping.

Twisting can be done with the fingers, hackle pliers, or as shown above, an E-Z Hook pliers.

Step 3. Begin wrapping the material forward in touching, adjacent wraps. The portion of material nearest the hook shank will be twisted most tightly. When that portion of material is wrapped, pause to retwist the strands as necessary to maintain a uniform appearance to the body.

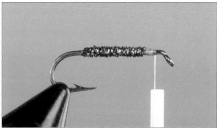

Step 4. Continue wrapping, retwisting the material as needed. Wrap to the tie-off point. Bind the strands and clip the excess.

Step 1a. A variation of this technique that is faster to tie employs a loop of material. Use half the number of strands that you would use for the method in the main sequence.

Loop the strands around the middle finger of your left hand, and pinch all the ends between left thumb and forefinger. Clip the ends to even them.

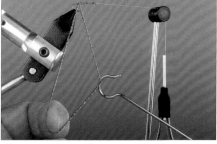

Step 2a. Tie in the ends directly atop the rearmost thread wrap, and bind them down to form a smooth, even underbody.

Insert a dubbing hook into the loop, twist the strands, and wrap the body. (If desired, a small amount of dubbing can be placed in the loop before spinning—see **Method #38: Trap-loop Dubbing**, p. 129, for further details about this technique.)

Oval and Round Tinsel Bodies

Oval and round (sometimes called "twisted") tinsels are manufactured from strands of metallic-finish Mylar wrapped around thread cores that are, respectively, oval and round in cross section. When wrapped, they give greater bulk and more distinct segmentation to a body than does flat tinsel. Primarily the province of tyers dressing steelhead and salmon patterns, these materials can nonetheless make effective bodies on trout streamers.

Two points are worth noting when tying oval or twisted tinsel bodies. First, as always, a smooth underbody gives the best results. Second, some heed should be paid to select a tinsel that is, at most, slightly larger than the hook shank diameter. If a large diameter material is wrapped around a very thin hook shank, the metallic strands on the exterior will separate slightly and create gaps that allow the core material to become visible.

Method #73:

Oval and Round Tinsel Bodies

The technique for wrapping these materials is quite straightforward, though again it should be emphasized that a smooth underbody will give the most pleasing results.

Step 1. Cut a length of tinsel. Pinch it tightly against the thumbnail as shown,

about ¼" from the end. Then strip off the exterior tinsel from the core. Pinching the material prevents the tinsel under the thumbnail from loosening or unraveling slightly during stripping.

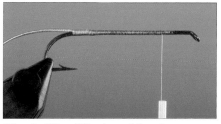

Step 2. Clip off the frayed tinsel.

Position the thread at the rearmost point of the body. Bind the exposed core of the material to the hook shank, and then take one wrap of thread over the exterior tinsel itself. This will ensure that the first wrap of material shows only the metallic coating, and not the core.

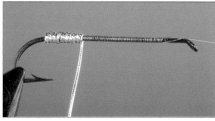

Step 3. Wind the tinsel forward in adjacent, touching wraps.

Step 4. Bind the material down at the tie-off point, angle-cut the tag, and bind down.

Wire Bodies

Wires of various sorts are sometimes used as a body material. They give distinct segmentation, add a small amount of weight to the fly, can produce a body with an extremely slim profile, and depending on the material chosen, may add a bit of flash to the pattern. Because of its handling simplicity, wire is often employed on very small nymph or chironimid patterns—perhaps most notably on Gene Lynch's Brassie Nymph—where tiny hook shanks can make the application of other body materials difficult.

Virtually any type of wire is suitable—gold, silver, copper, or brass fly-tying wire, colored craft wires, and so on. Many tyers have discovered an excellent source of fine, enamelled wire in used electrical components—old coils and small electric motors—and the same material is available in bulk from electrical supply houses.

As a rule, tyers tend to use relatively fine wire for wrapping bodies—anywhere from ¼ to ¾ the diameter of the hook shank. Thicker wires can pose problems in binding down and clipping excess material. If bulk is desired in the body, wrapping multiple layers of finer wire generally gives better results than a single layer of excessively thick wire.

As always when working with wire, a pair of fine-tipped sidecutters for clipping and trimming material is infinitely preferable to dulling a pair of good tying scissors.

Method #74:
Single-layer Wire Body

This is one of the simplest of all fly bodies. If a tail is used, bind down the butts of the tailing material to make a smooth underbody, as fine wire will conform to any bumps, gaps or irregularities and produce an uneven body. If desired, flattened thread can be used to taper the underbody for a more realistic silhouette on nymph patterns.

Step 1. Position the tying thread at the rearmost point of the body. Clip a length of wire and mount it atop the hook shank at the last thread wrap.

Smoothly and evenly bind down the excess wire, moving toward the hook eye.

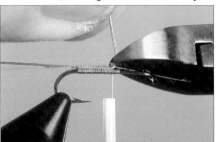

Step 2. Stop the tying thread one or two wraps short of the tie-off point of the body. Clip the wire here and bind down the tag. Trimming the wire short of the tie-off point will ensure that the last few wraps of the wire body are seated against the hook shank, and will simplify binding down the body wire.

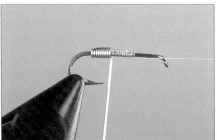

Step 3. Wrap the wire forward in adjacent, touching wraps to the tie-off point. Here, wire is used for the abdomen only. If extra weight is desired, the wire may be wrapped along the entire shank and thorax material applied over it.

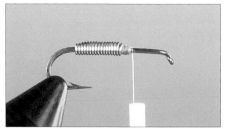

Step 4. Tie off the wire, clip the excess, and bind down the tag.

Method #75:
Double-layer Wire Body

This method gives both greater bulk and weight to the fly body.

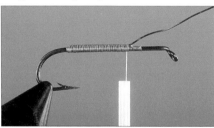

Step 1. Position the thread at the body tie-off point. Mount a piece of wire with the tag toward the hook bend, and bind the wire tag to shank as described above in **Method #74: Single-layer Wire Body**, Steps 1-2.

Return the thread to the tie-off point.

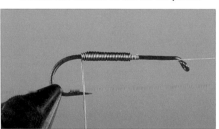

Step 2. Wrap a layer of wire to the rearmost point of the body.

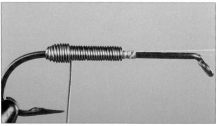

Step 3. Reverse the direction of wrapping, seating the second layer of turns in the "V-shaped" grooves between the wraps on the first layer.

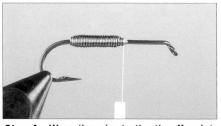

Step 4. Wrap the wire to the tie-off point. Bind down and clip the excess.

Method #76:
Thorax-wrapped Wire Body

This technique produces an enlarged thorax area. An entire nymph body can be made solely of wire in this fashion, or the extra wire in the thorax area can serve as an underbody, adding weight and bulk beneath dubbing or other body material.

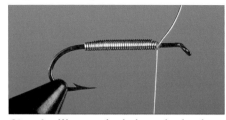

Step 1. Wrap a single-layer body along the entire length of the shank as described above in **Method #74: Single-layer Wire Body**, Steps 1-3. Do not clip off the excess wire.

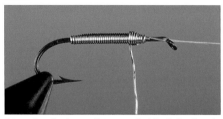

Step 2. A short distance behind the hook eye, reverse the direction of wrapping. Angle the wire back toward the bend, placing the first wrap of the second layer a short distance behind the front edge of the first layer. Note above how this creates a short "step" between the layers and will facilitate finishing the fly body.

Wrap the wire back to the rearmost point of the thorax.

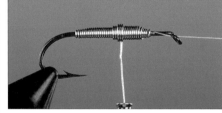

Step 3. Reverse direction again, creating another "step" between the second and third layers of wire that helps approximate a taper.

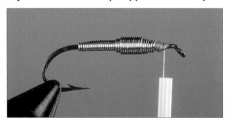

Step 4. Wrap the third layer forward, completely over the second layer and right down the "step" created at the front of the body. Keep the wraps tight and close to one another.

Wrap down to the hook shank. Take one or two turns of wire around shank, directly ahead of the first layer of wire. Bind down and clip the excess.

Woven-tubing Bodies

Woven tubings are made of flat Mylar strips woven over a core of thread or yarn, and indeed the material is sometimes called Mylar tubing or Mylar piping. Woven tubings come in a variety of metallic finishes and colors, and there is even a "glow-in-the-dark" type. In tying, the tubing is typically sleeved over an underbody of some kind—yarn, chenille, lead wire, or metal tape (see "Underbodies," p. 41) to create a body with pronounced bulk or a distinct, often minnow-like, shape. But woven tubing can also be drawn lengthwise down the sides of the hook shank to create a slim, reflective, streamer body. Since this process more closely resembles the method for forming pulled bodies than it does other techniques for tinsels, it is explained in **Method #87: Pulled Tinsel Body**, p. 173.

Woven tubing is available in a small selection of sizes, and when the material is to be sleeved over an underbody, choose a tubing size that gives a relatively snug fit. Using tubing that is too large not only creates a baggy appearance in the body, but makes binding down and tying off the tubing more difficult. Once the core is removed, the tubing has a tendency to unravel. Thus it's best to clip a length of tubing and remove the core immediately prior to mounting it on the hook shank, avoiding any unnecessary handling of the material which further encourages fraying. To this same end, it's prudent to clip a length of tubing about one inch longer than is required for the body. The extra length not only simplifies handling, but ensures that if the material does begin to fray at the front end, the weave at the tie-off point will still be intact.

Method #77:

Woven-tubing Body

This is the most common method of employing woven tubings and is used on such patterns as the Zonker and Janssen Minnow, which use a metal tape underbody (see **Method #11: Metal-tape Underbody**, p. 48); it can be used as well on patterns incorporating a frame underbody as shown in **Method #9: Frame Underbody**, p. 46.

On weighted streamer patterns, woven tubing can be substituted for flat tinsel, which can be difficult to wrap over lead-wire underbodies.

On unweighted patterns, a thick strand of chenille can be wrapped to form a simple underbody that fills the interior of the tubing for a good profile, but adds no weight, as shown in the following sequence.

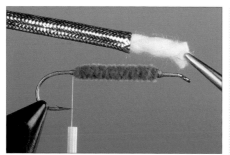

Step 1. Create the desired underbody—chenille is used here—and position the tying thread at the rearmost point. Note that a base of tying thread is laid ahead of the underbody. This foundation will help secure the front of the tubing.

Clip a length of tubing one inch longer than the finished body, and with a tweezer or hemostat, pull out the core.

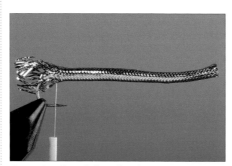

Step 2. Carefully slip the woven tubing over the hook eye. If the tubing begins to unravel, twist it slightly so that the tying thread slips between the frayed Mylar strips and abuts the tubing where the weave is still intact.

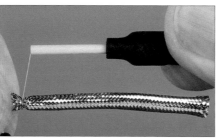

Step 3. Grip the end of the tubing in the left fingers to prevent it from fraying, and tightly wrap the tying thread around the tubing, cinching it to the hook shank with several firm wraps of thread.

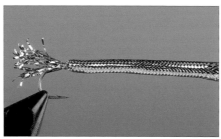

Step 4. When the tubing is securely mounted, tie off the thread with several half-hitches or a whip-finish and clip. If desired, fray the tag of the tubing to form a "skirt," which may be left long or clipped to length.

Step 4a. Or, if no skirt is desired, carefully clip the frayed strands at the rear and bind them down with thread. Secure the thread with half-hitches or a whip-finish, and clip.

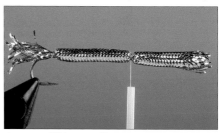

Step 5. With your fingers, carefully locate the front of the underbody. Remount the tying thread over the tubing at this point, using very firms wraps since the tubing is slippery.

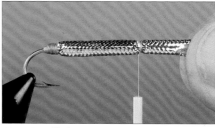

Step 5a. If there appears to be undesired slack in the tubing, or the body appears baggy, take only 4 or 5 tight wraps of thread and stop. Pull the excess tubing forward to tighten and smooth it around the underbody.

Then proceed to wind the thread tightly back to the front of the underbody.

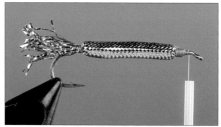

Step 6. When the tubing is secure, clip off the excess and bind down the butts.

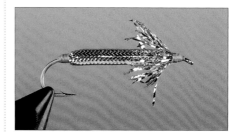

Step 6a. For a particularly flashy fly, you can unravel the excess material so that it is frayed into individual strips. These can be folded back and the butts bound down to form a synthetic hackle, which may be trimmed to any length.

Latex, Plastic, and Vinyl Bodies

Latex, vinyl, and plastic materials produce bodies with two distinct characteristics that are typical of many aquatic food forms—distinct segmentation and translucence. For the most part, their use is confined to subsurface imitations, primarily nymphs, midge pupae, and crustaceans. Though the techniques for tying them are varied, the materials themselves have a couple of properties in common. First is a certain elasticity that allows the tyer some latitude in controlling the body shape, and second, a consistent and predictable handling that comes from the uniformity of their manufacture.

Latex

The latex used in making artificial flies is sold in sheets specifically for fly tying. Its use as a body material owes much to the efforts of Poul Jorgensen, who popularized the material and devised a number of patterns incorporating it. Jorgensen himself credits Raleigh Boaze, Jr. with pioneering the use of latex and bringing it to the attention of the fly-tying world.

As sold to tyers, latex sheets are a natural cream color, but the material can be readily tinted with waterproof marking pens, which results in especially pleasing highlights on segmented bodies. The only real drawback to latex is that it will deteriorate some over time. Heat and direct sunlight are the principal culprits, though they pose less threat to latex-bodied flies than to the tyer's unused latex sheets, which should be stored in a dark place.

In general, latex is not a difficult material to tie, demanding only that the tyer control the wrapping tension with a bit of care in order to form a uniform body or one with the desired taper. Because of its elasticity, however, latex sheets can be a bit tricky to cut into strips for tying. Jorgensen recommends sandwiching the latex between two sheets of cardboard, which can then be cut with a sharp razor blade and a straightedge or a lever-type paper cutter. With a little patience, however, a latex sheet can be cut into strips with a pair of sharp paper shears.

Pre-cut elastic strips, both clear and dyed, have recently become available under the name Scud-Back. This highly translucent material is a bit thicker than sheet latex, though its handling characteristics are identical, and the pre-cut strips are handier to use. This material, however, is manufactured in a limited range of widths, and it is difficult to cut lengthwise if a thinner strip is needed.

The width of the strip, either latex or pre-cut material, should be roughly half the hook gap. Strips much thinner than this wrap too slowly; thicker ones can pose a problem in tying off the material. Because latex is translucent, the tying thread or underbody material will partially show through wherever the latex is stretched tightly or applied in a single layer—as for instance, on the first wrap of material at the rear of the body. Using tying thread to match the final body color will minimize this problem.

Method #78:
Smooth Latex Body

Latex can be used to form a smooth, translucent body, either tapered or straight. The technique for wrapping latex in this fashion most closely resembles a method for wrapping another very different material—floss. Both materials go on the hook shank in flat bands, and the best way to build bulk or taper is to work back and forth across the shank, building up material in the desired area. The techniques for forming tapered bodies in this fashion are presented in "Chenille, Floss, and Yarn Bodies," p. 99, and readers unfamiliar with these procedures may wish to consult that section. The instructions given below for tapering are an abbreviated version of those more detailed procedures.

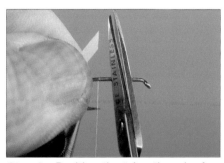

Step 1. Position the tying thread a few thread-wraps ahead of the rearmost body point.
Cut a strip of latex, and with tying scissors, carefully trim one end at an angle, as shown above.

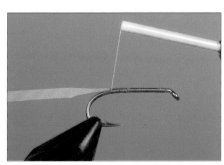

Step 2. Mount the latex strip by the point, with the straight edge along the shank. Trap the material against the hook shank with a couple of tight turns of thread. Then stretch the latex backward, and wrap the thread to the rearmost point of the body. This method will produce a flat tie-in.

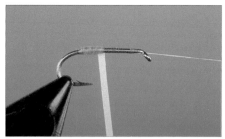

Step 3. Advance the thread in smooth, flat wraps to the body tie-off point.
Stretch the latex thin, but not to the breaking point. Wrap forward in smooth, overlapping layers. For the most uniform body, keep the pressure on the latex consistent.

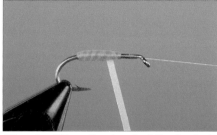

Step 4. When the front of the body is reached, the latex can be tied off if the body has the proper thickness.
If more bulk is desired, reverse the direction of wrapping, and wind the latex back to the rear of the body, applying another layer of material.
Then advance the material back to the front of the body, as shown here. These layers can be repeated until the desired body thickness is obtained.

Step 4a. If a taper is desired, wrap the latex back and forth across the shank to build up bulk in the appropriate area, such as the rear of the hook shank as shown here.

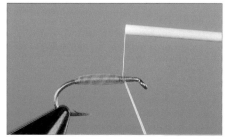

Step 5. When the body is completed and the latex strip is positioned at the tie-off point, stretch it very thin, and secure it with a few tight wraps of the thread. Trim the material and bind the excess.

Method #79:
Segmented Latex Body

Latex is perhaps at its best in forming segmented bodies, since few materials can match its realistic appearance. Both straight and tapered bodies can be formed.

The main sequence shows the procedure for producing an untapered body. The alternate steps demonstrate the construction of two different types of tapers.

Step 4. Maintain tension on the latex strip and clip it at the tie-off. Bind down the excess.

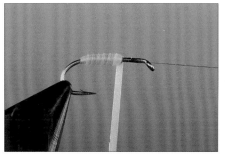

Step 4a. Under a relaxed tension, wrap the latex forward as described in Step 2.

Solid Cords

Solid cords of vinyl, nylon, or other plastics that are circular or semicircular in cross section can be used to make nicely segmented bodies with a glossy appearance. Moreover, some of the materials are translucent, giving the body an unusually lifelike appearance. The materials most commonly used for this application are Swannundaze, Nymph Rib, and V-Rib. All three come in a variety of sizes and colors, though Swannundaze is available in thicker widths better suited to larger nymphs. Nymph Rib and V-Rib are sold in smaller sizes, and because of their greater elasticity, can be stretched thin for bodies on tiny midge patterns. Stretching solid plastic cords to produce a narrower strand is made simpler if the material is first immersed in hot water for a few moments, then stretched while it is warm.

These materials can be wrapped directly around the hook shank or over a formed underbody to create a taper. Indeed, the translucence of some materials may be enhanced by an underbody of reflective or colored material—tinsel, floss, Mylar strips, wool, and so forth. Wrapping them over a dark hook shank or tying thread tends to mute the color of the material.

One of the most easily available materials in this category is ordinary nylon monofilament line. The wide variety of diameters make it useful for a broad range of hook sizes. Because of its translucence, mono is generally wrapped over a colored underbody—floss, tying thread, tinsel, and so on.

Perhaps the one drawback to solid cords is that, as fly-tying materials go, they are rather stiff and bulky. Care must be taken to fashion a smooth underbody to avoid bumps or unevennesss in the overbody, and the material must be bound tightly to the hook shank.

Step 1. Prepare and mount a strip of latex as described in **Method #78: Smooth Latex Body**, Steps 1-2, p. 164.

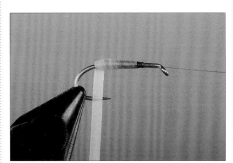

Step 1a. The simplest way to taper a latex body is to use the material to fashion the appropriately shaped underbody.

To produce a caddis-type taper, mount the material as shown in Step 1. Stretch the latex very thin and build a "bulge" at the rear of the hook shank. When the underbody is finished, the latex strip should be positioned at the rearmost point of the body.

Step 2. To produce a straight body, begin wrapping the strip forward under a very light pressure. A heavy hand here will stretch the latex too thin, and the body segments will not be well defined. Maintain an even spacing between the edges of the latex strip for a uniform segmentation.

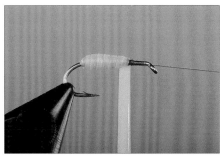

Step 2a. Under a relaxed tension, wrap the latex forward as described in Step 2.

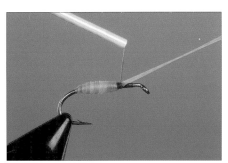

Step 3. When the tie-off point is reached, bind down the latex with 2 tight turns of thread.

Pull the latex strip until it is thin, and bind down with additional wraps. Stretching the material like this will produce a very low-bulk tie-off.

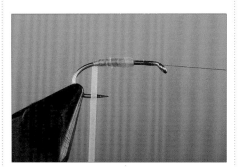

Step 3a. To form a mayfly-type taper, mount the latex strip at the body tie-off point. Stretch the material thin, and form a smooth underbody of the desired shape. When the underbody taper is completed, wrap the latex tightly to the rearmost point of the body.

Method #80:
Solid Cord Body

This technique demonstrates the basic wrap for solid cord bodies, for wide and narrow material, with or without an underbody.

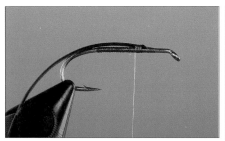

Step 1. Position the thread at the tie-off point of the body.

Cut a length of material—we're using Swannundaze here. Fly tyer Randall Kaufmann recommends briefly stretching the material to remove some of its elasticity, which makes for more consistent handling and a more uniform body, particularly when a compressible underbody material like yarn or dubbing is used.

Mount the material on top of the hook shank, at the frontmost point of the body, with the curved side up. Take a few tight wraps at the tip of the material.

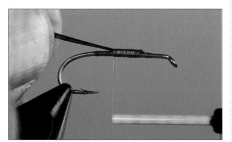

Step 2. As you begin to bind the material down the hook shank, pull to stretch it, lashing the taut material to the top of the shank with closely spaced wraps. Stretching the material like this provides a firmer tie-in and more consistent underbody.

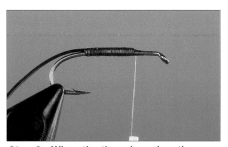

Step 3. When the thread reaches the rearmost point of the body, take a couple of tight wraps.

If an underbody material is used, either to highlight the body color or to form a taper, it is applied at this point. Otherwise, return the thread to the tie-off point, taking care to lay a smooth even foundation.

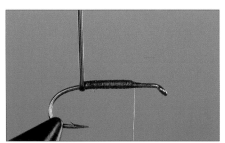

Step 4. Begin wrapping the material forward. The first wrap should made perpendicular to the hook shank to conceal the rearmost thread wrap.

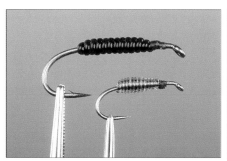

Step 5. Continue winding forward. When the tie-off point is reached, take a couple of tight turns of thread.

To help form a neat, low-bulk tie-off, stretch the material and secure with a few more wraps of thread. Clip the excess and bind down the tag.

At the top is the Swannundaze body dressed in this sequence. Beneath it is a body of monofilament line wrapped over an underbody of green floss. The floss provides the color; the mono gives a natural-looking segmentation and translucence.

Vinyl Tubing

While solid plastic cords have been around for some time, vinyl tubing is a relatively new fly-tying material that has gained wide acceptance for its versatility. Perhaps the most widely used type is Larva Lace, a translucent, thin-walled, elastic tubing sold in a variety of colors and two different diameters. Other materials, either vinyl or polyurethane, are occasionally available, and these can be employed in the methods described below.

The techniques for tying vinyl tubings vary, but the glossy, segmented bodies they produce are similar in appearance to those achieved with solid plastic materials. Vinyl tubing, however, is considerably more elastic than solid plastic strands, making it particularly well suited to smaller flies. It can be wound directly around the hook shank or wrapped over an underbody, much like the solid plastic materials described in the preceding section.

Because the tubing is hollow, some unusual applications are possible. A thin strip of reflective or colored material can be inserted inside the tubing before the body is wrapped to produce interesting rib effects, as shown in the following method. Or the tubing can be slipped over the hook shank and bound down to create a very narrow profile body. But certainly the most innovative technique of all is the liquid-filled body, detailed later in this section, in which vegetable oil is drawn into the tubing, and the filled tube is then wrapped around the hook shank.

Method #81:

Internal-ribbed Tubing Body

Vinyl tubing can be wrapped directly around the hook shank using the procedure shown in **Method #80: Solid Cord Body**, p. 165.

More unusual effects, however, can be obtained by using a version of this body style devised by tyer Phil Camera in which a strand of colored or reflective material is inserted through the tubing to create a ribbed effect on the wrapped body.

In the main sequence, clear Larva Lace is given a ribbing of copper wire, but Krystal Flash, oval or round tinsel, floss, yarn, monofilament, and almost any strand of material thin enough to fit inside the tubing can be used.

The alternate step demonstrates how limper materials can be used for ribbing.

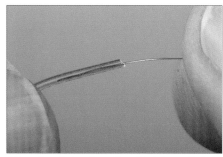

Step 1. Cut a length of tubing slightly longer than is required to form the body. There should be enough excess material to handle during wrapping, but not much more than that. Feeding the ribbing through long lengths of tubing can be difficult.

Stretch the tubing gently a few times to help straighten it, but do not pull too vigorously or you can deform the tubing and reduce the inside diameter.

Relatively stiff materials, such as the wire used here, Krystal Flash, oval tinsel, monofilament, and so forth can simply be pushed through the tubing. It helps, however, to twist either the ribbing or the tubing—whichever is the softer or limper of the two materials—when feeding the rib strand through the tubing.

Very limp rib materials such as floss require the different approach shown in Step 1a.

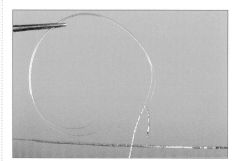

Step 1a. To rib with soft or limp materials, such as the piece of holographic tinsel shown here, cut a length of tippet material about 3 times as long as the tubing. Double it over, and feed the tag ends through the tubing. This will produce a loop of mono at one end of the tubing and the two tags projecting from the other.

The mono is used like a bobbin threader. Insert one end of the rib material through the mono loop, as shown at the top.

Pull the tag ends to draw the material through the tubing, as shown at the bottom.

10

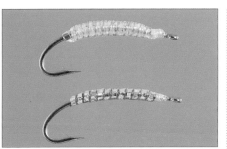

Step 2. Mount, secure, and wrap the tubing as explained in **Method #80: Solid Cord Body**, Steps 2-5, p. 166.

Both the bodies shown here have been wrapped over a light-colored thread underbody to emphasize the ribbing.

Method #82:
Slip-over Tubing Body

To our knowledge, this technique was first described by Phil Camera, a fly tyer widely known for his innovations with synthetic materials. The method is simple and can produce very slim-profile bodies, particularly useful on midge larvae and pupae.

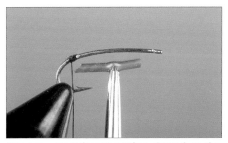

Step 1. Position the tying thread at the rearmost point of the body. Cut a piece of tubing ¾ the length of the finished body, and trim one end to a 45-degree angle.

This tubing length is important. When the material is ribbed and bound with thread, the thread pressure will squeeze the tubing forward, producing a finished body that is actually longer than the cut piece of tubing. Thus you must compensate by cutting the tubing shorter than the desired body length. Camera notes that some experimentation here is necessary, as hook-wire diameter and thread pressure determine how much the tubing is squeezed forward. Since the material is sleeved over the hook, trimming any excess material is cumbersome, though still possible.

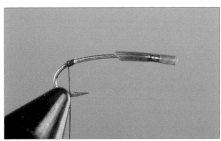

Step 2. Slip the angle-cut end of the tubing over the hook eye.

While the vinyl will stretch to fit over

hook eyes slightly wider than the inside diameter of the tubing, larger hook eyes may pose a problem. Camera recommends lubricating the tubing with a drop of vegetable oil. Use only a small amount of oil and wipe the excess from the shank.

Step 2a. If the tubing will not fit over the hook eye even with lubrication, try this approach. Remove the tying thread and debarb the hook. Slip the tubing over the hook point, and slide it around the bend so that the angle-cut end is at the rear of the body.

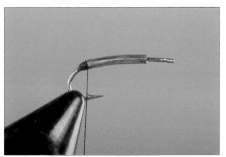

Step 3. When the tubing is mounted, position the point of the angle on top of the hook shank, and bind it down with a couple of tight wraps of thread.

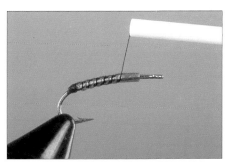

Step 4. Wrap the thread forward in an open spiral. The tubing will compress under the thread to form a segmented body.

Step 5. When the front of the body is reached, bind down the end of the tubing tightly.

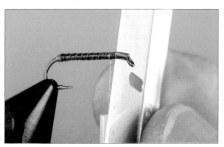

Step 5a. If a small amount of excess tubing remains, simply bind it to the hook shank where it will be covered by subsequent materials.

If a longer length of excess remains, you can trim it with a very sharp razor blade. Hold the razor blade perpendicular to the body at the cut-off point. Push the razor inward and roll the cutting edge around the hook shank to sever the material.

Method #83:
Liquid-filled Tubing Body

Filling vinyl tubing with a liquid to form fly bodies is one of those rare techniques that is in fact traceable to a single tyer—in this case Mike Tucker of Colorado, who developed the Liqui-fly design. Tucker maintains that the vegetable oil used to fill the tubing best reproduces the patterns of reflected and refracted light that are characteristic of subsurface insects, and such bodies do have a beautiful translucence. Moreover, the oil reduces the overall specific gravity of the fly and gives it both a more natural attitude and behavior underwater.

A variety of oils can be used, though Tucker has settled on various vegetable oils as most satisfactory. These come in a wide variety of viscosities and colors, from the greens of olive oils, to the deep gold of corn oil, to a number of paler types. These options, in conjunction with colored tubings, provide a wide range of color possibilities. Because the liquid-filled tubing is quite translucent, the choice of an underbody material is important in determining the finished appearance of the body. Darker-colored threads tend to mute the color. Tucker generally uses an underbody of white thread; if desired, it can be colored with a waterproof marker to produce a variety of color effects in the finished body. Reflective materials such as tinsels or Flashabou can be used as well.

Step 1. Cut a 6"-8" piece of tubing—we're using Larva Lace in this demonstration.

Fill a small container with vegetable oil. Using the tubing like a straw, insert one end into the oil and draw up enough liquid to fill the tubing.

Tie an overhand knot at each end of the tubing. The tubing diameter is small enough, and the oil viscous enough, that the liquid will not run out as these knots are formed. Clip the excess tubing beyond the knots.

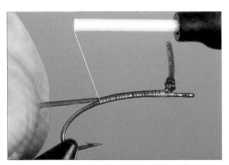

Step 2. Mount white tying thread at the front end of the body, and position the tubing atop the shank so that the knot lies ahead of the mounting point.

Take 4 or 5 tight thread wraps around the tubing at the rear base of the knot.

Gently stretch the tubing toward the rear of the hook, and bind it to the top of the shank with tight thread wraps. When the rearmost point of the body is reached, take another 4 or 5 tight thread wraps.

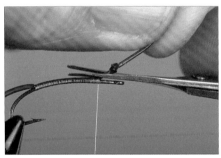

Step 3. Return the tying thread to the front edge of the body. Grasp the knot, and pull it slightly to stretch the tubing. Clip off the knot and bind down the tag of tubing with thread.

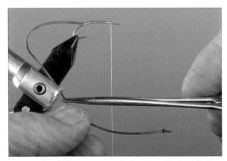

Step 4. With your right hand, hold the knot at the free end of the tubing.

With your left fingers, pinch the tubing tightly, and slide your pinched fingers up the tubing about halfway, forcing the oil from the lower half of the tubing into the upper half.

Hold the left fingers in the position, and with the right hand clamp the tubing in a hemostat directly above your left fingers to hold the oil in the upper portion of the tubing.

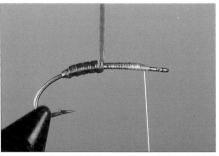

Step 5. For the first wrap of the body, stretch the tubing and take a tight wrap around the shank; this tapers the rear of the body.

As you wrap the tubing forward, relax the stretch to form body segments that increase in diameter.

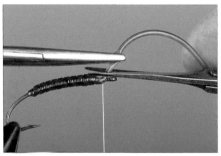

Step 6. When the front edge of the body is reached, bind down the tubing with 4 or 5 tight thread wraps. Lift the tubing and take one half-hitch of thread around the shank only, directly at the front base of the tubing.

Remove the homostat from the lower portion of the tubing and reclamp it around the tubing about ⅛" beyond the tie-down wraps.

Clip the tubing and bind down the excess. Tucker applies a bit of liquid CA glue to the thread wraps.

Step 7. Shown here is a completed caddis body.

SECTION NINE

Pulled, Bubble, and Brushed Bodies

Pulled, bubble, and brushed bodies are formed from long-fibered materials, either natural or synthetic, that are drawn lengthwise along the hook to produce, capsule-like, and in some instances, hollow bodies that fully or partially encircle the shank. Generally, the methods employed use comparatively little material to produce bodies with the appearance of bulk and substance.

Pulled and Bubble Bodies

In pulled and bubble bodies, materials are affixed at one point of the shank, pulled along the shank to encircle it partially or fully, then bound down. The result is a "capsule" of material. Pulled bodies are generally elongated or bullet-shaped. On floating flies dressed with a buoyant material such as hollow hair—the most conspicuous examples of which are the Humpy and the Crowe Beetle—a pulled body aids in floatation. On subsurface patterns, the relatively small amount of material fashioned into a hollow body produces a fly that sinks rapidly and possesses a lifelike translucence that is characteristic of many aquatic creatures, from nymphs to baitfish.

Bubble bodies are really a particular style of pulled body, usually more spherical in shape and more sparsely dressed. When tied as an overbody around another material, they are often used to represent the transparent sheath and bubble of air that surround an emerging caddis—as in Gary LaFontaine's Sparkle Pupa pattern—or the nymphal shuck of a hatching mayfly. Other body styles, however, are possible; egg patterns tied in the bubble style are an unusual and effective fly.

Method #84:
Pulled Fiber Body

This simple style of body is constructed on the top half of the hook shank only. It can be fashioned from any long-fibered material—hairs, yarns, twisted Mylars, tail-feather barbs, and so on—but deer hair is commonly used on floating patterns. It incorporates the superior buoyancy of hollow hair without the somewhat time-consuming process of spinning and clipping a body.

Pulled bodies tied from natural materials like deer hair and feather barbs do have one shortcoming. The "shell" of material drawn over the hook shank is vulnerable to a trout's teeth, and these bodies may not be especially durable.

The main sequence shows the procedure for tying a beetle body of deer hair; other materials can be tied in exactly the same fashion to produce bodies for other types of patterns.

The alternate sequence demonstrates one of the most common applications of pulled bodies—in tying the Humpy. Again, deer hair is used, though other materials, most notably poly yarn, can also be employed.

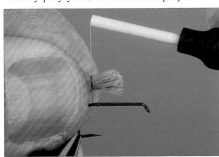

Step 1. Lay a thread foundation on the section of the hook shank that will be covered by the body. This thread base will help prevent the body material from spinning around the shank when binding it down. Position the thread at the rearmost point of the body. In this beetle pattern, the body extends the entire length of the shank.

Clip and clean a small clump of deer hair as described in **Method #2: Preparing and Cleaning Hair**, p. 68. Do not stack the hair, but rather clip the butts so that they are even.

Position the material above the hook shank, with the butts extending a short distance past the mounting point. Take one wrap of tying thread around the butts of the hair only, as shown. The wrap of thread should be just barely snug, not tight.

Step 2. While holding the bobbin above the hook shank, slide the bundle of hair down the thread until it rests on top of the hook shank.

Take a second wrap of thread, this time around both the hair and the hook shank, ending with the bobbin held, once again, above the hook. The thread should be snug, but not tight.

Step 3. Maintain a grasp of the hair tips in your left hand, and position your left fore-

finger behind the hook shank, pressing inward on both the hair and hook wire. Your finger will act as a backstop to prevent the hair from slipping around the shank when thread pressure is applied.

Pull the tying thread very firmly upward. If the hair begins to roll to the far side of the shank, use your index finger to prevent it from doing so. This wrap of thread should be quite tight.

Step 4. Take two or three more tight wraps to further bind down the hair. If the flared hair butts are long, they can be clipped close to the shank and bound down. If they are short, simply bind them down with thread, and advance the thread to the tie-off point of the body.

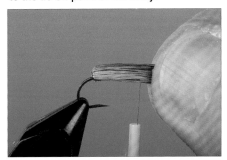

Step 5. Grasp the hair tips in the right hand and pull them forward over the top of the hook shank. If any of the hairs are crinkled or bent, readjust your grip and smooth them forward. The goal here is to exert equal tension on the hairs so that the "shell" formed is smooth and uniform.

The amount of tension you apply on the hair determines the shape of the body. A strong tension that pulls the hair tightly over the hook will give a body with a slim profile, as shown here. If you relax the tension, allowing the hair to slacken a bit, the body will be rounder and fuller in appearance.

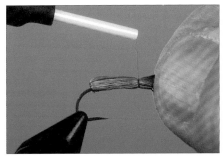

Step 6. With the left hand, pass the tying thread directly over the tie-off point. Bring

the thread beneath the hook, and raise it above the shank as shown. (You'll need to release the bobbin after each turn when using your left hand.)

Pull the bobbin firmly upward to cinch down the hair. Use your right fingers to prevent the hair from slipping around the shank.

Take 3 or 4 more tight wraps with your left hand.

Step 7. When the hair is firmly secured, release the tips. You can now take additional wraps with the right hand if they are needed.

The excess hair can now be clipped as desired. It can be cut close to the shank, with the excess bound down if additional materials are to be applied.

Or it can be trimmed to leave a short tuft of hair to serve as the head of the fly, as shown here.

Or a few fibers can be pulled outward and locked in position to form legs using the approach shown in **Method #9: Wingcase Legs**, Steps 3-4, p. 419.

In the interest of greater durability, some tyers apply a coat of head cement to the top of the body. Very thick head cement should be used, and even then applied only sparingly to the top layer of hair. Thinner cement will penetrate the deer hair and destroy its buoyancy.

Step 1a. In tying a Humpy, the natural hair tips are used to form the wings, and the key to a successful dressing is to use hair trimmed to the correct length.

Mount a tail of the desired material; it should be equal in length to the hook shank.

Position the tying thread about two thread-wraps behind the exact midpoint of the shank, as shown.

Prepare a clump of deer hair as explained in **Method #2: Preparing and Cleaning Hair**, p. 68, and align the hair tips as explained in **Method #3: Stacking and Aligning Hair**, p. 69.

Trim the butts so that the length of the hair is equal to the distance from the back of the hook eye to the tips of the tail fibers, as shown.

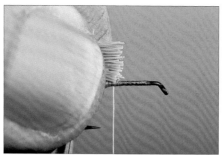

Step 2a. With the left fingers, position the hair above the hook so that the butts are at the exact midpoint of the shank.

Step 3a. Secure the hair atop the shank as described in Steps 2-4. The last thread wraps securing the hair should lie directly atop the rearmost thread wraps securing the tail.

Typically, the hair butts are bound down with colored tying thread or floss to form an attractive underbody.

Position the tying thread just ahead of the bound-down hair butts at the midpoint of the shank.

Step 4a. Fold the hair toward the hook eye as shown in Steps 5-6, and secure it to the top of the shank, as shown.

The hair tips can now be fashioned into wings using one of the techniques presented in "Divided Bundled-fiber Wings," p. 268.

Method #85:
Hollow-hair Capsule

This style of pulled body completely encircles the hook forming a capsule around the shank. While this technique is possible with almost any long-fibered material, hollow hair is among the easiest to use because it distributes itself readily around the hook shank, forming a body of consistent density and uniform appearance.

When tied using hooks with extra-long shanks, as shown in the main sequence, the capsule can be used as a body on caterpillar, inchworm, grasshopper, and adult stonefly patterns. Tied on a standard shank, it is often used for ant bodies, as shown in the alternate sequence.

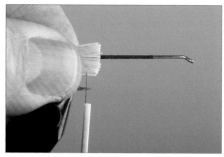

Step 1. Lay a thread foundation and prepare a clump of deer hair as described in **Method #84: Pulled-Fiber Body**, Step 1, p. 169.

Position the clump of hair so that the butts extend slightly past the mounting point. Work the hair downward around the shank, so that it is evenly distributed around the hook wire, as shown.

Step 2. Take one loose wrap of thread around the hair. Begin another wrap. As the bobbin passes over the top of the shank and down the far side of the hook, apply tension to the thread to cinch down the hair. Use very firm pressure.

Step 3. Take 3 or 4 additional wraps toward the hook eye to secure the hair. Clip the flared hair butts close to the shank, and bind them down securely with the thread.

Note the position of the bobbin. We're tying a segmented body here, and the distance between the thread and the rearmost point of the body establishes the width of the segments. To tie an ant body as described in the alternate sequence, advance the tying thread to the middle of the hook shank.

Use a dubbing needle to free or straighten any hairs that are trapped or twisted at the hook bend. Each hair should flare out straight from the shank.

Step 4. Use your index finger to push into the base of the hair, flaring it out from the shank.

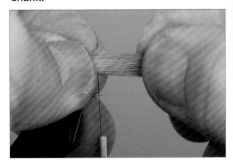

Step 5. Use your left fingers to push all the hair forward toward the hook eye, maintaining its even distribution around the shank.

Gather the hair in the right fingers, and pull it forward to form a smooth, uniform capsule. You may need to readjust your grip a few times to preen the hair evenly forward.

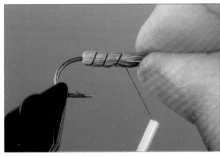

Step 6. Maintain your grip on the hair tips with the right hand. Use the left hand to spiral the thread forward. You'll need to release the bobbin after each turn, as the vise stem poses an obstacle to uninterrupted left-hand wrapping.

Snug the thread down after each spiral turn, forming even, symmetrical body segments.

Step 7. When the final body segment is formed, take 3 or 4 very tight turns of thread to bind down the hair. You can now release the hair tips and take additional wraps in the normal fashion.

The excess hair can now be clipped, and the remainder of the fly dressed.

Step 1a. To form an ant body, mount the body material as shown in Step 1 and position the thread at the middle of the shank.

Draw the hair forward. Use the left hand to bind the hair tightly at the middle of the shank, forming the "waist" of the ant.

Release the hair in the right hand, and advance the tying thread to the front of the body.

Step 2a. Recapture the hair in the right hand, and pull it forward. Bind it down as you did in Step 1a, forming a second body segment slightly smaller than the first. Clip the excess hair.

Hackle or other material can be applied at the waist to represent legs.

Method #86:
Pulled Bullet Body

The basic technique here—reverse-tying materials at the head of the fly and drawing them back toward the bend—is generally attributed to the famous fly dresser Carrie Stevens. It has been applied widely since her time, most notably by Keith Fulsher in his Thunder Creek bucktails (details of this style are presented in **Method #60: Bullet-head fiber Wings**, p. 308).

Though almost any long-fibered material can be used to create this style, most natural hairs lack sufficient length. Some very long hairs, such as Icelandic wool, may be suitable, but in general, artificial materials are the most practical. Provided they have sufficient length and enough stiffness to hold their shape, nearly any artificial fiber can be used—certain craft furs, the synthetic hairs used by saltwater tyers, even Krystal Flash.

Many variations of this basic style are possible. Barbell, stick-on, or doll eyes can be added. A separate tail material such as marabou can be used. Pectoral fins can be fashioned from hen saddle. To add color, flash, or weight inside the capsule-like body, an underbody can be tied from almost any of the conventional materials—lead

wire, tinsel, floss, tinsel-chenilles, and so on. Finally, light-colored bodies can be tinted or marked with waterproof pens to produce the desired effect.

The technique presented in the primary sequence below comes to us from Boyd Pfeiffer who uses this reverse-pulled technique to fashion streamer bodies.

The steps in the alternate sequence illustrate a number of variations of the technique: using material of a different texture; shaping a fuller body; using two or more materials for contrasting colors or textures; and a method for tying off the material that produces a bulkier body with a "floating" tail that is not attached to the hook shank.

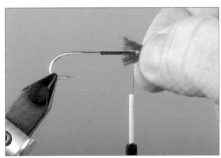

Step 1. Since the materials used for this style are often stiff or coarse, it is best to use a heavy tying thread. Attach the thread at the middle of the shank, and wrap it forward laying a tight thread foundation that will help secure the material. Position the thread directly behind the hook eye.

Clip a bundle of fibers about twice the length of the hook. The thickness of the bundle depends upon how dense or sparse you wish the finished body to appear. As a starting point for experimentation, try a bundle that, when tightly twisted, is about 4 times the diameter of the hook shank.

To form this type of body, the material must be evenly distributed around the hook shank. There are two basic techniques for accomplishing this. First, if the material is somewhat slippery or smooth, such as a natural or synthetic hair, you can use **Method #6: The Taut Distribution Wrap**, p. 28.

For thick, stiff, or crinkled fibers, use the following procedure, which is illustrated in the photo above. Grip the bundle of fibers in the right hand so that about ½" projects from the fingertips. Grip the bundle rather loosely, and center the hook eye in the base of the bundle. Push the fibers toward the hook bend, keeping the eye centered, so that the fibers evenly surround the shank.

Step 2. Use the left hand to grip the fibers, maintaining their distribution around the shank. Bind them down directly behind the

eye with several very tight wraps of thread. Taper-cut the material and secure the butts tightly to the shank.

At this point, barbell eyes can be added to the pattern. If a tail is desired, tie in the tailing material in the usual fashion. When it is securely bound, return the thread to the rearmost tailing wrap.

If an underbody is desired, mount the material directly behind the hook eye, and advance the tying thread to the rearmost point of the body. Wrap the underbody back toward the hook bend, and tie off.

Regardless of what additional materials are applied, the tying thread must end up at the rearmost point of the body.

Step 2a. To form a two-toned body, clip a bundle of fibers that is half the thickness required for the body. Bind these on top of the hook shank directly behind the eye, allowing the fibers to fan around the top of the shank only.

Clip a second bundle of fibers (equal in thickness to the first) of a contrasting color or texture. Bind these underneath the hook, allowing them to spread around the bottom half of the shank only. (To make a three-color body, tie a smaller bundle of a third material to each side of the shank.)

Step 3. You can form the body with your fingers, with a bullet-head tool, or with a simple hollow tube. We're using the empty barrel of a ballpoint pen here.

Push the tube over the hook eye, forcing the fibers toward the bend of the hook. If the fibers push the tying thread backward, gently wiggle the bobbin to slip the tying thread between the strands of material. The bobbin should hang freely at the rearmost point of the body

Step 4. Grip the protruding fibers with your left hand and remove the tool. You

should exert an even tension on all the fibers to maintain uniformity in the body. If the resulting bullet-shaped body is not symmetrical, or stray fibers project outward, repeat Step 3 until a smooth profile is obtained.

Here a very slim body is formed by drawing the fibers back close to the hook shank.

Step 4a. A fuller body can be formed by pushing the material forward slightly to "balloon" it around the shank.

When the desired profile is created, bind the fibers at the rear of the body as shown in Step 5.

Note the material used here is a softer synthetic hair, that is finer and less reflective than the stiff, glossy material used in the main sequence.

Step 5. Bind down the fibers against the hook shank, maintaining an even distribution, with several tight turns of thread. Secure with a few half hitches or whip-finish, and apply a drop of head cement or CA glue.

The tail can also be tied to form a different style of body as shown in the alternate sequence that follows.

Step 6. The tail can now be trimmed to any shape desired. It can be clipped vertically to form a straight tail (top); trimmed to a fish-like V-tail (center); or the butts can be clipped away entirely if the fly has been dressed with a separate tailing material (bottom).

Step 5a. Oregon tyer Bill Black uses an interesting variation of the tie-off technique in which the body material is bound behind the hook bend.

To dress this style, mount the body material as described in Steps 1-2, or Step 1a. Eyes, tail, and/or underbody can be tied in as well. When all the materials are securely bound to the shank, tie off the thread with a few half-hitches and apply a drop of cement to the windings.

Reverse the hook in the vise as shown. Form the body as described in Steps 3-4, but now working from left to right. Grip the protruding fibers in the right hand, exerting a uniform tension to produce a smooth body.

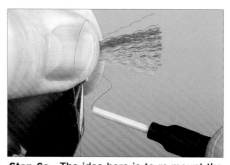

Step 6a. The idea here is to re-mount the tying thread beyond the bend of the hook, binding together the fibers only.

To accomplish this, grasp the materials in your left hand, pinching them together tightly behind the hook bend. Lay the tying thread over your left hand as shown, and slip it between your thumb and index finger so that it is pinched together with the bundle of fibers.

With your right hand, take a few tight wraps directly ahead of your fingertips, binding the fibers together and locking down the tag of tying thread. The procedure is identical to mounting the tying thread on a bare hook shank.

Step 7a. When the fibers are tightly bound together, secure the tying thread with a few half hitches. Clip both tags of thread and apply a drop of CA glue.

This teardrop-shaped body can be left as is, or given a more minnow-like profile as shown in Step 8a.

10

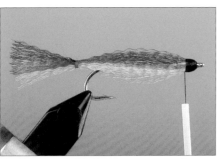

Step 8a. To change the body profile, re-mount the hook in the vise. Attach the tying thread directly behind the eye of the hook.

With the left hand, preen back the body material, and begin wrapping thread over the front edge of the body. These wraps will compress the fibers, and make the body slimmer and more symmetrical. When the desired shape is achieved, whip-finish the head.

Method #87:

Pulled Tinsel Body

This technique has appeared in the work of Dick Talleur, who credits Matt Vinciguerra, a fly tying photographer, with the invention of this method for a fly called the Beady Eye. The tying procedure is quite simple and yields a very slim, flashy, minnowlike body. We've reproduced here only the technique for fashioning the body. Readers interested in the full dressing should consult Talleur's *Mastering the Art of Fly Tying.*

The original method called for a single bead at the head, but bead chain, lead eyes, or any barbell style eye can be used in dressing the single pulled strand illustrated in the main sequence below. The alternate sequence shows a double pulled body, and only a single bead is suitable for this technique.

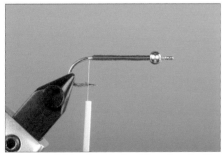

Step 1. Slide the desired bead onto the hook shank, and position it about ⅛" behind the eye. (For more information on beads, see the section on "Bead Heads," p. 428).

Wrap the desired body—we've used floss here—tying off the body material behind the bead. To secure a counter-drilled or tapered bead, slide it forward and build a thread bump just ahead of the body. Put a drop of CA glue on the bump, and push the bead back, seating the thread bump inside the counterdrilled or tapered hole. Allow to dry.

Remount the tying thread at the rear-most point of the body.

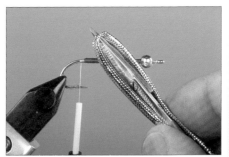

Step 2. Cut a piece of woven-Mylar tinsel tubing about one inch longer than twice the length of the hook shank. Remove the fiber core.

With a scissor point, poke a hole in the center of the braid.

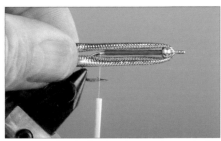

Step 3. Push the hook eye through the hole. Draw the two ends of the Mylar tubing back to the bend—one should be over the top of the shank and one underneath, as shown above.

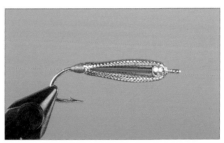

Step 4. Bind the tubing to the shank, taking care to keep one strand atop the shank and one below it. Clip the excess tinsel, and bind down the butts.

Step 4a. A more solid-looking body can be fashioned by mounting two cut pieces of tubing ahead of the bead. Prepare two lengths of material and mount each one as described in Steps 2-3. Pull the first piece of tubing (gold in the photo) back as described in Step 3—one strand above the hook, one below. Secure with a few wraps of thread.

Draw the second piece of tubing (pearl in the photo) along the sides of the hook shank. Bind down all four pieces of tubing with several tight wraps of thread.

The tubing can be clipped and the butts bound with thread as shown in Step 4, or they can be left long and frayed to form a tail, as shown here.

Method #88:

Double-strand Antron Bubble

This style of fly and dressing technique was devised by Gary LaFontaine for his Sparkle Pupa design, and both are explained in detail in his book, *Caddisflies.* From a technical standpoint, almost any yarnlike material can be used to fashion this pupal bubble, though LaFontaine argues persuasively for the particular effectiveness of Antron, a trilobal filament whose light-reflecting properties most closely imitate those of the natural insect.

The Antron suited to this technique generally comes in two forms: a twisted yarn, usually of 3 or 4 plies; or a single-ply, untwisted, spooled yarn. Both types have their advantages. Multi-ply yarns give a tyer the convenience of selecting one or more strands to match a given hook size, but they are especially well suited to flies of about #16 or smaller, since a single ply of yarn is roughly the right quantity of material for these small hooks. Larger hooks require preparing separate plies and then combining them. Spooled material is more convenient for larger hooks, #12 and #14, since the yarn can be used directly from the spool and requires no untwisting of strands. But this material is less handy for small flies, as it must be split lengthwise into two or more sparser yarns, and this procedure can be tedious.

Not all spooled Antrons are created equal. The best have fine filaments that are crinkly in texture. Less desirable are those with thicker, straighter fibers—they have less reflectivity and sparkle, and are a bit more difficult to work with.

The carded yarn on the left is a multi-ply Antron. The spool in the middle is the type preferred by many tyers. Notice, in comparing it with the spool on the right, that the fibers are finer, more crinkled, and glossier. The texture and finish of this type of Antron is well-suited to all flies, but particularly smaller ones where less material is used. The spooled Antron on the right is best for larger patterns.

The main sequence below reproduces the original method for tying the Antron bubble as it appears in LaFontaine's book. Readers interested in the various applications of this style should consult *Caddisflies.* The alternate sequence presents a variation that many tyers find a bit simpler and faster. Still other techniques are presented in **Method #89: Single-strand Antron Bubble**, p. 175.

Step 1. Lay a thread foundation on the rear half of the hook shank, continuing slightly down the hook bend. The final position of the tying thread, as the bobbin hangs, should be slightly behind the hook barb.

Cut a length of Antron yarn about twice the length of the hook shank. The thickness of the yarn depends upon the desired density of the finished bubble. We're using a #14 hook and a length of yarn cut directly from a spool of Antron, but more or less material can be used as preferences dictate. Using a small comb or a dubbing needle, fray the yarn to untwist and separate the individual filaments. Work both ends of the yarn until the filaments form a loose bundle.

Bind these fibers to the top of the hook shank as shown.

Step 2. Prepare a second length of yarn, identical to the first. Bind it beneath the hook shank.

Step 3. Create the fly body. We're using dubbing here, but whatever the material, the body should end well behind the hook eye to leave enough room for the fly head.

When the body is completed, draw the piece of Antron mounted atop the hook shank over the top of the body. As you do so, flatten the Antron slightly, spreading the fibers around the top and sides of the body. Pull evenly on all the filaments so that a smooth, even covering is formed over the body. Secure this piece of Antron with a few wraps of thread.

Step 4. Pull the second piece of Antron forward, beneath the hook shank, to cover the underside of the body. Again, attempt to flatten and spread the filaments, distributing them over the bottom and sides of the body material.

Secure this yarn with a few thread wraps.

Step 5. Before trimming the Antron, use a dubbing needle to pull slack into the bubble, where needed, to make the capsule symmetrical in appearance and to distribute the fibers uniformly around the body.

Step 6. Clip the excess Antron and bind the butts down tightly. The head of the fly—usually ostrich herl or dubbing—can now be dressed.

Step 1a. Wrap a thread base and prepare a length of Antron yarn as described in Step 1.

Bind the yarn to the far side of the hook shank (rather than the top). When the yarn is properly positioned, take a wrap or two of thread to secure it.

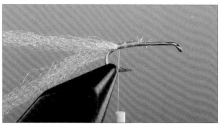

Step 2a. Mount the second piece of Antron yarn on the near side of the hook shank.

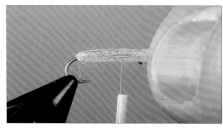

Step 3a. Dress the fly body as described in Step 3.

Draw both strands of yarn forward, covering the sides of the fly body. Pull the strands snugly to form a close-fitting covering for the body. Pinch the yarns together with the right thumb and forefinger slightly ahead of the hook eye.

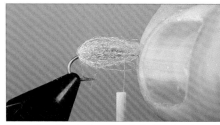

Step 4a. Push the yarn into the hook eye. The slack created should form a bubble-like capsule around the body. More slack will create a larger-profile bubble; less slack will create a tighter, slimmer one. The left fingers can be used to push or roll the filaments to fill any gaps in the bubble.

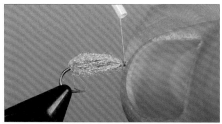

Step 5a. Once the bubble has the desired configuration, hold it in place with the right hand.

With the left hand, take a wrap of thread around the tie-off point, ending with the bobbin raised above the hook shank. Pull upward on the bobbin to tighten the thread and secure the Antron.

Release the Antron and check the body for a uniform distribution of yarn filaments. If there are thin spots, you may be able to slacken the thread tension, and redistribute the fibers to fill in any gaps. If the gaps are large and the bubble is significantly asymmetrical, you'll need to start over at Step 4a.

If the bubble appears properly formed, pinch the Antron against the body once again, and secure it at the tie-off point with several additional tight wraps of thread.

Method #89:

Single-strand Antron Bubble

The two techniques shown here involve forming Antron bubbles from a single strand of yarn. Note that for larger hooks or a denser bubble, the "single" strand may actually consist of two or more lengths of yarn combed and consolidated, but tied in as one piece.

The main sequence demonstrates an approach that is quick and that promotes an even distribution of fibers around the shank. The alternate sequence shows a technique we first saw in the work of Al Beatty. The use of a dubbing needle helps form a bubble of uniform diameter.

Note that yet another procedure for forming single-strand bubbles is presented in **Method #102: Bead Bubble Sheath**, p. 188, where the technique is demonstrated on a bead-body fly. It is equally practical, however, for flies with bodies of any material.

The method in the main sequence is quicker than the techniques demonstrated in **Method #88: Double-strand Antron Bubble**, p. 173, but it does take a bit of practice to master. It is not well-suited to tying bead-head flies, as the presence of a bead interferes with the tying procedure. Though we have seen a few tyers use versions of the following procedure, the one presented here was shown to us by Skip Morris.

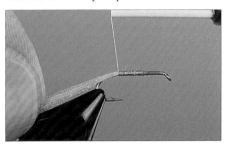

Step 1. Attach the tying thread at the middle of the hook shank. Cut a length of Antron yarn about 2½ times the length of the hook shank. Prepare the yarn by combing or teasing as described in **Method #88: Double-strand Antron Bubble**, Step 1, p. 174.

Bind down the yarn tightly at the middle of the shank. Begin wrapping the thread toward the bend of the hook. As you do so, use your left hand to pull the yarn back and slightly down, so that the fibers surround the hook shank. When the rearmost point of the bubble is reached, take a few tight turns of thread to secure the material.

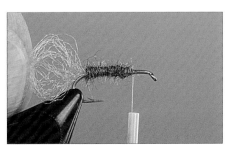

Step 2. Form the body of the fly—we're using dubbing here—stopping well behind the hook eye to allow space for the head.

With thumb and forefinger of the left hand, pinch the yarn about one shank-length behind the hook. Pull slightly, and readjust your grip as necessary to put an even tension on all the fibers. Now begin pushing the yarn directly into the hook shank. Notice that the fibers begin to balloon evenly outward, forming an evenly distributed bubble or "cage" of filaments, as shown. If the fibers are not uniformly distributed around the bubble, try pushing from a slightly different angle or readjusting your grip and trying again. This is one of the parts of the technique that takes a bit of practice.

Step 3. Continue pushing forward, sliding the bubble over the body. The fibers beneath your fingers should be taught and evenly distributed.

Step 4. Continue pushing forward, sliding your left fingers over and beyond the hook eye, until finally they are gripping the very end of the yarn.

Step 5. Transfer the end of the yarn to the right fingers. If necessary adjust your grip on the yarn to put an even tension on all the filaments.

Now push the yarn slightly into the hook eye, causing a bubble to form around the body.

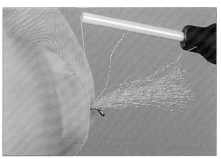

Step 6. When you have fashioned a bubble of the desired profile, pinch the Antron fibers against the fly body with the left hand. Take a slack wrap over the fibers, then pull the bobbin upward to tighten the thread.

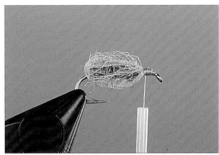

Step 7. Check the bubble for a uniform distribution of fibers, then secure the Antron with additional thread wraps.

Trim the excess fibers and bind the butts down tightly.

Step 1a. This approach uses a dubbing needle to help size the bubble.

Cut a length of yarn about 3 times the shank length, and use a dubbing needle or comb to separate and untangle the filaments so that they form a loose bundle.

Position the tying thread at the rearmost point of the body. Secure the yarn to the top of the hook shank, wrapping forward to bind down the tag of yarn.

Dress the fly body—dubbing is used here—and position the tying thread at the front edge of the body.

Form a loop in the yarn over the top of the shank, and secure the front of the loop with 2 or 3 thread wraps under moderate tension. Do not bind the yarn tightly; it must be able to slip beneath the thread wraps in a later step.

The loop can be formed by simply doubling the yarn over, but to maintain a good separation of the yarn filaments (which will simplify splitting the loop in Step 2a), fold the yarn over a dubbing needle, as shown here.

Do not clip the tag end of the yarn.

Step 2a. Use a dubbing needle to split the yarn loop into two loops of the same size, as shown in this top view.

After dividing the loop with the needle, use your fingers to pull the two new loops outward to the sides of the hook shank.

Step 3a. Pass a dubbing needle over the top of the loop on the near side, under the hook shank, and over the top of the loop on the far side, as shown.

Position the needle in the bend of the hook, perpendicular to the shank. Holding the needle lower in the bend will form a larger-diameter bubble. Holding it higher in the bend will form a narrower bubble.

Pull the tag of yarn toward the hook eye and slightly upward to tighten the two yarn loops around the shank of the needle.

Step 4a. Withdraw the needle. Use your fingers to separate the fibers in the two loops, preening them outward so that they are distributed evenly around the shank.

Step 5a. When the loop fibers have been preened to encircle the shank, secure the yarn at the front of the body with several tight thread wraps.

Clip and bind down the excess.

Method #90:
Hackle-bubble Body

In the United States, the use of hackles to form bubble-type bodies is traceable to the work of tyers Tom Light and Neal Humphrey, who first described the technique in *The Steelhead Fly Tying Manual*. Though a similar technique originated in Europe (and is presented below in **Method #91: Feather Capsule**), Light and Humphrey's work with steelhead patterns gave the method a new direction and application.

The best feathers for this style of body are long, heavily webbed hackles. Feathers from the butt end of a domestic neck, saddle hackles, or schlappen are most suitable as they have sufficient barb length for forming the body. From the many variations of this style, we've chosen two to present below. The primary sequence shows an egg-style body formed by wrapping the hackle in collar fashion and drawing the barbs forward to form the bubble. The alternate sequence shows an elongated body formed by palmering the hackle and drawing the barbs toward the rear of the hook. We've used black thread here for visibility, but in general a thread color that matches the hackle will produce a more pleasing result.

Step 1. Attach the tying thread at mid-shank, and wrap back toward the bend until the thread is directly above the hook point.

Prepare and tie in a hackle of the desired color using either the cross-mount or parallel-mount technique as described in **Method #2: Single-hackle Mounts**, p. 347.

Advance the thread to the hook eye.

Step 2. Wrap the hackle in close, adjacent turns toward the hook eye as described in **Method #5: Single-hackle Wet-fly Collar**, p. 352, being careful not to trap any barbs beneath the hackle stem as you wrap.

Tie off the feather and clip the tip.

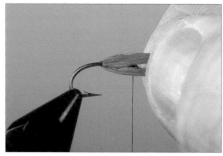

Step 3. Again, check to make sure that all hackle barbs are standing perpendicular to the hook shank. If necessary, use a dubbing needle to free any trapped or tangled barbs.

Preen all of the barbs forward to form a smooth, close-fitting shell around the hook shank.

Step 4. Take two wraps of tying thread, under light tension, around the barbs. Let the bobbin hang.

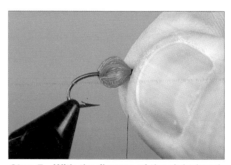

Step 5. With the fingers of the right hand, pinch the barbs directly ahead of the tie-down point, and push them back toward the hook bend. The barbs will balloon outward forming a bubble. When the bubble achieves the desired shape—spherical in this case—stop pushing.

Step 6. Secure the hackle barbs at the tie-off point with several additional tight wraps of thread. Clip the excess and bind down the butts.

Step 1a. To form an elongated bubble with a palmered hackle, attach the tying thread at mid-shank, and wrap it forward to the front point of the body. For a dry fly, the thread should be positioned slightly behind the winging point, as shown here; for a nymph, it should be positioned at the rearmost point of the thorax; for a streamer, the thread can be brought just behind the hook eye.

Prepare and tie in a hackle of the desired color using either the cross-mount or parallel-mount techniques described in **Method #2: Single-hackle Mounts**, p. 347.

Wrap the tying thread back to the rearmost point of the body.

Step 2a. Using the technique shown in **Method #17: Reverse Palmer Hackle**, p. 365, wrap the hackle in evenly spaced turns back to the tie-off point. Closely spaced wraps of hackle will produce a dense body; a more open spiral wrap will yield a sparser one.

When the hackle is wrapped, tie off the feather and clip the tip.

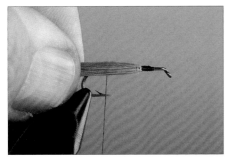

Step 3a. Preen the barbs toward the hook bend, and grip them in the left fingers. A dubbing needle or scissor points will help you preen and gather barbs beneath the shank that are obstructed by the vise jaws.

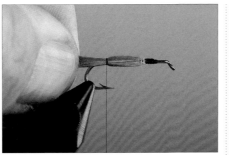

Step 4a. Take two wraps of tying thread, under light tension, around the barbs. Let the bobbin hang.

Step 5a. With the fingers of the left hand, pinch the barbs directly behind the tie-down point, and push them toward the hook eye. When the bubble achieves the desired shape, bind down the hackle at the tie-down point with additional tight wraps of thread.

Note that the excess hackle barbs can be used to form a tail here. If the hackle is palmered from bend to eye, the excess barbs can be elevated and split to form wings.

Method #91:

Feather Capsule

This is an older version of the hackle-bubble body that we were first made aware of in *Chalkstream Chronicle*, the work of the English writer and fly designer Neil Patterson, who also originated the Funneldun. Patterson says the style was devised by French tyers shortly after WWII; his version of it is named the Andelle, after a chalkstream in Normandy. In this method, feather barbs form a loose overbody capsule to imitate the nymphal shuck of a hatching mayfly. The use of gold wire to bind down the barbs and form the bubble is an interesting innovation. Patterson says the wire can be unwrapped at streamside, allowing the barbs to flare back and form a collar hackle, transforming the fly into a low-floating, damp dun.

Step 1. After the tail and body of the fly have been dressed, prepare the desired feather as you would a hackle, and attach it in front of the body using either the cross-mount or parallel-mount technique described in **Method #2: Single-hackle Mounts**, p. 347. Patterson uses dyed mallard flank, but any feather can be used provided it has sufficient length to extend over the body.

Step 2. Wrap the hackle as described in **Method #5: Single-hackle Wet-fly Collar**, p. 352.

When the hackle is complete, trim the feather tip and bind down the excess.

Take a piece of thin gold wire and attach it at the juncture of tail and body. Just a few wraps will hold the wire in place.

Step 3. Preen most of the barbs back toward the hook bend, pulling them snugly and uniformly around the fly body. Pinch the barbs in the left fingers directly behind the tailing point. The barbs nearest the hook eye should be left standing upright to form a very sparse collar.

Step 4. Push the barbs toward the hook eye to balloon them outward slightly and form a capsule. Take a few turns of the gold wire over the barbs and finish with a half-hitch.

Method #92:

Krystal Flash Bubble

This technique uses Krystal Flash, or any similar twisted Mylar material, to form bullet-shaped streamer bodies or spherical egg patterns. It is unusual in that it requires that two bobbins be used. The procedure takes a bit of practice and works best if the thread nearest the hook bend is kept long, so the bobbin hangs low in the tying field, while the thread nearest the hook eye is kept short, so the bobbin remains higher up. This precaution prevents the two bobbins from twisting together.

Step 1. Attach the thread from the front bobbin at the midpoint of the shank, and advance it toward the eye about 4 or 5 turns.

Snip a clump of Krystal Flash about 5 inches long. The clump should be about 3 times the diameter of the hook shank. Clip the butts of the strands to make them even.

Position the clump over the hook eye so that the butts reach to the midpoint of the shank. Using either **Method #6: The Taut Distribution Wrap**, p. 28, or the procedure described in **Method #86: Pulled Bullet Body**, Step 1, p. 171, tie in the Krystal Flash so that the strands are distributed around the hook shank. Bind the butts down tightly, but do not advance the thread more than 4 or 5 wraps ahead of the midpoint of the shank.

When finished, adjust the bobbin so that the tube nearly touches the hook shank.

Step 2. Attach the thread from second bobbin at the midpoint of the shank. Keep this thread long so that the second bobbin will pass beneath the first when wrapping. Take 4 or 5 wraps toward the hook bend.

Preen the Krystal Flash back toward the hook bend. Note that you will need to work the material around both tying threads. That is, when all the fibers are pulled back toward the hook bend, both bobbins should be hanging freely.

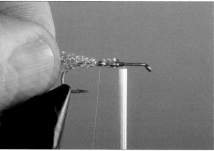

Step 3. With the rear bobbin, take several tight wraps of thread around the clump of Krystal Flash. If the material is unevenly distributed around the hook, you can use these thread wraps to help deploy the material more uniformly around the shank.

Notice that the front thread is now "inside" the capsule formed by the Krystal Flash. Maintain your grip on the Krystal Flash with the left hand, and using your right hand, gently pull the front bobbin toward the hook eye. Take 2 or 3 wraps of thread abutting the Krystal Flash, and advance the front bobbin 4 wraps toward the hook eye.

Step 4. Preen the Krystal Flash forward toward the hook eye, forming a second capsule over the first. Do not pull the material too tightly, or you will collapse this second bubble on top of the first.

Take several tight wraps around the material with the front bobbin.

Notice that the rear thread is now "inside" the capsule formed by the Krystal Flash. Maintain your grip on the Krystal Flash with the right hand, and using your left hand, gently pull the rear bobbin toward the hook bend. Take 2 or 3 wraps of thread abutting the Krystal Flash, and advance the rear bobbin 4 wraps toward the hook bend.

Step 5. Repeat Steps 2-4, building layers of Krystal Flash, forming capsule on top of capsule, each slightly larger in diameter and longer than the previous one.

When the desired number of layers are formed, or the desired length of hook shank is covered, bind down the material tightly. This can be done with either the front or rear bobbin. Clip the excess

Krystal Flash and bind down the butts. Put a drop of head cement or CA glue at each end of the material.

Here we've formed an elongated, bullet-shaped streamer body.

Step 6. To form a spherical egg fly, use the thumb and forefinger of each hand to push the ends of the bullet-shaped capsule simultaneously toward the center of the hook shank. As you shorten the capsule this way, the middle will balloon out and become spherical. Put a drop of head cement or CA glue at each end.

Brushed Bodies

Brushed bodies are formed from longer fibers that are affixed to the shank by only one end, then brushed or combed lengthwise down the shank to produce a full, usually bullet-shaped silhouette. Originally a style dressed by saltwater tyers, brushed bodies have, in recent years, made their way into trout-fly tying. As in saltwater tying, they are used almost exclusively for baitfish imitations, but other uses will almost certainly be found as tyers experiment more with this relatively new style.

As brushed bodies have become more popular, new materials suited to dressing them have appeared. The material itself is the real key to tying brushed bodies, and most tyers use synthetic hairs or furs of a specific type. For trout flies a medium- to fine-textured hair is used, and the fibers are typically kinked or crinkled rather than straight. The crinkled hair fills out the body silhouette more densely than a straight fiber, and the kinked fibers tend to intermix even after brushing to help the body hold its shape. The fibers must be soft enough to comb or brush into a flowing body shape, but stiff enough to retain the profile when submerged. A number of such fibers are available in a wide range of colors. Many tyers, however, dress flies from a single color of material, usually white or cream, and add stripes, bands, bars, spots, or other patterns with a marking pen.

For flies in trout sizes, natural wool on the hide, of the type used for stacked wool bodies (see "Stacked Wool and Yarn," p. 151) is an excellent brushed-body material, though the fiber length is much shorter than synthetics and is thus generally restricted to smaller patterns.

Method #93:

Brushed Body

Brushed bodies allow the tyer to dress baitfish imitations with broad, full silhouettes while using a relatively small amount of material that promotes both rapid sinking and an undulating action when stripped through the water. The body style is often dressed with barbell eyes, or a bead head, and if desired, a separate tail material such as marabou can be used to give added movement in the water.

There are a couple of approaches to dressing brushed bodies. The main sequence below shows perhaps the most popular method in which the fibers are mounted behind the hook eye. With this technique, nearly any type of underbody can be dressed on the hook shank—tinsel, Flashabou, Krystal Flash, sparkle chenilles, and so on. Because of the translucence of the body, these underbody materials can be made to show through on the finished fly, adding flash, color, or highlights to the pattern.

The method shown in the alternate sequence uses bundles of material staggered along the hook shank. More complex patterns of color and fiber density can be created with this technique, though it is more time-consuming. The method is well-suited, however, to larger hooks, where securing a sufficient quantity of material behind the hook eye alone can produce excessive bulk at the head of the fly. Typically, bundles of material are staggered at 2 or 3 points along the hook shank, but unusual bodies can be created by dressing the fly in the double-Aztec style, as explained in **Method #61: Aztec Wing**, p. 309. A sample of such a body is shown in Steps 1a-2a. In fact, the Aztec wing could rightfully be considered a form for a brushed body; it is presented in Chapter 12: "Wings," however, to preserve tyer Dick Nelson's original terminology.

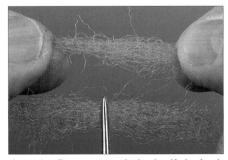

Step 1. Dress an underbody, if desired. We've omitted it here. Position the tying thread a short distance behind the hook eye. The precise distance depends upon the number of fiber bundles that will be mounted to form the body; adequate room must be left to mount all the bundles and form a head behind the hook eye.

There are a few different approaches to mounting the body material; in the following steps, three bundles will be mounted, each is handled in a slightly different way. The approaches can be used singly or in combination.

The materials used to form brushed bodies generally come in long hanks, and bundles used to form the body require a bit of preparation. The material must be cut to form a bundle of the proper length; yet the fibers within the bundle should not be equally long. Rather, fibers of random lengths give a tapering appearance to the body. There are a couple of ways to randomize the fiber length, both demonstrated in this sequence.

The fly shown here will have a thin lateral band of body material, in this case Aqua Fibers.

Separate out a bundle of the desired thickness, and clip a section 1½ to 2 times the body length, as shown at the bottom.

To randomize the fiber length, pinch the bundle loosely between the right fingertips. Use the left fingers to draw out a few fibers at a time to different lengths; pull a few fibers out ⅛", a few out ¼", and so on. You need not be perfectly exact in this. Just draw out fibers until the bundle has a tapered, flowing look, as shown at the top.

Step 2. Mount the bundle atop the shank. Angle cut the butts and secure with thread.

Position the tying thread just ahead of the bound-down butts.

Step 3. The next bundle of material will be mounted to form a portion of the body both above and below the shank. The material used here is Polar Aire, a slightly finer-textured fiber.

Separate out a bundle of material of the desired thickness, and clip a section twice as long as the body length.

The fiber length can be randomized as shown in Step 2, but tyers who regularly dress brushed bodies often use a pair of "taperizer" scissors—a type used by barbers. The scissor blades are cut with slots so that only some of the fibers pinched in the blades are trimmed; others are pushed into the slots and thus left long.

Cut crosswise through the bundles at various distances from the tip of the bundle until the fiber length is randomized and the bundle gradually diminishes in density from the middle to the tip. Prepare both ends of the bundle this way.

Note: some tyers will simply mount clipped bundles of material, and use the scissors to taper the body after all the bundles have been mounted. Both approaches give good results.

Step 4. Position this bundle atop the shank, and take 3 or 4 tight thread wraps over the center of the bundle.

Step 5. Take the end of the bundle extending over the hook eye, and draw half of this bundle down each side of the shank, below the hook, as shown.

Secure the fibers in this position (as shown in Step 6) with tight thread wraps.

Position the thread ahead of the bound-down butts.

Step 6. Cut a third bundle of material twice the body length, and randomize the fiber length.

Mount this bundle atop the shank with 3 or 4 tight thread wraps over the middle of the fibers.

Step 7. Fold the fibers extending over the hook eye, back to the hook bend.

Secure with tight thread wraps.

Form a head on the fly, whip-finish and clip. Apply a drop of cement or CA glue to the fly head.

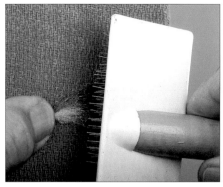

Step 8. Almost any comb or brush can be used to brush the body, but the flat, wire-toothed type sold in pet stores works well.

Hold the fly by the eye, and lay it flat against your pant leg. Working from the eye to the bend, brush the body several times to smooth and straighten the fibers, and form a tapered, flowing body.

Step 9. Shown at the top is the finished fly. Many styles are possible. At the bottom is a rainbow trout streamer.

Step 1a. Brushed bodies can also be tied in a staggered style by mounting material at intervals along the shank using any of the mounting approaches shown in the main sequence.

The fly at the left is dressed with 6 bundles of material mounted at 3 points on the shank. The fly at the right is dressed in the double-Aztec style.

Step 2a. When these bodies are brushed, there is a more uniform distribution of material over the length of the shank, and very dense bodies can be created if desired.

SECTION TEN

Bead Bodies

The use of metal, glass, or plastic beads to form bodies or parts of bodies on flies is a technique more common among European than American tyers—largely, it would appear, because of a certain bias among American fishermen against flies constructed of such non-traditional components. In this country, beads seem more an element of lure making than fly tying. The recent and enormous popularity of bead-head nymphs, however, is tempering this bias; bead-bodied flies are beginning to appear regularly, and beads themselves have become more readily available from suppliers of tying materials.

While some of the techniques for tying bead-head flies closely resemble the methods for tying beaded bodies, we have chosen, primarily as a matter of systematic reference, to detail bead-head techniques in the section "Bead Heads," p. 428. The following methods present the use of beads to fashion abdomens, thoraxes, full bodies, and emerger bubbles and sheaths.

Bead bodies are confined exclusively to subsurface flies, where their virtues are many. Beads add weight (for relative weights of different bead sizes and materials, see the chart on p. 37), bulk, color, and in some cases, flash or sparkle to a fly. Bodies made of several beads have the appearance of distinct segmentation, and those using certain types of glass or plastic beads have a lifelike translucency. Note, however, that bead-bodied flies of any material may not be legal on some catch-and-release or fly-fishing-only waters, and as always, it's best to consult local regulations to be on the safe side.

Beads themselves are available in a variety of materials and styles. Metal beads are typically made of brass, nickel, or copper, and may be shiny, dull, or even black. Glass and plastic beads may be clear, translucent, opaque, or pearlescent; they can be smooth or faceted, round or oblong. A few points about glass beads are worth noting. They are available in a wider variety of sizes and colors, and are more readily obtainable than any other type of bead. Glass-beads are reasonably durable under most circumstances, but if flies dressed with them are fished deep and bounced along rocky bottoms, the beads can break. But in general, they are both practical to tie and effective in fishing.

The techniques for tying beads depend less on the bead material than on the size of the hook, the diameter of the bead, and the size and type of hole drilled through it. This last consideration is probably the most important. Obviously, the hole in the bead must be sufficiently large to fit over the hook wire, but often this isn't enough. The bend of the hook poses a particular problem in mounting beads. All glass and plastic beads, and many metal ones, have a straight, uniform-diameter hole drilled through them. When such a bead is slipped over a de-

barbed hook point and reaches the hook bend, the wire begins to form an arc inside the bead hole. If the hole is small, it will not provide enough clearance for the curved wire, and the bead will bind up on the bend. The larger the bead in relation to hook gap, the bigger this problem becomes. Larger beads have longer holes and require a correspondingly greater clearance.

There are a number of solutions to the problem, the most obvious of which is to use a bead with a hole diameter large enough to pass around the hook bend. Sometimes, however, the hole required is large enough so that the bead can finally be slipped over the hook eye instead. In either case, you're faced with the subsequent problem of securing a bead with a big hole on a thin wire shank; the technique for doing so is presented below. The second solution is to use a hook with a finer wire or with an extra-wide gap where the radius of the hook bend is not so extreme that the bead binds up.

The last solution is to straighten the hook wire enough to let the bead pass around the bend. Since this technique is most commonly used with bead heads—which generally require larger beads than do bodies—it is explained in **Method #4: Slip-on Bead Head**, Step 1a, p. 430.

With some metal beads, a different alternative presents itself. Instead of having straight, uniform-diameter holes, they are drilled with tapered or countersunk holes. The large opening at one end of the bead provides enough clearance to pass around the hook bend, while the small hole at the other end prevents the bead from slipping over the hook eye. This style of bead is most useful in fashioning bead heads and thoraxes.

One important concern in bead-body flies is the size of bead in relation to the hook. A very large bead on the shank of a very small hook can significantly reduce the effective hook gap and render the fly almost useless in catching fish. Conversely, very small beads may not fit on the wire of a large hook. Methods for mounting oversize or undersize beads are shown below.

The final consideration in using beads is the underbody of the fly, which serves two functions. Since the bead hole must be larger than the diameter of the hook wire, a bead on a bare shank will fit loosely. Bodies using multiple beads may appear crooked or uneven. Securing the beads snugly to the hook shank requires building up an underbody on the shank that holds the beads firmly. With metal beads, or opaque glass or plastic ones, this bulk can be built up of tying thread, which is ultimately hidden beneath the beads. Clear or translucent beads, however, will allow the tying thread to show through and influence the appearance of the finished body. With such beads, underbodies can be fashioned from colored tying thread,

floss, tinsel, Mylar materials—almost anything—that not only disguise the dark color of the hook shank, but produce an attractive, two-toned translucence in the body. A few of the many possibilities are illustrated in the following methods.

Method #94:

Straight Bead Body

We were first made aware of this technique in the Seed-Bead Midge Pupa devised by Joe Warren ("seed" refers to the very small glass bead used in that dressing). But other styles and sizes of beads can be used to form entire bodies on caddis larvae and pupae patterns, and some nymphs. Some interesting nymph abdomens can be made by covering only the rear half of the hook shank. Tails or trailing shucks can be added to bead bodies (see **Method #96: Tailed Bead Body**, p. 183) as can gills (see **Method #97: Feather-gill Bead Body**, p. 183, and **Method #98: Dubbed-gill Bead Body**, p. 184), and bubble-type overbodies (see **Method #102: Bead Bubble Sheath**, p. 188).

Some bead and hook combinations will require an underbody of thread or some other material to make the beads fit snugly; others will not. The two cases vary only slightly in the method of dressing. We're using a thread underbody here. When using translucent or transparent beads, be aware that the thread may be visible through the beads, and choose a thread color accordingly.

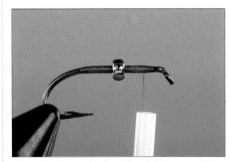

Step 1. Determining the thickness of the underbody needed involves a bit of trial and error at first, but once it is determined, dressing subsequent flies of the same type will go quickly.

Begin by slipping one bead on the hook shank and mounting the hook in the vise. Slide the bead around the hook bend so that it rests against the vise jaws.

Attach the tying thread at front point of the body. Wrap the thread in smooth, even wraps back to the rearmost point of the body, and then forward again to the front.

Slide the bead onto the thread underbody. The fit need not be perfectly snug, but it should not be so loose that the bead can sit crooked on the hook shank. All you are trying to do is provide a sufficiently thick underbody to hold all the beads centered on the shank.

If, after the initial trial, the underbody is too thick and the bead won't slip over the thread, slide the bead back down the hook bend and unwrap the thread. Re-attach the thread at the rearmost point of the body; wrap a single layer of thread to the front of the body, and test the fit again.

If, after the initial trial, the bead is still too loose, slide it back down the hook bend; wrap the tying thread back to the rearmost point of the body, and then forward again, thickening the underbody. Try the bead again, applying more layers of thread until the bead fits.

Make a note of the number of thread layers required for future use of the same bead-hook combination.

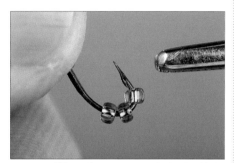

Step 2. When the proper underbody thickness has been determined, secure the tying thread with a few half-hitches, and clip it.

Remove the hook from the vise, and slide the desired number of beads onto the shank.

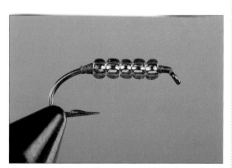

Step 3. When the appropriate length of shank is covered with beads, re-mount the hook. Attach the tying thread behind the rearmost bead, and use the thread to build a small bump or button to prevent the beads from sliding backward.

Note that this rear bump can be fashioned from tying thread of the same color as the beads to create the appearance of an additional body segment. Or it can used, as we've done here, to form a neat taper at the rear of the body.

Secure with a whip finish or a few half-hitches, and apply a drop of head cement or CA glue to the thread bump.

The beads can still slide forward on the hook shank, but the materials used to dress the head or thorax of the fly will be abutted against the front bead, thereby securing the bead body.

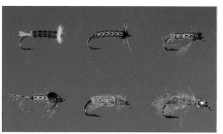

Shown here are a few examples of the types of bodies and abdomens that can be constructed with straight-bead bodies.

Top row: Seed-Bead Midge Pupa, Green Rockworm, Gold Caddis Larva.

Bottom row: mayfly nymph, Green Caddis Pupa, Green Bead-Pupa (the body on this fly is fashioned from green beads.)

Method #95
Tapered Bead Body

The tapered profile of bodies on some aquatic insects can be reproduced with beads. The success of the technique, however, relies on finding beads of roughly the same color and shape in 3 or 4 graduated sizes—all of which will fit on the desired hook shank. Given the beads that we have found commercially available, the smallest hook size on which it is practical to form a tapered body is about a #16. The largest hook size depends upon the largest beads you are able to locate.

The technique for making a tapered body is very similar to that for forming straight bodies, except that the underbody must be tapered so that all the beads are centered on the hook shank to produce a symmetrical body.

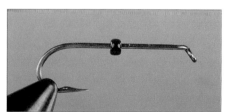

Step 1. Slip the smallest bead over the de-barbed hook point to determine if a thread foundation will be required under the smallest body segments. If the fit is snug, as it is here, no thread underbody will be required under this bead or any others like it. If the bead is loose, one or more layers of the thread will be needed.

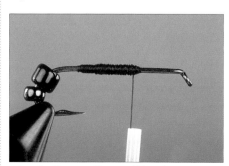

Step 2. Remove the small bead.

Slide the largest bead onto the hook,

followed by the second largest bead. Mount the hook in the vise, and position the beads against the vise jaws, as shown. These beads dictate the diameter of the thread foundation and will be test-fit as shown in **Method #94: Straight Bead Body**, Step 1, p. 181.

Attach the tying thread at the front point of the body, where the largest bead will sit. Form a tapered thread foundation (see **Method #2: Tapered Thread Underbody**, p. 42) by taking a few thread wraps toward the hook bend, then returning the thread to the original position. Test fit the beads.

If they are too loose, take a few more thread wraps toward the bend, extending beyond the first layer, then return the thread to the front of the body. Continue traversing the hook shank back and forth like this, building a tapered underbody that will hold all the beads snugly.

Again, the first fly will be a matter of trial and error, but if you take note of the number of thread layers created, subsequent flies of the same type will go rapidly.

For very large beads with large holes, this tapered underbody can be created more efficiently by using floss, dubbing, or some other material that builds up more quickly than thread on the hook shank.

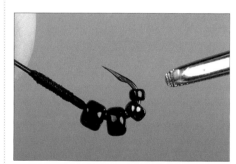

Step 3. Once you've fashioned an underbody of the proper taper, secure the tying thread at the front of the body with a few half-hitches, and clip it off.

Remove the hook from the vise and, starting with the largest bead and working to the smallest, thread the beads over the hook point and snug them against the underbody. Here we are making a beaded abdomen for a small stonefly nymph.

Step 4. Re-attach the tying thread behind the rearmost bead, and form a small thread bump to prevent the beads from sliding backward, as described in **Method #94: Straight Bead Body**, Step 3, p. 182.

Materials used to dress the thorax will be seated firmly against the front bead and thus secure the body on the front end.

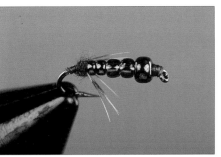

The tapered body described above is typical of mayfly and stonefly nymphs. A reverse taper typical of caddis bodies—thicker at rear, thinner at the front—is laborious, and sometimes not possible, using the technique described above.

The simplest solution to forming caddis tapers is to dress the fly backwards, as shown here. Form a tapered body using the method detailed above, but position the largest bead directly behind the hook eye. Then dress the head of the fly on the rear of the hook.

Method #96:
Tailed Bead Body

Because the beads must slide around the hook bend, it is impractical to mount the tails before the body is constructed, and two techniques for affixing the tails after the beads are in place are presented here.

On straight bodies, room is left at the front of the body to form a thorax or head; hence the beads can be slipped forward on the shank, giving room to tie in the tail after the body has been mounted, as shown in the main sequence.

The beads on a tapered body, however, cannot be slid forward as the smaller beads will not pass over the thick end of the underbody. A different approach must be used, and this is presented in the alternate sequence.

In both cases, however, the appearance of the finished fly is improved if the color of the tying thread is chosen to match the bead color as closely as possible.

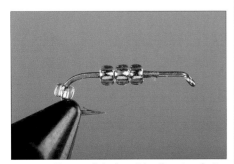

Step 1. For straight-bead bodies, begin by fashioning a thread underbody as described above in **Method #94: Straight Bead Body**, Steps 1-2, p. 181, except do not lay a thread foundation beneath the last bead. When the beads are mounted, the rearmost bead should be positioned on a bare hook shank.

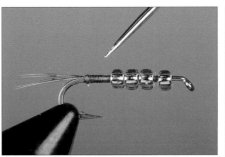

Step 2. Slide the beads toward the eye of the hook. Mount the tying thread at the tailing point, and secure the desired tailing material against the bare hook shank with a few tight turns of thread. Try to hold thread wraps to a minimum; if too much bulk is created the rearmost bead will not slide backward to cover the tail-mounting thread wraps.

Build a small thread bump directly over the rearmost thread wrap. It should be just large enough to prevent the beads from sliding backward. Secure the thread with a whip-finish or a few half-hitches, and clip. Apply a small drop of head cement or CA glue to the thread bump.

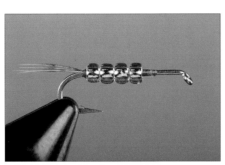

Step 3. Slide the beads backward until they abut the thread bump.

Step 1a. For tapered bodies, dress a tapered bead body as described above in **Method #95: Tapered Bead Body**, p. 182. Do not, however, form a thread bump behind the rearmost bead to secure it.

Re-attach the thread behind the last bead. Mount the tailing material as closely behind the rearmost bead as possible, using the minimum number of thread wraps that will tightly secure the tail.

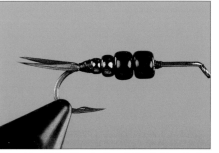

Step 2a. Trim the butts of the tail material as closely as possible to the hook shank, and build up a thread bump that covers the butts of the material. The thread bump can be used to form an additional body segment, or be tapered for a neat finish to the rear of the body.

Secure the thread with a few half-hitches or a whip-finish and clip. Apply a small drop of head cement or CA glue to the thread wraps.

Method #97:
Feather-gill Bead Body

Certain nymphs are more accurately imitated with fringe-like gills between the abdominal segments—structures often imitated on bodies of conventional materials with ribbing of herl or trimmed hackle stems. But ribbing materials wrapped over the bead bodies will partially obscure the segmented appearance and are difficult to hold in position on the slippery surface of the bead. Instead, a strand of herl or a feather can be wrapped around the shank prior to mounting the beads.

Because this technique requires that the bead be slipped not only over the hook shank, but also over an underbody of herl or hackle, the beads themselves must have relatively large holes—a fact which makes very small beads and hooks impractical. A #14 hook is about the smallest that can be used; larger hooks work better. It pays to experiment with hook styles, particularly the use of dry-fly hooks made of fine or extra-fine wire, which helps minimize bulk in the shank.

In the main sequence below, we're using a #12 hook with an ostrich herl gill and a seed-bead body. On larger flies, afterfeather (see "Afterfeather," p. 11), marabou blood feathers (see **Method #6: Marabou Collar Hackle**, p. 353), and hackle, as shown in the alternate sequence, can be used instead of herl. Hackle can be left long on the finished fly, which gives the appearance of a palmered hackle over the body for attractor-type patterns, or it can be clipped to form gills. The use of hackle is also effective in creating legs between beads used to dress the thorax of the fly (see **Method #101: Bead Thorax**, p. 187).

Regardless of the style used, there are a few points worth noting. First, choose and apply an underbody material such that the bulk on the shank is kept low enough to allow the beads to slide over it. Second, on the underbody material, either hackle or herl, the barbs should have a length greater than the diameter of the bead in order to produce distinct gills. Lastly, using very fine thread, 8/0 or 12/0, helps prevent the buildup of material, particularly at the mounting point of the underbody.

(In addition to the techniques shown below, feather barbs can be used to form lashed gills as explained in **Method #3: Tuft Gills**, p. 93. Though a bit laborious, it nonetheless produces a quite realistic effect on patterns that require a fringe of gills down either side of the abdomen. Since the procedure has been demonstrated in that method, we'll merely note here the few changes required to adapt this technique to bead bodies. Slip the desired number of beads on the shank, using no thread underbody. Add a tail if desired, and build a thread bump behind the last bead. Mount the gills as shown in **Method #3**, Steps 1a-5a, tie off and clip the thread. Slide the next bead toward the rear of the hook, pinching the gill material between the two beads. Mount the next pair of gills, and continue until the body is complete.)

Step 1. Mount the tying thread at the rearmost point of the body. Wrap a single strand of herl as explained in **Method #26: Single-herl Body**, p. 117.

Do not, however, overlap the quill stem when wrapping to produce a dense body as described in that sequence. This may produce so much thickness that the bead will not slide over the underbody. Instead, wrap the herl so that the turns of quill are laid in touching, edge-to-edge wraps.

Wrap the herl forward to the front end of the body. Tie off the material and use the thread to construct a bump large enough to prevent the bead from sliding over it. When the bump is formed, secure the thread with a few half-hitches, and clip it.

Step 1a. If using hackle, it's best to choose a saddle hackle (either rooster or hen, depending on the effect desired) with a very thin stem. To keep mounting bulk to a minimum, it helps to flatten the stripped

portion of the hackle stem as explained in "Preparing Feather-tip Downwings," p. 292.

Mount the hackle at the rearmost point of the body and spiral it forward. Two approaches can be used, the one described in **Method #16: Forward Palmer Hackle—Tip Mounted**, p. 364, or the one explained in **Method #15: Forward Palmer Hackle—Stem Mounted**, p. 363, and shown here.

Some trial-and-error may be required here. Beads with larger holes may slip over a body made of closely spaced, or even touching wraps of hackle, and a thread underbody may be required. Beads with smaller holes may require a hackle wrapped in a more open spiral, as shown here, to help reduce bulk on the hook shank.

Wrap the hackle forward to the front end of the body. Tie off the material and use the thread to construct a bump large enough to prevent the bead from sliding over it. When the bump is formed, secure the thread with a few half-hitches, and clip it.

Step 2. Remove the hook from the vise and slide the first bead over the underbody; butt it against the thread bump. Notice that some fibers of the underbody material are trapped underneath the bead. With the point of a dubbing needle, carefully free these trapped fibers so that they stand erect. Work close to the base of the bead and all the way around the hook shank.

Step 3. When the fibers are free, mount the second bead and abut it against the first. The fibers pinched between the two beads will form the gills. Again, free the fibers trapped by the second bead as described in Step. 2.

Step 4. Continue adding beads and freeing any trapped fibers until the body is completed.

Step 5. Re-mount the thread behind the rearmost bead. Working toward the hook eye, build up a thread bump that pushes the beads together. The bump should be large enough to prevent the last bead from slipping back toward the hook bend, as shown on the fly at the bottom. (Note that this bump can be fashioned during the application of tailing materials as described above in **Method #96: Tailed Bead Body**, Steps 2a-3a, p. 183.)

When the thread bump is complete, apply a drop of head cement or CA glue.

The fly at the top shows the hackle-barb gills dressed in Step 1a.

Method #98:
Dubbed-gill Bead Body

Gills on bead-body flies can be formed by applying a small quantity of dubbing material between each pair of beads. This approach allows a greater latitude in color, texture, length, and density of gill material than does the previous method. It is, however, a bit more time-consuming, as the thread must be tied off and remounted between each pair of beads. Still, when the overall number of body segments is small, as on most trout flies, the technique is practical.

This same approach can be used with long-fibered dubbings to form legs between two or more beads used to form the thorax of a fly and on scud patterns, as shown in Step 3.

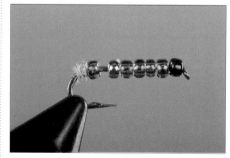

Step 1. If necessary, build a thread foundation as explained in **Method #94: Straight Bead Body**, Step 1, p. 181. Tie off and clip the thread.

Slide the desired number of beads on the shank up to the hook eye, and remount the thread at the rearmost point of the body.

If desired, tails can be applied at this point as explained in **Method #96: Tailed Bead Body**, Steps 1-2, p. 183. (We've omitted the tails here.)

To prevent the beads from slipping around the hook bend, wrap a small ball of dubbing over the rearmost thread wraps, as shown here, or build a bump of tying thread large enough to hold the bead on the shank.

When the bump is complete, secure the thread with a whip-finish or a few half-hitches, and clip it.

Slide the rearmost bead tightly against the bump.

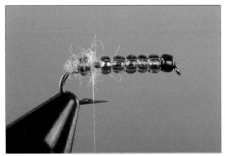

Step 2. Remount the tying thread ahead of the bead.

Apply a small amount of dubbing to the thread, and wrap it directly abutting the front of the bead. The quantity of dubbing used should be large enough to prevent the bead from sliding forward.

Secure the thread with a whip-finish or a few half-hitches, and clip.

Step 3. Slide the next bead forward, dub the gills, secure and clip the thread. Repeat until the body is complete, as shown on the fly at the top.

If desired, a dubbing needle or teaser can be used to pick out fibers between the beads for more pronounced gills.

The fly at the bottom is a scud pattern in which the sections of dubbing are broader, and made of a longer-fibered material. The dubbing is teased out beneath the hook shank to simulate legs; fibers on the sides and back of the fly have been trimmed flush with the beads to give a shellback appearance.

Method #99:
Bead-chain Body

This technique was first shown to us by one of the West's most innovative tyers, Bill Black, who uses bead chain and chenille to dress streamer and large nymph bodies. Because the beads are partially concealed by the body material, the flashiness is muted, and the top of the body has an almost spotted pattern. Smaller bead chain can also be used; gold beads will produce an interesting shell-

back effect on scuds or shrimp, and black chain will give a glossy segmentation to nymph abdomens.

Body materials are not restricted to chenille. Dubbing loops or brushes spun with herls, long-fibered chopped dubbing, fur chenilles—just about any material that produces a somewhat fuzzy body is practical. The fuzziness is important, though, as it fills in the gaps between the beads and gives the body a more uniform appearance.

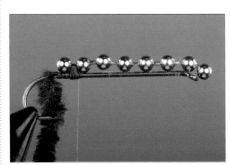

Step 1. Attach the tying thread behind the hook eye, and lay a foundation of thread as you wrap toward the tailing point. Mount whatever tails are desired, and tie in the body material—in this case, chenille. If a dubbing loop is to be used, form the thread loop at this point and hold it out of the tying field in a material clip.

Cut a length of bead chain about equal to the length of the hook shank; this is a bit more material than you will need, but it makes handling easier. Bind down the chain ahead of the rearmost bead, leaving about one bead's distance between this last bead and the tail. This spacing will allow the first wrap or two of body material to be placed between the tail and the rearmost bead.

The chain is mounted so that the beads sit atop the hook shank. Use tight wraps of thread abutting the front of the bead. If the chain tends to slip when binding it in, put a thin film of tying wax on the top of the thread foundation to help hold the beads.

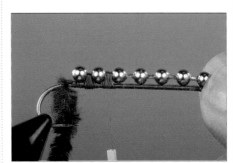

Step 2. Bind down the second bead as you did the first. On larger chain, there is a fair amount of slack in the wire that connects the beads, giving some latitude in the final spacing of the beads.

If you draw the chain tight when binding the second bead (as we're doing here), you will increase the distance between them, and fewer of them will be used on the body. If you push the second bead toward the first, you will decrease the spacing and use more beads on the body.

Step 3. Bind down each subsequent bead until the front of the body is reached. Whatever bead spacing is chosen, take care to maintain it as you bind down each bead.

When you reach the front of the body, use a wire cutter to clip any excess beads. (If there are more than one, these can be saved for bead-chain eyes.) By clipping the excess beads, you've now determined the precise number required for the body. On all subsequent flies of the same style and size, you need only mount the exact number of beads that you need.

Step 4. Wrap the body material forward. Take the first turn or two behind the rearmost bead. Then bring the body material underneath the hook shank and up in front of the rearmost bead. If the bead spacing is wide, or the body material sparse, you may need to take a second wrap of material directly ahead of the first.

Step 5. Continue winding forward, always taking the same number of turns of body material between each pair of beads.

When the front of the body is reached, bind down the body material ahead of the last bead, and clip.

Method #100:
Strung-bead Body

The bead-chain technique described in the previous method is somewhat limited because bead chain is available in a very small selection of sizes and colors. The same type of body, however, can be produced from loose beads of glass, plastic, or metal, by stringing them on a piece of thin monofilament, heavy tying thread, or wire, as shown in the following sequence—in essence, creating a piece of bead chain.

This approach is particularly helpful when using beads that are too small to slip over a large hook wire, or when using larger beads on smaller hooks, where slipping the bead over the shank would interfere significantly with the hook gap.

As explained in **Method #99: Bead-chain Body**, p. 185, any number of body materials are suitable for strung beads. But again, they must be fuzzy enough to fill the gaps between the beads for a uniform body. As a rule of the thumb, the body material should have a thickness equal to or greater than the diameter of the beads used. In the following demonstration, we're using peacock herl spun in a dubbing loop.

Step 1. Attach the tying thread behind the hook eye, and lay a foundation of thread as you wrap toward the tailing point.

Mount whatever tails are desired, and tie in the body material—in this case, we're binding in several strands of peacock herl. These are held in a material clip to keep them out of the tying field.

Form a dubbing loop as explained in **Method #29: Loop-twisted Herl Body**, p. 120.

Clip about a 4-inch length of fine monofilament, heavy tying thread, or as shown here, soft wire. Very thin wire can be used with small beads; slightly thicker wire works better with larger beads.

Lay the wire along the top of the hook shank, and bind it in about one bead's distance from the tail. Advance the tying thread to the hook eye, binding down the wire tag as you go.

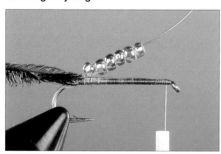

Step 2. String several beads on the wire; their combined length should be about ½ to ¾ the length of the hook shank. That is, when you come to bind down the wire in the next step, about ¼ to ½ of the wire should be bare. There must be enough room on the wire to slide the beads forward slightly to allow for wraps of body material between them. (You may at this point have more beads than are actually required for the body. The extra beads will be removed later.)

Step 3. When the desired number of beads have been added, draw the wire toward the hook eye over the top of the shank, and bind down the wire directly behind the hook eye.

Do not bind the wire tightly. As you wrap the body material between the beads, you will exert a downward pressure on the wire. The wire should be bound just loosely enough so that the downward pressure draws slack wire beneath the wrappings. The chain may appear loose and irregular at this point; it will even out as the body is wrapped.

Step 4. Begin forming the body by taking a wrap or two of body material behind the last bead.

Maintain tension on the body material, and use the fingers of the left hand to draw the rearmost bead backwards, seating it tightly against the wire. You may need to tug slightly on the wire tag with the right hand to prevent excessive slack from developing.

Now take a turn of body material (or more if desired) in front of the rearmost bead.

Step 5. Again, maintain tension on the body material, and using the fingers of the left hand, draw the second bead backward tightly against the first. Take a turn of material in front of this second bead.

Step 6. Continue drawing the beads backward, one at a time, and placing a wrap of body material between them. Work to maintain a uniform spacing between the beads.

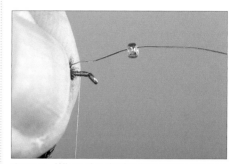

Step 7. When the desired body length has been created, maintain tension on the body material with the left hand.

With the right hand, unwind the tying thread to release the wire tag. Raise the tag and remove any excess beads.

Step 8. With the tying thread, bind down both the body material and the wire at the front point of the body.

With the first fly you tie, you will determine the exact number of beads and their spacing. On subsequent flies of the same style and size, you need merely mount the exact number of beads needed on the wire.

This photo shows various possibilities for strung-bead bodies: a crayfish (top); a scud formed from fuzzy dubbing, with a clipped back (lower left); and a tapered black nymph abdomen made of ostrich herl and trimmed to follow the body taper (lower right).

Method #101:
Bead Thorax

One or more beads, of any material, can be used to fashion the thorax on a nymph pattern, adding weight, gloss, or flash. The finished fly appears and behaves very much like a bead-head nymph, but the use of a wingcase or hackle, as well as the placement of the bead behind the head of the fly properly makes this a thorax technique. Any of the customary materials—sections of quill from a wing or tail feather, bundles of feather barbs, hairs, yarns, herls, or synthetics like Krystal Flash and Flashabou—can be used for the wingcase.

The main sequence shows a wingcase mounted behind the hook eye and folded rearward over the bead thorax, a technique that produces a very trim appearance at the head of the fly and is preferred by many tyers. The alternate sequence shows the reverse approach; this method produces a standard thread head on the fly, and if desired, the tips of some wingcase materials such as hair or feather barbs can be used to form legs on the fly.

With both approaches, however, fragile materials, such as the pheasant tail fibers used in the following demonstrations, may require measures to prevent the wingcase from fraying or breaking against a trout's teeth. Two preventative techniques are illustrated in Steps 4a-5a. Tougher materials, particularly synthetic fibers, need no reinforcement.

The following instructions pertain to beads with holes small enough that they must slipped over the hook point to be mounted on the shank. Beads with holes large enough to pass over the hook eye can be used to make the thorax in the usual fashion—dress the tail and body; tie in the wingcase as shown in either **Method #1: Folded-strip Wingcase**, p. 229, or **Method #4: Bundled-fiber Wingcase**, p. 232. Slide the bead(s) over the eye, draw the wingcase forward, and complete the fly.

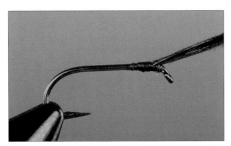

Step 1. Mount the wingcase material directly behind, and extending out beyond, the hook eye as shown.

If a hackle is to placed between the bead thorax and the front of the wing case, mount and wind the hackle at this point.

On thoraxes fashioned from two or more beads, feather-barb legs can be dressed at this point as described in **Method #97: Feather-gill Bead Body**, p. 183; apply the feather underbody material on thorax section of the fly only.

If the hole in the bead is quite large in relation to the hook wire, build up an underbody of tying thread on the shank directly behind the wingcase.

When the case is mounted and underbody (if needed) is wrapped, secure the tying thread with a whip-finish or a few half-hitches and clip.

Step 2. Slide a bead onto the hook shank and seat it against the base of the wing case. If desired, additional beads can be added and dubbing-fiber legs formed as explained in **Method #98: Dubbed-gill Bead Body**, p. 184.

When all the beads are mounted, re-attach the tying thread behind the bead.

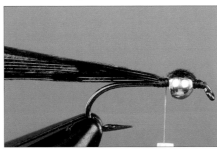

Step 3. Draw the wingcase material over the top of the bead, distributing it evenly over the surface of the bead to form a smooth, uniform wingcase. If fragile materials are used, they can be reinforced as shown in Steps 4a-5a.

Bind down the rear of the wingcase, working toward the hook eye in order to seat the bead securely.

The remainder of the fly can now be dressed. When the fly is complete, the thread is tied off directly behind the bead. To conceal these finish wraps, many tyers use **Method #13: Dubbed Whip-finish**, p. 24.

Step 1a. In this version, the bead is mounted first and slipped to the eye of the hook.

Mount the tying thread in the middle of the shank, and wrap toward the bead, stopping about 4 or 5 thread-wraps behind the rear of the bead. Since the wingcase will be tied off behind the hook eye, there must be enough room to slide the bead rearward.

Mount the wingcase material, in this case pheasant tail fibers, directly over the frontmost thread wrap, and bind the material down toward the rear of the hook, as shown.

Step 2a. Dress the remainder of the fly. When it is complete, tie off the thread atop the frontmost thread wrap securing the wingcase. Clip the thread.

Remount the thread behind the hook eye.

With your right fingers, draw the wingcase material over the top of the bead. As you do so, use your fingertips to push the bead rearward, abutting it against the front of the body to create space for the thread head. If fragile materials are used, the wingcase can be formed using one of the approaches used in Steps 4a-5a.

Step 3a. Bind down the wingcase material directly ahead of the bead, using thread wraps to force the bead back into the front of the body.

The excess wingcase material can be clipped and covered with thread, or used to form legs as explained in **Method #9: Wingcase Legs**, p. 418.

Step 4a. Wingcase materials drawn tightly over the bead may break or tear in a fish's mouth. There are two ways to prevent this.

The first is to pull back the wingcase material loosely, leaving some slack in the wing case that forms a shell over, but not in contact with, the bead. This slack allows the material to flex, and it will not break as readily.

Step 5a. This method of reinforcement was described to us by tyer Skip Morris. Before drawing the wingcase back, place a small drop of epoxy or gel-type CA glue on top of the bead. Pull the wingcase tightly over the bead into the drop of adhesive. Secure the wingcase in the usual fashion. If epoxy is used, another drop can be placed on top of the wingcase.

This photograph illustrates various styles of bead thoraxes. In the top row are a soft-hackle fly and a stonefly nymph. In the bottom row are a Hare's Ear nymph with a throat hackle, and a caddis pattern with both body and thorax made of beads.

Method #102:

Bead Bubble Sheath

Flies tied with beads and sheaths or bubbles of the type typically used on caddis emergers can be tied using two, almost entirely opposite approaches. Since both approaches produce essentially the same type of imitation, they are included in this method.

The main sequence shows such a fly dressed with a conventional body material, dubbing in this case, and a translucent, football-shaped bead to represent the sheath. This technique was developed by tyer Ken Ligas, who distributes such beads under the name "Scintillator Bubbles," but suitable substitutes may be found in craft stores; the key requirement is that the bead has a hole large enough to fit over the hook eye. Because this type of bead can extend significantly below the hook shank, it's best to use hooks with wide gaps so that hooking capability is not diminished.

The alternate sequence shows the converse approach—a body dressed with beads and a sheath made of more conventional tying material, in this case Antron yarn, tied

in a style devised by Gary LaFontaine for his Sparkle Pupa design. The technique shown in the alternate steps is the one most practical for bead bodies, since the other methods for forming such bubbles, (shown in **Method #88: Double-strand Antron Bubble**, p. 173, and **Method #89: Single-strand Antron Bubble**, p. 175) generally produce so much thread bulk on the shank that the body beads will not slide over the mounting wraps. The technique shown in the alternate sequence can be used on flies with other types of bodies as well.

Step 1. Mount the tying thread near the rear of the hook, and spin a little dubbing of the desired color on the thread. Wrap a ball of dubbing at the rearmost point of the body. The ball should be just large enough to prevent the bead from sliding backward when it is mounted.

Step 2. Create a body of the desired material and color. Almost any material can be used here—dubbing, floss, micro-chenille, Antron, twisted Mylar, herl, and so on. The only requirement is that the body be thin enough to permit the bead to slide over it. The finished body length should be equal to the length of the bead.

When the body is completed, secure the thread with a few half-hitches and clip.

Step 3. Slide the bead over the hook eye, and seat it against the dubbing ball at the rear of the hook.

Step 4. Finish the head of the fly. We've used a simple dubbed head here, but you can also use afterfeather, herl, hackle, or other materials. In any case, however, the head should be large enough to prevent the bead from slipping forward.

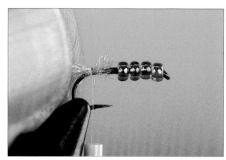

Step 1a. To construct a bead body with an Antron sheath, prepare the hook as you would for tailing a bead-body fly as explained in **Method #96: Tailed Bead Body**, Step 1, p. 183. That is, create a thread foundation under all but the rearmost bead on the shank. Tie off and clip the thread. The sheath material will be mounted on this bare portion of the shank.

Slip the beads on the hook shank, and slide them up to the hook eye.

Cut a length of Antron yarn about 3 times the shank length, and comb the fibers so that the individual strands are not tangled. The thickness of the yarn strand used depends upon the diameters of the hook and bead hole, since the bead must be slipped over the thread wraps used to mount the yarn. It takes a bit of experimentation to determine this amount; here, we're using a #14 dry-fly hook and one strand of spooled Antron.

Re-mount the tying thread at the rear of the shank. Place the trimmed end of the yarn atop the hook, and work the fibers downward so that they encircle the shank evenly.

When the yarn fibers are distributed, take one thread wrap around the yarn, cinching it to the shank. Note the short tag of yarn that will be bound down.

Step 2a. Bind down the yarn with a minimum of tight thread wraps to avoid bulk on the shank.

Secure the tying thread with a whip-finish or a few half-hitches, and clip. If desired, a small drop of CA glue can be placed atop the mounting wraps to help secure the material.

With a dubbing needle and your fingers, preen the yarn fibers so that they stand straight outward from the shank, as shown here viewed from the hook eye.

Step 3a. Slide all the beads rearward. The last bead should cover the thread wraps used to secure the Antron.

Remount the thread ahead of the beads.

Preen the Antron fibers forward to form a bubble, and secure them directly ahead of the frontmost bead.

Slip the bead on the hook and let it rest against the vise jaws, as shown.

Lay a thread foundation at the rear of the hook, just where the shank begins to bend. The length of the thread foundation should be equal to the diameter of the bead. You may need to test fit the bead a few times to get the proper thickness in the foundation. The fit should be snug.

Once the foundation is laid, apply a drop of CA glue to the thread.

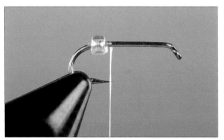

Step 2. Slide the bead up and seat it on the thread wraps. Allow it to dry, and finish dressing the fly.

Method #103:

Rear-mount Bead

Some fly patterns call for a bead mounted at the rear of the body, and most notable among these are dressings that imitate waterboatmen and backswimmers—species that trap a tiny bubble of air at the rear of the body to be used as an oxygen supply when they swim underwater. A small metal or glass bead suggests this bubble.

Rear-mount beads can be dressed in exactly the same fashion as bead heads except, of course, that they are mounted at the opposite end of the hook shank. These techniques are detailed in the section on "Bead Heads," p. 428.

Rear-mount beads can be affixed as either the first step in the dressing, as shown in the main sequence, or as the last step in the dressing, as shown in the alternate sequence.

Step 1a. To mount the bead last, dress the desired fly pattern. Slide a bead over the hook point and snug it against the body. Note that if using counterdrilled or tapered-hole beads, the large hole should face the fly body.

Step 1. We first saw this method for attaching beads on waterboatmen and backswimmers on the E.T.'s Corixia pattern designed by E.W Tainton.

Step 2a. Mount the tying thread behind the bead, and build a thread bump thick enough to prevent the bead from slipping backward.

Secure the thread with a few half-hitches or a whip-finish, and clip. Apply a drop of head cement or CA glue to the wrappings.

Foam Bodies

Foam is a relatively new fly-dressing material, though tyers have been quick to take advantage of its virtues—it is relatively easy to handle, can be cut to a variety of shapes, and is fairly inexpensive. Perhaps the most attractive property of all, however, is the exceptional buoyancy of some foams. Though the material is occasionally used in constructing wings, wingcases, float pods, and other fly components, its principal application is in bodies. The various techniques for tying foam bodies are detailed in this section, with one exception—extended foam bodies—which are presented in "Extended Bodies," p. 204.

The chemistry of foam and the manufacturing techniques involved are complex, and there are literally hundreds of different types that vary in composition, density, and texture. Only a few of these are readily available to tyers, though there is still plenty of room for confusion. While certain foam compositions do have trade names—Ethafoam, for instance—the actual products bearing these names may have widely different densities, and hence different fly-tying properties, making generalizations difficult. Moreover, the materials sold in fly shops are often identified by distributors' product names—like Float Foam—rather than the actual foam-industry designations, and it is often not apparent which specific material you are buying. Readers interested in more thorough or technical discussions of foam should consult Phil Camera's *Fly Tying with Synthetics*, *Tying Foam Flies* by Skip Morris, or *Modern Fly-Tying Materials* by Dick Talleur.

For our purposes here, a few broad distinctions will serve, and the first of these is between rigid foams (such as the material used to make foam coffee cups) and flexible foams, which are the most common type used in tying. Of the flexible foams, there are again two basic categories. "Open-cell foam," as the name implies, is a material honeycombed with connected openings, much like an ordinary sponge. And like a sponge it will absorb water, making it suitable for sinking flies—not because the material itself sinks, but rather simply because it does not prevent sinking. "Closed-cell foam," by contrast, is composed of individual, self-contained, closed chambers that may contain air, nitrogen, or some other gas that is produced in the manufacturing. Such foams are buoyant and, obviously, best suited to floating flies.

Not all closed-cell foams are equal, however. They vary in the size and wall thickness of the cell, and thus in overall density. These variables are important in that they govern characteristics important to the tyer—buoyancy, durability, and flexibility. Each type of closed-cell foam represents tradeoffs among these properties. Generally speaking, large-celled, thin-walled foams, which are often

translucent with a pebbly exterior texture, offer the greatest buoyancy and flexibility, but are the least durable. Finely grained, small-celled foams, on the other hand, are tougher, but stiffer and less buoyant. And in the end, it makes more sense to select a foam based on these characteristics rather than any name assigned to it by a manufacturer or distributor.

Shaping and Coloring Foam

Closed-cell foams can be cut simply with a razor blade or tying scissors, provided these tools are very sharp. When forming irregular shapes—teardrops, for instance, to use as beetle bodies, cardboard templates can be created and placed over a foam sheet for a cutting guide.

Cylindrical bodies, however, are more difficult to cut with a razor or scissors, but they can be fashioned from medium-density foams by flame shaping. As always, when using fire in fly tying, a certain caution is prudent. To create a cylindrical body, begin by cutting a strip of foam that is square in cross-section. Hold the foam at one end, and with the flame of a butane lighter, stroke lengthwise down one corner of the strip. Position the foam strip to the side of the flame, not above it, and do not allow the material to contact the flame itself. Mere proximity is enough to soften the edge of the corner. The movement of the flame should be like a smooth, gentle, and relatively brisk brushstroke—imagine yourself "painting" the corner of the foam with the flame.

Run the flame down all four corners of the foam in sequence. Then roll the foam crosswise between the fingertips to round it into a cylinder. The foam should not be so hot that you cannot touch it. The key here is to exercise restraint. You are emphatically not trying to burn away material, but merely getting it warm enough to re-shape with the fingers. While perfect cylinders are difficult to achieve, it is a relatively simple matter to smooth out the corners on the rectangular material for a body that is more natural in shape. Finally, some foams work better than others in this regard, and experimentation is the best way to determine which materials are suited to the technique.

Half of this rectangular strip has been flame-shaped into a cylinder.

While certain types of foams are available in a variety of colors, these are often bold primary colors or pastels—not exactly lifelike shades for most insects. Thus many tyers choose to color the foam, either before or after it is tied in. Waterproof marking pens work well here, but eventually the colors will fade or wear away. Richard Bunse, a painter, illustrator, and fly tyer has devised a solution for this problem. Bunse colors the foam with marking pens, and then brushes the material very lightly with a thinned solution of Flexament (one part cement to three parts thinner). This light coat of cement seals in the color and adds additional toughness to the exterior of the foam. Spray fixative can also be used as a color sealant, but it must be applied to the foam prior to tying or to a foam body mounted on a hook that contains no other dressing materials.

Tying Foam

The very properties that make flexible foam easy to handle—its softness and compressibility—are also limitations in tying. Excessive thread pressure applied when mounting, segmenting, or tying off a foam body can sever the material, either immediately or over time. Reducing thread tension for these procedures minimizes the risk of cutting the foam, but may well produce a body that is not firmly anchored to the hook shank.

There are two basic techniques for binding in and tying off foam bodies that will secure the material while reducing the risk of cutting it. The procedures can be used with both open- and closed-cell foams.

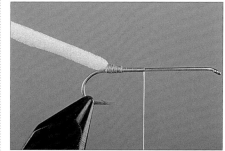

This technique is widespread among foam tyers. When mounting the material, secure and cover the tag end with tight wraps of thread, thus anchoring the foam to the hook shank. Then wind the thread a short distance up the foam, decreasing tension with each wrap. These snug, but not tight, turns of thread take some pressure off the "hinge" created by the very tight wraps and help prevent the foam from separating. The same procedure can be used in tying off the material.

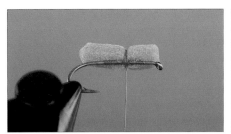

This method was shown to us by Skip Morris. When binding in or tying off material, or using thread to create a body segment as you would for an ant body, place a small drop of epoxy or gel-type CA glue on the hook shank, on the underside of the material, on the thread, or on all three. Then secure the foam with snug, but not tight, turns of thread. In essence, you're gluing the foam to the shank and using the thread to hold it in position.

The compressibility of foam becomes a problem when closed-cell foam is ribbed with thread to form body segments. A tight thread pressure will rupture the hollow chambers inside the material, and if very narrow body segments are created by using closely spaced wraps, enough cells may be destroyed that the foam loses it buoyancy. This is particularly true when ribbing relatively slender bodies, which incorporate smaller amounts of material and hence are less buoyant to begin with. It's worth remembering that the solid material in the foam does not account for the floatation; the small cell-like voids do, and the more of these that can be kept intact, the greater the buoyancy.

Method #104:
Lashed Foam Body

This simplest of foam techniques is generally used to form bodies on terrestrial imitations such as beetles and ants. Pieces of foam can be lashed directly to the shank, as shown in the main sequence.

As demonstrated in alternate steps 2a-2b, pieces of foam to be used for bodies can be encased in plastic wrap to help form them into more rounded shapes, to improve durability, and to give a glossy sheen to the finished body. We first saw this approach in the work of Veli Autti from Finland, who uses ordinary sandwich bags or heavy plastic wrap to enclose the foam. Mesh material of the type shown in **Method #90: Suspender Pod**, p. 340, can also be used.

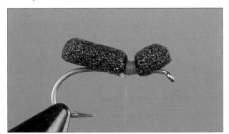

Step 1. We're forming an ant body here. Cover the center portion of the hook shank with a base of tying thread. If desired, a

small drop of epoxy or gel-type CA glue can be placed on the thread wraps.

Lash a strip of foam that is cylindrical or square in cross-section to the center of the hook shank. When the lashing is secure, one or both ends can be trimmed to the desired proportions. A hackle to simulate legs, or a piece of bright yarn to improve visibility can be tied in over the thread lashings.

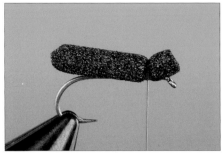

Step 1a. Varying the shape of the foam, the placement of the lashing, and the length of the thread wrap, will produce different body profiles.

Here, a flatter piece of foam has been attached closer to the eye of the hook with a narrow lashing to produce a beetle body.

Step 2a. Cut a piece of foam the size required for the body, as shown at the lower left, and a piece of clear plastic wrap, as shown on the lower right.

Place the foam in the center of the plastic, and pull the plastic around the foam to produce a tight shell with as few wrinkles as possible, as shown in the upper left. The enclosed body here is bound with thread only to give a clearer view of the assembly. In tying, simply use your fingers to gather the plastic wrap firmly around foam, and lay it atop the hook shank.

Step 2b. Secure the body by binding the plastic film to the hook shank. Make sure that the thread wraps tightly abut the base of the foam contained inside, as shown here.

A second, smaller body segment would be mounted ahead of the first to complete this ant pattern.

Method #105:
Segmented Lashed-foam Body

This technique simultaneously binds the foam to the shank and forms body segments. Because the foam is highly compressed at each tie-down point, this method is best suited to larger pieces of foam (to maintain buoyancy) and hence larger flies. And in fact it produces an elongated, blocky body characteristic of bigger insects such as grasshoppers and adult stoneflies.

The foam can be bound directly to a thread-covered hook shank, or atop an underbody of hackle, chenille, or herl. We're using an ostrich herl underbody, preferred by tyer Phil Camera in his P.C. Hopper, to demonstrate both the technique and effect of using an underbody.

Step 1. Dress the underbody, working from the hook eye to the bend. When the underbody is complete, the tying thread should be positioned near the hook bend. (If no underbody is used, wrap a thread foundation from the eye of the hook to the rear of the shank.)

Take a strip of foam and bind it tightly over the rearmost thread wrap. The butt end of the foam should extend to, or slightly beyond, the bend of the hook. The thread wraps used to secure the foam should be placed directly atop one another to create a very narrow, pinched segment joint.

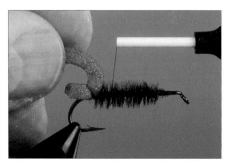

Step 2. Lift the foam, and advance the thread in a broad, open spiral about ¼ of a shank-length toward the eye. Wiggle the thread as you wrap to seat it between the herl fibers and prevent binding them down.

Step 3. Lay the foam down on top of the hook shank, and create another body segment by binding the foam with 4 or 5 tight wraps of thread.

Repeat Steps 2-3 to form another body segment.

Note that a greater number of narrower segments can, if desired, be created with this method — it depends upon hook size, shank length, and type of insect being imitated. But in general, fewer segments are better than more, as the formation of each segment compresses the foam and reduces the overall buoyancy of the fly.

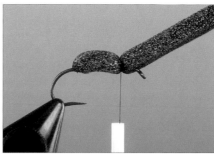

Step 2. Fold the foam over the top of the hook shank, and bind it securely at the tie-down point with several tight wraps of thread. It is important not to pull the foam too tightly over the shank. Stretching the material will reduce the buoyancy of the fly and will make the foam more susceptible to tearing or splitting. If a narrow body is desired, use a thinner piece of foam rather than stretching the material.

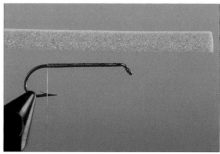

Step 1. Lay a foundation of thread from the tie-off point of the body to the rear of the shank. Cut a strip of foam about 2 ½ times the total hook length. The foam strip should be about as wide as the hook gap and about half as thick, though this latter dimension is not particularly critical and may be governed by the thickness of the foam stock you're using.

Step 4. When the final segment has been formed, clip the foam and bind the tag down tightly. The rest of the fly can now be dressed.

Step 3. The foam can now be cut, leaving a tag to form the head of the fly, as shown here. Or it can be clipped close to the shank and the excess bound down, leaving a foundation for subsequent materials.

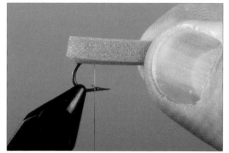

Step 2. Fold the foam in half along the length of the hook shank. Notice that the folded end of the foam extends to, or just beyond, the bend of the hook. The amount of extension here, that is, the distance between the end of the foam and the tying thread, determines the width of the body segments. For wider segments, increase the "overhang" of foam past the hook bend. For narrower segments, decrease it.

Method #106:
Folded Foam Body

This technique is both widely used and easy to execute. Its primarily application is in tying terrestrials—such as the beetle illustrated below—but it can be employed in other patterns as well. One of the more inventive uses comes from Phil Camera, who uses the method to form very buoyant bodies on Humpies.

Step 1. Lay a thread foundation, working from behind the eye to the rear of the shank.

Over the rearmost thread wrap, tightly bind in a strip of foam by the tip. If an underbody material is used, it should be tied and wrapped forward at this point. If no underbody is used, advance the thread to the tie-off point of the body.

Method #107:
Segmented Folded-foam Body

This technique, which secures and segments the foam simultaneously, offers two advantages. First, because a double thickness of foam is bound to the shank, the body has significant buoyancy. And second, a single strip of foam that is rectangular in cross-section will, when it is folded double, form a length of material that has an almost square cross-section; the compressing action of the thread will draw in the edges of the foam to produce a body that is nearly cylindrical. Typically, this style of body is used on larger flies with thick bodies—grasshoppers, crickets, and adult stoneflies.

This same basic approach can be used to form segmented extended bodies as explained in **Method #136: Folded Foam Extension**, p. 221.

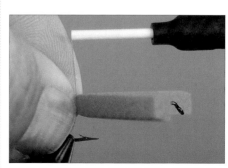

Step 3. With the left fingers, pinch the folded end of the foam against the hook shank, directly behind the tying thread. Take several tight wraps of thread around both halves of the foam, securing them to the sides of the hook shank. Use the left fingers to prevent the foam from twisting or rolling under thread pressure. These thread wraps should lie directly atop one another to create a thin, well-defined body segment.

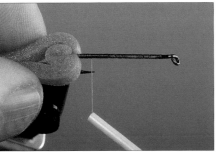

Step 4. Pull the ends of the foam back beyond the hook bend to get access to the hook shank. Advance the tying thread a distance that is equal to the width of the first body segment you've just created.

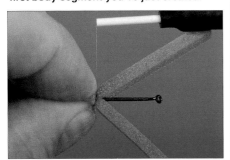

Step 5. Fold the ends of the foam forward, again sandwiching the hook shank between them, as shown here from the top. Create a second body segment by taking several tight wraps of thread as you did in Step 4.

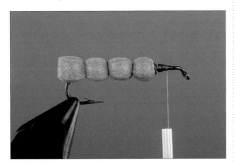

Step 6. Repeat Steps 4-5, creating uniform body segments, until the desired length of hook shank is covered.

When the final body segment has been created, and the foam secured tightly, clip the two tags of foam and bind the excess tightly to the shank.

Method #108:
Wrapped Foam Body

Bodies (and underbodies) can be fashioned by wrapping foam around the hook shank in much the same way as more conventional materials are wrapped. There is, however, one important difference. If closed-cell foam is stretched tightly during wrapping, the hollow chambers inside the material that provide floatation may be ruptured; the air will be forced from the cells, reducing the buoyancy of the material. The key in wrapping foam bodies is to use enough pres-

sure to form a secure body that does not twist around the shank, but not so much that floatation is reduced.

Step 1. Lay a thread foundation over the area of the shank to be covered with the body material.

For bodies with a relatively uniform diameter, cut an untapered strip of material as shown by the orange foam. The width of the strip governs the thickness of the finished body; the strip shown here is about ⅔ the width of the hook gap. Trim the end of the strip to a point, as shown.

For bodies with a steeper taper, cut a tapered strip of material, as shown by the gray foam.

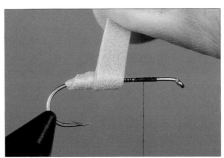

Step 2. Mount the foam by the point, and advance the thread to the body tie-off point.

Apply a moderate, consistent pressure on the foam strip, and wrap it forward in overlapping turns. The degree of overlap determines the spacing of the body segments and the thickness of the finished body.

Note: if desired, the body can be secured more firmly to the hook shank by applying a thin layer of gel-type CA glue to the thread foundation. Wrap the foam forward immediately, snugging it against the adhesive.

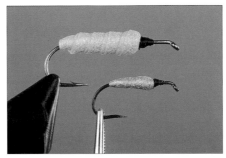

Step 3. Tie off the foam at the frontmost point of the body. First secure the foam tag. Then bind down the very front edge of the last body segment formed; overwrapping this edge with thread produces a neater, more symmetrical body segment and more secure tie-off.

The fly at the bottom shows a tapered body wrapped from the wedge-shaped strip shown in Step 1.

Method #109:
Threaded Foam Body

Because this technique keeps foam compression at a minimum, it produces a highly buoyant body. But since only one end of the foam is secured with tying thread, this type of body is somewhat more fragile than other styles, particularly where the body extends beyond the hook bend. This method is customarily used with cylindrical foam that is either rounded at the rear, or angle cut.

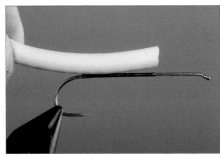

Step 1. This technique works best with a de-barbed or barbless hook, as the hook barb can damage the foam.

Lay a foundation of thread on the portion of the hook shank that will be covered by the foam body. When the foundation is complete, whip-finish the thread and clip it off.

Cut a piece of cylindrical foam about ⅛" longer than the finished body. The extra bit of material is bound to the hook shank and covered with thread.

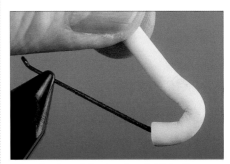

Step 2. Insert the hook point into the center of the foam cylinder. Begin threading the cylinder onto the hook, working it around the bend—much as you would (perish the thought) thread a worm on a hook. For a symmetrical body, take care to keep the hook centered as much as possible inside the foam.

194

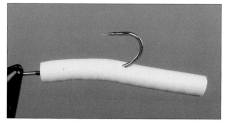

Step 3. Bring the point of the hook through the underside of the foam. Just where you bring the point through will determine how much of the foam cylinder is threaded on the shank and how much overhangs the rear of the hook. Here, we've brought the hook through the foam at the midpoint of the cylinder; half the body lies on the hook shank, and half extends behind.

Other styles, however, are possible. The body can be thread only a short distance onto the shank to produce an extended-body effect, or the entire length of the foam can be slipped onto the hook for no overhang of material at the rear of the shank.

Note: for a more secure hold, the foam can be slipped on a hook shank that has been wrapped with an open-spiral thread foundation. Apply a drop of gel-type CA glue to the rear of the thread wraps, and push the foam onto the shank. The foam will push the adhesive into the gaps between the thread wraps, where it will glue the body to the hook shank.

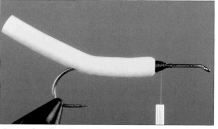

Step 4. Reattach the tying thread at the front of the body. Bind down the front end of the foam tightly for a distance of about ⅛".

For added durability, apply a drop of head cement or CA glue just at the point where the rear of the shank exits the foam.

Method #110:
Glued Foam Body

The technique described here is best suited to high-density foams. Lower-density foams, with relatively large hollow cells, do not offer sufficient contact area with the glue to give good adhesion. Denser foams, like the Rainy's Float Foam used here, will glue securely.

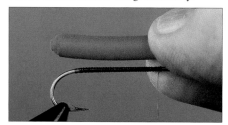

Step 1. Lay a thread foundation on the portion of the shank that will be covered

by the body. Position the tying thread at the front of this foundation.

Cut a piece of foam ⅛" longer than the finished body. You can, if you wish, use scissors or a razor blade to trim the foam to the desired shaped. We've cut a taper at the rear here to form a bullet-shaped body.

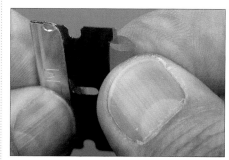

Step 2. With a very sharp razor blade, make a longitudinal slit on the underside of the body about ⅓ of the way through the foam.

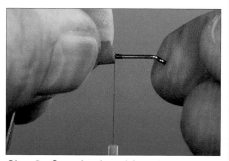

Step 3. Coat the thread foundation with a thin film of gel-type CA glue. Insert the hook shank into the slit that's been cut in the foam.

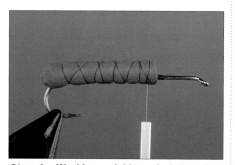

Step 4. Working quickly, spiral the tying thread snugly (but not tightly) over the body from front to rear. This pressure will help push the foam against the glued shank for good adhesion.

The thread should be left in this position for only a few seconds. The glue will set quickly, and any excess adhesive forced out of the slit may glue the thread to the foam.

After a few seconds, unwrap the thread. The body will be secured to the shank.

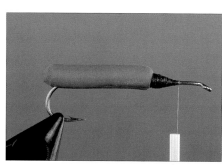

Step 5. Bind down the front ⅛" of the body to form a tapered thread foundation over which other materials can be applied.

Woven Bodies

Fly bodies can be fashioned by weaving or knotting strands of material on a hook shank. As with most fly-tying techniques, the precise origin of fly weaving is difficult to determine, but it is safe to say that the method is most closely associated with two American tyers, Franz Pott and George Grant, both of Montana. That Pott was trained as a barber and wigmaker probably explains his unique approach to fly tying, and in the 1920s and 30s, he was in fact granted two patents for his fly patterns and methods of weaving bodies and hackles. Grant, intrigued by the design, studied and dissected Pott's flies until he had worked out weaving processes of his own. Both men were commercial fly tyers, and by the middle of the century, woven-body flies such as Pott's Sandy Mite were a standard on Montana rivers. Pott was highly secretive about his methods (he and Grant never met), but George Grant shared his own techniques and dressings in two books—*The Art of Weaving Hair Hackles for Trout Flies* and *The Woven Hair Hackle: Montana's Contribution to the Art of Flytying*.

The weaving of fly bodies and hackles are arguably two of the few indigenous American fly-tying techniques, but the fly styles and methods to produce them are no longer as popular as they once were. While the weaving of hackle is admittedly a bit complicated (see "Hackle," **Method #25: Woven Hackle**, p. 374), woven bodies are reasonably simple to construct and not nearly as time-consuming as they might first appear. Though perhaps not feasible for the commercial fly dresser, many woven bodies are nonetheless practical for those who tie on a smaller scale.

Woven bodies have two principal virtues—they produce lifelike color patterns that are virtually unachievable with any other method, and they are extremely durable even when tied with relatively fragile materials. Almost any stranded material can be woven, provided that it is sufficiently long. Practically speaking, the strand should be at least 8" for all but the smallest flies. Though Pott favored horsehair, other materials will serve—chenilles and flocked yarns; fly-tying and embroidery flosses (these are often waxed to simplify handling); natural or synthetic yarns, particularly crewel yarns; dyed monofilament; fly line; Larva Lace and tubings; raffia; and even wire. Moreover in some techniques, materials can be combined not only for color patterns, but for variations in texture as well to produce bodies, for instance, that are shaggy on top and smooth underneath.

Moreover, each weaving strand can itself be composed of other strands, as shown in the following photo.

Note the combination of materials in these two flies dressed by German tyer Henning von Monteton. The weaving strand used to form the back of the fly at the top is composed of a light brown thread, a dark brown one, and a strand of Spektraflash (similar to Krystal Flash).

The underside of the fly at the bottom is woven from a strand containing one cream, one yellow, and one tan thread. These flies were woven using the technique shown in Method #114: The Overhand Weave, p. 198.

Woven bodies are generally restricted to subsurface patterns, primarily nymphs, as the density of the woven material is not well-suited to a floating fly. (As always, there are exceptions; see **Method #139: Woven Extended Body**, p. 225, for a woven body design for dry flies.) Weaving techniques that produce relatively simple color patterns—contrasting bands, or a stripe on the dorsal or ventral side of the body, for example—can be performed on a bare hook shank. But those that produce more complex patterns are generally tied over an underbody of some sort. On a thin hook shank, more complicated color schemes tend to run together, rendering the pattern indistinct. Some fly patterns, such as the Pott's Mite, have entire bodies constructed by weaving, but more commonly, only the abdomen of a nymph is woven, and the underbody should be constructed to the appropriate dimensions. George Grant preferred flattened underbodies made of lashed pins—and indeed these broad foundations tend to show the weaving designs to best advantage—but any of the conventional underbody materials and designs are acceptable (see "Underbodies," p. 41). Tyer Darrel Martin, a skilled weaver, prefers leather underbodies. In the following instructional sequences, we've used latex as an underbody material. Regardless of material, however, the underbody should be kept as smooth as possible, as some weaving materials, particularly thin-stranded types such as floss, will reveal any inconsistencies in the underbody. Note that thicker weaving materials will add significant bulk to the body, and to maintain proper proportions in the finished fly, the underbody may need to be kept rather thin.

Some of the techniques detailed in this section are, strictly speaking, knotting rather than weaving methods—**Method #114: The Overhand Weave**, p. 198; **Method #116: The Half-hitch Weave**, p. 199; and **Method #120: The Crochet Weave**, p. 202. While the manipulation of materials and types of bodies formed may be similar to weaving, knotting has some unique advantages. Because the strands are secured to the shank with a knot after each step, tension can be relaxed without the body unraveling. Thus the strands can be released to apply other materials—legs, gills, wingcases, hackle, and so on—to the hook, and then the knotting can be resumed to create another section of body.

There are two points to bear in mind when weaving or knotting. The first is to maintain a consistent tension on the strands of material. Except for those techniques that actually knot the material to the hook shank (**Method #114: The Overhand Weave**, p. 198, is one example), color patterns and separations are formed by tension and countertension on the weaving strands. Varying this tension will produce irregularities in the body—crooked stripes, uneven bands of color, asymmetrical ribbing. In most cases, the manipulation of the strands is reasonably straightforward; the consistency of tension is probably the part of weaving that requires the most practice.

The second point is to snug each turn or weave of material tightly against the preceding ones. Again, this produces a body that is uniform and neat in appearance, and prevents gaps that will allow the underbody to show through.

Method #111:

The Banded Weave

This is perhaps the simplest of all weaving techniques; it produces distinct, alternating bands of color. We're using high-contrast chenilles of different diameters for the purposes of illustration, but any combination of colors, sizes, types, and textures of materials can be employed.

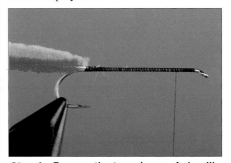

Step 1. Prepare the two pieces of chenille by stripping the ends. Twist the thread cores together as shown, and bind down the combined cores at the rearmost thread wrap.

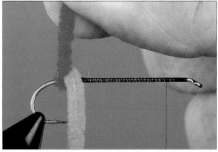

Step 2. Using one of the chenille strands—the red strand in this picture—take one wrap at the rear of the hook shank. When the wrap is completed, transfer the strand to the right hand and hold it vertically as shown.

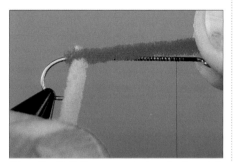

Step 3. Pull the second strand—the pink one in this picture—out from the hook shank, toward you. Bring the red strand down toward the hook eye, parallel to the shank. It should cross over the pink strand.

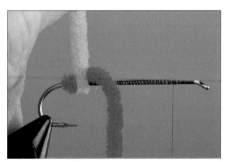

Step 4. Now take a wrap with the pink strand. It will cross over the red strand, and bind it down as shown. Once the red strand is crossed and held against the hook shank, it can be released, freeing both hands to use in wrapping.

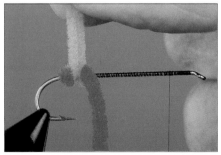

Step 5. When the pink wrap is completed, transfer the pink strand to the right hand and hold it vertically as shown.

You are now in the same configuration as described in Step 2, though the colors are reversed.

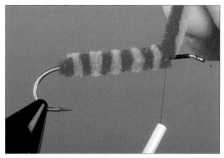

Step 6. Repeat Steps 3-5, alternating strands with each wrap until the tie-off point is reached.

When the tie-off point is reached, hold both strands in the right hand as shown, and take a wrap of tying thread over the point where both strands of chenille meet against the hook shank. This will bind down both strands at the same time.

After the first thread wrap is secured tightly, take one or two more wraps, clip the chenille strands, and bind down the butts.

Method #112:
The Parallel Weave

This is a common and relatively simple technique, made easier by the fact it does not require exchanging materials from hand to hand during the weave. Here the strand used for the bottom of the body—tan Vernille—is always held in the right hand; the strand for the top—red Vernille—is always held in the left. The finished weave produces a fly body that has one color on top, another color on the bottom, and short rib-like bands along the side. It's commonly used to weave dragonfly and stonefly nymph bodies.

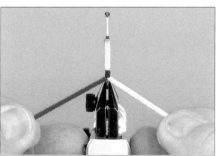

Step 1. With the vise in the normal position, mount the tying thread at the rear of the underbody. Bind in a strand of material, about 8 inches long, for the bottom of the body (tan in the photo) on the near side of the shank. Bind in a second strand of material, again about 8 inches long, for the top of the body (red in the photo) on the far side of the hook shank.

Bind down the butts of the material, using the thread to form a smooth transition from the tie-in point to the underbody. Tie off the thread with a few half-hitches or a whip-finish at the rear of the underbody, and clip it. Weaving is easier when the bobbin is not hanging in the tying field.

Re-position the vise so that the hook eye is pointing directly away from you.

Hold the red strand in your left hand, and position it to the left of the hook shank. Grasp the tan material in the right hand and hold it to the right, as shown.

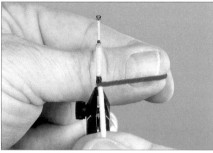

Step 2. Pull the tan strand toward you.

Pass the red strand over the top of the shank, in front of the tan strand, and extend it straight to the right, perpendicular to the hook shank. Note the position of the left hand—it is beneath the hook shank. This position is important, as it will allow the right hand an unobstructed motion in subsequent steps.

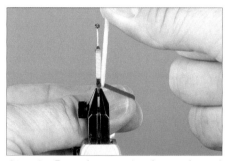

Step 3. Pass the tan strand over the red strand, so that the right hand extends beyond the hook eye and the tan strand is parallel to the hook shank.

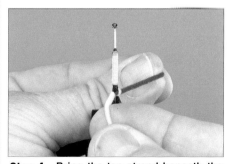

Step 4. Bring the tan strand beneath the hook shank, to left side, and raise it vertically above the hook as shown.

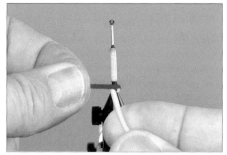

Step 5. Bring the red strand across the top of the hook shank, tightly in front of the tan strand, and over to the left.

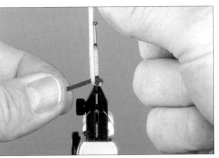

Step 6. Pass the tan strand over the red strand, so that the right hand extends beyond the hook eye, and the tan strand is parallel to the shank.

Step 7. Bring the tan strand beneath the hook shank to the right side, and raise it vertically.

The strands are now in the original position, as in Step 1.

Step 8. Repeat Steps 2-7, laying each weave of material tightly against the previous one to avoid gaps in the body. Tension on either strand can be adjusted to maintain a uniform and symmetrical pattern. When the desired length of hook shank is covered, pull both strands to the bend of the hook and maintain tension on them.

Remount the tying thread at the front of the body. Pull both strands forward, still maintaining tension. Tie them off, clip and bind down the excess.

Method #113:

The Mossback Weave

This technique was popularized in the Mossback series of nymphs tied by Dan Bailey. It is in fact quite similar to **Method #112: The Parallel Weave**, p. 196, but since it requires that strands be exchanged between hands, and because the vise orientation is different, it is presented as a separate technique.

It produces a body with differently colored dorsal and ventral sides, and "notched" or "toothed" edges on the body.

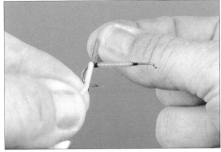

Step 1. Prepare a hook by tying two strands of weaving material at the rear of the underbody, as described in **Method #112: The Parallel Weave**, Step 1, p. 196. Here, olive Vernille will form the top of the body and is bound on the far side of the shank; tan will be used on the belly and is bound to the near side of the shank. The vise is positioned in the normal tying orientation.

With your left hand, hold the tan strand straight to the left and elevated to a 45-degree angle. With the right hand, pass the olive strand behind the tan strand, taking a loop around its base. Finish by holding the olive strand on the far side of the hook shank, pulling directly away from you.

Now pull the tan strand directly toward you.

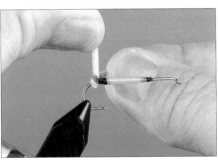

Step 2. Pass the tan strand beneath the hook shank to the far side. When it reaches the far side, it should be in front of the olive strand, as shown. (This position of the tan strand in front of the olive strand on each weave is the small, but important difference, between the Mossback Weave and the Parallel Weave.)

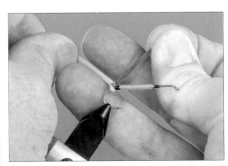

Step 3. Bring the tan strand back toward the hook bend, over the top of the olive strand. Note that the second and third fingers of the right hand form "scissors," ready to grasp the tan strand.

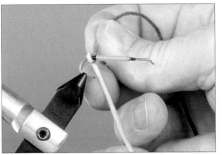

Step 4. Momentarily grasp the tan strand between the second and third fingers of the right hand. Bring your left hand around to the front of the vise, reach underneath it, and take the tan strand from the fingers of the right hand.

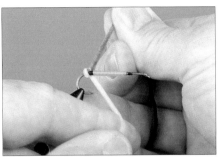

Step 5. Bring the tan strand beneath the shank and pull it toward you.

Step 6. Pass the olive strand over the top of the shank. Note once again that the olive strand is behind the tan strand.

Note as well that the second and third fingers of the right hand are pinching the tan strand so that the hands can be repositioned for the next weave.

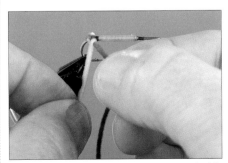

Step 7. Pinch the olive and tan strand with the right thumb and forefinger. Both strands are now held in the right hand.

Bring your left hand from the rear of the hook, reach over the olive strand, and grasp the tan strand. Bring the tan strand back toward the hook bend, over the base of the olive strand, and finish by pulling it downward as shown.

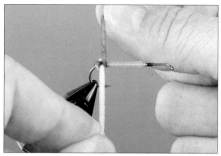

Step 8. Pass the olive strand over the top of the shank, and pull it directly away from you.

Pull the tan strand directly toward you. The materials and hands are now positioned as they were in Step 1.

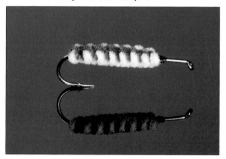

Step 9. Repeat Steps 2-8 until the desired body length is achieved.

When the weave is complete, maintain tension on both strands. Reattach the tying thread, bind down both strands of material, and clip.

Method #114:

The Overhand Weave

This technique is sometimes called the "edge weave," (and sometimes erroneously called the "half-hitch weave," which is in fact a different technique described in **Method #116: The Half-Hitch Weave**, p. 199). This method is actually just a series of overhand knots tightened around the hook shank. It is quite simple, and unlike weaving techniques, the strands can be released during tying without having the body unravel.

Two different patterns are in fact possible, depending on how the knots are formed. A bi-color body is shown in the main sequence below; a banded body is shown in the alternate sequence. Both styles, however, produce a body with a distinct ridge around the perimeter that gives it a somewhat flattened shape.

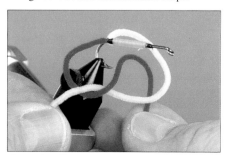

Step 1. Prepare a hook by tying two strands of weaving material at the rear of the underbody, as described in **Method**

#112: The Parallel Weave, Step 1, p. 196. The top color (red here) is mounted on the near side of the shank. The belly color (tan) is mounted on the far side.

Position the vise so that the hook eye points toward you.

With the two strands of material, form a loose overhand knot as shown. Note particularly the "loop" that is created by the two strands of material. The strand forming the top color of the fly body (red, in this case) must also form the top strand of the loop.

Step 2. Insert the hook eye into the loop, and tighten the knot at the very rear of the underbody. Tighten the loop as shown above, by pulling evenly outward on each of the strands. Note that the strands are now reversed from their original positions; red is now on the left and tan on the right.

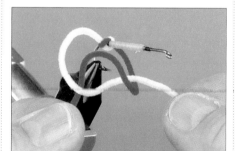

Step 3. The next overhand knot must be fashioned so that the red strand again forms the top of the loop, as shown here.

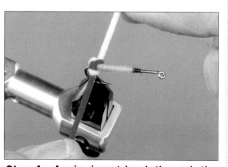

Step 4. Again, insert hook through the loop, and tighten the strands against the first knot formed in Step 2. The materials and hand positions are now identical to those pictured in Step 1.

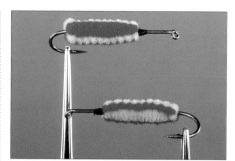

Step 5. Repeat Steps 1-4 until the desired body length is obtained.

When the body is complete, remount the tying thread, tie off the strands, clip and bind down the excess.

The upper fly shows the top of the woven body; the lower fly shows the underside of the same weave.

Step 1a. To create a banded body, form and tighten a knot as shown in Steps 1-2.

Then form a knot similar to that in Step 3, but this time when the loop is formed by the crossing strands of material, the tan strand should form the top of the loop.

Step 2a. Slip this loop over the hook eye as described in Step 2.

When the knot is tightened, a band of tan material will appear on the top of the shank.

The materials and hand positions are now identical to those pictured in Step 1.

Step 3a. Repeat Steps 1, 2, 1a, and 2a. When the body is complete, remount the thread, tie off the strands, clip and bind down the excess.

Method #115:
The Pott's Weave

Franz Pott used this weave with long strands of horsehair to tie his Mite series of flies. The sequence below will produce a body with a longitudinal band along the back. This band can be woven into the belly of the fly instead, either by performing the "loop wrap" underneath the shank, or more simply, by inverting the hook in the vise and following the instructions below.

In this technique, the two strands of material must be switched from hand to hand during the weave.

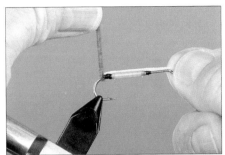

Step 1. Prepare a hook by tying two strands of weaving material at the rear of the underbody, as described in **Method #112: The Parallel Weave**, Step 1, p. 196. The body color (olive here) is mounted on the near side of the shank; the contrasting band color (tan here) is mounted on the far side. The vise is positioned in the normal tying fashion.

Begin by laying the tan strand along the hook shank toward the eye. Now take a full wrap around the hook shank, at the rear of the underbody, with the olive strand. This wrap should conceal the butts of both materials at the tie-in point. When the wrap is completed, the olive strand should be held vertically above the shank, as shown.

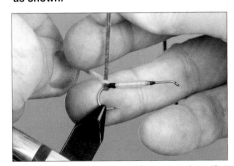

Step 2. Transfer the olive strand to the right hand. Hold the olive strand vertically, gripping it about 2 inches above the hook shank. Note that it is positioned behind the tan strand.

With the left hand, take the tan strand and rotate it from the hook eye toward you, then on toward the hook bend, behind the olive strand, and finally to the far side of the hook shank, partially encircling the base of the olive material. The tan strand should be projecting directly away from you as shown.

Note the position of the second and third fingers of the right hand, ready to grasp the tan strand, as detailed in the next step.

Step 3. Grip the tan strand between the second and third fingers of the right hand, maintaining tension on it. Now grasp the olive strand in the fingers of the left hand. You have now exchanged the strands between hands.

Continue wrapping the tan strand around the base of the olive one. You have now made a complete loop of the tan material around the base of the olive material.

Maintain tension on the tan strand, holding it out beyond the hook eye and slightly below the shank, as shown.

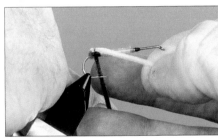

Step 4. With the left hand, begin making another wrap around the hook shank with the olive material. Note in the photo that the second and third fingers of the right hand are positioned to momentarily trap the olive strand and maintain tension on it so that the left hand can be re-positioned in front of the vise to continue the wrap of olive material.

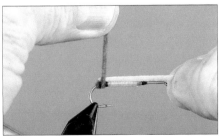

Step 5. Continue the wrap of olive material, ending with the strand held vertically above the hook shank.

Both the strands of material and the hand positions are now in the original configuration pictured in Step 1.

Step 6. Continue repeating Steps 2-5 until the desired length of hook shank is covered.

When the body is complete, maintain tension on both strands of material. Re-attach the tying thread, bind down both strands, and clip the excess.

Method #116:
The Half-Hitch Weave

This simple weave is actually a series of half-hitches cast around the hook shank with alternating strands of material. Because the strands are knotted, they can be released during the weave without unraveling.

The technique described in the main sequence results in a banded body that has a solid-color stripe down each side. The method in the alternate sequence produces a true banded body in which alternating colors completely encircle the shank, much like the body shown in **Method #111: The Banded Weave**, p. 195.

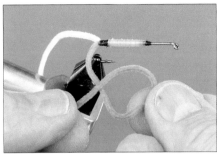

Step 1. Prepare a hook by tying two strands of weaving material at the rear of the underbody, as described in **Method #112: The Parallel Weave**, Step 1, p. 196. Here the brown strand which forms the top of the body is mounted on the near side of the hook; the tan strand for the belly is mounted on the far side. The vise is positioned in the normal tying fashion.

Beginning with the brown strand bound on the near side of the shank, form a simple loop as shown.

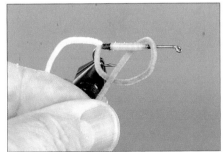

Step 2. Pass it over the eye of the hook.

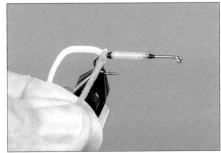

Step 3. Seat it tightly at the rear of the underbody by pulling the tag end directly toward you.

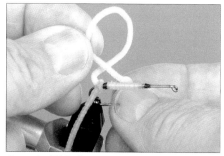

Step 4. With the tan strand on the far side of the shank, form a loop as shown.

Pass it over the eye of the hook as in Step 2. Seat this tan loop firmly against the previous wrap of brown material, and tighten the knot by pulling the tan tag directly away from you.

Step 5. Repeat Steps 1-4 until the desired length of hook shank is covered. The key here is to make sure that the brown half-hitches are always tightened by pulling the tag directly toward you, and the tan knots tightened by pulling tags directly away. This lays a uniform band of color along each side of the shank.

When the body is complete, reattach the tying thread, bind down the strands, and clip.

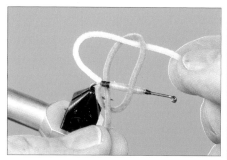

Step 1a. To weave a true banded body, form a loop as in Stem 1.

As in Step 2, pass the brown loop over the eye of the hook. Before tightening the loop, take the tan strand and pass it through the brown loop toward the hook eye.

Tighten the half-hitch at the rear of the underbody as shown in Step 3, snugging the brown material down and binding the tan material against the far side of the shank.

Pull the brown tag directly toward you to seat the knot.

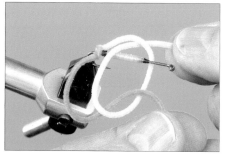

Step 2a. With the tan strand on the far side of the shank, form a loop and pass it over the eye of the hook as shown. Before tightening, pass the tag of brown material through the tan loop and toward the hook eye.

Seat the tan loop firmly against the previous wrap of brown material. Tighten by pulling the tan tag directly away from you, and binding the brown strand to the near side of the hook shank.

Step 3a. Repeat Steps 1, 2, 1a, and 2a until the body is complete.

Reattach the tying thread, bind down the strands, and clip the excess.

Method #117:

The Crisscross Weave

This simple technique actually involves wrapping two strands of material simultaneously around the hook shank, in opposite directions. The strands are crossed as they meet above the shank and below it. The method produces an asymmetrical weave with a banded pattern on one side and a horizontal division of colors on the other.

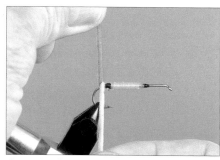

Step 1. Prepare a hook by tying two strands of weaving material at the rear of the underbody, as described in **Method #112: The Parallel Weave**, Step 1, p. 196. The belly color (tan here) is attached on the far side of the shank. The top color (brown here) is attached on the near side. The vise is positioned in the conventional manner.

Begin by holding both strands vertically above the hook shank. The brown strand is in the left hand.

Bring the tan strand toward you, over the top of the hook shank. It should pass in front of the brown strand. Continue downward until the strand is held directly below the shank.

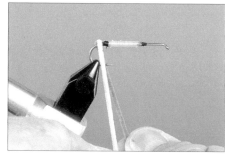

Step 2. Bring the brown strand over the top of the hook shank and down the far side, ending with the brown strand held directly below the shank, parallel to the tan strand.

At this point you will have to switch the strands to the opposite hands. The tan strand should now be in the left hand and the brown one in the right.

Step 3. Bring the brown strand toward you, underneath the shank, and in front of the tan strand. Finish by raising the brown strand vertically.

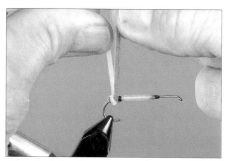

Step 4. Bring the tan strand around the far side of the hook shank and raise it vertically, as shown.

Now exchange the strands from hand to hand so that the brown strand is in the left hand, the tan strand in the right.

After the exchange, both your hands and the materials will be in the original position shown in Step 1.

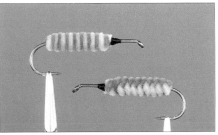

Step 5. Repeat Steps 1-4 until the desired length of hook shank is covered.

When the body is complete, remount the tying thread, bind the strands, and clip.

This weave is asymmetrical, producing a different pattern on each side of the body, as shown here.

Method #118:
The Spotted Strip Weave

This technique is a version of one used by George Grant. It produces a broken stripe pattern running lengthwise down the back of the body (as shown below) or along the belly if the hook is inverted.

This is an extremely versatile weave that admits many variations. For instance, by using three strands of material, two spotted stripes can be woven—one down each side of the body, or one on top and one on the bottom. Similarly if two or more strands, woven as a single piece of material, are used to form the stripe pattern, the spots become broad bands.

Unlike most weaving techniques, where all the materials used must be of a similar diameter and bulk, this method allows combining materials of different sizes and textures. Using chenille and floss, for instance, will create a fly with a fuzzy body and flat, glossy spots, or a flat, glossy body with fuzzy chenille bumps. Samples of the variety of styles obtainable with this weave are pictured at the end of the tying sequence.

One of the more interesting variations of this technique produces a mottled pattern. This is detailed in **Method #119: The Mottled Weave**, p. 201.

Step 1. Prepare a hook by tying two strands of weaving material at the rear of the underbody, as described in **Method #112: The Parallel Weave**, Step 1, p. 196. The strand for the body color (here it is brown) should be tied directly atop the hook shank; the strand for the stripe color (tan here) is mounted directly atop the brown strand. The vise is positioned in the normal tying fashion.

Take one complete turn of the brown strand, *behind* the tan strand, at the rear of the body.

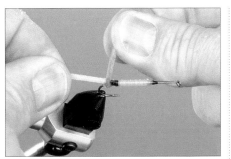

Step 2. Take a second wrap of the brown strand in *front* of the tan strand. Finish the wrap by pulling the brown strand to the far side of the hook shank.

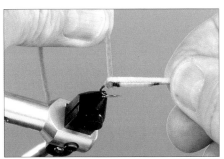

Step 3. At this point, you must switch hands on the strands—tan in the right, brown in the left.

Draw the tan strand down the length of the hook shank toward the eye, pinching it against the shank with the right hand.

Step 4. With your left hand, take another turn of the brown strand around the hook, binding the tan strand to the top of the shank. Again, finish by holding the brown strand to the far side of the hook shank, as shown.

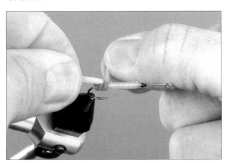

Step 5. Since the tan strand is now held in place, you can release it. Transfer the brown strand to your right hand. With your left hand, raise the tan strand toward the rear of the hook.

Continue winding the brown strand. On this wrap, it will *not* pass over the tan strand. Again, finish the wrap by pulling the brown strand to the far side of the shank.

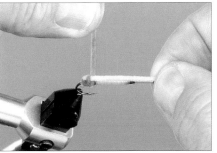

Step 6. Release the tan strand. Bring the left hand in front of the vise stem and transfer the brown strand to the left hand. Again use the right hand to draw the tan strand across the top of the hook and pinch it against the eye.

The materials and hand positions are now identical to those described in Step 3.

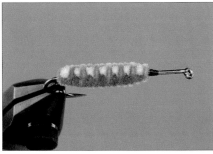

Step 7. Repeat Steps 4-6 until the desired length of shank is covered.

When the body is complete, maintain tension on both strands. Remount the tying thread, bind down both strands, and clip the excess.

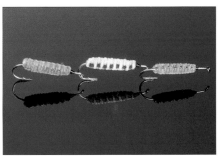

The fly on the left has a double strand of brown Vernille that forms a wide band across the back. The fly in the middle has a row of spots down each side of the body. The fly at the right has a row of Krystal Flash spots along the back.

Method #119:
The Mottled Weave

This variation of **Method #117: The Spotted Strip Weave**, p. 200, was shown to us by Darrel Martin. It is a three-strand weave that involves weaving two spotted strips, side-by-side, down the back of the body to produce a kind of checkerboard pattern. For the purposes of illustration, we are using three different colors—brown for the body, orange and red for the spotted pattern on the back. More often, the two strands forming the spots are of the same color. While the body pictured below certainly resembles nothing in nature, choosing more subdued colors with less contrast—combinations of olives, tans, browns, and grays—can produce a very lifelike variegated effect.

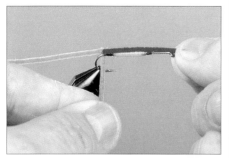

Step 1. Prepare a hook by tying three strands of weaving material at the rear of the underbody, as described in **Method #112: The Parallel Weave**, Step 1, p. 196. In this case, all three strands are tied in directly atop the hook shank. The brown strand will form the primary body color; the orange and red strands will form the checkerboard mottle. The vise is positioned in the conventional fashion.

Draw the orange strand rearward, out of the tying field. Pull the red strand forward toward the hook eye. With the brown strand, take one complete wrap around the hook shank. The brown strand will pass between the red and orange ones. Finish by pulling the brown strand directly toward you as shown.

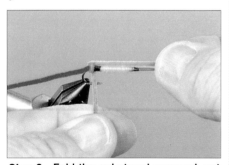

Step 2. Fold the red strand rearward, out of the tying field. Fold the orange strand forward toward the hook eye; it should lie against the top of the shank, slightly to the far side.

Wrap the brown strand directly in *front* of the red strand and over the orange strand. Bring the brown strand underneath the shank and finish by pulling it directly toward you.

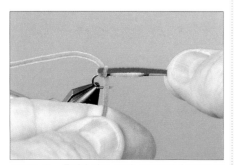

Step 3. Fold the red strand forward toward the hook eye; it should lie against the top of the shank, slightly to the near side. Fold the orange strand back toward the bend, out of the tying field.

Wrap the brown strand over the red strand and directly in front of the orange one. Bring the brown strand underneath the hook shank, and pull it directly toward you.

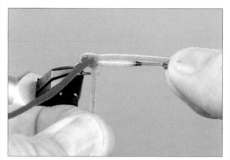

Step 4. Fold the red strand back toward the hook bend, and the orange strand forward toward the eye.

The materials and hands are now in the position described in Step 2.

Step 5. Repeat Steps 2-4 until the desired length of shank is covered.

When the body is complete, maintain tension on all three strands. Remount the tying thread, bind down the strands, and clip the excess.

Method #120:

The Crochet Weave

This technique was devised by Norwegian tyer Torill Kolbu, who uses a crochet hook to produce unusual fly bodies. Though it may appear arcane and difficult at first, the method is really no more than a series of overhand knots placed, alternately, around and below the hook shank. The crochet hook makes the process more efficient with some materials, but in fact such bodies can be fashioned simply by tying the knots with your fingers.

Materials of different sizes and types can be knotted together to produce not only variegations of color, but contrasts in texture. The finished body has a solid color on the dorsal side and longitudinal stripes on the belly, though these of course can be reversed by inverting the hook in the vise.

The size of the crochet hook used depends upon the thickness of the materials being knotted. The crochet hook must have a gap that is wide enough to hold the material securely. In the sequence below, a size E crochet hook is used to make a Vernille body; the same tool would be suitable for chenilles, yarns, and other bulky materials. For thinner materials, a crochet hook with a smaller gap, size D or E, would be appropriate.

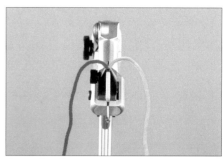

Step 1. Prepare a hook by tying two strands of weaving material at the rear of the underbody, as described in **Method #112: The Parallel Weave**, Step 1, p. 196. The material used for the top of the body (gray, in this sequence) is tied to the far side of the shank; the contrasting strand (red, here) is tied on the near side.

Position the vise so that the hook eye points directly toward you.

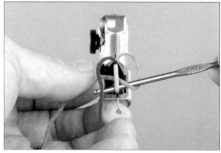

Step 2. Make a loop beneath the shank with the gray strand. Note that it passes underneath the red strand.

Insert the crochet hook through the loop by first passing the crochet hook over the gray strand and then underneath it. Trap the red strand in the crochet hook.

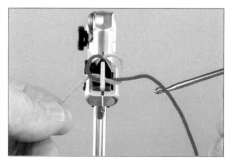

Step 3. Maintain tension on both strands. Pull the red strand through the gray loop. As it passes through the loop, rotate the crochet hook slightly toward you. This motion will help prevent the red strand from slipping out of the crochet hook. A constant, but moderate tension on the red strand will also help keep it in place.

Note that what you have really done is to tie an overhand knot beneath the hook shank.

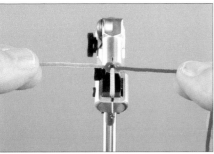

Step 4. Tighten the knot by pulling both strands outward with an even tension.

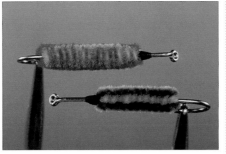

Step 8. Repeat Steps 2-7 until the desired length of shank is covered. When the body is complete, remount the tying thread, bind down the strands, and clip the excess.

The upper fly was woven in this sequence. The lower fly body was woven with the hook inverted to place the longitudinal stripes on the back.

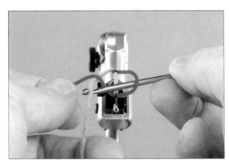

Step 5. Make a loop beneath the hook shank with the red strand. Note that the red strand passes over the gray strand. Insert the crochet hook into the red loop by first passing it under the red strand, then over the hook shank, and finally over the red strand. Grasp the gray strand in the crochet hook.

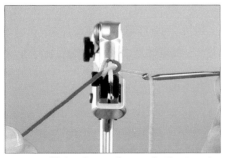

Step 6. Maintain tension on both strands, and pull the gray strand through the red loop. Again, rotating the crochet hook toward you slightly will help keep the gray strand secure.

Note that what you have done here is cast an overhand knot around the shank.

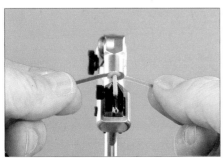

Step 7. Tighten the knot by pulling strands outward with an even tension.

The materials are now in the original position described in Step 1.

Extended Bodies

An extended body—as the term is used in this book—is one that is fixed in position to project rearward beyond the hook shank and is thus distinguished from the articulated or "wiggle" body, which is tied to allow some movement in the extension (see "Wiggle Bodies," p. 49). Where articulated bodies are used typically on subsurface patterns, extended bodies can be dressed on either floating or sinking flies. The principal function of the extended body, of course, is imitative, but the proper choice of materials can lend floatation to a dry fly.

Techniques for tying extended bodies range from the simple to the complicated, but as a rule, extensions are dressed on short-shank hooks. Longer shanks, which typically form the foundation for conventional bodies, are simply unnecessary; the shorter shank reduces the overall hook weight in a floating fly and allows the use of a wider gap for better hooking. A few methods for extended-body construction require, or are simplified by, the use of an extended-body tool to maintain tension on the materials that form the cores for certain types of body extensions. The use of such a tool is explained in the section on "Cored Extensions," p. 208.

By and large, tying extended bodies is more involved and time consuming than dressing conventional bodies, and many tyers avoid them altogether. They are, without question, a specialty style and certainly not a necessity under most conditions. By the same token, however, there are times, places, and circumstances—flat water, hard-fished and fussy trout, difficult hatches—under which extended bodies are undeniably more effective than traditional types.

Simple Extensions

This most basic of all extended-body styles simply entails lashing to the hook a body extension formed from a material that requires little or no advance preparation. Most materials suited to this type of extension lack buoyancy and thus are used chiefly to fashion extensions on subsurface flies. Chenilles and Vernilles, for instance, can be used to form abdomens on damselfly nymphs, for example, or New Dub employed as an extension on Brett Smith's Palomino Midge pattern. Some materials, however—foam strips or cylinders, hollow vinyl tubing, or even a length of floating fly line—can be used to lend buoyancy to dry flies. And should a dry-fly pattern contain enough other buoyant materials, the lack of floatation in the body extension becomes relatively unimportant, and virtually any material can be used. Brett Smith, for instance, uses New Dub on a caddis dry dressed with elk-hair wings; braided leader butt material (appropriately colored with marking pens) is often used to make the thin body extension on a damselfly adult. The

only real requirement for simple body extensions is that the material be sufficiently stiff to maintain its shape while fishing and thus serve its representational function.

Method #121:
Lashed Extension

This elementary technique merely entails lashing a length of material to the hook to form the body extension, as shown in the main sequence. It is also used, however, as the final step in attaching more complicated body extensions that require advance preparation and are detailed in many of the methods that follow. Some materials that form simple lashed extensions can also be used to create part or all of the remaining body on the hook shank. Techniques for doing so are presented in the alternate sequence.

While this style is quite simple, it does have its limitations. It is virtually impossible to create this type of extension and incorporate tails, ribbing, segmentation, or any of the more subtle imitative elements. As a rule, it is generally suggestive rather than precisely representational.

Step 1. We're using Vernille here as a representative material for creating a lashed body.

Lay a thread foundation on the rear half of the hook shank, and position the tying thread at the rear of the foundation.

With Vernille, micro-chenille, New Dub, and similar materials, body extensions of this type are frequently flame-shaped to a point. This process is suited only to a small range of materials, and even then is optional. To flame-shape the tip, cut a length of the appropriate material. Bring the end near the side of a flame from a butane lighter or candle, as shown above. The goal here is merely to singe the material, not to set fire to anything. When the material nears the flame, rotate it to taper the end evenly.

Step 2. Hold the material atop the hook shank so that the desired length of body extends beyond the hook bend. Bind the body material in over the rearmost wrap of the thread foundation, and secure it with a series of tight wraps up to the mid-point of the hook shank.

Clip the excess and bind down the butt.

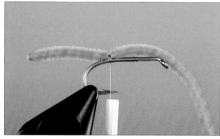

Step 1a. To use the material to form other body components, bind in the extension with a few tight wraps directly atop the rearmost point of the foundation only.

Step 2a. To wrap a body, advance the thread to the tie-off point. Wrap the material around the shank, bind down, and clip. Or . . . .

Step 3a. To form a shellback, create a body of the desired material—we're using dubbing here—leaving the thread at the front of the body. Fold the tag of body-extension material over the top of the dubbed body. Bind down the material and clip. This technique is often used with foam body extensions, as the shellback incorporates greater buoyancy in the fly.

10

Method #122:
Slip-over Extension

A single length of a thicker material can be used to form the entire fly body—both the extension and the portion on the hook shank. To achieve this, the material is threaded on the hook shank, often glued, and bound at the front end. Foam bodies and those made of macrame yarns, as shown here, are the materials most commonly tied in this fashion.

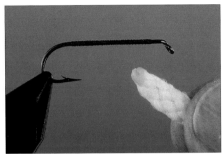

Step 1. Macrame yarn is used to create bodies on adult stonefly, grasshopper, and other thick-bodied imitations.

Prepare a hook by laying a secure thread foundation along the shank. Secure with a few half-hitches or whip-finish, and clip the thread.

To prevent the yarn strands from unraveling, they are melted at the end to seal them together. Cut a length of yarn. Bring the end of the yarn near the side of a flame, just close enough to begin melting the fibers. As the fibers begin to melt, rotate the yarn continually to produce a uniform end to the body.

Some tyers allow the melted material to cool slightly, then gently roll the pliable material between well-moistened fingertips to shape the end of the body. Care should be exercised here for the obvious reason.

Step 2. Measure the yarn against the hook shank to determine the total body length desired.

Step 3. Clip the extension to length.

Insert the hook point into the yarn and work the point down the length of the material. When the hook reaches the point along the yarn where the body extension begins, push it through the material.

As shown here, the yarn that will form the portion of the body on the hook shank itself is now threaded on the bend. The portion that forms the body extension is unthreaded and extends beyond the bend.

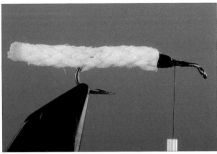

Step 4. Remount the hook in the vise. Before advancing the yarn to the straight portion of the shank, apply a coat of gel-type CA glue to the thread foundation.

Slide the yarn up the shank until it is properly positioned for the fly body. Allow the glue to set for about 30 seconds.

Re-attach the tying thread at the front of the body. Bind down the end of the yarn securely.

Method #123:
Quill Extension

Fashioning body extensions from porcupine quills is a technique generally attributed to Vince Marinaro, who described it in *A Modern Dry-Fly Code*. Though not seen much anymore, the style still produces attractive bodies that add buoyancy to a dry fly, particularly to sparsely dressed spinner patterns.

Two types of quill can be used. Porcupine quills are relatively easy to work with, but difficult to obtain in diameters suitable for larger fly bodies. The smooth, translucent end of a feather quill or stem (the "calamus," as it is called—see "Feathers," p. 5), usually from the flight feathers of ducks, geese, and game birds, can also be used. These make more durable bodies. Unfortunately, large-diameter feather stems are almost impossible to work with; they are tough and inflexible, difficult to bind to the hook shank, and prone to splitting. Feather stems about ⅛" in diameter are about the maximum practical size, and even these can be tricky to work with. Both types can be easily colored with marking pens to imitate specific insects.

This body style requires specific tailing techniques. Marinaro's original method is presented in the main sequence; a second method is shown in the alternate sequence. Tails, of course, can be omitted if desired.

Step 1. Select a porcupine quill of a diameter appropriate to the body extension you wish to create. (Note, however, that larger quills are easier to work with; the tailing procedure described in these steps may be difficult with very thin quills.)

Notice the small, hairlike structure at the base of the quill (at the upper left of the photo); this end of the quill will become the body extension.

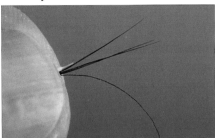

Step 2. To tail the body, select the desired tail material, in this case, three strands of moose mane. Clip a 7" length of tying thread that matches the quill color (black thread is used here for better visibility).

With the left thumb and forefinger, pinch together the quill, the tailing fibers, and the length of thread. Adjust the tail fibers to protrude beyond the quill to the desired length.

Using the left thumbnail, pinch the quill directly below the hairlike root against the left forefinger, trapping the tail fibers and thread against the quill.

Step 3. Take 5 or 6 turns of the thread, binding the tail fibers directly to the hairlike root of the quill.

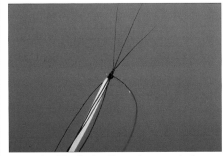

Step 4. Pinch the thread wraps between thumb and forefinger to keep them from unraveling. With the right hand, cast 3 or 4 half-hitches around the thread windings to secure them.

Clip both ends of the thread and the butts of the tail fibers. Apply a drop of head cement or CA glue to the wrappings.

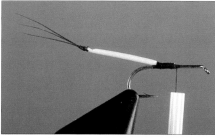

Step 5. Lay a short thread foundation on the hook, and position the thread at the rearmost wrap. Position the quill atop the shank.

Bind in the quill extension and tails as described in **Method #121: Lashed Extension**, Steps 1-2, p. 204.

Clip the end of the quill and bind down the butt. The quill can be colored with a marking pen, if desired, and the remainder of the fly dressed.

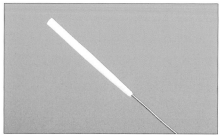

Step 1a. This alternate tailing method can be used with either porcupine quills or feather stems.

If using a porcupine quill, clip the hair-like tip off the end. Then clip off the sharp end of the quill, leaving a section of the quill about 1/16" to 1/8" longer than the desired extension length. This excess length of material will be bound to the shank.

Push the point of a fine needle (or thin piece of wire) down lengthwise into the narrow end of the quill. Insert the needle gently, rotating it as you push it farther into the quill. Don't advance the needle too far—perhaps 1/8" at most—or the quill will begin to split. The object here is to clear a pathway for the tailing fibers that will be inserted later.

If using a feather stem, clip it about 1/4" longer than the body extension. Use a needle to bore a hole in the tip and, at the same time, push out from the interior of the quill the small flakes of material adhering to the inside surface.

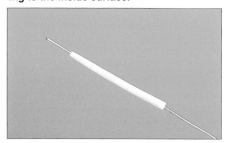

Step 2a. Now work the needle into the large end of the porcupine quill, again rotating it to create a hollow space. Since the quill is tapered, and you're now working at the wide end, you'll be able to push the needle through the quill without splitting the material.

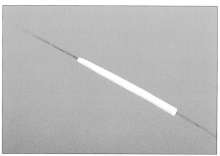

Step 3a. Select the desired tailing material. It should be a relatively stiff fiber—we're using Microfibetts here.

Insert the butts of the tailing material into the narrow end of the quill. Work the fibers through the quill until the tail butts project completely through and exit the wide end of the quill.

You can now grasp the fiber butts to adjust the length of the tail. Do not clip the butts.

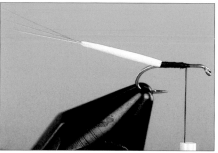

Step 4a. Lay a short thread foundation on the hook, and position the thread at the rearmost wrap. Position the quill atop the shank.

Bind in the quill extension as in Step 5. Secure the quill to the shank, and extend the thread wraps slightly beyond the end of the quill to bind the butts of the tailing material to the shank. These wraps will prevent the tails from pulling out.

After the quill is lashed to the shank, carefully bend or preen the tailing fibers to the desired position. Applying a small drop of head cement or CA glue to the end of the body extension will fix the tailing fibers in position and prevent the hollow quill body from admitting water.

The quill can now be colored with a marking pen and the rest of the fly completed.

Method #124:
Tubing Extension

Vinyl, plastic, and similar tubings can make simple and effective body extensions of various styles. The tubing can be left open at the rear of the body, which allows tailing material on the extension, or it can be sealed off to create a buoyant air capsule at the rear of the fly. Using the tubing in its manufactured form, that is, with a uniform diameter, simplifies tying, but the tubing can be tapered to produce a more realistic and elegant mayfly body, as shown in the main sequence; untapered tubing can be used to

form a tailed body using the procedure shown in Steps 4-6.

The alternate sequence demonstrates the construction of a simple, buoyant, untailed extension fashioned from sealed tubing. Larva Lace is used in both demonstrations.

Step 1. To taper the tubing, you'll need a candle or alcohol lamp. Cut a length of tubing about 4" long, and grip it at the ends between the thumb and forefinger of each hand.

Position the middle of the tubing close to the base of the flame, but not touching it. Just how close depends upon the tubing thickness—thin tubings, which soften faster, may be held as much 1/4" from the flame; thick tubings can be held closer. Hold the tubing moderately taut, but do not stretch it.

As you hold the tubing near the flame, rotate it slowly and evenly between the fingertips of both hands. The object here is to heat a section of the tubing. If you watch closely, you may begin to see the tubing soften and deform.

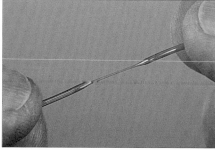

Step 2. At this point, take the tubing away from the flame and pull evenly on both ends. The soft center section will stretch and become thin. Hold this position for a few moments, and then relax the tension.

The resulting strand will assume an hourglass shape, a horseshoe bend, or even a curly pigtail in the middle. In all cases, however, you will have created two tapered lengths of tubing connected by a very thin middle section.

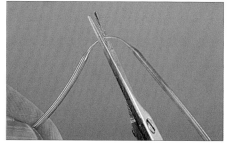

Step 3. Simply separate the two bodies by cutting the thin center section. The ends of the bodies can be trimmed further to decrease the length of the taper.

This technique requires a bit of practice, and the first few attempts may not be entirely successful. Aside from practice, there are a few keys here. First, work slowly. Getting the tubing too near the flame will cause it to burn in half. Second, rotate the tubing evenly in both hands to prevent it from twisting. Third, if you are unable to see the tubing soften, simply give a "test stretch" after 5 or 10 seconds; if the tubing is not soft enough, simply return it to the flame. Finally, if the tubing is heated in one section only, it will create a body with a rather abrupt taper. If, however, the tubing is moved back-and-forth across the flame as it is rotated, a longer section of material will soften. Stretching the tubing will result in a longer, more gradual taper.

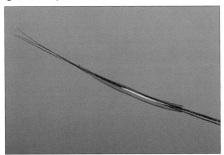

Step 4. Take the desired tailing material—we're using three strands of moose mane here—and insert them, tip first, into the large end of the tubing. Push them through so that they project out of the small end; adjust the fibers so that the tails are of the desired length. Do not clip the butts.

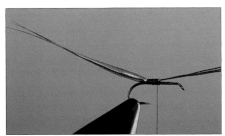

Step 5. Lay a thread foundation on the rear half of the hook shank, leaving the thread positioned at the rearmost wrap.

Hold the tubing atop the hook shank, and bind in as described in **Method #121: Lashed Extension**, Steps 1-2, p. 204. Bind the tubing tightly, as it is slippery.

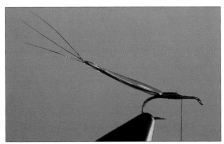

Step 6. Trim the excess material, and cover the butts with thread.

With a dubbing needle, separate and arrange the tail fibers in the desired position. Then place a very small drop of head cement or CA glue at the tip of the body, making sure that the small hole through which the tail fibers project is completely covered. This drop of glue will help fix the tail in the correct position and seal the hole at the end of the tubing, creating an airtight capsule that will help float the fly.

Step 1a. To create a closed, untailed body, you'll need to seal the end of the tubing with a flame. We're using a straight piece of tubing here, but a tapered one will certainly work as well.

To seal the tubing, bring one end near the base of a flame from a candle or alcohol lamp. Rotate the tubing slowly, heating the end. In a short time, the softened walls will collapse inward, forming a small bead that will seal the end.

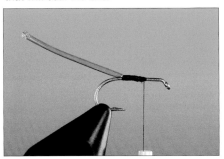

Step 2a. Lash the tubing atop the shank as described in **Method #121: Lashed Extension**, Steps 1-2, p. 204. Here we're using a straight section of tubing for an extended-body adult damselfly.

Method #125:
Feather Extension

The renowned Catskill tyer Harry Darbee is generally given credit for developing the feather extension as part of his "two-feather fly." More recently, in *Modern Fly Dressings for the Practical Angler*, Poul Jorgensen has revived the style and added a variation of his own.

Feather extensions are graceful, realistic, and when formed with an adhesive, reasonably durable. But since the feather extension adds no buoyancy, flies dressed in this style do not float particularly well and are best reserved for calmer, flatter waters.

There are a few particular requirements in the feather used to form the extension. First, it should have a noticeable natural curvature in the stem, which produces an upswept extended body. Second, the barbs must be long enough so that when they are drawn back down the length of the stem toward the base of the feather, all the barbs reach to the tie-in point of the body. This ensures that all barbs will be trapped beneath the tying thread preventing the extension from fraying. Given these provisions, almost any feather can be used—flank feathers, hen hackle, spade hackle (Jorgensen's preference), and so on. A rooster body feather is used in the sequence below.

The main sequence shows the method for creating a feather extension treated with adhesive. The type of glue used is important. Ordinary head cement, and even thicker types such as Flexament, are still too runny for this procedure. A thick silicone or vinyl glue, almost toothpaste-like in consistency, is satisfactory. We're using ordinary Duro Household Cement in the following procedure.

The alternate sequence demonstrates the procedure for forming a feather extension without the use of adhesive.

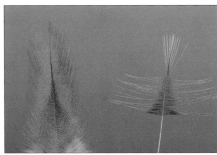

Step 1. Select a feather and strip the fuzz from the base. A short distance below the tip of the feather, begin preening the barbs on both sides down toward the base of the feather so they stand out perpendicular to the quill. The distance below the feather tip at which you begin to preen the barbs back depends upon the desired length of the tails. The lowest barbs at the tip that are still left in the natural position will become the tails, and hence define the tail length.

After the barbs are stroked downward, begin stripping off the lowest barbs on the quill until the section of preened out barbs that remain on the quill is slightly shorter than the desired length of the body extension (excluding the tails).

Step 1a. Poul Jorgensen offers an easy alternative method that does not involve the glue used in subsequent steps. The resulting body, however, is not as durable.

Prepare a feather as described in Step 1, but leave a section of preened barbs equal in length to the finished body extension (excluding tails). Clip the barbs along the stem, forming a tapered body extension as shown.

This extension can now be lashed to the hook shank as described in **Method #121: Lashed Extension**, Steps 1-2, p. 204, and shown below in Step 6.

Step 2. Take a dab of glue and place it on the hackle stem as shown.

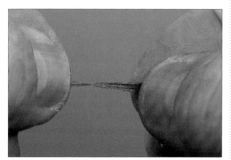

Step 3. Hold the tip of the feather in the left hand, and use the thumb and forefinger of the right hand to stroke the hackle barbs repeatedly toward the base of feather, distributing the glue throughout the barbs.

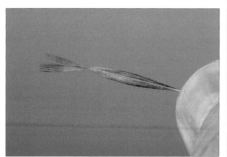

Step 4. At this point the body extension may be disproportionately wide. To thin it, cradle the glued portion of the feather in the first joint of the right index finger. Pull the feather, by the tip, through the joint, lightly squeezing the finger joint to crease the feather as it passes through. Repeat this process until the feather barbs lie downward against the stem, and the body is narrowed.

Step 5. Lay a thread base on the rear half of the hook shank, leaving the tying thread at the rearmost wrap. Lash the extension to the hook as described in **Method #121: Lashed Extension**, Steps 1-2, p. 204.

Step 6. Clip away the very tip portion of the feather, leaving one or two barbs on each side for tails.

　　The fly on the left was fashioned using the technique demonstrated in this sequence. The fly in the center has an extension formed as described in Step 1a. The fly on the right has an extension formed as explained below in Steps 2a-5a.

Step 2a. The body can be fashioned without using glue, and the resulting extension is quite graceful and elegant, though somewhat fragile.

　　Begin by laying a thread foundation on the rear half of the hook shank. Position the tying thread at the rearmost thread wrap. Take one half-hitch of thread around the shank at this point. This knot will help keep thread and feather in position when the body is formed in Step 4a.

　　Prepare a feather as described in Step 1. With the right fingers, preen the barbs toward the base of the feather.

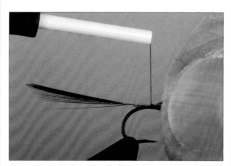

Step 3a. Using the bobbin in the left hand, trap the feather (still held in the "preened" position by the right hand) with two loose wraps of thread.

Step 4a. Grasp the rear of the body and gently pull, sliding the feather beneath the thread wraps until it projects beyond the hook bend for the desired distance. As you are drawing the body back, you may need to apply a bit of pressure to the tying thread by pulling on the bobbin, as sliding the body may disturb the position of the thread wraps.

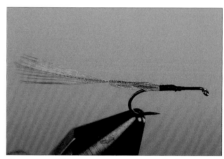

Step 5a. When the body has been drawn out the desired distance, bind down the feather tightly and clip the excess. To form the tails see Step 6.

Cored Extensions

　　Cored extensions are body extensions tied on a core of some type that furnishes a foundation for the body materials. This style of dressing has been around at least since the time of dry-fly pioneer Frederic Halford, and many techniques have since evolved for dressing flies in this fashion. Since the core material functions essentially as an extension of the hook shank, all of the customary body materials can be used to dress it. Moreover, tails, ribs, and overbodies, can be applied to the extension as well, which makes this particular approach to tying extended bodies one of the most versatile of all, particularly in dressing adult mayfly patterns.

　　The core material itself can be just about any fiber or strand that is stiff enough to tolerate the kind of thread tension applied during wrapping—hackle quills and other feather stems, stiff synthetic hair of the type often used by saltwater tyers, and so forth, but probably the most widely used materials are wire, monofilament line, and fly line. Though each of these latter three core materials is demonstrated in one of the sequences below, the particular material finally makes less difference in tying than the specific technique by which core and body materials are handled.

　　There are basically two approaches to tying cored extensions. In one technique, the core material is first bound to the hook shank, and the rear end of the core is left free-standing during tying, as shown in **Method #126: Free-standing Core Extension**, below. In the second type of technique, the core material is supported at both ends, providing a relatively taut and hence somewhat more stable foundation for the body materials. Versions of this approach are detailed in **Methods #127: Hand-held Core Extension**, p. 210, **Method #128: Double-vise Core Extension**, p. 212, and **Method #129: Extended Body Tool**, p. 212. The advantages and drawbacks of each approach are explained in the corresponding instructional sequences. There is no question, however, that dressing cored body extensions is one of the fussier, more meticulous procedures in fly tying. But it does create bodies achievable in no other way.

The methods below are organized primarily to show different ways in which the core material is handled. But in each case, almost any body material can be applied to the core, and we have chosen various types of dressings here to suggest both the range of materials that are feasible and how these may be handled. Thus, for instance, while **Method #127: Hand-held Core Extension**, p. 210 is primarily designed to provide instructions for using a core material that is supported by the left hand during tying, it also illustrates the way in which an extended body can be fashioned from a wrapped strand of material—floss, quill, herl, or as we have chosen, yarn—as well as how to create an overbody and/or rib. Thus the following four sequences might best be viewed as a kind of "mix and match" set of instructions—the technique for manipulating the core material may appear in one sequence, and the method for applying a specific body material in another.

Method #126:
Free-standing Core Extension

This is, in a sense, the most basic core-extension technique since it requires no additional tools or apparatus. The manipulation of both the materials and the bobbin are familiar to the tyer. The technique does have its difficulties, however, primarily in the lack of firm support for the core material. The tyer must furnish this support for the free-standing core in order to provide enough resistance to allow for wrapping tension of the thread.

To offset this difficulty, at least partially, this technique is best suited for stiffer core materials—stiffer wires, bundles of stiff hair, hackle stems, or fly line. Oregon tyer Gene Trump recommends what is certainly one of the more unusual, but still highly practical, core materials—bristles clipped from an ordinary toilet brush (preferably unused). Such a core is light, strong, rigid enough to apply body materials easily, inexpensive, and buoyant.

In the following demonstration, one of the most common core materials is used—monofilament line. In general, when using monofilament, it is best to select a size approximately the same diameter as the hook shank. This similarity will give the smoothest transition when wrapping certain kinds of material, such as floss, from the extension onto the hook shank. However, relatively thin, limp monofilaments, used on smaller hook sizes, are difficult to tie as free-standing extensions, and while it can be done, one of the techniques presented in subsequent methods will generally prove more efficient.

Once you begin dressing the body extension, one of your hands will be almost continually occupied in supporting the core material. Thus this method works best when all materials are prepared in advance and placed conveniently near the vise. If tails are used, as shown below, keep them handy in a hair stacker, which will keep the tips even. Body materials, like the dubbing we're using, should be kept near at hand.

As noted earlier, ribbing and/or overbody materials can be dressed on this type of extension. The procedure for doing so is explained in **Method #127: Hand-held Core Extension**, Steps 1a-4a, p. 211.

Step 1. Select a 3" piece of monofilament of the desired diameter. Most monofilaments take a "set" on the spool, and you can take advantage of this curvature to make an upswept mayfly body extension.

With a pair of needle-nose pliers or hemostats, mash down the last ¼" or so of the monofilament, crimping it in a direction perpendicular to the curl of the line. This flat section will aid in binding the mono to the shank, prevent it from rolling, and help maintain the proper orientation of the curl.

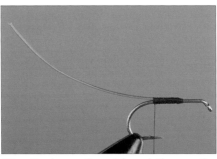

Step 2. Lay a thread foundation on the rear half of the hook shank and bind in the crimped portion of the monofilament, taking care to keep the direction of the line curl upward and the monofilament in line with the hook shank.

When the mono is bound in, return the tying thread to the rearmost thread wrap and secure with 2 half-hitches. These hitches are important, as the hook will be reversed in the

vise in the next step; this new orientation will reverse the direction of the thread wraps. Without the half-hitches, each turn of the bobbin will unwrap the thread.

Finally, clip the end of the monofilament to a length about ½" longer than the finished body extension.

Step 3. Reverse the hook in the vise jaws as shown.

Grasp the tailing material by the butts. The amount of tailing material projecting beyond the fingertips is equal to the length of the finished body extension plus the length of the finished tails. (Remember, that the monofilament is about ½" longer than the finished body extension.)

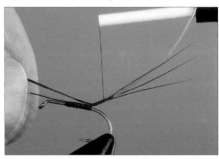

Step 4. Lay the tails atop the shank. With the tying thread, begin securing the tailing material to the top of the monofilament core, beginning at the base of the extension and working toward the tip. (Some tyers prefer to wax the thread at this point to give better adhesion on the slippery mono.)

Use close, adjacent wraps to lay a smooth thread base on the extension as you proceed. This base will provide a firm, non-slip foundation for the body materials, particularly if smooth, slick materials such as floss are used. Take care to keep the tailing fibers on top of the mono as you wrap; thread tension will want to draw them to the far side.

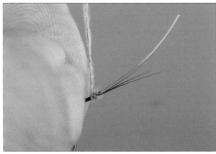

Step 5. As you advance the thread toward the tip of the body extension, the monofilament will wobble and bend under thread pressure. Pinch the extension in your left fingers to help keep it rigid as you wrap.

When the tailing point is reached (about ½" from the end of the mono), take two or three very firm turns of thread.

Now begin applying dubbing to the thread using any of the direct dubbing methods (dubbing loops aren't terribly practical with this technique). The trick here in applying dubbing is to keep just enough tension on the bobbin to allow for spinning the material, but not so much pressure that the monofilament bends and deforms.

Now begin wrapping the dubbed thread down the body extension, again supporting the mono with the fingers of the left hand to provide rigidity.

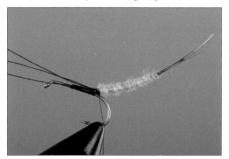

Step 6. Wrap the dubbing right up to the juncture of the mono and the hook shank.

When the extension is completely dressed, take a couple of half-hitches ahead of the dubbing.

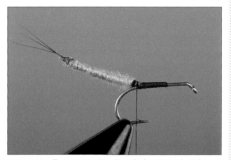

Step 7. Reverse the hook in the vise jaws as shown. Clip the butts of the tailing fibers.

Using scissors or clippers, cut the excess monofilament from the rear of the extension. Be very careful not to clip the mono so close to the tails that you risk cutting the tying thread or the body extension will be rendered worthless. Instead, leave a very small tag of mono projecting from beneath the tail. Apply a small drop of head cement or gel-type CA glue to the rear of the body to help secure the thread wraps against the mono and prevent them from slipping off the end.

At this point, the extension is complete. You can continue dubbing the rest of the body on the hook shank, or apply other materials required by the dressing.

Method #127:

Hand-held Core Extension

This technique is a good compromise in that it requires no additional tools, but still makes provisions for supporting the core material at the rear. It is, however, limited to longer-stranded materials such as wire, monofilament, or the fly line used in the following demonstration (see note below).

The trick in this method is wrapping the core material around the middle finger of the left hand in just such a way that the thumb and forefinger are properly positioned to pinch the tailing material around the core.

The main sequence below shows the wrapping of a simple stranded body material—poly yarn, in this case. The alternate sequence demonstrates how to apply rib and/or overbody materials, and the technique shown here can be used with any of the various cored extensions described in this section.

Lastly, this technique can be performed with the vise jaws positioned in the ordinary fashion, but the vise head will interfere significantly with the wrapping of material since the bobbin must be passed behind the vise stem with each wrap on the extension. Re-positioning the vise so that the jaws are vertical, or slightly beyond the vertical, greatly simplifies this method. If your vise will not permit this adjustment, position the vise head with the jaws pointing to the left. Once the extension is complete, you can return the jaws to the normal position to dress the rest of the fly.

Again, since one hand is continually occupied in holding the line it is best to have all materials prepared in advance and conveniently placed on the tying bench.

A note on fly lines: Obviously, an old fly line can be cut up for the purpose of making extended bodies, and various diameters can be obtained from the belly sections of weight-forward or double-taper lines of different weights. Thin sections of line, however, can be obtained from the thin, running line portion of a weight-forward line that you are currently using. In most cases, shortening the rear section of such a line will not diminish its performance.

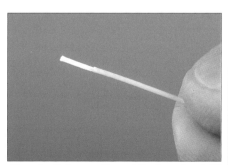

Step 1. Cut a section of fly line about 7" inches long. Using a razor blade or scissors, carefully scrape away the exterior coating from the last ¼" of the line to expose the fly line core. This core will give a firmer grip when bound to the hook shank.

You can also dip the end of the fly line in acetone, which will soften the exterior coating and make it easier to remove.

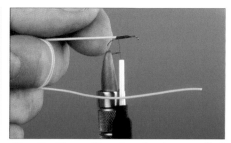

Step 2. Re-position the vise jaws so that they are vertical, or beyond the vertical, tilting to the left, if possible, and mount the hook as shown.

Lay a thread foundation on the rear half of the hook shank. Bind in the exposed core of the fly line, taking care to position the fly line so that any curve it has sweeps upward.

Pinch the thumb and forefinger of the left hand around the fly line directly behind the bend. With the right hand take the tag end of the fly line and wrap it firmly around the middle finger of the left hand a few times. If done correctly, this procedure will put the thumb and forefinger in position to grasp the tailing material at the correct point and still allow enough "reach" for the fingers to grasp materials around the hook shank.

After taking a few turns of line around the middle finger, you can remove the thumb and forefinger from the line and concentrate on securing the wrapped line. A simple overhand knot or half-hitch around the middle finger will prevent the

Step 3. With the middle finger of the left hand, put firm, but not excessive, tension on the fly line to help keep it steady and relatively rigid. This same tension should be maintained throughout the tying procedure.

Begin wrapping the thread toward the end of the body extension. Since the vise obstructs the wrapping, the right hand will need to be repositioned once for each full turn of thread. Note, as shown above, that you can use the ring finger of the left hand to support the bobbin and keep it from swinging as you re-position the right hand to continue wrapping.

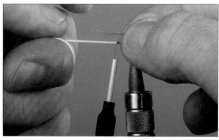

Step 4. When the thread reaches the tailing point, grasp the tailing material in the right hand. Position it on the extension so that the tips of the tail fibers extend the desired distance beyond the tail-mounting point.

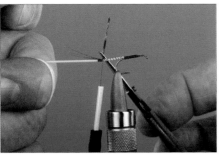

Step 5. Pinch the tailing material at the tail-mounting point with the left thumb and forefinger.

Begin wrapping the thread back down the extension, securing the tailing fibers as you go. After the material has bound down with 5 or 6 tight wraps, the butts can be clipped as shown. If desired, a drop of head cement or CA glue can be applied to the tailing wraps.

Continue wrapping the thread down the extension and onto the hook until the extension tie-in point is reached.

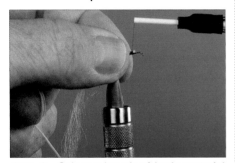

Step 6. Select a length of body material about 7" long. Note that the material will be wrapped up the body extension and back down to the hook, creating a double-layer body. Thus the body material should be half the thickness that would normally be used to create a single-layer body.

With the left thumb and forefinger, position the body material atop the hook shank. The point along the shank at which the material is bound in depends upon whether the complete body, or the extension only, is to be dressed. Here, the entire body will be fashioned from yarn, so the material is bound in at the frontmost point of the body with several tight turns of thread. The tying thread is left at this location. If only the extension is to be dressed, the body material is tied in directly over the rearmost thread wrap on the shank, and the bobbin left at that position.

To add a rib and/or overbody to the extension, see Step 1a.

Step 7. Begin wrapping the material toward the bend of the hook. When the extension is reached, take one wrap of material around the base of the fly line only, and tuck it up between the fly line

and hook shank as shown. This will help elevate the extension.

Continue wrapping up the extension. Pass the yarn momentarily to the left thumb and forefinger to allow repositioning the right hand during each wrap.

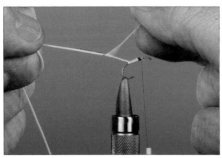

Step 8. When the tailing point is reached, reverse the direction of wrapping, and wrap the body material back down the extension.

Step 9. When the tying thread is reached, bind down the body material, clip the excess, and wrap over the butt ends.

Carefully raise the tails, and with scissors or clippers, trim the excess fly line. Be very careful not to cut any of the tail-mounting thread wraps or the body will unravel. It is better to leave a small tag of line projecting beyond the body.

When the excess fly line has been trimmed, apply a small drop of head cement or gel-type CA glue to the end of the body. The glue will help secure the tailing wraps and will seal the end of the fly line to make a watertight extension.

Step 1a. To create a ribbed extension, or one with an overbody, use the same finger positions described in Step 6 to mount the ribbing material atop the shank. Then mount the overbody material—red yarn, in this case—atop the ribbing. Finally, mount the body material, yellow yarn is used here, atop the overbody material. Again, the precise mounting point depends upon the overall length of the body to be dressed with these materials, as described in Step 6.

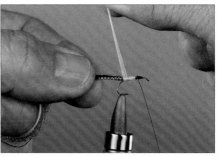

Step 2a. Lay the ribbing and overbody material atop the fly line extension. Use the thumb and forefinger of the left hand to draw them taut and pinch them slightly beyond the tailing point.

Begin wrapping the body material as described in Step 7. As you wrap up the extension, it is important that the overbody material be kept atop the fly line.

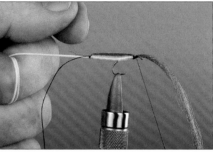

Step 3a. As in Step 8, reverse the direction of wrapping and wind the body material down the extension. Secure it tightly to the desired position on the hook shank.

Lay the overbody material down on top of the body extension, and secure it to the shank with several tight turns of thread.

Step 4a. Wind the ribbing in evenly spaced turns down the body extension.

When the body tie-off point is reached, secure the ribbing.

Finish the body as described in Step 10.

Method #128:
Double-vise Core Extension

This technique is quite popular because of the relative ease with which extended bodies can be made—both hands are free to manipulate tools and materials. Two vises support the core material and provide a firm, taut foundation on which to dress the extension. In fact, a second vise to hold the core material isn't really necessary; any vertical post or a screw-eye mounted in a vertical surface can serve as a substitute.

When two vises are used, dressing the extension is made easier if the front vise, the one holding the hook, is positioned so that the jaws are vertical, as shown below. This orientation provides better hand clearance. If the vise jaws cannot be adjusted in this way, position the front vise head so that the jaws point to the left. Once the extension has been completed, the vise can be returned to the normal position to complete the fly.

Once the core material is secured between the two supports, the extension can be dressed as though it were an ordinary hook shank—with a couple of exceptions. First, uninterrupted, one-handed wraps with the bobbin are not possible, so the bobbin must be passed from hand to hand as it is wrapped around the extension. Secondly, though it is possible to mount body, overbody, and rib materials directly on the extension core—as you would on an ordinary hook—it is simpler to follow the procedure detailed in **Method #127: Hand-held Core Extension**, Steps 1a-4a, in which all of these materials except tails are mounted on the hook shank. Given this similarity, we've abbreviated the instructions below; for more details, consult **Method #127: Hand-held Core Extension**, p. 210.

There are two principal variations of this technique. The first, shown after Step 3, involves securing the core material to the hook shank and supporting it at the rear with a second vise. In essence, the body extension is dressed as part of the complete fly.

The second approach, shown after Step 3, is one espoused by Ernest Schwiebert; it involves stringing a core between two vises and dressing several body extensions in sequence. The extensions are then cut apart, and each is lashed to a hook shank. The advantage is that the core need only be strung once for several body extensions, producing a certain economy in setting up the apparatus and in handling materials.

Though monofilament line and fly line can form the core, wire is used in both demonstrations. Ordinary fly-tying wire can be used for very small flies, but it is rather soft, and the force generated merely by casting the fly can cause longer extensions on larger hooks to bend out of position. A better choice for longer extended bodies are the stiff, springier stainless steel wires of the type used to fashion articulated or wiggle bodies. These provide a less malleable body

extension and stiffer foundation on which to tie. (For more information about wire materials, consult the chapter on "Wiggle Bodies, Tandem Hooks, and Weed Guards," p. 49.)

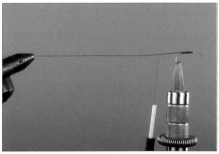

Step 1. Secure a hook in the front vise and lay a thread foundation on the rear half of the shank. Securely bind in a length of core material—stainless wire in this case. It should be at least 3 or 4" long to provide adequate hand clearance when tying. Excessively long lengths of wire, however, will not stretch tautly enough to give a solid tying foundation.

When the wire is secure, stretch the tag end firmly back to the second vise and clamp it in the jaws. The jaws of the rear vise can be positioned in line with the jaws of the front one, in which case the wire is strung in a horizontal position, as shown here. Or the rear vise can be elevated slightly, angling the wire upward in the attitude of a finished mayfly body. The actual application of materials is the same in either case.

Wrap the tying thread up the wire, laying a smooth foundation, to the tailing point. If desired, you can apply a drop of head cement to the thread wraps to help secure them to the wire.

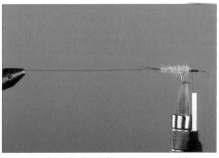

Step 2. Attach the tails as you would to an ordinary hook shank.

If the body is to be dubbed, dubbing can be applied to the thread at this time and the body wrapped, as shown here. (If the rear vise is a rotary type, and ordinary fly-tying wire is used as the core material, you can apply the dubbing by using **Method #46: Single-wire Spun Dubbing**, p. 135. You may find this technique easier in some instances. Stainless wire, however, is usually too stiff to be spun easily in this fashion.)

If the body is to be made of a material other than dubbing, such as floss or yarn, or a ribbing or overbody is to be used, wrap the thread back to the hook shank. Bind in and wrap the desired materials as described in **Method #127: Hand-held Core Extension**, Steps 6-9 or 1a-4a, p. 210.

Step 3. When the body material has been applied to the core material (and hook shank, if desired), raise the tails slightly, and with a pair of sidecutters, clip the wire core close to the end of the body. Be careful not to clip any of the tailing wraps or the body will unravel.

Apply a drop of head cement or gel-type CA glue to the rear of the body to secure the tailing wraps and prevent them from sliding off the extension.

To create a number of separate body extensions on a separate wire, stretch a length of wire 8" long between two vises positioned so that the jaws face one another. This orientation gives the most working room.

Dress the core as you would a hook shank, though as a rule, such body extensions are usually dubbed; affixing separate body materials, such as floss, directly to the core can be fussy and difficult, though it can be done. Note, however, that using the spun-wire technique referred to in Step 2 is not really suitable for creating multiple bodies. The cumulative twisting will usually fatigue and break the wire.

First dress the body farthest to the left, then work to the right as subsequent extensions are fashioned. Leave an inch or so of bare wire between the separate extensions to provide enough foundation to lash to the hook shank. When the extensions have been clipped apart, apply a drop of head cement or CA glue to the tailing wraps.

Lash the extension to the hook shank as described in **Method #121: Lashed Extension**, Steps 1-2, p. 204.

Method #129:
Extended-body Tool

If you tie large numbers of extended-body patterns, you may wish to consider an extended-body tool, a device designed specifically to support body-core materials. It functions essentially as the second vise in the double-vise method described above, but it offers certain advantages. It is easier to use and adjust, can remain installed on the vise stem even when other types of patterns are being tied, is more portable and less expensive. The type pictured in the sequence below is manufactured by Dyna King and doubles as a gallows tool for parachute hackling.

When an extended body tool is used, dressing the extension is made easier if the vise is positioned so that the jaws are vertical, as shown in **Method #127: Hand-held Core Extension**, Step 2, p. 210. This orientation provides better hand clearance. If the jaws of your vise are fixed in position and will not allow this adjustment, try positioning the vise head with the jaws pointing to the left. When the extension is complete, you can return the vise to the normal position and dress the remainder of the fly.

In addition to presenting the use of this tool, the sequence below also describes an interesting extended-body material—spun deer hair—that is certainly one of the most unusual and painstaking to tie. The result, however, is a durable, high-floating extended-body pattern. The best core materials for such a body are either stainless wire or monofilament (fly line is not recommended), and of these two materials, thicker diameters work better than thinner ones as they offer a firmer foundation for the somewhat heavy thread tension needed to spin hair. Because of this thicker core, a spun deer-hair extension is best suited to larger flies—bigger duns, stoneflies, or the grasshopper body shown below. Moreover, trimming the hair very close to the core, for a thin extension on a small fly, will reduce its buoyancy.

With care, deer hair can be spun on extensions of the type shown in **Method #127: Hand-held Core Extension**, p. 210, and **Method #128: Double-vise Core Extension**, p. 212. And, of course, other types of body materials can be, and in fact typically are, applied to cores supported by extended-body tools.

Since detailed instructions for spinning deer hair are provided in **Method #58: Spinning Hollow Hair**, p.145, the instructions below are abbreviated.

Step 1. Cut about 12" of monofilament, and bind it to the hook shank as described in **Method #126: Free-standing Core Extension**, Steps 1-2, p. 209.

Secure the free end of the monofilament in the extended body tool, as per the manufacturer's instructions. With some types of materials, you may wish to position the extended body tool so that the core angles upward from the hook shank. In this case, however, spinning hair is made easier if the tool is positioned so

that the core material is held horizontally. Advance the tying thread to the rearmost point of the body.

If a tailing material is to be used, secure it to the core as explained in **Method #127: Hand-held Core Extension**, Steps 4-5, p. 210. Return the thread to the rearmost point of the body.

Step 2. Clip and prepare a small bundle of deer hair as described in **Method #2: Preparing and Cleaning Hair**, p. 68. Cut off the tips of the hair so that the bundle is about ¾" long.

Pinch the bundle of hair against the top of the core, with the middle of the bundle directly atop the rearmost thread wrap.

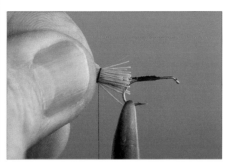

Step 3. Take two complete wraps of thread, directly atop one another, around the middle of the hair bundle. The thread should be just tight enough to snug against the hair, but not so tight that the hair begins to flare or is disturbed from its position atop the core. Finish these wraps with the bobbin hanging beneath the core.

Step 4. Apply moderate tension to the thread. You may need to adjust your left thumb and forefinger slightly to help support the core material and counteract the thread pressure.

Slowly begin taking another wrap of thread around the core. As you do, relax tension on the hair bundle and use your thumb and forefinger to encourage the hair to distribute itself around the core. As you continue the wrap, increase the thread pressure to flare the hair and secure it tightly to the core.

Step 5. Continue wrapping the thread tightly, until the hair is well-flared and resists any further migration around the core.

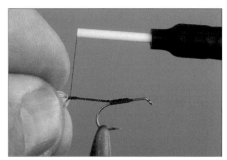

Step 6. When the hair bundle is secure, draw the tying thread to the front of the flared clump. Preen back the hair as shown, and take a few tight wraps of thread against the base of the hair.

Step 7. Repeat Steps 2-6 until the body extension (and any part of the hook shank desired) are covered.

Secure the thread with a few half-hitches. If desired, the thread can now be clipped to facilitate trimming the body.

Step 8. Trim the body to shape as described in **Method #67: Clipped Bodies**, p. 155.

Clip off the core material at the rear of the extension and apply a drop of head cement or gel-type CA glue to the core stub.

Furled Extensions

Simple body extensions can be made by "furling" a strand of material. A length of material is first twisted and then allowed to curl up on itself, or furl, creating a single length of material that is now doubled in thickness. The countertwist tension is maintained, and the material is affixed to the hook shank. Nearly any relatively supple material can be used—flosses, yarns, dubbed threads, fly line, even monofilament tippet material. The thickness of the material used is governed by the desired diameter of the body extension.

Furled bodies have a number of advantages. They are relatively easy to make; they can be fashioned from a variety of materials; they're durable; and they produce a nicely segmented appearance on the extension.

Method #130:

Simple Furled Extension

This technique can be used when tails are not needed in the dressing—for caddis, adult stonefly, and terrestrial patterns.

There are two ways to achieve this kind of body extension. The furling can be done before the extension is lashed to the hook, and this is explained in the main sequence below. Or one end of the material can be lashed to the hook before furling—a method some tyers find easier to use with smaller flies—and this is presented in the alternate sequence. As shown in Step 4, combining strands of different colors prior to furling can produce some interesting effects in the body.

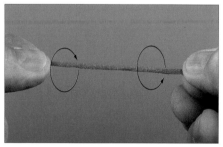

Step 1. We're using poly yarn here to make a furled extension for an adult stonefly pattern. Pinch the ends of a strand of material between the fingertips of each hand, as shown. The distance between the fingertips should be at least 2½ times the length of the finished body extension.

Roll the material between the fingertips of each hand. The ends of the strand should be rolled in opposite directions.

The tightness of the twist depends upon two factors: the desired appearance of the finished body, and the material itself. A tightly twisted strand will furl tightly, producing a thinner extension with more segments. Less twist will produce a looser, thicker body with fewer segments. There is, however, a maximum twist for each type of material. Over-twisting the strand will cause it to furl in more than one spot, or to furl on itself more than one time. Only experimentation can determine this maximum limit.

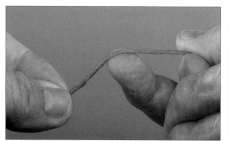

Step 2. Once the strand is twisted, press the middle finger of one hand into the center of the strand. This will encourage the material to furl in the middle.

Step 3. Relax pulling tension (but not the twist) by moving your hands closer together. The strand will twist or furl upon itself, forming a double thickness of material.

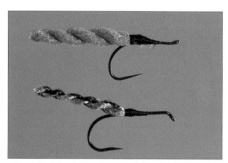

Step 4. Pinch the base of the furled extension in the fingertips of the left hand, taking care to maintain the twist so that the body does not unfurl. The extension can now be lashed to the hook shank as described in **Method #121: Lashed Extension**, Steps 1-2, p. 204, and shown at the top.

The extension at the bottom shows the effect created when two materials of different colors are stacked and then furled.

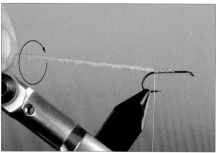

Step 1a. Some tyers prefer this approach.

Lash one end of the body extension material to the top of the hook shank. The rearmost thread wrap is located at the mounting point of the finished extension. The material projecting beyond the hook bend should be about 2½ times the length of the finished extended body.

With the left thumb and forefinger, pinch the free end of the material, pull it in line with hook shank, and twist. See Step 1 regarding the tightness of the twist.

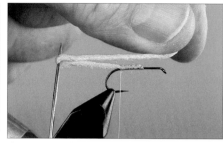

Step 2a. When the desired twist is obtained, fold the strand around the shank of a dubbing needle. The point of the fold will become the rearmost point of the body extension, so position the needle to obtain proper extension length.

Step 3a. Remove the needle and the body will furl on itself.

The free end of the material can be lashed atop the material already on the hook shank to complete the extension.

Method #131:

Furled and Tailed Extension

Creating furled extensions for adult mayfly patterns, or other patterns requiring a tapered body and/or tails, requires a more specialized approach than free-hand furling. The technique for doing so was shown to us by Darrel Martin. Almost any suitable furling material can be employed, but Martin uses a dubbing loop, and we've reproduced his procedures here to demonstrate how furs and other dubbing materials can make furled extensions.

On larger fly patterns, the extension can be created directly on the hook that will be used to tie the finished fly. On smaller fly patterns, however, manipulating the material in a very limited amount of room becomes difficult. In this case, the extension is formed according to the instructions given below, and then cut to length and lashed to a smaller hook.

Almost any fibers can be used for the tail, provided they are long enough. The fibers not only form the visible tail, but they run through the center of the entire furled body and are ultimately bound to the hook shank to hold them in place.

The following demonstration focuses primarily on getting the tails properly positioned inside the furled strand. Readers unfamiliar with the basic furling technique may wish to consult **Method #130: Simple Furled Extension**, for a more detailed explanation of the procedure.

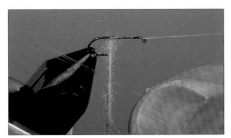

Step 1. Spin a quantity of dubbing sufficient to make the body as explained in **Method #38: Trap-loop Dubbing**, p. 129. In spinning the loop, the strand of body material is formed and simultaneously twisted for furling.

Select the desired number of tailing fibers, such as the Microfibetts shown here.

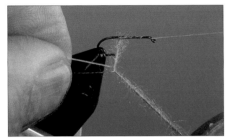

Step 2. Fold the tailing fibers around the dubbed strand. The point at which the fibers are folded is where the furling will begin, so they must be positioned at a point to form an extension of the desired length.

The fingers in the photo are drawn back in order to show the folded tailing fibers. In actual tying, the left fingers should pinch the folded tailing fibers very close to the dubbed strand; the fingertips should actually touch the dubbing.

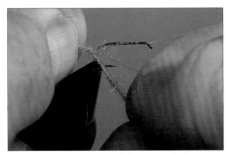

Step 3. This is the tricky part. Relax tension on the tail fibers slightly and move the ends of the dubbed strand close enough together to start it furling. Allow the material to furl once, forming a loop around the folded tailing fibers.

Sneak the left fingertips forward just far enough to pinch the loop formed from furling.

Then release the butts of the tailing fibers, maintaining your hold on the fiber tips.

Bring the two ends of the dubbing strand closer together to continue furling. As the two strands of dubbing twist together, the tail-fiber butts should be encircled by the spiraling strands.

This coordinated material handling takes some dexterity in the left fingers and some practice. But when you succeed and see the procedure work once, the technique becomes much easier as you know what you are attempting to accomplish.

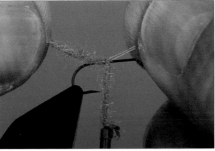

Step 4. Continue letting the dubbed strand furl around the tailing butts until the entire extension is furled.

Pinch the furled extension in your left fingers and bind both the dubbed strand and tail butts to the shank with two or three thread wraps under only moderate tension.

At this point, tail length can be adjusted by pulling on the fiber tips or butts, as shown here.

Step 5. When the tails have been adjusted to the proper length, secure the extension and tail butts with several tight thread wraps. Clip the excess materials.

For very small flies, the extension can be created on a larger hook for easier handling. Then pinch the extension tightly in the left fingers and clip it from the hook. It can then be remounted on a smaller hook to form an extension of the proper length.

Rolled-tape Extensions

Certainly one of the more unusual materials to form body extensions is double-sided tape, that is, tape that is sticky on both surfaces. Two tyers, Darrel Martin and Gary Warren have showed us versions of this technique, and it produces simple, nicely shaped bodies. Both tyers, however, are emphatic about the proper material. For slender body extensions on mayfly or adult damsel patterns, they recommend Scotch Wallsaver Removable Poster Tape (product #109). This is a more substantial material than ordinary Scotch tape, more like a thick membrane than a thin plastic film, and it has the added benefit of buoyancy. For larger body extensions on terrestrial or adult stonefly patterns, Darrel Martin recommends Scotch Heavy Duty Mounting Tape (product #111), a double-sided foam tape that adds bulk and buoyancy to larger flies.

Though these bodies may sound fragile, they are in fact surprisingly tough and springy. But since the use of this material is relatively new, the long-term durability of flies that are fished repeatedly throughout a season is still something of a question. Nonetheless, they are not difficult to tie.

Method #132:
Rolled Tape Extension

Cutting and rolling tape works best on a small plate of clean glass, as the smooth surface doesn't diminish the adhesiveness of the tape.

Step 1. Tear a piece of tape from the dispenser about 1½ times the length of the finished body extension. The tape is sticky on one side and has a paper backing on the other. Press the sticky side against the glass.

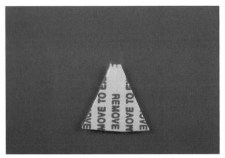

Step 2. You can roll a simple cylindrical body from this piece of tape, but here we'll demonstrate rolling a tapered, tailed extension for a mayfly body.

With a sharp razor blade, trim the tape (with the backing still attached) to the shape shown—a triangle with the point cut off to form a short straight section about 1/16" to 1/8" wide.

Note that the tape need not be used full-width. For small flies, it can be split lengthwise to form a narrower strip. For larger flies, two or more pieces of tape can be laid edge-to-edge, with a slight overlap to form a single piece of material.

Step 3. Carefully peel away the backing. Since the tape is transparent, we've colored it here with a green marking pen for better visibility. Such tinting, of course, can also be used to color the fly body to match specific insects. The body can be colored in this way either before or after the tape is rolled.

Select a tailing material—stiff hairs

such as moose, artificial fibers such as Microfibetts, or hackle barbs. Mount the tail fibers by pressing them against the tape as shown. The distance that the fibers project past the small end of the triangle will determine the finished length of the tails.

Two points to bear in mind here: first, the two outside fibers are positioned slightly inside the tape edges, leaving bare adhesive surfaces at the very edge of the tape to secure the rolled body. Second, the tailing fibers cross one another at a point beyond the tip of the tape, which helps keep them fanned apart and separate when the body is rolled.

When the tail materials are mounted, trim the base of the tail fibers flush with the base of the triangle. Rolling the body is easier without these fiber butts in the way.

Step 3a. If desired, a small amount of dubbing, a length of floss or yarn, or other material can be pressed against the tape at this point. Adding material here will darken the color of the finished body.

If dubbing is used, it should be finely chopped and pressed lengthwise down the center of the tape. Do not allow the dubbing to extend to the edges of the tape, or the rolled tape will not adhere to itself well.

Step 4. With the razor blade, raise the edge of the tape from the glass, forming a flap about ¹⁄₁₆" wide.

Fold this flap over creating a double-thickness of material at the edge of the triangle to give you a start on rolling the body.

Step 5. The trick in rolling is to maintain a relatively tight, uniform body, particularly at the tail end.

When the flap is folded over, use the

fingertips of both hands to push the tape, rolling it on to itself. Try to maintain a uniform pressure.

Note, however, that since the piece of tape is wider at the base, there is more material to roll at this end. The fingertips rolling the base of the body extension must work "faster" in order to compensate for the excess material. The object is to roll the piece of tape into a thin cone.

Step 6. Continue rolling until the body is complete. The exterior of the body is still sticky, allowing dubbing to be applied for color and texture. To preserve the adhesiveness, avoid excessive handling of the extension. Hold it by the base, which will be trimmed away when the extension is mounted. The best dubbing for this technique is fine, long-fibered material. Chopped or coarse dubbings do not adhere well.

Tease out a small amount of dubbing, making a relatively sparse skein of fibers. Press the dubbing against the body extension. Using thumb and forefinger, roll the dubbing onto the exterior of the body, pressing firmly but not hard enough to deform the extension. If the body still feels slightly tacky, add a bit more dubbing.

Step 7. When all the dubbing has been applied, roll the extension tightly at the tail end to emphasize the taper. A small drop of head cement can be applied to the base of the tails to help secure them and to seal the end of the body to form a waterproof capsule. Trim away any stray dubbing fibers that have not adhered to the tape.

Only the dubbing in contact with the tape will adhere, so it isn't possible to apply a large quantity of material. The resulting body extension will always be a bit light in color and somewhat translucent. If a darker color is desired, it is best to color the tape with a marker as described in Step 3 or apply interior dubbing as shown in Step 3a.

The finished body can now be lashed to the hook as described in **Method #121: Lashed Extension**, Step 2, p. 204.

Needle-formed Extensions

Extended bodies can be fashioned by applying materials to an ordinary sewing needle, which functions as a temporary core; when the body section is complete, the needle is removed and the extension lashed to a hook. There is much to recommend this approach. The needle provides a solid foundation, which simplifies tying, and its standard orientation in the vise eliminates the unfamiliar bobbin-handling often required with cored extensions. A reasonably wide range of materials can be used, and because the needle is removed, the resulting extension is quite light. Needle-formed extensions, however, do take extra time and steps to dress. Still, only a few of the techniques presented are at all complicated and, in general, these needle methods are far simpler than most tyers believe.

Almost any type of needle can be used. Ordinary sewing needles are available in a wide range of diameters, making them useful in techniques such as **Method #137: Dubbing Shell Extension**, p. 222, where the needle diameter governs the finished body size. For the most part, however, very thin needles are the most useful, as their removal from the finished extension causes only a minimal slack in the thread wraps. Sewing needles, however, often lack the length necessary for dressing larger bodies. Here, longer "beading needles" are useful, and some tyers prefer this style for all extensions, as the extra length allows them to work further away from the vise jaws and get better finger clearance.

The eye of the needle is mounted in the vise, as drawing the body down the tapered shank and off the point helps loosen the thread wraps a bit and facilitates removing the extension. Mounting the needle in this way, however, means that your fingers constantly work around the needle point; even if you're careful, drawing a little blood is not out of the question. Blunting the needle point with a whetstone is a wise precaution, particularly if a number of body extensions are to be formed.

Method #133:

Needle-formed Fiber Extension

Body extensions can be formed from any fiber, natural or synthetic, that has sufficient length. But the most popular choice is undoubtedly deer hair (or similar fibers such as elk and moose), which is used in the instructions that follow. The hollow hairs make for a buoyant extension that helps float the fly. Moreover, it is available in a variety of colors and textures, and it is easy to work with. The one drawback is durability; hollow hairs are rather fragile and easily broken in toothy jaws.

While the most common method for tying deer-hair extensions is to use a free-standing, coreless extended body (detailed in

Method #140: Bundled-fiber Extension, p. 226, and Method #141: Reverse-tied Bundle Extension, p. 227), such bodies require a substantial number of fibers to provide tying rigidity in the extension, and hence are best suited to somewhat larger flies. The needle-formed extension, however, permits the use of fewer hairs and is practical for dressing smaller patterns.

This type of extension can be ribbed in two ways, using either a continuous spiral (shown in the main sequence), which simulates body segments, or by using a true segmentation (shown in the alternate sequence Steps 1a-1c) that reproduces the actual independent body segments of a natural insect.

Alternate Steps 2a-2d show an unusual approach taken by Finnish tyer Veli Autti, in which the natural hair tips are used to form tails on the body extension. Shown as well is an unusual mounting method to dress a fly that floats upside-down.

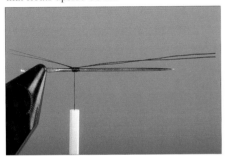

Step 1. Secure a needle by the eye in the vise jaws. Attach the tying thread with 4 or 5 firm wraps around the shank of the needle. The wraps should be firm enough to hold the thread without slipping, but not excessively tight, as they must be pulled from the needle when the extension is complete.

Select a tailing material. Virtually any type of tail can be used, with one provision—the tailing fibers themselves must be long enough that the butts project beyond the end of the body extension. This excess tailing material will be bound to the hook shank along with the extended body and prevent the tails from slipping out.

Mount the tail fibers atop the rearmost thread wrap on the needle and bind them down with 4 or 5 tight turns of thread. Do not clip the butts of the tail material.

Return the thread to the rearmost tailing wrap. At this point, you may help secure the tailing wraps by applying a small drop of head cement to the windings. CA glue isn't recommended here, as the strong adhesion and quick drying time may actually glue the thread to the needle.

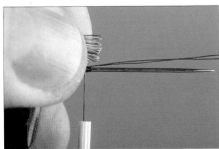

Step 2. Clip and prepare a clump of deer hair as described in **Method #2: Preparing and Cleaning Hair**, p. 68. Use the longest hair possible, as it will prove easier to

handle. The number of hairs used will determine the thickness of the finished body. Small flies may require only a couple of dozen hairs; larger flies will take more.

Align the tips as explained in **Method #3: Stacking and Aligning Hair**, p. 69. Cut off the very fine, pointed tips.

Grasp the clump near the tip and position it directly atop the rearmost thread wrap, with the hair butts pointing toward the vise.

Step 3. Take two wraps of thread—snug, but not tight—over the bundle of hair, directly atop the rearmost tailing wrap.

Begin a third wrap, drawing the thread more tightly, flaring the hair, and distributing it evenly around the needle. If necessary, use the fingers of the left hand to help work the hair around the needle. (For more detail on mounting deer hair in this fashion, see **Method #58: Spinning Hollow Hair**, p. 145).

Note that the butts of the hair will not distribute themselves around the needle, as the vise jaws are an obstruction. You must observe the hair near the mounting point to make sure it is evenly spread around the shank.

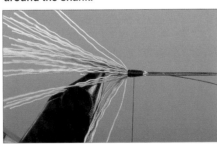

Step 4. Bind down the tips of the deer hair. Note that it is important that the rearmost wrap of thread holding the deer hair be directly atop the rearmost wrap of thread securing the tail. This will ensure the most secure hold for the tail material and the tailing wraps on the needle.

Position the tying thread at the point on the needle where you wish to create the first body segment.

Use a dubbing needle to preen the butts of the hair so that they encircle the hook shank, without being twisted or trapped behind the jaws.

Step 5. Draw the hair along the needle shank, work it past the tying thread, and pull it toward the needle point; it should

form a smooth, even capsule around the needle shank. Hold it in position with the right hand.

With the left hand, spiral the tying thread toward the point of the needle, creating evenly spaced segments as you go. These thread wraps should be snug enough to form a well-defined segmentation, but not so tight that they twist or deform the hair.

To form true, independent body segments, see Step 1a.

Step 6. When the desired length of extension is ribbed with thread, secure the thread at the last body segment with 2 or 3 half-hitches.

If desired, the thread can be clipped at this point and another extension formed. Or the thread can be left attached if the extension is to be mounted immediately on a hook shank.

Step 7. Using the thumb and finger of the right hand, pinch the needle behind the tailing point. Your fingernails should be directly against the needle shank, as they will help draw the underlying thread wraps off the needle. Simply pulling on the body extension itself may leave these underlying wraps on the needle, causing the body to unravel.

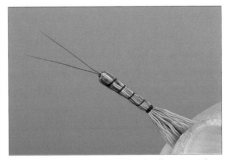

Step 8. Carefully draw the body extension off the needle. Put a drop of head cement or CA glue at the rear of the body to help secure the tailing wraps.

To improve the durability of the finished fly, the body extension can be given a light coat of spray fixative or flexible glue.

The extension can now be lashed to a hook shank.

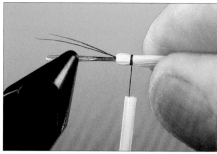

Step 1a. To create true body segments, draw the hair along the needle toward the point as described in Step 5; it should form a smooth, even capsule around the needle shank. Hold it in position with the right hand.

With the left hand, take two firm wraps of thread, one atop the other, to create the first body segment.

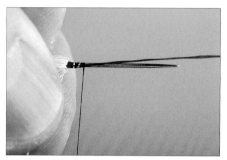

Step 1b. Draw the hair back toward the vise jaws. Advance the tying thread down the needle the distance of one body segment.

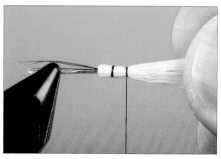

Step 1c. Fold the hair forward toward the needle point, again forming a smooth capsule. Form a second body segment as you did in Step 5a.

Repeat this procedure, forming the desired number of body segments.

Proceed to Step 6.

Step 2a. Autti's approach is similar to the one shown in the preceding sequences, but there are important differences. In this method, two layers of hair form the body, and thus correspondingly fewer fibers are needed. And because the hair tips form the tails, the fibers must be cut to an exact length to produce tails of the proper proportion.

Cut, clean, and stack a bundle of hair as explained in Step 2. Cut the butts of the hair so that the fibers are equal to twice the length of the body extension plus the tail length. (On larger flies, this may require rather long hair, and bucktail can be used if hollow hair of sufficient length is unavailable.)

Mount the thread as shown in Step 1, and secure the bundle of hair by the very butt ends directly over the mounting wraps.

Spiral the thread up the needle, securing the hair. Stop when you have bound down a length of hair equal to the length of the body extension (not counting the tails), as shown here.

Take 2 or 3 tight thread wraps at this point, and wrap the thread back a short distance, leaving it at the point where you wish to create the first body segment.

Step 2b. Using the right fingers, fold the hair tips over the top of the tied-down hair. Using the technique shown in Steps 1a-1c, create the desired number of body segments.

The last segment should be bound down directly atop the thread wraps initially used to mount the hair.

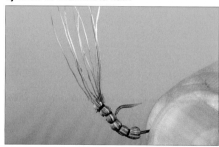

Step 2c. Slide the extension off the needle, and clip off any flared hair butts that may remain from mounting the bundle.

If there are too many hair tips for the tail, clip off the excess until the desired number remain.

Autti uses a scud-style hook for his inverted fly style. Insert the hook point into the front of the body extension, and thread the extension onto the shank for the desired distance. Here, about ⅔ of the extension is threaded; the remaining ⅓ will project beyond the hook bend.

Step 2d. Here is a finished fly tied by Autti. Note that it is designed to float upside-down.

In this inverted style, the wings are of special importance. They are in-line with the hook gap, and overly stiff wing materials, such as hair, can be a significant obstacle in hooking fish. Very flexible wings, like these film wings dressed from stretched plastic, as shown on p. 281, are supple enough to fold back and expose the hook point to a striking fish.

The hackle barbs on the underside of the fly can be trimmed away to form a "V"-shaped notch to help the fly float in the proper orientation.

Method #134:

Betts' Poly Extension

This technique—one of the more interesting applications of poly yarn—was originated by synthetic-materials guru John Betts, who was seeking a practical, effective, good-floating body extension for spinner patterns.

The quantity of poly yarn must be adjusted according to the fly size, and Betts suggests 1 to 1½ plies of poly yarn for larger flies and 1 to ⅓ ply for medium to small flies. Colors of yarn can be mixed for more specific imitations, and using two unmixed plies can produce a body extension with differently colored dorsal and ventral sides.

The following sequence demonstrates how to make a tailed poly extension. Untailed extensions are easily made simply by heating the end of the poly yarn (no needle is required) and rolling the soft material between the fingers as described in Step 4. The extension can then be lashed to a hook.

Step 1. Cut a length of poly yarn, and stretch it tightly to straighten the fibers. With a dubbing needle or small comb, preen the strands so that they are straight and loose.

Cut a piece about 3" long, and trim one end to make the fibers even.

Step 2. Insert a needle, eye first, into the strand. Try to keep the needle centered so that the poly fibers are evenly distributed around the needle. Betts advises beginning

with a larger needle, a #5 sewing needle, for example. Once you get the feel of the technique, smaller needles can be used.

Insert the needle until the point is flush with the end of the poly fibers.

With the left fingers, grip the needle and yarn together, about an inch from the point, and preen the fibers forward so they conform as closely as possible to the needle shank.

Step 3. With a butane lighter in your right hand, bring the side of the flame toward the needle point. Do not touch the yarn with the flame; the mere proximity of the fibers to the heat will begin to melt them.

As the ends of the fibers melt and the tip of the needle becomes visible, move the flame toward the yarn, "following" the fibers as they melt and recede up the needle shank.

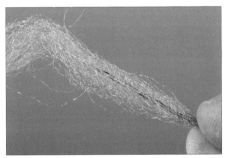

Step 4. When about ¼" to ⅜" of the needle point is exposed, set down the lighter and moisten the pads of the right thumb and forefinger.

Gently roll the softened material between thumb and forefinger to form a cone-shaped "bead" at the end of the poly yarn.

This can be a bit tricky, and a few pointers here might help simplify matters. First, when you begin rolling the softened material between your fingers, don't try to hold the needle stationary and roll the material around the shank. Rather, release the needle and material from your left hand, and roll the melted fibers and the needle together. Second, timing is important. There is a brief window in which the consistency of the melted material is just right for molding. Try to roll it too soon and the material will mash flat; wait too long and the material will harden. Betts recommends about 1½ seconds from the time that the flame is withdrawn to the time the material is rolled—just about as long as it takes to set down the lighter and moisten the fingertips. Lastly, the fingertips need only be moistened. If they are too wet, the material will slide between them rather than roll. Despite how it might appear, the risk of burning the fingertips is really rather low if the instructions are followed.

There's no question that mastering this procedure requires a bit of practice. But each attempt takes only a few seconds, and acquiring the touch really takes less time than might be imagined.

Step 5. When the tapered "bead" is formed, remove the needle.

Insert tailing material, butts first, into the hole in the end of the body extension. Any material can be used, but the butts should be long as they will be bound to the hook shank along with the extension.

Step 6. The extension can now be bound to the hook shank as described in **Method #121: Lashed Extension**, Steps 1-2, p. 204, and the rest of the fly dressed. Betts sometimes uses the excess poly yarn to create a shellback style body as described in **Method #121: Lashed Extension**, Step 2c, p. 204.

Method #135:
Rolled Foam Extension

In this needle-formed foam extension, a single strip of foam is temporarily lashed to a needle to form a segmented body. The tyer doesn't really "roll" the foam; rather, thread torque used in creating the segment draws or rolls the edges of a flat strip of foam around the needle to create a body that is rounded in appearance.

There are a number of variations of this technique that involve different preparations of the foam, different tailing methods, and different ways in which the finished extension is mounted on the hook shank. The main sequence below shows a method devised by tyer and illustrator Richard Bunse. Bunse uses a thin Ethafoam sheet to form not only a tapered body extension, but the body on the hook shank as well. Foam of this type is generally not sold specifically for fly tying, but it is widely used as a packing material for home electronic equipment. The large, thin-walled cells make the material highly buoyant and easily worked. It is manufactured in a variety of thicknesses, Bunse recommends a foam ³⁄₆₄" thick for hook sizes 18 and 20; ¹⁄₁₆" foam

for sizes 16 and 14; and ³⁄₃₂" foam for size 12 and larger. Some sheet foams sold for tying are thin enough to form the tapered mayfly bodies shown in the main sequence; most of them can easily form the larger body shown in the alternate sequence.

The alternate steps also show variations in tailing and mounting the foam extension.

In addition to the tailing procedures shown in both the main and alternate sequences, this body style can be tailed using the approach shown in **Method #136: Folded Foam Extension**, Steps 1a-3a, p. 222.

Step 1. The foam is first cut to the diamond shape pictured here. The length of the diamond is approximately 3 times the total hook length, and one hook-length wide. The flat ends of the diamond are about ½ to ¾ the hook gap.

Since Ethafoam is milky white it is ordinarily tinted at this point—see "Shaping and Coloring Foam," p. 190.

Step 1a. Eventually, slits must be cut in the foam to accommodate the wing. The slits can be cut now, or later, as shown in Step 13.

To form them now, use a pair of scissors to cut a crosswise slit on each side of the foam strip at its widest point. Each slit should be cut about ⅓ of the way through the foam strip.

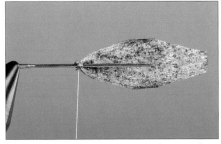

Step 2. Mount a needle by the eye in a vise; Bunse prefers a long, thin beading needle for this technique.

Using moderate tension, mount the tying thread at the center of the needle.

Bind in one tip of the foam over the thread-mounting wraps. Note that a small bump of foam is formed at the rear of the fly.

Step 3. Mount the desired number of tail fibers (two are used here) directly over the thread wraps used to affix the foam. The tails can be split at this point, or mounted as a bundle and divided when the fly is complete.

Do not trim the tail butts.

Step 4. Fold the foam back toward the vise jaws, and advance the tying thread toward the needle point, binding the tailing fibers to the needle under light pressure. The distance the tying thread is advanced determines the width of the first body segment formed.

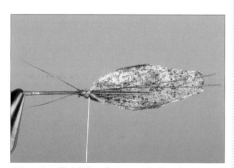

Step 5. Fold the foam strip back toward the needle point, and take two firm thread wraps around the foam to create the first body segment. Notice how the edges of the foam roll together to give the body a rounded appearance.

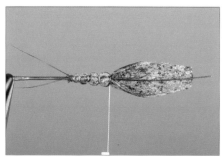

Step 6. Repeat Steps 4-5 until the desired number of body segments are formed.

When the last segment is created, secure the tying thread with a couple of half-hitches.

Step 7. Clip the tying thread.

Pinch the needle behind the rear of the extension and push the foam from the needle shank. Do not grasp the foam and pull or the body may be damaged.

Step 8. Since Bunse's particular dressing of the remainder of the fly is not well-suited to a hackled pattern, he uses arc wings for additional floatation and balance. The deer-hair wing shown here can be tied as explained in **Method #27: Hollow-hair Arc Wing**, p. 274. Other types of arc wings can also be used, as shown in **Method #28: Solid-fiber Arc Wing**, p. 276; **Method #29: Gathered-hackle Arc Wing**, p. 277; and **Method #30: Clipped-hackle Arc Wing**, p. 278.

When the wings are mounted, position the tying thread behind the wings a distance equal to the width of one body segment. Insert the hook point through the center of the foam strip, just ahead of the last body segment created on the needle.

(Note that the foam extension can be mounted in other ways, see Step 4a.)

Step 9. Tightly lash the foam extension to the hook shank. The tying thread should bind the foam directly over the half-hitched thread that secures the frontmost segment on the extension.

Step 10. Draw the foam rearward and advance the tying thread to the rear base of the wings, binding down the butts of the tailing fibers as you go.

Step 11. Fold the foam strip around the sides of the hook shank so that the edges of the foam meet atop the shank.

Take 2 or 3 tight turns of thread to form a body segment directly behind the wing.

Step 12. When this segment is formed, draw the tying thread forward on the near side of the shank so that it is ahead of the wing.

Step 13. Take one tight turn of tying thread ahead of the wing.

Bring the thread to the near side of the shank, then back behind the wing, forming a crisscross wrap (visible at the point of the scissors in the photo) on the near side of the shank.

Then bring the thread to the front of the wings and take several tight wraps to secure the foam ahead of the wings. Note that in doing so, you can create one additional body segment at the head of the fly, as shown here.

If slits in the foam were not cut in Step 1a on p. 219, they must be cut now, since the edges of the foam that are rolled to the top of the shank compress the wing into a bundle. Use a pair of scissors, as shown here, to cut a small vertical slit in the foam on each side of the wing base. Be careful in cutting this slit not to cut the crisscross wrap of thread on the side of the body.

Step 14. After the slit is cut, tie off the thread at the head of the fly and clip it.

Fan the wing fibers downward into the slits to restore the arc-wing shape, as shown here from the front.

Step 15. If necessary, preen the tail fibers to the desired angle. Apply a drop of head cement over the rearmost thread wraps to secure them and hold the tail fibers in position.

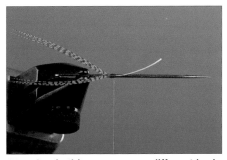

Step 2a. In this sequence, a different body and tail style are used.

Secure the thread to the shank as described in Step 2.

Affix the tail fibers—here, wood duck barbs left on the feather stem—directly over the thread-mounting wraps.

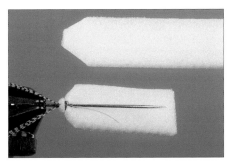

Step 3a. Here, a wider, untapered strip of foam will be used to form a larger body. The foam is tapered abruptly at the tip to facilitate mounting, as shown.

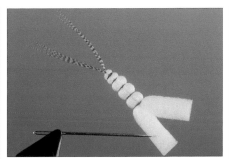

Step 4a. The body is formed as described in Steps 4-7.

In addition to the mounting method shown in the main sequence, there are a couple of other ways to handle a rolled-foam extension.

It can be lashed to the hook shank and the excess material trimmed away as explained in **Method #121: Lashed Extension**, p. 204. The remainder of the body is typically formed from dubbing. Using this approach on mayfly patterns allows almost any wing and hackle style to be used on the fly.

Or the unsegmented foam tag at the front of the body extension can be split lengthwise with a scissors, as shown here, and affixed to the hook as shown in **Method #136: Folded Foam Extension**, Steps 7-8, p. 222. On mayfly patterns, this mounting approach allows the use of almost any upright wing style in conjunction with a parachute hackle.

Method #136:
Folded Foam Extension

Folded foam techniques are among the most versatile of all needle-formed extensions. They can be used on larger flies such as adult stoneflies and grasshoppers (shown in the main sequence below); to form tapered, tailed mayfly body extensions (shown in the alternate sequence); and even slender, untapered adult damselfly bodies. Almost any foam is suitable with this technique.

Step 1. Mount a needle in the vise as shown. To form an adult stonefly body, cut a strip of foam about 4" long, ½" wide, and ¼" in thickness. Naturally, these dimensions can be varied for fly size, but to produce a rounded, symmetrical extension, the foam should be about twice as wide as it is thick. That is, when the foam is doubled over, it will be approximately square in cross-section.

Push the needle point through the very center of the foam, as shown in this top view. Mount the tying thread on the needle,

just ahead of the foam, with firm, but not excessive, tension.

Slide the foam forward until it touches the rearmost thread wrap. Position the tying thread so that the distance from the rear edge of the foam to the tying thread is equal to the desired width of the body segment.

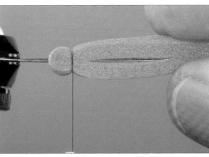

Step 2. Fold both halves of the foam forward, sandwiching the needle between them, as shown here from the top.

Take a loose wrap of tying thread around the foam. When a full wrap is complete, apply pressure to the thread to collapse the foam evenly and form the first body segment. Take 3 or 4 firm wraps, directly atop one another, to help secure the segment further.

Tyer Gary Warren, who first showed us this technique, now secures the segment with a couple of half-hitches. Though not strictly necessary, these knots improve the durability of the extension.

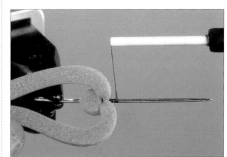

Step 3. Fold the halves of the foam back toward the vise jaws and hold them in place with the left hand as shown in this top view. Advance the tying thread toward the point of the needle a distance equal to the width of the first body segment. Again, these wraps should not be excessively tight.

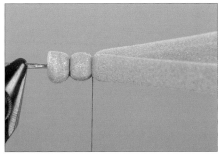

Step 4. Fold the foam forward and form another body segment as described in Step 2.

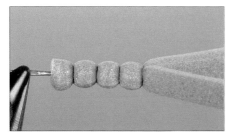

Step 5. Repeat Steps 2-4 until the desired number of segments have been created. When the last segment is finished, secure the thread at the last segmentation point with 3 or 4 half-hitches. Clip the thread.
Do not clip the tags of foam.

Step 6. Using thumb and forefinger, pinch the needle behind the rear of the body, and carefully slide the body extension off the needle. If any loose thread projects from the rear end of the extension, simply clip it off. Apply a drop of head cement to thread wraps that form each segment.

The body can be lashed to a hook as described in **Method #121: Lashed Extension**, Steps 1-2, p. 204. Or it can be mounted on the shank to create additional body segments as described in the optional steps below.

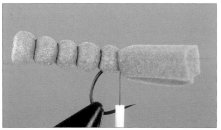

Step 7. Mount the tying thread on a hook shank, and position it at the rearmost point of the body. Fold the two halves of the foam around the hook, sandwiching the shank between them. The foam should be positioned so that the distance between the last segmentation wrap formed on the needle and the tying thread is equal to the width of one body segment.

Form a body segment as described in Step 2. These wraps will secure the extension to the shank.

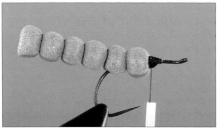

Step 8. Continue forming segments until the desired length of shank is covered. When the last segment is complete, trim the foam, and bind down the excess.

Step 1a. To form a tailed mayfly body, cut a strip of foam into the "bow-tie" shape shown here.

Mount the foam and tying thread as described in Step 1.

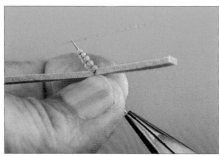

Step 2a. In tapered bodies, or thin bodies in which it is possible to bind down the foam by the very tip and create a small foam bump at the rear of the body, tails can be formed using the tail-mounting technique shown in **Method #135: Rolled Foam Extension**, Steps 2-3, p. 219.

The approach shown here, however, can be used with bodies of any size.

Using the procedure shown in the main sequence, form the body extension. Note for this mayfly body, the segments gradually increase in size.

When the extension is complete and thread half-hitched, remove the needle from the vise. Insert the butts of the desired tailing material through the eye of the needle; note the butts project only a short distance beyond the eye.

Pinch the front of the extension tightly; grip the point of the needle in a pair of pliers.

Step 3a. Draw the needle through the body, threading the tailing fibers down the inside of the extension.

When the extension is mounted, make certain to bind the tail butts tightly to the shank. The tail fibers can be preened to the desired position, and affixed with a drop of head cement or CA glue.

Method #137:
Dubbing Shell Extension

This technique came to us from Oregon tyer Bill Black. It is extremely simple and fast, produces lifelike bodies (with or without tails) of reasonable durability, and unlike many other extended body methods, is quite well-suited to smaller flies. Black's technique is demonstrated in the main sequence below.

We discovered a second version (presented in the alternate sequence) in the work of Swedish tyer Tomas Olsson; this variation is just as easy, but any tailing material must be added afterward. Because this alternate method uses no thread foundation on the needle, the body extension is more easily removed, and thus the technique lends itself nicely to creating longer body extensions, such as those used on adult damselflies. If sewing needles prove too thin to form a body of sufficient diameter, a steel or aluminum knitting needle can be used.

Both techniques rely on an adhesive to form a matrix for the dubbing. When removed from the needle, the finished body is a light, hollow shell of dubbing which can be lashed to a hook shank. A variety of adhesives can be used. CA glue dries quickly and yields a body that is useable within minutes. However, the finished body is quite rigid, and CA glue sets so rapidly that the body must be dressed quickly or it will become permanently affixed to the needle. Silicone- or vinyl-based glues give a longer working time and produce a more flexible body, but the extension must be allowed to dry before it is mounted on a hook. Most silicone or vinyl glues are too viscous as they come from the tube and must be thinned—usually with acetone—to an almost watery consistency. Whatever the adhesive, a small jar of the appropriate solvent should be kept handy. In the event that some adhesive makes its way onto tying tools, they should be wiped down immediately with solvent.

Finally, not all dubbings are equally suited to this method. The most satisfactory results are obtained with long-fibered, very finely textured synthetic dubbings.

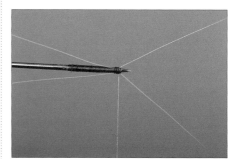

Step 1. Secure a needle in the vise as shown. Mount the tying thread on the needle shank; the distance from the needle point should be about 1½ times the desired length of the finished body extension. Lay a smooth, gapless foundation of thread almost to the point of the needle.

If tails are required, select a tailing material, and lash one fiber to each side of the needle. Crisscross wraps can be used to splay the tails. If three tails are used, lash the third fiber to the top of the shank. Or you can use any of the methods for creating divided, triple, or fan tails described in Chapter 8: "Tails and Trailing Shucks," except those techniques that employ a dubbing ball to divide the tails. If desired, tails can be omitted at this step and added later. The procedure for doing so is described in Step 5a.

Position the tying thread at the rearmost thread wrap.

Step 2. Using any of the direct dubbing methods, apply dubbing to the thread. Dub a length of tying thread sufficient to cover the entire length of the thread foundation on the needle.

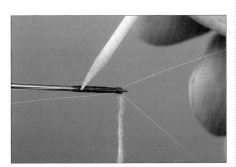

Step 3. Apply a drop of adhesive to the thread foundation on the needle. Use a toothpick to spread the adhesive evenly up, down, and around the foundation. Make certain to cover all thread wraps used for tailing. You want to use enough adhesive to saturate the thread foundation, but not so much that drops of glue begin to form on the underside of the needle.

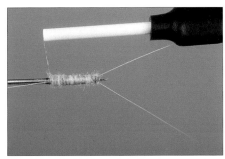

Step 4. Wait a few moments for the adhesive to set just a bit. With CA glue, this may take only a few seconds; with silicone or vinyl glues, it takes a bit longer.

Then with a firm, but not excessively tight thread pressure, dub the body over the thread foundation.

When the end of the body extension is reached, quickly secure the tying thread with a couple of half-hitches.

Step 5. Immediately remove the body extension from the needle. This is best accomplished with a pair of flat-jawed, needle-nose pliers. With the pliers, grip the needle shank (not the body extension itself) ahead of the body extension. Push the pliers toward the needle point. The sides of plier jaws will butt up against the base of the body and force it from the needle.

Allow the extension to dry.

Step 6. If desired, the body can shaped while the adhesive is still workable, forming, as we've done here, an upswept extension for a mayfly body.

If desired, a drop of head cement can be applied at the base of the tail fibers to seal the end of the capsule-like extension.

The finished extension can now be lashed to a hook shank as described in **Method #121: Lashed Extension**, Steps 1-2, p. 204.

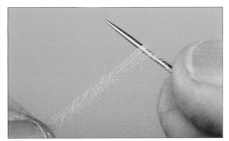

Step 1a. To form an extension with no thread foundation (to which tails may be added later), grip the eye of the needle in the right thumb and forefinger. Take a pinch of dubbing in the left fingers and tease out a sparse, narrow skein of material. Trap the end of the skein in the right fingers, pinching it against the needle shank.

Using the right fingers, roll the needle slowly, in one direction only, drawing more dubbing from the left fingers onto the needle shank. Try to keep the skein of dubbing coming from the left fingers relatively sparse and narrow for best control of the body shape. As you twirl the needle, work the dubbing up the needle shank a distance of about 1½ times the length of the finished body extension.

If a thicker body is desired, continue rolling the needle, reversing the direction of the dubbing, and applying more material toward the needle point. By working up and down the needle shank, you can dub a nicely tapered body.

Step 2a. When the body has the desired thickness, draw the needle away from the dubbing in the left hand. Use your fingers to roll any stray fibers of dubbing around the needle shank. You should now have a smooth, even layer of dubbing around the needle.

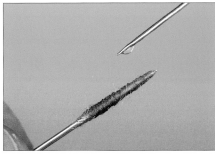

Step 3a. There are two options here. You can dip the needle momentarily into a jar of adhesive, making sure that all the dubbing is coated with glue. Wipe off any drips of adhesive against the lip of the jar.

Or you can use a toothpick to apply drops of glue to the dubbing. You must ensure, however, that the dubbing is completely saturated with adhesive.

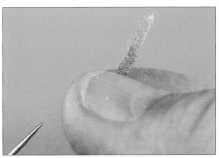

Step 4a. If desired, the body can be smoothed by rolling it gently between the fingertips. If a rougher-textured body is desired, omit this rolling.

Immediately pull the body extension from the needle. Since there is no thread foundation, this can be accomplished simply by using your fingers, or you can use a pair of pliers as described in Step 5.

The body can be shaped, if desired, as explained in Step 6.

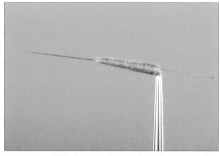

Step 5a. If tails are desired, select a material long enough to project completely through the dubbed shell. When the extension is mounted on the hook shank, the thread wraps will secure the tail butts as well.

Trim the front end of the shell so that the body extension is about 1/16" longer than the desired length. Insert the tailing material, butt first, through the small hole at the rear end of the dubbed shell. If fibers of dubbing obscure the hole, use a pair of scissors to snip off the very end of the body so that the hole is clear.

Step 6a. The body can be lashed to a hook shank as described in **Method #121: Lashed Extension**, Steps 1-2, p. 204.

Or, as shown here, you can thread the hook point a short distance through the hollow extension—a bit like you'd thread a worm on a hook—and work the shell around the shank up to the straight portion of the hook shank. You may need to readjust the tails before lashing the body down.

Once the body extension is attached to the hook shank, apply a small drop of glue at the rear tip of the extension to help secure the tail fibers and hold them in position.

Method #138:
Ribbed Tubing Extension

Plastic and vinyl tubings, such as the Larva Lace used in the following sequence, can be used to make durable, buoyant needle-formed extensions. (Such tubing can also be used to form lashed extensions as explained in **Method #124: Tubing Extension**, p. 206.) The technique is both simple and versatile, and some of the many possible variations are presented in the alternate sequence.

Selecting a needle with the proper diameter can make this technique a bit easier. When the tailing fibers are passed through the tubing, and the tubing slipped on the needle, the fit should be tight enough so that the tubing

does not spin easily around the needle shank.

Since plastic and vinyl tubings are usually translucent, dark-colored tailing materials, such as the moose hair used here, will be visible through the extension, particularly if the tubing is a lighter color. This can produce a lifelike effect in the body, but if a purer translucence is desired, use tailing fibers that are light in color or that match the tubing color. When the body is completed, the finished tails can be colored with a marker if desired.

Lastly, if the body is not dubbed, thread wraps will be visible at the tailing point of the body extension. You may wish to use a thread color that matches the color of the tubing.

The main sequence shows the basic technique for ribbing the tubing with tying thread. The alternate steps show various dressing options possible with this method.

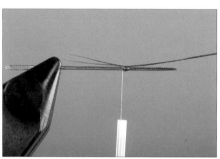

Step 1. Mount a needle in the vise as shown, and attach the tying thread on the shank. The distance from the thread-mounting point to the point of the needle should be about 1½ times the desired length of the body extension.

Form a foundation with 4 or 5 tight wraps of tying thread.

Select a tailing material. Almost any material can be used, but the fibers must be long enough to extend about ½" beyond the needle point. Secure the fibers over the thread foundation only (that is, take no thread wraps against the bare needle shank). You can use any of the methods for creating divided, triple, or fan tails described in Chapter 8: "Tails and Trailing Shucks," except those techniques that employ a dubbing ball to divide the tails. However, it is really simplest to mount the tail fibers as a bundle. This method is faster, and the tails can be divided at a later point in the tying procedure to form split, triple, or fan tails.

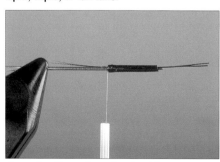

Step 2. Cut a length of tubing that will reach from the tail-mounting point to the point of the needle.

Slip the tubing first over the butts of the tailing fibers, and then over the shank of the needle. Position the end of the tubing directly over the rearmost thread wrap used to mount the tails.

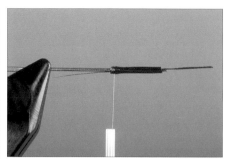

Step 3. Bind the end of the tubing over the tail-mounting wraps. The tubing can be slippery, and thread pressure may simply cause it to spin around the needle. If this is the case, take a loose turn of tying thread near the end of the tubing. Hold the tubing stationary with the right hand, and pull downward on the bobbin with the left hand. The thread pressure will pinch the tubing to the shank. Maintain tension on the thread, and take additional wraps. After a few turns of thread, the tubing will no longer slip.

Using 5 or 6 tight wraps of thread, bind down the very end of the tubing. Again, take care to wrap around the tubing only; do not place any wraps around the bare needle shank.

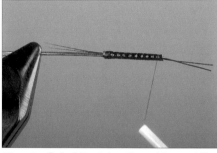

Step 4. Spiral the tying thread toward the point of the needle. Exert just enough thread pressure to compress the tubing slightly, giving the extension a segmented appearance.

Spiral the thread down the entire length of the tubing. Keep tension on the bobbin at all times. If pressure is relaxed, the springiness of the tubing will push outward against the thread and the compressed body segments will disappear.

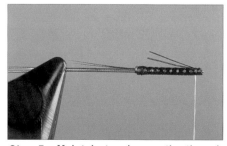

Step 5. Maintain tension on the thread. Fold the butts of the tailing material toward the rear of the extension. Bind them down against the tubing. Securing the butts in this way will lock the tails in position. Without these wraps, the tailing fibers can shift position. This is really a temporary measure. When the extension is mounted, the tailing butts will be cut away when the excess tubing is trimmed.

When the tail butts are tied down, secure the tying thread with a few half-hitches, and clip it.

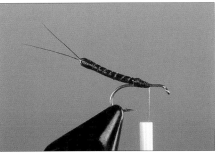

Step 6. Pinch the extension at the tailing point and carefully slide it from the needle.

Arrange the tails in the desired configuration, and apply a drop of head cement to the rear of the body to help lock the tail fibers in position and secure the thread wraps. The cement also seals off the end of the tubing, creating a hollow capsule of air for buoyancy.

The extension can now be lashed to a hook shank as described in **Method #121: Lashed Extension**, Steps 1-2, p. 204. Note that the when the extension is mounted, the excess tubing and tailing butts will be clipped away. The tailing material will be secured by the thread wraps used to mount the extension.

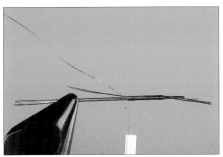

Step 1a. Two variations of the method are shown here. If you wish to rib the extension with a thread different in color from the tying thread, or you wish to use a different material such as tinsel or wire, mount the ribbing material along with tailing fibers. Like the tailing fibers, the rib material should extend all the way through the tubing.

Then, you can add color to the body inside the tubing with tying thread. After the tails are mounted, lay a thread foundation along the needle shank. The foundation need not extend to the needle point, but rather, should be only as long as the finished extension. Use firm, but not excessively tight, wraps; wrap the thread first toward the needle point, then reverse direction and return the thread to the tailing point.

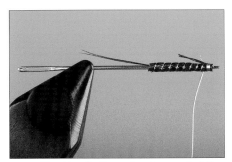

Step 1b. To rib the extension, spiral the ribbing material down the body as described in Step 4. Use the rib material to

bind down the tail butts as described in Step 5. This may produce a bulky tie-down if tinsel or wire is used, but it doesn't matter since this part of the tubing will be cut away as excess when the extension is mounted on a hook.

The extension can be slipped from the needle and mounted as shown in Step 6.

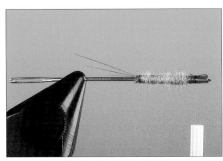

Step 2a. If desired, the tubing can be dubbed to produce a more conventional extended body that is still quite durable and buoyant.

Mount the tails and tubing as shown in Steps 1-3.

Using a direct dubbing method, spin the dubbing material on the thread and simply wrap the thread down the tubing. Dub only a length of tubing equal to the desired length of the finished extension.

If a separate ribbing material has been used, spiral the ribbing over the dubbing, and tie off the rib material with the tying thread.

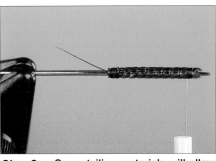

Step 3a. Some tailing materials will allow for the creation of an overbody on the extension. For the material to be suitable, however, the tail fibers must be long enough to fold back over the entire extension.

To create the overbody, dress the extension as shown in Steps 1-3.

Fold the butts of the tailing material back along the top of the tubing toward the tail. Secure them with a few wraps of thread at the tailing point, then spiral the thread toward the point of the needle, simultaneously lashing down the overbody and segmenting the tubing.

When the tying thread reaches the end of the tubing, secure with a couple of half-hitches and trim the excess tail butts at the rear of the extension.

Note that if a separate ribbing material has been tied in as described in Step 1a, this type of overbody can be fashioned on a dubbed extension.

Method #139:
Woven Extended Body

All of the techniques presented under the section "Woven Bodies," p. 195, can also be employed to tie body extensions by using a needle as a temporary core. Knotting techniques, however, work particularly well, and most tyers find these easier to execute.

Poly yarn is perhaps the best choice of weaving materials for floating flies, though other materials can certainly be used. Both the thickness of the needle and the density of the weaving strands can be varied to produce different body diameters. Thick needles and yarns will produce big, blocky bodies for grasshoppers and adult stoneflies. Thin needles and sparse weaving strands, composed of only a few dozen filaments each, will give thin extensions for mayflies or damsels. Woven extensions are a bit time consuming, but they are enormously durable and can produce a wide variety of color patterns and markings. Single-color bodies, of course, can be fashioned by weaving strands of the same color.

The weaving techniques for body extensions are identical to those for woven bodies, though the initial mounting of materials differs slightly and is presented below.

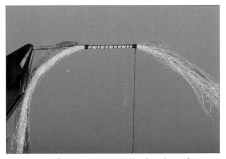

Step 1. Secure a needle in the vise as shown. Mount the tying thread near the point of the needle. Spiral a thread foundation along the shank; the foundation should be as long as the finished body extension.

If tails are to be used, they should be mounted according to the instructions presented above in **Method #137: Dubbing Shell Extension**, Step 1, p. 222.

The weaving material, in this case poly yarn, should be mounted directly over the rearmost thread wraps. The particular placement of the strands during mounting depends upon the weaving method selected. Regardless of method, however, the strands should be mounted so that the tags of material extend about 1" beyond the point of the needle.

Secure the strands tightly, and bind down the tags of material down the length of the needle shank. Note the overhang of material at the needle point. These "core strands" should not be trimmed. Secure the tying thread with a few half-hitches.

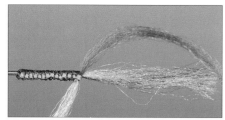

Step 2. Clip off the tying thread.

Weave the body according to the instructions provided for the method selected.

When the desired length of body is completed, you have two options. The tying thread can be remounted, and all strands—both core strands and weaving strands—can be tied off at the front of the extension. Secure the thread with a few half-hitches, and the extension can be slipped from the needle and set aside without unraveling. But again, do not clip any tags of material.

If the extension is to be bound to a hook immediately, you can tightly pinch all the strands of material at the front of the extension. The extension can then be slipped from the needle and mounted directly on a hook shank.

In either case, it is vital when mounting the extension that all strands—both core strands and weaving strands—be affixed securely to the hook shank with tying thread.

Once attached to the hook, the excess material can be clipped and the butts bound down. Or the core strands can be bound down along a length of hook shank, and the weaving strands used to continue weaving a body on the hook shank itself.

Bundled-fiber Extensions

Extended bodies can be tied from bundles of natural or synthetic fibers, primarily animal hair and yarn. This style of extension is quite versatile: a material can be used to tie only the body extension or to dress the entire fly body; it can be tied with or without a core; and combinations of materials can produce two-color bodies. Deer hair tied in this fashion is perhaps the most widespread and popular of all extended body types; the material is easy to handle and gives buoyancy to the fly.

Method #140:
Bundled-fiber Extension

The taper of natural hair lends itself well to forming a tapered body extension for mayfly patterns using this technique. Since the fiber bundle must provide a certain resistance to thread pressure, however, this method is most commonly used on larger dry flies that incorporate more substantial bundles of material. Smaller extensions of this type are generally dressed using **Method #133: Needle-formed Fiber Extension**, p. 216. By the same token, while it is certainly possible to dress bulkier extensions for terrestrial or adult stonefly patterns using the approach described here, such bodies are ordinarily tied using **Method #141: Reverse-tied Bundle Extension**, p. 227, which creates larger-diameter bodies without using an excessive amount of material.

The main sequence below illustrates the construction of a typical deer-hair extension. The alternate steps that follow are not intended to illustrate a single, continuous tying method, but rather to demonstrate some of the many variations in dressing style or technique that can be employed at specific stages of the tying procedure.

Step 1. Lay a base of tying thread on the portion of the hook shank that will be covered by the extended-body materials. The thread wrap nearest the hook eye will determine where the front end of the body extension will be located. Once the thread base is laid, it is important that the tying thread be positioned at the front edge of this foundation, as the thread location will be used in determining the proper hair length.

Clip, and clean a bundle of deer hair as described in **Method #2: Preparing and Cleaning Hair**, p. 68. The quantity of material depends upon the thickness of the desired body extension and the diameter of the particular hair used, but as a starting point use a bundle of material about 4 to 6 times the diameter of the hook shank.

Align the tips of the hair as explained in **Method #3: Stacking and Aligning Hair**, p. 69.

In this particular method, some of the natural deer-hair tips will be used to form the tail, so it is important that the bundle of hair be bound in at just the right point, as no trimming or adjustment is possible later. To determine the mounting point, position the bundle of hair above the hook shank, with the hair butts pointing toward the hook bend. Adjust the bundle so that the distance between the tips of the hair and the tying thread (located at the front of the thread foundation) is equal to the combined length of the body and tail.

When the hair is adjusted to the proper length, take two slack wraps of thread around the hair butts and proceed to spin the bundle of hair around the hook shank as described in **Method #58: Spinning Hollow Hair**, Steps 4-5, p. 146. The hair can, instead, be mounted using the technique shown in **Method #59: Flaring Hollow Hair**, Steps 1-3, p. 147.

When the hair is securely fastened to the shank, clip the flared butt ends of hair and bind them down with thread.

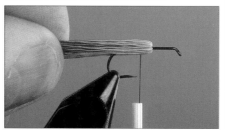

Step 2. The tying thread will now be used to bind the hair together and in so doing create body segments. Position the tying

thread behind the mounting point of the hair a distance equal to the width of the desired body segment. Note in the photo the position of the thread relative to the front of the body.

With the fingers of the left hand, gather the hairs together and preen them toward the hook bend, pulling evenly and gently until the left fingertips are holding the hair bundle by the very tip. Since the tying thread will be in the way, you must work the hairs around the thread so that the bobbin is hanging freely. As you draw the hair back with left hand, pull down slightly on the bobbin with the right hand to hold the tying thread in position. Try to form a smooth capsule over the hook shank, exerting an equal tension on all hairs to create a uniform body extension.

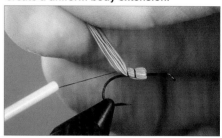

Step 3. Maintaining a consistent pressure on the hair tips, elevate the bundle slightly. Spiral the tying thread back toward the hook bend. Use a firm thread pressure to help secure the body and create the segments, but do not apply excessive tension; overly compressed deer hair will lose its buoyancy. The distance between wraps determines the width of the body segments.

When you reach the rear of the hook, take one wrap of thread around the hair only. In order to make this wrap, you'll need to release the bobbin, and reposition your hand in front of the vise stem.

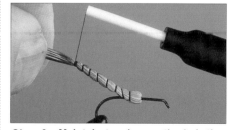

Step 4. Maintain tension on the hair tips with the left hand. Continue spiraling the thread up the hair bundle, creating segments as you go. For each wrap, you'll need to reposition your hand, since the vise stem will not allow continuous wrapping. Again, do not use excessive thread pressure.

When the rearmost point of the body is reached, take 2 or 3 thread wraps directly atop one another. These wraps are located at the base of the tails.

Step 5. Maintain tension on the hair tips, and spiral the thread back down the extension. The thread will make a crisscross

pattern. When the front of the body is reached, continue wrapping the thread onto the hook shank.

Since deer-hair extensions can be fragile, some tyers apply a light coating of spray fixative or flexible cement to the extension. This should be done before any other materials are affixed to the hook. Head cement is sometimes used, but it can penetrate the hairs and reduce buoyancy.

At this point, other components—wings, thorax dubbing, hackle—can be mounted.

Step 6. When the fly is complete, use fine-pointed scissors to trim away some of the deer hair tips from the center of the bundle, leaving intact whatever tips you wish to form the tail. You can clip all but one or two hairs from each side of the body, forming a split tail. You can leave an additional hair in the center for a triple tail. Or, all the tips can be left intact.

When the tail is complete, put a drop of head cement on the rearmost thread wraps to help secure them.

Step 1a. Several variations of the initial setup are possible. Three such options are illustrated here, and three more in the following photo. They can be used individually or in combination.

First, the extended body material can be used to form the entire fly body, as in the Paradrake design. The hair is mounted directly behind the hook eye, and the wing, such as this post-type wing, is then attached. A feather is mounted for parachute hackling (it is omitted here). When the hair is preened back, as described in Step 2, the body fibers must be drawn around either side of this wing post.

Second, while the main sequence illustrates an extension in which the natural deer-hair tips are used to form the tail, it is possible to use a separate tailing material, in this case, fibers of moose hair. If a separate tailing material is used, the clump of deer hair should be trimmed about ⅛" shorter than the length described in Step 1. When the deer hair is preened back as described in Step 2, the tailing material is drawn back along with it and incorporated into the bundle that forms the body. Once the body is formed, the tailing material will extend about ⅛" beyond the deer-hair tips; this differential in length will simplify trim-

ming the deer-hair tips to leave only the moose hair for the tails.

Third, some tyers dress this body extension over a monofilament core, which provides extra rigidity in the extension for simpler tying and greater durability. This core is affixed to the shank as described in **Method #126: Free-standing Core Extension**, Steps 1-2, p. 209. The mono is then clipped to a length about ¹⁄₁₆" shorter than the extended body (excluding tails). Trimming the mono like this will ensure that it remains concealed within the deer-hair extension. When the deer hair is preened back to form the body, the mono is drawn right along with it and is incorporated into the bundle that forms the extension.

Step 2a. This photo illustrates three other variations of the technique.

First, the hair need not be mounted with the tips toward the hook eye as shown in Step 1, but rather can be affixed to the hook in the conventional fashion, as shown above. The thread wraps binding down the hair butts are subsequently covered by other components of the fly, usually thorax dubbing or hackle. The procedure for mounting the hair in this fashion is identical to that described in Step 1, except the hair is reversed from the position shown in that photo.

Second, as shown above, the entire body can be fashioned atop the hook if the hair is stacked on top of the shank rather than spun around it.

Third, two-color bodies can be formed by simply stacking two bundles of material one atop the other. Note as well that materials can be mixed. Dick Talleur, for example, ties a body extension using poly yarn for the underside and deer hair for the top, as shown here.

Method #141:
Reverse-tied Bundle Extension

This technique produces thick body extensions typically used on grasshopper, caterpillar, or adult stonefly imitations. Hollow hairs are the most popular material employed in this method, though poly yarn can certainly be used. However, since the material is doubled over on itself in creating this extension, the length of natural hair can pose a limitation. While deer hair is suitable for mid-size hooks, for larger patterns, tyers often use longer hollow hairs from moose or elk.

Step 1. Lay a thread foundation on the portion of the shank that will be covered by the body. Position the tying thread about 3 thread-wraps behind the front of this foundation.

Clip, and clean a bundle of deer hair as described in **Method #2: Preparing and Cleaning Hair**, p. 68. The quantity of material depends upon the thickness of the desired body extension, but as a starting point use a bundle of material about 6 times the diameter of the hook shank. It is not necessary to stack the hair, but care should be taken to remove excessively short hairs, as they may not be sufficiently long to double over. Clip the butts of the hair even.

Secure the hair to the shank. You can allow the hair to spin around the shank, as we've done here, so that the resulting body capsule will be formed around the shank. Or you can stack the hair on the top of the shank only, in which case the body capsule will sit atop the hook shank.

When the hair is secure, trim the flared butts and bind them down completely with thread, as shown.

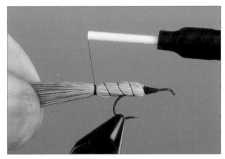

Step 2. Preen the hair back and grasp the bundle by the tip.

Spiral the tying thread back to the rearmost body point as described above in **Method #140: Bundled-fiber Extension**, Steps 3-5, p. 226. Take 3 or 4 very tight turns of thread at the rearmost point of the body.

Step 3. Reverse the direction of thread wrapping and spiral it forward to the front of the body.

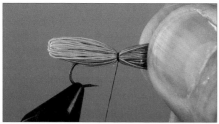

Step 4. With the right fingertips, draw the hair forward over the extension and the hook shank, finally pinching the bundle of hair around the hook shank behind the eye. You will need to work the hair past the tying thread so that the bobbin remains hanging freely. Try to form a smooth, even capsule of hair.

With the left hand, take two wraps of tying thread around the hair, and pull the thread tight.

Step 5. Take additional thread wraps to secure the hair. Trim the excess hair and bind down the butts.

Step 6. To further secure the hair and create segments, once again spiral the tying thread to the rear of the extension, and then back again.

If desired, the body extension can be reinforced with spray fixative or flexible cement. The remainder of the fly can now be dressed.

Braided Extensions

Braiding materials to produce extended bodies is a technique that has been, at best, only partially explored by tyers. But such extensions have advantages. Materials such as ostrich, marabou, and peacock herls can be braided to produce a body that is more compact and durable than a simple lashed extension tied of individual strands of these materials. The tightness of the braid can be varied—tighter to produce a more rigid body, looser for a more flexible one. Variegated patterns can be created by using strands of different colors, and different types of materials can be braided together to produce unusual textures or to enhance the durability of more fragile strands. And finally, the braiding technique is really quite simple.

The braided extensions we have seen, such as in the work of English tyer Peter Gathercole, are primarily used for bodies on damselfly nymphs and are fashioned from herls. But there

is no reason that other materials—rubber leg material, latex strips, floss, microchenilles, Antron, long hairs (especially synthetics), and so forth—could not be used. Braided extension for mayfly duns and adult damsels could be made from braided poly yarn.

Method #142:
Braided Extension

We're using ostrich herl here to braid a body extension for a damselfly nymph. With very thin, fragile materials—marabou herl, for instance—a thicker and more durable body can be created by braiding groups of strands rather than individual ones. Three colors are used here to simplify the braiding instructions. Though a needle is used here, this is not, technically speaking, a needle-formed extension, since the needle is used primarily as an anchor for the materials rather than a temporary core for the entire body.

Step 1. Mount a very fine needle in the vise as shown. Mount the tying thread near the point of the needle, and lay a thread foundation of 5 or 6 firm wraps.

Tie in the herl, letting the tips extend beyond the thread wraps to form tails of the desired length. It is important that the herl be mounted directly atop the thread foundation, not against the bare needle shank. If the mounting wraps do not lie atop the thread foundation, the wraps will unravel when the extension is slipped from the needle.

Step 1a. Thicker, sturdier materials, like the rubber leg material shown here, need not be bound to a needle. Simply group the strands together and tie an overhand knot in the material. Tighten it firmly. If necessary, clip the tails to length.

The knot can now be clamped in a vise jaws or, as shown here, pierced with a needle held vertically in the vise.

Step 2. When the tails are mounted, secure the tying thread with a few half-hitches or a whip-finish, and clip it. It is crucial to apply a small drop of head cement all around the tailing wraps; without cement, these wraps will unravel when the extension is removed from the needle.

Turn the vise so that the needle is pointing directly at you. Separate the strands. Note that the olive strand is on the left, white in the center, black on the right.

Step 3. Begin by passing the left strand (olive) over the middle strand (white).

Step 4. Now pass the right strand (black) over the middle strand (olive).

Step 5. Repeat Steps 3-4, alternately passing the right-hand strand over the middle strand, and then the left-hand strand over the middle strand.

Step 6. When the extension is braided to the desired length, pinch the braid in the right fingers. With the left fingers, force the extension off the needle point by pushing against the tailing wraps.

The extension can be mounted on a hook as described in **Method #121: Lashed Extension**, Steps 1-2, p. 204.

CHAPTER 11

Wingcases and Overbodies

Though wingcases and overbodies are dressed on different parts of the hook shank, both are tied to cover or partially cover another component of the fly, and thus the techniques used to fashion them are often similar.

Wingcases are tied over the thorax of a nymph pattern to represent the hard, rather smooth, often glossy immature wings of the natural insect. To the angler's eye at least, wingcases, or "wingpads" as they are sometimes called, are one of the more conspicuous features of nymphs and play a correspondingly important role in their representation. On larger patterns such as stonefly nymphs, wingcases are often tied to imitate the size, shape, color, and number of cases of the natural, often with strikingly realistic results.

"Overbody" is a somewhat less precise term, used in various ways by different tyers. The word is sometimes used to designate a body material that is applied over a foundation on the hook shank; in this usage, "overbody" is distinguished from "underbody." It is also occasionally used to specify materials that are tied or distributed downwing style over the primary body material. For our purposes here, "overbodies" are formed from materials lashed over the top, bottom, or sides of the primary body material to form a shell-like covering or sheath. Some types of overbodies, such as shellbacks on scud or shrimp patterns, are intended to represent an anatomical feature of the insect. But more often an overbody material is applied to create a contrast in color or texture on the abdomen of the fly, giving the pattern, for instance, a more realistic separation of color on the dorsal and ventral sides, or producing a lateral line. Overbodies are perhaps more typically tied on subsurface patterns, but they can be tied on dry flies as well.

Wingcases

As used in this chapter, the term "wingcases" is used to designate a component tied over the thorax of a nymph pattern and is distinguished from "wing buds" or "float pods" that represent the larger, more conspicuous thoracic distension or emerging wings of a hatching insect—imitations of which are presented in "Emerger Wings, Wing Buds, and Float Pods," p. 331. The distinction is admittedly a fine one, and probably means more to the tyer than to the insect or the fish.

Because wingcases are such prominent features on nymphs, tyers have shown great ingenuity in their construction and have enlisted a wide range of materials to represent them. Strips of flat material—segments of feather barbs; whole lacquered feathers; raffia; biots; and synthetics such as Swiss Straw, latex, wing films, and foam—can be folded over the thorax or cut to shape to form wingcases. Bundled fibers such as natural or synthetic hair, clumps of feather barbs, yarns, and colored Mylars such as Krystal Flash and Flashabou can be drawn over the thorax for the same purpose. Even epoxy and head cement can be used to represent wingcases.

Because wingcase materials are often pulled or drawn over the top of the thorax, they present a vulnerable surface to toothy jaws, and many tyers apply a coat of head cement or flexible cement to the finished wingcase to add durability.

The methods shown in the following section can be used for virtually any nymph except those constructed with a bead thorax. Techniques for mounting wingcases on these patterns required a slightly more specialized approach that is presented in **Method #101: Bead Thorax**, p. 187.

Method #1:

Folded-strip Wingcase

This is probably the most common technique for forming wingcases, since a strip of material already approximates the flat, smooth surface of a wingcase. Such materials generally tie with little bulk at the head of the fly and are relatively simple to dress. As indicated earlier, many materials of this type are available to the tyer and provide a wide range of textures and colors. Sections of feather barbs and whole feathers—particularly body and flank feathers from game birds, or hen neck and saddle hackles—can make particularly attractive mottled or figured wingcases. Whole feathers should first be treated with a flexible cement to glue the barbs together, as explained in **Method #50: Feather-tip Flatwing**, p. 299, which simplifies handling and improves durability. Feathers reinforced with a mesh backing (see **Method #45: Mesh-backed Feather Wings**, p. 294) make excellent wingcase material as well. On very small nymphs, a turkey biot can be used for the wingcase.

A section of barbs cut from a feather, such as the turkey tail used in the following demonstration, can profit from reinforcement, and most tyers treat such materials with a thin coat of adhesive. A single strip of barbs or a portion of a whole feather can be reinforced by smearing flexible cement over the front and back surfaces. If a larger number of nymphs are to be tied, the most efficient process is to mist an entire feather, on both sides, with a spray fixative, and reserve the feather exclusively for tying wingcases.

The main sequence that follows presents the basic method for forming a simple wingcase by drawing a flat strip of any material over the thorax of the fly. The alternate steps show some common variations on the basic technique—folding rather than drawing the wingcase, and creating a double-folded wingcase.

The complete alternate sequence shows a method for forming a split wingcase.

Step 1. All components that lie behind the thorax of the fly are first dressed. Lay a thread foundation up to the rear of the hook eye, and return the thread to the front of the abdomen.

Cut a strip of wingcase material of the desired width. The preferred width varies with the specific pattern and the individual tyer. But as a general rule, making the wingcase as wide as the hook gap is a serviceable guideline. When using a section of barbs, the wingcase strip can be formed by using a pair of dividers, as shown in the photograph on p. 244, which sizes and separates the strip simultaneously.

Step 2. Position the wingcase material lengthwise atop the hook shank as shown. The surface of the strip placed against the

abdomen will ultimately form the visible side of the wingcase, and with natural materials, most tyers place the most attractively marked or distinctly colored side of the strip downward, so that it shows on the finished fly.

When using a strip of barbs, particularly those from wing feathers, you will notice that the base of the barbs are rather thick and have a soft, spongy texture (see "Wings," p. 243). This section tapers to form the finer shaft of the barbs. When tying a strip of barbs, it's best to establish the mounting point of the barbs beyond this spongy material so that it is bound down or trimmed away. A wingcase that incorporates the soft, spongy base of the barbs is difficult to fold and is more apt to split since this material is relatively thick and inflexible.

The length of the strip extending toward the rear of the fly is not important, provided it is long enough to grasp and fold over the thorax. If, however, the strip is used to dress a separate head on the fly (Steps 8-9) or second wingcase on the fly (Step 9a), it should be sufficiently long to form these other components.

Finally, note that the wingcase strip is curved over the top of the abdomen and pinched against the sides. Holding the strip in this fashion will prevent the fibers from bunching up during mounting.

Step 3. Hold the strip firmly with the left fingers to prevent it from shifting position, and secure it to the shank with tight wraps of thread. Take a wrap or two of thread toward the rear of the hook to abut the wingcase strip firmly against the front of the abdomen; when the thorax is dressed, no gap will be visible at the front of the abdomen.

Clip the butts of the wingcase material and bind down with thread.

Step 4. Dress the thorax of the fly—we're using dubbing here, and position the thread at the front of the thorax. Note that a short section of the hook shank (covered with a thread foundation) is visible behind the hook eye. The wingcase material will be tied off on this portion of the shank; crowding it with thorax material will make it difficult to bind down the wingcase strip neatly.

Step 5. With the right fingers, draw the wingcase forward over the thorax. Pay particular attention to the edges of the wingcase strip at the rear of the thorax. If they are bunched or folded, use your fingers to preen or straighten them out so that the wingcase forms a smooth, shell-like covering when drawn forward.

When drawing the strip forward, apply a uniform tension on the strip so that no wrinkles or bulges form.

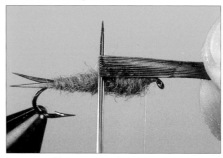

Step 5a. To create a wingcase with a sharper, more distinct rear edge—which better approximates the silhouette of some natural insects—fold the strip over a dubbing needle positioned crosswise atop the shank.

Pull the needle rearward and the front of the strip forward to crease the wingcase and form the rear edge.

Step 6. With the right fingers, hold the strip in position at the front of the hook eye. Use the left fingers to take two tight wraps of thread directly against the front of the thorax.

Step 7. To create a simple wingcase, release the material, and use the right hand to take a few tight turns of thread atop the first wraps.

You can clip the excess wingcase material as close as possible to the tie-down wraps, and cover the butts with thread, forming a neat head on the fly simultaneously, as shown on the left.

Or you can trim the wingcase butts to leave a tag of material that forms a head on the fly, as shown on the right.

Wingcase material can also be used to create a broad head on the fly, as shown in Steps 8-9, or a double wingcase as shown in Step 9a.

When the fly is complete, you can apply a drop of head cement, flexible cement, or epoxy (as shown in **Method #6: Epoxy and Varnish Wingcases**, p. 234), to the top of the wingcase to give it a more glossy appearance and improve its durability.

Step 8. To use wingcase material to form a head on the fly, bind down the strip in front of the thorax as shown in Steps 6-7.

Then use the thread to continue binding the wingcase strip to the shank, moving forward to a point directly behind the hook eye.

Step 9. Return the thread to the front of the thorax. As shown above, you can apply a bit of dubbing to conceal the thread wraps.

Fold the strip toward the rear of the hook, and bind it down directly ahead of the thorax.

Clip the wingcase material short, and if desired, take a few wraps of dubbed thread over the tie-down point.

Or you can clip the strip to leave a longer tag for a double wingcase, as shown in Step 9a.

Step 9a. To form a double wingcase, bind the strip of material forward as shown in Step 8. Fold the strip toward the rear of the hook. Bind down the folded front edge of the wingcase strip, and form the fly head simultaneously.

Clip the second wingcase slightly shorter than the first.

English tyer Oliver Edwards uses this split-wingcase style to imitate the clearly divided wingpads characteristic of some insects—certain species of *Ephemerella*, for instance. In *Flytyers Masterclass*, Edwards identifies this component as "wing buds"; in the terminology of this book, they are wingcases.

Step 1a. The technique used to form this wingcase style is very similar to the Edwards' method for fashioning a split cuticle as shown in **Method #81: Split Cuticle**, p. 331. Thus the instructions here are abbreviated, and readers seeking more detailed information should consult **Method #81**.

All components that lie behind the thorax are dressed first.

Cut two strips of wingcase material, such as the reinforced quill segments used here, each about ½ the hook gap in width.

Secure the strips at the upper sides of the thorax, as shown.

Step 1b. Dress the thorax, leaving room behind the hook eye to tie off the wingcase material.

Lay a short thread foundation behind the hook eye.

Pull the strip of material on the near side over the hook eye, and secure it behind the eye with 2 tight thread wraps.

Step 1c. Repeat the procedure with the strip on the far side.

Clip the wingcase tags and secure with thread, forming the fly head.

Method #2:
Multiple-fold Wingcase

The nymphs of some species—most notably stoneflies—have more than one distinct wingcase, and these can be imitated with a flat strip of material that is mounted with a series of folds, each of which suggests one of the cases. While natural stoneflies have only two wingcases, tyers often dress a third wingcase as a way of simulating the prothorax, a prominent shell-like structure on the nymph. We have included this third "wingcase" in the following demonstration.

The most practical materials for this technique are segments of feather barbs (though these must be long enough to form all the wingcases), raffia, and some synthetic films, since all of these materials take a crease well.

This method is generally used on larger flies, often ones that are weighted, sometimes quite heavily. On larger flies, many tyers prefer to dress the fly with an underbody material (see "Underbodies," p. 41) or use lead wire or strips to fashion the underbody (see "Weighting Hooks," p. 37). In the following demonstration, a simple underbody has been formed from orange yarn.

Because this wingcase technique alternates folds of the wingcase strip with wraps of thorax material, certain types of legs (thorax-palmered hackle, for example, or drawn feather legs) are not compatible with the method. Most tyers simulate legs by picking out long dubbing fibers on the thorax, using rubber legs, or employing some type of bundled-fiber leg (see "Bundled-fiber Legs," p. 415).

Step 1. Mount all the fly components behind the thorax.

Dress the thorax of the fly until it is just narrower than the finished diameter. The wingcase material (Swiss straw is used here) must be mounted over a base that is nearly the size of the finished thorax; if too narrow a thorax is used, the folded wingcases will slant upward in an unnatural position rather than lying flat across the back of the fly.

Using the procedure explained in **Method #1: Folded-strip Wingcase**, Steps 2-3, p. 229, mount the wingcase strip at the rear of the thorax.

Position the tying thread at the rearmost thread wrap, securing the wingcase strip.

Step 2. Dress the rear ¼ of the thorax; we're using dubbing here. Note that relatively little material has been added to this portion of the thorax—just enough to cover the underbody material and bring the thorax to its final size. Position the tying thread at the front edge of this thorax material.

To fold the first wingcase, use the left hand to position a dubbing needle crosswise atop the wingcase strip at the rear edge of the abdomen.

Fold the strip over the needle toward the hook eye. Note that the rear edge of the wingcase extends just slightly beyond the back of the thorax.

With the right fingers, pinch the strip in position at the hook eye, as shown.

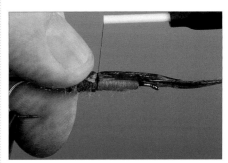

Step 3. Withdraw the needle. With the left fingers, pinch the fly from top to bottom to hold the first wingcase in position.

Bind down the wingcase material. Note that the wraps securing the strip are taken directly against the front edge of the dubbing. When securing the strip, take care to keep it centered atop the hook shank, with no wrinkles or folds.

Step 4. Fold the wingcase strip back over the body of the fly, and dress the second quarter of thorax to its final dimensions.

The materials are now once again in the configuration shown in Step 2.

Step 5. Repeat Steps 2-4 to form the middle wingcase and the third quarter of the thorax.

Step 6. Repeat Steps 2-4 to form the last "wingcase" or prothorax.

After folding and binding the wingcase strip, you can clip the excess material, and dress the final quarter of the thorax to form the head on the fly, as shown here.

Or you can use the procedure shown in **Method #1: Folded-strip Wingcase**, Steps 8-9, p. 230, to use the wingcase strip to form a head on the fly.

Method #3:
Reverse-folded Wingcase

Wingcase material can be mounted behind the hook eye, then folded rearward and secured. Strip materials, of the type indicated in **Method #1: Folded-strip Wingcase**, p. 229, or cut or burned wingcases are all suitable for this technique; bundled fibers work poorly.

The main sequence shows the procedure for creating a double wingcase of this type using a strip of material. The alternate sequence demonstrates another common application of this method in forming both head and wingcase on a dragonfly nymph, though the style can be adapted to other nymphs as well.

Step 1. Dress the entire nymph, leaving room behind the hook eye to attach the wingcase material. Lay a thread foundation behind the eye.

Cut a strip of material, such as the quill segment shown here, about equal in width to the hook gap. If a quill or feather tip is used, bind it down with the front or shiny side of the material against the hook shank.

Step 2. Fold the front strip of material rearward, smoothing it to make sure it is not creased or wrinkled

Secure it in this position with tight thread wraps, forming the head of the fly at the same time.

Step 3. You can raise and clip the two strips of material simultaneously to form a wingcase in which both sections are of equal length.

Or, as shown here, you can clip the top strip shorter than the lower one, to form a double wingcase.

Step 1a. In this reverse-mount technique, the material is generally used to form both head and wingcase.

Dress all fly components, leaving enough room behind the hook eye to dub a head or, or to mount a pair of barbell eyes, or both as shown in Step 2a.

Mount the wingcase material—we're using mesh-backed feather here (see **Method #45: Mesh-backed Feather Wings**, p. 294). The shiny or front side of the feather is placed downward, against the hook shank.

Step 2a. As shown in this top view, affix a pair of barbell eyes to the shank (see **Method #7: Barbell Eyes**, p. 431) behind the hook eye; we've added a dubbed head as well. The eyes or dubbing can be used alone if desired.

Position the tying thread at the front of the thorax.

Step 3a. Fold the wingcase material rearward, and bind it down with several tight thread wraps. Half-hitch or whip-finish the thread, and clip.

Trim the wingcase to shape.

Method #4:
Bundled-fiber Wingcase

A wingcase can be formed by drawing a bundle of individual fibers over the top of the thorax and binding them behind the hook eye. This approach gives the tyer a whole new, and rather large, category of materials with which to form wingcases—from feather barbs and natural hairs, which produce wingcases with very natural colors or markings, to Mylar-based materials such as Flashabou and Krystal Flash used to dress highly reflective wingcases in the "flashback" style. Many bundled-fiber materials, particularly hairs and synthetics, are much tougher than strip materials used to form folded wingcases and can make a more durable fly.

The basic technique is shown in the main sequence; the alternate sequence demonstrates how a bundle of fibers can be used to form both tail and wingcase.

Step 1. All fly components that lie behind the thorax should be dressed. Lay a thread foundation to a point just behind the hook eye, and return the tying thread to the front of the abdomen.

Prepare and mount a bundle of fibers—we're using Krystal Flash here. (If using yarns such as Antron, comb the bundle prior to mounting it in order to separate the fibers and make it easier to distribute them over the thorax in a later step.) When mounting the bundle, keep it atop the hook shank so that no fibers stray beneath the hook. If the tips of the wingcase fibers will be used to form legs, consult **Method #9: Wingcase Legs**, p. 418, for information about sizing the wingcase fibers.

Take a few tight turns of thread at the very rear of the bundle, forcing the fibers into the front of the abdomen.

Step 2. Dress the thorax of the fly. Do not apply materials all the way to the rear of the hook eye, but rather leave an exposed portion of the shank about 4 or 5 thread-wraps wide, as shown here, to provide space for tying down the wingcase fibers.

If the fiber bundle is very tightly consolidated, you may need to preen the sides of the bundle outward so that the fibers project in a narrow "fan" from the top of the thorax, as shown here. Distributing the fibers like this will produce a uniform, shell-like coverage of the thorax.

Step 3. Draw the fibers forward over the thorax to the hook eye.

In order to maintain a flat spread of fibers, it helps to use the right thumb to pinch the fibers against the pad of the right index finger, as shown here. This technique aids in drawing all the fibers forward under equal tension and maintaining a uniform distribution of material over the thorax.

Step 4. With the left hand, secure the fibers with 3 or 4 tight thread wraps at the front of the thorax.

As you make these wraps, do not let the fibers be drawn around the hook shank. Rather, keep them consolidated atop the shank to produce a neat, symmetrical wingcase.

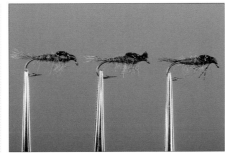

Step 5. At this point, you can clip the excess wingcase fibers, cover the butts with thread, and form the head of the fly, as shown on the left.

Or you can leave a tag of wingcase butts to form a head on the fly, as shown in the middle.

Or you can use the fiber tips to make legs on the pattern, as explained in **Method #9: Wingcase Legs**, p. 418, and shown on the right.

Step 1a. Almost any bundled fibers can be used to form both tails and wingcase, provided they are long enough. Pheasant tail barbs are used here.

Prepare a bundle of fibers by aligning the tips. The bundle should be large enough to form the wingcase. There will quite likely be more fibers here than needed to form the tail; the excess fibers will be trimmed later.

Secure the bundle at the rear of the shank to form tails of the desired length.

Then bind the fibers to the hook shank, stopping at the point where the rear of the thorax will be located.

Step 2a. Dress the abdomen, and any ribbing, gills, or other materials that lie behind the thorax.

Clip off any excess tail fibers until the desired number remain.

The butts of the tailing fibers are now in the position shown in Step 1. They can be folded rearward while the thorax is dressed, then folded forward to form the wingcase, as shown in the main sequence.

11

Method #5:
Cut and Burned Wingcases

A wingcase (or more than one wingcase on some patterns) can be cut or burned to a lifelike shape before it is mounted.

Burned wingcases are usually formed from very webby feathers—body or flank feathers, or hen neck or saddle hackles. Because the web contributes to the solid, shell-like appearance of the wingcase, web-free rooster hackle is generally unsatisfactory. Burning feathers is a relatively simple procedure, though readers unfamiliar with using burners may wish to consult **Method #6: Burned Wings**, p. 251, where the use of burning tools is discussed in greater detail.

Currently, the only wingcase burners commercially available are manufactured by Renzetti for use with stonefly patterns, though the double-lobed wingcase produced by these tools can certainly be used on other nymphs. Tyers interested in other burner shapes should consult Dick Talleur's *The Versatile Fly Tyer*, which contains instructions for making burners.

Shown here are a hen saddle feather, a Renzetti wingcase burner, and the finished product. The only real key in burning wingcases is to keep the feather stem centered in the burner, as off-center stems are a bit more difficult to mount symmetrically on the thorax.

Burned feathers can be treated with a thin coating of head cement or flexible cement to give them a glossier appearance and help them maintain their shape during fishing.

Cut wingcases can be made from a slightly larger variety of materials—feathers, strips of feather barbs, raffia or Swiss straw, synthetic film wing material, mesh-reinforced feathers (see **Method #45: Mesh-backed Feather Wings**, p. 294), or as Poul Jorgensen prefers, latex.

Wingcases can be cut to almost any shape desired, but most tyers favor relatively simple forms. A common approach

234

involves folding a strip of wingcase material lengthwise, and angle-cutting the rear to
produce a "V"-shaped wingcase as shown
on the barb strip at the left.

Webby feathers, of the type used for
burned wingcases, can also be cut to
shape, as shown on the wingcase in the
middle. Treating the feather with head
cement or flexible cement prior to cutting
can help simplify shaping the wingcase.

Synthetic materials can be cut to highly realistic shapes, such as the latex wingcase shown at the right. Using a paper
template or wingcase burner as a guide to
cutting helps give uniform results. Latex
and other synthetics are usually colored
with waterproof pens to give a more realistic appearance, as shown here. Such coloring can be done either before or after the
wingcase is mounted.

Cut or burned wingcases are typically
used on larger patterns such as stonefly or
dragonfly nymphs, since forming and handling the very small pieces of material necessary for smaller hooks can be difficult. In the
following demonstration, a pair of burned
wingcases are applied to a stonefly nymph,
but the technique is identical regardless of
the number of cases.

Step 1. Dress the fly as described in
Method #2: Multiple-fold Wingcase, Step
1, p. 231. As in that method, the thorax
here must be dressed—either with an
underbody or thorax material—to very
nearly its final diameter in order to prevent
the wingcases from flaring unnaturally
upward.

After completing the abdomen, dress
the rear ½ of the thorax to its finished size.

Step 2. Prepare wingcases of the desired
style. Center the first wingcase atop the
thorax so that the rear edge of the case
extends just beyond the back of the thorax.

Step 3. Hold the wingcase in position with
the left thumb by pinching the fly from top
to bottom, as shown.

Secure the wingcase with several tight
wraps of thread.

Step 4. (Optional) For added security in
mounting the wingcase, you can fold the
butt end of the wingcase toward the rear of
the hook, and take a few additional wraps
over the tag end, as shown.

Step 5. Clip and bind down the butts of
wingcase material.

Dress the next ½ of the thorax to its
finished size.

The configuration of materials is now
identical to that shown in Step 2.

Step 6. Repeat the mounting procedure,
adding a second wingcase

Step 7. Clip the wingcase butts and bind
down with thread.

Dub a head on the fly, and whip-finish.

Method #6:
Epoxy and Varnish Wingcases

While head cement is often used to reinforce folded-strip or bundled-fiber wingcases, adhesives can also be used to form the
wingcase itself.

The most modern approach to this technique, shown in the main sequence, was
devised by California tyer Mike Mercer for his
"Poxyback" series of nymphs. The resulting
wingcase is a glossy, bead-like shell over the
thorax that is quite durable. Because the epoxy
is clear, the material beneath is visible and
lends its coloration to the wingcase. Quick-setting, 5-minute epoxy is used with this technique and the pot life is relatively short; thus
the greatest efficiencies are obtained by mixing the epoxy in a small batches and using it to
form wingcases on several flies already prepared and ready at hand. These flies can be
mounted on a piece of foam or other material,
but care should be taken to position them so
that the wingcases are level, ensuring that the
epoxy will form a neat bead over the wingcase
and will not run or drip to the sides of the fly.

The alternate sequence shows a much
older version of this method, in which ordinary
head cement is used to form a wingcase over a
dubbed thorax. While head cement does not
form a wingcase that is as thick or rounded as
one fashioned from epoxy, it is less troublesome to use, can be applied to each fly as it is
tied, and gives acceptable results.

Either of these techniques can also be
used to create overbodies.

Step 1. The epoxy method is generally
used on flies that already have a wingcase
formed from another method, such as
Method #1: Folded-strip Wingcase, p. 229, or
Method #4: Bundled-fiber Wingcase, p. 232.

These wingcase materials form a base that contains the epoxy in a well-formed drop, and they give the wingcase its finished color as well. However, satisfactory results can be achieved by applying the epoxy directly atop a dubbed thorax; the dubbing is usually trimmed first, as shown in Step 1a.

Whatever type of wingcase is used, it is important to prepare each fly by preening any stray fibers—dubbing, legs, gills—downward and away from the wingcase. Stray fibers will adhere to the epoxy and make it difficult to form a neat bead.

Five-minute epoxy works best for this technique; it's liquid enough to apply to the fly, but thick enough to form a non-running bead atop the thorax, and it dries rapidly.

Mixing the epoxy on a doubled square of aluminum foil and stirring with a toothpick helps minimize the mess, since these items can be disposed of when you're finished. As always when working with epoxy, keeping a small jar of lacquer thinner and a rag close at hand is good insurance against accidents.

Step 2. After mixing the resin and hardener thoroughly, collect a small drop of epoxy on the tip of a toothpick. Apply to the wingcase, as shown.

On small flies, a single drop placed in the center of the wingcase may suffice. On larger flies, you may need to spread the epoxy to the edges of the case for complete coverage.

Once the wingcase is covered with the drop of epoxy, lift the toothpick vertically. A "string" of epoxy will be formed between the wingcase and the toothpick. Twirling the toothpick slowly as you raise it will break this string and pick up the excess adhesive on the tip of the toothpick.

Step 3. Here's the finished wingcase on the left. It should be kept level until it hardens.

The epoxy on the foil will quickly thicken and become more difficult to work with after 3 or 4 minutes. Attempting to use overly viscous adhesive gives poor results; you're better off mixing another small batch.

The remaining flies in the photo show other wingcase materials treated with epoxy; note how the material shows through. The fly in the middle has a Flashabou wingcase; the one on the right a Krystal Flash wingcase.

Step 1a. A wingcase can be formed by using head cement to mat down and fix into position dubbing fibers that lie atop the thorax. This approach works best with a thorax formed from a dubbing loop or dubbing brush (**Method #41: Fur Chenille Dubbing Loop**, p. 131; **Method #42: Hide-strip Fur Chenille**, p. 132; and **Method #44: Wire-core Dubbing Brush**, p. 133). With these techniques, the individual dubbing fibers project outward from the hook shank and are easily coated and smoothed down with head cement. Softer furs give better results than very stiff ones, which resist matting.

Once the thorax is formed, trim the wingcase area shorter than the surrounding fibers. Do not clip too close to the hook shank, or the short fibers will be too stiff. Trimming helps define the wingcase area and provides a flatter foundation for applying the cement.

Step 2a. With a dubbing needle, apply a drop of head cement to the wingcase area, smoothing it from the head of the fly to the rear and creating a flat, shell-like wingcase. Thickened head cement works best for this purpose, as it resists bleeding into the thorax away from wingcase fibers.

You may need to apply several drops of head cement before the fibers will lie flat, as shown here.

Step 3a. If the dubbing fibers are long, the cemented, flattened tips will extend back over the abdomen. These can be left long, as shown in the previous step, or clipped at the rear of the thorax, as shown here.

Overbodies

Overbodies are fashioned by flat strips of materials or bundled fibers tied lengthwise over part of the fly body. While one common type of overbody is, as the name suggests, tied atop the hook shank over the dorsal surface of the fly body, others are tied along the ventral side to form a "belly strip" or over the sides of the fly. In all of these cases, overbody materials are applied longitudinally over the primary body material, and the techniques for dressing them are quite similar. Though overbodies are sometimes tied to mimic a specific anatomical feature, such as the segmented exoskeleton on scuds or shrimp, they are generally used to add a strip of contrasting color or texture to the fly body, and hence have a broader range of applications than do wingcases. They can be tied on nymphs, dry flies (typically on mayfly duns), and on streamers.

In design, appearance, and construction, overbodies are similar to some wingcase styles, and most of the same materials can be used to dress them. Thus overbody materials can be selected to imitate natural colorations or markings, or to add flash and sparkle to a fly. Because they are dressed lengthwise along the hook shank, the materials used to tie overbodies are occasionally used to tie other longitudinally oriented fly components at the same time, primarily tails and wingcases. These combination techniques are presented in the section that follows.

Finally, overbodies can be created simply by applying epoxy or head cement in a strip along the desired portion of the fly body using the procedure explained in **Method #6: Epoxy and Varnish Wingcases**, p. 234.

Method #7:

Strip Overbody

This very common style of overbody can be formed from nearly any flat strip of material, such as segments of feather barbs, foam, biots, and so forth, but probably the most widely used materials are lacquered feathers (see **Method #1: Folded-strip Wingcase**, p. 229) to form dorsal overbodies on nymph patterns, and plastic or latex strips used to form shellbacks on scud and shrimp patterns, as shown in the main sequence.

The alternate sequence demonstrates two variations of this technique: first, forming a belly strip, and second, reverse-dressing the fly body to form a thread rib on pattern.

A strip of overbody material mounted on top of a nymph body can also be used to form the wingcase. This variation of the method is shown using bundled fibers in **Method #8: Bundled-fiber Overbody**, Steps 5-6, p. 237, but the technique is identical when a strip overbody is used.

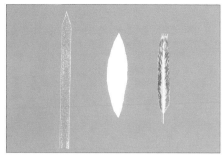

Step 1. Preparation of the overbody varies with the specific material used, the pattern, and the preferences of the tyer. Some tyers find that mounting the overbody is simplified if the material is trimmed to a point at one end, as shown on the elastic material at the left, which will be used to form the shellback on this scud pattern. Since this piece of material is a straight strip, it will form an overbody of uniform width over the back of the fly.

Other tyers prefer, when possible, to trim the overbody material to match the contours of the fly body. Shown in the middle is a piece of sheet latex cut to a football shape to form an overbody on a scud pattern dressed with a body that is thickest in the middle. On the right is a lacquered feather that has been trimmed to create a narrow overbody on the abdomen of a mayfly nymph.

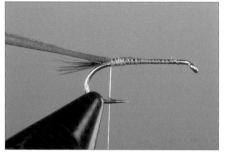

Step 2. Mount the tail of the fly, and position the tying thread 4 or 5 wraps ahead of the rearmost tail-mounting wrap.

Secure the overbody material to the top of the shank. Wrap the thread toward the rear of the hook so that the last thread wrap binding the overbody material lies directly atop the rearmost wrap securing the tail. When the overbody is folded forward, no thread wraps at the tail will be visible.

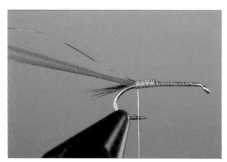

Step 3. The overbody is secured with ribbing material, which simultaneously creates the body segmentation.

Mount the ribbing material—wire is used here—so that it is bound atop the thread wraps securing the overbody strip.

Step 4. Dress the fly body. We've dubbed the entire body on this scud pattern. On a nymph, ordinarily only the abdomen would be dressed.

Position the tying thread at the front edge of the body material.

Step 5. With the right fingers, pull the overbody strip forward over the hook eye. The strip should be drawn directly along the top of the shank and curve evenly down either side of the body, with no wrinkles or creases.

With your left hand, take 2 or 3 tight thread wraps, securing the overbody strip directly at the front edge of the body.

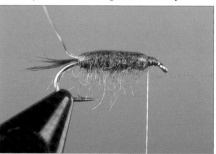

Step 6. When the overbody is secured, use the right hand to take additional tight turns of thread.

Clip the tag of overbody material and bind with thread. Position the tying thread again at the front edge of the body.

(On mayfly nymphs, you can use the tag of the overbody strip to form the wingcase as well. See **Method #8: Bundled-fiber Overbody**, Step 4, p. 237.)

Step 7. Wrap the ribbing material forward in an open, even spiral. Some tension on the rib material is necessary to secure the

overbody and create the body segments. On some materials, this tension may cause the overbody to be pulled to the far side of the hook shank.

If this occurs, use the left fingers as shown to pinch the overbody strip against the sides of the fly as each turn of ribbing is taken.

Step 8. When the front of the body is reached, bind down the ribbing and clip the excess material, as shown on the fly at the bottom.

The fly at top shows a nymph dressed with an overbody strip on the abdomen; the material is a feather-tip reinforced with vinyl glue.

Fragile overbody materials, such as strips of feather barbs, can be given a thin coat of head cement after the fly is complete to improve durability.

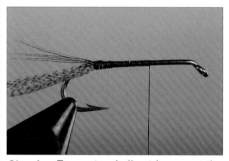

Step 1a. To create a belly strip, mount the overbody material on the underside of the shank directly atop the tail-mounting wraps.

Position the tying thread at the front edge of the abdomen.

Step 2a. In this version of the technique, tying thread is used in place of a separate rib material to secure and segment the body. Thus the body of the fly is dressed in reverse, moving from the hook eye to the bend so that the tying thread ends up at the tail of the fly, in the proper position for spiraling forward.

11

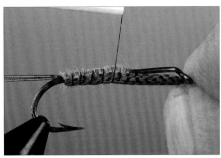

Step 3a. When the body is complete, use the right hand to draw the overbody strip forward directly on the underside of the shank.

Because the tying thread is now located at the rear of the fly, it isn't possible to secure the overbody strip ahead of the body. It must be held in position with the right fingers as the left hand spirals the tying thread forward.

Method #8:
Bundled-fiber Overbody

Bundled-fibers overbodies are a versatile style, partly because of the wide variety of fibers at the tyer's disposal, and partly because bundled-fibers permit a number of combination techniques in which the overbody material is used to form more than one component on the finished fly. Natural materials such as hairs and feather barbs produce overbodies with lifelike coloration or markings, while synthetic materials such as Krystal Flash or Antron yarn add sparkle and reflectivity to the fly.

The main sequence shows the technique for creating a basic bundled-fiber overbody that is pulled forward, much the way a strip overbody is created. This sequence also shows the method for using the overbody material to fashion the wingcase.

The alternate sequence shows a method used by tyer Skip Morris for a reverse-tied overbody in which the fibers are used to create tails on the pattern.

In either of these methods, the primary body material can be dressed in reverse fashion in order to use the tying thread as the ribbing material, as explained in **Method #7: Strip Overbody**, Steps 2a-3a, p. 236.

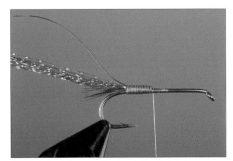

Step 1. Mount the tailing material and position the tying thread at the rearmost mounting wrap.

Prepare a bundle of fibers by aligning the tips. Natural hairs are prepared as described in **Method #3: Stacking and Aligning Hair**, p. 69; feather barbs are aligned on the stem, then clipped; synthetic fibers, such as the Krystal Flash used here, are simply trimmed on one end.

The thickness of the fiber bundle depends on the fly size, but in general, the bundle should be kept relatively sparse. The fibers will spread over the body material when they are drawn forward, making a thin shell-like covering. An overly large clump of material is more difficult to handle.

Mount the fibers so that they extend beyond the bend of the hook, as shown. (Hair and feather barbs should be mounted by the tips.) The mounting wraps should be taken directly above the wraps securing the tail, and the fibers should be kept atop the hook shank.

When the fibers are secure, mount the ribbing material; it should be bound in so the rearmost thread wrap securing the rib lies atop the rearmost mounting wrap on the overbody material, as shown.

Step 2. Dress the body—in the case of this nymph pattern, only the abdomen is formed.

Lay a short thread foundation in the thorax area to help in tying off the overbody, and return the thread to the front of the abdomen.

Step 3. With the right fingers, pull the overbody fibers forward over the top of the abdomen. Gather them carefully in the fingers so that you can draw them to the hook eye and apply a uniform tension on all the strands.

With the left hand, take 2 or 3 tight wraps of thread, securing the overbody fibers at the front of the abdomen.

Step 4. Use the right fingers to secure the fibers with 3 or 4 additional tight thread wraps, moving toward the hook eye.

At this point, the fiber butts can be clipped and bound with thread. If they are to be used to form the wingcase as shown in Step 6, leave the butts intact, as shown here.

Return the tying thread to the front of the abdomen, as shown.

Take the ribbing material and wrap it forward under moderate tension in uniform, open spirals over the fibers. If the tension begins to pull the fibers to the far side of the shank, use your left fingers to hold them atop the body during each wrap of the rib, as shown.

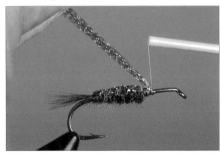

Step 5. When the entire overbody is ribbed, bind down the ribbing material and clip the excess.

With fragile materials, such as feather barbs and some hairs, the durability of the overbody can be improved by treating it with a light coating of head cement or flexible cement.

If the overbody fibers are to be used for the wingcase, wrap the thread forward, and take one turn around the hook shank ahead of the fiber butts, as shown here.

Step 6. With the left fingers, fold the fibers back across the top of the abdomen. When folding them back, try to spread and hold them in a uniform layer atop the abdomen; this will help position them to form a smooth, even wingcase.

Wrap the tying thread back to the front of the abdomen, tightly securing the fibers to the shank.

The components are now the configuration pictured in **Method #4: Bundled-fiber Wingcase**, Step 1, p. 232. The wingcase is formed using the procedure shown in the subsequent steps of that method.

Step 1a. Reverse-dressing the overbody is useful when the fibers are used to form tails on the fly.

Begin by attaching a piece of ribbing material at the tailing point.

Form the fly body, such as the dubbed abdomen on this nymph pattern, and lay a short thread foundation at the thorax area. Position the tying thread at the front of the abdomen.

Prepare a bundle of fibers as described in Step 1; we're using pheasant tail barbs here. With the right fingers, position the bundle atop the abdomen, as shown. Adjust the bundle so that the tips of the fibers project beyond the rear of the fly far enough to form tails of the desired length.

Step 2a. With the left fingers, pinch the fibers atop the shank and bind them down directly in front of the abdomen.

If the fibers are not used to form the wingcase, they can be clipped now and the butts bound with thread, as shown here.

If the fibers will form the wingcase, bind them to the shank with 4 or 5 turns of thread toward the hook eye as shown in Step 4.

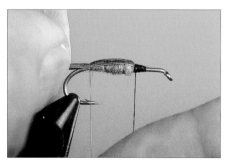

Step 3a. With the left fingers, draw the fiber tips out beyond the rear of the body, taking care to exert equal tension on the fibers for a uniform overbody.

Take one turn of the ribbing material and pull it toward you under moderate tension, as shown.

Step 4a. Skip Morris recommends using the left fingers to spread the tail fibers to the sides of the shank. As you pull fibers toward each side, maintain tension on the rib material with the right hand.

Note at this point there may well be a greater number of tailing fibers than you desire on the finished fly. These will be clipped later.

When the tail fibers are roughly fanned, pull more tightly on the rib material. If wire rib is used, do not apply too much tension or you will cut the overbody fibers.

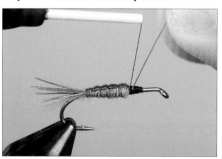

Step 5a. Spiral the rib material forward and tie it off at the front of the abdomen, as shown in Steps 4-5.

If the wing butts have been left long to form the wingcase, proceed to Step 6.

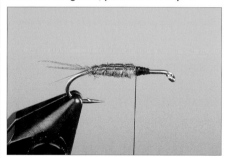

Step 6a. Trim the excess fibers from the tail until the desired number remain.

Method #9:
Side-mount Overbody

Side-mounted overbodies, which create bands down the sides of a fly, are occasionally used on streamer patterns to represent the lateral lines found on many species of baitfish. More often, however, tyers incorporate side-mounted material to give a flashy accent to less strictly imitative patterns such as the Woolly Bugger shown in the main sequence below.

Side-mounted overbodies can be dressed using the technique presented in the main sequence of **Method #8: Bundled-fiber Overbody**, p. 237, except that a strip or bundle of overbody material is secured to each side of the shank, drawn forward, and secured with ribbing material. The technique demonstrated in the main sequence that follows, however, is really a version of the alternate sequence shown in **Method #8**, in which the overbody material is incorporated into the tail of the fly. We're including it here both to illustrate the dressing style and to demonstrate that, on many patterns, the overbody can be secured with palmered hackle rather than a separate ribbing strand.

The alternate sequence demonstrates an unusual side-mounted overbody devised by Dick Talleur for his pattern The Alternative. In this approach strips of material, rather than the bundled fibers used in the main sequence, are used to form broader overbody sides to the fly that completely enclose the primary body material, giving an interesting minnowlike silhouette that can be adapted to many streamer patterns. (Readers interested in the complete dressing for this fly should consult *Mastering the Art of Fly Tying*.) The technique also illustrates the fact that overbody materials need not necessarily be bound to the hook shank along their full length; they can simply be secured at the ends to form an unribbed overbody. A strip of material bound over the top of the body in this fashion, for instance, is often used to form the shell on beetle patterns.

Step 1. Here we're dressing lateral accents on a Woolly Bugger pattern. The tail and body are dressed, and the hackle is tip-mounted at the rear of the body. The tying thread is positioned at the front edge of the body.

Gather a few strands of overbody material such as the Flashabou used here, and position them against the near side of the hook shank directly in front of the body material.

Step 2. Secure the strands to the side of the shank with several tight wraps of thread. Clip the excess material and bind with thread.

Mount an equal number of strands on the far side, as shown in this top view.

Step 3. With the left fingers, grasp the overbody strands on the far side of the shank and draw them directly down the side of the fly body. Apply moderate tension to keep them straight, and hold them at the base of the tail.

With the right fingers, draw the overbody material down the near side of the body, and transfer them to the left fingertips, as shown.

Step 4. The left fingers should pull the overbody strips firmly down either side of the shank.

Wrap the hackle forward as explained in **Method #16: Forward Palmer Hackle—Tip Mounted**, p. 364.

Maintain tension the strands as you wrap to prevent them from being pulled around the hook shank by the wraps of hackle.

Step 5. When the hackle is wrapped, tie it off, and complete the head of the fly. Trim the overbody strands even with the tail.

Note that this style of fly can be dressed by mounting a length of ribbing material at the rear of the fly and wrapping the hackle from the head of the fly rearward (see **Method #17: Reverse Palmer Hackle**, p. 365). The hackle feather is tied off with the ribbing material, which is then wrapped forward.

Step 1a. On this version of the side-mounted overbody, the tail of the fly is again dressed first. Talleur uses the tips of two very webby feathers—body or flank feathers, or hen hackle—mounted as described in **Method #21: Split Feather Tail**, p. 82, and as shown here.

Take a second pair of very webby feathers, and strip away the barbs at the base of the stem until the remaining feather is equal in length to the hook shank.

Prepare the feathers with a thin coat of flexible cement as explained in **Method #50: Feather-tip Flatwing**, p. 299. Allow the feathers to dry. Mesh-reinforced feathers (see **Method #45: Mesh-backed Feather Wings**, p. 294) can also be used.

Step 2a. Position a feather against the near side of the shank, with the tip at the rearmost tail-mounting wrap. The convex side of the feather is placed against the shank, and the feather stem is in line with the hook shank.

Secure it with tight thread wraps, and return the thread the to rearmost wrap.

Step 3a. Mount the second feather in the same fashion against the far side of the hook shank.

Dress the body of the fly. Talleur's pattern calls for a tinsel body; we're using twisted Krystal Flash.

Tie off the body material and position the thread at the front edge of the body.

Step 4a. Fold both feathers forward toward the hook eye. The feather stems should run directly along the sides of the fly body.

With the right fingers, pull the feather stems straight. With the left fingers, pinch the feathers against the sides of the body.

Step 5a. Secure the two feathers at the front of the body, binding down the feather stem only. The feathers should be parallel to one another, in a vertical plane, as shown.

The feather stems can now be clipped and the head of the fly dressed.

Wings

Few other components of fly construction have summoned more fly-tying ingenuity, inventiveness, and creativity than wings. And for good reason—wings are probably the single most conspicuous and defining feature of nearly all adult aquatic insects. In mature flies, wings largely determine fly profile, its attitude on or in the water, and the overall appearance of the insect. In artificial flies, tyers seek not only to replicate these qualities, but to use specific wing materials and styles to achieve other aims—visibility, floatation, and even lifelike movement in subsurface and emerger patterns. Given these manifold and significant functions, it is hardly surprising that tyers have devised dozens of wing designs using scores of materials.

It is equally unsurprising that a few problems in nomenclature have developed as well. For instance, tyers routinely speak of streamer "wings," though the food items imitated—

primarily baitfish and leeches—possess no such appendage. "Winging" materials contribute more to the impression of body profile and color than anything else. In other streamer styles—the Grey Ghost, for example—wings are actually fashioned from a number of materials which, according to custom in tying salmon patterns, have separate names—topping, shoulder, and so forth.

In an attempt to preserve ordinary fly-tying terminology, this chapter details methods for dressing materials that are attached at the winging point and are normally referred to among tyers as "wings." The chapter is divided into four sections, based primarily on the orientation of the wing and silhouette produced—"Upright Wings," which are primarily characteristic of adult mayflies; "Downwings," a defining feature of both adult caddis and stoneflies, as well as a style generally used to dress streamer

patterns; "Spentwings," which are characteristic of the spent mayfly imago and adult damselfly; and "Emerger Wings and Wing Buds," which appear on hatching mayflies, caddis, and midges. This last category involves some judgment calls, as the line between a wingcase on a nymph and the wing buds on an emerging fly is by no means clear cut. Here again we've tried to rely on traditional distinctions made by tyers, and the techniques explained in this section are aimed at producing emerging wings that are more distinct and exaggerated in profile than the immature wings suggested by the wingcases on nymph patterns, which are covered separately in Chapter 11: "Wingcases and Overbodies." In the interest of both efficiency and fly-tying custom, each of these four sections is subdivided according to the type of material used in the dressing.

SECTION ONE

Upright Wings

As the name suggests, upright wings are mounted so that they stand perpendicular (or nearly so) to the hook shank. They are used almost exclusively on dry flies, primarily those imitating mayfly duns.

While dressing techniques depend largely upon the specific material used, for most upright wing styles the tyer has options in three particular procedures: the orientation of the mount; the technique for mounting the wing material on the shank; and the method for "posting" the wing, that is, raising it to a vertical, or near-vertical, position. To some extent, mounting techniques differ with the choice of wing material, and the methods suitable for any given material are presented in the individual sections devoted to specific materials.

Mounting orientation and posting, however, are somewhat less dependent on wing material and style. Rather than repeat the available options for these procedures in each tying method, they are presented as a set of generalized techniques in **Method #1: Mounting and Posting Upright Wings**, p. 241. This introductory method is intended to provide a group of options that can be used with practically any of the materials and techniques used for upright wings. Thus, for

instance, while most of the upright-winging instructional sequences in this chapter picture a standard wing-mount, that is, one in which the wing butts are positioned toward the bend of the hook during mounting, the tyer is free to use the reverse-mount method described in **Method #1**. Similarly, when wings are posted upright, the tyer may choose any of the techniques presented in **Method #1**; in some cases, additional posting options are discussed as they pertain to specific materials.

The tyer has one final option. A minor, but persistent, controversy in fly tying has centered on the question of dividing upright wings, that is, whether the winging material should be mounted to form a single, undivided wing on the back of the fly, or whether wings should be divided, with a slight angle between them to give the impression of two distinct wings. One theory holds that most mayflies drift downstream with wings folded together, and an undivided wing best imitates this silhouette. And some fly styles, like Vince Marinaro's thorax ties, proceed from this assumption. Others argue that some important mayfly species do just the opposite, holding the wings slightly apart, and many fly patterns incorporate this wing style.

In our experience, there is little practical

difference—the trout seem not to care much—but the tyer is at liberty to choose. In this section on upright wings, most of the techniques for dressing wings of quill or feather tips show a divided wing. These materials exhibit a natural curvature, and mounting the wing halves with their convex sides together will cause them to flare away from one another and create the impression of two individual wings. Dressing an undivided wing is simply a matter of placing the concave sides together, causing both wings to curve inward and giving the appearance of a single wing. When using fibers to create wings, it is merely a matter of deciding whether or not to divide the bundle of fibers and using the appropriate quantity of material.

Method #1:

Mounting and Posting Upright Wings

The instructions shown here demonstrate a number of tying options in mounting and posting upright wings. Unless otherwise indicated, they are suitable for use with any upright wing style and any material. There is one additional procedure not shown since its use is restricted to wings formed from bundled fibers. Thus it is presented as a generalized technique at the beginning of the section "Upright Bundled-fiber Wings" in **Method #15: Bundled-fiber Post**, p. 263.

There are 3 procedures shown, each identified by a number/letter combination, in which the number indicates the tying sequence and the letter specifies the step within that sequence. That is, Steps 1a-1c constitute one method; Steps 2a-2c, a second method; and so on.

The first sequence illustrates the general technique for standard wing-mount orientation—with wing butts positioned toward the hook bend. This standard mounting orientation is used by most tyers. The bulk formed when tying in the winging material is positioned behind the wing, where it may be used in conjunction with tailing butts to form a smooth underbody. This orientation also keeps the shank directly behind the hook eye free for hackling and for forming a small, neat head.

This same sequence also illustrates the common "thread bump" technique for posting upright quill and feather-tip wings. (A variation of this technique used to elevate bundled-fiber wings is presented in **Method #15: Bundled-fiber Post**, p. 263, since it is restricted to bundled materials.)

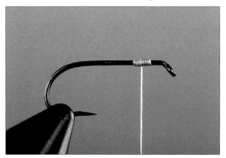

Step 1a. Mount the tying thread at the winging point (usually ¼ to ⅓ of a shank-length behind the eye, though this depends on the particular fly style).

If necessary, spin the bobbin (counter-clockwise when viewed from above) to flatten the tying thread. Take 5 or 6 adjacent turns toward the hook bend.

Then spin the bobbin (clockwise when viewed from above) to twist the thread into a cord. Wind the thread in adjacent wraps back to the mounting point. This "corrugated" foundation of twisted thread will provide a rough, non-slip surface for affixing the wing material.

Step 1b. Grasp the wing butts in your left hand. Your fingers should hold the material

directly behind the mounting point. Position the wings atop the shank so that the mounting point is directly above the tying thread.

Mount the wings, here a pair of hackle tips. (Mounting feather-tip wings is detailed in **Method #7: Feather-tip Wings**, p. 252. For instructions about preparing and mounting other winging materials, see the subsequent sections that correspond to those materials.)

Step 1c. With the left fingers, grasp the wing tips; gently pull them up and back toward the hook bend, slightly beyond the vertical.

At the front base of the wing, begin building a bump of twisted thread that will keep the wing elevated. Wind the first few wraps of thread tightly against the base of the wing. If you attempt, however, to place too many thread wraps directly atop one another, the bump will collapse. Instead, build a wedge-shaped "ramp" or cone of thread as shown, always butting the rearmost wraps tightly against the wing, and tapering the thread bump toward the hook eye.

To avoid bulk, you want to use as few thread wraps as possible to post the wing, so periodically release the wing to check your progress. When the wings stand vertically on their own, you're finished.

If desired, a small drop of head cement can be applied to the thread wraps at the base of the wing for added security.

The next sequence illustrates "reverse-mount" winging. Nearly all types of upright wings can be mounted in reverse, that is, with wing butts extending over the eye of the hook. Because the wing itself is pinched between the fingers during mounting, some tyers find that this method gives better control of the material and prevents some types of materials from twisting, rolling, or deforming under thread pressure. Since the wing butts are bound down behind the hook eye, there is no buildup of material behind the wing, making reverse-mounting useful in patterns with very slender bodies, such as those formed from quill or floss. Reverse-mounting is sometimes necessary when the wing materials are too short to grasp reliably by the butts. Very short feather tips, small slips of quill, short clumps of hackle barbs—all of which are typically used on smaller flies—may be mounted more easily in the reverse direction. (Feather-tip wings in particular are often reverse-mounted, and tyers have devised a few specialized techniques specifically for this material. These are presented separately in **Method #8: Reverse-mount Feather-tip Wings**, p. 253.) Finally,

some professional tyers routinely reverse-mount wings; because the wing butts are clipped only once, the handling of tools and materials is more efficient.

For the most part, reverse-mounting is best suited to quills, feather-tips, and very compressible bundled fibers such as hackle barbs. Most natural hairs and thicker synthetic fibers are too bulky to bind down securely in the short distance behind the hook eye and still give a neat appearance on the finished fly.

This sequence also shows the use of a thread-bump to post the reverse-mounted wings. Reverse-mounted quill wings can also be posted using the technique shown in **Method #3: Downs Mount Quill Wings**, p. 245.

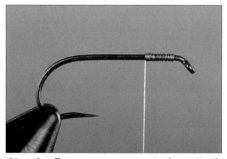

Step 2a. For a reverse-mount wing, attach the tying thread at the winging point. Flatten the tying thread, and wrap it toward the hook eye. Then twist the thread and wind a foundation of adjacent wraps back to the rearmost thread wraps.

Step 2b. Grasp the wing material—here, a pair of quill segments—in your left hand. Your fingers should hold the material directly behind the mounting point. Position the wings so that the mounting point is directly above the tying thread and the butts extend over the hook eye.

Mount the wings, here a pair of quill segments. (Mounting quill wings is detailed in **Method #2: Upright Quill Wings**, p. 244. For instructions about preparing and mounting other winging materials, see the subsequent sections that correspond to those materials.)

Step 2c. With the right fingers, pull the wing tips up and forward toward the hook eye, slightly beyond the vertical.

With the bobbin in the left hand, build a thread bump against the rear base of the wing. The procedure is identical to that described in Step 1c, except that the vise stem will interfere with continuous wrapping. You must release the bobbin once during each full wrap.

Release the wings periodically to check your progress. When they remain in the vertical position the posting is complete.

Wings fashioned from a variety of materials—quills, feather tips, and bundled fibers—can be posted to the vertical by casting a loop of tying thread around the wing base, drawing the wing upright under tension from the loop, and then securing the loop. It is particularly useful on hair wings, as it avoids the overly bulky thread bump at the wing base that is sometimes required to post up stiff materials. This technique has been around for some time, though it is not well-known among tyers. Recently, however, Randall Kaufmann has reintroduced the method to a wider audience in his book *Tying Dry Flies.*

The following sequence demonstrates the technique using calf-body hair mounted in the standard orientation. This posting method is not really suitable for reverse-mounted wings, as the buildup of bulky materials behind the hook eye makes finishing the fly neatly rather difficult.

Step 3a. Here the winging material is bound to the top of the hook shank in the standard orientation with several tight wraps of the thread. The butts have been clipped, but not covered with tying thread. The tying thread is positioned at the rearmost thread wrap.

Step 3b. Grasp the tip of the wing in your fingers, and with the bobbin in your left hand, bring the thread horizontally around the wing as shown. The thread wrap begins on the far side of the shank; the thread is brought in front of the wing, then toward the tyer, then back toward the bend.

Note that the thread contacts the wing at a point just about even with the tops of the wing butts that are bound to the shank. This thread wrap must be high enough up the wing to hold it upright, but not so high that the wing slips out from under the wrap.

With some smooth, slick materials such as natural hairs, the thread may have a tendency to slip up or down the wing and refuse to stay in position. Waxing the thread will help reduce slipping.

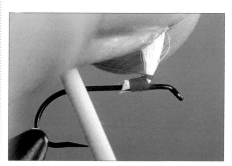

Step 3c. When working with extremely slippery materials, such as many natural hairs, or large quantities of material, a single loop taken around the front of the bundle may not sufficiently consolidate the fibers. To help gather and post slippery materials or large bundles, take one or more thread wraps horizontally around the base of the fiber bundle, as shown.

Then proceed to form the thread wrap shown in Step 3b.

Step 3d. Now slip the tying thread between the exposed hair butts. You've now made a full wrap that encircles the wing. The thread is hooked in the hair butts and cannot slip forward.

Step 3e. Now take 3 or 4 tight turns of thread, moving toward the wing, to lock the horizontal wrap in place.

Step 3f. The exposed wing butts should be bound down with thread wraps as the thread is moved to the rear of the shank to attach the tailing material.

Upright Quill Wings

Quill wings are a style with a long history in fly tying, and they have some advantages. The material produces nicely shaped wings that are naturally divided and cut a clean, clear silhouette. With appropriately chosen feathers, quill wings can be dressed on a wide range of hook sizes and fly patterns, and with practice, they are reasonably simple to tie. The principal drawback to quill wings is durability. Because they are fashioned from interlocking feather barbs, such wings split or tear rather easily, though as most fishermen have discovered, a tattered wing generally matters little to the trout. And the durability of the material can in fact be improved by using one of the procedures described in **Method #2: Upright Quill Wings**, p. 244.

For a more detailed explanation of feathers suited to quill wings, see "Wing Feathers," p. 9.

Preparing Quill Wings

Quills are among the easiest materials to prepare for winging; all that is required is that identical segments of material are cut from matched feathers. There are, however, a few points to bear in mind that will simplify winging or improve the results.

First, as it is important to match the pair of feathers, so it is important to match the segments of the feather cut to form the wings. The material cut from the feather should be taken from the same position along the feather stem, as shown in the following sequence.

Second is the matter of proportion. Regardless of wing style—upright or downwing—the width of the quill segment cut from the feather should be approximately equal to the hook gap. There is, of course, some latitude here. Wider segments of material will give a broader wing profile. But overly wide material is difficult to secure neatly to the shank, and the excessive bulk at the tie-in point may cause the segment of quill to split at the base. Wings narrower than the hook gap are easier to tie in, but do not offer the pronounced silhouette that is one of the chief virtues of quill. Again, see the photo sequence below.

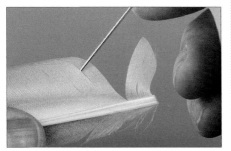

To prepare segments or "slips" of quill for winging, hold one of the feathers with the convex side up. The barbs nearest the base of the feather may be rather short and have ragged or uneven tips. This section of the feather isn't really suitable for wings and can be removed or simply preened downward, as we've done here.

Insert a dubbing needle into the feather to separate a segment of quill that—at its widest point—is equal in width to the gap of the hook being used. The widest point of the quill segment will be near the middle; do not size the quill segment at the feather stem. The base of the barbs are compressed and measuring the quill segment here may produce a wing that is too wide.

Slide the dubbing needle along the length of the barb, creating a "split" from the barb tip to the feather stem.

Clip this segment of quill near the feather stem.

Repeat the process for the other feather. Place the feathers with the convex sides together, and check to make sure they are of identical width. If one quill slip is wider, use a dubbing needle to peel off a single barb. Repeat as necessary until the wings are equal in width, as shown.

Not all of the feather will be useable. If you inspect the convex side of a wing feather,

you'll notice that a portion of the feather along the stem is somewhat shiny in appearance, as shown above. This "ventral ridge" (see "Wing Feathers," p. 9) is not suitable for wings, as it lacks curvature, is excessively thick and spongy, and prone to splitting when mounted. This glossy band poses little problem when slips of quill are cut from the lower half of the feather, as the shiny material will be cut away as excess when the wing is mounted.

Near the tip of the feather, however, this spongy material extends much closer to the barb tips, and it is more difficult to dress a quill wing without incorporating at least some of this undesirable portion of the feather. For this reason, and the fact that the barbs near the tip lack the desired curvature, the tip portion of the feather is seldom used for winging.

Here, a pair of wings cut from the upper portion of the feather are shown. Notice that the two segments do not flare away from one another.

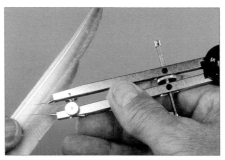

To simplify measuring wing width, many tyers use some sort of gauge. A pair of compass-type dividers can be set to the desired gap, then used in place of a dubbing needle to split the barbs. When fashioning multiple sets of wings, a pair of dividers like this makes the process faster and the resulting wings more consistent.

If your tying calls for a large number of quill wings, it may be easier to peel an entire strip of barbs from the feather stem and cut them into segments of the correct size. To strip a feather in this fashion, see **Method #3: Downs Mount Quill Wings**, Step 1a, p. 245.

Mounting Quill Wings

There are several techniques for mounting quill wings, but most of them share two common features. First, the quill is held edgewise atop the hook shank. And second, the thread is manipulated in such a way that thread pressure is exerted vertically, so that the barbs of the quill segment are drawn directly down on top of the shank. The rationale becomes apparent in the following photo.

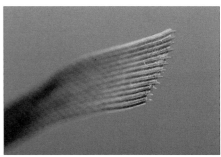

This photo shows the base of a cut segment of quill. Notice how the interlocking barbs form a "column." When thread pressure is exerted vertically, these barbs are "crushed" downward, collapsing one on top of the other in a neat stack. The barbs are not allowed to roll around the shank. Compressing the barbs in a stack like this preserves the shape of the wing.

Several of the general material-mounting techniques presented earlier in this book are suitable for quill wings. In fact, quill segments were deliberately used in those instructional sequences to make repeating them here unnecessary. The techniques best suited to mounting quill wings are identified in Step 2 of the following instructional sequence.

Method #2:
Upright Quill Wings

As explained in the preceding section, the tyer has options at various stages of dressing upright quill wings. The sequence that follows is primarily intended to provide a general picture of dressing quill wings by indicating where in the process those options apply. In addition, some techniques for improving the durability of quill wings are presented.

The photo at the end of the sequence illustrates an unusual wing style devised by René Harrop in which trimmed biots are dressed using the procedure shown in this method.

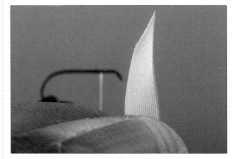

Step 1. Mount the tying thread and create a thread foundation for the wing as described in **Method #1: Mounting and Posting Upright Wings**, Step 1a, p. 242. (If the wing is to be reverse-mounted, consult Step 2a, p. 242.)

Cut a matching pair of quill segments as explained in "Preparing Quill Wings," p. 243. With the left fingers, pinch the quill segments, convex sides together, just behind the mounting point. (For an undivided wing, pinch the quill segments with the concave sides together.) Once the quills are pinched together, align the tips of the wings by sliding the fingertips against one another to push or pull the quill segments into alignment. Longer segments of quill can be aligned using the approach shown in **Method #40: Paired Quill Downwings**, Step 1, p. 287.

Notice that the quill segment is not symmetrical, but rather tapers to a point at one edge—on the right as shown in the photo below. This point is at the front of the wing.

Step 2. Hold the wings atop the hook as shown, with the front of the wings against the shank and the tips of the wing out the beyond the hook eye. (For reverse-mounted wings, hold the quills in the opposite orientation, with the back edge of the wing against the shank and the butts projecting over the hook eye.)

Affix the wings to the shank using any of the following mounting techniques: **Method #9: The Pinch Wrap**, p. 30; **Method #10: The Bobbin Loop**, p. 31; or **Method #11: The Langley Loop**, p. 32. After the initial mounting wrap is made, take one or two additional tight turns of thread at the mounting point to further secure the material.

Then take 4 or 5 tight, adjacent wraps of thread toward the hook bend (or toward the hook eye if the wing is reverse mounted), binding down the wing butts.

Step 3. Clip the quill butts, using an angle cut or other technique designed to create a smooth underbody when mated with the butts of the tailing material.

Post the wing to the vertical position using one of the techniques shown in **Method #1: Mounting and Posting Upright Wings**, p. 241.

Bind down the clipped butts tightly with thread.

Step 4. Quill wings can be reinforced in three ways. The most common is to apply a drop of flexible cement to the base of the wings—either between the two wings or at the outside of each wing base. Flexible cement is preferable to rigid adhesives such as CA glue or head cement, since a certain pliancy and resilience in the wing helps reduce air resistance during casting.

Second, with a needle or toothpick, apply a thin line of gel-type CA glue along the tip edges of the wing, as shown here. This adhesive essentially glues the quill barbs together at the tips to prevent splitting. It must, however, be applied sparingly and carefully, and not be allowed to bleed down into the main portion of the wing.

Finally, some tyers prefer to spray a light coating of workable fixative on the wing material. The wings can be coated before they are mounted or after they are mounted provided, of course, that no other materials have yet been affixed to the shank. Or whole feathers can be sprayed before the quill segments are cut. Spray fixative, however, has its drawbacks. The adhesive stiffens the wings, adding to air resistance in casting which may cause light tippets to twist. Where a wing made of untreated quill can sometimes be preened back to shape if it splits, a quill treated with workable fixative cannot; the adhesive mats the tiny barbules that cause the barb fibers to mate and adhere.

Step 5. Tyer René Harrop dresses upright wings from turkey biots trimmed to shape, as shown here. The technique for mounting and posting these wings is identical to the one shown in the preceding demonstration, except that they need not be reinforced with adhesive. Biots that lack a natural curvature may require a few crisscross wraps between the wings to separate them.

Biots are rather narrow, and thus this style is best suited to smaller hooks; the #16 shown here is about the largest practical size.

Method #3:
Downs Mount Quill Wings

Darrel Martin, who details this reverse-mount technique in his *Fly-Tying Methods*, named it for Donald Downs, the English tyer who demonstrated it for him. As he notes, it is the winging method advocated by Frederic Halford. While this technique is well suited to viseless tying—a traditional method not practiced much now—it is appropriate as well for use with a vise. Though the wing is reverse-mounted, the butts are tied off behind the wing, avoiding a bulky buildup of material behind the hook eye.

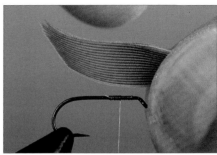

Step 1. Mount the tying thread and form a thread foundation that spans the winging point. Position the thread at the wing-mounting point, as shown.

Cut a pair of quill segments as described in "Preparing Quill Wings," p. 243.

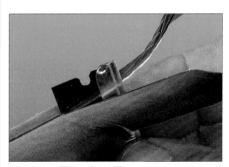

Step 1a. Though quill segments prepared in the ordinary fashion can be used, Martin suggests that tying is simplified and results improved if the quill segments are cut so that a small portion of the feather stem is attached at the base.

To prepare quill slips in this way, use a very sharp razor blade to shave the barbs from the feather stem. Work from the tip of the feather to the base, peeling the barbs from the feather. Note in the photo that a strip of the stem is peeled from the feather shaft and holds the barbs together at the base.

The wing slips are then misted with a workable fixative to improve handling during tying and increase durability. Feathers prepared in this way are easier to work with in viseless tying.

Finally, segments of quill of the desired width are simply snipped off the strip, as shown in the photo on p. 244.

Step 2. The wings are affixed to the shank, in a reverse mount using any of the following mounting techniques: **Method #9: The Pinch Wrap**, p. 30; **Method #10: The Bobbin Loop**, p. 31; or **Method #11: The Langley Loop**, p. 32.

After the initial mounting wrap is made, take one or two additional tight turns of thread at the mounting point to further secure the material.

Step 3. This procedure is the unusual part of the technique. Fold the feather butts back, one on each side of the hook shank, sandwiching the wings between them. Keep the butts above, and parallel to, the hook shank as shown.

Step 4. Holding the butts in this position with your left hand, grasp the wing tips in the right hand and raise them to the vertical position.

Now readjust your left fingers, grasping the wing butts closer to the wings and pinching them tightly. This will help the wings maintain their vertical position.

Step 5. Take 3 or 4 wraps of thread directly behind the wing, posting the wing and binding down the butts simultaneously.

If the wing is not vertical, pull it toward the hook eye by the tips, and take a few additional turns of thread close to the wing base toward the hook eye.

When the wing stands vertically, clip the butts and bind down the excess.

Method #4:
Side-mount Quill Wings

As the name suggests, side-mounted quills are a type of upright wing mounted to the side of the hook shank rather than bound to the top. Since the wings project from the side of the hook, they behave, to some extent, like pontoons or outriggers to support and balance the fly on the water. Typically, such flies are not dressed with hackle.

The most famous pattern incorporating this style is unquestionably the No-Hackle Dun made popular in *Selective Trout*, by Doug Swisher and Carl Richards. Swisher and Richards experimented with a variety of materials and styles in their No-Hackle design, but the version of this wing that is most familiar to modern tyers—broad, perfectly matched upright quill wings mounted on the sides of the shank—comes largely from the work of Idaho tyer René Harrop. The absence of hackle makes for a low-floating fly best suited to calmer waters. Such wings are quite fragile, however, and though a fly with tattered wings may still catch fish, excessively damaged wings may destroy the balance of the fly, which may cease to land upright on the water.

The main sequence illustrates a widely used method for dressing side-mounted wings. The alternate sequence demonstrates two separate procedures. The first is a method of wing preparation advocated by Dick Talleur. While these added steps do take a bit more time, they greatly simplify wing-mounting, and in fact tyer Bill Blades used this technique for preparing quill segments to dress the more conventional upright and downwing styles. The second procedure, which some tyers prefer, is an alternate technique for affixing the wings to the shank. The last photo shows a double side-mounted wing designed by René Harrop.

In either case, however, these wings can be tricky to dress; proper proportion, precise mounting, and symmetry are crucial to the performance of the fly on the water. The best results are obtained with quills of high quality—smooth, even tips, and feathers well matched in curvature. Secondary wing feathers or larger coverts (see "Wing Feathers," p. 9), with their finer texture, tend to produce better wings than primary feathers, particularly on smaller flies. Finally, this style of winging is really restricted to hooks of #14 and smaller. Larger hooks are difficult to wing, and the heavier wire makes a poor-floating fly.

Some tyers prefer to affix side-mounted wings after the tail and rear portion of the body have already been dressed. To assist in floating the fly, divided or fan tails are generally used and the body is dubbed. This approach has two advantages. First, the wings are not disturbed when dubbing the body, and second, the tying thread is wrapped a turn or two back over the dubbing to establish the wing-mount position. Mounting the wings over the forward edge of the dubbing provides a slightly broader base for attachment and can simplify winging a bit.

Other tyers, like Dave Whitlock, advocate dressing only the tail first and affixing the wings on a thread base laid on the hook shank. This approach allows for slightly easier adjustments of the wing position during tying.

Step 1. Prepare the hook by affixing tails and either dubbing a body up to the wing-mount position or laying a thread foundation at this same point. The wing-mount position is about ⅓ of a shank-length back from the hook eye. Take 4 or 5 turns of thread ahead of the wing-mount position to lay a foundation for binding the quill butts.

Then wrap the thread back over the front edge of the dubbed body, as shown, to provide a broader wing-mounting foundation. Position the thread at the wing-mounting point.

Cut a matching pair of quill segments as explained in "Preparing Quill Wings," p. 243, except that the width of the quill segments should be about ⅓ to ½ the length of the hook shank—somewhat wider than is customary on other styles of quill wing. If desired, mist these segments with a spray fixative to improve the durability of the finished fly; allow them to dry.

Pinch the quill segments together at the base, convex sides together, with the thumb and forefinger of the right hand. Once the quills are pinched together, even the tips of the wings by sliding the fingertips against one another to push or pull the quill segments into alignment.

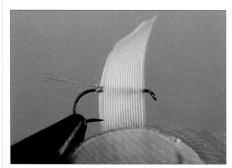

Step 2. From beneath the shank, slip the quill segments upward so that they are sandwiched around the hook shank at an angle of about 90 degrees, as shown. Adjust the wings so they are about one shank-length in height.

12

SECTION 1

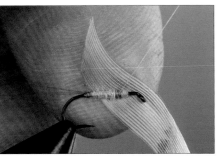

Step 3. Rotate the wing tips rearward until the quill segments make an angle of about 60 degrees with the hook shank.

Adjust the quill segments so that they *straddle* the wing-mounting point. That is, half of each wing should be ahead of the wing-mounting point (and the tying thread which is positioned there), and half of each wing behind it. The wing on the near side of the shank has been temporarily removed to illustrate the wing placement in relation to the mounting point.

Raise the tying thread between the wings, angling toward the hook eye, as shown above.

Step 4. Mounting the wings is the tricky part, and researching techniques used by various tyers has turned up two basic approaches. Both are versions of the pinch-wrap technique (see **Method #9: The Pinch Wrap**, p. 30) but they differ in the specifics of thread handling. The version described here uses thread wraps that are perpendicular to the *hook shank*. A second version is described in Steps 2a-2c.

With the fingers of the left hand, pinch both quills around the hook shank at the mounting point. Make certain that the entire width of the quill is pinched flat between the pads of your thumb and forefinger or the material will buckle when thread pressure is applied.

Begin with the bobbin raised above the hook shank. Slip the tying thread between the quill on the far side and your index finger.

Now bring the thread underneath the shank and up between the quill on the near side and your thumb. Do not tighten the thread, but rather form a slack loop beneath the shank.

Now bring the thread over the top of the shank and back down between the quill on the far side and your index finger. Again, do not tighten the thread, but form a slack loop above the shank.

In this photo, red wire shows the configuration of the thread wraps pinched between thumb and forefinger.

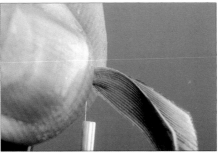

Step 5. Maintaining a firm pinch on the quill segments and hook shank, pull directly downward on the tying thread.

Without releasing the quills, take two more firm wraps around the quills, again by slipping the thread between the quill segments and fingers.

Step 6. Release the quills. If all has gone well, the wings will be raised to an angle of about 60 degrees with the hook shank, and will project from the sides of the shank, not the top. If the position is correct, bind down the butts and clip the excess. Reinforce the wings, if desired, using any of the procedures described in **Method #2: Upright Quill Wings**, Step 4, p. 245.

If the wings have rolled around the shank or are asymmetrical, you can adjust them at this point. Very slightly slacken the thread pressure and readjust the wings. Then pinch the wings against the shank, and tighten the thread.

If the wings are not raised vertically enough, but are satisfactory in other regards, bind down the butts and clip the excess. The wings can be raised slightly by putting a few turns of dubbing (or a few additional turns of dubbing if the body is already dressed) directly behind them.

Step 7. Here is a front view of the wings. Note that they project symmetrically from the sides of the shank. The bottom edges of the wings are flush with the bottom of the hook shank. The rear edges of the wing flare slightly outward, and the front edges tilt inward. This inward slant of the wing helps shed the wind and prevent tippet twist.

Dick Talleur uses a technique in which the wings are prepared in advance to simplify mounting.

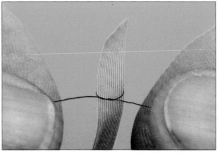

Step 1a. To prepare quill segments by "pre-crimping" them as Dick Talleur suggests, cut a pair of quill segments as described in Step 1.

Affix one end of a 12" length of tying thread to a hook. Tie an overhand knot in the middle of the thread, but do not tighten.

Insert one of the quill segments into the knot. Adjust the position of the quill so that the tip section extends beyond the knot a distance equal to the desired wing height.

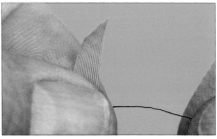

Step 1b. Pinch the quill tightly between thumb and forefinger. With the other hand, tighten the overhand knot.

Step 1c. The barbs will collapse at the knot point.

Put a small droplet of gel-type CA glue at the knotting point, and trim the ends of the thread close to the quill.

Repeat Steps 1a-1c with the other quill segment to pre-form a pair of wings. Proceed to Step 2.

In this version of the pinch wrap, the thread is not wrapped perpendicular to the hook shank, but rather almost perpendicular to the quill segments themselves.

Step 2a. Position the quill segments as shown in Step 2, and pinch them against the shank as explained in Step 4.

248

Begin by drawing the tying thread toward the hook point. Bring the thread up the near side of the shank, and slip it between the thumb and quill segment on the near side.

Then bring the thread over to the far side of the shank. Draw it toward the hook point, slipping it between the index finger and quill segment on the far side of the shank. You've now made a slack loop completely around the wings.

Make another such loop directly atop the first. The red thread here shows the configuration of wraps that is pinched between the thumb and forefinger.

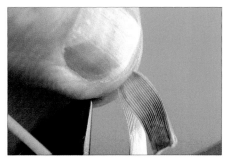

Step 2b. Maintaining a firm pinch on the quill segments and hook shank, pull the thread toward the rear of the fly and slightly downward.

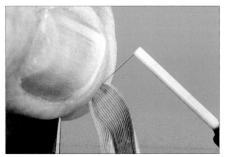

Step 2c. Without releasing the quills, bring the thread between the quill segment on the near side and your thumb, and pull the thread toward the hook eye, angling upward.

Step 3a. Tyer René Harrop devised a double side-mount wing for use on the No-Hackle Dun. While this wing style takes more time to tie, the finished wings are a bit more durable than the single side-mount.

The shorter, second pair of wings (tied from a darker feather for better visibility here) can be mounted after the longer first pair by using the techniques described above. Or the pair of wings on each side of the hook, one long wing and one short, can be mounted simultaneously.

Upright Feather-tip Wings

Upright wings can be fashioned from the tips of feathers—hackle or body feathers—in which the feather stem is left intact to become part of the wing. (Barbs stripped from the stems of these same feathers can be used for wings as well, and this style is described in the section "Upright Bundled-fiber Wings," p. 262.) Perhaps the most famous example of this wing type is in the Adams, in which grizzly hackle tips are used, but the style is gaining popularity on many other fly dressings, often as a replacement for quill or other materials. Feather-tip wings cut a clean, well-defined silhouette; they can be used with either conventional or parachute hackles on a wide range of hook sizes; the material is available in a variety of colors as well as barred and variegated patterns; and most of the dressing techniques are not difficult. Above all, however, such wings are extremely durable, despite their delicate appearance.

Still another advantage to this style is that the wings can be formed in a number of ways. Perhaps the simplest and most common is to tie in the natural tips of the feathers, such as on the Adams, to create the wings. However, feathers can also be cut or burned to specific shapes, giving the tyer greater latitude in wing profiles and a somewhat larger repertoire of suitable feathers from which to choose. Thus the range of plumage and the variety of preparation techniques make this wing an enormously versatile style.

Selecting Feathers for Feather-tip Wings

A variety of feathers are, or at least can be, suitable for fashioning feather-tip wings. Flank feathers, particularly from waterfowl such as mallard and teal, are sometimes used when wings with a barred or mottled appearance are desired. Such feathers, however, are rarely used to tie natural-tip wings; some of the feathers are long and spearhead-shaped, and these are severely asymmetrical about the center quill, producing thin wings of uneven appearance. Other feathers are shorter, fanlike, and more symmetrical, but they tend to produce wedge-shaped wings with straight, even tips that are not particularly realistic in appearance. These feathers, however, are occasionally used to dress fan wings. Flank feathers are more satisfactory when cut or burned to yield the desired wing profile, but even then, problems can arise. The difficulty with plumage from the flank (and other areas of the body) is that the feathers often have thick stems and narrow barb angles which, as discussed below, limit their acceptability for winging. But tyers who select these feathers with care can turn out wings that are strikingly attractive and practical.

Breast feathers (again, usually but not necessarily from waterfowl) are relatively short, fanlike in appearance, and quite curved. Their principal use in winging is for dressing natural-tip fan wings. When selecting breast feathers, choose the largest feathers and use only the very tip portion, where the stem is thinnest, to dress wings.

Small covert feathers (see the photo on p. 10) taken from the wings of smaller birds or from the leading edge of the wing on larger birds, are sometimes used as well. These feathers are short, webby, and symmetrical, and they make excellent winging material, provided the stems are not too thick. The one problem is that they are not readily available from commercial sources. The best bet for obtaining wing coverts is to buy whole, paired bird wings, or cultivate the friendship of a waterfowl or upland-bird hunter.

Of the materials suitable for feather-tip wings, the overwhelming favorite among tyers is hackle, particularly feathers from hen necks or saddles. Hackle tips from rooster capes and saddles were once commonly used for winging, but they are employed far less frequently now for a couple of reasons. First, most tyers today buy genetic hackle from birds raised exclusively for fly tying. Such feathers are expensive, and to use them for wings when a less costly alternative would serve just as well seems to most tyers a waste of material. Secondly, wings fashioned from rooster-hackle tips present a narrower, less distinct silhouette than hen-hackle tips; when they become wet, the barbs on rooster hackle tend to mat together, further narrowing the profile. Perhaps the one advantage of rooster hackle is that the feathers from variant necks, such as grizzlies, often have narrower bars of contrasting color than are found on hen hackle, which gives the wings a more mottled appearance. Inexpensive rooster capes or those of wet-fly grade can certainly be used. But many tyers find that hen hackle generally makes a superior winging material, and there is probably none better than the genetic hen necks and saddles that are essentially a byproduct of breeding for dry-fly hackle.

Even with a given type of plumage, however, not all individual feathers are equally useful. Exercising some care in selecting materials will ensure a wing that ties well, casts easily, and performs properly on the water. One of the most important criteria in choosing feather-tip winging material is stem thickness. Feathers with very fine, flexible stems make the most satisfactory wings. Thick stems make the wing overly rigid, creating substantial air resistance during casting, which causes the fly to spin and twist the tippet. A thinner, more pliable stem will flex during casting and reduce air resistance, yet spring back to an upright position when the fly is on the water. Unfortunately, less experienced tyers tend to gravitate toward feathers with thicker stems because the rigidity of the quill makes them slightly easier to tie. But such flies will be miserable to cast, and once the tippet becomes twisted, these flies often fail to land upright on the water.

Thickness of the quill is a relative measure. A #12 Adams, for example, can tolerate a thicker-stemmed wing than a #18 because the larger fly is delivered on a heavier tippet, which will resist twisting. In general, the practice is to choose the smallest feather that will still provide the desired width in the wing, thus ensuring the thinnest feather stem.

The second consideration is the amount of web in the feather. A webby feather produces a very well-defined wing; the interlocking barbules help the wing maintain its shape and create the appearance of a single, translucent panel. Most body, breast, and flank feathers are heavily webbed and pose little problem in this regard. Hackle, however, is a different story. Feathers from a rooster neck or saddle, particularly dry-fly grade, have somewhat indistinct edges when they are tied as wings and do not present a clear, nicely edged silhouette. Hen hackle, which is naturally rather webby, is a better choice, though there is still some variation here. The best winging feathers from a hen cape or saddle are webby right out to the edge of the barbs, and these are particularly useful when tying wings of natural hackle tips. Other hen hackles show webbiness only close to the stem; at the edges of the feather, the barbs are not interlocked and more closely resemble rooster hackle. However, such feathers can produce perfectly satisfactory cut or burned wings, which are discussed below.

Top row: The feather on the left is an excellent hen saddle hackle for winging. Notice that the webbiness extends to the very tip of the feather, making it suitable for a natural-tip wing, as shown in the center, or for a burned or cut wing, as shown on the right.
Middle row: The feather on the left has web that extends to the tip of the barbs, but the stem is quite thick. A wing made from such a feather is apt to twist the tippet during casting. The feather on the right has a very thin, flexible stem, but the lack of webbiness near the edges of the feather would make a natural-tip wing with a poorly defined profile.
Bottom row: The rooster hackle on the left appears as though it would make a nice wing, but when the barbs are preened back, as shown on the right, the resulting wing is a poor one—very narrow and lacking density for a distinct silhouette.

A commonly overlooked criterion in selecting winging feathers is the angle between the barbs and the feather stem. In some feathers, this angle is quite acute; the barbs lean sharply toward the feather tip, making a very narrow angle with the stem. When such feathers are sized for the fly and the excess barbs preened back toward the butt of the feather, the resulting wings will

appear as little more than thin slivers of material, insufficiently broad to create a clearly defined, well-proportioned wing. Many flank, body, and breast feathers exhibit this shortcoming, and such plumage must be selected carefully to produce a wing of satisfactory shape. The best feathers have barbs that project outward from the stem at 45-degrees or more; when the feather is sized and the barbs preened back, the feather tip will maintain its broad, winglike shape.

Top row: Both the dun body feather on the left and the mallard flank feather on the right seem well-suited to winging. But when the feathers are preened to size the wings . . .
Bottom row: The very narrow angle between the barbs and the feather stem becomes apparent. The wings formed with these feathers, shown on the left and in the middle, offer only sliver-like silhouettes as compared to the broader, more distinct profile of the wing on the right.

The final consideration in selecting feathers is symmetry. The barbs on each side of the stem should be of the same length and project from the stem at the same angle. This is particularly true if the feather is used to create natural-tip wings. A certain amount of asymmetry can be tolerated or compensated for if the wing is to be cut or burned.

The matter of symmetry extends to the pair of feathers used for winging as well. When the wings—either natural-tip, cut, or burned—are prepared, the two wing halves should be identical. Matching the wings is a fairly simple matter when using hackle; simply select feathers from the cape or saddle that are immediately adjacent to one another. In general, a pair of feathers that grow close together on the skin are very similar in color, stem thickness, web, barb angle, and symmetry. Body or breast feathers can be selected in the same way if you are removing them from the skin of a bird. Flank feathers, however, are generally asymmetrical—there are "left" and "right" feathers, much like wing quills. If the feathers are on the skin, choose one from each side of the bird. However, body, breast, and flank feathers are more commonly sold loose and packaged in bags. Choosing identical feathers is a matter of laying out all the feathers and attempting to pair them as closely as possible. Sorting them by size first simplifies this somewhat tedious process.

Preparing Feather-tip Wings

Feathers used to create natural-tip wings—that is, wings formed simply by

using the tip ends of the feathers—require little or no preparation other than sizing the wing to the hook and establishing the mounting point. The techniques for doing so are presented below in **Method #7: Feather-tip Wings**, p. 252.

Many tyers, however, prefer to wing their flies with feathers that have been shaped in advance, either by cutting or burning. Preparing wings in this fashion has some advantages. Because the edges of the feather (which often lack webbing) are removed, the wings exhibit a more sharply edged, distinct profile. Moreover, the wings can be given a greater variety of shapes and profiles to approximate more closely the appearance of the natural insect. But perhaps the single greatest advantage is that the tyer has a far greater latitude in the choice of feathers. With natural-tip wings, the width and profile of the feather must be matched to the hook size to give wings of the proper proportion, which limits the choice of feathers. With cut- or burned-wing styles, the feather can be shaped to the proper dimensions. Thus, for instance, the beautiful, thin-stemmed, webby feathers from a hen saddle—which are often too wide for natural-tip winging on smaller patterns—are made useable for almost any hook size. Body, breast, and flank feathers, which often have very lifelike markings, rarely produce a natural-tip wing with a realistic silhouette. Cutting or burning can remedy this problem.

The tradeoff, of course, is that cutting or burning wings is a time-consuming process, and forming symmetrical wings can take a bit of practice. But such wings are certainly among the most realistic and durable of any style, and many tyers find them worth the extra effort.

The techniques presented below for cutting and burning wings are generalized, and wings fashioned from these procedures can be used on patterns that call for natural-tip wings, such as the Adams, or they can replace wings of other materials, such as quill, on almost any dressing. Some dressings, such as the Iwamasa Dun, however, call for rather specialized cut or burned wings and unusual tying techniques, and these are detailed separately in subsequent methods.

Method #5:

Cut Wings

Though perhaps not as simple or as fast as burning, cutting wings requires no specialized tools and gives the tyer greater control over the shape of the finished wing. While wings can be cut with very sharp tying scissors, the scissoring action of the blades tends to push the feather barbs out of position during cutting, resulting in a wing that lacks a clean edge. Scissors with serrated blades help minimize this problem. And you can mist the feathers with a workable fixative which prevents the barbs from shifting, though the added stiffness from the adhesive may produce a wing that twists tippets.

Many tyers, however, prefer to use a sharp pair of ordinary fingernail or toenail clippers for shaping part or all of the wing. The clamping action of such clippers does not disturb barbs during the cut.

Feathers can be trimmed to a variety of shapes to form upright wings which are used almost exclusively on mayfly dressings. These shapes, however, fall into two general categories—symmetrical and asymmetrical. When the barbs are trimmed to be symmetrical around the feather stem, the two wing halves are identical. The stem runs up the center of the cut feather, and there is no "left" or "right" wing. Two feathers can be trimmed simultaneously without much difficulty. Some anglers argue that placing the stem in the middle of the wings increases their tendency to twist the tippet. But this is a problem only when the feather stem is too thick. Choose wing feathers with very fine stems and you'll experience few difficulties with twisted tippets.

Still, some tyers prefer to cut the wings asymmetrically, placing the feather stem very close to the leading edge of the wing. Wing feathers with slightly thicker stems can be made practical when trimmed this way, and unusually lifelike silhouettes can be produced. Cutting well-matched wings in this fashion, however, is more painstaking.

Wings can be cut singly or in pairs. Cutting each wing separately simply requires trimming each feather to shape as shown below. Producing identical wings, however, can be a bit tricky, and more experienced tyers generally cut both feathers at the same time.

In the main sequence below, two symmetrical wings are formed simultaneously using clippers. The alternate sequence illustrates a method used by Poul Jorgensen, a proponent and creative tyer of cut-wing flies, for shaping a pair of asymmetrical wings simultaneously.

Step 1. Begin by selecting a pair of matched feathers. Strip away the fuzz and barbs at the base of the stem until the feather is about twice as long as the finished wing.

Place the feathers together, front to back—that is, so that the feathers curve in the same direction and "nest" together.

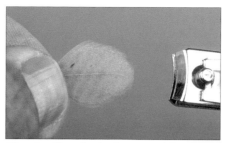

Step 2. Align the feathers carefully so that the stems lie directly atop one another. (Holding the feathers up against a light will make both stems visible.) They should look like a single feather. Maintaining this alignment is crucial to producing matched wings.

With a pair of clippers, cut straight across the feather tip. Note the location of the cut—very close to the tip of the feather. The object here is to trim away only the scraggly barbs at the edge so that the tip of the wing will be formed from a webby portion of the feather. You want to form the wing as close as possible to the tip of the feather. Removing too much material from the feather tip means that the wing will be formed farther down the feather, where the stem is thicker.

Step 3. Now trim the leading and trailing edges of the feather, roughing out the wing to the desired width. Remember to keep the cuts symmetrical about the feather stem, which should run exactly up the middle of the wing.

Step 4. Now round the wing tips.

Step 5. When the wings are paired and sized, they will look like this. Note that since the wings are identical, either feather can be mounted on either side of the hook shank.

To mount cut wings, see **Method #7: Feather-tip Wings**, p. 252, or **Method #8: Reverse-mount Feather-tip Wings**, p. 253.

Step 1a. To form asymmetrical wings using Jorgensen's technique, select two feathers as described in Step 1, and strip the fuzz from the base of the stem. Place the two feathers back-to-back, that is, with the concave sides together. In cutting asymmetrical wings, the curvatures must oppose another to produce a "left" wing and a "right" one.

At this point, Jorgensen strips the barbs from the base of the stems until both feathers are about ¼" longer than the finished wing, as we've done here. When prepared in this fashion, the finished cut wings will be of exactly the right length.

Such wings, however, will be mounted by binding in the stripped stems which can a bit tricky. Cut wings can be formed by leaving the lower barbs intact and then sizing the wings later, as described in **Method #7: Feather-tip Wings**, Steps 1 or 2a-3a, p. 252. Wings formed in this way can be a bit less troublesome to mount, but require extra steps to size and prepare.

Step 2a. If necessary, realign the feathers, and clip the stems together with a pair of hackle pliers or hemostats. With a small brush or dubbing needle, apply a thin band of head cement to one *edge* of the feather, gluing the barbs together at the very tips. Do not allow the cement to bleed down the barbs close to the stem. Apply a drop of cement at the very base of the barbs to glue the stems together.

Let the cement dry.

Step 3a. When making the initial cut, you can use the hook shank as a gauge to establish the finished wing height, but like many tyers, Jorgensen uses a winging gauge. A winging gauge can be made easily by cutting a strip of cardboard or stiff

paper; at one end, draw a line that is one "wing-height" in distance from the edge.

Lay the glued feathers across the gauge so that the barbs at the base of the stem are flush with the line. Pinch the feathers tightly against the gauge with the left hand. Now clip the tip of the feather flush with the edge of the gauge.

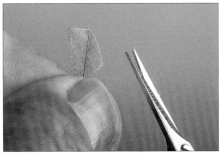

Step 4a. Using scissors, shape the trailing edge of the wing by trimming the edge of the feather that has not been treated with head cement.

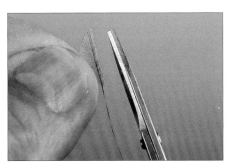

Step 5a. With scissors, shape the leading edge by cutting the barbs close to, and parallel to, the feather stem.

Step 6a. Trim the wing tips to give a rounded profile. Separate the glued stems.

Note that the wings are not identical, but rather, mirror images of one another.

To mount cut wings, see **Method #7: Feather-tip Wings**, p. 252, or **Method #8: Reverse-mount Feather-tip Wings**, p. 253.

Method #6:
Burned Wings

Many tyers find cutting wings to be a somewhat tedious process and prefer instead to shape them by using one of the commercially available wing burners. Burning wings is a bit faster than cutting and, when tying a quantity of flies, produces more uniform results. The primary drawback is that you are restricted to the wing shape produced by the burner itself. Most commercial burners are designed to produce asymmetrical wings, which means that each wing must be burned separately—as shown in the main sequence—or that the pair of feathers must be glued and prepared in advance, as shown in the alternate sequence.

Dick Talleur, however, suggests reshaping commercial wing burners to produce symmetrical wings, and in *The Versatile Fly Tyer* he provides instructions for making your own wing burners to yield symmetrical wings of any shape desired.

Renzetti wing burners, one of the most widely available types, are used for both of the following demonstrations.

Step 1. Begin by selecting a pair of matched feathers. Strip away the fuzz and barbs at the base of the stem until the feather is about twice as long as the finished wing.

Step 2. Hold one feather with the convex side facing you, and clamp it in the wing burner. Note that the feather barbs visible at the edges of the burner project evenly from all sides, indicating that the feather stem is centered inside the burner. Hold the wing burner firmly to keep the feather from shifting.

Note as well the shape of the wing burner. One side, here on the right, is almost straight. This side is the leading edge of the wing. The other side slopes away from the wing tip. It is important that once the orientation of the wing burner is established that the tool remain in this position and not be accidentally turned

backwards. Maintaining a consistent orientation of the burner will ensure that "left" and "right" wings will be formed.

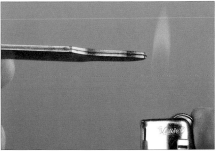

Step 3. If the feather is very wide and a substantial amount of material projects beyond the edge of the wing burner, trim this excess material with scissors to within ⅛" of the burner edge. Trimming like this allows you to burn as little feather material as possible, keeping the wing burner cleaner, minimizing the singed material on the feather, and producing a wing with a sharper profile.

Hold the wing burner horizontally above, and to the side of, a "clean" flame from an alcohol burner or butane lighter; candles produce excessive soot. Move the wing burner around the flame to burn away the exposed edges of the feather.

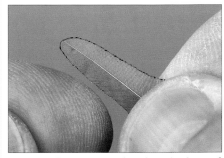

Step 4. Brush away the singed edges of the feather.

Remove the feather from the wing burner. If necessary, brush away any singed edges that remain.

Step 5. Hold the second feather with the *concave* side facing you. Make certain that the wing burner is in the same orientation as it was in Step 2, that is, with the straight edge of the burner facing right.

Clamp the feather in the burner as you did in Step 2, making certain that the barbs project evenly from all sides and that the feather stem is centered.

Burn the feather as described in Steps 3 and 4 to produce the second wing.

Step 6. The finished wings look like this.

To mount cut wings, see **Method #7: Feather-tip Wings**, below, or **Method #8: Reverse-mount Feather-tip Wings**, p. 253.

Step 1a. To burn two feathers simultaneously, prepare them as described in **Method #5: Cut Wings**, Steps 1a-2a, p. 250. There are two differences, however. First, cementing the quills at the base may not be necessary since pinching the feathers in the wing burner will help hold them in alignment. And second, do not strip the feather barbs from the base of the stems. It is easier to burn the wings to shape and size them afterward as described in **Method #7: Feather-tip Wings**, Steps 1, or 1a-3a, p. 252.

Note that the feathers used here must be wide enough so that the cemented edge projects beyond the edge of the wing burner. If any portion of cemented feather lies inside the burner, the wing halves will be difficult or impossible to separate without damage.

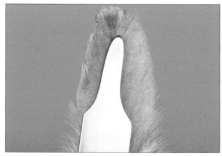

Step 2a. Clamp the pair of feathers inside the burner so that the stem is placed in the desired position. The stem may be centered or, as shown above, placed near the leading edge of the wing.

Unfortunately, the design of most commercially available wing burners makes the precise placement of the quill difficult to determine since it is concealed between the burner halves. The feather edges projecting beyond the burner are the only real reference point for positioning the quill.

Step 3a. Burn the wings as explained in Step 3.

Separate the wing halves. When the wings are paired and sized, they will look like this.

To mount cut wings, see **Method #7: Feather-tip Wings**, below, or **Method #8: Reverse-mount Feather-tip Wings**, p. 253.

Mounting Feather-tip Wings

Whether wings are formed from natural-tip, cut, or burned feathers, the techniques for mounting them are by and large identical. But there are several options available during specific stages of tying, depending upon the hackling style of the finished fly, wing-mounting orientation, the way the wings are sized and prepared, and, of course, personal preference. In fact, the number of options is large enough so that they cannot be conveniently explained in a single tying sequence. Thus the various options are explained in the following three methods: the first covers standard mounting (wing butts to the rear); the second deals with reverse mounting (wing butts toward the hook eye); and the last details the specific preparation of wings used as a base for parachute hackling.

These methods, however, are not mutually exclusive. The procedures for wing preparation, for example, or wing posting that are presented in one method may well be used in another. The following three methods, taken together, should be seen as a reservoir of alternatives from which the tyer may pick and choose in order to best accommodate a specific pattern or tying style.

Method #7:

Feather-tip Wings

This technique for attaching feather-tip wings is used when a standard collar-style hackle is used. The main sequence illustrates what is perhaps the most common way of preparing feather-tip wings for mounting—by preening back the excess barbs that will not be incorporated into the wings. The alternate sequence shows two methods of preparation preferred by some tyers—clipping the excess barbs before mounting, and stripping the excess barbs from the feather stem.

All of the techniques illustrated below involve "sizing" the wings in advance by preening, clipping, or removing the excess feather barbs. This approach minimizes stray barbs bound in with the wing that may

require clipping afterwards. However, sizing in advance is not strictly necessary; natural-tip, cut, or burned wings can also be tied in a standard mount, using the approach detailed in **Method #8: Reverse-mount Feather-tip Wings**, p. 253.

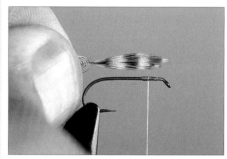

Step 1. Mount the tying thread and create a thread foundation for the wing as described in **Method #1: Mounting and Posting Upright Wings**, Step 1a, p. 242.

Before mounting, the wings are sized to the hook shank. On larger wings, particularly those formed from natural tips, sizing can be accomplished simply be preening back the barbs below the mounting point and holding them in position as the wing is attached. The advantage of this method is that some of the excess barbs are bound to the hook shank alongside the feather stems. The extra bulk furnished by these barbs helps prevent the feather stems from rolling under thread pressure, which simplifies the mounting procedure.

On natural-tip wings, or those shaped symmetrically by cutting or burning, both feathers can be sized simultaneously. Lay the feathers with the convex sides together, just as they will be oriented on the finished fly. Adjust them so that the tips are even and the stems lie directly atop one another.

To size the wings, use the hook shank as a guide; wings are generally one shank-length in height. Grasp the very tips of the feathers in the right fingers. Use the left fingers to pinch the stems at the mounting point and draw the barbs below the mounting point downward toward the feather base, as shown.

The feathers can be mounted at this point, or they can be prepared further as described in Steps 1a-3a. Asymmetrical wings or very small feathers can be sized as described here, but many tyers find that the wings are more easily handled using the procedures described in the alternate steps.

Step 2. Once the feathers are paired and sized, position the wings atop the shank so that the mounting point is directly above the tying thread, as shown.

Take a turn of thread under very light tension over the mounting point. Pull the thread tight, using the index finger of your left hand as a "backstop" to prevent the wings from rolling to the far side of the shank. Notice that this first wrap is taken over the stems directly below the lower-most feather barbs on the wings.

If you encounter difficulties in keeping the wings positioned atop the shank, particularly when mounting wings with stripped feather stems, you can employ the same slack-loop techniques used in mounting quill wings: **Method #9: The Pinch Wrap**, p. 30; **Method #10: The Bobbin Loop**, p. 31; or **Method #11: The Langley Loop**, p. 32. **Method #7: The Cradle Loop**, p. 28, can also be helpful in positioning the thread accurately.

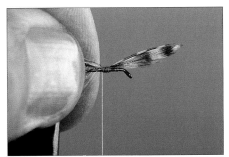

Step 3. Take 2 or 3 more tight turns of thread over the mounting point, again using the left index finger to keep the wings directly atop the shank.

Bind in the wing butts by taking 4 or 5 tight, adjacent turns toward the hook bend.

Step 4. Clip the excess feather material and bind down the butts. Bring the tying thread to a point directly in front of the wings.

Post the wing to the vertical position using the thread-bump technique explained in **Method #1: Mounting and Posting Upright Wings**, Step 1c p. 242. The modified lash-wrap described in **Method #8: Reverse-mount Feather-tip Wings**, Steps 3a-6a, p. 254, can be used as well, but the instructions must be reversed since the wings shown here are mounted in the opposite direction. (The loop-posting technique described in **Method #1** does not provide entirely satisfactory results with feather-tip wings, particularly those to be dressed with parachute hackle.)

If desired, place a small drop of head cement at the base of the wing.

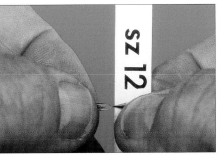

Step 1a. Many tyers size feather-tip wings by using a winging gauge. Winging gauges are particularly useful for very small feathers, which can be hard to grasp and manipulate with the fingers alone. For the same reason, a gauge is useful on wings where cutting or burning has shortened the barbs and made them difficult to handle. And finally, a pair of wing feathers shaped with a pronounced asymmetry can be difficult to size simultaneously. It is often easier to size them individually, and a wing gauge ensures consistency.

A winging gauge can be made easily by cutting a strip of cardboard or stiff paper that is equal in width to the wing height. A different gauge can be made for each hook size.

Place the feather crosswise against the gauge so that the feather tip is even with one edge of the paper. With the right thumb and forefinger, pinch the feather tip against the gauge. Use your fingers or a dubbing needle to stroke the barbs at the lower edge of the gauge downward. Once these lower barbs have been preened outward from the stem, and the mounting point established, you can use your fingers to preen them further toward the base of the feather.

The feathers can be mounted at this point, or they can be prepared further as described in Steps 2a or 3a.

Step 2a. On extremely small feathers, where it can be difficult to hold the very short barbs in the "preened" position during mounting, you can trim the barbs below the mounting point close to the stem, as shown. Trimming the barbs like this ensures that enough barb material will be bound to the shank to prevent the stems from rolling under thread pressure. At the same time, the barbs are short enough so that they require no trimming after the wing is mounted.

Steps 3a. Some tyers prefer to completely strip away the barbs below the mounting point. On natural-tip wings, the mounting point is located, and the excess barbs are simply stripped away, as shown on the left. On cut- or burned-wings, it is often easier to size the wing and remove the barbs before the feather is shaped, as shown on the right. Grasping and stripping the very short barbs that are left after cutting or burning can prove difficult.

Wings with stripped stems are most often used when the wing shape is highly asymmetrical. Such wings are often reverse-mounted so that the feather tips slant back toward the bend rather than projecting vertically (see **Method #8: Reverse-mount Feather-tip Wings**, p. 253). Stripping the stems in advance simplifies this type of mount.

However, stripped stems tend to roll and twist under thread pressure, and can be fussy to mount. For the most part, wings with stripped stems are best used only when absolutely necessary.

Method #8:
Reverse-mount Feather-tip Wings

Nearly any feather-tip wing can be reverse-mounted, though in most cases there is little to be gained in doing so. Feather tips tie in with relatively little bulk, and the butts on standard-mounted wings do not appreciably affect the body profile.

Reverse mounting, however, is very useful in two instances. Wings prepared by stripping the stems (see **Method #7: Feather-tip Wings**, Step 3a, p. 253) are usually reverse-mounted, since positioning the wing atop the hook by grasping the stripped feather stems, which would be required for a standard mount, can be difficult. It is easier to hold and position the feathers by grasping the wing tips, and the procedure for doing so is explained in the main sequence below.

Reverse mounting is also useful for dressing feather-tip wings that have not been "pre-sized" using one of the techniques explained in **Method #7: Feather-tip Wings**, p. 252. While pre-sizing feathers makes for a very neat mount, it is a time-consuming process, particularly for the production tyer whose livelihood depends upon efficiency. A.K. Best's technique for dressing feather-tip wings, shown in the alternate sequence, is a quick and reliable method that requires cutting the winging feathers to their final length before mounting. Since there are no wing butts to grasp, the feathers must be reverse mounted.

In addition, this alternate sequence shows Best's method of using a fast, modified lash-wrap to post the wings to vertical. This technique can also be used with any of the feather-tip wing styles described in **Method #7: Feather-tip Wings,** p. 252, though the instructions will need to be reversed to post a wing mounted in the standard orientation.

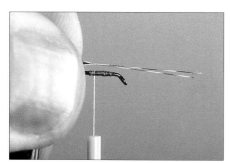

Step 1. Attach the tying thread and create a thread foundation for the wing as described in **Method #1: Mounting and Posting Upright Wings,** Step 2a, p. 241.

Prepare stripped-stem wings as explained in **Method #7: Feather-tip Wings,** Step 3a, p. 253. Pinch the wings with the convex sides together (place the concave sides together for a single, undivided wing). Adjust the wings so that the tips are even and the stems lie atop one another.

Position the wings atop the hook shank, with the base of the wing directly above the tying thread and the butts extending over the hook eye.

Step 2. Mount the wings with 2 or 3 thread wraps.

If you encounter difficulties in keeping the wings positioned atop the shank, particularly when mounting wings with stripped feather stems, you can certainly employ the same slack-loop techniques useful in mounting quill wings: **Method #9: The Pinch Wrap,** p. 30; **Method #10: The Bobbin Loop,** p. 31; or **Method #11: The Langley Loop,** p. 32. **Method #7: The Cradle Loop,** p. 28, can also be helpful in positioning the thread accurately.

Stripped hackle stems have a distinct tendency to roll under thread pressure, which often twists the wings on the hook shank. After the initial mounting wraps have been tightened, release the wings as shown here. If they remain in the desired position and are not twisted, grasp them again and bind them tightly to the shank. If the wings are crooked, pinch them

again in the left fingers, loosen or unwrap the turn of tying thread, and try mounting them again. Individual hackle stems vary a good deal in cross-sectional size and shape, and it may take a few attempts to secure the wings in the desired position.

Step 3. When the wings are satisfactorily mounted, take 4 or 5 tight, adjacent turns of thread toward the hook eye. Clip the excess stems and bind down the butts.

Step 4. Post the wing to the vertical using a thread bump behind the wings (see **Method #1: Mounting and Posting Upright Wings,** Step 2c, p. 241), or use the modified lash-wrap explained here in Steps 3a-6a.

If desired, place a small drop of head cement at the base of the wings.

Step 1a. To reverse-mount the wings using A.K. Best's method, attach the tying thread and create a thread foundation for the wing as described in Step 1.

Grasp a pair of wing feathers—cut, burned, or natural—with the convex sides together. Adjust the wings so that the tips are aligned and the stems lie atop one another. Using the hook shank or a winging gauge, establish the mounting point for a wing of the desired height.

Pinch the pair of wings in your left fingers so that the fingertips are located exactly at the mounting point.

Clip the feathers about ⅛" beyond the fingertips. This extra ⅛" length will be bound to the shank during mounting.

Position the wings so that the feather butts straddle the hook shank and project ⅛" beyond the tying thread, as shown.

Step 2a. Mount the wings using any of the methods noted in Step 2. When the wings are securely mounted, bind down the feather butts.

Position the tying thread at the front base of the wings. If the wings cling together, use your fingernail or a dubbing needle to separate them.

Step 3a. To post the wings to the vertical position, bring the tying thread toward you. Begin raising it above the hook shank. As you do, angle the thread toward the hook bend and pass it between the wings.

Step 4a. Bring the thread down on the far side of the hook shank so that it abuts the base of the wing on the far side. The pressure of this thread wrap should be enough to raise the far wing to the vertical position. If the wing is not vertical, tug the thread slightly toward the hook eye to elevate the far wing.

When the wing position is satisfactory, take one complete thread wrap ahead of the wings to anchor this posting wrap.

Step 5a. Now bring the thread up behind the wing on the near side of the shank. As you do so, angle the thread toward the hook eye and pass it between the wings.

Step 6a. Bring the thread down on the far side of the hook shank so that it abuts the base of the wing on the near side. Again, the pressure of the thread abutting the wing feather should be forceful enough to raise the near wing to the vertical position. If the wing is not fully elevated, apply more pressure to the thread to position the wing properly.

When the wing is satisfactory, take a complete wrap of thread ahead of the wings to anchor this second posting wrap.

If there are any stray or wayward barbs projecting from the wing base, trim them off.

Method #9:
Feather-tip Wings with Parachute Base

Fly patterns with feather-tip wings and a parachute hackle are among the most delicate and realistic of adult mayfly dressings. But one of the most desirable characteristics of the winging feathers—thin stems—works against parachute hackling. Even the relatively low torque of winding a parachute hackle can twist the wings out of position since the fine stems do not offer the kind of rigid base that simplifies parachute hackling.

There are two solutions. The first lies in reinforcing the wing base, and the main sequence below shows how such reinforcement can be accomplished using only tying thread. The technique shown in the alternate Steps 3a-3c, shown to us by Montana tyer Al Beatty, is an innovative solution that incorporates tail butts into the parachute post; it is, however, restricted to patterns with tailing materials that are sufficiently long. (A third technique that incorporates the hackle stem into the parachute post is presented in **Method #30: Parachute-hackle Mounts,** Steps 3a-3c, p. 382.)

The second solution, shown in Step 4a, is to wind the hackle around wings that have been deliberately twisted out of position during the application of the thread foundation. The torque of the hackle wraps draws the wings back into proper alignment.

Step 1. Wings used in parachute hackling are sized and prepared just as described

above in **Method #7: Feather-tip Wings**, p. 252. The difference comes in mounting. Instead of tying in the feathers precisely at the base of the wing, they are affixed to the shank a short distance below the base of the wing, as shown above. Here we're using wings that have been prepared by clipping the barbs below the mounting point close to the stem. We've elevated the wing slightly to show the section of feather stem between the mounting point and the base of the wing. This section of stem will be wrapped with tying thread for reinforcement in the parachute hackle base.

The length of this reinforced section varies with hook size, but it must be long enough so that the thread-wrapped base projects far enough above the *body material* to allow for 3 or 4 wraps of hackle. If this bare section is too short, the post created by the thread wraps will be entirely concealed by dubbing or other body materials, and the parachute hackle will overwrap the barbs at the base of the wings, distorting their shape.

To mount clipped hackle stems, see **Method #7: Feather-tip Wings**, Steps 2-4, p. 252. Wings with stripped hackle stems can be used as well, but must be reverse mounted (see **Method #8: Reverse-mount Feather-tip Wings**, p. 253.)

To mount wings prepared by preening back the barbs, see Step 1a, below.

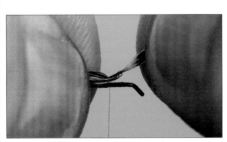

Step 1a. When tying in wings by preening back the barbs below the wing base, mounting the feathers by simply binding them down can be difficult. The preened-back barbs do not form a solid base over which to wrap the thread, and the wings tend to shift around.

Instead, you can use a version of **Method #7: The Cradle Loop**, p. 28. Place one wrap of thread directly over the feather stem at the base of the wing, and let the bobbin hang. Grasp the wing butts in the left fingers and the wing tips in the right fingers. Lift the wings very slightly and slide them forward beneath the thread wrap until the proper mounting point is reached.

Proceed to Step 2 or 3a.

Step 2. Secure the wing butts and clip the excess. Post the wings upright as explained in **Method #1: Mounting and Posting Upright Wings**, Step 1c, p. 241.

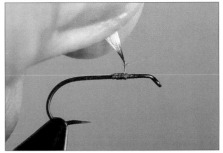

Step 3. These first thread wraps are the trickiest. Counterspin the bobbin to flatten the tying thread. Grasp the wing tips in the left fingers. (If using the Beatty method described in Steps 3a-3c, grasp the tail butts along with the wings, drawing all the material upward under even pressure.) With the tying thread under moderate tension, wrap the thread (clockwise as viewed from above) in adjacent turns up to the base of the wing. You'll need to release the wing tips once during each wrap of thread.

During wrapping, you'll need to maintain enough tension on the tying thread to keep the thread from loosening or unraveling, but not so much pressure that the thread slips over the top of the wing. If the wings are twisted out of position during this procedure, that's fine. It will be remedied later.

Step 4. With the tying thread flattened, increase thread pressure slightly, and wrap the wings back down to the hook shank. The wings will be twisted out of position now, having rotated toward you. They'll be straightened in a moment.

This is important: take one complete turn of thread around the hook shank ahead of the wings.

From this point, there are two ways you can proceed. The following steps in this main sequence show how the wings are straightened by applying a second thread foundation over the feather stems.

The procedure shown in Step 4a uses the hackle feather itself to straighten the wings.

Step 4a. At this point, you can mount a feather using any of the techniques explained in **Method #30: Parachute-hackle Mounts**, p. 381. The feather, however,

should be mounted to wrap in a counter-clockwise direction.

After the feather is mounted, the tail and body of the fly are dressed.

Wrap the hackle feather counterclockwise as explained in **Method #31: Single Parachute Hackle—Horizontal Wrap**, p. 383. As you wind the hackle, use the wrapping torque from the feather to twist the wings back into proper alignment. Do not try to straighten the wings with a single wrap of the hackle; rather, straighten them gradually, during a series of hackle wraps taken around the wings, as shown.

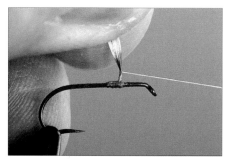

Step 5. If necessary, counterspin the bobbin to the flatten the thread. Wrap up the feather stems again to the base of the wing, but this time in a counterclockwise direction (as viewed from above). The "locking wrap" you took around the hook shank in Step 4 will allow you to reverse direction.

Because the first sequence of thread wraps has stiffened the feather stems a bit, you can increase thread pressure slightly.

Step 6. When you reach the base of the wing, wrap the thread back down the feather stems to the hook shank. As you approach the base of the feather stems, increase pressure as necessary to torque the wings back to their normal position. When the tying thread reaches the base of the stems, the wings should be perfectly straight on the hook shank. ("Sight down" the hook from the eye to ensure that the wings are correctly oriented.)

Lock in these counterwound wraps with another complete turn of tying thread around the hook shank ahead of the wings. If desired, apply a drop of head cement to the thread post.

The wings are now held in position by the tension and countertension of 4 layers of thread and will provide a reasonably firm base over which to wrap the parachute hackle.

Step 3a. Al Beatty uses the following technique to reinforce his reverse-hackle "wonder wings" (see **Method #13: Reverse-hackle Wings**, p. 260). It is equally useful for feather-tip wings.

Mount and secure the wings as described in Steps 1-2, but do not post the wings to the vertical position.

Wrap the thread to the tailing point, and tie in the tails. Bind the tail butts to the top of the hook, working up the shank until the base of the wing is reached. The last wrap of thread should secure the tailing butts directly over the wing-mounting point.

Step 3b. With the left fingers, raise the wings tips and tail butts to the vertical. Take a few turns of thread ahead of the wings to post them to the vertical position.

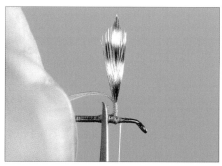

Step 3c. Form a thread base as explained in Steps 3-6.

Using Beatty's techniques, you will have wrapped a thread foundation over the feather stems and tailing material. The tailing material adds bulk and stiffness for a firmer parachute-hackle base.

When the thread base is complete and the wings positioned correctly on the shank, lock in the counterwound wraps with another complete turn of tying thread around the hook shank ahead of the wings.

Carefully trim the butts of the tailing material flush with the top of the thread post. If desired, apply a drop of head cement to the thread post.

Method #10:

Ogden Wings

We are indebted to tyer John Betts for pointing out that this wing style first appeared in the literature of fly tying in 1876 and was attributed to British tyer James Ogden. Most tyers are probably more familiar with the modern incarnation of this wing style as it has appeared in the work of Colorado tyer Ken Iwamasa and, more recently, Tatsuhiro Saido, who incorporate this highly realistic wing into their fly designs. Because the feather quill is placed low in the wing and angles to the rear, wind resistance against the wing is reduced.

The Ogden wing is used on the Iwamasa Dun, which is supported on the water by deer-hair cross-hackle (see **Method #29: Cross Hackle**, p. 378), and on a family of mayfly patterns devised by Saido which use either collar or parachute hackles. This wing can also be side-mounted to create a feather-tip version of the No-Hackle Dun as described in **Method #11: Side-mounted Feather-tip Wings**, p. 258. Iwamasa mounts the wings with concave sides together, forming a single vane atop the fly; Saido mounts them with the convex sides together to form a divided wing, as in Ogden's original design. Either mounting orientation, however, can be used on either pattern; the tying technique is identical.

The wings can be formed by cutting (Ogden's original method) or by burning. The main sequence below illustrates the wing-burning and mounting methods used by Ken Iwamasa.

Burning Iwamasa wings is easiest with a burner of the proper shape designed for the purpose. Though once commercially available, Iwamasa wing burners are now difficult to find. As indicated earlier, Dick Talleur describes in his book *The Versatile Fly Tyer* a procedure for making wing burners.

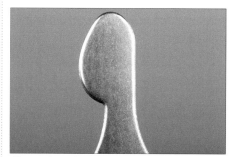

Shown here is an Iwamasa burner. Note its shape and proportions.

Though this type of burner is most efficient for producing Iwamasa wings, a conventional wing-burner can also be used, though some trimming will be required afterwards. This procedure is also illustrated in the main sequence.

The alternate sequence shows the cut-wing design and unusual mount of Saido's patterns. However, either type of fly can be dressed with either cut or burned wings.

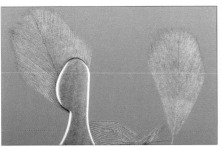

Step 1. Select a pair of winging feathers. The best feathers for this winging style are wide, webby, thin-stemmed hen saddles. Very broad feathers give the best results, as they allow you to form the wing very close to the tip of the feather to minimize stem thickness.

Place the wing burner in the orientation shown on the left. Move it is as close to the feather tip as you can, while still allowing the very ends of the barbs to project beyond the tip of the burner. This will ensure that any scraggly barb ends will be burned away and the wing itself formed from only the webby portion of the feather. When this position has been located, strip away all the barbs below the burner on both sides of the stem, as shown in the feather on the right.

Step 2. Use the stripped feather as a guide to preparing a second, matching feather.

Place the feathers back-to-back, that is, with the concave sides together. For this type of burning, make certain that the lowermost barbs on each feather are aligned and the stems lie atop one another. It is not necessary that the tips be matched precisely since they will burned away.

If the feathers have relatively little curvature, you may be able to clamp them in the wing burner at this point, making certain that the stems at the base of the barbs are aligned. Feathers with pronounced curvature are difficult to keep aligned while clamping, as the opposing curves tend to push the feathers sideways. In this case, additional measures are required.

To hold the feathers in the proper orientation, Ken Iwamasa recommends placing a drop of CA glue below the lowermost barbs to fasten the bare feather stems together. This can be a bit tricky, and equally good results can be obtained by gluing one edge of the paired feathers as shown here and explained in **Method #5: Cut Wings**, Step 2a, p. 242.

If you choose to glue the edge of the feathers, note the position of the wing burner in Step 1, and place the glue only on edges of the feather that will be removed by burning.

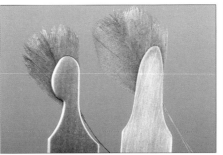

Step 3. Taking care to keep the feathers aligned, place them in an Iwamasa burner in the orientation shown on the left.

If using a standard wing burner, such as the Renzetti type, position the feather as shown on the right. Place the straightest edge of the wing burner (here, the edge on the right) parallel to the edge of the barbs on the right of the feather.

Burn the wings as explained in **Method #6: Burned Wings**, Steps 3-4, p. 251.

Step 4. The wings produced by the Iwamasa burner, on the left, are ready for mounting. In the middle is a feather shaped by the Renzetti burner. On the right is this same feather with the trailing edge trimmed to a curve with a pair of scissors or clippers. It is ready for mounting.

Step 5. The Iwamasa dun calls for a split tail, a dubbed body with a deer hair overbody, and deer-hair legs or cross hackle. These are applied before the wings, but have been omitted here for clarity of illustration.

The wings can be mounted in a couple of ways. Iwamasa places the wings with the concave sides together and mounts them by taking two wraps of thread over the hackle stems directly below the lowermost barbs, as shown here. With the wings held in position like this, they can be adjusted to the proper orientation. Then a drop of CA glue is applied to the two wraps of thread and allowed to dry. By using only two wraps of thread and essentially gluing the wings in position, you eliminate the tendency of the bare feather stems to roll under thread pressure.

However, the wings can also be mounted without glue by using the tech-

nique described in **Method #8: Reverse-mount Feather-tip Wings**, Steps 1-3, p. 254.

In Ogden's original technique, the wings flare outward and are secured as shown above with 4 or 5 thread wraps toward the hook eye. The feather stems are then pulled back along the sides of the shank and secured there with 2 or 3 wraps of thread (see **Method #1: Lock Wraps**, p. 25). This lock-wrap keeps thread bulk to a minimum while preventing the slippery stems from sliding loose.

Step 6. After the glue has dried, clip the excess feather stems and bind down the butts tightly.

Step 7. On the right is a finished Iwamasa dun tied by Ken Iwamasa; on the left is a Saido Trimmed-Hackle Dun from the alternate sequence.

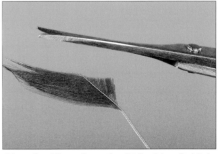

Step 1a. The wings for Tatsuhiro Saido's flies can be burned, but the following procedure shows the method for cutting them.

Prepare a pair of feathers by stripping the excess barbs as explained in Steps 1-2. The wings can be cut individually or, as we're doing here, in pairs to ensure symmetry.

To cut a pair of wings, mate and prepare the wings by gluing the edges as described in Step 2, taking care to keep the glue on the outermost edge of the feather.

Make the first cut by removing the feather tip. The width of the remaining barbs should be equal to the width of the finished wing.

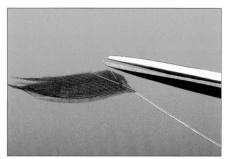

Step 2a. The following sequence of cuts can be made in virtually any order, but the sequence shown delays trimming the glued edge until the end, which helps keep the feathers aligned.

Trim the lower corner as shown. Round the sharp edges for a smooth profile as shown in Step 3a.

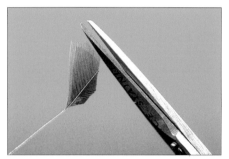

Step 3a. Now trim the wing to the proper height by cutting as shown. The wing height is equal to the shank length.

Step 4a. Now round the corners left by the cut in Step 3a to produce a smooth wing shape.

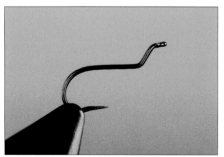

Step 5a. Part of Saido's unusual technique is to use a hook with shank that has been bent. With a pair of needle-nose pliers, bend the hook upward at the angle shown. The "elbow" that has been bent in the hook is ⅖ of the way down the shank from the eye.

Step 6a. The wings are affixed after the tail has been mounted, and a body dubbed. Saido uses a variety of hackling techniques. A collar hackle can be mounted on the straight portion of the shank immediately behind the bend. A "V" notch is trimmed from the hackle on the top of the shank to make room for the wings. A second "V" notch is then cut in the hackle on the underside of the shank. We've omitted these components for the sake of clarity, but a finished fly is pictured in Step 7.

Saido's dressings use a divided wing, so place the feathers front-to-front, with the convex sides together. The wings are mounted on the bent portion of the hook shank using either of the techniques noted in Step 5. Note the position of the wing; the bare hackle stem is mounted just ahead of the elbow in the hook shank.

Method #11:

Side-mounted Feather-tip Wings

In *Selective Trout*, Doug Swisher and Carl Richards explore many No-Hackle Dun patterns incorporating various winging materials, including feather tips, feather barbs, and wing quills. Of these, the side-mounted quill (see **Method #4: Side-mount Quill Wings**, p. 246) has probably gained the most popularity among fishermen. The tendency of the wing quill material to flare outward when mounted against the side of the hook creates a natural pontoon or outrigger effect that helps the fly land and float upright.

In their feather-tip No-Hackle Duns, Swisher and Richards primarily used hen-hackle tips and duck shoulder feathers mounted directly atop the hook shank. Such wings create a precise silhouette, but they do create some problems in the balance of the fly, which must rely primarily on the widely divided tail to remain upright on the water. This original style of fly can still be dressed by using the techniques detailed in **Method #7: Feather-tip Wings**, p. 252, and **Method #8: Reverse-mount Feather-tip Wings**, p. 253.

However, a fly that has better balance and lands upright more reliably can be fashioned from feather tips mounted on the sides, rather than the top, of the hook shank. Such flies are still somewhat tricky to dress properly, but they can be well worth effort. Feather-tip wings are far more durable than the quill wings often used for No-Hackle

Duns, and taking pains to tie these side-mounted wings produces an effective, long-lasting pattern. The key in dressing side-mounted feather-tip wings is in choosing a wing shape that provides the same outrigger effect as quill. In order to achieve this effect, the wings should flare slightly outward from the body, and the lowermost barbs on the wing should rest flush against the surface of the water. Most natural-tip wings are poorly suited to these requirements; to get the lowermost barbs in contact with the water requires angling the wings so severely backward that they cease to imitate effectively the upright silhouette of a mayfly dun. Cut or burned wings function much better, and of these, the Ogden style is perhaps the best. The lower edge of the wing can be set almost parallel to the hook shank, and the wing will still retain its upright profile.

We're using wings shaped in an Iwamasa burner for the following demonstration, but other cut- or burned-wing styles can be used.

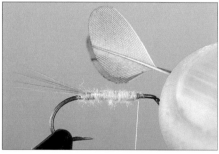

Step 1. Like patterns using side-mounted quills, those using feather-tip wings still rely heavily on widely split tails for balance on the water.

Mount any divided, triple, or fan tail described in Chapter 8: "Tails and Trailing Shucks."

Dub a slender body. The body material should be applied prior to the wings, since the dubbing helps flare the wings outward slightly; moreover, the wing position makes applying body materials difficult once the wings are mounted.

When the body is dressed, lay a foundation on the bare shank using 4 or 5 turns of thread. Then return the thread to front end of the dubbed body.

Cut or burn a pair of feathers as described in **Method #10: Ogden Wings**, p. 256. If a different style of cut or burned wings is used, you can prepare the feather by stripping off the barbs from the stem below the mounting point or by trimming these same barbs very close to the stem as shown in **Method #7: Feather-tip Wings**, Step 2a, p. 253.

The prepared feathers can be mounted in one of two orientations. Placing the concave sides together will create a fly with a narrower profile and less wind-resistance in casting, but it also produces a less pronounced pontoon effect in the wings. Mounting the wings with the convex sides together, as we're doing here, will produce a more exaggerated pontoon support in the wings for greater stability, but it does increase wind-resistance.

Step 2. Using the left fingers, pinch the wing tips together. Position the wings as shown, so that the stems straddle the hook and the bottom edge of the wing is parallel to the hook shank.

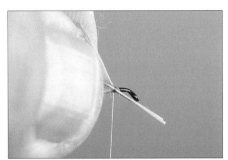

Step 3. Take two or three turns of thread, under moderate tension, to affix the wings to the sides of the hook shank. Do not place these first thread wraps over the bare stems, but rather, take the first 2 wraps over the very base of the lowermost barbs. Wrapping over the barb bases along with stem provides a kind of "cushion" for the feather and helps prevent the wings from twisting out of position during mounting.

Step 4. Release the wings and check their position. The bottom edge of the wing should sit parallel to the hook shank, as shown, and the wings should be symmetrical when viewed from the hook eye. If the wings are not in the correct position, you can adjust them by pulling gently on the tips or stems, or using your finger to position them exactly on the sides of the shank.

When the wing position is satisfactory, you can affix them permanently in one of two ways. You can pinch the wings again, and bind down the butts using tight thread wraps. However, the thread pressure can still cause the wings to twist out of position. A simpler way is to place a drop of CA glue over the mounting wraps and allow it to dry.

Step 5. When the glue is hardened, you can bind down the stems, and clip them, without fear that the wing will shift position.

From the side, the wings should appear as they do in Step 4. Here is a front view showing the symmetrical flare and position of the finished wings.

Method #12:

Fan Wings

Though early in this century, fan-wing flies enjoyed great popularity, the style is rarely seen now. Despite their elegant and graceful appearance, fan wings are highly wind resistant, owing to their broad surface area. In the days when heavier gut leaders were used, wind resistance was less of a consideration, but in this age of thin, high-strength monofilament, fan wings can twist tippets unmercifully. Yet fan wings do make a lovely fly, and if a tippet somewhat heavier than usual is used, and the feathers selected and dressed with care, the style is still practical.

Fan wings are typically fashioned from breast feathers, particularly of waterfowl, though other feathers can be used provided they exhibit the pronounced front-to-back curvature that causes the wings to flare away from one another when mounted.

Thin-stemmed feathers can be mounted and posted using **Method #7: Feather-tip Wings**, p. 252, but such material is rare. Ordinarily, fan-wing feathers are short, with thick, relatively stiff stems that cause problems for the tyer. Since the wing is prepared by stripping the barbs from the feather stem, the bare quill tends to roll and twist on the hook shank.

A better mounting method, shown in the technique below, involves lashing the feathers vertically to either side of the hook shank. The procedure may appear complex, but it is in fact fairly simple.

Step 1. Select a pair of feather—we're using duck covert feathers here—that are closely matched in size and curvature. It is important that the feathers have a broad

---

barb angle (see "Selecting Feathers for Feather-tip Wings," p. 248) so that when the excess barbs are stripped from the stem, the remaining wing will have a broad, fanlike shape.

Identify the mounting point of the wing, and strip the barbs from both sides of the stem below this point, leaving a wing of the desired height.

Prepare a hook by laying a short foundation of twisted tying thread that spans the mounting point on the shank. Position the thread at the mounting point.

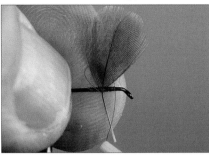

Step 2. In this technique, each feather is mounted individually, beginning with the wing on the far side of the shank.

Pin one feather against the far side of the shank with your left index finger as shown. It should be positioned directly behind the tying thread.

Bring the thread toward you, then above the shank. Angle the thread behind the wing. Bring the thread around the base of the wing, slipping it between your index finger and the feather, as shown here. Then seat it firmly against the shank.

The thread should end up being pulled directly toward you.

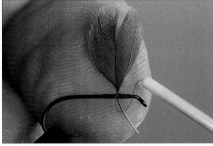

Step 3. Angle the tying thread toward the hook point, and bring it around the feather stem below the hook shank.

The thread should end up below the shank, angled toward the hook eye as shown.

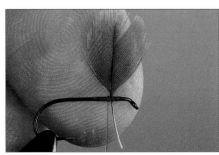

Step 4. Bring the tying thread toward you and up the near side of the shank. Then bring it down behind the wing again.

Take one full turn around the shank only to lock in the wing mounting wraps. The thread should now be positioned behind the wing.

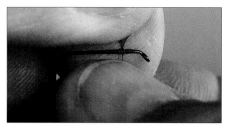

Step 5. Note that the thread pressure may have pulled the stem on the underside of the shank toward you. If this is the case, position your index finger as shown in Step 2. With your left thumb, pinch the wing tip to hold it in position.

Use your right thumbnail to force the feather stem back to the far side. It should project almost straight below the shank. Adjusting the stem like this will keep it out of the tying field when mounting the second wing.

Step 6. Position the second feather on the near side of the shank, holding it in place by the tip.

Bring the tying thread under the hook. Angle it toward the hook eye, across the base of the near wing, pinning the feather stem to side of the shank.

Step 7. Now bring the thread down the far side of the shank ahead of the wing.

When the thread is beneath the shank, angle it back to the hook point, passing it between the two feather stems. The thread should end up in the position shown—angled toward the rear of the hook and slightly toward you.

Step 8. Now bring the thread up the near side of the shank. Pass it between the two feathers on top of the shank, ending with the thread held below the shank, in front of the wings, as shown.

Step 9. Bring the thread beneath the shank. As the thread comes up the near side of the shank, cross over the wing on the near side, again pinning the feather stem to the shank with a lashing of thread. This wrap should be very tight.

Continue bringing the thread behind both wings, taking a wrap around the shank only to lock in the second wing mount.

Step 10. Now take the feather stems and fold them back along either side of the hook shank.

Bind them in with several tight wraps.

Step 11. Clip the excess feather stems. View the wing from the front, and adjust them for symmetry and the desired angle of spread.

When the wings are satisfactorily positioned, they can be locked in this configuration by using the wraps described in **Method #20: The Figure-eight Wing Split**, Steps 5-8, p. 269, or by using a series of tight crisscross wraps between the wings.

When the wings are secured, place a drop of head cement or CA glue at the base.

Method #13:

Reverse-hackle Wings

Strictly speaking, reverse-hackle wings are not true feather-tip wings, nor are they necessarily made of hackle. But we've included them here because they bear a structural resemblance to other styles in this section since the wings are formed from barbs with the feather stem attached. Reverse-hackle wings, sometimes called

"Wonder Wings," appear to have made their way to this country from Europe in the early 1950s. Despite their advantages, they never gained much popularity among American tyers, with a few notable exceptions—Chauncy Lively and, more recently, Montana tyer Al Beatty, who favors this wing style tied with a parachute hackle. A thread base for the parachute hackle can be formed using either procedure shown in **Method #9: Feather-tip Wings with Parachute Base**, p. 255, or the technique shown in **Method #30: Parachute-hackle Mounts**, Steps 3a-3c, p. 381.

The reverse-hackle style produces interesting, realistic wings notable for their translucency and suggestion of venation. A wide variety of feathers are practical, as there are only two real requirements: first, the feather stem should be relatively thin, and second, the barbs must be sufficiently long to form the wings. Breast, body, and flank feathers, and neck and saddle hackles from hens or roosters can all be used. Solid colors such as duns and creams are, of course, useful, as are feathers with pronounced markings such as mallard flank or grizzly hackle, that suggest mottled wings. CDC feathers are sometimes tied in this style on smaller hooks to produce a light, translucent, low-bulk wing.

These wings are relatively easy to tie, and if they have a drawback it is durability. The feather-barb "loops" formed in these styles are somewhat fragile, though they are still more durable than quill wings.

Step 1. Mount the tying thread and create a thread foundation for the wing as described in **Method #1: Mounting and Posting Upright Wings**, Step 1a, p. 241.

Select a pair of feathers, we're using large rooster hackles here, and clip off the stems just above the fuzzy barbs at the base.

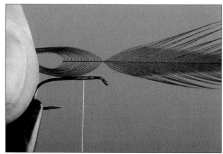

Step 2. Place the feathers front-to-front, that is, convex sides together with the butt ends of the feathers even. From the cut end of the feather, locate the point on the stem that is ¾ the length of the hook shank. Al Beatty

advise this proportion to ensure a wing of adequate length and density.

With the left fingers, preen the barbs back toward the base of the feather. Continue pulling the barbs downward beyond the base of the clipped stems. Pinch and hold the barbs firmly when wings of the desired height have been formed. (We're using only one feather here for a clearer illustration.)

Note that the mounting point established by pinching the barbs is below the feather stem; none of the stem will be bound to the hook shank.

Step 3. Affix the wings to the shank using any of the mounting techniques indicated in **Method #7: Feather-tip Wings**, Step 2 p. 252.

Clip the excess material behind the mounting wraps and bind down the butts.

Step 4. Grasp the feather tips and raise them vertically. Secure the wings in the upright position using either of the techniques shown in **Method #1: Mounting and Posting Upright Wings**, p. 241.

Step 5. When the wings are in the proper position, clip off the excess feather at the top of the wing; it can now be used to fashion another pair of reverse-hackle wings. If desired, apply a small drop of head cement at the wing base.

Note that if using a parachute hackle, leave the wings tips intact; you can hold the tips to support the wing while wrapping the hackle. The tips are trimmed afterward.

Method #14:
Half-hackle Wings

We first saw half-hackle wings in the work of Robert Jorgensen, who advocates them as a substitute for quill wings. Such wings can be tied from the same materials as reverse-hackle wings and offer many of the same advantages, (see **Method #13: Reverse-hackle Wings**, p. 260), but they are more durable since the feather barbs are not bent against the direction of their natural growth and the feather stems are incorporated into the finished wings.

The main sequence shows half-hackle wings mounted in the standard fashion, which places the feather stem at the front of the wing.

The alternate sequence shows a half-hackle wing that is reversed, that is, the feather barbs are preened and mounted against the natural direction of growth, and the feather stem is placed at the rear of the wing. While somewhat less durable than the wing shown in the main sequence, this reversed style can produce a beautifully shaped, delicately veined wing. Tyers who use this style generally dress the fly with a single wing. Since the feather stem and barb tips are bound to the shank at two different points, dividing a pair of wings dressed in this fashion is difficult. Because the mounted feather spans a long length of the hook shank, a collar hackle is not really practical with this wing design. Instead, most tyers use a parachute hackle without a post (see "Postless Parachute Hackle," p. 393), an inverted parachute hackle (see "Bottom-mounted Parachute Hackle," p. 400), or a cross hackle (see "Cross Hackle," p. 376). This wing style can be formed from any feather with sufficiently long barbs, though the best results are obtained by using a larger, relatively web-free rooster saddle. Barbs without web give a more pleasing venation in the wing.

Step 1. Mount the tying thread and create a thread foundation for the wing as described in **Method #1: Mounting and Posting Upright Wings**, Step 1a, p. 241.

Select a pair of feathers, such as the rooster saddles used here. Place them front-to-front, that is with the convex sides together. Adjust the feathers so that the tips are even and the feather stems lie atop one another.

Robert Jorgensen recommends cementing the very tips of the feathers together with a drop of head cement or CA

glue to keep the feathers aligned throughout the tying procedure, but the wings can be formed without this additional step.

With the feather stems aligned, snip away the fuzzy butt sections of both feathers.

Step 2. Now remove the barbs from one side of both feathers.

Step 3. Adjust the feathers if necessary to ensure that the stems are aligned.

With the fingers of the left hand, pinch the feathers together near the base. With the right fingers, grasp the butt of the feather and draw it slowly through the left fingertips until a portion of the feather—very slightly longer than the desired wing height—projects beyond the left fingertips. That is, the left fingers are now pinching the wings slightly behind the mounting point.

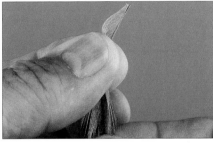

Step 4. Maintain your pinch on the feathers. With the right fingers, grasp the tips of both feathers. Pull gently, very slightly sliding the feathers back through the left fingertips. The barbs will bulge upward, forming a winglike shape, as shown here.

Step 5. Affix the wings to the shank using any of the mounting techniques indicated in **Method #7: Feather-tip Wings**, Step 3 p. 252.

Clip the excess material behind the mounting wraps and bind down the butts.

Note that the clipped feather is ready to use for another set of wings.

Step 6. Grasp the wings and raise them vertically. Secure them in this position using either of the techniques shown in **Method #1: Mounting and Posting Upright Wings**, p. 241, or the technique described in **Method #8: Reverse-mount Feather-tip Wings**, Steps 3a-3d, p. 253.

If desired, apply a small drop of head cement at the wing base.

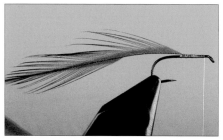

Step 1a. For the reverse-mounted style, the tails are dressed (we've omitted them here), and the tying thread positioned at a point anywhere from ½ to ¾ the shank-length behind the hook eye—considerably farther back than the mounting point for most upright wings.

Prepare a feather by snipping away the fuzzy barbs at the base. Strip most of the barbs from one side of the stem; leaving barbs on both sides of the stem at the feather tip helps simplify handling.

At the base of the feather stem, strip away a few of the lowermost barbs to provide a bare stem for mounting the feather.

Secure the base of the stem at the mounting point, as shown.

Step 2a. At this point, the hackle and body are dressed (we've omitted them for a clearer illustration, though a finished fly is shown in Step 6a).

When these components are complete, position the tying thread behind the hook eye.

With the left fingers, hold the feather vertically, as shown. With the right fingers, pinch a section of barbs equal to the height of the finished wing.

Preen these barbs outward and downward, keeping them aligned in a vertical stack so that they are not twisted, as shown. With the right fingers, pinch the barb tips and hook eye simultaneously.

Step 3a. The barb tips are secured using a pinch wrap as shown in **Method #9: The Pinch Wrap**, p. 30. The material can pinched in either the left fingers, in the conventional fashion, or in the right fingers, as shown here, which is generally a bit easier.

With the left hand, form a slack loop of thread over the top of the barb tips, pinching the tying thread between the right fingers.

Step 4a. Draw the thread downward, trapping the barb tips against the shank behind the eye.

The feather stem may be pulled severely forward at this point and the wing poorly shaped. This will be remedied in the next step.

Step 5a. In the right fingers, grasp all the barb tips projecting over the hook eye. With the left fingers, grasp the feather tip.

Lift slightly upward with both hands simultaneously, drawing the feather stem to the vertical position. This lifting will redistribute the barbs in an even, vertical stack to produce the wing veins as shown.

Step 6a. Bind down the barb tips; clip and secure them; and trim away the excess feather tip, as shown at the left.

The fly on the right has been dressed with a postless parachute, and a wing of the style demonstrated in this sequence. Notice that the parachute hackle barbs projecting over the hook eye can pose an obstacle in securing the front of the wing. These barbs can be pushed out of the way in Step 2a, or clipped to form a "V" over the hook eye to give better access to the shank during wing-mounting.

Upright Bundled-fiber Wings

As the name suggests, this wing style is formed from a clump or bundle of stranded or fiberlike material—natural or synthetic hair, yarns, or feather barbs. Such wings can be formed as a single, upright post (a standard for parachute hackling), as a pair divided wings (such as hair wings), or as an arc wing (the style used on Caucci and Nastasi's Comparaduns). Moreover, the tyer can select from a wide range of materials to accomplish a variety of purposes—natural colors or markings, buoyancy, and visibility—and such materials can be used in combination as well. But perhaps the greatest advantage of bundled-fiber wings is their durability. Properly tied, they are virtually indestructible.

Such wings do have a couple of drawbacks, though these are more or less manifest depending upon the material and wing style. First, unlike quill and feather-tip wings, which produce a clear outline and realistic shape, bundled-fibers produce a softer, less-distinct profile and a more impressionistic wing. The wing silhouette is further obscured when the standard, collar-style hackling is used. However, a single-post wing used for parachute hackling can be clipped to a more natural shape, and arc wings are typically used on dressings without hackle, which improves the visibility of the wing silhouette. The second drawback is bulk, particularly when using natural hairs. Because natural hair tapers toward the tip, achieving a sufficient density of material at the wing tip can result in a bulky tie-in and a correspondingly thick body. But materials with relatively little taper, such as yarns and feather barbs, pose far less problem in this regard.

Selecting and Preparing Bundled Fibers

A material can be chosen for its lifelike coloration or marking, and perhaps the most pleasing in this regard are feather barbs.

Mallard flank; breast feathers from game birds or waterfowl; dun, grizzly, or variant hackles; and a variety of other plumage can create wings with natural shades and mottlings. The best feather barbs for the purpose are heavily webbed. A bundle of webby barbs, produces an impression of greater density than does a bundle of smooth, unwebbed barbs, and thus less material is required for winging. Webby hackle, however, does absorb water, making it somewhat less suitable for dressings in which a high degree of buoyancy is desirable. Because feather barbs are a compliant material, soft, compressible, and not prone to slip or roll under thread pressure, they are among the easiest bundled fibers to tie. They require little preparation other than aligning the tips, removing them from the stem, and consolidating them into a bundle as explained in **Method #1: Preparing Feather Barbs**, p. 67. CDC barbs (and marabou used for downwings) can be stripped and bundled in this way as well, though they are generally easier to handle using one of the techniques demonstrated in **Method #9: Preparing Marabou and CDC**, p. 73.

Since bundled-fiber wings are basically impressionistic, many tyers pay little attention to imitating precise colors or markings, and choose a material instead on the basis of high visibility—particularly for patterns fished in rough water, such as the Wulff flies, or for very low-floating dressings, such as the Parachute Adams. Probably the most widely used natural materials for high-visibility wings are calf tail and calf body hair, usually in white, but sometimes dyed yellow or orange.

Hair from a calf tail is stiff and kinky or crinkled in texture. Because the hairs are kinked, they tend to "fill out" a wing, making it appear denser and broader than a wing fashioned from an equal amount of straight hair. Thus a wing with good volume and fullness can be created with a relatively small quantity of calf-tail hair, which reduces the tie-in bulk and generally simplifies handling. Moreover, calf tail provides long hairs suitable for winging large flies. When choosing calf tails, look for long, straight hair. That is, while the fiber itself will be kinked, the hair should not bend or arc along its length. The hairs very near the tip of the tail are almost always corkscrewed or twisted, and these should be avoided when tying. Choose hair from further down the tail.

Unlike calf tail, calf body hair is a very short, straight, smooth hair which stacks quite easily. A wing fashioned from this straight hair does not have the same broad, flared appearance as a calf-tail wing, but is more dense with a somewhat better-defined profile. The principal drawbacks of calf body hair are its slipperiness, which makes it a bit more difficult to handle than calf tail—particularly when larger quantities of hair are used—and its relatively short length. Calf body hair is impractical as a winging material for hooks much larger than #12. Moreover, some tyers feel that a tight bundle of this straight hair encourages a "wicking"

action that draws water into the wing. When selecting a patch of calf body, look for long, straight hairs that are dense on the hide. Some calf body that is commercially sold is somewhat crinkly—almost like calf tail—and the hair is quite sparse on the skin. Such material is cumbersome to use.

Some synthetic materials can also make highly visible wings—particularly Antron and poly yarns, reflective Mylars such as Krystal Flash, or some combination of these materials. These synthetics have the advantage of requiring almost no preparation, and they tie quite easily. With the exception of poly yarn, however, most synthetic fibers add little to the floatation of the fly.

One of the great advantages of bundled-fiber wings is that the material used can be selected to give the fly buoyancy. Here, few materials serve better than hollow hairs such as deer or elk hair. Because of the tendency of hollow hairs to flare under thread pressure, tying wings of this material can be tricky, as the fibers splay when tied tightly instead of consolidating into a more compact, winglike shape. There is, of course, a technique for controlling flare in the wings, and this is described in **Method #15: Bundled Fiber Post**, p. 263. But choosing the proper hair from the start will greatly simplify the matter; hollow hairs and their tying properties are discussed in greater detail in the section "Hollow Hair," p. 2. Of the synthetic fibers commonly used to dress wings, poly yarn is frequently selected for flies requiring buoyant wings. Though poly fibers are not hollow, and do not provide the degree of floatation afforded by deer hair, many tyers prefer poly yarn for ease of tying.

The specific materials mentioned in the foregoing discussion are the most widely employed in bundled-fiber wings, but certainly not the only ones. Squirrel, bear, mink, badger, woodchuck, and others are often used, depending upon the fly type or style, and the tyer's needs or preferences. The only requirements are that the guard hairs—which are the hairs most often used for winging—are relatively uniform in length and texture, reasonably abundant, and long enough to be handled when the wing is mounted.

It is difficult to offer ironclad advice about the precise amount of any given material to use for winging. The quantity of fibers determines wing breadth and density and thus are almost wholly at the discretion of the tyer. Al Beatty, however, offers a method for gauging the quantity of material to be used on dressings with hair wings and tails. He selects a clump of fibers and, holding them between the fingertips, rotates his hands to give the bundle a half-twist. For a hair tail, the thickness of the bundle at the twisted point should be equal to the outside diameter of the hook eye. A bundle of this same size is used for each half of a divided hair wing. Thus a fly with a hair tail and hair wings would use three bundles of material, one for the tail and two for the wings. For an undivided wing, the material is simply posted up; for a divided wing, it is separated into two bunches. If these proportions do not suit

the preferences of every tyer, they are at least a reasonable starting point for experimentation. If there is a general caution, it is to avoid using excessively thick bunches of material, particularly slippery fibers such as natural hairs. Thick bundles are difficult to tie in reliably and the bulk of the tied down butts can produce a disproportionately thick body.

Beatty confines his method to natural hairs only, and many tyers would find that using his proportions for other materials—particularly feather-barbs—would produce overly bulky wings. With barbs and synthetic fibers, experimentation is the best way to establish the quantities of material that seem pleasing and proportionate.

Synthetic fibers such as yarn require no preparation beyond combing the material to separate and untangle the filaments. Natural hairs are prepared by removing the underfur as explained in **Method #2: Preparing and Cleaning Hair**, p. 68; the hair tips can be aligned using the techniques shown in **Method #3: Stacking and Aligning Hair**, p. 69.

Single Post Bundled-fiber Wing

Dressing the wing as a single, undivided, upright post is perhaps the most common technique for dressing bundled fibers. In addition to suggesting the wing outline, the post wing is often used in conjunction with a parachute hackle since consolidating the fibers at the base of the wing with tying thread forms a firm foundation for the hackle wraps.

Most bundled-fiber posts are dressed in similar ways, and the basic techniques are presented below in **Method #15: Bundled-fiber Post**, p. 263, which illustrates the fundamental steps using natural hair. Other materials, such as feather barbs and yarns, differ in the preparation, handling, and finishing of the wing, and these are presented in the methods that follow.

Method #15
Bundled-fiber Post

Upright wings formed from a bundle of fibers are typically mounted in the standard orientation, with the butts of the wing material bound toward the tail of the fly, though thinner, less bulky bundles or more compressible materials can be reverse-mounted, if desired (see **Method #1: Mounting and Posting Upright Wings**, Steps 2a-2c, p. 241).

The sequence below illustrates the basic methods for mounting and posting a bundled-fiber wing, and as such functions as a basis for the other methods presented in this section. In addition to illustrating the general steps for dressing such wings, this method also shows hows these procedures apply specifically to tying natural hair posts.

Wings of synthetic fibers, particularly yarns, can be mounted using this same approach, but many tyers prefer the more efficient techniques shown in the alternate steps following the main sequence. For synthetic materials, these methods are a bit faster, and because there are no trimmed butts to bind down, they produce virtually no bulk on the shank.

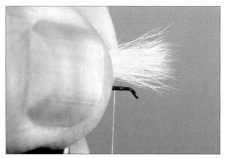

Step 1. Mount the tying thread as described in **Method #1: Mounting and Posting Upright Wings**, Step 1a, p. 241.

Clip and clean a bundle of hair as explained in **Method #2: Preparing and Cleaning Hair**, p. 68, and align the hair tips as shown in **Method #3: Stacking and Aligning Hair**, p. 69. If a different material is used, consult the section "Selecting and Preparing Bundled Fibers," p. 262, for the appropriate method of material preparation.

Position the hair atop the hook shank with the tips extending over the hook eye. The wing-mounting point on the bundle of hair should be directly over the tying thread.

Step 2. There are a number of methods suitable for mounting bundled-fiber materials. **Method #2: The Soft Wrap**, p. 26; **Method #3: The Angle Wrap**, p. 27; and **Method #5: The Compensation Wrap**, p. 27, are all useful. Any of the slack-loop techniques presented in Chapter 4: "Mounting and Trimming Materials" can also be used.

For purposes of illustration in this sequence, we are using **Method #12: The Noose Loop**, p. 32, a procedure that is especially useful for bulky or slippery materials such as hair since the initial wrap around only the winging material helps consolidate the bundle and prevent it from rolling around the shank.

Take one complete turn of thread—firm, but not tight—around the clump of hair only. The thread should encircle the fibers at the mounting point. When the thread wrap is complete, the bobbin should be positioned above the hook shank as shown.

Step 3. Apply very slight tension to the bobbin to tighten the thread loop. As you do so, slide or "roll" the bundle of hair down the tying thread so that the hair rests atop the hook shank.

Pinch the hair atop the hook shank, and bind it down using 6 or 7 very tight, adjacent turns of thread, working toward the hook bend.

Clip the excess hair. The wing is now ready to be posted to the vertical position using the loop-posting procedure explained in **Method #1: Mounting and Posting Upright Wings**, Steps 3a-3f, p. 241. Or you can use the thread-bump technique explained in the following steps.

Step 4. To post the wings with a thread bump, bind down the exposed hair butts tightly and return the thread to the wing-mounting point.

Gather the tips of the hair in the left fingers and pull them back toward the hook bend.

At the front base of the hair, build a bump of thread that will keep the wing elevated. Force the first wraps tightly against the very base of the fiber bundle. If you attempt to place several thread wraps directly atop one another, however, the thread bump will eventually collapse. Instead, build a wedge-shaped "ramp" or cone as shown that abuts the wing material and helps raise it perpendicular to the shank.

As you build the thread bump, periodically release the wings and observe your progress. When the fibers stand up upright, stop wrapping. (The fibers may be splayed at this point, but they will be consolidated in the next step.) The exact number of wraps required to raise the fibers varies with the type and quantity of material. Use as few as possible to avoid extra bulk on the shank.

Step 5. Grasp the tips of the hair once again in the left hand, and hold them

upright. Take 2 or 3 tight wraps of thread horizontally around base of the wing to consolidate the fibers. As you wrap the thread around the wing, you'll need to release the hair in order to let the tying thread pass by your fingers. Release it only momentarily, then grasp it again. The tension provided by your grip is necessary to make tight thread wraps.

When these wraps are complete, take a turn of thread around the hook shank only to lock in the horizontal wraps. If the wing leans slightly forward, take a few additional wraps around the thread bump to force the wings into a vertical position.

If desired, a drop of head cement at the base of the wing will help secure the thread wraps. The wing is now complete.

Step 5a. When using hollow hair for the wings, such as the deer hair shown here, the tight horizontal wraps will cause the fibers to flare. To reduce the flare and consolidate the fibers into a more wing-like silhouette, take 2 or 3 tight, horizontal wraps around the wing base as described in Step 5.

Then relax tension on the thread slightly, and take another horizontal turn of thread above the preceding ones. Relax the tension again, and take another turn of thread above the previous one. Continue decreasing thread tension as you wrap up the wing until the fibers are gathered into more compact bundle.

Now reverse direction, gradually increasing tension as you wrap the thread back to the base of the wing. Apply a drop of head cement to thread foundation on the wing to help secure the wraps.

Step 6. (Optional) The wing as shown in Step 5, whether achieved by the thread-bump method or loop posting, is suitable as a base for parachute hackle, but many tyers find that parachute hackling is simpler and more secure if the hackle is wrapped around a thread foundation rather than the wing fibers alone.

The foundation is formed by simply extending the thread base created in Step 5. After taking 2 or 3 tight wraps around the wing base, take 3 or 4 additional tight, adjacent wraps of thread working up the wing post. Then wrap the thread back down to the base of the wing to create a foundation as shown above. Note that if the wing is formed of hollow hair, these additional thread wraps should be snug, but not tight or else the hair will flare and splay.

The thread wraps here may appear to extend rather high up the wing, but remember that the lower portion of this thread foundation will be hidden beneath the body material. A short foundation of thread will project above the body to serve as a base for the parachute hackle.

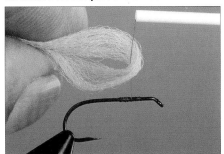

Step 1a. Synthetic fiber posts are more easily constructed. Prepare a thread foundation as in Step 1.

Cut a 1"-2" length of wing material, such as poly yarn shown here. Since the wing is formed from a double thickness of this yarn, the cut length of yarn should be half the thickness or density desired in the finished wing.

With a dubbing needle or small comb, comb through the fibers at both ends of the bundle to separate and untangle the individual filaments.

With the right hand, hold the tying thread vertically above the shank. With the left hand, fold the yarn around the thread as shown.

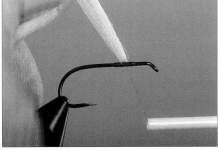

Step 1b. With the left fingers, put tension on the yarns tips; with the right, put counter tension on the bobbin.

Slide the yarn down the thread to the top of the hook shank. Maintain tension on the tips to hold the yarn in position as you bring the thread very firmly to the underside of the shank, as shown.

Step 1c. Release the yarn. Take 2 or 3 tight thread wraps around the center of the yarn bundle to secure it atop the shank.

Raise the two ends of the yarn vertically, and take 3 or 4 tight, horizontal thread wraps around the base of the fibers to consolidate the yarn halves, as shown in Step 5. (If a parachute hackle is to be used, see Step 6.)

Step 1d. Pull the yarn vertically, and clip the wing to length.

Step 2a. Gary Borger uses this approach in winging with synthetic yarns and strands.

Prepare a thread foundation and length of yarn as explained in Step 1a, and position the tying thread at the wing-mounting point.

Fold the yarn around the underside of the shank directly ahead of the tying thread, as shown.

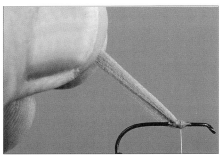

Step 2b. Pull upward on the yarn tips firmly, and tilt them rearward, as shown. Take 4 or 5 tight thread wraps to secure the fold in the yarn to the underside of the shank.

Step 2c. Take horizontal thread wraps as explained in Step 1c to consolidate the yarn halves, then clip them to length as shown in Step 1d.

Method #16:
Rolled-barb Post

This is a very old winging style that is both serviceable and simple to fashion. Webby barbs tie in more easily than slippery hairs, and the feather barbs can be chosen to give the wings a specific coloration or, in the case of the mallard flank used below, a distinct mottling.

Barbs are fairly compressible, creating a minimum of bulk when tied in, and thus are often used on patterns with a slender profile, such as quill- or floss-bodied flies.

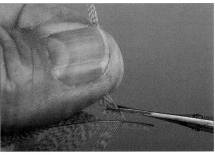

Step 1. Mount the tying thread as described in **Method #1: Mounting and Posting Upright Wings**, Step 1a, p. 241.

Prepare a bundle of barbs by first aligning the tips and removing the barbs from the feather quill as described in **Method #1: Preparing Feather Barbs**, p. 67. (If CDC barbs are used, gathering a sufficient bundle is easier if you use one of the procedures shown in **Method #9: Preparing Marabou and CDC**, p. 73, or the technique described in **Method #36: Stalcup CDC Parachute Hackle**, p. 391.)

Step 2. Stripping or cutting the material from the feather stem will produce a flat section of barbs with aligned tips. If you have more than one such section, stack them atop one another, making certain that all the tips are aligned.

To bunch the fibers together, first lay the flat sections of barbs on the tying bench. With the right fingers, pinch the sections together from the sides, squeezing the barbs into a bundle.

Step 3. Pinch the bundle in the right fingertips, and gently roll the barbs back and forth to further consolidate the bundle. Be careful not to pinch or roll the material too aggressively, as the barbs are soft and can easily be bent or damaged.

Step 4. When the barbs are bundled, mount and post them as described in **Method #15: Bundled-fiber Post**, p. 263.

Method #17:
Folded-barb Post

This technique is similar to the rolled barbs described in the preceding method, except that the material is prepared in such a way that the barbs are not rolled and randomized. Rather, the integrity of the flat barb section is maintained to produce a flat wing with a broad, distinct silhouette that in many ways resembles a feather-tip wing. Such wings can be used with a conventional collar hackle or parachute hackle, but perhaps their most famous application is in the Thorax Dun patterns devised by Vince Marinaro.

Since there are two ways to prepare feather barbs for this style of winging, the choice of plumage that can be used is quite broad. The main sequence shows how some feathers, turkey flats in this case, can be folded with the barbs on the stem. The alternate sequence demonstrates the technique for folding barbs that have been removed from the stem.

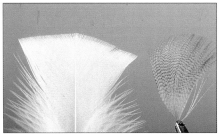

Step 1. Folding barbs on the stem is a quick and simple method, but its success depends upon using the proper feather. A suitable feather is one in which a substantial number of barbs on the stem extend all the way to the tip of the feather. When the

barbs are preened toward the feather tip, they should form a straight, almost squared-off end on the feather.

On the left is a turkey flat feather, and on the right a dyed mallard flank feather. Notice the alignment of the barbs at the feather tip; both of these feathers are suitable.

Step 2. Clip the feather stem near the tip, leaving a "V" between the barbs. How much of the tip of the feather is cut away depends upon the wing height. Once this "V" is formed, the uppermost feather barbs must be slightly longer than the height of the finished wing, so that no stem is incorporated into the wing.

Now preen the lower barbs toward the base of the feather to leave a section of barbs on either side of the stem. The width of these sections determines the width of the finished wing.

(Note that you can cut away the lower barbs rather than preening them downward. But on some feathers, these lower barbs will still have sufficiently aligned tips to form another wing, and you may wish to keep them on the stem for this purpose.)

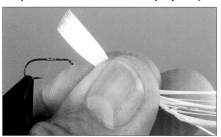

Step 3. Mount the tying thread as described in **Method #1: Mounting and Posting Upright Wings**, Step 1a, p. 242. For thorax style winging, as shown here, the thread base should begin at about the middle of the hook shank and extend toward the bend. Position the thread at the winging point.

Using the thumb and forefinger of the left hand, carefully fold the two sections of barbs together. In folding, you are trying to accomplish two things. The first is keeping the tips of the barbs aligned. The second is keeping the two sections of barbs flat; they should be folded together to form a flattened section of barbs of double thickness.

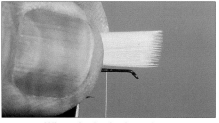

Step 4. When the barbs have been properly folded, momentarily grasp the barb tips in the right fingers, and reposition the left

fingers so that they pinch the wing at the mounting point.

Unlike other bundled-fiber materials, folded barbs must be mounted in a way that preserves their flat shape. The situation is very much like that encountered with quill wings. Pinching the wings at the mounting point will allow you to use any of the appropriate slack-loop techniques.

Step 5. Affix the wings to the shank using any of the following mounting techniques: **Method #9: The Pinch Wrap**, p. 30; **Method #10: The Bobbin Loop**, p. 31; or **Method #11: The Langley Loop**, p. 32.

Step 6. You can post the wing using either of the techniques shown in Method #1: **Mounting and Posting Upright Wings**, p. 241.

If the fly is to be dressed with a parachute hackle, a thread base should be created on the wing as explained in **Method #15: Bundled-fiber Post**, Step 6, p. 264. When forming this thread base, pinch the wings together sideways during each horizontal wrap of thread, and do not use excessive thread pressure. Failing to do so may cause the barbs to collapse together into a bundle and ruin the flat wing profile.

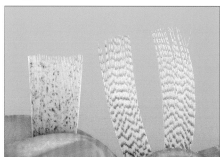

Step 1a. There are actually two ways to form a folded-barb wing by removing the barbs from the feather stem.

You can carefully cut a section of feather barbs as described in **Method #16: Rolled-barb Post**, Steps 1-2, p. 265. This flat section of barbs should be twice as wide as the finished wing, as shown on the left.

If the peculiarities of the feather do not allow cutting a double-wide section of barbs, you can cut two flat sections of barbs each of which is exactly as wide as the finished wing, as shown on the right.

12

Step 2a. With a double-wide section of barbs, carefully fold the section in half lengthwise, keeping the tips aligned and the folded barb section flat. If the barbs are curved, fold the concave sides together.

When using two separate barb sections, simply stack them atop one another, keeping the tips aligned. If the barbs are curved, place the concave sides together.

Once the wing is prepared, proceed to Step 4.

Step 3a. If the wing is deliberately dressed longer than necessary, the barb tips can be trimmed away to give greater density and a more distinct profile to the wing.

Method #18:
Trimmed-fiber Wing

Bundled-fiber wings can be trimmed to give them a more natural, wing-like shape, and the most commonly used materials for this style are synthetic fibers such as the poly yarn shown in the following demonstrations. Though it may run contrary to fly-tying custom and the prejudices of many tyers, natural-fiber wings fashioned from hackle barbs or hair can also be trimmed for a more realistic silhouette.

The main sequence below shows the mounting and trimming of an upright poly yarn wing. The alternate sequence illustrates a particular style of trimmed fiber wing designed by Gary Borger that uses a reverse-mount wing angled slightly rearward.

Step 1. Mount an upright post wing using any of the techniques shown in **Method #15: Bundled-fiber Post**, p. 263.

Use your fingers to flatten the sides of the wing and preen the yarn fibers to form a flat, fan-shaped wing as shown above. Try to distribute the fibers evenly so that the wing density appears uniform throughout.

Place a small drop of head cement, flexible cement, or CA glue at the very base of the wing to help hold the fibers in this flattened configuration. You can, if desired, use your fingers or a pair of flat-jawed pliers to squeeze the sides of the wing at the very base to help distribute the glue and further flatten the yarn.

Allow the glue to set.

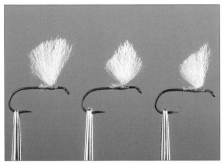

Step 2. The wing can now trimmed to the desired shape; a very sharp pair of serrated tying scissors are best for the purpose. Various shapes can be fashioned, as shown above.

Step 1a. Tying the trimmed-fiber wing designed by Gary Borger for his Yarn-Wing Dun patterns requires that tail, body, and hackle be dressed first. (Borger uses a dubbed body and thorax-palmered hackle, see **Method #18: Thorax Palmer Hackle**, p. 366.) We've included the dubbed body here because it is necessary for properly forming the wing, but the hackle has been omitted for greater clarity in the photographs.

After the other components of the fly have been dressed, lay a thread foundation between the front of the body and the hook eye. Position the tying thread about 3 thread-wraps ahead of the front edge of the body.

Prepare a 1-2" length of poly yarn. Mount the yarn atop the shank. Since this is a reverse-mount, only a short section of yarn should project over the hook eye; the bulk of the yarn should extend toward the hook bend.

Secure the yarn with 2 or 3 thread wraps.

Step 2a. Grasp the wing in the left fingers and elevate it about 30-45 degrees above the hook shank.

Wrap a few turns of tying thread tightly toward the hook bend, using thread pressure to butt the yarn against the front edge of the dubbed body. The "shoulder" of dubbing will help support the wing in the proper orientation.

When the wing is elevated 30-45 degrees above the shank, stop wrapping the thread.

Step 3a. Trim the wing by making a vertical cut, perpendicular to the hook shank, as shown.

You can trim the head by leaving short yarn butts, as we've done here, or you can trim the yarn close to the shank and bind the excess with tying thread.

Method #19:
Wedge Wing

This wing style was devised by Darrel Martin specifically for flies size 16 and smaller. The unusual technique uses a wing of bundled reindeer hair that is cemented and flattened into a thin panel. The wing can incorporate the natural hair tips, but highly realistic silhouettes can be obtained by dressing an oversize wing that is trimmed to a more lifelike shape, as shown in the main sequence.

Martin is emphatic about the use of reindeer hair, noting that it has precisely the right texture for this method. The wings can be dressed sparsely or densely for a variety of dressing styles. Wings formed from upright posts of hair allow the use of a collar hackle, while those tied to slant rearward over the fly body can be dressed with a parachute or crosshackle, and in the latter case, can be made to resemble an Iwamasa Dun (see **Method #10: Ogden Wings**, p. 256).

Step 1. Clip and clean a small bundle of reindeer hair as explained in **Method #2: Preparing and Cleaning Hair**, p. 68. Some hairs on the reindeer are quite long, with thin, threadlike tips; discard these. If the tips of the hair are to be incorporated into the wing, align the hair as described in **Method #3: Stacking and Aligning Hair**, p. 69. If the wing will be clipped to shape, as demonstrated here, stacking is unnecessary, though all very short hairs should be discarded.

The exact thickness of the bundle depends upon the hook size and desired density of the wing, though in general a somewhat sparse bundle is used. Martin, for example, notes that a bundle of 35 hairs or so will create a dense wing on a #18 hook.

The hair can be mounted and posted upright as explained in **Method #15: Bundled-fiber Post**, p. 263, but Martin prefers to reverse-mount the hair so that it slants toward the hook bend and allows trimming a wing with a more realistic silhouette.

To reverse-mount the bundle, lay a thread foundation ahead of the wing-mounting point, and position the tying thread at the rear of the foundation. Secure the bundle at the mounting point with several tight thread wraps; use your left fingers to keep the hair positioned atop the shank.

Clip the flared hair butts and bind down with thread.

Note that the fibers are much longer than the finished wing height. Mounting the hair in this fashion incorporates more of the thicker hair shafts into the wing, which simplifies forming the wing "panel" on wings that will trimmed to shape.

Step 2. Apply a small drop of flexible cement at the base of the wing.

Allow the cement to dry a few moments until it is slightly tacky. With a pair of needle-nose pliers or your fingers, squeeze the wing from side-to-side, flattening the fibers and distributing the cement.

Work from the base of the fibers to the tips, flattening the wing and pushing the excess cement upward.

The object here is to shape the fibers in a thin flat panel.

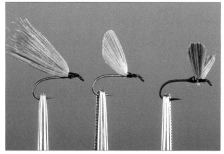

Step 3. On the fly at the left, the wing has been cemented and shaped as explained in Step 2.

After the cement dries, the wing can be clipped to shape as shown on the fly in the middle.

Double wedge wings can be fashioned by dressing a reindeer-hair wing using one of the techniques described in "Divided Bundled-fiber Wings," p. 268. After the wings are posted upright and divided, each wing half is cemented and flattened individually. Trimmed wings are shown here, but if desired, the wings can be formed with the natural tips intact.

Divided Bundled-fiber Wings

As with quill and feather-tip wings, there is some disagreement among tyers about the necessity for dividing fiber and hair wings. Some argue that divided wings make little difference to the fish and require extra tying steps. Others disagree, claiming that divided wings are more visible to the fish and are an aid in balancing the fly so that it lands properly on the water. About the only conclusion that can be drawn with certainty is that a single-post wing is necessary for dressings tied with a parachute hackle, but beyond that, the matter pretty much rests on individual tying preferences. Still, there is no question that divided bundled-fiber wings are quite widely used and have proven effective.

Most divided-fiber wings begin as a single, undivided wing that is posted and separated into two distinct wing halves. The amount of material used for the wings varies among tyers (see "Selecting and Preparing Bundled Fibers," p. 262). The crux of this winging style, of course, is the way in which wings are divided into equal bundles. There are several techniques for doing so, and these are presented in the methods that follow.

Method #20:

The Figure-eight Wing Split

This is probably the most common technique for dividing bundled-fiber wings and can be used with virtually any material. The method has two distinct procedures: first, dividing the wing material in half, and second, consolidating the fibers in each wing half to form a more compact bundle. The fibers on each half of the wing are gathered together by continuous thread wraps that resemble the character "8" and encircle the

base of each wing half. The number of wraps varies with the degree of wing consolidation desired by the tyer and by the material itself. Soft, compliant materials such as feather barbs may require only one gathering wrap; stiff materials, such as most natural hairs, may require more. When several wraps are used, many tyers mount the wings using thread of a color that matches the wing material since some of the gathering wraps at the base of each wing may be visible on the finished fly.

The main sequence illustrates the technique using calf tail. The alternate sequence shows the procedure for controlling flare when tying divided wings of hollow hair.

Step 1. Mount and secure a bundled-fiber post using the technique described in **Method #15: Bundled-fiber Post**, Steps 1-3, p. 263. (If you are using feather barbs for the wing, you may wish to consult **Method #16: Rolled-barb Post**, p. 265.)

Begin posting the wing to the vertical position using the thread-bump technique explained in **Method #15: Bundled-fiber Post**, Step 4, p. 264. Note that it isn't necessary to raise the wing completely upright at this point. It need only be elevated above the hook shank far enough to give some working room for the thread—about 45 degrees or so, as shown.

If desired, you can use instead the technique described in **Method #1: Mounting and Posting Upright Wings**, Steps 3a-3f, p. 243, in which case the single post will be fully upright.

In either case, leave the tying thread at the forward edge of the wing base.

Step 2. Using a dubbing needle and your fingers, divide the single clump of fibers into two equal halves. Try to make these two smaller bundles as equal in bulk as possible.

Pinch the tips of the bundle of fibers on the near side of the shank, and pull them toward you as shown.

Bring the tying thread up the near side of the shank, between the wings, then down the far side of the shank behind the far bundle.

12

SECTION 1

Step 3. Bring the thread beneath the shank and up the near side of the shank behind the near wing.

Pass the thread between the wings and down the far side of the shank ahead of the far wing, as shown in this top view.

Step 4. Bring the thread beneath the shank and make one full wrap of thread around the hook shank only behind both wings.

This crisscross of thread has now separated the two wing halves.

The bobbin should be hanging on the far side of the shank, behind the wings. This thread position is important for executing the next steps.

Step 5. The next few steps show how the two bundles of fibers forming the wings are consolidated by taking thread wraps at the base. It is worth noting that during this entire procedure, Steps 5-8, the thread never passes beneath or around the hook shank. The entire process takes place above the hook shank, around the base of the two fiber bundles only.

Grasp the tips of the far wing in your left fingertips. Raise them to the vertical (if they are not already vertical) and adjust the bundle so that it is in the desired position of the finished wing. Hold it in this orientation under moderate pressure.

To take a turn of thread around the base of the far wing, bring the thread forward around the outside of the far wing, toward the hook eye. Try to keep this wrap low on the wing, as shown in this top view.

Bring the thread between the wings toward the hook bend. You will need to release the fibers in your left hand momentarily. Snug the wrap down into the base of the wing.

Pinch the wing tip again and bring the thread forward on the outside of the wing, toward the hook eye. Again, try to keep the thread low on the wing.

You've now made a complete turn around the base of the outside wing in a clockwise direction. The wrap should be quite snug to draw the fibers together.

Note: if the wings are not sufficiently gathered into a bundle of the desired compactness, repeat Step 5, placing additional wraps around the bundle. Each subsequent wrap should be above the previous one. If hollow hairs are used, consult Step 5a.

Step 5a. When using deer, elk, or other hollow hairs that tend to flare, additional thread wraps will be needed to control the splay of the hair. The method for making these wraps is identical to that described in **Method #15: Bundled-fiber Post**, Step 5a, p. 264. That is, after the first wrap, each subsequent wrap is taken above the preceding one, under decreasing thread tension. Slackening thread pressure like this will gather the individual hairs together without causing them to flare.

Then wrap the thread back to the base of the fiber bundle, gradually increasing thread pressure and proceed to Step 6.

The wraps around the near wing, described in Step 7, are taken in just this same manner.

Step 6. The bobbin is now above the hook shank, ahead of the far wing. Bring the thread between the wings and toward you, so that the bobbin is above the shank and behind the near wing, as shown here from the top.

In this technique, thread tension holds the wings in position. Apply pressure to the thread until the far wing remains in the proper position when you release your grasp.

Maintain this pressure while you grasp the tips of the near wing with the left hand. Adjust the near fiber bundle until it is in the proper, final position of the wing.

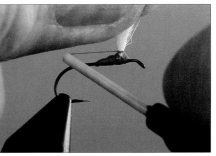

Step 7. It is important, as you work with the near wing, not to relax the thread pressure that is holding the far wing upright.

Now take a complete wrap around the base of the near wing. As you're looking down at the tips of the wing, the thread wrap will encircle the wing base in a counterclockwise direction. Keep this wrap snug against the base of the wing. Again, you'll have to release the fiber tips momentarily to complete the wrap.

When you've completely encircled the wing base, the thread should have just passed between the wings to finish the wrap around the near wing. The bobbin should be positioned above the shank, behind the wings, as shown. Do not yet release the wing tips held in the left fingers.

Note: As in Step 5, additional wraps can be taken, working up the wing bundle, if the fibers are not sufficiently consolidated by this single turn of thread.

Step 8. Apply enough pressure on the thread to hold the near wing in the final upright position. When the tension is sufficient to hold the wing upright, take a wrap of thread around the hook shank behind the wings to lock in the figure-eight wraps.

If the wings slant forward slightly, you can take a few more wraps atop the thread bump ahead of the wing base to raise them to the vertical.

If desired, place a drop of head cement or CA glue at the wing base.

Method #21:
Loop-split Wings

A version of the loop posting technique shown in **Method #1: Mounting and Posting Upright Wings**, p. 241, can be used to divide bundled fibers into a pair of wings using thread tension alone. Once mastered, the technique is faster than the figure-eight wraps shown in the preceding method and produces less thread bulk on the finished fly.

Loop-splitting, however, is best suited to softer fibers that are more easily controlled, such as feather barbs and yarns. Since no

such as feather barbs and yarns. Since no thread wraps directly consolidate the individual fiber bundles in this technique, wings fashioned from stiff hairs tend to splay and do not have a neat, wing-shaped appearance.

Step 1. Mount and secure a bundled-fiber post using the technique described in **Method #15: Bundled-fiber Post**, Steps 1-3, p. 263. (If you are using feather barbs for the wing, as shown above, you may wish to consult **Method #16: Rolled-barb Post**, p. 265).

Trim the wing butts but do not cover them with tying thread.

Using the thread-bump technique explained in **Method #15: Bundled-fiber Post**, Step 4, p. 264, elevate the wing. It need not be fully vertical, just raised enough to simplify handling the fibers.

When finished, the thread should be positioned tight to the wing base in front of the wing.

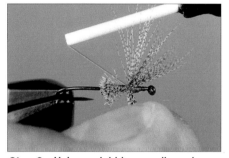

Step 2. Using a dubbing needle and your fingers, divide the single clump of fibers into two equal halves. Try to make these two smaller bundles as equal in bulk as possible.

Pinch the tips of the bundle of fibers on the near side of the shank, and pull them toward you as shown here from the top.

Bring the tying thread up the near side of the shank, between the wings and toward the hook bend. (Note that red thread is now used for better visibility)

As you bring the thread between the wings, you can force it into the front base of the near wing to stand the wing upright if it is not yet vertical.

Step 3. Bring the tying thread around the back of the wing butts, atop the hook shank. As you do so, slip the thread between the exposed wing butts.

Then bring the thread under the hook, and up through the wing butts on the near side of the shank. Wrap with pressure to lodge the thread tightly into the wing butts, as shown in this top view.

Step 4. Bring the tying thread between the wings, toward the hook eye, and down the far side of the hook shank directly against the front of the far wing, as shown here from the top.

You can force the thread into the front base of the far wing to stand it upright if it is not yet vertical.

Step 5. As shown here from the top, take 2 thread wraps directly against the base of the wings at the front edge to lock in the "X-shaped" wrap that divides the wing halves and to force the wings fully upright.

The wing butts can now be bound down with thread.

Method #22:

Forced-split Wings

In this technique, the butts of the winging material are drawn through the wings and bound to the shank, dividing and elevating the wings in one continuous procedure. The method is fairly quick and simple, but does have its limitations. First, the method works best with soft fibers such as feather barbs and yarn. Stiff hairs tend to splay, producing poorly defined wings, though they can be consolidated easily by adding a few figure-eight wraps. Second, the fibers used for winging must be long enough so that the butt ends can be easily grasped and manipulated after the wing has been tied in.

This same type of wing division can be achieved by using a separate material, mounted behind the wing and subsequently drawn forward between the wing halves to separate them. This approach makes the

forced-split practical with short-butted wing materials. In *Micropatterns*, Darrel Martin notes that Swiss tyer Marc Petitjean divides a clump of CDC that is used for the wings with a second CDC feather that is mounted separately; a loop formed of tying thread can be used as well. Both approaches are shown in alternate steps.

Step 1. Mount and secure a bundled-fiber post using the technique described in **Method #15: Bundled-fiber Post**, Steps 1-3, p. 263. If you are using feather barbs for the wing, as shown here, you may wish to consult first **Method #16: Rolled-barb Post**, p. 265. Do not bind down or clip the butts.

When the fiber bundle is tied in, position the tying thread at the forward base of the wing, though you need not be concerned about posting up the fibers.

Using a dubbing needle and your fingers, divide the single clump of fibers into two equal halves. Try to make these two smaller bundles as equal in bulk as possible.

With your *left* hand, pinch the tips of the bundle of fibers on the near side of the shank, and pull them toward you and slightly below the hook shank, as shown.

With your *right* hand, grasp a small clump of butt fibers from the top of the bundle, and pull them away from you to the far side of the shank, as shown. The number of fibers you grasp will determine the angle between the finished wings. A larger clump will spread the wings more widely; a smaller number of fibers will keep the wings closer together.

Step 2. Bring the fiber butts in your right hand between the two wings and pull them straight down, forcing the butt fibers into the base of the wing.

Step 3. With your left hand, grasp the bobbin and take one turn of thread over the butt fibers held in the right hand. This wrap will temporarily hold the butt fibers while you transfer the bobbin to the right hand.

Step 4. Transfer the bobbin to the right hand, and begin taking a series of very tight, adjacent wraps toward the wing base.

As you approach the wing base, preen the wings back toward the hook bend. Continue wrapping the thread against the base of the wings. These wraps will bind the folded wing butts down, pushing them firmly into the "V" between the wings and forcing them apart and upright, as shown.

Step 5. When the wings remain upright, clip the butt fibers ahead of and behind the wing.

If desired, the wings can be bundled more tightly with figure-eight wraps as shown in **Method #20: The Figure-eight Wing Split**, Steps 5-6, p. 269.

Apply a drop of head cement to the wing base.

Step 1a. If the wing fibers are too short to manipulate the butt ends easily—as with the CDC barbs shown here—use the following procedure.

When the wing bundle (shown here in black) is mounted, clip the butts and bind them down. Secure a separate CDC feather (shown here in white) by the tip directly behind the wings. (If a material other than CDC is used, tie in a small clump of the same fibers from the which the wing is fashioned.)

Note that the tips of this separate CDC feather point toward the *rear* of the hook during mounting. This mounting orientation eliminates the need to fold the feather over itself when using it to split the wings, and thereby reduces bulk on the shank.

As in Step 1, divide the wing fibers in half and pull the near wing toward you and slightly down with the left hand.

Grasp the CDC feather in the right fingers and proceed to Step 2.

Step 2a. Wings can also be divided by using a loop of tying thread to force them apart.

Form a thread loop about 3" long behind the wing, using the procedure described in **Method #38: Trap-loop Dubbing**, Steps 1-2, p. 129. We've changed to red thread here for better visibility, but in actual tying, the loop is fashioned from the working thread.

As in Step 1, divide the wing fibers in half and pull the near wing toward you and slightly down with the left hand.

Grasp the thread loop in the right fingers and proceed to Step 2.

Method #23:
Thread-split Wings

The approach shown here is really a version of **Method #22: Forced-split Wings**, p. 270, in which a separate loop of tying thread is used to force the wing halves apart. The technique is fast and builds little bulk on the hook shank. With soft fibers, such as feather barbs, the wings may be satisfactorily divided this way, but stiffer fibers may require additional figure-eight wraps to consolidate the wing halves into more compact bundles.

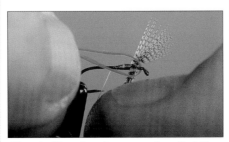

Step 1. Mount and secure a bundled fiber post using the technique shown in **Method #15: Bundled-fiber Post**, Steps 1-3, p. 263. (If using feather barbs for the wing, you may wish to consult first **Method #16: Rolled-barb Post**, p. 265.)

Clip and bind down the wing butts, and position the tying thread at the rearmost wrap securing the butts.

Cut an 8" length of tying thread, and fold it in half to form a loop.

With the right fingers, draw half the bundle of winging fibers toward you and slightly downward.

With the left fingers, slip the loop of thread over the hook eye. Position the loop threads between the wings.

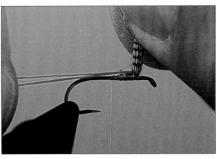

Step 2. With the right fingers, pinch both wing halves and draw them upward.

With the left hand pull the thread loop firmly toward the hook bend, holding it parallel to the shank.

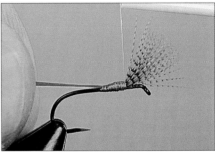

Step 3. Maintain tension on the thread loop, and use the right hand to bind the thread loop securely to the shank, right up to the rear base of the wings.

Step 4. When the rear base of the wings is reached, use the left fingers to preen both wings back toward the hook bend.

Build a thread bump ahead of the wings to post them to vertical.

Step 5. The wings will be elevated and split. If the individual wings are not consolidated to your satisfaction, you can bundle them more tightly with thread wraps as shown in **Method #20: The Figure-eight Wing Split**, Steps 5-6, p. 269.

Method #24:

Split Synthetic-fiber Wings

Wings fashioned from yarns and synthetic hairs can be mounted, posted, and divided using any of the preceding techniques in this section, but because such wings are trimmed to their final length, there is a simpler approach that can be used. In addition to its speed, it produces virtually no bulk on the hook shank from clipped wing butts.

Step 1. Lay a thread foundation that spans the wing-mounting area, and position the tying thread at the wing-mounting point.

Clip a length of wing material 2"-3" long. The bundle of material should be the thickness of one wing. Use a dubbing needle or comb to work through the fibers to untangle and separate them if necessary.

Lash the yarn crosswise atop the shank and secure it with 2 or 3 tight crisscross wraps using the technique shown in **Method #8: The Lash Mount and Crisscross Wrap**, p. 29. (You can also use the "slide-mount" approach shown in **Method #15: Bundled-fiber Post**, Steps 1a-1b, p. 265.)

Step 2. With the left fingers, raise both wings vertically, and take a few tight horizontal thread wraps around the base of the wings to angle them upward.

Step 3. Hold the wings by the tips, and clip them to length.

Method #25:

Side-mount Bundled-fiber Wings

Bundled fibers can be affixed to the sides, rather than the top, of the hook shank to create wings for a No-Hackle Dun pattern. The tips of the fibers can be left natural or trimmed to produce a more realistic silhouette. Even with trimming, however, this style of wing does not produce the kind of distinct profile that can be achieved with side-mounted quills (see **Method #4: Side-mount Quill Wings**, p. 246) or feather tips (see **Method #11: Side-mount Feather-tip Wings**, p. 258). But it is far easier to tie and more durable than either of these other materials.

One of the best materials for this purpose is poly yarn. Unlike quill, feather tips, or most other bundled fibers, poly yarn resists water absorption, contributing to the floatation of this no-hackle fly design. However, other bundled fibers, CDC barbs in particular, can be used as well.

Since dressing the body is difficult once the wings are mounted, and in fact the proper positioning of the wing is aided by the body material, it is first necessary to mount the tails and dub the body before dressing the wings. Typically, a split tail and finely textured dubbing such as polypropylene are used.

Step 1. Cut a section of poly yarn about 3" long. Each wing will be formed from a section of this piece of yarn, so the thickness of the yarn strand should be gauged accordingly. On larger flies, you may be able to form each wing from a full thickness of the yarn; on smaller flies, you may need to split the yarn lengthwise to avoid disproportionately bulky wings.

Run a dubbing needle or comb lengthwise through the yarn several times to separate and untangle the fibers. Cut the section of yarn in half, into two 1½-inch pieces.

Mount a divided, triple, or fan tail and dub the body about ⅔ of the way up the hook shank. Notice in the photo above that the body has a distinct "shoulder" at the front edge; this will assist in positioning the wings.

After the body is dressed, lay a thread foundation of 4 or 5 tight wraps ahead of the body. Position the tying thread about 2 thread-wraps ahead of the front edge of the body.

Step 2. The first piece of yarn is affixed to the far side of the hook shank.

The yarn can be mounted using any of the techniques indicated in **Method #15: Bundled-fiber Post**, Step 2, p. 264, but since it is important that the fibers be consolidated as much as possible on the sides of the hook shank, the noose-loop mount, as we're using here, (see **Method #12: The Noose Loop**, p. 32) is particularly useful.

Position the first piece of yarn along the far side of the hook shank, and take a single turn of thread around the yarn only.

Step 3. "Slide" the yarn down the thread and position it against the side of the hook shank. Bind it with 2 or 3 tight, adjacent wraps, moving toward the hook eye.

Return the tying thread to the rearmost thread wrap.

Step 4. Mount the near wing in the same fashion.

When both wings are mounted, clip the excess material and bind the butts to the shank.

During the mounting, use as few thread wraps as possible to avoid excessive bulk at the head of the fly.

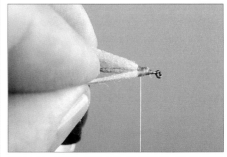

Step 5. Now grasp both wings as shown in this top view, pulling them back and up

until they are elevated about 60 degrees above the hook shank. Note that the grip pictured here helps keep the wings positioned on the sides of the shank.

Tightly wrap the tying thread back to the front of the body, forcing the wing base into the dubbing. The shoulder of the dubbing will help keep the wings elevated.

Step 6. When properly mounted, the lower edge of the wing should be flush with the bottom of the hook; the upper edge of the wing is elevated about 75 degrees above the shank; and the angle between the wings should be 30-45 degrees.

If the wings are not in the correct position, gently pull, tug, or preen them until they sit properly. Then take one crisscross wrap of thread between the wings.

Step 7. Run a dubbing needle lengthwise a few times through both wings to separate and untangle the fibers. Use your fingers and a dubbing needle to preen each wing into a flat "panel," which will later be trimmed to a more winglike profile.

When the wing fibers are fanned and spread thinly, put a drop of liquid-type CA glue between the wings, allowing a bit of the glue to bleed up into the base of each wing. When the glue sets, it will lock the fibers into the panel-like shape.

Step 8. While the glue is drying, thinly dub a short section of tying thread. Make one or two crisscross wraps between the wings to cover the exposed thread wraps with dubbing. Then dub the remaining portion of the body ahead of the wings, and whip-finish the fly.

CA glue dries quickly, and you can now trim the wings. The trimming is identical to that used for Gary Borger's Yarn-

Wing Dun, shown in **Method #18: Trimmed-fiber Wing**, Step 3a, p. 267.

The wings can be left in this shape or altered as desired by rounding the tips or lower edge.

After the wings are trimmed to shape, cut away any stray or overly short wing fibers to neaten up the profile.

Method #26:
Divided Fur Wings

This very unusual technique was shown to us by Finnish tyer Veli Autti, who uses a piece of fur on the hide to construct the tails, body, and wings. Ultimately the wings are formed from the underfur and have a soft texture and lifelike translucence. This style of wing could probably be formed from a bundle of fur clipped from the skin, but the strip of hide left intact during dressing simplifies handling the material.

Not all types of fur are suitable. In this technique, the tails are formed from the guard hairs that extend beyond the underfur. The distance that the guard hairs project beyond the underfur is important for proportioning the fly since this distance establishes the tail length and thus the suitable hook size, as shown in the following photo.

Shown at the left is a strip of muskrat fur used in main sequence. The dotted line shows the distance between the tips of the underfur and the tips of the guard hairs—a distance equal to the tail length. For the customary proportions, in which the tail length is equal to the shank length, this fur is sized for a #14 hook, also shown at the left.

On the right is a strip of beaver fur. Notice the much longer projection of the guards hairs—in this case, proportioned for the #10 hook shown at the right.

Both strips of fur, however, can be used for a range of hook sizes if the technique shown in the alternate sequence is employed.

There is certainly some leeway in this regard, however, depending upon the hook style, desired tail length, and so on. Notice for instance in Step 5, on the finished fly tied by Veli Autti, the tails may seem disproportionately long to American tyers, but it reflects the general preference among European tyers for longer tails. Note as well that Autti uses a short-shank hook, and it is possible that the long bundle of fibers repre-

sent not only the tails of the insect but the rear portion of the body as well. In Autti's original technique, shown in the main sequence below, a single patch of fur may be suitable for two or perhaps three hook sizes. The alternate sequence shows a version of the method in which separate tail and body materials are used, and the underfur alone forms the wings.

Even so, some types of fur work better than others. In his original technique, Autti uses muskrat fur, as shown in the main sequence, which is really ideal for the technique—it has long, straight, stiff, somewhat sparsely distributed guard hairs that extend well beyond the dense underfur. We experimented with other types of fur and found that woodchuck, beaver, and nutria are all suitable, and mink body fur would probably work well also. Rabbit fur generally lacks guard hair that is stiff enough to form tails, while squirrel and otter fur is generally too short to be practical with this approach.

Finally, fur on dried, rather than tanned, skins is better suited to this technique since it is more easily cut into the narrow strips required. Both, however, can be used.

Step 1. Begin by cutting a narrow strip of fur, about ¹⁄₁₆" to ⅛" wide, using the technique shown in **Method #42: Hide-strip Fur Chenille**, p. 132. If you have a choice, a cross-cut strip is slightly simpler to handle than a longitudinally cut strip (see "Fur-strip Bodies," p. 142), though either can be used.

Cut a section of the strip that is about twice the hook gap in length, though this dimension varies with the width of the strip and the density of the fur. On some strips of fur, a few of the guard hairs may be unusually long for the desired tail length; these can simply be plucked out so that the remaining guard hairs are more uniform in length.

Lay a thread foundation at the winging point of the fly. Comb or preen the fur so that it stands perpendicular to the hide.

Mount the fur at the winging point with two moderately tight wraps of thread.

With the left fingers, pinch the tips of the fur and hold them atop the shank. With the right fingers, grasp the patch of hide and pull it toward the hook eye until the guard hairs form tails of the proper length.

Step 2. When the proper tail length is established, wrap the tying thread back to the tailing point in an open spiral over the

fur, binding it atop the shank.

Take two tight thread wraps at the tailing point, then spiral the thread back to the wing-mounting wraps.

In Autti's original approach, the hair bound to the shank with these "X" wraps forms the fly body and ribbing, so do not place the thread wraps too close together or the fur will be entirely concealed beneath the tying thread.

Step 3. At this point, a hackle is mounted at the customary point behind the wings using either the cross mount or parallel mount shown in **Method #2: Single-hackle Mounts**, p. 347. We've omitted it here for a clearer illustration.

Take a pinch of the same type of fur used to form the wings, and dub a short length of the tying thread.

Use the dubbing to form a thorax, as shown. This dubbed thorax is necessary since the dubbing is used to post the fur upright. It is difficult to raise the wing material vertically using a thread-bump alone. When dubbing the front portion of the thorax ahead of the wings, pull the wing fur toward the hook bend, and place wraps of dubbing tightly against the front base of the wing fur to hold it upright.

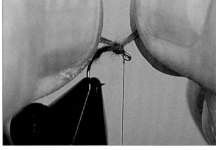

Step 4. Carefully trim away the strip of hide. The fur left on the shank should be equal to the finished wing height.

With a dubbing needle or your fingers, divide the elevated bundle of fur into two halves.

As shown here, use your fingers to pull the bundles apart to form the wings. On very soft, dense underfur such as muskrat, pulling the wings firmly apart is enough to keep them separated on the finished pattern. If desired, however, you can place a crisscross wrap of dubbed thread between the wing halves to help separate and consolidate them.

Step 5. Once the wings are divided, the hackle is wrapped forward in an open spiral over the thorax as shown in **Method #18: Thorax Palmer Hackle**, Steps 1-4, p. 366.

The finished fly shown here was tied by Autti. Notice the soft, fine texture and the translucence of the wings.

Step 1a. This variation of the original technique can make a patch of fur suitable over a larger range of hook sizes by using separate materials for the tail and body.

Here, a fly has been dressed with a hackle-barb tail and quill body. The wings are dressed using the approach shown in the main sequence, except that all of the guard hairs are plucked from the fur strip. The strip is simply mounted at the winging point, posted upright, clipped, and divided.

The hackle (omitted here) is then wrapped.

Arc-style Bundled-fiber Wings

Arc wings are fashioned from fibers that are raised perpendicular to the hook and spread in an arc of about 180 degrees over the top of the shank, forming a semi-circular fan. The best known arc-wing style is undoubtedly the Comparadun devised by Al Caucci and Bob Nastasi, which is itself a modified version of an earlier fly, the Haystack, designed by Fran Betters. Typically, arc wings are made of hollow hair—usually deer, sometimes elk—which flares under thread pressure and thus aids in distributing the hair over the top of the hook shank and, of course, contributes to the buoyancy of the fly. Other fibers, however, can be used as well: feather barbs (usually hackle), CDC, other types of hair, and synthetics such as Z-lon, Antron, or poly yarn.

The arc-wing design offers a number of advantages. The bottom edges of the wing act as outriggers, balancing the fly upright and supporting it on the water. At the same time, the fan shape creates a distinct wing impression when viewed from any angle. Such flies are tied without a hackle, which makes for a low-floating dressing and an unobstructed silhouette. Yet the broad, high

wing makes the fly visible to the angler. These wings are relatively easy to dress, can be adapted to imitate a variety of mayfly species, are quite durable, and create a highly effective dry fly.

Specific winging materials have their own particular virtues. Deer hair, commonly used on the Comparadun, is highly buoyant and will float a fly in surprisingly turbulent water. Other fibers such as feather barbs and yarn, while not as buoyant as hollow hair, give the tyer greater latitude in selection for wing colors or markings that match the naturals. Combinations of materials can also be employed. Colorado tyer Shane Stalcup, for instance, combines CDC with mallard flank to produce a fly with excellent floatation and mottled wings to imitate the *Callibaetis* dun, as shown in **Method #28: Solid-fiber Arc Wing**, p, 276. In much the same fashion, a bit of brightly colored hair or Antron can be added to a dull colored wing to increase its visibility to the fisherman.

Because flies dressed with arc wings rely primarily on the wing itself for floatation, they are often dressed with split, divided, or fan tails to help support and balance the fly, and many tyers often incorporate a non-absorbent or buoyant body dubbing such as finely textured poly.

Method #27:

Hollow-hair Arc Wing

Deer hair is the most popular material for this type of wing, though suitable elk hair can be used as well. Tyers differ in the types of hair they prefer for this wing style. Some choose hair that is less hollow and flares less, which is easier to control during tying; others prefer hair that flares readily and produces a buoyant wing. For more details on these types of hair, see "Hollow Hair," p. 2.

The actual quantity of material used depends largely on the tyer's preference, though sparser wings are generally used for flatter, calmer waters, and bulkier wings incorporating more material float more reliably in fast or broken water. As a starting point for experimentation, you may wish to use Al Beatty's method of gauging hair quantity; use the same amount of material that he recommends for a divided hairwing fly, as explained in the section "Selecting and Preparing Bundled Fibers," p. 262.

The widespread use of this winging style has resulted in a number of approaches to its dressing, as tyers have sought to overcome perhaps the one obstacle in tying this wing—hollow hair is resilient and, over time, the upright wing fibers may tend to lean in the direction they were originally mounted.

There are 4 procedures shown below, each identified by a letter/number combination in which the number indicates the tying sequence and the letter specifies the step within that sequence. That is, Steps 1a-1d constitute one method; Steps 2a-2c another; and so on.

The first sequence shown is the original dressing technique for Comparaduns devised by Caucci and Nastasi.

Step 1a. The initial wing mount is identical to that for a bundled-fiber post.

Mount the tying thread, and clip, clean, stack, and mount a clump of deer hair as described in **Method #15: Bundled-fiber Post**, Steps 1-3, p. 264.

During mounting, it is helpful to use the left thumb and forefinger to pinch the hair from the sides as the mounting wraps are tightened. Pinching the hair will help keep the bundle atop the hook shank.

When the wing is mounted, clip and bind down the butts. If a few stray fibers have made their way to the underside of the shank, ignore them.

Position the tying thread directly in front of the wing.

Step 1b. The wing is posted to vertical using a bump of thread. With the fingers of the left hand, pinch the wing fibers from the sides and draw them back toward the hook bend. It is important that the left fingers keep secure hold of the wing fibers; when you begin wrapping the thread against the wing base, thread pressure will drag some fibers beneath the shank if they are not held in position.

Begin building a bump of thread in front of the wing as explained in **Method #1: Mounting and Posting Upright Wings**, Step 1c, p. 242. Abut the thread wraps tightly against the wing base, forcing the deer hair to stand vertically. Do not try to stack too many wraps of thread atop one another, or the bump will collapse. Instead, the bump should be cone-shaped, wide where it abuts the wing and tapering toward the hook eye. Deer hair can be stiff, and thread wraps should be tight and butted firmly against the wing base.

Periodically release the wing to check your progress. You want to use the minimum wraps necessary to post the wing to avoid excessive bulk in the fly. When the wing stands vertically, posting is complete.

Step 1c. View the wing from the front. The deer hair fibers should fan out evenly, about 180 degrees around the top of the hook shank.

If the fibers are not uniformly distributed, use your fingers to pull or preen hairs from more dense areas to less dense ones. If the wing does not fan fully around the top of the shank, use your fingers to preen the fibers on the sides of the wing downward, as shown above, forming "pontoons" or "outriggers" to support the fly.

Step 1d. If adjusting the fibers has caused the wing to tilt forward, take a few additional wraps of thread on the thread bump to force it upright again.

If any stray hairs project beneath the shank, clip them off.

Place a drop of head cement or CA glue at the base of the wing, where it meets the thread bump. This glue will help the fibers maintain an even distribution and stay erect.

Note the finished wings here. The wing on the right shows a side view—the hair forms a relatively narrow, upright band, with no fibers leaning excessively toward the hook bend or eye. The wing on the left, the front view, shows the arc of fibers evenly distributed and reaching to the horizontal on both sides of the shank.

Al Caucci notes that some tyers dress arc wings with a reverse mount. Since the hair tips are mounted toward the tail of the fly and raised toward the eye, the body dubbing can be used to help secure the material in the vertical position. Should the wing eventually lean, it will slant toward the rear of the body, much like the wing of a natural mayfly.

Step 2a. Lay a thread foundation that spans the winging area, and position the thread at the wing-mounting point.

Prepare and stack a bundle of hair as explained in Step 1a. Trim the hair butts so that the bundle is ⅛" to ¼" longer than the finished wing height.

Grasp the hair tips and position the bundle atop the shank. Take a loose wrap over the mounting point of the bundle, then pull firmly downward to flare the hair butts. Keep a firm hold on the hair tips so that they do not roll around the hook shank.

If the head of the fly is to be dubbed, take several tight wraps over the hair butts, then clip and bind them down.

To form a clipped head on the fly, as we're doing here, take 3 or 4 very tight thread wraps over the first mounting wrap. Then take 2 or 3 tight wraps at intervals through the butts, working toward the hook eye. Finally, take 2 or 3 more wraps back through the butts toward the wing, ending with the tying thread positioned behind the wing. These wraps will flare the hair butts around the shank.

Step 2b. With the right fingers, preen all the hair (including the spun butts) forward over the hook eye.

With the left hand, build a thread bump, as explained in Step 1b, behind the wing to post it upright. (If a large clump of wing material is used, you can partially post the wing upright using either of the approaches shown in Steps 3a-3c or 4a-4c below.)

Step 2c. When the wing is posted upright, preen the fibers to shape as explained in Step 1c and apply a drop of CA glue to the rear base of the wing.

Dub the body (this step has been omitted here), and if necessary, use a few wraps of dubbing to force the wings further upright.

On smaller patterns, the flared wing butts may be sufficiently dense to form the head. On larger patterns, you can, if desired, spin or flare an additional small clump of hair (see **Method #58: Spinning Hollow Hair**, p. 145, or **Method #59: Flaring Hollow Hair**, p. 147) to complete the head.

Finally clip the head to shape.

Larger clumps of hair can be difficult to post up using a thread bump, and you may wish to use a posting technique recommended by tyer Al Beatty. In this method, smaller clumps of hair are partially posted, one at a time, then the entire wing is elevated to the vertical.

Step 3a. Mount a bundle of fibers as explained in Step 1a. Position the tying thread at the frontmost wrap securing the bundle.

Using the left fingers, grasp the tips of a bundle of hair fibers on the far side of the shank. The bundle should be about ¼ the total amount of hair. Raise the bundle and pass the thread between the small bundle and the remainder of the hair.

Step 3b. After passing the thread between the two bundles, hold the bobbin beneath the hook shank, pulling firmly downward and slightly toward the hook bend. This tension will force the small clump of hair to elevate slightly, though it will not be fully vertical. Maintain moderate tension on the thread.

Step 3c. Repeat Steps 3a-3b three more times, each time grasping and raising the next "quarter bundle" of hair. When the final clump of hair, the one nearest you, is raised, the tying thread will be drawn forward on the near side of the hair bundle and end up in front of the wing, as shown here.

The wing will not yet be vertical, but the thread tension against the smaller clumps of hair will make it easier to post them with a thread bump, and the wing will hold its position and shape more reliably.

Now finish raising the wing to the vertical by building a thread bump as shown in Step 1b-1d.

This last approach is very much like the one in the preceding sequence except that smaller clumps of hair are posted in increments working from the rear of the wing forward, rather than side to side.

Step 4a. Mount a bundle of hair as explained in Step 1a, and position the tying thread at the frontmost wrap securing the bundle.

With the left fingers, grasp ¼ to ⅓ of the fibers at the rear of the wing and pull them back toward the hook bend.

Take a slack wrap of thread at the base of the preened-back hair. Complete the wrap by raising the bobbin vertically above the shank, and pulling firmly to seat the wrap. (Making this wrap under tension from the beginning may cause some of the front fibers to roll around the hook shank.)

Step 4b. Repeat Step 4a with successive small bundles working toward the front of the wing.

When the front of the wing is reached, build a thread bump, shape the wing, and apply a drop of cement as explained in Steps 1b-1d.

Method #28:
Solid-fiber Arc Wing

Though hollow hair is a favorite material for arc wings because of its buoyancy, solid fibers—yarns, solid hairs, or feather barbs—can also be used. In general, however, these materials will not provide the same degree of floatation as hollow hair, and flies dressed with them are best suited to calmer waters.

If solid hairs are used, the material should be prepared as explained in **Method #2: Preparing and Cleaning Hair**, p. 68, and the tips aligned as explained in **Method #3: Stacking and Aligning Hair**, p. 69. If yarn is used, the strand of yarn should be combed to untangle the individual fibers so that they will fan out over the top of the hook shank.

The main sequence shows the use of wet-fly hackle barbs to create an arc wing (dry-fly hackle barbs can be dressed in the same fashion). The alternate sequence illustrates two unusual variations, both of which come to us from Colorado tyer Shane Stalcup. The first is the use of CDC to fash-

ion the wing. The second is the construction of a "double" arc wing in which two different materials are employed. Here, CDC is used to provide floatation and a smaller amount of mallard flank is used to give a mottled appearance to the wing. The mallard flank can be omitted, of course, if desired. This same technique can be used with any winging material, and the mallard flank can be replaced by a small quantity of brightly colored hair or yarn to increase the visibility of the fly to the angler.

Step 1. Create a firm thread foundation over the winging area of the hook, and position the thread at the mounting point.

Prepare a bundle of hackle barbs as explained in **Method #1: Preparing Feather Barbs**, p. 67.

Mount the bundle of hackle barbs as described in **Method #15: Bundled-fiber Post**, Steps 1-3, p. 263.

During mounting, use the left thumb and forefinger to pinch the fibers from the sides as the thread wraps are tightened. Pinching the hackle barbs will help keep the bundle atop the hook shank.

When the wing is mounted and the butts clipped and bound down, position the tying thread at the frontmost thread wrap. If a few stray fibers have made their way to the underside of the shank, ignore them.

Step 2. Because of its tendency to flare, hollow hair distributes itself over the top of the hook shank quite readily. Solid fibers, on the other hand, may resist spreading evenly, particularly if the quantity of material used is large. To assist them, use the left thumbnail (or a pair of needle-nose pliers) to gently "crush" the bundle downward directly at the mounting point. The goal here is to force some fibers to the sides of the hook shank so that a wing of uniform density will result after posting.

12

SECTION 1

Step 3. The wing can now be posted up with a thread bump and preened to a uniform density as described above in **Method #27: Hollow-hair Arc Wing**, Steps 1b-1d, p. 274.

As with all arc wings, you are striving here for an even distribution of fibers and an arc that is approximately 180 degrees over the top of the hook shank.

Step 1a. To tie Stalcup's CDC arc wing, mount a small bundle of mallard flank barbs according to the instructions in Step 1. The exact amount of material depends upon just how visible and distinct you wish the mallard flank to appear in the finished wing. As a general guideline, try for a quantity of mallard flank that is about ¼ to ⅓ the total amount of wing material.

Step 2a. The CDC used for the main part of the wing can be prepared in one of two ways. For flies approximately #16 and smaller, you can use barbs stripped from the stem. Stripping barbs like this has the advantage of creating a wing with no feather stem material contained within it, which reduces bulk and wind resistance. For larger flies, however, the method is tedious; tyer Shane Stalcup, who showed us this technique, uses feather tips instead.

To prepare such a wing, stack the desired number of feathers atop one another with the tips even. If the feather stems are curved, stack them so that the curvatures match, that is, so the feathers "nest" into one another neatly, as shown above.

Step 3a. Mount the bundle of CDC feathers directly atop the mallard flank by using the instructions given in Step 1.

Clip and bind down the butts as shown, and proceed to Step 2.

Step 4a. When the wing is posted, the mallard flank will appear in front of the CDC and give the wing a mottled appearance.

When using CDC, however, omit the drop of head cement at the wing base, as it may bleed into the feather barbs and diminish the floatation they provide the fly.

Method #29:

Gathered-hackle Arc Wing

We first saw this arc-wing design—fashioned from a collar-style hackle—in the work of Datus Proper, who prefers hackle to deer hair for its sheen, natural color, and resistance to matting. Proper prefers this style especially for smaller flies, where the coarseness of deer hair is a limitation in fashioning a neat, visible wing with good floatation.

The following sequence shows Proper's method of gathering the hackle into an arc wing using tying thread alone, and it is the basis for his Barb-Wing Dun design. The hackle used should be of dry-fly quality, but it need not be top-grade material. The hackle barbs should be about as long as the entire hook.

Dick Talleur uses a similar approach for tying hackle arc wings on his Drakeburger patterns. His technique is identical to that shown in **Method #11: Modified Thorax Hackle**, p. 360, except that the separate wing material used in that demonstration is omitted; the hackle barbs are used instead to represent wings on the fly.

Step 1. The application of hackle depends to some extent on the hook size. For hooks of about #16 and smaller, attach a hackle feather slightly behind the winging point—usually about ¼ to ⅓ of a shank-length behind the hook eye—and wrap it forward in 4 or 5 tightly adjacent turns as described in **Method #4: Single-hackle Dry-fly Collar**, p. 351.

Larger flies require a more dense wing fashioned from a greater number of hackle barbs. Here, the tyer has two choices. If a long, thin-stemmed hackle is used, you can wrap it in layers, winding it forward with 4 or 5 turns, then reversing direction and wrapping the hackle back over the initial wraps (see **Method #9: Overwrapped Collar Hackle**, p. 356). If a still denser wing is desired, the feather can again be wrapped forward. Or two or more hackles can be used to fashion the wing; these should be wrapped as described in **Method #7: Multiple-hackle Collar**, p. 354. Regardless of which approach is used, the goal is to confine the wraps of hackle to a relatively small area of the hook shank—layers of hackle should be built upward rather than outward along the hook shank. Finally, wrapping layers of hackle like this may cause some barbs to splay outward; don't be concerned with these as they will be pushed back into position when the wing is gathered above the shank.

Once the hackle(s) has been wound, tie off the feather, clip the tip, and position the tying thread in front of the wrapped hackle.

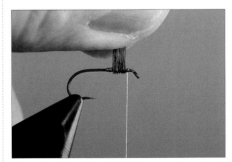

Step 2. The object in this procedure is to gather all the hackle barbs and raise them above the hook shank.

Begin by using your left thumb and forefinger to pinch the tying thread below the lowermost barbs. Slide your fingers up the thread, pushing the hackle barbs that are beneath the shank upward. Continue sliding your fingers upward around the hook shank, drawing the hackle barbs up until you are pinching all the barbs by their tips above the shank as shown.

Step 3. The barbs will be secured in this position with crisscross wraps formed beneath the shank.

Maintain your grasp of the barb tips. Bring the tying thread beneath the hook shank and cross it over the hackle wraps. Raise the thread vertically. It should now be above the shank and behind the hackle, as shown.

Step 4. Now bring the thread down the far side of the shank. You'll need to release the hackle tips momentarily.

After the thread passes over the shank, grasp the hackle tips again. Bring the thread underneath the shank, crossing over the hackle wraps. Draw the thread upward, in front of the wing.

Step 5. Take one wrap of thread ahead of the wing, around the shank only. This will lock in the crisscross wraps you've made.

Now inspect the wing from the front. The barbs should all be gathered atop the shank in a fan-like shape. The width the arc will vary with the thread tension used on the crisscross wraps. Very slight tension will gather the wing into an arc of about 180 degrees; greater tension will consolidate the wing into a tighter angle. The spread of the wing depends largely upon the tyer's preference. Datus Proper prefers an angle of 60-90 degrees; Talleur, a somewhat broader spread.

If stray barbs project, or a tighter wing is desired, repeat Steps 2-5 until the desired configuration is achieved.

Method #30:
Clipped-hackle Arc Wing

A simple arc wing can be constructed from wrapped hackle that has been clipped on the underside. The method is quick and easy but it produces a rather sparse dressing best fished in calmer waters. Since half of the hackle barbs are lost to trimming, fewer of them are available to support the fly.

Step 1. In order to yield a sufficient number of barbs to support the fly, this wing is best fashioned from multiple layers of hackle as explained in **Method #29: Gathered-hackle Arc Wing**, Step 1, p. 277.

Once the hackle(s) has been wound, tie off the feather, clip the tip, and position the tying thread in front of the wrapped hackle.

Step 2. View the feather from the front, and carefully trim away the barbs from the underside of the shank until the desired wing spread is obtained. Here, we've trimmed the wing to an arc of about 180 degrees.

The rest of the fly can now be dressed. Some tyers prefer to take a crisscross wrap of dubbing beneath the wing to conceal the trimmed stubs of hackle barb on the underside of the shank.

Upright Loop Wings

Tyer Andy Puyans is generally credited with developing the loop-wing style, a design that might be accurately described as "pure silhouette." The wing is formed from a teardrop-shaped loop of material that clearly and cleanly defines the outer perimeter of the wing. Since such wings are "hollow," they are light in weight and offer little wind resistance in casting. The loop style is versatile as well. It can be tied as a single, upright, post-type wing or as a pair of divided wings. It can be used to dress duns, as in the methods described below, for spinners (see **Method**

#79: Loop Spentwing, p. 329), or for emergers (see **Method #86: Fiber-loop Emerger Wing**, p. 336); and it can be used with flies incorporating either a collar or parachute hackle.

Loop wings can be formed from virtually any material composed of strands or fibers that are long enough to form the loop and rigid enough to maintain the loop shape when posted upright. Puyans originally used mallard flank feathers, and barbs from body feathers, wing quills, and tail feathers from turkey and pheasant are still popular for the design. These materials are relatively soft, easy to work, light in weight, and low in wind resistance; feather barbs, however, are fragile, and a toothy jaw can tear them. A more durable loop wing can be made from Antron or poly yarn. Natural hair, provided it is long enough, would seem to be suitable, though apparently tyers have not explored this material much for loop wings. Stiffer materials—clipped or stripped hackle stems and monofilament line—are sometimes used; such wings are a bit more wind resistant but quite durable.

Method #31:
Loop Wings

There are a number of approaches to tying loop wings, but most are slight variations of the technique shown below. The wings here should be kept sparse. When using body feathers, such as the mallard flank shown below, Puyans recommends a total of 6 fibers for flies up to #16, and 4 fibers for anything smaller. Wings made of yarn can be dressed a bit more heavily if desired. Note that if yarn will be used to create divided wings, it should be combed prior to mounting to remove any twists or tangles. Separating the fibers like this in advance will make dividing the wing much easier.

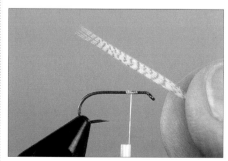

Step 1. Wrap a short thread foundation over the wing-mounting area, and position the thread at the mounting point.

Align the tips of the desired number of feather barbs and clip them from the stem as described in **Method #1: Preparing Feather Barbs**, p. 67. When cutting the barbs from the feather stem, try not to twist or roll the barbs, but rather leave them in a flat, interlocking strip. Preserving this flattened strip during the tying process will make dividing the wings easier.

Step 2. Mount the section of feather barbs atop the hook shank as shown. Take the first wrap of thread directly over the mounting point on the hook shank, and then bind the barbs down by wrapping the thread toward the hook bend. Don't try to mount the barbs by the very tips; these are thin and fragile and can easily break. Rather, take the first mounting wrap of thread about ⅛" to ¼" back from the barb tips.

Note: if the winging material is curved, mount it so that the convex side faces the hook shank. When the wing loop is formed, it will take advantage of the natural curvature of the material.

When the fibers are bound in, return the thread to the frontmost thread wrap.

Step 3. With your right hand, hold a dubbing needle directly above the wing-mounting point. With your left hand, fold the feather barbs back over the dubbing needle to establish the wing loop.

There are a few points to bear in mind during this procedure. First, the dubbing needle should be held precisely crosswise above the hook shank as shown. Angling the needle may cause the wing fibers to twist. Second, when folding the feather barbs, try to keep the strip of barbs flat and untwisted to simplify dividing them later on. Third, when forming the wing, apply a uniform tension on each fiber to produce an even wing. Lastly, the height of the wing when doubled over the needle should be twice the hook gap. When the needle is withdrawn and the wings relax, they will decrease in height slightly and be of the proper proportion.

When the proper wing height is established, pinch the barbs against the hook shank at the mounting point.

Step 4. Withdraw the dubbing needle, and bind the feather barbs to the shank. Take the first wrap of thread directly atop the mounting point and wrap toward the hook bend.

Clip the butts and bind them down. Return the tying thread to the frontmost thread wrap on the wing material.

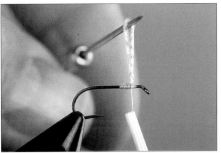

Step 5. Manipulating the wings to the proper position can be done with the fingers, but feather barbs are fragile and it is easier to handle them with a dubbing needle.

Insert the dubbing into the loop and raise the wings perpendicular to the hook shank. Post the wing to the vertical by creating a thread bump at the forward base of the wing as described in **Method #1: Mounting and Posting Upright Wings**, Step 1c, p. 241.

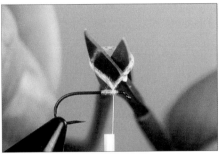

Step 6. Withdraw the needle. If the wing has been pulled into an excessively tall, thin shape, it can be widened at this point. Puyans recommends inserting closed scissor points into the loop, then opening them gently and pushing the blades against the interior sides of the wing to broaden the loop, as shown.

At this point, you have three alternatives. If you desire a single, undivided wing (as shown above) on the finished fly, simply apply a small drop of head cement at the base of the loop and proceed to dress the remaining materials. This wing style, however, must be tied with a collar-style hackle. If you desire a parachute hackle, consult Step 6a. If you wish to fashion a pair of divided wings, proceed to Step 7.

Step 6a. Forming a thread foundation on which to wrap parachute hackle can be tricky on loop wings formed of very soft materials such as feather barbs or yarn. With care, however, it can be done, and the best approach is to use the "tension/countertension" wraps explained in **Method #9: Feather-tip Wings with Parachute Base**, Steps 3-6. p. 255. Again, handling the loop wings with a dubbing needle is easier than using your fingers.

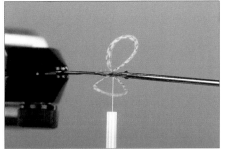

Step 7. The ease with which the wings are divided depends upon the care taken in preparing the feather barbs and folding them over the dubbing needle. If they have been allowed to twist excessively, dividing the wing will be difficult. If the strip of fibers has been kept relatively straight and flat, splitting the wings is a simple matter.

As shown in this top view, hold a dubbing needle parallel to the hook shank and, beginning at the top of the wing, press the needle downward, dividing the loop into two wings, each containing the same number of feather barbs. Continue bringing the needle down through the wing. When the base of the wing is reached, push the needle into the butts of the feather barbs to crimp them, which will temporarily maintain their separation.

Step 8. Take a crisscross wrap of thread between the wings to divide them permanently.

Take a turn of thread directly around the shank to lock in the crisscross wrap. Apply a small drop of head cement to the base of the wing.

Method #32:
Slip-loop Wings

Stiffer materials such as hackle stems or monofilament line may be formed into loop wings using the procedure described in **Method #31: Loop Wings**, p. 278, but that technique is not always successful. The severe bend require to post the wings upright may fracture hackle stems, and even if the material remains intact, the method often produces a bulky tie-in. The technique described below is easier to use with smooth, incompressible materials, and can be employed as well with softer materials, such as yarn, that are reasonably strong and slippery.

We're using stripped hackle stems in the sequence below, though cut lengths of monofilament line can be used as well. Darker-colored materials create a more distinct profile than clear mono.

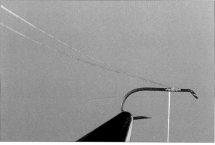

Step 1. Wrap a short thread foundation over the winging area and position the tying thread at the wing-mounting point.

Prepare a pair of hackle stems by stripping the barbs from both sides or by burning off the barbs using one of the procedures explained in **Method #12: Hand-stripped Quills**, p. 108, or **Method #13: Bleach-stripped Quills**, p. 109. Trim away the very tip portion of the hackle stem, as this thin material is prone to break.

Mount both hackle stems side-by-side atop the hook shank. Take the first wrap of thread at the wing-mounting point, and bind the down the stem tips by wrapping toward the hook eye.

If the material is curved, as these hackle stems are, mount it so that the convex side faces the hook shank. This orientation will allow you take advantage of the natural curvature when forming the loop wings.

When the hackle stems are bound in, position the tying thread directly behind the stems.

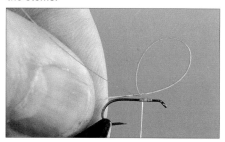

Step 2. Grasp the butt end of the hackle stem on the far side of the hook shank. Form the stem into a loop as shown. Keep the loop larger than the finished wing size.

Note that in forming the loop, the butt end of the stem passes to the outside of the mounted end of the stem.

When the loop is formed, pinch the hackle stem against the hook shank behind the mounting point.

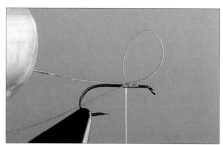

Step 3. Under light tension, take 2 turns of thread over the butt of the hackle stem, directly behind the point where the tip is tied in. The butt of the hackle should be on top, and slightly to the far side of the hook shank.

Pull the butt end of the hackle stem gently toward the hook bend, making the loop smaller, and stopping when it has formed a wing of the desired size.

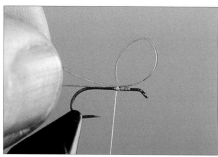

Step 4. Repeat Steps 2-3 for the hackle stem on the near side of the shank. Form a loop and take 2 turns of thread over the stem butt, securing it lightly to the top and slightly to the near side of the hook shank. Draw the loop closed to size the wing.

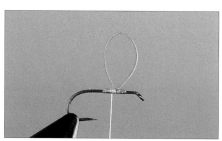

Step 5. When both wings have been properly sized, secure the butts of the hackle stems tightly with tying thread. Clip and bind down the excess.

Step 6. The angle of division between the two wings can be adjusted by using the crisscross wraps described above in **Method #20: The Figure-eight Wing Split**, Steps 2-4, p. 268. When the wing angle is satisfactory, put a drop of head cement at the base of the wings.

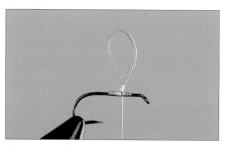

Step 6a. The two loops can be drawn together to form a single, undivided wing to be used for a parachute style fly. To form a thread foundation for the parachute hackle, see **Method #15: Bundled-fiber Post**, Step 6, p. 263.

Method #33:
Multiple-loop Wing

This technique was devised by Gary Borger to create a loop wing with a veined appearance for his Loop Wing Dun patterns. The style is dressed from feather barbs to form a single, undivided wing. It produces a more open, horseshoe-shaped wing, and in Borger's design, a collar-style hackle is wrapped around the hook shank inside the space between the wing attachment points. We're showing the wing only; for full dressing instructions, readers should consult Borger's *Designing Trout Flies.*

As with the Puyans loop wing, this one should be kept sparse. Borger ties the style in small sizes only and recommends using 5 feather barbs for hook sizes #18-22, 4 feather barbs for hooks #24-26, 3 barbs for size 28. However, a proportionately greater number of barbs could be used to dress larger hooks.

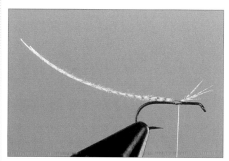

Step 1. Lay a short thread foundation at the middle of the hook shank, and position the tying thread at the center of the shank. (In Borger's Loop Wing Dun pattern, the tail has already been mounted and the abdomen dubbed.)

Prepare and clip the desired number of feather barbs—we're using mallard flank here—as described in **Method #31: Loop Wings**, Step 1, p. 278.

Mount the section of feather barbs atop the hook shank as shown. Take the first wrap of thread directly over the center of the hook shank, and then bind the barbs down by wrapping the thread toward the hook eye. Don't try to mount the barbs by the very tips; these are thin and fragile and can easily break. Rather, take the first mounting wrap of thread about ⅛" to ¼" back from the barb tips. Note the orientation of the barbs here—if the winging material is curved, mount it so that the convex side faces the hook shank. When the wing loop is formed, it will take advantage of the natural curvature of the material.

(In Borger's pattern, a hackle is mounted directly ahead of the feather barbs, and wrapped forward. It is tied off a short distance behind the hook eye.)

When the fibers are bound in, position the tying thread a short distance behind the hook eye.

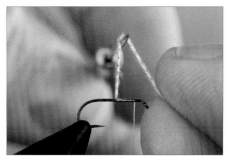

Step 2. With your left hand, hold a dubbing needle directly above the wing-mounting point. With your right hand, fold the feather barbs forward over the dubbing needle to establish the wing loop.

There are a few points to bear in mind during this procedure. First, the dubbing needle should be held precisely crosswise above the hook shank as shown. Angling the needle may cause the wing fibers to twist. Second, when folding the feather barbs, try to keep the strip of barbs flat and untwisted to simplify forming the interior loops later on. Third, when forming the wing, apply a uniform tension on each fiber to produce an even wing. Lastly, the height of the wing when doubled over the needle should be twice the hook gap. When the needle is withdrawn and the wings relax, they will decrease in height slightly and be of the proper proportion.

When the proper wing height is established, use your right fingers to pinch the barbs against the hook shank directly behind the eye.

Step 3. Carefully transfer the feather barbs to the left fingers, and take two wraps of thread, under light tension, over the butts of the feather barbs. Do not clip the excess barb material that extends over the hook eye.

Step 4. Using a hackle pliers, grasp a single feather barb, and pull gently. It will begin to form a smaller loop inside the wing. As this small loop begins to form, insert the dubbing needle inside the large wing loop to help hold the other fibers in position as this small loop is formed.

Continue pulling the single fiber until the small loop is ⅓ the height of the large wing.

Step 5. Use a hackle plier to grasp the butts of two more hackle fibers. Repeat Step 4, creating another loop from these fibers. This loop should be about ⅔ the height of the large wing.

(Note: for hook sizes smaller than #22, Borger recommends forming only one "interior" loop that is ½ the height of the larger wing.)

Step 6. When the interior loops are satisfactorily formed, tightly bind down the feather barbs behind the eye of the hook. Clip the excess and finish the fly head.

Upright Foam and Film Wings

The use of closed-cell foams and synthetic films—plastics, Mylars, woven materials, and others—is relatively new territory in fly tying. While foam is widely used as a body material, its use in winging is largely to confined to fashioning an upright post for parachute hackling, and this technique is described below. But the general bulkiness and difficulty in shaping foam makes the material poorly suited to more complex or realistic wing designs.

Synthetic films are considerably more versatile, but discussing such films presents a number of difficulties because of the rather wide variety of materials that can be used for winging. Perhaps the most readily available material is polyethylene cut from ordinary food-storage bags. It ranges in thickness from about .0015" to .003", with the thinner material being more pliable and the thicker more durable, and it is almost always clear.

The thin, .5 mil plastic used for some types of garbage bags also makes a satisfactory wing material.

Thin plastic garbage bags work best if the material is stretched before it is used for winging.

Cut a strip about 3 times as wide as necessary for the finished wing. Stretch the strip carefully to make it thinner and more translucent, as shown here.

Wings formed from this material are pictured in **Method #133: Needle-formed Fiber Extension**, Step 2d, p. 218.

Beyond these common materials, we enter the realm of specific products marketed to fly tyers for making film wings. These vary rather widely in their handling properties, and it can be something of a problem to speak of them as a group. Most such products are packaged with tying instructions for wing styles that are suited to the specific material.

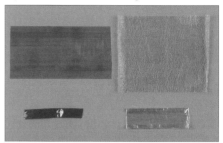

Synthetic films for winging tend to come and go from the market rather regularly. The types pictured here have been around for a few years now.

Scintilla Spinner Wing Film (upper left) has a slick texture with a pearlescent finish. Despite the name, it can be used to fashion upright wings. Shimazaki Airthru (upper right) is a soft, woven, almost felt-like material with a veined appearance. It is available in several colors. Wings & Things Fly Film (lower left) is a clear, plastic-like ribbon that has been given a mottled finish; it too is available in different colors. Zing (lower right) is a very thin, nearly clear material, with a very smooth finish. It can be tinted with marking pens, though eventually the color will wear off and require a touch up.

Note that some films—Zing and Shimazaki in particular—have a "grain" to them; that is, the material behaves differently in the lengthwise and crosswise directions. Wings should be formed with the grain of the material running from the base to tip of the wing.

Despite differences among the materials, there are some general techniques for constructing film wings, and the methods detailed below represent approaches that can be used with a reasonably wide variety of materials. Many tyers have "discovered" winging materials disguised as ordinary household products—tapes, packaging materials, and so on—and the only way to determine the best method of dressing such materials is to experiment. The physical characteristics vary significantly among different synthetic films; any given material may tie well with some of the techniques described below and poorly with others.

The principal advantage of film wings is that the materials have a natural transparent, translucent, or sometimes veined appearance, and can be trimmed to lifelike shapes. Because such products are manufactured, they are more consistent in character than natural materials and handle more predictably, and sometimes more easily. The one significant drawback is that upright film wings tend to be highly wind resistant, and their tendency to spin, twist leaders, and land improperly on the water has, perhaps, been the most substantial obstacle to a widespread acceptance among fishermen. To a certain extent, these problems are real, but in some cases they are caused by flies that are tied improperly or dressed with unsuitable materials. A correctly designed and dressed wing will minimize twisting, though perhaps not eliminate it altogether, and at least two materials have characteristics that help minimize wind resistance. Shimazaki Airthru is a soft, meshlike material that allows air to pass through. Zing, a film brought to the fly-tying world by John Betts, is dressed to promote longitudinal splitting during casting, which reduces wind resistance.

Even given the limitations, synthetic films can and do make useful and effective flies. And in a craft that is moving, slowly but inexorably, toward synthetic materials, it is reasonable to expect that improved materials and tying techniques will make this style of wing more practical still.

Method #34:
Foam Post

A foam post is a simple and effective way of creating a base for a parachute hackle. The compressible closed-cell material produces a low-bulk tie-in, and foam is generally easy to handle. The buoyancy of such a wing can also help re-float a fly that has become submerged. Foam is available in a variety of colors, and using brighter shades can increase the visibility of the fly with patterns that are very small or fished in low-light conditions. For specific details about mounting foam components and improving durability, see "Tying Foam," p. 190.

Step 1. Tying a foam post is very similar to tying a bundled-fiber post. Mount the tying thread as described in **Method #1: Mounting and Posting Upright Wings**, Step 1a. p. 241.

For a post, you can use a pre-cut foam cylinder (shown on the right), or a strip of foam cut to be square in cross section (on the left). When using cylinders or strips, the width of the wing should be about ½ the hook gap, and the post need not be cut to the finished wing height at this point.

Step 2. Mount the foam at the winging point as shown, and secure the butt end with thread wraps, working toward the hook bend. Clip and bind down the excess.

Step 3. Post the foam to the vertical position by using the thread-bump technique described in **Method #1: Mounting and Posting Upright Wings**, Step 1c, p. 241.

Clip the wing to the proper height. This post is now finished and ready for parachute hackling.

Step 3a. Some tyers prefer to wind the parachute hackle over a firmer, more rigid foundation fashioned from tying thread. The thread base is wrapped as described in **Method #15: Bundled-fiber Post**, Step 6, p. 264.

If desired, apply a drop of head cement to the wraps.

Method #35:
Post-mount Film Wings

This technique, devised by Montana tyer Al Beatty, is one of the simplest and most universally useful in mounting upright film wings. Because the wings are lashed at the base to an upright post, they are especially well-suited to forming the foundation for a parachute hackle.

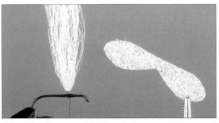

Step 1. Prepare the hook by mounting and posting a fiber bundle at the winging point. The post can be fashioned from any material, but there is really little advantage in using natural hair, since most of the post is even-

tually trimmed away. Synthetic fibers, such as the poly yarn shown here, are simpler to handle and mount with less bulk using the technique shown in **Method #15: Bundled-fiber Post**, Steps 1a-1d or 2a-2c, p. 265. Take 2 or 3 tight horizontal thread wraps around the base of the post to consolidate the fibers. Leave the post fibers long.

The wing material is shaped before it is mounted. We've cut these mayfly wings from Aire-Flow. To cut wings from sheets of material, see **Method #37: Front-fold Film Wings**, Step 1, p. 284, which describes the use of a cardboard template to form wings. The wings can be cut to any shape desired; the only requirement is a narrow "throat" between the wings, as shown here, which is necessary for mounting.

Step 2. Working from underneath the shank, fold the wing around the hook and up against the sides of the fiber post.

With the left fingers, pull upward on the wings and pinch them against the fiber post, as shown.

Take 3 or 4 tight horizontal thread wraps around the base of the wings, securing them to the fiber post. If a parachute hackle is to be used, build a taller thread foundation as explained in **Method #15: Bundled-fiber Post**, Step 6, p. 263.

Step 3. With the left fingers, pull upward on the post fibers. Use the scissor blades to force the wing tips downward, and clip off the fiber post just above the uppermost thread wrap.

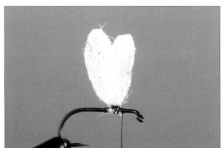

Step 4. The finished wing is solidly mounted with very little bulk on the hook shank. If desired, apply a drop of head cement to the thread post at the base of the wings.

Method #36:
Crossmount Film Wings

This simple method of tying film wings is one recommended by John Betts for tying Zing, but it can be used with many films provided they are not excessively stiff. Different materials, however, require slightly different preparations as discussed below. The chief virtue of the technique is its simplicity; its major drawback is that wings set in this fashion are not especially aerodynamic and may produce more leader twist than other designs. Wind resistance can be minimized, however, by taking care to make the wings as symmetrical as possible.

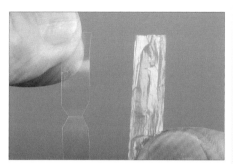

Step 1. To prepare the wing, cut a strip of material as wide as the desired width of the finished wing (usually about one hook-gap in width) and three times as long as the finished wing height. Softer, more compressible materials such as Zing and Fly Film can be used in this form, as shown on the right.

Stiffer materials such as polyethylene cut from food-storage bags, Shimazaki material, or Scintilla film require an extra step in preparation. After cutting the strip, fold it in half crosswise. Clip the corners of the folded end at a 45-degree angle. When unfolded, as shown in the wing material on the left, the strip will have a "bow-tie" shape. The wing will be mounted at the narrow center, which helps prevent an excess of material from bunching up at the mounting point.

Step 2. Form a short thread foundation over the wing-mounting area and position the tying thread at the mounting point.

Lay the strip of material crosswise and centered over the mounting point. Take two crisscross wraps under moderate tension to hold the material to the top of the shank, as shown in this top view.

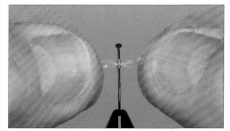

Step 3. Since some material is bunched beneath the lash wrap, it is important to straighten the wing to make the creases at the base as symmetrical as possible.

Grasp the wing tips as shown in this top view. Make sure to keep the fingers of both hands parallel to the wing material to exert an even, longitudinal pressure on both wing halves. Pull both wing halves under moderate pressure, but do not lift the wing or you will loosen the lash wrap.

Step 4. Pull the thread to tighten the wraps, and make 2 or 3 additional crisscross wraps atop the original ones to secure the wing tightly to the shank.

When the wing material is locked in, fold the wing halves upward, pinching them at the base to crease them and hold them in the elevated position shown here. Folding like this does not secure the wing upright; it is an aid to making the next set of wraps which will hold the wing in this position.

Step 5. The wings will be secured by using a version of the figure-eight wrap.

Begin by holding the tying thread vertically above the shank directly in front of the wing. Bring the thread down between the wings, around the base of the wing on the far side of the shank, and then back between the wings again. The thread should end up as shown, on the near side of the shank and behind the wing closest to you.

Step 6. Continue bringing the thread around the base of the wing on the near side of the shank. Then pass the thread

between the wings again, until the tying thread is as shown—behind the wing on the far side of the shank.

Step 7. Pinch the two wing halves together by the tips and let the bobbin hang beneath the hook. (The thread should still be positioned behind the far wing.)

Simultaneously pull upward on the wing tips and downward on the bobbin. The downward thread pressure will cause the figure-eight wraps to compress inward. The more thread tension used, the closer together the wings will be drawn.

Apply pressure to the thread slowly, and periodically release the wing tips to check the angle between them. If the angle is too shallow, grasp the wing tips again, pull upward on them, and pull tighter on the thread. If the wings are too close together, grasp the tips, pull upward and slacken the thread pressure.

Step 8. When the desired angle between the wings is obtained, take a wrap of thread around the hook shank only to lock in the figure-eight wraps.

Step 9. To shape the wings, pinch the two halves together by the very tips. Cut the wing tips parallel to the hook shank to the desired height.

Then position your left fingers beneath the hook shank and pinch the wings together at the base allowing access to the tips. Trim the tips to the desired shape.

Method #37:
Front-fold Film Wings

According to John Betts, versions of this type of wing have been developed by a number of tyers—Betts himself, Chauncy Lively,

Monty Montplasir, Leon Hansen, and European tyers Roman Moser and Rudi Heger. What the wings have in common is that they are formed from a single piece of material folded along the front edge and mounted atop the hook. This folded front produces a more aerodynamic, wedge-shaped edge that, if cut symmetrically and tied carefully, sheds the wind past the wing and reduces tippet twist. Where these tyers differ is in the methods used to raise the wing to the vertical position.

These wings require some practice to tie—or more accurately, practice to fabricate. Film materials are slippery and sometimes difficult to cut with precision, particularly in very small sizes. It is best to begin with simple wing shapes until you develop a feel for the material.

Step 1. The fabrication of the wing begins with making a paper template of the wing shape. Take a 2"x2" piece of stiff paper—a note card or old file folder—and fold it half. Trace out the shape of one wing on the paper; the front of the wing should lie along the folded edge, as shown. Note as well that the drawing narrows to a thin tab below the base of the wing. The wing will be mounted by this tab.

Step 2. Cut the wing pattern from the paper. Fold a strip of film wing material large enough for the finished wing. Sandwich the wing material inside the paper template as shown. Make sure that the folded edge of the wing material lies against the folded edge of the paper template.

To help prevent slippage, you can clamp the template around the wing material with hackle pliers, as we've done here.

Cut the wing material using the template as a guide. Be careful not to cut into the paper template or the wing will be undersize.

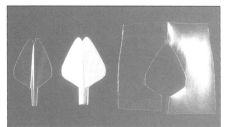

Step 3. Remove the wing material from the template.

Step 4. Prepare a hook by attaching the tails and dubbing the body up to the wing-mounting point. Lay a short thread foundation toward the hook eye, and return the thread to the wing-mounting point.

Place the cut wings, folded edge forward, atop the hook shank. The inside of the wing should butt up against the forward edge of the dubbing. The body material will cushion the wing and help keep the wing halves separated as the wing is tied in.

Secure the wing with several tight turns of thread, moving toward the hook eye.

When the wing is firmly attached, clip and bind down the excess wing material, and return the thread to the rearmost thread wrap.

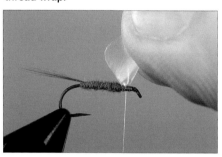

Step 5. With the right fingers, grasp the tip of the wing and pull it upward lightly. Maintain this upward tension, and fold the wing forward toward the hook eye. The object here is to crease the wing at the very base, forming a pivot point for raising the wing to a more vertical position.

Step 6. John Betts describes three techniques for posting the wing to a vertical position. The first, shown in this step, simply involves building up the dubbing directly behind the wing. The bulk formed by the dubbing will force the wing to a more upright position and hold it there.

This particular approach will produce a wing that slants slightly toward the rear of the hook, as it is difficult to build up enough dubbing to force the wing to a vertical position without creating a disproportionate bulk in the fly body. If a more vertical wing is desired, there are two other techniques that can be employed. The first is shown in subsequent Steps 7-9; the second in the alternate sequence.

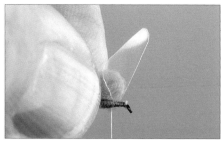

Step 7. Betts credits Michigan tyer Leon Hansen with the following technique.

Position the tying thread directly behind the wing. Take short length of poly yarn and double it over. Use the right fingers to raise the wing to the desired position and hold it there. With the left fingers, insert the folded end of the yarn into the rear base of the wing, between the wing halves. Push the yarn forcefully enough so that the wing stands in the desired position when it is released from the right fingers.

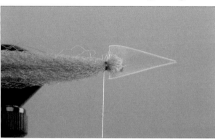

Step 8. Bind the poly yarn down directly behind the wing. As shown in this rear view, a ball of poly yarn will be formed between the wing halves and hold them upright.

Step 9. Trim off the excess poly yarn and bind down the butts.

Step 6a. John Betts devised this technique. Because it pulls, rather than pushes, the wing forward, a smaller amount of material can be used to raise the wing, which reduces the overall bulk of the fly.

Position the tying thread directly ahead of the wing. Take a strand of Z-lon yarn, and loop it around the rear of the wings, with the free ends of the yarn extending out beyond the hook eye. Take two wraps of thread, under light tension, over the yarn directly ahead of the wing.

Step 7a. Pull the free ends of the yarn, pulling the loop closed behind the wing and around its base. Keep drawing the yarn strands forward until the wing reaches the desired position.

Step 8a. Secure the yarn tightly with tying thread. Clip the excess yarn and bind down the butts. The rest of the fly can now be dressed.

Method #38:

Bottom-mount Film Wings

This technique for mounting film wings was designed for use with Shimazaki material, shown in the following demonstration, but can be used with other films as well. Because these bottom-mounted wings flare outward, they provide a pontoon-like support to the fly and can be used to dress No-Hackle style patterns, provided that some type of divided or fan tail and a buoyant dubbing are used. Or a conventional collar hackle can be wrapped ahead of the wing. As always, symmetrically fabricated wings and careful tying are required for balance.

Step 1. Take a piece of film material and fold it. Cut a triangle as shown on the left, with the fold at the bottom.
    Cut the points off the triangle as shown in the middle. The width along the folded edge should be equal to the width of the finished wing. The height of the material should be equal to the finished wing height.
    Finally, trim the corners to the desired wing shape, as shown on the right.

Step 2. Form a loop of monofilament tippet material about 4 inches in diameter.
    Fold the wing around the loop so that the monofilament sits in the fold.

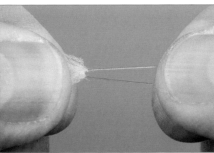

Step 3. Grasp the wings by the tips and pull on the loop so that the monofilament line seats tightly into the fold. This procedure creases the base of the wing, putting symmetrical pleats into the material and simplifying mounting.
    Note that some of the more elastic films will deform if stretched in this way. For such materials, this step should be omitted. Films vary widely in their elastic properties and behaviors, and the only way to determine if this particular step is suitable for any given material is to experiment and observe if the material stretches out of shape.

Step 4. Prepare a hook by mounting the tails and body material, usually dubbing. Dub the body up to the wing-mounting point. Lay a short thread foundation ahead of the body, and return the thread to the wing-mounting point.
    Fold the wings around the hook from underneath so that the underside of the hook shank rests against the fold of the wing material. The tying thread should be behind the wing. Hold the wings by the tips and position them at the desired spot on the shank.

Step 5. Holding the wings by the tips in your left fingers, apply upward pressure to hold them in position.
    Bring the tying thread underneath the hook shank, crossing the underside of the wing material, to the near side of the shank ahead of the wing. Pull the thread rather tightly when making this cross wrap, but do not disturb the wing position.

Step 6. Bring the tying thread over the top of the shank ahead of the wing, then down the far side.
    Pass the tying thread beneath the shank, across the underside of the material again, to the near side of the shank behind the wing, as shown. Again, use tight thread pressure.
    You've now mounted the wing with a crisscross wrap of tying thread on the underside of the shank. Take a wrap of thread around the hook shank only, behind the wing, to lock-in this crisscross wrap.

Step 7. Inspect the wings from the front, and notice their position. The rear edges of the wings should flare slightly outward, and the front edges should point slightly inward. This slanting orientation of the wing helps shed the wind and prevents the fly from spinning.
    If the wings do not slant properly, take a crisscross wrap of tying thread between the wings to force the rear edges outward. If tying a No-hackle Dun pattern, this crisscross wrap between the wings can be made with a sparsely dubbed thread to apply body material between and beneath the wings.

Method #39:

Top-mount Film Wings

This technique, developed for the Shimazaki material used in the following sequence, is also suitable for other films. Unlike **Method #38: Bottom-mount Film Wings**, p. 285, this method does not produce a wing suitable for use on No-hackle Dun patterns; a collar-style or thorax hackle should be used.

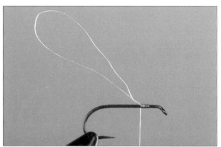

Step 1. Prepare a hook by wrapping a short thread foundation that spans the wing-mounting point, and position the tying thread at the front of this foundation.

Form a loop in the tying thread about 2 inches long, exactly as you would form a dubbing loop (described in **Method #38: Trap-loop Dubbing**, Steps 1-2, p. 129).

Raise the loop to the top side of the shank, and wrap the tying thread back toward the hook bend, binding the loop to the top of the shank, until you reach the wing-mounting point.

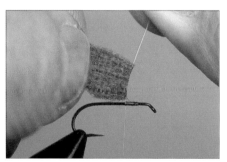

Step 2. Prepare a wing as described in **Method #38: Bottom-mount Film Wing**, Steps 1-3, p. 285.

Fold the wing around both strands of the loop so that the two loop strands are seated in the fold of the wing.

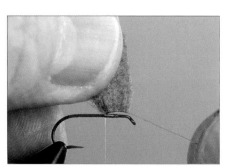

Step 3. Slide the wing down the loop until it meets the hook shank.

Fold the loop forward, atop the hook shank, extending over the hook eye, as shown.

Step 4. Reposition the left fingers to grasp the wings near the base. Bind down the loop threads, directly ahead of the wing, with 3 or 4 tight wraps of tying thread.

Step 5. Position the tying thread behind the wing.

Bring the loop threads back between the wings, toward the hook bend.

Step 6. Hold the loop threads against the top of the hook shank, and apply moderate tension. Take 3 or 4 tight wraps of thread to bind the loop securely to the top of the shank, directly behind the wings.

Step 7. Clip off the excess loop thread. Take 2 or 3 firm crisscross wraps between the wings; make these wraps rather tight, as they will secure the wings to the shank.

Inspect the wings from the front and notice their position. The rear edges of the wings should flare slightly outward, and the front edges should point slightly inward. This slanting orientation of the wing helps shed the wind and prevents the fly from spinning.

If the wings do not slant properly, use crisscross wraps to force the rear edges of the wings outward.

When the wings are properly positioned, take a wrap of thread around the hook shank only to lock in the crisscross wraps.

Downwings

Wings that are dressed to slant back along the hook shank toward the bend, or lie flat atop the shank, are often called "downwings." Where the upright style is confined largely to dressing mayfly adults, the downwing has a number of different applications, making it one of the most versatile and widely used wing types in fly tying. Downwings are dressed on patterns that suggest adult caddisflies, stoneflies, craneflies, midges, damselflies, and terrestrials such as grasshoppers and flying ants. Materials tied in the downwing style are also used on patterns imitating food forms that, in fact, have no actual "wings," such as streamers that represent leeches and baitfish, and they are used on general attractor flies as well. A broad range of materials can be used to dress this winging style, and specific materials can be chosen not only for their imitative properties—silhouette, color, lifelike movement underwater—but for other characteristics such as buoyancy, water absorption, durability, ease of handling, and so on.

As in the preceding section on upright winging techniques, this section is organized by the types of materials used to fashion downwings: quills, feather tips, bundled fibers, synthetic films, and fur strips.

Quill Downwings

Though quill downwings are used on streamer patterns such as the Muddler Minnow and on some dry flies, primarily those that imitate adult caddis and terrestrials, they are most often dressed on wet flies. Anglers have debated the precise representational function of these subsurface patterns—emerging nymphs or pupae, diving caddis, drowned adult flies, even small baitfish—but the fact remains that quill downwing patterns are highly effective. A readily available material, quill produces wings with a sharp and substantial profile while keeping bulk and weight to a minimum. The biggest drawback is durability; quill splits easily, though a tattered wing seldom compromises a fly's effectiveness.

The type of quill suitable for downwings and its method of preparation are identical to those used for upright wings, and these are detailed in the sections "Wing Feathers," p. 9 and "Preparing Quill Wings," p. 243.

Method #40:
Paired Quill Downwings

This is the basic winging style for wet flies, streamers such as the Muddler Minnow, and dry flies such as the Henryville Caddis. The main sequence shows quill segments mounted in the traditional orientation, which produces a wing that is slightly

upswept at the rear. The alternate sequence illustrates a simple method for reshaping the quill segments to produce a wing with a more rounded tip.

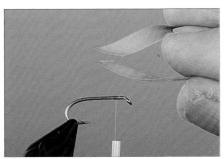

Step 1. Lay a thread foundation that spans the winging point, and position the tying thread at the wing-mounting point. For downwing flies, the exact winging point varies with the pattern. Typically, wet-fly quill wings are mounted a short distance behind the hook eye, as shown here. On streamer or dry-fly dressings, they may be mounted farther down the shank to accommodate materials at the head of the fly.

Cut a pair of quill segments as described in the section "Preparing Quill Wings," p. 243. Place the quill segments with the concave sides together so that the tips are even.

You can align the quill segments by "sliding" them against one another as explained in **Method #2: Upright Quill Wings**, Step 1, p. 244, or by holding the quills in the grip picture here. Hold the quills loosely at first, adjusting them until the ends of the feather project an equal distance beyond the fingertips. When the quill segments are aligned, squeeze your fingertips together to make the quill tips meet, as shown.

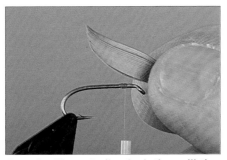

Step 2. Momentarily pinch the quill tips together in your left fingers, then grasp the butt ends of the segments in the right hand as shown.

Note the orientation of the quill—the rear edge sweeps upward in the traditional mounting position.

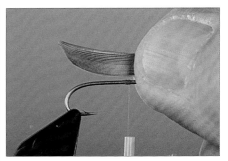

Step 3. Position the wings atop the hook shank and adjust them to the desired length. Most tyers prefer the tip of the wing to extend to the midpoint of the tail, or slightly beyond the bend of the hook

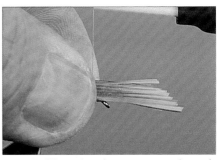

Step 4. When the wings are properly positioned, pinch both the quill segments and the hook shank directly at the mounting point.

The actual mounting of the wings can be accomplished with a variety of methods: **Method #9: The Pinch Wrap**, p. 30; **Method #10: The Bobbin Loop**, p. 31; and **Method #11: The Langley Loop**, p. 32. All of these procedures are demonstrated using quill downwings, and you should refer to one of these methods for detailed instructions on mounting the wings. **Method #7: The Cradle Loop**, p. 28, can also be used if you experience difficulty in properly positioning the thread at the mounting point.

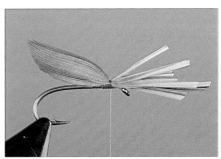

Step 5. A properly dressed wing will appear as a flat panel that is pleated at the mounting point where the quill barbs are crushed in a vertical stack.

Step 6. When the wing is satisfactorily mounted, clip the excess quill and bind down the butts with thread.

The hook on the left has wings dressed in the traditional manner; the hook on the right has wings shaped according to the procedure described in the alternate sequence.

Step 1a. If a more rounded wing is desired, you can reshape the quills before mounting.

Grasp the butt of one quill segment in your right fingertips. Note the orientation here—the rear edge of the quill sweeps upward.

Step 2a. With the fingertips of the left hand, pinch the quill very close to the fingertips of the right hand.

Slide your left fingers down toward the tip of the quill. As you do so, draw the quill downward in an arc, as shown.

Step 3a. In drawing the quill downward like this, you slide the feather barbs against one another and realign the tips.

Repeat with the second quill segment, and then pair the two wing halves together as explained in Step 1.

Method #41:

Married Quill Wings

Certain types of paired quill wings can be fashioned by joining together or "marrying" thinner segments of barbs taken from different feathers. Typically, a married wing will be composed of a main quill segment topped with barb strips of contrasting colors. Though largely the province of the salmon-fly tyer, married wings are very much a part of trout-fishing tradition. In *Trout*, Ray Bergman writes about several of his favorite patterns—some trout flies, some reduced versions of salmon dressings—that use married wings. Most are of the brightly colored variety of wet fly designed for brook-trout fishing.

The actual dressing of married wings is virtually identical to the procedure used in tying standard paired quill downwings. The difference, of course, is in the advance preparation of the winging materials. Married wings are possible in the first place by the somewhat unusual structure of feathers. The feather barb itself is fringed with tiny hairlike structures called "barbules" (see "Feathers," p. 6). The barbules on the edges of adjacent barbs lock together, almost like a zipper, and are responsible for holding the barbs in an orderly row and giving the feather a flat, panel-like appearance. If two adjacent barbs are separated from one another, they can be preened back to shape so that the barbules are once again interlocked. In essence, the barbs can be "unzipped" and then "zipped" back together. Married wings rely on the fact that with well-chosen material, barbs from different feathers can be zipped together to produce a smooth, attractive wing. The ease with which strips of different quills can be married together, however, depends almost entirely on the material used.

In constructing married wings, you are actually asking the barbs of one feather to join smoothly and evenly with barbs of a different feather. It's a little like an organ transplant, and the greatest insurance of success lies in the best possible match between donor and recipient. With feathers, this match is achieved in two ways. The first is texture, which is, as a rule, closely related to feather size. It is difficult to marry a wide, coarse quill segment to a fine, narrow one; the width of the barbs and length of the barbules differ enough that a good union is almost impossible. The second criterion is that the feathers must match in curvature. Joining a segment of very straight barbs to one that is very curved, for example, is difficult. The adhesion provided the barbules is not strong enough to overcome the tendency of the curved barbs to pull away from the straight ones.

This matter of matching curves is what makes many flight feathers poorly suited to married wings. Flight feathers (see "Wing Feathers," p. 9) of the type ordinarily used in paired quill wings—particularly duck quills—may have a rather exaggerated "cupping," or front-to-back curvature, and finding

two feathers with very similar contours from different birds is not an easy task. With persistence and a discerning eye, however, it can be done. Flight feathers from geese, turkeys, and swans—particularly secondary feathers—as well as covert and shoulder feathers, are somewhat more regular in their curvature and can be employed more successfully. Even if a good match is obtained, however, some flight feathers have another problem. The front is the most vividly colored or marked side of the feather, but it is often the side with a concave curvature. Thus when the wing halves are placed with concave sides together, as is necessary for mounting, the most attractive faces of the feathers are hidden on the inside. This does not preclude their use, or necessarily diminish the effectiveness of the fly, but such wings are duller in appearance than those made with more suitable materials. Flight feathers from some larger birds, however, may have a convex front side and can be used successfully.

These feathers from a swan wing (left), a goose wing (middle), and a turkey tail (right) are all suitable for married wings.

For many tyers, goose shoulder feathers are an overwhelming favorite for constructing married wings—good specimens are relatively consistent in texture, not excessively curved, and show a nice smooth edge. The best feathers are symmetrical about the stem, which allows one wing half to be cut from each side of the feather stem. The front of the feather is convex, which means that paired wings will have the most attractive side facing outward. Goose shoulder is not terribly expensive, but prime feathers are difficult to find; those of lesser quality will have a fair amount of waste material. Goose shoulder is a standard for dressing salmon flies and most readily available from sources catering to these tyers.

The swan flight feathers used in the following sequence are a good substitute for goose shoulder and share many of the same desirable physical characteristics.

Step 1. In fashioning married wings, it is best to have the feathers arranged beforehand. If the plumage is sufficiently sym-

metrical so that quill segments for the left and right wings are formed from the same feather, all is well. If not, the feathers should be separated into groups for the left and right wings.

The finished wing should be about the width of the hook gap. The wing we are forming here uses three quill sections of equal width, two of white, one of red. Begin by separating a section of barbs of the desired width, here, ⅓ the hook gap. For patterns in the trout sizes, it's best to use the barbs nearer the tip of the feather, where the texture of the barbs and their degree of curvature is better proportioned to smaller hooks.

You can use a dubbing needle to separate this section of barbs from the rest of the feather, but using a pair of compass-type dividers, as we're doing here, has a number of advantages. First, because the gap between the divider points can be set by measuring them against the hook shank, there is less guesswork involved in sizing the quill segment. But more importantly, once the correct gap is set, you can use the dividers to measure out sections of barb for each wing, knowing that the sections will be identical in width, which saves time and ensures that the halves will be uniform. When the barb section is separated, carefully clip it from the stem with scissors.

Continue clipping out the barb sections from all feathers that will form the married wings. Make sure to keep the strips of barbs to be used for the right wing separate from those to be used for the left.

Step 2. When all the quill sections are cut, they can be assembled. Marrying the strips is actually rather simple once the proper material is selected and cut. The object in forming the married wing is to reproduce as closely as possible the contours of a natural quill segment, and it may be helpful to have a properly sized section of ordinary wing quill in front of you as a model.

Begin by taking the section of barbs that will form the bottom of the wing (here a white strip) and joining it to the section of barbs above it (here a red one). The most crucial area in marrying the strips is the tip. Take a section of quill in each hand and align the tips carefully. Then press together the middle portions of the barb strips until they adhere.

It would seem that if tip alignment is important, the most logical procedure would be to join the quill segments at the tip first. But the very tip of the barb often lacks the zipperlike barbules that hold the feather segments together. Joining the barbs at the tips is difficult. Working from the middle to both ends is simpler.

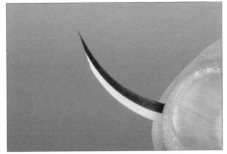

Step 3. Grasp the butt ends of the quill sections and stroke the barbs toward the tip, joining them as you go.

Dick Talleur, in *The Versatile Fly Tyer*, recommends two procedures that may prove helpful. First, as you stroke the barbs, bend them in the direction of their natural curvature, as shown here. Second is to join and separate the barb sections a couple of times. He notes that repeatedly locking and unlocking the barbules like this before the final mating produces a more secure union between the two strips.

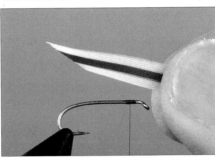

Step 4. Repeat Step 3 with the next section of barbs. Continue marrying strips of barbs until one wing is complete, as shown here.

When the wing is completed, measure it against the hook gap to make certain it is the proper size. If the wing is too wide, determine which segment of barbs needs to be narrowed. Carefully separate the wing at that segment and use a dubbing needle to peel off barbs until the segment is of the proper width; then remarry the strips. Before assembling the second wing, peel an equal number of strips off the corresponding barb segment for the other wing in order to produce a properly sized wing on the first attempt.

Then assemble the second wing.

Dick Talleur also observes that any scraggly tips that refuse to mate because they lack barbules can be trimmed away with a pair of very sharp, curved scissors. Though heresy in some fly-tying circles, this procedure can neaten up the wing.

Step 5. Mounting married wings is identical to mounting any quill, and an explanation of the technique can be found in **Method #40: Paired Quill Downwings**, p. 287.

Method #42:
Folded Quill Downwing

A single segment of quill can be folded or curved over the back of the fly to form a wing that hugs the top of the body. Wings of this type are ordinarily used on dry flies like the King's River Caddis and numerous grasshopper and cricket dressings. Because of the tendency of quill to split, this type of wing is often reinforced with a thin coat of flexible cement or spray fixative. Durable wings of this style can be formed as explained in **Method #45: Mesh-backed Feather Wings**, Steps 1a-3a, p. 294.

The main sequence shows the basic procedure for mounting a folded downwing on a narrow-bodied fly. Flies with thick or bulky bodies require a slightly different approach, shown in the alternate sequence.

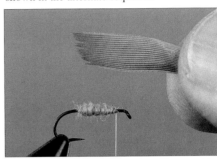

Step 1. Cut a section of quill equal in width to the hook gap. The quill segment should be long enough to form the entire wing from the thinner, more pliable section of barbs near the tip; it should not incorporate any of the thick, spongy base of the barbs that lie close to the feather stem.

With a dubbing needle, apply a thin coating of flexible cement to the top of the quill segment, or mist the quill with a spray fixative. (If several wings are to be made, it is faster to treat the entire feather with flexible cement or spray fixative and cut individual quill segments as needed.) Let the quill segment dry.

Folded wings are mounted after the body materials have been applied. Dress the body of the fly—here we've dubbed a body for a caddis—and leave the tying thread at the very front of the body, which will become the wing-mounting point.

Step 1a. If a wing with an untrimmed, natural tip is desired, the barbs can be manipulated to form a more symmetrical wing segment. Cut a quill segment as described in Step 1, then preen the barbs to shape as explained in **Method #40: Paired Quill Downwings**, Steps 1a-3a, p. 288.

The quill segment can be reinforced with glue as described in Step 1, or left untreated.

Step 2. To form a caddis wing, fold the section of quill in half lengthwise. Trim the tip at an angle, as shown on the wing at the left, giving it the characteristic tent-shaped caddis wing.

To form the wing for a grasshopper pattern, hold the quill flat and trim the tip to a rounded shape as shown on the right.

Step 3. With the left fingers, fold the wing and pinch it together at the mounting point. Then slip the quill segment over the top of the hook so that the shank is inserted about halfway into the fold, as shown here from underneath. Do not mount the wing directly atop the hook shank, as you would with paired quill downwings, or the folded wing will flare upward and refuse to lie flat over the body.

Step 4. The wing can be mounted using a variety of techniques: **Method #9: The Pinch Wrap**, p. 30; **Method #10: The Bobbin Loop**, p. 31; and **Method #11: The Langley Loop**, p. 32.

Mount the wing with one tight turn of thread, and then release your fingers to check the wing position. If the wing slants upward in the rear instead of lying flat, unwrap the mounting wrap of thread and reposition the wing—this time folding the wing around the hook so that the shank is seated up against the fold in the quill. Then remount the wing. It should lie close over the top of the body as shown.

If the wing still slants upward, the body may be too thick for the wing to lie flat. If this is case, see Step 4a.

Step 5. When the wing is properly positioned, grasp the quill again with the left fingers to prevent it from shifting around. Then add extra thread wraps to secure the wing. Clip the excess quill and bind down the butts.

Or the butts can be used to form the base for a parachute hackle as explained in **Method #38: Postless Parachute Downwing**, p. 393.

The caddis dressed in the main sequence is on the left; the grasshopper wing formed in the alternate steps is on the right.

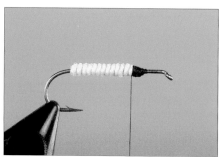

Step 4a. To mount a grasshopper wing, as shown here, or any wing placed over a relatively thick body, you will need to use a different wing-mounting position. If you attempt to mount the wing directly on the hook shank ahead of the body, the bulky materials will force the wing upward in the rear.

Begin by dressing the body—we're using poly yarn for a grasshopper body—and lay a short thread foundation toward the hook eye. Return the thread back to the front edge of the body, and then take 3 or 4 wraps back over the front edge of the body material itself. The wings will be mounted atop this thread foundation laid on the body.

Step 5a. Fold the wing over the top of the body as shown, and mount with any of the methods noted in Step 4.

Method #43:
Quill Flatwing

Flatwings—mounted to lie flat over the fly body—are most often used on adult stonefly imitations and are typically fashioned from feather tips. Recently, however, John Betts re-introduced tyers to a quill flatwing designed a century ago by British angling author Charles Edward Walker for stonefly patterns. It is an unusual and practical use of quill segments, and the general shortcoming of the material, its lack of durability, can be overcome in this winging style by applying a thin coat of flexible cement or spray fixative to the quill. Obviously, such reinforcement was not used in Walker's original dressings.

Nearly any quill material is suitable, though it must be long enough to form the wings without incorporating into them any of the thick, spongy material at the base of the barbs (see "Wing Feathers," p. 9).

Quill flatwings can also be fashioned by using the technique shown in **Method #69: Folded Film Flatwing**, p. 317. In this method, the quill segment must reinforced with a light misting of spray fixative, a thin coat of flexible cement, or a mesh backing as explained in **Method #45: Mesh-backed Feather Wings**, Steps 1a-3a, p. 294.

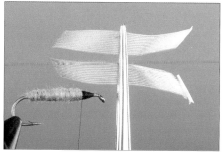

Step 1. All fly components that lie behind the winging point are dressed first. Lay a short thread foundation on the shank ahead of the body.

On slender-bodied flies, position the tying thread at the front edge of the body. On flies with thick or bulky bodies, wrap the thread over the front edge of the body as explained **Method #42: Folded Quill Downwing**, Step 4a, p. 290, to prevent the wing from flaring upward when mounted.

Matched quill segments are required for this technique. They can be cut from the stem as explained "Preparing Quill Wings," p. 243, in which case the finished wings will have rounded rear tips. In Walker's original technique, a small strip of the feather stem is left at the base of the barbs, as shown here; to prepare quill in this fashion, see **Method #3: Downs Mount Quill Wings**, Step 1a, p. 245. Quills cut in this fashion will produce wings with pointed tips.

The width of each segment is approximately one hook-gap.

Step 2. Lay the quill segments atop one another so that curvatures match. The tips of the segments should form a narrow "V".

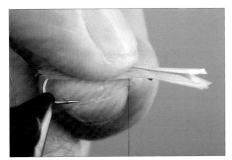

Step 3. Place the quill segments atop the shank over the wing-mounting point. It is easiest to mount the quill using the finger position shown here; the left thumb pinches the quill segments to the top of the shank, while the index finger supports them from underneath.

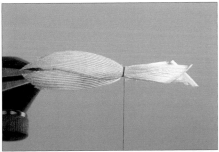

Step 4. Secure the quill segments with 2 or 3 tight thread wraps, using the left fingers to keep them centered atop the hook shank.

When the segments are affixed, check their position and make any necessary adjustments. Here, the wings form a very narrow angle; from a trout's eye view beneath the fly, the two quill segments will appear as a single, broad wing. But the angle between the wings can be altered to suit the tyer's taste or the demands of the particular imitation.

Step 5. When the wing position is satisfactory, secure the butts with additional tight turns of thread. Clip and bind down the excess.

Feather-tip Downwings

Effective downwings can be fashioned from feather tips—that is, a portion of a feather in which the stem is left intact. (Wings can also be made from stripped feather barbs, and methods for doing so are explained in the section on "Bundled-fiber Downwings," p. 305.) Feather tips are quite a versatile downwing material and can be tied in a number of configurations for both floating and subsurface patterns. In general, the material offers a well-defined wing silhouette, a wide range of colors and markings, and good durability.

Selecting Downwing Feathers

The particular criteria for selecting feather tips vary somewhat depending on the wing style. Feather tips can be used to tie "tentwings," a "V"-shaped style used primarily for caddis, and the principles governing the choice of materials for tentwings are virtually identical to those for upright feather-tip wings (see "Selecting Feathers for Feather-tip Wings," p. 262). Hen hackle, from either capes or saddles, is the most commonly used material, though flank feathers, wing coverts, and a variety of body feathers can also be employed. Feathers that are heavily webbed right to the ends of the barbs provide the sharpest profile and best hold their shape; for these reasons, rooster hackle is rarely used. Feathers with less web and somewhat ragged barb ends can still be used for burned or cut wings.

Broad, densely webbed feathers are also used on flatwings, folded wings, and Matuka styles of dressing. Flatwings, as the name suggests, are laid flat across the back of the body and are often used on beetle, jassid, and occasionally adult stonefly dressings. Folded feather-tip wings can be used on both caddis and grasshopper patterns. For small flatwings and folded wings, small hen hackles, body feathers, or wing coverts from smaller birds, such as starling, are all useful materials. Larger flatwings and folded wings can be fashioned from large hen neck hackles, hen saddles, shoulder feathers, and body feathers. Matuka-style streamer wings are typically tied in larger sizes, and long, symmetrical, heavily webbed feathers generally come from only one source—hen saddles. For all three types of wings, however, look for plumage on which the barbs are of equal length along either side of the hackle stem and the stem itself is straight.

Feather-tip delta wings are usually tied from the tips of a good grade of rooster hackle. These somewhat thin tips better represent the narrower wings on adult midge and cranefly patterns, spent caddis, and flying ants. Many of these imitations float low in the water, and the web-free rooster hackle helps support the fly in the surface film.

There is some latitude in choosing materials for feather-tip streamer wings, as individual tastes vary. Some tyers prefer wings with rounded ends, others with pointed tips; some dress wings with a broad profile, others like a narrower one; some choose dense, webby, panel-like wings, while others favor

the more muted impression that results from a relatively web-free feather. In almost all cases, however, tyers use large neck hackle or saddle feathers. (A few patterns call for other materials. The Hornberg, for instance, is dressed with mallard flank wings, though whether this is a streamer or a dry fly depends, in the end, on who's fishing it.) Hen-hackle streamer wings cut a broad, bold underwater profile, somewhat blunt in shape since the feather tips are often quite rounded. Rooster saddle hackles (or the long feathers from the end of the cape) tend to have less web and a more tapered, spearlike shape for a thinner underwater profile; the springy feather stems help the wings maintain their shape.

Regardless of the wing style or the plumage used to tie it, there are two important considerations in selecting material for any style of feather-tip downwing. The first is the thickness of the feather stem. Thin-stemmed feathers are preferred for tying upright feather-tip wings because they flex during casting, reducing wind resistance and tippet twisting. But feather-tip downwings generally lie flat against the top or sides of the fly body; they offer a more aerodynamic profile than do upright wings and reduce the problem of twisted tippets. Since the downwings need not flex during casting, stem thickness is not a consideration in selecting feathers—at least theoretically. Practically speaking, thick stems pose more of an obstacle in tying than in casting. Many feather stems, those found on hackles in particular, are not round in cross-section; they are elongated and oval-shaped, with the barbs projecting outward from the long sides of the oval. When you attempt to mount such a feather to lie flat down the back or sides of the fly body, you are actually trying to bind it edgewise, with the narrow point of the oval against the hook shank; it may twist and roll during mounting, and the wing refuses to sit in the proper position. It's a bit like trying to balance an egg on the end—it will naturally roll on its side to a position of greater stability. This type of rolling can be a problem even with some thin-stemmed feathers, but it is more common and more pronounced with thick-stemmed ones. There are techniques to minimize this difficulty, and those are presented below in "Preparing Feather-tip Downwings." But the first step is to choose material with relatively narrow stems. Some feathers, by nature, have thinner stems than others, and these are a good choice for feather-tip wings. You can also get good results with thicker-stemmed feathers by choosing the longest feathers and using only the very tip portion, where the stem is narrower, to form the wings.

The second consideration in choosing feathers for downwings is front-to-back curvature. In tying upright wings, some curvature is desirable, as it causes the feathers to flare away from one another and produce divided wings. For downwings, the feather should be reasonably flat. Excessively curved feathers can be troublesome to mount and cause the wings to bulge outward at the middle of the fly body. A slight curvature is not a problem, and as a rule, most hackle feathers are relatively flat. Body and flank feathers, however, often have a pronounced arc in the stem, and a method for reducing this curvature is presented below.

Preparing Feather-tip Downwings

Preparing relatively flat, thin-stemmed feathers involves little more than sizing the wings. The most common sizing method is simply to strip away the barbs from below the mounting point, leaving a bare feather stem. Bare stems, however, can increase the tendency of a feather to roll or twist during mounting. Clipping the barbs below the mounting point, instead of stripping them, helps reduce twisting, though it takes a bit more time.

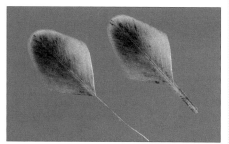

The feather on the left has been stripped of barbs and is ready to mount. The feather on the right has had the barbs clipped; the stubble that remains on the stem adds bulk at the mounting point that helps prevent the feather from twisting under the pressure of the tying thread.

If feathers with stripped stems prove difficult to mount and resist lying in the proper position, you can take measures to improve their behavior by flattening the stem. The oval-cross section of the stem thus becomes a ribbonlike band that will tie in properly.

For feather-tip wings that are intended to lie flat across the back of the fly or along the sides of the body, flatten the stems as follows:

Lay the feather flat on a hard surface such as glass or formica. Using the rounded, outside edge of a pair of tying scissors, press directly downward against the stem at the mounting point. Holding moderate pressure on the scissors, run the edge down the length of the feather stem, flattening it as you go. Thicker stems may require more than one pass of the scissors over the quill.

Unfortunately, not all feather stems can be flattened in this manner. Excessively thick stems, or those with a highly exaggerated oval cross-section, will tend to roll rather than flatten. But in many instances this technique does help to tame unruly feather stems.

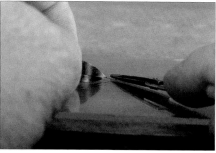

Many streamer patterns call for wings mounted atop the shank so that the feather-tips rest vertically, as shown in **Method #53: Feather Streamer Wings**, p. 301. In this case, the stem must be flattened in a direction perpendicular to the feather barbs.

Hold the feather vertically, on its edge, and use a pair of scissors to flatten the stem as described in the preceding photo.

Excessive curvature in a feather can pose a problem in mounting and setting the wings. Curved feathers can be partially straightened by using the technique shown in the following sequence.

This mallard flank feather, like many body feathers, shows a pronounced front-to-back curve. To straighten the feather, first size the wing.

Using your thumbnail or hackle pliers, pinch the stem directly at the mounting point as shown. Pressure from your thumbnail or pliers must be applied directly against the front of the stem.

With your fingertip, push the back of the feather forward, levering the stem around your thumbnail. Don't push the feather too far, or it can fracture. Rather, you are just trying to crease the stem at the mounting point.

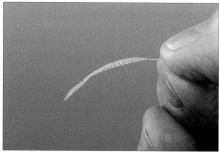

Here, the feather has been partially straightened and will mount more easily.

Feathers with excessive curvature can also made useable by using a mesh backing as explained in **Method #45: Mesh-backed Feather Wings**, p. 294, or a tape backing as shown in **Method #46: Tape-backed Feather Wings**, p. 295.

Method #44:

Cut and Burned Tentwings

The tentwings used to imitate adult caddis can be dressed from natural feather tips, but some tyers prefer to cut or burn the wings to shape. Forming wings in this fashion not only produces a more realistic silhouette, but makes available to the tyer a wide range of feathers that may not be suitable for natural-tip wings. Any of the materials specified in the preceding section, "Selecting Downwing Feathers," can be used, and tyers who possess entire skins from game birds, waterfowl, or other birds may find an abundance of feathers suitable for making tentwings. The procedures for cutting or burning tentwings are very similar to those used for shaping upright feather-tip wings, and readers may wish to consult the previous explanations in **Method #5: Cut Wings**, p. 249, and **Method #6: Burned Wings**, p. 251 for additional information.

Burning feathers, shown in the main sequence that follows, has the advantage of producing uniformly shaped wings, even if the feathers are burned individually rather than in pairs, and it is probably slightly faster than cutting wings. But burning does confine the tyer to the wing shape formed by the wing burner. The main sequence below illustrates the use of a Renzetti wing burner, but in *The Versatile Fly Tyer*, Dick Talleur provides instructions for making your own wing burners in any shape desired.

Cutting wings, as shown in the alternate sequence, requires no special tools and allows the tyer to trim feathers to any shape. Because caddis wings are highly asymmetrical, however, it is best to cut wings in pairs, which requires some additional preparation of the feathers. If the feathers are cut individually, it can be difficult to produce a pair of wings that are closely matched in shape. Both natural feathers, mesh-backed ones (see

Method #45: Mesh-backed Feather Wings, p. 294), and tape-backed ones (see **Method #46: Tape-backed Feather Wings**, p. 295) can be used.

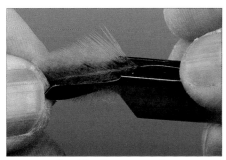

Step 1. In this demonstration, we are burning the wings individually for clarity of illustration. A pair of wings can be burned simultaneously by preparing the feathers as shown in Step 1a.

Select a pair of feathers, we're using hen hackle here, and strip the fuzz and lower barbs from stem, leaving a feather tip about twice as long as the finished wing. If the lower portion of the stem is excessively thick, trim it away.

Place one feather, concave side down, in the wing burner. The feather stem can be placed at the top edge of the burner, the bottom edge, or in between; each position will yield a wing of a slightly different shape as shown in Step 4. Generally speaking, placing the stem at the top edge of the burner produces a wing that sits lower over the body, with a slightly wider angle between the wing halves. Moreover, the straight upper edge of the burner gives a good reference point for the stem placement, making it easier to burn wings individually and still produce a matched pair. Positioning the stem at the lower edge of the burner yields a wing that sits higher over the body with a narrower angle between the wing halves.

But in either case, the stem must be completely concealed inside the burner or the flame will burn it in half.

Step 2. After positioning the feather in the desired orientation, clamp it in the burner. If the feather barbs project significantly beyond the burner edge, you may wish to trim the waste material with scissors, since the quantity of ash produced by burning an excessive amount of material can interfere with a clean wing profile.

Hold the burner horizontally as shown, and burn away the exposed barbs with the side of a flame from a butane lighter.

Step 3. Remove the feather from the burner and brush away any ash or residue at the tip to produce a clean edge.

Repeat Steps 1-3 with a second feather. You must, however, turn the second feather over to produce the opposing wing half. Positioning the feather tip with the convex side down will ensure that you produce a left and a right wing, as shown above.

They are ready for mounting using the procedure explained in **Method #47: Feather-tip Tentwings**, p. 295.

Step 4. The pair of wings on the left show a pair of feather tips burned with the feather stem placed close to the top edge of the wing. Note that when the feather stem is positioned near the top of the wing, the wings can be mounted to produce a wide angle between the halves, for a pronounced tent shape. The wings in the middle show the effect produced when the stem is placed lower in the wing. These wings ride higher on the body with a narrower angle between them. The fly on the right shows the pair of wings cut to shape in the alternate sequence.

Step 1a. Feather tips can be cut individually, but since caddis wings are highly asymmetrical in shape, it can be difficult to produce a matched pair of wings by cutting the feathers one at a time. Better results are obtained if the two feather tips are shaped simultaneously, as shown in the following steps.

(Note that the same method for preparing feathers can be used to burn two wings at once, except that the feather tips need not be trimmed as described below. The feathers can be prepared beginning with Step 2a.) Prepare 2 feathers by clipping off

¼"-½" of the tip, perpendicular to the feather stem. Trimming the feather like this will ensure that the barbs near the tip are wide enough to form the rear of the wing.

Size the wing by stripping the barbs below the mounting point as explained in "Preparing Feather-tip Downwings," p. 292. In sizing the wing, you can use the hook shank as a guide as we're doing here, or use a winging gauge (see **Method #5: Cut Wings**, Step 3a, p. 250, and **Method #7: Feather-tip Wings**, Step 1a, p. 253, for constructing winging gauges).

Here, one feather has been trimmed and sized.

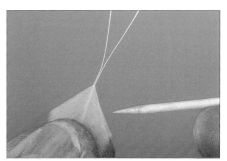

Step 2a. Now glue the two feathers together as shown in **Method #5: Cut Wings**, Steps 1a-2a, p. 250. Note the orientation of the feathers—they are placed back-to-back, that is, with the concave sides together. Placing the feathers in this orientation will ensure that cutting will produce a left wing and a right wing. Note that in temporarily gluing the feathers together, the cement is placed only on the outer edges of the barbs and is not allowed to bleed into any portion of the feather that will form the wing. When the cemented portion is trimmed away in the final cut, the wing halves will separate easily.

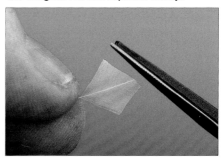

Step 3a. Trim the rear of the wing to the desired shape, as shown. Typically, this is a "V"-shaped cut.

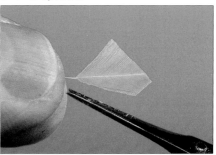

Step 4a. Trim the bottom edge of the wing. Note that this slanting cut does not taper right up to the feather stem. Rather, we've left the barbs at the mounting point about ¹⁄₁₆" long. This will give the wing some breadth at the front for a more realistic imitation.

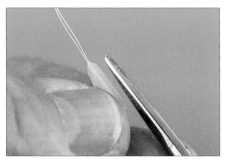

Step 5a. Trim the top edge of the wing. We've chosen to place the feather stem high in the wing, so this cut is made parallel, and close to, the stem. At the same time, the glued tips of the feather are trimmed away.

Step 6a. The wing halves can now be separated as shown. They are ready for mounting using the procedure explained in **Method #47: Feather-tip Tentwings**, p. 295.

Method #45:

Mesh-backed Feather Wings

Both feather-tip wings and certain types of quill wings can be reinforced by gluing them to a mesh backing—an approach that is particularly popular among European tyers. Wings fashioned in this manner are extremely durable, though their use is typically confined to downwing or flatwing styles; mesh-backed feathers are quite stiff, and if used for upright wings they can cause problems with tippet twist.

The method shown in the main sequence is generally credited to Slovenian tyer Dr. Bozidar Voljc. Any webby feather—hen neck or saddle hackles, body or flank feathers—is suitable for this method. And as shown in the following demonstration, reinforcing the mesh with adhesive and using no feather at all can create a synthetic winging film. Perhaps the best adhesive for this application is PVC glue, which dries quite quickly, though other flexible, tacky glues such as vinyl cement may also be suitable.

The technique shown in the alternate sequence was shown to us by German tyer Henning von Monteton, who uses a mesh backing on wing and tail feathers and makes these larger feathers practical for many cutwing applications. He uses cut sections of these feathers for wings on his Be Ge design of caddis and stonefly adults. They also make a very durable wingcase material.

In both methods, a woman's stocking furnishes an excellent backing material.

Note that both techniques involve the use of PVC glue. This adhesive is loaded with solvents and should be used in a well-ventilated area.

Step 1. It's best to assemble all the required materials first. You'll need an embroidery hoop of the type pictured; mesh material; PVC glue; a piece aluminum foil; cardboard, or scrap lumber; a pair of scissors; and the feathers. The feathers should be stripped of all the fuzzy barbs at the base of the stem, but do not clip off the stems.

Begin by sandwiching the mesh material between the two embroidery hoops, and tighten the outer hoop; typically, it has a screw closure. The mesh should be tight, but not extremely taut or else the mesh and feathers will curl when the cement dries.

Apply a thin coat of PVC glue over the entire surface of the mesh; ordinarily, PVC glues come with a dauber of the type pictured, but a small brush will work as well.

Step 2. When the entire surface of the mesh is coated with cement, use the left fingers to pick up a feather by the very base of the stem.

Lay the feather against the aluminum foil, cardboard, or scrap wood, and use the dauber to apply a thin film of cement on both sides of the feather. Spread the cement from the base of the feather toward the tip to keep the barbs preened flat.

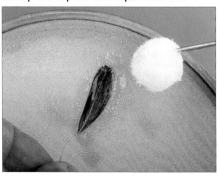

Step 3. Immediately place the *back* of the feather against the mesh. Hold the stem away from the mesh with the left fingers, as shown.

Use the dauber or brush to smooth the

feather against the mesh, again working from the base of the feather to the tip. Do not cement the feather stem to the mesh.

Step 4. When the feather is pasted flat, elevate the stem and clip it off at the base of the barbs. Cutting off the stem makes additional room for more feathers on the mesh.

Step 5. Continue applying feathers until the mesh is covered. If desired, leave some of the mesh uncovered; the cemented mesh alone can be trimmed and tied as a synthetic film.

After all the feathers are applied, turn the hoop upside down and check to see if there are any air bubbles beneath any of the feathers; they will appear as lighter spots. Working from the underside, use a dowel or your fingertips to push the bubbles toward the feather tip and out from beneath the feather.

When the glue is dry, remove the mesh from the hoop. If some of the adhesive has bled and glued the mesh to the hoop, cut the mesh material from the hoop first, then remove any cemented mesh from the edge of the embroidery hoop. Store the sheet of wings flat.

When a feather is needed, trim it from the sheet as shown. The cemented mesh that has no feather applied over it can be used to tie film downwings.

Flight and tail feathers are often too large and curved to use successfully with the method shown in the main sequence. The approach shown here works well.

Step 1a. Again, assemble all the materials—the feathers; a length of nylon stocking material large enough to cover each feather; PVC cement; and a spray contact cement (von Monteton recommends 3M Spray Mount, used here).

Mist the underside of the feather with a film of the spray cement. Though the mesh is eventually glued to the feather with PVC cement, this film of contact cement holds the mesh material in place.

Step 2a. Press the nylon material against the cemented side of the feather, smoothing out all wrinkles.

Step 3a. Coat the mesh backing with a thin film of PVC cement. Allow the glue to dry.

When the feather is dry, the wing material can be cut to shape, usually in strips following the grain of the feather barbs.

Method #46:

Tape-backed Feather Wings

Finnish tyer Veli Autti uses this simple technique to reinforce hen hackle, body, and flank feathers for fashioning caddis wings. It can be used as well for hoppers, delta wings, and just about any other type of downwing application. The reinforced feathers, however, are too stiff for upright winging.

Because clear or frosted tape is used, the natural translucence of the feather is maintained and produces a handsome wing.

Step 1. Prepare a feather by stripping away the fluffy barbs at the base.

Place the back side of the feather against a strip of Scotch tape. Press firmly and repeatedly to ensure a complete, tight bond.

Trim away the edges of the tape.

If desired, the front of the feather can be given a thin coating of spray fixative or flexible cement.

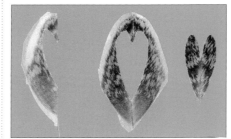

Step 2. To fashion a wing, fold the feather in half lengthwise along the stem, and trim out the desired wing shape as shown at the left.

The elongated, heart-shaped wing cut here and shown at the right is used to dress caddis patterns.

Step 3. The fly at the left was dressed using a feather similar to the one shown in the preceding steps. The fly at the right shows another example of the same reinforced-wing style used on a smaller fly. Both patterns were tied by Autti using the technique shown in **Method #48: Folded Feather-tip Wing**, p. 297.

Method #47:

Feather-tip Tentwings

The distinctive, tent-shaped wings on an adult caddis can be imitated by using feather tips—either left natural; cut or burned to shape; reinforced with mesh as shown in **Method #45: Mesh-backed Feather Wings**, p. 294; or reinforced with tape as shown in **Method #46: Tape-backed Feather Wings**, p. 295.

In the following demonstration, we're using natural hen-hackle tips to illustrate both the mounting technique and the appearance of the finished wings. Cut and burned feathers are dressed in exactly the same way, and the type of tentwings they produce are shown in **Method #44: Cut and Burned Tentwings**, Step 4, p. 293.

The alternate sequence shows an unusual technique in which the feather is reverse-mounted to create a tentwing with distinct venation. Almost any type of feather can be used. A web-free dry-fly hackle produces a delicately veined appearance, though such feathers can be slippery and more difficult to work with. Webby feathers produce a denser wing and are less trouble to handle. The durability of the wing depends largely on the type of feather used. CDC is used in the demonstration; it is easy to handle and,

---

unlike other feathers, ultimately contributes to the floatation of the fly. CDC, however, is more fragile than other feathers dressed in this style.

Step 1. Prepare a pair of wings by stripping the feather tips to the proper length or by trimming the barbs below the mounting point as described in the section "Preparing Feather-tip Downwings," p. 292. If using cut or burned wings, follow the procedure explained in **Method #44: Cut and Burned Tentwings**, p. 292. If the feather is excessively curved, straighten it by crimping the stem at the base of the barbs, again as shown in "Preparing Feather-tip Downwings," p. 292.

Because tentwings lie over the hook shank, any body materials must be dressed prior to mounting the wings. In this sequence, we've dubbed a simple body.

Lay a foundation of tying thread beginning at the wing-mounting point and extending 4 or 5 wraps toward the hook eye. Return the tying thread to the mounting point—here, at the very front of the dubbed body.

Both wings can be mounted simultaneously, but it is easier to produce symmetrical, correctly positioned wings if the feather tips are mounted separately. Begin by positioning one feather against the far side of the hook shank, as shown. The lowermost barbs on the wing should be directly behind the mounting point, and the feather stem parallel to the hook shank. The feather should not be perfectly vertical, but rather the top edge should be angled toward the tyer, so that it tilts over the back of the fly to make half of the tent wing, as shown here from the front.

Hold the feather firmly in this position with the tip of your left index finger.

Step 2. Using moderate tension, take a wrap of thread around the far wing. The thread should not be wrapped directly over the bare stem, but rather should just cross the base of the frontmost feather barbs. Binding down a very small portion of these first barbs will help minimize any roll or twist in the feather. (If you have prepared the feather to leave a stubble of clipped barbs below the wing, simply take the first wrap of thread directly over these clipped barbs.) When the wrap is complete, the bobbin should be pulled directly toward the tyer.

296

Holding the feather in position with moderate thread tension, slide your left index finger forward, and roll it slightly beneath the hook shank so that the tip of the finger is supporting the feather stem from underneath, as shown. In this position, the finger acts as a backstop to prevent the feather from being drawn beneath the shank when additional thread pressure is applied.

When the index finger is proper positioned, pull the tying thread toward you under increased tension.

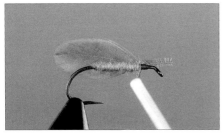

Step 3. Now lift your left index finger from the hook shank and check the position of the wing. The stem should be held against the far side of the hook and parallel to the shank. The top of the wing should slant toward the tyer, and when viewed from directly above, the top edge of the wing should run down the centerline of the hook shank.

If the feather has rolled or twisted, place your index finger in the position explained in Step 2. Relax the thread tension, and adjust the feather to compensate for the direction of twist. If it has rolled too far over the top of the hook, move the wing very slightly down the far side of the shank; if it has rolled outward, slide it a bit more toward the top of the shank. Then reapply thread pressure and check the wing position.

It may (or may not) take a few attempts to get the proper wing position; some feathers behave well, others badly. If, after a few attempts, the feather refuses to sit in the proper position, you may need to flatten the stem as explained in the section "Preparing Feather-tip Downwings," p. 292. With feathers that absolutely refuse to cooperate, try repositioning the wing at a slightly new location on the far side of the hook shank.

When you can hold the wing in the correct position using thread tension alone, as shown above, maintain the thread pressure, lightly grasp the wing again in the left fingers, and take one additional turn of thread around the base of the wing.

Maintain tension on the bobbin as you prepare to mount the second wing in the next step.

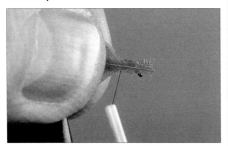

Step 4. Position the second feather on the near side of the shank, as shown. The top of the wing should slant away from the tyer, and when viewed from directly above, the top edge of the wing should run down the center line of the hook shank.

Step 5. Using moderate thread pressure, take one wrap over the very base of the frontmost barbs. The wrap should end with the bobbin pulled directly toward the tyer.

Release the near wing and check its position. It should match the far wing precisely. When viewed from the bend, the two wings should make a symmetrical, inverted "V" over the top of the body.

If the near wing has twisted out of position under thread pressure, relax the thread tension just a bit, and adjust the position of the feather to compensate for the roll or twist. Hold the feather firmly and reapply thread pressure. Then check the wing position once again.

When the wings are satisfactorily positioned, bind down the stems with tight wraps, moving toward the hook eye. You can clip the stems and bind down the butts, or clip them to length to form antennae.

Step 1a. In this reverse-mount technique, all fly components that lie behind the wing are dressed first; we've omitted them here for a clearer illustration. Position the tying thread at the wing-mounting point.

Select a matched pair of feathers; we're using CDC here. Locate the point along one feather stem where the barbs are slightly longer than the desired length of the finished wing. You can locate this point by preening the barbs toward the feather tip, as shown here. The curved section of barbs beyond the fingertips will form the wing.

Take the barbs below this point and preen them toward the butt of the feather, or strip them off as shown here.

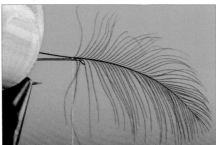

Step 2a. In normal tying, the wing on the far side of the shank would be mounted first. We're mounting the near wing for better visibility of the procedure.

Place the feather along the hook shank as shown. Most feathers are curved and the concave (or back) side of the feather faces the hook shank, and the glossiest or most attractively marked side faces outward.

The feather should not be perfectly vertical, but rather the top edge should be angled toward the hook shank so that it slants over the back of the fly body to produce one half of the tentwing.

Take 2 wraps of thread under moderate tension directly over the feather stem at the base of the barbs.

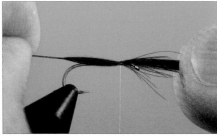

Step 3a. With the left fingers, grasp the butt of the feather stem; with the right fingers, grasp the feather tip.

Pull with the left fingers to slide the feather beneath the mounting wraps and produce a wing of the desired length.

At this point, the wing is rather narrow. It can be left as is, or broadened as shown in the next step.

Step 4a. To make the wing wider and the venation more distinct, maintain your hold on the butt of the feather. With the right fingers, grasp the barb tips that project forward from underneath the mounting wraps, as shown.

Pull the barb tips slightly toward the hook eye. This will cause the barbs in the wing to bulge outward on either side of the stem, as shown.

Step 5a. Mount the second wing in precisely the same way.

When the wings are mounted and properly positioned, pinch them in the left fingers and secure them with several tight thread wraps toward the hook eye. Clip the excess feather at the tip and clip the bare feather stem at the rear of the wing.

The fly on the right has wings made of CDC feathers. We've dressed a body on the fly to give a better idea of its finished appearance. The fly on the left has wings made of rooster hackle.

To promote good flotation, the flies can be finished with a collar hackle, crosshackle, or spun-hair head.

Method #48:
Folded Feather-tip Wing

Like quill segments, feather tips can be folded to form tent-shaped caddis wings or wings on grasshopper and cricket patterns. Feather tips, however, give the tyer a greater range of choices in color, markings, and mottlings, and can produce downwings that are quite striking in appearance.

In order to fold the feather tip and make a durable wing, it must be reinforced in some fashion. This style is commonly dressed with mesh-reinforced feather tips (see **Method #45: Mesh-backed Feather Wings**, p. 294), as shown in the main sequence, where they are used to dress a tent-shaped caddis wing. Feathers can also be misted with a spray fixative, or treated with a coating of flexible cement as shown in the alternate sequence, where a folded wing is dressed on a thicker-bodied grasshopper pattern.

As shown in **Method #46: Tape-backed Feather Wings**, Step 3, p. 296, feathers reinforced with tape can be used with this technique as well.

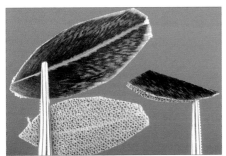

Step 1. Select a feather and fold it lengthwise so that the crease lies along the feather stem. Feather tips that have been coated liberally with cement or prepared with a mesh or tape backing can be stiff and may resist taking a crease at first. Getting a permanent fold in the wing is largely a matter of persistence, pinching the feather repeatedly up and down the feather stem until it remains folded.

The natural feather tip can be left intact if desired, but this wing style is more commonly trimmed to shape. Clipping the feather while it is folded will ensure symmetrical wings. Trimming the feather is simplified if the fold of the feather is held in a pair of hackle pliers to give more working room.

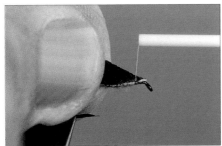

Step 2. All fly components behind the winging point are dressed first. Lay a short thread foundation toward the hook eye, and return the thread to the front edge of the body material.

Center the wing atop the hook so that the crease in the feather rests against the shank.

Pinch the sides of the feather against the sides of the shank, and secure it with 2 or 3 thread wraps taken under moderate pressure.

Step 3. Release the feather and make any necessary adjustments in position.

Then secure the feather with additional tight thread wraps; clip and bind down the excess.

Step 1a. On flies with thicker bodies, the feather must be mounted atop the body material to prevent the wing from flaring upward.

Dress all components behind the wing-mounting point, and position the tying thread over the front edge of the body material, as explained in **Method #42: Folded Quill Downwing**, Step 4a, p. 290.

Generally, grasshopper wings are dressed so that they are of uniform width throughout. The feather can be left untrimmed, as shown on the left, or clipped to produce a wing of uniform width, as shown on the right.

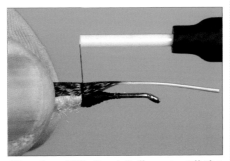

Step 2a. With the left fingers, roll the sides of the feather downward so that they follow the contour of the body.

Secure the feather with several tight thread wraps.

Step 3a. Clip and bind down the butts.

Method #49:
Feather-tip Delta Wing

Delta wings are dressed flat over the back of the fly body to form a narrow "V" and are typically used on patterns that imitate spent caddis, midges, and craneflies.

This wing style is commonly dressed from the tips of rooster neck hackle, as shown in the main sequence. These narrower feathers yield a more distinct "V" shape than do broader hen hackles and give better support in the surface film.

The alternate sequence shows a shortcut method of producing delta wings from a single feather; the procedure is fast, but does not allow for any adjustment of the angle between the wings.

Step 1. Delta flatwings are dressed after the body materials, such as the dubbing used here, have been applied. Lay a foundation of 4 or 5 thread wraps ahead of the body, and return the tying thread to the very front edge of the body material.

Prepare a pair of feathers—we're using rooster hackle here—by stripping or clipping the barbs below the mounting point, as explained in the section "Preparing Feather-tip Downwings," p. 292. Typically, delta wings are sized to be as long as the entire hook.

The feathers are mounted individually, beginning with the wing on the far side of the shank. Pinch the feather, shiny side up, directly behind the mounting point and lay it across the top of the hook to make an angle of about 25 degrees with the rear portion of the shank. The top-view photo here shows the proper feather position, though for actual mounting, you use the hand position shown in Step 2.

298

Step 2. Using light tension, take one wrap of thread over the wing, ending with the bobbin pulled toward you. The thread should not be laid directly over the bare feather stem, but rather should cross the base of the lowermost feather barbs. Trapping the base of the barbs beneath the thread like this will help prevent the feather from rolling or twisting.

Step 3. Apply tension to the thread and release your fingers from the feather. A properly mounted feather will remain in a horizontal position, as shown above. If the angle between the feather and the hook shank changes slightly, don't be concerned; it can be remedied later.

If the feather has rolled or twisted, grasp it again with the left fingers. Relax the thread pressure and adjust the feather to compensate. If the feather has rolled away from you, reposition it by rotating it slightly toward you; if it has twisted toward you, reposition it by rotating the feather slightly away from you. Then apply tension to the thread again, and check the wing position. It may take a few attempts before the wing lies flat. If the feather refuses to behave, you may need to flatten the stem as explained in "Preparing Feather-tip Downwings," p. 292.

Step 4. When the wing is properly positioned, grasp the very tip, as shown in this top view. Bind down the feather stem, toward the hook eye, with two or three wraps of thread. As you do so, pull the tip of the wing away from you, as binding the stem will cause the wing to swing toward the hook shank; pulling on the tip will compensate for this movement and maintain the proper wing angle.

Step 5. Return the tying thread to the front edge of the body. Take the second feather and position it over the shank, as shown here from the top. The photo here shows the proper wing position; for actual mounting, you will need to grip the feather closer to the mounting point, as shown in Step 6.

Step 6. Pinch the feather behind the mounting point, and mount the near wing by using the procedure described in Steps 2-3.

Step 7. When the wing position is satisfactory, bind down the stem with 2 tight wraps. As you do so, pull the tip of the wing toward you to maintain the proper angle with the hook shank.

Step 8. After 2 wraps, stop and check the wing position. They should appear as they do in this top view—flat across the back of the body, with a 45-degree angle between them. If one or both wings are slightly out of position, adjust them by pulling the tips until a symmetrical delta wing is formed. Then continue binding the stems.

The stems can be clipped, and the butts bound down, or left long to form antennae, as shown here. A drop of head cement or CA glue can be applied to the wing-mounting wraps to secure the feather tips.

Step 1a. To form delta wings from a single feather, prepare the hook as explained in Step 1.

Select a feather with barbs as long as the finished wing length. Almost any type of feather can be used; web-free rooster hackle will produce a very sparse wing, while webby feathers, such as the hen hackle shown here, will produce a denser one.

Snip away the tip of the feather at the point along the stem where the barbs are as long as the finished wing length.

Preen most of the remaining barbs toward the base of the feather, leaving a section of barbs on either side of the stem. The width of the barb sections is the width of the finished wings.

When the wing width is established, strip away the excess barbs.

Step 2a. Position the feather atop the hook shank.

Take one thread wrap over the very base of the frontmost feather barbs to prevent the feather from rolling under thread tension. Then secure the feather with additional tight thread wraps taken toward the hook eye.

Step 3a. Clip the feather stem, and bind down the excess.

Method #50:
Feather-tip Flatwing

As the name suggests, flatwings are formed from one or more feather tips that are mounted to lie flat across the body. A single feather can be mounted directly over the top of the body to imitate the shell of a beetle, and this style is shown in the main sequence. A stack of feathers may also be dressed in this fashion to produce a denser, more opaque wing for larger flies such as the adult stonefly illustrated in the alternate procedure.

Flatwings are usually constructed from natural feather tips, though nothing prohibits the tyer from using feathers that have been clipped to shape. On stonefly or beetle patterns, hen neck or saddle hackle is probably the most common material, as these wide, webby feathers give the impression of greater substance in the wing. Hen-hackle flatwings may appear disproportionately broad when they are dressed, but when fished, the wings will become slightly matted and decrease in width.

Other feathers can of course be used, most notably the jungle cock nails used in Vince Marinaro's Jassid pattern. Wing coverts, and some types of back and body feathers, may also prove acceptable; CDC feathers can produce a flatwing with an interesting veined appearance.

Flatwings can be mounted in one of two ways. The barbs below the mounting point can be stripped or clipped, and the feather bound in directly over the very lowermost barbs. This method produces a teardrop-shaped wing that tapers toward the mounting point, and is shown in the main sequence. Or the feather can be bound in a short distance above the lowermost barbs, which creates a wing that is more uniformly broad throughout its length, as shown in the alternate sequence.

If desired, the winging feathers can be reinforced with spray fixative or with flexible cement, as shown in the main sequence. Feathers reinforced with mesh as explained in **Method #45: Mesh-backed Feather Wings**, p. 294, are commonly used to dress this downwing style as well. But natural, untreated feathers can certainly be used, as shown in the alternate sequence.

Step 1. After dressing the body materials, such as the peacock herl used here, lay a foundation of 4 or 5 wraps of thread ahead of the body. Then return the thread to the wing-mounting position—usually immediately ahead of the body.

Prepare and size the feather tip by stripping or clipping the barbs below the mounting point as explained in "Preparing Feather-tip Downwings," p. 292. The length of the wing depends upon the particular pattern, but wings that are not reinforced with cement or mesh should project only slightly beyond the hook bend. Excessively long wings may wrap around the fly body and catch on the hook bend during casting. Reinforced wings can be left somewhat longer as they better resist twisting.

Treating the wings with adhesive is a simple matter. After sizing the feather, put a drop of flexible cement at the base of the lowermost feather barbs. As shown here, pinch the feather flat and draw it slowly between thumb and forefinger, distributing the cement over the entire length of the feather. Repeat this pinch-and-draw procedure until the entire feather is covered with a thin coating of cement. Allow the feather to dry.

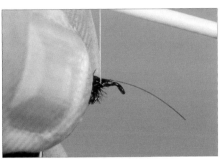

Step 2. Regardless of whether the wings are treated with cement or left untreated, the mounting procedures are the same. With the left fingers, position the feather directly atop the hook shank over the fly body. Hold the feather close to the mounting point and pinch it slightly from the sides to prevent the feather from shifting under thread pressure.

Using moderate tension, take a thread wrap over the base of the very lowermost barbs—not over the bare feather stem—and complete the wrap with the bobbin held above the hook shank as shown.

Step 3. Apply pressure to the thread to seat the wing firmly against the hook shank. Release the wing and check its position. It should lie flat across the body, with the feather stem in line with the hook shank.

If the wing is twisted or tilted, grasp the feather again as shown in Step 2, relax the thread tension enough to manipulate the feather, and then shift the wing slightly in a direction that will compensate for the twist or roll. Increase thread tension again, and re-check the wing position. It may take a few attempts to set the wing properly, and particularly stubborn feathers may need to have their stems flattened as explained in "Preparing Feather-tip Wings," p. 292.

If the wing does not lie flat over the top of the body, but rather slants upward, remove the feather from the hook and remount it closer to the front of the body. If the body is excessively thick, you may need to mount the wing atop the front edge of the body material as shown in Step 1a.

Step 4. When the wing position is satisfactory, grasp the feather again and secure it to the shank with tight wraps moving toward the hook eye.

The stem can be clipped and bound down, as shown here. If 2 feathers are used, the stems may be left long for antennae as shown in **Method #49: Feather-tip Delta Wing**, Step 8, p. 298.

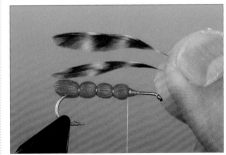

Step 1a. Larger flies may require more substantial wings made of two or more feathers.

Prepare a body and position the thread at the mounting point as explained in **Method #42: Folded Quill Downwing**, Step 4a, p. 290. We're using a pulled deer-hair body here.

Select 2 or more winging feathers, such as the hen saddle shown, that are closely matched in size and curvature. Strip the barbs from the stem, leaving the feather tip ¼" longer than the desired length of the finished wing. This extra ¼" of barbs will be bound down with thread, and the resulting wing will have a relatively uniform width throughout, which better imitates adult stonefly wings.

Stack the feathers front to back, that is, so that the curvatures match and the feathers "nest" together.

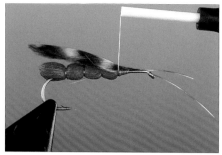

Step 2a. Place the stacked feathers atop the hook shank so that the lowermost feather barbs extend ¼" past the mounting point toward the hook eye.

Mount the feathers as explained in Steps 2-3. Don't be concerned that the stems be bound directly atop one another. One stem will probably shift slightly to the side, but the appearance of the finished wing will be unaffected.

Release the feathers and check their positioning. Because the thread is binding down a quantity of barbs along with the feather stem, twisting or rolling is not generally a problem. If the feathers are not properly aligned, slacken the thread tension, adjust the wing, and tighten the thread once again.

Once the wing position is satisfactory, grasp the feathers again, and secure them with tight wraps toward the hook eye, binding down both barbs and feather stem. Clip the excess or leave the stems long to form antennae.

Method #51:
Reverse-hackle Flatwing

A simple and realistic downwing can be dressed by tying a hackle feather in the reverse style, where the gaps left between the preened-back barbs suggest wing venation. This wing type is most often used on smaller stonefly patterns, though it can be adapted to other imitations. Many types of feathers can be used—breast, flank, wing coverts, hen hackle—but the style is typically dressed with relatively web-free rooster hackle, either large neck feathers or saddles. The absence of web allows the barbs to separate and produce a more distinct veined appearance.

There are a few limitations with this wing. As a rule, it is restricted to somewhat smaller flies, as it is difficult to obtain suitable feathers with sufficient barb length to dress large patterns, such as salmonflies. Moreover, these wings are rather fragile since the barbs are bent against the natural direction of growth and can break away from the feather stem. Finally, reverse-hackle wings contribute little to the buoyancy of the fly, though the one exception here is CDC. If the barbs are sufficiently long, CDC feathers can tie an attractive reverse-hackle wing that aids in floating the fly.

The technique for dressing this wing style is similar to a tying body with a feather extension, and readers may wish to consult the section on "Extended Bodies," **Method #125: Feather Extension**, p. 207.

Step 1. Dress the body of the fly. Counterspin the bobbin to flatten the tying thread, and lay a short thread foundation toward the hook eye. Keep the thread flattened, and return it to the front edge of the body. This smooth foundation will simplify sliding the feather in a later step.

Take one half-hitch with the thread directly at the mounting point and snug it down securely. This knot will prevent the thread from shifting position at a later stage of the dressing.

Select a rooster hackle with barbs sufficiently long to form the wing. Strip the fuzzy barbs from the base of the feather stem.

Step 2. Hold the feather flat, with the shiny side up. With the right fingers, pinch the feather stem front to back. Exactly where along the feather to pinch the stem and begin the forming the wing depends upon the size of the fly. You want to begin at a point where the barbs are long enough to form the wing, but contain as little web as possible.

With your left hand, pull the tip of the feather slowly, drawing the hackle through the right fingers and preening the barbs back toward the base of the feather. Stop when about ¼" of preened barbs extends beyond the right fingertips, as shown.

Step 3. Position the feather atop the hook shank by sliding the feather over the hook eye, so that the thumb and feather are on top of the shank and the index finger below it. Essentially, you are now pinching both the feather and the hook shank.

Apply pressure with your thumb as necessary to keep the preened barbs as flat as possible. The barbs should be lined up side-by-side rather than bunched into a clump.

Step 4. Here, you must manipulate the bobbin with your left hand.

With a flattened tying thread, take 2 loose wraps over the feather at the mounting point, as shown in this top view. Pressing your index finger upward will help prevent the barbs on the far side of the hook from rolling underneath. These turns of thread should be quite light, and every effort made not to disturb the position of the barbs. Since the feather must be slipped beneath these 2 wraps of thread, there should be no more tension on them than is supplied by the weight of the hanging bobbin.

Step 5. Do not release the feather from the right fingertips. Grasp the tip of the feather in the left hand, and draw it carefully beneath the thread wraps until a wing of the desired length is created.

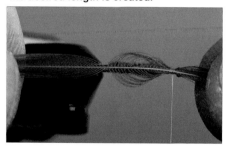

Step 6. (Optional) If the wing that is formed is too narrow for the pattern, use the right fingertips to gently and very slightly draw the feather back beneath the thread wraps toward the hook eye. This will cause the barbs on each side of the wing to flare outward and produce a wider profile.

Step 7. When the wing has the desired shape, take 4 or 5 tight turns of thread toward the hook eye. Clip the excess material and bind down the butts.

Finally, clip away the feather tip from the rear of the wing.

Method #52:
Biot Downwings

Obviously, biots are not feather tips, but we have included them in this section of the chapter because the techniques for dressing them are virtually identical to those employed in dressing feather-tip downwings, and in some instances, the wings produced are quite similar.

The use of biots as a winging material is largely attributable to tyer René Harrop, who has also helped popularize the use of biots as a body material. Harrop prefers turkey biots because of their large size, which makes them easier to handle and suitable for a larger range of hook sizes. Even the largest biots, however, are rather narrow, which ultimately limits the size of the hook on which they may be dressed.

Biots can be dressed in the tentwing style, particularly for dressing microcaddis patterns, and in the delta-wing style, both of which are shown in the following photograph.

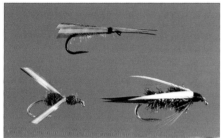

Step 1. At the top is a biot tentwing. It is dressed using exactly the same procedure described in **Method #47: Feather-tip Tentwings**, p. 295; note that the biot tips are left intact to form antennae, an option that can also be used when tying delta wings. At the lower left is a biot delta wing, and at the right is a delta wing dressed with the biots in the reverse orientation—a style used almost exclusively on the Prince nymph, shown here. Both types of delta wings are tied using the procedure explained in **Method #49: Feather-tip Delta Wing**, p. 297.

Method #53:
Feather Streamer Wings

Perhaps one of the most widespread styles of feather-tip downwing is the type used to dress conventional streamer patterns. Here, one or more pairs of feathers are tied atop the hook shank to produce a long, flexible wing.

As discussed in the section "Selecting Downwing Feathers," p. 291, the choice of feathers for this wing style varies among tyers, but regardless of the specific material, it is important that the feathers be chosen to match one another as closely as possible in shape and barb length. The simplest way to achieve this match is to select adjacent feathers from a neck or saddle. If loose or strung hackle is used, it's best to sort through the

feathers to get matching pairs and thereby ensure a symmetrical, well-balanced wing.

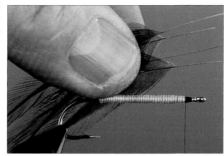

Step 1. Dress the body of the fly. In this style of winging, it's worth taking pains with the tie-off of the body material. There should be no abrupt "ledge" at the front of the body, but rather the thread should be used to make a smoothly tapering tie-off—a cone-shaped "ramp" that tapers toward the hook eye. Use as little thread as possible for the tie-off of the body material to avoid excessive bulk at the head of the fly. Return the tying thread to the rearmost thread wrap of the body tie-off, that is, the thickest part of the thread "cone."

Select one or two pairs of feathers—we're using 2 pairs of rooster saddle, though the technique for tying a single pair is identical. Strip off the fuzzy barbs at the base of the feathers.

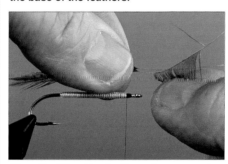

Step 2. Size the feathers by measuring them against the hook shank or by using a winging gauge (see **Method #5: Cut Wings**, Step 3a, p. 250, and **Method #7: Feather-tip Wings**, Step 1a, p. 253, on making and using wing gauges). The feathers can be sized individually, but if they are carefully stacked so that the tips are even, two or more feathers can be sized simultaneously. In any case, avoid excessively long wings, as they can wrap around the hook shank during casting.

Strip away the barbs below the mounting point. All the feather tips should now be of equal length.

Step 3. Take 2 of the feathers and stack them, front-to-back, so that the curvatures match and the tips are even. Stack the second pair of feathers in the same fashion.

Now take the 2 stacks, and place them with the concave, or dull, sides together. The tips of all 4 feathers should be aligned.

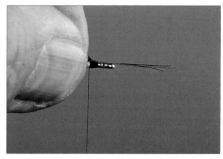

Step 4. Pinch the entire stack of 4 feathers in the left fingers, directly behind the mounting point, as shown. The stems should lie in row across the top of the thread base and should not be bunched together or crossed.

Step 5. Take a turn of thread directly below the lowermost barbs on the feathers. The wrap should fall on the bare feather stems; trapping any barbs beneath the thread will distort the front edge of the wing. The wrap of thread should be tight, but made carefully enough so that the side-by-side alignment of the stems is not disturbed.

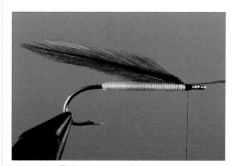

Step 6. Take 2 more tight turns, moving toward the hook eye, and release the wing. Check its position. The feathers should be perfectly vertical and the silhouettes aligned; that is, from the side, they should look like a single feather.

If one or more of the feathers has rolled out of position, remove the feathers and remount them. You may try altering the mounting point very slightly in attempt to reduce twisting or rolling. If the feathers prove particularly unruly, you can flatten the stems as explained in "Preparing Feather-tip Downwings," p. 292.

Step 7. When the wing position is satisfactory, grasp the wing again and bind down the feather stems very tightly.

You can angle-cut the feather stems and bind down the excess or lock them in as shown in Step 7a.

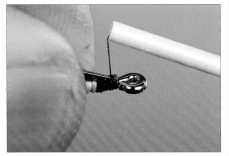

Step 7a. Bare hackle stems are slippery, and some tyers prefer to lock in the wings and reduce the possibility that they may pull out.

To form this lock-wrap, grasp the bare feather stems and preen them back over the top of the wing, as shown. Take 2 or 3 very tight wraps back over the folded stems.

When the stems are locked in position, clip them at an angle that matches the front edge of the wing, and bind down the butts.

Method #54:

Streamer Cheeks and Shoulders

Streamer cheeks (sometimes called "shoulders" or "sides") are fashioned from one or more feathers affixed flat against each side of a streamer pattern. The terminology among tyers is a bit inconsistent. If a single feather is tied to each side of the fly, it is often called a "cheek" regardless of the material. If two feathers are tied to each side, the inside feather, which is usually larger, is sometimes referred to as a "shoulder" and the smaller, outside feather as a "cheek." Other tyers simply refer to the combination of two feathers as the "cheek."

Though largely the province of the Atlantic salmon dressings, cheeks have a venerable history in the tying of trout flies, most notably in the patterns of Carrie Stevens. Stevens favored a combination of silver pheasant and jungle cock (used in the sequence below) on streamer patterns such as her Grey Ghost, where the materials suggest the gill plates and eyes of a small baitfish. Though streamers of this style are less commonly used today, they nonetheless remain beautiful and effective patterns.

If a single feather is used on each side of the fly, the procedure for dressing cheeks is identical to that presented in **Method #47: Feather-tip Tentwings**, p. 295. If two feathers are used on each side of the fly, as shown in the following sequence, they can be affixed separately, atop one another, but it is generally easier to employ the method advocated by Carrie Stevens and glue the feathers together, after which the assembly can be dressed as though it were a single feather.

A word about these somewhat specialized materials is in order. Silver pheasant body feathers, though expensive, are still within the means of most tyers. The feathers are generally available in packages of a dozen. Obtaining a matched pair of cheeks from a pre-packaged assortment, however, can prove troublesome at times, as both the markings and the angle between barbs and stem may differ from feather to feather. Within reasonable limits, though, a mismatched pair makes little difference in a fly to be used for fishing. Tyers who are serious about silver pheasant (and can afford to be) buy whole skins; choosing matched feathers is easiest when they are supplied in the bird's own packaging.

But the price of silver pheasant doesn't begin to compare with the cost of jungle cock eyes, particularly in the top grade. For the most part, real jungle cock eyes (or "nails") are used by tyers dressing flies for display rather than everyday use. However, suitable (if far less elegant) substitutes can be purchased or made. One of the most common of these are images of jungle cock eyes photo-imprinted on a Mylar sheet. These are at least distantly realistic, but do not tie up as nicely as the genuine article. A reasonable substitute can be made from a strip of barred wood duck. The strip is trimmed to shape at the tip, and a black waterproof pen is used to imitate the markings of the jungle cock eye. Some tyers have used waterproof enamel paint to apply markings to a small, dark feather—from a starling or crow—and make a passable imitation.

The feather at the left is a natural jungle cock eye. The next two feathers are strips of barred wood duck, the first one natural, the second trimmed and colored as a jungle cock imitation. The feather second from the right is a starling body feather painted to resemble a jungle cock. The feather at the right is a guinea fowl body feather burned to shape as explained in the next two photos.

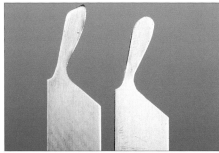

Nicely shaped substitutes for jungle cock eyes can be made by burning a feather to shape. A burner can be fashioned specifically for the purpose, or a commercial wing burner can be modified.

On the left is a standard Renzetti caddis wing burner; on the right, an identical burner has been filed to a more symmetrical shape for burning eyes.

The key to good results lies in selecting the right type of guinea feather. It should have a white spot in the center of the feather near the tip. When properly placed in the burner, as shown, this spot will become the "eye." For details on burning feathers to shape, see **Method #6: Burned Wings**, p. 251.

There is little doubt that authentic jungle cock eyes make striking and distinctive cheeks; it is less clear that they make a more effective fly, and we have used all of the substitutes noted here with good results in both fishing and tying.

Step 1. Real jungle cock eyes, or feathers used as substitutes, can profit from reinforcement. Though the practice would send shivers through any tyer who dresses flies for display, treating the eyes with adhesive greatly improves the durability of patterns tied for fishing.

There are two ways to reinforce real or imitation jungle cock feathers. Lightly misting the feathers with a spray fixative is perhaps the fastest method, but greater durability is obtained by treating the feather with a flexible cement. Silicone glue is good for this purpose, though it may require a drying time of up to 24 hours. Vinyl cement sets more quickly.

In either case, smear a small dab of glue between the fingertips, and lightly stroke the feather lengthwise as shown here to spread the glue in a thin coat over all the barbs. Allow the feather to dry.

Step 2. Prepare a pair of silver pheasant body feathers by stripping away the barbs below the mounting point. Proportions vary a bit among tyers, but generally the tip of the silver pheasant should extend to about the midpoint of the hook shank.

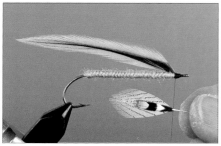

Step 3. Affixing the jungle cock to the silver pheasant to make a single assembly simplifies mounting and improves durability.

Place a small dab of silicone or vinyl cement on the back of the jungle cock eye or substitute. Do not use head cement, liquid-type CA glue, or any runny adhesive that will bleed into the absorbent barbs of the silver pheasant, as this will mar the appearance of the finished fly. Using your fingertip, carefully spread the cement in a thin layer over the back of the feather only.

Press the back of the jungle cock feather against the front of the silver pheasant. The stems of both feathers should be aligned, as should the lowermost barbs.

Step 4. A neat and secure mount of the cheeks and shoulders depends in part on a fly body that is properly tied off, with no abrupt changes in diameter or ledges, as explained in **Method #53: Feather Streamer Wings**, Step 1, p. 301.

When the assembly is dry, or nearly so, it can be mounted using the technique explained in **Method #47: Feather-tip Tentwings**, p. 295, except that the feathers are mounted flat against the sides of the body, not angled to form a "tent" above the hook shank.

Method #55:
Matuka Feather Wing

In Matuka winging, one or more feathers are lashed along the top of the body with ribbing material. Such a wing will not wrap around the hook bend when casting (as is sometimes the case with conventional streamer wings) and is highly durable.

Probably the most common material for Matuka wings is hen saddle, used in the main sequence that follows. These wide, webby feathers give a broad wing with a pronounced, rounded trailing edge. Other feathers, however, can be used to create much different effects. Rooster saddle is used by many tyers and results in a somewhat narrower, spear-shaped profile. Marabou, either the tip of a plume or a long blood feather, can be tied Matuka-style to make a slim, leech-like fly with a very mobile wing. Emu and rhea feathers create a wing with an almost spiny appearance, as will very small ostrich plumes.

If hen or rooster hackle is used, a pair of feathers is mounted with the concave sides together to produce a symmetrical wing; some tyers use four feathers, a pair on each side. With marabou, emu, ostrich, and other relatively straight materials, a single feather can be used, though two or more feathers make a fuller wing.

Typically, a Matuka dressing actually forms both the wing and tail, but these two parts of the fly can be fashioned from separate materials. In this case, shown in the alternate sequence, the tail is tied in first and the Matuka wing is formed from the midsection of a feather rather than the tip.

Metal wire is ordinarily used for ribbing and is the most durable material. But strong tying thread, monofilament leader material, fine oval tinsel, fine flat materials such as Mylar tinsel or Krystal Flash—indeed almost any stranded material of sufficient length and strength—can form the ribbing.

Step 1. Tie in the ribbing material at the bend of the hook, and fashion the body. Take care to form a neat, smoothly tapered body tie-off as explained in **Method #53: Feather Streamer Wings**, Step 1, p. 301; position the tying thread at the mounting point described there and shown as well in the photo above.

Prepare and size a pair of hen saddles by placing the feathers back-to-back, that is, with the concave sides together, and stripping the barbs from below the mounting point. The exact wing length is variable, but as a guide you may wish to make the overall length of the winging feathers 1½ to 2 times the length of the hook shank.

Step 2. From the underside of the pair of feathers, strip off a section of barbs that is equal in length to the fly body. Accuracy in this regard will produce the most attractive wing. If the body is curved or bulky, it is best to lay the feathers directly atop the body to establish the proper length of the stripped portion of the feather stem. Notice here that the bare feather stem extends exactly from the rear of the body to the tie-off point at the head.

Step 3. Position the feathers over the top of the shank so that the bare feather stems lie directly along the center of the body.

Mount the feathers at the front by using the technique explained in **Method #53: Feather Streamer Wings**, Steps 3-6, p. 301.

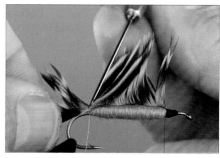

Step 4. With the left fingers, grasp the tips of both feathers and draw the wings back over the top of the body, applying a light pressure to hold them in this position.

With the right fingers, preen the barbs above the feather stems upward.

Slip a dubbing needle between the feather barbs that are directly above the rear edge of the body. Use the needle to push the barbs behind the body back toward the tail; push the barbs that lie over the body toward the hook eye. Dividing the barbs like this will expose a small portion of bare feather stem at the rearmost point of the fly body. When making this division, keep a light but consistent pressure on the feather tips and part the barbs on both feathers at exactly the same point.

Step 5. While maintaining a light pressure on the feather tips, take one turn of the ribbing material through the division in the barbs, binding both feather stems to the hook.

As shown here, use the middle finger of your left hand as a backstop to prevent wrapping torque from pulling the feathers to the far side of the shank. The feathers should remain vertical and centered along the top of the fly body.

Complete the wrap by holding the ribbing material below the shank.

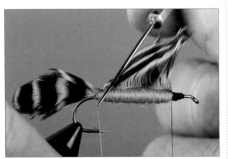

Step 6. Preen the barbs upward again, and use the dubbing needle to form another division, just as you did in Step 4, about ⅛" ahead of the first. If you are using wire as a ribbing material, as we are here, you may be able to release the wire momentarily and use the left fingers to assist in creating this second division; the wire will hold its shape and prevent the first wrap of ribbing from unraveling. If you're using a limp material such as oval tinsel, you will need to maintain moderate tension on the ribbing at all times.

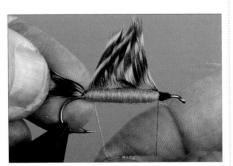

Step 7. Take another wrap of ribbing material through the new division you have created, again making certain to keep the winging feathers vertical, side-by-side, and centered along the top of the body.

Step 8. Repeat Steps 6 and 7 at evenly spaced intervals until the front of the wing is reached. The last turn of ribbing material should be brought ahead of the wing, where it is tied off with thread, clipped, and the excess bound down.

Step 1a. A Matuka style fly can be dressed with a separate tailing material, if desired.

Tie in the tail, we're using marabou here, the ribbing, and dress the body. Form a neat tie-off and position the thread as indicated in Step 1.

Prepare a winging feather, or a pair of feathers such as the emu shown here, by stripping away any short, broken, or otherwise unsuitable barbs from the base of the stem.

Step 1b. From one side of both feather stems, strip the barbs to leave a bare quill that is about ⅛" longer than the fly body.

Secure the feather as explained in Steps 3-7.

Step 1c. Complete the fly as shown in Step 8, then carefully clip away the excess feather that extends beyond the rearmost wrap of ribbing material, leaving only the feather sections bound atop the body.

Method #56:
Feather-tip Downwing

Downwings are often dressed by mounting an entire feather tip with the stem left intact. The practicality of this technique, however, depends upon the particular material used. The feather must, first, have a large number of barbs that extend evenly right to the tip, thereby providing sufficient material to make the wing. Such a feather will appear to be "squared off" rather than rounded at the tip. Second, the feather stem should be rather thin and flexible at the tip. Using a thick-stemmed feather will produce an excessively rigid wing and a bulky mount. The feathers that typically exhibit the most desirable characteristics are marabou blood feathers (see "Marabou," p. 11), CDC feathers (see "CDC," p. 11), and some body and flank plumage.

In the following sequence, we're using the tips of CDC feathers to produce a high-floating wing. Since the feather is affixed to the hook in the downwing style, flies dressed in this manner can be used to imitate caddisflies and midges. But the tendency of CDC barbs to flare or fluff up when mounted gives this wing a somewhat higher profile than that produced by other materials; thus CDC can be used effectively to represent upright wings on some mayfly species, particularly Pale Morning Duns and Blue-wing Olives. (CDC can, of course, be tied as a true upright wing; see **Method #28: Solid-fiber Arc Wing**, p. 276.) This same downwing, dressed quite short, is often used to imitate mayfly emergers as described in **Method #84: Tuft Emerger Wing**, p. 333.

Note that a downwing identical to the type shown here can be formed by stripping the barbs from the quill and employing the technique described in **Method #57: Solid-fiber Downwing**, p. 305. But using the feather tips is a considerably faster method, provided the right type of material is chosen.

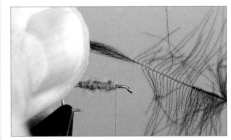

Step 1. Any tail, rib, or body materials must be dressed prior to mounting the wing. Position the tying thread at the front edge of the body.

Select a CDC feather. (If a denser, fuller wing is desired, or you are using a larger hook, stack 2 or more CDC feathers atop one another so that the curvatures match; treat them as a single feather in the following procedures.)

With the left fingers, preen the barbs upward and pinch them at the very tip of the feather. Not all the barbs will reach the tip. Use the right fingers to preen these short barbs toward the base of the feather. The barbs tips in the left fingers will be used for winging.

Step 2. Momentarily transfer the feather tip to the right fingers, and position it atop the body to size the wing, as shown.

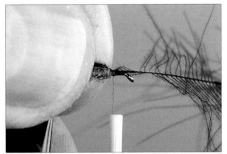

Step 3. Pinch the feather tip at the mounting point in the left fingers. Bind in the feather tip with tight turns of thread, moving toward the hook eye. Use the left index finger as a backstop to prevent the feather from rolling to the far side of the shank.

Step 4. Clip the excess material and bind down with thread.

Bundled-fiber Downwings

For the most part, downwings constructed of bundles of natural or synthetic fibers do not possess the realistic appearance of many quill or feather-tip downwings; the rather indistinct edge formed by the fiber tips does not offer the cleanly edged profile characteristic of many natural insects or baitfish. Thus bundled fibers are often used to tie wings on more impressionistic patterns.

But fiber materials offer the tyer many advantages, and chief among them is ease of tying. Generally, such wings are simpler and faster to dress than either quill or feather tips and are more durable. Moreover, materials can be selected for characteristics other than visual realism—buoyancy or absorbency; lifelike movement in the water; ease of handling; availability; and so on. It is a testimony to the usefulness of bundled fibers that they are the single most common type of material used in fashioning downwings.

Here, as in other chapters of this book, a

distinction is drawn between fibers that are solid and those that are hollow. Solid fibers form the larger of the two categories and include barbs from flank, body, and tail feathers; CDC and marabou; hairs such as bucktail, calf tail and body hair, woodchuck, bear, squirrel, mink, and indeed just about any type of fur with guard hairs sufficiently long to form wings and sufficiently plentiful to make it practical; natural and synthetic yarns, particularly polypropylene; a large number of synthetic hairs; twisted Mylars such as Krystal Flash; and other stranded synthetics. Solid fiber materials are most commonly used in subsurface patterns, particularly streamers, but a few materials such as poly yarn, mink hair, woodchuck, and calf have applications in floating flies.

The hollow hairs used for winging are far fewer in number. Deer and elk are the most common (see "Hollow Hair, p. 2"); caribou is sometimes used, and moose could conceivably be employed. As a rule, antelope hair is rather brittle; frequently the hair tips are bent or broken off, making the material unsuitable for most wing styles.

Method #57:
Solid-fiber Downwing

This is the basic technique for mounting any bundle of solid fibers in the downwing style. A useful distinction can be drawn among the various suitable materials. On one hand are relatively soft and compressible materials, such as barbs from body, flank, and hackle feathers, including CDC and marabou, and softer strands such as wool and poly yarns. Such materials are relatively easy to affix securely to the hook.

The second category consists of hard, relatively incompressible, rather slippery fibers—a category that includes most synthetic hairs, Mylar materials, and most natural hairs. Because they are smooth and slick, these materials can pose a problem in achieving a wing mount that securely holds all the fibers. Many of these fibers are also stiff, which can make trimming the materials after mounting somewhat cumbersome. The main sequence below shows a method of mounting bundled fibers that is particularly useful when the downwing is the last material dressed on the hook, as in many bucktail and hairwing streamer patterns; the proximity of the wing to the hook eye gives unencumbered access to the fiber butts for trimming.

Wings placed further back on the hook shank to allow for the placement of hackle or other materials close to the hook eye may be difficult to trim because of the stiffness of the material. In this case, the wing fibers can be angle-cut to length before mounting, and this procedure is shown in the alternate sequence.

In patterns that require a very full wing, or a wing composed of more than one material, a number of smaller clumps of material—rather than a single large one—are mounted at the winging point, and the methods for

doing so are also shown below. Tightly securing a very large bundle of slippery, incompressible fibers is difficult, and the finished wing often lacks durability.

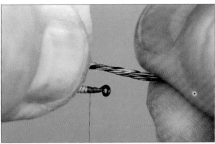

Step 1. All body materials must first be dressed, and care taken to produce a neat, tapered tie-off as explained in **Method #53: Feather Streamer Wings**, Step 1, p. 301. Position the thread at the rearmost thread wrap of the body tie-off.

Clip and prepare a bundle of fibers using a method appropriate to the material as explained in "Selecting and Preparing Bundled Fibers," p. 262.

Part of the key to a durable wing in which all fibers are locked firmly in position is to avoid using too much material, particularly slippery fibers such as squirrel tail (shown here), mink tail, woodchuck, and to a slightly lesser extent, bucktail. As a rough guideline, the bundle of fibers, when twisted to compress it, should be no thicker than the outside diameter of the hook eye, as shown here, though some materials may permit slightly larger quantities. For the most part, however, if a fuller wing is needed, mount two or more bundles of material separately.

Step 2. Using the hook shank or a winging gauge to establish the proper wing length, pinch the clump of material directly behind the mounting point.

Cast a turn of tying thread around the bundle only, as explained in **Method #12: The Noose Loop**, p. 32. Using a noose loop to mount the fibers will help keep them consolidated into a tight bundle on top of the hook shank.

Step 3. Roll or slide the bundle of material down the thread to the top of the shank, and bind it in with 6 or 7 very tight wraps of thread. Use the maximum tension you can obtain without breaking the thread.

Wings made of very slippery fibers or large bundles can be further secured by using one of the approaches shown in **Method #62: Hollow-hair Downwing**, Step 5 or 5a, p. 311.

Step 4. Trim the butts using the angle of the hook eye as guide.

Step 5. (Optional) With very slippery fibers, the durability of the wing can be increased by using a dubbing needle to force head cement or CA glue into the exposed fiber butts.

Step 6. Cover the butts with thread.

To mount a second of clump of material—we're using bucktail here for better visibility, return the tying thread to the mounting point. Prepare a second bundle of fibers and use the noose loop to mount it over the first bundle.

Wrap the thread forward, again very tightly, until you reach the rear edge of the angle-cut made on the first clump of material.

Step 7. Trim the second bundle of fibers, following the angle establish by the hook eye and the cut on the first bundle, as shown.

Step 8. Again, head cement or CA glue can be forced into the exposed fiber butts if desired.

Bind down the butts with tying thread.

If a third bundle of material is required, repeat Steps 6-8.

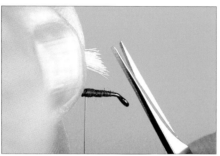

Step 1a. On the body pictured here, the bucktail downwing is mounted farther back on the hook shank to allow for a hackle. The shank can pose on obstacle to angle-cutting the mounted wing, so here the fiber bundle will be trimmed in advance.

After preparing the clump of material and establishing the wing length, pinch the bundle of fibers tightly at the mounting point. With a sharp pair of serrated scissors, trim the fiber butts at an angle, as shown.

Note that the left fingertips extend right to the mounting point, and the angle cut begins about ⅛" beyond.

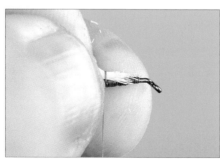

Step 2a. With pre-trimmed materials, preventing the fibers from rolling to the far side of the shank under thread pressure can be a bit tricky. A noose loop is impractical since tension on the noose will cause the fibers to twist and distort the angle cut.

Instead, position the wing atop the shank and take a wrap of thread under light tension over the fiber bundle. Press the middle finger of the left hand against the far side of the hook shank to act as a backstop that will prevent the fibers from migrating to the far side.

Apply thread pressure to seat the bundle firmly, while using the middle finger to keep the fibers atop the shank.

Step 3a. Bind the fibers tightly and mount additional bundles, if needed, as shown in Steps 5-8.

Form a smooth thread foundation. The long tapered tie-off wraps shown here provide a base for the front hackle on a Stimulator type pattern or for a spun-hair head.

Method #58:

Staggered Wing

Some interesting winging effects can be created by tying a series of downwings along the length of the hook shank rather than a single wing near the head of the fly. Staggering winging material along the shank has a number of applications. It can be used to create a full wing when using soft, thin materials such as the marabou shown in the following sequence. It can be used to create a shaped wing by varying the lengths of the individual wing segments, also shown below. And it also allows you to employ rather short materials, such as CDC barbs, to dress a wing on a longer hook shank.

Unlike other downwing styles in which the body is dressed first, here the body material is tied in first, but not wrapped until the wing is complete.

Step 1. If a tail is used, it should tied in first and care taken to bind the butts so that a smooth underbody is formed. A short tuft of marabou is used here.

Tie in the body material—chenille here—over the rearmost tailing wraps, and bind it along the length of the hook shank, again forming a smooth underbody.

Position the tying thread at the mounting point of the rearmost wing section.

Step 2. Clip and prepare a bundle of fibers using a method appropriate to the material as explained in "Selecting and Preparing Bundled Fibers," p. 262. The marabou barbs used here can be gathered into a bundle using the techniques shown in **Method #9: Preparing Marabou and CDC**, p. 73.

Determine the length of this wing segment. To form a tapered wing, as we're doing here, this segment should be short.

If the wing material is a relatively soft fiber—marabou, CDC, or other types of feather barbs; poly yarn; and so on—it can be mounted using the simple technique shown in **Method #56: Feather-tip Downwing**, Steps 3-4, p. 305.

If the wing material is stiffer—natural hair, Krystal Flash, and the like—use the procedure shown in **Method #57: Solid-fiber Downwing**, Steps 2-5 or 2a-3a, p. 305.

After this wing segment is mounted, the butts clipped, and the excess bound down, position the tying thread at the mounting point for the second segment. This mounting point varies depending on the desired number of wing segments and hence the density of the finished wing. But the wing segments should be spaced far enough apart to allow for at least one wrap of body material between them since the body material will be used to conceal the wing-mounting wraps.

Step 3. Continue repeating Steps 3-4, mounting additional wing segments. For a tapered wing, each segment is slightly longer than the preceding one.

When the frontmost wing segment is bound in, wrap the body material forward. With fluffy materials like marabou, dampening the wing and preening the segments upward will prevent the feather barbs from tangling with the body material, as shown here.

Wraps of body material can help establish the appearance of the finished wing. If the body material is abutted against the rear of each clump of marabou, the wing will project upward from the hook shank, giving it a broader profile. If the material is wrapped tightly over the front of the marabou segments, the wing will lie closer to the hook shank.

Step 4. Tie off the body material ahead of the frontmost wing segment, clip, and bind down the excess.

Method #59:

Reverse-mount Fiber Downwing

Mounting smooth, slippery winging fibers often results in a bulky and insecure wing tie-in, since the material itself compresses poorly and requires a fairly large number of thread wraps to affix the bundle and cover the butts. In some cases, the problem can be solved by reverse-mounting the fibers, burying the wing butts beneath the body material. This solution works well provided that the wing is relatively sparse. A large clump of hair will give substantial bulk at the folding point and prove difficult to secure. But when a smaller bundle of fibers is used—as in a sparsely dressed wet fly or streamer—the reverse mount makes a wing with a reasonably neat tie-off and firmly secured fibers.

Reverse-mounting winging fibers is also the basis for forming bullet-head patterns shown in **Method #60: Bullet-head Fiber Wings**, p. 308.

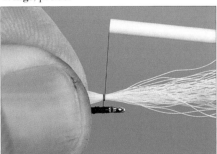

Step 1. Lay a thread foundation on the hook so that the frontmost thread wrap lies directly over the wing-mounting point on the shank.

Clip and prepare a bundle of fibers using a method appropriate to the material as explained in "Selecting and Preparing Bundled Fibers," p. 262.

Using the hook shank or winging gauge as a guide, determine the proper wing length. Grasp the butts of the fibers in the left hand, with the fingertips pinched at the mounting point.

Because the wing will be folded and the base of the fibers bound down, a short length of the wing will actually be covered tying thread, which effectively decreases the overall wing length by about ⅛" or so.

You can compensate by extending the length of the fibers beyond the left fingertips by about ⅛".

You can bind the fiber bundle directly or, as shown here, use the technique explained in **Method #12: The Noose Loop**, p. 32, to cast a turn of thread around the fiber bundle only. This wrap will help keep the fibers consolidated on top of the shank.

Step 2. Proceed to bind in the wing fibers with very tight wraps, moving toward the hook bend.

When the wing is secure, after 7 or 8 tight wraps, you can angle-cut the butts and bind them down.

Or you can bind more of the fiber butts down the length of the hook shank, as shown here, clipping them closer to the hook bend where they can be mated with body, tail, or rib materials to form a smooth underbody (see **Method #6: Spliced Underbody**, p. 44).

Step 3. At this point, the tail, body, rib, and hackle materials that lie behind the wing must be dressed. Tie these materials off about ⅛" behind the frontmost thread wrap securing the wing material. Leaving this short gap means that the wings will not, in the next step, be folded and bound down on top of any body materials, thus reducing bulk at the tie-down.

After the body and other materials have been tied off, bring the tying thread to the front of the wing as shown.

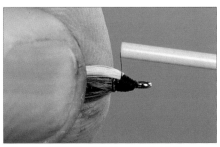

Step 4. With the left fingers, fold the wing fibers back over the body, making sure to keep all the fibers on top of the hook shank. Pinch the fibers tightly against the top of the body.

Begin taking close, tight wraps of thread directly ahead of the folded wing

308

fibers. You will need to form a small thread bump ahead of the wing base. When this bump is thick enough, the thread will "climb up" the base of the wing.

Step 5. Take 4 or 5 tight wraps over the base of the wing and release the fibers to check the wing position. If the wing sits too high, add a few more thread wraps toward the hook bend to lower the wing.

When the wing position is satisfactory, whip-finish and clip the thread or proceed to add any materials that lie ahead of the wing.

Method #60:
Bullet-head Fiber Wings

This is one of the many tying techniques that is difficult to categorize, since the method simultaneously produces two components of the finished fly—a bundled-fiber downwing and a bullet-style head. Since the tying method closely resembles other techniques in this section, we've chosen to present it as a winging procedure. A similar style of head, however, that does not necessarily involve forming wings is shown in **Method #2: Bullet Head**, p. 427.

Typically, this technique is used with either solid or hollow natural hair, but a few patterns such as the Krystal Bullet (which has a wing and head formed of Krystal Flash) use synthetic fibers. The main sequence below shows a head and wing formed of hollow hair, a very buoyant dressing used on patterns such as the Madam-X. The same method, however, can be employed using solid hairs, synthetics, or even marabou barbs.

The alternate sequence illustrates a slightly different approach in which two bundles of hair form the head and wing. This method is particularly useful if the body has dorsal and ventral sides of fashioned from different colors or materials. This particular wing style is perhaps most widely used in Keith Fulsher's Thunder Creek streamer dressings.

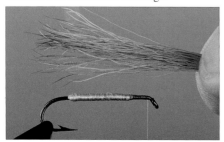

Step 1. Any tail, body, or rib materials should be applied prior to dressing the wing. The body materials should terminate

¼ to ⅓ of a shank-length behind the eye. Lay a tight thread foundation over the bare shank, and position the thread behind the hook eye.

If using natural hair, such as the deer hair shown here, or marabou barbs, clip and prepare a bundle of fibers using a method appropriate to the material as explained in "Selecting and Preparing Bundled Fibers," p. 262. If synthetic fibers are used, simply clip a bundle and trim the rear tips even.

Use the hook shank or a winging gauge to establish the proper wing length.

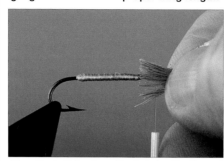

Step 2. In this step, the hair is distributed 360 degrees around the hook shank. Hollow hairs can be spun around the shank to distribute them evenly. The butts of the hair clump are held in the left hand, directly behind the mounting point, and the material can be spun as explained in **Method #58: Spinning Hollow Hair**, p. 145. When the hair is distributed and securely bound to the shank, the butts are clipped and covered with tying thread.

The method demonstrated here, however, works equally well with hollow hairs and with solid fibers, which are more difficult to spin. Begin by reversing the fibers, pinching them at the mounting point with the right fingertips so that the butts extend outward. Trim the butt ends of the fibers so that they extend ¼ to ⅓ of shank-length beyond the mounting point.

Push the center of the bundle into the hook eye so that the fiber butts are uniformly distributed around the shank. Push the bundle down the hook shank just far enough so that you feel the hook eye beneath your right fingertips; the mounting point of the material should lie just behind the hook eye.

With your left hand, you will need to pull the bobbin downward, wiggling it from side to side, so that the fiber butts slide past the tying thread. When the hair is properly positioned, the bobbin should be hanging straight down from behind the hook eye.

Step 3. Carefully grasp the butts of the material in the left fingertips. Take one wrap of thread, under light tension, completely around the material at the mounting point.

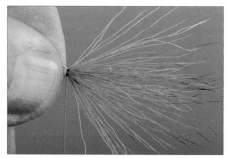

Step 4. Pull the thread downward tightly to compress the fibers, and immediately take 2 or 3 turns of thread directly atop the first wrap to secure the fibers tightly behind the hook eye.

Step 5. Under tight tension, wrap the thread toward the hook bend, binding down the material as you go. Eventually, you will need to release the butts from the left fingers, but the winging fibers should now be securely bound to the shank and resist spinning or shifting under the wrapping pressure.

If any stray fibers project from the wrappings, clip them off and cover with thread.

Position the tying thread at the front edge of the body.

Step 6. There are a couple of methods for consolidating the wing and fashioning the bullet head. You can preen the fibers back toward the hook bend with your left fingertips, drawing the fibers smoothly over the front of the hook shank.

As you preen the fibers back, you will need to maintain tension on the bobbin with the right hand to keep the thread in position. As you draw the fibers toward the bend, slide your fingers around the tying thread.

On dry flies, the fibers are ordinarily drawn back toward the bend and above the shank, as shown here. This method places the entire wing atop the hook shank. On streamer patterns, the fibers can be drawn back so that they completely encircle the hook shank, as shown in Step 8.

When the wing is properly formed, the head is smooth and uniform in shape.

Step 7. You can also form the wing and head by using a bullet-head tool (shown here), or in fact any cylinder—the empty barrel of an old ballpoint pen, for example—that has a hole large enough to fit over the hook eye and fiber bundle.

When using solid fibers which don't flare you may first need to preen the hair backward with your fingers a few times so that the fibers stand away from the hook eye.

Push the tool over the hook eye, as shown. The tying thread will also be pushed backward, but it will be repositioned in the next step.

Step 8. After the bullet head is formed, grasp the bundle of hair directly behind the front edge of the body. Remove the bullet-head tool, and work the thread forward again so that it hangs straight below the front edge of the body.

The wing can be bound in this position, or the fibers can be drawn carefully above the shank to form the type of wing shown in Step 6.

Step 9. After the bullet head is formed, take several tight wraps of tying thread around the wing, forming a short "neck" or "throat" that defines the head and secures the wing.

Step 1a. A bullet-head style streamer, such as the Thunder Creek minnow, is formed from two reverse-mounted clumps of fibers, one above the shank and one below.

Lay a thread base on the hook as explained in Step 1. Prepare a bundle of fibers (white bucktail is used here) and measure them to establish the wing length. Pinch the fibers in the left fingers so that the fingertips pinch the fibers at the mounting point.

It is easiest to mount the clump on the shank underside first, and the simplest way is to invert the hook in the vise. If you have a rotary vise, you can simply turn the jaws until the hook is upside down.

Mount the fibers as explained in **Method #59: Reverse-mount Fiber Downwing**, Steps 1-2, p. 307.

When the fibers are secure, return the tying thread to the frontmost thread wrap.

Step 2a. Return the hook to the normal position in the vise. Prepare a second clump of material (brown bucktail in this instance), and measure the wing length.

Mount this clump of material as shown in Step 1a.

Position the tying thread at the point on the shank where you wish to form the "neck" or "throat" of the bullet head.

Step 3a. If the winging fibers are all the same color or same material, you can form the bullet head by using either of the procedures shown in Steps 6-8.

If you wish to maintain a horizontal division between materials or colors, as we're doing here, the two fiber bundles will need to be manipulated separately.

Begin by grasping the tips of the upper fiber bundle and drawing them over the top of the body toward the hook bend.

Keep all the fibers on top of the shank. You may need to smooth the fibers by preening them back toward the hook bend alternately with the left and right fingertips.

When the fibers are smoothly drawn back, pinch them as shown.

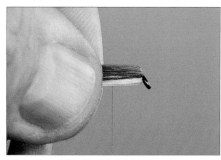

Step 4a. With the right fingers, grasp the lower bundle and preen it back toward the hook bend. Again, you may need to smooth the fibers a few times before they lie neatly together.

When the fibers form a smooth bundle, slip them upward into the left fingertips as shown.

Step 5a. If the fibers have been preened carefully, the wing may now be secured. If, however, the wing and head are not smooth and uniform, you can further shape them by preening them alternately with the left and right fingers, stroking them toward the hook bend. Or you can use a bullet-head tool, as shown in Step 7. In either event, make certain that bundles stay separate to form a well-defined horizontal division down the side of the body.

When the wing and head are satisfactorily formed, pinch the fibers tightly against the hook shank to prevent them from twisting. Take 5 or 6 very tight wraps of thread to compress the fibers and form the head of the fly.

Method #61:

Aztec Wing

This unique, inventive, and versatile wing was devised by tyer Dick Nelson for his Aztec fly, a streamer designed primarily for bass, though the winging style can make excellent trout flies as well. Though superficially similar to a staggered wing, the Aztec is tied differently, with body and wing materials applied simultaneously. Moreover, unlike a staggered wing in which materials are mounted to angle back toward the hook bend, the Aztec wing is tied so that materials stand vertically from the hook shank. The result is a much fuller silhouette.

Nelson's original dressing calls for acrylic yarn for both body and wing materials, but other types of yarn can be used, such as the Antron used in the following demonstration. If a multi-ply yarn is used, the strands should be separated and only a single ply used for the wing; the body can be wrapped from the full thickness of yarn. Other winging materials, however, are possible: clumps of synthetic hair, twisted strands such as Krystal Flash, and even marabou as shown in the alternate steps. Different colors or types of material can be combined as well. A very full wing—indeed, almost a body very much like the brushed body shown in **Method #93: Brushed Body**, p. 342—can be formed by tying a double-Aztec wing, mounting strands alternately above and below the shank, which is shown in the alternate steps.

A variety of different body materials can be used: Antron yarn (used in the main sequence), tightly twisted floss, twisted Krystal Flash, thicker oval tinsels, a dubbed thread or dubbing loop, twisted herl, vernille (used in the alternate sequence), and others. There are two primary requirements for the body material. First, it must have some thickness since the body material abuts the wing strands and holds them upright; a flat material such as tinsel will not perform this function. Second, it must be reasonably strong; wrapping pressure of the body material affixes the wing strands to the shank, and some tension must be applied for a secure wing mount.

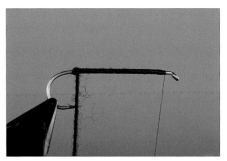

Step 1. The tail of the fly must be tied in first; we've omitted it here for a clearer illustration. The original Aztec pattern calls for a brushed yarn bundle, but other materials can be used as well. Whatever type of tail is dressed, however, care should be taken to bind in the tail butts so that a smooth underbody is created.

The strand of body material must also be tied in. Mount it over the rearmost tailing wrap, and secure it along the length of the shank, again forming a smooth underbody. Position the thread at that point on the shank where you wish the front edge of the wing to be located.

Since the body material is used to secure the winging strands to the shank, and thus tension must be maintained on the strand once tying begins, it is difficult to pause during the procedure to cut the individual winging strands. It's best to prepare these materials in advance. The exact number of winging strands required depends upon the thickness of the materials and the size of the hook, but as an estimate you'll need about 6-8 strands of material for every inch of hook shank covered.

Cut the strands at least twice as long as the height of the finished wing. Longer strands are a bit easier to handle, and can be trimmed later. Place these cut strands within convenient reach of the left hand.

Begin dressing the wing by taking a complete turn of body material directly over the tailing point, covering the rearmost thread wraps and creating a bump of material at the rear of the shank. This bump is necessary to post the first winging strand upright.

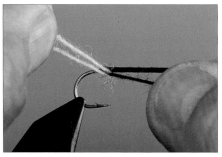

Step 2. Twist the body material rather tightly, and pinch it in the right fingers to maintain the twist. The twist will add bulk to the material for posting up the winging strands and add strength for wrapping. Pull the body strand toward you and slightly upward.

With the left hand, fold one of the winging strands over the top of the body material near the hook shank, as shown.

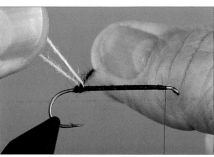

Step 3. Begin wrapping the body material over the shank. As you do so, slide the folded winging strand down the body material until it is positioned on top of the hook shank. The body strand should now be on the far side of the hook, pulled directly away from you.

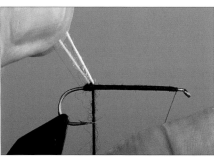

Step 4. To secure this segment of the wing, pull the body material directly downward under some tension. At the same time, pull the winging strand upward, and slightly toward you to prevent it from rolling to the far side of the shank under the wrapping pressure of the body material.

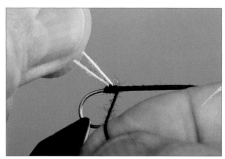

Step 5. Maintain your grasp on the winging strand, and draw it back slightly toward the hook bend. Take one turn of body material around the shank only, tightly abutting the base of the winging strand so that it stands upright. The body material should be pulled directly toward you and slightly upward.

Note that for a sparser wing, you can take two wraps of material ahead of the winging strand, which effectively reduces the overall number of strands that will be mounted on the shank.

Step 6. Repeat Steps 2-5 until the desired length of hook shank is covered.

When the wing is complete, take a wrap of body material ahead of the last wing strand to post it upright.

Step 7. Tie off and clip the body material, and bind down the excess.

If the wing is too high, or you wish to shape it, use a pair of sharp scissors to trim the strands to the desired length or contour.

Step 8. Some materials, especially single strands of multi-strand yarns should be fluffed out by combing them upward to separate the individual filaments and make a fuller wing with a softer appearance, such as the fly on the left. The fly on the

right is tied with spooled Antron which need not be combed; it produces a stiffer, brushlike wing.

Step 1a. Materials such as marabou can make an effective and unusual Aztec wing, though they are not as easily handled as yarn. A very full, good-quality marabou plume works well for this application.

To form the winging strands, strip away any short or scraggly marabou barbs at the base of the feather. Dampen the plume, and preen the barbs outward from the stem. Beginning at the base of the quill, cut a section of barbs about ¼" wide and twice as long as the height of the finished wing. Continue cutting identical sections of barbs until you have a sufficient number to form the wing.

Dress the marabou bundles as shown in Steps 2-7.

Step 1b. If a marabou wing requires shaping, you can trim it with scissors, but most tyers prefer to break the marabou tips to produce a slightly uneven, more natural-looking silhouette.

To shape the wing, pinch it lengthwise as shown between the right thumb and forefinger. Use the left fingers to break the marabou tips to the desired length or shape.

Step 1c. The fly on the left has a marabou wing that has had the tips broken to shape; the fly on the right has a double-Aztec wing formed into a minnow-like shape, as shown in the following steps.

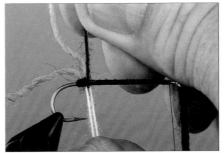

Step 2a. You can form a double-Aztec by binding winging strands alternately above and below the shank. (Naturally, twice the number of winging strands will be required.)

After the first wing strand is mounted atop the shank, as shown in Steps 2-4, and the body material is pulled downward, fold a second wing strand around the body material and slide it upward against the underside of the shank.

Secure this wing strand by pulling the body strand up and toward you, while simultaneously pulling the wing strand downward and away from you.

Step 2b. Alternate Steps 2-4 with Step 2a, mounting strands above and below the hook until the desired length of shank is covered. When the wing is complete, take one wrap of body material ahead of the last winging strand to post it upright.

The wing can now be trimmed and combed as in Steps 7-8.

Method #62:
Hollow-hair Downwing

A downwing tied of deer or elk hair is one of the most popular methods of imitating adult caddis, as in patterns such as the Elk Hair Caddis, where the hair flares to suggest the characteristic tent-shaped profile of the caddis wing. This same winging style is often used to represent the blurred silhouette of whirring wings on an adult stonefly attempting to escape the surface of the water. In either case, the hollow hair provides excellent floatation.

Standard, hollow-hair downwings, as shown in the main sequence, are relatively simple to dress, though some tyers have difficulty securing the fibers tightly enough so that the wing stays positioned atop the shank. Unless the hair is firmly affixed, it will, under the stresses of casting and fishing, rotate to the side or underside of the shank. One technique to remedy this common problem is presented in the main sequence below.

The two techniques presented in the alternate steps are particularly useful for securely fastening a large clump of hair to the shank to make a very high-floating wing.

Though typically the wing butts are bound down or trimmed to form a head, they can also be used to form a parachute post; this option is explained in **Method #38: Postless Parachute Downwing**, p. 393.

Tyers differ in the types of hollow hair they prefer for dressing downwings; see "Hollow Hair," p. 2.

Step 1. All tail, body, and rib materials should be dressed prior to winging. Lay a thread foundation of about 6 or 7 wraps ahead of the body tie-off, toward the hook eye, and return the tying thread to the rear of the thread foundation

Prepare a bundle of hair, we're using elk hair here, as explained in **Method #2: Preparing and Cleaning Hair**, p. 68. The exact quantity of hair is variable. A thinner bundle will produce a sparse wing of somewhat more realistic proportions, but only moderate buoyancy. A thick bundle will give an exaggerated wing profile, and prove slightly more difficult to secure tightly, but will provide excellent floatation for fishing heavy water.

Align the hair tips as shown in **Method #3: Stacking and Aligning Hair**, p. 69.

Use the hook shank or a winging gauge to establish the proper length of the wing—usually just to, or slightly beyond, the hook bend.

Step 2. Transfer the bundle to your left hand with the fingertips pinching the fibers at the mounting point.

Cast a wrap of thread around the mounting point of the hair bundle only as explained in **Method #12: The Noose Loop**, p. 32. This wrap of thread will help keep the hair consolidated atop the hook shank.

Step 3. Roll or slide the hair down the tying thread to the top of the shank. Pinch it tightly between the left fingertips to prevent it from rolling to the far side of the shank under thread pressure.

Bind in the hair with very tight thread wraps, moving toward the hook eye. With thicker bundles of material, you may wish to wind the thread back over this first layer of thread wraps for extra binding pressure.

Step 4. After this point, additional thread wraps do little to secure the wing further. To check for a solid wing mount, release the wing tips and pull the bobbin directly downward, exerting significant thread pressure. If the wing begins to slip to the far side of the hook shank, it isn't mounted securely enough and the additional measures shown in Step 5 or Step 5a should be taken.

If the wing does not slip, proceed to Step 6 or Step 7.

Step 5. To secure the wing fibers further, consolidate the hair butts in your left fingers and raise them vertically. Bring the tying thread ahead of the hair butts. Take several tight thread wraps, beginning directly at the point where the hair meets the hook shank and working toward the hook bend. As you wrap toward the bend, you will have to force the thread wraps into the hair. Essentially, you're pinching the hair between these wraps and those wraps formed in Step 3, which will prevent the wing from rolling around the shank.

Step 5a. An alternate method for securing the wings uses thread wraps taken horizontally around the wing fibers.

With the left fingers, raise both the wing-fiber tips and butts upward above the shank.

Take 3 or 4 tight, horizontal turns of thread around the base of the wings. These turns of thread squeeze together the wraps used to mount the hair, causing them to compress tightly against both the hair bundle and the hook shank.

Step 6. To make a trimmed head, draw the hair butts out over the hook eye and clip them following the angle of the hook eye as a guide.

Step 7. To make a thread head, or a base for adding hackle or other materials, clip the hair close to the shank and cover the butts with tying thread.

Step 2a. This method is useful in securing thicker bundles of hair for bushy downwings.

Determine the wing length as in Step 2, and trim the hair butts even with the hook eye.

Step 2b. Take a slack wrap of thread around the wing-mounting point of the hair bundle.

Pinch the hair very tightly to keep it on the top of the shank.

Tighten the thread to flare the hair. When this first wrap is tight, take additional wraps to secure the hair further.

Step 2c. Now take a tight wrap of thread through the rear section of the hair butts. As you wrap, wiggle the thread back and forth to prevent binding the hair butts down, seating the thread instead at the base of the butts and anchoring them to the shank.

Take a second wrap, shown above, through the middle the butts, again wiggling the thread to work it down to the base of the butts.

Finally, take a third wrap close to the front of the butts to secure them.

These additional wraps secure sections of the hair butts and prevent the wing from shifting position.

The flared hair can be left as is, or trimmed to form a smaller head.

Method #63:

Tip-mount Hollow-hair Downwing

An unusual type of hollow-hair downwing is obtained by mounting the hair by the tip rather than the butts. Though not commonly seen, this approach to winging can eliminate any excessive flare in the hair. Because it puts the most buoyant part of the hair near the rear of the fly where it supports the heaviest part of the hook, this wing style can be dressed with less material than is required for the more familiar type of hollow-hair downwing (see **Method #62: Hollow-hair Downwing**, p. 311). The rear of the wing can be trimmed to shape for a well-defined silhouette.

Deer hair is used in the following demonstration, though elk is also highly suitable. Hair fibers that are relatively uniform in diameter throughout their length and have short, abruptly tapering tips will flare more to produce a higher wing. Hair with more

12

gradually tapering tips will lie closer to the shank (see "Hollow Hair," p. 2).

The main sequence shows the dressing for the basic tip-mount wing in which the fiber tips are secured and covered with thread, forming a foundation for a collar hackle or spun head. The alternate sequence shows a variation in which the hair tips are left intact to form a crosshackle on the finished fly.

Step 1. All tail, body, and rib material should be dressed prior to winging. Lay a thread foundation of about 6 or 7 wraps ahead of the body tie-off, toward the hook eye, and return the tying thread to the rear of the thread foundation

Clip and clean a bundle of hair as explained in **Method #2: Preparing and Cleaning Hair**, p. 68, and align the hair tips as shown in **Method #3: Stacking and Aligning Hair**, p. 69.

In the left fingers, consolidate the hair into a bundle. Trim off the hair tips about ⅛" from the end.

Position the hair atop the shank as shown. Pinch it tightly between the left fingertips and use the middle finger as a backstop against the hook shank to prevent the hair from rolling to the far side of the shank under thread pressure.

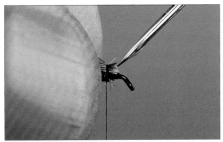

Step 2. Bind in the hair with 2 very tight thread wraps, moving toward the hook eye.

The hair tips can be very slippery. After a couple of wraps you can, if desired, apply a drop of cement for added strength. Use a dubbing needle to work some head cement or liquid CA glue into the exposed portion of the tips.

Step 3. Typically, a hackle is applied over the wing tie-in, and so the thread wraps should be smooth and even. Counterspin the bobbin to flatten the thread, and continue binding in the tips with very tight, even wraps until the rear of the hook eye is reached.

If any hair tips project beyond the tying thread, clip them off and cover them with thread.

Step 4. If the hair shows a tendency to roll around the hook shank under thread pressure, secure it as follows:

Raise the wing fibers and take 2 or 3 thread wraps against the rear base of the wing. Abut these wraps tightly against the wing fibers to pinch them against the mounting wraps.

Step 5. Finally, clip the rear of the wing to the desired length. Here, the cut has been angled to reproduce the silhouette of a natural caddis wing.

Step 1a. To form the wing and a crosshackle from the same bundle of fibers, prepare a clump of hair as in Step 1, but do not trim the hair tips.

Position the bundle of hair over the shank so that the hair tips extend beyond the mounting point a distance equal to the length of the crosshackle—about one hook gap.

Secure the hair with 5 or 6 very tight wraps of thread.

Step 2a. Using crisscross wraps, divide the fiber tips to form a crosshackle as explained in **Method #29: Cross Hackle**, p. 371. If desired, the crisscross wraps can be concealed with dubbing.

Trim the rear of the wing to the desired shape.

Method #64:
Flat Barb Downwing

Barbs from hackle, body, and flank feathers are frequently tied as "rolled" down-wings by consolidating the fibers into a bundle and dressing them as explained in **Method #57: Solid-fiber Downwing**, p. 305. However, flat sections of barbs can be mounted to form a panel-like downwing that is much like quill in appearance. Such wings can be used on traditional wet-fly dressings, and they are highly effective on patterns designed to imitate diving caddis.

One advantage of this technique is that the tyer may choose from feathers with a wide range of colors and markings. Body and flank feathers, as well as hen saddle, are typically used, but regardless of the particular plumage, the best feathers are webby right to the barb tips. The webbiness helps keep the individual barbs married together, preserving the panel-like appearance of the wing.

Even so, such wings are relatively fragile—much like quill wings in this respect—and are easily mangled by fish. For this reason, you may wish to treat the winging feathers with a misting of spray fixative to improve durability.

There are two basic approaches to preparing feathers for winging, the first shown in the main sequence, the second in the alternate sequence.

Step 1. If the plumage chosen is symmetrical, that is, if the barbs on either side of the stem are of equal length and curvature and make the same angle with the quill—such as the hen saddle shown on the left—both wings can be taken from a single feather.

Begin by stripping away the fuzzy barbs at the base of the stem. If desired, mist the entire feather lightly with a spray fixative, as we've done with the feather in the middle.

When the fixative is dry, use a pair of fine-pointed scissors, clip the stem so that the sections of barbs that remain on each side are equal in width to the hook gap, as shown on the right. Note that the feather tip that remains may have barbs long enough to form another pair of wings.

Step 2. With the thumb and forefinger, carefully fold the sections of barbs together, back-to-back, that is, with the dull sides together, as shown.

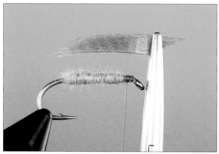

Step 2a. If the feathers chosen are highly asymmetrical, you will need a "left" feather and a "right" one, much as you would for a pair of quill wings.

Begin by stripping away the fuzzy barbs from the base of each stem, and misting the feather with a light film of spray fixative.

When the fixative is dry, cut a section of barbs from each feather, equal in width to the hook gap. Place the barb sections together, back-to-back, that is, with the dull sides together. The procedure here is identical to forming quill wings as explained in "Preparing Quill Wings," p. 243.

Step 3. The wings can now be mounted, much as you would quill wings, using any of the suitable techniques: **Method #9: The Pinch Wrap**, p. 30; **Method #10: The Bobbin Loop**, p. 31; **Method #11: The Langley Loop**, p. 32.

Step 4. When the wing is mounted, clip the butts of the barbs and bind them down with thread.

Method #65:
Bundled-fiber Delta Wing

Modern tyers seem to have abandoned bundled fibers in favor of feather tips and synthetic films in dressing delta wings. While these latter materials create a more clearly defined wing silhouette, bundled fibers give excellent support to a fly on the water and reproduce the pattern of scattered light that is characteristic of insect wings lying flush in the surface film.

Almost any material, solid or hollow hairs, synthetic fibers, and yarn, as shown in the following sequence, is suitable for this simple technique.

Step 1. If using hollow hair, you can dress a downwing as explained in **Method #62: Hollow-hair Downwing**, p. 311. But the technique shown in **Method #63: Tip-mount Hollow-hair Downwing**, p. 312, is especially effective for converting to a delta wing for a couple of reasons. The wing has less tendency to flare when divided, and the wing tips are formed from the hollowest portion of the hair which gives the fly excellent buoyancy.

If using solid fibers, such as the poly yarn shown here, dress a downwing as explained in **Method #57: Solid-fiber Downwing**, p. 305. Regardless of the material, it is best to keep the wing somewhat sparse.

When the wing is secure, use your fingers or a dubbing needle to divide the wing fibers into two equal bundles, one on the near side of the shank, and one on the far side.

With the left fingers, pull the bundle on the near side toward you. Take 2 or 3 crisscross wraps between the bundles to separate the wings, as shown.

With some materials, the wing bundles may be sufficiently consolidated at this point. With other materials, particularly hollow hair, the fibers may be splayed. To consolidate splayed fibers, take a few thread wraps around the base of each wing bundle to compact the hairs. If using hollow hair, these wraps should be snug but not tight; tight wraps will flare the hair.

After the crisscross and consolidation wraps are complete, take a wrap of thread around the hook shank only ahead of the wings. If desired, apply a drop of head cement or liquid CA glue to the thread wraps.

Step 2. If it is necessary to slant the wings further toward the rear of the hook, use the left fingers to preen the wings toward the hook bend. Take 2 or 3 tight thread wraps over the front base of the wings to force them rearward.

Step 3. If synthetic fibers or tip-mounted hair has been used, the wings can be trimmed to shape. Here, pointed wings have been fashioned, but the tips could be rounded if desired.

Film Downwings

Synthetic film materials lend themselves well to forming downwings. Because wings fashioned from these materials tend to be highly wind resistant, broad-profile, upright wings can spin during casting and twist tippets if they are not carefully dressed. The more aerodynamic, slant-back style of the downwing, however, sheds wind and greatly reduces twisted tippets. And film materials nicely reproduce the delicate translucence of wings on caddis, stoneflies, and midges, that are typically imitated in the downwing style.

A number of synthetic films are sold specifically for tying, and others—polyethylene storage bags, for example—are used by home tyers on a more improvisational basis. Further information about these materials can be found in the section on "Upright Foam and Film Wings," p. 281. Virtually all of them are suited to downwings. The downwing design also adds to the tyer's repertoire two types of materials that are generally not suited to upright winging. The first are very stiff films, such as the reinforced mesh fabric shown in **Method #45: Mesh-backed Feather Wings**, Step 5, p. 294, that are too wind-resistant for dressing in the upright style. The second are very flexible materials, such as Swiss straw, which often lack the rigidity to form upright wings.

Most film materials, however, lack any real buoyancy, and while they may not work to sink a fly, they do not materially contribute to its floatation. Thus patterns dressed with film downwings generally incorporate other materials—a foam body, for instance, or a hackle—that will help keep the fly on the surface.

Film upright wings can be somewhat fussy to tie, particularly if close attention is paid to achieving balance and an aerodynamic profile, which may explain why film materials are not more widely popular among tyers. But film downwings are relatively easy to dress. The material is easy to shape and behaves predictably under the tying thread, and the wings formed are both realistic and durable.

Method #66:
Folded Film Downwing

This is perhaps the simplest winging technique suited to films. The main sequence demonstrates how the material can be folded and cut to produce the characteristic tent shape of a caddis wing. The alternate sequence shows a film wing that can be used for grasshopper, adult stonefly, and midge patterns.

Virtually any film can be used with this method, though those materials that take a permanent crease—such as the Fly Film used in the following demonstration—produce the most attractively shaped wings.

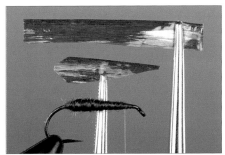

Step 1. All tail, body, and rib materials must be dressed prior to winging. Lay a short thread foundation ahead of the body, and return the thread to the front edge of the body material.

Cut a section of film that is twice as wide as, and slightly longer than, the finished wing. Note that many films are not manufactured to have identical properties in the lengthwise and widthwise directions. That is, they have a "grain," as described in the section on "Upright Foam and Film Wings," p. 281. If using such a material, the grain should run lengthwise along the wing.

Fold the material in half lengthwise, and with a pair of sharp scissors, trim the wing to the desired shape. Do not trim away the folded edge; the crease gives the wing its tent shape. You can trim the wings free-hand, as we've done here, or you can cut them using a paper template of the desired shape, as shown in **Method #37: Front-fold Film Wings**, Steps 1-3, p. 284.

Note that the cut wing tapers toward the front edge. The narrow width here simplifies mounting and prevents an overly bulky tie-in.

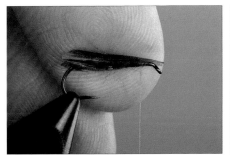

Step 2. Fold the film around the fly body, positioning it so that the wings are of the desired length and the crease runs directly down the top of the fly body.

Note that at the mounting point, the film material is sandwiched around the hook shank.

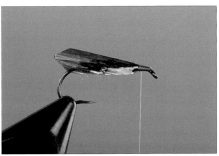

Step 3. With the left fingers, pinch the film tightly from the sides at the mounting point. A firm grip here will ensure that the wing remains in position as it is tied in.

Secure the wing with 4 or 5 tight, adjacent wraps, moving toward the hook eye. Clip the excess material and bind down the butts.

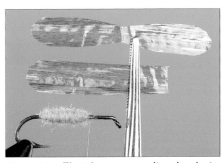

Step 1a. Flatwings are quite simple to fashion from film. Cut a strip of material as wide as the finished wing.

Many film materials are quite translucent, and two layers of material may be needed to produce a wing that is sufficiently dense in appearance. A simple double-layer wing can be fashioned by cutting a strip of material slightly longer than twice the length of the finished wing. Fold it in half crosswise, and trim the tips to shape as shown at the top.

To form a single wing, as shown on the bottom, simply cut a strip that is slightly longer than the finished wing, and trim the tip to the desired shape.

Step 2a. Prepare a body and mount the wing by using the technique shown in **Method #42: Folded Quill Downwing**, Steps 4a-5a, p. 290.

On some patterns, a slightly splayed wing may be desirable. To form the wing, use a folded strip of material cut to shape as in Step 1a, and slightly separate the tips as shown above. Hold the wings in this configuration during mounting.

Method #67:
Film Backwing

This technique was devised by John Betts for tying caddis wings of Zing film, but it can be used with a variety of materials. However, because Zing has some particular properties—it is quite thin, compressible, and easily trimmed—it is well suited to the technique shown in the main sequence. Materials that are thicker and crease less easily may be better suited to the technique shown in the alternate sequence.

This method produces a tent-shaped downwing formed of trimmed wing halves, very much like the effect obtained using cut or burned feather tips.

Step 1. Tail, body, and ribbing materials can be dressed prior to winging, or they can be applied after the wing material has been positioned in Step 2, as we're doing here. If these other components are to be dressed later, lay a short thread foundation along the winging area of the hook shank and position the thread at the wing-mounting point.

If the body is dressed first, lay a thread foundation of about 6 wraps toward the hook eye, and wind the thread back, leaving it about 2 thread-wraps ahead of the front edge of the body. The wing material will be mounted at this point; the wings will eventually be affixed in position directly at the front of the body.

Cut a strip of wing material, such as the Zing shown here, that is about one hook-gap in width and about 3 times as long as the finished wing. If the material has a "grain," (see "Upright Foam and Film Wings," p. 281), the grain should run lengthwise along the strip of material.

Mount the strip crosswise as explained in **Method #36: Crossmount Film Wing**, Step 2, p. 283.

The creases at the mounting point must be equalized to produce symmetrical wings. To accomplish this, use the thumb and forefinger of each hand to pinch the wing halves and pull them directly outward, as explained in **Method #36: Crossmount Film Wing**, Step 3.

Step 2. After equalizing the creases, add 2 or 3 more sets of tight crisscross wraps to secure the material to the shank.

If the tail, body, and rib materials have not yet been applied, dress them at this point. Note that the front edge of the body stops about 2 thread-wraps behind the wing-mounting point.

Position the thread directly behind the wings.

Step 3. John Betts positions the wings with a dubbed thread, as we're doing here, which produces a dubbed head on the fly. If a hackle is to be dressed at the head of the fly, the wings can be positioned with bare thread as shown in Steps 4a-6a.

Apply dubbing to a short length of thread. With the left fingers, draw the near wing back toward the hook bend. The upper edge of the wing should slant away from you, so that it lies directly down the top of the body, forming one half of the "tent."

To secure the wing in this position, take one wrap of the dubbed thread over the base of the near wing. As it is wrapped around the shank, the thread should pass behind the far wing. The wrap should be snug but not excessively tight.

Step 4. Pull the far wing back toward the hook bend, slanting the upper edge toward you so that it meets the upper edge of the near wing along the top of the body, thereby completing the tent shape, as shown here from the top

Secure the far wing with two snug wraps of the dubbed thread directly atop the wrap that secures the near wing.

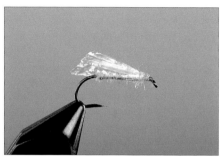

Step 5. If desired, another turn or two of dubbing can be added toward the eye of the fly. Whip-finish and clip the thread.

The wings can now be trimmed to the desired length and shape, as shown.

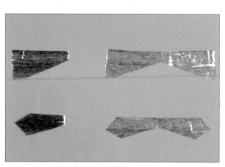

Step 1a. For this alternate procedure, it's best to dress any tail, body, or rib materials prior to mounting the wing, and then position the thread as noted in Step 1.

Cut a strip of film to the dimensions given in Step 1. Thicker film materials, such as the Fly Film used here, will tend to bunch up at the mounting point and be difficult to set in the final position if a full-width strip is used. Trimming them to narrow the mounting point will alleviate the problem.

Fold the material in half crosswise, and trim one corner of the fold, as shown at the upper left of the photo. Trimming like this produces a narrow "throat" in the middle of the material when it is unfolded, as shown at the upper right of the photo.

If desired, the entire wing can be shaped at this point by cutting the folded material to the finished wing length and shaping it to the desired profile, as shown at the lower left. Trimming the wings to shape while the material is folded will ensure symmetrical wings, as shown in the strip of material at the lower right.

Step 2a. Mount the wings—we're using a strip cut to the finished shape—flat across the top of the hook shank, as explained in Steps 1-2. Use snug, but not extremely tight wraps. Note that the straight edge of the strip, the one that was not trimmed to narrow the mounting point, is positioned toward the rear of the fly.

Step 3a. Pinch the wing halves close to the mounting point as shown, and pull to equalize the creases. Pull gently, and apply pressure as close as possible to the crisscross wraps, as shown here, not near the tips; some materials are slightly elastic, and pulling on the tips may cause the wings to stretch out of shape. The goal here is to get the wings to sit flat and symmetrically atop the shank.

When the wings are properly seated, take 2 or 3 more tight crisscross wraps to secure them firmly. Position the thread directly behind the wings.

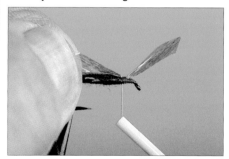

Step 4a. If the fly is to be dressed with a dubbed head, the wings can be set and completed by following Steps 3-5.

If a hackle or other material is to be added at the head of the fly, the wings must be set in position with bare tying thread.

Begin by grasping the tip of the near wing and pulling it back to the hook bend so that the straight edge of the film strip forms the top edge of the wing. The upper edge of the wing should slant away from you, so that it lies directly down the top of the body, forming one half of the "tent."

Secure the wing in this position by taking one very snug wrap of thread over the base of the near wing. The thread should pass behind the far wing as it is wrapped around the shank.

Step 5a. Pull the far wing back toward the hook bend, again making sure that the straight edge of the film strip forms the top edge of the wing. This far wing should be slanted toward you, so that it meets the upper edge of the near wing along the top of the body, thereby completing the tent shape.

Secure the far wing with two very snug wraps of thread. These wraps should lie directly atop the wrap that holds the near wing.

Step 6a. If the wings are set in the desired position—forming a symmetrical tent over the body—wrap the thread forward tightly. Bind down the film butts, as shown.

If the wings are slightly out of position, they can be altered at this point. Adjust the wings to sit properly. Pinch them tightly behind the mounting point. Take one snug wrap of thread toward the hook bend, which will secure the wing in the new desired orientation. Then wrap the thread forward, trim the film, and bind down the butts.

If the wings were not pre-trimmed to the finished shape, as shown in Step 1a, trim them to the desired length and shape.

Method #68:
Film Delta Wing

Synthetic films can be used to make delta wings for midges, craneflies, and flying ants. Though they take some advance preparation, such wings are less fussy to tie than feather-tip delta wings and, with the right materials, quite realistic in appearance.

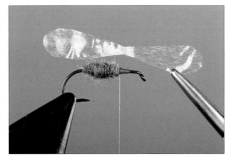

Step 1. All tail, body, and rib materials behind the winging point must be applied

prior to dressing the wing. We've dubbed an abdomen for a flying ant pattern here.

Wrap a short foundation of tying thread ahead of the body and return the thread to rearmost thread wrap, directly ahead of the body tie-off.

Cut a strip of film material as wide as, and twice as long as, the finished wing. If the material has a "grain," (see "Upright Foam and Film Wings," p. 281), the grain should run lengthwise along the strip of material.

Fold the strip in half crosswise, and use scissors to trim the wing to the desired shape. We're making teardrop-shaped wings.

Step 2. Position the wings over the top of the mounting point, as shown in this top view. The near wing is pointing rearward, making an angle of about 45 degrees with the hook shank.

Take 2 wraps of thread over the middle of the wing.

Step 3. Since films tend to bunch up under thread wraps you may need to straighten the creases in the material. Use the fingertips of each hand to pinch the film as near as possible to the thread wraps, then pull gently outward on each wing to seat it flat atop the hook shank, as shown.

When the wing is properly seated, take 2 more tight wraps of thread over the mounting point.

Step 4. Fold the far wing over the top of the body, using the mounting wraps as a hinge point.

Pull the wing tip to the far side of the hook, again making an angle of about 45 degrees with the shank. The two wings should form a symmetrical "V" shape.

Step 5. Holding the far wing in the correct position, take 2 wraps over the wing base.

Release the wing tip and check its placement. If it has twisted or rolled under thread pressure, reposition it.

When the wing is in the proper position, bind down the excess film with tying thread.

Method #69:
Folded Film Flatwing

Because they are easily trimmed to shape and are highly translucent, film materials make excellent flatwings on a variety of patterns. The technique shown in the following sequence is particularly useful for forming flatwings that extend beyond the rear edge of the body, as is characteristic of adult stoneflies and midges. But because the film is secured at the rear of the hook, the wing cannot twist around the shank and catch in the hook bend.

While this type of wing is easily formed with film materials, such as the Swiss straw shown in the following demonstration, other materials can be used. Darrel Martin, for instance, uses a quill segment clipped from a flight feather and reinforced with a light misting of spray fixative or flexible cement. If a quill segment is used, it should not be trimmed to shape as shown in Step 1; doing so will cause the barbs to separate when the wing is folded. Instead, the tips of the quill segment are secured at the rear of the hook, and the material is used full-width throughout the tying procedure.

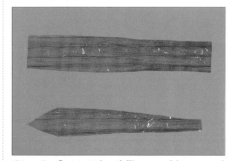

Step 1. Cut a strip of film as wide as, and twice as long as, the finished wing, as shown at the top.

Taper the front of the material as shown at the bottom. The wing is tied off at the narrow edge in the front. The shape of the taper cut into the material at this step will determine the shape of the finished wing.

Trim the rear edge to a more abrupt taper, also as shown at the bottom. The distance between the widest point of the wing material and the point at the rear is twice the length that the wing overhangs the rear of the body.

Note: some synthetic films are quite thin, and two layers of material trimmed to an identical shape and mounted as a single piece will produce a denser wing.

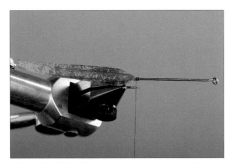

Step 2. If tails are desired, mount them first and position thread at the rearmost tailing wrap. If no tails are used, lay a short thread foundation at the rear of the shank, and position the tying thread at the rearmost point of the body.

Secure the wing material at the back of the hook by the point cut at the rear edge of the film.

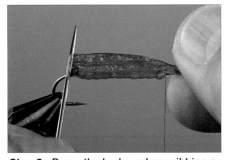

Step 3. Dress the body and any ribbing or other materials that lie underneath the finished wing. Position the tying thread at the front edge of the body.

With the left fingers, position a dubbing needle crosswise at the rear of the hook, and with the right fingers, fold the film over the needle. The fold should be formed at the base of the rear taper, at the widest point of the wing, as shown.

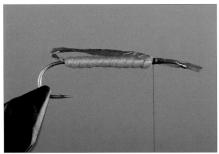

Step 4. Remove the dubbing needle and use the left fingers to pinch the film at the front edge of the body.

Secure the wing with several tight thread wraps.

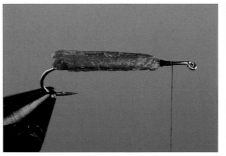

Step 5. Clip and bind down the excess. If desired, the rear edge of the wing can be clipped to shape, as shown. If a quill segment is used, do not trim the wing.

Fur-strip Downwing

Strips of fur on the hide can make highly effective wings on streamer and leech patterns. If the proper fur is chosen, such wings have excellent movement underwater—much like marabou, but considerably more durable. The best furs for this application are quite soft and supple, since stiffer furs, calf body for example, lack the flexibility to produce a wing with an attractive undulation. Rabbit is the most commonly used material; it is relatively inexpensive and available in a range of natural and dyed shades. Moreover, pre-cut strips of rabbit fur are readily available in fly shops, which simplifies the preparation of materials. Note, however, that hides can be cut either lengthwise or crosswise (see "Fur-strip Bodies," p. 142), and the distinction is important. Strips cut crosswise, often sold as "cross-cut rabbit" or "bunny hackle," are intended for dressing wrapped fur-strip bodies and are not suitable for fur-strip wings. The fur on a crosscut strip will lean to one side of the fly rather than slant back along the top of the body. Longitudinally cut strips, suitable for winging, are often sold as "Zonker Strips."

You can, of course, cut your own fur strips, which gives you some flexibility in controlling the width of the wing, and hence the quantity of winging material and its appearance in the water. The technique for cutting fur strips is detailed in **Method #42: Hide-strip Fur Chenille**, p. 132.

On smaller flies, however, rabbit fur may be too long to make a well-proportioned wing, and other soft furs—mink, squirrel, otter, and the like—can be used, though you must cut these yourself since materials of this type are generally not available pre-cut.

Regardless of the type of fur, however, the hide should be tanned, not dried, to give maximum movement in the water.

As explained in "Fur-strip Tails," p. 87, there is some overlap in tying terminology when dressing fur strips. In some cases, the fur strip is used to form two components simultaneously, such as a wing and tail or a body and tail; in other cases, the precise name of the fur-strip component varies from pattern to pattern. For instance, a fur strip tied on a Zonker pattern is ordinarily termed a "wing," whereas a fur strip dressed in a very similar fashion on a leech pattern is typically called a "body." Instead of grouping these technically similar tying methods together, we have attempted to preserve the most familiar tying terminology and have presented these techniques in separate sections of this book. Tyers dressing fur-strip wings may wish to consult related fur-strip techniques presented in **Method #30: Fur-strip Tail**, p. 88, and **Method #56: Lashed Fur-strip Body**, p. 143.

Method #70:
Fur-strip Downwing

The most popular application for a fur-strip wing is on the Zonker pattern, where it actually forms both wing and tail, as shown in the main sequence. The wing style, however, can be dressed on almost any type of body. Fur-strip wings can also be mounted Matuka style, as shown in Step 8.

A much fuller wing—one might even call it a body—can be formed by tying a double fur-strip wing, as shown in the alternate sequence. The technique shown here for producing the bottom-mounted wing can also be used to form a top wing on a fly in which a separate tailing material is desired.

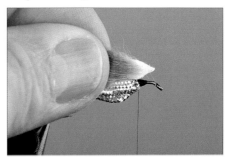

Step 1. Any body or ribbing material (or a separate tailing material, if desired) must be dressed prior to mounting the wing. Here, the body has been formed as shown in **Method #77: Woven-tubing Body**, p. 163. A similar type of body can be tied using the approach shown in **Method #9: Frame Underbody**, p. 46.

Position the tying thread at the wing-mounting point—here, the rearmost thread wrap of the body tie-off.

Select or cut a strip of longitudinally cut fur (see "Fur-strip Bodies," p. 142), such as the rabbit shown here. The width of the strip may vary with hook size and the tyer's taste. But as a rule, a strip ³⁄₁₆" wide is about right for streamers of size 2-8. The length of the strip depends upon the desired length of the "tail," or that portion of the wing that extends beyond the rear tie-off. For Zonkers and similar patterns, the strip should be slightly longer than the entire hook.

Notice that the fur has a natural curvature, slanting away from one end of the strip. This end is the front of the wing. With a razor blade or sharp scissors, trim the hide at the front of the wing to a point, as shown.

Clip off or pluck the hair from this point. Shaping the front edge of the hide and removing the hair simplifies mounting and makes a less bulky tie-in.

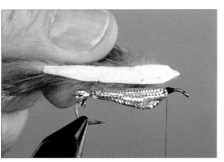

Step 2. Again using scissors or a razor blade, trim the hide at the rear of the wing to a slight taper. As shown above, this rear taper is formed on the section of wing that will project beyond the rear tie-off. Its purpose is to make this free end of the wing more mobile for a better action in the water.

Step 3. Position the strip atop the shank so that the rear edge of the shaved point is directly above the tying thread.

Using very tight thread wraps, bind down the end of the hide strip, working toward the hook eye. As you bind down the tip of the hide, work to create a smooth, tapering tie-in, since these thread wraps not only secure the wing but may also form the head of the fly or function as the base for a hackle to be added afterward.

When the wing is securely attached, whip-finish and clip the thread.

Step 4. Fold the fur strip forward over the hook eye and re-attach the tying thread at the rear of the body. If Mylar tubing or a similar material has been used for the body, as we've done here, re-attach the thread directly atop the wraps that were used to secure the tubing. If dubbing, chenille, or other material has been used, re-attach the thread directly behind the rearmost wrap of body material. The red thread shown here is traditionally used for the rear tie-down on Zonkers.

Step 5. Draw the fur strip back over the top of the shank. Pull it gently to keep the strip straight.

Use a dubbing needle to part the fur directly above the tying thread, as shown. Make this division perfectly crosswise to the hide strip, so that when the strip is bound down, no fur will be trapped beneath the thread. It may help to dampen the fur, as we've done here.

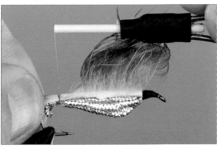

Step 6. Take 4 very tight turns of thread around the point on the hide where the hair has been parted, taking care not to bind down any fur. Make these wraps almost directly atop one another. You want a tight, narrow band of thread.

Step 7. When the rear of the wing is secure, tie off the rear thread with 2 or 3 half-hitches and clip. Apply a drop of head cement to all thread wraps.

Step 8. A somewhat different effect can be created by mounting the fur strip in the Matuka style, as shown here. The strip is bound to the body by spiraling turns of ribbing material.

The procedure is identical to that for binding in feather-tip Matuka wings, as shown in **Method #55: Matuka Feather Wing**, p. 303.

Step 1a. To create a double fur-strip wing, begin by mounting the top strip as shown in Step 3, but secure it with only 2 very tight wraps, as shown.

Prepare a second strip of fur for the lower wing, to be dressed on the underside of the shank, by clipping the front end to a point and removing the fur, as in Step 1. Since this lower wing will not extend beyond the body tie-off it need not be tapered at the rear. This fur strip should be slightly longer than the hook shank; a small amount of excess material is necessary for holding the strip during dressing. It will be clipped later.

Step 2a. Position the lower wing on the underside of the hook shank, as shown. Secure it with 2 tight wraps of thread. View the fly from the hook eye to ensure that the wings are in a vertical plane, directly atop and underneath the shank.

If necessary, adjust the position of the wings. When the alignment is satisfactory, bind in both tips of hide simultaneously, again working to create a smooth, tapered head.

When both strips are secure, whip-finish the thread and clip it, as shown here.

Step 3a. Fold both strips of fur forward toward the hook eye, and remount the tying thread at the rear of the body, as explained in Step 4.

Fold the upper wing strip back toward the hook bend, and use a dubbing needle to part the fur directly above the tying thread, as shown in Step 5.

Secure the upper wing with one tight wrap of thread, as shown.

Step 4a. Draw the lower wing along the underside of the hook shank. Pinch the very end of the fur strip against the hook bend to hold the strip in position.

Use a dubbing needle to part the fur at the tying thread.

Secure upper and lower wing strips simultaneously, with 4 tight wraps of thread.

Step 5a. When the strips are secure, tie off the thread with a few half-hitches and clip.

Clip the tag of material on the lower wing that projects beyond the rear tie-down.

Note that the lower wing has been dressed so that it doesn't form a "tail," but rather has been clipped off at the rear of the body. This same technique can be used to dress an upper wing if a separate tailing material for the fly is desired. The fly on the bottom, for example, is dressed with a fur-strip wing and marabou tail.

Method #71:

Woven-tubing Downwing

A simple downwing for attractor-style flies can be fashioned from a length of woven Mylar tubing that is mounted and frayed. Though this wing style is more typically used on steelhead patterns, it is sometimes incorporated into stillwater and sea-run trout flies. A version of this technique can also be used to hackle flies as shown in **Method #24: Mylar Hackle**, p. 373.

Step 1. All materials behind the winging point are dressed first. Position the tying thread at the front edge of the body.

Mount a length of woven tubing using very tight thread wraps; the material can be slippery. If a hackle or other components are to be applied ahead of the wing, form a smooth thread foundation with the mounting wraps.

Clip the tubing to the desired length.

Step 2. With a dubbing needle, fray the tubing to separate the individual strands.

SECTION THREE

Spentwings

Spentwings are dressed to lie in a horizontal plane, extending perpendicularly from either side of the hook shank. As the name suggests, they represent the outstretched wings of an exhausted or "spent" adult insect floating on the surface film. Their most common use by far is in tying mayfly spinners but spentwings are occasionally used as well in dressing adult damselfly imitations, craneflies, and even flying ants.

Like other wing styles, spentwings are tied with a wide range of materials, not all of which are necessarily chosen for the same reason. Some materials are selected primarily to imitate the delicate, glassy, cellophane-like appearance of the natural wings. Others may do only a workmanlike job of representation but offer other advantages such as visibility or buoyancy. These two characteristics are of particular importance to the angler. Since spentwing dressings rarely incorporate hackle—that is, apart from hackle that may be used to form the spentwings in certain techniques—the floatation of the fly must be borne entirely by tail, body, and wing materials. And because spentwing patterns float flush on the surface of the water, they can be difficult to see. The extent to which these are problems for the angler depends upon the specific fishing circumstances—water type, presentation distance, fly size, and so forth—but they are certainly common enough to make the judicious selection of winging material important. And in fact, some tyers occasionally use spentwing designs that incorporate a combination of materials to serve more than one of these purposes.

Nearly any of the materials used to tie upright or downwings can be dressed in the spentwing style, with one exception—quill segments. The structure of the material makes it difficult (though not impossible) to tie quill segments in the spentwing configuration, and in any case, such wings would prove extremely fragile.

The selection and preparation of most of the materials used to fashion spentwings have been discussed earlier in this chapter and are cross-referenced as necessary in the individual methods presented in this section.

Because the spentwings on an artificial fly have two distinct halves, they are closely related in terms of tying technique to upright, divided wings. Indeed many of the techniques for dressing spentwings incorporate procedures used in upright winging; such spentwings begin life as a vertical wing and are subsequently altered to lie in a horizontal plane.

Feather-tip Spentwings

Spentwings are often formed from the tips of hackle, flank, and body feathers. Any plumage suitable for upright winging can also be used for spentwings (see "Selecting Feathers for Feather-tip Wings," p. 248), but

hen-hackle tips, with their broad silhouette and rounded tips, are probably used most often by tyers. However, feathers that have been cut or burned to shape also make excellent spentwings and bring into the tyer's repertoire materials such as body and flank feathers that may not be suitably shaped when the tips are left natural. Techniques for creating such cut wings are explained in **Method #5: Cut Wings**, p. 249; **Method #6: Burned Wings**, p. 251; and **Method #10: Ogden Wings**, p. 256.

Feather tips tied spent produce a wing that is at once substantial and sparse. Because the feather tips lie flat on the water, the trout sees the full wing "imprint," yet the wing itself is only one feather-barb in thickness. Each barb contributes to both the shape of the wing and the support of the fly. Thus a relatively small amount of material is quite efficiently used. Moreover, feather-tip spentwings offer a profile that is realistic in appearance, and when the fly is resting on the water, light-colored feathers become quite translucent, much like the glassy wings of a mayfly spinner. For this reason, white feather tips are often used, as in Swisher and Richard's hen-spinner patterns. Some mayfly spinners and adult damsels, however, have wings with mottling or a distinct dark venation, and grizzly or other variant feathers, or patterned body feathers such as mallard flank, can be used to imitate these species.

Like most feather-tip winging styles, spentwings offer good durability; they are tougher than the very fragile loop spentwings, but not as sturdy as most bundled-fiber types. Their chief disadvantage is that they contribute little buoyancy to the fly. Recently many tyers, most notably René Harrop, have begun using CDC feathers tied spent to remedy this problem. Such wings greatly improve floatation, though they lack the clean, wing-shaped edges of other types of feather tips and in some ways more closely resemble bundled-fiber wings. Since CDC feathers are uniform in color, tyers sometimes secure a small quantity of synthetic fiber—usually Antron or Z-lon—across the top of the finished CDC wing to simulate mottling or venation, as shown in **Method #75: Lashed Fiber Spentwing**, Step 5, p. 325.

While natural, cut, or burned feathers are perhaps the most common feather-tip spentwing materials, almost any style of upright feather-tip wing can be tied spent, as shown in the following sequence.

Method #72:

Feather-tip Spentwing

This basic method is used to form spentwings from virtually any type of upright, feather-tip wing. Natural hackle tips, shown

in the following demonstration, cut wings, or burned wings are perhaps most commonly used, but as shown in Step 6, attractive spentwings can be formed from reverse-hackle or half-hackle upright wings.

The technique shown here results in a wing-mounting point with very low bulk, which simplifies dressing the very slender bodies characteristic of many mayfly spinners as well as damselfly adults.

Note that feather tips can also be tied spent using the procedure shown in **Method #74: Forced-split Spentwing**, Step 1a, p. 324.

Step 1. Begin by tying a pair of upright feather-tip wings using either **Method #7: Feather-tip Wings**, p. 252 (the technique shown here); **Method #8: Reverse-mount Feather-tip Wings**, p. 253; **Method #13: Reverse-hackle Wings**, p. 260; or **Method #14: Half-hackle Wings**, p. 261.

When the wings are complete, position the tying thread in front of the wing base. The wings in the photo have been mounted with black thread; for better visibility, red thread will be used to tie them spent.

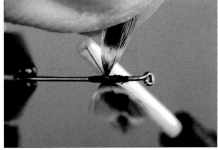

Step 2. Setting the wings in the spent position requires two sets of crisscross wraps, one to position the far wing and one for the near wing.

Use the left fingertips to pull the far wing directly outward, so that it lies in a horizontal plane, perpendicular to the hook shank as shown.

Raise the bobbin above the hook shank and begin passing the tying thread between the wings, toward the far side of the shank. As you do so, wrap the thread up against the feather stem of the far wing, pushing the wing down and toward the hook eye, as shown in this top view.

When the wrap is complete, the bobbin should end up beneath the hook shank directly behind the far wing.

Step 3. Bring the tying thread underneath the shank and up behind the near wing. Pass the thread between the wings toward the far side of the shank, this time abutting the thread against the front of the feather stem on the far wing. The thread pressure should force the wing further downward and back toward the hook bend, so the wing is now horizontal and perpendicular to the shank, as shown here from the top.

The far wing is now set in position.

Step 4. To set the near wing, use the left fingertips to pull the feather tip directly toward you. Hold the wing tip firmly with your left fingers since the torque of the tying thread will tend to push the wing upward as you complete the next wrap.

Bring the thread under the shank and raise it vertically. Now repeat Step 2, passing the thread between the wings, but this time wrap the thread against the feather stem on the near side, forcing the near wing toward the hook bend and partially holding it in the horizontal position, shown here from the top.

Step 5. Bring the thread under the shank behind the wings and up the far side. Repeat Step 3, bringing the thread between the wings toward the far side of the shank, but this time abutting the thread against the back of the feather stem on the near side. This wrap will push the wing tip toward the hook eye into its final position perpendicular to the shank, and hold it in the horizontal position, as shown in this top view.

Larger wings or thicker quills may require an additional set of wraps to set the wings in position. If so, repeat Steps 2-5.

When the wings are satisfactorily set,

take a wrap of thread around the hook shank only to lock in the crisscross wraps and prevent the wings from shifting.

A small drop of head cement can be placed at the wing-mounting point.

Step 6. Shown here are spentwings tied from reverse-hackle upright wings (left) and half-hackle wings (right).

Bundled-fiber Spentwings

Virtually any material that consists of fibers or strands can be tied in the spentwing style, though different types of materials, of course, permit or demand different techniques. This wide range of materials is one of the principal advantages of bundled-fiber spentwings, giving the tyer considerable latitude in selecting for certain wing characteristics. Wings with mottled markings or dark veins can be imitated by choosing appropriately marked feather barbs. Higher-visibility wings can be fashioned from light-colored hairs or a highly-reflective material such as Antron or Z-lon. Good floatation can be achieved with poly yarn, bundled CDC barbs, or hollow hairs.

Many anglers have observed that the spent wings of a natural insect lying flush in the surface film are less conspicuous for their wing-like shape than for the impression they produce of reflected and scattered light. They theorize that the trout's "search image" or recognition pattern of a spent fly centers more upon the quality of this glittery light pattern than on the characteristic clean-edged, rounded wing shape. Individual fibers resting in the surface film produce similar reflections and scatterings, and thus may appear more "realistic" to the trout than do more conventionally shaped feather-tip or film spentwings. This, at least, is the theory—as plausible as any, and it does account for the fact that bundled-fiber spentwings do make highly effective flies.

In any event, bundled-fiber spentwings are probably the most durable of any type and the techniques for tying them are among the simplest, provided the wings are kept sparse. Large clumps of materials are more difficult to affix securely to the hook shank. But more importantly, the purpose of the spentwing is twofold—first, to create the imprint of the wing on the surface film, and second to support the fly. Since both of these purposes are accomplished primarily by those wing fibers actually in contact with the water's surface, relatively little material is necessary. Unlike upright or downwings, where larger amounts of material may help to produce a desired

bulk or opacity in the wing, spentwings are generally more delicate and transparent—qualities better served by less material.

Method #73:
Thread-split Fiber Spentwing

Strictly speaking, this style of wing could be tied from any bundle of strands or fibers, natural or synthetic. In reality, it is largely restricted to natural hairs and feather barbs. Synthetic materials such as yarns are easier to tie using **Method #75: Lashed-fiber Spentwing**, p. 324.

Feather barbs tied in this style make an attractive spentwing and can make use of rooster neck or saddle hackles that are too large for other applications. Hen hackles, flank, and body feathers can be used as well. Any hair suitable for other wing styles (see "Selecting and Preparing Bundled Fibers," p. 262) can be used to tie spentwings. But hair that has a crinkly texture, such as natural wool or the calf tail used in the main sequence, is especially well suited to spentwings. The kinked fibers give the impression of density and support the fly well on the water even when a sparse amount of material is used.

Spentwings tied with hollow hair such as deer and elk add buoyancy to the fly. The tendency of the hair to flare under thread pressure has the advantage of spreading the fiber tips to make a broad wing with a relatively small amount of material. However, extra tying steps are necessary to consolidate the hair into a nicely shaped wing, and this technique is presented in the alternate sequence.

An unusual type of hollow hair spentwing can be formed by tip-mounting the hair as shown in Step 7a.

Step 1. Begin by preparing and mounting a bundle of fibers as shown in **Method #15: Bundled-fiber Post**, Steps 1-3, p. 264. The thickness of the bundle depends upon both hook size and the desired density in the wing, but as a point of departure for experimentation, try using a slightly smaller clump of fibers than you would use for a bundled-fiber post.

When the bundle is mounted and the butts bound down, position the tying thread at the frontmost mounting wrap, as shown. The wing fibers have been mounted here with black thread; for better visibility, red thread will be used to tie the wings spent.

Step 2. With your fingers or a dubbing needle, separate the bundle into 2 halves—one on the far side of the shank, one on the near side.

With the left fingers, swing the far clump 180 degrees, so that it lies alongside the hook shank with the tips pointing toward the hook bend.

Take two tight wraps of thread between the wing halves, forcing the thread tightly into the base of the far wing to set it in the spent position.

Step 3. Now draw the bundle of fibers on the near side toward the hook bend.

Bring the thread beneath the shank and take two tight wraps between the wings, this time forcing the thread tightly into the base of the near wing, as shown in this top view, to set it in the spent position.

Step 4. The wings will be roughly positioned at this point. Repeat Steps 2-3 until the wings lie in a horizontal plane, perpendicular to the shank as shown.

When the wings are properly set, take a wrap of thread ahead of the wings around the hook shank only.

If desired, apply a drop of head cement to the wing-mounting wraps.

Step 5a. After dividing the bundle with thread wraps as shown in the preceding steps, wings made of hollow hair (or those made from large bundles of solid fibers) probably won't be well consolidated; the splayed fibers won't have a winglike shape.

To neaten up the wing, grasp the hair tips of the far bundle and draw them into the spentwing position on the far side of the shank. Flatten the tying thread, and take 2 or 3 wraps around the base of the far wing, as shown here. These wraps should be made under relatively light thread pressure—just enough to consolidate the fibers into a tighter bundle. Too much thread tension will simply cause the hair to flare even more.

After the last wrap is taken, bring the bobbin beneath the shank to the front of the wings. Take a wrap of thread around the hook shank only.

Step 6a. Execute the same procedure with the near wing, pulling the tips toward you and taking 2 or 3 wraps of thread under light pressure around the base of the near wing, as shown.

When these wraps are completed, bring the thread above the hook shank and between the wings. Take a wrap of thread ahead of the wings around the shank only.

Step 7a. Preen the wings into a flat, fanlike shape, and apply a drop of head cement or liquid CA glue to the thread wraps at the wing base. Let a bit of cement bleed into the base of the wings to help hold them in position.

Step 8a. Here, a spentwing is fashioned by mounting the hair by the tip. Not only do the hollow hair butts provide good floatation near the wing tips, but the hair can be trimmed to shape, as shown here.

Method #74:
Forced-split Spentwing

This technique is identical to the one described in **Method #22: Forced-split Wings**, p. 270, for creating upright wings. Here, however, a smaller bundle of fibers is used for the wing, and the material drawn between the wing halves is used to force the wing into the spent position, creating at the same time a humped thorax. The method is most practical with feather barbs or natural hairs, since synthetic yarns and stranded materials are more easily tied as spentwings using **Method #75: Lashed-fiber Spentwing**, p. 324.

If the winging fibers are sufficiently long, such as the calf tail used here, the untrimmed fiber butts can be used to divide the wings, and this approach is shown in the main sequence.

The approach shown in the alternate sequence—using a separate piece of material to force the wings into the spent position—has a number of applications. It can be used when the winging fibers are not long enough to apply the technique shown in the main sequence. Or it can be used to improve the buoyancy or visibility of low-floating spinner patterns. Materials such as CDC, deer hair, poly yarn, and closed-cell foam (used in the alternate sequence) can be used to increase floatation, while brightly colored material can be used to make the fly more visible.

This use of a material to force bundled-fiber upright wings into the spent position can be also be used to fashion feather-tip spentwings; an example is shown in Step 6.

Step 1. Begin by mounting the winging material as shown in **Method #22: Forced-split Wings**, Step 1, p. 270.

In this technique, it is not possible to apply body materials to the underside of the thorax area once the wings have been secured in the spent position. There are two options for forming this area of the body. You can fashion it from tying thread, shown in the hook on the left, in which case the thread used to mount the winging fibers should be of the appropriate color (we're using black here for better visibility). Or, once the wing fibers are secured, you can apply dubbing to the thread and cover the wing-mounting wraps; when the frontmost thread wrap is reached, raise the wing fibers and take a turn or two of dubbing immediately ahead of the wing, as shown on the hook at the right.

After the desired thorax has been formed, position the tying thread ahead of the wings.

Step 1a. To split the wing fibers with a separate material, mount the wing (we're using barbs from a mallard flank feather) as in Step 1. In this case, however, trim the butts and bind them down with thread.

Mount the material that will be used to divide the wing directly atop the wing butts. This material can be positioned in one of two ways. The fly on the left shows a strip of foam wrapped directly up to the base of the wing. When affixed in this position, the foam will form a relatively small and inconspicuous hump between the wings, and allow you to dub the remainder of the thorax after the wings have been set in position.

On the hook shown at the right, the foam strip is bound in toward the hook bend. When material mounted in this fashion is folded over, it creates a more pronounced and visible hump. The farther the material is bound toward the hook bend, the larger this hump will become. This approach, however, does not allow for applying any body materials to the thorax area after the wings are set. As explained in Step 1, a suitably colored tying thread should be used or dubbing should be applied over the wing butts and ahead of the wing.

The technique for affixing the wing in position is identical to that shown in the main sequence. Proceed to Step 2.

Step 2. Divide the bundle of wing fibers into two smaller clumps, and fold the butts toward the hook eye and down between

the wing halves as shown in **Method #22: Forced-split Wings**, Steps 1-2, p. 270.

Pull the wing butts firmly with your right hand to force the wing halves down into a horizontal plane, as shown.

Step 3. With your left hand, grasp the bobbin and take 2 tight wraps of thread over the butt fibers, directly ahead of the wing.

Step 4. With your left hand, preen the wing halves back against the hook shank toward the bend.

Take 4 or 5 tight wraps over the fiber butts moving toward the base of the wing.

Step 5. Release the wings and check their position. They should lie in a horizontal plane, extending perpendicular to the hook shank, as shown. If the wings lean toward the hook eye, repeat Step 4, adding additional wraps toward the wing base, forcing the hump of wing-butt material more tightly into the wings.

Step 6. When the wing position is satisfactory, clip the fiber butts and secure with tying thread. If the body has not been dubbed, you can apply a drop of head cement to the thread wraps beneath the wings on the underside of the shank.

The finished wings are on the upper

left; the fly on the upper right shows the effect of dubbing the body, as explained in Step 1. The flies at the lower left and lower middle show the folded foam strips from Step 1a; the fly on the lower right suggests how the technique shown in the alternate sequence can be used to divide other types of spent wings—here, a pair of feather tip wings have been dressed with a "bright spot" of orange poly yarn.

Method #75:
Lashed-fiber Spentwing

This may well be the single most popular way of dressing spentwings. The technique is compatible with almost any stranded synthetic material, though poly yarn is a favorite among tyers for its buoyancy, durability, and ease of tying.

The lashing technique described here can also be used to secure a sparse bundle of strands over spentwings of other types, as shown in Step 5, where a CDC feather-tip wing has been topped with lashed strands of Z-lon to suggest venation when the wings are viewed from underneath.

Two suitable techniques for lashing synthetic fibers atop the hook have been presented in **Method #8: The Lash Mount and Crisscross Wrap**, p. 29, and **Method #15: Bundled-fiber Post**, Steps 1a-1d, p. 265. A slightly different version is shown below.

Step 1. Lay a short thread foundation over the winging area, and position the thread at the wing-mounting point.

Clip a bundle of fibers slightly longer than the total wing length. The extra material will be trimmed away to shape the wing tips.

Lay the material directly along the top of the hook shank so that the center of the fiber bundle is directly over the mounting point. Secure it with three tight wraps of thread.

Step 2. Pull the rear section of material toward you, perpendicular to the hook shank. Bring the tying thread up behind the near wing, angling it forward over the top of the shank and crossing the base of wing fibers to hold the wing in position.

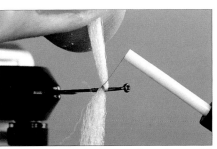

Step 3. Pull the other section of material away from you, perpendicular to the shank, and continuing the wrap begun in Step 2, bring the tying thread down ahead of the far wing. Again, cross the base of the fibers to hold the far wing in position.

Step 4. Add several tight crisscross wraps over the wing-mounting point, pausing a few times to pull the wing tips directly outward and squaring them perpendicular to the hook shank.

Step 5. When the wing is secure, trim the wing tips to length and, if desired, shape them; the wings on the left have been rounded slightly.

The fly on the right shows a few strands of Z-lon lashed over a pair of CDC feather-tip wings dressed using the technique in **Method #72: Feather-tip Spentwing**, p. 321. The lash and crisscross wraps can be used to combine materials like this on almost any spentwing style.

Step 5a. Synthetic fibers allow for trimming the wing to more realistic shapes. Austrian tyer Roman Moser clips spentwings, particularly on larger mayfly patterns, to the shape shown here. The "notches" at the rear of the wings simulate the smaller hind wing found on most mayflies. Moser also uses waterproof markers to create mottling or markings on the wings when it is appropriate to the species imitated.

Method #76:
Gathered Collar-hackle Spentwing

Spentwings that are very light and delicate in appearance can be fashioned by consolidating the barbs of a hackle wrapped collar style. This approach eliminates the extra steps required to strip barbs from the feather stem and mount them separately as in other bundled-fiber techniques. Stripping and bundling fibers, however, allows the use of oversize hackle barbs, since the butts can be clipped; gathering barbs requires that the correct size of hackle be used at the outset.

Though any type of hackle can be employed, most tyers prefer top-quality rooster hackle, either neck or saddle, for the purpose. The stiff, glossy, web-free barbs resist water absorption and better support the fly in the surface film. While it is possible to fashion spentwings in this manner from a spun-hair hackle (see **Method #22: Spun-hair Collar Hackle**, p. 370), most tyers prefer to dress hair spentwings using **Method #73: Thread-split Fiber Spentwing**, p. 322 or **Method #74: Forced-split Spentwing**, p. 323. Either of these methods is more direct and requires fewer steps.

There are two basic approaches to this technique. In the main sequence, hackle barbs are gathered together with tying thread, a technique that produces a slightly neater wing and gives the tyer some latitude in the selection of materials used to dress the thorax. Since the barbs must be gathered and held in the fingertips, the method is best suited to hook size 16 and larger, though a nimble-fingered tyer may find that smaller sizes are feasible. The alternate sequence shows how a dubbed thread can be used to consolidate the hackle barbs. The wing formed is somewhat less tidy than the one formed in the main sequence, but in the overall dressing of the fly, this method is somewhat more efficient since the wings and thorax are formed simultaneously. It does, however, restrict the tyer to dubbing as the thorax material.

Step 1. Select a hackle feather with barbs approximately equal in length to the hook shank. Wrap a collar hackle that spans the wing-mounting point, as explained in **Method #4: Single-Hackle Dry-fly Collar**, p. 351. The precise number of wraps of hackle varies some with hook size, feather quality, and the desired wing density, but with a good grade of hackle, about 5 or 6 wraps is sufficient for a #14 hook.

If a denser wing is desired, do not take additional wraps along the hook shank;

the hackle collar will become too wide to form the wing easily. Instead, begin by mounting and wrapping 2 hackles as explained in **Method #7: Multiple-hackle Collar**, p. 354. If a sufficiently long saddle hackle is used, two or three layers of barbs can be wrapped as explained in **Method #9: Overwrapped Collar Hackle**, p. 356. Wrapping multiple hackles or overwrapping a single hackle will, however, produce additional width in the thorax.

Whether wrapping one or more feathers, the hackle collar should occupy no more than about ⅓ of the length of the hook shank, and should be centered around the wing-mounting point.

After the collar is formed, wrap the tying thread back through the collar, wiggling it as you wrap to avoid binding down any barbs, and position the thread at the middle of the collar, as shown.

Step 2. The near wing will be formed from the hackle barbs on the near side of the shank. That is, if you view the collar from the hook eye, all the barbs from the 6 o'clock position to the 12 o'clock position will form the near wing.

Using a dubbing needle, your fingers, or a combination of both, gather these barbs together into a bundle and pull them directly toward you, as shown in this front view. The wrapping procedure in Step 3 is easiest if the hackle tips are held in the right fingers and the bobbin manipulated with the left hand.

Step 3. Take 4 or 5 tight wraps of thread around the base of the gathered barbs, as close to the hook shank as possible, as shown in this bottom view. This wrapping is a bit awkward since the bobbin must be released once during each wrap.

Rooster hackle is very slippery, and one problem you may experience is that the wing-binding wraps will slide toward you, seating themselves some distance from the hook shank. There are a couple of measures that help counteract this tendency. First, do not pull the barb tips too tightly in the right fingers. Barbs near the front and back of the collar must "stretch" to the middle to become part of the wing bundle. Thus the tips of these barbs must be allowed to slip just a bit through the right fingers as thread pressure compresses the bundle. Pinching the barb tips too tightly inhibits the barbs from consolidating under the binding wraps. Second, elevate the barb tips in the right fingers slightly above the hook shank, since the tying thread cannot slide uphill. Finally, you can apply a small amount of dubbing wax to the portion of thread used for the binding wraps to prevent slippage.

Step 4. When these wraps are complete, raise the tying thread above the hook, bring it over the thorax, and down through the center of the barbs on the far side of the shank. Positioning the thread this way will ensure that the far wing is formed at the proper location.

Grasp the remaining hackle barbs in the left fingertips and pull them outward from the hook shank, directly opposite the far wing, as shown. Again, take 4 or 5 tight wraps of thread—shown here from the top—as close to the hook shank as possible.

Step 5. When the hackle barbs have been gathered to form the far wing, take a couple of crisscross wraps across the thorax, as shown in this top view, to lock in the wing-binding wraps.

At this point, the hackle barbs may form a bundle that is almost cylindrical. They must be fanned to give a more wing-like shape that better supports the fly. Using the fingertips of both hands, grasp the barb tips of the far wing. Pull about ⅓ of the barbs toward the hook bend, another ⅓ toward the hook eye, leaving the middle ⅓ perpendicular to the shank. Continue pulling and preening until the barbs are evenly spread into a fanlike shape.

Repeat this process with the near wing.

When the wings are satisfactorily fanned, apply a drop of head cement to the thread wraps, allowing a small amount of cement to bleed into the base of each wing to affix the barbs in position.

Step 1a. This alternate technique works best if only a single feather is used; two feathers can be wrapped, or a single feather overwrapped, but the resulting wings will not be as neat as those formed by a single hackle.

Wrap a collar hackle as explained in Step 1.

Position the tying thread at the front of the collar and dub about 2 inches of the thread. The dubbing should be applied in a moderate density. Too thinly applied, the dubbing will not give adequate coverage on the thorax; too much dubbing will build up disproportionate bulk in the thorax.

Take one turn of dubbing ahead of the collar, firmly abutting the base of the hackle barbs.

(Optional) Dick Talleur recommends clipping a small "V" notch lengthwise through top of the hackle collar and again through the bottom. These notches facilitate gathering the barbs to form the wings. We're omitting this step.

Step 2a. The hackle barbs are consolidated into wings using crisscross wraps above and below the hook shank. The wrap below the shank is formed first.

Bring the tying thread beneath the hook shank, crossing the hackle collar, and dividing the barbs so that half the barbs are on the far side of the dubbing and half on the near side. Dividing the barbs evenly is easiest if you "sight down" the hook from the bend when bringing the dubbing beneath the shank and across the hackle collar.

Finish this wrap by holding the dubbed thread vertically on the near side of the shank, behind the hackle collar, as shown.

Step 3a. Pass the dubbed thread over the top of the shank and down the far side.

Bring the dubbing underneath the shank, through the division in the hackle barbs, and crisscrossing the first wrap.

Finish the wrap with the dubbing raised vertically on the near side of the shank, ahead of the hackle collar, as shown.

Step 4a. To form the crisscross wrap atop the hook shank, use your left fingertips to pull half the hackle barbs toward you, as shown in this top view.

Pass the tying thread over the top of the shank through this division, and down behind the far wing. As you make this wrap, hold the barb tips in position.

Step 5a. Bring the thread beneath the hook shank and up the near side, behind the near wing.

Gather the hackle barbs on the far side of the shank and then pinch them by the tips. Pull them away from you, and maintain your grasp.

Bring the thread across the top of the shank, between the wings, and crisscross the first wrap, as shown here from the top.

Step 6a. Take a turn of dubbing around the hook shank ahead of the wings.

If the wings are not sufficiently consolidated, or the thorax not adequately covered by the dubbing, repeat Steps 2a-5a. Make certain to hold the wing tips in position as you perform these additional crisscross wraps.

Method #77:

Gathered Parachute-hackle Spentwing

Like collar hackles, parachute hackle can be gathered to form a spentwing, a process that is in fact easier since parachute hackles are already mounted in a horizontal plane. Since the barbs are only partially or loosely gathered, however, spentwings formed from parachute hackle are not quite as tidy as those formed from stripped, bundled fibers or from collar hackle as demonstrated in preceding methods.

There are 3 procedures shown below, each identified by a number/letter combination, in which the number indicates the tying sequence and the letter specifies the step within that sequence. That is, Steps 1a-1e constitute one method; Steps 2a-2d another; and so on.

The first two sequences demonstrate how the parachute post can be used to gather the hackle fibers into a spentwing. In both cases, the post material serves as the wrapping base for the hackle, but it can be chosen to serve other purposes as well. A piece of brightly colored material such as Krystal Flash, or the Antron yarn shown in Step 1a, can be used to make flush-floating spinner patterns more visible to the angler. A buoyant material, such as poly yarn, CDC, or the foam shown in Step 2a, can be used to give additional floatation to the fly. Both of these techniques are particularly useful on smaller flies, where very short hackle barbs can prove troublesome to manipulate when using the bundled-fiber or gathered collar-hackle methods.

The last procedure shows the use of a dubbed thread to divide a postless parachute hackle.

This first sequence illustrates a technique we first saw in Gary Borger's work where he uses the method to dress a wing for an adult damsel pattern. It produces a spentwing that is roughly semi-circular in shape.

Step 1a. Tie in a parachute post; the post should be left at least one inch high.

Wrap a parachute hackle as explained in **Method #31: Single Parachute Hackle—Horizontal Wrap**, p. 383. Position the tying thread ahead of the parachute post.

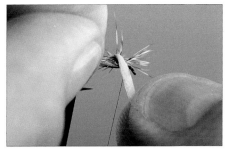

Step 1b. With your left fingers, grasp the tips of the hackle barbs that lie ahead of the parachute post on the near side of the hook shank, and preen them toward you as shown.

With your right fingers, fold the post forward and pull it downward through the gap you've made in the hackle barbs. Holding the post firmly below the hook shank will keep the barbs on the near side of the shank in position, freeing your left fingers for the next step.

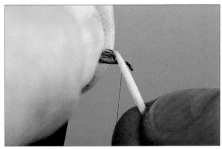

Step 1c. With your left thumb and index finger, lightly pinch the hook shank just behind the eye. Slide your fingers toward the hook bend, preening back the barbs on both sides of the parachute post and holding them against the hook shank, as shown.

Step 1d. Position the parachute post material atop the hook shank, and use the fingertips of the left hand to hold it in position, as shown.

Bind the post material to the top of the shank with 4 or 5 tight wraps of thread.

Step 1e. Release the barbs in your left hand and check the wing position. The frontmost barbs should be perpendicular to the hook shank and lying in a horizontal plane. If the barbs lean toward the hook eye, preen them back as shown in Step 3,

and take additional wraps of thread toward the hook bend, binding the post material more tightly against the hackle barbs to stand them outward.

Clip the excess post material and bind the butts with thread.

In this approach, a separate piece of material is bound in behind the parachute post and folded over to consolidate the hackle fibers into a more conventionally shaped wing—a technique we have seen several tyers use.

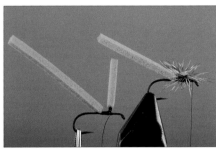

Step 2a. The most efficient way to dress this style of spentwing is to form the parachute post and leave the butt end of the post material long enough to fold over and consolidate the hackle barbs. If desired, separate materials can be used for the wing post and the folded strip, but since the wing post will eventually be clipped off, there is little to be gained by using two materials.

The hook on the left shows a strip of foam mounted in the proper position. The foam is bound in at the post-mounting point very tightly, and secured to the top of the hook shank with 4 or 5 tight wraps toward the hook bend. The thread is returned to the post, and wrapped horizontally up the post a short distance to create a base for the parachute hackle (see **Method #34: Foam Post**, p. 282).

At this point, body materials are applied, making certain to cover the thread wraps between the parachute post and the strip of material at the rear. We're omitting this step for a clearer illustration.

After the post is formed, wrap a parachute hackle as explained in **Method #31: Single Parachute Hackle—Horizontal Wrap**, p. 383. Finally, clip off the excess parachute post just above the topmost wrap of hackle, as shown on the right, and apply a drop of head cement to the top of the post, letting a bit of cement bleed down to the hackle stem and into the base of the barbs.

Step 2b. Use your fingertips to preen the barbs behind the post, on the near side of the shank, directly toward you, as shown. This will create a gap in the hackle through which the strip of foam is folded.

Bring the strip of foam forward

through the division in the hackle barbs, as shown.

From this point, the barbs are further consolidated and the foam strip bound down by using the technique shown in Steps 1b-1d.

Step 2c. When the strip has been bound in ahead of the parachute post, use your fingertips to spread the hackle barbs evenly in a horizontal plane, making narrow, fan-like wings of uniform density.

If necessary, additional thread wraps can be taken as shown in Step 5.

Step 2d. When the barbs are satisfactorily positioned, clip the excess material and bind down the butt.

The following technique was used often by Pennsylvania tyer Chauncy Lively to dress spentwings from a postless parachute hackle.

Step 3a. The fly is dressed with tails, abdomen, and a postless parachute hackle. Any of the techniques shown in "Postless Parachute Hackle," p. 393, can be used, but this technique works best with a low-bulk "hub" on the parachute hackle. Lively favored the approach shown in **Method #40: Folded-post Parachute Hackle**, p. 395, but **Method #41: Stem-loop Parachute Hackle**, p. 395, or **Method #42: Mono-loop Parachute Hackle**, p. 397, are suitable as well.

Position the tying thread directly ahead of the parachute hackle base, and dub a length of the thread.

With the left fingers, gather all the barbs on the near side of the shank, and draw them toward you, as shown in this top view.

Bring the dubbing thread over the top of the parachute-hackle "hub," and down the far side of the shank behind the hackle. This wrap partially separates the barbs

gathered on the near side of the shank from those on the far side.

Step 3b. Bring the thread beneath the shank and toward you. Take a wrap of the dubbing over the top of the hub again, completing a crisscross wrap.

Step 3c. Repeat Steps 3a-3b as necessary to consolidate the hackle barbs into a spentwing configuration and, simultaneously, dress the thorax.

Method #78:
Clipped Hackle Spentwing

This is a simple, shortcut method to creating spentwings. The wings produced are not quite as neat, well-shaped, or dense as those formed with other techniques, but the method is quite fast and produces perfectly useable flies.

The main sequence shows how spentwings are produced from collar hackle, and the alternate sequence shows the technique for trimming parachute hackle. In both cases, the key to producing good spentwings is to hackle the fly heavily in the beginning, since most of the barbs will be lost to trimming.

For flies about size 14 and larger, a collar hackle of spun hair can be dressed and clipped, as shown in Step 3. This style of wing has a strongly veined appearance when viewed from underneath and gives exceptional floatation to spinner patterns.

Step 1. Wrap a collar hackle that spans the wing-mounting point. The hackle cho-

sen should have barbs equal in length to the hook shank, and the collar can be formed, as we're doing here, from two rooster neck hackles dressed as explained in **Method #7: Multiple-hackle Collar**, p. 354. If a sufficiently long saddle hackle is used, two or three layers of barbs can be wrapped as explained in **Method #9: Overwrapped Collar Hackle**, p. 356. More or fewer wraps of hackle can be used depending upon the desired density of the finished wing and the characteristics of the particular hackle used.

If hollow-hair spentwings are desired, dress a hackle as explained in **Method #22: Spun-hair Collar Hackle**, p. 370.

Step 2. Sighting down the shank from the hook eye, trim away the barbs that project upward from the top of the shank. Clip them very close to the hackle stem.

Notice the broad angle between the uppermost remaining barbs. These barbs do not lie in the horizontal plane, and hence will not materially aid in supporting the fly. But they do add density in the appearance of the finished wing.

Step 3. Repeat Step 2, clipping away barbs from below the shank. You may find it easiest to invert the hook in the vise to get access to the underside of the hook.

The fly on the left has been dressed in this sequence. Notice that the angle between the barbs remaining below the shank is equal to the angle between the barbs above it, and that the resulting wings are symmetrical.

The fly on the right shows the spentwings produced by clipping a spun-hair hackle. Note that the clipped butts have been left slightly long to form a thorax and aid in fly floatation. The butts can also be clipped flush with the body and a thorax formed from dubbing or other body materials.

Step 1a. Parachute hackles can be clipped to form spentwings as well.

Dress a parachute hackle as explained in **Method #31: Single Parachute Hackle—Horizontal Wrap**, p. 383. For extra density in hackling, you can use two or more feathers as explained in **Method #34: Multiple-hackle Parachute**, p. 389.

The parachute post can be left long, or clipped, as we've done here, just above the topmost wrap of hackle. Apply a drop of head cement to the stem of the topmost hackle wrap, letting the cement bleed down the post and into the base of the hackle barbs.

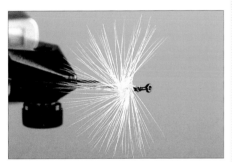

Step 2a. View the hook from above the shank, and clip away the barbs that project forward toward the hook eye. Trim them close to the parachute post.

Notice the broad angle left between the frontmost barbs. These help create a fan-shaped wing.

Step 3a. Repeat Step 2a, this time clipping away the barbs behind the parachute post that project toward the hook bend. The angle between these rearmost barbs should match the angle between the frontmost barbs to create a symmetrical wing.

Loop Spentwings

Loop-style wings can be tied spent to create a silhouette with a well-defined shape and clear edge when resting on the surface film. Like the upright version, the basic loop spentwing defines only the wing perimeter and has a hollow interior. The particular requirements of a spentwing, however—most notably that it must assist in floating the fly—limits the materials that can be used for the basic loop. The mallard flank fibers used for upright wings in **Method #31: Loop Wings**, p. 278, are not entirely practical for spentwings, at least on larger patterns. The barbs lack sufficient stiffness to support the fly and tend to absorb water as well. Moreover, these barbs are rather fragile, and without the protection of the collar hackle used with the upright wings, would be reduced to shreds in short order. Stripped hackle stems and monofilament tippet material shown in **Method #32: Slip-loop Wing**, p. 279, are rather heavy and, again, lack the necessary buoyancy.

The best material for loop spentwings is poly yarn, though Antron or Z-lon may also be used. With yarn, a number of thin filaments form the wing, providing additional surface area of material to help support the fly. Poly yarn is also sufficiently buoyant to help float the fly.

As shown in the following method, a basic loop wing can be overlaid with lashed strands of a second material—usually strands of poly yarn, Antron, Z-lon, or Krystal Flash. This "overwing" suggests wing venation and provides additional surface area to aid in floatation.

Method #79:
Loop Spentwing

This sequence shows the technique for tying a basic loop wing in the spent position. Since these wings must help support the fly in the surface film, you may wish to use a slightly larger amount of material—we're using poly yarn here—than would be used for an upright loop wing, which has no real structural function in the dressing.

Optional Steps 5 and 6 describe the procedure for making an overlaid wing, which gives a veined appearance to the interior of the loop wing and additional support to the fly.

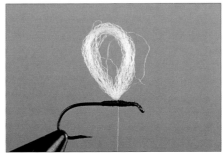

Step 1. Mount a pair of upright, divided loop wings as explained in **Method #31: Loop Wings**, p. 278. After mounting one

end of the yarn strand used to form the wings, comb the fibers to untangle them; when forming the loop wings, take care to fold the yarn so that the fibers maintain a flat, ribbon-like shape. Both of these procedures will facilitate dividing the wings in Steps 7-8 of the aforementioned tying sequence.

When the wings are mounted, position the tying thread directly in front of the wing base. Black thread has been used to mount the wings; for better visibility, red thread will be used to tie them spent.

Step 2. The procedure for tying the wings in the spent position is identical to that used in **Method #72: Feather-tip Spentwing**, p. 321. In the interests of brevity, the instructions here are condensed, and readers requiring more detail should consult **Method #72**.

This technique involves two sets of crisscross wraps, one at the base of each wing.

Begin by pulling the far wing outward into the spent position. Bring the tying thread over the top of the hook shank, and angle it back between the wings. Continue bringing the thread down behind the far wing so that the thread just crosses the wing base. This wrap will force the wing slightly downward and forward.

Pass the thread beneath the shank and up behind the near wing. Bring the thread above the shank and angle it forward between the wings, again wrapping just over the base of the far wing. This wrap will push the wing further downward and back perpendicular to the hook, as shown in this top view.

Take one wrap ahead of the wings around the shank only to lock the crisscross wrap in position. If the far wing is not yet exactly in the spent position, it can be adjusted later.

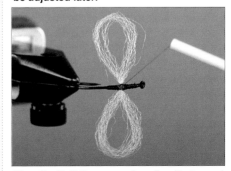

Step 3. Pull the near wing directly toward you. Make a crisscross wrap as described in Step 2, but this time as you bring the thread between the wings, it should just cross over the base of the near wing. The first wrap will force the wing downward and toward the bend; the crossing wrap will force the wing further downward and back toward the eye, as shown here from the top.

If the wings are not yet in spent position as shown, additional crisscross wraps can be made. Adjust the tension and position of these added wraps so that the thread abuts the wing base and forces the wings into the proper position.

When the wings are satisfactorily positioned, take a wrap of thread ahead of the wings around the hook shank only.

If desired, apply a drop of head cement or CA glue to the thread wraps.

Step 4. (Optional) If an overlaid wing is desired, cut a length of yarn about 2" longer than the total wingspan. Here, we're using Antron.

Using the techniques described in **Method #75: Lashed-fiber Spentwing**, p. 324, lash the yarn crosswise at the wing-mounting point, taking care that the new thread wraps do not disturb the position of the loop wings.

Step 5. Pull the length of yarn on the far side of the shank gently outward, and trim it to be even with the inside edge of the loop wing.

Repeat this procedure with the near wing.

Film Spentwings

Most of the many types of synthetic winging films available will tie a spentwing that is realistic in appearance, and the very thin, glossy, translucent, and delicate materials can produce wings almost indistinguishable from natural ones. (For a more detailed discussion of film materials, see "Upright Film and Foam Wings," p. 281.)

The thin films with plastic or cellophane-like appearance and texture can in fact be rather heavy, and while they may help to support a fly on perfectly calm water, such wings ride rather low; should they become awash in the surface film, they can begin to sink the fly. These films can still be practical if buoyant materials are incorporated into the tail and body, and the fly itself fished in relatively still water.

Better success can be obtained by using softer, slightly thicker materials with a "woven" or "spun" texture and appearance

such as Airthru and Aire-Flow. These materials, though not as durable, are generally lighter, accept floatant well, and tend to ride somewhat higher in the water. Even so, choosing materials and dressing styles that promote floatation in the tail and body is still wise.

Method #80:
Lashed Film Spentwing

Where tying upright wings from film can be rather tricky, tying spentwings is fairly simple. The following technique can be used with virtually any type of synthetic film, though as noted above, the degree of floatation and durability can vary significantly with different kinds of material.

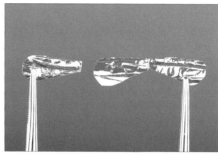

Step 1. Cut a strip of film slightly longer than the total finished wingspan, and slightly wider than the width of the finished wing. Note that if the particular film material has a "grain," as explained in "Upright Foam and Film Wings," p. 281, this grain should run from wing tip to wing tip.

Fold the strip in half crosswise, and either cutting freehand or using a paper template as explained in **Method #37: Front-fold Film Wings**, p. 283, trim the wings to shape.

While you can trim the wing to any shape, there is one provision—it should be cut with a rather narrow "throat" at the folded edge, as shown on the left. The folded edge will form the center of the wing, as shown on the right, and the throat is the point at which the film will be lashed to the hook shank. A full-width of material at this mounting point will cause most film materials (Zing is perhaps the one exception here) to bunch up and can inhibit a neat, flat spentwing. Cutting some of this material away to narrow the wing at the center will make the film easier to work with. Moreover, a narrow width at the base of the finished wing will allow the film to flex at this point during casting and somewhat reduce its propensity to twist tippets.

There's a hitch, however. If the throat is too narrow, pressure from the tying thread will weaken or cut the film material, and the wings may separate during fishing. Since each material has different properties, it's difficult to generalize about how narrow this throat can be. You want the throat to be as thick as possible, but still achieve a neat wing mount. As a starting point for experimentation, try making this throat half the width of the finished wing.

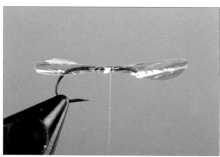

Step 2. Lay a short thread foundation that spans the wing-mounting point. Lash the wings to the top of the hook shank, as shown. Use only two wraps under light thread tension—enough to hold the wings atop the shank but still allow them some mobility beneath the thread, since they must still be adjusted.

Step 3. Grasp one wing tip in each hand, and pull gently, directly outward from the hook shank. Pulling the wing helps flatten it and straighten out any material that may have bunched up beneath the thread wraps.

Take care not to pull too hard, since some materials are elastic and can deform if stretched too far.

Step 4. Take tight crisscross wraps to secure the wings firmly to the top of the shank. As you apply these tighter wraps, pause periodically if necessary to straighten the wings as described in Step 3.

SECTION FOUR

Emerger Wings, Wing Buds, and Float Pods

Emerger wings are dressed on patterns that represent newly hatched aquatic insects, though only species that metamorphose on or in the water are of importance to anglers. Stoneflies, damselflies, and dragonflies, for instance, undergo this transformation in a terrestrial environment, crawling from the stream or lake to brush on the bank or objects that project above the water's surface, where they emerge from the nymphal skin. Insects of this type in the transition stage from nymphs to adults, that is, emergers, are available to trout only incidentally, and flies representing this brief phase of the life cycle are rarely imitated by tyers.

Mayflies, caddis, and midges, however, which emerge on or in the water, are available to trout and hence of importance to the angler and tyer. They swim or float to, or just beneath, the surface; the nymphal or pupal skin splits open and the adult wriggles free, its wings bent or crumpled from confinement within the shuck. Because most emergences take place at the water's surface, emerging flies are typically dressed to float on, in, or just under the surface film, and the required buoyancy may be provided by the winging material.

What emerger wings of most types have in common is that they tend to be undersize representations of the adult wings, often fully or partially laid back against the body to simulate the wing attitude of an insect emerging from a nymphal shuck or pupal case or skin. Thus many emerger winging styles, even for mayflies and midges, are related in a technical sense to downwing dressings.

But because emergence is a process rather than an instantaneous event, the wings can be imitated at any stage of this transformation. Though many tyers and anglers speak generally of "emerger wings," others, particularly when speaking of mayfly imitations, draw a distinction among "float or wing pods," "wing buds," and "emerger wings." Tyer René Harrop differentiates even further among the stages of emergence, and ties patterns imitating "captive duns" and "transitional duns," which represent particular points of the metamorphosis. The terminology and tying rationales for these various versions of wings on emerging flies is hardly fixed, but if nothing else, they represent the complexity of imitating an insect in the process of change. Still, there are some rough consistencies. In general, "float pods" are usually constructed of a small clump of buoyant material attached at the winging point of a mayfly nymph or midge pupa, which positions the fly directly beneath the surface film in the attitude of a natural insect ready to emerge. Their primary physical function is to provide buoyancy to the fly, but their imitative purpose is not always so unambiguous. On midge patterns, a float pod may actually represent the filamentous gill structures on the thorax of the pupa. Or it may suggest, on mayflies as well as midges, an enlargement or distension in the thorax area just prior to emergence. Or it may in fact imitate wings and thorax emerging from the pupal or nymphal skin. Exactly how the trout interprets the wing pod is a matter of conjecture.

"Wing buds" generally refer to the swollen emerging base of the wings, just as they are breaking free from the nymphal shuck; buds tend to be small and rather unwinglike in appearance, and the flies dressed with them may more closely resemble a nymph than an adult imitation. "Emerger wings," by contrast, refer to wings partially or wholly freed from the nymphal case, though these may still be short and crumpled or irregular in shape, and not yet in the full configuration of the adult wing. Even here, however, the terminology is not entirely precise. Caddisflies and midges actually undergo two "emergences." The insect first emerges from a cocoon-like pupal case anchored to the stream or lake bottom. The wings, though held close to the sides of the body, are prominent structures particularly in caddis, and in the artificial fly they are typically called "emerger wings." The pupa rises to the surface, where the pupal shuck splits and the adult insect emerges. Representations of wings at this stage of transformation are also called "emerger wings."

This particular "double-emergence" of most caddis and midges give rise to what is perhaps the most useful distinction for tyers—emerger wings that are dressed on the sides of the fly body, and those dressed atop the body. In this latter category, there is an interesting representational possibility that has not been addressed much by American tyers. The nymphal skin or cuticle splits along the back of the thorax, and from this opening the wings and thorax of the adult fly emerge. With a few exceptions, American tyers have not sought to imitate in any detail the nymphal skin of the hatching insect beyond a general, impressionistic representation of the nymphal skin of the insect as it trails from the body in later stages of emergence (see "Trailing Shucks," p. 89). But the splitting membrane or cuticle over the thorax of the fly may be a conspicuous component of the hatching fly, and English tyer Oliver Edwards has devised a technique for representing it as shown in the following method.

Method #81:
Split Cuticle

Oliver Edwards, known for his meticulous imitations, particularly of subsurface flies, uses a technique to represent the split cuticle or nymphal skin around the thorax of the hatching fly. Edwards ties this component in conjunction with a pair of CDC emerger wings (see **Method #84: Feather-tip Emerger Wings**, p. 333), on his *Emphemeroptera* imitations. But the split cuticle has broader applications and can in fact be tied on any emerger pattern that has wings mounted atop the hook shank. Thus we are presenting it as a generalized technique that can be used with any of the top-mounted wing styles shown in this section.

To represent this component, Edwards uses a thin foam, such as the Ethafoam used in the following demonstration. This material not only reproduces the translucence of the nymphal skin, but adds buoyancy to the thorax area and gives the fly a lifelike, semi-horizontal position in the water.

Step 1. Dress any components that lie behind the thorax of the fly. Lay a thread foundation over the thorax area, and position the tying thread at the front edge of the abdomen.

Cut 2 strips of shiny translucent or clear foam, about ¹⁄₁₆" thick and about ½ the hook gap in width.

Secure a strip of foam on each side of the hook shank, as shown.

Step 2. Dress the desired style of emerger wing and the thorax of the fly. Make certain to leave room behind the eye of the fly to tie off the foam strips and to add any legs or hackle that may be used.

Here, a loop-style CDC emerger wing is used, as described in **Method #86: Fiber-loop Emerger Wing**, p. 336.

Step 3. After the wing and thorax are dressed, use the right fingers to pull the foam strips forward along the sides of the thorax. Snug the strips against the thorax, but do not stretch them.

With the left hand, take a slack loop of thread around the foam strips just ahead of the thorax.

Tighten the loop gently, but do not use too much pressure or you can cut the foam.

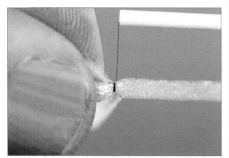

Step 4. With the left fingers, pinch the foam against the sides of the shank.

With the right hand, add additional thread wraps, under increasing tension, to secure the foam.

Step 5. Trim the foam and cover the butts with thread, either forming a head on the fly or laying a foundation for other components that may be applied behind the hook eye.

Quill Emerger Wings

Though flight feathers, or quills—primarily from waterfowl—are generally used for upright or downwing styles, they make effective emerger wings as well. Though perhaps more commonly used for wings on emerging caddis, quill segments can also be tied on mayfly emerger patterns.

The two chief virtues in using quill for this wing style are its realistic appearance and the relative simplicity of dressing. Quill makes unusually lifelike wings, particularly on caddis pupae, as the contours of the quill quite nicely reproduce the shape of the natural wing. Because the wings are mounted

against the sides of the body or hook, instead of atop the hook shank, the slightly fussy procedures used to dress quill in the upright or downwing style are not required, and the tying techniques are quite straightforward. The main weakness of quill, as always, is its fragility; quill wings are easily split or torn. Tattered wings, however, particularly on emergers, do not seem to reduce the effectiveness of the fly, and if desired, the wings can be reinforced using a workable fixative or flexible cement to forestall damage.

Any quill material suitable for upright or downwings can be used for emerger wings. Information about quill materials can be found in the section on "Wing Feathers" p. 9, and "Preparing Quill Wings," p. 243.

Method #82:

Paired Quill Emerger Wings

No tyer has probably done more to popularize the use of quill for emerger wings than Poul Jorgensen in his caddis pupa patterns. (Complete dressing for this simple but realistic dressing can be found in his *Modern Fly Dressing for the Practical Angler.*) Jorgensen's basic approach is demonstrated in the main sequence below. The alternate sequence shows how to dress paired quill segments for a mayfly emerger.

Film materials such as raffia or Swiss straw can be substituted for quill if desired. They are somewhat simpler to handle, though extra time is required to trim the entire wing to shape before mounting.

Step 1. Fashion a body of the desired material, and position the thread at the body tie-off point.

Cut a matched pair of quill segments as explained in "Preparing Quill Wings," p. 243. The width of the wings should be about ½ the hook gap, as shown. If desired, the quill segments can be reinforced for greater durability by misting them with a spray fixative or giving them a light coat of flexible cement (see **Method #2: Upright Quill Wings**, Step 4, p. 245).

Note that the pair of wings here are held in the position they will occupy on the finished fly. The concave sides are together and the quill tips point downward. Positioning the wing together like this will allow you to determine which quill segment belongs on the near side of the fly and which on the far side.

Step 2. The wings can be mounted simultaneously, but easier and more accurate placement can be obtained by mounting them individually.

Begin with the near wing. Determine which quill segment belongs on the near side of the shank, as shown in Step 1, and position it alongside the fly body as shown. Note the orientation in the photo. The wing quill extends about ⅔ the length of the body and slants downward slightly.

Take one wrap of thread around the near wing under just enough tension to hold the wing in place. While maintaining slight tension, make any adjustments necessary to the wing position.

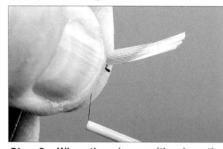

Step 3. When the wing position is satisfactory, pinch the wing firmly against the shank with the left fingers, as shown. Your thumb should lie over the thread wrap made in Step 2 to prevent the wing from shifting when the thread is tightened.

Pull on the thread to seat the wing firmly against the shank.

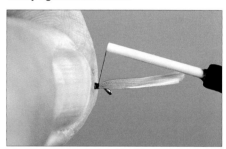

Step 4. Slide the left thumb and forefinger back just enough to expose the thread wrap, and take 2 or 3 additional wraps to secure the wing.

Step 5. Mount the far wing by repeating Steps 2-4.

Trim the quill butts and bind down with thread.

Step 1a. To form quill wings on a mayfly emerger, begin by dressing any tail, trailing shuck, body, and rib materials. Position the thread at the body tie-off point.

Cut a pair of quill segments as explained in Step 1. Note in the photo that the orientation of the quill segments in forming the wing is reversed from that shown in Step 1. The convex sides are placed together and the tips of the quill point upward. This is a typical wing configuration for a mayfly emerger.

Step 2a. Position the near wing as shown, and take one wrap of tying thread around the quill under light tension, as explained in Step 2.

Note here that the wing position differs from that shown in Step 2. The wing is shorter—about ⅓ to ½ the body length—slants slightly upward, and is positioned closer to the top of the body. When both wings are mounted, the top edges of the quill segments should meet, or nearly meet, along the back of the body as shown in Step 3a.

The wings are mounted using the procedures described in Steps 3-5.

Step 3a. Here, both wings have been mounted. Notice the upper edges of the wings lie close together down the back of the fly.

Legs, head, or any other component on the pattern are dressed over the wing-mounting wraps.

Method #83:
Folded Quill Emerger Wings

A single piece of folded quill can be used to fashion emerger wings, and though they are somewhat less elegant in appearance than paired quill wings, they are simpler and faster to construct. We're demonstrating this technique on a caddis emerger, but quill cut to the appropriate shape can be used on mayfly emergers as well.

The technique is virtually identical to that for forming a quill tentwing as described in **Method #42: Folded Quill Downwing**, p. 289, so the following instructions are abbreviated. Readers seeking greater detail should consult **Method #42**.

Other materials such as Swiss straw and raffia can be substituted for quill if desired.

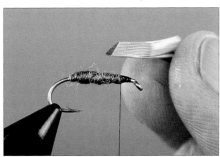

Step 1. Any body or rib materials should be applied prior to dressing the wing. Position the tying thread at the frontmost point of the body.

Cut a section of quill about equal in width to twice the hook gap. If desired, the quill can be reinforced by misting it with spray fixative or applying a thin coat of flexible cement (see **Method #2: Upright Quill Wings**, Step 4, p. 245).

Fold the strip of quill in half lengthwise, and trim the rear edge. We've made a simple angle-cut here, but more realistic, winglike shapes can be cut if desired.

Step 2. Sandwich the quill around the hook shank so that the top of the fly body is seated up into the fold of the quill section. The fold should be positioned to run directly down the top of the fly body to make the wings symmetrical.

Mount the wing with 3 or 4 tight wraps of thread.

Note that in these caddis emerger wings, the wing length is approximately equal to ⅔ the body length.

If the wing flares upward, take a turn or two of thread toward the hook bend, securing the wing atop the very front edge of the fly body.

Step 3. When the wing is properly positioned, secure it with a few more thread wraps, trim the butts, and bind with thread.

The wing can be left in this tentlike shape, as shown on the left, or you can take dubbing needle or scissor points and carefully split the wings down the center to form separate wing halves, as shown on the right. In splitting the wings, work from the rear of the wing forward to ensure that the wing halves are identical in size.

Feather-tip Emerger Wings

Though feather tips are probably used less frequently than other materials, they nonetheless make highly satisfactory emerger wings. The range of available colors and markings give tyers a broad choice in this regard, and because feather tips can be left natural, or cut or burned to shape, the material offers the tyer still more options.

There is no question that feather-tips are slightly more difficult to tie than some other materials, but the durability and attractiveness of these wings make them worth the effort.

Any feather suitable for making feather-tip upright or downwings can be used for emerger wings (see the section on "Upright Wings," "Selecting Feathers," p. 248). And in fact because stem thickness—a major factor in choosing feathers for upright wings—is of little concern in this winging style, still more types of plumage are available to the tyer. Even so, as with most feather-tip wing styles, hen hackle is probably the single most commonly used material. The tips can be left natural or cut or burned to shape, though for the latter process, tyers will be forced to improvise a bit since commercial burners specifically for emerger wings are not available.

Recently many tyers, most notably René Harrop, have been using CDC feathers for emerger wings—a useful material that adds floatation to the pattern and positions the fly almost horizontally in the surface film, much like many natural emergers.

Method #84:
Feather-tip Emerger Wings

This type of wing is generally tied in one of three ways. In the first style, shown in the main sequence, feather tips are mounted atop the shank, slanting back, and slightly splayed. Probably the best known uses of this approach are in Randall Kaufmann's Timberline Emerger, a generic pattern using natural hackle-tip wings that suggests an emerging mayfly or midge, and in René Harrop's transitional flies, which incorporate wings of paired CDC feather tips. Swisher and Richards also use a version of this technique, however, in which the wings are not splayed, for their Emerging Dun pattern, as noted in Step 1.

In the second style, shown in the alternate sequence, feather tips are mounted alongside the body, slanting slightly downward to suggest wings on a caddis emerger. For this demonstration, we're using feather tips that have been cut to shape.

A third, rather unusual style, is used by Oliver Edwards who mounts CDC feathers in a broad fan-shape facing the hook eye, as shown in Step 6.

Step 1. Any tail, trailing shuck, body, or hackle materials that lie behind the wings must be dressed first. Position the thread at the front edge of the body (or directly ahead of the hackle, if one is used).

Select a pair of feathers for the wings. These can be sized by trimming the barbs below the mounting point to leave a stubble along the feather stem that will help prevent the feathers from rolling or twisting when tied in (see **Method #7: Feather-tip Wings**, Step 2a, p. 253). Preparing feathers in this way makes for a more precise mounting and a low-bulk tie-in.

Generally, however, it is faster to omit this preparation and mount feathers that have not been trimmed, as we're doing here. Because some barbs are bound to the shank along with the feather stem, the tie-in bulk is greater and the method not quite as tidy, as some stray hackle barbs will require trimming afterward.

For this technique, it is necessary only to strip away the fluff at the base of the feather stem. Hold the feathers with the tips aligned and the convex sides together, so that the wings flare away from one another, as shown.

Note that for the Swisher/Richards Emerging Dun, the feathers are held with the concave sides together, for an undivided wing. Otherwise, the dressing technique is identical to that shown in the following steps.

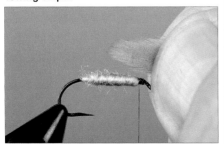

Step 2. With the tips aligned, pinch the feathers in the right fingers and position them along the top of the fly body to establish the wing length. Typically, the wings are tied ¼ to ½ the body length.

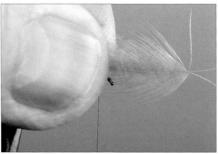

Step 3. Hold the feathers in the orientation shown in Step 2, and with the left fingers, simultaneously pinch the feather tips and the hook shank, as shown. Note that the fingertips extend beyond the mounting point toward the hook eye. Positioning the fingers like this enables mounting the wing using one of the slack-loop techniques noted in the next step.

Step 4. Mount the wing using any one of the slack-loop methods described in the Chapter 4: "Mounting Trimming Materials." **Method #9: The Pinch Wrap**, p. 30, is perhaps the quickest, but **Method #10: The Bobbin Loop**, p. 31; and **Method #11: The Langley Loop**, p. 32 are suitable as well.

Regardless of the specific method used, secure the wing with 2 or 3 firm wraps of thread.

Release the wings and check their position. The feather tips should not have rolled or cocked, but have remained in a vertical plane and flared away from one another.

Step 5. When the wings are properly positioned, grasp the tips in the left hand and secure the butts with 2 or 3 tight wraps of thread.

Clip the excess material and trim away any stray hackle barbs. Bind down the butts with thread.

Step 6. Shown here is the CDC feather-tip emerger wing used by Oliver Edwards. The feathers are mounted flat against the front edge of the body, and slightly fanned. These wings are dressed, as Edwards does, using the split cuticle shown in **Method #81: Split Cuticle**, p. 331.

Step 1a. To tie feather-tip caddis emerger wings, all materials behind the wing-mounting point are dressed first.

Select and shape a pair of feathers for the wings.

For cut wings, as shown here, the feathers can be trimmed individually or glued together and trimmed simultaneously as explained in **Method #5: Cut Wings**, p. 249.

Burned wings can be fashioned using the procedure shown in **Method #6: Burned Wings**, p. 251. Though no wing burners are available specifically for emerger wings, the Renzetti caddis wing burners can make a passable substitute, and even mayfly burners can be used if necessary. For any given hook size, however, the burner used for emerger wings should be narrower than that used for wings on an adult pattern.

Size the wings by stripping away all the hackle barbs below the mounting point. Typically, the wings are ⅔ to ¾ the body length, as shown.

Step 2a. Wings of this type are mounted on the side of the fly. The way in which the mounting point is prepared will determine the degree to which the wings flare away from the body. If the wings are mounted against a simple thread base laid on the hook shank, they will be splayed outward by the bulkier body materials directly behind the wings.

Building a thicker foundation of tying thread ahead of the body materials or wrapping the thread back over the front edge of the body, as shown here, will reduce the splay, and the wings will lie closer to the body.

The wings are easiest to mount individually. Begin with the wing on the near side. With the right fingers, hold the feather by the stem and position it in the desired attitude, usually with the wing slanting slightly downward, as shown. The very base of the lowermost hackle barbs should lie over the mounting point.

Step 3a. While holding the wing in the position shown in Step 2a, pinch the wing against the shank with the left fingers, as shown.

Mount the wing with 3 firm wraps of thread. The first wrap or two should cross the base of the lowermost barbs on the stem. Binding in the base of the barbs will help prevent the wing from rolling under thread pressure, as often happens when the thread binds down the bare stem only.

Step 4a. Release the wing and check its position. Make any adjustments necessary. Many wing orientations are possible, but the one shown here is typical.

Step 5a. Mount the far wing by repeating Steps 2a-4a.

Clip the feather stems and bind down the butts.

Bundled-fiber Emerger Wings and Float Pods

It's likely that the most widespread style of emerger wing is fashioned from bundled fibers—natural or synthetic hairs; yarns, particularly Antron and Z-Lon; and hackle barbs, especially CDC, are the most popular, but virtually any stranded material can be used. Wings constructed of bundled fibers are relatively simple to tie and generally quite durable. Moreover, the wide variety of fiber materials allows the tyer to select for coloration or markings, visibility, floatation, or combinations of these characteristics.

Bundled-fiber emerger wings fall into one of two general designs. The "tuft" style wing is really just a short version of a bundled-fiber downwing, though it is often dressed more sparsely. Like most bundled-fiber wings, it tends to be impressionistic, at least compared to the more realistic effects achieved with quill and feather tips. In its most common form, the tuft wing is used on flies that float on or in the surface film. A longer wing may suggest a freshly emerged fly, while a shorter clump of material may suggest the wing buds of an insect just beginning transformation.

Loop emerger wings are formed from a bundled of fibers bound at both ends to form a loop at the winging point. As with the tuft style, the loop can be varied in size for different representational purposes. A long loop can be dressed on a floating fly to imitate the wings on a newly hatched insect, but more often, the loop is tied shorter to suggest wing buds or partially emerged wings and thorax. The remainder of such a fly is often dressed more in the nymph style than as a dry fly. When the loop wings are dressed with a buoyant material, the fly rides just in or on the surface film.

Method #85:

Tuft Emerger Wing

This style is perhaps the most basic, and easiest to tie, of all emerger wings. Though more widely used for mayfly emergers such as Caucci and Nastasi's Compara Emerger, the tuft wing is also used in some caddis emerger patterns, most notably Gary LaFontaine's Emergent Sparkle Pupa.

Except for wing length and density of dressing, the style is virtually identical to a bundled-fiber downwing, and hence the instructions here are abbreviated. Readers seeking more information should consult earlier portions of this chapter: if using solid fibers such as natural or synthetic hair, see **Method #57: Solid-fiber Downwing**, p. 305; if using deer or elk hair, see **Method #62: Hollow-hair Downwing**, p. 311. The method shown in the main sequence, using stripped CDC barbs, is suitable for all feather barbs. (CDC feather tips can also be used to dress the wing style; information about suitable feather tips and the procedure for tying

them are explained in **Method #56: Feather-tip Downwing**, p. 304.)

The alternate sequence shows a reverse-tuft dressing that simultaneously forms a shellback wingcase and a tuft that extends out over the eye. The style is perhaps most familiar to tyers as a component on the Tom Thumb pattern; it can, however, be used on many emerger patterns. The representational function of this tuft is debatable. Since its forward orientation suggests emerging wings only in the broadest, most impressionistic sense, the deer-hair tuft may actually function more like a float pod to keep the fly just under the surface film. In either case, there's no denying that emergers tied in this style are extremely effective.

Step 1. All tail, trailing shuck, body, and rib materials must be dressed prior to winging the fly. Lay a short thread foundation ahead of the body, and return the thread to the front edge of the body material.

Prepare a bundle of CDC barbs as explained in **Method #1: Preparing Feather Barbs**, p. 67; **Method #9: Preparing Marabou and CDC**, p. 73; or **Method #36: Stalcup CDC Parachute Hackle**, p. 391. Consolidate the section of barbs into a bundle.

Since CDC barbs are often of inconsistent length, the bundle may be a bit scraggly. You can neaten it up by breaking off the tips of the longer barbs to make the entire clump more uniform in length. Most tyers avoid clipping the bundle to length, claiming that the somewhat irregular tip ends formed by breaking the barbs are more natural in appearance than the very squared-off ends produced by scissor trimming.

Even the barbs by using the left thumbnail to break off the longer barbs.

Position the clump atop the hook shank as shown to determine the wing length—usually ¼ to ¾ the body length.

Step 2. Grasp the tips of bundle in the left hand, and bind in the wing with 4 or 5 tight wraps of thread. Use the middle finger of the left hand, as shown, as a backstop during wrapping to prevent fibers from migrating around the shank under thread pressure.

Step 3. Clip the wing butts. The butts can be left a bit long to serve as the head of the fly, or as shown here, bound down with thread. Any materials forming the head of the fly can then be applied.

Step 1a. The reverse tuft is usually dressed on a nymph-style fly. All tail, trailing shuck, abdomen, and rib materials should be dressed. Lay a thread foundation over the thorax area, and return the thread to the front edge of the abdomen.

Clip and clean a bundle of hair as explained in **Method #2: Preparing and Cleaning Hair**, p. 68, and align the hair tips as shown in **Method #3: Stacking and Aligning Hair**, p. 69.

The thickness of the bundle will determine the density of the tuft, and varies with the taste of the individual tyer, but as a starting point, use a clump of hair about the size that would be used for a tail—see "Tailing Styles and Proportions," p. 65.

Establishing the right mounting point for the material is important, as the point at which the deer hair is tied in ultimately determines the length of the tuft wing. Preferences vary here, but the method shown in the photograph is a starting point for experimentation.

Assuming that the abdomen of the nymph has been dressed on the rear half of the hook shank, that is, the front edge of the abdomen terminates at the middle of the shank, position the clump of hair atop the hook so that the tips extend to the end of the hook bend, as shown.

The right fingers are pinching the hair at the mounting point.

Step 2a. Hold the bundle of hair in this position, and grasp the tips with the left fingers.

Bind in the deer hair directly at the front edge of the abdomen; then take additional binding wraps moving toward the hook eye. Use the middle finger of the left hand as a backstop to prevent any fibers from rolling around the shank. All the hair should be secured atop the hook.

When the hair is secured, clip the butts and bind down with thread.

Step 3a. At this point, dress the thorax of the fly.

With the right fingers, grasp the hair bundle and draw it smoothly over the top of the thorax and out beyond the hook eye. You may need to preen the hair a few times to grasp all the hairs and pull them with an even, consistent tension.

Step 4a. With the left hand, grasp the bobbin and lay the thread over the bundle directly behind the hook eye. Release the bobbin so that the thread wrap is held in place only by the weight of the hanging bobbin. Adjust the position of thread wrap if necessary.

Maintain a firm hold on the hair tips with your right hand. With the left hand, pull the bobbin to cinch this thread wrap tightly. Keep tension on the bobbin with your left hand.

Step 5a. Maintaining tension on the bobbin, release the hair tips and transfer the bobbin to your right hand. Grasp the folded hair just behind the mounting point and take 4 or 5 more tight thread wraps to secure the hair.

Step 6a. When the hair is secure, whip finish and clip the thread.

If a higher wing angle is desired, lift the hair tips with the left hand and place two or three thread wraps around the hook shank only, forcing the wraps into the base of the tuft to post it up slightly.

Method #86:
Fiber-loop Emerger Wing

Though somewhat similar in dressing to upright loop wings, the emerger version is considerably simpler to dress, since there's no need to post or divide the wings. The style has been advocated by many tyers; Swisher and Richards have used hen-hackle fibers to tie wings on emerging mayfly duns, and in his Iris Caddis, Craig Mathews uses Antron yarn, as we're doing in the main sequence here.

CDC makes a particularly effective loop wing. Stripped CDC barbs (prepared using the techniques indicated in **Method #85: Tuft Emerger Wing**, Step 1, p. 335) can be used, but a more interesting, veined appearance can be given to the wing by using a whole CDC feather, as shown in the alternate sequence.

The wing can be tied in one of two ways. The entire loop can formed at a single point on the hook shank—behind or ahead of the thorax, or in the middle of the thorax as shown in the main sequence. Or the wing can be tied to loop over the thorax, as shown in the alternate sequence. Either style, however, can be used with any material.

Step 1. Dress any tail, trailing shuck, abdomen, and ribbing materials. To place the wing in the middle of the thorax, as we're doing here, dress the rear half of the thorax. Lay a short thread foundation toward the hook eye, and return the thread to the front of the thorax material.

Clip a one-inch length of Antron yarn, and secure it tightly to the top of the shank. The rearmost thread wrap should push the yarn tightly against the thorax material, as shown.

Step 2. With your left hand, hold a dubbing needle crosswise over the hook shank. With your right hand, fold the yarn over the needle to form a loop of the desired size.

When the loop is formed, pinch the yarn against the top of the shank with the right fingers.

Step 3. Holding the yarn in position, pinch the loop wing with the left fingers, directly behind the mounting point.

Take 4 or 5 tight wraps, binding this end of the yarn directly atop the section of yarn already affixed to the shank.

Step 4. Clip the excess yarn and bind down the butts. Dress the remainder of the thorax.

Step 1a. Dress any tail, trailing shuck, rib, and abdomen materials. Position the tying thread at the front edge of the abdomen.

Select a CDC feather. The best feather for this application is the same type used for a CDC downwing and pictured in **Method #56: Feather-tip Downwing**, p. 304. Two feathers can be used, if desired, and they should be positioned, front-to-back, nested together so that the curvatures match and the tips are aligned.

With the right fingers, preen the barbs upward and pinch them at the very tip. Not all the barbs will reach the tip; use the left fingers to preen these short barbs toward the base of the feather.

Step 2a. Transfer the feather to the left hand, taking care to keep the barb tips aligned.

Position the feather atop the shank, and bind in the feather tip directly ahead of the abdomen material. The feather should mounted by the very tip so that no trimming of excess material is necessary. The rearmost mounting wrap should force the feather tightly against the front edge of the abdomen.

If you have difficulty securing the feather by the very tip, take two thread wraps, medium tight, over the feather stem at the base of the preened barbs. Then pull the feather to slide it beneath the thread wraps until the tip of the feather is reached. Secure the tip with additional tight wraps.

Step 3a. At this point, dress the thorax of the fly, and any legs, gills, or other components on the pattern.

Form a loop of material as shown in Step 2, though in this case, the front of the loop is positioned ahead of the thorax, directly behind the hook eye.

Step 4a. Bind down the front of the loop as described in Step 3. Clip the excess feather, and bind down the butt.

Method #87:
Funnel Wing

This unusual CDC winging technique was shown to us by German tyer Henning von Monteton. The CDC barbs are distributed in funnel-shapes atop the hook shank with a clump of shorter barbs at the base a kind of cross between a float pod and a parachute hackle. This style makes excellent use of the CDC barbs, since each fiber is in contact with the surface film to help support the fly. Von Monteton uses this style to wing woven-body caddis patterns, as shown in Step 10, but inventive tyers may well find other applications for this unique style.

With a bit of practice, this technique is not at all difficult, but there is one crucial element—the pair of CDC feathers must be closely matched in size and of good quality, with a minimum of short or broken fibers.

Step 1. All components of the fly behind the winging point are dressed first. Lay a short thread foundation over the winging area, and position the thread at the winging point.

Using one of the techniques shown in **Method #38: Trap-loop Dubbing**, p. 129, form a dubbing loop about 3"-4" long. Do not wax the loop. Advance the tying thread to the rear of the hook eye.

Take 2 closely matched CDC feathers, and preen the barbs to stand perpendicular to the feather stem.

Lay the feathers atop one another, front-to-back so that the curvatures match. Place them tip to butt, as shown here, with the stems aligned.

Step 2. Pinch the barbs on one side of the stack of feathers in a paper clamp. The distance from the edge of the clamp to the feather stem should be about ¼".

Trim the barbs from the stem.

Step 3. Carefully insert the strip of barbs into the dubbing loop so that the barbs project about ¹⁄₁₆" beyond the loop threads, as shown. For a well-defined wing, it is important the butts not be inserted too far through the loop. Pull the loop closed with a dubbing twister or hook.

Note that a very short length of loop thread—about ¹⁄₃₂"—is left bare between the hook shank and the first barbs.

Step 4. With the left hand, pull the dubbing twister to close the loop.

With the right fingers, push the barbs upward, sliding them inside the loop toward the hook shank to form a compressed stack, as shown. Take care to keep all the barbs perpendicular to the loop threads. (This is why unwaxed thread is used; wax would inhibit sliding the barbs upward.)

Step 5. Spin the dubbing twister about 10 times to lock in the fibers.

Maintain tension on the loop, and use the right fingers to push the barbs upward again, forming an even tighter stack.

Step 6. Now spin the dubbing loop very tight.

With the right hand, raise the dubbing twister and loop above the hook shank.

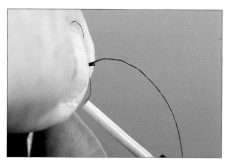

Step 7. With the left fingers, preen all the barbs toward the rear of the hook.

Using a pinch wrap (see **Method #9: The Pinch Wrap**, p. 30), secure the dubbing loop thread with three tight pinch wraps at the front base of the preened-back CDC clump.

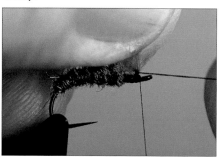

Step 8. With the left fingers, raise all the fibers vertically.

With the right hand, use the *dubbing loop thread* to make one wrap, under light tension, directly around the base of the CDC bundle.

Step 9. Now preen all the barbs toward the hook eye. With the dubbing loop thread, take 3 tight turns against the rear base of the bundle, as shown.

Step 10. Wrap the dubbing loop thread to the hook eye; secure it with the tying thread and clip the excess.

Release the fibers and fluff them upward to shape the wing, as shown on the left. You can clip any excessively long CDC barbs that project upward. The thorax of the fly can now be dubbed.

On the right is a funnel-winged Lamonte pattern, dressed by Henning von Monteton.

Method #88:
Dubbed Float Pod

Float pods are often made of foam, since the great buoyancy of the material is capable of supporting even a large fly in the surface film (see "Foam and Film Float Pods and Wing Buds," p. 339). Foam, however, is not a terribly durable material, and dubbing can be used instead in a method shown to us by Darrel Martin, who first saw it in the work of European tyer Klaus V. Bredow. If a suitable material is used—fine poly dubbing or chopped CDC barbs—the pod will easily float small to medium-size patterns.

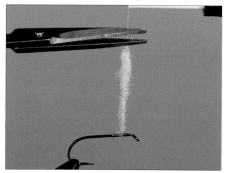

Step 1. Any tail, trailing shuck, body, and rib material should be dressed. We've omitted these components for a clearer illustration. Position the tying thread at the desired location of the float pod—usually at or near the head of the fly.

Firmly, but not tightly, dub a short length of thread. The amount of dubbing applied will determine the size of the finished float pod. Notice the teardrop shape of the dubbing. Applying material in this fashion helps create a more spherical float pod.

When the dubbing is applied, raise the thread vertically above the shank.

Maintain tension on the bobbin with the right hand. With the left hand, carefully position a pair of scissor blades around the tying thread above the dubbing.

Two particular points are worth observing in the photo. First, the scissor blades are angled about 45 degrees off the horizontal. This angling helps prevent the thread from contacting the sharp edge of the blade. Second, notice the relatively small amount of clearance between the thread and the inside edges of the scissor blades. In subsequent steps, this spacing will help produce a neat, compact float pod.

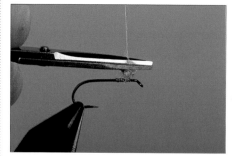

Step 2. Maintaining the proper blade angle, slide the scissor blades down the thread, pressing the dubbing into a ball on top of the hook shank. Naturally, take care not to nick the thread with the scissor blades.

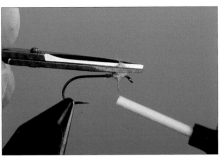

Step 3. Wrap the thread around the rear scissor blade, beneath the shank, and pull the bobbin directly toward you.

Step 4. Maintaining tension on the thread, carefully withdraw the scissors. Thread tension will snug the ball of dubbing to the shank.

Step 5. (Optional) If the float pod is to be used as the base for a parachute hackle, take 3 or 4 wraps of thread horizontally around the base of the dubbing to act as a foundation for the hackle.

Foam and Film Float Pods and Wing Buds

In many regards, closed-cell foam is an ideal material for forming float pods and wing buds. Because it is highly buoyant, relatively small amounts of material—that is, quantities in proportion to the natural insect—will float a fly rather easily. Many foams have a lifelike translucency, can easily be trimmed to shape, and are reasonably simple to tie. (See "Foam Bodies," p. 190 for further information on foam types.)

The one shortcoming of foam is a lack of durability; it tears relatively easily, and the pressure of the tying thread during mounting can exacerbate the problem by creating a weak spot in the foam. Some closed-cell foams are tougher than others, but these types gain durability by incorporating smaller air cells into the material, which means a greater proportion of cell walls and, ultimately, less buoyancy. Nonetheless, foam is a practical and popular material.

Synthetic films are occasionally used for emerger wings, though such materials would seem to warrant more attention than tyers have given them. The primary drawback to films—their wind resistance—is of little consequence on emerger wings, and many of the materials do have good durability and a lifelike appearance. Two techniques are described in the section that follows, and most of the films noted in "Upright Foam and Film Wings," p. 281, are suitable for these methods.

Method #89:
Folded Foam Float Pods

This simple technique of folding a strip of foam to form a float pod is both widely used and highly practical. Folding the foam not only produces a hump-shaped wing pod that is reasonably natural in appearance, but also gives a lower-bulk tie-in than would using a single, larger piece of foam. The height of the folded foam can be varied for representational purposes, and the resulting float pod can also be used as a base for a parachute hackle.

There are many versions of this technique. The main sequence shows an interesting method preferred by Skip Morris for midge pupae. The foam not only forms the float pod, but is also incorporated into the body and trailing shuck for additional floatation and efficiency of tying. The alternate sequence shows a pair of more conventional approaches to forming the float pod only.

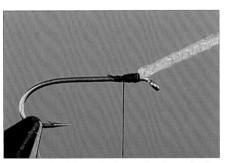

Step 1. In this technique, the foam is the first material applied. Lay a short thread foundation at the wing-mounting point.

Cut a strip of closed-cell foam about twice the length of the hook shank. The foam strip can be round, square, or rectangular in cross-section, but since it is lashed to the hook shank, it should be kept relatively thin—about ¼ to ⅓ of the hook gap in the largest cross-sectional dimension—to avoid excessive bulk in the fly body.

Bind one end of the foam at the winging point, with the butt of the foam extending over the hook eye as shown. With thin strips of foam, or fragile types such as Ethafoam, it is best to follow the procedure explained in "Tying Foam," p. 190; the tip of the foam is bound in with 3 or 4 tight wraps of thread, and then two or three more wraps are taken toward the hook eye, each under decreasing thread pressure. These looser wraps help prevent the tying thread from cutting the foam.

Return the tying thread to the rearmost mounting wrap.

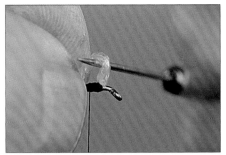

Step 2. With the right hand, place a dubbing needle crosswise over the top of the hook shank, and fold the foam over the needle, forming a float pod of the desired height.

When the fold is complete, pinch the butt end of the foam against the top of the hook shank with the left fingers, as shown.

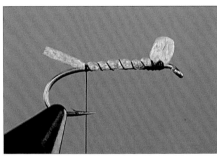

Step 3. Bind the strip of foam to the top of the shank with firm wraps in an open spiral if more buoyancy is desired. Placing the wraps closer together will compress the foam and decrease the amount of floatation it provides.

When the rear of the fly is reached, take 2 or 3 firm wraps directly atop one another to secure the foam at the end of the hook shank.

The tag of foam can be clipped to the desired length to form a trailing shuck. If a tail or shuck of a different material is desired, clip off the foam entirely, and bind down the tag. The fly is ready to be dressed with other components.

Step 1a. In this more typical approach, all materials behind the winging point are normally dressed first. Lay a short thread foundation at the winging point.

Cut a strip of foam. Since the foam will not be bound down along the length of the entire hook shank, it can be somewhat larger in cross-section than that used in the main sequence.

Bind in the tip of the foam with the butt extending toward the hook bend, as shown. As explained in Step 1, tie in the tip tightly, and decrease thread pressure as you wrap toward the hook bend.

Step 1b. The foam can be used to form a post-type float pod by folding it over the dubbing needle, as shown here. Note that the foam is doubled completely over.

When the foam is folded, use the right fingers to pinch the butt end tightly to the top of the hook shank.

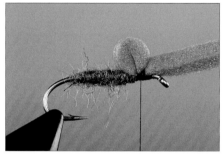

Step 1c. Secure the foam, moving toward the hook bend so that both ends of the foam are bound to the hook shank at the same point, as shown.

This type of float pod can be used as the base for a parachute hackle, and some tyers prefer to take several wraps of thread horizontally around the base of the float pod to form a foundation for hackling.

Step 2a. To form a more compact float pod, really more like a distended wing-case, mount the foam as shown in Step 1a. Then dress any thorax and/or leg materials, as shown here.

Fold the strip of foam over the thorax and pinch it against the shank directly behind the hook eye.

Secure it with thread wraps.

Step 2b. Clip the excess and finish the head of the fly.

Method #90:
The Suspender Pod

The unusual technique shown here is the basis of John Goddard's Suspender Hatching Midge and Charlie Brooks's Natant Nymph. It can be used for both emerging midge and mayfly nymph patterns designed to float suspended just beneath the surface film. Because the foam is contained inside nylon mesh, this style of float pod is fairly durable.

(Note that a similar, but simpler, suspender pod—and one quite commonly used—can be dressed from a foam post, and the technique is identical to that shown in **Method #33: Foam Post**, p. 280. The foam can be left slanting over the hook eye or raised to the vertical.)

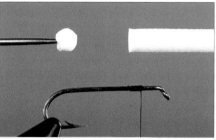

Step 1. This float pod is usually the first component of the fly to be dressed. Because of the peculiarities of this technique, the float pod itself will ultimately be positioned on the hook shank a short distance ahead of where it is actually mounted.

Determine where on the hook shank you wish the float pod to be positioned, and lay a short foundation of tying thread behind that point. Position the tying thread at the frontmost wrap of the thread foundation.

The suspender pod requires a small, roughly spherical piece of foam. There are two ways to produce this. First, ordinary closed-cell foam can be trimmed to a ball of the proper size—with a diameter about ⅓ to ⅔ the hook gap. When trimming, it helps to hold the foam on the point of the needle, as shown. Even so, this method is somewhat tedious, particularly when cutting foam for very small flies.

If the size of the fly permits it, ready-made foam balls can be used as shown in Step 1a.

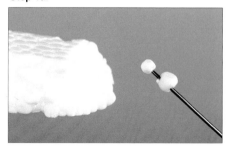

Step 1a. Ready-made foam balls can be found in expanded polystyrené material of the type molded to protect audio gear, computer equipment, and so on, as well as in some soft-drink cups.

Note in the photo that the "solid" piece of foam is actually composed of numerous small pellets of material. With care, the foam can be separated into small, individual balls, as shown.

The one shortcoming with this material is that while the balls vary somewhat in diameter, most are relatively small and hence confined to small hooks.

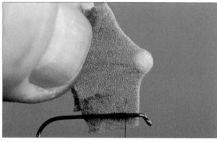

Step 2. One rather unusual fly-tying material is required for this technique—a section of fabric cut from a woman's stocking. How one acquires such a material is, of course, an entirely personal affair; we simply assume you have obtained some. Cut a section of material about 1-inch square.

Again, it's easiest to handle the foam ball by sticking it on the point of a needle. Place the foam ball in the center of the nylon material as shown.

Step 3. Draw the nylon material around the foam ball and withdraw the needle. Twist the nylon at the base of the ball to form a tight-fitting sheath for the ball.

Step 4. Mount the pod by binding the twisted "throat" of the nylon material to the top of the hook shank. Take a couple of tight wraps toward the hook eye to tighten the nylon around the foam ball, then reverse direction and bind the excess nylon to the shank moving toward the bend.

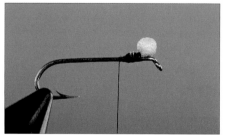

Step 5. Clip the excess fabric, and bind down the butts.

If the suspender pod is to be used as the foundation for a parachute hackle, you may wish to take 2 or 3 thread wraps around the base of the pod as explained in **Method #88: Dubbed Float Pod**, Step 5, p. 339.

Method #91:
LaFontaine Halo

According to Gary LaFontaine in *Trout Flies*, a hatching insect escaping through the bulging nymphal skin shows a "halo" of light at the thorax area, "created by the edges of the stretched skin and the natural air bubbles surrounding the thorax." Strictly speaking, then, these foam "wing buds" may in fact have little or nothing to do with the wings themselves. But since they are a conspicuous feature on this emerger design and are located at the winging point of the fly, we have included them in this section. Halos can be dressed on both mayfly and midge emergers.

Though any type of closed-cell foam can be used, the soft translucence of Ethafoam makes it ideal for this purpose. Moreover, because the technique produces two foam loops, the halo itself is constructed of a double thickness of material. The foam used should thus be rather thin—another argument for Ethafoam, which is often manufactured in thin sheets.

Step 1. All materials behind the winging point of the fly must be dressed prior to mounting the halo. Lay a short thread foundation that spans the wing-mounting point, and position the tying thread in the middle of this foundation.

Cut a narrow strip of foam—about ⅓ the hook gap in width, and about 2 inches long. The extra length here makes the material easier to handle.

Using the technique described in **Method #8: The Lash Mount and Crisscross Wrap**, p. 29, lash the foam strip crosswise atop the hook shank, as shown in this top view.

Step 2. With your right hand, position a dubbing needle on the far side of the hook, parallel to the shank, as shown in this top view. Fold the foam around the needle, making a doubled-over section of material that projects outward from the hook shank a distance equal to ¼ to ⅓ the shank length.

With the left fingers, pinch the folded piece of foam just beyond the mounting wraps.

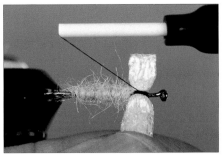

Step 3. Using 2 or 3 crisscross wraps, secure the folded tag of foam directly atop the wraps used to mount the foam strip.

Step 4. Pull the tag end of the foam gently toward you, and clip it close to the crisscross wraps.

Step 5. Repeat Steps 2-4 with the strip of foam on the near side of the shank, folding, binding and clipping it. The short tags of foam at the crisscross wraps are covered with thorax material, usually dubbing.

Method #92:
Twisted Film Wing Buds

This unique method of forming wing buds from synthetic film was originated by the makers of Shimazaki wing material. The technique involves twisting the material to reproduce the folded, crumpled appearance of emerging mayfly wings. Both the softer films and the thinner, more translucent materials, shown in the following sequence, can be used, and the twisted construction makes these wing buds quite tough. However, since few films are naturally buoyant, emergers dressed with this wing style must rely on other components for floatation.

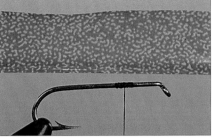

Step 1. The twisted film wing buds are the first material applied to the hook. Lay a short thread foundation that spans the winging area and position the tying thread at the wing-mounting point.

Cut a strip of film material about twice as long as the hook and about as wide as the hook gap. Note that if the film has a "grain" (see "Upright Foam and Film Wings," p. 281), the grain should run lengthwise on the strip.

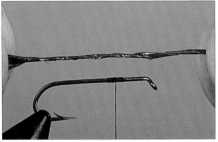

Step 2. Using the fingers of both hands, twist the material into a tight rope.

Step 3. Position the strip crosswise atop the hook shank, so that the middle of the strip sits at the mounting point.

Using the procedure shown in **Method #8: The Lash Mount and Crisscross Wrap**, p. 29, bind the twisted material to the top of the hook shank, as shown in this top view.

When the material is secure, position the thread behind the twisted film.

Step 4. With the left fingers, grasp the tip of the material on the far side of the shank. If it has unraveled, twist it tight.

With the right fingers, position a dubbing needle as shown. Fold the twisted material around the needle to the back of the mounting point, as shown here from the top. The length of the wing bud should be about ⅓ the shank length.

Step 5. Withdraw the needle, and pinch the twisted film tight to the hook shank.

Secure it directly behind the mounting point, with 5 or 6 tight wraps of thread, moving toward the hook bend.

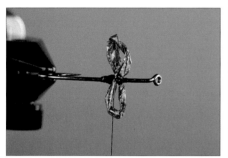

Step 6. Repeat Steps 3-5 to form the near wing bud, matching it in size to the far one.

When the near wing bud is formed, clip the tags of material at the rear and bind down with thread.

Position the thread behind the wing buds.

Step 7. Take 3 or 4 tight wraps around the base of the far wing.

Step 8. Take 3 or 4 tight wraps around the base of the near wing.

When these are complete, pinch the wings together from underneath the hook shank to elevate them about 45 degrees up from the horizontal. Apply a drop of head cement or CA glue to the thread wraps.

Method #93:

Folded Film Emerger Wings

We saw this approach to forming caddis emerger wings in the work of English tyer Oliver Edwards. Edwards uses Swiss straw, as shown in the following demonstration, but any film material that takes a crease well can be used. The technique is quite simple and produces durable wings.

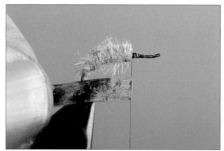

Step 1. All fly components that lie behind the thorax are dressed first. Lay a short thread foundation over the thorax area and return the thread to the front of the abdomen.

Cut a piece of film material about 2" long and about as wide as the hook gap. Fold the film in half lengthwise to make a thinner strip of double thickness.

Hold the tying thread beneath the hook shank, and fold the film around the thread, as shown. The fold should face the hook eye.

Step 2. Slide the film upward to the underside of the shank, and secure it there with 2 or 3 tight thread wraps.

When the film is mounted, unfold the two halves and draw them outward from either side of the hook shank as shown.

Step 3. Draw the ends of the film rearward around the sides of the abdomen and slightly downward. Pinch them together beyond the hook bend, as shown. Pull the film taut.

Secure the film in this position with tight thread wraps at the front of the abdomen.

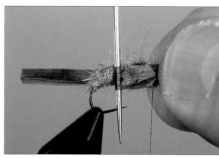

Step 4. At this point, dress the thorax of the fly and any other components that lie behind the wing tie-off point. Make certain to leave sufficient room behind the hook eye for any legs or other components that will be applied after the wings are tied off.

To form the wing on the near side of the shank, use the left hand to position a dubbing needle vertically at the midpoint of the abdomen, as shown.

With the right hand, fold the film around the needle and toward the hook eye.

Step 5. With the left fingers, pinch the folded wing tightly against the side of the thorax. Secure it to the shank with 2 moderately tight thread wraps.

With the right fingers, grab the tag end of the film material and pull it upward. This helps compress and gather the film beneath the tie-down wraps to make the wing narrower at the front.

Do not clip the film tag yet.

Step 6. Repeat Steps 4-6 using the remaining film strip to form a wing on the far side of the shank. Take care to make the wings of equal length.

When the far is wing formed, pinch both wings against the sides of the thorax, and secure both film tags with tight thread wraps. Clip and bind down the excess. The fly can be finished with a thread head, or other components added.

Hackle

Certainly no other material in fly dressing calls forth from tyers more discussion, debate, interest, wonder, admiration, longing, covetousness, lust, or hard cash, than hackle. There is no mystery about this—good hackle is as beautiful to work with as it is to look at. Moreover, in decades past, it was the Holy Grail of tying. Top-grade dry-fly hackle was difficult to find; it existed, but in quantities so small that the average tyer stood little chance of acquiring some, and the search for it was a consuming passion among many tyers. In recent decades, however, the situation has changed dramatically, and tyers now may choose from among half-a-dozen different suppliers of rooster capes and saddles that vary in quality from the merely very good to the superb. To our knowledge, in fact, hackle is the only natural material whose bearers are bred solely for the purpose of supplying fly tyers—further testimony to the enduring appeal of these feathers.

While rooster hackle tends to get the lion's share of attention from tyers, there are, of course, other types of hackle, and one byproduct of modern genetic hackle breeding that often goes unremarked is the wide availability of excellent wet-fly hackle from hen necks and saddles. Some tyers are under the largely mistaken impression that any hackle feathers that are unsuitable for dry flies automatically make good wet-fly material. But this is not necessarily the case; there are distinct differences among feathers that make some top-grade wet-fly hackling material and others nearly worthless for the purpose. For a more detailed explanation about the types, characteristics, and selection of hackle feathers, capes, and saddles, see "Hackle," p. 6.

Like many of the terms in fly tying, "hackle" is one with multiple meanings. The word "hackle" describes a feather, and by fly-tying custom, a feather than comes from the neck or saddle of a bird. But "hackle" is also a term used to designate a component of a finished fly—a group of fibers that extend or radiate outward from the hook shank, as in a collar hackle or crosshackle, or from another component of the dressing, such as a wing post in parachute hackling. Hackles on flies are often formed from hackle feathers, but not always. Wet-fly hackles may be dressed from rump, breast, flank, or body feathers, and indeed almost any feather with a stem sufficiently thin and pliable to be wrapped around a foundation. To complicate matters further, not all hackles are made of wrapped feathers; some are tied from feather barbs that have been removed from the stem. And some "hackles" contain no feather barbs at all; they are fashioned from hair or synthetic fibers. This chapter details these various types of "hackle" and the methods for dressing them.

Sizing Hackle

In most fly styles, the proportions of the fly components—tail, abdomen, thorax, wing or wingcase, legs, and so on—are in part based upon representation; they attempt to reproduce the relative sizes of these parts on the natural insect. On dry flies, however, proportion has an added dimension. A prevailing theory in fly tying holds that a dry fly with a collar hackle is supported on the water by the tail and tips of the hackle, and these two components must be properly proportioned if the fly is to balance and sit properly.

John Betts, one of tying's most learned historians, has traced the history of dry-fly proportions from the time of Frederic Halford, one of dry-fly fishing's first and still most eloquent exponents, to the modern age. Halford worked out careful proportions and relationships among dry-fly components in a way that accommodated both their structural and imitative functions. As Betts shows, hook styles changed over time, from the approximately 2XL shanks used by Halford to the "standard" length shanks used today, and thus introduced corresponding changes in the proportions of dry-fly components, which incidentally, Betts feels has somewhat diminished their imitative value.

At any rate, in a combination of trial-and-error and tradition, modern tyers have adopted the following proportions for standard dry flies:

Tail = length of the hook shank
Hackle barbs = 1 ½ times the hook gap

It is interesting to note that proportions of the hackle and tail are expressed in terms of specific hook dimensions—quite understandably since the hook is a tyer's most convenient reference point. However, since only the tail and hackle are the primary structural components of a standard dry fly, all that is really required is that the hackle and tail be in proportion to one another to achieve a well-balanced fly. And in fact, at least one fly style, the Variant, acknowledges this. Its extra-long tail and oversize hackle violate conventional notions of dry-fly proportions, yet the pattern itself sits perfectly well on the water.

This relation of hackle and tail sizes is, it should be emphasized, the governing theory of modern dry-fly design. But as many fishermen have observed, reality often falls short of this theory for various common reasons—water absorption in the dressing materials, broken or turbulent water, and so forth. Dry flies often do not float on the tips of the hackle and tail, but rather, ride lower with the body and tail lying on the surface and supported by the hackle fibers that extend directly outward from the sides of the shank. And in fact, a fly with the body lying on the surface film may present the trout with a more realistic silhouette. As some tyers have argued, a fly that rests on the tips of hackle and tail elevates key components of the fly, such as body and wings, above the surface where they are visually less distinct to the trout. Natural flies float much lower.

In the end, the precise manner in which a collar-hackled fly rides in the water depends upon a rather large number of variables: the quantity and quality of hackle; the length of time a fly has been fished; the type of water; the skills of the caster; whether the hackle wraps are bunched near the wing or palmered over the body; and other such considerations. But in many cases, dry flies do not float as advertised.

Still, there is no question that collar-hackled dry flies catch trout quite handily, and for practical purposes, the customary proportions of hackle and tail certainly work well enough. Even so, there is some latitude in this regard. One need only look at dry flies dressed by master tyers to notice discrepancies in tail and hackle length; many skilled tyers in fact dress tails and hackle slightly longer than standard proportions would demand.

Sizing a hackle, that is determining the length of the barbs relative to hook gap, is a simple matter and will be explained momentarily. But it's important to note that choosing a "properly" sized hackle feather does not necessarily guarantee a correctly proportioned hackle on the finished fly. The most obvious exception, for instance, is in palmering a hackle over a body, as one might do on an Elk Hair Caddis. Wrapping the hackle over a relatively thick body effectively increases the length of the barbs; that is, they project further beyond the hook point than they would if dressed on a bare shank. The results are not negligible. A #14 Elk Hair Caddis dressed with a hackle that is measured to be a size #14 may well produce a hackle length on the finished fly that is really a #12 or even #10. The same effect can be seen to a slightly lesser degree on collar-style hackles wrapped over bulky body materials or thick wing butts. In these cases, the effective hackle radius is increased, and the resulting fly may appear out of proportion according to standard relationships. We hasten to add, that unless proportions are radically violated, such flies float and catch fish perfectly well.

Moreover, some patterns deliberately violate the customary hackle proportions. This tends to occur in two types of flies. First, on parachute patterns, tyers quite often use hackle that is slightly oversize, providing a broader radius of support that prevents that fly from tilting to one side. The second instance is, again, in palmer hackling. As noted earlier, a conventional collar hackle theoretically functions as a fulcrum; the rear of the hook shank "pivots" around the hackle tips, lowering the abdomen of the fly closer to the water's surface. A body dressed with palmer hackle that has been sized to the customary proportions, however, sits parallel to the water, and the fly is elevated above the surface. In some case— flies designed to skate on the water, for instance—this elevation is desirable. In other flies, it is not. Randall Kaufmann's Stimulator patterns, for example, are dressed with significantly undersized hackle to lower the fly body closer to the water. Many tyers in fact dress other palmered patterns such as the Elk Hair Caddis in this same way, or dress them with a hackle of the "proper" size, then trim the barbs beneath the hook shank so that the fly body rides closer to, or flush against, the surface.

All of this is to say that sizing the hackle, using either the hook gap or a hackle gauge as a guide, is really a starting point for proper fly proportions. This is doubly true, in fact, when using hackle gauges, which often show discrepancies in sizing hackle; a #14 hackle on one gauge, for instance, may read as a #12 on a different one. The best way to compensate for all these variables is simple: dress a fly using a hackle "correctly" sized for the hook, using whatever sizing method you prefer. Then observe the result. Note the length of the hackle barbs that project beneath the hook shank and the relationship with the hook gap. (The barbs projecting above the hook shank will probably be longer since they are wrapped atop the wing butts, body tie-off, and so forth; and they are, in any event, immaterial to the floatation of the fly.) If you have, for instance, dressed a #14 hook with a #14 hackle, and the final result shows barbs that extend downward to a length twice the hook gap, dress the next fly with a hackle sized to #16 and check the result. If, on the other hand, the hackle barbs are too short, use a larger one on the next fly. Make a mental note between the "gauged" size of the hackle feather and the finished length of the hackle since this relationship will quite likely hold for most of the flies you tie.

Still, one must have a starting point, and there are three basic ways of measuring hackle feathers.

Here, a hackle feather is flexed, and the hook point positioned in the crotch between barb and stem. Note the hackle should project above the hook shank a distance equal to ½ the hook gap.

This method is relatively quick, but lighter colored hackles can be difficult to see, and the technique is cumbersome to use with feather still attached to the neck or saddle skin.

The post-type hackle gauge is employed as shown here. The feather is folded over the post and the barb dimensions read from a scale. The rigidly held gauge is simple to use with individual feathers, but measuring feathers on the skin, particularly small ones, is awkward.

In our experience, this style of gauge routinely results in oversize hackles: that is, a true #12 hackle reads as a #14 on the gauge. But this is easily compensated for, and this device is the fastest method for sizing hackles when an entire neck or saddle is stripped and feathers bagged according to size.

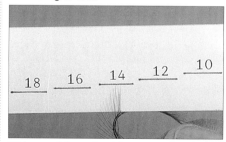

This card type hackle gauge is a good compromise. The edge of the card positioned at the base of the hackle barb, and the barb tip matched against the sizing scale. It is easily used with feathers still on the skin or with individual hackles.

The gauge can be made quite simply by ruling lines on thin, stiff paper card, and the lines can be adjusted to give exact readings for an individual tyer's preferences or tying style. The one in the photo is laminated in plastic to improve durability.

Hackle feathers can be selected for size and prepared for tying as demanded for each fly. But most tyers find that the repeated han-

dling of material for each fly requires additional time, and they prefer the efficiency of sizing and preparing in advance all the hackles to be used at a single tying session. One of the best approaches, though it seems practiced by few tyers, is to strip an entire dry-fly neck (or at least that portion containing feathers in the commonly used sizes) and bag the feathers according to size. Ultimately, the total time spent handling materials is greatly reduced.

Wet-fly hackle sizing is both far less crucial and far more variable than sizing dry-fly hackle. On wet flies with collar or beard hackles, most tyers use feathers with barbs long enough to reach from the hackling-point to the hook point, or slightly longer. But since wet-fly hackle has no real structural function in the pattern, there are innumerable exceptions. Soft-hackle flies for example, use hackles with barbs that are twice the hook gap, or more. The best guide in this respect is to pay close attention to a sample or photograph of the particular pattern you wish to dress.

Preparing Hackle Feathers

There are a number of methods for preparing hackle, depending upon how the feather will be wrapped. The techniques shown in the following method are used as a basis for the hackle-wrapping methods demonstrated in this chapter.

Method #1:

Preparing Hackle Feathers

Since most techniques for preparing hackle are fairly simple, we have grouped them together under a single method in the interests of economy. There are 4 methods shown below, each identified by a number/letter combination, where the number identifies the tying sequence, and the letter specifies the step within that sequence (or in some cases, a variation of the method). That is, Steps 1a-1b constitutes a one method; Step 2a another method; and so on.

Step 1a. This sequence shows the method for preparing hackle that is tied in by the *feather stem*. Dry-fly hackle prepared in this fashion is used in both collar and parachute dressings, as well as in stem-mounted hackles for both palmer and reverse-palmer techniques. This method is also used for a

wet-fly hackle, either collar or palmer, that is tied in at the butt of the feather.

The hackle is prepared by stripping away the barbs below the mounting point. On dry-fly hackle, the exact mounting point along the feather stem depends upon the amount of web that the tyer is willing to tolerate in the hackle (see "Hackle," p. 6). Opinions vary on this matter, but as a general rule, the lowermost hackle barbs on the stem—which are the webbiest ones— should have web over no more than about 25% of their length. That is, the first useable barbs for hackling have web on no more than the bottom quarter of the barb. Less web is better, but stripping barbs closer to the tip may reduce the useable length of the feather so much that it will not provide an adequate number of hackle wraps.

The two feathers on the left in the last photo on p. 344 are rooster hackles. The long feather has an unacceptable amount of web at the base. This web is stripped away to produce a shorter feather which is ready for mounting.

Strip these waste barbs away and clip the feather so that there is about one-half inch of bare stem.

On hackle intended for a wet fly, web is not a problem. Strip away any fuzz and scraggly barbs at the base of the feather, as shown on the two hen hackles at the right in the last photo on p. 344. On some feathers, you may need to strip additional barbs until you reach a point at which the stem is thin enough to wrap. However, such thick-stemmed feathers are often mounted by the tip, as shown in Step 2a.

Step 1b. With dry-fly hackle, many tyers take an additional step by stripping away two or three additional barbs from the side of the feather stem that will contact the hook shank during wrapping. Which side of the stem is stripped depends upon whether the hackle is to be wrapped with the dull (back) side or the shiny (front) side facing the hook eye.

In this photo, the hackle on the left will be wrapped with the back of the feather facing forward, and so a few barbs are removed from the left side of the stem, as the feather is viewed from the front.

Removing barbs from the side of the hackle that first contacts the hook shank helps prevent barbs from splaying during the initial wrap of hackle.

Wet-fly hackle can be prepared in this way, but since the hackle on a wet fly is not usually dressed to stand perpendicular to the hook shank, splaying is seldom an important consideration.

There are some tyers who prefer to clip, rather than strip, the barbs at the base of the feather, as shown here at the right. The stubble at the base helps secure the hackle and prevents it from slipping out from beneath the thread wraps.

Step 2a. This photo shows the method for preparing hackle that is to be mounted by *the tip* of the feather. A dry-fly hackle is shown at the left, a wet-fly feather at the right. On both wet and dry flies, palmered hackle that is wrapped from the rear of the fly toward the eye is sometimes mounted by the tip. On wet flies, tip-mounting is often used when forming hackle collars from very short feathers—such as the grouse hackle used on soft-hackle patterns—on which the stems taper dramatically. Mounting such a feather by the butt end would require wrapping a rather thick, stiff stem around the hook shank. Tip-mounting allows the tyer to take advantage of the thinnest portion of the feather stem.

At the tip of the feather, use your left fingers to pinch any barbs that are too short for the hook size used. Preen the barbs below the tip so that they stand perpendicular to the stem. Preening the barbs in this fashion not only gives better access to the feather tip for mounting and a neater tie-in, but also helps position the barbs for more convenient hackling.

Do not clip the butt of the feather; in many cases, it will provide enough extra length to allow wrapping the hackle with the fingers instead of using a hackle pliers.

Step 3a. This photo shows the method for preparing feathers to be tied in the *half-hackle* style. On dry flies, half-hackles are sometimes mounted by the tip and wrapped from the rear of the fly forward. This style of hackle preparation eliminates the barb splay that sometimes results from foward-palmering an intact hackle feather. On wet flies, half-hackles are used for both palmered and collar-style hackle, primarily to keep the dressing neat and sparse.

Prepare the feather as shown in Step 1a. Then beginning just below the tip of the feather, strip away all the barbs on one side of the stem. Which side of the stem that is stripped depends upon whether the hackle will be wrapped with the front side or back side facing forward.

The dry-fly hackle on the left will be mounted by the tip and palmered forward with the back side of the feather facing the hook eye. The wet-fly hackle on the right will be mounted by the butt and wrapped collar style with the front side of the feather facing the hook eye.

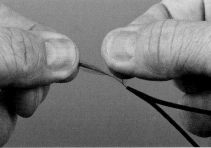

Step 4a. This sequence shows the preparation for a folded hackle. On both dry flies and wet flies, folded hackles are sometimes mounted by the tip at the rear of the fly and palmered forward; the folded hackle reduces the barb splay that sometimes results with unfolded feathers. On wet flies, folded hackles are dressed collar-style; the folded barbs are wrapped to lean toward the rear of the hook, reducing the need for using tying thread to slant the barbs rearward and producing a neater tie-off. The techniques pictured here are best used with longer hackles. Shorter feathers can be folded as they are wrapped, a technique illustrated in **Method #5: Single-hackle Wet-fly Collar**, Steps 2a-4a, p. 353.

For a stem-mounted feather, begin by trimming away the butt end so that the feather is slightly longer than the length needed for wrapping. For tip-mounted feathers, leave the stem untrimmed, as the butt portion may provide length to wrap the feather without using hackle pliers. Grasp the butt of the feather stem in a pair of hackle pliers, and loop the pliers around the little finger of the right hand, as shown. Grasp the tip of the feather in the left fingers.

The barbs can be folded in either direction, that is, back-to-back or front-to-front, but most tyers prefer folding the feather so that the backs of the barbs meet, leaving the more attractive front side to face outward. To fold in this orientation, hold the feather horizontally, so that the front of the feather faces the floor.

Use the left fingertips to maintain a moderate tension on the feather stem. Use the right thumb and forefinger to pinch the barbs on both sides of the stem and stroke them upward, as shown.

The barbs may need to be preened in this fashion several times before they will maintain a fold. Work up and down the stem, folding and pulling the barbs. Moistening the right fingertips can help with pinching very slippery barbs.

Step 4b. With feathers that are extremely long (making the grip shown in Step 1a impractical) or with extremely stubborn feathers, some tyers use a book—either to fold the feather or to help get the barbs crimped in the right direction, after which the technique in Step 4a is employed.

Lay a fairly substantial book, like a dictionary, on a table, and hold the feather by the tip and butt so that barbs are vertical, as shown, and the front of the feather faces one corner of the book.

Step 4c. Maintain the vertical orientation. Apply some tension to the feather stem,

and slide the feather between the pages, beginning at the corner of the book. In the photo, the feather has been inserted part way.

Continue slipping the feather farther into book until it is completely enclosed between the pages. Release the feather and press down firmly on the top of the book for a few seconds to crease the feather barbs.

Then remove the hackle and inspect it. Some feathers may be completely folded at this stage; others may require repeating the procedure a few more times. Once the feather is partially folded, the procedure shown in Step 4a can be used to complete the fold.

Step 4d. Here is a finished, folded hackle. Notice that the folded barbs do not actually meet, but rather form an angle. A folded hackle can be wrapped once the angle between the barbs reaches about 45 degrees or so.

SECTION ONE

Collar Hackle

Collar hackles are formed by wrapping feathers or distributing bundled fibers around or partially around the axis of the hook shank. The most familiar collar hackles are those fashioned from feathers wrapped in adjacent turns around the winging point (as in a standard dry fly) or behind the hook eye (as in a wet fly). Collar hackle on a dry fly is dressed so that the barbs stand perpendicular to the stem to help support the fly on the water. On a wet fly or streamer, the hackle barbs are typically swept back toward the rear of the fly, and they may perform any of several functions: adding color or movement to the fly, imitating legs, or even trapping small bubbles of air like those often generated during insect emergence.

Because of their similarities in structure and tying technique, we have included other hackle styles in this section as well—palmer and thorax hackle, and those fashioned from bundled fibers, such as spun hair and distributed collar hackle.

Mounting Hackle Feathers

Mounting a hackle feather actually entails two considerations: the feather orientation, that is, whether the hackle will be wrapped with the concave (back) side or the convex (front) side facing the hook eye; and mounting position, that is, the location at which the feather is mounted and the direction it points relative to the hook shank. There is significant variation among tyers about both of these matters, and many tyers use more than one approach depending upon whether the pattern is floating or subsurface, incorporates wings or not, the style of wings, and the type of hackle feather. The advantages, drawbacks, and typical uses of these orientation and mounting options are noted below.

However, in dressing traditional, wrapped-collar hackles such as those used on winged dry flies and wet-fly patterns, there is

an additional matter that deserves the tyer's attention before mounting the feather—that is, the foundation over which the hackle is wrapped. Some tyers have difficulties with feather barbs that splay outward when the hackle is wrapped, and the principal cause is usually an uneven foundation that has resulted from dressing other fly components, such as wings. A feather stem will tend to twist, and consequently cause the barbs to splay, when two successive wraps of the feather are taken around significantly different foundation diameters, as shown in the following photos.

The fly pictured here has a typical divided upright hairwing and mounted hackle feather. Notice the bulk and large diameter created by the bound-in wing butts, compared to the small diameter of the hook shank directly ahead of the wings. This discrepancy can cause wrapping problems, as shown in the next photo.

The hackle will wrap smoothly to a point just behind the wings. When the next wrap

is taken directly in front of the wings, and the diameter of the wrapping base changes markedly, the hackle will twist and the barbs will splay as shown.

The solution to this problem lies in preparing the foundation before wrapping the hackle. Add wraps of tying thread to build up and extend the thread bump used to post the wings. The thread foundation ahead of the wings can be slightly smaller than the diameter of the foundation behind the wings, and it should taper toward the hook eye.

A hackle wrapped on this gradually tapering foundation will resist twisting and splaying.

13

The same problem can be encountered on downwing flies. Here, the bound-in butts of a hair wing form an abrupt "ledge" where the hair has been cut, again causing a sudden change in the diameter of the foundation.

Wrapping a hackle over this ledge will again cause the barbs to splay outward and leave a gap in the hackle collar.

The solution to this problem lies, first, in carefully angle-cutting the wing butts before they are bound in (see **Method #17: The Angle Cut**, p. 35). Second, any smaller ledges can be smoothed out with tying thread. Third, if the angle-cut is steeply tapered, lay a base of tightly twisted thread for the foundation. The ridged or corrugated base created by the twisted thread will help prevent the hackle wraps from sliding down the foundation.

Like so many elements of fly tying, feather orientation—the side of feather that is wrapped facing the hook eye—is the subject of debate. That it's an issue at all owes to the fact that most hackle feathers are not flat, but rather cupped from front to back. The front of the feather (the glossy side on a dry-fly hackle) is convex and the back of the feather (the dull side) is concave, though the degree of cupping varies to some extent among different feathers. When a hackle is wrapped with the back side facing the hook eye, the barbs will often lean slightly toward the eye. The "fulcrum" formed by the barb tips that pivots the fly back on its tail is thus placed slightly forward, and many tyers believe that feathers wrapped in this fashion produce dry flies that land upright more reliably and have a wider base of support. In fact, it's probably safe to say that for dry flies, the majority

opinion holds that feathers dressed both collar and palmer style should be mounted and wrapped with the dull side facing the hook eye, and this orientation is used throughout the following section. Still, many other tyers, and there are certainly experts among them, prefer mounting and wrapping a dry-fly hackle with the front of the feather facing the hook eye, arguing the hackles wrap better when mounted in this orientation.

There are additional justifications for both side of the question, but finally, two conclusions might be ventured: first, both orientations produce flies that land and balance on the water perfectly well, and second, wrapping modern genetic hackle, with its thin stems, straight barbs, and long useable length, quite often results in barbs that stand almost perfectly perpendicular to the hook shank no matter which orientation is used. Individual tyers are free, of course, to mount hackles as they choose, but in many instances, it really makes no difference.

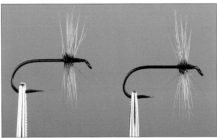

On the hook at the left, the hackle is wrapped with the concave, dull, back side of the feather facing the hook eye; the hook at the right is hackled with a feather wrapped in the opposite orientation—the shiny, front side of the feather faces the hook eye. The difference in the finished hackle is quite slight.

In the end, the appearance of the finished hackle may owe more to the particular feather and the individual tyer who wraps it than to the mounting orientation. Regardless of which direction the feather is positioned, the preparation and mounting techniques are the same.

There is far greater agreement on the orientation of wet-fly hackles, which are almost always dressed—collar or palmer—with the front of the feather facing the hook eye. Because the front of the feather is convex, wrapping the hackle with this side forward encourages the barbs to lean toward the hook bend, if only slightly, and most wet flies are dressed with the barbs sweeping rearward. Moreover, wrapping the hackle in this fashion places the front of the feather barbs—the most distinctly colored or marked side—on the outside, making them more visible to the trout.

Method #2:
Single-hackle Mounts

There are a number of approaches to mounting single hackle feathers. In some cases, the particular technique chosen is strictly a mat-

ter of the tyer's preference, while other methods are reserved for specific types of hackling. The techniques shown here are used as a basis for the hackle-wrapping methods demonstrated in the section on "Collar Hackle".

Mounting methods are relatively simple, and for the sake of economy of presentation and the comparison of techniques, we are presenting them as a group. There are 4 methods shown below, each identified by a number/letter combination, where the number specifies the tying sequence, and the letter indicates the step within that sequence (or in some cases, a variation of the technique). That is, Steps 1a-1e constitute a one method; Steps 2a-2d another method, and so on.

In all of the methods that follow, the hackle can be mounted in almost any position on the hook shank. That is, a cross-mounted feather can be mounted with the tip pointing in any direction—up or down, toward or away from the tyer, or anywhere in between. A parallel-mounted feather can be affixed to the top, bottom, or either side of the shank, or at any position in between. However, a great number of tyers prefer the particular orientations shown in the following sequences when hackling a dry fly, because feathers positioned in these ways put the maximum number of hackle barbs beneath the shank with a minimum number of wraps. On dry flies, hackle barbs above the hook shank serve no real purpose; the best support is afforded the fly when the maximum number of barbs project below the hook. Thus a feather-mounting orientation in which the first half-wrap of hackle deploys barbs beneath the shank, rather than above it, is preferred. In much the same way, the last half-wrap of dry-fly hackle is best taken underneath the shank, and the feather tip tied off on the near side, or on top, of the hook shank. This tie-off technique is explained in detail in **Method #4: Single-hackle Dry-fly Collar**, Steps 7-9, p. 352.

On wet-fly or streamer hackles, there is no particular need to place the first barbs beneath the shank, and the feather can be mounted in any orientation convenient for the tyer.

Step 1a. The *cross mount* method is widely used for mounting feathers used for simple collar hackles on wet and dry flies, as well as both forward-tied and reverse-tied palmer hackles. The virtue of this approach is that the hackle is mounted perpendicular to the hook shank in the proper orientation for wrapping. There is no need to bend or twist the quill into position as wrapping commences. Except for

forward-wrapped palmer hackle, which is mounted prior to the wrapping the body material but not itself wrapped until the body is complete, cross-mount hackles are typically tied in and then wrapped immediately. Cross-mount hackles, however, could conceivably be tied in at any stage of the dressing, but since the feather projects into the tying field, it can become a nuisance if you must work around it to dress other fly components.

Position the tying thread directly behind the hackle-mounting point. Prepare a hackle feather using one of the appropriate techniques shown in **Method #1: Preparing Hackle Feathers**, p. 344. Lay the feather crosswise against the shank. The feather tip can point in any direction; we've mounted it vertically here for a better view of the thread wraps. The side of the feather, back or front, that faces the hook eye during mounting will remain facing the hook eye during wrapping.

Take one wrap of thread over the top of the hackle stem and continue down the far side of the shank. This wrap should be made under firm pressure; if the thread tension begins to pull the feather around the shank, lift up on the feather tip as you wrap to counteract the thread torque.

Notice that the lowermost barbs of the hackle are not touching the hook shank; rather, a short length of bare stem separates these barbs from the hook shank. This bare stem allows small adjustments in the feather position during the first wrap without causing the barbs to splay.

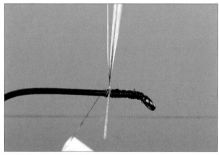

Step 1b. Bring the thread beneath the hook shank and up the near side, in front of the stem. Now wrap the thread over the feather stem and down the far side of the shank behind the feather tip.

Again, make the wrap tight and counteract any tendency of the feather to be pulled around the shank by lifting the hackle tip as you wrap the thread. This crisscross wrap of thread atop the hackle stem locks the feather perpendicular to the hook shank.

Step 1c. Bring the tying thread beneath the shank and toward you. As you begin to wrap over the top of the shank, angle the thread slightly toward the hook eye, and

catch the base of the hackle stem, where it protrudes from the crisscross wrap, under the thread. Use thread pressure to fold the stem against the shank, toward the hook eye as shown.

The amount of thread pressure will determine where the stem lies against the shank. Moderate pressure, as shown here, will fold the stem along the side of the shank. With less pressure, you can position the stem underneath the shank.

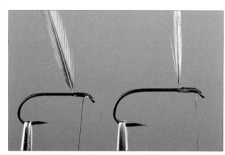

Step 1d. Bind the stem with close, even wraps of thread. This thread foundation should be smooth, with as few bumps or ridges as possible, since the hackle will eventually be wrapped over it. You may wish to counterspin the bobbin to flatten the thread for a smooth, low-bulk mount.

There are two basic methods tyers use to finish the mount. In the first, the stem is bound down to a point about halfway between the mounted hackle and the hook eye. There it is clipped, as shown in the fly on the right, and the tying thread advanced to the rear of the hook eye. The tip of the feather is tied off directly against the hook shank, behind the eye, forming a small, neat head.

Some tyers prefer to bind the feather stem along the entire shank and angle-cut it directly behind the eye, as shown on the left, forming a smooth, consistent foundation for hackle wrapping. There is no need at this point to cover the stem butt with thread. When the hackle is wrapped, tied off, and clipped, the excess tip and the stem butt can be covered with thread simultaneously.

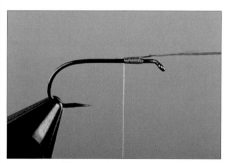

Step 2a. The *parallel mount* is used by many tyers, primarily for collar hackles wrapped in either the standard or reverse methods, and in reverse-palmer hackles. The advantage of this approach is speed and simplicity; its drawback is that the feather must be drawn perpendicular to the hook shank before wrapping. Bending the hackle stem like this may cause the feather to twist or roll, splaying the barbs during the first wrap.

There are innumerable variations of this mount. A few are shown in the following photos to give some notion of the flexibility of this approach.

Position the tying thread at the hackle-mounting point. In this version of the method, the feather is placed flat atop the hook shank, with the feather tip extending over the eye of the hook. (In a typical dry fly, the wings would be mounted first; we've omitted them here for clarity.) The side of feather—either the convex front side or concave back side—that faces upward will face toward the rear of the hook when the hackle is wrapped.

Place the first wrap of thread a short distance below the lowermost hackle barbs, as explained above in Step 1a, leaving a short section of bare stem between the mounting wrap and the first barbs on the feather.

Continue binding down the complete hackle stem in smooth adjacent wraps.

The particular approach pictured here places the hackle stem beneath the body material, eliminating bulk from the hackling area of the fly.

Step 2b. When the tail and body are dressed, the hackle is drawn vertically. It can now be wrapped as a conventional collar hackle or back to the rear of the hook using the reverse-palmer technique.

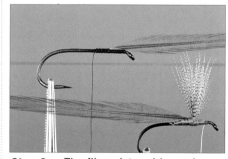

Step 2c. The flies pictured here show a number of variations of this technique and options available to the tyer for the placement of the feather tip and stem.

The upper fly shows a feather mounted much like the one pictured in Step 2b, except that it is not laid flat atop the shank, but "edgewise," so that the barbs are in a vertical plane. Because of the cross-sectional shape of the hackle stem, many feathers are easier to bind to the shank in this orientation.

After body and tail are dressed, the feather tip is drawn to the far side of the shank and wrapped—either forward for a collar, or back for a reverse-palmer hackle. The side of the feather mounted to face the tyer will end up facing the hook eye when the hackle is wrapped.

The lower fly shows a mount used for conventional collar hackling. The feather is again placed edgewise, but the side of the feather facing the tyer will this time end up facing the hook bend when the hackle is wrapped. The feather is laid atop the hook, in line with the shank, and the feather stem passes between the wings. The stem is bound tightly to the shank to a point directly behind the wings; the thread is then brought beneath the hook shank to the front of the wings, where the rest of the stem is bound. Many tyers prefer this method as it creates a very symmetrical hackle foundation, and the hackle stem that passes between the wings is not part of the actual hackle foundation, thus eliminating some bulk. Since the stems are bound toward the hook eye, the tie-in bulk is removed from the body area, and this approach is useful with very slender-bodied flies, such as those dressed from quill.

To wrap the hackle, the feather tip is first pulled to the far side of the shank.

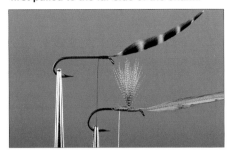

Step 2d. The last major variation of this technique is a mount used for reverse hackling.

The fly on top shows the a typical mount for a reverse-hackled wet fly. Here, the feather is mounted flat (though it could be mounted edgewise as well) and the side facing up will face the rear of the hook when the hackle is wrapped.

The lower fly shows a typical mount for a reverse-hackled dry fly. Here, the feather is mounted edgewise (though it could be mounted flat as well), and the side of the feather facing the tyer will face the hook eye when wrapped. Note that the stem here is bound to the top of the shank, and clipped off at the front base of the wings. Binding the stem in this fashion helps equalize the bulk in the hackle foundation that lies ahead of and behind the wings.

Note that in both of the mounts pictured here, the hackle can, if desired, be tied in before any wing materials are applied to the shank.

Step 3a. A few types of hackle are affixed to the shank with a *tip mount*. Probably the most common instance is in wrapping a wet-fly hackle from a feather on which the stem is quite thick at the butt end—many types of body feathers, for instance, and some of the grouse or partridge hackle used on soft-hackle patterns. Wrapping the thick stem would pose difficulties and produces unnecessary bulk in the fly. Some forward-palmer hackles are also mounted by the tip, but since palmer hackling entails additional considerations, it is presented separately in Steps 4a-4b.

Position the tying thread at the hackle-mounting point. Prepare a wet-fly hackle as explained in **Method #1: Preparing Hackle Feathers**, Step 2a, p. 345.

For a collar wrapped in the standard fashion, as shown on the top fly, lay the feather atop the shank with the front of the feather facing upward. Preen back the uppermost barbs that will be incorporated into the hackle, exposing only the tip portion. Take the first wrap of thread a short distance ahead of the preened barbs, leaving a small section of the feather tip exposed. As in virtually all hackling techniques, this "bare" area permits the tyer to adjust the position of the feather during first wrap.

Bind in the tip with several tight wraps of thread, laying a smooth thread foundation for the hackle as you go. Clip the feather tip, and bind down the excess material.

Tip-mounted feathers are often reverse-wrapped, and are mounted as shown on the lower fly. Note the feather is placed with the concave or back side facing upward; this orientation will put the front side of the wrapped hackle toward the hook eye.

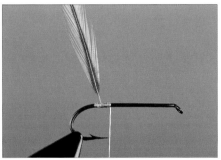

Step 4a. Palmered hackles can be wrapped in either the forward direction, that is, from the bend of the hook toward the eye, or in the reverse direction, from the front of the body toward the tail. Reverse-wrapped palmer hackle poses little difficulty, as the feather is usually tied in by the stem, and either the cross-mount or parallel-mount methods described in preceding steps can be used.

Forward-wrapped feathers can be mounted by the hackle stem using either the cross-mount (shown here) or parallel-mount method, or by tip of the hackle, in which case the tip-mount procedure is used. There are, however, some slight differences in mounting that can simplify hackle wrapping and give better results on the finished fly.

First, in a palmer mount, the hackle should be affixed at a position on the rear of the hook shank that will allow one wrap of body material behind the hackle. If the first wrap of hackle is taken around the hook shank or tail butts, and the second wrap taken over the body material, the abrupt change in diameter of the hackle foundation often causes the barbs to splay rearward.

Second, as in all hackle-mounting, a portion of bare hackle stem or feather tip should be left between the mounting wraps and the first hackle barbs to help prevent the barbs from splaying on the first wrap of hackle. But since some of this bare stem or feather tip will be concealed by the body material, it must be made long enough so that a short section of it is visible after the body has been wrapped.

Step 4b. The palmer hackle shown in this photograph is correctly mounted. Notice that one wrap of body material is taken behind the feather. When subsequent wraps of body material are taken, a small portion of bare hackle stem still projects beyond the body.

Method #3:
Multiple-hackle Mounts

A substantial number of dry-fly patterns (and a few wet-fly patterns) call for two or more hackles to be mounted and wrapped collar-style. On dry flies, the matter of feather orientation is again the tyer's choice. All feathers can be mounted with the convex (front) side or the concave (back) side facing the hook eye. Or the orientation can be mixed, with one or more feathers positioned with the front side toward the hook and the remaining feather(s) with the rear side facing the eye; tyers who favor this approach contend it provides the widest possible base of support for the fly. The mounting procedures are identical, regardless of orientation.

Multiple hackles can be mounted exactly the same way as single feathers, using any of the cross-mount techniques explained in **Method #2: Single-hackle Mounts**, Steps 1a-1d, p. 347, or any of the variations of the parallel mount shown in Steps 2a-2d, p. 348. In both of these approaches, as shown in the following demonstration, all feathers are mounted simultaneously. The technique shown in Steps 3a-3d, however, comes to us from tyer Skip Morris, who mounts the feathers separately.

There are 3 methods shown below, each identified by a number/letter combination, where the number specifies a tying sequence and the letter indicates the step within that sequence. That is, Steps 1a-1d constitute one method; Steps 2a—2c, another method; and so on.

In all of the following demonstrations, we're using 2 feathers for the sake of clearer illustration. The procedures for mounting 3 or more feathers are identical. The feathers in a multiple hackle are usually wrapped one at a time, and their mounting position determines which feather is wrapped first. There are two considerations in deciding the order in which feathers are wrapped. Many tyers position the feathers so that the shortest feather is wrapped first, and the longest feather last since it must traverse the longest section of hook shank and be wrapped around the largest diameter. Hence, extra feather length is desirable. This approach is particularly advisable if the feathers are all of the same color.

If the hackles are of different colors, the finished hackle collar will tend to show a bit more prominently than the color of the hackle that has been wrapped last.

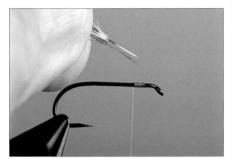

Step 1a. Position the tying thread at the hackle tie-in point, and prepare the feathers as explained in the section "Preparing Hackle Feathers," p. 344.

Place the feathers together in the desired orientation, and align the lowermost barbs on the stems, as shown.

Step 1b. Place the feather stems crosswise against the hook shank, as shown. Note the hackle stems lie next to one another, and are not crossed.

In cross-mounting multiple hackles, the feather closest to the hook eye (grizzly in this case) is wrapped first; the one nearest the fly body (the brown hackle here) is wrapped last.

Step 1c. As explained in **Method #2: Single-hackle Mounts**, Step 1a-1b, p. 347, take a tight crisscross wrap over the top of the feather stems. Note again that stems are not bound to the shank directly at the lowermost barbs, but rather, a bare section of stem is left between the lowermost barbs and the first mounting wrap.

Step 1d. Bind the hackle stems against the hook shank, working for smooth, even wraps of thread.

As explained in **Method #2**, Step 1e, p. 348, the feather stems can be clipped ahead of the wing and bound with thread, or clipped directly behind the hook eye to be bound later. In clipping the stems on multiple hackles, however, it is important that the stems be either angle-cut, or trimmed so that the clipped butts are staggered, as shown here. Trimming both stems to the same length can cause an abrupt "ledge" to form in the hackle foundation or behind the hook, which can interfere with hackling or finishing the fly.

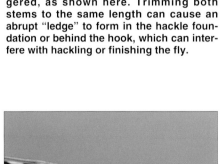

Step 2a. For a parallel mount, position the thread and prepare the feathers as indicated in the section "Preparing Hackle Feathers," p. 344. Stack the feathers with the lowermost barbs aligned.

Position the feathers parallel to the hook with the stems lying against the shank. Again, the tyer has options. You can orient the hackles with the tips pointing toward the rear of the fly and the feathers laid edgewise against the top of the hook shank, as shown on the left. (On a divided-wing dry fly, the stems would pass between the wings.) When the hackles are mounted in this orientation, the feather farthest from the tyer is wrapped first; the feather nearest the tyer is wrapped last.

The fly on the right shows the hackles laid flat against the top of the shank with the feather tips projecting over the hook eye. (Again, the feather stems would be positioned between the wings on a divided-wing pattern.) Note that the hackle stems do not lie atop one another; rather, thread pressure causes them to sit side-by-side; the stems will be concealed by the body material. In this case, the top feather is wrapped first, and the bottom feather last.

In both mounts, note that the first wrap of tying thread is made a short distance below the lowermost feather barbs, leaving a short section of bare stem, and that the clipped stems are staggered.

Step 3a. Tyer Skip Morris uses a technique in which 2 hackles are mounted independently. The thread is positioned at the hackle tie-in point, and the feathers prepared as indicated in the section "Preparing Hackle Feathers," p. 344.

The feather to be wrapped first is laid edgewise, with the barbs in a vertical plane, at an angle across the top of the shank as shown. The tip of the feather points away from the tyer and forms a 45-degree angle with the body of the fly. It is secured in this position with 2 or 3 tight thread wraps.

Return the tying thread to the rearmost thread wrap on the feather.

Step 3b. The second hackle is positioned edgewise beneath the shank, as shown in this bottom view. The tip points toward the tyer and again makes a 45-degree angle with the body.

Secure the feather with 2 or 3 tight wraps.

Step 3c. Begin binding the stems to the shank. As you approach the wing, draw the stem of the first feather to the near side of the shank; draw the stem of the second feather directly along the underside of the hook shank.

Continue binding the stems in these positions. Take one thread wrap ahead of the wing and trim the stem of the first feather, which is on the near side of the shank. Bind it down directly ahead of the wings, as shown.

13

Step 3d. Take 2 or 3 more thread wraps and trim the second stem, which is beneath the shank.

Continue wrapping to a point just behind the eye of the hook.

Method #4:

Single-hackle Dry-fly Collar

This basic hackling style is used on count-less dry flies, and its widespread use has given rise to equally widespread (but not unani-mous) ideas about what constitutes a well-dressed collar hackle. Many of these ideas are really more aesthetic than functional, but a neatly dressed hackle is one of the more sig-nificant criteria when tyers assess the quality of a finished fly. In general, tyers regard a "properly" dressed hackle as one in which no barbs splay outward toward the bend or eye of the hook, in which the feather is wrapped in uniform, adjacent turns, in which no barbs are trapped or bound down beneath the feather stem, and in which the barbs radiate perpen-dicular to the hook shank. The technique for dressing hackle in this fashion is shown in the following demonstration.

Other tyers, while they may appreciate the trim appearance of hackle wrapped in this manner, believe that from a functional standpoint, hackle that actually splays some-what toward the front and rear of the hook, gives a broader base of support to the fly on the water. **Method #9: Overwrapped Collar Hackle**, p. 356, shows a couple of techniques for dressing single feathers in which the hackle is wrapped over itself, both to increase the number of barbs that support the finished fly, and to splay them slightly.

On winged dry flies, there is some dis-crepancy among tyers about the number of hackle wraps taken behind the wing and the number taken ahead of it. The number of wraps taken behind the wing is really estab-lished by the body tie-off point, as this deter-mines the amount of space left free behind the wings for hackling. Some tyers prefer to take an equal number of wraps ahead of and behind the wing; others prefer to place more wraps ahead of the wing. The matter is large-ly one of taste, but few tyers place the bulk of the hackle behind the wings. Doing so shifts the "fulcrum" of the hackle barbs back toward the center of the fly, and the weight of the wings, particularly bulky ones of hair or other bundled fibers, can cause the fly to land "nose down" on the water.

The main sequence below shows the com-mon "finger-loop" method for wrapping hack-le. This technique is relatively fast, but gives the tyer somewhat less control over the feath-er if it should begin to twist or roll on the hook shank. The alternate sequence shows the "hand-to-hand" method for manipulating the hackle pliers. While somewhat slower, it does enable the tyer to compensate more easily if the feather begins to twist during wrapping.

Step 1. Prepare a hackle as explained in **Method #1: Preparing Hackle Feathers**, Steps 1a-1b, p. 344. Mount the feather as shown in **Method #2: Single-hackle Mounts**, using either the cross mount or parallel mount, p. 347. Position the tying thread directly behind the hook eye.

Grasp the feather tip in a pair of hackle pliers so the plies are in line with the feath-er stem, as shown. Grasping the feather tip crosswise in the pliers increases the risk of breaking the stem during wrapping.

If the hackle has not been mounted at a right angle to the hook shank, draw the feath-er perpendicular to the shank. Some tyers momentarily fold the hackle feather over the hook eye to put a bend or crimp in the stem at the mounting point, which helps coax the feather into a perpendicular orientation.

Rotate the hackle pliers a quarter-turn so that the index finger can be inserted into the loop of the pliers. You must use the index finger to apply a light outward tension on the feather at all times during wrapping in order to position the wraps of hackle accurately. The tension must be gentle, however, or the hackle tip may break or the pliers may slip off the feather. Moreover, the pliers must be able to rotate around the finger during wrapping.

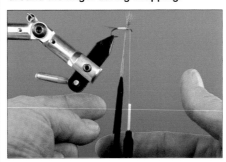

Step 2. Begin wrapping the feather by orbiting the index finger around the hook shank. Note that the index finger is held parallel to the shank at all times. Note as well the position of the left fingers beneath the hook shank ready to grasp the hackle pliers, in Step 3.

At first, only the bare stem left during mounting will be wrapped. As this bare

stem is applied to the hook, carefully observe the base of hackle feather. If it begins to twist or roll off the perpendicular, use the hackle pliers or your fingers to gen-tly twist the stem to compensate, so that the first hackle barbs wrapped stand direct-ly outward from the shank, as shown here.

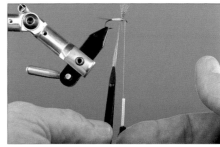

Step 3. When the right hand reaches the underside of the hook, the pliers are momentarily transferred to the left fingers. The right hand is then repositioned in front of the bobbin.

Step 4. The index finger is again slipped in the pliers loop, and wrapping resumes. Notice that on each wrap of hackle, the feather stem touches, but does not over-lap, the stem on the previous wrap. The wraps should be firm, but not excessively tight, as too much pressure may break the tip of the feather.

If the barbs begin to splay during a wrap, unwind the splayed wrap, and repo-sition the feather stem very slightly on the hook shank. Very small changes in place-ment of the feather stem can remedy the problem of splayed barbs. If the barbs continue to splay, unwrap the splayed barbs and use your fingers or the hackle pliers to twist the feather very gently in a direction opposite to the splay. Be very cautious about twisting the feather too far, or too often, with the hackle pliers, as the feather tip is easily sheared.

Continue wrapping until you reach the rear of the wings. The last wrap of hackle behind the wings should be placed as closely as possible to the base of the wings, as shown.

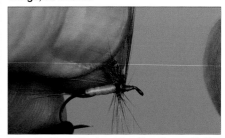

Step 5. Pass the hackle pliers beneath the shank, and take the next wrap of hackle directly against the front base of the wings. If necessary, you can use the left fingers to tilt the wings back, as shown here, to lay this wrap of hackle directly against the wing base.

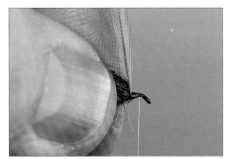

Step 6. Continue wrapping toward the eye. If the barbs begin to splay and they cannot be straightened using the procedures described in Step 4, there is another remedy.

Leave the splayed wrap on the hook shank. With the fingers of the left hand, draw back all the hackle fibers, as shown, and place another wrap of hackle directly abutting the preceding one. This new wrap of hackle often pushes the splayed wrap back into the vertical position. (This technique is impractical to use with wraps of hackle behind the wing, however, as it is difficult to draw the hackle barbs rearward without trapping the wings in your left fingers.)

Step 7. The hackle tie-off point varies among tyers, but is generally considered to be about the length of one hook-eye behind the very front of the shank. Tying off the hackle at this location will ensure enough room for tying off the feather tip and forming the head of the fly.

When the tie-off point is reached, hold the hackle pliers vertically above the hook shank with your left hand.

With your right hand, unwrap the tying thread until the thread is exactly adjacent to the last wrap of hackle. This is important; if the thread is left directly behind the hook eye and then simply angled back to tie off the feather tip, the barbs will splay.

Step 8. A neat and secure tie-off is obtained when the hackle tip is bound down by the stem only, and no barbs are trapped beneath the tie-off wraps.

To achieve this, use your right fingers to wrap the hackle another quarter turn, until it extends straight outward from the far side of the shank. This extra quarter-

turn flares the hackle barbs on the top of the stem so that the tying thread can be slipped between them.

With the left hand, bring the thread over the top of the shank, between the barbs, and down atop the feather stem. Do not yet use the thread to bind the hackle stem to the shank. Just position the thread against the stem.

Step 9. Now pull the feather tip toward you. This flares the barbs on the underside of the stem, allowing you to pass the thread between those barbs.

After drawing the feather tip toward you, use the left hand to wrap the thread down the far side of the hook, binding the hackle stem to the shank.

Step 10. Take two more tight turns of thread directly over the first. Clip the tip of the feather close to the shank, and bind down the excess. Complete the head of the fly.

Notice the absence of any splayed barbs and the vertical orientation of the finished hackle.

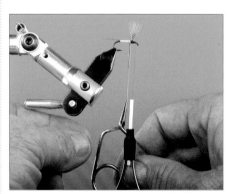

Step 1a. Shown here is another technique for handling the hackle pliers. The tips of the pliers, like the feather itself, have been kept in a vertical position and wrapped down the far side of the shank with the right hand. When the right hand comes beneath the shank, the hackle pliers are shifted to the left hand, as shown in Step 2a.

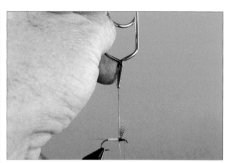

Step 2a. Transfer the hackle pliers to the left hand, and complete the wrap.

Continue wrapping the hackle, maintaining a light tension on the feather at all times. transferring the pliers from hand-to-hand on each wrap.

The specific details of placing the wraps and tying off the feather are identical to those shown in the main sequence.

Method #5:
Single-hackle Wet-fly Collar

Wet fly hackles that are wrapped in the forward direction are generally dressed in one of two ways. (Reverse-wrapped wet-fly hackles are explained in **Method #8: Reverse Collar Hackle**, p. 355). The first method, shown in the main sequence below, is nearly identical to the shown in **Method #4: Single-hackle Dry-fly Collar**, p. 351, and the instructions below are abbreviated. However, at the completion of hackling, thread wraps are used to slant the barbs rearward.

The alternate sequence shows the technique for wrapping a tip-mounted hackle, where the barbs are folded rearward as the hackle is wrapped. Such an approach is frequently used when the butt of the feather stem is too thick to wrap easily.

Hackle that has been folded in advance, as explained in **Method #1: Preparing Hackle Feathers**, Steps 4a-4d, p. 344, can be mounted by either the butt or the tip, but it is wrapped using the technique shown in the alternate sequence.

Step 1. Prepare the feather—we're using a hen saddle hackle here—as explained in **Method #1: Preparing Hackle Feathers**, Step 1a, p. 344, and tie it in using either the cross-mount or parallel-mount technique shown in **Method #2: Single-hackle Mounts**, p. 347. Notice the hackle orientation here; the convex, or front side of the feather, faces the hook eye.

Step 2. Wrap and tie-off the hackle as explained in **Method #4: Single-hackle Dry-fly Collar**, Steps 7-9, p. 352. With wet-fly hackle, there is rarely a need to contend with upright wings, and the feather is wrapped in adjacent turns. Typically, wet flies are hackled more sparsely than dries; we've taken 3 wraps here.

In tying off the hackle, the webbiness of the feather may present a problem. When the feather is flexed to spread the barbs and expose the feather stem for tie-down, the barbs may adhere to one another and refuse to flare. If this is the case, try gently blowing crosswise on the barbs, against the natural direction of growth. Often this will separate the barbs enough to admit the tying thread.

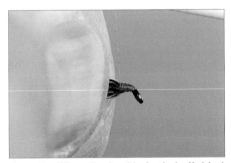

Step 3. When the hackle is tied-off, bind down the excess material and return the thread to the frontmost hackle wrap.

With the left fingertips draw all the hackle barbs toward the rear of the fly, as shown. With the tying thread, take a few wraps over the frontmost hackle wrap, forcing the barbs rearward.

Step 4. Release the hackle, if the barbs are not slanted sufficiently, draw the barbs back again and add thread wraps until the barbs slope rearward at the desired angle. The slant shown here is typical, though it may vary from tyer to tyer and pattern to pattern.

Step 1a. For a tip-mounted hackle, prepare the feather as explained in **Method #1: Preparing Hackle Feathers**, Step 2a, p. 344, and mount it as shown in **Method #2: Single-hackle Mounts**, Step 3a, p. 349, as shown on the fly at the top.

The lower fly shows the correct position for a hackle that has folded prior to mounting. The feather is mounted so that the barbs face the rear of the hook. In this example, the hackle is mounted by the stem, but folded hackles can be mounted by the tip as well.

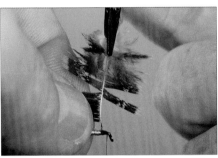

Step 2a. Grasp the feather stem with a pair of hackle pliers; insert your right index finger into the hackle pliers loop, and raise the feather vertically above the shank, as shown. Be careful not to apply too much tension, as the thin feather stem bound to the hook is rather fragile.

Position your left hand as shown, with the heel of the hand resting on the vise head. With the left thumb and forefinger, stroke a section of barbs nearest the hook toward the bend. The barbs are folded with the concave, or back, sides together.

Step 3a. While holding the barbs in this folded position, wrap the hackle until the right hand is beneath the shank, as shown here.

When the right hand is underneath the shank, release the hackle barbs. Momentarily grasp the hackle pliers with the left fingers, and reposition the right hand in front of the tying thread.

Grasp the pliers in the right hand again, and use the left fingers to stroke another section of barbs rearward, as shown.

Step 4a. Continue wrapping in this fashion, always pulling rearward on the barbs until the desired number of wraps have been taken. Folding the barbs like this prevents them from being trapped beneath the feather stem and gives them the rearward slant characteristic of wet-fly hackle.

Step 5a. The feather is tied-off using the procedure explained in **Method #4: Single-hackle Dry-fly Collar**, Steps 7-9, p. 352.

Method #6:
Marabou Collar Hackle

A wet fly or streamer hackle can be wrapped from a short, fluffy, plumulaceous feather such as a marabou blood feather (see "Marabou," p. 11), a dressing style designed by tyer Jack Gartside for use in his Soft-hackle Streamer. Gartside actually called this component a "wing" since the long, flowing marabou barbs on his pattern more closely resemble streamer wings. But the technique for producing it is virtually identical to wrapping hackle, and smaller feathers such as the short, marabou-like plumage from a chicken (sometimes sold as "grizzly marabou") or afterfeather (see "Afterfeather," p. 11), will produce a more hackle-like appearance. And in fact this particular use of afterfeather was another style devised by Gartside.

Step 1. All components behind the hackling point are dressed first.

One of the keys to success in this method lies in preparing the feather. Marabou blood feathers have stems that are quite thick at the base, making them difficult to wrap. Strip away the barbs at the base of the stem until you reach a point on the stem that is relatively thin and flexible, as shown here.

Mount the feather using either the cross-mount or parallel-mount technique shown in **Method #2: Single-hackle Mounts**, p. 347.

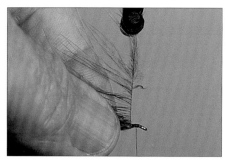

Step 2. Bind down the feather stem and position the tying thread at the hackle tie-off point.

The feather is wrapped using the procedure explained in **Method #5: Single-hackle Wet-fly Collar**, Steps 2a-5a, p. 353.

There are, however, a couple of points worth noting. First, dampening the marabou barbs, as shown here, gives better control over the material. It is easier to place the wraps of hackle accurately, since the feather stem is more clearly visible, and dampening the barbs mats them together and prevents them from becoming trapped beneath the feather stem during wrapping.

Second, wrap with a light touch, particularly when using shorter feathers that must be clipped in a hackle pliers. The feathers typically dressed in this fashion have very thin, fragile tips and are easily broken.

Step 3. When tying off the marabou, it is almost impossible to slip the thread between the barbs (particularly if they are wet) and secure the feather by the stem alone. Instead, simply bind down the feather, barbs and all; any barbs trapped beneath the tie-off wraps will contribute to the hackle.

The finished marabou hackle is shown on the left; the hook in the middle was dressed using chicken marabou; the one at the right has a short "hackle" collar wrapped from afterfeather.

Method #7:
Multiple-hackle Collar

Many dry flies (and a few wet-fly patterns) have collar hackles wrapped from two or more feathers. Indeed, in the days before genetic hackle, using two feathers to dress

most dry flies was commonplace (at least among American tyers) since a single hackle feather often lacked sufficient length to fully hackle the fly. Even today, tyers who use genetic neck hackle to dress size 8 and 10 hooks often employ two feathers, as hackle in these sizes, even on top-grade genetic capes, are often of somewhat lower quality than the smaller feathers. In fact, much hackle of middling quality can be made useable by wrapping a collar from two or more feathers. Not only are more hackle barbs put beneath the fly to support it, but multiple hackling packs the barbs rather tightly together on the shank, giving the collar an aggregate stiffness that could not be obtained by a single feather alone, particularly a feather with more than average webbiness.

More often, tyers today use good quality feathers for multiple hackling on dry flies designed for fast or heavy water. The bushy collar that results gives these flies the added floatation needed under such circumstances.

Another reason for using multiple hackles is to mix feather colors, producing a color effect in the collar that would be difficult to achieve with a single feather. The most conspicuous example is the Adams, which is dressed with one brown and one grizzly feather. An Adams can in fact be dressed with a single Cree feather, but good-quality Cree is not easily found. And many tyers, of course, use multiples hackles to achieve both purposes simultaneously, producing a bushy, high-floating fly with a mixed-color hackle.

The matter of color mixing has not been explored much by modern tyers, with one exception—Eric Leiser, in *The Metz Book of Hackle*, details the ways in which combining hackle feathers can produce unusual color effects or imitate colors that are otherwise obtainable only by single feathers in shades that are relatively scarce. Leiser has kindly allowed us to reproduce some of these color-mixing recipes, and they appear at the end of the following sequence.

The most common way to dress multiple hackles is to wrap the feathers individually. When the feathers are wrapped in tight, adjacent turns, as shown in the main sequence, the maximum number of hackle wraps are placed in the space allotted, and a very dense, bushy hackle results. The feathers can also be wrapped in more open turns, as illustrated briefly below, to allow color mixing in a sparser collar. In the following demonstration, two hackles are used, but the procedure is identical for dressing 3 or more feathers.

Some tyers wrap both feathers simultaneously, as shown in the alternate sequence—a procedure that is faster, but more limited. First, the method is really only practical with two hackles; the process can get out of control with more than two feathers. Second, the hackle feathers themselves must be closely matched in length, stem thickness, and curvature. Third, simultaneous winding puts only a single layer of wrapped hackle on the shank, and thus is really suited only to color mixing. The total amount of hackle wrapped on the fly is identical to that produced by using a single feather. Finally,

the technique is best suited to feathers that are long enough to wrap without the aid of hackle pliers. Using pliers to grasp the tips of two feathers at once is an uncertain proposition at best; one of them usually slips out. Moreover, as the two feathers are wrapped, slight inconsistencies in the wrapping foundation can cause one feather to shorten more quickly than the other. Slack develops in the stem of the longer feather, and the hackle does not wrap firmly to the shank. There is no way to compensate for slack with pliers; using the fingers, the feathers can be drawn taut to maintain a consistent wrap.

Step 1. Prepare two feathers as explained in **Method #1: Preparing Hackle Feathers**, Steps 1a-1b, p. 344. Mount the feathers as shown in **Method #3: Multiple-hackle Mounts**, using either the cross mount or parallel mount, p. 349.

The feather with the stem nearest the hook eye is wrapped first. For a very dense, bushy hackle, wrap the feather as explained in **Method #4: Single-hackle Dry-fly Collar**, p. 351, as shown on the fly at the left. Here, the wraps of hackle are taken immediately next to one another. After dressing the first hackle, the feather tip can be clipped, as we've done here, or left intact to be trimmed later along with the second hackle tip.

To mix feather colors without producing an excessively bushy hackle, wrap the first feather in a more open spiral, allowing space between the wraps to place the second feather stem, as shown in the fly on the right.

Step 2. Grasp the tip of the second feather so that the pliers are in line with the feather stem. Begin by wrapping the second feather behind the first. Bring the feather down the far side of the hook, around the shank, pausing when the feather is pointed straight toward you, as shown in this top view.

13

SECTION 1

Step 3. As you continue this wrap over the top of the shank, angle the feather very slightly toward the hook eye and lay the wrap over the stem of the first feather. The angle must be slight, or barbs will splay toward the rear of the hook.

As the second feather "enters" the projecting barbs of the collar, wiggle it slightly from side to side, pushing away the barbs of the first feather to seat the wrap directly against the stem of the first feather without binding down or trapping any hackle barbs.

Step 4. Continue wrapping the second feather forward, wiggling from side to side as you go, "weaving" this second feather between the barbs of the first.

If the first feather has been applied in an open spiral, place the wraps of this second feather in the gaps left between the wraps of the first feather.

Step 5. The final wrap of the second hackle is placed directly ahead of the last wrap of the first hackle; that is, this last wrap is closest to the hook eye.

Tie off the second hackle as explained in **Method #4: Single-hackle Dry-fly Collar**, Steps 7-9, p. 352.

Trim the second feather tip and bind down the excess material.

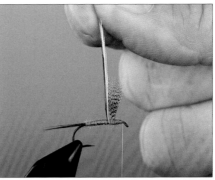

Step 1a. To wrap both feathers simultaneously, prepare and mount the feathers as noted in Step 1. When mounting the feathers, take extra care that the stems are bound in immediately next to one another. (Dubbing has been applied to the shank over the hackling area to give better visibility of the feather stems during wrapping.)

Grasp both feather tips in the right fingers, as shown. Make certain to maintain the proper feather orientation as you grasp them; that is, the feather whose stem is mounted nearest the hook eye—here, the white feather—should be held closest to the eye of the hook. Do not cross the feather stems.

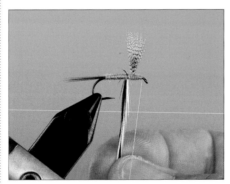

Step 2a. Begin wrapping both feathers simultaneously. As you do so, take care to put an even tension on both feathers and to keep the stems as close to one another as possible.

If the barbs begin to splay, unwrap the splayed wrap, and twist the feather tips with your fingers in a direction that compensates for the splay.

Wrap the feather until you reach the underside of the shank, as shown.

Step 3a. Transfer the feather tips to your left fingers, making sure to keep the feather barbs in a vertical plane.

Continue wrapping until you reach the top of the shank, as shown.

At the top of the shank, transfer the feather tips to your right fingers again.

Step 4a. Continue wrapping, placing the turns of hackle immediately adjacent to one another, but not overlapping, until the tie-off point is reached. Both feather tips are secured, clipped, and bound down simultaneously using the procedure noted in Step 5.

Note the alternating bands of black and white formed by the feather stems on the shank, indicating that the wraps are placed closely together without crossing or overlapping.

Multiple hackles can be wrapped to mix feather colors. Eric Leiser recommends the following combinations:

1 medium dun + 1 grizzly = medium speckled dun
1 white + 1 medium dun = pale dun
1 black + 1 medium dun = dark dun
1 medium dun + 1 dark ginger (or sandy brown) = medium bronze dun
1 dark dun + 1 dark ginger (or brown) = dark bronze dun
1 sandy dun + 1 brown (or dark-barred ginger) = dark bronze dun
1 black + 1 barred-ginger = rusty dun
1 white + 1 golden ginger (or light barred-ginger) = medium cream ginger
1 white + 1 cream ginger = cream

Method #8:
Reverse Collar Hackle

Reverse-wrapping a collar hackle, that is, winding the feather from the eye of the hook toward the rear, was more widely practiced in the past than it is currently. The few tyers who use the method now apply it almost exclusively to wet flies, though it is in fact equally useful with dry flies. It is unfortunate that this technique has been neglected since it offers some noteworthy advantages. After the hackle is wrapped and the tip secured at the front edge of the body, the tying thread is spiraled back through the hackle collar, binding the stem to the shank and reinforcing the hackle for greater durability. And because no hackle stems are tied behind the eye of the hook, a very small, neat head on the pattern can be fashioned.

The following sequence illustrates the technique with a dry fly, but the procedures are identical for a wet-fly hackle.

Step 1. Prepare a hackle as explained in **Method #1: Preparing Hackle Feathers**, Steps 1a-1b, p. 344. Mount the feather using either the cross-mount or parallel mount explained in **Method #2: Single-hackle Mounts**, p. 347. Note that the feather is not mounted immediately behind the hook eye, but rather a short section of bare hook shank is left ahead of the mounting wraps for finishing the fly head.

Position the tying thread at the front edge of the body material.

Step 2. The technique for wrapping the hackle is identical to that explained in **Method #4 Single-hackle Dry-fly Collar**, p. 351, except that the hackle is wrapped in the reverse direction, moving toward the body.

As in standard forward-wrapping, the turns of hackle should be placed in close, adjacent wraps and the feather adjusted as needed to maintain a vertical orientation of the barbs. When the wings are reached, as shown here, a wrap of hackle should be placed as closely as possible to the front base of the wings.

Step 3. The hackle is brought beneath the shank and another wrap of the feather is taken as closely as possible to the rear base of the wings.

The hackle is then wrapped to the front edge of the body. The last wrap of the feather should be placed immediately in front of the tying thread, as shown here.

Step 4. The feather tip is tied off using the technique explained in **Method #4: Single-hackle Dry-fly Collar**, Steps 7-9. p. 352.

The tip should be bound down with two very tight thread wraps, and it is important that the feather tip be tied off against the thread foundation, not against the body material itself. Tying off the feather against a cushiony base, like a dubbed body, will not secure it tightly, and the hackle tip may work loose.

Clip the hackle tip very close to the tie-off wraps.

Step 5. Begin spiraling the thread forward through the wrapped collar. As the thread is wrapped forward, wiggle the bobbin slightly from side to side, "weaving" the thread between the hackle barbs so that it lays firmly against the feather stem and does not bind down or splay any barbs.

Note: when spiraling the thread through a wet-fly hackle, extra care must be taken since very webby barbs tend to adhere to one another. They do not separate as well as dry-fly barbs, and thus are more apt to be bound down by the thread. In this case, it helps to fluff the hackle outward and toward the hook eye to encourage the barbs to separate.

Step 6. When the front of the fly is reached, take a turn of thread ahead of the frontmost hackle wrap. Then form a small, neat head on the fly, as shown here.

Method #9:

Overwrapped Collar Hackle

It is possible to fashion a dense, bushy collar hackle on dry flies, much like the ones produced using **Method #7: Multiple-hackle Collar**, p. 354, by wrapping a single feather back on itself and creating two or more layers of wrapped hackle. The method does have its limitations, however. Naturally, it doesn't lend itself to mixing hackle colors, as you can using two feathers, and the technique requires a feather with an unusually long useable length—which pretty much restricts it to high-quality saddle hackle. The method, however, is faster and more efficient than using multiple hackles and produces a somewhat smaller head on the fly since only one feather is tied off behind the eye.

The main sequence shows a simple, double-layer overwrap of hackle. The alternate sequence shows a technique used by A.K. Best on dry flies to produce an extremely dense collar hackle. Dick Talleur uses a similar technique for hackling Wulff patterns.

Step 1. Prepare a hackle as explained in **Method #1. Preparing Hackle Feathers**, Steps 1a-1b, p. 344. Mount the feather, as shown above, using either the cross mount or parallel mount explained in **Method #2: Single-hackle Mounts**, p. 347. Note that the feather is not mounted immediately behind the hook eye, but rather a short section of bare hook shank is left ahead of the mounting wraps for finishing the fly head.

Position the tying thread directly behind the hook eye.

Step 2. Using the procedure described in **Method #8: Reverse-Collar Hackle**, Steps 1-3, p. 356, wrap the feather in adjacent turns back to the front of the body. The last wrap of hackle taken in this direction should tightly abut the front of the body, as shown.

Step 3. Bring the feather beneath the hook shank. As you wrap the feather up the near side of the shank, angle it slightly toward the hook eye to reverse the wrapping direction. The angle must be slight, or barbs will splay toward the rear of the hook when you begin wrapping over the first layer of hackle.

Bring the feather over the top of the shank, laying this wrap of feather over the first layer of hackle. As the feather "enters" the projecting barbs of the collar, wiggle it slightly from side to side, pushing away the barbs to seat the wrap directly against the stems on the first layer of wraps without binding down or trapping any hackle barbs.

Step 4. Continue wrapping the hackle forward, wiggling the hackle pliers to "weave" the second layer of wraps between the barbs of the first.

The last wrap of hackle should be taken directly ahead of the very first wrap of hackle laid on the hook shank in Step 2.

Tie-off, trim, and bind the feather tip as explained in **Method #4: Single-hackle Dry-fly Collar**, Steps 7-9, p. 352.

Step 1a. The hackling technique used by A.K. Best requires a somewhat unusual feather mount. The hackle is tied in between the wings, but the stem is only bound to the shank ahead of the wings. A portion of bare feather stem is left between the lowermost barbs and the first mounting wrap.

We've drawn the mounted hackle forward here to show these specifics more clearly.

Step 2a. The hackle is drawn directly away from the tyer and down the far side of the shank, ahead of the far wing. Note that when the hackle reaches the underside of the shank, the feather is angled slightly toward the rear of the fly.

Step 3a. Complete the wrap by placing one wrap of hackle directly behind the wings. The hackle stem should touch the base of the wings.

Step 4a. Take another wrap of hackle behind the first. The wrap should be firm, but not excessively tight, and immediately adjacent to the first wrap.

Step 5a. The next turn of hackle is made exactly between the first two. As this wrap is made, the feather is wiggled a bit from side to side to prevent binding down any barbs from the previous wraps. Notice that this wrap of hackle forces some of the barbs on the previous turn to splay toward the rear of the hook.

Step 6a. Cross the hackle beneath the hook shank, and take the next wrap directly ahead of the wings. The feather stem should touch the base of the wings.

Step 7a. Take another turn of hackle directly in front of the previous one.

Step 8a. Take the next turn of hackle squarely between the previous two wraps, causing some barbs to splay toward the hook eye.

Step 9a. Continue wrapping the hackle forward to the tie-off point. Clip and secure the hackle tip as explained in Step 4.

Here is the finished hackle. Notice the spread of the barbs beneath the shank; the splaying produced by this method gives a broader base of support for the fly.

Method #10:

Thorax Hackle

The term "thorax hackle" is often used by tyers to refer generally to any dry-fly collar hackle wrapped at or near the midpoint of the hook shank. Some patterns use a standard collar hackle, wrapped in either the forward or reverse directions directly around the hook shank. Others use a hackle that is palmered over a base of dubbing, as shown in **Method #18: Thorax Palmer Hackle**, p. 366. Still others use some version of **Method #11: Modified Thorax Hackle**, p. 360.

But the term "thorax hackle" more specifically applies to a technique devised by Vince Marinaro and explained in *A Modern Dry-Fly Code*. This hackling style was designed to be used in conjunction with split tails and with feather-tip wings mounted at the midpoint of the hook shank (though many tyers now use other winging materials, most notably turkey flats). This unusual technique produces a hackle that is widely splayed from front to back, giving a broad foundation of support for the fly and placing the fly body closer to the water for a more distinct profile.

In Marinaro's original instructions, two hackles are used, one wrapped in each direction, and this approach is presented in the main sequence below. Marinaro does note, however, that a tyer fortunate enough to possess very long feathers can form the hackle from a single feather. Most modern tyers are indeed this fortunate, and the single-feather technique is presented in the alternate sequence.

Step 1. The wings are mounted at the midpoint of the shank. A tail is dressed, and a body material—such as the dubbing shown here—is applied.

Two important points for successfully dressing thorax hackles are creating the thorax itself and mounting the hackle feathers, and tyers who have difficulty dressing thorax hackle may not be giving these two procedures sufficient attention.

The thorax itself must be dressed to a larger diameter than the abdomen, as on the natural insect, but the thickest part of the thorax must lie directly at the front and rear base of the wings, both above and beneath the shank. That is, the thorax should taper or curve up to the wings, which then project from the thickest part of the thorax.

The shape of the thorax is important because it forms a "shoulder" behind and in front of the wings. This helps the hackle maintain the proper orientation when wrapped, and prevents the feather stem from sliding into the wing base and bending the wings out of alignment.

Step 2. To hackle the fly with two feathers, Marinaro recommends that one feather have slightly longer barbs than the other. For a clearer illustration, we're using hackles of two different colors. The feather with the longer barbs—here, the black feather—is mounted on the near side of the shank. Marinaro doesn't specify the feather orientation, but the logic of the design suggests that the feather is mounted with the dull or back side facing upward. The stem crosses the thorax at a 45-degree angle and is bound to the near side of the shank, or to the underside, directly ahead of the dubbing. The stem should be secured to the shank, not bound over the body material.

The feather on the far side of the shank—here, the white feather—is mounted in exactly the same way, crossing the thorax at a 45-degree angle, bound to the shank ahead of the thorax, and mounted with the dull or back side of the feather facing upward.

When the feathers are mounted, clip the excess stems and position the tying thread directly ahead of the thorax.

Step 3. The feather on the near side of the shank is wrapped first. Grasp the tip of the feather with hackle pliers so that the pliers are in line with the feather stem. Elevate the feather as shown, so that it makes a 45-degree angle with the rear portion of the hook shank. This angle is maintained throughout the wrapping.

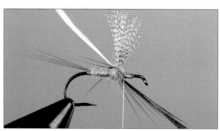

Step 4. Wrap the hackle around the back of the thorax, passing beneath the second feather, until it reaches the underside of the shank. If the correct wrapping has been maintained, the feather will now form a 45-degree angle with the front portion of the hook shank.

Note here the hackle placement. It crosses the thorax behind the wing, and is prevented from abutting the wing base by a "shoulder" of dubbing.

Step 5. Pass the hackle beneath the tying thread, and up the near side of the shank, until it again makes a 45-degree angle with the rear of the shank.

Step 6. Repeat Step 4, taking another half-wrap of hackle around the far side of the shank.

Bring the feather tip to the near side of the tying thread.

Lift the feather slightly so that it contacts the underside of the shank, and secure the tip of the feather tightly at the front of the thorax with 2 or 3 wraps of thread, as shown.

Step 7. Return the tying thread to the front of the thorax.

Grasp the tip of the second hackle with the pliers. This feather is wrapped in the opposite direction. Elevate the feather, as shown, so that it makes a 45-degree angle with the front of the shank. This angle is maintained during the entire wrapping procedure.

Step 8. Wrap the feather in front of the wings and angle it down across the near side of the thorax, crossing the stem of the first hackle to make an "X" against the side of the thorax. As you cross the first hackle with the second, wiggle the hackle you're wrapping to slide it between the barbs of the first feather to avoid binding them down.

Note again the position of this second feather stem, held away from the wing base by the shoulder of dubbing.

13

SECTION 1

Step 9. Continue the wrap around the far side of the thorax, again wiggling the pliers when you cross the first hackle, until the feather is again in the position shown in Step 7.

In making this wrap, you will have to dip the hackle pliers downward to pass the hook point. In doing so, maintain enough tension on the feather so that it does not shift position on the thorax.

Step 10. Repeat Steps 8-9, taking another turn of hackle around the thorax.

Lay the feather stem across the top of the shank, and secure it at the front of the thorax with 2 or 3 tight thread wraps, taking care not to bind down any hackle barbs.

Step 11. Clip the feather tip, and bind down the excess with thread.

The fly can now be finished by dubbing the body forward to the hook eye.

Step 1a. To wrap with a single feather, affix it to the top of the hook shank, directly ahead of the thorax, using the cross-mount technique shown in **Method #2: Single-hackle Mounts**, Steps 1a-1d, p. 347. Position the feather with the dull side facing upward.

Step 2a. Wrap the feather downward and toward the hook bend, crossing the far side of thorax. The feather should end up beneath the hook, making a 45-degree angle with the rear portion of the shank, as shown.

Step 3a. Maintaining this angle, bring the feather up the near side of the shank, crossing the thorax, and ending above the hook, making a 45-degree angle with the front of the shank.

Step 4a. Repeat Step 2a, making a second wrap of hackle against the far side of the thorax, and ending with the feather held directly toward you, as shown.

Step 5a. Bring the feather directly up the near side of the thorax, and hold it vertically behind the wings, as shown.

Step 6a. Now reverse wrapping directions, bringing the feather downward across the far side of the thorax, making an "X" with the stems of the first wraps, and angling it toward the hook eye. The feather should end up, as shown, beneath the hook at a 45-degree angle to the front of the shank.

Step 7a. Maintaining this angle, bring the feather up the near side of the shank until it is once again behind the wings.

Step 8a. Repeat Step 6a, taking another wrap of hackle around the far side of the thorax.

The feather will be positioned ahead of the thorax on the near side of the shank. Secure the feather to the side of the shank with 2 or 3 tight turns of thread.

Step 9a. Clip the feather tip, and bind down the excess with thread

The fly can now be finished by dubbing the body forward to the hook eye.

Method #11:
Modified Thorax Hackle

Many tyers like the broad hackle-base and lowered body profile provided by the Marinaro-style thorax dressing shown in **Method #10: Thorax Hackle**, p. 358, but find the technique overly difficult and time-consuming. Instead, they reproduce the same effect in a simpler fashion. Where Marinaro's thorax dressing spreads the hackle barbs from front to back, a modified thorax hackle spreads them from side to side, forming "outriggers" from the hackle barbs and lowering the body closer to the water.

The easiest way to achieve this effect is to trim a "V" from the underside of a collar hackle. This approach, simple as it is, tends to remove a rather large number of useful hackle barbs from the fly. Dick Talleur offers a different solution, using a dubbed thread to divide the hackle beneath the shank and spread it to the sides.

Where Marinaro's technique relies on wings mounted at the center of the hook shank, Talleur's modified thorax hackle works equally well with center-mounted wings or with wings and a collar hackle mounted in the standard position, as shown in the following sequence.

Note that the wings can be omitted altogether and their representational function performed by the hackle instead. The procedure shown in the following demonstration then results in an arc wing very similar to the one shown in **Method #29: Gathered-hackle Arc Wing**, p. 277.

Step 1. Dividing the hackle is in fact the last step in dressing. Wings, tails, and abdomen are applied to the hook shank. A collar hackle is wrapped. Talleur recommends overwrapping the hackle, as shown in **Method #9: Overwrapped Hackle**, Steps 1a-4a, p. 357. Wrapping the hackle in this fashion concentrates the barbs near the base of the wing and makes dividing them easier.

After the hackle is wrapped, clip away the barbs that project directly downward from the hook shank beneath the fly. The object here is not to shape the finished hackle, but merely to create a "slot" through which to pass the dubbed thread.

After the hackle is wrapped and tied off, the thread is positioned at the front of the hackle collar. Apply dubbing very thinly to a short length of the tying thread.

Step 2. Angle the dubbed thread beneath the shank, through the slot cut in the hackle collar.

Step 3. Bring the dubbed thread over the top of the shank to the far side, directly behind the hackle collar.

Step 4. Bring the thread back beneath the hook shank, toward the hook eye, again passing through the slot cut in the hackle collar.

Step 5. Take one wrap of the dubbed thread tight to the front of the hackle collar.

Step 6. Repeat Steps 2-5 until the hackle barbs beneath the hook shank are spread into a wide angle and the thorax is dubbed to the proper proportions, as shown here.

Method #12:
Skater Hackle

Judging by the research material, it appears that tyers are not in total agreement about the precise meanings of the terms "skater" and "spider" in fly tying. What consensus exists indicates that "spider" refers to a fly dressed on a 1X or 2X short shank; it has an extra-long tail and oversize hackle, and may or may not have a body. "Skater" refers to a fly dressed from two oversize hackles, usually on a 2X short hook.

These two fly types have a couple of features in common. First, the oversize dressings, particularly in the hackle, make them particularly well adapted to skittering, skating, and rolling on the surface of the water, under the influence of the wind or a motion imparted by the fisherman. Second, both fly styles were once far more popular than they are today. The modern fly angler's notion of an attractor pattern seems largely restricted to larger, sometimes brightly colored, heavily dressed dry flies fished on a dead drift. The idea that a fly can be an attractor by virtue of its behavior rather than its appearance seems to have fallen out of favor somewhat. But, again according to some anglers, dapping, sliding, and skittering these flies can produce aggressive strikes, perhaps representing to the trout an insect on the verge of escaping.

Spiders are dressed from one or more hackles tied in the conventional dry-fly collar fashion. Skaters, however, take a different approach to hackling. Two feathers are wrapped collar style, with the concave sides facing, a short distance apart on the hook shank. They are pushed together so that the hackle tips interlace and form a brushy perimeter.

Skater hackles are indeed large—from 2 ½ to 4 times the hook gap. Tyer Larry Duckwall says that Catskill fly dresser Walt Dette liked to fashion skaters from very stiff spade hackles (see "Hackle," p. 6). But the modern hackle-breeder's penchant for small, long feathers has produced correspondingly small spade hackles. Finding them with barbs long enough to dress a skater is difficult, and few tyers would probably sacrifice so much excellent tailing material to a single fly. Good-quality saddle hackles, used in the following demonstration, are a passable substitute. Since only a few wraps are taken with each hackle, long feathers are not necessary.

Skaters can also be hackled with deer hair using the technique explained in **Method #21: Reverse-distributed Collar Hackle**, p. 368 or **Method #22: Spun-hair Collar Hackle**, p. 370.

Step 1. Prepare a hackle as explained in **Method #1: Preparing Hackle Feathers**,

Steps 1a-1b, p. 344. Mount the feather as shown in **Method #2: Single-hackle Mounts**, using either the cross mount or parallel mount, p. 347.

As noted above, the hackle barbs should be 2½ to 4 times the hook gap. The feather should be bound to the shank so that it can be wrapped with the dull or concave side facing the hook eye, and it should be mounted near the very end of the hook shank. Do not yet clip the stem.

Using the procedure explained in **Method #4: Single-hackle Dry-fly Collar**, p. 351, wrap the hackle forward. On hooks of size 12, you may wish to take 4 or 5 wraps, depending upon the barb density of the hackle; on smaller hooks 3 or 4 wraps will suffice. Keep the wraps of hackle very close together.

After wrapping the feather, tie it off using the technique explained in **Method #4: Single-hackle Dry-fly Collar**, Steps 7-9, p. 352.

Now clip both the feather tip and the feather stem at the same point, as shown above, and bind down the excess. By trimming the feather stem at this point, rather than earlier in the procedure, you ensure that no portion of the stem is bound down ahead of the last hackle wrap. Confining the bound-in stem to that portion of the shank underneath the hackle wraps will facilitate sliding the hackle along the shank in a later step.

Step 2. When the first hackle is tied off, advance the thread in an open spiral to a point about one-third of the shank length behind the hook eye. The open spiral is important here. If you densely pack the thread wraps on the shank as you advance to the mounting point for the second hackle, you'll make it difficult to push the two hackles together; the tight thread foundation will prevent the hackles from moving.

Mount the second hackle about one-third of the shank-length behind the hook eye. This feather should be mounted so that it can be wrapped with the dull or concave side facing the rear of the hook.

Step 3. Wrap this second hackle toward the hook eye, taking a number of wraps equal to that taken with the first feather.

Tie-off the feather tip. Clip the tip and feather stem, and bind with tying thread. Whip-finish the fly.

Step 4. Using the fingers of both hands, as shown above, pinch the hook shank directly at the base of each hackle. Push the hackles together, taking care to apply pressure as near the base of the barbs as possible.

Push the feathers together only until the barb tips interlace. It isn't necessary that the bases of the two hackles are compressed together.

Step 5. Here's the finished skater; note the interlaced barb tips.

Method #13:

Deveaux Hackle

This unusual hackling technique was devised in France by tyer Aime Deveaux in the 1930s. The technique uses two collar hackles—one wrapped directly behind the hook eye, the second a short distance back. The barbs on the second hackle are pushed forward by the application of body material so that the tips interlace with the barbs on the first hackle. The theory here is that the interlaced barbs support and stabilize one another for superior floatation, and their position far forward on the hook shank keeps the hook gap less obstructed for more reliable hook-ups.

Deveaux dressed flies with this hackle style on short hooks. We're using a 2X short shank in the following demonstration.

Step 1. Wrap a short thread foundation at the front of the hook, and position the tying thread directly behind the eye.

Select two hackle feathers and prepare them as explained in **Method #1: Preparing Hackle Feathers**, Steps 1a-1b, p. 344. One feather should have barbs about 1½ times the hook gap—a cream feather, sized properly for the #12 hook in the photo, is used here. The second feather should have a barb length that is oversize by 1 or 2 hook sizes—in this case, #8 hackle. We're using a brown feather for a clearer illustration, but for actual dressing, two hackles of the same color would normally be used.

Mount the first feather directly behind the hook eye and take 4 or 5 wraps of hackle toward the hook bend, as explained in **Method #8: Reverse Collar Hackle**, Steps 1-4, p. 355. The concave side of the feather should face the hook eye. Tie off and clip the tip.

Mount the second, larger, feather next to the last wrap of the first hackle. Again, the concave side of the feather faces the hook eye. Using the same reverse-collar method, take 4 or 5 wraps of this second feather toward the hook bend. Tie off and clip the tip.

Wrap the thread back to the tailing point, and secure a tail of the desired material and style.

Thinly dub a short length of tying thread.

Step 2. To form the hackle, you need a short length of tubing. A ¼" section of drinking straw will work, as will a strip of stiff paper, rolled and taped.

Slip the tubing over the hook eye, down the shank, and down the bend. If the hackle fibers are trapped beneath the tubing, use a dubbing needle to free them.

Step 3. Move the tubing forward again, as shown, so that all the hackle barbs are pushed forward over the hook eye.

Dub the body. When the base of the rear hackle is reached, take a few wraps of dubbed thread over the base of the hackle barbs to push the rear hackle barbs forward. These barbs should make an angle of about 45-degrees with the front of the hook shank.

In order to obtain this angle, you may have to remove the tubing to check the barb position. If the barbs do not slant far enough forward, replace the tubing and take another wrap of dubbing forward over the base of the hackle.

362

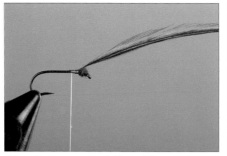

Step 4. When the barbs lie in the correct position, tie off the thread directly ahead of the body, using a whip-finish or series of half-hitches. It helps to have the tubing in place when finishing the fly to avoid binding down any hackle barbs.

Slip the tubing off, and the fly is complete. Note the brown barbs from the rear hackle. Though originally oversize, these barbs slant forward and the tips are aligned with those on the front hackle.

Method #14:

Funneldun Hackle

The Funneldun hackle is actually one component of the Funneldun fly design devised by the highly innovative English tyer Neil Patterson. In his fascinating book, *Chalkstream Chronicle*, Patterson describes his frustration with dressing some of the more complicated dun patterns and his desire to use the only hackle at his disposal—somewhat webby feathers with long barbs and a relatively short useable length. His resulting design bears some similarity to the Deveaux hackle, but is even more extreme in its departure from traditional collar hackles. Angling the wrapped barbs over the hook eye in a "funnel" shape gives the fly a very broad foundation of support from front to back and allows the tyer to use an oversize feather without upsetting the balance of the finished fly. Indeed, because the projecting barbs makes the artificial fly appear somewhat longer than normal, Patterson dresses his imitations on a hook one size smaller than the natural. Thread wraps over the base of the hackle cover the webbiest portion of the barbs, leaving only the stiffer barb tips to float the fly. This is an inventive way of productively using the larger feathers on a hackle cape, which are typically somewhat webby.

While a Funneldun hackle can be dressed on almost any pattern, it is really intended to be used in conjunction with the Funneldun tail (see **Method #8: Funneldun Tail**, p. 355). The downward-angling tail places the hook's center of gravity so high that the fly rolls over and floats with the hook point upward—which Patterson argues is a much more convincing approach to imitation, especially with selective trout.

Step 1. Lay a short thread foundation at the front of the hook and position the thread directly behind the hook eye.

Build a small ball of dubbing—about 2-3 times the diameter of the hook eye—directly behind the eye of the hook.

Select a hackle that is about 2 sizes larger than would normally be used for the hook. Some web at the base of the barbs is perfectly acceptable. Strip away barbs from the base of the feather; the remaining tip of the feather need only be long enough to provide 3 or 4 wraps of hackle.

Mount the feather as shown in **Method #2: Single-hackle Mounts**, using either the cross mount or parallel mount, p. 347. The feather should be mounted directly behind the ball of dubbing, as shown, with the stem bound toward the bend of the hook.

Step 2. The feather is wrapped reverse style, using the technique shown in **Method #8: Reverse Collar Hackle**, p. 355. Take 3 or 4 close turns of hackle, moving toward the hook bend.

Tie off the feather using the procedure explained in **Method #4: Single-hackle Dry-fly Collar**, Steps 7-9, p. 352. Leave the thread at the tie-off point.

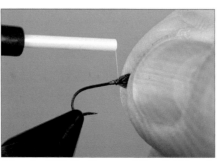

Step 3. With the fingers of the right hand, draw all the hackle barbs forward, over the ball of dubbing and beyond the hook eye, as shown.

Using the left hand, spiral the thread tightly over the base of the hackle barbs until it reaches the ball of dubbing. Take 2 tight turns of thread directly behind the dubbing.

Step 4. Release the hackles, and take additional thread wraps over the hackle base, covering it with tying thread.

Note the finished hackle. Though the barbs are oversize, the angled orientation makes the actual vertical distance between the hook shank and the barb tips just about the same as that on a traditional dry-fly collar—that is, about 1½ times the hook gap.

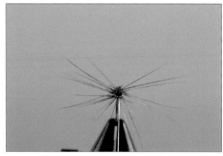

Step 5. To make the Funneldun Fly, clip away some of the barbs atop the hook shank, making a "V"-shaped notch in the Funneldun hackle.

Step 6. Here are two completed Funnelduns dressed with the appropriate tailing style. Notice when the fly is positioned "upright," as shown at the left, the center of gravity is so high that it will cause the fly to roll 180 degrees and float with the hook point upward, as shown at the right on a Funneldun tied by Neil Patterson. The notch cut in the hackle provides a broad, pontoon-like base of support for the fly.

Method #15:
Forward Palmer Hackle—Stem Mounted

Forward palmering, that is, wrapping the hackle from the rear of the fly forward, is a technique used on many flies, both wet and dry. As noted in the section on "Sizing Hackle," p. 343, the relation between barb length and hook gap may vary considerably with the specific pattern, from the "undersize" hackle often dressed on dry flies to the "oversize" hackle frequently used on streamers.

There are two basic approaches to forward palmering. The first, in which the feather is tied in by the butt end of the stem, is shown in the main sequence below. The second, in the which the feather is tip-mounted, has enough variations and unique problems that it is presented separately in **Method #16: Forward Palmer Hackle—Tip Mounted**, p. 364.

Forward palmering can produce one of two hackle shapes on the finished fly. If the feather used has a long section of barbs that are uniform in length, the hackle on the finished fly will be untapered. If the feather lacks this section of uniform barbs, or is prepared in a way that will allow the tyer to incorporate the very tip of the feather into the wrapped hackle, the resulting palmer hackle will have a tapered shape with the longest barbs at the rear of the fly and the shortest at the front.

There are a number of variations for this hackle style, depending upon how the feather is prepared and whether the hackle is dressed on a floating or subsurface pattern. The main sequence shows two of these approaches. The first, and probably most common, is the method for wrapping a full palmer hackle. We're using a dry-fly hackle in the following demonstration, but the wrapping procedure is identical for a wet-fly hackle. Also shown in the main sequence is the method for mounting and wrapping a half-hackle, which produces a sparser dressing on either wet or dry flies.

The alternate sequence shows the method for applying a folded hackle for both floating and subsurface patterns. Though sometimes used on dry flies, folded hackles are more often dressed on wet-fly patterns, and the hackle is wrapped so that the barbs sweep toward the hook bend.

While all of the following demonstrations incorporate a body material into the fly, at least one pattern—the venerable Bivisible—uses hackle wrapped along the entire length of the hook shank, and uses no body material at all. Though the hackle is dressed palmer style in the sense that the feather is wrapped from the rear of the fly forward, the technique for actually applying the hackle is identical to that shown in **Method #4: Single-hackle Dry-fly Collar**, p. 351, except of course that the feather is mounted at the rear of the hook shank.

Finally, because palmer hackling exposes so much vulnerable feather stem to a trout's teeth, many tyers prefer to reinforce the hackle by using a thin wire counter-rib as shown in **Method #2: Counter-ribbing**, p. 92.

Step 1. For a standard palmer hackle on either a dry fly (shown at the left) or wet fly, prepare a feather as explained in **Method #1: Preparing Hackle Feathers**, Steps 1a-1b, p. 344.

To dress a half-hackle palmer, as shown on the right, prepare a feather by stripping the barbs from one side of the stem as explained in **Method #1**, Step 3a, p. 345.

Mount the feather as shown in **Method #2: Single-hackle Mounts**, using the procedure shown in Steps 4a-4b, p. 347. Note particularly the orientation of the half-hackle; the stripped side of the stem is mounted against the shank so that the barbs project perpendicular to the hook.

Dress the fly body. At least one wrap of body material is taken behind the mounted hackle to help prevent splayed barbs. Both hackles pictured here have a short length of bare feather stem that projects beyond the body material.

Step 2. Grasp the feather with your fingers if it is long enough, or with hackle pliers otherwise. Use the procedure described in **Method #4: Single-hackle Dry-fly Collar**, p. 351, and begin wrapping the hackle forward in a uniform, open spiral. If necessary, twist the hackle pliers gently to compensate for a feather that wishes to roll or twist, and maintain the perpendicularity of the barbs as you wrap.

The distance between the hackle wraps varies with both the specific pattern and the individual tyer. Here, we're wrapping a rather dense dry-fly hackle.

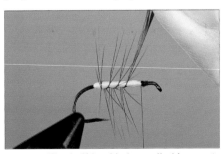

Step 3. The half-hackle is applied in exactly the same way. The stripped side of the feather stem is laid against the body. Here, we're dressing a more sparsely hackled fly, and so are using fewer turns of hackle with a greater spacing between them.

Step 4. Wrap the hackle forward. When the front of the body is reached, tie off the feather using the technique explained in **Method #4: Single-hackle Dry-fly Collar**, Steps 7-9, p. 352.

The fly on the left shows the finished full-feather, dry-fly palmer; the one on the right shows the half-hackle palmer.

Step 1a. To dress folded hackle, prepare a feather as explained in **Method #1: Preparing Hackle Feathers**, Steps 4a-4d, p. 344.

Mount the feather as explained in **Method #2: Single-hackle Mounts**, Steps 4a-4b, p. 347.

Note the two different mounting orientations. The key in mounting folded palmer hackle is to affix the feather to the shank in such a way that the barbs point in the direction that you wish them oriented on the finished fly. Thus for the dry-fly hackle on the left, the feather is mounted so that the barbs project upward. For the folded wet-fly palmer on the right, the hackle is mounted so that the barbs point toward the bend of the hook.

Step 2a. As in Step 2, wrap the hackle forward in a uniform, open spiral with the desired spacing between wraps.

Notice the feather orientation on this dry-fly hackle. The folded feather has a "V" shape, and the point of the "V" is laid against the shank to keep the barbs perpendicular.

Step 3a. The wrapping technique for the wet-fly hackle is identical, except that the "V" made by the folded hackle is laid on its side against the hook shank, with the barbs pointing toward the hook bend.

Feathers wrapped in this fashion often show a tendency to twist so that the point of the "V" lies against the hook and the barbs project perpendicular to the shank. Use your fingers or the hackle pliers to counter-twist the feather to compensate. Or . . . .

Step 4a. You can use the procedure explained in **Method #5: Single-hackle Wet-fly Collar**, p. 352, in which the left fingers draw the barbs toward the hook bend as you lay down the hackle wraps.

Step 5a. Continue wrapping forward until you reach the front of the body. Tie off the hackle using the procedure described in **Method #4: Single-hackle Dry-fly Collar**, Steps 7-9, p. 352.

The fly on the left shows the finished, folded dry-fly hackle. The fly on the right shows the folded wet-fly palmer; note the sweep of the barbs toward the hook bend.

Method #16:

Forward Palmer Hackle—Tip Mounted

Tip-mounted feathers are used when the tyer wishes the finished hackle to be tapered with shorter barbs at the rear of the fly and longer ones in front. If an untapered body is desired, that is, one with uniform barb length

throughout, it is generally easier to wrap a stem-mounted hackle as explained in **Method #15: Forward Palmer Hackle— Stem Mount**, p. 363, or to wrap the feather in reverse, as shown in **Method #17: Reverse Palmer Hackle**, p. 365.

Palmered hackles that are mounted by the tip can present some obstacles to the tyer, and the ease of wrapping the hackle depends upon the way in which the feather is prepared and the type of body over which the hackle is applied.

Wrapping hackle over soft, compressible materials such as dubbing or chenille, is relatively simple. The feather is mounted and wrapped "flat," as shown in the main sequence. The stem sinks or "bites" into the soft body material, which forces barbs on both sides of the stem upward, resulting in a neat hackle with barbs that stand perpendicular to the shank.

Wrapping a tip-mounted feather over hard, smooth, incompressible body materials, such as floss, is a bit more difficult, for two related reasons. First, in winding the hackle, the tyer is actually wrapping the feather against the natural direction of barb growth. In a sense, the hackle is wrapped "against the grain." When a feather is mounted by the stem, the barbs slant toward the tip of the feather, away from the hook shank. During wrapping, the stem contacts the hook shank first, and barbs flare outward from the base in an orderly fashion. When a feather is mounted by the tip, however, the barbs are pointed toward the fly body. As the feather is wrapped, the tips of the barbs are forced into the body material; the barbs will exert resistance against the body and push the feather stem to one side or the other. Because the feather stem is so thin at the tip, it is unable to exert enough counter-torque to overcome the resistance from the barbs, and so the stem tends to twist or lean and splay the hackle at the rear of the fly. As wrapping continues, the stem becomes thick enough to resist the pushing from the barbs, and the hackle lies down more neatly.

The problem of stem twist and barb splay can be mitigated somewhat by stroking the barbs perpendicular to the stem before the feather is mounted. But even then the shafts of the barbs contact the hook before the base and exert enough resistance to twist the feather.

The alternate sequence shows three approaches to wrapping hackle over an incompressible body. The first is the "brute force" technique that simply relies on the fingers to countertwist the feather to compensate for any splaying barbs. The second approach is to use a half-hackle, which lies neatly against an incompressible body, though incorporates fewer barbs into the fly with each wrap of hackle. The third employs a folded hackle, which takes advantage of the full number of barbs on the feather and wraps reasonably easily.

Finally, because palmer hackling exposes so much vulnerable feather stem to a trout's teeth, many tyers prefer to reinforce the hackle by using a thin wire counter-rib as shown in **Method #2: Counter-ribbing**, p. 92.

Step 1. Prepare a feather as explained in **Method #1: Preparing Hackle Feathers**, Step 2a, p. 344. We're using a wet-fly hackle here, but the technique for dressing a dry-fly hackle is identical.

Mount the feather as shown in **Method #2: Single-hackle Mounts**, Step 3a, p. 349. Note that the feather can be mounted either flat, as shown here, or edgewise. The wrapping procedure and results are the same in either case, but most tyers find the flat-mounted feather a bit easier to wrap.

Dress the body of the fly; chenille is used here. Notice that at least one wrap of body material should be taken behind the hackle-mounting point, and that the feather is mounted so that a small section of the tip, free of projecting hackle barbs, extends beyond the body of the fly.

Step 2. Grasp the feather with your fingers if it is long enough, otherwise use a hackle pliers. Using the technique shown in **Method #4: Single-hackle Dry-fly Collar**, p. 351, wrap the feather forward in a uniform open spiral. Again, wrap spacing is a matter of a specific fly pattern and the tyer's preference.

If necessary, twist the feather to maintain the original orientation of the feather; if it was mounted flat, keep the feather flat during wrapping; if it was mounted edgewise, maintain this position during wrapping.

Step 3. If the barbs tend to catch under the hackle wraps, use your left fingers to preen them gently toward the hook bend during each turn of hackle, as shown here.

Step 4. Continue wrapping until the front of the body is reached. Tie off and trim the feather tip as explained in **Method #4: Single-hackle Dry-fly Collar**, Steps 7-9, p. 352.

Step 1a. The three flies shown here demonstrate three approaches to tip-mounted palmer hackles wrapped over incompressible bodies. All three flies use dry-fly hackle; wet-flies are hackled in a similar fashion.

For a standard palmer hackle, as shown at the left, prepare a feather as explained in **Method #1: Preparing Hackle Feathers**, Step 2b, p. 345.

To dress a half-hackle palmer, shown in the middle, prepare a feather as explained in **Method #1**, Step 3a, p. 345. This will produce a sparser dressing; on dry flies, tyers may wish to compensate for the "missing" hackle barbs by spacing the hackle wraps more closely together.

To dress folded-hackle palmer, shown at the right, prepare a feather as explained in **Method #1**, Step 4a-4d, p. 344.

Mount the feather as shown in **Method #2: Single-hackle Mounts**, using the procedure shown in Steps 4a-4b, p. 349.

Note the orientation of each feather. The full feather is mounted "edgewise," so that the barbs lie in a vertical plane. The half-hackle is mounted with the stripped side of the stem against the shank so that the barbs project perpendicular to the hook. The folded feather forms a "V" shape; the point of the "V" is mounted against the shank. (On a wet fly or streamer, the folded feather is mounted with the barbs pointing toward the tail of the fly.)

Dress the fly body. At least one wrap of body material is taken behind the mounted hackle to help prevent splayed barbs. All the hackles pictured here are mounted so that a small section of the tip, free of projecting hackle barbs, extends beyond the body of the fly.

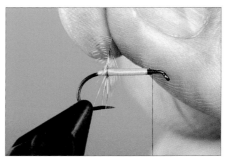

Step 2a. To wrap the tip-mounted full hackle, as shown here, grasp the feather very close to the mounting with your right fingers. Begin wrapping the feather slowly, laying it edgewise on the body. Observe the behavior of the barbs; if they begin to splay, unwrap the turn of hackle slightly, and twist the stem gently in a direction that will straighten the barbs. The manipulation of the feather must be done with care, as too much pressure or an excessive amount of twisting can break the very thin stem at the feather tip.

The half-hackle is wrapped using the technique shown in **Method #15: Forward Palmer Hackle—Stem Mounted**, Step 3, p. 363.

The folded hackle is wrapped using the procedure explained in **Method #15**, Step 2a, p. 363.

Step 3a. Continue wrapping, again paying heed to any twist exhibited by the stem. These first few wraps are the one most likely to twist and splay the barbs, and for a neat, uniform palmer hackle, it pays to go slowly.

Step 4a. Continue wrapping until the front of the body is reached. Tie off and clip the feather as explained in **Method #4: Single-hackle Dry-fly Collar**, Steps 7-9, p. 352.

The fly on the left shows hackle wrapped in this sequence. The fly in the middle shows a palmered half-hackle, and the fly on the right shows the folded palmer hackle.

Method #17:
Reverse Palmer Hackle

For many tyers, reverse-palmer hackling has taken the place of forward-palmering in most applications on both floating and subsurface patterns. The technique requires that the hackle be tied off and reinforced with ribbing material, which adds to the durability of the dressing. Moreover, the feather can be mounted after the body material is applied; should the hackle break during wrapping—as sometimes happens—it can simply be removed and a new feather put in place. With forward-palmering, a broken feather means unwrapping the body material and essentially beginning the fly anew.

Perhaps the most widespread use of reverse-palmering is in the Elk Hair Caddis, but many tyers use it on patterns, such as the Woolly Bugger, that originally called for a forward-palmer hackle. Wrapping the feather in reverse allows the tyer to introduce a slight taper to the hackle without the more troublesome use of a tip-mounted, forward-palmer hackle, since the shape of the finished hackle is identical in both cases.

Step 1. Begin by mounting a length of thin ribbing material at the tailing point. A thin metal wire is typically used, but the rib can also be fashioned from a separate piece of tying thread, a strand of Krystal Flash or other twisted Mylar, or any material thin enough to lay against the feather stem without pushing the barbs out of position.

Dress the tail (if required) and the body; we're using dubbing here.

Prepare a hackle as explained in **Method #1: Preparing Hackle Feathers**, Steps 1a-1b, p. 344. Mount the feather as shown in **Method #2: Single-hackle Mounts**, using either the cross mount or parallel mount, p. 347. The hackle should be mounted immediately ahead of the front edge of the body, as shown above.

Position the tying thread at the rearmost mounting wrap.

Step 2. Grasp the tip of the feather with a pair of hackle pliers so that the pliers are

in line with the feather stem, as shown.

Using either one of the techniques for manipulating the hackle pliers shown in **Method #4: Single-hackle Dry-fly Collar**, p. 351, wrap the hackle in a uniform spiral to the rear of the body. The distance between hackle wraps is a matter of the tyer's taste or the requirements of the particular pattern.

Step 3. When the tail is reached, use the left hand to hold the feather tip above the hook shank at angle, as shown.

With the right hand, bring the ribbing material over the top of the shank, slipping it between the barbs so that it lies atop the feather stem.

Step 4. Take another wrap of ribbing material over the first. As the rib is brought down the far side of the shank, angle it toward the hook eye and begin wrapping it forward.

As you wrap the ribbing material forward, wiggle it slightly from side to side to avoid trapping any hackle barbs and to place the ribbing material directly against the feather stem.

Step 5. Wrap the ribbing material to the forward edge of the body. Note that the spacing of the rib material is approximately the same as the spacing between hackle wraps.

When the front edge of the body is reached, tie off the ribbing material. Clip or break off the excess ribbing and bind down the tag with thread. Trim off the feather tip.

Method #18:
Thorax Palmer Hackle

Palmered hackle need not be wrapped the entire length of the hook shank. Closely spaced, spiraling wraps of hackle can be placed over a thorax area that has been dressed with a body material. The technique shown in the main sequence is used by many tyers, most notably Rene Harrop in his Hair-wing Dun design. Palmering hackle over a relatively soft body material, like the dubbing shown below, has a couple of advantages. First, the barbs are more reliably positioned perpendicular to the hook shank since the soft body helps prevent the feather stem from twisting during wrapping. Second, such hackle is less apt to break in a trout's jaw since it is wrapped over a "padded" foundation and can endure rougher treatment.

The style of palmer hackling shown in the alternate sequence was devised by Gary Borger for his Yarn Wing Dun patterns. The feather is actually palmered over the hackling area three times, splaying the barbs outward to provide, as Borger notes in *Designing Trout Flies*, "a very secure platform to support the fly on the water."

In both case, it will probably be necessary to use a hackle that is undersize for the hook if you wish to observe the customary dry-fly proportions. Wrapping hackle over the body material effectively increases the radius of the hackle barbs.

Step 1. Dress the wings, tail, and abdomen of the fly. As in other thorax hackling styles, the hackle is placed somewhat farther back on the hook shank than a collar hackle would be. Here, we've finished the abdomen at about the midpoint of the shank.

Prepare a feather as explained in **Method #1: Preparing Hackle Feathers**, Steps 1a-1b, p. 344. Mount the feather as shown in **Method #2: Single-hackle Mounts**, using either the cross mount or parallel mount, p. 347. The hackle should be mounted immediately ahead of the front of the abdomen, leaving a section of bare hackle stem long enough to project slightly beyond the body material.

Step 2. Apply body material to the thorax area. If using dubbing, as shown here, it's

best to dub the thread rather thinly and wrap two or three layers over thorax rather than making a single layer of thick dubbing. The thorax should be firm and uniform, with no gaps or high spots.

Position the tying thread at the front of the thorax.

Step 3. Using either one of the techniques for manipulating the hackle pliers shown in **Method #4: Single-hackle Dry-fly Collar**, p. 351, begin wrapping the hackle forward in uniform, spiraling wraps to the front of the thorax. The wraps are spaced at the tyer's discretion, but on a dry-fly pattern, as shown here, there should be enough hackle applied to support the finished fly.

Step 4. Tie off and clip the feather tip as explained in **Method #4: Single-hackle Dry-fly Collar**, Steps 7-9, p. 352.

The head can now be dubbed and the fly completed.

Step 1a. To dress an overwrapped hackle, prepare a fly as shown in Step 2.

Using either one of the techniques for manipulating the hackle pliers shown in **Method #4: Single-hackle Dry-fly Collar**, p. 351, take two or three evenly spaced wraps of hackle, ending at the front of the thorax, with the feather held down at the far side of the hook.

Angle the feather toward the hook bend, and begin wrapping up the near side of the shank.

Step 2a. Take an equal number of turns—2 or 3—back to the hackle mounting point. The forward and reverse wraps of hackle intersect to form crisscrosses on the thorax.

Step 3a. Wrap the feather forward again, taking as many evenly spaced wraps as the feather length will permit.

Tie off and clip the feather as explained in **Method #4: Single-hackle Dry-fly Collar**, Steps 7-9, p. 352.

Method #19:

Buried Palmer Hackle.

We have seen many tyers use this palmer-hackling technique, most notably Norm Norlander, who produces this body/hackle combination in a matter of seconds using a rotary vise, and Darrel Martin, who coined the term "buried hackle." Because the hackle is twisted around a core-strand of body material, the resulting dressing is extremely durable.

This technique is perhaps more widely used on subsurface patterns, particularly Woolly Buggers and Woolly Worms, but it is well-suited to dry flies such as Elk Hair and Deer Hair Caddis, as shown in Step 5.

German tyer Henning von Monteton uses an interesting variation of this technique that incorporates a "mock palmer" hackle of the type shown in **Method #23: Loop-spun Hackle**, Steps 1a-4a, p. 372. CDC barbs are partially spun in a dubbing loop as shown in that method. The body material is then drawn alongside the dubbing loop, and the loop-spun hackle and body are twisted and wrapped forward using the technique shown in the following demonstration.

Step 1. Tie in a strand of body material, such as the chenille shown here, at the rear of the hook shank. (Note: it is possible to form a dubbed body by using the tying thread as a foundation, but this technique is easier if the dubbing is applied to a separate length of thread attached at the rear of the shank. This approach greatly simplifies twisting body and hackle together and tying them off at the end of the procedure.)

Prepare a feather as explained in **Method #1: Preparing Hackle Feathers**, Steps 1a-1b, p. 344. Mount the feather as shown in **Method #2: Single-hackle Mounts**, Steps 4a-4b, p. 349. (Generally, the feather is mounted at the base of the stem; a feather affixed by the tip will probably break during twisting.) As indicated in **Method #2**, make sure to mount the hackle far enough forward on the shank to leave room for one wrap of body material behind the feather.

Advance the tying thread to the body tie-off point.

Step 2. Take one wrap of body material behind the mounted hackle feather, and complete the wrap with the body strand pulled downward below the hook shank, directly behind the hackle feather.

Draw the hackle feather downward alongside the body strand, and pinch both materials together at the feather tip, as shown.

Step 3. Twist the body strand and hackle together. If the feather is too short to manipulate easily with the fingertips, clip both materials together in a hackle pliers.

Step 4. Wrap the twisted strand forward, using the left fingers to preen the feather barbs toward the rear of the hook each time the strand is wrapped around the shank.

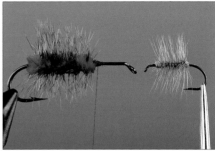

Step 5. When the body tie-off point is reached, secure the twisted strand; clip and bind down the excess.

The hook dressed in this sequence is shown at the left; at the right is a hook dressed with dry-fly hackle and a dubbed body in a style typically used for caddis patterns.

Method #20:

Distributed Collar Hackle

This technique is used to form a wet-fly or streamer collar from a bundle of individual fibers. It allows the tyer to fashion hackle from oversize barbs that would form too long a hackle if the feather itself was wrapped, or from barbs on feathers that are too thick-stemmed to wrap. It is also useful for materials other than feathers—hairs, twisted Mylars such as Krystal flash, or other synthetic fibers.

The method involves "spinning" fibers around the hook shank, and to some extent resembles spinning deer hair. But the bundled fibers typically used in this technique are solid; they do not flare or distribute themselves as readily around the hook shank as hollow hair. Thus they require more precise control and a more careful manipulation to spin them around the shank. (Hackle can in fact be formed from hollow hairs such as deer and elk, but the unusual spinning properties of these materials make them better suited to **Method #21: Reverse Distributed Collar Hackle**, p. 368, and to **Method #22: Spun-hair Collar Hackle**, p. 370).

Fashioning a hackle from individual bundled fibers has in fact been used as a demonstration of a generalized technique in

Method #6: The Taut Distribution Wrap, p. 28, and readers unfamiliar with this technique may wish to consult that earlier method.

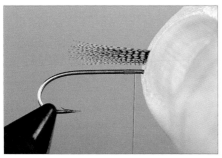

Step 1. Normally, all the fly components behind the hackling point—tail, rib, body, and so on—would already be dressed. We've omitted them here for a clearer illustration.

Advance the tying thread to the hackle-mounting point; then unwrap one turn of thread. Unwrapping the turn of thread like this leaves the hook shank bare at the mounting point, which facilitates distributing the fibers.

Clip a bundle of material of the desired thickness—we're using woodduck flank here. The number of fibers in the bundle, of course, will determine the density of the finished hackle.

With the right fingers, place the bundle of fibers atop the hook shank, as shown, adjusting their position so that the fiber tips project rearward the desired distance.

Step 2. Transfer the bundle to the left fingertips, as shown. Using moderate tension, bring the thread to the top of the shank.

As you begin wrapping the thread over the top of the hook and it contacts the fibers, do not wrap the thread over the bundle. Rather, use the taut thread to "push" some of the fibers down the far side of the shank.

As the thread begins to push the hackle fibers down the far side of the hook, use the left fingers to help roll the fibers and encourage their distribution around the shank.

Step 3. Keeping tension on the thread, continue wrapping around the hook shank, pushing the fibers ahead of the thread and helping them along with your left fingers. The goal here is to place a layer of barbs around the shank.

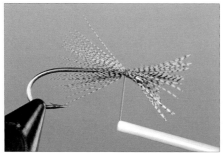

Step 4. When one complete wrap has been taken, the fibers should be distributed more or less evenly around the shank.

To distribute them more uniformly, release the materials from your left hand, and take one tight wrap of thread toward the hook bend, immediately behind the first mounting wrap. This tight wrap will often redistribute the fibers enough to thin out any thick spots and fill in the sparse areas.

If this wrap is taken tight against the front of the fly body, it will also cause the hackle to flare outward a bit. If desired, an additional wrap or two can be taken toward the hook bend to further distribute the fibers or increase the degree of flare.

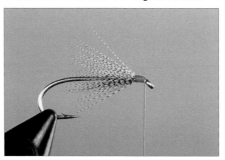

Step 5. When the fibers are satisfactorily distributed, take a few more tight thread wraps over the mounting area. Clip the butts and cover with thread.

Method #21:

Reverse Distributed Collar Hackle

Like the preceding method, this technique enables tyers to make use of oversize hackle barbs as well as hairs and synthetic fibers for constructing collar hackles. The reverse technique shown here, however, is considerably more versatile since it can be used to form hackles on dry flies as well as wet flies and streamers. Moreover, the fibers are tied in with the butts toward the hook bend, and they can be concealed beneath the body material, making a neater head on the fly.

We first saw the technique for fashioning dry-fly hackle in the work of John Betts, who used synthetic yarn. Tyer Al Beatty is perhaps the best-known proponent of this hackle style using deer hair, though we have seen other tyers employ the same technique. Hollow hairs are easier to work with, but solid hairs can be used provided they are not excessively crinkly in texture, such as calf

tail. Many hairs make excellent hackle since they tend to be stiff, and hollow hairs have the added advantage of buoyancy. (Note that a second technique for dressing hackle from hollow hair is shown in **Method #22: Spun-hair Collar Hackle**, p. 370.)

There are, however, a couple of limitations to this style of hackle. First, the fibers must be long enough so that the butts can be held in the left hand as the material is distributed around the hook shank; some natural hairs may be limited to smaller hook sizes. Second, there is a limit to the quantity of material that can be used. Excessively large bundles are not only difficult to secure to the shank, but also prove troublesome to post upright. And a thick bundle of fiber butts that must be bound to the shank may create a disproportionately bulky body on the fly. Thus fiber hackles of this type tend to be sparser than wrapped-feather hackles. However, on dry flies, the additional stiffness of the hair helps offset this problem, since fewer fibers are required to support the fly.

The main sequence illustrates the technique for using hair or synthetic fibers to hackle dry flies—a method that may be under-appreciated by tyers, since it is relatively simple and forms a serviceable collar hackle with inexpensive materials, such as the calf body hair used in the demonstration.

The wet-fly collar shown in the alternate sequence is used by many tyers and can be fashioned from hair, synthetic fibers or, most commonly, hackle barbs. The technique is often employed in tying soft-hackle patterns, since many of the hackles on a grouse or partridge—the most widely used soft-hackle materials—are too large to dress in conventional collar fashion. This technique makes such oversize feather useable.

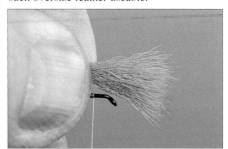

Step 1. Attach the thread at the middle of the hook shank, and wrap it to the hackle-mounting point.

Clip and clean a bundle of hair as explained in **Method #2: Preparing and Cleaning Hair**, p. 68, and align the hair tips as shown in **Method #3: Stacking and Aligning Hair**, p. 69. Take extra care in stacking the hair as it is important that the tips be as even as possible. If using synthetic fibers, such as Antron or poly yarn, comb the fibers carefully to untangle them.

With the left hand, position the fibers atop the shank, as shown, so that the tips extend the desired distance beyond the mounting point—as with feather hackles, about 1 ½ times the hook gap.

Momentarily remove the material and clip the fiber butts; they should be short enough to clear the hook bend when they are distributed around the shank, but still long enough to hold easily.

13

SECTION 1

Step 2. Employing the technique shown in **Method #20: Distributed Collar Hackle**, p. 367, use thread tension, aided by a rolling motion of the left fingers, to distribute the fibers around the shank, as shown.

It is important in distributing the fibers that the fiber butts be allowed to migrate around the shank as well. If the butt ends of the fibers are bunched together on top of the hook shank, their bulk will make it almost impossible to secure the fibers tightly, and the body will end up with a disproportionate bulge on one side.

When the first thread wrap is complete, view the fly from the hook eye to check the fiber distribution. If the fibers are not uniformly distributed, pinch the bundle at the mounting point. Slacken thread pressure just a bit; while pinching the hair bundle, roll it slightly between thumb and forefinger to even out the layer of hair around the shank. Then tighten the thread wrap and check the result.

Do not release the fiber butts yet.

Step 3. Using tight turns of thread, bind down the fiber butts until they are secure.

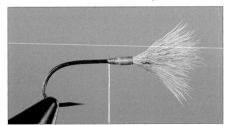

Step 4. Angle-cut the fiber butts and secure with thread.

If wings are desired on the pattern, they are mounted behind the hair bundle and posted to vertical at this point. The wing-mounting point should be about one thread-wrap behind the frontmost thread wrap on the fiber bundle. This short space provides a necessary clearance; when the hackle is raised to the perpendicular, it will not push the wings out of position.

Once the wings are mounted, bring the thread to the tailing point, attach the tails and dress the body to a point directly behind the wings. If using dubbing, a thinly dubbed wrap of thread can be placed ahead of the wings, but a thicker material will interfere with raising and posting the hackle fibers.

We've omitted these components for a clearer illustration.

Step 5. Using your fingers, a bullet head tool, or half-hitch tool, push the fibers back from the hook eye. Attempt to push them back so that each fiber projects directly outward from the hook shank and is not twisted, bent, or angled to one side. Each fiber should radiate outward, perpendicular to the shank.

When all the fibers are properly arranged, preen them back toward the bend, against the fly body. A bullet-head tool, or half-hitch tool as shown, simplifies this procedure, though the fingers can be used instead.

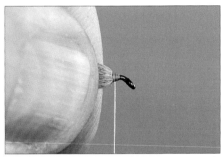

Step 6. With the left fingers, pinch the hair against the body of the fly.

Slip the tying thread forward, between the preened-back fibers, until it is in front of the fiber bundle.

Build a bump of tying thread abutting the base of the fibers, as shown, to stand the fibers perpendicular to the shank.

Step 7. Periodically release the fiber tips to check their position, and when they stand perpendicular to the shank, the hackle is complete. The two hooks here show the side and front views of the hair hackle.

A drop of thinned head cement can be applied to the base of the hair to help fix the collar in position.

You can add a bit of dubbing ahead of the hackle, if desired, then build a small, neat head on the fly.

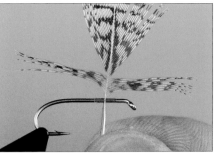

Step 1a. There are actually two approaches to mounting the fibers for a wet-fly hackle. You can clip a bunch of the desired fibers and distribute around the hook shank using the procedure explained in the main sequence, Steps 1-4. After the fibers are distributed and the butts bound down, proceed to Step 5a.

To form a hackle with an oversize feather, you can take the approach shown here. Prepare a suitable feather as explained in **Method #1: Preparing Hackle Feathers**, Steps 1a, p. 344.

To determine the mounting point for the feathers, preen the lowermost barbs perpendicular to the stem, and place the feather against the hook as shown. Adjust the feather position so that the barbs extend beyond the hook eye at a distance equal to the desired hackle length on the finished fly. Note the location of the feather stem. This is the mounting point for the hackle, and the tying thread should be positioned at that spot.

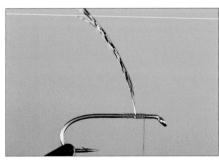

Step 2a. Mount the feather as shown in **Method #2: Single-hackle Mounts**, using either the cross mount or parallel mount, p. 347.

Step 3a. Using the technique described in **Method #4: Single-hackle Dry-fly Collar**, p. 351, take 2 or 3 wraps of the feather, very close together, toward the hook eye.

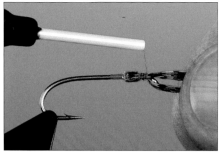

Step 4a. Tie off and clip the feather tip.

With the right fingers, draw all the barbs forward, pulling them tight to the hook shank. Pinch them at the eye, as shown.

With the left hand, wrap the thread snugly in an open spiral, stopping just behind the hook eye, as shown.

Step 5a. Wrap the thread back to the hook bend, placing addition wraps on the hackle barbs, binding them firmly to the shank.

At this point, dress any tail, rib, body, or other materials. We've dubbed a simple body here. Note that the body is not dressed right up to the base of the hackle barbs; a small space is left at the front of the body to facilitate folding and secure the barbs in subsequent steps.

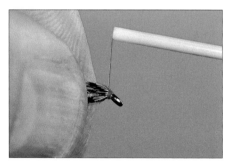

Step 6a. Fold all the hackle barbs back along the sides of the body. Pull them evenly and snugly, and pinch them against the body as shown.

Slip the tying thread between the barbs, and position it on the bare shank behind the hook eye.

Build a small thread bump abutting the base of the hackle barbs, and then take 2 or 3 turns of thread over the front of the hackle base to slant the barbs toward the rear of the hook in typical wet-fly style, as shown. Periodically release the barbs in your left hand to check your progress.

Step 7a. When the barbs are secured at the desired angle, the hackle is complete.

Method #22:

Spun-hair Collar Hackle

In this technique, a hackle is actually spun from hollow hair, either deer or elk. It is somewhat faster to execute than the procedure shown in **Method #21: Reverse Distributed Collar Hackle**, p. 368, and results in a collar that occupies a longer section of the hook and provides a wider base of support.

The one limitation with this method can be in using hooks smaller than about size 14. On larger hooks, flaring the hair to form the collar poses no problem because the hair itself is mounted far enough from the tip that the thread binds down a hollow area of hair shaft and the hair will flare, as shown in the main sequence. On smaller hooks, however, the proper hackle length may prove so short that the hair is not bound down at a point where it is hollow, and the tips will not flare. Thus when using smaller hooks, care must be taken to choose hair that is hollow close to the tips (see "Hollow Hair," p. 2). Bundles of hair used for smaller hooks are more easily handled using the technique shown in the alternate sequence.

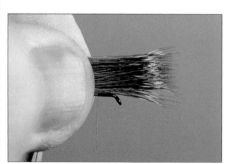

Step 1. Mount the thread near the mid-point of the hook, and lay a foundation forward, stopping the thread at the point on the shank where you wish the hackle collar to begin.

Clip and clean a bundle of hair as explained in **Method #2: Preparing and Cleaning Hair**, p. 68, and align the hair tips as shown in **Method #3: Stacking and Aligning Hair**, p. 69. The quantity of hair depends upon the size of the hook and the desired density of the finished wing. As a starting point for experimentation, use of bundle of hair that, when given a tight half-

twist, is about twice the diameter of the hook eye.

Using the hook gap or a hackle gauge as a guide, establish the length of the hackle fibers. Then clip the fiber butts; they should be short enough to clear the hook bend when spun around the shank, but long enough to grasp easily.

Pinch the clump in the left fingers directly behind the mounting point, and position it atop the shank, as shown, so that the hair extends beyond the tying thread at a distance equal to the desired length of the finished hackle.

Step 2. Take one complete turn of thread around the hook shank and hair bundle at the mounting point, ending with the bobbin held directly away from you, on the far side of the shank, as shown. When taking this wrap, use just enough tension to hold the clump in position, but not enough to flare the hair.

Step 3. Pull the thread tightly, directly away from you, to flare the hair. As you put pressure on the tying thread, coax the butts of the hair around the shank by rolling them with your left fingers.

As the hair begins to flare and spin around the shank, "follow" it with the thread, taking 3 or 4 additional tight turns atop the first.

It's important that the hair butts be allowed to spin around the shank along with the tips. If the butts are long and catch on the bend of the hook, pause periodically during the hair spinning to free them. If they are not allowed to spin, the butt ends of the fibers will be bunched together on one side of the hook shank; their bulk will make it almost impossible to secure the fibers tightly, and the body will end up with a disproportionate bulge on one side.

13

Step 4. Release the hair, and take 4 or 5 tight turns of thread through the hair butts toward the hook bend to secure the hair bundle to the shank.

Wrap the thread back to the mounting point, securing the butts with additional wraps.

Step 5. Trim the hair butts and bind them down with tying thread. It isn't necessary to completely cover all the exposed hair butts with thread; attempting to do so may make the underbody excessively thick. Take enough thread wraps to secure the hair firmly, and let the body material conceal the very tag ends of the hair.

If wings are used on the fly, make a smooth, even foundation of thread at the wing-mounting point.

If desired, wings are mounted and posted to the vertical at this stage of the procedure. The wings should be mounted a distance of about one thread-wrap behind the frontmost mounting wrap on the hair.

Bring the tying thread to the tailing point. Dress the tail and the body. Position the tying thread directly atop the frontmost thread wrap that secures the hair hackle.

Step 6. Spin the bobbin to twist the tying thread. Begin winding the thread tightly through the hair tips. The wraps of thread should be placed quite closely together. As you wrap the thread, wiggle it slightly to avoid binding down any hair tips.

Each wrap of thread serves two purposes. First, it helps distribute the hair tips more evenly around the shank, and second, it raises them perpendicular to the shank.

The photo here shows two thread wraps taken through tips. Notice the hair tips behind the thread have been flared perpendicular to the shank.

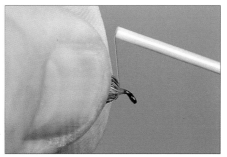

Step 7. After 4 or 5 very closely spaced wraps have been taken through the hair, most of the tips will have flared. A small amount of hair will still project over the hook eye, but additional thread wraps will do little to raise them to the perpendicular.

Instead, preen these hairs back toward the hook bend, and build a small thread bump ahead of them to hold them upright.

Step 8. Here is the finished hackle. You can apply a drop of thin head cement at the front base of the hair hackle, allowing it to bleed into hair butts throughout the collar. The cement adds durability and stiffness to the hackle.

Step 1a. You may find it easier, particularly when working with smaller hooks, to mount the hair bundle while holding it by the tips and pushing the hair butts into the hook eye, as shown here. The eye of the hook should be centered in the bundle.

Step 2a. With the left hand, take 2 snug, but not tight, wraps of thread over the mounting point of the hair bundle.

Step 3a. Maintaining your hold on the hair tips, pull the thread to flare the hair, and take an additional thread wrap or two over the mounting point.

Once these additional wraps are made, the hair will be affixed securely enough so that you can release the tips and proceed to Step 4.

Method #23:

Loop-spun Hackle

A collar hackle, primarily for wet flies, can be formed from natural hair, synthetic fibers, or feather barbs such as marabou, mounted and spun in a dubbing loop. Natural fur is probably the most commonly used material, and the method for spinning a fur hackle is shown in the main sequence below. In general, the hackle is formed from either the guard hair or the underfur, since what we term "hackle" customarily consists of fibers of approximately uniform length. A mixture of guard hairs and underfur can certainly be spun in a dubbing loop, though this technique is typically used to form collars and legs on nymph patterns and is explained in **Method #13: Dubbing-loop Legs**, p. 422.

Ordinarily, spun-loop hackles are not used to dress dry flies. The spinning process splays the fibers 360 degrees around the thread core, and wrapping a neat, perpendicular dry-fly hackle from such fibers is difficult. There is an exception here, however, shown in the alternate sequence. Clipped CDC barbs are spun in a loop and used to form what Darrel Martin calls a "mock palmer" hackle—a method best suited to smaller hooks. The spun hackle can be wrapped in close, adjacent turns over a thread foundation to make a simple hackle fly—something like a CDC Bivisible—or palmered over a body, as shown in the following demonstration, for a pattern resembling a Griffith's Gnat.

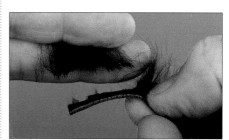

Step 1. Position the tying thread at the hackle-mounting point, and form a dubbing loop as explained in **Method #38: Trap-loop Dubbing**, p. 129. Wax the loop, and advance the thread to the hackle tie-off point.

The method for clipping the hair and mounting it in the loop is identical to that shown in **Method #41: Fur Chenille Dubbing Loop**, p. 131; thus the instructions here are abbreviated; and readers seeking a more detailed explanation should consult that method. As explained in **Method #41**, use a paper clamp or, as shown, form "scissors" with the left hand and clamp the hair tips crosswise. We're using a strip of rabbit fur here.

Cut a section of fur about 1"-2" long, close to the base of the hide. Since wet flies are, as a rule, sparsely hackled, not much fur is required.

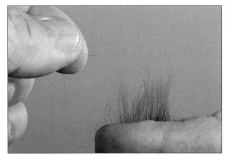

Step 2. Again form "scissors" with the fingers of the right hand, and clamp the clipped fur tightly at the base, as shown.

Use the fingers of the left hand to draw out the guard hairs. The left fingers should now have the guard hairs held by the tip and the right fingers have the underfur held by the base.

The hackle will be formed from the underfur. If you wish to fashion the hackle from the guard hair, simply discard the underfur and clamp the butt ends of the guard hairs in the right fingers.

Step 3. Insert the hairs into the loop, as shown. The tips should project beyond the thread a distance equal to the desired length of the hackle fibers.

When the hair has been mounted to the proper length, insert a dubbing twister, whirl, or crochet hook into the loop, and pull it closed, trapping the hair between the two loop threads.

Step 4. Holding the loop taut, carefully clip the hair butts close to the thread.

Step 5. Spin the dubbing loop tightly to trap the hair securely in the thread core.

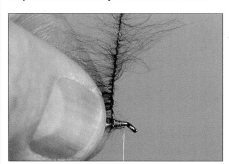

Step 6. Begin wrapping the spun hair. With each wrap, use the left fingers to draw the hair back toward the hook bend, as shown, so that no fibers are trapped beneath the thread core. This preening will also help position the hackle to sweep back toward the hook bend.

Step 7. When the desired amount of hackle has been applied, tie off the dubbing loop and clip the excess.

If the frontmost fibers do not slant back at the proper angle, preen them back with the left fingers and take a few thread wraps over the base of the fibers to secure them in the desired position.

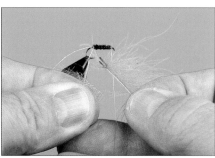

Step 1a. To form a "mock palmer" hackle from CDC, form a dubbing loop (see **Method #38: Trap-loop Dubbing**, p. 129) at the rear of the hook shank. The loop should be at least 7 times longer than the hook shank. Wax one of threads well.

Mount and wrap the body material. We're using peacock herl here. (If the fly is to be dressed entirely with adjacent turns of the spun barbs, no body material is required.)

Advance the tying thread to the rear of the hook eye.

Take two CDC feathers and place them together so that the curvatures match and the stems are aligned.

Strip or cut a section of barbs from the two stems simultaneously.

Step 2a. Trim the base of the barbs so that the remaining fibers are twice as long as the desired length of the finished hackle.

Mount the barbs in the loop by placing them crosswise on the waxed thread. The fibers extending outward from each side of the thread should be equal in length.

Do not yet close the loop. The fibers will adhere to the waxed thread and be held in position.

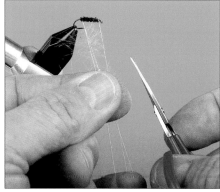

Step 3a. Insert the little finger of the left hand into the base of the loop to hold it open, as shown, freeing the rest of the fingers.

Strip another section of barbs, clip them to length, and mount them.

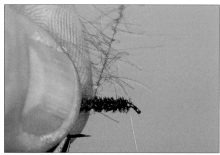

Step 4a. Continue cutting sections of CDC barbs, trimming to length, and mounting them in the loop.

When you have mounted barbs on a section of thread about 6 times as long as the hook shank, spin the loop tightly.

Wrap the hackle as shown in Step 6, preening the barbs toward the hook bend with each turn of hackle. Here, the hackle is wrapped forward in an open spiral to let the body material show between the wraps.

13

Step 5a. When the hackle is wrapped up to the tying thread, tie off the loop and clip the excess.

Any long barbs can be trimmed to make a hackle of uniform diameter.

Method #24:

Mylar Hackle

Collar hackle for attractor-style wet flies and streamers can be fashioned from woven Mylar tubing of the type often used to make bodies on streamers such as the Zonker. Metallic-finish tubing can be used for the purpose, but some interesting effects are obtained by using colored pearlescent Mylars.

There are a couple of approaches to forming this hackle, depending upon the preferred mounting technique and the desired density of the finished hackle.

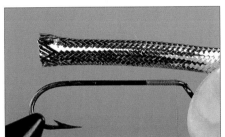

Step 1. Normally, this style of hackle is the last component dressed on the fly. After applying tail, body, wings, and so on, lay a thread foundation at the hackle-mounting point if such a base has not already been formed by tying off other materials. We've omitted the other fly components here for clarity of illustration and laid a simple thread base on the hook shank.

Cut a length of tubing about ½" longer than the desired length of the finished hackle. Remove the core.

Step 2. In this particular approach, the thread is first tied off with a whip-finish or several half-hitches, and clipped.

Slip the tubing over the hook eye, and slide it back toward the bend until the butt end of the tubing is positioned over the hackle-mounting point, as shown.

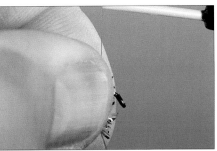

Step 3. With the left fingers, tightly pinch both the loose end of the tying thread from the bobbin and the Mylar tubing against the hook shank.

Remount the tying thread at the hackle-mounting point, as shown.

Bind in the tubing with several very tight wraps of thread, moving toward the hook eye.

Step 4. Trim the tag end of tying thread and the tags of Mylar material behind the eye. Cover the butts with thread.

With a dubbing needle, unravel the strands of Mylar.

Step 5. Continue unraveling the tubing until all the strands are separated, as shown.

The strands can now be clipped to the exact length.

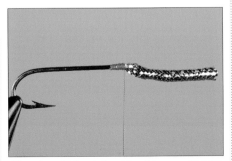

Step 1a. This style of hackle can also be mounted in reverse. Position the tying thread a few wraps behind the actual hackle-mounting point.

Cut a length of tubing as in Step 1, and slip the butt end of the tubing over the hook. Secure the tubing with several tight wraps of thread, moving toward the hook eye.

When the tubing is secured, clip the Mylar tags, and cover with thread. Then clip the tubing to the desired length of the finished hackle.

Position the thread at the frontmost mounting wrap.

Step 2a. With a dubbing needle, completely unravel the Mylar strands.

Step 3a. When the tubing is unraveled, fold the strands back alongside the fly body.

Slip the tying thread between the Mylar strands so that it is positioned in front of the hackle, as shown. Build a thread bump at the base of the Mylar strands to force them back toward the hook bend.

Step 4a. If a small thread bump is built, the strands will project more directly outward from the shank. If a larger thread bump is built, as we've done here, or if the thread is wrapped over the front edge of the collar, the hackle will lie closer to the body for a more streamlined appearance.

Step 5a. A denser collar can be created by mounting two or more lengths of tubing. We've mounted three pieces here, but whatever the number, they should distributed equally around the hook shank to give a uniform density of strands in the finished hackle. Three different types of tubing are used here to show their relative placement around the shank.

374

Step 6a. When all the strands are secured, use a dubbing needle to unravel them completely.

Method #25:

Woven Hackle

It is probably safe to say that hackle weaving is one of the more obscure techniques in fly tying. Few tyers have probably heard of it, and far fewer are familiar with the procedure. As far as we can determine, hackle weaving originated with German immigrant Franz Pott, whose fly designs such as the Mite series incorporated woven bodies (see **Method #115: The Pott's Weave**, p. 199) and woven hackles. Though Pott's hackle weave, which incorporated a 3-strand thread core, was patented in the 1930s, the exact technique has remained something of a mystery to tyers. About the same time, master fly-weaver George Grant devised his own technique using a 2-strand core, and his method has predominated among tyers who weave hackles.

The materials preferred by both Potts and Grant are difficult and expensive to obtain for the modern tyer—ox ear hair, Chinese boar bristle, and imported badger. Grant later turned to synthetic materials and these are perhaps more practical for today's tyer. The two requirements in hackle-weaving fibers are stiffness and length. The original flies dressed with such hackle were designed for fishing in big, fast, Western rivers, and they were often swung on a tight line. The stiff fibers would maintain their shape against the resistance of fast-moving water where a softer fiber would simply be pressed back against the fly, obscuring the body. The fiber length, at least 2" or so, is necessary for handling during the weaving procedure.

While preparing the materials is a bit time-consuming, the weaving technique itself is in fact not particularly difficult.

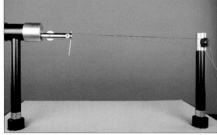

Step 1. To set up the core strands, take a length of thread 3/0 or thicker (we're using a

size A in this demonstration). Double the thread to form a loop in one end, and then tie an overhand knot about 2" or 3" from the loop.

Secure a pin in the vise jaws, as shown, and slip the thread loop over the pin.

The other ends of the thread are secure to a vertical support on the tying bench positioned about a foot away from the vise jaws. A second vise could be used for this support. We're using a rotary Nor-Vise in this demonstration which has a thread post. The two loose ends of thread are secured to a rubber button on the post.

Notice the angle between these two threads. Don't make the angle too large, or securing the hairs to the core threads is more difficult. Too small an angle makes weaving the hair more complicated. The angle shown here is about right.

The top strand here has been colored black to distinguish between the two threads in the following steps.

Step 2. Individual hairs are not actually woven; rather, clumps of 3-5 hairs are used, and weaving is simplest if the hair butts are cemented together.

Select 3-5 hairs and align the tips; we're using badger hair here. Apply cement to the last ½" of the hair butts by dipping them in a jar of head cement or applying it with a dubbing needle.

Form a loop of masking tape and secure it to the edge of the tying bench as shown. Press the tips of the cemented hairs lightly to the tape, letting butts overhang the tying bench. The tape holds the hair clumps while they dry and keeps them handy for weaving.

You'll need about 15-20 bundles of hair for the hackle.

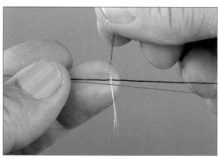

Step 3. Take a bundle of hair, and insert it tip-downward into the loop. Notice that the bundles passes in front of the top (black) strand and behind the bottom (red) one. With your left middle finger, press the bundle against the loop from behind.

Use your right hand to adjust the length of the tips projecting beneath the lower thread—this establishes the length of the finished hackle.

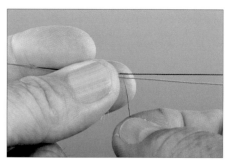

Step 4. Once the length of the hackle is established, pinch your left thumb against your left middle finger to hold the bundle firmly in place. This pinch is maintained throughout the entire weaving process to ensure that the tips don't shift position and the finished hackle fibers will be of uniform length.

With the right fingers, fold the hair butts back over the top thread. Pull the butts downward, snugging the fold against the top thread.

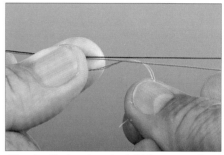

Step 5. Notice that the fold formed in Step 4 is now pinched between left thumb and middle finger to hold it in place.

Wrap the hair butts once around the lower thread only.

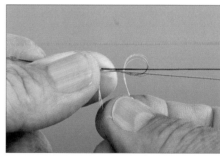

Step 6. Slide the wrap formed in Step 5 toward the left fingertips.

Now take the hair butts and simply form a half-hitch around both threads, as shown.

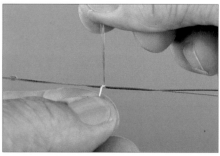

Step 7. Snug the half-hitch against the threads, pulling the hair tips with the left fingers and hair butts with the right fingers. Pull firmly, but not too tightly or the hair may break.

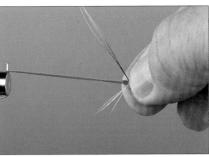

Step 8. Now using the right fingers, slide the woven bundle down the thread and abut it against the overhand knot.

Step 9. Repeat Steps 3-8 with the remaining bundles. When inserting a new bundle into the loop, as in Step 3, use the previously woven hair tips as a gauge for each new bundle in order to make all the hair tips equal in length on the finished hackle.

After each new bundle is woven, slide it against the previously woven hair, as shown here.

When about ½" of the thread core is woven with hair, repeat the weaving process using a length of waxed tying thread. This will secure the core strands, and the hackle can be removed and mounted on a fly.

Step 10. When the hackle is complete, clip the hair butts close to the core threads.

The woven hackle strand is mounted and wrapped exactly as though it were a wet-fly hackle (see **Method #5: Single-hackle Wet-fly Collar**, p. 352). Only one complete wrap of the woven hackle is used.

Grant typically dressed these woven hackles on woven-body flies, as shown here.

Throat and Cross Hackle

Throat hackle (sometimes called "beard" hackle) consists of fibers bound behind the hook eye on the underside of the shank. On streamers, throat hackle may be used to give some density near the head of the pattern or to imitate gills or gill plates. On wet flies and nymphs, such hackle is typically used to imitate legs, as very soft fibers will undulate underwater. In fact, many of the techniques shown below could logically be placed in the chapter on "Legs," but since it is the custom among tyers to refer to this component as a type of hackle, we have included the methods for dressing it in this chapter.

Typically, throat hackle on wet flies and nymphs is fashioned from very soft hackle barbs. Streamers are sometimes dressed with this same material, but many tyers prefer a throat hackle with slightly stiffer barbs that will hold their shape when submerged. In either case, the dressing techniques are identical.

Cross-hackling involves mounting fibers—usually hair or feather barbs—that stand outward at right angles on either side of the hook shank, forming "pontoons" to support the fly. In many regards, they resemble spentwings and in fact are tied in much the same fashion, but cross hackle is usually dressed shorter and frequently used in conjunction with upright or downwings. Again, cross hackles are sometimes referred to as "legs," but since their function is to float a dry fly, we have included them in this chapter.

Method #26:

Bundled-fiber Throat Hackle

This simple and widely used method for throat hackling is typically employed on nymphs and, to a lesser degree, wet flies. Though strands of almost any material can be used—synthetic fibers, hair, or twisted Mylars—the soft, webby barbs from hen hackle or body feathers are the most common.

The main sequence shown below illustrates the procedure for mounting the fibers on the underside of the shank with the hook in the standard position. Many tyers, however, prefer to invert the hook in the vise jaws and mount the fibers as though dressing a bundled-fiber downwing. In this case, the procedure described in **Method #57: Solid-fiber Downwing**, p. 305, is used, though there is no need to gather the material with a noose loop as described in that method, as some flaring or "fanning" of the fibers on the underside of the shank is desirable.

The technique shown in the alternate sequence, used by many professional tyers, is a form of distribution wrap in which the fibers are initially mounted atop the shank

and then rolled to the underside using thread tension. It takes a bit of practice, but once mastered is quite fast.

Step 1. Any components of the fly behind the hackle—tail, body, rib, etc.—should be dressed first. We've omitted all of these except the body, since the body materials can play a role in the final position of the throat hackle.

Position the thread at the hackle-mounting point, here about one thread-wrap ahead of the body material.

Select a clump of fibers. Hen hackle is shown here, but other fibers can be used. Prepare the bundle as explained in **Method #1: Preparing Feather Barbs**, p. 344, so that the fiber tips are aligned, or approximately so; some tyers feel that a slight inconsistency in fiber length makes for a more attractive hackle.

Size the bundle by pinching it in the right fingers and holding it on the underside of the shank against the mounting point so that the fiber tips extend the desired distance toward the hook point. The exact fiber length depends upon both the tyer's preference and the specific pattern.

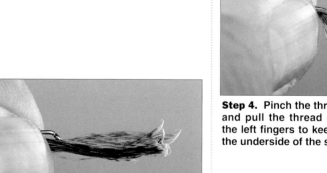

Step 2. Hold the hackle fibers, now sized to the proper length, beneath the shank. With the left thumb and forefinger pinch the bundle against the underside of the hook shank. The left forefinger also pinches the tying thread against the far side of the shank.

Note the finger position here. Thumb and forefinger are nearly parallel to the shank. The shank is held in the upper half of the pinched fingers, and the hackle fibers in the lower half.

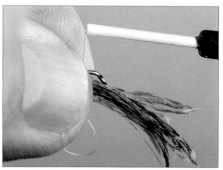

Step 3. The bundle is actually mounted using a pinch wrap formed on the underside of the shank (see **Method #9: The Pinch Wrap**, p. 30).

Form a loop of thread beneath the shank, and slip the tying thread between the left thumb and the hook shank, and raise the bobbin above the shank, as shown. The thread should cross the near side of the shank directly at the hackle-mounting point.

Though we've used a pinch wrap here, other slack-loop techniques, **Method #10: The Bobbin Loop**, p. 31; **Method #11: The Langley Loop**, p. 32, can be used. In all cases, however, the instructions must be adjusted so that the slack loop is formed beneath the shank.

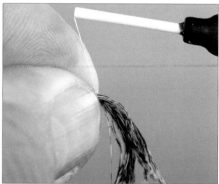

Step 4. Pinch the thread and fibers tightly, and pull the thread directly upward. Use the left fingers to keep the fiber bundle on the underside of the shank.

Step 5. Here is the result of the pinch wrap; the fibers are held to the underside of the shank with a single thread wrap.

Step 6. Pinch the fibers directly behind the mounting point and take one firm wrap of thread toward the body.

The fibers are secured to the shank, but not tightly. If desired, the fibers on the edges of the bundle can be gently pulled outward to distribute the fibers in arc around the underside of the shank, as shown here.

Step 7. When the fibers are spread or fanned to the desired degree. Bind them tightly with additional thread wraps.

If the wraps are taken further toward the front of the body, thread tension will force the fibers into the front edge of the body material and flare them downward for a more distinct hackle profile.

If the additional wraps are taken toward the hook eye, the fibers will lie closer to the underside of the body for a more streamlined appearance.

After the additional wraps are taken, trim the butts and bind with thread.

Step 1a. In this technique, the fiber bundle is initially mounted atop the shank.

Size the fibers as shown in Step 1. Transfer the fibers to the left fingertips.

Take one snug, but not excessively tight, thread wrap over the mounting point of the bundle, ending with the bobbin held vertically, as shown. Before releasing the fibers, shorten the tying thread so that only about an inch of thread extends beyond the bobbin tube. More precise thread control is achieved when the thread is shorter.

Step 2a. Begin taking a second wrap under increased thread tension. The object here is to use thread pressure to roll the fibers beneath the shank. As you take this second wrap, observe the fibers carefully. If they seem to be rolling too slowly—that is, if it appears that the thread wrap will be completed before the bundle reaches the underside of the shank—increase thread tension. If they seem to be rolling too quickly, and will move beyond the underside of the shank, decrease thread pressure.

Here, half a turn has been taken. The thread is beneath the shank and the fibers have rolled to the far side of the shank.

Step 3a. Continue wrapping the thread, adjusting tension as necessary to draw the fibers beneath the hook.

Here, one complete wrap has been made.

Step 4a. Maintain tension on the bobbin, and take 2 or 3 more wraps toward the front of the body. The object of these wraps is both to secure the fibers and to spread them more evenly on the underside of the shank.

Again, thread-tension control is necessary. Use enough pressure to flare the fibers, but not so much that they begin to roll to the top of the shank.

Step 5a. When the proper spread of fibers is obtained, clip and bind down the butts.

Method #27:
DeFeo Throat Hackle

Legendary tyer Charles DeFeo used a simple method for throat hackling salmon patterns with feather barbs, and the technique works equally well on trout flies. Because the barbs are left attached to the feather stem, handling the material is simplified, and the barbs are naturally distributed on the sides of the shank. The length of the barbs used is not critical, since it is adjusted during tying, but the hackle barbs on either side of the stem should be equal in length.

Step 1. All fly components behind the hackle should be dressed. We've omitted all but the body for a clearer illustration. Position the tying thread at the hackle-mounting point—here, directly at the front edge of the body.

Select a feather such as the mallard flank shown here. Clip away the tip of the feather so that the uppermost remaining feather barbs are longer than the finished hackle length.

Strip away the lower barbs, leaving a section of fibers on either side of the feather stem. The total number of fibers left on the stem depends upon the desired density of the finished hackle.

Step 2. Position the feather on the underside of the shank. Notice that most feathers will have some natural curvature. The feather can be positioned so that the barb tips curve toward the fly body, as shown here, or away from the body. The orientation chosen will be preserved in the finished fly.

Using either a pinch wrap formed on the underside of the shank as shown in **Method #26: Bundled-fiber Throat Hackle**, Steps 2-4, p. 367, or the procedure described in **Method #4: Bottom Wrap**, p. 27, affix the feather stem to the underside of the shank with 2 turns of thread under moderate tension.

Step 3. Maintain a slight tension on the bobbin. Draw the feather stem toward the hook eye, sliding the hackle barbs beneath the thread wraps until they are of the proper length.

Step 4. When the feather barbs are of the correct length, bind the feather to the shank with additional tight thread wraps. Clip and bind down the excess.

Method #28:
Gathered Throat Hackle

Throat hackles can be formed by fibers that have already been distributed around the hook shank. The following sequence shows the procedure for forming a throat hackle from a wrapped feather, or from fibers distributed around the shank in the standard or reverse directions.

This technique is useful for forming a denser throat hackle or one that is broadly fanned around the underside of the shank.

Step 1. All fly components behind the hackle should be dressed first. We've omitted all but the body for a clearer illustration.

This technique begins with a collar hackle. If using a feather, wrap a hackle as described in **Method #5: Single-hackle Wet-fly Collar**, p. 352, and shown on the fly at the left. If using bundled feather barbs, hair, or other fibers, dress a collar as shown in **Method #20: Distributed Collar Hackle**, p. 367, as shown on the middle fly.

You can also mount the fibers using **Method #21: Reverse Distributed Collar Hackle**, Steps 1-4 or Steps 1a-5a, p. 368, as shown on the right.

Note that all the fibers forming these collars will eventually form the throat hackle, so use a quantity of fibers that will produce the desired hackle density in the finished fly.

Position the tying thread at the front edge of the collar.

Step 2. Pinch the left thumb and forefinger together and position them over the hook parallel to the shank as shown. The fingertips should extend beyond the hook eye.

Step 3. Maintain the pinch and draw the fingers downward over the hackle fibers and hook shank, pulling the fibers beneath the shank and toward the hook point.

The object is to draw all the fibers downward and back. You may need to repeat this stroking motion a few times before all the fibers are pulled evenly into position.

Take several tight wraps over the front edge of the collar.

The placement of these wraps will determine the position of the fibers in the finished hackle. If only a few thread wraps are taken toward the hook bend, the finished hackle will form a wide arc around the underside of the shank. If more wraps are taken toward the bend, the fibers will be consolidated into a tighter bundle directly beneath the shank.

As you wrap, periodically release the fibers to check their position.

Step 4. When the fibers are affixed in the proper position, the fly can be finished or additional materials applied.

Method #29:
Cross Hackle

Cross-hackling is not an extremely well-known style, but it is used on dry flies by some tyers who find that the bushiness of a standard collar hackle unduly obscures the silhouette of the fly. Perhaps its best-known use is in the Iwamasa Dun, which incorporates a deer-hair cross hackle. But other tyers, most notably Oregon tyer Bill Black, use CDC barbs for cross-hackling on a variety of patterns. Since cross hackles are typically somewhat sparse, patterns hackled in this style often employ other buoyant materials in the dressing. Cross hackling is particularly well suited to smaller flies.

In both appearance and tying technique, cross hackles most strongly resemble short, sparse spentwings. And in fact, virtually all of the methods shown in the section "Spentwings," p. 321, could theoretically be used to fashion cross hackles. However, in practice, only two techniques are typically employed, and these are demonstrated here.

The main sequence shows a widely adaptable method for cross hackling, which involves mounting a bundle of fibers and separating it into halves with crisscross wraps. It can be used with almost any stranded material—natural or synthetic hairs, yarns, or feather barbs—though buoyant materials are most commonly chosen.

The alternate sequence shows a cross hackle formed from a bundle of fibers lashed crosswise atop the hook shank. This method is faster, but since the ends of the hackle fibers are eventually trimmed, the technique does not take advantage of the inherent taper of materials such as natural hair or most feather barbs; it is most commonly employed with CDC barbs or synthetic fibers such as poly yarn.

Step 1. This approach to cross hackling is virtually identical to the technique for creating spentwings shown in **Method #73: Thread-split Fiber Spentwing**, p. 322, and so the instructions here are abbreviated. Readers seeking a more detailed explanation should consult that method.

Lay a thread foundation along the hackling area, and position the thread at the hackle-mounting point.

Prepare a clump of hair or feather barbs (yarns are more easily dressed using the technique shown in the alternate sequence). The size of the clump varies with the tyer's preference and the hook size; larger hooks require thicker bundles for floatation. But in general, the clump should be about as thick as that used for a spentwing.

Mount the bundle atop the hook shank with the tips extending over the hook eye, as shown. Position the tying thread at the frontmost mounting wrap.

13

Step 2. Using a dubbing needle and your fingers, divide the clump of fibers into two halves—one on the far side of the shank and one on the near side.

Grasp the tips of the clump on the far side, and draw it outward away from you, as shown in this top view, so that the fibers are perpendicular to the shank.

Bring the thread up behind the bundle of fibers on the near side of the shank, then over the top of the shank between the two bundles. Finally, bring the thread down the far side of the shank ahead of the far bundle, forcing the thread tightly into base of the fibers on the far side of the shank.

Make another wrap identical to the first.

Step 3. Pull the near clump of fibers directly toward you.

Bring the thread underneath the shank and up the near side ahead of the fiber bundle on the near side. Take the thread over the top of the shank, between the two bundles, forcing the thread into the base of the fibers on the near side. Finally, bring the thread down the far side behind the far bundle.

Take another wrap identical to the first.

Step 4. Repeat Steps 2-3 until the two bundles lie in a horizontal plane, perpendicular to the shank as shown.

If the fiber bundles are not sufficiently consolidated, take a wrap or two of thread at the very base of each bundle, as shown here. If the cross hackle is formed from hollow hair, take these wraps under light tension to avoid flaring the fibers excessively.

Step 5. Very stiff fibers may still tend to lean toward the hook eye. If this is the case, preen the bundles toward the rear of the hook, and build a small thread bump at the front base of the bundles as shown here to hold the fibers perpendicular to the shank.

Step 6. The cross hackle can be left in a horizontal plane, and the crisscross wraps covered with a thinly dubbed thread.

On some patterns, such as the Iwamasa Dun, the cross hackle is drawn slightly downward, as shown here from the front. A drop of glue is applied to the wraps to hold the fibers in this position.

Step 1a. This approach to cross hackling is virtually identical to the technique for creating spentwings shown in **Method #75: Lashed-fiber Spentwing**, p. 324, and so the instructions here are abbreviated. Readers seeking a more detailed explanation should consult that method.

Lay a thread base over the hackling area, and position the tying thread at the hackle-mounting point.

Prepare a clump of material—we're using CDC barbs here. Do not yet clip the material to length; longer fibers are easier to handle.

Lay the material crosswise atop the shank at the hackle-mounting point. Mount the bundle using a lash wrap, and secure it with tight crisscross wraps as explained in **Method #8: The Lash Mount and Crisscross Wrap**, p. 29.

Step 2a. Repeat Steps 1a-2a until the bundle is firmly affixed. Then trim the fibers to the desired length.

Parachute Hackle

Once considered something of a novelty, perhaps owing to the perceived difficulty in tying, parachute hackling has gained enormous popularity in the past few decades. A wide variety of imitations—mayflies, caddis, stoneflies, midges, damsels, even ants and hoppers—are now dressed with parachute hackles. The advantages are significant. As the name suggests, parachute hackle causes a fly to land lightly on the water, and because the hackle is wrapped in a horizontal plane, the barbs form a broad, pontoonlike base of support for the fly and, in most parachute styles, give the trout an unencumbered view of the fly body.

Contrary to what some tyers still believe, parachute hackles are not particularly difficult to dress—at least not all of them. There are really two styles of such hackle. The first, what are termed in this section "Wing-post Parachutes" use hackle wrapped around the base of single or divided wing, and as a rule, this style is relatively easy to tie. Some wing materials, of course, such as feather-tip wings, provide a less rigid base than others, such as bundled-fiber posts, and are a bit trickier to handle, but the dressing techniques are identical and generally quite manageable.

The second type, "Postless Parachutes," are dressed so that no wing or post remains on the finished fly. As a rule, these are used on flies imitating species that do not hold their wings upright or that have no wings at all. The hackle is wrapped around a base, but there are various techniques by which this base or shortened, minimized, or removed. Postless parachute hackles can be dressed atop the hook shank or beneath the hook shank as shown in "Bottom-mounted Parachute Hackle," p. 402.

Parachute hackles are, of course, restricted to dry flies and, to a lesser extent emergers, and the criteria governing the selection of appropriate feathers are discussed in "Hackle," p. 6. However, many tyers feel that because the horizontally positioned hackle barbs provide such an efficient base of support for the fly, the quality of the feather used need not be quite as high as one used for a collar hackle. The weight of the fly on the water forces the lowermost hackle barbs upward; they in turn press against the layer of barbs above them, and a kind of aggregate stiffness is gained simply by virtue of the hackle design. As a result, a somewhat "softer" feather, that is, one with more web at the base of the barbs, can be used successfully. While a poor quality feather will still tie a poor quality hackle, it isn't always necessary to use perfectly top-grade feathers for parachute hackling. The one exception here is in stem thickness. The parachute hackle foundation, whether it be the base of a wing post, a monofilament loop, or any of the other foundation types shown in the following methods, is nowhere near as rigid as a hook shank, and wrapping the hackle will be much easier if the feather itself has a fine stem.

Since parachute hackles are always mounted by the feather stem, rather than the tip, preparing the feather is a rather simple matter and is identical to the preparation used for collar hackles and shown in **Method #1: Preparing Hackle Feathers**, Steps 1a-1b, p. 344.

The matter of feather size is, or at least can be, slightly different. Because the barbs lie horizontally, their length is far less important for fly balance than barb length on a collar hackle, and there is far more variation in sizing parachute hackle, depending upon the tyer's preference and the particular pattern. Many tyers, of course, use hackles that are "properly" sized for the hook, as explained in "Sizing Hackle," p. 343. Others prefer a parachute hackle that is one size larger than would be used on a collar hackle. For large flies, those bigger than size 10 or so, some tyers go the opposite direction, and use a hackle one or more sizes smaller, hackling, for instance, a #4 hopper with size 6, 8, or even 10 feather—a choice that probably has as much to do with the individual tyer's sense of proportion than with the performance of the hackle on the fly. In short, the horizontal design of the hackle gives more latitude in sizing the feather, though it's worth bearing in mind that feathers wrapped around a thick foundation, such as a bundled-fiber post, will appear larger on the finished fly since the thickness of the post adds to the effective diameter of the wrapped hackle.

Wing-post Parachute Hackle

Of the two categories of parachute hackling, the style that incorporates wings or a wing post in the finished fly is by far the most common. Not only is this style easier to tie, but the wings or post do double duty—structurally, as a hackle foundation, and imitatively, as a representation of wings on the finished pattern.

Efficient parachute hackling begins with a well-prepared foundation, usually a series of horizontal thread wraps at the base of the wings or wing post—to stiffen them; to provide a smooth, uniform foundation that will help prevent the hackle stem from twisting or rolling; and to help anchor the hackle wraps more securely on slippery wing materials. Nearly any material from which wings are made can be used as a base for parachute hackle, and a number of techniques for preparing hackle foundations have been presented in the chapter on "Wings." Creating a base on feather-tip wings is shown in **Method #9: Feather-tip Wings with Parachute Base**, p. 255; on bundled-fiber upright wings, **Method #15: Bundled-fiber Post**, Step 6, p. 264; on loop wings **Method #31: Loop Wings**, Step 6a, p. 279, and **Method #32: Slip-loop Wings**, Step 6a, p.280; and on foam posts **Method #34: Foam Post**, Step 3a, p. 282.

This thread foundation should be high enough to accommodate 4 or 5 turns of hackle—after the body is dressed. Since the thread foundation is generally wrapped immediately after the wings or wing post are dressed, body materials that are subsequently applied will cover up the lower portion of this foundation. A sufficient section of the foundation should extend above the body material to accommodate the desired number of hackle wraps.

Parachute hackles can also be applied around float pods—**Method #88: Dubbed Float Pod**, p. 338; **Method #89: Folded Foam Float Pods**, p. 339; and **Method #90: Suspender Pod**, p. 340. However, floating nymph and emerger patterns that incorporate a float pod and parachute hackle are typically very sparsely hackled—one or two wraps of the feather—and ordinarily no thread base is required.

There is substantial diversity among tyers in the technique used to mount feathers for parachute hackle, and these are detailed in **Method #30: Parachute Hackle Mounts**, p. 381. There is, however, greater agreement on the question of feather orientation. The vast majority of tyers mount the feather so that the hackle will be wrapped with the shiny or front side of the feather facing upward and the dull or back side of the feather facing downward. If the feather is slightly cupped, the barbs on the finished hackle will arc downward just a bit, toward the surface of the water, and advocates of this orientation feel that it provides a more stable base of support and makes better use of the full barb length. A few tyers mount the feather in the opposite orientation, and with very flat feathers that show little cupping—often the case on genetic hackle necks—this reverse orientation is satisfactory.

There is one final matter in parachute hackling that is not an issue in collar hackles—the direction of wrapping. Tyers seem equally divided on whether parachute hackle should be wrapped clockwise or counterclockwise (when viewed from above). While the finished hackle is identical regardless of wrapping direction, there are slight differences in hackle mounting and tie off. If a cross-mount technique is used, the feather should be positioned on the hook shank so that the tip points in the wrapping direction. If a hackle is mounted ahead of the wings with the feather tip pointed away from the tyer—the natural direction for a counterclockwise wrap—but then wrapped clockwise, the feather stem is folded back on itself, and it may weaken or break. With other mounting techniques, however, the feather can be wrapped in either direction.

Wrapping direction makes a somewhat bigger difference in binding down the feather tip after the hackle has been applied. When a feather is wrapped counterclockwise, the feather tip is pulled away from the tyer when it is bound down, and the thread torque pulls the feather tip in the same direction in which the hackle was wrapped. Many tyers believe that this better secures the hackle around the foundation and provides a more secure tie-off. The drawback to this approach is that it is difficult to place the tie-off wraps directly against the feather stem, since the thread wraps tend to trap the barbs against the feather stem. As a result, some hackle barbs are bound down to the shank when tying off the feather tip, and a bulkier fly head is formed. When a feather is wrapped clockwise, the stem is pulled toward the tyer during the tie-off, making it much easier to slip the tying thread between the barbs and bind only the stem to the shank. The disadvantage to this approach is that the thread torque tends to push the feather tip against the direction of hackle wrapping; it may slightly loosen the hackle, and some tyers feel that the tie-off is less secure. In the end, however, both techniques can be used successfully if they are well executed.

Method #30:
Parachute-hackle Mounts

Many of the techniques for mounting parachute-hackle feathers are similar to those for mounting collar-hackle feathers. In all of the methods illustrated here, the tyer has the option of mounting the feather either before or after the fly abdomen has been dressed. If a feather is mounted immediately after the wings or wing post have been set upright, the feather stems can be bound to the hook shank toward the tail of the fly and concealed beneath the body material, which removes bulk from the head area of the fly. If the feather is mounted after the abdomen of the fly has been dressed, the stems are bound down toward the hook eye. Mounting in this direction keeps a minimum of bulk in the body area, which can be a consideration in dressing slender quill or biot bodies. Moreover, mounting the hackle feather after applying the tails and abdomen keeps the tying field clear to dress these components.

One of the most important considerations in the first two methods shown here is that the feather be affixed with a section of bare quill between the mounting wraps and the lowermost feather barbs. In most hackling methods, the first wrap of the feather is taken at the top of the hackle foundation, and the feather is then wrapped downward toward the hook shank. Thus as wrapping begins, the feather must first be spiraled upward around the wing base to position it for the uppermost hackle wrap. If the feather is properly mounted, with a section of stripped stem between the hook shank and the lowermost hackle barbs, this upward spiraling will lay the bare feather stem against the wing-base foundation; the feather barbs will begin to flare outward only when the first, uppermost horizontal wrap of the hackle is taken.

If, however, the feather is mounted directly at the lowermost barbs, this upward spiraling will begin to flare the hackle barbs before the feather reaches the top of the foundation. When the hackle is then wrapped downward, these first flared barbs may cause others to splay, producing a parachute hackle that has barbs angling upward, where they contribute nothing to the support of the fly and create an untidy appearance.

This photo shows a feather mounted directly at the base of the lowermost barbs. We've exaggerated the height of the thread foundation wrapped up the base of the wing post to illustrate the point more clearly. When this feather is wrapped to the top of the thread foundation to take the first wrap of hackle, barbs flare outward as the feather is spiraled up the thread foundation. These barbs can cause splaying in the finished hackle.

Here a hackle is correctly mounted with a section of bare stem between the mounting wraps and the lowermost feather barbs. When this feather is spiraled upward to the top of the thread foundation, no barbs are deployed, and the first wrap of hackle taken at the top of the foundation spreads the barbs neatly in a horizontal plane.

For the sake of economy in presentation and the comparison of techniques, we are showing the mounting methods as a group. There are four methods shown below, each identified by a number/letter combination. The number indicates the tying sequence and the letter specifies the step within that sequence. Thus Steps 1a-1e constitute one method, Steps 2a-2d another, and so on.

For better visibility in all of the sequences, the thread used to mount the hackle feather is different in color than the thread used to mount and post the wing material.

For all of the methods below, the feather should first be prepared by using one of the techniques shown in **Method #1: Preparing Hackle Feathers**, Steps 1a-1b, p. 344.

Step 1a. The feather can be affixed to the shank using a simple *cross mount*. It is perhaps most common in this approach to mount the feather ahead of the wings or wing post with the feather tip pointing away from the tyer and the stem bound toward the hook eye. The feather is thus in the natural position for counterclockwise wrapping; to mount it for the clockwise wrapping, the tip should point toward the tyer. The feather can be mounted in this fashion immediately after the wing is posted to the vertical or after the abdomen of the fly has been dressed.

Position the tying thread at the *rear* base of the wings or wing post. Beginning with the thread here will ensure that the first thread wrap over the feather will pull the stem close to the wing base. Lay the feather crosswise directly against the "elbow" formed by the hook shank and the front of the wing post, with the feather tip pointing directly away from the tyer, as shown. Take two thread wraps over the feather stem. The shiny or convex side of the feather faces upward.

Two points are worth noting here. The stem is bound as closely as possible to the front base of the wings or wing post, which simplifies positioning the feather for wrapping. And as described earlier, a length of bare feather stem is left between the mounting wraps and the lowermost feather barbs. This section of bare quill is slightly longer than the height of the thread foundation laid on the wings or wing post.

Step 1b. Hold the feather tip in the left hand and elevate it slightly to counteract the torque from the tying thread. Begin wrapping toward the hook eye, using thread pressure to bend the feather stem forward against the hook shank.

Step 1c. Bind the stem down until it is a few thread-wraps behind the hook eye. Clip the excess stem and bind down the butt.

Step 1d. After the feather is mounted, you can lift it vertically and prop it against the front of the wings to minimize its interference with dressing the remainder of the fly.

Step 1e. The same mount can be used to affix the feather behind the wing post, as shown here. In this case, the stems are bound toward the tail of the fly and will be hidden beneath the body materials.

Notice that this feather is positioned for wrapping in a clockwise direction—around the far side of the wing post and toward the eye of the hook. If this feather were wrapped by first drawing it toward the tyer, the stem would be doubled over on itself and could break. To use this mount with a counterclockwise wrap, the feather tip should point toward the tyer.

Step 2a. Some tyers prefer to use a *parallel mount*. Typically, this technique is used to mount the hackle after the body has been dressed, but if the feather is affixed in the reverse direction, as shown in Step 2d, it can be mounted prior to applying the body materials.

Begin by positioning the tying thread at the rear base of the wing. Lay the feather atop the shank with the tip pointing toward the rear of the hook and angled slightly upward; the shiny or convex side of the feather is facing upward, as shown. The feather stem angles downward alongside the wing. If the stem is placed against the near side of the wing, as shown here, the feather is positioned for wrapping in the clockwise direction; if the stem is placed against the far side of the wing base, it can be wrapped in the counterclockwise direction.

Take one turn of thread over the feather stem as close as possible to the rear base of the wing, as shown here. Again, notice that a length of bare feather stem extends beyond the mounting wrap.

Step 2b. Bring the tying thread beneath the shank, and take a second wrap over the stem and as close as possible to the front base of the wing.

Step 2c. Continue binding the feather stem forward until it is a few thread-wraps behind the hook eye. Clip the excess stem and bind down the butt.

Step 2d. Here is a parallel-mounted feather positioned in the reverse direction. The stem is bound to the shank toward the hook bend and will be covered by the body materials. Note that this feather is positioned for counterclockwise wrapping.

Step 3a. The *wing-post mount*, in which the feather stem is bound against the thread foundation on the wings or wing post, is becoming increasingly popular among tyers. It presents a couple of significant advantages. When using wings with a very flexible base, such as feather-tip or loop-style wings, binding the feather stem to the base of the wings adds extra rigidity to the hackle-wrapping foundation. The hackle can be more easily wrapped without twisting these delicate wings out of position. Moreover, on any style of wings or wing post, this mount positions the lower-

most feather barbs at the top of the thread foundation, where the first wrap of hackle will be taken. Thus there is no need to spiral a bare feather stem up the wing post prior to wrapping the first turn of hackle. In general, tyers who use this method find that the feather is better positioned for wrapping and produces a neater parachute hackle.

The following method can be used with relatively rigid wing posts, such as those formed from bundled fibers. Feather-tip or loop-style wings, however, may prove too flexible to secure the feather using the technique shown here, and a different procedure is illustrated in Steps 4a-4d.

With the right hand, spiral the tying thread to the very top of the thread foundation on the wings or wing post, and hold the thread out beyond the hook eye.

With the left hand, hold the stem of a feather, and position the feather vertically against the near side of the wing post, as shown. The shiny or convex side of the feather should be facing the wing.

Step 3b. Take a horizontal wrap around the feather stem, binding it to the very top of the thread foundation on the wings or wing post. Notice here that a small section of bare quill is left between this mounting wrap and the lowermost feather barbs.

Step 3c. Continue taking horizontal thread wraps moving downward, to the base of the wings, securing the feather stem to the thread foundation on the wings or wing post.

Step 3d. At this point, the feather stem can be bound toward the hook bend, as we're doing here, or toward the hook eye, depending upon the tyer's preference and the demands of the pattern.

Draw the feather stem toward the bend and secure it with several tight wraps of thread.

Step 3e. Clip the excess stem and bind down the butt. Notice that the uppermost thread wrap binds the feather stem directly against the side of the thread foundation on the wing post. The feather can be wrapped in either the clockwise or counterclockwise direction with no danger of bending the stem back on itself and breaking it.

To wrap the hackle, simply pull the feather tip downward so that the shiny or convex side of the hackle faces upward, as shown here.

Step 4a. A second type of *wing-post mount* is more practical with very flexible hackle foundations, such as the feather-tip wings shown here. Note that a thread foundation—formed from red thread in this photo—has already been applied to the base of the wings

Position the tying thread directly behind the wings, and lay a prepared feather crosswise over the hook shank in front of the wings. Notice the feather orientation; it is laid "edgewise" on the shank, with the shiny or convex side facing the rear of the fly and the tip pointing away from the tyer.

Take three tight wraps of thread over the feather stem. Because the thread must be drawn forward from behind the wings, the feather stem will be pulled tightly and as close as possible to the base of the wings. Note that a section of bare stem is left between the mounting wraps and the lowermost feather barbs. The length of this bare section is slightly longer than the height of the thread foundation around the base of the wings.

Step 4b. Now raise the feather tip vertically, so that the shiny side of the feather lies against the wings, as shown. Hold the hackle in this position.

Begin wrapping horizontally up the base of the wings, binding the feather stem against this base as you go.

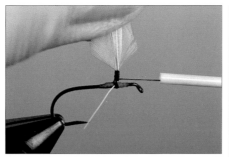

Step 4c. As you wrap, pull upward gently on the feather tip to help steady the wings and provide a more rigid foundation against which to wrap. You'll need to release the feather tip momentarily once during each wrap.

When you reach the top of thread foundation formed around the wing base, wrap the thread back down to the hook shank.

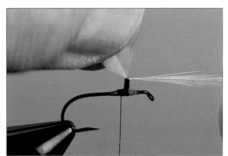

Step 4d. When you reach the base of the wings, take a wrap of thread around the hook shank. Clip the excess feather stem, and cover with tying thread if desired.

When it is time to wrap the hackle, grasp the wing tips in the left fingers and the feather tip in the right fingers. Holding the wings steady, bend the feather so that it lies in a horizontal plane, with the shiny side up, as shown here. You many need to pull the feather almost straight downward to crease the stem so that the feather will lie flat.

Method #31:

Single Parachute Hackle—Horizontal Wrap

Wrapping parachute hackle is a relatively simple procedure, though there are a number of variations for certain steps in the process—primarily in the way that the hackle pliers are manipulated and the feather tied off. These alternatives and options are presented in the following sequences.

There are, however, a couple of matters that are essentially independent of the hackle wrapping, and in order to keep the instructional sequences as uncluttered as possible, we will present those here.

First is the matter of the hackle tie-off point. After the wings and abdomen have been dressed, and the hackle feather mounted (in whatever order you prefer to dress these components), the tie-off point is establish and the thread positioned there. Some tyers

prefer to bind down the hackle tip directly ahead of the wings or wing post. In this case, no body materials are applied to the hook shank between the wings or wing post and the hook eye. The feather is then tied off using one of the techniques shown below, and typically a bit of dubbing is applied over the tie-off wraps and the fly finished directly behind the eye, as shown in the following photo. Other tyers prefer to dress the body completely, and tie off the hackle behind the hook eye, again shown in the following photo, as they find applying additional body materials once the hackle is wrapped to be a cumbersome procedure. Either technique, of course, can produce fine flies. The former procedure creates a bit neater head on the fly, since the feather tip tie-off is entirely concealed beneath body materials. The latter procedure is a bit simpler. In either case, however, the techniques for hackle wrapping and tie-off are identical.

The fly on the left shows a hackle that has been tied off directly in front of the wing. The excess material is then trimmed and covered with thread. The fly is finished by lifting the hackle barbs that extend toward the front of the fly and dubbing the forward portion of the body. The thread is tied off behind the hook eye.

The fly on the right shows a hackle that has been wrapped after the entire body has been dubbed. The tip of the feather is drawn to a point just behind the eye, and tied off there.

Many tyers, particularly less experienced ones, find wrapping parachute hackle around rather flexible foundations, such as those produced by feather-tip or some loop-style wings, to be difficult. And indeed it is one of the more delicate tasks in parachute hackling. The torque exerted by the relatively stiff feather stem often bends the wings out of position—so much so that sometimes the first hackle wrap will slide up and off the wing tips. To alleviate this problem, some tyers employ a "gallows tool" or "parachute tool" which functions as a third hand, holding the wings in position while the hackle is wrapped. While a gallows tool is not exactly standard equipment for most tyers, it can nonetheless be a useful aid, particularly for those who tie a large number of parachute patterns, and a few words about its operation are in order.

Though many styles of gallows tool are available, they all share a couple of common features. First, they have an extension that hangs downward from a vise-mounted frame (hence the name "gallows"). This hanging extension usually has a hook from which a pair of hackle pliers can be suspended. The tips of the wings are then grasped in the plier jaws and held in position while the hackle is wrapped. Second, this hanging extension has some provision, usually a spring, for controlling the amount and consistency of the upward tension placed on the wings. The gallows-tool set-up for feather-tip wings is shown in the following photo. With loop-style wing-posts, the gallows hook is used without hackle pliers as shown in **Method #41: Stem-loop Parachute Hackle**, Step 4a, p. 396.

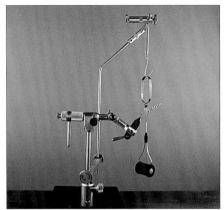

Here is a typical gallows tool, this one manufactured by Dyna-King. When using a gallows tool, there are a couple of points to bear in mind. First, the hackle pliers should be positioned directly over the wings; if they are off-center, the wings may be crooked on the finished fly. Second, the spring tension on the hackle pliers should be relatively light—just enough to hold the wings in position. Pulling the wings upward too forcefully can deform them or break the tips.

Once the wings are clamped in the gallows tool, the hackle tip is clipped in a second pair of hackle pliers, and wrapped by passing the plier from hand to hand, as explained in the main sequence that follows.

The following two demonstrations, one in the main sequence and one in the alternate sequence, illustrate the different ways of handling the hackle pliers during wrapping. The main sequence shows the procedure for wrapping a hackle around a relatively stiff, rigid wing post, such as one formed from bundled fibers, and it illustrates as well a common approach to tying off the feather against the hook shank. The alternate sequence shows a technique for wrapping a feather around a more flexible foundation, such as one formed from feather-tip wings.

Once a parachute hackle is wrapped, the hackle tip lies beneath several layers of flared barbs, and tying off the feather without trapping flared hackle barbs beneath the tie-off wraps takes some care. In addition to the method shown here, tyers have devised other techniques for binding down the feather tip, and these are presented in **Method #32: Parachute-hackle Tie-offs**, p. 386. Any of the wrapping techniques shown in the following procedures can be used in conjunc-

tion with any of the tie-offs demonstrated in **Method #32**.

As with other hackle styles, parachute hackles can be dressed sparsely or densely. The number of hackle wraps ultimately taken depends upon the fly size, pattern style, the water in which the fly is to be fished, and the tyer's preference. By and large, however, most tyers prefer parachute hackles that are dressed more sparsely than collar hackles. On a collar hackle, barbs projecting beneath the hook shank on each turn of the feather rest against the water and contribute to the support of the fly. Thus the more turns of hackle, the greater the support. On parachute hackle, however, only the barbs on the lowermost wraps of hackle, those closest to the water, are actually in contact with the surface. Adding extra wraps of hackle contributes little to the support of the fly, and in fact may serve only to obscure the wing silhouette. As a rule, 3-5 turns of hackle are sufficient.

Finally, in this sequence and throughout this section of the book, we are demonstrating hackle-wrapping techniques by using hackle pliers. Long feathers, such as those from top-grade rooster saddles, can and should be wrapped by omitting the pliers and using the fingers only. But even the longest feathers eventually become too short to wrap with the fingers; sooner or later the tyer must resort to pliers, and thus we are demonstrating their use.

Step 1. Dress the wings or wing post, tails, abdomen or entire body, and any ribbing material. At the desired point during the dressing, mount the hackle feather using one of the techniques shown in **Method #30: Parachute-hackle Mounts**, p. 381. Position the thread at the tie-off point, either directly ahead of the wings or directly behind the hook eye, as shown here.

The wrapping methods shown in this sequence are best adapted to fairly rigid wing posts, such as the calf tail shown here. The thread foundation on the wing post has been fashioned from red thread to make the placement of the hackle on the foundation more readily visible.

Grasp the tip of the feather in hackle pliers so that the pliers are in line with the stem; grasping the feather tip crosswise in the pliers puts undue strain on the stem, which can break.

If you have tied in the feather with a cross mount or parallel mount, spiral the feather to the top of the thread foundation in about one-half of a wrap, so that only the bare feather stem lies against the thread foundation. As you spiral the feather upward, make any adjustments necessary by twisting the feather gently so that

when the feather reaches the top of the foundation, it is positioned horizontally, with the shiny or convex side pointing upward, as shown. (If you have used the wing-post mount, the feather will already be positioned at the top of the thread foundation and there is no need to spiral it to the top.)

Depending upon the type and orientation of the mount used, the feather tip may not necessarily be pointing in the direction shown here. It makes no difference for the finished hackle.

Step 2. In hand-to-hand wrapping, the hackle pliers are passed from one hand to the other as the feather is wrapped around the wing post. The left hand manipulates the pliers on the half-turn at the rear of the hook, and the right takes over for the half-turn at the front of the hook. This wrapping method is suitable for stiffer wing posts and wings supported by a gallows tool.

Since the feather tip shown in Step 1 lies behind the wing, we'll begin with the left hand. Grasp the hackle pliers and make one-half of a wrap around the very top of the thread foundation. We're wrapping counterclockwise here. Stop when the feather is pointing directly toward you.

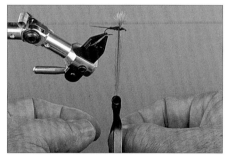

Step 3. When the feather reaches the near side of the wing post, transfer the pliers to the right hand, as shown here. Maintain the original orientation of the pliers, so that the feather remains in a horizontal plane.

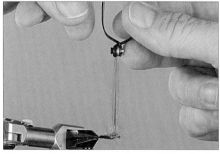

Step 4. Continue wrapping until the feather points away from you again, as shown in this top view.

13

Step 5. Again transfer the pliers to the left hand and make another half-wrap. This wrap should be placed directly below the first wrap.

There are two objectives in wrapping. First is to keep each wrap of hackle *below* the previous one and to avoid binding down any hackle barbs from a previous wrap. There is simple way to accomplish this. Each time the hackle is wrapped around the far side or near side of the wing post, drop the hackle pliers slightly below the horizontal plane, as shown in this front view. Lowering the pliers like this will ensure that the wrap being taken will slip beneath the wrap above it. At the front and rear of the wing post, the hook shank will not allow you to lower the pliers in this way; during this part of the wrapping, just keep the pliers as low as is practical.

The second goal is to keep the feather barbs horizontal, so that they flare directly outward from the wing post. If the feather begins to roll or twist at any time during wrapping, gently countertwist the hackle pliers to compensate and bring the barbs back to the horizontal plane. If barbs begin to splay, tilting upward or downward, unwrap half-a-turn of the feather and slightly reposition the wrap on the thread foundation. Small differences in positioning the feather stem can often remedy any flaring barbs.

Step 6. The entire feather can be wrapped using the hand-to-hand approach, in which case Steps 2-5 are repeated until the desired number of wraps are applied to the wing post, and the feather tip points toward the hook eye as shown in Step 8.

But some tyers take a different approach and wrap the hackle using the right hand only, and this "finger-loop" method is demonstrated in the next few steps. If the wing post is sufficiently stiff, this technique can be employed from the beginning. If the wing post is a bit more flexible, you may need to seat the first wrap or two of hackle using the hand-to-hand technique; when the hackle stem becomes thinner, you can employ the finger-loop approach.

Rotate the hackle pliers one-quarter of a turn so that they are in the horizontal plane. Insert the right index finger down-

ward into the loop of the hackle pliers, as shown. Apply just enough tension on the feather to keep the pliers from sliding off your index finger. Note that the right hand is held well above the hook shank.

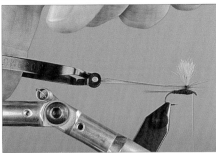

Step 7. Continue wrapping the hackle by orbiting the hand around the wing post. You must maintain a light but consistent outward pressure on the feather to keep the pliers from slipping off the index finger. As you wrap around the far side and near side of the shank, dip the pliers below the horizontal plane to seat the new wrap beneath the previous one.

This finger-loop wrapping is relatively fast, but the tyer has less control over the position of the feather. Should it begin to twist and cause the barbs to flare, you will need to use the hand-to-hand approach to countertwist the feather and keep the shiny side facing up.

Step 8. As you finish the last and lowermost wrap of hackle, draw the feather tip toward the hook eye, and angle it downward.

Raise the tying thread vertically so that it crosses the feather stem, as shown.

Step 9. Pull the feather tip directly toward you, bending the stem against the tying thread. This flares the barbs on one side of the feather stem and prevents them from being caught beneath the tying thread, making a neater tie-off.

Bring the tying thread to the far side of the shank. Do not wrap the thread directly over the top of the hook, but rather angle it slightly toward the hook eye, so that you can slip the thread between the flared hackle barbs and avoid binding them to the shank.

Pull the thread tightly to cinch the feather tip to the shank.

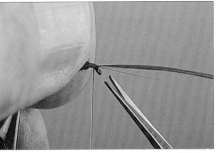

Step 10. Take two more wraps of tying thread directly over the first. Release the feather tip from the pliers.

With the left fingers, gently raise the barbs that project over the hook eye. Clip the feather tip, and any stray barbs that may be trapped beneath the tying thread.

Step 11. Bind down the exposed end of the feather tip, and finish the head of the fly.

Step 12. Apply a drop of head cement or liquid-type CA glue to the point where the topmost hackle wrap meets the wing post. The cement should be thin enough that it bleeds downward, securing the feather stem to the wing post and ensuring that the hackle wraps will not separate or slide off during fishing.

Some tyers clip a "V" notch in the barbs that extend to the front of the fly, as shown here. This gap gives better access to the hook eye for tying the fly to the leader.

Step 1a. This wrapping method is used when the hackle foundation is rather flexible, such as that produced by feather-tip or loop-style wings. A parachute base of this type requires some support during

wrapping, and though a gallows tool may be used, the wings can be held in the fingers as shown in the following demonstration.

Here, we've affixed the hackle with a wing-post mount to a pair of feather tips wings, which helps strengthen and stiffen the hackle foundation. This foundation can be reinforced further if the butts of the tailing material are incorporated into the wing base, as explained in **Method #9: Feather-tip Wings with Parachute Base**, Steps 3a-3c, p. 256. Wrapping is simplified enormously if a very thin-stemmed feather is used for the hackle.

Grasp the tip of the hackle feather in a pair of hackle pliers as shown in Step 1, and position the feather so that it lies in a horizontal plane with the shiny or convex side facing up.

Grasp the wings in the left fingers and pull them gently upward as shown.

Step 2a. In this technique, the hackle is wrapped almost solely with the right hand; the left fingers hold the wings, releasing them momentarily during each wrap so that the right hand can be repositioned and resume wrapping.

The first wrap is the most difficult because the hackle stem is thickest. With the left fingers, maintain a gentle upward tension on the wings. With the right hand, begin taking a wrap of hackle at the very top of the thread foundation. Wrap the hackle around the far side of the wings and as far toward the tail of the fly as you can. Seat the wrap firmly to help bend the feather stem in the wrapping direction.

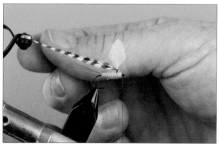

Step 3a. Now slacken tension on the hackle. For hackle feathers with rather stiff stems, you may need to slacken tension so much that the feather is no longer seated tightly against the thread foundation, but just barely touches it.

Momentarily release the wing tips and transfer the hackle pliers to the left hand, as shown here. It is important that the hackle feather be under relatively little tension when you release the wing, or the torque of the stem will bend the unsupported wings backward and the hackle will slip off. The wings may well bend out of position, but this can be remedied in the next step.

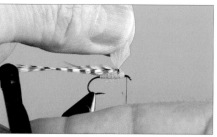

Step 4a. Reposition the right hand on the near side of the hook shank, and take the hackle pliers from the left hand.

With the left fingers, grasp the wing tips once again and pull upward gently.

Now increase tension on the feather slightly, to seat the feather stem against the thread foundation.

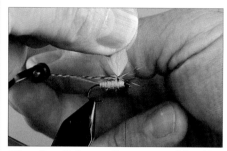

Step 5a. Take another wrap of hackle, directly beneath the first wrap, again bringing the right hand around the wings as far toward the rear of the fly as possible.

If the feather begins to twist or roll, countertwist the hackle pliers to compensate so that the barbs project directly outward from the wings and do not tilt upward or downward.

Note: if the wings were mounted using the approach shown in **Method #9: Feather-tip Wings with Parachute Base**, Step 4a, p. 255, they will be twisted toward the tyer. In this case, wrap the hackle using more tension; each wrap of the feather should twist the wings slightly away from the tyer until they finally reach the proper alignment.

Step 6a. Repeat Steps 3a-5a, laying each wrap of hackle beneath the preceding one, and slackening tension on the feather each time the pliers are transferred to the left hand.

These hackle wraps should be made under minimal tension—just enough to seat them against the thread foundation, but not enough to torque the wings out of position. It takes a light touch with the hackle pliers, but as the stem grows thinner with each turn of the feather, the wrapping grows easier.

Continue wrapping. The last and lowermost wrap should end with the feather tip pointing toward the hook eye and angled downward, as shown here. The feather is tied off and the fly finished as described in Steps 8-12.

Method #32:
Parachute-hackle Tie-offs

Though the tie-off technique illustrated in **Method #31: Single Parachute Hackle—Horizontal Wrap**, Steps 8-11, p. 385, is commonly used, tyers employ a number of other useful methods, which are shown in the following demonstrations.

For the sake of economy in presentation and the comparison of methods, we are showing these tie-off techniques as a group. There are four methods shown below, each identified by a number/letter combination. The number indicates the tying sequence and the letter specifies the step within that sequence. Thus Steps 1a-1f constitute one method, Steps 2a-2c another, and so on.

Step 1a. We were first shown this unusual technique by Al Beatty, who ties off a parachute hackle around the base of the wing post. The method is quite fast and produces a neat tie-off, with none of the trapped or splayed hackle barbs at the hook eye that sometimes results from other techniques.

This approach is best suited to stiff wings or wing posts, as some thread pressure must be exerted to secure the feather tip. With care, however, it can be accomplished with more flexible types of wings.

Any hackle mount can be used, but Beatty prefers one of the wing-post mounts shown in **Method #30: Parachute-hackle Mounts**, p. 381. Prior to hackling, the entire fly body is dressed, which eliminates the need to lift the hackle after wrapping in order to dress the forward portion of the body.

Beatty wraps the parachute hackle in a clockwise direction, as is shown in the following steps. The hackle can be applied counterclockwise, and the slight adjustments needed to wrap in that direction are explained below.

Prepare the fly by dressing all fly components and mounting the hackle feather. Any type of abdomen can be dressed, but the thorax and head of the fly should be dubbed. When dubbing ahead of the wing post, apply a thin layer of dubbing to a point just behind the hook eye; then dub back over the same area, ending with one turn of dubbing behind the wing post. The thread should be positioned behind the wings, hanging down the far side of the hook shank, as shown here.

(Note: if the hackle is to be wrapped in a counterclockwise direction, position the tying thread ahead of the wing post, and let it hang down the far side of the hook shank.)

Step 1b. Wrap the hackle using either of the approaches explained in **Method #31: Single Parachute Hackle—Horizontal Wrap**, Steps 1-7 or 1a-6a, p. 384.

When the last and lowermost wrap of hackle is complete, the feather tip should be pointing toward the tail of the fly, as shown here.

(Note: if wrapping in a counterclockwise direction, the feather tip should point toward the hook eye.)

Step 1c. Grasp the bobbin, and bring it horizontally to the front of the wing post, beneath the lowermost wrap of hackle. Continue bringing the bobbin around the near side of the shank toward the tail of the fly, holding the bobbin low enough to slip the thread between the lowest wrap of hackle and the fly body.

(Note: if wrapping in a counterclockwise direction, bring the thread around the back of the wing post, then forward toward the hook eye on the near side of the shank.)

Step 1d. Bring the thread around the back of the wing post and to the far side of the hook. As you do so, cross *over* the tip of the hackle feather, trapping the feather stem against the wing post with the thread.

Once the thread has crossed the feather tip, draw the feather slightly downward as shown here, to simplify subsequent wraps.

(Note: If using a counterclockwise wrap, the feather tip is trapped beneath the thread as the thread is brought around the front of the wing post.)

Step 1e. Take 2 or 3 more firm wraps over the first, making certain that the thread remains below the lowermost hackle wrap and crosses the feather tip, further securing it to the wing post.

Conclude the binding wraps with the tying thread held ahead of the wing post, slightly toward the tyer, as shown.

Step 1f. You can use a half-hitch tool to secure the thread directly behind the hook eye, as shown here. Take 4 or 5 half-hitches.

Or you can half-hitch or whip-finish the thread at the base of the wing post, beneath the lowermost wrap of hackle.

Clip the feather tip and apply a drop of head cement or CA glue to the finish wraps.

Step 2a. In this tie-off technique, shown to us by Skip Morris, the hackle pliers are draped over the hook shank directly at the tie-off point—which is behind the eye in this demonstration—and left hanging there.

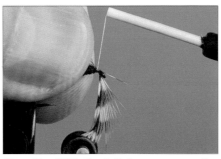

Step 2b. With the left fingers, grasp the hackle barbs that project over the hook eye, and lift them upward to gain better access to the hook shank.

Take 2 or 3 tight wraps of thread over the feather tip to secure it to the shank.

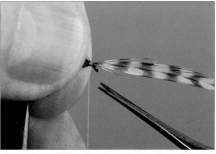

Step 2c. With the hackle barbs still elevated in the left hand, clip the feather tip and secure it with additional thread wraps.

Step 3a. In this tie-off technique, the barbs at the feather tip are preened back so that the tying thread binds only the feather stem to the shank.

When the last wrap of hackle is complete, draw the feather toward the hook eye and angle it slightly downward, as shown.

Step 3b. Position the left thumb and forefinger under the hook shank, directly beneath the tie-off point. Pinch them together and raise them upward simultaneously, preening back the barbs behind the tie-off point on the feather and the wrapped hackle barbs. As you draw the left fingers upward, pull downward slightly on the feather tip to help separate the barbs.

Take 3 or 4 tight wraps around the feather stem, taking care not bind down any stray barbs.

Step 3c. Before releasing the barbs in the left fingers, clip the feather tip away and cover the excess material with a few additional thread wraps.

Step 4a. Tyers who have difficulty with parachute hackles that slide up the wing post or are pulled from the wing post by trout often use this technique, in which a strand of material is folded over the wrapped hackle to secure it.

The most common approach is shown on the fly at the left. After the wing post material is mounted and set upright, a loop is formed in the tying thread as shown in **Method #38: Trap-loop Dubbing**, p. 129. The loop is then lashed to the wing post as the thread foundation for the hackle is formed. Here, for better visibility, we've used a separate loop of red tying thread. Ordinarily, this loop would be formed from the working thread itself. The hackle feather is then mounted.

In the version of this technique shown at the right, the hackle stem itself is lashed to the wing post.

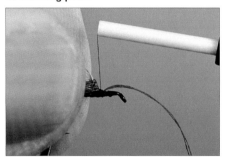

Step 4b. The hackle is wrapped and the feather tip is tied off using the technique shown in **Method #31: Single Parachute Hackle—Horizontal Wrap**, Steps 8-11, p. 385. (Or the tip can be tied off using one of the methods shown in the preceding sequences.)

With the right fingers, draw the loop threads (or hackle stem) forward toward the hook eye, slipping it downward between the flared hackle barbs.

Use the left fingertips to draw the wrapped hackle toward the rear of the hook and to pinch the loop threads against the hook shank.

Secure the loop threads with 3 or 4 tight wraps, as shown.

Step 4c. The excess threads are clipped and the hackle fibers preened back to a horizontal position.

Method #33:
Single Parachute Hackle—Vertical Wrap

For parachute hackling, some tyers find it easier to reposition the fly, by rotating the vise jaws so that the wing post is nearly horizontal, and by turning the vise stem so that the eye of the hook faces the tyer. When the fly is oriented in this manner, the wing post lies approximately in the position of the hook shank during ordinary tying, and the actual wrapping of the feather becomes very much like wrapping a collar style hackle.

There are two approaches to vertical wrapping. The main sequence shows a feather wrapped in the conventional fashion, from the top of the wing post down to the fly body, and secured at the base. The alternate sequence shows a more unusual approach that we've seen used by both British and American tyers in which the feather is wrapped up the wing post and tied off at the top.

Both techniques, however, are most feasible with relatively rigid wings or wing posts, since the torque of hackle wrapping and the thread tension needed for the wing-post tie-off can distort a more flexible type of wing.

To position the fly for vertical wrapping, it isn't necessary to have a true centerline rotary vise, but it is necessary that the vise head or jaws can be turned 90 degrees.

Step 1. Since the feather will ultimately be tied off using the technique shown in **Method #32: Parachute-hackle Tie-offs**, Steps 1a-1f, p. 386, the fly body is prepared as described in Step 1a of that sequence; wings, tails, and body are dressed, the hackle is mounted, and the tying thread positioned directly behind the wing post.

The hackle feather can be mounted using any of the techniques shown in **Method #30: Parachute-hackle Mounts**, p. 381, but this wrapping style is particularly well suited to one of the wing-post mounts demonstrated in that method.

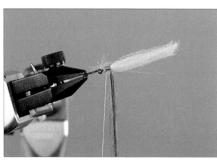

Step 2. Rotate the vise head or jaws so that the wing post is pointing away from

you. Do not rotate the vise a full quarter-turn, however, so that the wing post is perfectly horizontal. The tip of the wing should slant upward slightly; this angle will help keep the hackle wraps from sliding toward the tip of the wing post during wrapping.

Rotate the vise stem so that the hook eye is pointing toward you, as shown here.

Grasp the tip of the feather with hackle pliers so that the pliers are in line with the stem, as shown here.

Step 3. The technique for wrapping the hackle is identical to that explained in **Method #8: Reverse Collar Hackle**, p. 355.

At the conclusion of the last hackle wrap, that is, the one closest to the fly body, the feather tip should be pointing toward the tail of the fly, as shown here.

Step 4. The feather is tied off using the procedure explained in **Method #32: Parachute-hackle Tie-offs**, Steps 1c-1e, p. 387, in which the feather stem is bound to the base of the wing post.

Step 5. Return the vise jaws and stem to their normal tying position. Secure the thread with half-hitches and clip the feather as explained in **Method #32: Parachute-hackle Tie-offs**, Step 1f, p. 387.

Step 1a. In this sequence, the feather is wrapped up, rather than down, the wing post.

Prepare the fly as shown in Step 1. In this case, however, the feather must be mounted using either the cross-mount or parallel-mount technique, and the feather must be oriented for clockwise wrapping, as shown in **Method #30: Parachute-hackle Mounts**, Steps 1a-1e or 2a-2d, p. 381. (A wing-post mount positions the feather improperly for this technique.) Again, note that the tying thread is positioned behind the wing post.

We're using red thread here for a clearer illustration. For a neat appearance, however, the thread color should be chosen to match the color of the wing-post material, since a few tie-off wraps will be visible at the top of the hackle when the fly is complete.

Step 2a. Rotate the vise head or jaws and the vise stem as shown in Step 2.

When the vise is properly positioned, wrap the tying thread up the thread foundation at the base of the wing post.

Step 3a. Leave the thread at the topmost wrap and let the bobbin hang.

Grasp the tip of the feather in a hackle pliers, and begin wrapping. The technique for wrapping the hackle is identical to that described in **Method #4: Single-hackle Dry-fly Collar**, p. 351.

Take the wraps of hackle very close together, moving toward the tip of the wing post.

Step 4a. Continue wrapping until the top of the thread foundation is reached. At the conclusion of the final wrap, the feather tip should be pointing directly toward the tyer, as shown.

Step 5a. With the left hand, raise the tying thread vertically so that it crosses the feather stem and traps it against the wing post.

Step 6a. Take 2 or 3 more thread wraps to secure the feather tip. After the last thread wrap is taken, grasp the tip of the wing post in the right fingers, and pull the tying thread firmly to tighten these wraps.

Step 7a. Clip the feather tip and secure with a few half-hitches, as shown here, or a whip-finish. Try to keep these wraps to a minimum number and confined to a small area of the wing post for a neat appearance.

Step 8a. After the tie-off is complete, apply a drop of head cement or liquid-type CA glue to the thread wraps at the top of the hackle.

Method #34:
Multiple-hackle Parachute

Two or more feathers are occasionally wrapped parachute style, and probably the best-known instance is the Parachute Adams. Unlike collar hackle, where two or more feathers are often used to increase the density of the finished hackle, multiple-hackle parachutes are tied primarily to mix feather colors (for more information on mixing hackle colors, see **Method #7: Multiple-hackle Collar**, p. 354). The added turns of hackle from a second feather do little to increase the number of barbs in contact with the water and hence do not materially improve the support given the fly. When wrapping multiple-hackle parachutes, the total number of wraps taken with all feathers should not much exceed the number of wraps that would be taken if only one hackle feather were used.

Step 1. Select and prepare two feathers. The neatest results and best color blend are obtained if the feathers match one another as closely as possible in barb length and thickness.

Place the feathers together, front to back, so that the curvatures match and the lowermost barbs on each stem are aligned. The stacking order will make some small difference; the feather that is wrapped last will very slightly dominate the color mix since these barbs will form the topmost hackle wrap and this stem will be more visible against the wing post. Which feather is wrapped last depends upon how they are mounted.

The feathers are mounted simultaneously, using one of the techniques described in **Method #30: Parachute-hackle Mounts**, p. 381. If using a cross-mount, or parallel mount as shown here, the feather on the bottom will be wrapped last. If one of the wing-post mounts is used, the outside feather is wrapped last.

Step 2. Wrap the first feather using any of the techniques explained in **Method #31: Single Parachute Hackle—Horizontal Wrap**, p. 383 or **Method #33: Single Parachute Hackle—Vertical Wrap**, p. 388.

The topmost wrap of this feather is not taken at the very top of the thread foundation on the wing post. Rather, enough room is left at the top of the foundation to take one wrap of the second feather; in general, the hackle will have a neater appearance with less barb splay if the topmost hackle wrap is taken with the second feather.

Tie off the feather using the technique shown in **Method #31: Single Parachute Hackle—Horizontal Wrap**, Steps 8-9, p. 385, or any of the techniques explained in **Method #32: Parachute-hackle Tie-offs**, p. 386. The excess feather tip can be clipped now, as we've done here, or left long to be trimmed along with the second feather tip.

Step 3. We've taken 3 turns of the first feather and will take 3 turns with the second.

Begin wrapping the second hackle. If a cross-mount or parallel mount has been used, you will need to first spiral the second feather to the top of the thread foundation on the wing post. As you wrap this feather upward, wiggle it up and down slightly to seat the bare feather stem between the barbs of the first hackle to avoid splaying them.

When the top of the thread foundation on the thread post is reached, take one wrap of the second feather at the very top of the foundation, as shown here.

Step 4. Begin wrapping the second feather downward. As you wrap, wiggle it up and down slightly, seating the second feather directly against the stem of the first to avoid binding down or splaying any hackle barbs.

Step 5. After taking the desired number of wraps, tie off the second feather stem directly atop or adjacent to the first.

Clip the feather tip(s) and bind down the excess material with thread.

Apply a drop of head cement or liquid-type CA glue to the point where the topmost hackle wrap meets the wing post. The cement should be thin enough that it bleeds downward, securing the feather stem to the wing post and ensuring that the hackle wraps will not separate or slide off during fishing.

Method #35:
Water Walker Hackle

The unusual Water Walker dressing was devised by Montana tyer Frank Johnson, and the hackle style is actually a kind of hybrid, with elements of both collar hackling and parachute hackling. The fly is supported on the water by the tips of the hackle barbs, and in this regard closely resemble a collar hackle. But since a hackle is wrapped around the base of each upright wing, the actual dressing technique more closely resembles a parachute hackle—which is our rationale for including it here.

Because one hackle is wrapped around the base of each wing, the barb tips splay widely, providing a broad base of support and good stability for flies dressed in this fashion.

Step 1. Dress a pair of wings using any of the techniques and materials explained in the section "Divided Bundled-fiber Wings," p. 268. We're using calf tail here. Position the thread directly behind the wings.

Select and prepare two matched feathers. The barb length should be one or two sizes smaller than would normally be used for the hook size. Place the feathers so that front or glossy sides are together, that is, so the feathers flare away from one another, and so that lowermost hackle barbs on each feather are aligned, as shown.

Step 2. There are 3 approaches to mounting the feathers. Because each hackle must be wrapped in a specific direction, it is important that the feathers be mounted properly. In the method shown here, the hackles are mounted immediately after the wings are dressed and the stems are concealed beneath the body material. The other two methods are noted in Step 3a.

Lay feathers "edgewise" atop the hook shank so that the stems lie between the wings and point toward the tail of the fly.

The stems are bound to the hook shank until secure, then clipped and covered with thread.

Note that a length of bare stem has been left on each feather between the frontmost mounting wrap and the lowermost barbs.

Step 3. Mount the tail and dress the body—usually dubbing—up to the rear base of the wings.

With the left fingers, elevate the feathers slightly and complete the body. Leave the tying thread directly behind the hook eye.

Step 3a. Some tyers prefer to mount the feathers after the wings and tail have been affixed to the shank, and the body dressed up to the rear base of the wing. The tying thread is then positioned directly in front of the wing base.

In this case, the feathers are mounted in the reverse direction. The near feather is laid flat against the side of the hook shank, with the dull side facing the tyer. The feather stem passes on the outside of the wing, and is secured in this position with two wraps of thread in front of the wings. Note again that a length of bare stem has been left between the rearmost mounting wrap and the first hackle barbs on the stem.

The other feather is laid flat against the far side of the shank with the glossy side facing the tyer. The feather stem passes to the outside of the far wing.

Both feather stems are secured with several tight wraps ahead of the wings. The stems are clipped and covered with thread.

Once both hackles are mounted, the front of the body is dressed and the tying thread positioned directly behind the hook eye.

The last method, not shown, is to affix each feather to a wing using the wing-post mount shown in **Method #30: Parachute-hackle Mounts**, Steps 3a-3c, p. 382. The feathers are usually mounted before the body is dressed.

Step 4. The direction of hackle wrapping is important, since on the last wrap of

hackle, the tip of the feather is brought forward between the wings to be tied off.

Begin with the feather on the far side, as shown in this top view. Grasp the tip of the feather with hackle pliers, and wrap the feather counterclockwise (as viewed from the wing tip, looking down). Begin at the top of the thread foundation, and wrap down to the base of the wing, as explained in **Method #31: Single Parachute Hackle—Horizontal Wrap**, p. 383.

Unlike other parachute dressings, Water Walkers are supported on the surface by the barb tips, so added turns of hackle do in fact increase the amount of support for the fly. Typically, 4 or 5 wraps of hackle on each wing are sufficient, but more may be added if desired.

When the last wrap of hackle is complete, draw the feather tip between the wings pointing toward the hook eye, as shown.

Step 5. The feather tip is tied off directly behind the hook eye, using the technique shown in **Method #31: Single Parachute Hackle—Horizontal Wrap**, Steps 9-10, p. 385, or one of the techniques shown in **Method #32: Parachute-hackle Tie-offs**, Steps 2a-2c or Steps 3a-3d, p. 387.

The feather tip can be clipped, as shown here, or left long and trimmed with the second feather tip.

Step 6. Wrap the near feather clockwise around the wing base (as viewed from the wing tip, looking down). Take the same number of hackle wraps that were used on the far wing.

When the last wrap is complete, draw the feather tip between the wings and toward the hook eye, as shown.

Step 7. Tie off the feather tip as you did in Step 5. Clip the tip(s) and bind down the excess with tying thread.

Step 8. Here is the finished fly as shown from the front. Note the broadly splayed barbs beneath the hook shank.

Method #36:

Stalcup CDC Parachute Hackle

This innovative method for parachute hackling with CDC barbs comes from Colorado tyer Shane Stalcup. Because CDC barbs are quite soft and flexible, they can be made to migrate around a wing post under thread pressure and produce a uniform parachute hackle. CDC is well-suited to such hackling, since the radial, pontoonlike distribution of fibers traps a large number of air bubbles for good floatation (see "CDC," p. 11).

Because the wing post must be folded in this procedure, natural hairs, as a rule, are not suitable. Stalcup uses poly yarn (shown in the following demonstration), but other synthetic fibers can work.

Step 1. The tail is mounted and the abdomen of the fly dressed prior to hackling. Lay a thread foundation ahead of the abdomen, and position the tying thread at the hackling/winging point.

Select two CDC feathers, and strip away the fuzz at the base. Align the lowermost barbs on the hackle stems.

Pinch the feather tips in the left fingers, and with the right fingers, preen a section of barbs outward on both sides of the quills, as shown. The section of barbs should be ½"-1" long, depending on the fly size.

Step 2. With the right fingers, grasp the section of barbs on the lower side of the stem, and strip them by pulling toward the butt of the feather.

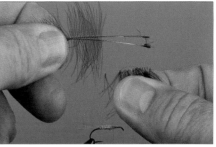

Step 3. Turn the feathers over. While still holding the bundle of barbs in the right fingers, carefully slip the second section of barbs between the right fingertips on top of, or adjacent to, the first bundle.

Strip away this second section of barbs. The right fingers should now be holding a bundle of aligned barbs.

Step 4. Take a piece of poly yarn about 3" long. The thickness of the yarn should be half the thickness desired in the finished wing.

Slip the middle of the yarn between the fingertips so that it lies on top of the CDC barbs, as shown. Do not allow the CDC barbs to creep around the sides of the yarn. You want to maintain a stack of material with the CDC on the bottom and the yarn on top.

Step 5. Transfer the bundle to the left fingers, with the fingertips pinching the stack of material at the center. This is the mounting point for the hackle/wing assembly. Again, the yarn is on top and the CDC on the bottom.

Lay this bundle of material atop the hook shank at the mounting point. Take one firm wrap of thread to hold it in position, as shown.

Step 6. Carefully turn the bundle of material crosswise atop the shank, as shown in this view from above, taking care to keep the CDC barbs on the bottom and the yarn on top.

Secure it in this position with a series of crisscross wraps, as though binding a spentwing (see **Method #75: Lashed-fiber Spentwing**, Steps 1-4, p. 324.

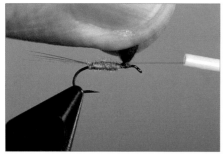

Step 7. Preen both sides of the lashed bundle upward, so that the yarn halves are folded together and sandwiched between the clumps of CDC barbs.

Take 3 or 4 tight turns of thread around the base of the clump, as shown.

After taking this wrap, you can further distribute the CDC fibers as follows: Slip the left fingers up the wing post until the CDC barbs are released. Carefully take one tight wrap of thread beneath the CDC barbs (not through them). The thread pressure will "drag" the fibers around the base of the wing and distribute them evenly.

Step 8. When you release the bundle, the two halves of yarn should have folded together to make a single wing with the CDC fibers distributed around the base. If the CDC barbs are not uniformly spread around the wing, use your fingers to pull and draw the fibers evenly around the wing base.

Step 9. At this point, the CDC barbs are again raised upward and the thorax of the fly fashioned from dubbing. The head is whip-finished or half-hitched and the tying thread clipped off.

With the right fingers, pull only the yarn directly upward. With the left fingers, preen all the CDC barbs downward beneath the hook shank. Try to exert a uniform tension on all barbs simultaneously, creating a smooth, even bundle beneath the shank.

Release the yarn and clip the CDC barbs even with the hook point.

Step 10. Pull the yarn upward and clip the wing to length.

Shown here are the side and top views of the finished hackle.

Method #37:
Umbrella Hackle

This very unusual hackling style was designed by Tatsuhiro Saido for use on emerger patterns. The body is dressed to sink below the surface, suspended by the parachute hackle placed high on the wing post. The section of the wing post between the body and hackle represents the emerging wings of the fly. A tuft of post material projects above the surface, enabling the angler to track the fly and detect strikes.

The method shown below is an adaptation of Saido's technique that uses a loop of material for the wing post, which simplifies wrapping the hackle. Though theoretically any material could be used for the wing post, a long synthetic strand such as the poly yarn shown in the following demonstration, makes hackling easier. Tyers intrigued by this design may wish to experiment with foam wing posts as well.

Step 1. Cut a length of poly yarn 4" to 5" long. Since the yarn will be doubled, the thickness of the strand should be half that of the finished wing post.

Double the yarn over to form a loop. Mount the ends of the yarn at the winging point and post the loop upright as explained in **Method #15: Bundled-fiber Post**, p. 263, and shown here.

The hackle feather preparation is somewhat unusual. Strip away the barbs from the lower ⅓ of the feather.

Then strip away the barbs from a second area of the feather nearer the tip, this stripped upper section should be at least as long as the hook shank, as shown.

A section of barbs in the middle of the feather is left intact. The length of this section in part determines the number of

hackle wraps taken around the post. The number of wraps varies as well with post thickness, tightness of the wraps, and so on, but as a general rule, a ¾-inch section of barbs will give 4-6 wraps.

Step 2. Mount the feather using either the cross mount or parallel mount shown in **Method #30: Parachute-hackle Mounts**, p. 381.

Note here where the hackle has been mounted. The length of bare feather stem between the mounting wraps and the first hackle barbs is about one shank-length. This will allow the first wrap of hackle to be placed about ¾ of a shank-length up the wing post. Saido points out that the position of the hackle on the post is variable. Mounting it closer to the body will keep the fly just under the surface film; placing it higher on the post lets the fly ride a bit deeper. In any case, the bare stem left during mounting must be long enough to reach the desired point on the wing post.

At this point, tails, ribbing, body and other components can be dressed; we're omitting them here for greater clarity.

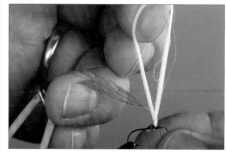

Step 3. Insert your left index finger into the wing loop and apply upward tension to provide a firmer base for wrapping the hackle.

Use your right hand to spiral the hackle stem upward around the wing post; wrap as far toward the rear of the hook as you can. Then momentarily transfer the hackle pliers to the left fingers, as shown here, while you reposition the right hand in front of the hook to re-grasp the pliers and continue wrapping.

Step 4. The hackle is wrapped using the technique explained in **Method #31: Single Parachute Hackle—Horizontal Wrap**, p.

383. Each wrap of hackle is taken below the preceding one. Maintain a constant upward tension on the loop with your left index finger.

Step 5. When the last of the barbs are wrapped around the post, spiral the bare hackle stem back down to the base of the wing.

Tie off the hackle behind the hook eye as shown in **Method #31**, Steps 8-12, p. 385, and clip the tip.

Trim the wing post to leave a tag of yarn. Apply a drop of head cement or CA glue to the base of the topmost hackle wrap and allow it to bleed down into the lower wraps.

Postless Parachute Hackle

Some patterns with parachute hackles are dressed so that no wing post is visible on the finished fly. This approach is most often used to imitate insects that do not have upright wings—caddisflies, stoneflies, damselflies, ants, grasshoppers, and so on. Flies dressed in this fashion gain all the advantages of parachute hackling—soft landing on the water, good floatation, and an unobstructed body silhouette—but they are not encumbered by the unnatural profile of upright wings or wing posts.

The most direct approach to creating postless parachutes is to hackle the fly around a wing post, and once the hackle is complete, clip the wing post just above the topmost hackle wrap. Though almost any material could be used to fashion the wing post, three materials in particular stand out for the advantages they offer, as shown in the following photo.

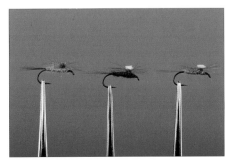

The fly on the left has a clipped wing post made from hollow hair. If such a post is bound tightly with horizontal thread wraps to form the hackle foundation, the hair immediately above the thread foundation will flare. When clipped, it produces a small "button" of hair that prevents the hackle from sliding off the tip of the post.

The fly in the middle shows a wing post dressed with yellow poly yarn. Though the yarn flares somewhat less than hollow hair, the bright color makes low-floating flies more visible to the angler. Antron yarn can be used for a similar effect.

The fly on the right has been dressed with a bright-colored foam post. Like hollow hair, the foam will flare, producing a button to help secure the hackle, and the color gives the fly a bright spot for visibility on the water.

In all cases, however, a drop of thinned head cement or liquid-type CA glue is applied to the topmost hackle wrap before the post is clipped. The thin cement will bleed down the post into the lower wraps of hackle and secure the stems to the post.

A fourth type of post material favored by tyer Chauncy Lively is a knotted monofilament loop as shown in **Method #40: Folded-post Parachute Hackle**, Step 2, p. 395.

An unusual type of postless parachute can be formed from synthetic fibers using **Method #47: Bottom-mounted Synthetic Parachute Hackle**, p. 405. In that demonstration, the hackle is mounted beneath the shank, but it can easily be formed atop the hook instead.

One particular category of fly patterns—those dressed with bundled-fiber, quill, or synthetic-film downwings—can be hackled parachute style without taking the extra steps required to mount and clip a separate wing post. A couple of techniques use the wing material to form a parachute post as well, and these are presented in the first two methods that follow.

There are a number of other options in dressing postless parachute hackles in which no remnant of the post is visible on the finished fly, and these technique are presented in the remainder of this section.

Method #38:

Postless Parachute Downwing

In this technique, the excess material at the butt of the wing is used to form the parachute post. Its most familiar application is probably in tying parachute caddis patterns, though it can be used equally well on stoneflies and grasshoppers.

The main sequence shows the method forming a parachute post from a fly tied with bundled-fiber downwings; the alternate sequence shows the technique for using quill or synthetic film material to form the post.

Step 1. The fly pictured here has been dressed with a downwing of elk hair as explained in **Method #62: Hollow-hair Downwing**, p. 311. Other materials, however, such as poly yarn, mink tail, or any fiber suitable for dry-fly wings could also be used, and fashioning wings from these materials is explained in **Method #57: Solid-fiber Downwings**, p. 305.

The wing butts have not been clipped, and the tying thread is positioned at the frontmost thread wrap securing the wings to the shank.

Step 2. Raise the wing butts and post them to vertical using the approach explained in **Method #1: Mounting and Posting Upright Wings**, Steps 3a-3f, p. 242, or by using a thread bump as explained in **Method #15: Bundled-fiber Post**, Step 4-6, p. 264, as we're doing here.

Create a thread base for wrapping the parachute hackle by wrapping the thread horizontally up the wing butts, and back down to the hook shank. Cinch the topmost wrap tightly to flare the wing butts outward.

Clip the wing butts to be about the length of the hook shank. They will be trimmed again when the fly is complete, but shortening them at this point of the procedure makes them more manageable during tying.

Finally, mount a hackle feather using one of the techniques shown in **Method #30: Parachute-hackle Mounts**, p. 381.

Step 3. Wrap the hackle as explained in either **Method #31: Single Hackle Parachute—Horizontal Wrap**, p. 383, or **Method #33: Single Hackle Parachute— Vertical Wrap**, p. 388.

Tie off the feather tip using the technique shown in **Method #31**, Steps 8-12, p. 385, or any of the techniques shown in **Method #32: Parachute-hackle Tie-offs**, p. 386.

Apply a drop of head cement or liquid-type CA glue to the point where the top-most hackle wrap meets the wing post. The cement should be thin enough that it bleeds downward, securing the feather stem to the wing post and ensuring that the hackle wraps will not separate or slide off during fishing.

Step 4. Clip the wing butts, leaving a short bunch of flared fibers to help keep the hackle positioned on the wing post.

If desired, an additional drop of head cement or liquid-type CA glue can be applied to the top of the clipped wing-post fibers.

Step 1a. The fly shown here has been dressed with a folded quill downwing as explained in **Method #42: Folded Quill Downwing**, p. 289. A similar type of wing made of synthetic film and explained in **Method #66: Folded Film Downwing**, p. 315, can also be used.

Again, the wing butts have been left untrimmed and the tying thread positioned at the frontmost thread wrap securing the wings to the shank.

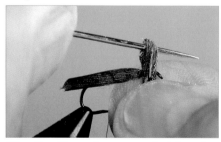

Step 2a. Grasp the very end of the wing butt in the right fingers and gently twist it into a "rope." Do not twist too tightly, just enough to consolidate the wing butt into a rolled strand.

With the left fingers, position a dub-bing needle crosswise above the hook shank. Fold the rolled wing butts forward over the needle and back down to the hook shank, making a doubled strand of material. The two ends of the doubled strand should be as close as possible to one another on the shank.

Step 3a. Pinch the doubled strand with the left fingers, and bind the free end tight-ly to the shank.

Step 4a. Clip the excess and bind with thread.

Create a thread base for wrapping the parachute hackle by wrapping the thread horizontally up the folded wing butt, and back down to the hook shank. Cinch the topmost wrap tightly to flare the wing butts outward.

Mount a hackle feather using any of the techniques explained in **Method #30: Parachute-hackle Mounts**, p. 381.

If desired, a small amount of dubbing can be applied to the shank ahead of the downwing to conceal the thread wraps that secure the wing post and hackle stem.

Step 5a. Wrap and tie off the hackle as explained in Step 3.

Step 6a. Clip the wing post as shown in Step 4.

Method #39:
Folded Downwing Parachute

This postless parachute technique appears in Darrel Martin's *Fly-Tying Methods* as a way of dressing microcaddis. The method is best suited to flies dressed on hooks size 16 and smaller, which require only a few turns of hackle.

The wings can be dressed from natural or synthetic hair, yarn, or feather barbs such as the pheasant tail fibers used in the following demonstration. We're dressing the hackle with a dry-fly feather, but a tip-mounted CDC feather could also be used.

Step 1. The fly shown here has been dressed with a wing of pheasant tail fibers as explained in **Method #59: Reverse-mount Fiber Downwing**, Steps 1-3, p. 306. The wing fibers should extend beyond the mounting wraps a distance equal to about 1½ times the length of the hook shank.

Mount a hackle feather directly atop the frontmost mounting wrap securing the wing. Use either the cross-mount or paral-lel mount technique explained in **Method #30: Parachute-hackle Mounts**, p. 381. Though the feather can be wrapped in either direction, a clockwise wrap is easi-est to tie off in this method, and you may wish to mount the feather so that it is posi-tioned for clockwise wrapping.

At this point, a thinly dubbed body may be dressed. We're omitting the body for greater clarity in the demonstration.

Position the tying thread immediately behind the mounted feather stem.

Step 2. With left fingertips, grasp the wing tips and raise them vertically, as shown. Wrap the hackle using the technique shown in **Method #31: Single Parachute Hackle—Horizontal Wrap**, Steps 1a-6a, p. 383. About 2-4 wraps of hackle are suffi-cient.

Step 3. Tie off the feather behind the wing using the technique shown in **Method #31: Single Parachute Hackle—Horizontal Wrap**, Steps 8-11, p. 385. Though the hackle tip is behind the wing rather than in front of it as illustrated in **Method #31**, the tie-off procedure is identical.

Position the tying thread about ¼ the shank length behind the hook eye.

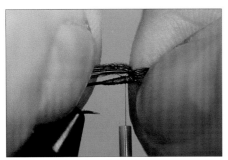

Step 4. With the right fingers, preen the hackle barbs toward the hook eye. With left fingers, fold the wing fibers toward the rear of the hook.

Step 5. Bind the wing fibers atop the hook shank. Take care when wrapping to not bind down any hackle barbs.

The fly is completed with a series of half-hitches or a whip-finish directly atop the wing tie-down point.

Method #40:
Folded-post Parachute Hackle

If a parachute hackle is wrapped around a sufficiently thin post material, the post can be folded forward and bound to the hook shank to secure the hackle.

Different post materials can be used—a knotted monofilament loop, as shown in this demonstration; the stem from the hackle, as shown in the alternate step; a loop of tying thread; a single strand of mono; even a thin strand of Antron or poly yarn.

As noted in **Method #32: Parachute-hackle Tie-offs**, Steps 4a-4c, p. 388, this same approach can be used to give added security to a parachute hackle that is wrapped around a wing post.

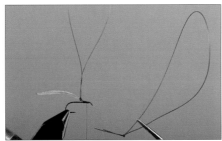

Step 1. Lay a thread foundation over the hackling area, and secure the desired type of post. Shown here is the type of post favored by tyer Chauncy Lively. A 6" length of monofilament is knotted to form a loop, as shown on the right. In order to show it more clearly, the mono used here is somewhat heavier than would normally be used in this technique.

The loop is then tied in as a wing post, as shown on the left. Note the placement of the knot here—the wraps of hackle will be taken beneath the knot, which helps prevent the hackle from sliding up the loop and facilitates wrapping.

Mount a hackle feather using any of the techniques shown in **Method #30: Parachute-hackle Mounts**, p. 381.

Step 1a. Tyer Bill Blades preferred using the stem of the hackle feather to form the wrapping foundation.

Note that a parallel mount is used here, and the feather is affixed with 3 or 4 very tight thread wraps confined to a small area of the shank.

To dress the hackle, the stem is held vertically with the left fingers and the feather is wrapped around it using the technique shown in **Method #31: Single Parachute Hackle—Horizontal Wrap**, Steps 1a-6a, p. 383. A gallows tool, shown on p. 384, can also be used.

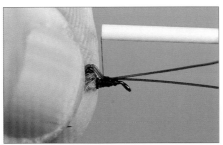

Step 2. At this point, the tail, abdomen, ribbing, and if desired, the thorax can be dressed. We've omitted them here.

Wrap the hackle using either of the techniques shown in **Method #42: Mono-loop Parachute Hackle**, p. 397.

After the hackle is wrapped, tie off the feather tip using the technique shown in **Method #31: Single Parachute Hackle—Horizontal Wrap**, Steps 8-11, p. 385, or one of the approaches shown in **Method #32: Parachute-hackle Tie-offs**, p. 386.

Fold the loop downward toward the hook eye, slipping it between the flared hackle barbs.

Use your left fingers to preen the wrapped hackle back toward the hook bend, and to hold the strands of mono against the hook shank, as shown here. Take 3 or 4 tight turns of tying thread over the monofilament.

Step 3. Trim the tags of mono and preen the hackle back to the horizontal position.

Method #41:
Stem-loop Parachute Hackle

This is perhaps one of the better-known methods of postless parachute hackling and one of several techniques that uses a loop of material to cinch down the feather tip after the hackle has been wrapped, thereby eliminating the need for a separate tie-off.

In most cases, the hackle can be wrapped using the fingers alone, but with excessively fine-stemmed feathers or very small flies, a gallows tool can be helpful for some tyers. Its use is demonstrated in the alternate sequence.

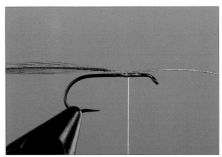

Step 1. Any materials that lie behind the hackling point—tail, rib, abdomen—should be dressed first. We've omitted these components for greater clarity in the photos.

Prepare a feather by stripping away all the barbs below the useable portion of the hackle, but do not clip the stem.

Affix the feather to the top of the hook shank using the parallel mount shown in **Method #2: Single-hackle Mounts**, Step 2a, p. 348. The glossy or convex side of the feather faces upward, and the feather tip points to the rear of the fly. Secure the feather using only 3 or 4 tight thread wraps, as shown here.

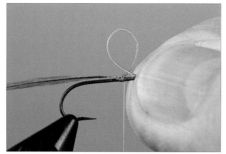

Step 2. Form a loop in the hackle stem that is about ½" in diameter.

Step 3. Pinch the loop in the left fingers, and bind the free end of the feather stem to the top of the hook shank. Take the first wrap of thread as close as possible to the thread wraps that secure the feather to the shank. Then take 3 or 4 more wraps toward the hook eye. All of these wraps should be moderately tight, but not excessively so, as the feather stem must be slipped beneath these thread wraps later in the procedure.

If desired, these wraps can be taken with a thinly dubbed thread to complete the thorax and head of the fly.

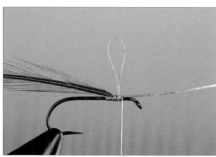

Step 3a. (Optional) While an average number of wraps for parachute hackling—4 or 5—can be taken without constructing a thread base on the loop, a larger number of wraps for a denser hackle may require a thread foundation around the stem loop to prevent excessive barb splay.

Bind the two portions of the hackle stem together with a series of horizontal wraps, first wrapping up the loop the desired distance, then wrapping back down to the shank, as shown.

Again, don't use excessive wrapping pressure as the feather stem must be able to slide beneath these wraps.

Step 4. Wrap the hackle as explained in Method #31: **Single Parachute Hackle—Horizontal Wrap**, 1a-6a, p. 383.

The loop shown here has no thread foundation, so the first wrap of the feather is taken directly around the base of the loop. On each subsequent wrap, lower the feather tip each time it passes on the far side and the near side of the shank. This will push each new wrap of hackle underneath the previous one, and slide the previous wraps up the stem loop very slightly.

The barbs may splay somewhat at this point, but cinching down the feather loop later in the procedure will help coax them neatly into a horizontal plane.

If a thread foundation as shown in Step 3a has been formed, first spiral the feather to the top of the thread foundation, and then wrap the hackle down to the hook shank.

Step 4a. Most gallows tools are furnished with a hook of some type precisely for the purpose of supporting loop-style parachute foundations. Shown here is the set-up for wrapping hackle around a loop. For additional information on the gallows tool, see **Method #31: Single Parachute Hackle—Horizontal Wrap**, p. 383.

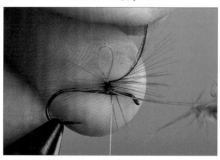

Step 5. When the last hackle wrap is completed, the feather tip should be pointing directly toward the tyer.

Position the middle finger of the left hand on the far side of the shank, and pinch inward on the wrapped hackle, pinning it against the stem loop to prevent it from unraveling when the feather is released from the hackle pliers.

Release the tip of the feather from the hackle pliers and grasp it with the thumb and forefinger of the left hand, as shown.

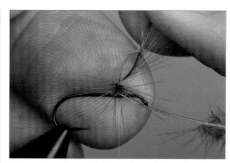

Step 6. Insert the tip of the feather through the stem loop, and grasp it in the right fingers.

Step 7. Put enough tension on the feather tip to prevent the hackle from unraveling. Transfer the feather tip to the left fingers.

Grasp the butt of the stem in the right fingers.

Step 8. Pull the feather stem to close the loop. At the same time, gently pull the feather tip to remove any slack and seat the hackle firmly around the foundation.

When the loop is closed, raise the feather tip vertically, as shown here, and pull the stem firmly to cinch the feather tip tightly.

Step 9. Clip the feather tip. With the left fingers, elevate the barbs extending over the hook eye.

Secure the stem with a few additional tight turns of thread, and clip the excess.

Apply a drop of thinned head cement or liquid-type CA glue to the exposed portion of the stem loop that secures the feather tip.

13

Step 9a. (Optional) For added durability, some tyers bind the feather tip to the hook shank.

With the left thumb and forefinger, preen all the hackle barbs rearward. Draw the feather tip into the "pinch" formed by the left fingers, and lay it against the top of the shank. Secure it with a few tight thread wraps.

Clip the excess feather tip and preen the barbs back into their original position.

Method #42:

Mono-loop Parachute Hackle

As in the previous method, this technique employs a loop of material to secure the hackle tip after the feather is wrapped. In this case, however, the loop is formed from a length of monofilament leader material rather than the feather stem. This approach gives the tyer somewhat greater control over the loop characteristics. Larger, stiffer loops can be formed if desired, and there is almost no chance for breakage during tying, as is sometimes the case with thin or brittle hackle stems. Mono-loop techniques, however, do require extra tying steps.

The main sequence that follows shows two approaches to wrapping hackle around a loop. Steps 1-3 show the basic technique for forming the monofilament loop. In these steps, a relatively small loop is formed. If the monofilament is sufficiently stiff, a small loop like this can be wrapped by hand; a loop of any size monofilament can be supported by a gallows tool, as shown in **Method #41: Stem-loop Parachute Hackle**, Step 4a, p. 396. However, a gallows tool isn't necessary, and Steps 7-12 demonstrate how a larger mono loop can be supported by the fingers to form a reasonably rigid base while the hackle is wrapped. This approach allows the use of thin monofilament to create a very compact hackle, especially on smaller flies.

The method shown in the alternate sequence is somewhat unusual. The general approach originated with tyer Ned Long, and the specific version of the technique demonstrated here was devised by noted California tyer Terry Hellekson. In this technique, the hackle pliers are actually passed through the loop during wrapping. This technique works best with rather thin-stemmed feathers which will not twist the monofilament loop when they are wrapped.

The size of monofilament used varies with the hook size and the dexterity of the individual tyer. For hooks #14 and larger, tippet material of about 1x (.010") is generally satisfactory, and thinner diameters are used for smaller flies. Stiff monofilaments give a firmer wrapping foundation than softer types, though either can be used.

Because the monofilament forms such a thin-diameter foundation, relatively few feather barbs are deployed with each turn of the hackle. Thus the customary 4-6 wraps of parachute hackle may not be enough to hackle the fly; you may need to wrap the feather 8-10 times around the mono to produce a sufficient density of barbs in the finished hackle.

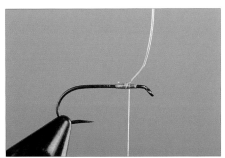

Step 1. Lay a thread foundation that spans the hackle-mounting area, and position the tying thread at the hackling point.

Cut a 6" length of monofilament, and with a pair of needle-nose pliers, crimp a flat in one end of the line. This flattened portion simplifies tying the line in.

Lay the mono atop the hook shank so that the flattened portion points toward the tail of the fly. Secure it in this position with several tight turns of thread taken toward the rear of the fly.

When this end of the mono is secure, position the tying thread directly ahead of the tied-in monofilament, as shown.

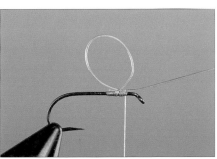

Step 2. Form a loop in the mono about ½" in diameter, and secure the free end of the mono to the forward portion of the hook shank, as shown. Take the first wrap of thread as close as possible to the thread wraps that secure the rear portion of the mono to the shank. Then take 3 or 4 more wraps toward the hook eye. All of these wraps should be moderately tight, but not excessively so, as the mono must be slipped beneath these thread wraps later in the procedure.

If a dense hackle is desired, you may wish to form a thread foundation on the loop as explained in **Method #41: Stem-loop Parachute**, Step 3a, p. 396.

Step 3. Mount a hackle feather using either the cross-mount or parallel-mount technique explained in **Method #30: Parachute-hackle Mounts**, p. 381. The glossy or convex side of the feather should face upward.

The feather can be mounted in front of, or behind, the loop, but the stem should be secured toward the tail of the fly. Binding the stem toward the hook eye puts extra thread wraps over the tag end of the monofilament, which may inhibit pulling the mono loop closed later in the procedure.

Step 4. At this point, the tail is mounted and the body dressed to the rear base of the loop. We've omitted these components for a clearer illustration.

The procedure for wrapping and securing the hackle is identical to that shown in **Method #41: Stem-loop Parachute**, Steps 4-9, p. 396.

Step 5. After the feather is wrapped, the tip is inserted into the mono loop, and the loop closed. Clip the feather tip and any barbs that splay upward.

The remainder of the body can be dressed.

Step 6. A different approach is required to wrap a hackle around a loop of very thin

monofilament that is not rigid enough to permit the technique shown in the previous steps.

Here a loop has been formed, as shown in Steps 1-3, using a section of monofilament about 10" long; the loop formed here is 2-3" tall. A feather has been mounted as shown in Step 4.

Insert your left index finger into the loop, as shown, and apply tension upward, holding the loop in a vertical position.

Grasp the tip of the hackle with hackle pliers, and wrap the feather around the base of the loop until the feather tip is pointing as far as possible toward the rear of the fly, as shown. We're wrapping in a counterclockwise direction.

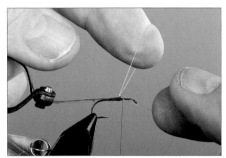

Step 7. Transfer the hackle pliers to the thumb and third finger of the left hand, and reposition the right hand in front of the vise.

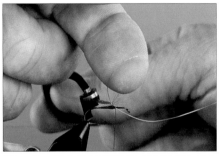

Step 8. Pass the pliers to the right hand, and resume wrapping back to the far side of the shank.

Continue wrapping, placing each wrap of hackle beneath the preceding one, and passing the pliers from hand to hand once during each wrap. Maintain upward tension on the loop at all times.

Step 9. When the last wrap of hackle is taken, use the middle finger of the left hand to pinch the hackle against the base of the loop to prevent it from unraveling.

Withdraw your index finger from the loop.

With the right fingers, pass the hackle pliers through the loop.

Step 10. Once the pliers have passed through the loop, draw the feather tight. Transfer the hackle pliers to the left thumb and forefinger. The finger pinching the hackle can now be withdrawn.

Begin pulling the mono loop closed. As the loop grows smaller; maintain light tension on the feather.

Step 11. Pull the loop closed firmly. Clip the feather tip and any barbs that project upward.

Trim the mono and secure with tight thread wraps. The remainder of the body can now be dressed.

Place a small drop of head cement or liquid-typo CA gluc on the small bump of mono at the center of the hackle.

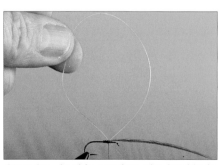

Step 1a. In this version, the hackle is wrapped around only one of the loop strands.

Form a loop and mount a feather as shown in Steps 1-4 (if desired, two hackle feathers can be mounted). In this case, however, cut a section of monofilament about 12" long, and form a loop about 5" tall.

The body and tail can be dressed (we've omitted these steps for a clearer illustration) and the tying thread is positioned in front of the mono loop.

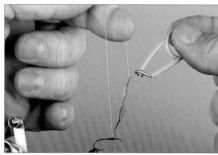

Step 2a. With the left index finger, raise the mono loop vertically and hold it open. The loop is now elongated, with two vertical strands. Pull the tag end of the mono a short distance, and determine which of these vertical strands is pulled downward. It is crucial to determine which of these strands is the "moving" one, as the feather must be wrapped around this strand.

Wrap the feather around the strand of the monofilament most directly attached to the tag end. You can accomplish this wrapping with the right hand only, or use the right hand to pass the hackle pliers through the loop. Then momentarily pass the pliers to the thumb and third finger of the left hand. Reposition the right hand in front of the loop, take the pliers from the left hand and continue wrapping.

Make no attempt to wrap the feather so that the hackle barbs flare in a horizontal plane, as would normally be done in parachute hackling. The feather is simply spiraled upward around the strand of monofilament, as shown.

If two feathers are used, they are wrapped simultaneously by grasping both feather tips in the pliers at the same time.

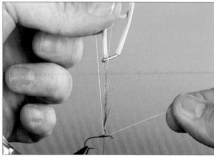

Step 3a. When the desired number of wraps have been taken, pinch the hackle pliers with the left thumb, as shown. With the left forefinger maintain moderate upward tension on both the feather stem and the mono loop

With the right fingers, grasp the tag end of the mono.

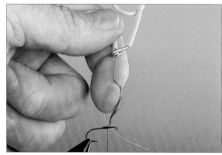

Step 4a. Begin pulling the tag end to close the loop. As the loop grows smaller, "follow" it down to the shank with your index finger. A moderate tension should be kept on both the feather tip and loop.

Step 5a. Continue pulling the loop closed. As it begins to tighten around your fingertip, withdraw your index finger. Continue to maintain a bit of tension on the feather tip, and pull the loop completely closed.

When the loop is fully closed, pull firmly on the mono to cinch down the feather tip.

Step 6a. Clip the end of the mono tag and secure with additional tight thread wraps. Clip the feather tip and apply a drop of head cement to the mono hub. The forward portion of the body can now be dressed.

Method #43:
Olsson Parachute Hackle

This technique, developed by Swedish tyer Tomas Olsson, uses hackle wrapped around a poly yarn wing post that is subsequently trimmed and melted, producing a small button of material that prevents the hackle from sliding upward. The method is quite simple and creates a durable, strong fly.

A heat shield is used to avoid burning the hackle barbs when the post is melted. Such a shield can be fashioned from a thin sheet of brass, aluminum, or even rigid plastic, and the technique for doing so is described in Step 4.

Olsson uses poly yarn for his wing post, but any synthetic yarn that will melt can also be employed.

The main sequence below shows the Olsson method used on a fly hackled and tied off using conventional methods. The alternate sequence shows a technique for forming the melted post and securing the hackle tip simultaneously.

Step 1. To facilitate slipping the heat shield over the wing post, the poly yarn

wing material requires some advance preparation.

Cut a length of poly yarn about 1" long. The thickness of the yarn varies with fly size, but is generally somewhat thinner than would normally be used for a wing post. For a #14 hook, the strand of yarn, when compressed, should be about as thick as a toothpick.

Trim one end of the yarn so that the fibers are very even.

Using a butane lighter, carefully heat the end of the yarn just enough to melt the fiber tips together, as shown.

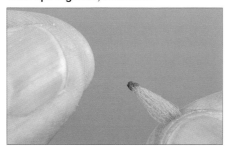

Step 2. While the melted end of the yarn is still warm, roll it between thumb and forefinger to compact the melted end and form a rough point.

Step 3. Mount the poly yarn at the winging position, and post it upright as explained in **Method #15: Bundled-fiber Post**, p. 263. The wing height is not important since the poly yarn will be trimmed later, but the melted end of the yarn must form the tip of the wing post.

Dress the remainder of the fly, wrapping and tying off the parachute hackle using the procedure explained in **Method #31: Single Parachute Hackle—Horizontal Wrap**, p. 383, or **Method #33: Single Parachute Hackle—Vertical Wrap**, p. 388. If the fly uses more than one hackle feather, wrap them as shown in **Method #34: Multiple-hackle Parachute**, p. 389.

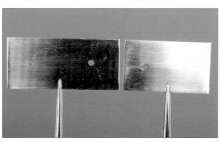

Step 4. Making the heat shield is a relatively simple matter, and a couple of different styles are possible. We're using a thin sheet of brass here, but aluminum works just as well; in fact, if caution is used when melting the wing post, even rigid plastic can be used to form the heat shield. If the wing post is heated carefully, the shield will not become so hot that it melts.

The simplest type of shield, shown on the left, is formed by drilling a hole in the sheet of material. Here we've drilled two holes with different diameters—1/16" and 1/8"—for use on flies of different sizes; the particular hole used must be small enough in diameter to protect the hackle, but large enough to slip over the button formed by melting the wing post.

The shield shown on the right has a slot cut in the side and a 1/16" hole. With this type of shield you can create a wide, flat button of melted material and still remove the shield by sliding the wing post through the slot.

Step 5. Slip the heat shield over the wing post, and press it down, lightly but firmly, on the hackle.

Clip off the wing post so that about 1/8" of yarn projects above the heat shield, as shown.

Step 6. With a lighter, carefully melt the ends of the yarn fibers.

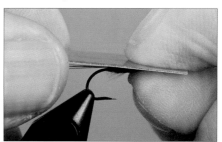

Step 7. As soon as they begin to melt, withdraw the lighter. Moisten your fingertip and press down on the melted wing stump to form a flat button.

Step 8. Immediately remove the heat shield. Apply a drop of thinned head cement or liquid-type CA glue to the top of the button and let it bleed down the wing post to further secure the hackle.

Step 1a. In this approach, the wing post is melted and the hackle tip secured at the same time.

Cut a piece of yarn of the same length and thickness as shown in Step 1, but divide it lengthwise into two equal strands.

Using the procedure shown in Steps 1 and 2, melt one end of each strand.

Step 2a. Stack the two pieces of yarn so that the melted tips are even. Mount them together at the hackling point, and post them upright. Take a few tight turns of thread around the base of the yarn strands to consolidate them into a single wing post.

Mount a hackle feather, but do not wrap it yet.

Step 3a. Complete the rest of the fly.

Wrap the hackle *up* the wing post, placing the first turn of the feather closest to the body, and each subsequent turn above the previous one. You can use the technique described in **Method #31: Single Parachute Hackle—Horizontal Wrap**, p. 383, and adjust the instructions to wrap up the wing post rather than down. Or you can use the approach shown in **Method #33: Single Parachute Hackle—Vertical Wrap**, Steps 1a-8a, p. 389.

When the last wrap of hackle is taken, split the two halves of the wing post, and bring the hackle tip between them. Let the hackle pliers hang down to hold the feather tip in the "V" formed by the wing halves.

Step 4a. Slip both pieces of yarn through the heat shield. Clip the wing post short and melt it as explained in Step 4.

Step 5a. Remove the burner and clip the excess feather tip, which is now secured between the melted halves of the wing post.

Bottom-mounted Parachute Hackle

Flies with parachute hackle mounted on the underside of the hook shank are hardly standard fare in most fly boxes, but the design offers some interesting advantages. Chief among them is the ability to produce a dry fly that is at once sparsely dressed and high floating. No other hackle design, conventional top-mounted parachutes included, take such full advantage of hackle barbs in supporting the fly. Because the hackle is mounted beneath the shank, the entire length of the barbs lie on the surface of the water, providing a large contact area to support the fly. At the same time the body of the fly, supported by these leg-like barbs, rides high on or above the surface. Moreover, some techniques for bottom-hackling allow the use of upright divided wings, making some intriguing fly styles possible—a parachute fly, for instance, with upright quill wings or divided hair wings.

It is possible, as some have argued, that bottom-mounted hackles obscure the body profile of the fly, a claim that may be relevant in some instances and not others. Proponents of the design, however, claim that the pattern of scattered light created by the hackles, when viewed from under water, is quite similar to that produced by the legs of a natural insect, again a point that may have merit in some circumstances and not others. Much can be advanced theoretically both for and against the hackling style, but it seems safe to venture two observations: first, flies dressed with bottom-mounted hackles catch trout; and second, most tyers steer clear of the design less from any doubts of its

effectiveness than from the perceived difficulty of dressing it. Based on these two points, one might conclude that the design is somewhat underutilized and could prove valuable particularly to anglers who fish clear, glassy waters such as spring creeks.

Bottom-mounted parachute hackles are in fact no more difficult to dress than top-mounted parachutes (indeed the techniques are in many cases identical), but they are generally more involved, requiring a great number of tying steps and more time. Most of the methods shown below are in some way restrictive—practical only with certain hook sizes, fly types, or materials. But as a group, they are fairly comprehensive and allow a tyer to use bottom-hackles on a wide range of fly types and styles.

Method #44:

Inverted Parachute Hackle

This might well be termed the "brute-force technique," since it involves dressing a standard postless parachute and merely twisting the fly body until hackle lies on the underside of the shank. It is crude and limited, but simple and effective as well.

The main sequence that follows demonstrates this method with an unwinged fly. In this case, we're dressing a simple beetle pattern to show how the inverted hackle is applied in conjunction with other fly components. When dressing a parachute hackle that is to be inverted, it is best to wrap the hackle around a stem loop (see **Method #41: Stem-loop Parachute Hackle**, p. 395) or monofilament loop (see **Method #42: Mono-loop Parachute Hackle**, p. 397) or use the melted-post technique shown in **Method #43: Olsson Parachute Hackle**, p. 399. One might wrap the hackle around, for instance, a hair post and then clip away the top of the post leaving only a stub of wing for the parachute base; but when the hackle was inverted, the wing stub would project downward and significantly narrow the hooking gap. Either of the loop techniques or the Olsson method produces a much shorter wing post with minimal gap interference.

The alternate sequence shows an ingenious version of this approach devised by Swedish tyer Tomas Olsson that incorporates his melted wing-post technique. It produces a fly with an upright poly-yarn wing post and bottom-mounted hackle. Theoretically, this approach could be used to produce a fly with wings of any type—hair, feather tips, and so on. But practically speaking, wings of these other materials are more easily dressed in conjunction with a bottom-mounted parachute by using the technique shown in **Method #45: Bottom-wrapped Parachute Hackle**, p. 402.

13

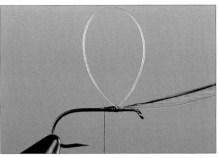

Step 1. Wrapping and inverting the hackle is a relatively simple procedure, but a few tricks do make it easier.

We're using a monofilament loop here to demonstrate the technique. Mount a mono loop and hackle feather as explained in **Method #42: Mono-loop Parachute Hackle**, Steps 1-4, p. 397, and shown here. Note that the butt end of the mono is bound only to about the halfway point of the hook shank. The feather stem is bound atop or alongside the monofilament butt. Thus the whole loop/feather assembly is now restricted to this portion of the hook shank, forming a somewhat independent unit that will make rotating it to the underside of the shank easier.

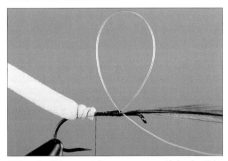

Step 2. The next fly component(s)—in this case the foam beetle shell—are affixed to the shank *behind* the butt end of the mono, not atop it. If the foam were bound atop the mono, not only might the tension from the extra thread wraps make rotating the hackle difficult, but the foam may follow when the hackle is twisted to the underside of the shank.

We're using brightly colored foam here for better contrast among the various dressing components, and have bound it with open thread wraps on the shank to show the placement of the material. In dressing an actual fly, the foam would be bound with tight, adjacent thread wraps (as shown in the next step) and no material would be visible between the turns of thread.

Step 3. The body material is now applied. Virtually any material can be used—herl is popular in patterns of this type—but we're using dubbing. The entire body must be completed at this stage; note here that the dubbing extends all the way up to the

most thread wrap on the monofilament tag.

Even though applying the body material has placed additional thread wraps over both ends of the monofilament, these wraps are neither so tight nor so numerous that they will inhibit rotating the hackle.

Step 4. Wrap the hackle and secure the tip as explained in **Method #41: Stem-loop Parachute**, Steps 4-9, p. 396. (If very thin monofilament is used, consult the wrapping technique explained in **Method #42: Mono-loop Parachute**, Steps 7-11, p. 398).

When the loop is drawn closed and the feather tip secured, bind the tag end of mono tightly to the hook shank and clip the excess, as shown here.

Step 5. Place the right index finger flat atop the wrapped hackle, and the right thumb beneath the shank, as shown. Pinch the hackle from over the hook eye to avoid catching your fingers on the hook point.

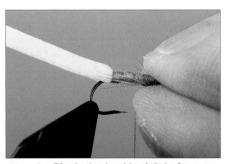

Step 6. Pinch the hackle tightly from top to bottom, and twist the hackle *away* from you, to the far side of the shank, then underneath it. It is important that the hackle be rotated in this direction, as the twisting motion will tighten, rather than loosen, the thread wraps and body material previously laid on the shank.

Step 7. Inspect the hackle from the hook eye to ensure that it sits directly beneath the shank with the barbs radiating outward parallel to the top of the tying bench.

If the hackle is not properly positioned, pinch it again and twist it to make the necessary adjustment.

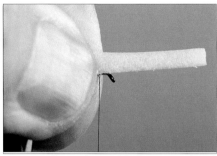

Step 8. Once the hackle is wrapped and inverted, only the simplest tying operations performed directly behind the hook eye are possible since the barbs now project into the tying field. In this case, we'll tie off the foam beetle shell, but it is also possible, for instance, to mount a bundled-fiber downwing for a caddis pattern.

Pinch the left thumb and forefinger out ahead of the hook eye, and pull them back along the shank, pinching and drawing the hackle barbs toward the rear of the hook.

With the right fingers, fold the foam strip over the top of the shank, and press it into the pinched left fingers to hold it in position.

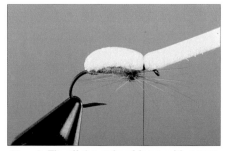

Step 9. Tie off the strip of foam with several tight thread wraps, as shown.

Step 10. Clip the foam to leave a head on the fly. Whip-finish and the fly and apply a drop of head cement or CA glue to the "hub" of the hackle.

Step 1a. To dress a fly with a bottom-mounted hackle and poly wing—what Tomas Olsson calls the Reversed Polyparadun—begin by melting the end of a length of poly yarn as explained in **Method #43: Olsson Parachute Hackle**, Steps 1-2, p. 399. In this case, you may wish to use a bit thicker strand of yarn to give greater density to the finished wing.

Lay a short thread foundation at the winging point. Position the yarn atop the shank with the melted end extending over the hook eye, and secure it at the mounting point with a wrap or two of tying thread, as shown.

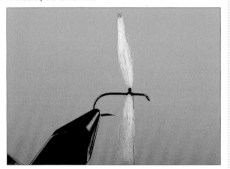

Step 2a. Simultaneously pull the melted end of the yarn upward and the unmelted end downward, so that the yarn is now positioned vertically on the near side of the shank, as shown.

Secure the yarn to the side of the shank with a series of crisscross wraps laid against the near side of the shank.

Form a thread foundation on the base of the melted end of the yarn, as shown.

Step 3a. Prepare and mount a hackle feather using any of the techniques described in **Method #30: Parachute-hackle Mounts**, p. 381.

Once the hackle is mounted, dress the remaining components of the fly. The abdomen can be fashioned from any material, but the thorax should be dubbed. When dressing the thorax, take a few crisscross wraps of dubbing over the thread wraps securing the yarn post to the side of the shank to ensure that the entire thorax is covered with dubbing. (We've omitted these wraps to give a better view of the wing/hackle mount.)

Step 4a. Wrap the hackle and melt the wing post as explained in **Method #43: Olsson Parachute Hackle**, Steps 5-8, p. 399.

Step 5a. Using the procedure explained in Steps 5-7, invert the hackle.

Step 6a. Clip the yarn post to length, shape it to a more winglike profile if desired, and the fly is complete.

Method #45:

Bottom-wrapped Parachute Hackle

In some respects, this is the most direct approach to a bottom-mounted parachute hackle, as the feather is wrapped directly around a foundation mounted on the underside of the shank. It is a highly versatile technique since it allows the use of almost any winging style: upright feather-tip or quill wings, divided hair wings, loop wings, and virtually any type of downwing. Some unusual and effective patterns are made possible.

It does entail its difficulties, however. First, some attention must be paid to the coordinated application of the fly components; that is, dressing the fly takes a bit of planning. Second, because materials are applied, sometimes alternately, to both the top and bottom of the hook shank, the hook must be inverted and then returned to its nor-

mal position a number of times during tying. A true, in-line rotary vise greatly facilitates this procedure, but a conventional vise can be used. Third, the bend of the hook will interfere with wrapping the parachute hackle on the underside of the shank. A technique for working around this problem is presented below.

The hackle here should be formed using **Method #40: Folded-post Parachute Hackle**, p. 395; **Method #41: Stem-loop Parachute Hackle**, p. 395; **Method #42: Mono-loop Parachute Hackle**, p. 397, or **Method #43: Olsson Parachute Hackle**, p. 399. (Note, however, that when using the Olsson parachute, you may need to construct a rather narrow heat shield that will slide over the wing post and fit inside the hook bend.) These techniques produce the most compact hackle foundations to minimize interference with the hook gap. It should be noted here that probably the simplest method for bottom-wrapping hackle is the technique shown in **Method #42: Mono-loop Parachute Hackle**, Steps 1a-6a, p. 398. Because this method involves twisting the hackle upward around one strand of the mono loop, the hook bend does not interfere with wrapping. However, it is not necessary to employ this approach, and in the sequence that follows, we're using the stem-loop method to illustrate the way in which hook-bend interference can be dealt with.

Step 1. Mount and post upright the desired style of wing using the appropriate method in the section "Upright Wings," p. 241. We're using burned feather-tip wings here. Position the tying thread directly behind the wings.

Step 2. Invert the hook. The technique for mounting the hackle has been presented in **Method #41: Stem-loop Parachute**, p. 395, so the instructions here are abbreviated. Readers seeking a more detailed explanation should consult that method.

Prepare a hackle feather and lay the dull side upward on what is now the top of the hook shank; the feather tip should point toward the hook bend. Secure it with 2 or 3 tight thread wraps directly behind the rear of the wing.

Raise the feather stem and take 4 wraps of thread toward the hook eye around the shank only.

Form a loop in the stem, and secure it with 3 or 4 moderately light thread wraps, moving back toward the hook bend. Do not make these wraps overly tight, as additional turns of dubbed thread will be taken over the feather stem later. If the aggregate pressure of all these wraps is too great, the feather stem will not slide beneath the wraps to secure the hackle tip.

Step 3. Return the hook to its normal position. If desired, pull the feather stem to make the loop smaller and minimize its interference during tying the remaining fly components. When it is time to wrap the hackle, the loop can be pulled open again.

Grasp the feather tip and pull it to the far side of the shank to expose the rear portion of the hook for dressing. If desired, the feather can be brought to the front of the hook and trapped beneath the eye, as shown here, to remove it from the tying field.

Wrap the thread to the tailing point. As you wrap back through the thorax area, manipulate the thread carefully around the wings, stem loop, and feather to avoid disturbing their position.

Step 4. Dress the tail and entire body of the fly. The abdomen can be fashioned from any material—floss, quill, biots, or the dubbing used here—but the thorax should be dubbed. When creating the thorax, use a thinly dubbed thread and take a few criss-cross wraps against the sides of the hook shank between the wings and stem loop to cover this area with body material. Work carefully to ensure that all exposed thread wraps are concealed by dubbing. (A few thread wraps may still show at the base of the stem loop, but these will be concealed when the hackle is wrapped.)

Dub all the way to the head of the fly, just behind the hook eye.

Step 5. Invert the hook again. If the stem loop was closed to facilitate tying, insert a dubbing needle into the loop and pull it open again.

The hackle is wrapped using the finger-loop technique shown in **Method #31: Single Parachute Hackle—Horizontal Wrap**, Steps 6-7, p. 385. The feather can be wrapped in either direction; we're wrapping it clockwise in the following steps.

Begin by inserting the right index finger downward into the loop of the hackle pliers, and wrapping the feather as far toward the bend of the hook as possible.

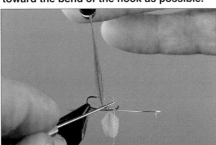

Step 6. With the left hand, position a dubbing needle over the hook shank directly behind the wing post. Rest the needle atop the feather stem, and draw the feather tip upward so that it is vertical. Apply enough downward tension on the dubbing needle to hold the hackle wrap in place as the feather tip is raised.

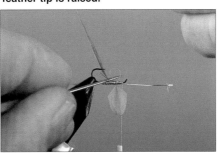

Step 7. Without moving the dubbing needle, bring the feather tip around the hook point.

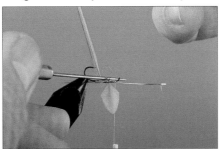

Step 8. Take another wrap of hackle beneath the first, until the hackle is once again obstructed by the hook bend.

Again, place the dubbing crosswise as in Step 6. Exert a slight downward pressure to ensure that this wrap slips beneath the previous one.

Step 9. Repeat Steps 7-8 until the desired number of wraps are taken.

Step 10. Secure the hackle as explained in **Method #41: Stem-loop Parachute Hackle**, Steps 4-8, p. 396.

Clip the excess feather tip. Put a drop of head cement or liquid-type CA glue at the "hub" of the parachute hackle, and whip-finish the head of the fly.

Method #46:

Pittendrigh Parachute Hackle

This unusual and somewhat specialized technique was devised by Montana tyer Sandy Pittendrigh for his BMP (bottom-mounted parachute) Dun. This hackling method is used with a detached, extended body—that is, one in which the body extension is attached, at the front end only, to the hook shank. Typically, such detached extensions are formed in advance, and then lashed to the shank—see, for example, any of the methods in "Extended Bodies—Needle-formed Extensions," p. 204. But other types can be used as well.

The technique is actually an interesting hybrid in that the hackle is wrapped partially above and partially below the hook shank. But because the entire parachute hackle is dressed below the body itself, we have included it in this section on bottom-mounted parachutes.

The main sequence shows Pittendrigh's original method in which the hackle is wrapped around a localized point beneath the hook shank. The technique is pictured using a split, needle-formed, foam body extension (see **Method #136: Folded Foam Extension**, p. 221), though it can also be used with any type of body extension that has enough excess material at the front to fold around the hook shank and form a thorax, as in Steps 3-4 (see, for instance, **Method #133: Needle-formed Fiber Extension**, p. 216). The method shown in the main sequence is suited as well to a simple lashed extension and dubbed thorax of the type pictured in the alternate sequence.

The alternate sequence shows a variation of Pittendrigh's technique in which the hackle is wrapped around the thorax itself. This method is a bit simpler to master and produces a broad, well-distributed hackle. Wrapping around the thorax, however, effectively increases the barb radius, and it may be necessary to use a feather from 1-3 times smaller than normal to achieve proper proportions in the fly. We're using a simple lashed extension and a dubbed thorax in this demonstration; the foam type used in the main sequence is poorly suited to this method, as the foam thorax does not descend below the hook shank far enough to provide a firm base for wrapping the hackle.

Virtually any upright-wing style can be used with this alternate hackling technique, and as with other types of extended-body flies, a short-shank hook is generally used.

Step 1. Lay a thread foundation at the winging point, and mount an upright wing.

The wing can be fashioned from almost any material—we're using poly yarn—but with the foam body used here (or any type body in which the front of the extension is folded forward to form the thorax), there are two restrictions. First, the wing should be of the undivided style, such as a simple post. When the extension material is folded forward to form the thorax, divided wings will be pinched between the sides of the thorax and forced together, essentially resulting in a single, undivided wing anyway. Second, the wing must be reverse-mounted (see **Method #1: Mounting and Posting Upright Wings**, Steps 2a-2c, p. 242), or the bound-down wing butts will be visible on the finished fly.

Prepare a hackle feather and use the parallel mount described in **Method #2: Single-hackle Mounts**, Steps 2a-2d, p. 248, to affix the feather to the underside of the hook shank, directly beneath the wing, as shown. The hackle is positioned with the shiny, or front, side facing upward and the tip pointed toward the hook eye.

When the hackle is mounted, position the tying thread about two thread-wraps behind the wing.

Step 2. Take the body extension (this one was formed by using the technique shown in **Method #136: Folded Foam Extension**, p. 221) and position it atop the hook shank so that the last set of thread wraps on the extension are directly above the tying thread on the hook.

Lash the extension firmly to the shank with 3 or 4 tight turns of thread.

Step 3. Fold the halves of the body extension rearward, and wrap the tying thread forward to the point on the shank where the front edge of the thorax will be located.

Fold the two halves of the body extension forward, sandwiching the wing between them. Pinch them at the hook with the right fingers.

With the left hand, bend the hackle feather backward out of the tying field. (If you wish, you can temporarily wedge it against the vise jaws or underneath the body extension to hold it out of the way.)

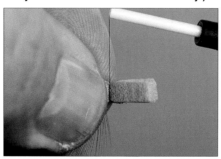

Step 4. Grasp the thorax with the left fingers and bind the foam to the hook shank.

Step 5. Clip the excess foam tags, and cover with tying thread.

Under light tension, pull the tying thread over the top of the thorax, and take

one tight turn of thread over the wraps securing the body extension to the shank. (Note: we're using a contrasting color of thread for better visibility. Normally, thread color would be selected to match the body color, and this short length of thread over the thorax would not be visible.)

Pull the hackle to the far side of the hook shank.

Step 6. With the right hand, clip the feather tip in a pair of hackle pliers. Insert the right index finger downward into the loop of the pliers, as shown.

With the left hand, draw the tying thread toward the hook eye and downward, so that it makes a 45-degree angle with the underside of the shank, as shown.

Throughout the hackle-wrapping procedure, maintain a firm, consistent tension on the tying thread with the left hand.

Step 7. The hackle is wrapped using the finger-loop technique explained in **Method #31: Single Parachute Hackle—Horizontal Wrap**, Steps 6-7, p. 385.

Begin by bringing the feather around the front of the hook, *beneath* the shank but above the tying thread. Seat the feather stem in the "V" formed by shank and thread.

Step 8. Continue wrapping the feather. As you approach the rear of the hook, bring the feather *above* the hook shank but *below* the extended body. Seat this wrap in the "V" made by hook shank and body extension.

Step 9. Repeat Steps 5 and 6, taking additional wraps and placing each subsequent wrap of hackle, as best you can, above the previous one. Three to five wraps are usually sufficient.

Step 10. When the last hackle wrap is complete, pull the feather tip toward you.

With the left hand maintain tension on the bobbin, raise the thread so it is in line with the hook shank. Take 2 or 3 turns of thread around the shank behind the eye. At this point, your hands are crossed, and taking these wraps is a slightly awkward movement.

Note that you are not binding the feather tip to the shank. Raising the thread "pins" the wraps of hackle to the underside of the shank; a few turns of thread around the shank secures them in this position.

Step 11. Clip the excess feather tip, and any wayward barbs that project downward beneath the shank. Whip-finish behind the hook eye.

Apply a small drop of head cement or liquid-type CA glue to the "hub" of the parachute hackle beneath the shank.

Step 1a. In this version of the technique, the hackle is wrapped around the middle of the thorax rather than underneath it.

Mount and post upright the desired type of wing, such as the burned feather-tip wings shown here.

Prepare and mount a hackle feather as shown in Step 1. In this case, however, the feather is mounted at the point on the shank where the front edge of the thorax will be located.

Position the tying thread at the point on the shank where the body extension will be lashed and the rear of the thorax begun.

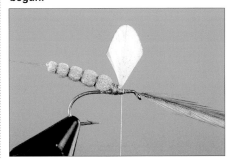

Step 2a. Lash the body extension tightly to the shank.

Clip the excess tags on the extension and bind them down.

Step 3a. Dub the thorax area, and position the thread at the front of the thorax.

Step 4a. The hackle is wrapped using exactly the same procedure described in Steps 6-9. Note here, however, that because the tying thread is positioned in front of the body, the wraps of hackle encircle the thorax.

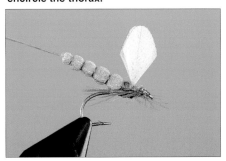

Step 5a. Continue wrapping the hackle. When the last wrap is complete, secure the feather and finish the fly as explained in Steps 10-11.

Apply a drop of head cement to the area where the feather stem crosses the underside of the hook shank at the front edge of the thorax for added durability.

Method #47:

Bottom-mounted Synthetic Parachute Hackle

This technique was devised by tyer John Betts for forming a bottom-mounted hackle from synthetic fibers; it can, however, be used equally well to create a top-mounted postless parachute.

This highly unusual method works quite well, though the particular synthetic material used must be of type that takes a "set" when heat is applied. Poly yarn and Antron are both good for the purpose; the suitability of other types of fibers or yarns can only be determined by experimentation.

The fibers are fixed in the final position by the application of a heated metal tool to the hub of the hackle. Exactly how much heat is required depends upon a number of variables—the number and type of hackle fibers, the size and type of metal tool, the type of heat source. Only trial-and-error can determine how long the tool is heated before it is applied to hackle. Too little heat and the fibers will not be fixed in position; too much heat and they will fry. In experimenting with different amounts of heat, we suggest dressing the hook with the yarn only, as shown in the following demonstration, rather than completing the entire fly. Once the proper heating time is established, the hackle can be heated on a fully dressed pattern without the risk of destroying the fly.

Step 1. Cut a bundle of synthetic fibers about 2 inches long, such as the poly yarn shown here. The thickness of the bundle varies with fly size, but in the following procedure, the bundle will be doubled over; thus the original bundle should contain half the number of fibers that are desired for the final hackle.

Comb the yarn strand to separate the fibers.

Lash the yarn crosswise atop the shank and secure it with a series of criss-cross wraps (see **Method #8: The Lash Mount and Crisscross Wrap**, p. 29).

406

Step 2. Pull both ends of the yarn upward. Take a series of tight horizontal wraps around the base of the yarn to consolidate the two halves into a single yarn post.

Step 3. Reach over the hook eye with the right thumb and forefinger and pinch the yarn post where it meets the hook shank. Twist the post away from you (that is, clockwise as viewed from the hook eye) until it is directly beneath the shank. Rotating the material in this direction will tighten, rather than loosen, the thread wraps already on the hook shank.

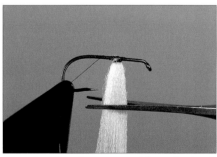

Step 4. View the yarn post from the hook eye to make certain that it projects directly downward from the underside of the shank. Make any necessary adjustments in its position. If desired, add a few thread wraps directly ahead of and behind the post to secure it further.

With the left fingers, pull all the yarn fibers directly downward, and clip them to the desired length—usually about 1½ times the hook gap.

At this point, the remainder of the fly is dressed. Virtually any wing style, body material, and tail type can be applied. After the fly is complete, whip-finish the head, and clip the tying thread. We've omitted these components for a clearer illustration of the hackle-forming technique.

Step 5. Invert the hook in the vise, and comb the yarn fibers again to separate them.

Push the tip of your index finger into the center of the bundle to splay them outward.

Step 6. Inspect the fibers. Each fiber should project straight outward from the center of the bundle, and the fibers should be evenly distributed, as shown here.

If the fibers are not straight or uniformly splayed outward, use your fingers to pull them outward or redistribute them.

It is not necessary that the fibers lie perfectly flat in a horizontal plane at this stage, only approximately so.

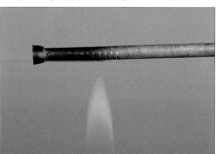

Step 7. This is the tricky part. The fibers can be fixed in position with any piece of heated metal—a narrow wing burner, for example—but the best tool we have found is an ordinary finishing nail, shown here, with the head filed smooth to make a uniform contact surface.

The nail can be heated with a butane lighter, as shown here, but it is important that the heat be applied behind the head of the nail. If the flame contacts the head of the nail directly, soot will be deposited and subsequently transferred to the hackle fibers. The same caution applies to any type of tool used for this purpose; do not directly heat the part of the tool that will come into contact with the synthetic fibers.

Just how long to heat the nail is a matter of experimentation, but you might take our experience as a starting point. With the number of hackle fibers shown in Step 6, the finishing nail shown here, and a butane lighter, the nail head will reach the proper temperature in about 5 seconds.

It is better to be cautious and err on the side of too little heat rather too much. If the nail head is not hot enough, the fibers won't set and you will simply have to try again. If it's too hot, the hackle will melt and the entire fly will be ruined.

Step 8. Press the head of the heated nail directly downward onto the "hub" of the hackle. Hold it there for 1 or 2 seconds.

Step 9. Withdraw the nail. If all has gone well, the hub of the hackle will now be permanently flatted and the fibers fixed in position, as shown at the left.

The fly at the right shows a fully dressed pattern using this style of hackle.

CHAPTER 14

Legs

The inconsistencies of tying terminology produce some slight complications in speaking about legs on artificial flies. On the one hand, tyers use the term "legs" to designate a component applied to the hook specifically to imitate this feature of a natural insect—the large rear legs on a grasshopper pattern, for example. In other cases, "legs" is used to describe the representational function of a material or component that is designated by some other term; a few turns of a feather at the middle of an ant pattern or a few guard hairs teased out from the thorax of a nymph are said to represent legs, though most tyers would refer to these components as "hackle" and "dubbing." "Legs" of this second type—those customarily designated by another term—are discussed elsewhere in this book and are cross-referenced in the appropriate sections that follow. This chapter is devoted primarily to legs of the first type, in which deliberate, usually separate, tying steps are devoted to applying materials whose sole function is to represent legs.

Though almost all aquatic insects possess legs, the representation of legs on artificial flies is largely confined to subsurface patterns. There are, of course, exceptions—cross hackles, for instance (discussed in **Method #29: Cross Hackle**, p. 378) are commonly used on terrestrial patterns, and to a lesser extent on caddis and mayfly adults; grasshoppers are typically dressed with large rear legs; and some large dry flies, such as adult stonefly patterns, are occasionally dressed with rubber legs. It could be argued, as many have done, that hackle—essentially a structural component—on any dry fly also represents legs, though this claim sounds suspiciously like making a virtue from a necessity. Hackles are necessary to float the fly; fly tying is the craft imitation; thus hackle must represent something, like legs. Perhaps. But given the remarkably un-leglike number, density, and length of hackle barbs on a dry fly, the argument is not entirely convincing, particularly given the distinct success of unhackled (and hence legless) flies like the No-Hackle Dun on hard-fished, discriminating trout.

A more likely reason that tyers add legs primarily to subsurface patterns is that adult flies tend to have more conspicuous identifying features—primarily wings, but also bodies and on some species, tails. As objects of representation, legs seem somewhat insignificant in comparison to these other

features, and tyers devote their labors accordingly. Subsurface food forms—nymphs, pupae, scuds, aquatic beetles, and so forth—certainly have their identifying characteristics, but in general lack the large, showy, even dramatic features of adult insects, and so some anatomical parts such as legs or antennae that are often ignored on adult representations assume a larger importance in subsurface imitations. And in fact, some tying materials compound this imitative function, representing not only the appearance of legs, but their liveliness and movement as well.

The value of legs, even on subsurface flies, is by no means a settled issue. Some tyers omit them altogether and claim no loss in effectiveness of their patterns. Others consider them indispensable, and still others will dress only legs of an exaggerated style, such as rubber legs on a large nymph or rear legs on a grasshopper, believing that only these more conspicuous types add to the appeal of a fly. Even conceding the effectiveness of legs on fly pattern, the angler will never know whether these components are perceived by the fish as "legs," or whether they merely add, for instance, a bit more bulk in the thorax or a little movement or contrasting color to the pattern. The fish, of course, are largely silent on all of these questions. When it comes to legless or legged patterns, or what materials or styles are used, the trout ultimately votes with its mouth, but it is seldom obvious exactly what the ballot is cast for, or against.

Legs may be tied with almost any stranded or fiber material, including yarns, artificial hairs, synthetic fibers such as Microfibetts, twisted Mylars, and so on, but in practice tyers tend to rely on a relatively small group of materials—rubber leg material, monofilament or braided Dacron line, feather stems, feather barbs, feathers, natural hair, and to a lesser extent, flocked yarns such as New Dub or microchenille. Generally, the choice of leg styles determines which of these materials are feasible.

Single-fiber Legs

Legs of this type are fashioned by lashing or binding individual strands of material to the hook shank. Because the total number of legs (usually six) and their placement at the thorax are characteristic of natural insects, single-fiber techniques are capable of producing legs that, generally speaking, are

more realistic in appearance than those fashioned with other techniques. Tying the individual legs or pair of legs can be a somewhat tedious process, especially with very thin or short fibers, and most tyers tend to employ single-fiber legs on larger patterns. The thicker, longer strands required by larger hooks are simpler to handle, and the greater spacing between legs more easily allows for wraps of thorax material to divide and position the leg fibers. Single-fiber legs are sometimes knotted or crimped, before or after attachment to the hook, to give the appearance of a jointed appendage and add to the realism.

One of the most popular materials for single-fiber legs are strands of rubber sold specifically for the purpose. While not particularly leg-like in appearance, rubber leg material will flex and undulate in the water, giving lifelike movement to the fly. To produce this motion, however, the thickness of the rubber material must be considered in relation to the length of the finished legs. A length of material that feels supple and lively in the tyer's hands may, when lashed to a hook and trimmed to ¼" legs, be stiff and lifeless on the finished fly.

"Rubber leg material" was once an accurate description of a single product, but more recently it has become something of a generic term, identifying a category of materials that includes silicone, latex, and other types of elastic strands. All of these can produce satisfactory legs, and the principal difference is the shape and thickness of the manufactured strand. Finding thicker elastic materials for legs on larger flies has never posed a problem for tyers, but very thin, flexible strands suitable for use on smaller patterns have been difficult to come by until fairly recently. The very fine latex strips currently available have made patterns such as the Rubber-leg Hare's Ear more practical to tie and more popular among fishermen.

Rubber-type strands are widely used for single-fiber legs, but they are not the only suitable material. Monofilament tippet material and hackle stems, which are quite durable, are often lashed and crimped to produce bent legs, though these lack the mobility of rubber. Feather barbs, usually the long fibers from the tail of a pheasant or turkey, can be knotted to produced quite lifelike legs with a moderate flexibility, though these are less durable than those fashioned from other materials.

Method #1:
Straight-lashed Legs

This basic lash technique can be used to secure virtually any material crosswise atop the hook shank. Because each strand of material produces a pair of legs, the method is relatively quick and efficient, but generally restricted to materials with a uniform diameter throughout their length, which ensures that each leg of the pair will be identical. As a rule, this means that synthetic or manufactured materials are used. Tapered fibers such as natural hairs affixed in this fashion tend to produce a thick leg on one side of the shank and a thin leg on the other. However, long strands of deer hair that maintain a relatively consistent diameter are occasionally used with this technique, particularly to produce legs on terrestrial patterns.

The main sequence below illustrates the lashing method using monofilament line. Some tyers prefer synthetic bristles from a hairbrush; they are straight, rigid, and fairly easy to handle.

The alternate sequence shows an approach suited to more elastic materials such as rubber or latex strands, or to very supple materials such as flocked yarn.

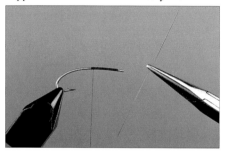

Step 1. Lay a thread foundation over the leg-mounting area—usually the thorax—and position the tying thread at the mounting point for the rearmost pair of legs.

Cut a strand of leg material, in this case monofilament line, that is about 2"-3" long. Longer strands are easier to handle and can be cut to exact length later.

Most leg materials can be affixed to the hook shank without further preparation, but monofilament is rather slippery and has a tendency to roll around the shank under thread pressure, particularly if the strand is thick. To avoid this problem, use a pair of needle-nose pliers to crimp a small flat in the center of the strand, as shown.

Step 2. Lash the mono crosswise atop the shank and secure it with a series of tight crisscross wraps as explained in **Method #8: The Lash Mount and Crisscross Wrap,** p. 29.

Advance the tying thread to the mounting point for the second pair of legs. The spacing between the legs depends largely on the particular pattern and taste of the individual tyer. But generally, the legs are placed far enough apart to allow for at least one wrap of body material between them. If the legs are mounted quite close together, the wrap of body material behind the legs and the wrap ahead of them will compress the strands into a single bundle, and the impression of individual legs will be reduced.

Step 3. Repeat Steps 1-2, to mount and secure a second and then third strand of material.

You may wish to put a small drop of CA glue or head cement atop the lash wraps on each pair of legs, particularly if the monofilament was not flattened with pliers, as shown in Step 1.

Step 4. It is usually best to trim the legs to length before applying the body material to the shank. Shortening the legs first minimizes their interference when wrapping the body or affixing other materials to the hook.

To trim the legs to a uniform length, form "scissors" with the fingers of the left hand. Preen all six strands upward simultaneously. Clip them parallel to the hook shank.

If desired, the legs can be crimped to form "elbows" as shown in **Method #5: Crimped-fiber Legs,** p. 413.

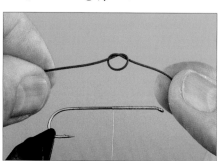

Step 1a. Rubber strands can be affixed to the shank using the technique shown in the main sequence, but their elasticity can pose a problem for the tyer. The material will deform under thread pressure, and

unless the crisscross wraps are formed under a very uniform tension, the legs may sit unevenly on the shank.

The problem can be remedied by first forming an overhand knot at the center of the strand.

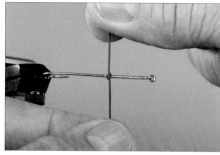

Step 2a. Slip the knot over the hook eye, and position the strand at the mounting mount.

Pull directly outward on the rubber strand, tightening the knot around the shank.

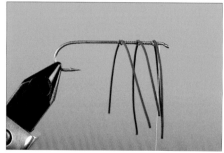

Step 3a. Lash wraps are now taken over the knot to secure the legs to the hook. You can use these thread wraps to force the legs to sit perpendicular to the shank, though this positioning can also be accomplished by using wraps of body material when the body is dressed.

In addition to helping position the legs, the knotting method helps prevent the legs from pulling out, provides a firmer foundation for the crisscross wraps, and allows the tyer to mount and position all the legs on the shank before binding them in with thread, which reduces handling time of the materials.

Method #2:
Loop-lashed Legs

When using long strands, usually of a manufactured material such as rubber or monofilament, tyers can dress legs more efficiently by mounting a single length of material that is looped and lashed to form all the legs, rather than mounting each pair of legs separately. Preparation and handling time are both reduced.

In this method, the two ends of the strand are lashed to the sides of the hook, and their final position is not perpendicular to the shank; as shown in the main sequence below, they are angled to the eye of the hook. Some tyers prefer to maintain this angled orientation in the finished fly, as it gives greater separation to the legs. The leg strands, however, can be fixed perpendicular to the shank by forcing them directly outward with a wrap of body material abutting the front of the legs. Or as shown in Step 6, they can be used to form antennae on a four-legged fly.

With a slight variation of the method, shown in the alternate sequence using flocked yarn, the entire process can be reversed. The angled legs face rearward; they can left in this position, affixed perpendicular the shank with wraps of body material, or as shown in Step 6a, used to form tails on a four-legged fly.

Step 1. Lay a thread foundation over the leg-mounting area, and position the tying thread at the mounting point for the rearmost pair of legs.

Cut a 6-inch length of leg material (we're using a strand of rubber here).

As shown here from the top, center the material over the mounting point and lash it using the procedure explained in **Method #1: Straight-lashed Legs**, Steps 1-2, p. 408. If a relatively supple material is used, it can be knotted and lashed as explained in **Method #1**, Step 1a-3a.

Advance the tying thread to the mounting point for the middle pair of legs.

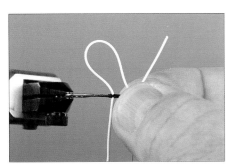

Step 2. Take the strand of material on the far side of the shank and double it over to form a loop. The length of the loop should be at least slightly longer than the length of the finished legs. When using any elastic leg material, take care not to twist the strand or you will introduce a twist into the loop itself, which can affect the position of the legs.

With the right fingers, pinch the strand against the far side of the hook shank, at the mounting point for the middle pair of legs. The material should form an open loop, with no twisting or furling, that projects outward as shown in this top view.

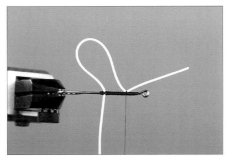

Step 3. Pinch the strand against the hook shank with the left fingers, and secure it to the far side of the shank with 2 or 3 wraps of thread, and let the bobbin hang.

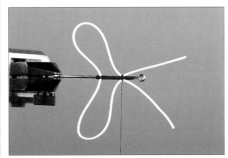

Step 4. Form a second loop just like the first, and secure it to the near side of the shank, and secure it with 3 or 4 tight turns of thread.

Note that when the loops are clipped in Step 7, the two front pairs of legs project from the hook shank at very nearly the same point. They can be left in this position on the finished fly, in which case all that remains is clipping the legs, as shown in Step 7.

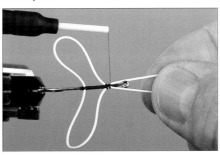

Step 5. If a greater distance of separation is desired between the two front pairs of legs, use the right fingers to draw the two front legs forward, along either side of the shank.

Take additional thread wraps to bind the strands to the sides of the shank and increase the distance between the two front pairs of legs, as shown.

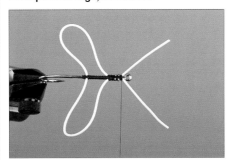

Step 6. By binding the two front legs to a point just behind the hook eye, they can be used to form antennae on a finished fly that has only four legs.

Step 7. After the front pair of legs has been lashed in the desired position, the loop is clipped to form two separate pairs of legs. The legs can be trimmed to their final length as shown in **Method #1: Straight-lashed Legs**, Step 4, p. 408.

On the finished fly, the legs are positioned at the desired angle using wraps of body material.

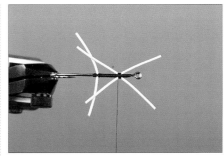

Step 1a. The procedure described in the main sequence can be executed in reverse in order to angle the rearmost legs toward the hook bend or to use them to form tails.

Lay a thread foundation over the leg-mounting area, and position the thread at the mounting point for the rearmost pair of legs.

Cut a 6-inch length of material—a flocked yarn, New Dub, is used here—and double it over to form a loop. Position the two ends of the loop on either side of the hook shank at the mounting point, leaving two tags of material projecting rearward. The tags should be at least slightly longer than the finished legs.

Step 2a. Pinch the two strands at the mounting point with the left fingers, and bind them tightly to the sides of the shank.

When the two tags of material are secured, wrap the thread toward the hook eye, binding the strands to either side of the shank as you go. Stop when you reach the position on the hook shank at which the middle pair of legs are to be located.

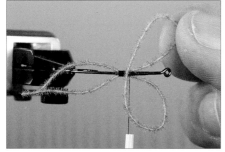

Step 3a. Grasp the front of the loop and fold it back so that it sits atop the front-most thread wrap securing the leg material to the shank.

Step 4a. Use a series of crisscross wraps at the base of the two loops to secure them tightly to the hook shank.

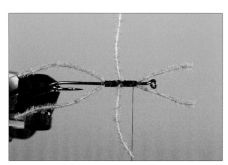

Step 5a. Clip the loops to form two pairs of legs. As explained in Step 5, the legs can be left in this position, or additional thread wraps can be used to give a greater separation between the two front pairs, as shown here.

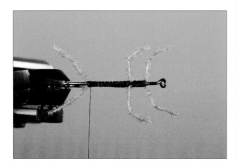

Step 6a. If the material is initially mounted at the rear of the hook shank, two of the leg strands can be used to form tails.

Note here that we have crimped the four front legs as explained in **Method #5: Crimped-fiber Legs**, p. 413, for a more realistic effect.

Method #3:
Side-mounted Legs

Affixing materials to the sides of the hook shank or fly body is one of the most common techniques for forming legs and is used on a variety of patterns. Legs can be mounted in this fashion so that they sit flush against the side of the fly body, as on the grasshopper pattern shown in the main sequence. Or they can be made to flare outward, as shown in the alternate sequence. In both cases, the key to accurate leg placement lies in preparing the fly body itself.

Step 1. Here we've dressed a simple grasshopper body of poly yarn. Notice that the body tie-off is finished with a smoothly tapering thread foundation, with no abrupt changes in diameter; creating a smooth foundation like this simplifies adding materials at the head of the fly that will cover the leg-mounting wraps.

After the body material is tied off, the thread is wrapped back over the front edge of the body to create a smooth thread foundation that is equal in diameter to the body itself. This thread foundation should be made with tight wraps to compress the body material—a particular consideration with foam bodies. If the legs are mounted over a soft or spongy foundation, thread pressure will cause them to flare outward rather than lie flush against the fly body.

Position the tying thread at the rear-most wrap of the foundation laid on the front edge of the body.

The legs pictured here have been made from knotted pheasant tail barbs as explained in **Method #11: Knotted-barb Grasshopper Legs**, p. 420.

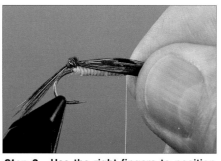

Step 2. Use the right fingers to position the leg against the near side of the shank, so that it rests at the desired angle and extends the proper length.

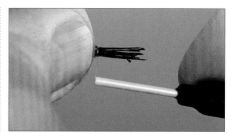

Step 3. While holding the leg with the right fingers, use the left fingers to pinch the leg against the side of the body without disturbing its orientation. The left thumb should pinch the leg directly behind the mounting point.

Take one wrap of thread over the leg, and pull the bobbin toward you tightly. Use the left thumb to prevent the thread pressure from pulling the leg around the shank.

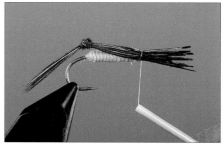

Step 4. Release the leg and check its position. Small adjustments can be made by slackening thread tension, altering the position of the leg, and re-tightening the thread.

Notice here that the leg has been affixed to the shank so that the barbs in the thick upper leg lie flat against the body rather than being consolidated into a bundle. Mounting these barbs as a flat panel gives a broader, more lifelike silhouette to the legs.

Step 5. When the leg position is satisfactory, pinch the leg again with the left fingers, and bind down the butt of the leg toward the hook eye with tight thread wraps. Do not yet clip the butt ends of the material.

Return the tying thread to the leg-mounting point.

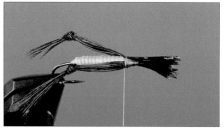

Step 6. Repeat Steps 2-4 with the far leg, positioning it so that the length and angle match those of the near leg.

Pinch the leg against the far side of the shank, and mount it with one tight wrap of thread.

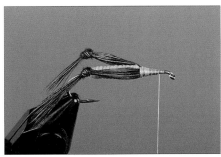

Step 7. Adjust the leg position if necessary, then bind the leg toward the hook eye.

Once both legs are secure, turn your attention again to the thread foundation ahead of the body. Angle-cut or stagger the leg butts, cutting one shorter than the other, to keep this foundation as smooth and even as possible.

Step 1a. Legs that flare away from the fly body, such as the biot legs on this backswimmer pattern, are typically mounted after the abdomen of the fly is dressed. The degree of flare is governed by the shape of the abdomen.

The fly shown here has a dubbed abdomen that tapers at the rear and has a rather thick, abrupt "ledge" at the front. Legs mounted with this type of body will flare almost directly outward from the shank, as shown in the following steps.

If the fly has a more football-shaped abdomen that tapers at both ends, the finished legs will slant more toward the hook bend.

After the body has been prepared, advance the tying thread 4 or 5 wraps toward the hook eye, laying a thread foundation as you go. The legs are actually mounted at this position, ahead of the body, where there is a bit more working room on the hook shank.

Prepare the legs—we're using goose biots here.

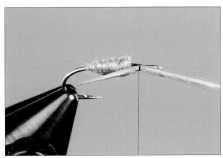

Step 2a. As explained in Steps 2-3, use the fingers to position the leg—parallel to the shank in this case—and then use the left fingers to hold it in position.

Take two tight thread wraps toward the front of the body to secure the leg.

Step 3a. Repeat Steps 2-3 to affix the far leg.

Note in this top view that the thread wraps do not yet abut the front of the body material and the legs slant toward the rear of the hook.

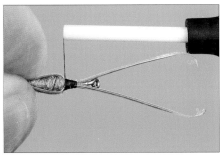

Step 4a. Preen the legs back along the sides of the body, and pinch them there with the left fingers, as shown here from the top.

Under moderate tension, wrap the thread toward the front of the body, taking care not to pull the legs around the hook shank.

When the front of the body is reached, take 2 tighter turns of thread, tightly abutting the front of the body.

Step 5a. Forcing the base of the legs into the front of the body causes them to splay outward. Trim the leg butts and bind them down. The remainder of the fly can now be dressed.

Method #4:
Knotted-fiber Legs

Strands of leg material can be knotted to form an "elbow" that gives the legs a more realistic appearance. (Knotted legs can also be formed from bundles of fibers as explained in **Method #11: Knotted-barb Grasshopper Legs**, p. 420, and from whole feathers, as shown in **Method #15: Feather**

Grasshopper Legs, p. 424.) Tyers employ a wide variety of fibers and strands to form such legs, but in general the materials fall into two categories—long strands, usually manufactured material such as monofilament or Dacron fishing line, rubber leg material, synthetics such as Krystal Flash, and so on; and short fibers, usually natural materials such as feather barbs, biots, and feather stems, though short synthetic fibers such as Microfibetts can also be used. The approaches to knotting and mounting legs differ somewhat for the materials in each category.

Knotting is usually performed prior to mounting the legs, since casting and accurately positioning a knot on material fixed to the shank is difficult. Because long strands of manufactured material are relatively easy to handle and maintain a consistent diameter or shape throughout their length, it is possible to knot a pair of legs from a single strand. The knotted strand is then mounted to form a pair of legs from a single tying operation.

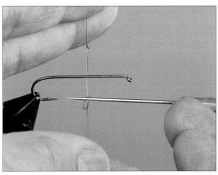

To produce a pair of knotted legs from a single strand, begin by tying a tight overhand knot about one inch from the end of the material.

Forming the second knot takes a bit more care, as it must be placed accurately to give the proper leg length. Begin by casting a loose overhand knot about one inch from the first knot. Pull the knot so that the loop is relatively small, but do not tighten it.

Using the fingers of the left hand, as shown, position the leg material crosswise so that the knots straddle the hook shank. Insert a dubbing needle into the loop of the second knot. With left fingers, maintain a light tension on the strand, and use the dubbing needle to "slide" the knot up or down the strand until it is properly positioned for the desired leg length.

The lengths of material between the hook shank and each knot will form the femur or upper portion of the leg. Note, however, when gauging this length, that once the leg is mounted, part of the upper-leg will be concealed by body material, effectively shortening its visible length. Thus you must compensate by leaving extra distance (a distance equal to the width of the body) between the knots.

When the proper distance between knots has been determined, remove the dubbing needle and tighten the second knot.

412

The knotted strand is lashed to the top of the hook shank using the technique shown in **Method #1: Straight-lashed Legs,** Steps 1-2. p. 408. The lower leg is then clipped to length, and additional knotted strands can be mounted.

When all legs are mounted and trimmed, apply a tiny drop of head cement or CA glue to each knot to secure it.

When using shorter fibers, each leg must be knotted individually. Some materials, such as stripped or clipped feather stems, may be long enough to knot using the fingers only. Other materials, such as feather barbs and biots, are too short to manipulate with fingers alone, and knotting them is most easily accomplished using a tool.

To tie an overhand knot in a short piece of material, such as the pheasant tail barb shown here, grasp the tapered end of the material in the left fingers and use the right fingers to form a loop as shown. Note that the tapered end crosses in front of the thicker middle portion of the fiber. The loop is formed most easily by holding the tapered end, since the thicker end is stiffer and is more readily brought through the loop.

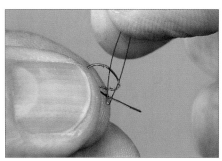

Pinch the loop at the base with the left fingers. Insert a bobbin threader from the back of the loop through to the front. (A length of tippet material, doubled over to form a loop, can be used in place of a bobbin threader.) Capture the free end of the strand in the bobbin threader.

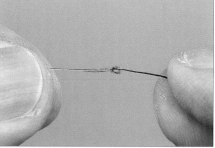

Pull the free end of the strand through the loop. Release the strand from the threader and tighten the knot to form the leg.

Knotted legs formed from relatively fragile materials such as pheasant tail or other feather barbs can be sprayed with a workable fixative to improve their durability.

Shown here are various types of knotted legs—pheasant tail barbs, biots, stripped and clipped hackle stems, and peacock herl.

There are innumerable variations in dressing knotted legs, depending upon the final orientation of the finished legs and whether the legs are all mounted before applying body material or legs and body material are dressed alternately. The largest distinction in technique, however, is that between side-mounted and top-mounted legs.

The main sequence below shows the method for affixing legs to the side of the hook shank. Typically, this approach is used with rather flexible materials, like the knotted pheasant tail used in the demonstration. Regardless of the final orientation, all the legs are mounted pointing over the hook eye prior to dressing the body. Mounting them in this direction keeps the tying field clear for applying other components to the shank. The legs are then fixed in their final position with wraps of body material.

The alternate sequence shows the method for lashing knotted legs to the top of the hook. This approach is generally reserved for stiffer materials, such as the biots used in the demonstration. The legs are mounted in the orientation they will occupy on the finished fly. Stiff materials are often brittle, and mounting them out of position and then forcing them into their final orientation with wraps of body material bends them around the mounting wraps, and the legs can weaken or break. Legs of this type can be dressed prior to, or alternating with, wraps of body materials.

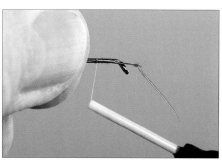

Step 1. Lay a foundation of thread over the leg-mounting area, and position the thread at the mounting point for the frontmost pair of legs.

Knot all the legs strands and place them conveniently at hand.

Begin with the frontmost leg on the near side of the shank. Grasp the butt end of the leg in the left fingers and pinch it against the shank at the mounting point so that the upper leg points toward the hook eye.

There are a couple of points to bear in mind here. First, the final orientation of the upper leg will be fixed by the body material; the lower leg or "forearm" can point forward, downward, or rearward on the finished fly, but this orientation must be established when the leg is mounted. Notice here that the lower leg points downward as the leg is mounted—its position on the finished fly.

Second, when the body is eventually dressed, the body material will partly cover the base of the leg, and the upper part of the leg will appear shorter on the finished fly than it does now. So mount the leg to be a little longer than desired on the finished fly to compensate for the portion concealed beneath the wraps of body material.

When the leg is properly positioned against the near side of the shank, bind it there with two tight wraps of thread, as shown.

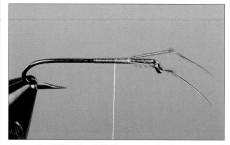

Step 2. With the left fingers, pinch a second leg against the far side of the hook shank, so that its orientation matches the first.

Secure it in position with 3 or 4 tight thread wraps.

Clip the leg butts, cover them with thread, and position the tying thread at the mounting point for the middle pair of legs.

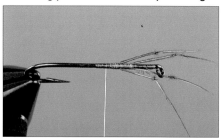

Step 3. Repeat Steps 1-2 to mount the middle pair of legs. Clip the butts and position the tying thread at the mounting point for the rear pair of legs.

14

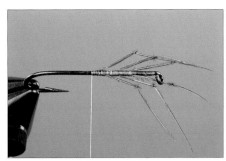

Step 4. Repeat Steps 1-2 and mount the rear pair of legs. Clip the butts and bind down the excess.

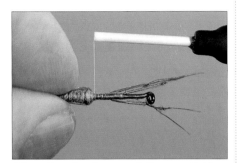

Step 5. Apply any tails or ribbing required, and dress the body (dubbing here) to the base of the rear legs.

From here, the legs can be positioned in their final orientation—facing rearward, forward, or perpendicular to the shank. We'll dress one in each orientation—a common configuration in dressing the adult cranefly or "Daddy Long Legs," as it is called by British anglers.

The rear legs here will be slanted toward the hook bend. Draw the rear legs back and pinch them to the sides of the abdomen.

For any legs that face rearward, take 1 or 2 tight wraps of thread over the base of the legs where they meet the hook shank. These thread wraps essentially "re-mount" any rearward-facing legs. Pulling the legs back folds the material back on itself, levering it around the original mounting wraps and potentially weakening it. These new thread wraps take the stress off the material.

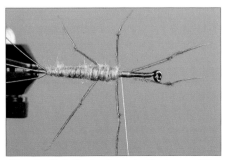

Step 6. Dub the body up to the base of the middle legs.

Temporarily fold the middle legs rearward, and take a few turns of dubbing at the front base of the legs to hold them perpendicular to the shank.

Step 7. Dub the body up to the base of the front legs. Pull the front legs far enough rearward to place a few wraps of thinly dubbed thread at the front base of the legs. The dubbing should not be so bulky that it pushes the legs directly outward, but rather it should spread them at a forward-facing angle.

When the fly is complete, a drop of head cement or CA glue may be applied to each leg knot.

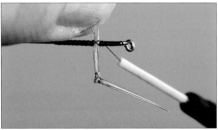

Step 1a. Legs lashed to the top of the hook shank are mounted in their final orientation. The final orientation of the legs determines the order in which they are mounted. If the lower leg portions or "forearms" on the finished fly point forward, as in this demonstration, the frontmost legs are mounted first to keep the projecting forearms out of tying field when mounting subsequent legs. (If the forearms point rearward, the rearmost legs are mounted first; if the forearms point downward, the legs can be mounted in either order.)

Lay a thread foundation over the leg-mounting area, and position the thread at the mounting point for the front legs.

Knot all the legs—we're using biots here—and place them conveniently at hand.

Begin with the leg on the near side of the shank. Grasp the leg in the left fingers, and position it crosswise atop the shank at the mounting point.

Take a few tight crisscross wraps over the leg material. These wraps may tend to pull the leg around the hook shank; if so, lift upward on the leg when wrapping to counteract the thread torque.

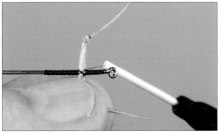

Step 2a. Clip the excess material at the base of the first leg very close to the hook shank.

Position the far leg directly atop the crisscross wraps securing the near leg.

Secure this second leg with 3 or 4 tight crisscross wraps.

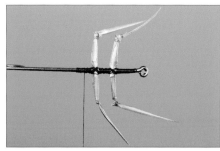

Step 3a. Clip the butts of the second leg close to the hook shank.

Position the tying thread at the mounting point for the middle legs.

Repeat Steps 1a-2a and mount the middle legs. Clip the butts, and position the tying thread at the mounting point for the rear legs.

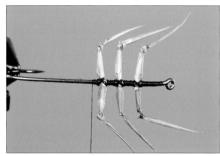

Step 4a. Repeat Steps 1a-2a to mount the rear legs.

Step 5a. Tail, rib, abdomen and other materials that lie behind the rearmost legs are now dressed.

The remainder of the body is dressed by carefully wrapping it on the shank between the legs. As you wrap up to the base of each pair of legs, take one or two crisscross wraps of body material over the leg-mounting wraps, as shown here, to conceal the tying thread.

Method #5:

Crimped-fiber Legs

Leg fibers can be crimped to produce an elbow similar to that obtained by knotting. Crimping is faster and easier than knotting, but it is restricted to certain materials.

Legs are generally crimped after the fly is complete, since straight, uncrimped lengths of material are more easily bound to the hook shank. It is, however, possible to crimp legs immediately after they are mounted, or even prior to mounting. The main sequence below shows crimped legs formed with needle-nose pliers—a method used primarily with clipped or stripped feather stems or stiff-cored flocked yarns such as New Dub. The alternate sequence shows two unusual heat-crimping techniques. Heat-crimping is most feasible with nylon fibers such as monofilament line or Microfibetts, with New Dub, with legs formed from clipped or stripped hackle stems, and with legs made of feather barbs, such as those shown in the alternate sequence of **Method #7: Side-mounted Bundled-fiber Legs**, p. 416.

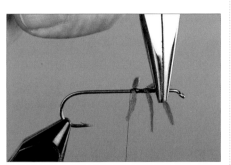

Step 1. Crimping legs with pliers is a simple operation, though there are 2 keys to getting good results. First is to grasp the *upper* portion of the legs with the plier tips. Bending the leg to form the crimp is actually done with fingers; the pliers merely hold one section of the leg stationary and provide a fulcrum around which to bend the lower leg. Holding the upper leg by the very tips of the pliers insures a neat, precise crimp.

Second, hold the plier jaws exactly perpendicular to the bending direction. Here, for instance, we will bend the forearm to extend toward the hook eye, so the pliers jaws are held vertically. (If the leg was to be bent downward, the jaws would be held horizontally.)

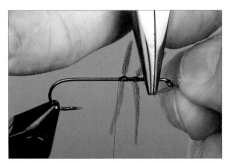

Step 2. With your free hand, bend the foreleg crosswise, at 90-degrees to the plier jaws. You will probably need to over-bend the leg, folding beyond the desired finished angle, as most materials will spring back and open the angle slightly.

For an extreme bend, as we're doing here, the leg is nearly doubled over on itself.

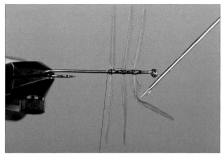

Step 3. Release the leg. If too much bend has been introduced into the leg, simply pull the forearm to the desired angle. If a greater degree of bend is needed, repeat Steps 1-2.

When the leg is crimped to the proper angle, apply a small drop of head cement or flexible cement to the elbow to lock the leg in position.

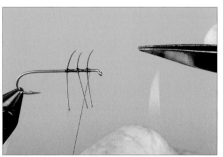

Step 1a. Heat-crimping can actually be accomplished in one of two ways. We saw this first approach in the work English tyer Oliver Edwards, who uses it to crimp monofilament legs. It can be used with feather-stem or feather-barb legs as well, as shown in Step 4a.

Heat a pair of tweezers over a lighter. Note that the flame is applied *behind* the tweezer tips. Heating the tips directly will deposit soot on them which will be transferred to the leg material. The exact amount of heat applied depends upon the size of the tweezers and the type of leg material, but generally a few seconds suffices. It is better to underheat, and be forced to repeat the process, than get the tweezers too hot and ruin the leg.

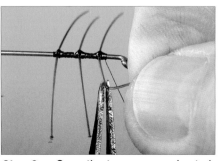

Step 2a. Once the tweezers are heated, simply grasp the leg at the crimping location, and bend the forearm to the desired angle, as shown.

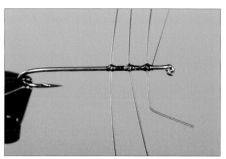

Step 3a. Here's the finished leg. No glue is required on the elbow as a heat-crimped joint will maintain its shape.

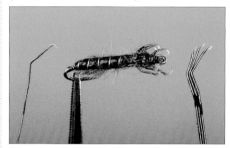

Step 4a. Feather barbs can be crimped in the same way and are especially effective on this unusual leg design shown to us by Veli Autti of Finland.

The legs are formed from pheasant-tail barbs that are stripped from the stem. Strip the barb by peeling it from the tip of the feather toward the base. A small portion of the stem is left attached to the base of the barb and forms a small, hooked "claw" at the end of the fiber, as shown on the left.

The fibers are mounted and then crimped; they make highly realistic legs such as those on the caddis larva (middle) tied by Autti.

Three fibers can be stripped simultaneously, as shown on the right, and mounted as a group of legs on each side of the body.

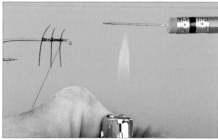

Step 5a. A second approach we have seen for heat-crimping uses a needle. Again, monofilament and New Dub are the most practical materials, but with care, feather stems can be used.

The degree of bend is more difficult to control than when using tweezers, but with some practice the method forms legs quite quickly. Since this technique requires heating the needle, it isn't advisable to use a good dubbing needle, since the heat will discolor the metal and may alter the temper, rendering the needle unsuitable for other purpose. An ordinary sewing needle will work, but some type of handle is necessary to protect your fingers from the heated metal. We've simply pushed the eye of the needle into the eraser of pencil.

Apply the flame for a few seconds behind the tip of the needle to avoid transferring soot should you inadvertently touch the leg material.

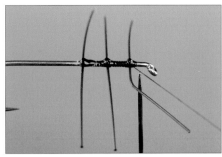

Step 6a. While the needle is still hot, bring it to within ½" of the leg, holding the needle perpendicular to the desired bending direction. Here, we're bending the mono toward the hook eye, so the needle is held vertically.

When the needle is positioned correctly, bring it slowly toward the leg. As you approach, the leg will begin to curl toward the needle. Do not let the mono material touch the needle. (With some materials, New Dub for instance, you can touch the needle to the leg without damaging it, and in fact doing so may be necessary to crimp the material.)

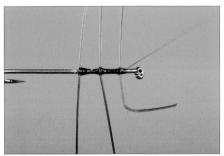

Step 7a. When the mono has bent to the desired angle, as shown here from the top, remove the needle. Again, no glue is necessary as this type of crimp is quite permanent.

Method #6:
Sewn Legs

This is a simple method for attaching rubber-type legs to a finished fly. It can be used to "retrofit" flies you may have already tied, or to produce legged patterns without the sometimes troublesome task of wrapping body material between shank-mounted legs—a particular problem on smaller flies, where working room is limited.

The technique, however, has a couple of drawbacks. First, it works best with elastic-type strands—rubber leg material, latex strips, and so forth—since the high-friction surface and stretchiness of the material helps keep the legs in position. Second, even with elastic materials, the legs are not as secure on the pattern as those lashed or knotted to the hook shank. But if mounted properly, they generally remain in place for the life of the fly.

Step 1. The only real difficulty in this technique can be locating the proper needle for sewing the legs. It should have an eye just large enough to admit the rubber leg material. It may be necessary to angle-cut the end of the leg material, as we've done here, to fit it through the needle eye, but the best results are obtained by using a needle eye just barely large enough for the leg material. The needle should also have a sharp point. Dull needles that are otherwise satisfactory can be sharpened with a file or whetstone.

Begin by feeding the leg material through the eye of the needle. Note in the photograph that a relatively small tag of material is pulled through the eye—about ¼" or so. This eliminates the need to pull a long length of doubled material through the fly body.

Push needle point through the leg-mounting point—here, the thorax of a nymph. Push the needle through the fly body, passing the needle point as close as possible to the hook shank. With a dubbed body, such as the one pictured here, the thorax material is most tightly compacted near the shank and will best hold the leg strand. If the body is constructed of a cored material, such as chenille, the needle must pass between the hook shank and at least one wrap of the body material in order to hold the leg strand.

Draw the needle completely through the body.

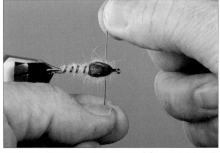

Step 2. Release the tag end from the hook eye, and pull additional material through the body to increase the leg length.

If desired, gel-type CA glue can be applied to the rubber strand, and the cemented section drawn inside the fly body.

When the leg length is satisfactory, grasp both ends of the leg strand and pull them tightly outward in a straight line, as shown here. This pulling stretches the rubber, and when tension is relaxed, the strand retracts inward to help hold the material in position.

Step 3. Note that the needle need not be inserted directly perpendicular to the shank. The fly pictured here has splayed legs formed by pushing the needle through the thorax at an angle.

Bundled-fiber Legs

As a rule, legs formed of bundled fibers tend to be more impressionistic and less precisely representational than single-fiber legs (though there are exceptions), and they generally incorporate a quantity of fibers that produces a greater density or number of legs. Most tyers find bundled-fiber legs faster and simpler to tie than single-fiber types, particularly on smaller flies.

Some of the methods presented in Chapter 13: "Hackle" can produce bundled-fiber legs. Throat or beard hackles are frequently used on nymph patterns to simulate legs, and the techniques for dressing them can be found in **Method #26: Bundled-fiber Throat Hackle**, p. 376; **Method #27: DeFeo Throat Hackle**, p. 377; and **Method #28: Gathered Throat Hackle**, p. 378. The technique shown in **Method #29: Cross Hackle**, p. 378, can be used to fashion legs on either floating flies or nymphs.

Most bundled-fiber legs dressed on nymph patterns tend to be tied in one of two styles. "Creeper" style legs extend outward, almost perpendicular to the hook shank, and suggest the strong, stout legs of crawling nymphs—stoneflies and certain species of mayflies. "Swimmer" style legs are generally dressed to sweep back toward the hook bend, and suggest legs held closer to the body in a more streamlined attitude that is characteristic of swimming mayfly nymphs. Most of the techniques for tying nymph legs presented in this section can be used to dress either style, depending upon the position in which the bundled fibers are affixed to the shank.

Probably the favorite material among tyers for bundled-fiber legs on subsurface patterns is feather barbs—primarily the soft, webby fibers from body or flank feathers, or hen hackle, though tail-feather barbs, marabou, and CDC are often used. Webby feathers absorb water readily to help sink the fly, and the soft, flexible barbs undulate and impart a lifelike movement to the imitation. Many feathers of this type are marked or mottled, and legs made from them have a broken-color or banded appearance that is quite natural. Other materials, however, can be used—reflective strands such as Antron or Krystal Flash, bundles of guard hairs from softer furs, and a variety of synthetic fibers.

Method #7:

Side-mounted Bundled-fiber Legs

This technique is probably the most direct approach for dressing bundled-fiber nymph legs. A clump of material, usually feather barbs, is bound to either side of the hook shank at the front, or middle, of the thorax.

The main sequence below shows the basic technique in which separate bundles of material are affixed to the shank.

The alternate sequence shows a method used by Oliver Edwards to dress sparser legs made of fewer fibers. Since smaller clumps of material can be more difficult to handle, Edwards uses a version of the DeFeo throat-hackle technique. This same approach, however, can be employed with larger bundles of material, and can be used to dress a single pair of legs or a series of legs, as shown in the demonstration.

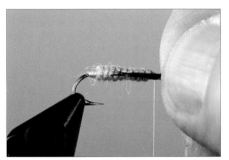

Step 1. This style of leg is the last, or nearly last, component to be affixed to the shank, so all other components—tails, gills, ribbing, abdomen, and thorax—should be dressed. The wingcase should be mounted using one of the methods shown in "Wingcases," p. 229. (The wing-case has been omitted here for a clearer illustration.) This style of leg can be dressed either before or after the wingcase has been secured, though mounting and positioning the legs prior to finishing the wingcase generally produces a neater head on the fly.

(Note: to tie these legs so that they project from the middle of the thorax, as shown in Step 7, dress only the rear half of the thorax at this point.)

Position the thread about 4 thread-wraps ahead of the front of the thorax.

Strip or cut a bundle of fibers—we're using hen hackle here. The thickness of the bundle depends upon the size of the fly and the individual tyer's preference, but in general, the legs should be kept sparse. If necessary, roll the fibers gently between the fingertips to consolidate them into a bundle.

Pinch the butts of the fibers in the right hand and position them against the near side of the shank, as shown, to establish the leg length. Like leg density, leg length varies considerably from one pattern or tyer to another. Some tyers maintain that shorter legs—about the length of the tho-rax—better approximate the proportions of the natural. Others prefer to exaggerate the length to make the legs a more con-spicuous feature of the dressing to give them more movement.

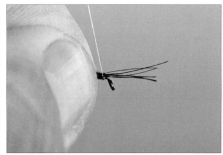

Step 2. Using the left thumb and forefin-ger, pinch the fibers firmly against the side of the thorax. Notice that the tip of the thumb presses the fibers against the hook shank directly behind the mounting point. Applying pressure to the fibers like this will help keep them positioned on the side of the shank when they are bound in.

Using very light tension—almost a slack thread—take one wrap of thread over the fibers. When the thread is beneath the hook shank, pull it tightly to seat the wrap and secure the fibers.

Maintain your grasp with the left fin-gers, and take a second tight wrap atop the first.

Step 3. Clip or strip a second bundle of fibers identical in thickness to the first, and position it on the far side of the hook shank so that the legs will be equal in length to those formed from the first bundle.

Again, use the left fingers to pinch the fibers against the side of the thorax. This time, the tip of the index finger should press the fibers against the side of the shank to prevent them from shifting posi-tion when they are mounted.

As in Step 2, make a loose wrap over the fibers. When the wrap is complete, tighten the thread.

When this first wrap is complete, make a second tight wrap atop it, as shown in this top view.

Step 4. Carefully trim the fiber butts close to the mounting wraps, and secure them with thread.

If swept-back, swimmer-style legs are desired on the pattern, the legs are now complete. The wingcase (if used) can now be folded and the fly finished.

If you wish the legs to extend more directly outward, proceed to Step 5.

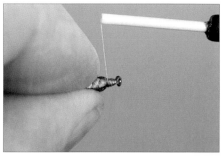

Step 5. To form creeper-style legs, pinch the legs tightly against the sides of the thorax, as shown.

Wrap the tying thread back toward the front of the thorax. Note that if the fibers are not pinched tightly in the left fingers, they will begin to twist around the shank.

Step 6. Each wrap taken back toward the thorax pushes the base of the fibers into the front of the thorax and causes the legs to flare outward. As you wrap the thread back, periodically release the legs and check their position until the desired degree of flare is obtained.

Here, we've tightly abutted the fibers against the front of the thorax so that the legs flare outward nearly perpendicular to the shank.

Step 7. The fly shown here has legs placed in the middle of the thorax. To dress this style, form only the rear half of the tho-rax. Mount the legs as described in the pre-ceding steps, and then complete the front half of the thorax ahead of the legs.

If a folded-style wingcase is used, fold and tie down the wingcase material.

Step 1a. In Oliver Edwards' technique, two legs are mounted simultaneously.

14

Dress the tail, rib, abdomen, and any other components applied behind the thorax. If a folded-style wingcase is used (see **Method #1: Folded-strip Wingcase**, p. 229; **Method #2: Multiple-fold Wingcase**, p. 231; and **Method #4: Bundled-fiber Wingcase**, p. 232), it should be mounted at this point. Position the tying thread at the front edge of the abdomen.

Select a feather to form the legs. The feather barbs should be longer than the desired length of the finished legs, and the barbs on each side of the feather stem should be equal in length.

Snip away the tip of the feather so that the uppermost remaining barbs are at least slightly longer than the finished legs.

Preen most of the barbs toward the base of the feather, leaving 3 or 4 barbs on each side of the stem at the very tip of the feather, forming a "V" as shown.

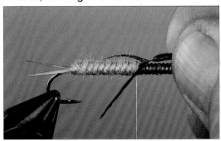

Step 2a. Using the right fingers, take the "V" tip of barbs and straddle the hook shank at the front edge of the abdomen. The barbs can be positioned parallel to the hook shank for legs that lie in a horizontal plane, or they can be angled slightly downward, as shown here.

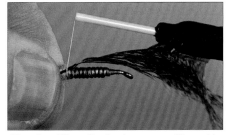

Step 3a. When the barbs are positioned in the desired orientation, pinch them against the sides of the abdomen with the left fingers, as shown.

Take 2 or 3 wraps of thread to secure the two clumps of barbs to opposite sides of the hook shank.

Note that if a feather with long barbs is used, the legs can be sized after they are mounted. Secure the feather as shown here, using two moderately tight thread wraps. Then pull the feather stem to slide the barb beneath the mounting wraps until they are of the correct length (see **Method #27: DeFeo Throat Hackle**, Steps 3-4, p. 377).

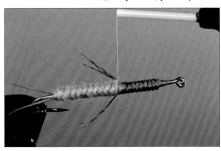

Step 4a. When the legs are secure, clip the excess feather, and wrap the tying thread

toward the abdomen, abutting the base of the fibers tightly against the front of the body material. These wraps further secure the feather and flare the barbs outward.

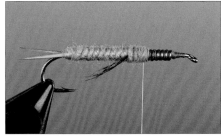

Step 5a. Build the thorax forward to the midpoint. The thorax material, in this case dubbing, can be used to position the pair of legs just mounted.

To sweep the legs rearward, as we've done here, take a wrap or two of body material over the front base of the legs, forcing them to slant back toward the tail of the fly.

If you wish the legs to extend outward perpendicular to the hook shank, take a crisscross wrap of body material atop the hook shank between the pair of legs. This wrap will conceal the thread used to mount the legs without forcing the barbs rearward.

When the hook is dressed to the midpoint of the thorax, position the tying thread directly in front of the thorax material.

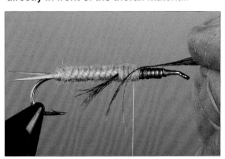

Step 6a. Take the same feather used to form the first pair of legs, and prepare it as shown in Step 1a, creating a second "V" of feather barbs equal in size to the first. You will need to snip off the small tag of material at the tip of the stem that was left when the feather was clipped away from the first pair of legs.

Straddle the hook shank at the front of the thorax, positioning this second pair of legs in the same orientation as the first.

Step 7a. Bind down these legs exactly as you did the first pair in Steps 3a-4a.

If a multiple wingcase is used (see **Method #2: Multiple-fold Wingcase**, p. 229, or **Method #5: Cut and Burned Wingcases**, p. 233), the first wingcase section is formed at this point.

Dress the remainder of the thorax, using wraps of body material, as shown in Step 5a, to position this second pair of legs so that they match the orientation of the first.

Step 8a. Repeat Step 6a to dress the third pair of legs (and the second section of a multiple wingcase).

If a folded-style wingcase has been used, it is now folded forward, tied off, and the fly finished.

Oliver Edwards suggests heat-crimping the legs using the tweezer method (see **Method #5: Crimped-fiber Legs**, Steps 1a-2a, p. 414), and treating the barbs afterward with a thin coating of flexible cement.

Method #8:
Gathered-fiber Legs

Legs can be fashioned by gathering into a bundle fibers that have been wrapped around or bound to the hook shank. Nearly any fiber can be used including Antron and Z-lon yarns and reflective materials such as Krystal Flash or Flashabou, but most tyers use either feather barbs or natural hairs.

The main sequence shows a method for forming legs from a bundle of fibers reverse-mounted on the hook shank. This method is particularly well suited to smaller flies, where handling very short leg fibers can be cumbersome.

Steps 1a-1c in the alternate sequence demonstrate how the same type of leg can be formed from distributed fibers, such as wrapped or distributed feather barbs.

Both approaches can be used to mount legs either in the middle or at the front of the thorax.

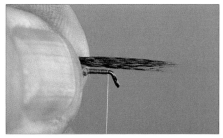

Step 1. Dress any fly components behind the thorax, and mount the wingcase, if one is used, employing one of the methods shown in "Wingcases," p. 229. (We've omitted the wingcase here for a clearer illustration).

Wrap the tying thread forward, laying a thread foundation over the thorax area as you go. Position the thread far enough behind the hook eye so that enough room remains to tie off any wingcase materials. If no wingcase is used, the thread can be positioned just behind the hook eye.

Prepare a bundle of fibers so that the tips are even. Feather barbs are used in this demonstration. (Note: if yarn is used, the strand should be combed thoroughly to separate the individual filaments.)

With the left hand, position the bundle atop the shank so that the tips project over the hook eye, as shown. The length of fiber extending beyond the mounting point should be slightly longer than the desired length of the finished legs. (When the fibers are folded back and tied down to form the legs, a small bit of length will be lost.)

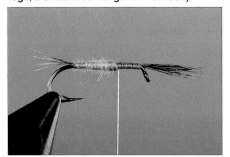

Step 2. Bind the bundle of fibers atop the shank with tight thread wraps, moving back to the rear of the thorax.

Clip any fiber butts that remain and bind down with thread.

Position the thread at the rear of the thorax.

Step 3. Dress the thorax—we're using dubbing here—but do not completely cover the thread wraps used to mount the leg fibers. Rather, when the thorax is complete, the 2 or 3 frontmost thread wraps securing the leg fibers should be visible beyond the thorax, as shown.

Position the tying thread at the front of the thorax.

Step 4. With your fingers or a dubbing needle or both, divide the bundle of fibers in half. On larger flies, dividing the fibers is a relatively simple matter. For smaller patterns with shorter legs, see Step 4a.

With the left fingers, grasp the tips of the half-bundle on the near side of the shank, and fold the fibers back along the side of the thorax into the desired position. The fibers can be laid parallel to the body, or angled slightly downward, as shown here.

Step 4a. On small flies with short leg fibers, dividing the bundle in half can be difficult. You can position the leg fibers for easier handling by pressing the right thumbnail into the base of the barbs where they meet the hook shank. This will bend them partially upright and flare the fiber tips, making them easier to divide and grasp.

Step 5. Take 2 tight turns of thread around the base of the fibers to secure them in position.

Step 6. Repeat Steps 4-5 with the bundle of fibers on the far side of the shank, fixing them in a position symmetrical with the first.

If no wingcase is used, cover the butts of the fibers with thread, forming the head of the fly simultaneously.

If a wingcase is used, it is folded over at this point and bound directly atop the thread wraps securing the leg fibers, covering them with thread and forming the head of the fly.

Step 1a. Legs can be formed by gathering fibers that have been distributed around the hook shank using methods illustrated in Chapter 13: "Hackle." Loose fibers can be distributed with procedures shown in

Method #20: Distributed Collar Hackle, p. 367, or Method #21: Reverse Distributed Collar Hackle, p. 368. Or, as shown here, a feather can be wrapped as explained in Method #5: Single-hackle Wet-fly Collar, p. 352.

Here, a hen hackle feather is wrapped at the center of the thorax (if desired, the fibers could be mounted at the front of the thorax instead). When placing the legs in the center of the thorax, the base of the fibers will eventually be concealed beneath wraps of thorax material and make the legs appear shorter. Make certain that the fibers used are long enough to produce legs of the correct length after the thorax is dressed.

Step 1b. Using the technique shown in **Method #76: Gathered Collar-hackle Spentwing**, p. 325, make a series of criss-cross wraps that gather and divide the fibers so that a bundle projects outward from either side of the shank, as shown.

Step 1c. Create the thorax. As explained in **Method #7: Side-mounted Bundled-fiber Legs**, Step 5a, p. 414, use wraps of thorax material, such as the dubbing shown here, to position the legs in their final orientation.

Method #9:

Wingcase Legs

This is one of the many "combination techniques" that abound in fly tying, in which two components are formed simultaneously. Here, a length of bundled fibers are folded over the thorax to create the wingcase, and the tip ends of the fibers are used to fashion the legs. This approach is suitable for flies of almost any size, but it is frequently employed to create legs on smaller flies, where mounting a separate bundle of short leg fibers can be difficult.

This technique can be used with almost

any fibers suitable for use as a wingcase (see **Method #4: Bundled-fiber Wingcase**, p. 232). Antron, Z-lon, Krystal Flash, and other synthetic fibers are suitable, but most tyers use natural hair or feather barbs, particularly the long tail-feather barbs such as the pheasant tail fibers used in the following sequence.

Step 1. Dress all fly components that lie behind the thorax of the fly.

Prepare a clump of bundled fibers for the wingcase and legs so that the fiber tips are even. Aligning the fiber tips is particularly important for smaller flies with shorter legs, since any small unevenness in the fiber tips will show up as a large discrepancy in length on the finished legs.

Mount the wingcase fibers as explained **Method #4: Bundled-fiber Wingcase**, Steps 1-2, p. 232. With natural materials, the length of the wingcase fibers extending beyond the mounting wraps will eventually determine the length of the finished legs. (With synthetic fibers, the legs can be clipped to length after they are affixed in position, so establishing the proper length of the wingcase is not critical.)

Exactly where to position the wingcase tips depends upon a number of factors: the length of the abdomen, the size and placement of the thorax, and the desired length of the finished legs. As a starting point for experimentation, however, you may try positioning the wingcase fibers so that the tips are aligned with the bend of the hook.

Once the wingcase fibers are mounted, dress the thorax of the fly, and position the thread at the front of the thorax.

Step 2. Using the procedure shown in **Method #4: Bundled-fiber Wingcase**, Steps 3-4, p. 233, fold and secure the wingcase fibers at the front of the thorax as shown.

Tie down the wingcase fibers with only 2 or 3 tight thread wraps. Additional wraps will be used to affix the legs in the position, and these will further secure the wingcase. Using too many thread wraps now to bind in the wingcase will merely add bulk to the head of the fly later.

Step 3. Dressing the legs from this point on is very similar to the technique shown in **Method #8: Gathered-fiber Legs**, Steps 4-6, p. 418. Readers seeking a more detailed explanation for the following steps should consult that method.

Fold half the fibers tips against the near side of the thorax, and bind them in position, as shown.

Note: if the total number of fibers used in the wingcase is large, and using all the fiber tips would result in excessively dense legs, see Step 4a.

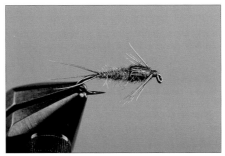

Step 4. Repeat Step 3, binding the remaining fiber tips to the far side of the shank.

Cover the leg butts with tying thread, and form the head of the fly.

Step 4a. When dressing a large fly that requires a substantial bundle of fibers to form the wingcase, using all the fiber tips may result in legs that are too numerous or bulky. In this case, form legs by folding back only the desired number of fibers on each side of the shank, as shown here.

After affixing the legs in position, clip the fibers that remain projecting over the hook eye, and cover the butts with thread as the head is formed.

Method #10:
Wingcase-split Legs

This method uses the wingcase material to divide a bundle of fibers mounted ahead of the thorax. The technique is quite efficient in that separate thread wraps are not required to

position the leg fibers prior to securing the wingcase. This approach is especially useful for very soft, fluffy fibers—such as marabou or CDC barbs—which can be a bit unruly and difficult to mount in 2 separate bundles, as is required by some methods in this section.

The main sequence shows the leg material mounted in the downwing style. The alternate sequence shows a bundle of fibers reverse-mounted over the hook eye. The butts of the leg fibers are concealed beneath the thorax, making for a very small, neat head on the pattern.

Step 1. Dress all fly components, including mounting the wingcase as explained in **Method #1: Folded-strip Wingcase**, p. 229, or **Method #4: Bundled-fiber Wingcase**, p. 232. (Note: if a wingcase is formed using **Method #2: Multiple-fold Wingcase**, p. 231, all wingcase segments except the final one should be dressed.)

Lay a short thread foundation toward the hook eye, and position the tying thread directly at the front of the thorax.

Prepare a bundle of leg fibers of the desired thickness so that the fiber tips are aligned.

Establish the desired leg length, and with the right fingers pinch the material at the mounting point. Position it over the tying thread as shown.

Step 2. Using the technique described in **Method #85: Tuft Emerger Wings**, Steps 2-3, p. 335, mount the leg material. When it is secured to the shank, clip the butts and bind with thread.

When mounting the leg material and binding down the butts, use as few thread wraps as possible to secure the material in order to avoid building bulk at the head of the fly. When the wingcase is folded, the thread wraps used to bind it down will also provide additional security for the leg fibers.

Step 3. With your fingers or dubbing needle or both, divide the leg fibers. (With very fluffy fibers such as marabou, it helps to dampen the material slightly.) Use your left fingers to fold half the fibers against the near side of the thorax, and slightly downward.

With your right fingers, fold the remaining half of the fibers against the far side of the thorax and slightly downward. Pull both fiber bundles firmly, as shown.

The object here is to temporarily pull the fibers away from the top of the thorax, clearing a space so that the wingcase can be folded forward.

Step 4. With your left fingers, grasp the fiber bundle on the near side of the shank.

With the right fingers, fold the wingcase over the top of the thorax and pull firmly.

Step 5. Hold the wingcase in position with the left fingers, and secure the wingcase with 2 or 3 tight thread wraps.

Step 6. If the legs are satisfactorily positioned, add 2 or 3 more tight thread wraps to the wingcase, clip and bind down the butts.

If the legs are not properly positioned, gently pull or preen them into the desired

orientation—slanting downward, for instance, or more outward from the hook shank.

With the left fingers, hold the legs in this new orientation, and take 2 or 3 tight thread wraps over the wingcase, moving toward the front of the thorax. Abutting the wingcase material against the base of the legs this way will help hold the leg fibers in position.

Clip and bind down the wingcase butts and form the head of the fly.

Step 1a. To create a small, neat head on a fly, mount the leg fibers with the tips extending over the hook eye, as explained in **Method #8: Gathered-fiber Legs**, Steps 1-3, p. 417. Dress all the components behind the thorax. Mount (but do not fold) the wingcase, and dress the thorax so that all the thread wraps binding the leg fibers are concealed beneath the thorax material, as shown.

Position the tying thread ahead of the leg fibers by lifting the bundle and taking one wrap of thread around the hook shank only.

Step 2a. Divide the fiber bundle in half, and fold each half-bundle of material over the sides of the thorax, pulling slightly downward, as shown in Step 3.

To complete the fly, proceed to Step 4.

Method #11:

Knotted-barb Grasshopper Legs

Forming legs for grasshopper and cricket patterns is probably the most common use of bundled-fiber legs on dry flies. (Grasshopper legs can also be made from knotted feathers as shown in **Method #15: Feather Grasshopper Legs**, p. 424.) Because the rear kicking legs of grasshoppers are relatively large, and knotting itself is difficult with shorter fibers, tyers generally use the long, straight barbs from the tail feathers of

various species of pheasants or from turkeys. However, wing quills from larger birds such as geese or turkeys can be suitable if the barbs are long enough.

It is possible to knot a bundle of fibers using the technique shown in **Method #4: Knotted-fiber Legs**, p. 411, but knotting the barbs while they are still attached to the feather stem, as shown in the main sequence, is generally faster and easier, and gives more consistent results. The feather stem acts as a "third hand," holding barbs and freeing the tyers own hands to manipulate the material and accurately position the knot. Knotting barbs on the feather stem is most easily accomplished by using a tool. In the main sequence, we're using Rainy's E-Z Leg Tool, a commercially available device specifically for knotting legs. But a small rug-hooking tool or splicing tool can also be used.

Whether formed individually or in groups on the feather stem, bundled-fiber grasshopper legs can be sprayed with a workable fixative or treated with flexible cement after they are knotted to make them more durable.

The techniques shown in the alternate sequence show procedures used by some tyers to produce a bundled-fiber upper leg with a rubber-strand lower leg, or a leg fashioned entirely from rubber strands. Such legs have a lifelike movement, particularly if the fly is fished with a twitch.

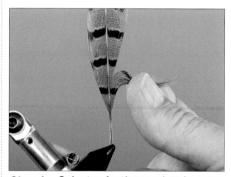

Step 1. Select a feather and strip away any fluff and short barbs at the base. Crush the stem flat with a pair of needle-nose pliers, and mount it upright in the jaws of a vise. The barbs to be knotted are on the right side of the feather stem.

Separate out a section of barbs—here about a dozen barbs are used to form a leg suitable for a #8 or #10 hook. Pull the barbs outward so that the tips are aligned.

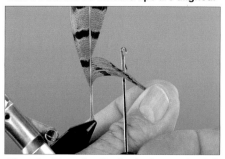

Step 2. Transfer the barb tips to the left fingers, as shown.

With the right hand, position the leg tool behind the barb section, as shown.

14

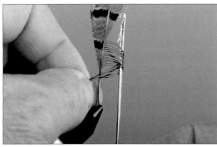

Step 3. With the left fingers, wrap the barb section around the tool, forming a loop of material around the shank.

Maintain moderate tension on the barb tips, and note that you can reposition the tool along the length of the barb section by "sliding" it closer to or farther from the feather stem. Position the tool at the point along the barb section where you wish to form the knot.

If you slide the tool, press the middle finger of the left hand against the feather stem to help steady the feather and prevent it from bending.

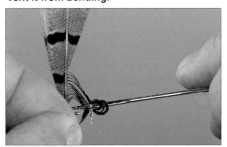

Step 4. Rotate the tip of the tool so that it angles downward; note that the hinged latch will fall open. Catch the barb tips in the hook.

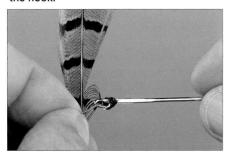

Step 5. Pull the tool to draw the tip of the material through the loop formed around the shank of the tool. The hinged latch will close as the tool is pulled through the loop.

Notice that the left fingertips maintain a slight tension on the tips of the barbs, and the third and fourth fingers of the left hand press against the feather stem to steady it as tension is applied to close the knot.

Step 6. Pull the tips of the barbs through the loop. As you do so, it may help to use your right thumb to push the loop of material off the end of the tool.

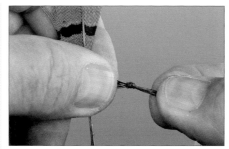

Step 7. Use your fingers to tighten the knot.

Step 8. It's easiest to form a series of legs while the feather is clamped in the vise. Once the legs are formed, they can be sprayed with a workable fixative or treated with flexible cement if desired.

Step 1a. To form a leg with a rubber-strand foreleg, insert the tip of a short length of rubber leg material through the knot formed in Step 6.

Step 2a. Tighten the knot firmly around the rubber strand.

Step 3a. Clip away the excess barbs at the knot, and trim the rubber strand to length.

It is important to apply a drop of head cement or flexible cement to the knot to prevent it from loosening.

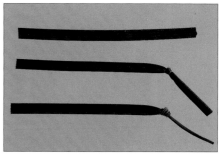

Step 4a. Some tyers prefer very active legs tied entirely from rubber strands.

Strip a section of rubber leg material that contains 4 or 5 strands, as shown at the top.

Tie an overhand knot as shown in the middle.

Then trim all but 1 or 2 strands from the lower leg to give it the proper shape.

Method #12:
Lacquered Legs

Legs can be created from a dubbed thorax by gathering the dubbing fibers into bundles and coating them with head cement or flexible cement. The technique is better suited to larger nymphs, where the greater spacing between legs affords more working room for gathering the fibers and applying the adhesive.

Lacquered legs can also be formed from feather-barb legs produced by **Method #14: Drawn Feather Legs**, p. 423.

Step 1. Getting good results with this method depends to a great extent on dressing the thorax properly. First, the dubbing material should contain a good quantity of longer fibers. Second, the fibers should not be twisted tightly around the thread, and the thorax should be roughly, not tightly dubbed. Taking care in forming the thorax will ensure that plenty of longer fibers are available to form the legs.

Probably the simplest way of meeting these requirements is to form the thorax using a dubbing or spinning loop, as we've done here, containing a mixture of underfur and guard hairs as explained in **Method #41: Fur Chenille Dubbing Loop**, p. 131; **Method #42: Hide-strip Fur Chenille**, p. 132; or **Method #44: Wire-core Dubbing Brush**, p. 133.

The fly is first completed. The legs are the last component to be found.

Step 2. We'll begin with the legs on the near side. Use a dubbing needle and your fingers to gather the fibers on the front third of the thorax into a rough bundle. Gather the fibers on the side of the thorax only.

Hold the dubbing needle vertically against the near side of the thorax, and work it outward through the fibers to create a "part."

With your right fingers, pull these fibers toward the eye of the hook and twist them into a loose bundle. Even on a large fly, it will probably not be possible to twist these fibers into a clearly defined strand. The object here is merely to create a rough separation between the fibers used for the front leg and those on the rest of the thorax.

Step 3. Repeat Step 2 for the fibers at the rear third of the thorax, pulling them toward the hook bend. Don't be concerned about trying to twist or consolidate the fibers in the middle of the thorax that will be used to fashion the middle leg. These will be gathered using the adhesive.

Step 4. Repeat Steps 2 and 3 to divide the dubbing fibers on the far side of the thorax, as shown here from the top.

Step 5. Glue is used to consolidate the fibers into legs. Generally, thicker adhe-

sives such as thickened head cement or flexible glue work best; they are viscous enough to remain on the leg fibers and resist the tendency to run down into the thorax.

Put a drop of adhesive on the point of a dubbing needle. Hold the needle vertically and place the cement at the base of the fibers that will form the front leg, and spread it toward the tips. It's best to work on the sides of the leg, using the needle to "paint" the glue from the base of the fibers to the tips.

Remember that you're working primarily with fibers on the side of the thorax, not the bottom. The bottom fibers will resist being incorporated into the leg bundle.

Step 6. Repeat Step 5 for the remaining legs, as shown here from the top.

The legs can be left in this configuration, or . . . .

Step 7. After the glue has had a chance to set, but not yet harden, you can use a pair of tweezers to crimp "elbows" into the legs for a more realistic appearance.

When the legs are dry, you can trim them to length and "manicure" the underside of the thorax, if desired, trimming away any excessively long fibers that obscure the leg silhouette.

Method #13:
Dubbing-loop Legs

Impressionistic legs can be fashioned by teasing out longer strands of dubbing from the thorax of any dubbed nymph. But tyer Poul Jorgensen uses a dubbing loop to form and dress legs in a somewhat more realistic and precise manner; at the same time, the dubbing loop forms the thorax of the fly. While Jorgensen uses this technique primarily for legs on caddis pupae, as shown in the following demonstration, it can be used with virtually any nymph.

Step 1. All components behind the thorax of the fly are dressed first.

Mount a section of fur in a dubbing loop as explained in either **Method #41: Fur Chenille Dubbing Loop**, p. 131, or **Method #42: Hide-strip Fur Chenille**, p. 132. (These legs and thorax can be fashioned as well from a separate dubbing brush, as explained in **Method #44: Wire-core Dubbing Brush**, p. 133. Using the dubbing brush may allow you to spin material for several flies at once.)

Note the placement of material, rabbit fur in this case, in the loop—the guard hair that will form the legs extends to the bend of the hook; the underfur is left intact to form the thorax.

Step 2. Spin the dubbing loop to lock in the fibers.

Once the loop is spun, raise it vertically above the hook shank. Moisten your fingers and preen all the fibers toward the rear of the hook, as shown.

Step 3. Wrap the dubbing strand forward, using your left fingers to preen the hairs back toward the rear of the hook and prevent them from becoming trapped under each new wrap of material.

Bind down the dubbing strand, and clip the excess.

Trim the long, trailing hairs from the top and sides of the thorax; leave them intact beneath the shank for legs.

Feather Legs

There are a couple of leg styles that are produced by using whole feathers. Depending on the type, either the feather barbs or the feather stem is the primary component in representing the legs.

A few of the techniques for dressing feather legs have been presented elsewhere in this book.

The fly on the left has legs formed from a hackle feather palmered over the thorax, as explained in **Method #18: Thorax Palmer Hackle**, p. 366. This style can be dressed with or without a wingcase.

The fly on the right has legs formed from a turn or two of a hackle feather ahead of the thorax, as explained in **Method #5: Single-hackle Wet Fly Collar**, p. 352. The wingcase is folded forward, forcing the uppermost hackle barbs to the sides of the fly.

Method #14:

Drawn Feather Legs

This simple technique is a common one for dressing legs on nymph patterns. Nearly any soft, webby feather can be used, provided the barbs on each side of the feather stem are equal in length. Many tyers, however, prefer mottled feathers that produce legs with distinct bands or markings.

Drawn feather legs are an excellent application for the many types of body feathers on game birds such as grouse or pheasants, since this plumage is often attractively variegated. Rooster hackle, even in poor grades, is ill-suited to this technique, as the barbs lack webbing and produce thin, indistinct legs.

As shown in the alternate step, drawn-feather legs can be made from the plumulaceous portion of a feather (see "Feathers," p. 5), a material that often is discarded by tyers.

Step 1. Dress all the fly components that lie behind the thorax, and mount the wingcase material as explained in **Method #1: Folded-strip Wingcase**, p. 229, or **Method**

#4: Bundled-fiber Wingcase, p. 232. (Note as shown in Step 6, the width of the wingcase will effect the position of the finished legs.)

Position the tying thread at the rear of the thorax.

Select a feather for the legs. The barb length depends upon the length of the finished legs. In this technique, the base of the barbs will be concealed beneath the wingcase, effectively shortening the length of the legs on the finished fly. As a rule, choose a feather with a barb length that is about twice the thickness of the thorax, though a feather with longer barbs can be used if longer legs are desired.

Prepare the feather by preening all the barbs except those at the very tip toward the base of the feather, as shown.

Step 2. Position the feather atop the hook shank, so that the dull side faces upward.

Bind the feather tip at the rear of the thorax. Note that the rearmost thread wrap securing the feather lies directly atop the rearmost thread wrap securing the wingcase.

Step 3. Dress the thorax—we're using dubbing here—and position the tying thread at the front of the thorax material.

With the right fingers, draw the feather over the top of the thorax, as shown here from above. Exert light tension on the feather—enough to keep the feather stem positioned straight down the middle of the thorax, but not enough to risk breaking the feather.

Step 4. With the left hand, grasp the bobbin and take two tight turns of thread over the feather stem, binding it to the hook shank.

In binding down the feather, slip the thread between the barbs, trapping only the feather stem beneath the thread.

Step 5. Clip away the butt of the feather. With the right fingers, fold the wingcase forward.

As you fold the wingcase, use the left fingers to pinch the feather barbs against the sides of the thorax so that they remain in position.

Step 6. Secure the wingcase and clip the excess wingcase material. Cover the butts with thread, forming the head of the fly at the same time.

The final position of the legs is determined by the width of the wingcase. A narrow wingcase will allow the feather barbs to project almost straight outward from the thorax, as shown on the left. A wider wingcase that curves down the sides of the thorax will force the feather barbs to angle downward, as shown on the right.

Step 1a. Here, legs have been dressed using the fuzzy base of a feather. Such legs are quite mobile in the water. The fly can be left as shown here, since the feather stem is quite thick and durable, or the stem can be covered with a wingcase, as shown in the preceding demonstration.

424

Method #15:

Feather Grasshopper Legs

Very realistic and durable grasshopper or cricket legs can be fashioned from a knotted feather with a clipped foreleg. The upper leg can be trimmed to shape, or pulled and mounted as shown in this sequence.

For this style of leg, most tyers prefer to use rooster saddle or large neck hackles. In either case, using a relatively inexpensive, poor grade of material is best, since some webbiness at the base of the barbs contributes to the leg silhouette. While any such rooster hackle is suitable, most tyers use grizzly feathers, often dyed yellow, to give the finished legs a banded appearance.

Step 1. Select a feather of the type shown at the left.

Tie an overhand knot in the stem. The knot should be formed closer to the feather tip than to the butt. Pull the knot closed, but do not tighten it firmly. Before fully tightening the knot, use a dubbing needle to pick out any feather barbs that are trapped in the knot. You won't be able to get them all, but try to free as many barbs as possible. Then tighten the knot in the feather stem, as shown in the middle feather.

Next, preen all the barbs on the feather so that they stand outward from the stem. Trim the barbs at the tip portion of the feather close to the stem, leaving a short stubble, and then trim any stray barbs projecting from the knot, as shown on the feather on the right.

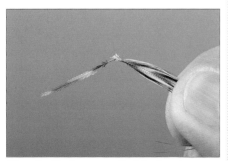

Step 2. To form a pulled feather leg, use the fingers of the right hand to preen back a section of feather barbs equal in length to the desired length of the finished leg. The right fingertips are located at the mounting point on the leg.

Step 2a. To form a clipped leg, trim the remaining hackle barbs into the shape shown here.
Proceed to Step 3.

Step 3. Without disturbing the position of the pulled barbs, transfer the feather to the left hand. The left fingertips should be pinching the feather at the mounting point.

Position the leg against the side of the body, and secure it there using the procedure explained in **Method #3: Side-mounted Legs**, Steps 1-5, p. 410.

The finished pulled leg is shown at the left; the clipped leg is shown at the right.

Repeat the procedure to fashion and mount the far leg.

Heads, Collars and Eyes

Because all of these components are tied at or near the rear of the hook eye, heads, collars, and eyes are presented together in this chapter.

Heads and Collars

Heads on artificial flies run the gamut from minimalist to elaborate and have a wide variety of purposes in fly construction. They may perform an imitative function, dressed to reproduce the appearance of the head on a natural food form or to help give the fly a realistic silhouette. Other types of heads, by contrast, may be dressed simply to add flash or sparkle to a pattern. Some head styles and materials lend floatation to the fly, while others promote sinking. And some heads serve a combination of these purposes.

A few styles of heads have been presented earlier in this book. One of the simplest and most common is simply formed from tying thread, and the procedures for constructing whip-finished or half-hitched heads are presented in Chapter 3: "Thread Handling." Other head styles are formed in conjunction with other fly components, particularly downwings and wingcases, since these are typically dressed near the front of the hook shank, and excess material behind the hook eye can be used to create the head on a pattern. One of the most common of these approaches is to use clipped wing butts on a downwing pattern, as shown in **Method #62: Hollow-hair Downwing**, Step 6, p. 311. Wingcase material can also be clipped, leaving the butts to form the head of the fly, or the wingcase can be folded over other materials or components such as a ball of dubbing or pair of barbell eyes to suggest the glossy head on some types of nymphs. These procedures are illustrated in **Method #1: Folded-strip Wingcase**, Steps 7-9, p. 230, and **Method #3: Reverse-folded Wingcase**, Step 3a, p. 232.

Most of the head styles previously presented are dressed on smaller patterns, and the heads themselves are comparatively minor or inconspicuous parts of the dressing. The focus of this section is on constructing larger heads that play a more prominent role in the fly pattern.

These types of heads are often dressed in conjunction with a "collar"—fibers secured radially around the hook shank behind the fly head and slanting toward the rear of the fly. The most common type of collars are those formed from feathers wrapped in the wet-fly style or a bundle of loose fibers deployed around the hook shank. Techniques for creating these types of collars are presented in **Method #5: Single-hackle Wet-fly Collar**, p. 352; **Method #20: Distributed Collar Hackle**, p. 367; and **Method #6: Marabou Collar Hackle**, Step 3, p. 353, where afterfeather is used. Aside from these methods, there are only a couple of techniques for fashioning collars, and in both, the collar is formed simultaneously with the head, as shown in the following two methods.

Method #1:
Clipped Head

The clipped-head style is commonly used on streamers, such as Muddlers and sculpin patterns, as well as on larger insects such as grasshoppers, crickets, and adult stoneflies.

Probably the most widely employed material is deer hair, particularly on floating patterns, where the spun head provides buoyancy. But deer hair is used as well on some streamer patterns, primarily because the material is easily worked.

A variety of other materials, however, can form clipped heads, though these are generally restricted to subsurface patterns since they tend to absorb water. The techniques for dressing these materials on the hook shank have been presented in earlier chapters. Wool (on the hide or spun into a rope) or egg yarn makes an excellent clipped head on streamers: it can be applied densely; it does not inhibit sinking; and colors can be mixed for banded, mottled, or multi-color heads. The wool head is formed by mounting the wool using one of the techniques shown in **Method #63: Wrap-around Wool Stacking**, p. 151; **Method #64: Single-stacked Wool**, p. 153; or **Method #65: Multi-stacked Wool**, p. 153.

Moreover, wool or synthetic fibers can be used to make a brushed head. The technique is identical to that shown in **Method #93: Brushed Body**, p. 179, except that shorter strands of material are used to form only the head portion of the fly.

Hackle feathers, usually from a hen neck or saddle, can be wrapped around the hook and clipped to shape. This approach is quite simple and feathers offer a broad range of natural and dyed colors. Using the technique described in **Method #5: Single-hackle Wet-fly Collar**, p. 352, a series of hackle feathers can be wrapped in very close turns over the head area. It may take several feathers to cover the shank, and even so, the head will not be as dense as one formed from deer hair or wool. Thus heads formed of clipped feather barbs are most satisfactory when they are small, since clipping the barbs close to the shank forms the head from the densest portion of the wrapped feather.

Marabou barbs can also be used to form a clipped head. Though somewhat more time-consuming to dress and lacking the density of other clipped-head materials, marabou can produce a mottled or multi-color head that is quite realistic in appearance. The soft material also gives some movement to the fly underwater. Marabou barbs are mounted over the head area using the technique shown in **Method #66: Stacking Marabou and CDC**, p. 154.

Lastly, fur spun in a dubbing loop or dubbing brush can form an attractive and durable clipped head. The fur is spun and applied as described in **Method #41: Fur Chenille Dubbing Loop**, p. 131; **Method #42: Hide-strip Fur Chenille**, p. 132; or **Method #44: Wire-core Dubbing Brush**, p. 133.

After dressing the head, all of the materials can be clipped to the desired shape using the technique shown in **Method #67: Clipped Bodies**, p. 155.

The main sequence below shows the procedure for forming a clipped deer-hair head with a collar, of the type commonly used on Muddler Minnow and grasshopper patterns. (For details on selecting the appropriate type of hair, see "Hollow Hair," p. 2.)

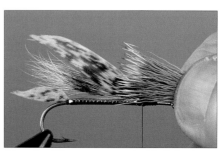

Step 1. All components behind the head of the fly are dressed first. When tying off these components, particularly wings and thick body materials, take care to form smooth, tapered tie-off wraps, as the head and collar material is mounted over this foundation. Position the thread at the rear-

most tie-off wrap securing the body or wings.

Clip and clean a bundle of hair as explained in **Method #2: Preparing and Cleaning Hair**, p. 68, and align the hair tips as shown in **Method #3: Stacking and Aligning Hair**, p. 69.

The size of the clump depends upon the desired density of the collar and head; as a rule, however, subsurface patterns using hollow hair tend to be dressed more sparsely to minimize buoyancy, while more material is used on floating patterns.

Step 1a. If no collar is desired, clip the butts so that the hairs are even, then clip away the tips, leaving a bundle about one inch long.

Step 2. The deer hair can be distributed around the shank in a variety of ways, two of which have been explained in the section on "Spun Bodies." Many tyers use the basic spinning technique shown in **Method #58: Spinning Hollow Hair**, p. 145. However, hair may not spin quite as readily around a thick thread foundation as it does around a bare hook shank, and uniformly distributing the hair takes a little lighter touch with the material and some encouragement with the fingertips in rolling it around the shank.

Other tyers prefer to use **Method #60: Stacking Hollow Hair**, p. 148. In using this technique, half the hair bundle prepared in Step 1 is secured atop the hook shank, and half on the underside. This approach permits constructing clipped heads of more than one color.

The technique shown here (see **Method #59: Flaring Hollow Hair**, p. 147) is used by many tyers for a variety of hair-flaring applications.

Begin by holding the butt end of the hair clump in the right fingers, as shown. Insert the eye of the hook into the center of the clump.

Step 3. Push the clump down the hook shank until the mounting point on the hair is directly above the tying thread and the tips of the hair extend behind the thread far enough to form a collar of the desired length.

Step 4. Grasp the hair tips with the left hand, maintaining their uniform distribution around the shank.

With the right hand, take 2 turns of thread under very light tension over the bundle, ending with the bobbin held below the shank.

Step 5. Maintain your grasp with the left fingers, and pull downward on the thread tightly to flare the hair.

When the thread is tightened and the hair flares outward, take another turn of thread over the first two to further secure the material.

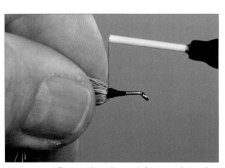

Step 6. Draw the thread forward to the front of the spun hair.

With the left hand, gather the flared hair butts and pull them toward the rear of the fly.

With the right hand, take 3 or 4 tight wraps of thread against the front of the spun hair to lock it in position.

Step 7. To complete the head, prepare another clump of hair as shown in Step 1a; mount and secure it as shown in Steps 3-6. Repeat until the hook shank is covered with flared hair.

Step 8. Begin clipping the head to shape by carefully trimming short the flared hair butts just in front of the collar. Take care not to trim away any hair tips from the collar.

Step 9. Final shaping of deer-hair heads, shown in the top row, can be accomplished using any of the techniques shown in **Method #67: Clipped Bodies**, p. 155; **Method #68: Razor-trimmed Bodies**, p. 157; or **Method #69: Flame-shaped Bodies**, p. 157.

On subsurface patterns, many tyers apply one or more coats of thinned head cement to the flared deer hair. The hair will absorb the cement and make the head less buoyant.

The flies in the middle row have heads and collars formed from feather barbs—marabou on the right, and hen hackle on the left.

In the bottom row, the fly on the left has a head formed from clipped-fur chenille; the fly head on the right is fashioned from clipped stacked wool.

Heads made of clipped deer hair, wool, or fur chenille can also be treated with vinyl or silicone cement as shown in **Method #10: Glued Eyes**, Step 1a, p. 436. Glue is not practical with clipped heads made from wrapped hackle or marabou barbs.

Method #2:
Bullet Head

Bullet heads are formed by reverse-mounting material (usually a bundle of fibers) behind the hook eye, drawing them rearward, and securing them a short distance behind the eye to form a hollow capsule or bubble for the head. This style of head is almost always formed in conjunction with a collar or wing.

Two bullet-head techniques are presented earlier in this book. The rather unusual approach shown in **Method #39: Folded Downwing Parachute**, p. 394, explains the construction of a combination bullet head/downwing that also serves as a post for a parachute hackle. **Method #60: Bullet-head Fiber Wings**, p. 308, demonstrates the techniques for forming bullet heads in conjunction with natural hair downwings—either wings that sit above the hook shank, or wings that completely encircle the shank. The technique presented below closely resembles the procedure for forming bullet-head downwings, and hence the instructions are abbreviated. Readers seeking a more complete explanation should consult **Method #60**.

Bullet heads can be fashioned from a variety of materials; natural hair, such as the deer hair used in the following procedure, synthetic hair, or stranded materials such as Krystal Flash are perhaps the most common. But other materials are sometimes used. A bullet head can be formed from a feather, wrapped collar style, and the technique for doing so is virtually identical to that shown in **Method #90: The Hackle-bubble Body**, p. 176. When forming a hackle bullet head, the feather must be chosen so that, once the head is formed, the barb tips form a collar of the desired length.

Gary LaFontaine forms bullet heads from strips of foam for his Airhead patterns. Six strips of foam are reverse-mounted behind the hook eye so that they encircle the shank. They are drawn back and secured as shown below in Steps 4-6, forming a large bubble of foam at the head of the fly. The strips on the underside of the shank are clipped just behind the thread wraps at the "throat" of the fly; those atop the shank are left long for wings.

Bullet heads are dressed on floating flies, where deer hair is probably the most widely used material, and on subsurface patterns, particularly streamers, where solid hairs or synthetic strands are used.

Step 1. Materials that form the bullet head can be mounted either before or after the other fly components. Mounting the head

materials last keeps the fibers out of the tying field while dressing the other fly components and is convenient in this regard. Dressing the head first, as we're doing here, gives better access to the hook shank for mounting the head materials and tends to produce a neater fly; the bound-down butts of the head material can be concealed beneath the fly body if desired.

Mount the tying thread about 1/3 of a shank-length behind the hook eye. Wrap forward, laying a foundation as you go, and stop about 2 or 3 thread wraps short of the hook eye. This will leave a small section of bare hook on which the bullet-head material is mounted. Most materials are more easily distributed around a bare shank than around a thread foundation.

Clip and clean a bundle of hair as explained in **Method #2: Preparing and Cleaning Hair**, p. 68, and align the hair tips as shown in **Method #3: Stacking and Aligning Hair**, p. 69.

Using the left hand, position the bundle atop the shank. With natural hairs, in which the tapered tips form the collar, the material must be positioned accurately so that the tips project beyond the hook eye a distance equal to the combined length of head and collar, as shown here. With synthetic materials, the strands projecting over the hook eye can be trimmed later if they are too long.

Step 2. Mount the deer hair, distributing it uniformly around the shank using any of the techniques noted in **Method #1: Clipped Head**, Step 2, p. 426.

(Solid fibers can be mounted using the technique shown in **Method #6: The Taut Distribution Wrap**, p. 28, or using the approach shown above in **Method #1: Clipped Head**, Steps 2-4, p. 425, in which the bundle of fibers is pushed over the hook eye to encircle the shank.)

Once the fibers are distributed around the shank, secure the fibers tightly behind the hook eye. Clip the butts and bind them down with thread.

(If synthetic fibers are used, they can be preened forward and clipped to the proper length for forming the collar.)

Step 3. Dress the remaining fly components. The tie-off point for the body and/or wing materials will determine the size of the bullet head. Generally, the body is tied

off ¼ to ⅓ of a shank length behind the eye.
Position the tying thread at the front edge of the body or wing material.

Insert the tip of the right index finger into the center of the fiber bundle, and preen the fibers outward so that they flare outward and stand nearly perpendicular to the hook shank. Preening the fibers to this position will make fashioning the bullet head easier.

Step 4. The bullet head can be formed in a couple of different ways.

You can use the left fingers to draw all the fibers rearward, pinching them against the body, as shown here. All the fibers should be drawn back uniformly, so that a smooth capsule is formed around the body.

In drawing the fibers back, the tying thread will be pulled along with them. Carefully work the thread between your fingers so that the bobbin once again hangs freely at the front edge of the body.

Or you can use a bullet-head tool of the type shown in Step 4a.

Step 4a. Bullet-head tools are commercially available, or you can make one from the empty barrel of a ballpoint pen or any tube large enough to fit over the hook eye and fiber bundle.

Slip the tool over the eye, pushing the fibers backward.

Once the fibers are pushed back, grasp them with the left fingers, as shown in Step 4, and position the tying thread at the front edge of the body.

Step 5. To form a very slim bullet head, pull the fibers back tightly so that they hug the hook shank, and take several turns of thread over the material, forming a "throat" at the front edge of the body.

To form a larger, hollower head, push the fibers forward slightly, and secure them.

Step 6. Tie off the thread with a whip-finish or series of half-hitches, and clip.

The fly at the top has a bullet head formed from the procedure in the main sequence; the fly in the middle, dressed in Steps 1a-1c below, has a Krystal Flash head with a larger "bubble" and bead inside; the fly at the bottom has a bullet head made of wrapped grizzly hackle.

Step 1a. Interesting subsurface patterns can be created by sliding a bead over the hook shank so that it abuts the base of the bullet head fibers. If a relatively sparse bundle of fibers or a translucent material is used, the bead will be visible beneath the finished head.

The bead, however, must have a large enough hole to fit over the thread-wrapped butts. With counterdrilled beads, you can reverse the normal mounting direction so that the larger hole faces the hook eye.

When mounting the bead, you can tie off the thread behind the head material, clip it, slide the bead up the hook shank, and remount the thread behind the bead. Or you can slide the bead into position over the thread and simply draw the tying thread to the rear of the bead and take a few wraps around the hook shank. The length of thread drawn over the surface of the bead will be concealed when the bullet head is formed.

Step 1b. Pull the fibers back as shown in Step 4 or 4a, and secure them.

Method #3:
Foam Head

We've watched a few tyers use this technique, but first saw it in print in the work of Dick Talleur. A short foam cylinder is slipped over the hook eye and cemented to the shank. It's used primarily to dress a very buoyant head on flies that imitate natural insects with large, blocky profiles, such as grasshoppers and adult stoneflies.

The cylindrical foam strips sold to tyers are well-suited to this technique, but such foam tends to be dense. If a more buoyant type is desired, a length of foam that is rectangular in cross-section can be trimmed with scissors or shaped with heat as shown in "Shaping and Coloring Foam," p. 190. White or light-colored foams can be tinted with a waterproof marker, then given a coat of flexible cement or spray fixative to help prevent the color from fading.

Step 1. Applying the head is the last step in tying the fly, and all other components should be dressed first.

Cut a piece of cylindrical foam to the length of the finished head. Insert a toothpick lengthwise, directly through the center of the cylinder. The toothpick forms a "starter hole" that simplifies mounting the foam.

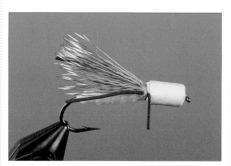

Step 2. Apply a drop or two of gel-type CA glue to the head area of the hook shank.

Remove the foam from the toothpick and slide it over the cemented portion of the shank.

Bead Heads

Though flies using heads made of glass and metal beads have been around for decades, they were for a long time a local style confined primarily to spin fishermen in Northern Italy and central Europe. Only in recent years have they become well-known in the fly-fishing and tying world, owing pri-

marily to the efforts of Austrian tyer Roman Moser. Dutch tyer Theo Bakelaar helped popularize the style, and today bead-head flies are standard inventory in fly boxes worldwide.

A bead head on a fly can serve many purposes. A shiny metallic or colored bead can suggest an air bubble on a caddis pupa or emerger pattern; or it can simply add an attractive flash or sparkle to the fly. A bead in a muted color or matte finish can more realistically imitate the head of a natural insect. Beads, particularly metal ones, add weight to the fly, and because it is concentrated at the head, this weight gives the fly a lifelike, erratic, jigging action when fished with a retrieve. Theo Bakelaar has even suggested that there may be some attractive property in the sound of a metal bead tapping against the riverbed when a fly is dead-drifted. (For relative weights of different types of beads, see the chart on p. 37.)

A similar versatility exists in the way beads have been incorporated into tying. Many tyers have designed patterns specifically around the use of beads, while others have "retrofitted" proven nymph patterns with bead heads. The result has been an enormous proliferation of bead-head dressings and, more to our purposes here, of beads themselves.

Glass beads are available in a large variety of sizes, colors, and finishes, and metal beads in a range of materials—brass, copper, nickel, steel, and tungsten. Even ordinary pinch-on split shot can be used to form a bead head. For the most part, however, beads can be divided into three categories—straight-hole beads, those with a tapered or counterdrilled hole, and pinch-on beads.

Straight-hole beads are formed with holes of a uniform diameter and include many types of metal beads and virtually all glass and plastic ones. This style of bead offers the tyer some advantages. It is available in a variety of materials and colors, is relatively inexpensive, and can be mounted on a hook in a number of different ways. When straight-hole beads are slipped over the hook shank to form the head, dressing the fly is somewhat simplified since securing the bead in place does not require filling a tapered or countersunk recess with body material. The primary drawback of straight-hole beads, particularly those of larger diameter, is that they are difficult, and sometimes impossible, to slip over the hook shank—the mounting method preferred by many tyers. The bead hole may be large enough to accommodate the hook wire, but the bead binds as it is slipped around the hook bend, since the straight hole does not provide adequate clearance to "turn the corner" on the hook bend.

Beads with counterdrilled or tapered holes are manufactured to eliminate this binding problem. The large diameter opening on one side of the bead provides enough clearance to slip it around the hook bend and up the shank. Aside from the somewhat greater cost, the main disadvantage of such beads is that they are mounted with the large-diameter opening facing the rear of the hook. In order to secure the bead, body material must be built up to a diameter larger than that of the rear hole in order to prevent the bead from sliding back over the body. On some hooks, building the body to this size may cause it to appear disproportionately bulky.

Pinch-on beads are split to the center and are simply clamped around the hook shank with a pair of pliers. They do not form quite as neat a head on a fly, since they produce a seam, though this of little consequence in actual fishing. Currently, however, the pinch-on beads specifically for use in fly tying are available in a limited range of sizes and only in brass. Lead and non-toxic split shot, however, can also be used.

Method #4:
Slip-on Bead Head

A large number of tyers prefer this approach; it is quite simple and forms a symmetrical dressing since the hook shank runs through the center of the bead. The relation of bead size to hook size is a limitation in this method, however. The bead must have a hole large enough to accommodate the hook wire, and the bead cannot be so large that it interferes with the hook gap. Some narrowing of the gap is inevitable, however, and offsetting the hook point, as shown in Step 9, can help compensate for the smaller gap.

The main sequence below shows the mounting of a counterdrilled or tapered bead, and a number of possible options—weighting the fly, securing the bead by "strapping" it with a strand of material, or securing the bead by abutting it with the body material.

The alternate sequence shows two approaches to the slip-on mounting of straight-hole beads and the use of a rear-mounted bead-head.

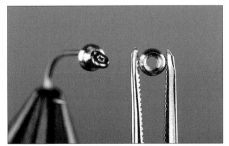

Step 1. Counterdrilled beads are mounted by slipping the hook point through the smaller of the two holes, as shown here.

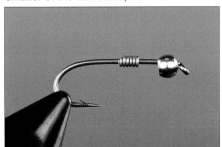

Step 2. The weight of the fly can be increased, and finishing the fly body simplified a bit, by taking a few turns of lead wire around the hook shank.

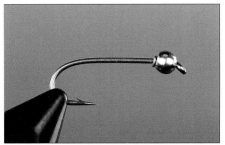

Step 3. The wraps of lead are then forced up inside the hole at the rear of the bead. Besides increasing the overall weight, these wraps of lead effectively decrease the diameter of the rear hole, and fewer wraps of body material are required at the back of the bead to prevent it from sliding rearward over the body.

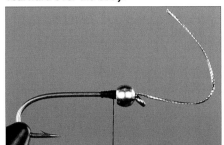

Step 4. The most common method of securing the bead is by abutting it at the rear with body material, forcing the bead forward and pinning it against the rear of the hook eye. This approach, however, sometimes necessitates a thickness of body material at the rear of the bead that is disproportionate to the hook size. To secure the bead on a fly with a trimmer body, you can use a method shown to us by Gary LaFontaine.

Secure a strand of material to the top of the hook shank directly behind the hook eye. LaFontaine uses oval tinsel, as we're doing here, but monofilament line or wire will also do the job. Multiple strands of a material like Krystal Flash can be used as well, in which case this method of securing the bead closely resembles the technique for creating bead thoraxes shown in **Method #101: The Bead Thorax**, p. 187. Regardless of the material, the bound down butts behind the hook eye must be small enough to permit the bead to slide over them.

After securing the material, clip the thread and slide the bead over the bound-down butts and up against the rear of the hook eye, as shown

Remount the tying thread behind the bead.

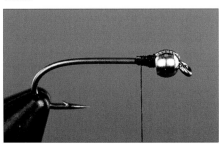

Step 5. Draw the strand of material over the top of the hook shank, and bind it to the hook shank, as shown. Wrap the thread directly up to the rear base of the bead to secure it in position. The rest of fly can now be dressed.

Step 6. The fly on the left has been dressed with a simple dubbed body. Note the thickness of the body directly behind the bead (which has not been plugged with lead wire). Enough body material must be applied to prevent the bead from slipping back over the body.

The fly on the right, a bead-head Prince, has a narrower body fashioned from twisted herl. A body of this type may not be thick enough to prevent the bead from sliding backward toward the tail. Forming a tapered underbody, or building up tying thread behind the bead, as shown here, will provide the width needed to secure the bead.

Step 7. Here, gold wire has been wrapped over the dubbed body and tied off. Note the exposed thread wraps used to tie-off the ribbing. Many tyers simply whip-finish or half-hitch the thread over these wraps and leave them visible on the finished fly.

There are, however, a couple of techniques for concealing these thread wraps for a neater body. You can use the approach presented in **Method #13: Dubbed Whip-finish**, p. 24.

Or you can use the technique shown here. Thinly dub a short length of tying thread. Do not twist the dubbing too tightly, it should be a bit loose.

Step 8. Wrap the dubbing over the exposed thread wraps.

Take two or three whip-finish wraps, or two or three half-hitches. When taking these wraps, lay the thread over the rear of the bead so that the thread slides down and sneaks beneath the dubbing wraps. Tighten the thread firmly to snug it further beneath the dubbing.

You can place a drop of head cement

atop the bead prior to taking the finishing wraps. With each whip-finish wrap or half-hitch, drag the thread through the cement, down the bead, and beneath the dubbing. This approach avoids getting head cement on the body material, as usually happens when you attempt to apply the cement with a dubbing needle in the customary fashion.

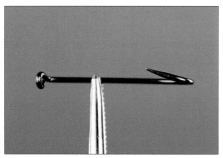

Step 9. The effects of offsetting a hook point are debated among tyers. Some feel that an offset point offers no advantages; others are equally convinced that it improves hooking performance, particularly with narrow gaps on small hooks or gaps partially obscured by fly components such as beads.

To offset the hook point, grasp the hook "spear"—the straight portion of the hook between the point and the beginning of the bend—in a pair of needle-nose pliers. Bend it slightly, about 15 degrees, to one side. The direction of bend makes no difference, though technically speaking, if the spear is bent to the right (when viewed from the hook eye with the hook bend downward), the hook is said to be "kirbed"; if the spear is bent to the left, the hook is said to be "reversed."

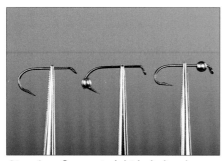

Step 1a. Some straight-hole beads may be small enough, or have large enough holes, that they can be slipped directly around the hook bend as shown in Step 1. Larger beads, however, may not slide around the relatively narrow radius of the hook bend. There are a couple of ways to address this problem.

First, you can use a pair of needle-nose pliers to bend the spear of the hook downward, decreasing the radius of the bend, as shown at the left.

Slip the bead over the hook, as shown in the middle.

Use the pliers to return the hook spear to its normal shape, as shown in the right.

This particular approach works better with some hooks than others. Some brands and styles of hooks are too brittle to tolerate this kind of bend. Slightly softer, thick-wire hooks work best, and despite appearances, this bending does not noticeably weaken the hook, and it will not bend open when a fish is hooked.

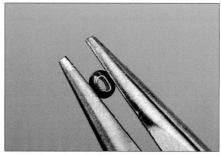

Step 2a. Darrel Martin has suggested a different approach to the problem. With a pair of needle-nose pliers, squeeze the bead so that it is no longer round, but oval. Do not squeeze so hard that you crush the bead flat and close the hole.

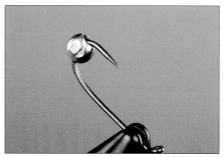

Step 3a. Squeezing the bead elongates the hole, providing enough additional clearance to slip the bead around the hook bend.

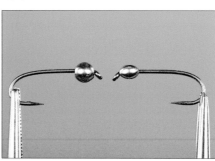

Step 4a. When the bead is positioned behind the eye of the hook, you can use the pliers to squeeze the bead round again, as shown on the left. Or you can position the bead to make a flattened head, as shown on the right. This flattened head also reduces the bead's interference with the hook gap.

Step 5a. As shown here, beads can form the head on a fly that is tied in reverse. The entire fly is dressed, and the tying thread half-hitched and clipped.

The bead is then slipped on the shank, the tying thread remounted, and a bump of thread is built at the front of the bead, as shown here, to secure it on the hook.

Method #5:
Pinch-on Bead Head

Slotted beads can be pinched around the hook shank to make a head. The method is fast and allows the angler to form bead heads from split shot, for a quick-sinking fly. (Split shot can also be used with the technique shown in **Method #6: Lashed Bead Head**, p. 431.) Removeable split shot, formed with two tabs that allow you to open the slot and remove the shot, can be used, but the round, non-removeable type makes a neater head.

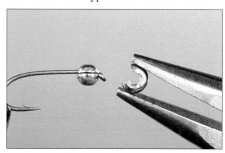

Step 1. Pinch-on beads made specifically for fly tying, such as the BT's Pinch-EZY beads shown here, are simply gripped in a pair of needle-nose pliers and squeezed around the hook shank.

Step 2. Split shot requires a slightly different approach. Both lead and non-toxic split shots are relatively soft. If they are merely pinched around the hook shank, they may in time loosen, open up, and fall off.

To avoid this problem, first use your thumbnail or the back of a pair of tying scissors, to open the split shot wide enough so that the hook shank will be seated deeply into the slot. When thicker hook wires are used, a neater and more secure mount is achieved if a groove is formed at the bottom of the slot using a needle file.

Lay a thread foundation behind the hook eye; the foundation should be as wide as the split shot. Apply a drop of CA glue to the thread.

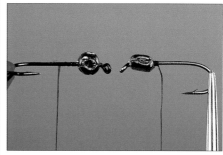

Step 3. With pliers, pinch the shot around the thread wraps. Make sure the hook shank is seated as far as possible into the

slot, and that the slot is pinched closed tightly, as shown on the left.

If desired, the shot can be flattened with pliers to minimize interference with the hook gap, as shown on the right.

When the glue dries, the head can be painted if desired (see **Method #9: Painted Eyes**, p. 435, for notes on paint).

Method #6:
Lashed Bead Head

The lashed-bead technique places the head of the fly atop, rather than around, the hook shank. Though it does not produces as neatly symmetrical a head as does **Method #4: Slip-on Bead Head**, p. 429, it is a versatile approach that has some distinct advantages. First, any size bead can be used with any size hook; beads with very small holes, for example, can be mounted on hooks with very thick wires. Second, there is no hook-gap interference from a bead mounted in this fashion. Finally, lashed beads cause the fly to ride upside-down, which can help reduce snagging on patterns that are fished very deep.

The main sequence shows how this technique can be used with a metal or monofilament post mount. The alternate sequence shows a strap-mount technique using monofilament line.

Lashed-bead heads can also be formed from using a version of **Method #8: Mesh-wrapped Eyes**, p. 434, in which only a single bead is enclosed in the nylon material.

Step 1. Beads and split shot can be mounted on a post made from an ordinary straight pin or a piece of monofilament line.

To prepare a straight-hole bead, insert a pin through the hole in the bead, as shown on the left; the pin head must be larger than the hole diameter.

To mount a piece of split shot on a pin, clamp the pin in a vise. Lay thread foundation directly behind the head, apply a drop of CA glue to the wraps, and crimp the split shot on the foundation as explained in **Method #5: Pinch-on Bead Head**, Steps 2-3, p. 430, and shown second from the left.

To mount a straight-hole bead on a section of monofilament, select a piece of mono that is just slightly thinner than the hole diameter of the bead. Insert the mono through the bead, and using the technique for melting mono shown in **Method #7: Barbell Eyes**, p. 431, melt the end of the mono into a ball larger than the hole diameter of the bead. If desired, use the side of

a razor blade or tying scissors to flatten the ball while the mono is warm and pliable, as shown second from the right.

To mount a piece of split shot on monofilament, insert the mono into the slot on the split shot. Apply of drop CA glue in the slot, and crimp the shot closed as shown on the right. Then melt a ball of mono on the end.

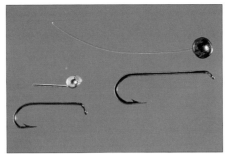

Step 2. To prepare the pin for mounting, bend an angle into the shank of the pin directly at the rear of the bead. Clip off the tip of the pin so that the remaining portion is slightly shorter than the hook shank, as shown on the left.

To prepare the monofilament for mounting, use a pair of needle-nose pliers to flatten the mono behind the split shot or bead. The flattened portion of mono should be about as long as the hook shank, as shown on the right. (Do not yet trim the excess mono behind the flattened section; this tag of material will help in handling.)

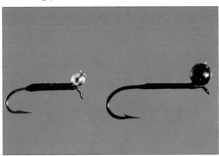

Step 3. Lay a thread foundation on the hook shank. Lay the pin or mono atop the shank so that the bead or split shot is directly over, or slightly behind, the hook eye.

Lash the pin or mono to the shank. When using mono, clip and bind down the excess, as shown.

Apply a drop of CA glue to the thread wraps.

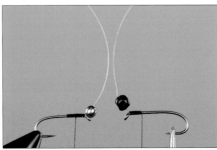

Step 1a. Beads and split shot can be "strapped" to the hook shank using monofilament line (as shown here), round or oval tinsel, or wire. If wire is used, it should be thick enough to resist bending easily, since any flexing of the bead during fishing could cause the wire to break.

For straight-hole beads, flatten one end of a piece of monofilament line of about 8-10 lb test. Secure the mono to the top of the shank; the frontmost thread wraps securing the mono should be just behind the hook eye. When the mono is secured, position the tying thread behind the eye a distance equal to the diameter of the bead. Thread the bead on the mono and position it above the hook eye, as shown on the left.

For split shot, crimp a piece of shot around the line as explained in Step 1. Flatten one end of the mono and bind it to the top of the shank so that the frontmost binding wraps are placed directly behind the hook eye and the shot is positioned with the closed slot facing downward, as shown on the right.

Note the short length of monofilament between the frontmost binding wraps and the rear of the split shot. This section of material is necessary to position the shot properly when the mono is folded rearward in Step 2a.

Step 2a. Fold the monofilament back over the hook shank. This will pull the bead or shot backwards and tip it upside-down atop the hook shank.

Secure the tag of the mono atop the shank with tight thread wraps. Wrap the thread directly up to the base of the bead or shot.

Eyes

In many ways, eyes are a component of fly dressings that most closely resemble bead heads in the variety of their functions. Eyes can be dressed to represent the corresponding anatomical feature on a natural food form, primarily nymphs and baitfish patterns. Eyes can also be used to add flash or sparkle to more general attractor patterns, and they can be used as well to give weight or even buoyancy to a fly. The selection of materials governs which function, or combination of functions, is served.

Method #7:
Barbell Eyes

This is the largest and most common category of eyes in trout-fly tying, and it is characterized more by the shape of the component tied to the hook than by the particular material used. As the name suggests, these eyes are shaped like barbells or an hourglass, with a larger diameter eye on each end of a narrow shank or throat.

Pre-formed barbell eyes are available in a range of sizes, styles, materials, and finishes, including eyes made of nylon or plastic, lead, brass, steel, aluminum, and cut lengths of bead chain. (For relative weights of different types of metal barbell eyes, see the chart on p. 37.) Some of these styles are available with countersunk eye sockets into which adhesive eye pupils are mounted.

While it is impractical for most tyers to fashion their own metal eyes, many other types of barbell eyes are easily made at the tying bench. One of the most common styles is made from a short section of monofilament line melted at each end to produce two eye-like beads. Synthetic hairbrush bristles are often used for the same purpose. This type of eye is generally used on patterns representing damselfly and dragonfly nymphs.

For the purposes of making eyes, there are really two types of monofilament; they behave differently when direct heat is applied and thus must be melted using slightly different techniques, both of which are demonstrated below. The first and largest category is composed of nylon and copolymer materials of the type ordinarily sold for spinning line, leader, and tippet material. These materials have a relatively low combustion point and when melted, tend to "bead up," forming a more or less spherical ball. Nylon line comes in a variety of colors, from clear to muted shades of olive to fluorescent shades of red, yellow, green, and purple. Colored mono in particular can make some unusual eyes.

The second type of material is the relatively new fluorocarbon leader material. This material has a somewhat higher combustion point, and when melted, tends to form a shallow mushroom-shaped eye when heated.

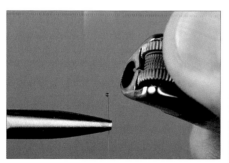

To form eyes of nylon or copolymer monofilament, begin by cutting a section of mono about 2 inches long. The diameter of the line will determine the size of the finished eye. When the mono is melted, a bead of molten material will form at the end, but there is a practical limit to the size that this bead will attain. After a molten ball forms, the mono begins to burn and vaporize, and though the length of mono line grows shorter and shorter with the continued application of heat, the bead itself actually becomes no larger. As a general rule, the maximum size of the eye that can be formed is about 2 or 2½ times the diameter of the mono used.

Grasp the section of mono crosswise in a pair of needle-nose pliers. Its position in the pliers is significant. The length of material that is concealed between the plier jaws will determine the distance between the eye beads. Thus the material should be placed in the plier jaws to form a shank or throat of the desired length—closer to the plier tips for smaller patterns, farther toward the plier hinge for larger ones. After the material is properly positioned in the pliers, clip each end to about ½" long. Generally, this is enough material to form eyes of the maximum size.

Hold the pliers so one end of the mono projects vertically upward. Hold the flame of a butane lighter above the tip of the mono, and slowly lower the flame until the mono begins to melt. Do not touch the material with the flame; rather, hold it just close enough to keep the material molten. As the mono begins to melt, it will shorten, and you must "follow" it downward with the flame.

Some tyers actually ignite the end of the mono, let it burn down, and blow out the flame when the eye is formed. This approach can work, but it is somewhat uncertain. The burning mono will form bubbles on the inside and "balloon" outward. Sometimes these bubbles burst and leave an irregularly shaped eye. And even if they remain intact, forming 2 eyes of identical size is difficult. It's best to melt the material more slowly.

Continue melting the mono until the molten ball reaches the edge of the plier jaws. Then withdraw the heat.

During the melting procedure, try to keep the mono as nearly vertical as possible. This will ensure that the melted ball will assume a spherical shape centered on the end of the mono.

Allow the material to cool for a few seconds, and the eye is formed.

Fluorocarbon monofilament must be treated a bit more delicately. If it is allowed to burn, it will carbonize, turn sooty, and refuse to form an eye with a symmetrical shape.

Grasp a length of material in a pair of pliers, as you would for ordinary nylon monofilament. In this case, however, clip the tags of mono on each side of the pliers to about ⅛" in length; less material is needed to form eyes from fluorocarbon mono.

Hold one tag of mono vertically and approach the tip with the bottom of a flame from a butane lighter. When you see the material begin to melt, immediately withdraw the flame. Then immediately lower the flame to the material again. When you see it begin to melt, remove the flame.

Keep repeating this procedure until the eye is formed. The motion here is one of "bouncing" the flame against the tip of the line so that the mono is heated in very short bursts. If heat is applied in this manner, the material will flatten and mushroom out, as shown here.

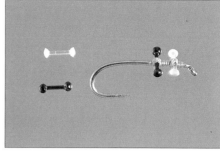

With either type of mono, turn the pliers over and melt an eye on the other end.

Before releasing the eyes, squeeze the pliers to crimp the section of mono between the jaws. Flattening the material in this way aids in mounting the eyes on the hook shank.

Here are the finished eyes and how they appear when mounted on a hook.

By melting monofilament, you can form other types of barbell eyes as well. Some attractive and useful eyes can be fashioned from glass, metal, or plastic beads, as shown in the following sequence.

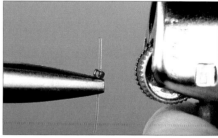

To form bead eyes, select 2 beads of the appropriate size. We're using glass beads here; if metal beads are used, they should have a straight hole rather than a counter-drilled or tapered hole (see "Bead Heads," p. 428). The size of the bead hole to some extent determines the diameter of the monofilament used. The mono should be very nearly the same diameter as the bead hole to ensure a melted mono ball large enough to prevent the bead from slipping off.

Cut a length of mono, position it in a pair of pliers, and trim the end to length as explained in the preceding sequence.

Hold one end of the mono vertically, and slip a bead over the end, as shown.

As described in the preceding sequence, melt the mono until the ball of molten material just touches the bead.

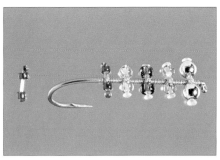

Let the mono cool for a few seconds, invert the pliers and form a second bead eye.

At the left are the finished eyes; at the right are various eyes formed from this technique mounted on a hook. The eyes nearest the front of the hook are fashioned from straight-hole brass beads.

Perhaps the simplest way of forming barbell eyes is by tying two overhand knots in a length of material, as shown in the following photo.

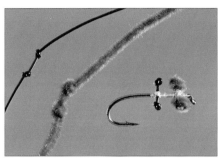

Here, eyes have been formed by casting two overhand knots in a length of material. At the upper left is knotted monofilament; in the middle is knotted Vernille. At the right are these eyes mounted on a hook.

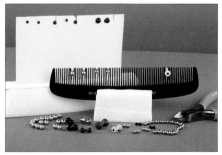

Some tyers prefer to paint barbell eyes made of melted or knotted mono, unfinished lead barbell eyes, or eyes formed from clipped sections of bead chain. It is easiest to paint several pairs of eyes at once. A piece of cardboard cut with slots, or an ordinary pocket comb, supported in a block of foam makes a convenient rack to hold the eyes for painting and drying.

The technique for mounting barbell eyes is nearly identical for all materials and is explained in the main sequence that follows. Eyes are normally mounted atop the hook shank. When lighter materials such as monofilament, small beads, or knotted strands are used, the fly will ride right-side up underwater. Heavier metal eyes mounted atop the hook shank will cause the fly to turn over and ride with the hook point upward,

which reduces snagging with flies fished deep. Because they become inverted, such flies are often dressed "upside-down." That is, a nymph pattern for instance, will have the wingcase and other dorsal components tied on the underside of the shank so that these features are visible to the trout when the fly is fished. The eyes, of course, can be mounted on the underside of the shank simply by inverting the hook in the vise for the following procedure. Such flies will ride in the normal position when fished, though the eyes will partially obscure the hook gap.

The alternate sequence shows a technique for mounting a modified type of barbell eyes that can be formed from melted mono, beads mounted on a monofilament stem, or knotted materials.

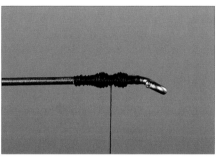

Step 1. For softer, more flexible materials such as flattened monofilament or knotted materials, lay a thread foundation behind the hook eye, and position the thread at the eye-mounting point.

Metal eyes can be a bit more difficult to mount over a smooth thread foundation, and many tyers find it easier to mount such eyes by constructing a notch or cradle from two bumps of tying thread flanking the eye-mounting point, as shown here. After forming the notch, position the thread between them.

Step 2. Position the eyes crosswise atop the hook shank at the mounting point. Brass eyes are shown here, but the technique is the same regardless of materials.

Secure the eyes to the shank using a series of crisscross wraps.

The first wraps should be made under moderate thread pressure, and they serve merely to hold the eyes in position. The next 6 or 7 wraps should be made under very heavy thread pressure to secure the eyes to the shank, as shown here from above.

Step 3. As shown in this top view, take 4 or 5 very tight wraps of thread horizontally, beneath the eyes but above the hook shank. These tight turns of thread will compress the crisscross wraps to hold the eyes more securely.

Step 4. Take a few more crisscross wraps between the eyes. Softer materials will be secured tightly at this point.

Metal eyes, however, have a greater propensity to twist around the hook shank even after being tightly bound with thread. The most secure mount is obtained by applying a drop or two of CA glue (either liquid or gel type) to the thread wraps.

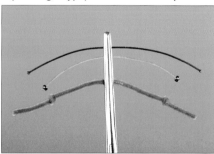

Step 1a. The eyes shown here are a modified barbell style. They are formed using the techniques shown in the introduction to this method, except that the shank or throat separating the eyes is about 2" long.

At the top are melted mono eyes; in the middle beads mounted on monofilament; and at the bottom, knotted Vernille.

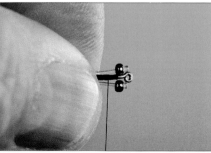

Step 2a. Lay a thread foundation behind the hook eye and position the thread at the mounting point.

Fold the eyes in half so that the eyeballs are aligned, and with the left fingers, straddle the hook shank with the eyes.

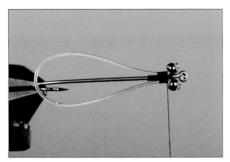

Step 3a. Tightly secure the eyes so that the two strands of material are bound to the sides of the shank.

Step 4a. Clip the excess mono and cover the butts with thread. The finished eyes are on the left.

With this technique, eyes can be mounted on top of the hook by binding the strands of material side-by-side down the top of the shank, as shown in the middle. By leaving an exposed section of the strand, you can create eyes on "stalks," as shown on the right, which are often used for crayfish or shrimp patterns; since these flies are often dressed reverse-style, the eyes here are mounted at the rear of the hook shank.

Method #8:
Mesh-wrapped Eyes

This is really an extension of the technique for fashioning suspender pods, in which material is wrapped in a piece of nylon mesh and then mounted on the hook shank. The result is very much like barbell eyes, and mesh-wrapping gives the tyer an interesting latitude of materials for the eyes. English tyer Peter Gathercole uses this approach to form eyes made of foam balls (see **Method #90: Suspender Pod**, p. 340, for information on foam balls) which add buoyancy to patterns fished on or just under the surface, such as damselfly nymphs. But almost any type of bead can be used for the eyes, including beads without holes. Weighted eyes, for instance, can be formed from the shot (lead or steel) found in shotgun shells; it comes in a wide range of sizes and is inexpensive. Colored glass and plastic beads can also be used. When coated with CA glue, most colors of mesh material will become transparent and the color of the eye beads will be quite visible. However, dark-colored nylon mesh over light-colored beads gives the eyes an interesting cross-hatched appearance.

Like metal barbell eyes, heavy mesh-wrapped eyes will cause the fly to ride upside-down in the water, and you may wish to dress dorsal components, such as wingcases, on the underside of the shank so they are visible to the trout when the fly is fished.

Using a single bead, this technique can also be used to fashion a bead head on a fly.

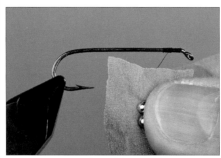

Step 1. Lay a thread foundation over the eye-mounting area, and position the tying thread 3 or 4 wraps behind the point on the shank where you wish the eyes to be located.

Cut a one-inch square of nylon mesh material. Women's stockings are excellent for this purpose, as the fabric has the proper amount of stretch and is relatively compressible for a neat tie-in.

Put 2 beads in the center of the square.

Step 2. Fold the mesh around the beads, pulling or twisting with the left fingers to pull the material into a smooth sheath around the beads, as shown here.

Step 3. To create eyes on top of the hook shank, pull the mesh very tightly around the eyes so that virtually all the stretch is removed from the material.

Position the mesh-wrapped eyes atop the hook, so that the beads flank the shank.

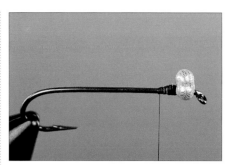

Step 4. Bind the nylon material tightly to the hook shank. Clip and bind down the excess nylon.

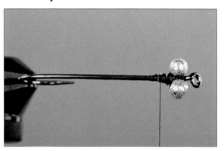

Step 5. Take a series of crisscross wraps between the beads to divide the eyes and give them better definition, as shown here. When the mesh is stretched tightly over the eye beads, they cannot slip to the sides of the shank but will remain atop the hook.

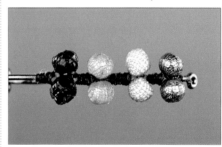

Step 6. If a very light material such as foam is used, the eyes are now completed.

Heavier eyes of metal or glass, however, can easily abrade the mesh material if the fly rubs against the streambed. In order to reinforce them, apply a thin coating of liquid CA glue or epoxy to the mesh over the eyes; use a toothpick or needle to spread the glue to the underside of the eyes as well, where they are bound to the shank. Treated in this way, the eyes become quite durable.

Shown here are mesh-wrapped eyes of various materials; moving from the bend to the eye of the hook, they are black glass, pearlescent plastic, foam, and brass. All but the foam eyes are coated with CA glue.

Step 1a. To position eyes on the sides of the shank, pull the mesh over the eyes to remove all the wrinkles from the material, but do not pull so tightly that all the

15

stretch is removed. Leaving a bit of "slack" will allow the eyes to slide to the sides of the hook shank in Step 2a.

Mount the eyes as shown in Step 4.

Step 2a. Use crisscross wraps placed close to the base of the eye beads to force them to the sides of the shank. The stretch in the mesh will allow the beads to slide into position.

Apply a coat of CA glue as explained in Step 6.

Method #9:
Painted Eyes

Many tyers paint eyes on some patterns. This approach, however, is generally restricted to streamers and bucktails that imitate baitfish, since the style of eye formed by painting is most appropriate to this type of food form. The "canvas" on which the eye is painted depends upon the fly style. Eyes can be painted directly on the thread head of a conventional streamer or bucktail pattern; they can be painted on the body material of some flies, such as the woven mylar bodies on Hal Janssen's minnow patterns; or they can be painted over a bullet head, such as the bucktail head on the Thunder Creek streamer shown in the following sequence.

Nearly any type of paint can be used. Several types are marketed for fly tying, and these give good results. But the small jars of enamel paint used by model-makers are good as well. The only requirements are that the paint must be waterproof when dry and thick enough to resist running or dripping when applied to a vertical surface. Paints that are thin, but otherwise acceptable, can be poured into a small dish, a bottle cap, or pan formed from aluminum foil, exposed to the air, and allowed to thicken to the proper consistency.

For greater efficiency, most tyers prepare a batch of flies and paint the eyes on, all at one sitting.

Step 1. Paint is applied with two wooden dowels of the proper diameter, a larger

one to form the iris, or colored part of the eye, and a smaller one to form the pupil. (Some tyers use ordinary carpentry nails instead.) Wooden dowels available from hobby or craft stores are fine for the purpose, particularly for the larger iris diameter. Round wooden toothpicks are excellent for the pupil since they are tapered and can be cut at a point to give a pupil of the proper size.

The ends of the dowels should be trimmed flat, as shown here.

Step 2. To form the iris, dip the very end of the dowel in the paint, and capture a small drop on the tip. Carefully apply the drop of paint to the side of the fly head.

The technique takes a little practice. Too much paint will drip; too little will not give sufficient coverage, though an additional coat can be applied. Do not press the dowel forcefully into the fly head, or rub or smear the paint. You're merely trying to apply a small, circular bead of paint to the fly head.

Step 3. Paint the other eye, and let the iris paint dry.

Repeat Step 2 with the small dowel, and apply a drop of paint in the center of the iris to form the pupil.

Step 4. When the eyes are dry, you can coat them with clear head cement, CA glue, or epoxy to seal the paint and help prevent chipping.

Method #10:
Glued Eyes

Pre-formed plastic eyes, often called "doll eyes," are sometimes glued to the heads of larger patterns. Though more commonly practiced by bass-fly tyers, this technique is occasionally used on trout flies. Doll eyes can be glued directly to the thread head on some streamer patterns, but the more common approach is to use them on flies dressed with substantial, bulky heads, such as the clipped heads described in **Method #1: Clipped Head**, p. 425. Doll eyes are better proportioned to such heads, and the foundation of clipped material provides a large gluing surface.

The main sequence shows the technique for mounting the eyes in a clipped socket so that they are flush with the head.

The alternate sequence shows Dick Talleur's method for mounting eyes on clipped heads made of wool, egg yarn, or fur chenille that may not be dense enough for clipping a socket. (This same approach, which involves laying a foundation of glue over the head, is occasionally used without eyes simply to reinforce clipped heads and make them more durable.)

The choice of adhesive varies among tyers. Five-minute epoxy, vinyl cement, or silicone glue are all good for the purpose, but whatever adhesive is used must be thick enough to avoid running down into the base of the head or being absorbed by the fibers.

Step 1. We're using a clipped deer-hair head for this demonstration. Eyes are applied to the finished fly.

Begin by using fine-pointed tying scissors to clip a socket of the same diameter as the eye.

Step 2. Use a toothpick to work some glue into the back of the socket.

Step 3. Put a drop of glue on the back of the eye, and with your fingertip, press the eye into the socket.

Step 1a. On very densely compacted wool or egg-yarn heads, eyes can be mounted using the method shown in the main sequence.

On sparser heads, however, the clipped wool may not provide a sufficiently stiff foundation or enough gluing surface to hold the eyes securely. Dick Talleur solves this problem by coating the wool or yarn head with silicone glue prior to mounting the eyes. He notes, however, that the film of glue can trap air inside the head and add buoyancy to subsurface patterns.

Using your fingers or a toothpick, simply smear a thin coating of glue over the surface of the head, taking care not to get the adhesive on other components of the fly.

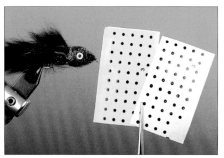

Step 2a. While the glue is still tacky, press an eye into either side of the head. Doll eyes, as shown in the main sequence, can be used, but here adhesive-backed "stick-on" eyes have been applied. These are normally available in sheets of the type shown here.

When the glue is dry, or nearly so, a second thin coat of glue can be applied over the first, sealing the eyes to the head.

Index